Discovering Imperialism

Historical Materialism Book Series

More than ten years after the collapse of the Berlin Wall and the disappearance of Marxism as a (supposed) state ideology, a need for a serious and long-term Marxist book publishing program has arisen. Subjected to the whims of fashion, most contemporary publishers have abandoned any of the systematic production of Marxist theoretical work that they may have indulged in during the 1970s and early 1980s. The Historical Materialism book series addresses this great gap with original monographs, translated texts, and reprints of "classics."

Haymarket Books is proud to be working with Brill Academic Publishers (http://www.brill.nl) and the journal *Historical Materialism* to republish the Historical Materialism book series in paperback editions. Current series titles include:

Alasdair MacIntyre's Engagement with Marxism: Selected Writings 1953–1974, edited by Paul Blackledge and Neil Davidson

Althusser: The Detour of Theory, Gregory Elliott

Between Equal Rights: A Marxist Theory of International Law, China Miéville

The Capitalist Cycle, Pavel V. Maksakovsky, translated with introduction and commentary by Richard B. Day

The Clash of Globalisations: Neo-Liberalism, the Third Way, and Anti-Globalisation, Ray Kiely

Critical Companion to Contemporary Marxism, edited by Jacques Bidet and Stathis Kouvelakis

Criticism of Heaven: On Marxism and Theology, Roland Boer

Criticism of Religion: On Marxism and Theology II, Roland Boer

Exploring Marx's Capital: Philosophical, Economic, and Political Dimensions, Jacques Bidet, translated by David Fernbach

Following Marx: Method, Critique, and Crisis, Michael Lebowitz

The German Revolution: 1917–1923, Pierre Broué

Globalisation: A Systematic Marxian Account, Tony Smith

The Gramscian Moment: Philosophy, Hegemony and Marxism, Peter D. Thomas

Impersonal Power: History and Theory of the Bourgeois State, Heide Gerstenberger, translated by David Fernbach

Lenin Rediscovered: What Is to Be Done? in Context, Lars T. Lih

Making History: Agency, Structure, and Change in Social Theory, Alex Callinicos

Marxism and Ecological Economics: Toward a Red and Green Political Economy, Paul Burkett

A Marxist Philosophy of Language, Jean-Jacques Lecercle, translated by Gregory Elliott

Politics and Philosophy: Niccolò Machiavelli and Louis Althusser's Aleatory Materialism, Mikko Lahtinen, translated by Gareth Griffiths and Kristina Köhli

The Theory of Revolution in the Young Marx, Michael Löwy

Utopia Ltd.: Ideologies of Social Dreaming in England 1870–1900, Matthew Beaumont

Western Marxism and the Soviet Union: A Survey of Critical Theories and Debates Since 1917, Marcel van der Linden

Witnesses to Permanent Revolution: The Documentary Record, edited and translated by Richard B. Day and Daniel Gaido

Discovering Imperialism

Social Democracy to World War I

Translated, edited, and introduced
by Richard B. Day and Daniel Gaido

Haymarket Books
Chicago, IL

First published in 2011 by Brill Academic Publishers, The Netherlands

Published in paperback in 2012 by
Haymarket Books
P.O. Box 180165
Chicago, IL 60618
773-583-7884
info@haymarketbooks.org
www.haymarketbooks.org

ISBN: 978-1-60846-235-3

Distributed to the trade in the US through Consortium Book Sales and Distribution (www.cbsd.com) and internationally through Ingram Publisher Services International (www.ingramcontent.com).

This book was published with the generous support of Lannan Foundation and Wallace Action Fund.

Cover design by Ragina Johnson.

Printed in the United States. Entered into digital printing March 2022.

Library of Congress Cataloging-in-Publication data is available.

To Natalie, Philip, Amelia, Monica and Mason

Contents

Introduction

Historical scholarship on the classical-Marxist theories of imperialism

In his recent book *Western Marxism and the Soviet Union*, Marcel van der Linden commented that 'in the history of ideas Marxist theories have not received the attention they deserve.'[1] In a previous volume, we have shown that this was true of the early history of Marx's theory of 'permanent revolution', which was reborn and elaborated as a result of the Russian Revolution of 1905.[2] It is also true of the other most important development in Marxism after Marx's death, the theory of imperialism, which originated during the Spanish-American and Boer Wars (1898–1902) and reached maturity with World War I, a decade and a half marked by the accelerating arms-race and mounting apprehension of disaster. This volume is the story of the 'discovery' of imperialism, followed by remarkable prescience on the part of European Social Democrats as they sounded the alarm on countless occasions over its bloody implications.

The standard historiography on imperialism relies exclusively on the canonical books by Hobson, Hilferding, Luxemburg, and Lenin and is therefore

1. van der Linden 2007, p. 2.
2. Day and Gaido (eds.) 2009.

unsatisfactory on the early stages of the theory.[3] The early German overviews of the origins of Marxist theories of imperialism, by Kurt Mandelbaum and Hans-Christoph Schröder, have been superseded by the much more fully researched book of Franco Andreucci, which is only available in Italian, deals exclusively with German Social Democracy and ends with the outbreak of the First World War.[4] R. Craig Nation's book on Lenin and the Zimmerwald Left contains an excellent chapter on the immediate intellectual background to publication in 1917 of Lenin's *Imperialism, the Highest Stage of Capitalism,* but its main interest lies elsewhere, in the 'origins of Communist internationalism'.[5] Finally, mention should be made of two collections of primary sources that include many documents related to the debate on imperialism: the socialist scholar John Riddell's anthology covering the period 1907–16 (an important and valuable work that tends, however, to exaggerate Lenin's international role before 1914) and the older anthology by Olga Gankin and Harold Fisher on the origins of the Third International, entitled *The Bolsheviks and the World War.*[6]

This volume includes, for the first time, English versions of the major articles and reviews on the theory of imperialism written before publication of Lenin's book. The documents come mainly from theoretical journals such as *Die Neue Zeit* and *Der Kampf,* to which we have added material from *Vorwärts,* from left-wing newspapers such as *Leipziger Volkszeitung* and *Bremer Bürger-Zeitung,* and from more ephemeral journals issued by the Zimmerwald Left after the outbreak of WWI such as *Lichtstrahlen, Neues Leben* and *Vorbote.* Given the period covered by this volume, it cannot be exhaustive. For obvious reasons, we could not include the most famous comprehensive texts – Hilferding's *Finance Capital,* Luxemburg's *The Accumulation of Capital,* and Lenin's *Imperialism, the Highest Stage of Capitalism* – all of which are available in English. We are persuaded, nevertheless, that the documents we have translated will provide readers with an accurate picture of the unknown origins and context of these classical-Marxist theories.

3. Brewer 1990.
4. Mandelbaum 1926, Schröder 1975 and Andreucci 1988.
5. Craig Nation 1989.
6. Riddell (ed.) 1984, Gankin and Fisher (eds.) 1940.

Hegel and Marx: the state and the world economy

In modern political usage, theories of imperialism are typically Marxist or substantially influenced by Marxism, although Marx himself never attempted such a theory. In response to Hegel's view of the *Rechtstaat* as the 'end of history', Marx did point out that, beyond individual states, lay the greater totality of the world market, ruled by the world 'law of value'. But the implications only began to be clarified in the years of imperialist expansionism that culminated in the Great War. It is no exaggeration to say that those same implications – different in form but thematically connected – remain central to today's debates, only now we speak of 'globalisation'. In that sense, the documents translated here represent a kind of 'pre-history' of globalisation, or the first chapter in a continuing story.

A fundamental difference between today's circumstances and those prior to WWI is that today the capitalist state-form, having originated in Western Europe, has become universal. It is on these grounds that some writers have revived Hegel's view of the modern state as the end (and purpose) of history. But, while the modern state was, for Hegel, the final political form, the purpose of states was also to make history, and the history of the world was 'the world's court of judgement'.[7]

Hegel believed that particular nations and states, at different periods, become 'world-historical' as they contribute novel forms of civilisation.[8] In his *Philosophy of History*, he explained the significance of nineteenth-century England in *commercial* terms: 'The material existence of England is based on commerce and industry, and the English have undertaken the weighty responsibility of being the missionaries of civilization to the world…'.[9] England's mission was 'to form connections with barbarous peoples, to create wants and stimulate industry, and first and foremost to establish among them the conditions necessary to commerce',[10] which meant extending the European form of state and thus establishing lawful 'respect for property' and 'civility to strangers'.[11]

7. Hegel 2003, p. 371.
8. Hegel 2003, p. 374.
9. Hegel 2001, p. 475.
10. Hegel 2001, p. 476.
11. Ibid.

Hegel praised the modern state for specifying the legal 'rights' and 'duties' of all its constituent elements. Marx, however, had a different view. In the *Communist Manifesto*, he famously declared that the executive of the modern state was but 'a committee for managing the common affairs of the whole bourgeoisie'. The 'single unconscionable freedom – free trade' then brought its universal opposite: 'naked, shameless, direct, brutal exploitation'.

In his *Philosophy of Right*, Hegel wrote that 'The civilized nation is conscious that the rights of barbarians are unequal to its own and treats their autonomy as only a formality.'[12] Marx amplified that remark, too, declaring that the bourgeoisie 'compels all nations, on pain of extinction, to adopt the bourgeois mode of production; it compels them to introduce what it calls civilisation into their midst, i.e. to become bourgeois themselves. In one word, it creates a world after its own image.'[13] For Marx, the mission of the bourgeoisie was to create a capitalist *world market* in preparation for universal civilisation that would lie beyond any and all states: communism, in which the unconscious phenomena of market transactions would be replaced by deliberate planning as the exercise of social reason.

In his original plan for the critique of political economy, Marx projected six books, the last of which was to deal with the world market and crises.[14] The first book was to be *Capital*, of which Marx finished only one volume in his own lifetime – Volumes II and III being pieced together by Engels from Marx's notes. Since Marx never completed his undertaking, his successors were left to interpret imperialism in terms of their own experiences and the projections first set out in the *Communist Manifesto*. However, there were really two themes in the *Manifesto*: on the one hand, the 'civilising' mission of capitalism to 'the barbarian nations'; on the other, the economic means by which capitalism would carry through the project of world-transformation.

In the *Manifesto*, Marx spoke of 'the cheap prices of commodities' as the 'heavy artillery' with which capitalism would batter down 'all Chinese walls'.[15] By the turn of the century, rival capitalist states were turning to a different kind

12. Hegel 2003, p. 376.
13. Marx 1970, p. 36.
14. Rosdolsky 1989, p. 56. Marx wrote that 'the scientifically correct method' of political economy must ascend 'from the simple relations, such as labour, division of labour, need, exchange-value to the level of the state, exchange between nations and the world market'. Marx 1973, pp. 100–1.
15. Marx 1970, p. 36.

of 'heavy artillery', militarised expansionism, in the struggle over markets, materials, and spheres of investment. In the institutionally 'vacant' corners of the world – the precapitalist periphery that many still regarded as 'barbarous' – access to markets and resources appeared to presuppose the conquest of territory, for only armed might could guarantee the security of investments against both capitalist rivals and indigenous peoples. In that context, imperialism was frequently rationalised in terms of racial and cultural superiority. Until Marxists could formulate more comprehensive theories, the first inclination of many was to fall back on the view that capitalism's worldwide expansion would carry 'civilisation' to backward peoples. In this volume, we trace the development of Social-Democratic literature on imperialism with reference to two themes: Eurocentric convictions of cultural superiority, followed by gradual emergence of more sophisticated economic theories in the spirit of Marx's *Capital.*

The origins of the term 'imperialism'

The early history of the word 'imperialism' has been explored by Richard Koebner and Helmut Dan Schmidt, who concluded that '*imperialism* was introduced into the English language as a gloss on a regime which had been established in France'; namely, Louis Napoleon's Second French *Empire* (1852–70).[16] The word *impérialisme* entered usage as a neologism side by side with *bonapartisme*, indicating the various ways by which the Second French Empire of Louis Napoleon maintained its hold on France. The word was twice used as a synonym for Bonapartism in *The Eighteenth Brumaire of Louis Bonaparte* (1852), where Marx argued that 'the parody of the empire [*des Imperialismus*] was necessary to free the mass of the French nation from the weight of tradition and to work out in pure form the opposition between the state power and society'.[17]

The term 'imperialism' began to be used more widely in Britain with passage of the Royal Titles Act of April 1876, which officially recognised Queen

16. Koebner and Schmidt 1965, p. 1.
17. Marx 1978a, p. 133. 'And this same bourgeoisie now decries the stupidity of the masses, the vile multitude, that has betrayed it to Bonaparte. It has itself forcibly strengthened the imperialism of the peasant class, it conserved the conditions that form the birthplace of this peasant religion.' Marx 1978a, p. 128.

Victoria as 'Empress of India'. She assumed this title at the encouragement of Prime Minister Benjamin Disraeli. In turn, Victoria elevated Disraeli to the peerage in August 1876, making him Earl of Beaconsfield. But Koebner and Schmidt note that 'The term Imperialism became associated in the British mind with the despised regime of Napoleon III...the term occasionally recurred to denounce an alien form of government that made use of direct appeals to the multitude, false military splendour, adventures abroad...and...arbitrary despotic rule; it all fitted so perfectly with what the Liberals felt Disraeli represented, the fraud, the charlatan, as *Punch* called him.'[18] By 1878, *Punch* portrayed 'imperialism' as an irritating buzzword:

> Imperialism! Hang the word! It buzzes in my noodle
> Like bumble-bees in clover time. The talk on't's mostly twaddle;
> Yet one would like to fix the thing, as farmers nail up vermin;
> Lots o'big words collapse, like blobs, if their sense you once determine.[19]

Almost two decades after Disraeli's tenure as Prime Minister, one author remarked that 'However much the imperialism of Lord Beaconsfield may be criticised in regard to details, there can be little doubt now that he laid down the general lines of policy which must be followed by the British race, if it is to hold a foremost place in the world.'[20] The Marxist writers whose works we have collected for this anthology associated the change in British attitudes not only with race and personalities but also with the fact that Britain's rivals were turning increasingly to protectionism. Lincoln had introduced a 44 per cent tariff in America during the Civil War to finance the Union armies, subsidise railways, and protect domestic manufacturing. France imposed prohibitive duties in 1860 on English pig-iron, machinery and woollen goods. In 1878–9, Bismarck levied tariffs on iron and all major grains to appease both emerging industry and the Junker aristocracy. British interest in a more coherent

18. Koebner and Schmidt 1965, pp. 147–8.
19. Punch, 23 November 1878, vol. 75, p. 233. Quoted in Koebner and Schmidt 1965, p. 156. The main documents of the early debate on imperialism in Great Britain are available in Cain (ed.) 1999, including reprints of 'English Imperialism', *Spectator*, (8 April 1876), pp. 158–62, Robert Lowe, 'Imperialism', *Fortnightly Review*, Vol. 24 (1878), pp. 453–65, and Frederic Seebohm, 'Imperialism and Socialism', *Nineteenth Century* (April 1880), vol. 7, pp. 726–36.
20. Rose 1898, p. 199, quoted in Koebner and Schmidt 1965, p. 212.

economic Empire grew as other countries sought to safeguard their markets against British goods.

The principal manifestations of the new British imperialism were the occupation of Egypt under Gladstone in 1882, which heralded the wholesale scramble for Africa in the 1880s, and the establishment of the Imperial Federation League in London in 1884. The League hoped to share the costs of imperial defence by establishing a federal state of all the colonies of the British Empire. The celebration of Queen Victoria's Diamond Jubilee in 1897 led to an outburst of imperialist sentiment, but the true apotheosis of British imperialism took place with the outbreak of the Boer War in 1899. That event prompted the 'New Liberal' John Hobson to write his famous book *Imperialism* and also resulted in several articles and pamphlets on the subject in the English socialist press, associating imperialism with the emerging imperatives of capitalist competition.[21]

The term was similarly given broader economic meaning when used to describe the new expansionist turn in American foreign policy, initiated in 1898 by the Spanish-American War. An American financial journalist and banking expert, Charles Arthur Conant (1861–1915), then editor of the New York *Bankers' Magazine*, welcomed the departure in American policy with an article in the September 1898 issue of the *North American Review* entitled 'The Economic Basis of Imperialism'.[22] Conant attributed the war to the imperative to expand markets and capital-exports in response to over-saving, growing inventories and falling profit-margins:

> It is the excess of saving, with the resulting accumulation of unconsumed goods, in the great industrial countries, which is one of the world maladies of the economic situation of today. It lies at the root of a large share of industrial discontent, and explains more logically than changes in the mere mechanism of exchange the conditions which set in about 1870, when the great civilized countries first appear to have become fully capitalized to meet all demands which consumers were willing to make out of their earnings. The world's economic history since that time – the intense industrial activity in machine production and railroad building up to 1873; the long period of

21. See the articles in *The Social Democrat* (Social-Democratic Federation 1900, 1901 and 1902).
22. Conant 1898.

> stagnation which followed, broken only by brief periods of activity after surplus goods had been consumed; the great accumulations of both capital and metallic money; the convulsions attacking the great capitalistic countries, without respect for their differences in tariff policies and money standards; and the steady fall in the earning power of capital – all these tendencies point to excess of saved capital beyond the effective demand of the community as their underlying cause.... [U]nder the present social order it is becoming impossible to find at home in the great capitalistic countries employment for all the capital saved which is at once safe and remunerative.[23]

An important role in the spreading use of the word imperialism, with its modern negative connotations, was played by the American Anti-Imperialist League, established in the United States in June 1898 to struggle against annexation of the Philippines. The League counted among its members leading personalities such as Carl Schurz and Mark Twain as well as the Democratic presidential candidate William Jennings Bryan, who in his address accepting the nomination for the Presidency, delivered on 8 August 1900, decried 'the swaggering, bullying, brutal doctrine of imperialism'.[24] The Democratic Party Platform stated that 'the burning issue of imperialism growing out of the Spanish war involves the very existence of the Republic and the destruction of our free institutions'. Democrats regarded the new imperialist policy of the United States as 'the paramount issue of the campaign' and warned 'that imperialism abroad will lead quickly and inevitably to despotism at home'.[25]

Early Marxist debates on the colonial question

In Germany, the first commentaries on imperialism were also influenced by domestic concerns. The Social-Democratic Party that emerged in 1875 had nothing in common with Bismarckian notions of German grandeur. Historian Carl Schorske notes that the Party remained committed to bourgeois-democratic revolutionary traditions of struggle for German national unity while opposing both Prussian militarism and tsarist military interventions in

---

23. Conant 1898, p. 330.
24. Bryan 1900, p. 44.
25. Democratic Party Platform of 1900. For early analyses of imperialism by American socialist writers, see for instance Boothman 1900; Wilshire 1901.

support of Western-European reaction. Russophobia was combined with a commitment to national defence, but Social Democrats thought responsibility for the latter must rest with the armed people in a democratically organised citizens' army or militia.[26] Only gradually did the new economic and diplomatic realities bring major changes in the foreign-policy convictions of the Social-Democratic Left, including abandonment of the slogan of national defence, which Friedrich Engels had advocated for Germany as late as 1892.[27]

The prehistory of Marxist theories of imperialism in Germany covers the period from 1884 to 1898, beginning with a heated debate over steamship subsidies [*Dampfersubventionsstreit*] in 1884–5. On 23 May 1884, a bill was submitted to the Reichstag proposing subsidies for steamship-companies to expand German trade by building maritime lines from Hamburg or Bremen to different points in Asia, Australia and Africa. A violent confrontation erupted among Social Democrats over their attitude towards the so-called steamer-subsidy bill, namely, whether the proposed subsidies should be treated purely as a question of transport, worthy of support in terms of creating employment in difficult economic times, or as a foreign-policy initiative that should be rejected on principle. The former view was defended by a majority of the Reichstag fraction (18 out of 24), while the latter was advocated by a minority led by August Bebel and Wilhelm Liebknecht, who appealed to party-members in the pages of the party organ *Der Sozialdemokrat*. The majority of the Reichstag group denied the right of the official journal to criticise their attitude and demanded control over the newspaper, but they were defeated on that issue. Nevertheless, their own view prevailed in parliament on 23 March 1885, as the Reichstag approved the steamer subsidies.[28]

In the course of the inner-party quarrel, Wilhelm Liebknecht gave a speech on 4 March 1885, that framed the issue of colonialism in political-economic terms and argued that it was merely a vain attempt to export the 'social question':

> Let us ask ourselves calmly: what is the actual purpose of so-called colonial policy? If we get to the root of it, its purpose is proclaimed to be to control overproduction and overpopulation. But what is overproduction, and

26. Schorske 1970, p. 67.
27. Engels 1892.
28. On the *Dampfersubventionsstreit*, see Mittmann 1975 and Schwarz 1884/85.

> what is overpopulation? These are very relative terms.... Overpopulation exists because we have poor social and economic institutions, and the same happens with overproduction. The manufacturers complain that they can't sell their products. Yes, gentlemen, why can't you sell them? Because the people cannot buy [them]...national wealth goes hand-in-hand with mass poverty.... [W]ill colonial policy achieve anything in this direction? No, gentlemen, you just export the social question and conjure up before the eyes of people a kind of mirage in the sands and swamps of Africa.[29]

Rejection of colonialism was characteristic not only of the SPD. For instance, a resolution on colonial policy, adopted at the thirteenth national congress of the Parti Ouvrier Français, held at Romilly in September 1895, read:

> Considering that colonial policy is one of the worst forms of capitalist exploitation, which tends exclusively to enlarge the *field of profits* of the proprietary class at the expense of the blood and money of the producing proletariat; considering that its expeditions undertaken under the pretext of civilisation and national honour lead to corruption and destruction of primitive populations and unleash on the colonising nation itself all sorts of scourges...; considering that the only really human way of securing outlets to modern mechanical production is to abolish class differences and enable the producers, masters of the social forms of the means of production, to consume themselves the wealth produced by their manual and intellectual labour; the thirteenth national congress of the French Workers' Party protests with all its forces against the colonial filibustering expeditions for which no conscious socialist will ever vote one man or one penny.[30]

---

29. Reichstag 1871–1918, VI. *Legislaturperiode*. I. *Sessionsabschnitt*, 58. Sitzung. Mittwoch den 4. März 1885, p. 1540, emphasis in the original (for the full text of Liebknecht's speech see pp. 1539–44). In 1900, Liebknecht dealt with the issue of imperialism in the English socialist newspaper *The Clarion* edited by Robert Blatchford, a supporter of the British government during the Second Boer War. However, Liebknecht used the word in Marx's old sense: 'Imperialism is the father of Militarism. I mean Imperialism in the only sense of the word I know – that is, in the sense of *violent extension of power*, of *subjecting other countries and nations* to the Empire – the *Imperium*.... Militarism does not lie in the *fighting*. It lies in the *political system* and aim. Its danger is in Imperialism. If you do not succeed in stemming the tide of Imperialism you will have Militarism, and you may bury freedom.' Liebknecht 1900c, emphasis in the original. (See also Liebknecht 1900a and 1900b.)

30. Parti Ouvrier Français 1897, pp. 47–8, emphasis in the original. See also Ageron 1973. The original usage of 'filibustering' referred to US attempts to take over countries formally at peace with America through privately financed military expeditions.

The colonial question in the revisionist controversy

Shortly afterwards, the question of colonial expansion played a prominent role in the famous revisionist controversy. The long spell of reaction that followed the crushing of the Paris Commune in 1871 had led to revival of bourgeois-democratic illusions in the socialist parties of the Second International and an attempt to revise Marx's doctrines along parliamentary-reformist lines. Eduard Bernstein personified this tendency in a series of articles published in *Die Neue Zeit* late in 1896 and subsequently in his book *The Preconditions of Socialism and the Tasks of Social Democracy*. Bernstein had originally been a close friend of Engels, but, after Engels's death, he stayed on in London and came under the spell of the reformist Fabian Society. It is therefore not surprising that he first clashed with an English Marxist, Ernest Belfort Bax, a member of the British Social-Democratic Federation. At that time, Bax's position on the colonial question was extreme not only in rejecting any sort of colonialism but also in advocating a joint armed struggle, together with the colonised peoples, against their European oppressors.[31]

On 14 October 1896, Bernstein published in *Die Neue Zeit*, the theoretical journal of German Social Democracy, an article on Turkey advocating diametrically opposed views. While some Social Democrats were already framing the discussion of colonialism in economic terms, Bernstein – and he was certainly not alone at the time – thought the issue could not be separated from questions of race and the cultural superiority of European civilisation:

> Races who are hostile to or incapable of civilisation cannot claim our sympathy when they revolt against civilisation. We recognise no right of robbery, no right of hunters against cultivators. In short, however critical our view of contemporary civilisation may be, we none the less acknowledge its relative achievements and take them as the criterion for our sympathy. We will condemn and oppose certain methods of subjugating savages. But we will not condemn the idea that savages must be subjugated and made to conform to the rules of higher civilisation.[32]

Bernstein's comments drew upon Marx's rhetoric in the *Communist Manifesto* regarding the bourgeoisie's mission to civilise 'barbarian' peoples. Bax's

31. See, for instance, Bax 1896 (available online at the Marxists Internet Archive).
32. Bernstein 1988a, pp. 52–3.

views seemed altogether extraordinary from that perspective, and Bernstein dismissed them this way: 'Some time ago, it was... suggested in the socialist camp that savages and barbarians be assisted in their struggles against the advancing capitalist civilisation, but that was an outcome of romanticism that needed only to be followed to its logical conclusion to be proved untenable.' He concluded: 'even among peoples capable of civilisation we cannot treat every revolt with equal sympathy. The freedom of an insignificant people in a non-European or semi-European region does not carry the same weight as the free development of the great and highly civilised nations of Europe.'[33]

The debate between Bernstein and Bax continued in the English journal *Justice* and in *Die Neue Zeit*. Bax replied that Bernstein's statements on 'a proposal made by myself as to supporting barbaric and savage communities against the inroads of aggressive capitalism' amounted to

> an allegation that only those risings deserve the sympathy of the Socialists which are likely to result in the expansion of capitalist civilisation! On the other hand, such peoples as show no disposition to be drawn within the vortex of the modern world market, who resist being smothered with duck-trousers, Lancashire 'shoddy', adulterated spirits, and other exhilarating products of the *höhere Kultur* [higher culture] with the aid of the Maxim gun – we are given to understand – are hostile to culture, or incapable of cultural development[34] and as such have no claim whatever to our sympathies.[35]

Bax introduced another issue, even more controversial, when he questioned the generally accepted Marxist view that all countries must pass through capitalism. In the *Manifesto*, Marx had written that the bourgeoisie 'draws all, even the most barbarian nations into civilisation'. Bax, to the contrary, explained that his wish 'to limit, as far as possible, the area of capitalistic exploitation' stemmed not only from his opposition to capitalism's attempt to secure 'a new lease of life of some decades' duration', but also from his conviction that in history's movement 'from capitalism to socialism it is not by any means essential that *all barbarian and savage peoples* and out-of-the-way corners of the earth should come under the dominion of capitalism, with the human misery

33. Bernstein 1988a, p. 53.
34. Bax spoke of such peoples as being 'kulturfeindlich, oder kulturunfähig'.
35. Bax 1988a, p. 61.

involved in it'.[36] In words that seemed the antithesis of Marx's *Manifesto*, he concluded: 'our duty as socialists is to fight tooth and nail against all advances of civilisation in barbarous and savage countries'. This also applied to the

> communities of Africa upon whom the curse of civilisation has not yet fallen. Their fight against the white man, against missions, traders, and settlers is our fight. We recognise no rights, under any circumstances whatever, for a civilised power to subjugate races living in a lower stage of social development and to force civilisation upon them. The specious humanitarian twaddle talked in press and upon platform to throw dust in our eyes and cover wanton aggression does not impose upon us.[37]

John A. Hobson's *Imperialism: A Study* (1902)

The British radical democrat John A. Hobson, best known today for his book *Imperialism: A Study*,[38] also played an unintentional role in the revisionist controversy. Bernstein's first article in his *Problems of Socialism* series, which initiated the debate, contained long quotations from an essay by Hobson, and the second article was actually a translation of a work by Hobson that appeared in the first number of the *Progressive Review*.[39] The *Review*, which lasted only two years (1896–8), was issued by the Rainbow Circle, a group of 'New Liberals' of which Hobson was a founding member. After the outbreak of the Boer War, the Circle's members divided into those who favoured imperialism and the 'anti-imperialists' or 'pro-Boers'.[40] The latter upheld the radical traditions of the industrial northern counties and regarded London financiers as appendages

36. Bax 1988a, p. 62.

37. Bax 1988a, p. 63. Bax summarised his ideas in a contribution to *Die Neue Zeit* that is particularly important because its emphasis on the possibility of skipping historical stages anticipated the later debate during the Russian Revolution of 1905 concerning the theory of permanent revolution. (See Bax 1988c). This brought forth an answer from Bernstein censuring Bax for proposing to furnish 'fire-arms to the savages in order to stiffen their power of resistance'. (Bernstein 1988b, p. 67). Bax responded by again insisting on the devastation caused by capital in the colonised areas. (Bax 1898. See also Kaarsholm 1988.)

38. Hobson 1902b.

39. Bernstein 1896a and Bernstein 1896b (a translation of Hobson 1896b).

40. The Rainbow Circle included Hobson's colleague and friend J.M. Robertson, who according to P.J. Cain, Hobson's main scholar, wrote 'the most comprehensive radical analysis of imperialism in the run-up to the Boer War'. Cain 2002, p. 89, referring to Robertson 1899.

of the aristocracy and the chief architects of imperialism. Hobson associated imperialism with maldistribution of income and wealth, creating the need to export excessive savings. While financial and trading interests supported the use of force to open up countries such as China, Hobson objected in 1898 that this would merely be 'the thin end of the wedge of empire as India, Egypt and Africa testify'. Free trade was a worthy ideal, but it should not be extended with 'kicks and blows upon others'.[41] The practical alternative to imperialist expansion was trade-unionism to raise domestic wages, and redistribution through progressive taxation of unearned incomes.

The outbreak of the South-African War offered Hobson the opportunity to study the workings of the colonial system at first hand. In the summer of 1899, he went to South Africa as special correspondent of the *Manchester Guardian*. After the journey, he published a book called *The War in South Africa*, which now injected a further variant of racism. Hobson described the conflict in South Africa as a 'Jew-Imperialist design'.[42] But Judeophobia was not an integral part of Hobson's world-outlook, and further reflection led him 'to revise his over-simplified account of the Jewish factor in South Africa. When he published his full-length study of imperialism in 1902, the references to a Jewish conspiracy had largely disappeared.' Nevertheless, the damage had been done by his earlier adoption of 'the comfortable tradition of *cherchez le juif*': 'so persuasive had he been that his original view of the Boer War as a Jewish plot became for a time conventional wisdom in anti-imperialist circles'.[43]

41. Quoted in Cain 2002, p. 68.

42. Hobson 1900c, p. 226. 'The stress which my analysis lays upon the Jew has reference to the class of financial capitalists of which the foreign Jew must be taken as the leading type.' Hobson 1900c, p. 189.

43. Hirshfield 1980, p. 629. 'Anti-imperialist' anti-Semitism spilled over into English socialist ranks and was upheld, for instance, by the Social-Democratic Federation leader Henry Hyndman and his successor as editor of the SDF's organ *Justice*, Harry Quelch. Belfort Bax denounced this conflation of anti-imperialism and anti-Semitism in strong words: 'I heartily agree with our friend [Theodore] Rothstein that this howl for the liver of the financing Jew, taking him as it were out of the category capitalist or even financier in general, and holding him up to special obloquy, is a disgrace to our movement; indeed, if it goes on much longer I would be disposed to borrow a classical phrase of Rothstein's and say it constituted an "indelible burning stain" on English Socialism.' The unsigned editorial comment on this piece, clearly written by Hyndman, reads: 'We gladly publish the above as showing how little fear there is of the Socialist movement here drifting into anti-Semitism.... But the Jew capitalists have been specially prominent in this nefarious business, and it is the Jew-owned yellow press which has been specially virulent in exciting the jingo mob here and inciting the rowdies to violence.' Bax 1899, p. 6.

In October 1902, Hobson published his major work, *Imperialism: A Study*, and attributed the new imperialist foreign policy no longer to a Jewish conspiracy but rather to the urge to invest capital abroad. 'It is not industrial progress that demands the opening up of new markets and areas of investment,' he wrote, 'but mal-distribution of consuming power which prevents the absorption of commodities and capital within the country.'[44] He believed the only way to eliminate excessive saving was to 'raise the general standard of home consumption and abate the pressure for foreign markets':[45]

> It is not inherent in the nature of things that we should spend our natural resources on militarism, war, and risky, unscrupulous diplomacy, in order to find markets for our goods and surplus capital. An intelligent progressive community, based upon substantial equality of economic and educational opportunities, will raise its standard of consumption to correspond with every increased power of production, and can find full employment for an unlimited quantity of capital and labour within the limits of the country which it occupies. Where the distribution of incomes is such as to enable all classes of the nation to convert their felt wants into an effective demand for commodities, there can be no over-production, no under-employment of capital and labour, and no necessity to fight for foreign markets.[46]

The intellectual roots of Hobson's reform programme lay with the late classical English political economists who, influenced by the growing strength of the labour-movement, tried to harmonise the postulates of political economy with the claims of the workers. The most famous among these writers, John Stuart Mill, argued that, while production was regulated by 'physical laws', the distribution of wealth was 'a matter of human institution' and could be politically altered.[47]

Hobson's *Imperialism* was subsequently held in high esteem by Lenin, but it should also be noted that Hobson did not have much immediate impact on

---

44. Hobson 1902a, p. 85.
45. Hobson 1902a, p. 91.
46. Hobson 1902a, p. 92.
47. Mill 1868, Vol. I, pp. 258–9. Cf. Kautsky's criticism of Hobson 1896b: 'The position of the workers is determined by their interests as producers, not as consumers, and the first concern of socialism is to abolish the exploitation of the workers, not of the consumers. This means that collectivism will certainly not be defined as Hobson defines it.' Kautsky to Adler, 12 November 1896, in Tudor and Tudor (eds.) 1988, pp. 81–2.

the continental socialist press. While researching the SPD periodicals, Hans-Christoph Schröder found just a single reference to Hobson's book: a review in *Vorwärts* written by the Austro-British Marxist Max Beer in 1906.[48] Hobson's influence on Lenin was therefore probably not mediated by the SPD-press but rather resulted from Lenin's own exile in London. Krupskaya notes in her memoirs that Lenin arrived in London in April 1902, shortly before Hobson published his book.[49] As he made notes in 1915–16 for his own work on the subject, Lenin commented that 'Hobson's book on imperialism is useful in general, and especially useful because it helps to reveal the basic falsity of Kautskyism on this subject.'[50] By 1915, Karl Kautsky famously dismissed attempts to explain imperialism in terms of economic necessity, believing instead that conflicts could be resolved by disarmament, free trade and peaceful arbitration of international disputes. Lenin thought Hobson's statistical data showed the unevenness of empire-building and thus proved the impossibility of 'extending cartel methods to the field of foreign policy', thereby also excluding any possibility of stable and general disarmament.

The first Marxist analyses of imperialism

The first pioneering analyses of imperialism in the continental socialist press came from two writers who remain virtually unknown to most historians: Max Beer (1864–1943), an Austrian émigré in London, and Paul Louis, a Frenchman whose real name was Paul Lévi (1872–1955). Since both authors have been given considerable space in this book, with appropriate biographical information attached to the translated documents, there is no need to summarise their views here.[51] We will just point out that they both initially used the term 'imperialism' in its customary meaning of the time; namely,

48. Beer 1906. For an English version see this anthology Chapter 16. See also Schröder 1970, pp. 104–22. In a previous article, Beer had analysed the theoretical basis of Hobson's radicalism (particularly his views on the theory of value) and his attempt to set up 'a reform party for workers and radicals – a party of "*socialism sans doctrines*"'. Beer 1902a. For an English version see this anthology, Chapter 14.

49. Krupskaya, 1959, Part I: Life in London, 1902–1903. See also Social-Democratic Federation 1902. Lenin had reviewed one of Hobson's works in Russian translation back in 1899 (Lenin 1899a, a review of Hobson 1894).

50. Lenin 1939, Notebook "β" ("Beta"): Note on K. Kautsky Versus Imperialism.

51. Paul Louis's book on colonialism (Louis 1905) is available online in French at the Marxist Internet Archive.

with reference to the advocacy of a British imperial federation, repudiation of free trade, and creation of a protectionist tariff-union. Later, they extended their analysis to other European countries and to the United States in the effort to probe imperialism's economic foundations. Their exploratory works appear tentative and inconclusive in view of the later books from Hilferding, Luxemburg and Lenin, but they nevertheless helped to initiate the debate that led to those more comprehensive texts. Another early analyst of imperialism, whose work we have rescued from oblivion, is the German socialist Heinrich Cunow (1862–1936), who pioneered use of the concept of finance-capital. In his article 'American Expansion Policy in East Asia' (included in this anthology), Cunow also referred his readers to the above-mentioned work by Charles Conant on the economic basis of American imperialism.[52]

Although Karl Kautsky never wrote a comprehensive study of imperialism, his name was frequently invoked and almost as frequently denounced in the literature, particularly as WWI approached. His contributions spanned more than forty years and involved several changes of emphasis and even of direction. According to his own self-flattering account in his booklet *Socialism and Colonial Policy* (1907), 'In the first volume of *Neue Zeit*, published in 1883, there appeared a longer essay of mine on "Emigration and Colonisation" in which I already formulated the view which has determined the position of our party on colonial policy from then up to the present.'[53] While Kautsky's article in 1883 was meant to encourage opposition to German colonial policy, favourably contrasting the democratic political institutions of the English settlement-colonies with the aristocratic and militaristic German political system, its disregard of the genocide practised in settlement colonies is striking to a modern reader. Kautsky contrasted the achievements of the 'work-colonies' of European settlement (the United States, Canada and Australia) with the grim record of 'exploitation-colonies' (such as India and the German colonies in Africa), where the native masses were exploited by a small group of European merchants, civil servants and military officials.[54] The Eurocentrism of many adherents to the Second International was particularly evident in a subsequent article by Kautsky on 'The Chinese Railways and the European

52. See the short biographical sketches of these three authors in the introductions to Chapters 1, 4 and 8.
53. Kautsky 1907b, p. 13.
54. Kautsky 1883.

Proletariat', published in 1886, in which he warned that more powerful than the armies of Xerxes and Genghis Kahn would be 'the army of those who, as a consequence of the construction of the Chinese railroads, will threaten our civilisation. A new Mongol invasion threatens us! And it is we ourselves who are forcing the Chinese to fall upon us, who are building the road for them.'[55]

By the turn of the century, Kautsky returned to issues of colonial policy in response to German naval preparations. In that context, he wrote several articles: 'Old and New Colonial Policy' (1898), 'Jiaozhou' (1898), 'The War in South Africa' (1899), 'Schippel, Brentano and the Naval Bills' (1900), and 'The Consequences of the Japanese Victory and Social Democracy' (1905).[56] The article 'Old and New Colonial Policy' was also part of the revisionist debate. In that connection, Kautsky rejected Bernstein's pro-colonialist position with the claim that, rather than promoting historical progress, modern colonial policy was pursued by *precapitalist* reactionary strata, mainly Junkers, military officers, bureaucrats, speculators and merchants, although Kautsky neglected to mention German banks and heavy industry.[57]

In this volume, we have included several articles by Kautsky, the first two of which were written under the immediate impression of the Boer War. In one of these, 'Germany, England and World Policy' (1900), he did mention the concept of finance-capital, but not in Rudolf Hilferding's later sense of a merger between banking and industrial capital. For Kautsky, finance-capital stood for money-capital and its protectionist, militarist and imperialist policy, which he distinguished from the free-trading, pacifist and supposedly democratic inclinations of industrial capital.[58]

The SPD Congress at Mainz (17–21 September 1900)

Among German Social Democrats, the first full-scale debate on imperialism came at a party congress held in Mainz on 17–21 September, 1900. The topic was 'world policy [*Weltpolitik*]', involving the implications of the Boer War

55. Kautsky 1886, p. 544.
56. Kautsky 1907b, p. 14, referring to Kautsky 1898a, 1898b, 1899c, 1900b, 1905. For an English version of 'The Consequences of the Japanese Victory and Social Democracy' see Day and Gaido (eds.) 2009, pp. 373–408.
57. Kautsky 1898a.
58. Kautsky 1900c.

and of Germany's colonial policy in China.[59] Specific issues were the creation of a German protectorate in Kiautschou (Jiaozhou), repression of the Boxer Rebellion by the Western powers, and Kaiser Wilhelm II's 'Hun speech' at Bremerhaven (27 July 1900).[60] At this congress, Rosa Luxemburg emerged as the most perceptive critic of imperialism and its catastrophic potential, portraying the struggle for colonies in world historical terms. She characterised events in China as 'a bloody war of united capitalist Europe against Asia' and nothing less than a 'turning point' in world history. She urged her comrades to take antiwar agitation to the streets: 'The Chinese war is the first event of the world political era in which all developed states have become involved, and this first thrust of international reaction, of the Holy Alliance, must be answered immediately by a protest of the united workers' parties of Europe.'[61] A similar view came from Georg Ledebour, who likewise described imperialism not in terms of contingent events but as a worldwide phenomenon that might vary in specifics from country to country 'but essentially is everywhere the same, in absolutist Russia as in constitutional England, in republican France and America as in Germany'.'[62]

The resolution adopted by the Congress declared that recent developments were 'world-encompassing', being conducted solely 'for the purpose of capitalist exploitation and the development of military power'. Imperialism's

59. Sozialdemokratische Partei Deutschlands 1900, *Protokoll über die Verhandlungen des Parteitages abgehalten zu Mainz vom 17. bis 21. September 1900*, pp. 154–70: 7. Die Weltpolitik. Berichterstatter: Paul Singer.

60. When a regiment of German troops was sent to China after the murder of the German ambassador, the Emperor Wilhelm II, in a speech of 27 July 1900, exhorted these troops: 'Just as the Huns under their king Etzel created for themselves a thousand years ago a name which men still respect, you should give the name of German such cause to be remembered in China for a thousand years.' This exhortation became known as *Hunnenrede*, or the 'Hun speech'.

61. Luxemburg 1972, Vol. I/1, pp. 800–1. 'The protectionist era is connected with imperialism and reaction.' (Luxemburg 1972, Vol. I/1, p. 804). During debates over a resolution on world policy submitted by Paul Singer, differences emerged over whether imperialism was a policy of 'reaction' or represented 'perhaps the last stage of development of capitalism', as the delegate from Karlsruhe, Anton Fendrich, put it. Sozialdemokratische Partei Deutschlands 1900, *Protokoll über die Verhandlungen des Parteitages abgehalten zu Mainz vom 17. bis 21. September 1900*, p. 166.

62. Sozialdemokratische Partei Deutschlands 1900, *Protokoll über die Verhandlungen des Parteitages abgehalten zu Mainz vom 17. bis 21. September 1900*, pp. 166–7. Ledebour criticised Bernstein, Max Schippel and the other *Sozialistische Monatshefte* writers as 'half-and-half supporters of such imperialism in our ranks'. Sozialdemokratische Partei Deutschlands 1900, *Protokoll über die Verhandlungen des Parteitages abgehalten zu Mainz vom 17. bis 21. September 1900*, p. 167.

principal causes were twofold: in the specific case of Germany, there was the military thirst for glory and the chauvinist passion of creating a 'Greater Germany', but, in more general terms, the resolution also spoke of capitalism's inherent contradictions and the resulting imperative to 'find new opportunities of investing' and to 'open up new markets for sales'. Imperialism [*Weltpolitik*] was condemned as a 'policy of overseas conquest and robbery' that brutalised indigenous peoples and threatened new international conflicts through an 'intolerable' arms-race on land and sea. The delegates at Mainz repudiated Germany's intervention in China and declared that military conquest could never be regarded as an instrument of civilisation:

> Social Democracy, as the enemy of any oppression and exploitation of men by men, protests most emphatically against this policy of robbery and conquest. It demands that the desirable and necessary cultural and commercial relations between all peoples of the earth be carried out in such a way that the rights, freedoms and independence of these peoples be respected and protected, and that they be won over for the tasks of modern culture and civilisation only by means of education and example. The methods employed at present by the bourgeoisie and the military rulers of all nations are a bloody mockery of culture and civilisation.[63]

The International Socialist Congress at Paris (23–7 September 1900)

Just days after the SPD party congress at Mainz, the same issues resurfaced at the fifth International Socialist Congress, held in Paris on 23–7 September, 1900.[64] According to the official record of the Congress, Rosa Luxemburg reported on the question of 'international peace, militarism, and suppression of standing armies. Citizen Luxemburg made an indictment against militarism and imperialism.'[65] On this occasion, too, Luxemburg warned that workers faced a 'new phenomenon of world policy' that 'in the last six years has brought about four bloody wars'. Its symptoms were everywhere identical:

63. Sozialdemokratische Partei Deutschlands 1900, *Protokoll über die Verhandlungen des Parteitages abgehalten zu Mainz vom 17. bis 21. September 1900*, p. 245: Resolution zum Referat über Weltpolitik.
64. International Socialist Congress 1901.
65. International Socialist Congress 1901, p. 94.

'The same militarism, naval policy, the same hunt for colonies, the same reaction everywhere, and above all a permanent international war danger or at least a condition of permanent animosity, in which all the important developed states are equally entangled.' The proletariat had to 'set against the alliance of imperialist reaction an international protest movement', not just to fight against militarism but also because 'it appears increasingly probable that *the collapse of the capitalist order* will be brought about, not by an economic, but by a *political* crisis, by world policy'.[66] Luxemburg's resolution, acclaimed by the Paris Congress, described imperialism as a *necessary* consequence of capitalism's newest contradictions, which brutalised the inhabitants of foreign lands and must be resisted in every manner by organised workers:

> Considering that the development of capitalism necessarily leads to colonial expansion, the cause of conflict among governments;
>
> That imperialism, which is its necessary consequence, excites chauvinism in all countries and forces them to make ever-growing outlays for militarism;
>
> That the colonial policy of the bourgeoisie has no other goal than to increase the profits of the capitalist class and maintain the capitalist system, squandering the blood and the product of the proletariat's labour, perpetrating countless crimes and cruelties towards the natives of the colonies conquered by armed force;
>
> The International Socialist Congress of Paris declares:
>
> That the organised proletariat must use all the means at its disposal to struggle against the colonial expansion of the bourgeoisie and must condemn, under all circumstances and with all its forces, the injustices and cruelties that necessarily take place in all parts of the world left at the mercy of rapacious, ruthless and shameless capitalism.
>
> With that aim, the congress recommends in particular the following measures:

---

66. Luxemburg 1972, vol. I/1, pp. 807–9, emphasis in the original. In her later book *The Accumulation of Capital*, Luxemburg would reverse this order of causality entirely to emphasise instead the *economic* contradictions of imperialism. In his report on the Paris Congress, Belfort Bax remarked that 'the great practical problem before Social Democracy at the present moment is the combating of imperialism in all countries in the interests of international solidarity.' (Bax 1900, p. 4.)

1.. That the different socialist parties, wherever economic conditions permit, apply themselves most urgently to the study of the colonial question.
2.. That everything possible be done to further the formation of socialist parties in the colonies, affiliated to the metropolitan organisations.
3.. The establishment of ties and close collaboration between the socialist parties of the different colonies.[67]

Analysing the Paris Congress for *Nieuwe Tijd*, the Dutch socialist Henriette Roland Holst commented that this resolution finally proved 'there is not, and cannot be, an imperialist minority in Social Democracy'.[68] Her remark was clearly directed against Bernstein, whose own conclusions were quite the opposite. In an article criticising the resolutions adopted at both Mainz and Paris, Bernstein remarked that their tone reminded him of his earlier exchange with Belfort Bax.[69] He also favourably quoted George Bernard Shaw's recent pamphlet on *Fabianism and the Empire*, which claimed that the British Empire could not be conducted on 'fixed-frontier ideals'.[70] Shaw added that 'if the Chinese themselves cannot establish order in our sense, the Powers must establish it for them'. Shaw's one worry was that 'if we meddle with China, and our interference does not relieve the poverty that produces emigration, we shall find ourselves in a Yellow Muddle that may bring the Chinese War into our own streets'.[71]

The next major forum for debating the issue of colonialism came at the Dresden Congress of the SPD, held on 13–20 September 1903, at which the party officially condemned Bernstein's revisionism and pledged 'to carry on more vigorously than ever the fight against militarism, against the colonial and imperialist policy, against injustice, oppression and exploitation of every kind'.[72] The Sixth International Socialist Congress, held in Amsterdam on 14–20 August 1904, also adopted a resolution that condemned colonialism

67. Internationaler Sozialistenkongress vom 23. bis 27. September 1900 in Paris, Resolution zur Kolonialpolitik, in Institut für Marxismus-Leninismus 1975 (ed.), Band IV: März 1898–Juli 1914, 1975, p. 61.
68. Henriette Roland Holst, 'Het Vde International Soc. dem. Kongres', *Nieuwe Tijd*, V (1900), pp. 290–1, quoted in Hansen 1973, p. 88, note 22.
69. Bernstein 1900c.
70. Shaw (ed.) 1900, p. 3.
71. Shaw (ed.) 1900, pp. 47 and 49.
72. De Leon 1904, pp. 96–7.

and was modelled on the SPD's Dresden resolution.[73] But colonial expansion became a far more immediate political issue, both for the SPD and for international socialism, following the German 'Hottentot elections' of 1907, which brought a disastrous setback for Social Democracy.

The 'Hottentot elections' in Germany (13 January 1907)

The Reichstag elections of January 1907 were conducted against the background of a colonial war and genocide in German South-West Africa (present-day Namibia), in which some 65,000 Hereros were massacred by German troops from 1904 to 1908.[74] Rosa Luxemburg later spoke of 'a paroxysm of imperialistic enthusiasm' and a 'spiritual pogrom atmosphere' that produced an earthquake in the otherwise placid life of the German party.[75] Although the SPD received 3,259,029 votes – almost a quarter of a million more than its total in the previous election of 1903 – the government mobilised large numbers of previously indifferent citizens by whipping up nationalist enthusiasm in support of colonial appropriations. The number of voters rose dramatically from 76.1% of those eligible in 1903 to 84.7% four years later. According to Nicholas Stargardt, 'the Herero uprising in West Africa in 1906 played a similarly polarising role in Germany to the Boer War in Britain'.[76] The SPD suffered severely from the surge of patriotic emotion, losing almost half of its Reichstag representatives (falling from 81 to 43 seats).

Karl Kautsky worried, with good reason, that the ruling class had countered the appeal of socialism with 'the fascinating effect of the colonial state of the future'.[77] In his preface to *Militarism and Anti-Militarism*, written seventeen days after the elections, Karl Liebknecht similarly remarked that the 'farcical elections' of 1907 had been fought 'over national cant, over colonial cant, and over chauvinism and imperialism', revealing 'how miserably weak'

73. International Socialist Congress 1976–85, tomes 14–15: VII. Congrès socialiste international, Amsterdam 14–20 août 1904 (see the Dutch revisionist Henri van Kol's report and draft resolution on colonial policy on pp. 36–63). See also van Kol's assessment of the Amsterdam Congress in van Kol 1904.

74. Drechsler 1980.

75. Luxemburg 1919, p. 40.

76. Stargardt 1994, p. 58.

77. Kautsky 1907, p. 588, quoted in Schorske 1970, p. 63. For a revisionist assessment of the elections see Calwer 1907.

was 'the resistance of the German people to the pseudo-patriotic rat-traps' laid by the 'contemptible business patriots'.[78] Seven years later, with the outbreak of WWI, the implications of these remarks would become dramatically obvious as workers everywhere rushed to the colours in the name of national defence.

In terms of the developing literature on imperialism, the German elections of 1907 also led to a major study by Parvus, *Colonial Policy and the Collapse*, two chapters of which we have included in this volume. Despite the major setback, Parvus confidently maintained that the world system of imperialism would be brought down by its own contradictions. The Kaiser and the bourgeoisie had presented their imperialist ambitions as a matter of 'national honour'. Parvus replied that 'If there is any matter of national honour involved, then in our opinion it can only be to keep our hands off these disgraceful proceedings.'[79]

The debate on colonialism at the Stuttgart Congress (18–24 August 1907)

Parvus published his book with a view to the International Socialist Congress that was scheduled to meet in Stuttgart in August 1907. Following the electoral reversal suffered in Germany, delegates were deeply divided at Stuttgart, and most German representatives quickly forgot the resolution against colonialism adopted in Paris just seven years earlier. The majority of them now supported a motion by the Dutch revisionist Henri van Kol, who thought colonial policy should not be condemned in principle because it could still play a civilising role – if not today under capitalism, then tomorrow under socialism. A minority in the congress commission, led by Georg Ledebour and including Polish and Russian delegates, replied that a 'socialist colonial policy' was nothing more than a contradiction in terms, to which right-wing members responded that Ledebour had a 'barren, negative' attitude and no 'practical' programme.

78. Liebknecht 1907, p. VI. On the Hottentot elections, see further the introduction to Chapter 21.

79. See Chapter 21 in this volume.

A draft-resolution, supported by the commission majority, proposed revising the anti-imperialist decision taken at Paris in 1900 at Rosa Luxemburg's prompting. That meeting had declared that 'the organised proletariat must use all the means at its disposal to struggle against the colonial expansion of the bourgeoisie and must condemn, under all circumstances and with all its forces, the injustices and cruelties that necessarily take place in all parts of the world left at the mercy of rapacious, ruthless and shameless capitalism'. This formulation was now to be replaced with the statement that 'Socialism strives to develop the productive forces of the entire globe and to lead all peoples to the highest form of civilisation. The congress therefore does not reject in principle every colonial policy. Under a socialist régime, colonisation could be a force for civilisation.'

In the debate over this new proposal, Henri van Kol posed as a mature politician who, like Bernstein, no longer 'believed in the theory of capitalist collapse'. Taking the long view – that is, assuming that the end of capitalism was nowhere in sight – he announced that colonies were necessary to relieve Europe's overpopulation and overproduction (although he also noted that two wars had already originated with colonial policy, so that 'the first duty of Social Democracy is to turn against imperialism, as the English workers fought against Chamberlain's imperialism').[80] His fellow revisionist, Bernstein, agreed (to calls of *Bravo!*) that

> we should not adopt a purely negative position on the colonial policy, but practice a positive socialist colonial policy. We must relinquish the utopian idea of simply abandoning the colonies. The ultimate consequence of such a view would be to give the United States back to the Indians [*Commotion*]. The colonies are here. Certain tutelage of the uncivilised peoples by the civilised ones is a necessity which also the socialists should acknowledge.[81]

Speaking for the minority view, Georg Ledebour opposed 'above all the first sentence of the majority resolution, which recognises in principle the need of colonies'. As for Bernstein, Ledebour remarked:

80. International Socialist Congress 1907, pp. 27–8. English passages in Riddell (ed.) 1984, pp. 10–14.
81. International Socialist Congress 1907, pp. 28–9.

> I remember that Bernstein, together with some Fabians and English socialists, sided with the English Jingoes during the Boer War [*Hear! Hear!*]. He was even more imperialistic than the English Liberals. He stood for the subjugation of Transvaal by England, like that comrade [Robert] Blatchford, who every evening during the Boer War wanted his daughter to play *Rule Britannia* on the piano [*Laughter*].[82]

Karski [Julian Marchlewski], a delegate from the Polish SDKPiL and author of several articles on imperialism, some of which have been included in this book, agreed with Ledebour that a socialist colonial policy was self-contradictory: 'one can speak as little about a socialist colonial policy as about a socialist state. [The revisionist Eduard] David has asserted the right of one nation to exercise tutelage over another. But we Poles know the real meaning of this tutelage, since both the Russian tsar and the Prussian government have acted as our guardians [*Very good!*].' In wake of the debate over permanent revolution during the Russian Revolution of 1905, it was noteworthy that Karski-Marchlewski also rejected the claim 'that every nation must go through capitalism.... What Marx said was that countries that had already begun capitalist development would have to continue the process through to completion. But he never said that this was an absolute precondition for all nations.' Responding to Bernstein, he added: 'We socialists understand that there are other civilisations besides simply that of capitalist Europe. We have absolutely no grounds to be conceited about our so-called civilisation or to impose it on the Asiatic peoples with their ancient civilisation.'[83]

During the debates at Stuttgart, Karl Kautsky also opposed the majority of delegates from his own party, wondering how the 'complete logical contradiction' of a socialist colonial policy could possibly command so many supporters:

> Until now we have never heard anything about a socialist colonial policy.... Colonial policy signifies the conquest and seizure by force of an overseas land. I contest the notion that democracy and social policy have anything to do with conquest and foreign rule [*Bravo!*].... Bernstein wants to persuade us that the policy of conquest is a natural necessity. I am quite astonished that he defended here the theory that there are two groups of peoples, one

82. International Socialist Congress 1907, pp. 29–30.
83. International Socialist Congress 1907, pp. 32–3.

> destined to rule and the other to be ruled, that there are people who are like children and incapable of governing themselves. That is only a variation of the old refrain, which is the foundation of all despotism, that some people are born into this world to be riders, with spurs on their feet, and others with saddles on their backs to carry them. That has always been the argumentation of every aristocracy; it was also the argumentation of the slave-holders in the American South, who said that culture rested on the forced labour of the slaves, and that the country would relapse into barbarism if slavery were abolished. We cannot adopt such an argumentation.[84]

Algie Simons, representing the Socialist Party of America,[85] took the identical view in light of the American experience in the Philippines: 'For us Americans the colonial question is extremely important, because we stand at the beginning of a new American colonial policy.' Simons denounced the brutal suppression of the Filipino Rebellion, in which an estimated 250,000 Filipinos had been killed: 'To be sure, America has sent a whole army of schoolteachers to the Philippines, but also [far] more soldiers and cannons. It has wrought a bloodbath in the Philippines at the service of civilisation [*Hear! Hear!*].... The resolution of the majority is in our view nothing but a vote in favour of Roosevelt.'[86]

When Henri van Kol returned to the podium, he again spoke in favour of socialist colonial policy and criticised Kautsky for upholding

> the thesis that colonial policy is conquest, is 'imperialism'. This formula is completely false. You should learn better grammar! Today, to be sure, colonial policy is imperialist, but it does not have to be so, it can be democratic as well. In any case it is a grave error on Kautsky's part to equate colonial policy conceptually with imperialism.... If we Europeans go there [to Africa] with tools and machines, we would be defenceless victims of the natives. Therefore we must go there with weapons in hand, even if Kautsky calls that imperialism.[87]

---

84. International Socialist Congress 1907, pp. 34–5.
85. The Socialist Party of America, formed in 1901 by a merger of the Social-Democratic Party of America with dissidents from the Socialist Labor Party, ran Eugene Debs as its presidential candidate against Theodore Roosevelt in 1904.
86. International Socialist Congress 1907, p. 35.
87. International Socialist Congress 1907, p. 37. The Congress witnessed other racist tirades, notably the American delegate Morris Hillquit's argument in favour of the

After long debate, Kautsky and his supporters prevailed. In its final resolution, the full congress resolved to strike the original sentence of the draft and to replace it with the following four paragraphs:

> The congress considers that by its inherent nature, capitalist colonial policy must lead to enslavement, forced labour, or the extermination of the native population of the colonised regions.
>
> The civilising mission that capitalist society claims to serve is no more than a veil for its lust for conquest and exploitation. Only socialist society will offer the possibility to all peoples of fully developing civilisation.
>
> Capitalist colonial policy, instead of increasing the world's productive forces, destroys the wealth of those countries where this policy is carried out by enslaving and impoverishing the native peoples as well as by waging murderous and devastating wars. It thus slows down and hinders even the development of trade and the export of industrial products of the civilised states.
>
> The congress condemns the barbaric methods of capitalist colonisation. In the interests of the development of the productive forces it demands a policy that guarantees peaceful, cultural development and that puts the natural resources of the earth at the service of the further development of all of humanity.[88]

Reflecting upon the 'extremely heated debate' at Stuttgart, in October 1907 Lenin summarised the proceedings this way for readers of the Russian newspaper *Proletary*:

> The opportunists rallied behind van Kol. Speaking for the majority of the German delegation Bernstein and David urged acceptance of a 'socialist colonial policy' and fulminated against the radicals for their barren, negative attitude.... [T]hey were opposed by Kautsky, who felt compelled to ask the Congress to pronounce *against* the majority of the German delegation. He rightly pointed out that there was no question of rejecting the struggle for reforms.... The point at issue was whether we should make concessions

legal restriction of Asian immigration into the United States. International Socialist Congress 1907, pp. 36–7.

88. Internationaler Sozialistenkongress vom 18. bis 24. August 1907 in Stuttgart, Resolution zur Kolonialpolitik, in Institut für Marxismus-Leninismus 1975 (ed.), pp. 212–13.

> to the modern regime of bourgeois plunder and violence. The Congress was to discuss present-day colonial policy, which was based on the downright enslavement of primitive populations. The bourgeoisie was actually introducing slavery in the colonies and subjecting the native populations to unprecedented outrages and acts of violence, 'civilising' them by the spread of liquor and syphilis. And in that situation socialists were expected to utter evasive phrases about the possibility of accepting colonial policy in principle! That would be an outright desertion to the bourgeois point of view.[89]

Though the Congress defeated the commission's original motion by 128 votes to 108 (with ten abstentions), presumably laying to rest the notion of capitalism's civilising mission, Lenin noted that the result was only due to the combined vote of delegates from small nations. Elsewhere, 'even the proletariat has been somewhat infected with the lust of conquest'. In a remark that foreshadowed his later account of the 'labour-aristocracy' in *Imperialism: The Highest Stage of Capitalism,* Lenin worried that Stuttgart had 'revealed a negative feature in the European labour movement', one that he attributed to 'socialist opportunism', 'bourgeois blandishments', and the privileged position of European workers in relation to 'the practically enslaved natives in the colonies'.[90]

Militarism and national defence at the Stuttgart Congress (August 1907)

The Stuttgart Congress debated a number of other issues in August 1907, including women's suffrage, emigration and immigration, and relations of socialist parties with the trade-unions. Apart from the question of colonialism, however, the most important resolution for present purposes dealt with anti-militarism. If imperialism was now linked inseparably with aggression and conquest in the interest of capitalist exploitation, it seemed obvious that use of military power must be just as forcefully condemned. The problem was that Marx and Engels had never been pacifists; they enthusiastically supported the defensive struggle of the Paris Communards against the government of Thiers following France's defeat in 1871 by Bismarck's Germany.

89. Lenin 1907, p. 76.
90. Lenin 1907, pp. 76–7.

Drawing upon revolutionary traditions dating back to the eighteenth century, they called for replacement of the standing army by the 'armed people' in the form of a permanent citizens' militia.

At the Suttgart Congress, such qualifications escaped the notice of Gustave Hervé, a Frenchman who submitted one of four resolutions on the subject of militarism. Lenin reported to his Russian readers that 'The notorious Hervé, who has made such a noise in France and Europe, advocated a semi-anarchist view by naively suggesting that every war be "answered" by a strike and an uprising.'[91] Hervé was a curious, even bizarre figure. He moved from semi-anarchism at Stuttgart to defence of 'the fatherland in danger' by 1914, and, ultimately, to admiration of Hitler and Mussolini in the 1930s.[92] This was Hervé's first encounter with the international socialist leadership, and his resolution seems to have been intended deliberately to pique the Germans. He regarded reformism as a peculiarly German vice and associated the SPD with 'authoritarianism, a bureaucratic mentality, materialism, conformism and a lack of revolutionary zeal'.[93]

The SPD, shaken by its recent electoral setback, had no intention of committing itself to a general strike in the event of war. As August Bebel put it, 'we must not allow ourselves to be pressured into using methods of struggle that could gravely threaten the activity and, under certain circumstances, the very existence of the party'.[94] In his clash with Hervé, Bebel invoked the notion of patriotic self-defence: 'Hervé says: "The fatherland is the fatherland of the ruling classes. It is not a concern of the proletariat." A similar idea is expressed in the *Communist Manifesto* which says: "The proletariat has no fatherland." But Marx's and Engels' students have declared that they no longer share the views of the *Manifesto*.'[95]

While Hervé addressed the question of war in class-terms, Bebel insisted that Social Democracy must determine its attitude towards any future war on the basis of whether it was aggressive or defensive: 'I maintain that it is easy now to determine in any given case whether a war is defensive, or whether it is aggressive in character. While previously the causes leading to

91. Lenin 1907, p. 79.
92. See Loughlin 2003.
93. Loughlin 2003, p. 523.
94. International Socialist Congress 1907, p. 83, Riddell (ed.) 1984, p. 26.
95. International Socialist Congress 1907, p. 82, Riddell (ed.) 1984, p. 24.

the catastrophe of war remained obscure even to the trained and observant politician, today that is no longer the case. War has ceased to be a secret matter of cabinet politics.' Besides, in purely practical terms Hervé's antimilitarist agitation and tactics were 'not just impossible but totally beyond discussion' for the SPD. 'The case of Karl Liebknecht shows how things stand today in Germany. Even though he clearly expressed his differences with Hervé in his book [*Militarism and Anti-Militarism*], and stated that Hervé's methods are unworkable, Liebknecht has been charged with high treason.'[96]

Hervé retorted that Bebel's support for national defence in case of a war of aggression against Germany would enable the German government to manipulate the SPD into a patriotic position in the event of an all-out European conflict:

> Bebel draws a fine distinction between offensive and defensive wars. When tiny Morocco is carved up, this is easily recognised as an offensive war of unconcealed brutality. But should war break out between the great powers, the only too powerful capitalist press will unleash such a storm of nationalism that we will not have the strength to counteract it. Then it will be too late to make your fine distinction.[97]

Holding the leadership of the SPD in contempt, Hervé explicitly attributed its weakness – dramatised in the 'Hottentot elections' – to its growing commitment to parliamentarism rather than revolutionary struggle:

> You have now become an electoral and accounting machine, a party of cash registers and parliamentary seats. You want to conquer the world with ballots. But I ask you: When the German soldiers are sent off to re-establish the throne of the Russian tsar, when Prussia and France attack the proletarians, what will you do? Please do not answer with metaphysics and dialectics, but openly and clearly, practically and tactically, what will you do?[98]

The SPD's resistance to antimilitarist agitation, he declared, would eventually lead it to 'go to war for your Kaiser, without offering any resistance': 'Today Bebel went over to the revisionists when he told us: "Proletarians of all

96. International Socialist Congress 1907, p. 82, Riddell (ed.) 1984, p. 25.
97. International Socialist Congress 1907, p. 84, Riddell (ed.) 1984, p. 25.
98. International Socialist Congress 1907, p. 84, Riddell (ed.) 1984, p. 27.

countries, murder each other!" [*Loud commotion*].'[99] In a final flourish, Hervé shouted to the infuriated August Bebel: 'Follow the flag of your Emperor, yes follow it. But if you enter France, you will see floating over our insurrectional communes the red flag of the International which you will have betrayed.'[100]

Hervé contributed flamboyant rhetoric to the Stuttgart meeting, but the final resolution of the Congress was more temperate. It began by endorsing 'the resolutions adopted by previous international congresses against militarism and imperialism'. Among other things, it reiterated the call for 'substitution of the people's militia for the standing army', a theme the left wing would later champion in opposing Kautsky's proposals for disarmament and international arbitration-courts. The unanimously adopted final resolution also tactfully ignored Bebel's distinction between 'aggressive' and 'defensive' wars, declaring that 'In case war should break out', socialists were duty bound 'to intervene for its speedy termination and to strive with all their power to utilize the economic and political crisis created by the war to rouse the masses and thereby hasten the downfall of capitalist class rule'.[101] In his report to Russian readers, Lenin emphasised the latter provision, commenting that Hervé had forgotten the proletariat's obligation to take up arms in the event of a revolutionary war: 'The essential thing is not merely to prevent war, but to utilise the crisis created by war in order to hasten the overthrow of the bourgeoisie.'[102]

In his book *German Social Democracy, 1905–1917*, the historian Carl Schorske summarised the role of SPD-representatives at the Stuttgart Congress by noting that on the two major issues – imperialism and militarism – the shattering experience of the 'Hottentot elections' was the decisive factor providing 'the external impetus for the accommodation of Social Democracy to the facts

---

99. International Socialist Congress 1907, p. 84, Riddell (ed.) 1984, p. 28. On Hervé see further Chapter 51, note 11.

100. Herve Quoted by Loughlin 2003, p. 522. Loughlin also reports (p. 523) that following this encounter at Stuttgart, Hervé summarised his experience as follows: 'I was excited at meeting personally German Social Democracy which I for years had only known and dismissed with a shrug of the shoulders, from its quibbling hair-splitting quarrels about the exegesis of Karl Marx. Now I've seen the German proletarians in the streets of Stuttgart. My naïve illusions are destroyed; they are all good, contented, and satisfied bourgeois.'

101. Stuttgart Resolution on 'Militarism and International Conflicts', in Joll 1974, pp. 206–8.

102. Lenin 1907, p. 80.

of life in the era of imperialism'. The powerful German trade-unions were 'the primary agency' pressing for moderation and peaceful social reform, which implied avoidance of any provocation to the powers that be. Behind the Stuttgart deliberations stood 'the triple alliance of trade-unionists, party revisionists, and party executive who pushed back the German radicals on the questions of war and colonialism as they had earlier defeated them on domestic tactic'.[103]

The debate on militarism and national defence at Essen (September 1907)

Despite the decisions taken at Stuttgart, the dispute over militarism and national defence resumed shortly afterwards at the SPD-congress held in Essen during 15–21 September 1907. The *Parteitag* met against the background of Karl Liebknecht's impending trial for statements contained in his pamphlet *Militarism and Anti-Militarism*.[104] The focus of renewed dispute was an address that Gustav Noske had made in the Reichstag on 25 April 1907, when debating Germany's military budget. Noske, who in January 1919, as self-appointed 'bloodhound' against the German revolutionaries, would be responsible for the murder of Karl Liebknecht and Rosa Luxemburg by the right-wing Free Corps, had argued that SPD representatives were not 'vagabonds without a fatherland'. He added: 'We wish Germany to be as able to defend itself [or to be as well armed, *wehrhaft*] as possible, we wish the whole German people to have an interest in the military establishment, which is necessary for the defence of our fatherland.'[105] At the Essen Congress Noske repeated this patriotic stand and quoted an earlier but still famous speech by Bebel. On 7 March 1904, Bebel had declared in the Reichstag that in a 'war of aggression', in which Germany's existence may be at stake, 'we will all, to the last man, even

103. Schorske 1970, p. 85.

104. Liebknecht's trial began on 9 October 1907 and lasted three days: the Imperial High Court found him guilty of advocating the abolition of the standing army and sentenced him to 18 months of imprisonment for high treason.

105. Quoted in Schorske 1970, p. 77. The Prussian war minister, Count Karl von Einem, rejoiced at this protestation of patriotism: 'I accept the assurance of the previous speaker, that the Social-Democratic Party is decided, in case of a war of aggression against the German Reich, to defend it with the same loyalty and devotion as the other parties.' *Vorwärts* (26 April 1907), cited by Paul Lensch in Sozialdemokratische Partei Deutschlands 1907, p. 263.

the oldest amongst us, be ready to take the rifles upon our backs and defend our German soil, not for your sake but for our own, and if necessary in spite of you. We live and struggle in this soil, for this fatherland, which is as much our fatherland, perhaps even more so, than yours.'[106]

The left wing of the Party emphatically rejected the patriotic attitude of Noske and Bebel. Paul Lensch, editor of the *Leipziger Volkszeitung*, argued that Bebel's readiness to 'shoulder a rifle' for national defence 'was correct fifty years ago, but today it is absolutely false' because the international political situation had changed completely:

> In the meantime an event has happened which Noske doesn't seem to have noticed – namely the Russian Revolution [of 1905]. As a result, Russian tsarism has been eliminated as an arch-enemy, as an effective enemy; it lies shattered on the ground. Russian militarism is no longer able to wage a large European war.... Due to this changed situation, the sharpest protest must be raised against those views, which are today as reactionary as they were formerly revolutionary.[107]

Karl Liebknecht also attributed the views of Noske and Bebel to 'the depressing effects of the election results', arguing that 'Noske has been most strongly taken in by the nationalist fuss made during the election campaign'. Liebknecht wondered at the fact that Noske's speech did not contain 'a single syllable about international solidarity, as if the tasks of Social Democracy stopped at Germany's border!'[108]

In his own speech at Essen, Bebel backed Noske and reaffirmed that

> we must defend the fatherland if it is attacked. In connection with this, I have been asked – and Comrade Kautsky, too, has harped upon this string – 'What is an aggressive war?' Well, it would be very sad if today, when larger and larger circles of the people are interested in everyday politics, we could still not judge in each particular case whether we are

106. August Bebel's speech to the Reichstag of 7 March, 1904. Reichstag 1904, *Stenographische Berichte über die Verhandlungen des Reichstags. XI. Legislaturperiode. I. Session, erster Sessionsabschnitt*, 1903/1904, Zweiter Band, p. 1588C (for the full text of Bebel's speech see pp. 1583C–1592A).

107. Sozialdemokratische Partei Deutschlands 1907, *Protokoll über die Verhandlungen des Parteitages abgehalten zu Essen vom. 15. bis 21. September 1907*, p. 233.

108. Sozialdemokratische Partei Deutschlands 1907, *Protokoll über die Verhandlungen des Parteitages abgehalten zu Essen vom. 15. bis 21. September 1907*, pp. 246–7.

> confronting a war of aggression or not. A deception in such a matter might have been possible in the 1870s, but is no longer possible today.

Bebel repeated that he was ready to 'shoulder his gun' if it came to war with Russia, 'the enemy of all culture and of all the oppressed, not only in her own country, but also the most dangerous enemy of Europe, and especially for us Germans'.[109]

Bebel's main critic at Essen was Karl Kautsky, whose speech Trotsky approvingly quoted after the outbreak of WWI in his work *The War and the International*.[110] Kautsky skilfully dismissed the question of aggressive and defensive war by arguing that workers had no responsibility to defend the fatherland unless 'a proletarian and democratic interest is in danger':

> Let us think for example of Morocco. Yesterday the German government was aggressive, tomorrow the French government will be, and we can't know whether the day after tomorrow the English government will be. That changes continuously. Morocco, however, is not worth the blood of a single proletarian. If a war were to break out over Morocco, we should reject it decisively, even if we were attacked. Indeed, a war wouldn't be a national but an international question for us, because a war between the great powers will become a world war, it would concern the whole of Europe and not only two countries. Some day the German government might make the German proletarians believe they were being attacked; the French government might do the same with the French proletarians, and we would then have a war in which the French and German workingmen would follow their respective governments with equal enthusiasm and murder each other and cut each other's throats. That must be avoided, and it will be avoided if we do not adopt the criterion of the aggressive war, but that of proletarian interests, which at the same time are international interests.... The German workers are united with the French workers, and not with the German war-mongers and Junkers.[111]

---

109. Sozialdemokratische Partei Deutschlands 1907, *Protokoll über die Verhandlungen des Parteitages abgehalten zu Essen vom. 15. bis 21. September 1907*, pp. 254–5. According to Karl Retzlaw, the remark was constantly cited by German workers during the war and did 'inestimable damage' by providing an 'alibi' for defencism. Retzlaw 1972, p. 29 quoted in Craig Nation 1989, p. 252, note 44.

110. Trotsky 1918a, pp. 149–50.

111. Sozialdemokratische Partei Deutschlands 1907, *Protokoll über die Verhandlungen des Parteitages abgehalten zu Essen vom. 15. bis 21. September 1907*, pp. 261–2. In a letter

Although Kautsky hoped to settle the matter by replacing the question of who started a war with the higher principle of 'a proletarian and democratic interest', years later the debate over war and defence of the fatherland still raged in the pages of left-wing SPD newspapers. To represent that ongoing dispute, we have included in this anthology an article entitled 'Social Democracy and Foreign Policy', published anonymously in the *Leipziger Volkszeitung* in December 1912, whose authorship we have tentatively ascribed to the editor of that journal, Paul Lensch. The article argued that the main task of German workers was to fight German imperialism rather than any foreign country. Lensch rejected the binding character of all alliances and treaties between capitalist states, particularly the Triple Alliance, as well as Bebel's distinction between aggressive and defensive wars. The only guarantee of peace, he claimed, was the bourgeois fear that war would bring revolution. Lensch also cautioned that German Social Democrats could never call upon German workers to take up arms against Russia because 'the International would be torn apart in that way'.[112]

The debate on colonialism at Essen (September 1907)

The Essen Congress of the German Social-Democratic Party showed that the unanimously adopted Stuttgart resolution on militarism had left a great deal of unfinished business. This was equally true of the other major issue debated at Stuttgart, the question of colonialism and its relation to both socialism and imperialism. In Essen, Paul Singer reported on the Stuttgart international congress and tried to diminish the differences expressed there over socialist colonial policy as merely 'a struggle over words'.[113] August Bebel also attempted

---

written on 25 September 1909 to the American socialist writer Upton Sinclair in rather awkward English, Kautsky further said: 'You may be sure there will never come the day when German socialists will ask their followers to take arms for the fatherland.... If there will be war today, it won't be a war for the defence of the fatherland, it will be one for imperialistic purposes, and such a war will find the whole socialist party of Germany in energetic opposition. That we may promise. But we can't go on so far and promise this opposition shall take the form of insurrection or general strike, if necessary, nor can we promise that our opposition will in every case be strong enough to prevent war.' Archiv des Vereins für Geschichte der Arbeiterbewegung, Wien. Quoted in Steinberg 1972, p. 26.

112. Lensch 1912c. See Chapter 41.

113. Sozialdemokratische Partei Deutschlands 1907, *Protokoll über die Verhandlungen des Parteitages abgehalten zu Essen vom. 15. bis 21. September 1907*, pp. 266–7.

to cover the tracks of the majority of the German delegation at Stuttgart, affirming that 'on this question there can be no serious differences' and dismissing the whole debate as 'hair splitting [*ein Streit um des Kaisers Bart*]': 'I consider the struggle over whether a socialist colonial policy is possible to be a totally idle struggle that is not worth the time and paper spent on it.' Bebel thought the prospect of a socialist colonial policy merited no further discussion because it was mere 'music of the future'.[114]

The left wing had no intention of letting the issue go that easily. Heinrich Laufenberg pointed out that 'the position of the majority at Stuttgart', in support of a socialist colonial policy, was 'incompatible with the Mainz resolution' adopted by the German Party as early as 1900 and that there was 'a clear contradiction between the Stuttgart majority resolution and the resolution finally adopted'. When Georg Ledebour had objected at Stuttgart to socialist colonialism, he had been criticised for 'a negative standpoint leading to the idea of giving up the colonies'. Emanuel Wurm, a Reichstag deputy since 1890, now ironically declared that the charge against Ledebour had been absolutely correct. He clarified by adding: 'We want to give up our own colonies as well.'[115] Karl Liebknecht also demanded an answer as to why socialists should 'combine the dirty and bloody word "colonial policy" with the sacred word "Social Democratic"'. Liebknecht continued:

> We want to pursue a policy of civilisation, of culture! The watchword 'socialist colonial policy' is a contradiction in terms, because the word 'colony' already includes the concept of 'tutelage', 'domination', and 'dependency'. That the question under discussion is not a philological debate, that the word 'colonial policy' was meant in that sense by the main advocate of the resolution, van Kol, is demonstrated by his emphasis on the need to treat lower peoples like children if necessary, indeed to confront them by armed force. Therefore it was not just a mere struggle over words, but a sober earnest debate.[116]

114. Sozialdemokratische Partei Deutschlands 1907, *Protokoll über die Verhandlungen des Parteitages abgehalten zu Essen vom. 15. bis 21. September 1907*, pp. 271–2.
115. Sozialdemokratische Partei Deutschlands 1907, *Protokoll über die Verhandlungen des Parteitages abgehalten zu Essen vom. 15. bis 21. September 1907*, pp. 281–2.
116. Sozialdemokratische Partei Deutschlands 1907, *Protokoll über die Verhandlungen des Parteitages abgehalten zu Essen vom. 15. bis 21. September 1907*, pp. 282–3.

When Karl Kautsky joined the debate, he reiterated his own opposition to a socialist colonial policy: the idea that it was 'necessary that the more cultured peoples should wield control over less cultured ones' contradicted the SPD's Mainz resolution of 1900, which 'demanded independence of the peoples'.[117] It is noteworthy that he also denied an assertion by the revisionist Eduard David that 'the colonies must go through capitalism'. Leon Trotsky and Parvus had already acquired both fame and notoriety in Russia for the theory of permanent revolution. Having helped to initiate the Russian debate on that subject, Kautsky was convinced that backward societies could skip historical stages and arrive at socialism without any need of first enduring the tribulations of capitalism.[118]

Kautsky's *Socialism and Colonial Policy* and Bernstein's criticism

The final chapters of the Essen dispute over colonialism were written in a new clash between Kautsky and Bernstein. Kautsky sparked the exchange with his brochure *Socialism and Colonial Policy*, published in September 1907 in a large edition of 11,000 copies. The essay was written immediately after Stuttgart with the intention that it should appear before the SPD resumed discussions at Essen. Kautsky used the essay to explain at greater length the possibility of colonial peoples skipping historical stages. He posed the question this way: 'Do van Kol and David wish to assert that every people reached their present stage of development along precisely the same path, and had to pass through all the same earlier stages of development as other equally developed or more highly developed nations?'[119] He answered that one glance at colonial policy was sufficient to refute such an argument:

> Present day colonial policy, depending on the export of capital, is distinguished by the fact that it carries capitalist exploitation and capitalist production into all the colonies whatever their level of development. Therefore it can well be said that there is no colony which does not consequently jump over one or more stages of development.[120]

---

117. Ibid.
118. Sozialdemokratische Partei Deutschlands 1907, *Protokoll über die Verhandlungen des Parteitages abgehalten zu Essen vom. 15. bis 21. September 1907*, p. 290. See Kautsky's articles in Day and Gaido (eds.) 2009.
119. Kautsky 1907b, p. 56.
120. Kautsky 1907b, p. 57.

Kautsky added that backward nations had always learned from the more advanced, and they had often 'been able to leap with one bound over several stages of development which had been climbed wearily by their predecessors'. In that way, limitless variations arose in the development of different nations, 'and these variations increase the more the isolation of individual nations decreases, the more world trade develops, and thus the nearer we come to the modern era'.[121] It followed that 'spreading capitalism to backward countries is definitely not a requirement for the spread and victory of socialism'.[122] To argue otherwise was merely to subscribe to the sort of 'European pride and megalomania' that divided 'mankind into lower and higher races'.[123]

After explaining his own problematic distinction between progressive settlement-colonialism ('work-colonies') in temperate areas and mere occupation ('exploitation-colonies') in tropical and subtropical areas, he then turned explicitly to 'the *imperialist idea*' of 'creating an Empire, economically self-sufficient, sufficiently extensive to be able to produce all its own raw materials and to sell all its industrial products on its own markets, so that it is absolutely independent'. This ambition had 'arisen simultaneously with the rise of cartels, the new protective tariffs, the combination of militarism and naval arms-race, and the new colonial era since the 1880s'. It was also

> the offspring of the same economic situation that has increasingly transformed capitalism from a means of developing the greatest productivity of labour into a means of limiting this development. The higher the tariff barriers between the individual capitalist states grow, the more each of them feels the need to assure itself of a market which no one can exclude them from, and to gain supplies of raw material which no one can cut off.[124]

Hence the incessant 'drive for colonial expansion by the great states', the accelerating arms-race and 'the danger of a world war'.[125]

Kautsky's explanation of imperialism followed closely an earlier article written by Parvus in June 1907, 'Colonies and Capitalism in the Twentieth Century', which we have included in this anthology. Like Parvus, he traced the quest for colonies to underconsumption on the part of the working class,

---

121. Kautsky 1907b, p. 58.
122. Kautsky 1907b, p. 59.
123. Kautsky 1907b, p. 46.
124. Kautsky 1907b, p. 65.
125. Kautsky 1907b, p. 66.

beginning in the 1880s when the capitalist mode of production 'seemed to have reached the limit of its capacity for expansion, and therefore to have reached its end'.[126] But the capitalists had found new expedients to prolong their rule. The first was to limit foreign competition through protective tariffs and to suppress internal competition by means of cartels and trusts. A second was to dispose of surplus-production through unproductive consumption by the state – the arms-race and militarism. The third was to export capital to backward agricultural countries, particularly to the colonies. 'In other words, the capitalists do not export their products as commodities for *sale to* the foreign countries, but as *capital* for the *exploitation* of the foreign countries.'[127]

The main vehicle of capital-export, Kautsky explained, was railway-construction, transforming modern means of communication into 'means of extracting more products from poorer countries than before'. But so great were these expenditures, with the attendant non-productive costs of defending against colonial uprisings and capitalist competitors, that the total effect was nothing more than 'a method of wasting resources and causing impoverishment'.[128] Colonial expansion began as 'a means of prolonging the existence of capitalism', but its negative consequences meant that it ultimately benefited no one but heavy industry and the bankers.[129] On those grounds, socialists 'must support equally energetically all native colonial independence-movements. Our aim must be: the emancipation of the colonies; the independence of the nations inhabiting them.'[130]

Yet Kautsky still equivocated, pointing out that this objective might not be immediately practical, for in most cases colonial uprisings would prove hopeless. This left one 'main practical implication': to reject any extension of colonial possessions and to

> work zealously for an increase in the self-government of natives. The native uprisings to throw off foreign domination will be always certain of the sympathies of the fighting proletariat. But the armed might of the capitalist nations is so immense that it is not to be expected that any of these uprisings could come anywhere near their aim. As much as we understand such

126. Kautsky 1907b, p. 35.
127. Kautsky 1907b, p. 39.
128. Kautsky 1907b, p. 41.
129. Kautsky 1907b, p. 44.
130. Kautsky 1907b, p. 45.

> rebellions, and as deeply as we sympathise with the rebels, Social Democracy cannot encourage them, just as it does not support pointless proletarian putsches in Europe itself.[131]

As Bebel feared confronting the armed might of the capitalist state, so Kautsky believed military force narrowly circumscribed the possibility of resisting imperialism and limited the workers' parties to traditional pursuits in parliament.

The conclusion Kautsky reached was that the colonies must be regarded simply as a matter of fact: they were not about to be abandoned by the capitalists, they could not be endorsed by the proletariat, and they were unlikely to achieve independence by their own efforts. Gradual change was the most for which one could reasonably hope. When Kautsky reiterated these views in another article in *Vorwärts* on 5 October 1907,[132] Eduard Bernstein rose to the challenge with his own essay on 'The Colonial Question and the Class Struggle'.[133] At Stuttgart, Bernstein had likewise said 'the colonies are here' and would evidently be inherited by socialism. Now he repeated his support for colonialism, referring once again to 'the right of peoples with a higher culture over those with a lower culture'. The corollary was that 'a certain guardianship of the cultured peoples over the non-cultured peoples' remained a duty to humanity that socialists must positively embrace:

> ...the colonial question is.... a human issue and a cultural issue of the first order. It is the question of the spread of culture and, as long as there are big cultural differences, it is a question of the spread, or rather the assertion, of the higher culture. Because sooner or later it inevitably comes to pass that higher and lower cultures collide, and with regard to this collision, this struggle for existence between cultures, the colonial policy of the cultured peoples must be rated as an historical process. The fact that it is usually pursued from other motives and with means, as well as in forms that we Social Democrats condemn, may lead us in specific cases to reject it and fight

---

131. Kautsky 1907b, p. 76.
132. Kautsky 1907c.
133. Bernstein 1907b. On this occasion, Bernstein added another gratuitous racial comment, referring this time not to Native Americans, as he had at Stuttgart, but to the Chinese: 'I am the last to exaggerate the Mongol peril. But I am not for that reason blind to the advances of Mongolism [*Mongolentums*] and the problems it involves.' Bernstein 1907b, p. 996.

against it, but this cannot be a reason to change our judgement about the historical necessity of colonisation.[134]

Austro-Marxism and the national question

Attempts to conceptualise imperialism remained divided at this point between those who argued in 'cultural' terms and those who wanted imperialism to be seen as an emerging world system with its own political-economic imperatives. These two themes were most closely connected in the literature of 'Austro-Marxism', which eventually produced the first coherent works on imperialism by Otto Bauer and Rudolf Hilferding. Austrian Marxists saw that the debates over *Weltpolitik* articulated cultural prejudices that were already quite familiar in discussions of the 'nationality-question' in Central Europe. This was especially true in the multinational state of Austria-Hungary, with its Germans, Hungarians, Poles, Czechs, Ruthenians, Slovaks, Slovenes, Croats, Italians and other minorities, many of whom regarded themselves as 'colonials' within the Habsburg domain. On the other hand, the bourgeois parties often spoke of the Habsburg state as an outpost of culture and a pillar of order in face of the quarrelsome Balkan remnants of the Ottoman Empire. Given this array of competing 'national' interests, Austrian Social Democrats found themselves compelled to address the relationship between nationality and social class. While their comrades in the German SPD were occasionally tempted by the ambitions of a 'Greater Germany', Austro-Marxists struggled with the more immediate problem of merely keeping the homeland intact.

The Austrian Social Democratic Workers' Party (Sozialdemokratische Arbeiterpartei, SDAP), was established in 1889 under the leadership of Victor Adler. At its Vienna Congress in 1897, the Party transformed itself into a federation – a 'little international' as Adler called it – comprising German, Czech, Polish, Italian and South-Slav parties.[135] In its Brünner programme of September 1899, the SDAP rejected the right of oppressed minorities to secede from Austria-Hungary but endorsed claims to national-cultural autonomy (involving self-administered but not necessarily contiguous national entities

134. Bernstein 1907b, p. 989.

135. Victor Adler claimed in 1900 at the Fifth International Socialist Congress in Paris that 'we in Austria have a little International ourselves'. Joll 1974, p. 120.

with their own national parliaments, state secretaries, schools, etc.). After general suffrage for males was granted in 1907, Social Democrats scored a significant electoral success as a by-product of a general strike inspired by the Russian Revolution of 1905. In elections to the Reichsrat, the SDAP won 87 of 516 seats, becoming the second strongest group in parliament. Just three years later, however, the Party began to break apart when Czech socialists proclaimed their independence of the federated party.

The multinational empire of tsarist Russia faced the same nationality-issues as Austria-Hungary, only multiplied several times over. Within Russian Social Democracy, the Austro-Marxist nationality-programme was advocated by the Bund, a Jewish organisation opposing both assimilation and Zionist territorialism – although, ironically, Otto Bauer, the father of the idea, devoted an entire chapter of *The Question of Nationalities and Social Democracy* to arguing that the demand for 'cultural-national autonomy' could *not* be applied to Jews. Lenin also opposed the Bund's claim to be the exclusive representative of Russian Jews[136] while simultaneously denouncing Austrian Social Democrats on two grounds: first, for advocating transformation of Austria-Hungary into a federation of nationalities rather than supporting the right of oppressed nations to break away; and secondly, for adopting a federal rather than a unified party structure.[137]

Austrian Social Democrats failed to resolve the nationality-question, but their unique experience of what many considered to be domestic 'colonisation' did yield a particular 'Austro-Marxist' perspective on the broader question of imperialism. In the Habsburg domain, imperialism was already a fact of domestic political life. Shortly after the outbreak of WWI, Karl Renner,

136. Lenin's attitude towards the Jewish question shifted between endorsement of Kautsky's dictum: 'The Jews in Galicia and Russia are more of a caste than a nation, and attempts to constitute Jewry as a nation are attempts at preserving a caste' and Lenin's own definition of the Jewry as 'the only extra-territorial (not having its own territory) nation'. Lenin 1913c, p. 248, and Lenin 1913d, p. 506.

137. Lenin 1914a, p. 398. Trotsky also argued that 'despite all the thorough investigations undertaken at the beginning of the century, the [Austrian] Party never made the distinction between oppressed and oppressing nations, which was the key to Bolshevik nationality policies.' (Trotsky quoted in Löw 1986, p. 14 and Kuhn 2007, p. 28.) Roman Rosdolsky noted that Austrian Social Democracy 'loudly proclaimed its commitment to internationalism and the right of peoples to self-determination but in practice supported a policy that left *the decisive positions of state power in the hands of the German minority*'. Rosdolsky 1987, p. 184, quoted in Kuhn 2007, pp. 27–8, emphasis in the original.

leader of the Party's right wing, wrote in *Der Kampf*: 'It is no coincidence that the so-called Austro-Marxists Otto Bauer, Rudolf Hilferding and Karl Kautsky recognised first and analysed most sharply the most recent phase of capitalist development, national imperialism.'[138] Austro-Marxists were among the first to recognise that the methods used to 'protect' the domestic market, which included the subordinate areas of the national minorities, were a miniature replica of imperialism's methods on the world scale. Austro-Marxism became an identifiable tendency with the launch in 1904 of the *Marx-Studien* series, in which both Bauer's and Hilferding's books were later published, and with the appearance of its theoretical journal *Der Kampf* in 1907.[139]

Marx on capitalist crises and foreign markets

Nationality and culture, class and civilisation, militarism and self-defence, underconsumption and capital-exports – all of these themes recurred continuously in early Social-Democratic attempts to conceptualise imperialism's causes and consequences. Further complicating these issues was the overriding concern of party establishments to tailor resolutions to an electoral context in which empire was associated by many voters not merely with

138. Renner 1915, p. 10, quoted in Leser 1968, p. 174. Although Karl Kautsky belonged to an older generation, lived in Germany and worked for the SPD, he was raised and educated in Vienna and after 1910 became leader of the Social-Democratic centre-faction, whose main theorists were Austro-Marxists.

139. In his study of Austro-Marxism, Norbert Leser wrote that the group 'appeared as a variety and tendency, in many ways as the leading tendency, of the Marxist centre, that political grouping that stood between reformism and Bolshevism and cemented this middle position theoretically as well' (Leser 1968, p. 177). In 1927, Bauer described Austro-Marxism as 'the international intellectual trend of the Marxist centre – not an Austrian speciality but an intellectual current within the International which has its representatives and supporters in every socialist party'. (Otto Bauer 1927, p. 550, quoted in Leser 1968, p. 177.) See also Bauer 1978 and 1927b. Lenin condemned Austro-Marxists for occupying the Social-Democratic 'centre' and trying 'to sit between two stools', pretending to disagree with the opportunists on everything in theory, but agreeing with them on everything essential in practice (Lenin 1919). Leon Trotsky, who lived in Vienna from 1907 to 1914, was even harsher. After the Russian Revolution of 1917, he called Kautsky, who became the most severe critic of Bolshevism, the 'founder and most consummate representative of the Austrian falsification of Marxism'. In Trotsky's settled judgement, Austro-Marxism was 'an erudite and stilted theory of passivity and capitulation'. Leo Trotski, 'Die Austromarxisten', in Kommunistischen Partei Österreichs (ed.) 1921, p. 7, quoted in Leser 1968, pp. 177–9. (See also Trotsky's assessment of Austro-Marxism in Trotsky 1920, pp. 177–87 and in Trotsky 1941, pp. 152–6.)

economic advantage but even more so with national pride and convictions of historical destiny. As with any great debate, clarification ultimately depended upon a return to first principles, and, for Marxists, this meant reinterpreting immediate issues with reference to the economic theory of *Capital*. Marx never wrote his projected volume on the world economy, but *Capital* did have a great deal to say about cyclical economic crises. Moreover, in Volume III, Marx explicitly linked the prospect of a falling rate of profit with countervailing tendencies arising from foreign trade and capital-exports to the colonies. The difficulty was that *Capital* itself left room for competing interpretations. Before continuing our exposition of Social-Democratic debates over imperialism, it will therefore be necessary to review briefly some of Marx's own thoughts on the reproduction of capital, which shortly became the principal theme of sophisticated theoretical works by Otto Bauer, Rudolf Hilferding and Rosa Luxemburg.

From the outset, the question of imperialism had been periodically linked with convictions of capitalism's inability to create a market sufficient to absorb total production. This was the view of Wilhelm Liebknecht in 1885, when he denounced capitalist attempts to export the 'social question'; of the American banker Conant in 1898, when he applauded American expansionism; of John Hobson in his advocacy of trade-unionism to redistribute national income; as well as of Karl Kautsky, Parvus and several others whom we have discussed. To many readers of *Capital*, it seemed that Marx, too, associated capitalism's periodic crises with underconsumption by the working class. Indeed, Marx did lend some credibility to this thinking. In Volume III of *Capital*, he wrote that the 'ultimate reason for all real crises always remains the poverty and restricted consumption of the masses'.[140] Yet, in Volume II, he explicitly dismissed underconsumptionist theories as follows:

> It is a pure tautology to say that crises are provoked by a lack of effective consumption.... If the attempt is made to give this tautology the semblance of greater profundity, by the statement that the working class receives too small a portion of its own product, and that the evil would be remedied if it received a bigger share, i.e. if its wages rose, we need only note that crises are always prepared by a period in which wages generally rise, and the working

140. Marx 1992, p. 615.

> class actually does receive a greater share in the part of the annual product destined for consumption. From the standpoint of these advocates of sound and 'simple' (!) common sense, such periods should rather avert the crisis. It thus appears that capitalist production involves certain conditions...which permit the relative prosperity of the working class only temporarily, and moreover always as a harbinger of crisis.[141]

How could Marx argue that a shortage of markets was the 'ultimate reason' for crises and simultaneously claim that underconsumptionist theories were tautological? The apparent inconsistency arose from the fact that the 'ultimate reason' – the contradiction between production and consumption – was one expression of a more general problem of 'disproportionalities' in the expanded reproduction of capital. Marx saw the absorptive capacity of markets varying over time: capitalists curtailed the market when they laid off workers and cut wages in a cyclical crisis; they created a market when they resumed investment, expanded production, and employed more workers. Market-creation and market-destruction were dialectically opposing tendencies in the singular process of the capitalist business-cycle.

At the peak of a cyclical expansion, shortage of labour created what Marx called 'a disproportion between capital and exploitable labour-power'.[142] Temporarily high wages meant workers did for a time receive 'a greater share in the part of the annual product destined for consumption', but this occurred at precisely the moment when falling investment would precipitate a new crisis. The final result must be mass-unemployment and the consequent restricted consumption of the masses. Marx believed that in capitalist society, where investments could never be co-ordinated in advance, and where 'any kind of social rationality asserts itself only *post festum*, major disturbances can and must occur constantly'.[143] Spontaneous regulation through the 'law of value' meant 'the proportionality of the particular branches of production presents itself as a process of passing constantly out of and into disproportionality'.[144]

Marx regarded the economic cycle as capitalism's distinguishing feature compared with every previous mode of production. To trace the require-

141. Marx 1978b, pp. 486–7.
142. Marx 1976, p. 770.
143. Marx 1978b, p. 390.
144. Marx 1992, p. 365.

ments of proportionality, and by implication the origins of disproportionality, in Volume II of *Capital*, he divided the whole of production into two departments, one producing means of production, the other consumer goods. By positing coherent investments in both departments, the 'reproduction-schemes' showed the *abstract* possibility of continuing capital-accumulation without cyclical crises.

The reproduction-schemes were an abstract model of pure capitalism, omitting all reference to non-capitalist production or foreign markets. Marx's concern was to establish the conditions necessary for crisis-free expansion of capitalist production in order, by implication, to see more clearly the potential causes of periodic crises. To some readers, however, including Eduard Bernstein, Marx's account of capitalism's laws seemed to have demonstrated the possibility of surmounting the system's inherent contradictions. 'In modern society,' Bernstein declared, 'our understanding of the laws of development, and particularly of economic development, is on the increase. This knowledge is accompanied . . . by a growing ability to *direct* economic development.'[145] Bernstein never attempted an *economic* explanation of imperialism because he remained convinced that imperialism *had* no insurmountable economic causes: only a subjective 'antagonism of interests' stood in the way of class peace, and with full parliamentary institutions the rival classes of modern society could moderate their demands and ultimately agree on the ethical superiority of socialism.

More careful readers of Marx's work were far less sanguine, and from 1905 through 1913, in the works first of Otto Bauer and then of Hilferding and Luxemburg, the reproduction-schemes figured prominently in increasingly elaborate economic debates concerning the role of imperialism as a response to capitalism's crisis tendencies. In the documents that we have translated, this applies particularly to Luxemburg's *Accumulation of Capital*. The great disputes over Luxemburg's work arose from her differences with Marx over his explanation of *periodic* crises in terms of disproportionate economic growth. Luxemburg believed, to the contrary, that capitalism suffered from a *chronic* problem of markets that could only be mitigated by continuously conquering new markets in precapitalist regions. Bauer and Hilferding, in contrast, connected the export of commodities and 'excess'-capital with attempts to

145. Bernstein 1993, pp. 18–19.

moderate the cycle and redress the secular trend towards a falling rate of profit. The weight of Marx's argument clearly supported Bauer and Hilferding, not Rosa Luxemburg. When Marx discussed the role of foreign markets he spoke of temporarily forestalling a decline in the rate of profit by investing in more lucrative ventures overseas and by importing low-cost food and materials.[146]

Otto Bauer: Austro-Marxism and imperialism

Among Austro-Marxists, Otto Bauer was one of the first to offer a lucid account of imperialism in terms that rejected the notion of chronic underconsumption and simultaneously linked capitalism's latest tendencies with national oppression. In 1905, five years before the appearance of Hilferding's *Finance Capital*, Bauer wrote an article on 'Colonial Policy and the Workers' that recalled Marx's comment on the underconsumptionist tautology. Some people had argued 'that capitalist society would be unfeasible without continuous colonial expansion. They claimed that capitalism's problem was underconsumption – the masses' inability to consume the goods they produced – and that capitalist society could overcome its internal contradictions only by opening up new outlets.' Bauer replied that this argument was 'basically mistaken'. Overproduction originated 'in the fact that each increase of the productivity of labour under capitalism is paid for with labour-displacement, with the elimination of human labour from production'. Consumption then fell with unemployment, but Bauer added that no worker and no fund of capital remained indefinitely idle: the reduction of wages during a crisis brought unemployed workers back into production at the same time as falling prices compelled capitalists to renovate the means of production through new investments, which in turn were eventually facilitated by declining interest-rates. It followed that colonial expansion was 'by no means an absolute need for capitalist production; periodically conspicuous underconsumption would be overcome even without it'. The real need for new markets arose from the fact that colonies offered the possibility of 'fending off the *fall in the profit-rate* and overcoming partial and general crises with fewer sacrifices'.[147]

---

146. Marx 1992, pp. 344–5.
147. Bauer 1905, pp. 415–16.

In *The Question of Nationalities and Social Democracy* (1907), Bauer elaborated on 'capitalist expansionism' in the sixth chapter by adding the concept of 'finance-capital'. In *Capital*, Marx had dealt mainly with competitive capitalism, while simultaneously predicting that successive crises would bring about the concentration and centralisation of capital as small firms were eliminated. When economic growth slowed in Europe during the last quarter of the nineteenth century, industrial concentration accelerated with the formation of trusts and cartels to regulate production and suppress competition with the aid of tariff-protection. Bernstein thought these new forms of capitalism would diminish the danger of crises by deliberately tailoring productive activity to the market.[148] Bauer replied that, along with industrial concentration, came also the 'centralisation of monetary capital in the modern major banks'.[149] Since the relation between banks and industry was becoming 'increasingly intimate', they had a shared interest in expanding output as far as possible behind protective tariffs, then using the high domestic prices to subsidise the 'dumping' of industrial commodities to win new markets for sales and investment in the colonies.[150]

Given the multinational context of Austria-Hungary, Bauer also related these economic changes to a transformation of political discourse on the role of state institutions. 'Cosmopolitan liberals', previously the advocates of free trade, were now becoming 'national imperialists', committed to replacing 'the old bourgeois principle of nationality' by a new imperialist-nationalist principle of state formation. In these circumstances, the might of the executive power had expanded at the expense of the legislative; 'the ideal form of the imperialist army' had become 'an army of mercenaries';[151] and 'the ideology of imperialism' increasingly glorified 'power, the pride of the master, the idea of the right of a superior culture'[152] – all of which pointed to 'a future imperialist world war'.[153] Imperialism seemed to represent the Austro-Hungarian Empire writ large:

---

148. See Bernstein 1993, pp. 79–97.
149. Bauer 2000, p. 378.
150. Bauer 2000, p. 392.
151. Bauer 2000, p. 390.
152. Bauer 2000, p. 391.
153. Bauer 2000, p. 405.

> It is no longer the liberty, unity, and state-independence of each nation that is the ideal of late capitalism, but the subjugation of millions of members of foreign peoples to the rule of one's own nation. No longer are the nations to vie peacefully with one another in the free exchange of commodities, but instead each nation is to arm itself to the teeth in order to be able to maintain its oppression of the subjugated peoples at all times and to keep foreign rivals away from its own sphere of exploitation. This complete transformation of the principle of state-formation within capitalist society ultimately springs from the fact that, with the concentration of capital, the methods of capitalist economic policy have changed.[154]

In a section of his book devoted to 'imperialism and the principle of nationality', Bauer related these conclusions directly to the Habsburg Empire by commenting that it was imperialism that explained the oppression of national-minority groups: 'The idea of the unity of one's own nation and its domination of foreign peoples in the service of industrialists lusting after cartel-profits, in the service of finance-capital craving the supplementary profits to be had in young foreign lands, in the service of stock-market jobbers hungry for speculation – this is imperialism's principle of nationality.'[155] The proper response was to reconcile minorities through the principle of cultural autonomy: 'The prime objective of the workers of all the nations of Austria' could not be 'realisation of the nation-state, but only...national autonomy within the given state framework'.[156] Bauer published *The Question of Nationalities and Social Democracy* one year before Austrian annexation of Bosnia-Herzegovina on 6 October 1908. The following year, he developed his arguments further in one of his most important theoretical essays, 'National and International Viewpoints on Foreign Policy', which we have translated for the first time in this volume.[157]

154. Bauer 2000, pp. 380–1.
155. Bauer 2000, p. 395.
156. Bauer 2000, p. 404.
157. Bauer 1909. See Chapter 25.

Rudolf Hilferding's *Finance Capital*

Bauer made a significant contribution to understanding the economics of imperialism, but probably the greatest theoretical achievement of Austro-Marxism came in 1910 with Rudolf Hilferding's monumental *Finance Capital: A Study of the Latest Phase of Capitalist Development*. Heinrich Cunow was one of many who hailed the work as 'a 'valuable supplement to the three volumes of Marx's *Capital*';[158] many others, including Kautsky, were even more effusive, praising the work as the missing fourth Volume that Marx himself might have written had he lived to do so.

Hilferding first began collaborating with Kautsky in *Die Neue Zeit* in 1902. For the next three years, he pursued his medical profession while continuing theoretical studies in Vienna. In 1906, Bebel called him to Berlin to teach political economy and the history of economics at the party school. During his stay in Berlin, he was initially on the left wing of the Party, and by 1914 he opposed war-credits although he was still a resident foreigner in Germany, not a Reichstag deputy. In 1915, he was drafted into the Austrian army. For a period after the War, he joined the Independent Social-Democratic Workers' Party. He strongly opposed a merger of the USPD with the Communist Party and instead supported merger with the SPD. Hilferding's commitment to parliamentary methods convinced him that socialisation must be gradual, beginning with the most 'mature' industries. He became a German citizen in 1920 and was briefly Finance Minister in 1923 and again in 1928–9. Still a Reichstag deputy when Hitler came to power in 1933, he predicted the Nazi government would last no more than six to eight weeks: once Hitler laid hands upon the Reichsbank, he would be overthrown. Hilferding died in 1941, evidently poisoning himself after the Vichy government turned him over to the Gestapo.

Since Marx had spoken of *cyclical* economic crises, in *Finance Capital* Hilferding dismissed any notion of explaining imperialism in terms of *chronic* underconsumption. Like Marx, he thought the level of consumption was always determined by changes in production: 'since the periodic recurrence of crises is a product of capitalist society, the causes must lie in the nature of capital'.[159] He began his study of capitalism's newest forms by focusing on Marx's theme of capital's concentration and centralisation, ending in the

158. Cunow 1910.
159. Hilferding 1981, p. 241.

emergence of gigantic firms in which displacement of labour by machinery tied up capital for a steadily lengthening turnover-period. Since fixed capital could not be readily reallocated elsewhere in the event of falling prices, large firms became more dependent on the banks in adjusting to short-run market changes, while the banks in turn protected their growing investments in industry through collaborating in the formation of trusts and cartels. The larger the trusts and cartels, the greater were their credit requirements, causing industrial combination to stimulate a parallel centralisation of banking capital and eventual merger of the banks with industry. 'I call bank capital,' wrote Hilferding, 'that is, capital in money form which is actually transformed in this way into industrial capital, finance capital.... An ever-increasing proportion of the capital used in industry is finance capital, capital at the disposition of the banks which is used by the industrialists.'[160]

Hilferding integrated his analysis of finance-capital with Marx's theory of the business-cycle, emphasising how cyclical variations in the rate of profit enhanced the trend towards trustification and cartelisation. In the reproduction-schemes, Marx had divided the entire economy into two departments, the first producing means of production, the second, consumer-goods. Following Marx, Hilderding noted that, during a cyclical expansion, prices and profits rose most quickly in Department I as it responded to new investment-demand. The rise in prices for machinery and materials would then tend to depress the rate of profit in Department II. Conversely, with a cyclical contraction, profits would fall most quickly in Department I as heavy industrial producers were forced either to produce for inventory or to slash prices. Industrial combination offered a way to stabilise profits for both groups. During a contraction, firms in Department I had an interest in combining with those in II that used their products; during an expansion, light industries in II could acquire means of production relatively cheaply if they were amalgamated with supplier firms. Thus the pressure to organise capitalist production grew steadily: 'It is, therefore, the differences in rates of profit which lead to combinations. An integrated firm can eliminate fluctuations in the rate of profit.'[161]

160. Hilferding 1981, p. 225.
161. Hilferding 1981, p. 195.

Finance-capital strove to surmount the law of value principally by means of centralised control over pricing and output. By restricting output in relation to demand, organised capital could artificially raise the profits of cartel-members at the expense of unorganised enterprises; the total surplus-value would then be redistributed to the benefit of the largest firms, with the result that 'cartel profit' represented 'nothing but a participation in, or appropriation of, the profit of other branches of industry'.[162] Knowing that they would drive down their own rate of profit if they expanded capacity too eagerly, cartels also faced narrow constraints on their domestic investment activity. Hilferding concluded that imperialist expansion had nothing to do with a chronically inadequate home market, resulting instead from the intensifying quest for a higher rate of profit: 'The precondition for the export of capital is the variation in rates of profit...'.[163]

Although he associated imperialism with structural changes aimed at sustaining finance-capital's rate of profit, Hilferding also remained convinced that Bernstein and the revisionists were mistaken in their belief that new institutions might avert cyclical crises. 'This view,' he declared, 'ignores completely the inherent nature of crises. Only if the cause of crises is seen simply as the overproduction of commodities resulting from the lack of an overall picture of the market can it be plausibly maintained that cartels are able to eliminate crises by restricting production.'[164] In reality, crises arose from the inter-industrial disproportionalities that Marx had discussed; and in spite of their commitment to regulating production, the new organisational forms of capitalism must inevitably break down in the struggle over surplus-value.

Individual cartel-members always faced the temptation to over-invest during a cyclical expansion. A cartel's central office typically allocated production-quotas on the basis of productive capacity, making an increase in capacity the obvious way for any single cartel-member to enlarge its allocated market-share. The result was that competition within the organisation always re-created a tendency towards overproduction. The greater the redundancy of productive capital, the more stubbornly the cartel would then attempt to maintain prices once the crisis arrived, and the more aggravated would be the

162. Hilferding 1981, p. 203.
163. Hilferding 1981, p. 315.
164. Hilferding 1981, p. 295.

consequences for unorganised capitalists. Yet, by contributing to bankruptcies elsewhere, cartels ultimately ended up undermining their own prices and were forced again to restrict output.

Given the high organic composition of capital in large firms, or their greater dependence on machinery and technology as opposed to labour, any drop in output would also significantly raise unit-costs of production in large firms with high fixed costs; smaller 'outsiders', with less advanced technology, would then intervene to compete with and even dissolve the cartel. The outcome was that cartels could never surmount the cyclical anarchy of capitalism. They neither prevented crises nor even reduced their severity; they could only 'modify' them to the extent that they might temporarily transfer the burdens of adjustment to unorganised firms. Bernstein and others, who thought business-cycles would disappear, were committing the logical error of confusing quantity with quality. A real end to capitalist cycles and crises would require nothing less than a single, universal cartel to manage the whole of capitalist industry in league with the biggest banks:

> Partial regulation, involving the unification of a branch of industry into a single enterprise, has absolutely no influence upon the proportional relations in industry as a whole.... Planned production and anarchic production are not quantitative opposites such that by tacking on more and more 'planning' conscious organization will emerge out of anarchy.... Who exercises this control, and is the owner of production, is a question of power. In itself, a general cartel which carries on the whole of production, and thus eliminates crises, is economically conceivable, but in social and political terms such an arrangement is impossible, because it would inevitably come to grief on the conflict of interests which it would intensify to an extreme point. But to expect the abolition of crises from individual cartels simply shows a lack of insight into the causes of crises and the structure of the capitalist system.[165]

The main point on which Hilferding diverged from Marx was with respect to monetary phenomena. Whereas Marx saw a financial crisis as the final phase of every industrial crisis, Hilferding believed that the concentration of bank capital and its union with large-scale industry made major financial disturbances highly improbable. Previous monetary and credit crises had

165. Hilferding 1981, pp. 296–7.

been due to excessive speculation followed by a credit crash. Controlling virtually the whole of society's money-capital, and with their far-flung domestic and international affiliations, large banks were now in a position to throttle speculation at will. The role of speculators was further circumscribed by the tendency for trusts and cartels to bypass commercial capital and deal directly with one another. These organisational changes had been accompanied by a corresponding change of capitalist psychology: 'The mass psychoses that speculation generated at the beginning of the capitalist era, in those blessed times when every speculator felt like a god who creates a world out of nothing, seem to be gone forever.'[166]

But, if cartelisation was a continuous process, drawing a new impetus from every cyclical crisis, the question must eventually arise as to how far the process might advance. On this question Hilferding allowed his imagination to wander:

> If we now pose the question as to the real limits of cartelization, the answer must be that there are no absolute limits. On the contrary there is a constant tendency for cartelization to be extended.... The ultimate outcome of this process would be the formation of a general cartel. The whole of capitalist production would then be consciously regulated by a single body which would determine the volume of production in all branches of industry. Price determination would become a purely nominal matter, involving only the distribution of the total product between the cartel magnates on one side and all the other members of society on the other.... Money would have no role. In fact, it could well disappear completely, since the task to be accomplished would be the allocation of things, not the distribution of values. The illusion of the objective value of the commodity would disappear along with the anarchy of production, and money itself would cease to exist.... This would be a consciously regulated society, but in an antagonistic form.... In its perfected form finance capital is thus uprooted from the soil which nourished its beginnings. The circulation of money has become unnecessary.[167]

In a fully organised society, the law of value would have no room to operate. The 'social division of labour', mediated previously by money and the

166. Hilferding 1981, p. 293.
167. Hilferding 1981, p. 234.

market, would be replaced by a 'technical division of labour', mediated by a central office governing the whole of production and distribution. For the first time in its history, capital would appear as a 'unified force'. In contrast to Kautsky, however, who eventually expected a phase of 'ultra-imperialism' to become a lasting reality, Hilferding always set limits to his own logical projections by emphasising that the final obstacle to organised capitalism lay in the class-struggle. Organised capitalism would pose the question of property in its 'clearest, most unequivocal and sharpest expression at the same time as the development of finance capital itself is resolving more successfully the problem of the organization of the social economy'.[168] The objective socialisation of production could begin within capitalist society, but the final stage of socialist planned economy would only arrive when the expropriators were expropriated. In the final chapter of *Finance Capital*, Hilferding wrote:

> The socializing function of finance capital facilitates enormously the task of overcoming capitalism. Once finance capital has brought the most important branches of production under its control, it is enough for society, through its conscious executive organ – the state conquered by the working class – to seize finance capital in order to gain immediate control of these branches of production. Since all other branches of production depend upon these, control of large-scale industry already provides the most effective form of social control even without any further socialization. A society which has control over coal mining, the iron and steel industry, the machine tool, electricity, and chemical industries, and runs the transport system, is able, by virtue of its control of these most important spheres of production, to determine the distribution of raw materials to other industries and the transport of their products. Even today, taking possession of six large Berlin banks would mean taking possession of the most important spheres of large-scale industry, and would greatly facilitate the initial phases of socialist policy during the transition period, when capitalist accounting might still prove useful.[169]

Hilferding never doubted that the planned economy of socialism was a logical consequence of capitalism's own organisational tendencies. The problem was that he expected a parallel progression of democratisation and economic

168. Hilferding 1981, p. 235.
169. Hilferding 1981, pp. 367–8.

rationalisation, so that socialisation of the means of production would finally coincide with proletarian capture of the state through parliamentary means. In the interim, however, he recognised that finance-capital had transformed the bourgeois state and brought radical intensification of inter-state rivalries. In Marx's day, the bourgeoisie wanted a liberal state; now finance-capital demanded a strong state.

> The old free traders believed in free trade not only as the best economic policy but also as the beginning of an era of peace. Finance capital abandoned this belief long ago. It has no faith in the harmony of capitalist interests, and knows well that competition is becoming increasingly a political power struggle. The ideal of peace has lost its lustre, and in place of the idea of humanity there emerges a glorification of the greatness and power of the state. The modern state arose as a realization of the aspiration of nations for unity. The national idea...regarded the frontiers of the state as being determined by the natural boundaries of the nation, [but it] is now transformed into the notion of elevating one's own nation above all others. The ideal now is to secure for one's own nation the domination of the world, an aspiration which is as unbounded as the capitalist lust for profit from which it springs.... These efforts become an economic necessity, because every failure to advance reduces the profit and the competitiveness of finance capital, and may finally turn the smaller economic territory into a mere tributary of a larger one.... Since the subjection of foreign nations takes place by force – that is, in a perfectly natural way – it appears to the ruling nation that this domination is due to some special natural qualities, in short to its racial characteristics. Thus there emerges in racist ideology, cloaked in the garb of natural science, a justification for finance capital's lust for power, which is thus shown to have the specificity and necessity of a natural phenomenon. An oligarchic ideal of domination has replaced the democratic ideal of equality.[170]

Exactly how these contradictions would develop was impossible to foresee. The costs of combat were enormous, but the more unequal were the contending forces, the more likely was armed conflict. Until the ultimate victory of socialism, it seemed the best hope for avoiding hostilities lay in the possibility

170. Hilferding 1981, pp. 335–6.

of 'international cartelization'. Protective tariffs served as an offensive weapon, but they also imparted greater stability to national cartels and thus facilitated inter-cartel agreements. 'The net result of these two tendencies is that these international agreements represent a kind of truce rather than an enduring community of interest, since every change in the tariff defences, every variation in the market relations between states, alters the basis of the agreement and makes necessary the conclusion of new contracts.'[171] International cartelisation was fully consistent with Hilferding's view of a world gradually becoming more rational and organised. The problematic implications became obvious, however, when Karl Kautsky later forgot Hilferding's qualifications regarding the instability of international cartels, deciding instead that 'ultra-imperialism' might avoid the use of force through international agreements that would allow the advanced countries to 'tap, in a far more vigorous and untrammelled way than before, the whole area of at least the Eastern Hemisphere'.[172]

Although Hilferding's political logic was strictly gradualist, his economic refutation of revisionism was decisive and earned his work a reception that was almost unanimously celebratory. In this anthology we have included two reviews of *Finance Capital* by Otto Bauer and Julian Marchlewski (published in the *Leipziger Volkszeitung*), representing, respectively, the centre and left wings of international Social Democracy.[173] Readers may also wish to consult the review by Miron Nachimson (Spektator) in the *Bremer Bürger-Zeitung*[174] as well as Kautsky's review in *Die Neue Zeit*.[175] The one review that expressed predictably less enthusiasm came from Eduard Bernstein.

Writing in *Sozialistische Monatshefte*, Bernstein commented that *Finance Capital* reminded him of an article already published fifteen years earlier in *Die Neue Zeit* by a Russian student writing under the pen name Kapelusz.[176] Both Kapelusz and Hilferding attempted 'to identify modern finance-capital – that category of capital dictating contemporary world policy – with a certain tendency in commercial policy', but they reached exactly opposite conclu-

171. Hilferding 1981, p. 313.
172. Kautsky 1912c, p. 108.
173. Bauer 1910b and Marchlewski 1910. See Chapter 28.
174. Nachimson 1910a and 1910b.
175. Kautsky 1911b.
176. Kapelusz 1897.

sions: 'according to Kapelusz the commercial policy of finance-capital was free trade and liberal, while according to Hilferding it is protectionist and imperialist'.[177] Bernstein contended that Hilferding would have to provide 'much more abundant empirical material' if he hoped to prove his thesis 'that finance-capital, represented by the banks, plays the decisive role in determining economic policy'.[178]

One of Bernstein's more bizarre criticisms involved a complete misrepresentation of Hilferding's view of politics. In *Finance Capital* Hilferding had written that since 'protective tariffs' were now 'the common demand of the ruling class', free trade must be regarded as 'a lost cause'.[179] He added that 'The proletariat avoids the bourgeois dilemma – protectionism or free trade – with a solution of its own; neither protectionism nor free trade, but socialism, the organization of production, the conscious control of the economy...by and for society as a whole.... Socialism ceases to be a remote ideal, an "ultimate aim"...and becomes an essential component of the immediate practical policy of the proletariat.'[180] Bernstein denied that finance-capital was interested in protectionism, citing examples of both cartelised industries and bourgeois politicians who advocated free trade. And since he always regarded socialism as merely an ultimate aim, he also decided that in current circumstances Hilferding's remark could only imply extra-parliamentary anarchosyndicalism: 'Naturally, if Social Democracy only fought extra-parliamentary battles, as revolutionary syndicalism wants it to, it could confront in a purely critical way the struggle over protectionism or free trade along with the closely related battle over aggressive imperialism or a consistent peace policy, over boundless naval construction or arms limitations. As a participant in legislation it cannot.'[181] He concluded that the principal flaw of Hilferding's work lay in its impractical implications, which he dismissively attributed to a 'hypostasis of concepts' and a lapse into 'the method of speculative dialectic' in place of a sober assessment of empirical data.[182]

177. Bernstein 1911a, p. 948.
178. Bernstein 1911a, p. 951.
179. Hilferding 1981, p. 365.
180. Hilferding 1981, pp. 366–7.
181. Bernstein 1911a, p. 954.
182. Bernstein 1911a, p. 953. A more realistic representation of Hilferding's own views came in his article on 'The Party Congress and Foreign Policy', written for the

Bernstein disapproved of *Finance Capital* because he denied the plausibility of 'economic determinism' and thought Marx had discovered only 'tendencies' of historical development. In *The Preconditions of Socialism*, he claimed that modern society 'is, in theory, more free of economic causation than ever before'.[183] Hilferding, in contrast, said in his preface that *Finance Capital* was dedicated to 'the discovery of causal relationships. To know the laws of commodity-producing society is to be able, at the same time, to disclose the causal factors which determine the willed decisions of the various classes of this society'.[184]

Marx and Hilferding both treated causality and determinism in terms of necessary outcomes implicit within existing contradictions. But, in *Capital*, Marx spoke of 'laws' and 'tendencies' interchangeably, taking account of the fact that, in the short run, every economic tendency entailed its own counter-tendency. In the third volume, Marx's heading for the section dealing with the falling rate of profit was 'The Law of the Tendency of the Rate of Profit to Fall'. In the long run, the profit-rate must fall; but within any particular business-cycle it would both rise and fall, depending on specific circumstances. Neither Marx nor Hilferding thought of economic laws in terms of unilinear movement. But, in Marx's sense of determinism, Hilferding did believe imperialism was an *economic necessity* of capitalism in its latest phase. Eventually, imperialism must so intensify the contradictions of bourgeois society that elements from other classes would join the workers in resisting the tax burdens of the armaments-race. 'In the violent clash of these hostile interests the dictatorship of the magnates of capital will finally be transformed into the dictatorship of the proletariat.'[185]

The Reichstag fraction's resolution on disarmament and Copenhagen

Karl Kautsky was not as rigorous as Hilferding in his use of words and concepts. He typically spoke of imperialism synonymously with 'colonial policy'

---

second Jena party congress of the SPD in September 1911 and translated for the first time for this anthology. See Chapter 34.

183. Bernstein 1993, p. 19.
184. Hilferding 1981, p. 23.
185. Hilferding 1981, p. 370.

and 'Weltpolitik' – meaning world policy or world politics. In 1909, a year before Hilferding completed *Finance Capital*, Kautsky wrote *The Road to Power* and declared that imperialism 'implies a *policy* of conquest.... [It] cannot be carried out without a strong arms race, without great standing armies, without being able to carry on battles on distant oceans.'[186] At that time, Kautsky also doubted any possibility of a successful peace programme:

> The contemporary arms race is above all a consequence of the colonial *policy* and imperialism, and so long as this *policy* is maintained it will do little good to preach peace.... This ought to suggest something to some of our friends who are mad about world peace and disarmament, attend all the bourgeois peace congresses, and at the same time consider the colonial *policy* necessary – to be sure, an ethical, socialist colonial *policy*....[187]

Kautsky thought imperialism was 'the single ideal' that capitalists could offer in opposition to socialism, and this madness would continue and grow 'until the proletariat gains the power to determine the *policy* of the state, to overthrow the *policy* of imperialism and substitute the *policy* of socialism'.[188]

Words have implications. Was imperialism merely a policy, or was it an integral element of the latest phase of capitalism? To be sure, the general argument of Kautsky's *Road to Power* treated imperialism as a consequence of the latest economic and political developments. Shortly thereafter, however, he began to argue that imperialism really was a matter of *policy* – not an historical necessity – and that the policy might conceivably be changed to avoid a world war. Although Kautsky was not a Reichstag deputy, he was regarded in the Party as an eminent authority, and it was his kind of thinking that motivated the SPD-caucus, on 29 March 1909, to submit a resolution calling for 'an international understanding of the great powers for the mutual limitation of naval armaments'.[189] Kautsky supported this move even though, mere weeks earlier, he had ridiculed 'all the bourgeois peace congresses'. Referring to decisions of the Hague Conferences of 1899 and 1907, which had been

---

186. Kautsky 1909b, p. 76 (emphasis added).
187. Kautsky 1909b, p. 90 (emphasis added).
188. Kautsky 1909b, p. 98 (emphasis added).
189. Reichstag 1909, *Stenographische Berichte über die Verhandlungen des Reichstags*, XII. Legislatursperiode, I. Session, Bd. 236, 29 March 1909, p. 7822A (for Ledebour's speech see pp. 7818A–7825C). The resolution was rejected by the Reichstag. For more details, see the introduction Chapter 38.

approved by the German government, the resolution proposed that Germany take steps 'in order to bring about an international understanding of the great powers for the mutual limitation of naval armaments'.[190] Two years later, on 30 March 1911, the SPD-deputies extended their proposal, calling for agreement on a general limitation of armaments.[191] Although both resolutions were rejected by the bourgeois majority in the Reichstag, they marked the beginning of internal divisions that split Social Democracy into factions of the Right, Left, and Centre, with Kautsky and Hilferding finding common ground in the emerging Centre. Hilferding certainly did not think of imperialism as a policy, although he did regard temporary international agreements as a counter-tendency to imperialist rivalries.

Little more than a year after the first SPD-resolution on disarmament, the Centre achieved an important victory at the Eighth International Socialist Congress, which met in Copenhagen from 28 August to 3 September 1910. At the Paris Congress in 1900, Rosa Luxemburg had promoted the resolution that condemned imperialism and called for determined opposition by workers' parties. At the Stuttgart Congress in 1907, van Kol's proposal for a socialist colonial policy had likewise been condemned. But the Copenhagen Congress in 1910 followed the SPD's lead and resolved to seek peace through disarmament. Just as Kautsky proposed, the Congress called for international agreements through compulsory arbitration:

> The Congress, reiterating the oft-repeated duty of Socialist representatives in the parliaments to combat militarism with all means at their command and to refuse the means for armaments, requires from its representatives:
>
> a. The constant reiteration of the demand that international arbitration be made compulsory in all international disputes,
> b. Persistent and repeated proposals in the direction of ultimate complete disarmament; and, above all, as a first step, the conclusion of a general treaty limiting naval armaments and abrogating the right of privateering,
> c. The demand for the abolition of secret diplomacy and the publication of all existing and future agreements between the governments,
> d. The guarantee of the independence of all nations and their protection from military attacks and violent suppression.

---

190. Reichstag 1909, Bd. 254, No. 1311, p. 7485; Ratz 1966, p. 198, note 4; Ledebour 1909.
191. Reichstag 1909, Bd. 278, No. 855, pp. 4106–7.

The resolution closed by quoting the final paragraph of the Stuttgart resolution in 1907, summoning socialists everywhere, in the event of world war, 'to arouse the masses politically and hasten the overthrow of capitalist class rule'.[192] Despite this gesture, protests from the Left were immediate. Karl Radek underlined the obvious fact that 'the calls for understandings about the extent of armaments are futile insofar as there is no international executive power able to enforce the agreements'.[193] Paul Lensch (editor of the *Leipziger Volkszeitung*) ridiculed disarmament as a utopia that could never be realised under capitalism. Similar criticisms followed from Radek and Pannekoek,[194] matched by articles supporting disarmament from Georg Ledebour (a Reichstag deputy who had promoted the SPD's original motion in 1909), Hugo Haase (who later reported on imperialism at the SPD's Chemnitz Congress in 1912), as well as from the Austro-Marxists Bauer, Hilferding and Gustav Eckstein.[195]

The debate between the Centre and the Left of the SPD on disarmament and the militia

Hostilities over disarmament quickly became entangled with another polarising conflict over parliamentarism and extra-parliamentary action. In March 1910, Rosa Luxemburg submitted an article to *Die Neue Zeit* urging the general strike as a means of securing universal suffrage in Prussia, while also posing the demand for a republic in the hope of promoting revolutionary action. Under pressure from the party executive, Kautsky refused to publish the article.[196] In *The Road to Power*, Kautsky had spoken of 'a new period of revolutions', possibly involving 'the *general strike*',[197] but he was fundamentally committed to parliamentary politics, believing that democracy 'cannot abolish the revolution, but it can avert many premature, hopeless revolutionary attempts and render superfluous many revolutionary uprisings.... The direction of development is not thereby changed, but its course becomes

192. Riddell (ed.) 1984, p. 70.
193. International Socialist Congress 1910, p. 99. See also Radek 1910a and 1910b.
194. Lensch 1911, Radek 1911a, Radek 1911b, Pannekoek 1911, Radek 1911c, and Radek 1911d.
195. Ledebour 1911 and 1912. Eckstein 1912b, see this volume, Chapter 39.
196. The article was finally published as 'Was Weiter?' in the *Dortmunder Arbeiterzeitung*, 14–15 March 1910 (Luxemburg 1910a, English edition: Luxemburg 1910b).
197. Kautsky 1909b, p. 110, emphasis in the original.

steadier and more peaceful.'[198] Repudiating Luxemburg's calls for a general strike, Kautsky now developed his so-called strategy of political 'attrition' – or 'exhausting the enemy [*Ermattungsstrategie*]' on small issues – as opposed to Luxemburg's strategy of 'defeating the enemy [*Niederwerfungsstrategie*]'.[199]

On 28 April 1911, in anticipation of May Day, Kautsky published an article supporting the Reichstag fraction's second disarmament and arbitration proposal and claiming that 'the aversion to war is increasing rapidly not only among the popular masses, but also among the ruling classes'.[200] It followed that 'the immediate task is to support and strengthen the movement of the petty bourgeoisie and bourgeoisie against war and the arms race'. Cautioning against any underestimation of the bourgeois peace movement, Kautsky continued:

> ...we should under no circumstances confront the demand for international agreements to preserve peace or limit armaments...with the remark that war is closely linked to the nature of capitalism and therefore inevitable. The matter is not so simple. And when proposals are made from the bourgeois side for the preservation of peace or the limitation of armaments, which are to some extent feasible, we have every reason to support them and to force governments to state their position on them. When our parliamentary fraction did that recently in the Reichstag, it acted in a completely correct way.[201]

Kautsky acknowledged that such agreements were no guarantee of a lasting peace, which would ultimately require 'the union of the states of European civilisation into a federation with a common commercial policy, a federal parliament, a federal government and a federal army – the formation of the *United States of Europe*'.[202] But, for the foreseeable future, any socialist committed to avoiding war would be compelled to seek common ground with progressive elements among the bourgeoisie.

One week later, Rosa Luxemburg answered with her own article on 'Peace Utopias', which we have included in this volume. Her views were exactly the opposite of Kautsky's; the task of Social Democrats was 'to show the

198. Kautsky 1909b, pp. 53–4.
199. Kautsky 1910a. See also Luxemburg 1910c, Kautsky 1910b, Luxemburg 1910d, Kautsky 1910c.
200. Kautsky 1911a, p. 99.
201. Kautsky 1911a, p. 101.
202. Kautsky 1911a, p. 105.

impracticality of the idea of a partial *limitation* of armaments' and 'to make it clear to the people that militarism is closely linked to colonial policy, tariff-policy, and world policy'. Imperialism was 'the highest and last stage of capitalist development', and militarism was the 'logical result of capitalism'. Social Democrats must therefore dismiss all 'disarmament antics' and ruthlessly 'smash all illusions about peace attempts made by the bourgeoisie'. As for the project for a 'United States of Europe', it represented nothing but the hope for 'a customs union for *trade-wars against the United States of America'*. The cornerstone of socialism was not 'European solidarity' but '*international* solidarity embracing all parts of the world, all races and peoples'.[203]

The dispute between Kautsky and Luxemburg continued on the occasion of the Second Moroccan conflict, or Agadir crisis (1 July–4 November 1911). In August 1911, Kautsky wrote, at the SPD-executive's request, an anonymous broadsheet called 'World Politics, World War and Social Democracy!' in which he argued that world policy was not in the interest even of most bourgeois strata: 'In Germany not even the interests of the propertied classes call for this type of world policy' because 'colonial policy and naval construction not only yield no profit, but are actually detrimental to the masses of the possessing classes'. Heavy industry benefited from the arms-race, selling weapons of war at inflated cartel-prices to governments willing to conclude long-term contracts, but Kautsky claimed that apart from banks and war-profiteers, it was 'in the interest not only of the proletariat, but of the entire German people, even the mass of its propertied classes, to prevent the government from continuing its world policy'.[204] If the workers' party could politically isolate the magnates of heavy industry, it could also undermine popular support for imperialism and resume pursuit of democratic social change.[205] Luxemburg contemptuously replied that the author of the broadsheet was trying to portray world policy simply 'as an absurdity, as an *idiocy*' and even 'a burden' for most of the propertied classes – 'the product of mere *ignorance*' and 'a *bad bargain* for everybody' – that could be reversed 'because it does not

203. Luxemburg 1911a. See Chapter 29.
204. Kautsky 1911d. See Chapter 32.
205. Stargardt 1994, pp. 120–1. Unlike Kautsky, Hilferding considered the conflict of interest among the imperialist powers economically necessary; he agreed, however, that Social Democracy should work for Anglo-German understanding and not content itself with protesting against imperialism as a whole. Hilferding 1913.

pay', meaning socialists were now expected to postpone revolution in order to 'enlighten' the bourgeoisie concerning their own real interests.[206]

In 1912 Kautsky produced another May Day article, this time directed against left-wing advocates of the militia system in place of a standing army. If disarmament was now being held forth as a plausible goal, Kautsky's critics thought socialists should also be taking up Marx's call to replace the instruments of offensive warfare with a strictly defensive force of armed citizens. Democratisation of the military would surely be the obvious way not only to promote peace but also to cripple the militarist German government and to help clear the way for socialist revolution. Kautsky responded that disarmament and militia proposals were not mutually incompatible but actually complemented each other. As a *political* demand, the call for a militia might democratise the military but would not necessarily be less expensive than a standing army, while international agreements to reduce armaments, particularly between Germany and Great Britain, represented an *economic* demand intended to ease the tax-burden of militarism upon the popular masses.

As for the revolutionary implications that the Left associated with the militia issue, Kautsky denounced his critics as 'worshippers of pure mass instinct' who mistakenly thought socialism was the one and only answer to imperialism.[207] In reality, there was a '*community of interests* between the bourgeois world and the proletariat on this issue',[208] and workers could 'find allies among more far-sighted bourgeois strata, leading to victory even before the proletariat is strong enough to conquer state power by itself'.[209] The arms-race, he insisted, resulted from economic 'causes' but was not an economic '*necessity*'; nor was its cessation 'an *economic impossibility*'.[210] Drawing on Hilferding's notion of a universal cartel, Kautsky imagined an entirely new stage of imperialism in which 'the competitive battle between states will be neutralised by their cartel-relationship. That does not mean the abandonment of the expansion of domestic capital, but only the transition to a less expensive and less dangerous method.'[211]

---

206. Luxemburg 1911a. See Chapter 29.
207. Kautsky 1912c, p. 99.
208. Kautsky 1912c, p. 105.
209. Kautsky 1912c, p. 101.
210. Kautsky 1912c, p. 107.
211. Kautsky 1912c, p. 108. Kautsky later famously called the policy of agreements between great powers for the peaceful division of the world and the economic exploi-

Kautsky's article was sharply attacked in two left-wing documents that we have included in this collection: Paul Lensch's 'Militia and Disarmament', and Karl Radek's 'Ways and Means in the Struggle against Imperialism'.[212] In another article, entitled 'The Nature of our Present Demands', the Dutch Marxist Anton Pannekoek argued that 'the debate turns around the question of whether, considering the strength and inner necessity of imperialist policy for the bourgeoisie, a containment of armaments is futile and impossible, as we believe, or whether, despite that, it still remains possible, as Kautsky and Eckstein assume.'[213] Pannekoek recounted his differences with Kautsky over the issue of a militia. Kautsky treated the questions both of a militia and of disarmament in terms of their implications for the tax-burden. Pannekoek made a finer distinction: while 'the demand for disarmament (in the sense of a constant limitation of armaments by the governments)' merely asked for 'a relief of capitalism's pressure upon the masses', the demand to replace the standing army by a popular militia was 'a force for the overthrow of capitalism' because it would 'place an important share of power in the hands of the proletariat' and accelerate the transition to socialism.[214] The outcome of these exchanges, however, proved to be of little consequence. When the SPD held its annual congress at Chemnitz in September 1912, it quickly became obvious that Kautsky's centrist views enjoyed the support of a large majority of delegates – including on this occasion even Karl Liebknecht, who in 1907 had been charged with treason over his denunciations of militarism.[215]

---

tation of colonial areas 'ultra-imperialism', defining it as a 'transfer of cartel policy into foreign policy'. Kautsky 1914b, p. 921. See Chapter 47.

212. See Chapters 38 and 40.

213. Pannekoek 1912c, p. 815. The article was a reply to Eckstein 1912a. It should be pointed out that not all left-wingers sided with Kautsky's critics on the disarmament-issue. For instance Julian Marchlewski, one of Rosa Luxemburg's closest collaborators and later co-founder of the Spartacus League, initially backed Kautsky's position while repudiating Radek's accusation of being *ipso facto* a supporter of the Reichstag-fraction (Marchlewski 1911a. Radek 1911a. Marchlewski 1911b). Similarly, according to Trotsky, Lenin at first supported Kautsky against Rosa Luxemburg on the issue of disarmament proposals (Trotsky 1932).

214. Pannekoek 1912c, pp. 815–16.

215. For an English version of the Chemnitz debate and resolution on imperialism see Chapter 42.

The International Socialist Congress at Basel (24–5 November 1912)

In November 1912, shortly after the outbreak of the first Balkan War, an Extraordinary International Socialist Congress was also convened at Basel with 545 delegates attending from 22 countries. On the surface, this international meeting appeared to soothe the conflicts we have been describing. Gankin and Fisher note that 'The Basel Congress was the last general session of the Second International before the World War, and it is significant that, in contrast to the previous resolutions of the International on militarism and international conflicts, this Congress declared for the first time that national wars in Europe had ceased and that a period of imperialist wars had begun.'[216] The Basel Manifesto spoke of workers in all countries 'bringing public opinion to bear' on all warlike ambitions and even 'simultaneously rising in revolt against imperialism'. It also repeated the Stuttgart summons in 1907 to exert every effort in order to prevent the outbreak of war and, if that proved unavailing, 'to utilize the economic and political crisis created by the war to arouse the people and thereby to hasten the downfall of capitalist class rule'.[217] But fiery declarations were belied by the fact that the Social-Democratic Centre was becoming increasingly estranged from the revolutionary left wing, who repeatedly demanded that words be replaced by deeds – by immediate mass-actions against capitalist domination and the threat of war. Forty years later Anton Pannekoek recalled that his comrade, Herman Gorter, had gone to Basel

> to provoke a discussion about the practical means of fighting against the war. Mandated by a certain number of elements of the left, he proposed a resolution according to which, in all countries, workers had to discuss the danger of war and consider the possibility of mass action against it. But the discussion was cut off because people said that the expressions of our differences about the means would weaken the great impression that our agreement made on the governments. Of course it was just the opposite: the governments, not misled by appearances, now knew that they had to fear no serious opposition from the socialist parties.[218]

216. Gankin and Fisher (eds.) 1940, p. 79.

217. Walling (ed.) 1915, pp. 100–3. On the Basel Manifesto see further Lenin and Zinoviev 1915, p. 17.

218. Pannekoek 1952. Gorter himself wrote in 1914, following the outbreak of war, that 'The Stuttgart Congress was the last Congress to seriously take a position against

Rosa Luxemburg's theory of imperialism

The most comprehensive left-wing response to theoretical conflicts over imperialism came with Rosa Luxemburg's *The Accumulation of Capital*, published in the spring of 1913. Luxemburg was the exemplary revolutionary internationalist. Born in 1871 in Russian-occupied Poland, she fled the tsarist police and emigrated to Zurich in 1889, where she received a doctorate in law and political economy in 1898. In the same year, she moved to Germany and, with her booklet *Social Reform or Revolution*, became Eduard Bernstein's most scathing adversary in the revisionist controversy. With the outbreak of revolutionary unrest in Russia in 1905, she became a leading figure in the debate over 'permanent revolution',[219] later returning to Germany, after brief imprisonment in Warsaw, to teach at the party school from 1907–14.

Luxemburg was a complex thinker and, in a way, even self-contradictory. In *The Mass-Strike, the Political Party and the Trade Unions* (1906), she discounted the significance of bureaucratic organisations and argued that mass-revolutionary consciousness would arise spontaneously in class-battles, like an 'electric shock'[220] from 'the whirlwind and the storm'.[221] During the German Revolution of 1918 she adopted Bakunin's anarchist slogan: 'In the beginning was the deed.'[222] Yet her economic theory of capitalist breakdown [*Zusammenbruch*] also had something of a mechanistic character, claiming to forecast with absolute certainty the final collapse of the world-capitalist system. In personal correspondence with a friend in 1917, Luxemburg recalled her exhilaration in writing *The Accumulation of Capital*:

> The period in which I wrote the *Accumulation* belongs to the happiest of my life. I lived in a veritable trance. Day and night I neither saw nor heard anything as that one problem developed so beautifully before my eyes. I don't know which gave me more pleasure: the process of thinking...or the literary creation with pen in hand. Do you know that I wrote the whole 900 pages in 4 months at one sitting? An unheard-of thing! Without checking the rough copy even once, I had it printed.[223]

---

imperialism. This attitude began to go into retreat at Copenhagen and was routed at Basel.' Gorter 1914, p. 21.

219. See Luxemburg's articles in Day and Gaido (eds.) 2009.
220. Luxemburg 1964, p. 27.
221. Luxemburg 1964, p.31.
222. Luxemburg 1966, p. 21.
223. Luxemburg 2003, p. x.

Luxemburg explained her view of capitalism's terminal flaw by arguing that Marx was mistaken in the reproduction-schemes when he portrayed the theoretical possibility of crisis-free economic growth. The reproduction-schemes were abstract because they assumed pure capitalism (no non-capitalist production) and a self-contained economy. Luxemburg objected that such abstractions could not possibly clarify 'the actual and historical process of accumulation'.[224] In fact, she argued, it was only possible in non-capitalist markets to realise the surplus-value that capitalists must accumulate for expanded reproduction:

> Realisation of the surplus value...requires as its prime condition...that there should be strata of buyers outside capitalist society. Buyers, it should be noted, not consumers, since the material form of the surplus value is quite irrelevant to its realisation. The decisive fact is that the surplus value cannot be realised by sale either to workers or to capitalists, but only if it is sold to such social organisations or strata whose own mode of production is not capitalistic.[225]

Marx had ignored these 'third parties', assuming that all incomes derived, directly or indirectly, from the capitalist production of commodities. In other words, all market exchanges were assumed to be financed by purchasing power put into circulation by the capitalist class itself. Marx then divided the social product into three components: the first representing expenditures on plant, materials and machinery; the second representing wage-payments; and the third, surplus-value. The first two parts of the social product were automatically realised in order that production might continue from one year to the next. Even a portion of the surplus-value represented no problem, since it provided for the capitalists' own consumption. The crucial issue concerned the remaining portion of surplus-value, that part intended for accumulation and reinvestment. Luxemburg's question was elegantly direct: Within the context of Marx's assumptions, who could possibly buy the commodities embodying this surplus-value?

The workers could not do so, because their wages were already accounted for. Yet, if the capitalists were to buy these commodities, they would have no

224. Luxemburg 1963, p. 348.
225. Luxemburg 1963, pp. 351–2.

incentive to embark upon expanded reproduction. The exchanges would all be financed, *ex hypothesi*, from the capitalists' own pockets. The total money-capital commanded by the collective capitalist would therefore remain constant. While production might expand in such circumstances, it could not be *capitalist* production (for profit) but merely production for its own sake. Even if the capitalists did realise the balance of the surplus-value themselves, they would, at best, postpone an insurmountable contradiction. In the next round of reproduction, the same problem would return on an even larger scale. If production for profit was to occur, a continually increasing source of new demand must be found. According to Luxemburg, no such source was evident in Marx's *Capital*:

> It cannot be discovered from the assumptions of Marx's diagram for whose sake production is progressively expanded. Admittedly, production and consumption increase simultaneously in a society. The consumption of the capitalists increases...the consumption of the workers increases as well.... And yet, the growing consumption of the capitalists can certainly not be regarded as the ultimate purpose of accumulation; on the contrary, there is no accumulation inasmuch as this consumption takes place and increases.... Rather, the question is: if, and in so far as, the capitalists themselves do not consume but 'practise abstinence', i.e., accumulate, for whose sake do they produce?.... [T]he maintenance of an ever-larger army of workers [cannot] be the ultimate purpose of continuous accumulation of capital.... And in any case, the workers can only consume that part of the product that corresponds to the variable capital [wages], not a jot more. Who, then, realises the permanently increasing surplus value? The diagram answers: the capitalists themselves and they alone. – And what do they do with this increasing surplus value? – The diagram replies: They use it for an ever-greater expansion of their production. These capitalists are thus fanatical supporters of an expansion of production for production's sake.[226]

Capital's real 'aim and goal in life', however, was always 'profit in the form of money and the accumulation of money-capital'. The reproduction-schemes did not explain – so Luxemburg believed – the source of any net addition to social purchasing power, without which *capitalist* economic growth was

226. Luxemburg 1963, p. 334.

inconceivable. One imperative conclusion seemed to follow: 'capitalism needs non-capitalist social organisations as the setting for its development'[227] and requires nothing less than the 'whole globe for untrammelled accumulation'.[228] *Militarism* was no answer; it might realise surplus-value for individual capitalists, but what was spent on armaments also came from taxes and made no net addition to the market. What some capitalists gained, others would lose. And, even when capitalism as a whole turned to imperialism in the quest for new markets, in its world-transforming role it must end up eliminating pre-capitalist forms by reproducing itself elsewhere, thus endlessly negating 'the very conditions which alone can ensure its own existence'.[229]

The need for new markets stretched out into infinity, yet the closer capitalism came to transforming the entire globe in its own image, the fiercer would be the struggle for markets and spheres of investment, bringing 'a string of political and social disasters and convulsions'. 'But even before this natural economic impasse…is properly reached it becomes a necessity for the international working class to revolt against the rule of capital.' In the *Manifesto,* Marx and Engels had predicted that capitalism would create the 'universal inter-dependence of nations'; Luxemburg wrote that universal capitalism, to the contrary, was an absolute theoretical and practical impossibility. Only socialism could develop the productive forces of the entire globe, for only socialism 'is by its very nature an harmonious and universal system of economy'.[230]

Among all the Marxist criticisms of imperialism, never before had such a forceful argument of predetermined collapse been made. Yet, despite its compelling rigour and the remarkable clarity of its conclusions, Rosa Luxemburg's theory ultimately depended upon her own misinterpretation of *Capital.* In an appendix to this book, we provide a more detailed explanation of this conclusion, relating Luxemburg's analysis directly to Marx's account of the reproduction-schemes. For present purposes, however, a brief summary will suffice.

227. Luxemburg 1963, p. 366.
228. Luxemburg 1963, p. 365.
229. Luxemburg 1963, p. 366.
230. Luxemburg 1963, p. 467.

In Volume II of *Capital*, Marx explained that some capitalists were always buying without selling; others were selling without buying.[231] Expressing the same point differently, some capitalists would always be investing their accumulated money-capital at the same time as others were accumulating. This was true because the lifetimes of various elements of plant and equipment differed and because investment opportunities were never uniform throughout the economy. Luxemburg posited an impossible situation when she assumed that expanded reproduction meant *all* capitalists were accumulating a cash-hoard simultaneously. What expanded reproduction actually required was a net addition to purchasing power (social demand), which could be achieved through a net expenditure from accumulation-funds. Luxemburg denied that these funds could be the source of new demand, since they were already committed to the replacement of currently functioning plant and equipment. She overlooked the fact, as Marx said, that fixed capital is like 'an animal whose average life is ten years, but this does not mean that it dies by one-tenth each year'.[232]

Luxemburg did not consider the possibility that accumulated money-capital could in fact be reinvested *before* the original fixed capital was worn out. She did not see that (leaving aside the question of an expanding money-supply) economic growth depended upon the simple condition that dis-hoarding (investment) exceed current hoarding (saving). If net depletion of accumulation-funds caused a significant increment to effective demand, then a wave of expansion would necessarily result without any recourse to 'third-party' markets. Should any individual capitalist contemplate an expenditure that exceeded his available resources, he would, as Marx observed, borrow the difference. Those capitalists who were not yet prepared to spend their accumulation fund would never permit it to lie idle. Surplus-value, Marx wrote, was 'absolutely unproductive in its monetary metamorphosis.... It is a "dead weight" on capitalist production.'[233] Funds would therefore move continuously from those capitalists with no immediate need to those desirous of expanding their operations, the relation between the two being mediated by the money market and the interest rate.

231. Marx 1978b, p. 537.
232. Marx 1863, II, pp. 479–80; cf. Marx 1978b, p. 573.
233. Marx 1978b, p. 574.

Marx abstracted from 'third-parties' because they were not essential to understanding the fundamentals of reproduction. There could be no doubt that it was theoretically possible to realise the surplus-value, provided inter-industry relations of proportionality were maintained. Should it happen that the distribution of production did not match the prevailing demand within and between sectors of the economy, then foreign trade might enter to redress the disproportions. Alternatively, trade might arise from considerations of comparative cost, from the export of capital in search of a higher return, or from the need to secure cheaper raw materials and food-supplies from backward countries. A full explanation of the penetration of capital into the non-capitalist environment required only the law of the falling rate of profit, a proper understanding of the business-cycle, and awareness of the need for access to natural resources. By reinterpreting *Capital* in terms of a theory of *chronic* market-inadequacy – or the chronic impossibility of realising surplus-value for accumulation – Rosa Luxemburg ended up obscuring the causes of capitalism's real, *cyclical* pattern of development.

If Rudolf Hilferding's *Finance Capital* received almost universal critical acclaim, the reviews of Luxemburg's *Accumulation of Capital* were almost universally negative, even including many from the Marxist Left. In this volume, we have included four reviews: two that were critical, coming from Social-Democratic centrists in Germany and Austria (Gustav Eckstein and Otto Bauer); another that was equally critical from Anton Pannekoek, representing the international left wing; and one that was supportive from Franz Mehring, representing the tiny fraction of SPD left-wingers associated with the Berlin group around *Die Internationale*, who later formed the Spartacus League. Since Luxemburg's book involved detailed commentary on Marx's reproduction-schemes, the reviews are complex and the critics' occasional frustration will be apparent. In the revisionist theoretical journal *Sozialistische Monatshefte*, Max Schippel, a leading revisionist, summarised his own distraction upon reading Luxemburg's work:

> Capitalism is treated [by Luxemburg] much like poor Argan in Molière's *Le malade imaginaire* (*The Imaginary Invalid*): 'I must now tell you,' his doctor railed at him, 'that I give you up to your bad constitution, to the intemperament of your intestines, to the corruption of your blood, to the acrimony of your bile, and to the feculence of your humours. And I will have you before four days in an incurable state. You shall fall into bradypepsia, from

> bradypepsia into dyspepsia, from dyspepsia into apepsy, from apepsy into lientery, from lientery into dysentery, from dysentery into dropsy, and from dropsy to the deprivation of life into which your folly will bring you.' Only in our case the explanation is couched [by Luxemburg] in 'orthodox'-Marxist economic terms – to be sure strictly technical – and is arrived at only after 446 pages. But perhaps capitalism will nevertheless be able somehow to find a way out; or maybe it is just a case, as in Molière's play, of an imaginary illness? Actually, a second 'orthodox' Marxist now appears on the scene, none other than Anton Pannekoek from Bremen, and amazingly proves in the twinkling of an eye that only a small improvement in the diagrams is necessary to dispose of the whole frightening problem.[234]

The hostile reviews by Pannekoek, and even by the centrists Eckstein and Bauer, were endorsed by Lenin, to whom the whole affair was *déjà vu*. In the 1890s, Russian populist-socialists (Narodniks) had argued that capitalism was impossible in Russia because it would first destroy the peasantry and then prove incapable of accumulating capital to compete in foreign markets. At that time, Lenin declared that he was perfectly satisfied that 'Marx proved in Volume II [of *Capital*] that capitalist production is quite conceivable without foreign markets, with growing accumulation of wealth and without any "third parties".'[235] Describing the Narodniks as hopeless 'romantics', Lenin interpreted Marx in exactly the same way as Hilferding did in *Finance Capital*:

> The various branches of industry, which serve as 'markets' for one another, do not develop evenly, but outstrip one another, and the more developed industry seeks a foreign market. This does not mean at all 'the impossibility of a capitalist nation realising surplus value'.... It merely indicates the lack of proportion in the development of the different industries. If the national

---

234. Schippel 1913, p. 148. This sarcastic review was penned by one of the main theoreticians (together with Gerhard Hildebrand, Ludwig Quessel and Karl Leuthner) of the current within revisionism that Charles Andler appropriately called 'imperialist socialism in contemporary Germany' (Andler 1918, pp. 124–5). Hildebrand went so far in his chauvinism that he was expelled from the SPD at the Chemnitz Congress; Schippel – the 'good Prussian', as Andler called him – was more circumspect, but he still openly called for military intervention in backward nations, the disciplining of the natives by force, and turning at least part of Morocco into a German settlement-colony (Schippel 1911 and 1912a).

235. Lenin 1895, pp. 498–9.

> capital were distributed *differently*, the same quantity of products could be realised within the country. But for capital to abandon one sphere of industry and pass into another, there must be a crisis in that sphere; and what can restrain the capitalists threatened by such a crisis from seeking a foreign market, from seeking subsidies and bonuses to facilitate exports, etc.?[236]

Apart from economic theory, however, there was also an important political sub-text to Rosa Luxemburg's argument. In *The Making of Marx's 'Capital'*, the Marxist scholar Roman Rosdolsky points out that the reproduction-schemes could actually be cited – and often were – by right-wing authors who wished to prove there would be neither a capitalist breakdown nor revolutionary crises. Luxemburg's task, unlike Lenin's, was to refute such claims that were being put forth on behalf of a powerful workers' bureaucracy interested only in gradual reforms.[237] After the collapse of the Second International and the decision by the SPD-leadership to support Germany's war-effort, in 1915 Luxemburg wrote her own *Anti-Critique* and made the sub-text explicit: those who claimed capitalist accumulation was possible in an 'isolated capitalist society' were the same people who portrayed imperialism as merely the 'wicked invention of a small group of people who profit from it'. In terms of political tactics, the consequence was an attempt to 'moderate' imperialism and 'draw its claws' by educating wide elements of the bourgeoisie to resist taxation and demand disarmament-treaties instead. A final confrontation between the proletariat and capital was to be postponed by utopian compromises.[238] Luxemburg's apprehension of class-compromises was emphatically justified by SPD Reichstag deputies at the moment when her *Accumulation of Capital* first appeared.

SPD-complicity in German military policy (1912–13)

Despite mounting internal conflicts, the German Social-Democratic Party had won a great electoral victory in January 1912: 113 deputies were elected out of a total of 397 seats, turning the parliamentary delegation into the largest group in the Reichstag. The SPD had become an organisational behemoth, with

236. Lenin 1895b, p. 66.
237. Rosdolsky 1989, Vol. 2, p. 491.
238. Luxemburg 1921, p. 148.

over 1,100,000 members, 86 daily papers, and support from three-quarters of Germany's trade-unionists. The salient question was how this apparent power would be used. In the spring of 1913, the German government submitted a new military budget demanding a peacetime increase of the standing army by 136,000. The government claimed expansion was warranted by the compelling facts of the First Balkan War and introduction of a three-year term of military service in France. The expenditure was to be financed, as were similar measures in Great Britain, by direct income and property-taxes. This meant two bills were under discussion in the Reichstag: an armament (or military-expenditure) bill, and a corresponding appropriation- (or military-taxation) bill. When the military-expenditure bill was passed despite SPD-opposition, the Reichstag group devised a clever ruse. They supported the taxation bill on the grounds that, in this case, the issue was not *whether* to spend on the military – which had already been decided – only *how* to raise the revenues, and socialists had always supported direct taxes because they fell more heavily on the bourgeoisie than on the workers.[239] The Party's long-standing slogan on military matters had always been 'For this system not one man, not one penny!', yet, on this occasion, its Reichstag members contrived to support militarism while washing their hands of any responsibility. Luxemburg denounced the betrayal as purchasing a 'limited reform' in taxation at the cost of a 'fundamental principle'.[240]

When the SPD met in congress at Jena in September 1913, the issue of military taxation become further entangled with the ongoing struggle over political tactics. A resolution in support of a political general strike was submitted by Luxemburg, Pannekoek, Liebknecht, and Geyer – and was promptly defeated by 333 votes against 142. Employing the terminology of the Convention during the French Revolution, Luxemburg attributed this dismal defeat to the 'swamp' of the Kautskyist Centre: 'If Bebel's course of action at [the first Jena congress in] 1905 was to thrust the party forwards in order to push the trade unions to the left, the strategy of the party executive at Jena in 1913 was to let itself be pushed to the right by the trade union officials, and to act as a batter-

239. On the debate over funding for the military budget [*Deckungsfrage*], i.e. the approval of taxes for military purposes by the SPD representatives in the Reichstag in 1913, see Walling (ed.) 1915, pp. 64–81.

240. Quoted in Riddell (ed.) 1984, p. 94. On this issue, see further Luxemburg 1913b.

ing ram for them against the left wing of the party.'[241] The stronger the party machine grew, the more effectively it marginalised internal critics and the more complicit it became in the tide of events leading to WWI.

The outbreak of the First World War and the Dutch 'Tribunists'

Although the outbreak of war in 1914 took many European diplomats by surprise, Social Democrats should have been the least likely group to share that reaction. For a decade and a half, the most far-sighted leaders of the international socialist movement had warned on literally thousands of occasions – in congresses, articles, and speeches in every conceivable forum – that imperialism was inextricably linked with the threat of war. Yet the outbreak of hostilities on 1–3 August 1914 – astounding though it may seem – caught many leaders of international socialism completely unawares. Perhaps the most remarkable indicator of this fact was a document drafted by Hugo Haase for an International Socialist Congress that was planned to meet at the end of August 1914 but had to be cancelled due to the War. Speaking for the SPD-executive, the document solemnly proclaimed that

> The feelings of enmity which existed between Great Britain and Germany and which the Basel Congress, in 1913, regarded as the greatest danger to the peace of Europe, have now given way to a better understanding and feeling of trust. This is largely due to the ceaseless efforts of the International and also to the fact that at last the ruling classes in both countries are gradually coming to realise that their interests are best served by bridging over the differences.[242]

The same Hugo Haase had declared in the Reichstag on 4 August, the very day when Great Britain declared war on Germany, that 'in the hour of danger we will not desert our fatherland'.[243]

---

241. Luxemburg 1913c, pp. 148–53.

242. Haase 1914.

243. Grünberg (ed.) 1916, p. 449. Haase spoke officially as party chairman and on behalf of the SPD parliamentary group. Rosa Luxemburg quoted him as follows: 'We are now facing the irrevocable fact of war. We are threatened by the horrors of invasion. The decision, today, is not for or against war; for us there can be but one question: by what means is this war to be conducted? Much, aye everything is at stake for our people and its future, if Russian despotism, stained with the blood of its own people,

Leon Trotsky later recalled that, when the issue of *Vorwärts* containing the report of the Reichstag debate arrived in Switzerland, Lenin thought it was a fake published by the German General Staff to deceive their enemies.[244] The Romanian Social-Democratic press referred to accounts of Haase's speech to the Reichstag as 'an incredible lie' and claimed 'the censors had changed the text in accordance with the desires of the government'.[245] The general disbelief was accompanied by equally astonishing political decisions. Benito Mussolini, editor of the Italian socialist newspaper *Il Popolo*, abandoned socialism to become a fascist. Gustave Hervé, the *enfant terrible* of French antimilitarism and anticolonialism, became a national socialist. In Belgium, Emil Vandervelde, former Chairman of the International Bureau, accepted membership in the Cabinet, as did Jules Guesde in France. Georgii Plekhanov, the father of Russian Marxism, who, during the Russo-Japanese War, had publicly shaken hands with the Japanese Marxist Sen Katayama, supported the tsarist government. Heinrich Cunow, formerly a fierce anti-revisionist who defended the theory of capitalist collapse and wrote some of the first Marxist analyses of imperialism (included in this anthology), likened anti-imperialism to Luddism and declared that imperialism was a necessary stage of capitalist evolution in which neither Europe nor the rest of the world were yet ripe for socialism.[246]

The first Marxist writer to react to these palpable betrayals of proletarian internationalism was Anton Pannekoek in his article 'The Collapse of the International', which circulated widely in German, English, Dutch and Russian versions and is included in this anthology.[247] Pannekoek categorically proclaimed that 'The Second International is dead.' Lenin affirmed that Pannekoek was 'the only one who has told the workers the truth': his harsh

should be the victor. This danger must be averted; the civilisation and the independence of our people must be safeguarded. Therefore we will carry out what we have always promised: in the hour of danger we will not desert our fatherland. In this we feel that we stand in harmony with the International, which has always recognised the right of every people to its national independence, as we stand in agreement with the International in emphatically denouncing every war of conquest. Actuated by these motives, we vote in favour of the war credits demanded by the Government.' Luxemburg 1915b, p. 20.

244. Trotsky 1930, p. 184.
245. Craig Nation 1989, p. 29.
246. Cunow 1915.
247. Pannekoek 1914b. See Chapter 48.

condemnation of Kautsky and other prominent leaders of international socialism were 'the only socialist words. They are the truth. Bitter, but the truth.'[248]

Pannekoek also participated on an editorial committee affiliated with the Dutch journal *De Tribune*, whose members – including David Wijnkoop and Willem van Ravestejn – collectively approved Herman Gorter's *Imperialism, the World War and Social Democracy*, the definitive response of 'Tribunist' Marxism.[249] Gorter saw imperialism as worldwide rule by monopolies and laid blame for the fighting on '*all* the states that pursue an imperialist policy and seek to expand their territories'.[250] Like Lenin and Pannekoek, he angrily criticised Kautsky for his utopian pacifism and even denial that the War was due to imperialist motives: after everything that had happened, Kautsky still imagined the world could be set right if only capitalism returned to political alliances, trade agreements, and 'peaceful means such as arbitration-tribunals and disarmament'[251] – a parade of nonsense compared to the Kautsky of 1909, who gave a far more respectable account of imperialism in *The Road to Power*. Crediting Hilferding's *Finance Capital* as the basis for his own views, Gorter saw imperialism as the axis around which 'the rise and the struggle of the proletariat, and finally the revolution itself revolve. Imperialism is the greatest issue [of our day], and it is upon its interpretation, as well as the fight against it, that the fate of the proletariat unquestionably depends for many years to come.'[252]

Since the established Social-Democratic parties had totally surrendered to nationalism, Gorter said the paramount duty incumbent upon socialists was to reveal to the masses the true character of the slaughter. Entirely new tactics were needed: parliamentarism must be replaced by direct mass-action;

248. Lenin 1914c, p. 168. The War and the collapse of the International gave rise to a flurry of analyses linking these events to imperialism. In chronological order, the most important were: Gorter's *Imperialism, the World War and Social Democracy* (September 1914), Trotsky's *The War and the International* (October 1914), Luxemburg's *The Crisis of Social Democracy* (April 1915) and Lenin and Zinoviev's *Socialism and War* (August 1915). We should also mention *Imperialism and Democracy* (1914) by Laufenberg and Wolffheim. Calling for a new International, they characterised the War as a 'natural product of imperialist development' that destroyed the foundations of reformism by making a broadening of democracy impossible, thus paving the way for a series of international crises and wars.
249. Craig Nation 1989, p. 49.
250. Gorter 1914, p. 7.
251. Gorter 1914, p. 105.
252. Gorter 1914, p. 39.

anti-imperialist struggle must be moved to the forefront of national and international politics; and a new International must be founded.[253] Gorter's ideas sounded much like those of Lenin, who read the Dutch original and congratulated Gorter for his insight. But the split in the 1920s between Lenin and the council-communists was already implicit in Gorter's aversion to the kind of tight organisation that Lenin would impose upon parties of the Third (Communist) International. Gorter thought the appalling experience of the Second International left one valuable lesson:

> From the passive struggle the proletariat must advance to the active struggle, from petty battles through representatives, the proletariat – itself, alone – must take the great step to waging a leaderless struggle, or a struggle whose leaders are in the background, to act alone against the most powerful capitalist creature, the strongest social force that ever existed: imperialist world capital.[254]

Responses to war: Trotsky, Luxemburg and Lenin

In October 1914, the same month when Pannekoek's 'The Collapse of the International' appeared, Leon Trotsky wrote *The War and the International* and also pronounced the end of the Second International to be a 'tragic fact': 'All efforts to save the Second International on the old basis, by personal diplomatic methods and mutual concessions, are quite hopeless.' Organised along national lines, the old Social-Democratic parties were themselves 'the main hindrance' to proletarian internationalism.[255] The German SPD was the worst offender of all: it 'subordinated the entire future of the International to the quite extraneous question of the defence of the frontiers of the class state because it felt itself first and foremost to be a conservative state within the state'.[256]

253. Gorter 1914, p. 116.
254. Gorter 1914, p. 77. On council-communism, see van der Linden 2004. On the Tribunists' further political evolution see Gerber 1989.
255. Trotsky 1918a, pp. 33, 36. American ed.: Trotzky, *The Bolsheviki and World Peace* (1918).
256. Trotsky 1918a, p. 209. Trotsky's specific analyses included the Balkan question (he repeated a demand of the Basel Manifesto, calling for the creation of a Balkan federation in the former territories of European Turkey), Austria-Hungary (he supported the dissolution of the Austro-Hungarian Empire), and a study of German

Trotsky understood imperialism in terms of a generalised contradiction between modern means of production and the limited confines of the national state. The working class had no further interest 'in defending the outlived and antiquated national "fatherland", which has become the main obstacle to economic development. The task of the proletariat is to create a far more powerful fatherland ... the republican United States of Europe as the foundation of the United States of the World.'

> The nation must continue to exist as a cultural, ideological and psychological fact, but its economic foundation has been pulled from under its feet. All talk of the present bloody clash being a work of national defence is either hypocrisy or blindness. On the contrary, the real, objective significance of the War is the breakdown of the present national economic centers, and the substitution of a world economy in its stead.... The War proclaims the downfall of the national state.... The War of 1914 is the most colossal breakdown in history of an economic system destroyed by its own inherent contradictions.[257]

Rosa Luxemburg also laid primary blame upon the SPD. Denouncing the Party for supporting war-credits, she wrote in *The Crisis of Social Democracy* (the *Junius Pamphlet*) that 'in the present imperialistic milieu there can be no more wars of national defence'.[258] Capitalism had buried the old socialist parties at the moment when the War, 'devastating culture and humanity', first erupted: 'And in the midst of this orgy a world tragedy has occurred; the capitulation of the Social Democracy. To close one's eyes to this fact, to try to hide it, would be the most foolish, the most dangerous thing that the international proletariat could do.'[259] 'The world had been preparing for decades, in

war-aims. He noted that Germany's main forces were not hurled against tsarism but against republican France; that Germany's main goal was to overcome England's naval supremacy by securing a gateway to the Atlantic through Belgium; and that the Kaiser ultimately wanted to reach a deal with Tsar Nicholas II to establish an alliance of feudal-monarchic states on the European continent. Trotsky rejected the distinction between wars of defence and aggression as a valid criterion for determining the position of socialist parties in the conflict, quoting extensively from Kautsky's 'splendid' answer to Bebel at Essen. Trotsky 1918a, p. 151.

257. Trotsky 1918a, pp. 21–3. In this volume, we have included Trotsky's 'The Nation and the Economy' (July 1915), which developed these ideas further in response to Kautsky's 'National State, Imperialist State, and Confederation' (published in February 1915 and also included here).

258. Luxemburg 1915b, p. 95. The *Junius Pamphlet* was written in April 1915 – while Luxemburg was in prison – but not published until January 1916.

259. Luxemburg 1915b, p. 8.

broad daylight, in the widest publicity, step by step, and hour by hour, for the world war.'[260] It was simply incomprehensible that the SPD-leaders should have been taken unawares. And now that the savagery was in full swing, German Social Democrats had the effrontery to object that their enemies were recruiting colonial peoples to participate in the blood-letting:

> Our party press was filled with moral indignation over the fact that Germany's foes should drive black men and barbarians, Negroes, Sikhs and Maoris into the war. Yet these peoples play a role in this war that is approximately identical with that played by the socialist proletariat in the European states. If the Maoris of New Zealand were eager to risk their skulls for the English king, they showed only as much understanding of their own interests as the SPD Reichstag fraction that traded the existence, the freedom and the civilization of the German people for the existence of the Hapsburg monarchy, for Turkey and for the vaults of the Deutsche Bank. One difference there is between the two. A generation ago, Maori negroes were still cannibals and not students of Marxist philosophy.[261]

The implications of Luxemburg's analysis of the War, including its sham rationalisations and its real causes, were summarised in the twelve 'Theses on the Tasks of International Social Democracy' that were adopted at a conference of the Berlin Internationale group (the predecessor of the Spartacus League) on 1 January, 1916, and were added as an appendix to the German edition of *Junius Pamphlet*. Thesis 5 declared that 'in this era of unleashed imperialism there can be no more national wars. The national interests serve only as means to deceive the masses of working people and make them subservient to their arch-enemy, imperialism.' Thesis 8 rejected calls from Kautsky and Trotsky for a United States of Europe as a 'utopian' or fundamentally 'reactionary project'. As Lenin would do a year later in his own *Imperialism*, Thesis 9 declared that imperialism was capitalism's 'last phase' and 'the common arch-enemy of the proletariat of all countries'.[262]

Although Lenin was not aware of who had authored the *Junius Pamphlet*, he welcomed it as 'a splendid Marxist work'. However, he did think it contained 'two mistakes': first, the author was wrong to claim there could be no

260. Luxemburg 1915b, p. 32.
261. Luxemburg 1915b, p. 65.
262. Luxemburg 1916 (January).

more national wars; and, secondly, there was not sufficient criticism of the Kautskyist Centre for its social chauvinism and opportunism. In fact, however, Luxemburg did write a truly devastating critique of Kautsky's 'National State, Imperialist State and Confederation'. We have included both Kautsky's article and Luxemburg's reply, 'Perspectives and Projects', in this collection. On the question of national wars, however, there was a genuine difference. The *Junius Pamphlet* dealt mainly with the European conflict, while Lenin was already seeing the revolutionary struggle in much broader terms. Whereas Social Democrats had for years regarded colonial peoples as subordinate, backward, and even culturally and racially inferior groups on the periphery of civilisation, Lenin believed national wars were inevitable in the colonies and would be both '*progressive* and *revolutionary*' in throwing off the domination of capitalist countries.[263]

In his own theses on 'The Socialist Revolution and the Right of Nations to Self-Determination', at the beginning of 1916 Lenin recast revolution in global terms. As a world system, capitalism had spread its contradictions to include all peoples and nations. National Social-Democratic parties had always conceived revolution mainly as a struggle against their own governments. Lenin replied that every movement that helped to break down the divisions imposed by imperialism would be a step towards ultimate reunification in socialism. Socialist revolution was neither a single act nor 'one single battle on a single front', but an entire series of battles on a global scale. The aim of socialism was to end all 'national isolation', and the way to achieve 'the inevitable merging of nations' was first through 'complete liberation of all the oppressed nations, i.e., their freedom to secede'.[264]

Lenin saw the entire world in terms of three types of countries: first, the advanced capitalist countries of Western Europe and the United States, where the workers' task was to emancipate oppressed nations within their own country and in the colonies; secondly, Eastern Europe, including Austria, the Balkans and particularly Russia, where the class-struggle in oppressor-nations must be merged with the struggle by workers in oppressed nations;

263. Lenin 1916a, p. 312. Lenin thought the *Junius Pamphlet* suffered from the same faults as the work of 'certain Dutch [i.e. 'Tribunists'] and Polish Social-Democrats, who repudiate self-determination of nations even under socialism' (Lenin 1916a, p. 313). See also Lenin 1919c.

264. Lenin 1916b, pp. 144, 146–7.

and thirdly, the colonies and semi-colonial countries, such as China, Persia, or Turkey, where even bourgeois-democratic movements had hardly begun. Here, socialists must 'render determined support to the more revolutionary elements in the bourgeois-democratic movements for national liberation... [and] assist their uprising – or revolutionary war, in the event of one – *against* the imperialist powers that oppress them'.[265]

Lenin: *Imperialism, the Highest Stage of Capitalism*

In *Imperialism, the Highest Stage of Capitalism*, completed shortly after the theses on self-determination, Lenin wrote:

> the characteristic feature of the period under review is the final partitioning of the globe – final, not in the sense that *repartition* is impossible; on the contrary, repartitions are possible and inevitable – but in the sense that the colonial policy of the capitalist countries has *completed* the seizure of the unoccupied territories on our planet. For the first time the world is completely divided up, so that in the future *only* redivision is possible, i.e., territories can only pass from one 'owner' to another, instead of passing as ownerless territory to an 'owner'.[266]

At the beginning of this essay, we spoke of the documents we have translated as a story of 'the discovery of imperialism'. Lenin intended to write the final chapter to that story: imperialism was the 'highest' and final stage of capitalism, a global system of moving contradictions that must be brought down by worldwide revolution.

Lenin's *Imperialism* has often been regarded as a secondary work, a kind of literature-review that repackaged data and ideas drawn from countless other sources, beginning with John Hobson and Rudolf Hilferding. In his subtitle to the book, Lenin himself called it 'a popular outline'. The work did synthesise the ideas and data of other authors, but one of its most important achievements was to relate the 'highest' stage of capitalism to Marx's account of capitalism in the late nineteenth century, and particularly to the analysis Marx gave of capitalism's *cyclical* development. Lenin saw the end of imperialism

265. Lenin 1916b, pp. 151–2.
266. Lenin 1970, p. 90.

not as the terminal collapse projected by Rosa Luxemburg in *The Accumulation of Capital*, but rather as an uneven process in which peoples everywhere would be on the move, simultaneously resisting exploitation even though their histories and stages of development might be radically different. Capitalism had finally achieved its universal form, but it also entailed universal contradictions.

In his early essays criticising the Russian Narodniks, Lenin had already concluded from Marx's reproduction-schemes in *Capital* that periodic crises were due to a 'lack of proportion in the development of the different industries'.[267] In *Imperialism*, he likewise attributed capitalist world policy to the need for resources, for periodic abatement of cyclical crises through exports, and most importantly to the export of capital in search of a higher rate of profit. But the decisive contribution came when Lenin translated Marx's description of capitalism's cyclical growth, with its continuous unevenness between different branches of industry, into *a global formula for the uneven development of imperialism as a whole*. At the beginning of his chapter on the export of capital, he wrote that 'The uneven and spasmodic development of individual enterprises, individual branches of industry and individual countries is inevitable under the capitalist system.'[268] Lenin applied Marx's insight into disproportionate growth within a single capitalist economy to the relations between nations and whole empires.

The fact that uneven development occurred on a global scale meant that the shifting balance of military and economic power would inevitably lead to imperialist wars to re-divide colonial possessions. With reference to Kautsky, Lenin commented: 'Certain bourgeois writers (whom K. Kautsky...has now joined) have expressed the opinion that international cartels...give the hope of peace among nations under capitalism. Theoretically this opinion is absolutely absurd, while in practice it is sophistry and a dishonest defence of the worst opportunism.'[269] Kautsky's 'silly little fable about "peaceful" ultra-imperialism' was nothing but 'the reactionary attempt of a frightened philistine to hide from stern reality' – from imperialist wars and their revolutionary implications.[270] Kautsky had failed to see that every monopoly or cartel was

267. Lenin 1899b, p. 66.
268. Lenin 1970, p. 72.
269. Lenin 1970, p. 88.
270. Lenin 1970, p. 115.

inherently unstable and must periodically disintegrate in the struggle to appropriate surplus-value. In this connection Lenin could have quoted Marx in *The Poverty of Philosophy*:

> In practical life we find not only competition, monopoly and the antagonism between them, but also the synthesis of the two, which is not a formula, but a movement. Monopoly produces competition, competition produces monopoly. Monopolists compete among themselves; competitors become monopolists. If the monopolists restrict their mutual competition by means of partial associations... competition becomes [more desperate] between the monopolists of different nations. The synthesis is such that monopoly can only maintain itself by continually entering into the struggle of competition.[271]

Without quoting Marx directly, Lenin did make the same point: 'the monopolies, which have grown out of free competition, do not eliminate the latter, but exist over and alongside of it, and thereby give rise to a number of very acute, intense antagonisms, frictions and conflicts'.[272] Preoccupied with the advances of capitalist organisation, Kautsky had forgotten 'the very profound and fundamental contradictions of imperialism: the contradiction between monopoly and free competition which exists side by side with it, between the gigantic "operations" (and gigantic profits) of finance capital and "honest" trade in the free market, the contradiction between cartels and trusts on the one hand, and non-cartelised industry on the other, etc.'[273] The statement that cartels could abolish either the business-cycle or imperialist conflicts was simply 'a fable spread by bourgeois economists'.[274]

Lenin agreed with Hilferding that large-scale capital had become temporarily more organised, but the 'privileged' positions of the biggest firms in heavy industry only created 'a still greater lack of coordination' elsewhere.[275] The 'privileged' sectors might try to alleviate capitalism's contradictions by creating a 'labour aristocracy' of more highly paid workers, supported by a share in 'superprofits' obtained both at home and in the colonies, but this

271. Marx 1977a, pp. 146–7.
272. Lenin 1970, p. 105.
273. Lenin 1970, pp. 141–2.
274. Lenin 1970, p. 28.
275. Lenin 1970, p. 29.

fact did nothing more than explain the political basis of Social-Democratic opportunism – the powerful trade-unions with no interest in revolution.[276]

Lenin's *Imperialism* drew heavily upon *Finance Capital,* but Lenin also thought Hilferding's greatest insights had been confounded by the excesses of his own imagination, ending with the idea that 'organised capitalism' might evolve into a single cartel as a 'unified force'. Lenin admitted that monopoly prices might in the short run reduce competition, thus forestalling technological progress, but these were the achievements of 'parasitic decaying capitalism',[277] and imperialism was parasitic capitalism on a world scale:

> Hence the extraordinary growth of a class, or rather, of a stratum of rentiers, i.e., people who live by 'clipping coupons', who take no part in any enterprise whatever, whose profession is idleness. The export of capital, one of the most essential economic bases of imperialism, still more completely isolates the rentiers from production and sets the seal of parasitism on the whole country that lives by exploiting the labour of several overseas countries and colonies.[278]

In *Capital,* Marx had abstracted from foreign trade and capital-exports to analyse reproduction in its 'pure' form. But Lenin regarded Hilferding's universal cartel and Kautsky's ultra-imperialism as far more than methodological abstractions, implying that *real capitalism* might emerge in a pure form, overcoming its own contradictions. According to Lenin, 'The very concept of purity,' if applied to real life, 'indicates a certain narrowness, a one-sidedness of human cognition, which cannot embrace an object in all its totality and complexity.'[279]

Some months prior to his own *Imperialism,* Lenin also wrote an introduction to Nikolai Bukharin's *Imperialism and World Economy*. Bukharin was a close comrade in the Bolshevik Party, but there were profound methodological differences between the two authors that Lenin subsequently made clear. Bukharin carried to the extreme all the speculative ideas that Lenin found objectionable in the writings of Hilferding and Kautsky. In 1915, Bukharin

276. Lenin 1970, p. 9. Marx had also foreseen an 'aristocracy of the working class' as early as Volume 1 of *Capital*.
277. Lenin 1970, p. 122.
278. Lenin 1970, p. 120.
279. Lenin 1915c, p. 236.

wrote an article 'Towards a Theory of the Imperialist State', claiming that the War had finally overcome divisions within the bourgeoisie when all parties signed up to patriotic national defence. The result was said to be a 'single finance-capitalist clique',[280] with the imperialist state now functioning as 'a collective, joint capitalist'.[281] The need to concentrate economic authority had converted each developed 'national system' of capitalism into a collective 'state-capitalist', or what Bukharin described as a 'new Leviathan beside which the fantasy of Thomas Hobbes appears as a child's toy'.[282] In *Imperialism and World Economy*, Bukharin declared that the concentration and centralisation of capital had reached the point where organised 'national economies' – each a 'company of companies' – were the principal contestants, reducing domestic competition 'to a minimum' in order to maximise fighting capacity in the world tournament of nations.[283]

Glossing over contradictions within the capitalist class, Bukharin thought each state-capitalist trust expressed the 'collective will' of its own national bourgeoisie, pursuing a 'mad orgy of armaments'[284] in which imperialist wars would henceforth play a role similar to previous cyclical crisis. World-capitalism must move 'in the direction of a universal state capitalist trust by absorbing the weaker formations'.[285] Kautsky was mistaken, of course, in thinking this process could ever reach its 'logical end' of ultra-imperialism, and, for his critical comments on Kautsky, Bukharin was congratulated by Lenin.[286] But, when he wrote his *Economics of the Transition Period* in 1920, Bukharin finally went too far:

> ...the reorganization of the productive relations of finance capitalism has followed a path towards universal state-capitalist organization, the elimination of the commodity market, the conversion of money into a unit of account, the organization of production on a nationwide scale, and the subordination of the entire 'national-economic' mechanism to the goals of international competition, i.e., mainly to war.[287]

280. Bukharin 1982, p. 25.
281. Bukharin 1982, p. 22.
282. Bukharin 1982, p. 31, cf. p 42.
283. Bukharin 1929, p. 120.
284. Bukharin 1929, p. 127
285. Bukharin 1929, p. 139.
286. Bukharin 1929, pp. 12–14 (Lenin's preface).
287. Bukharin 1982, p. 51.

Commenting upon *The Economics of the Transition Period*, Lenin worried that Bukharin had abandoned Marxist dialectics and lapsed into philosophical idealism: 'often, too often, the author falls into a scholasticism of terms.... and into idealism.... This scholasticism and idealism is in contradiction with dialectical materialism (that is, Marxism).'[288] When Bukharin proposed to include in the Bolshevik Party's new programme an integral picture of imperialism fashioned after his own writings, Lenin drew the line: no such integral picture was possible because imperialism could never be a 'pure' phenomenon. The fundamental regulator of capitalism's movement was the universal law of uneven development, meaning there were no pure monopolies, only 'monopolies in conjunction with exchange, markets, competition, crises'.[289] Lenin's *Imperialism* borrowed heavily from Hilferding, but Bukharin was borrowing Hilferding's most egregious mistakes along with his insights. As Lenin remarked:

> Pure imperialism, without the fundamental basis of [competitive] capitalism, has never existed, does not exist anywhere, and never will exist. This is an incorrect generalisation of everything that was said of the syndicates, cartels, trusts and finance capitalism, when finance capitalism was depicted as though it had none of the foundations of the old capitalism under it.[290]

'Globalisation' and imperialism

A full century after the Social-Democratic 'discovery' of imperialism, capitalist 'globalisation' is now being heralded as the latest and greatest novelty of our own time. But today's globalisation also has some old 'foundations' underlying it. Many writers have pointed to important similarities between twenty-first century globalisation and imperialism prior to WWI. One of the earliest such books came from Paul Hirst and Graham Thompson. In *Globalization in Question* (1996), they emphasised that in many ways the world economy before WWI was even more highly integrated than it is today. In 1914, all major currencies were freely convertible on the basis of a universal gold

288. *Leninskii Sbornik*, Moscow 1929, XI [Lenin's comments on the margins of his copy of Bukharin's *Economics of the Transition Period*].
289. Lenin 1917, p. 464.
290. Lenin 1919a, p. 165.

standard, whereas today there are a variety of currency-régimes – many floating currencies, some pegged, others subject to a 'moving peg', and still others switching periodically. But, despite these differences, trade-to-GDP ratios, for many major trading economies, are comparable for the two periods.[291] In the absence of significant restrictions on immigration, labour mobility before WWI was also much greater than it is today; and, in terms of foreign capital-investments, most international businesses are still, as in the time of the great colonial empires, nationally 'embedded' in their 'home'-countries rather than being truly 'globalised'.[292]

The war of 1914–18 disrupted the world-capitalist economy, but, during the 1920s, it was to some degree restored under British and American co-hegemony and with the help of new international institutions such as the League of Nations and the Bank for International Settlements. The final collapse of the international system came not with WWI, but with the Great Depression that began in 1929. In *The End of Globalization: Lessons from the Great Depression*, historian Harold James makes the case that the world system of capitalism, painstakingly reconstructed in the 1920s, broke apart with the failure of these new institutions to manage the conflicts inherited from WWI.[293]

The disruption of the 1930s, led in Europe by Nazi Germany's drive for autarchy, was itself in many ways a continuation of the imperialist ambitions that sparked WWI. An excellent recent study of Nazi Germany, by the British historian Adam Tooze, persuasively argues that the Nazi ambition to conquer *Lebensraum* in the East largely derived from Germany's continuing grievances over having been excluded from colonial conquests before 1914.[294] The Nazi government – like that of Imperial Japan – resented exclusion from 'great-power' status and believed that the future belonged only to those nations that could rival America and the British Empire in economic power and global reach. Hitler's ambitions for territory were not so different from the Kaiser's: both wanted the kind of empire that Karl Kautsky described in 1907 – 'a market which no one can exclude them from', and 'supplies of raw material which no one can cut off'.[295]

291. Hirst and Thompson 1996, p. 27.
292. Hirst and Thompson 1996, p. 98.
293. James 2001, pp. 4–5.
294. Tooze 2006.
295. Kautsky 1907b, p. 65.

Together with these historical parallels and continuities, of course, there are also great and obvious differences. The literature that we have been reviewing suggests that perhaps the most significant of these is the final universalisation of the European state-system, first projected by Hegel at the beginning of the eighteenth century and subsequently elaborated by Marx in *The Communist Manifesto*. The institutionally 'vacant' corners of the world are now limited to a handful of 'failed states' or those few countries that have yet to reach the modern state-form, being organised instead through precapitalist ties of kinship and faith. The Social-Democratic literature before WWI explained the rise of imperialism by the need to secure foreign investments – in the absence of a local state – with the armed might of the capitalist metropolis whence the capital originated. Of the articles that we have collected for this volume, the one that made this connection most persuasively is probably Anton Pannekoek's 'The Prehistory of the World War', published in 1915. Pannekoek wrote that

> ...extension of capitalist business over the undeveloped world demands at the same time extension of the political domination of European nations over those regions. The legal concepts and forms of primitive peoples do not fit with capitalist enterprise and must be replaced by European law; their freer attitudes and way of life do not correspond to the requirements of capitalist exploitation, which elicits a resistance that can only be broken through armed intervention, conquest and subjugation in favour of European capital. In countries that were already united into large states under despotic rulers, the existing governments are used for this political mastery.... That is what happened or is happening in Egypt, Persia, Morocco, Turkey, and China. Where such states are missing, however, as in Africa, the country is simply taken into possession as a colony; and if the black people are not satisfied, they are either subjected by violent means or eradicated.[296]

The world economy now presupposes European-style states, but this has come about through a final irony. It was the Russian Revolution of 1917, led by Lenin and Trotsky, that gave birth to Stalin's USSR, one of the greatest empires of the twentieth century. In addition to its conquests in Eastern Europe and its troubled sponsorship of the Chinese Revolution, the nominally 'socialist' Soviet Union spent four and a half decades after WWII in a

296. Pannekoek 1915. See Chapter 53.

worldwide rivalry with America to sponsor 'client-states' and replace the failing empires of Britain and France. Yet Stalin's USSR, like the tsarist régime before it, remained a 'prison of peoples' that ultimately collapsed due to its inability to solve the national question or to compete economically with the developed capitalist world.

We are now left with a declining America, a rising China and India, a European Union festooned in faded glory, and a multitude of states elsewhere, each claiming sovereignty while simultaneously co-existing with regional economic associations and the new institutions created after WWII: the United Nations, the World Bank, the International Monetary Fund (IMF) and the World Trade Organisation (WTO) that has recently succeeded the General Agreement on Tariffs and Trade (GATT). Within this new framework, America – the world's greatest creditor after 1945 – has become the world's greatest debtor; and export-led growth has moved from traditional metropolitan centres to more recently industrialising countries. Economic and institutional changes have also brought corresponding changes in ideology as 'civilising missions' have been replaced by universal 'human rights' that negate all cultural experiences foreign to the needs of capital.[297]

Despite vast changes, however, some patterns remain familiar: the universalisation of capital has continued, as Marx expected; the process has involved astounding unevenness, as Lenin predicted; and the outcome bears many features that Kautsky would recognise as 'ultra-imperialism' – beginning with the Cold-War division of the world and continuing with multinational manufacturing and banking alliances, who now discipline errant recipients of foreign investments primarily through recourse to the IMF or the WTO in place of imposing their own garrisons. But the most important concept arising from the Social-Democratic discovery of imperialism was probably *finance-capital.* As the world 'recovers' from the financial crisis of 2008–9 – commonly described as the greatest crisis of capitalism since the Great Depression – Rudolf Hilferding would not be surprised by the power of financial institutions to bend governments to their needs; and Lenin would surely see the gigantic rescue-plans, financed by working people to bail out their tormentors, as one more display of obscene parasitism in the 'highest stage' of capitalism.

---

297. This process was aided by the distinctive strategy of American imperialism, which sponsored both formal decolonisation as a weapon against British and French imperialism and the establishment of bourgeois-parliamentary régimes, including *democratic* counterrevolutions in Germany, the Soviet Union and elsewhere in the 1990s.

Chapter One

'Modern English Imperialism' (November 1897)

Max Beer

Max Beer (1864–1943) was a Jewish-Austrian journalist and historian, born in Tarnobrzeg, a little town in Galicia. He migrated to Germany in 1889, where he became editor of the *Magdeburger Volksstimme*. After eight months, he was arrested, charged with inciting class-struggle and insulting the German army and authorities, convicted and sentenced to fourteen months of imprisonment. In June 1894, Beer moved to London and studied at the London School of Economics in 1895–6. In December 1897, he left for Paris, where he covered the Dreyfuss affair. From there, he moved to New York, where he spent the crucial years 1898–1901 (the time of the Spanish-American War and the Filipino Rebellion) and witnessed the birth of American imperialism, which he analysed for *Die Neue Zeit* and *Vorwärts*, the main journals of German Social Democracy. Beer was also correspondent for the *Munchener Post* and the Jewish *Arbeiter-Zeitung* and collaborated in editing the *Encyclopaedia Judaica*. Max Beer's other major works include his massive *General History of Socialism and Social Struggles*, issued in English in five separate volumes, and his *History of British Socialism*.[1]

1. Beer 1919–25 and 2002 (first published 1919; revised ed. 1929; one vol. ed. with a new chapter 1943, reprinted in two vols. 1953).

When Eduard Bernstein left England in 1901 to return to Germany, Beer was asked to replace him in London as English correspondent for the *Vorwärts*, a position he occupied from 1902 to 1912. In 1915, he was deported to Germany as an enemy-alien, and from 1919 to 1921 he edited *Die Glocke*, a journal founded and financed by Parvus, who, at that time, belonged to the extreme right wing of the SPD (the Lensch-Cunow-Haenisch group). In his autobiography, *Fifty Years of International Socialism*,[2] Beer claims that he attempted to turn the paper away from the SPD and into a cultural and educational review, causing Parvus eventually to dismiss him. Beer later worked, at Ryazanov's request, at the Marx-Engels Institute in Moscow from 1927–9, and subsequently at the Institut fur Sozialforschung in Frankfurt am Main. In 1933, after the Nazis' rise to power destroyed his family, he went into exile once more in London, where he died in 1943.

In *Imperialism, the Highest Stage of Capitalism*, Lenin cited the article that we have translated here and commented as follows:

> In the most flourishing period of free competition in Great Britain, i.e., between 1840 and 1860, the leading British bourgeois politicians were *opposed* to colonial policy and were of the opinion that the liberation of the colonies, their complete separation from Britain, was inevitable and desirable. M. Beer, in an article, 'Modern British Imperialism,' [*Die Neue Zeit*, XVI, I, p. 302.] published in 1898, shows that in 1852, Disraeli, a statesman who was generally inclined towards imperialism, declared: 'The colonies are millstones round our necks.' But at the end of the nineteenth century the British heroes of the hour were Cecil Rhodes and Joseph Chamberlain, who openly advocated imperialism and applied the imperialist policy in the most cynical manner!
>
> It is not without interest to observe that even then these leading British bourgeois politicians saw the connection between what might be called the purely economic and the socio-political roots of modern imperialism. Chamberlain advocated imperialism as a 'true, wise and economical policy', and pointed particularly to the German, American and Belgian competition which Great Britain was encountering in the world market. Salvation lies in monopoly, said the capitalists as they formed cartels, syndicates and trusts.

2. Beer 1935.

> Salvation lies in monopoly, echoed the political leaders of the bourgeoisie, hastening to appropriate the parts of the world not yet shared out. And Cecil Rhodes, we are informed by his intimate friend, the journalist Stead, expressed his imperialist views to him in 1895 in the following terms: 'I was in the East End of London (a working-class quarter) yesterday and attended a meeting of the unemployed. I listened to the wild speeches, which were just a cry for 'bread! bread!' and on my way home I pondered over the scene and I became more than ever convinced of the importance of imperialism.... My cherished idea is a solution for the social problem, i.e., in order to save the 40,000,000 inhabitants of the United Kingdom from a bloody civil war, we colonial statesmen must acquire new lands to settle the surplus population, to provide new markets for the goods produced in the factories and mines. The Empire, as I have always said, is a bread and butter question. If you want to avoid civil war, you must become imperialists' [*Ibid.*, p. 304].
>
> That was said in 1895 by Cecil Rhodes, millionaire, a king of finance, the man who was mainly responsible for the Anglo-Boer War. True, his defence of imperialism is crude and cynical, but in substance it does not differ from the 'theory' advocated by Messrs. Maslov, Südekum, Potresov, David, the founder of Russian Marxism and others. Cecil Rhodes was a somewhat more honest social-chauvinist....[3]

This reference to Cecil Rhodes has been quoted countless times, but apparently always from the English translation of Lenin's *Imperialism*. In Lenin's original text, he gave a Russian rendering of Max Beer's shortened German version of the English original. We thank Ted Crawford for tracing the original quotation for us from W.T. Stead's book at the British Library. In our translation of Beer's article, we include this original quotation.

Beer, who had the advantage of having actually lived for some time in both London and New York, also wrote a pioneering analysis of American imperialism as well as reviews of John Hobson's work, as his other items in this anthology show. In this article he documents the *material and class-interests* that distinguished modern English imperialism from its great historical predecessors in the Macedonian, Roman and Napoleonic empires: 'All those epochs had in common the fact that they were governed by outstanding

3. Lenin 1970, p. 94.

personalities, men of authority whose actions overshadowed and dimmed all the material motives of these historical events.... Things are different with modern English imperialism. Here the material motives appear clearly.'

* * *

'Modern English Imperialism'[4]

I

Following the American Revolutionary War, Benjamin Franklin came on a diplomatic mission to England. Edward Gibbon, the historian of the *Decline and Fall of the Roman Empire*, was already then a famous man whom many people wanted to see. Franklin also asked whether he could receive him. Gibbon declined bluntly because he was reluctant to meet a rebel, whereupon the clever American sent him word that he only wanted to provide him with material for a new work – a history of the *Decline and Fall of the British Empire*.

Franklin's witty reply was by no means regarded merely as a clever reproof. It was then a generally held view that English colonial power, which the bold seafarers had been building since the time of Elizabeth, was about to end. The overseas possessions remaining in England's hands at that time were actually not many: the Eastern coast of Canada, Bengal, Gibraltar and some scattered islands. But even those possessions were of very doubtful nature. Bengal and Canada, barely conquered, were in open rebellion. Spain and France sent a navy to Gibraltar, and Holland also assumed a warlike attitude. And those were then powerful colonial empires. Spain owned Mexico, Central America and, alongside Portugal, almost all of South America; France, then stronger than England, owned Mauritius and many West-Indian islands, and Holland had major possessions in Asia, South Africa and South America. What could England, humiliated and reduced, amount to vis-à-vis those powers?

Two factors were at work in Great Britain that made possible the erection and consolidation of the worldwide 'Second Empire': the powerful Industrial Revolution, which led to the development of gigantic productive forces, and

4. Beer 1897.

the relatively free constitution, which enabled the Englishmen to take up the colonial policy again and continue it in the spirit of the new economic doctrines. The strong influence of Adam Smith's *Wealth of Nations* on the young Pitt is too well known to require further proof. Those factors enabled England to overcome the serious crisis and put together the elements of modern English imperialism. Spain, Portugal and Holland, the proud rulers of the seas in the seventeenth and eighteenth centuries, almost ceased to be colonial powers during the nineteenth century due to the lack of one or both of those two factors. 'Greater Britain', by contrast, encompasses today the greater half of North America; territories in East, South and West Africa; India; the Malaysian peninsula; countless islands and invaluable fortresses, which rule over the main routes of world trade; as well as Australia, Tasmania and New Zealand, which were colonised by peaceful means, free from any violent state-action.[5] The ratio of the English colonial territories to the motherland is 92.6:1 – an empire unrivalled in world history.

II

If there ever were statesmen able to learn from history, they are undoubtedly the English. Each energetic show of force, whether it ends in victory or defeat, is for them an occasion for reflection. Each revision, each forward movement of the political and social theories of England, had a national shock for a starting point. Even the loss of the United States was a significant lesson. The Englishmen rightly saw in that catastrophe the bankruptcy of the old colonial policy, based on [commercial] monopoly and the mercantile system.

Mercantilist doctrine was cruelly simple and fully corresponded to the needs of nascent capitalist production and the crude ideas of the 'primitive accumulators'. Could there be anything better than a distant monopolised market ruled by the state, which supplied cheap raw materials and bought expensive manufactured products? That was the principle of the old trade and colonial policy that ruled the world from the discoveries of Columbus and Vasco da Gama to the work of Washington and Adam Smith. According to the well-informed Thorold Rogers, that was the main goal of the papal

5. [Max Beer, like Kautsky and most of the theoreticians of the Second International, had a blind spot for settler-colonialism.]

bulls of Alexander Borgia. It led the Dutch in their successful, indeed, too-successful, struggles for the Spice Islands, and it was the reason for the charters of the Russian, Latin, Turkish and Hudson Bay companies.

At the end of the eighteenth century that doctrine was already obsolete, at least for the economic life of England; further adherence to it could only be harmful for the production- and exchange-relations resulting from the Industrial Revolution. In 1776, the *Wealth of Nations* appeared, attacking the entire system of monopoly and protection with extreme vehemence and shattering it; in the same year came the American Declaration of Independence, which proved even more emphatically the perniciousness of the old colonial policy.

From then on began a new era in the political history of England. Adam Smith and Washington were the Rousseau and the Robespierre of the English revolution of the eighteenth century. But their doctrines were only slowly introduced into real life. Even if the principle of economic and political freedom was generally granted *in abstracto*, seventy years passed before it was applied in practice. Only in the 1840s did England begin to support free trade, granting to the main colonies – Canada, Australia and South Africa – self-government and almost complete political independence from the mother-country. The disciples of Jeremy Bentham played a prominent role as supporters of the latter measure, those of Adam Smith as supporters of the former.

In the enthusiasm over the triumph of *laissez-faire*, which incidentally did much more for Great Britain than anything the *Kathedersozialisten* could possibly do for Germany, people believed that they had found in commerce the only factor necessary for the advancement of culture. All the other methods that the state had so far used were considered either useless or harmful. Already in 1836 Cobden declared that 'The colonies, army, navy, and church are, with the corn laws, merely accessories to our aristocratic government.'[6] John Bull employed the following fifty years to clean up his house from that rubbish. And the brilliant results of the free-trade policy, which paralysed the internal enemy – the Chartist movement – and gave an unexpected boost to England's foreign trade, seemed to confirm this assumption. Thus a complete indifference towards the colonial possessions set in. The English regiments in Canada, the West Indies, South Africa and Ceylon were disbanded, and the only concern seemed to be how to get rid of the colonies as quickly as possible.

---

6. Cobden 1886, p. 2, Letter to Thomas Dick, Manchester, 7th Oct., 1836.

It is very characteristic of this period that a statesman as well disposed to imperialism as Disraeli regarded the colonies as an evil. As Lord Rosebery recounted at the beginning of July 1893, on the occasion of the imperialist banquets in the National Liberal Club (London), Benjamin Disraeli wrote in 1852: 'These wretched colonies will all be independent, too, in a few years, and are a millstone round our necks.'[7] Those views became dominant right up until the 1880s.

III

Thomas Hardy and George Gissing are the only modern English novelists who know not only how to draw and analyse their characters sharply, but also how to reveal the social tendencies that set the individuals in motion. In *Jude the Obscure*, Hardy shows, with his usual psychological refinement, the type of modern worker who, rising from the depths of life, struggles to reach intellectual heights and a socialist worldview. Gissing, by contrast, shows us in his *Whirlpool* the transformation of the financially bankrupt, spiritually decadent bourgeois into a colonial politician and an imperialist. Rolfe, one of his main characters in *Whirlpool*, listens to the lecture of the *Barrack-Room Ballads* of Rudyard Kipling, which, together with his poems from *The Seven Seas*, gives vigorous artistic expression to the imperialist strivings and deeds of England.

> 'Here's the strong man made articulate,' cried Rolfe at length. 'It's no use; he stamps down one's prejudice – what? It's the voice of the reaction. Millions of men, natural men, revolting against the softness and sweetness of civilisation; men all over the world; hardly knowing what they want and what they don't want; and here comes one who speaks for them – speaks with a vengeance.... The Empire; that's beginning to mean something. The average Englander has never grasped the fact that there was such a thing as a British Empire. He's beginning to learn it, and itches to kick somebody, to prove his Imperialism. The bully of the music-hall shouting 'Jingo' had his special audience. Now comes a man of genius, and decent folk don't feel ashamed to listen this time. We begin to feel our position. We can't make money quite

7. Letter of Benjamin Disraeli to his Cabinet colleague Lord Malmesbury, 13 August 1852. Quoted in Malmesbury 1884, Vol. I, pp. 260–1.

> so easily as we used to; scoundrels in Germany and elsewhere have dared to learn the trick of commerce. We feel sore, and it's a great relief to have our advantages pointed out to us. By God! We are the British Empire, and we'll just show 'em what *that* means!'[8]

What a striking contrast between the vehement outburst of Gissing and the wistful remark of Disraeli! And this turnabout took place in less than two decades. The idea of a commercial, political and military federation of the colonies with the mother-country began to insinuate itself already in the 1870s, but it was in 1884 that it first began to assume concrete forms. At that time, the Imperial Federation League was created in London and was joined by many of the most important persons of England. In 1882, the Federal Council was established in Australia, its job being to confederate the Australian colonies upon the pattern of Canada and the West Indies. In 1886, New South Wales and Canada sent a number of volunteers to Egypt in order to participate in the Sudanese military expedition undertaken by England. In 1887 and 1894, colonial conferences were organised, dealing with the ways and means of preparing an imperial union. In South Africa, Cecil Rhodes worked for the conquest and confederation of huge territories in the interest of the British Empire, and in 1895 he organised a revolution against the Boer oligarchy as well as a military campaign against their country, which stood in the way of the British imperial plans in that region. And on 22 June 1897, came the 60th crown-jubilee of Queen Victoria, which turned into a gigantic demonstration in the streets of London for imperialism.

Canada, whose French-speaking population still unfurled the tricolour a decade ago, sent its first Francophone Prime Minister, Sir Wilfrid Laurier, to England in order to work for the imperial federation. He brought to the mother-country the greetings and thanks of a united and loyal Canada, as well as a tariff-reduction of 12.5, or 25 per cent. 'We are loyal,' said Laurier, 'because we are free, and we have to thank England for this luminous liberty.' The Cape colony donated to the English navy a first-class warship. And Mr. Joseph Chamberlain, the English Colonial Secretary, conferred for days with the seven prime ministers of the colonies about the methods of the federation. Only two colonies pronounced themselves in favour of a so-called

---

8. Gissing 1897, pp. 420–1.

Imperial Council, while the rest supported periodical imperial conferences. But all were in favour of abrogating the treaties with Germany and Belgium. Thus English imperialism, which signifies a centralisation of countless colossal forces, is advancing slowly but surely towards its realisation.

IV

Up to now, world history has seen three great momentous imperialist periods: the Macedonian, the Roman and the Napoleonic. All those epochs had in common the fact that they were governed by outstanding personalities, men of authority whose actions overshadowed and dimmed all the material motives of these historical events. Machiavelli, the gifted theoretician of imperialism, looked for a 'Prince' as the main agent of his imperialist plans.

Things are different with modern English imperialism. Here, the material motives appear clearly. Broad popular strata were set in motion by them; Chamberlain and Rhodes are only their instruments. Those motives are: the well-founded assumption that England's industrial and commercial supremacy has been shaken; the growth in political power, socialist strivings and class-consciousness of the workers; the rise of the German Empire, its colonial zeal and aggressive penetration into the world market; the reawakened colonial activity of France; and the rejuvenation of the Tories and their ideals by Disraeli, or rather their merging with the bourgeoisie. At the bottom of all those motives stands the frantic striving of the bourgeoisie to retain its economic and political power, which boils down to preservation of the capitalist mode of production. A tighter economic, political and military attachment of the colonies to the mother country would open up for English industry worldwide markets and enable it to brave the dangers that undoubtedly confront it; namely, a) the industrial and military threats of Europe, America and awakening East Asia, and b) the aspirations of the modern English proletariat.

How deeply people here are aware of these dangers is shown by the utterances of Rhodes and Chamberlain, who are generally acknowledged as the most capable agitators for imperialism. In his *History of the Mystery*, W.T. Stead, the famous editor of the *Review of Reviews*, described the South-African disturbances in 1895. In the first chapter his intimate friend Cecil Rhodes, who in February 1895 visited London and was received by the Privy Councillor, says the following about his imperialist ideas:

'Last night I went down to a meeting of the unemployed in the East End. I wanted to see for myself how things were. [...] The meeting last night, the wild speeches, which were nothing but semi-articulate wails for bread, and the hungry look on the faces of those present, gave me a bad turn, I can tell you. And your Little Englanders,' said he, suddenly halting, 'and, your Little Englanders are such fools they do not see it.' [...] 'Oh, you are all alike,' he said savagely – 'you are all alike! You are all so full of the politics of the parish pump, you have never a thought for the great problem which overshadows everything. They call it an Imperial question; a bread-and-butter question it is, or rather a bread-without-butter question for the people.' [...] 'My real idea is the solution of the social problem, which, being interpreted, means that in order to keep your forty millions here from eating each other for lack of other victuals, we beyond the seas must keep open as much of the surface of this planet as we can for the overflow of your population to inhabit, and to create markets where you can dispose of the produce of your factories and of your mines. The Empire, I am always telling you, is a bread and-butter question. If you have not to be cannibals, you have got to be Imperialists.'[9]

No less clear is Mr. Joseph Chamberlain. The English colonial minister, who organised the latest imperial conference, is at the same time the social politician of the current Conservative government. He is an assiduous reader of the publications of the Labour Department and a sharp observer of the socialist movement. His conception of history is outspokenly materialist, and, in his foreign and colonial speeches, the material foundations of modern English imperialism are suggested with unambiguous clarity: 'Empire is Commerce.' Chamberlain understands by commerce the whole of economic life:

In my personal opinion... [the commercial union of the Empire] is a question which dominates all other Imperial interests, to which everything else is secondary, and which is at the root of the problem with which we have now to deal. The establishment of commercial union throughout the Empire would not only be the first step, but the main step, the decisive step towards the realisation of the most inspiring idea that has ever entered into the minds

9. Stead 1897, Part I: On the Engaging of an Editor, Chapter I: The Ideas of Mr. Cecil [Rhodes].

> of British statesmen. (Cheers.) No one nowadays, in this country or outside of it, denies the enormous benefit it would be to the British race throughout the Empire if we could arrange some union which would lead to closer relations, and which would retain within the Empire, and for the benefit of the Empire, the trade and the subjects now diverted to foreign lands.[10] ... The fact is history teaches us that no nation has ever achieved real greatness without the aid of commerce, and the greatness of no nation has survived the decay of its trade.[11] ... we are actively pursuing that policy of developing the Imperial estate which I ventured to recommend to the House of Commons as the true, the wise, and the economical policy for this country to pursue. (Cheers.) If we pursue it, and if, like that of so many great empires that have passed away, our great dominion comes to an end, we shall at least have left behind us the material monument of our progress through the world. Just as the Romans left their roads which remain to this day to speak for their intelligence and their courage, so we shall leave railroads and means of communication which we have provided as permanent benefits to the country over which we have exercised Imperial sway.[12] ... Because, let the little Englanders say what they like, we are a great governing race, predestined by our defects, as well as by our virtues, to spread over the habitable globe, and to enter into relations with all the countries of the earth. Our trade, the employment of our people, our very existence, depend upon it. We cannot occupy an insular position, and we cannot occupy ourselves entirely with domestic matters – (hear, hear) – and therefore foreign affairs and colonial affairs will continue, as long as our country exists, to be the greatest and the pre-eminent interest to the people of the United Kingdom.[13]

Chamberlain warned the workers not to let themselves be led by the Little Englanders, who stigmatise as filibusterers those brave men who are opening up new lands for English industry.

---

10. Chamberlain 1897, p. 181: 'Commercial Union of the Empire', speech to the Congress of Chambers of Commerce of the Empire, London, 9 June 1896.

11. Chamberlain 1897, p. 102: 'A Noble Heritage', speech to the Congress of Chambers of Commerce of the Empire, London, 10 June 1896.

12. Chamberlain 1897, pp. 149–50: 'British Trade and the Expansion of the Empire', speech at the Birmingham Chamber of Commerce, 13 November 1896.

13. Chamberlain 1897, p. 235: 'A Year's Work', speech at the ninth annual dinner of the Birmingham Jewellers and Silversmiths' Association, 30 January 1897.

And Chamberlain is very well informed. On 28 November 1895, that is to say, immediately after joining the government, he sent a circular letter to the colonies asking them for statistical reports on the crowding out of English trade. The answers appeared in September 1897. This blue book effectively showed a constant decline in English imports and a constant increase in foreign imports into the English colonies. In 1883, the former amounted to 65,409,401 pounds sterling, the latter to 35,800,000. In 1894, the sums were 53,719,040 and 44,040,049 respectively. England's main competitors are Germany, America and Belgium.

In 'Greater Britain' the 'Little Englanders' have almost disappeared. Among the 'Little England' writers can be mentioned Olive Schreiner and John Morley.[14] The former, in her book *Trooper Peter Halket of Mashonaland*,[15] makes Jesus Christ come to Rhodesia to repeat there the Sermon on the Mount, and Morley preaches in his *Machiavelli* the necessity of ethics in foreign policy. Sir William Harcourt changed his dictum: 'We are all socialists now' for a new one: 'We are all imperialists.' Gissing's Rolfe, who some two decades ago was a cofounder of the Social-Democratic Federation and read William Morris and Francis Adam, is today an imperialist and reads Rudyard Kipling's *Barrack-Room Ballads* and *The Seven Seas*.

V

In this concluding section, I would like to point out briefly the difficulties facing the imperialist endeavours and their consequences. Since the seventeenth century, English colonial interests have virtually ruled the foreign policy of England. The conflicts with Holland and France, Chatham's support for Prussia in the Seven Years' War, Trafalgar, Waterloo – all these events had colonial interests as their *leitmotif*. On this point, there are almost no differences of opinion. And it is equally clear that the effect of modern English imperialism on European politics is already noticeable. Imperialist endeavours have placed England in opposition to Germany, France, Portugal and the United States. The English colonial interests intersect in Africa with the German ones; in Delagoa Bay [Maputo Bay, Mozambique], with the

14. See Aveling 1898, pp. 182–8.
15. Schreiner 1897.

Portuguese ones; in Egypt, due to its long-lasting occupation by England, with the French ones; and in Canada and the Bering Sea with those of the United States. By contrast, there has been no direct conflict of interests in colonial policy between England and Russia. As long as Russia makes no move on India, one can hear in England weighty voices in support of an Anglo-Russian agreement. 'The anti-Russian policy of Disraeli is outdated,' declared Lord Salisbury on 9 November 1896. The centre of gravity of English colonial policy lies in Africa: 'From Cairo to Cape Town' is today the watchword. In these endeavours, England clashes with Germany and France. The consequence of all this is the revival of militarism in England. Most poems and the best novels of Kipling are apotheoses of the English soldier, who obeys the 'Widow at Windsor'[16] and fights and dies for the world empire.

No less reactionary are the consequences of imperialism for domestic policy. In liberal and progressive circles, people are beginning to find fault with democratic institutions and even to call into question democracy itself. The liberal professor and parliamentarian Lecky gives literary expression to these voices in his work *Democracy and Liberty*.[17] He attacks general suffrage as the 'most asinine cult of numbers', extols the blessed government of a hereditary aristocracy, praises militarism and considers any reform in property-relations absurd and dishonest.[18]

Nevertheless, the realisation of imperialism still has to struggle against many material and formal difficulties. Chamberlain's notion of a 'commercial union of the empire' means free trade within and protectionism without. Lord Salisbury and the Duke of Devonshire find themselves in complete harmony with the views of their colleagues. Canada and New South Wales, on the contrary, spoke out against a protectionist tariff. Besides, the government-problem is far from having been solved. How should the colonies share in the government of this huge empire? The democratic colonies of Australia do not want to hear about sending delegates to the House of Lords. If an imperial parliament were formed, then Scotland, Ireland, Wales and England should

16. [*The Widow at Windsor* is a poem by Rudyard Kipling, part of the first set of the *Barrack-Room Ballads*. The eponymous 'widow' is Queen Victoria. Kipling 1893, pp. 179–81.]

17. Lecky 1899.

18. All the writings quoted in this article by Hardy, Gissing, Kipling, Stead, Schreiner, Morley and Lecky appeared in the last three years and are indispensable for understanding contemporary England.

have separate parliaments – and therefore home rule. The imperial parliament could not thus deal with provincial affairs.

No less important and difficult is the question of national defence. How should the army be organised in order to be able to defend those huge territories? Already now, when the military needs are smaller, the admiralty is unable to man the navy adequately, and the war-department cannot fill the contingents. The introduction of universal conscription seems to be the only way out; and that will not happen easily in England.

No less important is the question of leadership. Lord Salisbury is not equal to those tasks. Chamberlain, Rosebery and [Charles W.] Dilke, the most gifted living politicians of England, have neither the prestige nor the trust necessary to implement such gigantic plans.

All of those problems still wait for solutions. Their discovery would, on the other hand, realise a dream no less grandiose than the 'United States of Europe'. And such a political and economic centralisation would represent nothing but the last phase of the bourgeois world. To quote Bruno Bauer, the gifted researcher of the Roman Empire: 'Such a treasure of goods and funds portended something far more than legislation, which changes every year.'

Chapter Two

'The United States in 1898' (31 December 1898)

Max Beer

American imperialism[1]

There are few documents by great founders of nations that are more appealing to the modern mind than George Washington's Farewell Address to his compatriots. He wrote it in 1796 in order to describe his experiences for the benefit of the nation. He departed from public life in the same calm and cheerful mood he had shown in stormy circumstances, and the prize for his hard and dangerous work was the justified hope of having laid the foundations of a free and powerful republic.

He could imagine the growth of the Union: the North with its industry, the South with its production of raw material, and the East in lively commercial intercourse with the West. And this growth and change alarmed the otherwise so optimistic spirit of the American founding father. He feared that the strengthened Union would follow the way of the European states and mingle in their quarrels and intrigues. The consequence would be the introduction of 'overgrown military establishments which,

1. Beer 1898.

under any form of government, are inauspicious to liberty, and which are to be regarded as particularly hostile to republican liberty'. He therefore added: 'The great rule of conduct for us in regard to foreign nations is, in extending our commercial relations, to have with them as little political connection as possible.... Why by interweaving our destiny with that of any part of Europe, entangle our peace and prosperity in the toils of European ambition, rivalship, interest, humor or caprice? It is our true policy to steer clear of permanent alliances with any portion of the foreign world.'[2]

This advice by Washington represented the first principle of American foreign policy. The second principle was established by President Monroe in his famous message of 2 December 1823. The Monroe Doctrine consisted, as is generally known, of the following two points: 1) any attempt by European powers to extend their rule over any part of the American continent would be regarded by the Union as a hostile act; and 2) the American continent could no longer be regarded as an object of colonisation by any European power. Those principles of Washington and Monroe have until now been the basis of American diplomacy.

The year 1898 witnessed a complete turnaround. Dewey's cannons in Manila announced to the world the death of the Spanish colonial empire and birth of the new American diplomacy. American democracy, which Alexis de Tocqueville considered five decades ago so firmly established, gave way to imperialism. In the equality of conditions Tocqueville saw the source of American life, and this equality has now been wasted.

Political democracy presupposes a certain economic equality. And wherever we see democratic principles implemented in a complex society, we can be sure that a formerly oppressed class has become a powerful factor. But, as long as the struggle of that class is unsuccessful, it strengthens the tendency to imperialism created by economic inequality and accelerates its crystallisation. This phenomenon gives liberal writers the opportunity to complain that the social-revolutionary movement is the cause of imperialism. This reproach is, however, completely unfounded. It rests on the fallacy: *post hoc ergo propter hoc*.[3] Imperialism and socialism only go together to the extent that they spring from the same sources: the growing economic inequality. And the growing

2. Washington 1796.
3. 'After this, therefore because of this.'

economic inequality created by modern production also drives the United States to imperialism.

On 14 June 1898, the American Secretary of the Treasury laid before Congress a memorandum on the economic situation in the Union, which contains the following passages:

> A transformation has taken place in the foreign trade of the Union, which promises to have a deep influence on the whole economic future of the country. It is a well-known fact that the Union has joined the front row of industrial states. For a number of years already, its position as one of the greatest producers of industrial articles and raw materials has been undisputed. Busy as it was with internal development, and content with the home market of 70 million inhabitants, it did not trouble itself much to capture foreign markets. Recently this fact appeared more clearly, because the production of goods in the Union, developed with sensational speed by the remarkable inventiveness and industrial skill of our people, has reached a high degree of development that exceeds internal demand.... The possibilities of developing our productive forces further are so great that their only limits are the profits that we can obtain from them.... Clearly, therefore, the Union must be greatly interested in the partition of those regions where we could find markets for our commodities. This consideration refers specially to the Chinese kingdom. As is generally known, three European powers have seized significant areas in that kingdom, which will enable them to have a direct influence on its commercial fate.[4]

Here we have an official document that explains to us the causes of the new turn [in American foreign policy].

Even clearer, more resolute and instructive is a report of the London *Daily Chronicle* of 4 July 1898, which reveals to us the mainsprings of American imperialism. The report is based on Washington information and was written by a liberal anti-imperialist. 'The astonishing growth of our industry,' it says among other things, 'has perturbed the Washington cabinet. Thanks to the energy and inventiveness of our people the Union is today able to satisfy its annual demand for goods in *eight* months. Thus we have to choose between laying our machines idle during four months per year or overproduce and

4. [Retranslated from the German.]

face a crisis that will fill the streets of our cities with the unemployed in revolt. The government believes that the current situation must lead to a social revolution.'

Social revolution or imperialism! The government chose imperialism, and the revolution in Cuba gave it the opportunity of seizing the Philippines and stepping into East Asia as a great power.

The revolution in Cuba

When Monroe proclaimed his doctrine, Cuba was in a relatively peaceful and prosperous condition. During the Spanish wars against Napoleon, Cuba was loyal to the motherland. The defection of Spanish America and Santo Domingo in 1821 seems to have frightened Spain so much that it changed its Cuban policy. On 18 March 1825, a royal decree turned Cuba into a military dictatorship. This initiated in Cuba the period of insurrections and putsches. Revolts or attempted revolts took place in 1826, 1827–9, 1835, 1844, 1850, 1854, then in the decade between 1868 and 1878, and finally in the last insurrection, which began on 24 February 1895, and led to the downfall of the Spanish colonial empire. The last revolt originally had a local character and seemed to be only a traditional putsch. It would have been quickly suppressed if powerful economic factors had not intervened that gave it remarkable intensity and power of resistance. Those factors were: 1) *the triumph of beet-root over sugar-root*, and 2) *the Spanish mercantilist system*.[5]

Cane-sugar is Cuba's main industry. On it depends railroad-traffic, shipping, foreign trade and numerous small industries. The weal and woe of two thirds of Cuba's population is bound up with this industry. As long as modern technique had not mastered beet-root, sugar-cane was the victor. 'We read that by the end of the 1840s,' Schippel says, 'the struggle was decided against beet-root.' In the two decades from 1850 to 1870, sugar-processing was revolutionised by technical progress to such an extent that beet-root could take up the fight against sugar cane, supported by export-subsidies. In 1884, the production of beet-sugar was equal to that of cane-sugar. The consequence of this development was a fall in the price of sugar. While the European states,

5. Sources: Foreign Office 1895, 1897. Royal Economic Society 1897 (September). Yale University 1898 (October). Schippel 1891.

especially Germany, Austria and France, stimulated sugar-export through shipping subventions, Spain levied, in addition to domestic taxes, an export-tariff of 6 dollars per hogshead! It was calculated, according to the *Yale Review*, that taxes and tariffs on Cuban sugar amounted to 143 per cent. To this should be added import tariffs on basic foodstuffs that raised production-costs even more. The Spanish export-tariff, conceived wholly in the spirit of the mercantilist system, had disastrous consequences for Cuba's economy. [...] Under the blows of European competition, the most prosperous planters turned to large-scale exploitation with machines, and the small owners became proletarians or brigands.

The passage to large-scale plantations soon manifested itself in an increase of production. But this increase could not offset the effects of the fall in prices and the evils of the Spanish tariffs system. The situation became increasingly more critical. 'But even in the most critical situation, caused by the competition of Cuba with the European subsidies to exports, Spain continued to raise the export tariff', says the London *Economist* (supplement of November 1889).

Incidentally, Spain was driven to this suicidal policy by its financial distress. The numerous wars waged by Spain in Europe and America, the numerous revolts and putsches it had to suppress, together with the mismanagement, indolence and poverty of the country, have burdened Spain with relatively enormous debts. [...]

The evils of the Spanish tariff-system were joined by the corruption of Spanish customs-officers, which set even greater obstacles to foreign trade.

And the price of sugar fell continuously. In February 1895, it reached such a low level in Havana that many sugar-refineries ceased to work. The crisis was sharpened by the tariff-war that the Spanish waged at that time against American imports – especially foodstuffs. With these measures, Spain wanted to exert pressure on the United States, which in 1894 reintroduced an import-tariff for sugar.

In February 1895, in the midst of this acute crisis, the revolution broke out that paralysed Cuba's main industry. [...] In the course of a single year Cuba lost three fourths of its main production. The remainder disappeared as a consequence of the infamous command of Weyler[6] to the rural population,

6. [Valeriano Weyler y Nicolau, marquis de Tenerife (1838–1930), Spanish general. His early career was spent in Santo Domingo and Cuba, where he served during the

ordering it to 're-concentrate' in the cities (January 1896). This economic ruin drove even the most peaceful Cuban into the revolutionary camps.

The baleful tariff-system, which drove Cuba to desperation, was also felt very directly in the United States, which bought 94 per cent of Cuba's sugar and 90 per cent of all other Cuban exports. On the other hand, the American share in Cuba's imports was only 33 per cent, because the Spanish tariff policy hindered American exports to the island. [...] And how strongly could the trade between both countries develop if Cuba were free and open to the American spirit of enterprise! That was the heartfelt groan of the American press whenever it came to speak about the Cuban trade.

During the three years of the revolution, the exchange of goods was completely stopped, which aroused great dissatisfaction in American commercial circles. Discontent was even rifer among those Americans who bought property in Cuba and invested significant capitals in industrial enterprises. It is impossible to determine with certainty how high this sum is. According to an article in the March issue of *Forum*, it adds up to 50 million dollars. President Cleveland, in his message of December 1896, estimated it to be between 30 and 50 millions.

Let us recapitulate: the tangible economic interests of the United States, their vehement demands for new markets, as well as the traditional sympathies of the Americans for peoples struggling for bourgeois freedom, led to intervention on behalf of Cuba and the annihilation of the Spanish colonial empire.

That was the conclusion of the Cuban insurrection. No doubt, American capitalists supported the insurrection and contributed a good share to the defeat of Spain. European reaction – especially German and French – may be right in this regard; but they forget that the main cause of the revolution lay in the subsidies to sugar-exports supported by reaction, which gave the United

---

Ten Years, War. He returned to Spain in 1873 and fought against the Carlists (1875–6). While captain-general of the Canary Islands (1878–83) he was created marqués de Tenerife. Later he held a series of high posts, becoming captain general of the Philippines in 1888. In 1896 he replaced Arsenio Martínez de Campos in Cuba to suppress the rebellion there, but his cruel methods were protested against by the United States and he was recalled (1897). Weyler was war minister three times between 1901 and 1907. While captain-general of Catalonia, he suppressed the anarchist rebellion in Barcelona, which culminated in the execution of Francisco Ferrer Guardia (1909). In the mid-20s, he was accused of plotting against Primo de Rivera but was acquitted.]

States the opportunity to intervene. In light of the economic facts, the German and French conservatives and Centre Party supporters, who sympathised with Spain, appear as relentless destroyers of the Spanish colonial power.

The consequences of the War – the elections – anti-imperialism

The victories in Manila and Santiago de Cuba made public the tendencies to adopt an expansionist and great-power [foreign] policy, operating in the United States since 1886. In the intoxication of victory, even those social strata that always opposed the great-power strivings forgot their traditions and supposed interests. I mean the free-silver supporters. The free-silver movement always supported here a purely North-American, at most a pan-American policy, because they all too often had to hear from the gold supporters that foreign trade could only be conducted on the basis of gold [currency]. Limited as the silver-supporters were, they answered: 'Why should we have dealings with foreign countries? Let us remain Americans and let us make of our continent a silver-International!' This demand was regarded as a completion of the Monroe doctrine and was also in the spirit of American traditions.

In the exultation of victory those watchwords grew silent. Even the pan-Americanists [*Rein-Amerikaner*: isolationists] let themselves be carried away by the imperialist wave that swept the country. That is shown by the results of the latest congressional and state elections of 8 November 1898. Their final outcome was the annihilation of the free-silver supporters. It was certainly not to be expected that the Republicans could retain their majority of 1896, but, for the first time since 1886, the party of the president retained a congressional majority two years after its accession to power. In the last Congress, the Republicans had a majority of 55, now reduced to only 10. Apparently, this was a success for the Democrats; upon closer inspection, however, it indicates that the Democrats won only where the currency question was *not* an issue, as in the East. In the West, by contrast, where Democrats supported the free-silver demand, they were defeated by their Republicans rivals. The silver question, which in 1896 stirred the country so much, seems henceforth to be buried.

This appeared even more clearly after the state elections, which determined the composition of the Senate. The Senate, elected for six years, is a stronger legislative body than the House of Representatives. Among the 90 Senators, there were until now 44 Republicans and 46 Democrats, Populists and Silver-Republicans. As a result of the state elections, on 4 March 1899, 50 to 55 Republicans will join the Senate and will go with William McKinley through thick and thin. Gold and imperialism will find no serious opposition in the new Senate. The same will possibly be true of a tariff-revision, which is demanded especially by wholesale trade. Of the 42 states that held elections on 8 November 1898, 22 also had Senators to elect. The Republicans won majorities in California, Connecticut, Delaware, Indiana, Massachusetts, Michigan, Minnesota, Nebraska, New Jersey, New York, North Dakota, Pennsylvania, Washington, Wisconsin and Wyoming. The Democrats have majorities in Florida, Missouri, Montana, Tennessee, Texas, Utah and West Virginia.

These results must be especially depressing for the Democrats. There is no difference of principle between the two great parties. Their politicians must therefore look after electoral slogans. So far, free silver was the programme of the Democrats. Imperialism washed it away. The expansionist policy, in the wake of strengthened foreign trade, actually makes free-silver agitation impossible. The phrase-mongering Bryan and his supporters turned, therefore, to anti-imperialism, which, as we have seen, is logically connected with free-silver agitation. They were joined by customs-officers who feared a tariff-revision, sugar-producers, for whom the liberation of Cuba was inconvenient, and ideologists who clung to the traditions of the late Washington.

The War has therefore significantly modified the internal politics of the Union. But American foreign policy also experienced a turnaround. The traditional enmity against England is disappearing. England adopted a tolerant attitude towards the United States as soon as it realised that the significance of colonies does not lie in their rule but in peaceful trade with them. American policy towards England was, on the contrary, anything but cordial. In recent years, it was especially the free-silver supporters who agitated against England because they regarded London as the world-ruling gold city. To them should be added the Irishmen, who brought over their hatred of England to America. The Bering Sea fishery and the regulation of Venezuela's boundary[7] afforded them an opportunity to give political expression to their enmity.

---

7. [The Venezuela boundary-dispute was a diplomatic controversy over the boundary between Venezuela and British Guiana (now Guyana), notable for the tension it caused between Great Britain and the United States. Venezuela's claim, extending east to the Essequibo River (and thus taking in most of the settled areas of British

The Spanish-American War also brought about a transformation in this regard. The Americans saw that England was the only great power they could count on in a moment of danger. Germany was regarded here as an enemy. The news that Admiral Dewey allowed the American warships in Manila Bay to shoot at the German warship *Irene,* under the command of Admiral Diedrich, was received by the public opinion of the Union with unmixed satisfaction. France was also regarded as an enemy. Only good old England remained true to America. This attitude was immediately understood here and duly appreciated. After the end of the War, the government of the United States transferred to England compensation of 400,000 dollars for the confiscation of Canadian vessels in the Bering Sea, a sum that had been determined in 1890 by the Paris court of arbitration. Soon afterwards Senator Davis, chairman of the US Senate Committee on Foreign Relations, made the following statement: 'A conviction, until now only imperfectly felt and only partially recognized, has emerged and begins to operate clearly. I mean the conviction that 125 million English-speaking citizens, who all over the world established representative governments and personal freedom as well as a progressive civilization, are drawing near in a peaceful way under

Guiana), had been inherited from Spain, and that of Great Britain, stretching west to the Orinoco, was acquired from the Dutch in 1810. The controversy did not gain importance until Great Britain in 1841 had a provisional line (the Schomburgk Line) drawn. Discovery of gold in the region intensified the dispute. Great Britain refused to arbitrate concerning the settled area; Venezuela, however, maintained that the British were delaying in order to push settlements further into the disputed area. Venezuela sought aid from the United States and in 1887 broke off diplomatic relations with Great Britain. President Grover Cleveland's secretary of state, Thomas Francis Bayard, began negotiations, but the matter lapsed. In 1895, Secretary of State Olney, invoking a new and broader interpretation of the Monroe Doctrine, virtually demanded arbitration, basing the right of the United States to intercede on the ground that any state whose interests or prestige is involved in a quarrel may intervene. Lord Salisbury, the British prime minister, offered to submit some of the area to arbitration but refused to allow British settlements to be submitted to adjudication. That reply, a rebuff to Olney, brought Cleveland's momentous message to Congress on 17 December 1895, which denounced British refusal to arbitrate and maintained that it was the duty of the United States to take steps to determine the boundary and to resist any British aggression beyond that line once it had been determined. The president's message caused a commotion; Congress supported him, but while there was some war talk, neither nation desired to fight. Salisbury, involved in European troubles and disturbed by difficulties in South Africa, sent a conciliatory note recognising the broad interpretation of the Monroe Doctrine. An American commission was appointed, and the line that was finally drawn in 1899 made an award generally favourable to Great Britain. Venezuela has periodically revived its claims to the disputed territory, most recently in 2000 under President Hugo Chávez.]

the compulsion of historical development.' Influential journals and reviews also support an Anglo-American rapprochement. In the December number of the *Political Science Quarterly* Mr. Giddins, professor of sociology at Columbia University, pleaded for imperialism and an Anglo American alliance 'to confront effectively a powerful Russian-Chinese empire'.[8] And, in *Scribner's Magazine*, Joseph Chamberlain, English colonial secretary, wrote about 'the new political development in the United States and its significance for an Anglo-American alliance'. He interpreted Washington's farewell address as a warning against 'permanent alliances'. Chamberlain is not interested in a formal alliance, but in sympathetic cooperation on all questions where the interests of both empires are at risk. Chamberlain's wishes will surely be fulfilled if America resolutely pursues its imperialist policy.

Labour-movement and socialism

Socialists from the European continent, who at present direct a great part of their energy to the conquest of democratic liberties, would surely be astonished to hear that the consequence of those democratic freedoms has been to hinder the development of a politically class-conscious labour-movement in England and America. Nevertheless, European socialism is right in its present endeavours because democracy can only hinder the socialist movement when the former originated long before the latter, thus giving to the bourgeoisie the possibility of turning the democratic liberties into a conservative force. It would certainly be interesting to develop these ideas further and investigate more closely the psychological effects of democracy in England. But here I must confine my analysis to America, and the two countries have few points of contact politically and socially.

The main difficulty for the development of a politically class-conscious labour-movement in America is its party system. Political life is based here on two large parties, Republicans and Democrats. There is no difference of principle between them. A change of government is nothing more than a change of personnel. We have here only two party skeletons. But how do they manage to survive and set the country in motion despite the existence of a free press and free criticism?

---

8. [Giddings 1898 (December).]

In order to make my answer clearer, let us first compare American party-conditions with English ones. The Tories were considered for many years to be reactionary and hostile to freedom, while the Liberals were regarded as the shield of English liberties. As far as a party can fulfill its mission, the Liberals have done it. They have defeated the Tories intellectually. England offers today the peculiar spectacle of a progressive nation. There are no differences of principle between Tories and Liberals today. The consequence is the decay of the Liberal Party. If the Liberals want to stay in the political arena, they can do nothing else but turn to the Left and adopt from progressive trade-unionists and socialists a straightforward social-political and radical-democratic programme. The radical wing of the Liberal Party understood this well and therefore strives to unite the remains of the Liberal Party with the progressive labour-movement. Those who want to know more about the current domestic political situation in England can consult the last article of the September issue of the *Contemporary Review*, signed by 'New Radical'. The disappearance of principled differences between Tories and Liberals will be to the advantage of the labour-movement.

Here, in America, things are completely different. If the parties have no principles and programme to offer, they command in return a vast patronage and can reward their supporters with governmental and private posts because a change of government means a change of public servants. Here the rule is: To the victor belong the spoils! And the victors divide among themselves the greatest and smallest jobs: they dispose of the federal government, the state governments and the city administrations. The city of New York alone can dispose of 14 million dollars annually for jobs. The appointment of civil servants is not a question of qualifications or strength of character, but of political orientation. Even the 4,000 typesetters working at the government printing presses in Washington are appointed and dismissed according to their political conviction.

But that is not all. The party leaders are also connected with great industrial firms: railway-companies, telegraph-owners, street-car companies, etc. The recommendations of the almighty party bosses also count in the private sector. Bourgeois politics permeates all pores of social life – not the English, principled bourgeois politics, but petty and concrete politics based on momentary interests. And the country is covered with a net of such party organisations, led by ruthless, mostly uneducated but always brutal bosses. Theodore

Roosevelt, the famous leader of the Rough Riders in the Cuban campaign and today imperialist governor of the state of New York, described this boss-system in the *Century* (November 1886). He said:

> A Boss is able to procure positions for many of his henchmen on horse railroads, the elevated roads, quarry works, etc. Great corporations are peculiarly subject to the attack of demagogues, and they find it greatly to their interest to be on good terms with the leader in each district who controls the vote of the assemblyman and alderman; and therefore the former is pretty sure that a letter of recommendation from him on behalf of any applicant for work will receive most favourable consideration. The leader also is continually helping his supporters out of difficulties, pecuniary and otherwise: he lends them a dollar now and then, helps out, when possible, such of their kinsmen as get into the clutches of the law, gets a hold over such of them as have done wrong and are afraid of being exposed, and learns to mix bullying judiciously with the rendering of service.[9]

Thus wrote Theodore Roosevelt, one of the best connoisseurs of political life in America.

What can a poor labour-movement accomplish against these rich, widespread organisations, with countless job-hunters and job-offers, when it can offer nothing but ideals, struggles and persecutions! How morally strong must a class already be in order to be able to renounce all momentary advantages and impose on itself sacrifices in the name of social justice and human liberation! And where should that moral strength come from if political life is based on corruption and that corruption is legalised?

Under those conditions, the socialist movement, that is to say the independent political organisation of the proletariat, suffers most. But the trade-unions are also insignificant both in character and numbers. There are in the United States about half a million workers organised in unions. Numerous local, national and federal unions are united in the American Federation of Labor, which encompasses some 250,000 workers. That organisation is at present the most significant and active and must therefore be regarded as the representative of trade-union thought in America. It is led by Samuel Gompers and Peter J. McGuire. The latter was, as Julius Motteler told me in

9. [Roosevelt 1886, p. 81. Quoted in Bryce 1893, Vol. 2, p. 115, Note 1.]

London, in one of his informative private conversations on the international labour-movement, an intelligent socialist; Gompers was a member of the *Internationale* group [in New York]. Both are now keen to chain the American trade-unions to bourgeois politicians.

From 12 to 18 December 1898, the eighteenth congress of the American Federation of Labor took place in Kansas City. 230,000 dues-paying members were represented. Most of the time was taken up by endless debates on the internal affairs of the Federation, as well as by the reading of the twenty-pages-long report of President Gompers. Only twice did the congress rise to a certain intellectual height: on the occasion of the reports on imperialism and socialism. To give here extracts from Gompers's report is not feasible, because it would only lead to misunderstandings. Gompers wrote it in a grandiloquent, almost oriental style that enabled him skilfully to avoid decisive questions. In lofty words he celebrated the victory of American arms, and he became totally sentimental and maudlin when speaking about the consequences of the War – i.e. about imperialism. By contrast, he found no time to condemn the butchery of 13 miners in Virden,[10] or judge Hammond of Cleveland, who forbade and repressed the perfectly legal strike of 1,600 wire-pullers by means of an injunction. Gompers only found his courage again against the poor socialists, whose crime consisted of calling for meetings of striking workers in order to explain to them the immanent forces of the modern mode of production.

On the question of imperialism the following resolution was adopted

> *Whereas*, as a result of the war with Spain a new and far-reaching policy, commonly known as 'imperialism' or 'expansion', is now receiving the attention of the National Government, and if ratified by the United States Senate will seriously burden the wage-workers of our country, thrust upon us a large standing army and an aristocratic navy, and seriously threaten the perpetuity of our Republic, therefore be it

---

10. [On 12 October 1898, Illinois miners at Virden, Illinois, confronted armed guards in a battle that became one of the bloodiest class-conflicts in American history. Seven miners were killed and eight wounded. This battle was part of a longer struggle to organise miners known as the Illinois mine-wars of 1898–9. It is the reason why Mary Harris 'Mother' Jones, the famous American labour-leader, is buried in Mt. Olive (although she died in Silver Spring, Maryland), along with the miners who were killed in what became known as the 'Virden Massacre'.]

> *Resolved*, that this convention offers its protest against any such innovation in our system of government, and instructs our officers to use every honorable means to secure its defeat.[11]

In other words, the resolution called on the workers of the United States to vote in the next presidential elections for the Democratic candidate Bryan and against McKinley or Admiral Dewey.[12] The latter was already proposed as Republican candidate for 1900. All the speakers, with the exception of the typesetter Max S. Hayes of Cleveland, spoke for the resolution. Hayes argued that the American worker should not turn these questions into electoral slogans. 'The workers of this country have occupied themselves enough with questions like free trade and protective tariffs, free silver and gold, and in doing so have neglected their own interests. Imperialism also threatens to bring dangerous confusion into our ranks. The expansion policy is the logical consequence of the present capitalist system. We are not gathered here to support one of the two big bourgeois parties. As trade-unionists we should leave aside such questions.' The [anti-imperialist] resolution was accepted.[13]

The second important discussion concerned the socialist motions submitted to the AFL congress by the mechanics, brewers and the Cleveland Central Union. Their aim was that the congress should declare itself in favour of a socialist policy. The motions were first of all handed over for appraisal to the legislative commission of the Federation. The commission reported that the Federation was ready to accept help from reformers and socialists, but that 'the Federation should not introduce or endorse party programs…and it is not the duty of the unions to tell their members which party they should vote for.'

Delegate Tobin then introduced the following countermotion: 'The congress resolves that the labor question can only be solved by turning the land and the

11. [Gompers 1995, p. 43.]

12. [This is a peculiar reading of the anti-imperialist resolution of the 1898 AFL convention, though it is true that Gompers ultimately drove the AFL into the Democratic Party fold. The Democratic Party Platform of 1900 included an anti-imperialist plank that denounced 'the war of "criminal aggression" against the Filipinos' and warned the American people 'that imperialism abroad will lead quickly and inevitably to despotism at home'. Democratic Party of the United States 1900 (July 6), p. 5.]

13. [The prevailing sentiment at the convention was opposed to colonial annexations on the ground that this would involve competition from cheap native labour. Only three delegates voted against the resolution.]

means of production, distribution and exchange into common property, and that the union movement, together with class-conscious political action, is the best method to reach that goal. We therefore recommend to trade unionists that they vote only for political parties that make these principles their own.' This motion was supported by James F. Carey, the state-representative for Haverhill [for the Social-Democratic Party of America], and Max S. Hayes of Cleveland. Both revealed in their speeches a considerable knowledge of modern socialism. The motion was bitterly attacked by McGuire and Gompers. The former called socialism a theory that blinded and dimmed the eyes of the workers; Gompers turned especially against the Socialist Labor Party, whom he accused of trying to ruin the union-movement. Finally, Tobin's motion was rejected by 197,100 votes against 49,300.

All the speakers who opposed Tobin's motion were especially vehement in their attacks against the Socialist Labor Party. Hatred against that party grows in proportion to its successes. In the last elections, it put up candidates in 22 states who received some 80,000 votes, and in Holyoke it even succeeded in electing a town-councillor. The hatred of the pure-and-simple unionists against the Socialist Labor Party is due to the fact that, in 1896, the Party made an attempt to create socialist unions, and that the members of the Party within the old unions agitate for socialism.[14]

The question of whether socialists have the right to create oppositional unions is a burning one here. Even among the ranks of the party members there is no clarity on this issue, which gives rise to disagreeable disputes. There are few indications in socialist literature on this issue. The international socialist and union-congress, held in London in 1896, declared in its resolution on the 'economic policy of the working class' that 'political views should not be a cause for splits in the economic struggle, but it is the *duty* of the labour organisations, arising from the essence of the proletarian class struggle, to educate its members as *social democrats*'. But what is to be done when the unions deny the existence of the class-struggle and not only neglect their

14. [In 1896 the Socialist Labor Party, led by Daniel De Leon, endorsed 'dual unionism' by creating the Socialist Trade and Labor Alliance, the first attempt to build a revolutionary union-movement in the United States. By contrast, the union-leaders of the Socialist Party of America adopted a policy of 'boring from within' the AFL with some success: in 1912, Max Hayes, a prominent Cleveland Socialist who was running against Samuel Gompers for President of the AFL, obtained about one third of the votes cast.]

duty to educate their members as socialists but actually fight against socialism? Is it not at least excusable if there are comrades who decide to build counter-unions?[15]

That is the main cause of the disunity in the Socialist Labor Party. It is often accused of being intolerant and narrow-minded, much like the Social-Democratic Federation in England. This disunity gave rise to the appearance of Eugene Debs's Social-Democratic Party. Debsian Social Democracy was formed in 1897 in Chicago. Its original aim was to establish socialist colonies, but already at its first congress, held in Chicago in July 1898, it split. Those who opposed colonisation and supported political action left the congress, and Debs joined them. Thus was the Social-Democratic Party formed. In the last elections, it put forward candidates in five states who received some 9,000 votes.[16] In Haverhill, an industrial zone in Massachusetts, it succeeded in sending comrades Carey and Scates to the state assembly, as well as in electing comrade Chase as mayor and some comrades as town-councillors. The Social-Democratic Party has many similarities with the English Independent Labour Party, and like it is regarded as more tolerant and broad-minded vis-à-vis the reform attempts and the unions.

On the whole, it seems to me that the American labour-movement is to a certain extent following the same course as the English one. In America, too, the time has come when the unions must face up to the class-struggle and adopt socialist resolutions. Until then, the different socialist parties will also grow in numbers and political experience, which will enable them to overcome their contradictions and achieve unity.

---

15. ['Comrade Beer, while in America, was a De Leonite – what we call here an "Impossibilist". When he came over to this country his first note was, therefore, rank pessimism. He could find, outside the then rather limited body of the S.D.F., no Social Democratic movement in England nor even any such prospect.... The election of Mr. Shackleton – which, it will be remembered, was a walk-over – changed comrade Beer's state of mind as if by magic. The event, I well remember, was described by him in the *Vorwärts* as a 'new era', and ever since then he has been attached to the Labour Party, supporting it and the tactics of its leaders through thick and thin, and criticising the S.D.P. at the same time as sectarian and doctrinaire.' Rothstein, 1908, p. 6.]

16. According to reports that appeared after this article (whose publication was unfortunately delayed due to our chronic lack of space) was written, the number of votes of Debsian Social Democracy is larger. An American friend wrote this to us from Chicago on 31 January: 'A little band of 20 to 25 people formed in 1898 the nucleus of the new party. Through an exceptionally active agitation this handful of people recruited in five months 1,000 members, and in the elections obtained 12,000 votes in 5 states. In the past 60 days the membership has grown to 1,600.'

Chapter Three

'The United States in 1899' (19 November 1899)

Max Beer

The White Man's Burden[1]

In the course of this year, two poems have appeared here that quickly became popular and gave rise to countless imitations, rejoinders and travesties. One of them, called 'The White Man's Burden', stemmed from the imperialist pen of Rudyard Kipling, while the other, called 'The Man with the Hoe', was written by Edwin Markham, who spent his teens working as cowboy in the mountain-ranges of California and is today a university-professor and worker-poet.[2]

Those poetic voices are, so to speak, the artistic expression of the political and economic events of the passing year and of the moods evoked by them. Rudyard Kipling represented the mightily imposing imperialism; he summons the Americans to take upon themselves the 'burden' of spreading American rule and sticking to plans for the colonisation of the Philippines.

1. [Beer 1900. The article consists of five sections, of which only the first one has been translated here. The remaining four do not deal with American foreign policy but with American labour-politics.]

2. [Kipling 1899 (February), reprinted in Kipling 1908, pp. 78–80. Markham 1899a (January 15), reprinted in Markham 1899b, pp. 15–18.]

Markham, by contrast, speaks about the 'burden' of the working slaves, whom the modern economic system degrades into beasts of burden. We are much more interested in the 'man with the hoe' than in the burden of Kipling's 'white man' and the bourgeois policy of conquest, which was splendidly characterised by an anecdote recounted by John Fiske in his book *American Political Ideas*:

> Among the legends of our late Civil War there is a story of a dinner-party given by the Americans residing in Paris, at which sundry toasts concerning not so much the past and present as the expected glories of the great American nation. In the general character of these toasts geographical considerations were very prominent, and the principal fact which seemed to occupy the minds of the speakers was the unprecedented *bigness* of our country. 'Here's to the United States,' said the first speaker, 'bounded on the north by British America, on the south by the Gulf of Mexico, on the east by the Atlantic and on the west by the Pacific Ocean.' 'But,' said the second speaker, 'this is far too limited a view of the subject: in assigning our boundaries we must look to the great and glorious future which is prescribed for us by the Manifest Destiny of the Anglo-Saxon Race. Here's to the United States – bounded on the north by the North Pole, on the south by the South Pole, on the east by the rising and on the west by the setting sun.' Emphatic applause greeted this aspiring prophecy.[3]

For thirty years, this phrase about 'Manifest Destiny' was let rest, only in order to be resurrected this year. It was the *leitmotif* of the speeches that McKinley delivered across the country, and among the great majority of American citizens the conviction has established itself that their destiny is actually to rule over foreign countries. The excessive enthusiasm with which Admiral George Dewey was greeted in New York on 30 September 1899, was intended less for the victor of Manila Bay than for the man who dared to lift the curtain under which the future of the United States was hidden. There can be no doubt that the ruling classes are determined to keep the Philippines, and the higher the price that they have to pay for that country the stronger their determination. On 5 January 1899, General Otis issued a proclamation sent to him from Washington, which in unmistakable terms called upon the disappointed

3. Fiske 1902, pp. 101–2, Chapter III: 'Manifest Destiny'.

Filipinos to submit to the victor. On 6 February, the Senate ratified the Paris peace treaty [with Spain], and on 20 February Congress granted 20 million dollars for the campaign, which began on 4 February with a strong attack on the part of Aguinaldo. The elections that took place in 12 states on 7 November showed favourable results for the government and its policy.

The administration of the new colonial possessions met with constitutional difficulties but has been on the whole satisfactory. In Cuba and Puerto Rico, American generals stand at the head of the government, but they are advised by a cabinet composed of natives. The dispositions have been met for granting a good measure of local government to the islands. The Americans earned great merits with the sanitation of Havana. By contrast, the Hawaii islands, which were annexed on 12 August 1898, were thrown into the hands of sugar-speculators who import proletarians from all corners of the world to turn them into bound labourers. The working conditions there are utterly lamentable. The American colonial possessions were enlarged this year with the island of Guam. And had the situation in the Philippines been calmer, we would undoubtedly have witnessed much more far-ranging developments in colonial policy this year. The unrest in Venezuela, Colombia and Santo Domingo would have led to further annexations. The lust for expansion is growing here, and, in recognition of this tendency, Argentina, Brazil and Chile have made an attempt to pave the way for a federation of South-American republics.

In the foreign relations of the United States, further progress can be noticed in the friendship towards England, although Russia, through its cunning representative Cassini, has made extraordinary efforts to prevent that entente.

Presidential elections are due to take place in 1900. To all appearances, McKinley and Bryan will again face each other. And, if the Republicans remain at the helm, as seems very probable, the programme of the government will be: enforcement of the gold currency, construction of a Nicaragua canal or purchase of the Panama Canal, continuation of the colonial policy and construction of a great fleet.

Chapter Four

'Anglo-Saxon Imperialism' (March 1899)

Paul Louis

This article by Paul Louis was apparently the first analysis of imperialism to appear in the continental European socialist press. 'Paul Louis' was a pseudonym used by the French Socialist Paul Lévi (1872–1955). As a youth, he was opposed to militarism and became a member of the Blanquist Comité Révolutionnaire Central (CRC), later known as Parti Socialiste Révolutionnaire (PSR). In 1905, he joined the newly united socialist party (Section Française de l'Internationale Ouvrière or SFIO), representing the Seine area (greater Paris) in Socialist national congresses and sitting on the national council. At that time he wrote *Le colonialisme,* the major French-language book on the subject to appear during the entire period of the Second International.[1]

The historian Georges Haupt quotes Louis expressing a hope, on the eve of war in 1914, that German Social Democrats would save the International: 'As part at least of the French and British socialists are in favour of the proposal signed by Vaillant and Keir Hardie [calling for the declaration of a general strike in case of war], the eyes of the world – and not only

1. Louis 1905. Among his articles in the international socialist press should be mentioned Louis 1900b.

of the workers – are focused on Germany. It is up to German Social Democracy to help this proposal to victory or to bring about its defeat. On the Germans depend the International's decisions.'[2]

It was probably disillusionment with the SPD that fuelled his chauvinism when war began. During the War, he initially supported the *union sacrée,* a commitment by the French Left not to oppose the government or to start a strike for the duration of hostilities. After the October 1917 revolution in Russia, however, he actively backed the Bolsheviks. At the SFIO Tours Congress, held in December 1920, he endorsed affiliation with the Third International, later becoming a member of the French Communist Party's executive committee and of the editorial board of *L'Humanité.* In 1923, he was expelled and subsequently served as general secretary of the Parti d'Unité Prolétarienne (PUP), which reunited with the SFIO in 1936. He ceased all political activity during the Second World War.

Louis wrote several books on the history of socialism, including *Histoire du socialisme en France de la Révolution à nos jours (1789–1945)* and *Cent cinquante ans de pensée socialiste: de Gracchus Babeuf à Lénine,* as well as countless articles for *La revue socialiste, La revue bleue, La grande revue, La revue du mois,* etc.[3] In an article on 'Contemporary Colonisation', published in 1901, he attributed the British concern for markets to overproduction, which he regarded as 'the chronic evil of the modern world.... *Tout vient de la surproduction et tout y aboutit* [it all comes from overproduction and it all ends there]',[4] a conviction that reappeared in his 'Essai sur l'impérialisme' in April 1904. In the meantime, he wrote another essay in 1903 on 'The Bases of Imperialism'. There, he identified imperialism with protectionism and maintained that the growth of trusts and cartels in the United States and Germany resulted from their early adoption of high tariffs.

In the current article, he uses the term 'Anglo-Saxon imperialism' (which he borrowed from the English political lexicon) in reference to calls for a British imperial federation. Repudiation of free trade and creation of a protectionist tariff-union were being proposed to halt the decline in England's share of the world export market. Louis warned that plans to surround the British

2. Paul Louis, 'L'impérialisme', *Socialisme et Lutte de classe,* Vol. 13 (1–5 July 1914), p. 290, quoted in Haupt 1972, p. 167.
3. Sheila Tremlett, 'Paul Louis' in Lane (ed.) 1995, p. 736.
4. Louis 1901a, p. 163.

Empire with protectionist barriers inevitably entailed 'Jingoist' excesses in the drive for new colonial conquests and the recurrent threat of warfare. At the same time, however, he saw the hour approaching when 'the members of the trade-unions and the unions themselves will join the cadres of the incipient revolutionary parties'.

* * *

'Anglo-Saxon Imperialism'[5]

Anglo-Saxon imperialism has lately become one of the essential factors in world politics. It has contributed to darkening Europe's horizon more than any other element. Its influence on everyday events is growing and obvious. Its diffusion in Anglo-Saxon countries can have incalculable consequences, and it must be considered a principle of reorganisation for civilised humanity as a whole. Its effects may appear deplorable or excellent according to the way in which they are regarded. It is one of the most powerful and effective ferments of war and nationalist exaltation known to history, and it could unleash multiple conflagrations. On the other hand, by creating a federation of peoples, i.e. a less limited association than the fragmentary groupings of our era, it appears as a new type of enlarged political formation and a step forward towards the internationalist ideal.

Long before the formulation of the theory of Greater Britain (the title of a well-known book by Charles Dilke),[6] the advent of a system of races or large human societies had been foreseen by numerous German, Austrian and Russian publicists. Pan-Germanism and pan-Slavism are much older than Anglo-Saxon imperialism. One cannot say that they have been totally sterile: pan-Germanism resulted in the unification of Germany and in the Berlin-Vienna alliance, and pan-Slavism led to liberation of the Balkan countries. It would be an exaggeration to attribute to them outstanding qualities or great importance, because both seem to have been quickly relegated to the museum of antiquities. But to do it justice, British imperialism does not deserve to be likened to those two principles of association because its base is much larger, its reasons much more conclusive, and its effectiveness less contestable and

5. Louis 1899 (March).
6. [Dilke 1890.]

distant. Pan-Germanism and pan-Slavism were ideas of publicists and statesmen in search of arguments. When concrete motives were lacking, one could put forward pseudo-ethnographical arguments backed by that blissful sentimentality that carries away ignorant people, the pompous phraseology that is at bottom the last resort of politics among the uneducated masses.

Anglo-Saxon imperialism is a confused aspiration and an economic programme. It is a confused aspiration among part of the British working classes who, in the same way as part of our own working class, accept without further proof the coarse suggestions of an exasperated nationalism or the incitements of a skillful dominant oligarchy. It is an economic programme for the British industrial bourgeoisie, which is threatened for the first time after centuries of its universal rule, assailed by competition in its monopoly-outlets, and condemned to lose its social and political influence together with its admirable commercial prosperity.

Anglo-Saxon imperialism therefore shows three essential and, moreover, contradictory traits: it is the product of chauvinist exaltation; it is destined to save the privileges of the ruling class; and it aims at tearing down boundaries and forming the widest possible agglomeration of peoples, the largest unit of internationality known so far. It therefore clearly deserves the attention of socialism and merits careful examination and scrutiny.

* * *

For two centuries, colonial expansion has been the basis of the United Kingdom's foreign policy. Ever since English industry outweighed agricultural production, Great Britain has turned to distant countries in order to carry out uninterrupted annexations. Its wars with France and Spain during the eighteenth century had no other goal than to conquer those countries' foreign dependencies. The military campaigns of the British Empire thus resulted in vast colonial acquisitions. For [the past] twenty years, England has been making gigantic efforts in this task of progressive enlargement. It has not been successful everywhere; sometimes it had to retreat before too strong or well-armed peoples, but it succeeded in forming around it an agglomeration of territories next to which the empires of antiquity were child's play. During the most recent period, its activity centred in two continents where it pursued – with the tenacity, lack of scruples, and adaptation of means to ends that always characterised it – a work already partially consummated.

It attacked Africa from three angles: the Niger-River basin was penetrated by a chartered company that, after rendering eminent services to the motherland, clashed with its government. A vast extent of territories in the basin of that large river and outside it has been claimed by the London cabinet. Egypt has already been tacitly annexed, despite repeated protestations by certain great powers. In a few short military campaigns with relatively few casualties, the *sirdar* [commander of the Anglo-Egyptian army] Lord Kitchener went down as far as Southern Khartoum and regained control of all the regions formerly involved in the Mahdist revolt [in Sudan].[7] An Anglo-Egyptian convention in January placed all the Upper Nile, including Suakim and Assuan, under the actual domination of the agents of the Queen.

In Southern Africa, Cecil Rhodes established a colony of huge dimensions. Despite his brutal manoeuvres and criminal assaults, he was forced to temporise with the Boers of Transvaal and the Orange Free State. On the other hand, he conquered the areas previously occupied by the Matebele tribes and systematically destroyed those unfortunate peoples. He occupied the ancient capital of the most important of these tribes, Bulawayo, some 2,000 kilometres from Cape Town, and pursued his rapid march to Tanganyika.

---

7. [The Mahdist War (also called the Anglo-Sudan War or Sudanese Mahdist Revolt) was fought in Sudan in the late nineteenth century. In the early 1880s the British-backed Egyptian régime in Sudan was threatened by an indigenous rebellion under the leadership of Muhammed Ahmed, known to his followers as the Mahdi. In 1883 the Egyptian government, with British acquiescence, sent an army south to crush the revolt. Instead of destroying the Mahdi's forces, the Egyptians were soundly defeated. The occupation of Khartoum on 25 January 1885, and the execution of the Governor of Sudan, Charles Gordon, temporarily ended British and Egyptian involvement in Sudan, which passed completely under the control of the Mahdists. Muhammad Ahmad died soon after his victory in 1885 and was succeeded by the Khalifa Abdallahi ibn Muhammad, who proved to be an able ruler of the Mahdiyah, the Mahdist State. In 1898, in the context of the scramble for Africa, the British decided to reassert Egypt's claim on Sudan. An expedition commanded by Herbert Kitchener, the new *Sirdar* (commander) of the Anglo-Egyptian Army, was organised in Egypt. After defeating a Mahdist force in the Battle of Atbara in April 1898, the Anglo-Egyptians reached Omdurman, the Mahdist capital, in September. The bulk of the Mahdist army was cut down by British machine-guns and rifle-fire. The remnant, with the Khalifa Abdullah, fled to southern Sudan. During the pursuit, Kitchener's forces met a French force under Major Jean-Baptiste Marchand at Fashoda, resulting in the Fashoda Incident. They finally caught up with Abdullah at Umm Diwaykarat, where he was killed on 24 November 1899, effectively ending the Mahdist régime. 30,000 Sudanese were killed, wounded or captured, while British and Egyptian forces suffered approximately 700 casualties.]

For the completion of English plans in Africa, it would have been necessary to occupy a line of continuous possessions uniting the delta of the Nile to Table Bay and Port Natal. The programme could not be realised because the independent state of Congo and German East Africa[8] separated Tanganyika from Uganda. In 1894, Great Britain thought victory was at hand when it signed with the king of Belgium the famous agreement granting it lease to a strip of land alongside Tanganyika, on the edge of the Congolese possessions. But, in view of opposition from France and Germany, and in the face of an irrefutable legal argument, the agreement was terminated. London seemed resigned to accept this interruption, at least temporarily, but meant to remedy it by building a railway-line 10,000 kilometres in length across the African continent, stretching from Alexandria to Cape Town. The Northern section of the line is almost completed up to the Khartoum area; to the South, it leads to Rhodesia. In London Cecil Rhodes is seeking a guarantee for a loan to extend the line to Tanganyika. In order to extend it to Uganda, he will need, failing a very doubtful consent from Germany, an authorisation from the Belgian king. That is what he went to look for in Brussels when he travelled to Europe at the beginning of February 1899.

The designs of the United Kingdom and its leaders in the Far East are no less vast. There is at Westminster, alongside an African Party, a 'Far-East Party' whose programme is the conquest and progressive assimilation of China. This enormous mass will be attacked from several sides at the same time. First of all, from Wei-Hai-Wei [Weihai] in the Gulf of Petchili, which Lord Salisbury claimed and obtained shortly after the occupation of Port Arthur by the Russians and of Kiaotschau [Jiaozhou] by the Germans. To the South, the trading posts of Hong Kong and Shanghai will enable the United Kingdom to conduct multiple undertakings. Canton and the huge Yang-tse-Kiang [Yangtze River] valley, which the Peking court promised not to give away, are considered a future sphere of action by Great Britain. Finally, Burma [Myanmar] can serve as a base of operations against the rich provinces of Yunnan and Sichuan, which can be reached by relatively easy valleys. The appointment of George Curzon, a convinced imperialist, as Viceroy of India [in January 1899] clearly

8. [German East Africa (German: *Deutsch-Ostafrika*) was a German colony in East Africa, including what is now Burundi, Rwanda and Tanganyika (the mainland part of present-day Tanzania). It measured 994,996 km² (384,170 square miles) in size, or nearly three times the size of Germany today.]

shows the plans of the British cabinet. This powerful functionary will leave nothing undone to be ahead of France in Southern China and to push the Mandalay railway to Yunnan. No matter how strong Russia's position may be in the North, England has the advantage of encircling China from all sides. If, as expected, China is partitioned at the beginning of the twentieth century, Great Britain will again grab the largest and richest part. Alongside the almost accomplished African task, the Foreign Office's Asian work already makes a good impression, and the hour when Great Britain annexes several tens of million Chinese, or even more, is perhaps not as distant as some say.

This feverish expansion led England to make contact and to clash with several great powers. Jingoism has come to consider war – even a general conflagration – as a desirable, if not necessary, eventuality. Irrupting into official spheres as far as government councils, Jingoism has imposed on diplomacy a total desertion of traditions, an extraordinarily casual behaviour, a bearing never before seen in foreign relations.

On four occasions, the United Kingdom was on the verge of war with big countries whose own material and moral expansion clashed with British interests. The measures taken by the Foreign Office four years ago regarding Venezuela provoked an ultimatum from the United States Department of State.[9] Later, the invasion of Transvaal, planned by Cecil Rhodes with the

9. [A reference to the Venezuela boundary-dispute (1895–9), a diplomatic controversy notable for the tension caused between Great Britain and the United States. The long-standing dispute concerned the boundary between Venezuela and British Guiana (now Guyana). In 1876, Venezuela protested, broke diplomatic relations with Great Britain, and appealed to the United States for assistance, citing the Monroe Doctrine as justification for US involvement. In 1895, invoking the Monroe Doctrine, newly appointed US Secretary of State Richard Olney sent a strongly worded note to British Prime Minister and Foreign Secretary Lord Salisbury, demanding that the British submit the boundary-dispute to arbitration. Salisbury's response was that the Monroe Doctrine had no validity as international law. The United States found that response unacceptable, and, in December 1895, President Grover Cleveland asked Congress for authorisation to appoint a boundary-commission, proposing that the commission's findings be enforced 'by every means'. Congress passed the measure unanimously, and talk of war with Great Britain began to circulate in the US press. Great Britain, under pressure in South Africa with the Boers and managing an empire that spanned the globe, could ill afford another conflict. Lord Salisbury's government submitted the dispute to the American boundary-commission and said nothing more of the Monroe Doctrine. An American commission was appointed, and the line that was finally drawn in 1899 made an award generally favourable to Great Britain, causing Venezuela periodically to revive its claims to the disputed territory. Internationally, the incident marked the United States as a world power and gave notice that under the Monroe Doctrine it would exercise the prerogatives it claimed in the Western hemisphere.]

complicity of Chamberlain and Salisbury, gave rise to the famous dispatch of Wilhelm II,[10] and tension between London and Berlin became so great that, for the first time since the unification of Germany, the hypothesis of an Anglo-German war seemed plausible. One can easily see how everyday occurrences, above all economic rivalries, prevent any sincere rapprochement between those two great industrial countries. As we write these lines, a feeling of defiance and mutual hostility dominates relations between the British cabinet and the German Foreign Office, although according to certain reports an agreement has been reached to settle the question of Delagoa Bay [Maputo Bay in Mozambique],

There is no need to expand on the coolness of Anglo-Russian relations. The colossal development of Russian influence in China and Central Asia, the seizure of Port Arthur[11] and the Tsar's agreement with the Afghan Emir, exasperated British chauvinism.

But imperialism's influence is felt above all in Great Britain's relations with France. We will not go here into whether, at certain moments, war was about to break out between the two powers, whether Chamberlain was really reckless and inhuman enough to unleash such a calamity upon the world. Nor will we draw up the list of partial faults that France may have committed in Central Africa, among other places. We are the first to regret and condemn the provocations that Hanotaux,[12] in his narrow-mindedness, made against public opinion. It is very unusual in an international conflict for all the faults

10. [A reference to the Krüger Telegram: On 3 January 1896, Wilhelm II approved the dispatch of a telegram to Paulus Ohm Krüger (1825–1904), who led the Boer Republic of Transvaal against the British, after the latter had attempted to incite an uprising with the Jameson Raid. The dispatch, which criticised the British for launching the Jameson Raid, unleashed a flurry of anti-German sentiment in Great Britain.]

11. [Port Arthur (China): Former name (until 1905) of the port and city of Lüshun in northeast China, now part of Dalian. It was occupied by the Japanese, together with the rest of the Liaodong Peninsula, during the First Sino-Japanese War (August 1894–April 1895). After the European diplomatic initiative known as the Triple Intervention (April 1895), Germany, France and Great Britain took advantage of China's weakness to seize port-cities and expand their spheres of influence. To Japan's consternation, after the retreat of Japanese forces late in 1895 Russia moved to occupy the Liaodong Peninsula and fortify Port Arthur. This 'humiliation' was one of the direct causes of the Russo-Japanese War (1904–05).]

12. [Gabriel Hanotaux (1853–1944), French Minister of Foreign Affairs from May 1894 to January 1895, and again from 2 November 1895 to 14 June 1898. The Fashoda incident of July 1898 took place during his term of office, and Hanotaux's distrust of England is frankly stated in his literary works.]

to be concentrated on a single side. However, we think that the responsibility for the sombre situation of last winter fell above all upon the Foreign Office, and that Jingoism has been the cause of its criminal ambitions and relentless vanity.

It is unnecessary to recall events that are surely present in everybody's memory. The proof that the imperialist party led everything, pursuing the fixed idea of winning at any cost, is that it accumulated grounds for conflict without any real motive, concertedly placing at the same level grievances of very different value. Hardly had the Fashoda incident[13] been settled to the complete satisfaction of the London cabinet when Charles Dilke resuscitated the dispute over Newfoundland, and Lord Salisbury, against all rules, published without prior notice the Blue Book on Madagascar.

The detente that took place later, our debate on the foreign-affairs budget, the Queen's message to Parliament, and explanations from Salisbury and Balfour, have restored calm to public opinion and courtesy to the negotiations. The grave crisis that all the civilised countries feared has been momentarily averted, but who can say that, within six or eight months, another even more serious crisis will not develop, and that Anglo-Saxon imperialism, going further than it did this winter in its dreams of conquest and territorial greed, will not make war inevitable? We will describe later the essence, the ultimate reason of imperialism, showing more clearly the permanent danger of war it entails. We can summarise our apprehensions in a few words. At a banquet held at Guildhall at the end of 1898, [the British Prime Minister] Lord Salisbury talked in passing about an English protectorate in Egypt, not in order to advocate it but, on the contrary, to dismiss it. The quite large audience at first applauded frenetically, believing that the Prime Minister was going

13. [The Fashoda Incident (1898) was the climax of imperial territorial disputes between the United Kingdom and France in Eastern Africa and brought them to the verge of war. On 10 July 1898, a small French force reached Fashoda (Kodok, in the south of present-day Sudan) and occupied the fort there. Led by Lord Kitchener, the larger Anglo-Egyptian forces steamed up to the Nile, and on November 4th, 1898, the French government withdrew its forces. In the aftermath, a three-month negotiation was conducted by the British Prime Minister, Lord Salisbury, and the French ambassador in London, Paul Cambon, resulting in the Anglo-French Declaration of 21 March 1899. The Fashoda incident ended in a diplomatic victory for the British and gave rise to the so-called 'Fashoda syndrome' in French foreign policy (giving importance to asserting French influence in areas of Africa that may become susceptible to British influence).]

to proclaim the great change that the Jingoes awaited so much. But when, on the contrary, Salisbury described in a few words its inconveniences, the audience showed a coolness very rare on such solemn occasions. Imagine that tomorrow or in the near future England replaces *de facto* with formal sovereignty over the Nile Delta: will war once again be averted? Will not France, Russia, perhaps even Germany mobilise their troops straightaway? A sudden impulse of British chauvinism threatens to shatter the shaky peace that Europe keeps so precariously; it has become the fundamental element of perturbation at an historical period when one can never be sure about the next day or even the present hour.

* * *

Imperialism is not the weapon or instrument of a particular British party. It is much deeper, more stable and widespread than the nationalisms of the European continent, such as French and Austrian nationalism, for instance. It has nothing in common with them except being contemporary. It penetrates, to an almost equal measure, into all the parties currently represented in the British parliament. The doctrine of indefinite overseas expansion has taken over, carrying along Liberals and Conservatives, Radicals and Unionists. The new leader of the opposition in the House of Commons, Henry Campbell-Bannerman, is an imperialist just like Lords Kimberley and Rosebery, who hold the same political views in the Upper Chamber, or Lord Salisbury, Arthur Balfour and Joseph Chamberlain, the heads of the current Cabinet. Mr. Charles Dilke, radical MP from a mining constituency, is an imperialist just like the Duke of Devonshire, Henry Fowler, Michael Hicks Beach, Herbert Henry Asquith, Lord Hamilton or Sir Edward Grey. We are purposely mentioning here people from all fractions who play a considerable role in English political life and have a single fact in common: their deference for imperialism.

Among the bourgeois groups represented at Westminster, only two men stand out: William Vernon Harcourt and John Morley, the two best lieutenants of William Gladstone. Whatever divergences of ideas may separate these men from socialism, we pay them our respects because they dared to resist the current of national exaltation so worrying to the civilised world. It is true that they paid a high price for their brave fidelity to principles. One had to give up the leadership of the Liberal Party [in December 1898], and the other had to abandon the second place he occupied due to his eminent qualities. With the exception of the original and shrewd editor of *Truth*, Henry Labouchère,[14] all MPs have joined the Jingoes' chorus.

The only consolation from this moral imbalance is that this universal abandonment of principles by the bourgeois parties, this cowardice vis-à-vis the abusers of the flag, will eventually benefit British socialism. Only socialism, amidst unbridled chauvinist fury, appears as a nucleus of calm people who do not lose their heads in the storm. It has already rendered inestimable services in the sombre days of last winter, even if, unfortunately, the organisation of its cadres is not powerful enough to paralyse chauvinism, which can still commit abominable crimes before being broken by the democratic assault.

We will later show that this antagonism between socialists and bourgeois parties is linked to the historical struggle of the classes and is rationally necessary.

* * *

Joseph Chamberlain[15] is the *grand maître* of imperialism. Englishmen have historically liked to incarnate their opinions in a man. William Pitt, Lord Palmerston and Benjamin Disraeli had the honour of this acknowledged

---

14. [Henry Labouchère (1831–1912), a Radical-Liberal politician and journalist, drafted in 1885 the Labouchère Amendment outlawing 'gross indecency', i.e. any sexual activity between men (sodomy was already a crime). This amendment allowed for the prosecution in 1895 of Oscar Wilde, who was incarcerated for the crime.]

15. [Joseph Chamberlain (1836–1914) was the leading exponent of British imperialism. After a successful business career, he entered local politics and won distinction as a reforming mayor of Birmingham (1873–6). Entering Parliament as a Liberal in 1876, Chamberlain advocated radical social reform and served under William Gladstone as president of the Board of Trade (1880–5). In 1886, however, he broke with Gladstone, leading the defection from the Liberal Party of the Liberal Unionists (those Liberals who opposed Home Rule for Ireland). In 1895, he joined the Conservative government as colonial secretary. He pursued a vigorous colonial policy aimed at imperial expansion, co-operation, and consolidation. Although a parliamentary inquiry cleared him of complicity in the Jameson Raid, there is some evidence that he was at least aware of the conspiracy. His subsequent attempts to reach a settlement with the Boers failed, resulting in the South African War (1899–1902). Chamberlain's belief in the need for closer imperial union led him to espouse the cause of imperial preferential tariffs. However, this proposed abandonment of Great Britain's traditional free-trade policy provoked wide controversy, and, in 1903, he resigned from the Colonial Office to spend three years in an attempt, through the Tariff Reform League, to convert the country to his views. His campaign split the Liberal Unionist-Conservative bloc and contributed to its defeat in the election of 1906. Ill health ended Chamberlain's public life in 1906, but his tariff-policy was adopted (in 1919 and 1932) within the lifetime of his sons, Austen and Neville.]

preponderance. Neither Lord Salisbury nor William Gladstone inherited the sceptre, one because he has been accused of simultaneous weakness and violence, the other because he was too haughty intellectually, too disdainful of the brutal greed of an age of traders. Chamberlain was tailored to those merchants from Birmingham who wanted to subordinate English politics and measure everything by their own standard. He became their idol, their Messiah, their boss. He was not taken to task, quite the contrary, for his monstrous palinodes, which left far behind the most extraordinary volte-faces of our own politicians. Though an ex-Radical, he was not reproached for joining a Conservative government [in 1895 as Colonial Secretary]; and, although anti-religious and a partisan of democratic taxation, he was not criticised for having joined his efforts to those of the worst adversaries of democracy. It is true that he associated with so many noble personalities – Salisbury, Balfour and Hamilton – in order to subjugate them. [Chamberlain took formal charge at the Colonial Office on 1 July 1895.] In a few months, thanks to the timidity of the Prime Minister [Lord Salisbury], he became the head of the Cabinet. Imperialism was his instrument, his main slogan, his *raison d'être*. By means of it, he captivated the nobility, usually very hard on *parvenus*, and the bourgeoisie, usually defiant, except in Birmingham. The Colonial Secretary, relegating domestic, fiscal, social, educational, religious, etc. questions to the background, found a way of subordinating Great Britain's foreign relations to his field of competence. He crystallised, so to speak, in a single formula, the Jingoism that had been floating in the air for years. He announced to the country that it would become the main owner on the African Continent as well as the almost exclusive heir to the Chinese Empire; he pointed out that, in order to be strong, Great Britain had to group, syndicate around itself its multiple possessions disseminated around the globe, and overall set up the most formidable empire ever known. Imperialism became a poignant term, the most fascinating mirage yet presented to a nation. The bourgeoisie and the nobility, whose economic opulence and political privileges had been under threat, saw in Chamberlain and his programme a lifeline, the indefinite prolongation of their twin reign, and the MP from Birmingham had the luck and the glory of concentrating in his mind the goals of an entire country.

Whatever Lord Salisbury may do or say, Chamberlain is his master. It is he who proposes alliances to other states or affronts them; he who can liken

Tsar Nicholas II to Beelzebub or hold out his hand to the German Emperor Wilhelm II, appeal to America or offer friendship to France. His diplomatic proceedings are bizarre, to the chagrin of ambassadors and other diplomats. His insolence is only rivalled by his platitudes; the sudden turnabouts he imposes on British foreign policy can only be compared to the volte-faces of his own political life. But contemptible as he may seem, his personage is powerful, almost omnipotent. Imperialism is almost inconceivable in detachment from this curious individual. Chamberlain's own origins, his devotion to the city of Birmingham, its industry and appetites, give us the key to the psychological phenomenon triumphing on the other side of the English Channel, and into which almost any upper- and middle-class Englishman will give us a sufficient insight.

* * *

Anglo-Saxon imperialism is not at all a superficial phenomenon, and even less one of those mental epidemics from which some nations have suffered at certain times during the last centuries. It comes down to a few deep principles, a few strictly economic reasons, and even illustrates the socialist thesis affirming the subordination of political events to economic facts. Briefly, Anglo-Saxon imperialism can be explained by the decay of British foreign trade, the stagnation of British industry, and the apprehension that this unexpected fall created among the ruling class. [...][16]

The British ruling class has fallen into imperialism almost without exception: its sudden turnabout is understandable. Commercial stagnation compromises and ruins its social authority. Just as the feudal class lived from war, the power of the industrial plutocracy is based on commercial prosperity; the least attack on trade threatens its supremacy. The restriction of the colonial and Far-Eastern markets has, for the first time since the victory of the English Third Estate, disturbed its peace of mind and freedom from care. The Liverpool merchants, the great manufacturers of Sheffield, Leeds, Birmingham and Bradford, were reminded that their rise to political power coincided with the development of mechanisation and the blossoming of

16. [Here, Louis provides numerous statistics showing a slackening and even diminution in British exports and discusses the causes of British commercial stagnation, particularly the rise of international competition, including some British colonies such as Canada.]

British industry. It was natural that declining [foreign-trade] statistics would seem to them a gloomy omen of impending collapse.

In no other country is bourgeois pre-eminence so intimately linked to commercial wealth. The United Kingdom does not have, as France does, a numerous rural proletariat or a class of small peasants. Workers owning a small plot of land have long ago been expropriated to the benefit of the landlords.

The British industrial population is much denser than in any other country with the exception of Belgium. Unlike our bourgeoisie, the disciples of Jules Méline,[17] the British bourgeoisie will not be able to reckon upon an opposition, an eventual hostility between urban and rural workers. The number of urban workers has grown enormously. As soon as they begin to stir and go beyond the purely professional organisation of the trade-unions, they will turn to socialism and nothing will stop them.

Until 1880 or even 1884, the economic expansion of the United Kingdom enabled the employment of those millions of people and, through high wages, kept in strict dependence a proletariat that was at the same time organised and amorphous. Politically inorganic, it was strictly disciplined by its everyday material demands. The growth of markets and foreign trade facilitated dealings between the bosses and the unions. But those times are gone, and the situation cannot be regarded with the same optimism.

On the one hand, certain industries are experiencing growing unemployment. Lancashire is undergoing painful trials due to competition from the European continent, America, India, China and Japan. The reserve army of unemployed proletarians is growing and, with it, the workers' thrust against the ruling class.

Even more serious is the fact that, due to the influx of foreign competitors, British industry cannot keep its high wages and is forced to restrict its workforce. But British workers have acquired certain needs and habits that they will not give up willingly. Every reduction of salaries pushes them to socialism. British plutocracy feels the hour approaching when the members of the trade-unions and the unions themselves will join the cadres of the incipient revolutionary parties. This apprehension of a social war is at the bottom of the

17. [Félix Jules Méline (1838–1925) was a French statesman and Prime Minister from 1896 to 1898.]

imperialist movement and has dictated their vast expansion-programmes to the representatives of the big employers, among them Chamberlain.

Anglo-Saxon expansion can be conceived in two ways: either the United Kingdom, following the above-described tactics, carries on with its methodical conquest of Asia and Africa, or else it carries out the Imperial Federation, the commercial and political *Zollverein* that today haunts all British politicians. Moreover, these two lines of action are not mutually incompatible but complementary.

Chamberlain has been planning for more than a decade the creation of a syndicate of production and exchange unique in history. He aspires to group around the metropolis all its dependencies in the two hemispheres and to create a closed economic association. The British Empire would thus cease to be a partially fictitious term; it would become fully real, and Canada, Australia and India would be as intimately linked to England and among themselves as a French *département* to another French *département*. The English colonies would more or less have the monopoly of the British market, and the United Kingdom would reserve the monopoly of the colonies. Great Britain, which sells to its colonies two billion [pounds sterling] annually, would suddenly be able to triple, quadruple, or increase that figure five-fold. That is the ruling idea of imperialism. We insist that it is not a recent idea, that it has been incessantly spread and justified by a considerable section of the British press, and that, if its triumph in public opinion is recent, its slow penetration is much older. As far back as 1887, at a speech delivered [to the colonial conference held] in Toronto, Canada, Chamberlain set it out and examined it in detail.[18] And his later speeches show that he never abandoned it for a minute.

Two facts have clearly marked the imperialist campaign: the Colonial Conference held in London in 1897 on the occasion of the fiftieth anniversary of Queen Victoria's accession to the throne, celebrating her golden jubilee, and the recent vote in Australia for a Federation of Oceania. None of them

---

18. [Under the sponsorship of the British Colonial Office, four colonial conferences involving Great Britain and her colonies were held in 1887, 1897, 1902 and 1907 to discuss matters of mutual interest.]

has sanctioned the triumph of the Greater Britain programme, but they have brought the deadline considerably nearer.

Is the idea realisable, will the economic confederation of Anglo-Saxon countries prevail against the considerable obstacles it faces? It is certain that the project will not run smoothly or be accomplished rapidly, but nothing seems to preclude its success.

The difficulties are numerous. Up to now, the colonies of Africa, Australia and Australasia have remained separated. Cape Town and Natal have contradictory interests, and their ports fight for supremacy. New South Wales and Victoria do not want to give up predominance, and they also refuse to grant equal representation to younger or less prosperous colonies, such as West Australia, in a Federal Senate in Sydney or Melbourne. Finally, the economic régime is not uniform over all of Australia; New South Wales stands for free trade while the other states are ultra-protectionist. In America, if Canada is already confederated, Newfoundland shows an incessant hostility towards the Dominion of Canada: the parliament of that island even considered voting for annexation to the United States of America.

And there is more. How to blend into a single régime, or at least to create sufficient harmony, with countries as different in every respect as Scotland, the Antilles, India and New Zealand? Is a purely economic centralisation even compatible with such pronounced divergences in climate, race, interest and social organisation?

And beyond that, if one regards the *Zollverein* from a strictly commercial point of view, why impose on its members very unequal sacrifices? England does not have to revolutionise its customs-system to grant tariff-exemptions to colonial products. By contrast, Australia, which is strongly protectionist with the exception of New South Wales, will have to eliminate the taxes of 30 to 35 per cent that it levies on British imports. Such an innovation would threaten not only its industrial expansion but also its financial equilibrium. The abolition of tariffs that are providing most of its fiscal income will create a permanent deficit in Australia's budget. Will the United Kingdom be willing to fill these inevitable gaps and impose on itself burdens to which it has long been unaccustomed for the benefit of its dependencies?

These are some of the many problems raised by the imperialist programme. We can see that its adversaries can allege against it complex and numerous inconveniencies.

And yet the Anglo-Saxon Federation is more than a future possibility because it is in the logical order of things, and if one cannot predict on which precise bases it will be organised, its triumph is just a matter of time. It will appear as an ineluctable necessity for the British bourgeoisie, and the colonies will ultimately find in it enough transitory advantages to accept it despite all its difficulties. [...]

Chapter Five

'Imperialism in England and the United States' (September–December 1900)

Paul Louis

In this article, Paul Louis extended his previous analysis of 'Anglo-Saxon imperialism', which in 1899 he used as a synonym for British imperialism, to the United States. In a note that appeared early in 1901 in the same journal, under the title 'American Imperialism', he wrote:

> Alongside English imperialism there is an American imperialism that has been making itself felt more and more for some time. Its manifestations are already very numerous: it dictated first the war with Spain and then the definitive conquest of Cuba and Puerto Rico and the partial occupation of the Philippines; at the Congress in Washington it persuaded a big party to demand the formation of a standing army capable of dealing with any eventuality; and finally it also manifested itself in the relations of the United States with the great European powers.

In 1901, the United States and the United Kingdom signed the Hay-Pauncefote Treaty, nullifying the previous Clayton-Bulwer Treaty and giving the United States the right to create and control a canal across Central America, connecting the Pacific and Atlantic

Oceans. After pointing out the frictions between English and American imperialism caused by US plans to build an isthmoid canal, Louis concluded:

> American imperialism is a product of the same principles as English imperialism. The United Kingdom embarked upon colonial expansion to the utmost because it had to find an outlet for its threatened industries, and because its policy was dominated by the powerful money-syndicates. It is for the same reasons that the United States declared war on Spain, annexed the Spanish islands in the Caribbean, multiplied its nearly fruitless efforts in the Philippines, and adopted an aggressive attitude towards nations opposing its commercial ambitions and the designs of its great financiers.[1]

* * *

'Imperialism in England and the United States'[2]

It seems that imperialism is the dominant force of the last days of the century, for, with different degrees of intensity, it has dominated the policy of all peoples. Like the principle of nationalities during the golden age of liberal ideas, a ruling element has appeared characterising international relations. No country (except those deprived of any means of action) has been able to escape the influence of the new system or to resist the immoderate demands for territorial expansion. England, the United States, France, Italy and Japan have one after another turned to the method of thoughtless and limitless annexations.

Imperialism escapes a precise definition; it is not the same in Latin and Anglo-Saxon countries because ethnic, historical, intellectual and social conditions play a role in it and affect its functioning. Clearly, it cannot experience the same development in peoples with a long past and already vast overseas possession as in those that, being recently formed or unified, have not yet gone beyond their natural frontiers. But everywhere it arose from the capitalist structure of contemporary societies.

Does imperialism constitute progress or reaction? Must it be repressed or does it deserve our approval? The question does not seem very important to

1. Louis 1901b (January–April).
2. Louis 1900a.

us, because a moral judgement about such a generalised method cannot have serious consequences. It would be like passing judgement on the excellence of the principle of nationalities, or on the passage from the primitive community to the Hellenic city and the modern state. We find ourselves here before an organic phenomenon that depends on the physiology of the world and deserves to be examined by itself, like digestion or the circulation of blood in the individual.

The governments alone are not responsible for imperialist expansion. It would be rather childish to blame exclusively Ferry or Crispi, McKinley or Chamberlain.[3] That some of these politicians wanted at some point to

---

3. [Jules François Camille Ferry (1832–93) was a French politician who served twice as France's premier (18801 and 1883–5). Two important works are associated with his administration: the non-clerical organisation of public education, and the beginning of the colonial expansion of France. Intending to destroy the influence of the clergy in the university, Ferry succeeded in passing the law of 28 March 1882, which made primary education in France free, non-clerical and obligatory. Following France's military defeat by Germany in 1870, he also formed the idea of acquiring a great colonial empire, not to colonise it, but for the sake of economic exploitation. He directed negotiations that led to establishment of a French protectorate in Tunis (1881), prepared the treaty of 17 December 1885, for the occupation of Madagascar, directed the exploration of the Congo and the Niger region and, above all, organised the conquest of Indo-China. The excitement caused in Paris by a reverse for French troops at Lang-son caused his downfall (30 March 1885), but the treaty of peace with China (9 June 1885) was his work.

Francesco Crispi (1819–1901) was an Italian politician instrumental in the country's unification. He served as Premier from 1887 until 1891 and again from 1893 until 1896. A deputy in the Italian parliament from 1861, he was at first a republican but later became an outspoken monarchist. He became minister of the interior (1877–8) in the Depretis cabinet. A charge of bigamy hindered his political career for the next nine years, but he returned to the Depretis cabinet in 1887 and became premier upon Depretis's death. He strengthened Italy's commitment to the Triple Alliance with Germany and Austria-Hungary, but thereby also helped to cause Italian relations with France to deteriorate still further, leading to a tariff-war between the two countries from 1888 to 1892. He pressed a forward policy in North-East Africa and organised the colony of Eritrea. He was overthrown in 1891 by Giolitti, but returned to power in 1893 and was re-elected by a huge majority in 1895. However, resentment over his reactionary policies and, above all, the terrible defeat suffered at Adwa (1896) by Italian forces seeking to expand into Ethiopia, soon forced him from office.

William McKinley (1843–1901) was the twenty-fifth President of the United States. He was elected for two terms as Republican candidate for the presidential office, serving from 4 March 1897, to 14 September 1901, when he was assassinated by an anarchist soon after being re-elected. McKinley presided over the rise of American imperialism; major events during his presidency included the Spanish-American War (25 April–12 August 1898), the Annexation of Hawaii (7 July 1898), the beginning of the Philippine-American War (1899–1913), and US participation in repressing the Boxer Rebellion (November 1899–7 September, 1901). He was succeeded by Theodore Roosevelt in 1901.]

accelerate the movement and precipitate some conquest in order to escape a pressing embarrassment is not improbable, and we do not dispute it. But nowhere could the system have been practised so systematically if it had not had the support of the whole nation or, what amounts to the same thing, the consent of the ruling classes.

It cannot be disputed now that on both sides of the Atlantic it is the bourgeoisie, the omnipotent master, which has embraced imperialism most ardently. In France, the agrarian, clerical, royalist and Bonapartist aristocracy fought for more than ten years against colonial annexations before capitulating. One recalls the attitude of the Right in 1881, 1882 and 1885, during the famous debates on Tunis and Tonkin.[4] And if, during recent years, Dahomey and Madagascar[5] found numerous partisans in the ranks of the monarchist opposition, that is because it thought it could drown the Republic by means of the constant exaltation of militarism. Actually, the true supporters, the intransigent adherents of armed colonisation in France, have been the bourgeois opportunists who reached power with the collapse of 16 May and subsequently remained there.[6] Even in Italy, the apostles of megalomania have not been the grand lords, the latifundia-owners of the Midi (who only want to exploit their peasants peacefully, and whose tendencies Rudini and

4. [The French occupied Tunis, the capital of Tunisia, from 1881 to 1956, having established a protectorate system of administration that recognised the nominal authority of local government.

Tonkin, also spelled Tongkin or Tongking, is the northernmost part of Vietnam. Vietnam's independence was gradually eroded by France in a series of military conquests from 1859 onwards, until France assumed sovereignty over the entire country after the Sino-French War (1884–5). The French colonial government divided Vietnam into three administrative territories: Tonkin in the north, Annam in the centre, and Cochinchina in the south. France retained control of the country until 1954.]

5. [Dahomey was a French colony and part of French West Africa from 1904 to 1958. It is now the Republic of Benin.

From the seventeenth century, the British and French colonial empires competed for influence in Madagascar. The island became a French protectorate in 1890, a colony in 1896, and gained full independence from France in 1960.]

6. [The crisis of 16 May 1877, concerned both the role of the president and the contested dominance of royalist forces. The crisis was triggered by the royalist President Marshall MacMahon's dismissal of the moderate republican Prime Minister, Jules Simon, after a dispute concerning the relevant functions of the presidency and of the parliament. New elections brought an overwhelming victory for the Republicans, and the interpretation of the Constitution as a parliamentary system prevailed over a presidential system. The crisis ultimately sealed the defeat of the royalist movement and was instrumental in creating conditions for the longevity of the Third Republic, which lasted until France's defeat by the Nazis in 1940.]

Visconti-Venosta[7] have symbolised most clearly) but the capitalists of Lombardy, Piedmont and Florence, the old historical Left who demand outlets for their industry.

In England, the Lords, with the exception of some politicians like Rosebery, and of some financiers like Fife and Abercorn,[8] cared very little for the increase of the British Empire in Asia and Africa. Besides, they are more or less in the situation of constitutional monarchs: they only have a very limited authority in public affairs and leave their management in the hands of the manufacturers and merchants who, with Chamberlain, have definitively become the rulers of the United Kingdom. It is this bourgeoisie, formerly Whig and now Unionist, indifferent to political and economic liberalism, that has really launched Great Britain into the intemperate enterprises of recent years. Through its joint-stock corporations and its financial syndicates, it determines almost exclusively the foreign relations of the country. It organises a military expedition as a business transaction or an investment, as shown by the Jameson Raid five years ago, the occupation of the Ganda and the war in Transvaal.[9]

In America, finally, because one cannot prolong this enumeration indefinitely, the war with Spain was skilfully and methodically prepared by the yellow press, which expresses so faithfully and brutally the feelings of the

7. [Antonio Starabba, Marchese di Rudinì (1839–1908) was Prime Minister of Italy between 1891 and 1892 and from 1896 until 1898. Emilio, marquis Visconti-Venosta (1829–1914), was an Italian politician born at Milan, whose political-diplomatic career of more than 50 years spanned Italian history from the Risorgimento to the First World War.]

8. [Archibald Philip Primrose, Lord Rosebery (1847–1929), served as Prime Minister from 5 March 1894, to 22 June 1895. During the Boer War (1899–1902) Rosebery became estranged from most of the Liberal Party because of his enthusiasm for the British Empire. Late in 1905, a few weeks before the Liberals returned to power, he broke with them by declaring his opposition to Irish Home Rule. Abercorn and Fife were financiers linked to the British South-Africa Company and the Jameson Raid.]

9. [The Jameson Raid (29 December 1895–2 January 1896) was conducted against Paul Kruger's Transvaal Republic by a British colonial statesman, Leander Starr Jameson, and his Rhodesian and Bechuanaland policemen over the New Year weekend of 1895–6. It was intended to trigger an uprising by the primarily British expatriate-workers (known as Uitlanders) in the Transvaal, but failed to do so. The raid was ineffective and no uprising took place, but it did much to cause the Second Boer War and the Second Matabele War.

The Ganda people (also called Baganda or Waganda) inhabit the area north and northwest of Lake Victoria in south-central Uganda. They speak a Bantu language called Ganda or Luganda. The war in Transvaal refers to the Second Boer War (11 October 1899–31 May 1902).]

ruling class. The trusts and the kings of sugar, oil, iron, etc., who have such a powerful influence on the deliberations of the government in Washington, were powerful enough to force the conquest of the Philippines and the Spanish islands in the Caribbean. The masses, always fooled, applauded. The United States, already pushed beyond its boundaries by the adventure in Hawaii, has inaugurated a system that could result in the most unexpected developments.[10]

That imperialism is very intimately linked with capitalism is attested by the fact that it has been most evident in countries with a strong capitalist development. In Italy, a country with a weak industry, it sagged after the first defeat. In France, where the transformation has been less rapid than in the Anglo-Saxon states, is seems to back down somewhat today in face of the weariness of public opinion. It is in America and in the United Kingdom that it has manifested itself in all its vitality and has all the aspects of a durable and consistent historical phenomenon.

Imperialism serves as a dividing line for the political parties. In England, the old names of Whigs and Tories became obsolete a long time ago. After the first project for Home Rule was submitted by Gladstone,[11] the electorate divided between Liberals or Radicals and Unionists, and the old partitions were so shattered that one could witness the union of irreconcilable conservatives and semi-socialists like Chamberlain and his friends. Now imperialism has taken the place of opposition to Irish autonomy as a political platform. One is for or against the annexation of the South-African republics, for or against

10. [The Annexation of Hawaii took place on 7 July 1898.]

11. [William Ewart Gladstone (29 December 1809–19 May 1898) was a British Liberal Party statesman and Prime Minister (1868–74, 1880–5, 1886 and 1892–4). Gladstone is famous for his intense rivalry with the Conservative Party Leader Benjamin Disraeli. In 1886 Gladstone's party allied with Irish Nationalists to defeat Lord Salisbury's government. Gladstone regained his position as PM and combined the office with that of Lord Privy Seal. During this third ministry, he first introduced his Home Rule Bill for Ireland. The issue split the Liberal Party (a breakaway group went on to create the Liberal Unionist Party), and the bill was thrown out on second reading, ending his government after only a few months and inaugurating another headed by Lord Salisbury. In 1892 Gladstone was re-elected Prime Minister for the fourth and final time. In February 1893, he re-introduced a Home Rule Bill that provided for the formation of a parliament for Ireland, although it did not offer Ireland independence. The Bill was passed by the Commons but rejected by the House of Lords. On 1 March 1894, in his last speech to the House of Commons, Gladstone asked his allies to override this most recent veto. He resigned two days later, although he retained his seat in the Commons until 1895.]

the unification or federation of the British Empire, [as one was formerly] for or against the enfranchisement of Ireland. It is on this ground that the coming elections – which the current cabinet at Westminster, being sure of its victory, fervently anticipates – will take place. The British government knows that all or almost all the bourgeoisie is on its side. A Morley or Labouchère are so rare among the Liberals![12]

In the United States, the presidential elections of next November [1900] will be entirely dominated by the problem of imperialism. Formerly, Republicans and Democrats fought over free trade and protectionism, the gold-standard or bimetallism. This time, there are only imperialists and anti-imperialists. McKinley is the candidate of the first group and Bryan the candidate of the second.[13] The positions are so well drawn, and the division between the two parties is so brutal, that all the ambitious middlemen, such as Admiral Dewey, had to quit the race. And, in order to corroborate the character of the two rival programmes, Bryan made quite large concessions to the socialists, while McKinley, the servant of large capital, did not dare to condemn explicitly the trusts, against which a powerful clamour is arising in America.

In both England and the United States, the struggle that will take place this winter will therefore be of much greater importance than an ordinary electoral contest. It will not be simply a question of knowing whether some individuals will keep power or others, quite similar to them, will succeed them. It is a question of principle that will be settled: it is, we repeat, an organic

12. [Henry Labouchère (1831–1912) was a Radical-Liberal politician and journalist. John Morley (1838–1923), a prolific writer and newspaper-editor, was a prominent Gladstonian Liberal who denounced the Boer War of 1899–1902 and British imperial expansionism.]

13. [The Democratic Party Platform of 1900 read: 'The importance of other questions, now pending before the American people is no wise diminished and the Democratic party takes no backward step from its position on them, but the burning issue of imperialism growing out of the Spanish war involves the very existence of the Republic and the destruction of our free institutions. We regard it as the paramount issue of the campaign.' It argued that 'to impose upon any people a government of force is to substitute the methods of imperialism for those of a republic', and that 'no nation can long endure half republic and half empire', warning the American people that 'imperialism abroad will lead quickly and inevitably to despotism at home'. It denounced the Porto Rican law for imposing 'upon the people of Porto Rico a government without their consent and taxation without representation', thus committing the United States 'to a colonial policy, inconsistent with republican institutions'. It also denounced the continued occupation of Cuba and 'the war of "criminal aggression" against the Filipinos'. Democratic Party of the United States 1900 (6 July).]

phenomenon that will be decided upon. The people will have to say whether they will tolerate the indefinite expansion of imperialism, a corollary of capitalist development, or whether they want to check the latter by preventing the former. The people will inform us in quite striking terms about the prolongation of their servitude or about their emancipation – the strengthening of bourgeois dictatorship or the collapse of the last ruling caste... Some fear that imperialism, this time also, will not be condemned.[14]

14. [The campaign for the general election of 1900 in the United Kingdom was held from 25 September to 24 October 1900. Also known as the Khaki Election because the main issue was the Second Boer War ('khaki' was the colour of the relatively new military uniform of the British army that had been universally adopted in that war). The election returned the Conservative government of Lord Salisbury to office with an increased majority over the Liberal Party.

The United States presidential election of 1900 was held on 6 November 1900. It was a rematch of the 1896 race between Republican President William McKinley and his Democratic challenger, William Jennings Bryan. The return of economic prosperity and recent victory in the Spanish-American War helped McKinley to a decisive victory. His margins in the popular and electoral vote were both larger than in 1896, and he even carried Bryan's home-state of Nebraska.]

Chapter Six

'The War in South Africa' (November 1899)

Karl Kautsky

In this article, dealing with the Second Boer War (11 October 1899–31 May 1902), Kautsky argued that two forces arose out of the decline of 'Manchesterism' (liberalism) in England: socialism and imperialism. He pointed out that imperialism was making 'even more rapid progress than socialism' and was becoming 'the primary means of arresting the development of the latter'. It should be emphasised, though, that Kautsky still understood imperialism in its then-current meaning as 'the creation of a "Greater Britain", a huge world *empire*' surrounded by protectionist tariffs, which offered the prospect, although temporary at best, of improving economic conditions for the workers.

* * *

'The War in South Africa'[1]

The fortunes of war are changeable; and if, as we write, they stand now on the side of Transvaal, they may well stand on the side of the Englishmen by the time these lines reach our readers. But this much is

1. Kautsky 1899c.

already certain: the war will not be a military parade to Pretoria. If it is a life-and-death struggle for the Boers, it will not, in any case, be a mere frontier-war for their opponents, one that passes by like the campaigns against the Afridis and Matabeles without producing any deep impression. It is already an historical event that has imposed the greatest sacrifices on England and most profoundly aroused and stirred the entire civilised world. Such wars tend to be accompanied by profound consequences that their authors did not foresee and often did not wish for, consequences that suddenly impress a new character upon political and social development. Must we expect something similar from the Boer War?

If the Englishmen finally prevail, as is still likely given their enormous superiority, that would mean a triumph for the English capitalist clique that plotted the War; a triumph not only over the resistance of the Boers, who are not ready to give up willingly their land with its treasures, but also over the capitalists of other nations – the Germans, the French and the Russians, who grew so indignant about the encroachments of the Englishmen in South Africa because they could not take their place. But the defeat of the Boers would also mean, first of all, a strengthening of the position of the capitalist class within England itself.

To be sure, the power of the democratic states of Europe against absolutist Russia must grow at the same time. That aspect [of the question] could make us come to terms with [the prospect of] an English victory, but one must not overestimate it. Support is not to be expected from England for the democratic trends on the European continent. Then again, Russia is today no longer the most dangerous threat to European freedom. Its gaze hardly turns to the west, where it can grab nothing. Each territorial expansion westwards and even southwards in Europe would be for Russia a source of difficulties, an element of weakness, not of strength. And the tsarist régime has enough to do with its internal difficulties.

But, if Russia has become less dangerous for Western Europe, England has progressively ceased to be the most decided opponent of Russia, and for good reasons. At sea, England is a match for any enemy. But, up to now, it has not been given to any state over the long run – though many circles in Germany seem to have forgotten it – to be a military power of the first rank simultaneously on land and sea. England is weak as a land-power, and thus it is exposed above all to Russia, which already borders on India. There lies the

Achilles heel of England, and that is why it seeks to maintain peace with Russia, enabling her to encroach on China and Persia and enduring her presence on India's borders, although all those steps bring mischief ever closer. It is not to be expected that England's victory in South Africa would make it inflexible vis-à-vis Russia. Yet that would be the only reason that could impart to such a victory an aspect favourable to democratic development.

But, as things stand in South Africa today, we should contemplate the possibility not only of an English victory but also of an English defeat.

Certainly, no matter how magnificently the militia system can still prove itself vis-à-vis the [English] standing army, the instruments of power of greater Britain, with its almost four hundred million habitants, are so overwhelming that the little Boer people runs the risk of being crushed if left to its own resources. But it is precisely the huge extension of the British colonial empire that constitutes its weakness, because it offers numerous vulnerable points for foreign opponents or internal rebellions. The longer the War lasts, the more will England's prestige diminish and the sooner may complications arise that could force England to conclude peace before its has reached its goal, indeed, possibly even under humiliating conditions.

But that would mean a hard blow for that tendency that arose in England, alongside socialism, out of the wreckage of Manchesterism, and that today competes with socialism for mastery over the minds of the English proletariat: *imperialism*.

In an article published in 1885 in *Die Neue Zeit*, Engels wrote:

> The truth is this: during the period of England's industrial monopoly the English working-class have, to a certain extent, shared in the benefits of the monopoly. These benefits were very unequally parcelled out amongst them; the privileged minority pocketed most, but now and then even the great mass had at least a temporary share. And that is the reason why, since the dying-out of Owenism, there has been no socialism in England. With the breakdown of that monopoly, the English working-class will lose that privileged position; it will find itself generally – the privileged and leading minority not excepted – on a level with its fellow-workers abroad. And that is the reason why there will again be socialism in England.[2]

2. Engels 1885, p. 245.

As is generally known, that prophecy has come true. Manchesterism is no longer regarded as a panacea, and we have socialism again in England; socialist ideas are growing stronger with every passing year. In the big trade-unions, where socialism was still laughed at fifteen years ago, the most active and zealous elements are now devoted to it; and if, up to now, a rotten electoral law has prevented it from showing its force in parliament, it is making rapid and decisive progress in the elections for city-councils, counties and school-inspectors.

But, in addition to socialism, another power arose out of the decline of Manchesterism: *imperialism*. Driven by the needs of the ruling classes, imperialism is making even more rapid progress than socialism among the English people, and is today the primary means of arresting the development of the latter.

The colonies are the root of the economic superiority that England has maintained for so long. Plunder of the colonies was the principal means of furthering the development of capitalism in England in a hothouse fashion, and of bringing about the blossoming of large-scale industry there at a time when its puny beginnings were hardly noticeable in Germany.

Free trade was then for England the means to exploit its industrial monopoly to the full. It seemed no longer to need the colonies that helped to establish its greatness. They were therefore neglected, and they faded from the spotlights. The policy of colonial expansion meant war, while free trade aspired to freedom. As long as the industrial classes of England believed in free trade, they were peace-loving.

Then came the massive crisis of the 1870s and 1880s, as well as the industrial aspirations of Germany, America and Russia. England's industrial monopoly became increasingly untenable. At that time, the other European powers began to develop a lust for overseas possessions – not to open them up for international trade and international capitalist exploitation, but to secure a privileged position for their own trade and their own capital.

While England was losing its industrial superiority, it was also increasingly squeezed out of the world market by the protective tariffs and the colonial policy of its competitors.

The system of free trade (not merely the import of commodities without protective duties, but Manchesterism and *laissez-faire*) became untenable. From a proletarian standpoint, the consequence of this breakdown should have been the transition to socialism and, therefore, first of all the strengthening of the socialist movement.

For the ruling classes, however, the consequences of the collapse were very different. It was impossible to go on without the intervention of the state in economic life. The English capitalists had to put up with the idea of appealing to the power of the state. But the state should intervene neither in support of the proletariat nor for the benefit of society as a whole but in support of capitalist profits. Through *political* means, the shaking capitalist mode of production was to be strengthened again. This was to occur through centralisation of the colonies with the mother-country in a colossal empire, whose market would then be guaranteed for British industry by means of protective tariffs (a policy that England alone could not possibly implement); through the constant expansion of that empire, the permanent conquest of richer colonial regions that promised rich yields to plunder-seeking capital; in other words, through the creation of a 'Greater Britain', a huge world *empire* (hence the word *imperialism*), that would be completely dependent on the capitalist class of little Britain. In those ways, English capitalism would create for itself the possibility of developing further, after its industrial monopoly ceased to exist.

However, the new tendency, the imperialist one, has thus far encountered considerable obstacles. The bureaucratic-military elements that support it are weaker in England than elsewhere. To be sure, high finance, which has the greatest interest in imperialist policy, is also stronger; and the now decisive industry, the iron-industry, has no objection to armaments on land and sea. Nevertheless, Manchesterist views were until recently still deeply rooted among England's industrialists.

Among the workers, however, one could have expected that Manchesterist views would be replaced by socialist ones precisely in the field of foreign policy, especially colonial policy, where they [Manchesterism and socialism] differ the least. Like the Manchesterists, the proletariat is also a decisive opponent of wars of conquest, of exploitation and oppression – in the colonies no less than at home – as well as a decisive supporter of free international exchange and the abolition[3] of national rivalries.

To our bitter disappointment, the present mood in England shows us how much imperialism has also taken possession of the proletariat.

Wherever there was a fighting proletariat, it condemned an overseas as well as any other policy of conquest. Not only in Germany, but also in France,

3. [The original reads *Schaffung* (creation), but this is probably a misspelling of *Abschaffung* (abolition, annulment).]

Italy, Belgium, and even Spain the proletariat, to the extent that it had attained independent thinking at all, opposed any policy of colonial oppression. Only among the English workers, those role-models of our ethical social liberals and national socialists, do we find the lamentable spectacle of proletarian masses crazy about a war of conquest that serves purely capitalist interests more openly than any other. And that is happening in England, where even the bourgeoisie had a love of peace unsurpassed anywhere else in the world, a love of peace that was regarded as a sign of weakness by the bourgeoisie of 'more spirited' nations.

Nowhere is the proletariat stronger, nowhere is it in a better position to follow an independent policy, and nowhere does it show itself more dependent on bourgeois politics than in England!

The reasons for that attitude are, to be sure, not only the habits inherited from the golden age of the Manchesterian upswing, but also the material circumstances of the most recent period. The workers of England feel united with their capitalists as a privileged class vis-à-vis the population of the conquered territories. Those territories seem to the English workers to have been opened up not only for the capitalists' spirit of enterprise but also for the surplus proletarians, whose departure relieves the labour-market; not only for the rich to get even richer, but also for the poor to have a chance – surely no better than a lottery-ticket – of getting rich as well; to stimulate industry through broadening not only the foreign market, but also the home market by means of the war-industries, armaments and the expenditures of those who return home with the plunder amassed in the overseas possession; to increase the hosts of the propertied classes and their demand for commodities and services.

But, even if the English workers are today, for the most part, so intoxicated by imperialist phraseology that they jubilantly pull the wagon of Messrs. Rhodes and Chamberlain, they will also become disillusioned sooner than the ruling classes because the question of greater Britain and its exploitation is not a vital question for them. In the struggle for socialism, they have another means, more human and solid than colonial buccaneering, for protecting their interests and furthering the development of society.

When Rosebery, the 'workers' friend' and liberal, proclaimed support for the Tories in their present adventure to be the duty of any British patriot, he may have been right from a capitalist point of view. But, when people who call themselves socialists likewise declare that the patriotic duty of the British proletariat is to stand up for a bourgeois government, which plotted a war in the most frivolous and brutal way with the sole end of promoting the business of a band of capitalists with connections in high circles, they prove to have just as peculiar an idea about socialism as about patriotism. But the mass of English socialists condemned the War in the most decided way; and the longer it lasts, the more sacrifices it demands, the sooner must its course disillusion the non-socialist workers as well by showing them the reverse side of imperialist policy.

The more imperialism drives back Manchesterism, the more it becomes the foundation of the political and social system, the more social development depends on *military success*, the more powerful will become *militarism*, that sworn enemy of democracy, and the more will a military defeat threaten to lead to an economic catastrophe.[4]

But it is precisely imperialism that also increases the danger of military conflicts. Until recently, England still had not totally grasped that fact, and its colonial policy, even during recent years, was often more defensive than aggressive, as shown especially by the example of China. In spite of that, in Africa alone (including Egypt) the British Empire grew in the course of the last fifteen years by more than *six million* square-kilometres, a territory larger than half of Europe. The greater part of it was acquired in recent years. In 1871, Kolb calculated the number of inhabitants of the British Empire to be approximately 217 million. Hübner's statistical tables estimated it at 347 million in 1898. By contrast, the population of the ruling country only grew during the same period from 31,600,000 to 40,400,000 – an increase of less than 9 million compared with 130 million. The greater the Empire and the more numerous its weak points, the larger are the numbers of subjected peoples and malcontents and the greedier the competitors.

Today, England is the most bellicose country on earth. Almost every year it has to repress a 'rebellion' or wage a frontier-war in some part of its huge territory. Naval expenditures are growing too, because with the expansion of greater Britain the hostility of the other European great powers and competitors

4. [Two months later, Kautsky wrote an article on militarism and socialism in England, where he returned to this idea: 'Imperialism, which ought to have nipped English socialism in the bud, would thus be, as a consequence of its defeat, the most tremendous stimulus to socialism.' Kautsky, 1900, p. 593.]

also increases. As with France at the beginning of the nineteenth century, and Russia at the middle of the century when it coveted Turkey, greater Britain is today the object of general animosity among the ruling classes of the main European states.

The more British imperialism makes its development dependent on military success, and the more numerous its enemies become, the closer lurks the danger of a defeat and the more insecure will the foundations of its existence be.

Some people have pointed England out to us as the model of a country where social progress will henceforth take place only in the most peaceful way. Until recently, the domestic circumstances of England seemed to justify those expectations. But the growing imperialism has the effect of destroying the preconditions for that peaceful development. There is already talk of altering the constitution to restrict general suffrage, and of creating a large standing army to meet all the demands being made upon it. Chauvinism, brutality and military exaltation are spreading everywhere with the rising imperialist tide, and its boundless world policy is bringing closer the danger of military disasters and their accompanying social catastrophes. One need only think about the consequences of a world war ending in the loss of England's colonial possessions, especially India!

British democracy shows us today an image in many respects comparable to that of Athenian democracy before the Peloponnesian War. In both cases, we find a great influence of the lower classes on the state, together with an aristocracy at the helm of the state that satisfies the people through its foreign policy. Thanks to its naval power, Athens succeeded in turning into tributaries almost all the islands and coasts of the Aegean Sea; and their tribute, as well as the flourishing trade made possible by Athens' superiority, provided the means for enriching the aristocracy and at the same time for practising a democratic social policy corresponding to the conditions of that age, which granted to the masses of the people numerous small benefits. Hardly any other era offered such a brilliant sight as the era of Pericles. But the anger of the subjected and exploited on the one hand, and the greed of those excluded from the rich booty on the other, finally grew so strong that Athens's opponents waged a life-and-death struggle, under the leadership of Sparta, against the powerful coastal city, which in the Peloponnesian War lost all its overseas possessions and sank into complete insignificance.

Any historical analogy is imperfect, and the same applies to this one. History never repeats itself. Contemporary Great Britain differs from Athens in the fifth century BC, first of all in that it possesses large-scale industry and a powerful proletariat, which will not idly watch the collapse of the political and social system and also has the strength to regenerate the nation and place it on a new social basis. Naturally, it would be very hasty to maintain that the end of the capitalist system in England would be brought about by a new edition of the Peloponnesian War and the loss of its colonial empire, or even that the Boer War means the beginning of that end. Those are eventualities that *could* arise out of the current situation, but it would be silly to count on them. One thing, however, is certain and should be illustrated by that comparison: the situation of English capitalism will become increasingly precarious the more the superiority of its large-scale industry comes to an end, and the more England accordingly strives to replace its lost pre-eminence with the creation of a huge empire resting merely on the superiority of its navy and land-army.

The greater that [military] superiority appears to be, the more will imperialism thrive, and the harder will socialism have to struggle in England. By contrast, a defeat of the forces upon which imperialism is based must lead almost immediately to the disillusionment of at least those classes that have no direct interest in colonial exploitation, and must make clear to them the dangers that the boundless world policy of imperialism entails even for the nation with the most powerful navy in the world. The more that fact is recognised, the sooner will the mass of the British people be inclined to strive for the development of the current capitalist system in the direction of socialism, rather than in the direction of imperialism.

The progress of the Boer War must, therefore, be of the utmost significance for the course of social development in England, even if it does not cause any further complications and leaves the English colonial empire intact. If it ends with a brilliant victory of the British army, then we must expect in England an era of the most brutal jingoism and the wildest capitalist boom, which for a long time will also drag along the mass of the workers and will place our comrades there in a difficult position. In that case, Cecil Rhodes would triumph not only in Africa but also in England. After all, his programme has been to stifle the rise of socialism in England by means of his South-African policy.[5] But that would also inaugurate in England an era of development pregnant with catastrophes.

---

5. See the instructive article of Max Beer, 1897, p. 304. [See this volume, Chapter 1.]

If the policy of Messrs. Rhodes and Chamberlain is shipwrecked, that will give a powerful impulse to the cause of socialism and will also improve the prospects of development along democratic and relatively peaceful lines.

The whole of international Social Democracy, as far was we can follow its proclamations, has accordingly placed itself on the side of the Boers, and that is totally justified. If by doing so we find ourselves in the company of French and Russian reactionaries and chauvinists, that causes us a very unpleasant feeling, but our task is clearly delineated and we cannot change the situation at will.

The motives of our attitude are, however, completely different from those of the navy-enthusiasts, anti-Semites and similar supporters of freedom for the Boers in Transvaal and of the penitentiary for workers in their own mother country [Germany]. Those people hate England because they would like to swallow for themselves the fat morsels that it is snapping up, much like the land grabbers who condemn greedy Albion because it is a democratic community.

We, by contrast, condemn modern colonial policy everywhere, in our own country no less than among our neighbours, and we wish the Boers success not out of hatred for the English people but in the interest of their own social development.

Chapter Seven

'Germany, England and World Policy' (8 and 10 May 1900)

Karl Kautsky

In 1898, two years before the article translated here, Karl Kautsky wrote 'Old and New Colonial Policy'. In that article, he rejected Eduard Bernstein's support for German colonial ambitions on the grounds that colonial policy was driven by *precapitalist* strata, including the Junkers, the military caste and bureaucracy, speculators and merchants, etc. (a confusion partially explained by conditions in the semi-absolutist German Reich).[1] According to Kautsky in 1898, the project to build a colonial empire was 'a work of *reaction*' and was not determined primarily by 'the needs of industrial development':

> It is true that industrial capital, too, wanted to gain from this policy, but it does not constitute the driving force of the colonial movement. Militarism, yearning for activity and advancement; the bureaucracy, wishing for an increase in the number of lucrative posts; the decline of agriculture, which drives so many peasants off the land and forces so many younger sons of big landowners to look for positions requiring little knowledge but all the more brutality;

1. Kautsky 1898a.

> the growing greed of the Church, which wants to gain prestige and wealth in uncivilised countries [...]; and finally, the growing power of high finance and its growing need for exotic business – these are the principal driving forces of the latest phase of colonial policy.[2]

The article translated below marked a significant advance in Kautsky's thinking. Now he saw 'finance-capital' as the driving force, with the role of colonial markets for industrial goods receding 'far behind their importance as fields for the investment of capital'. Kautsky did not use the term 'finance-capital' in Rudolf Hilferding's later sense of a convergence between banking and industrial capital, but he did draw a clear connection between the export of capital and the need to protect foreign investments through a projection of state-power.

Once industrial exports were shipped abroad and paid for, the seller's interest was satisfied. But, with railways and mining operations, the case was different: the exporters of finance-capital demanded protection for their ongoing commitments. Militarism followed because 'a certain application of force' was indispensable 'to protect the exported capital'. This article cast militarism as a consequence of colonial ambitions. It also foreshadowed Kautsky's conclusion a decade later that the 'policy' of imperialism might be thwarted by a multi-class alliance of workers and bourgeois strata, all of whom bore the tax-burden of imperialism to support the profits of bankers and heavy industrialists.

* * *

'Germany, England and World Policy'[3]

For some time past, the German and English capitalist press have been exciting the public opinion of both countries and hurling invectives at each other.

---

2. Kautsky 1898a, pp. 811–12. According to Kautsky's grandson, Joseph Schumpeter shared with him the attribution of imperialism to precapitalist classes: Kautsky, John H. 1961.

3. Kautsky 1900c. A partial translation of this article appeared three months later in the organ of the British Social-Democratic Federation *The Social Democrat*: Kautsky 1900d. The translator, J.B. Askew, prefaced Kautsky's work with this comment: 'I feel that at a time when the problem of Imperialism has assumed so pressing a character, the following article, which appeared in *Vorwärts*...will be, on account of its dispassionate tone and the thoroughness of its analysis, of especial interest to comrades in England.'

The English press accused German newspapers of artificially manipulating public opinion in favour of the Boers by publishing mendacious reports about South-African conditions, and of spreading suspicions about English intentions out of envy of England's colonial successes. The German press, in turn, pointed out the nasty English utterances about German colonial policy and the advance of German trade in Asia, England's attitude in the Samoa affair, and the seizure of German mail-steamers.[4] Undoubtedly, certain events – such as the manifestations of sympathy for the Boers by German newspapers and the sharp tone of the German protest-notice against the seizure of the mail-steamers, recently published by the Foreign Office – have contributed to fanning the flames of mutual excitement. But this effect could only be achieved because a strong resentment has already existed for a long time between the capitalist circles of both countries. Otherwise, neither the foolish incitements of the *Times* and the *Observer* nor those of capitalist kindred German press-organs, the *Rheinische-Westfälische Zeitung*, the *Hamburg Nachrichten*, etc., would have found such an attentive audience. Actually, the reasons for the mutual suspicions that the English and German organs of certain interested circles heap on each other lie deeper. These phenomena are not new. They must be traced back to economic transformations that have taken place in the world market during approximately the last two decades, transformations that, on the one hand, have complicated the economic machinery and increased the mutual economic dependence of both nations and, on the other hand, have also sharpened the contradictions and awakened a previously non-existent rivalry.

It is in light of these facts that we must look at the attitude of the two governments. Measures and statements calculated to wound national sensitivity have not been lacking on either side. But, overall, the governments seem to have been more driven than driving. Neither the Salisbury-Chamberlain government nor the German Foreign Office would dare, out of respect for the important commercial and other interests at stake, to push matters too far. In the matter of the seizure of the German mail-steamers, for example, the English government only consented to this after those 'Hotspurs' of the English press,

4. [A reference to the mail-steamer affair of January 1900. In October 1899, the Boer War broke out. In January 1900, British cruisers stopped three German mail-steamers off the African coast and searched them on suspicion of carrying arms and ammunition to the Boers.]

the *Daily Mail* and the *Times,* had published long accounts of Prussian officers taking part in the Boer War, and of the smuggling of war-contraband through Delagoa Bay. In the same way, the German government, in spite of concessions to the desires of the colonial enthusiasts, tried to remain on friendly relations with Great Britain, as shown by its conduct in the Samoa affair, during the discussions over the seizure of the steamers, and by its attitude towards the various attempts at an anti-English intervention in the South-African War. In opposition to the emotional policy of three years ago, which found its expression in the famous telegram sent by the Kaiser to Kruger,[5] there is no lack of signs today that the sharp anti-English tone of the capitalist newspapers does not at all suit the leaders of German foreign policy. The warnings that have appeared repeatedly in official newspapers during recent months concerning the anti-English demonstrations policy, and the deliberate emphasis on the interest that France has in an estrangement between Germany and England, clearly betray, in both form and content, their source in government circles. If, nevertheless, the rivalry of England and her capture of German vessels were utilised in putting forward the Fleet Acts,[6] that was only because they had no other grounds that would appeal in the same way to the capitalist and petty-bourgeois classes. With the best will in the world, they could not base their fleet requirements on the success of Russia in Central Asia, or on the French colonial policy in Madagascar. In any event, the relative strength or weakness of France or Russia lends itself to new military demands for land-forces, and certainly, as on previous occasions, during the discussions on the

5. [The Kruger telegram was sent by Germany's Kaiser Wilhelm II to Stephanus Johannes Paulus Kruger, president of the Transvaal on 3 January, 1896. The Kaiser congratulated the president on repelling the Jameson Raid, a sortie by 600 irregulars from Cape Colony into the Transvaal under the command of Leander Starr Jameson. The Raid was intended to trigger an uprising by the primarily British expatriate-workers but was a fiasco with around 30 raiders killed and the rest surrendering. It was applauded by the German press, but caused huge indignation in Great Britain and led to a further deterioration in relations between the two countries. The telegram was taken to mean that the Kaiser endorsed the Transvaal's independence in a region seen by the British as their own sphere of influence.]

6. [The Fleet Acts were four separate laws passed by the German Empire in 1898, 1900, 1908, and 1912. These Acts, championed by Kaiser Wilhelm II and his Secretary of State for the Navy, Grand Admiral Alfred von Tirpitz, committed Germany to building a navy capable of competing with the Royal Navy of the United Kingdom. The First Fleet Act, passed in 1898, stated Germany's aim to build a navy for defensive purposes. However, the Second Fleet Act, passed in 1900, enunciated the German intention of creating a naval force capable of competing with that of Britain.]

next military proposals the French or Russian danger will be held up as the reason – but it would have been absurd to give this as a reason for expanding the fleet. Thus, the only semi-plausible ground that remains is the menace that England poses to our foreign trade. The provocative impression that this motivation will leave on England will certainly not be diminished as a result.

The agitation on both sides through the press is sustained, for the most part, by groups of interested capitalists. On the German side, in addition, the chorus of anti-Semitic feudal agrarians pipe in because of an instinctive hatred for England as an industrial state and as a representative of bourgeois self-government. Also, and not without reason, the capitalist engaged in the German export-trade, as well as the financiers – people who a few years ago made themselves ridiculous by their admiration for everything English – adopt a hostile attitude to England. Just as little are the recent remarks in English writings on the necessity of a defence against German commercial rivalry, or the need for tightening the bonds of interest between England and her colonies and for the enclosure of so-called spheres of interest, made without any object. As we have already said, transformations have taken place during the last twenty years that have essentially changed the relations of the two countries, and the situation can only be explained with regard to those changes.

The nature of colonial policy, as well as the means by which economically stronger races exploit weaker ones, has repeatedly changed in the last centuries. If we go back to the middle ages, we find that the aim of commercial policy of the powers who then had an overseas trade – the Italian city-republics, the Hanseatic League, Portugal and Holland – lay in securing for themselves a trade-monopoly with certain markets and in excluding other powers either by force or by artificial restrictions. Following the discovery of America, after Spain had founded her colonial empire and Holland had acquired large possessions in the East Indies, no foreign ship was allowed into colonial harbours, and special measures were taken to secure a monopoly of the colonial market and to prevent smuggling. For example, in the seventeenth century, the trade between China and Spanish America was allowed only by way of Manila and Acapulco, and, further, the combined import and export could not exceed a certain figure in order to secure high trading profits on the one hand and, on the other hand, to secure the exports from Spain against competition. Furthermore, the natives were forced to render certain services to the administrators or to settlers of the same nationality, to cultivate their lands, etc.;

the conquerors gave great landed estates to societies, missions, etc. – together with the natives settled on them – as *encomiendas*.[7] Similar trade-monopolies and tributes were imposed by England on her American and Indian colonies. The breaking away of the United States, nevertheless, produced a change. It showed, and the fact was further confirmed by the struggle of Spain with her American possessions, that a colony populated by white people could not be held in complete economic dependence on the mother-country and that a certain independence must be granted to it. England made greater concessions to her colonies from time to time; only in the possessions of the East India Company did the old method of colonial government remain – and indeed, it partly remains even today.

However, it was not only the loss of the New England colonies that produced the change. While, formerly, imports and the trade in colonial products were the principal business, towards the end of the eighteenth century, great industry began to develop in England, and exports became more important. Markets had to be provided for the national industry, for which the colonies had to become outlets. But the feudal conditions that prevailed in them, the oppression of the native population as slaves incapable of consuming, and the creation of a sort of planter-aristocracy, were a direct hindrance to this. Therefore, the old colonial system had to be destroyed and the consuming power of the colonies increased. The same industrial Liberal, who in England supported unrestricted exploitation of labour and was in favour of a *twelve-hour working day for nine-year-old children* in English factories, became a colonial philanthropist who waxed enthusiastic over human dignity and elevation of the natives in the colonies. In the year 1838, England abolished slavery in her colonies; during the transition-period under the Emancipation Acts, the hours of labour for an adult black man were fixed at 45 hours per week or 7½ hours daily.

Meanwhile, English industry, and with it the English export-trade, acquired a sort of market-monopoly not only in her own colonies but everywhere in the

7. [The Spanish Crown used the *encomienda* labour-system in colonising the Americas and the Philippines. An *encomienda* (from *encomendar*, 'to entrust') involved the grant of a specified number of Indians living in a particular area, from whom the grant-holder, the *economendero*, could exact tribute in kind or in labour. After the decline of the native population the haciendas, or large landed estates, replaced the *encomienda*-system.]

world. Large-scale industry in Germany and France was still in its infancy; the United States did not count. German overseas trade was carried out mainly with England, the Nordic countries and the Netherlands. Overseas commerce was very seldom conducted directly and went, for the most part, through England or Holland. England's position on the world market is explained, on the one hand, by the sympathy of the Hanseatic merchants for England from the 1830s to the 1860s (Hanseatic trade was, in a certain sense, only an auxiliary and an appendage of English world commerce), and, on the other hand, by the cool indifference with which Englishmen looked on the English colonies. As early as the 1830s, the view that colonial possessions were useless acquired more and more influence; they brought only anxieties, necessitated maintenance of a colonial army, and strengthened the bureaucracy and feudal-aristocratic elements in the state. Therefore, away with the colonies. As regards a market for her industry, England could find that in foreign states. As Benjamin Disraeli expressed himself in 1852, the colonies were merely a 'millstone' round the neck of the English people.

With the industrial development of Germany and the United States, and the accompanying competition in the industrial market, the estimation of the colonies among England's industrial capitalists again changed. German and American competitors came to the fore not only in foreign countries but even in the English colonial market, and German and American shipping lines drove back their English competitors. While the declared value of the total export of English products to her colonies stood in 1880 at exactly 75.3 million pounds sterling, as against 51.8 million sterling in 1870 (therefore 24½ millions higher), in 1890 the value was only 87.4 and in 1897 only 80.7 millions, although the total imports of the colonies continually rose. Therefore, in free-trade England, the idea of a customs-union with her colonies began to take root at the beginning of the 1880s, i.e., the encouragement of English industry in colonial markets. Already in 1884, the 'Imperial Federation League' arose in London, although the agitation remained confined to certain narrow capitalistic circles. It is only since 1895, and especially under the influence of the South-African War, that the idea of a closed British Empire, standing as a unity against foreign nations, or so-called imperialism, has gained considerable ground.

Simultaneously with this development of Germany and the United States into industrial and commercial rivals of England, another change took place in colonial and foreign markets. The capitals made by industry and trade do not find a sufficient number of good investment, opportunities in the home-market and the markets of industrial neighbours; they are pressing forward into the exotic countries. It is no longer a question merely of securing a market for the growing surplus of goods, but also of providing the increasing accumulation of capital with investment markets. Already under the old colonial system, we find individual cases of export of capital to found new commercial undertakings and plantations in the colonies, but these were quite exceptional. Now, on the contrary, the importance of overseas settlements as markets often recedes far behind their importance as fields for the investment of capital.

China is an example. In order to force her to receive East-Indian opium, in the years 1839–42 England waged the so-called Opium-War. To acquire the immense territory of the Chinese Empire for industry and commerce, with its vast population; to get the most important harbours opened for commodity-exports; and to free the great water-courses for navigation into the interior – these were the aims of the efforts undertaken by the industrial states. Today, too, much of their effort is directed to this end, but the actual struggle over the Heavenly Kingdom today turns on the question of acquiring certain territories as 'spheres of influence', i.e., as markets for capital-investments and as areas for exploitation, to get railway and mining concessions, to place capital as loans, etc. Moreover, we find similar struggles for fields of investment in Asia Minor, Egypt, and South Africa. The small republics of Central America are more important for the United States as territories for financial exploitation than as markets for commodities, just as India is for England.

From this new situation in the world market springs the new colonial policy, the hunt for new colonies, the new American expansionist policy, English imperialism and, at least partly, German world policy. As long as England's industry controlled the world market, colonial possessions were of little value – except, as with India for example, to the extent that they served for the subsistence of officers and officials and for squeezing out high taxes. The situation is different today as competition from other nations assumes a threatening character. Now, colonies have once again acquired great significance, since it is possible to favour imports from the mother-country at the expense of foreign imports not only through differential customs but also through differential application of customs-regulations, invoicing and harbour-dues, etc. It is natural for the colonial government to get from the old country the materials it requires for public works and administrative purposes. In the meantime, finance-capital, much more than industry, finds satisfaction in acquiring colonies. It is only possible to exclude foreign industrial competition from colonial markets to a limited extent if development of the colony is not to be artificially checked and if the colony itself is not to become economically opposed to the mother-country. On the other hand, it is of the utmost importance to finance-capital, looking for the most profitable investment, that its fields of investment should lie within its own state, which will secure them more or less forcibly. Since the state has to decide on granting railway, mining, and other concessions, by means of subsidies it can raise the value of industrial undertakings, of shipping companies etc., just as it can, on the other hand, limit or cut off their income altogether through legislation. Therefore, we find that capital invested in foreign countries, as soon as it becomes a powerful economic factor, always endeavours to bring these areas under the government of its own state. Examples can be seen in Egypt; in the annexation of the Hawaiian Islands by the United States at the instigation of American planters; in the war over Cuba as a consequence of the agitation of interested capitalists in America; in the French expedition to Madagascar to ensure profits on the loan of the Comptoir d'Escompte and the people behind it; and in the contemporary South-African War, whose purpose is to abolish the Boer peasant-régime as a hindrance to British finance-capital and to free the South-African market as a field for investment of British capital.[8]

Hence the newly-awakened passion of capitalist states for the acquisition of colonies, and the endeavour everywhere to create fields for the investment of surplus-capital and to acquire areas for exploitation in foreign countries as so-called 'spheres of interest'; hence, too, the rise of militarism in democratic countries such as England and the United States. In order to force through concessions for investments and to protect the exported capital, a certain application of force is indispensable. England, Russia and Germany succeeded in 'leasing' territories in China; Italy did not.

This altered economic situation explains the spirit of increasing jealousy between certain German, English, and North-American capitalist circles. Just as it is certain that the industries of England and Germany are mutually

8. [The references are to: America's annexation of Hawaii (July 1898); the Spanish-American War (25 April–12 August 1898); the occupation of Madagascar by French troops and abolition of the monarchy (1896); and the Second Boer War (11 October 1899–31 May 1902).]

dependent, and that an interruption of commercial relations between the two countries must have the most disastrous effects on their industrial development, so it is equally certain that finance-capital frequently has interests different from those of industrial capital. The intrusion of German manufactures into its overseas markets is not pleasant for English industry; nevertheless, constant expansion of these markets has hitherto taken away much of the intensity of the competition while, at the same time, the German market for England and the English market for Germany continually gains in importance. Moreover, many points of contact result from the interest that the leading industries of the two countries have in opening markets that are still more or less closed. On the other hand, finance-capital is by nature thoroughly monopolistic; it endeavours to assure for itself a monopoly in the exploitation of certain areas. In fact, English complaints about German industrial competition sound much less bitter than complaints over the intrusion of so-called German capital into foreign areas, the founding of German commercial undertakings and banks, the exclusion of English shipping companies, the establishment of German industries, etc.

Take China as an example. In 1898 the entire export of Germany to China amounted to only 48 million marks; on the other hand, from *German Capital Investments in Overseas Countries*,[9] a book recently published by the German Imperial Navy Department, there appear to be 105 German commercial houses in China, 43 in Shanghai alone and more than 20 in Hong Kong, with a joint capital and credit far in excess of 100 million marks. No less important are the investments of German capital in shipping, docks, bank undertakings, railways and mining. The English coastal-shipping trade has also been transferred completely into German hands through purchase of two English lines (25 steamers) that trade between Siam, the Dutch colonies and the Chinese harbours (especially the Yangtze harbour).

The above-mentioned book shows the importance of German capital invested abroad; the overseas investments alone amount to over 7½ billion marks, leaving aside the investments in foreign loans and speculative commercial paper, etc. In the proceedings over the Stock-Exchange Act,[10] the

9. [Reichs-Marine-Amte (ed.), 1900.]
10. [The first German Stock-Exchange Act (*Börsengesetz*) was drafted in June 1896 and came into force on 1 January 1897.]

latter were estimated at 10 to 12 billion marks. In addition, there are the German investments in European countries, so that the sum of German capital-investments in foreign countries is probably more than 25 billion marks. The amount of English capital invested abroad is naturally much greater.

The mutual estrangement of German and English capitalists is but a consequence of this development, as are those political tendencies that people today call imperialism, expansionist policy, world policy and so on. The working classes and manufacturers will certainly be told that it is a question of extending their markets; still, the decrease in the export of English industrial goods to the English colonies, the extraordinarily small value of Tonkin and Algiers for French industry, and the even lesser importance of the German colonies for German industrial development – all prove how much of this is merely idle talk. Under certain circumstances, the investment of German capital abroad can bring advantages to German industry. The German iron-industry may profit, for example, from German railway-building in foreign parts; the founding of German commercial undertakings may cause an increase of German exports. However, such limited advantages are balanced by at least equivalent disadvantages, for through the founding of industrial enterprises, shipping lines, and commercial undertakings in foreign countries, what German industry gains in one way it will lose in another. Let us look at the statistics. As we said above, in China we find 105 German commercial houses with a joint capital of 100 million marks. Whoever believes that these houses only concern themselves with the German-Chinese trade, which in 1898 only amounted to not even 70 million marks, must be very naïve. The majority of these houses neglect German imports in favour of foreign industries. The only beneficiary from the founding of colonies, from the modern expansion-policy, is finance-capital, which draws further advantages from the failings of colonial governments and the consequent expenditures and loans for colonial purposes.

Then there are the costs of world policy, which are now being so forcefully demonstrated to England in South Africa – the reaction in domestic politics, the inevitable strengthening of militarism, the continuous breeding of renewed colonial troubles, and the increase of warlike entanglements. As with every other policy, so the policy of imperialistic world power has certainly found not only its poet, Rudyard Kipling, but also its philosophers and sophists, who endeavour to prove that imperialism means the strengthening of democracy, a rise in the general well-being, and many other things besides. But there is nothing to be seen of these results thus far, only a repeat of colonial crimes and the colonial wars of previous centuries, and there is an abundance of these from which to choose. We only need look at the war of the United States with the Filipinos, at the last English war with the Indian frontier tribes, at the Matabele War and at the Boer War.[11] These are the most striking accomplishments of the imperialist world policy! The prospect of similar results for Germany is certainly not enticing.

11. [The references are to the Philippine-American War (February 1899–1913); the Tirah Campaign, or Tirah Expedition, an Indian frontier-war against the Afridis who controlled the Khyber Pass (18 October 1897–4 April 1898); and the Second Matabele War (March 1896–October 1897).]

Chapter Eight

'Trade Agreements and Imperialist Expansion Policy' (May 1900)

Heinrich Cunow

Heinrich Cunow (1862–1936) was a German Social-Democratic Party journalist and historian. From 1898, he served as one of the editors of the SPD theoretical journal *Die Neue Zeit*, and, from 1902 onwards, he also worked as editor of the SPD central organ *Vorwärts*, where, together with Henry Ströbel, he was considered an anti-revisionist spokesman for the Left. In 1907, Cunow became a lecturer at the SPD party school in Berlin, teaching alongside Franz Mehring, Rudolf Hilferding and Rosa Luxemburg. His theoretical works include several studies in anthropology and a history of the revolutionary press during the French Revolution.

In August 1914, Cunow and his editorial colleagues at *Vorwärts* opposed the Reichstag's approval for war-loans, but, in mid-October 1914, he shifted to the chauvinist position of the SPD-majority led by Friedrich Ebert. In 1915, he attempted a theoretical justification for war-loans, arguing that Marxists should not oppose imperialism because it represented a step forward compared to competitive capitalism, and neither Europe nor the rest of the world was yet prepared for socialism.[1]

1. Cunow 1915.

During the War, Cunow worked for the *Hamburger Echo* and Parvus's newspaper *Die Glocke*. After the split between the Independent Socialist Party of Germany (USPD) and the SPD in October 1917, he remained in the latter and succeeded Kautsky as editor of *Die Neue Zeit* from 1917 to 1923. In 1919, he was elected to the National Assembly; in the same year, he was appointed Extraordinary Professor of Ethnology at the Humboldt University of Berlin; and, from 1919 to 1925, he was a member of the Prussian State-Parliament.[2]

The articles by Cunow in this anthology show him pioneering the study of American imperialism,[3] but also, and more importantly, emphasising the central role of banks and finance-capital in imperialist expansionism. In the article preceding this one, Karl Kautsky remarked that colonial expansion was more directly connected with the interests of finance-capital than with those of industry. This article by Cunow makes the same argument in greater detail and more emphatically. Cunow thought industrial exporters clearly had no interest in what political régime prevailed in export markets, only in the competitiveness of the products they hoped to sell:

> The statement that the possession of colonies by a state secures their territory as a market for its industrial products is, as can be proven easily by statistical data, completely erroneous. What decides the colonies' imports is not who owns them but rather, in the first place, the quality and cheapness of the industrial products as well as the degree of development of competing industries, followed by the ease of trade, which basically depends again on geographical location and the quality of the means of communication.

For exporters of investment-capital, however, the situation was radically different:

> For capital seeking higher profits in foreign undertakings than in domestic ones, it is by no means immaterial to whom this or that territory belongs, because political rule is of decisive significance for the feasibility and security of investments. A state with large colonial possessions can not only grant franchises and subventions for plantations, mines, railways, etc., but the interests of capital invested in those enterprises are also naturally given

2. For biographical details, see Florath 1987.
3. Cunow's article 'American Expansionist Policy in East Asia' refers to the work of Charles Conant on the economic basis of imperialism that was published in *The North American Review* in September 1898. See Cunow 1902 and also the next item in this anthology.

> much more consideration than they would receive under a foreign political régime.... Hence the phenomenon that when foreign capital has become firmly established in a certain area, it subsequently attempts to bring that territory under the political rule of its own state.... And this, so to speak, *need for employment and expansion on the part of money-capital, is what finds expression in modern expansion and world policy.*

When Otto Bauer reviewed Rudolf Hilferding's *Finance Capital* in 1910, he acknowledged Cunow's contribution to this question.[4] In his own review of Hilferding's work, Cunow called it a 'valuable supplement' to Marx's *Capital* that 'undertakes a thorough examination, on the foundations of Marx's theory of value, of the new phase of development of capitalism', especially 'the progressive mobilisation of capital' through banking credit and joint-stock corporations and 'the influence of these reorganisations on trade-policy'.[5] In his famous later work on *Imperialism* as the highest stage of capitalism, Lenin – through Hilferding's influence – also adopted the idea, propounded by Cunow as early as 1900, that capital-exports in search of higher profit were the principal explanation of modern imperialism.

* * *

'Trade-Agreements and Imperialist Expansion Policy'[6]

I

On 30 July 1900, the German-English temporary commercial agreement, which has already been extended twice since England's abrogation of the earlier commercial treaty on 30 July 1897, expires again. The Federal Council [the upper house of the German parliament] will almost surely be empowered by the Reichstag once again to grant England preferential treatment for another year, even if probably not without some declamations of indignation by the agrarian trefoil[7] of Hahn-Rösicke-Wagenheim along with their always

---

4. Bauer 1910.
5. Cunow 1910.
6. Cunow 1900.
7. [The 'trefoil' refers to a plant leaf with three parts, coming from the Latin *trifolium*.]

faithful anti-Semitic Sancho Panzas. If those gentlemen could not fail to remonstrate in the sessions of 16 and 19 June 1899, after the failure of their *coup de main* against meat-imports, they will be even less inclined to let pass by this opportunity to use one of their well-known recipes for stirring up the country: scolding 'perfidious Albion'. But, apart from those elements who want a tariff-war, all political parties in the Reichstag agree that keeping open a peaceful settlement of the commercial and political relations with England lies in Germany's own economic interests, and people in England are equally clear that, under present conditions, it would not only be a crude economic mistake but an even greater political mistake for England to seek now to introduce changes in its commercial relations with Germany and in that way to isolate itself even more.

For the time being, therefore, everything will remain unaffected. However, this does not at all mean that England has begun to realise the dubious and dangerous character of its imperialist ambitions as they have emerged of late, being directed towards the creation of a British imperial customs-union – a tariff-union that, for the benefit of England's trade with its colonies, will hinder the import of foreign products into the area of the customs union. If anything, the South-African War heightened Jingoistic and imperialist aspirations even more, and the dream of a world-ruling British 'Empire' assumed even more diverse forms. If England emerges victorious from the South-African struggle, as in all probability it will, the already overexcited English national feeling will doubtless be further strengthened, and it is by no means excluded that, under the influence of this mood, England will take steps that could be extremely dangerous for her position in the world market – even more dangerous than for the nations against whose industrial and commercial competition they would be directed.

It is an exceedingly characteristic event of economic development in the 1880s and 1890s that, while German large-scale industry and trade increasingly converted to the theory of free trade, the same England that in the 1860s still regarded free-trade doctrines almost as religious dogma today willingly accepts protectionist projects. If one cannot yet speak about a crossover to a protectionist system, when one compares the economic-theoretical debates of the English commercial press forty years ago with its contemporary reflections on the state of the world market, the turnabout is unmistakable. If, formerly, people enthused about the peaceful effects of economic competition, which would make the political separation of peoples virtually meaningless and bring about a general brotherhood of nations, today they say that England cannot maintain its position as an industrial state without constantly expanding the export of its commodities. The first precondition for that, however, would be the preservation of old markets against competition by Germany and the United States, which could most easily be achieved by a customs-union with the colonies as a 'barrier against foreign countries'. Economic living conditions have changed, and, in their wake, the 'economic principles' respected for so long have also changed. Instead of enthusiasm for the era of commercial peace came the demand for energetic expansion; instead of tender care for the salvation of blacks in Africa, concern about allocation of spheres of interests on that continent; and, instead of Tennyson's sentimental lyrics, the soldier-lyrics of Kipling.

The system of mutual commercial favouritism between England and its colonies through differential tariffs began to crumble away in the 1840s under the agitation of the strengthening Manchester school, and its last remnants were eliminated in 1860. This trend corresponded to a turnabout in economic conditions. The meaning of agriculture for the economic life of the English nation had diminished more and more; England had become an industrial state that had actually achieved a monopolistic position in world trade and world industry. Even without special protective tariffs, its industrial products held their ground in colonial markets and, despite the tariff-walls erected by European countries, made constant headway in their domestic markets. The only country of any importance as an industrial competitor in the world market was France. Germany's large-scale industry was still in its early stages in the 1840s and 1850s, and the United States, whose industrial development today threatens England's supremacy much more than Germany does, was barely beginning to develop its industry. The interests of the Southern planting aristocracy still almost completely controlled the economic life of the North-American union. And the English monopoly of shipping traffic was even more complete. Insofar as trade between the European continental states and overseas countries existed at all, it was almost without exception an auxiliary trade annexed to English overseas trade. What they exported to Asia, Australia, Africa and America, or received from there, went on English ships and through English harbours to its destination. English merchants and intermediaries pocketed most of the profits.

Why, therefore, should England want to secure for itself, by protectionist means, a monopoly it already possessed? The locking up of its colonial markets against free trade would have only supplied the continental states with a pretext for surrounding themselves with protective duties in their turn. The interest of English export-industries was rather to assert unhindered their natural superiority in the foreign markets, that is to say, to obtain the freest possible access for their products. Differential colonial tariffs gradually disappeared. Together with free self-administration, the North-American, Australian and South-African colonies were also granted the right to formulate their commercial policy freely and therefore to practise free trade or protectionism at their discretion, even towards the English motherland, but they were forbidden to introduce differential tariffs. England only reserved to itself the right to conclude commercial treaties for its colonies with foreign powers. On the basis of that clause, Great Britain reached a commercial agreement with Belgium in 1862 that gave it most-favoured-nation status in the English colonies. In 1865, a similar treaty was concluded with the German customs-union [*Zollverein*].

That solution of the colonial question did not at all satisfy a significant portion of England's free-trade politicians. They would have preferred to see England withdraw from its colonies and leave them to their own resources. From their standpoint, the colonies were conceived only as sales markets for English industry, and because those markets and their trade would almost certainly have remained with England even if it relinquished its colonial possessions, the expenses on colonial administration, colonial troops, shipping stations, etc. seemed to them a pointless burden on the English budget. The maintenance of troops in the colonies demanded considerable sums; in 1859, for instance, they cost 4 million pounds sterling. With the triumph of industrialism, bourgeois self-confidence also grew, and the bourgeoisie regarded the presence of a colonial army and bureaucracy only as a prop of feudal tendencies. Already in the 1820s, voices of that kind could be heard. In 1823, David Hume declared in Parliament that the colonies could only weaken the English motherland and that the best thing would be to let them take care of themselves. Similar opinions were voiced by a whole series of economists and Whig party leaders, John Stuart Mill among them, not to mention the leaders of the extreme free-trade movement such as Cobden and Bright.

The impetus that the abolition of differential tariffs gave to exports to the colonies proved that the free-trade politicians were right. The development of

English export-trade from 1860 to 1880, and, to some extent, from 1880 to 1890, offers the image of annually increasing progress. [...] In the thirty years from 1860 to 1890, exports almost doubled, although, in the last decade, English exports were already beginning to lose ground before German and American competition. From 1890 onwards, English exports gradually decreased, while those of the United States and Germany grew. Even the period of prosperity that began in 1895 did not restore English exports to their former level. [...]

Understandably, such a result did not please English industrialists and exporters, especially since German and American competition was not limited to commodity-exports. Relatively more significant was the growth and competition of the German and American merchant-navy, and the penetration of American and German commercial and banking capital into regions that English capitalists were used to considering their own domain – above all in [Latin] America, whose central states, especially Mexico and Guatemala, fell into growing financial dependence on the United States, while German capital-exports flew particularly towards South America (Brazil, Chile, Argentina, Venezuela). According to the recent overview of German capital-investments in overseas countries issued by the royal admiralty, German capital invested in the above-mentioned countries alone amounted to more than 1,400 million marks, not counting the sums invested in state-loans and similar securities, and this amount was considered too low by German and American experts.

The consequence in England was that, even by the early 1870s, agitation began to develop, at first half-hidden and later public, for a tighter commercial and political union with its colonies. The old free-trade theories were revised, and a tariff-union of the motherland with the colonies was portrayed as a desirable goal. In 1884, the Imperial Federation League was created for propagation of those ideas, and, as early as the following year, the London Chamber of Commerce asked the government to consider the question of a customs-union with the colonies and to request their governments for comments on this issue. The consequence of this movement was that the Colonial Office actually called upon the colonies to state their position on the question of a customs-union, and, in April 1877, a conference was held in which the most important colonial representatives participated. The question of imperial federation was, to be sure, excluded from the discussions as not yet being ripe for decision, but most delegates declared themselves in favour of a tariff-union that would have secured for England certain preferential tariffs in its colonial markets. A considerable part of the English commercial class, however, totally disagreed with the protectionist tendency; they raised protests, and the customs-union plans were dropped for the time being. The decline of the English export-trade, events in East Asia, new tariff-legislation in the United States, expansion of the British spheres of influence in Africa, and differences with the Boer states – all brought the question of a customs-union to the surface again and again. Simultaneously with the projects for a future imperial federation, appreciation of the colonial possessions grew once more. One can say, without exaggeration, that England never, not even at the time of the great colonial acquisitions in the nineteenth century, felt itself to be a colonial power as much as it does today.

However, the English government would hardly have abrogated the commercial treaties with Germany and Belgium if certain colonies, particularly Canada, had not put pressure on it. The reason for this attitude of the colonies is also to be found in the economic transformations that took place since 1860. When England at that time reserved to itself the right to conclude commercial treaties with foreign powers for its colonies, without asking for their consent, the colonies' exports were relatively small and almost totally restricted to agricultural products; real industry did not exist in the English colonies at that time. Since then, however, many things have changed. For instance, English colonial sugar from Mauritius, Barbados, etc. was until recently (since last year the British West Indies have levied so-called compensation-duties) excluded not only from the market of the English motherland due to the competition of German, Austrian and French sugar (which received export-premiums), but also largely from English colonial markets, because the most-favoured-nation clause in the old commercial treaty that England signed with Germany and Belgium extended to all the colonies. It was especially Canada – where since the 1880s, under the tariff-policy of the Conservatives, a native large-scale industry began to develop after the model of the Northern states of the Union – that felt the most-favoured-nation clause as an obstacle to its commercial policy, because its result was that any tariff-treaty that Canada reached with another country was immediately applied to the benefit of German exports. And England saw itself forced, if it did not want to offend Canada, to take its interests into consideration, because despite all protestations of loyalty there was a strong party there that saw the future of the country in joining the United States and pleaded for the establishment of a tariff-union with the latter. When the McKinley tariff in 1890 seriously threatened Canadian exports, agitation for such a customs-union, which would have been directed mainly against England, assumed such proportions that at the elections the Anglophile Conservative Party had a very hard time.

It is understandable that, under such circumstances, England would feel its position in the world market threatened and decide to abrogate the treaties with Germany and Belgium. It is less obvious why it would decide to defend itself from threatening competition by means of a customs-union with areas whose economic interests not only frequently clash with its own but are often mutually incompatible.

It looks almost as if the popular fervour stirred by the current struggle in South Africa, with its enthusiasm for 'Greater Britain', had suffocated all pedestrian critical sense, because the important questions – how far conditions are given for such a union of Great Britain with its colonies in a tightly connected economic territory protected by tariff-walls, what influence such a unification would have on the commercial relations of particular countries and especially on England's contemporary position in the world market – were regarded as immaterial. There is no lack of sober individual voices, but the mass of imperialists have gradually worked themselves up into such a state of paroxysm that no matter how much their goals may diverge from those of the former free-trade propagandists, they still resemble them in their dreams about the ultimate establishment of peace on earth, the abolition of national disputes and the dissolution of all economic struggles into general goodwill. They see only the bright side of things, and the fact that Canada and Australia have voluntarily sent some thousands of troops to the South-African war-theatre – which, for the feasibility of the imperialist projects, is almost immaterial – is, in their view, already a half-realisation of their dreams.

England is an industrial state; its colonies are agrarian states whose exports consist mostly of raw materials and foodstuffs. A domestic industry has begun to develop in some states, which, however, at its present stage, stands in absolute need of protection against superior English industry if it is not to be condemned to atrophy from the outset. From those different economic conditions the most diverse contradictions result: there are the same antagonisms between agrarian and industrial interests that exist wherever agricultural areas are united into a customs-union with industrial ones, but they are even more diverse because the forms of agriculture and the conditions for their prosperity in the particular colonies are completely different. It may be theoretically correct to argue that England should supply its colonies with industrial commodities and that they should provide England in exchange with raw materials and foodstuffs. Unfortunately, such a so-called exchange faces in practice the most diverse obstacles. [...][8]

Industry is not able to profit from colonial possessions, or it profits only to a very meagre extent. It is completely false to argue that the plans of English imperialism are driven by the expansion needs of large-scale industry and by the workers' standard of living – as mendacious as the claim by German fleet-enthusiasts that the acquisition of colonies in Asia, Africa and Australia is required by German industrial development, although many fleet-agitators do believe that, to be sure. Fundamentally, however, it is not the interests of industry but totally different economic forces that stand behind contemporary colonial, world and expansionist policy. Even if industrial interests are not totally unconcerned, they play a completely subordinate role. *The driving force of contemporary world and expansionist policy is the need for activity and profit on the part of money-capital!*

II

The so-called Commercial Union of England with its colonies, through an imperial customs-union, is only one of two demands of imperialism. The other is the 'expansion of Empire'; that is to say, when translated from the glittering phraseology of imperialist politicians into dry German, the increase of English colonial possessions through new conquests. And this second demand is the one to whose realisation the imperialist efforts of the world powers are first of all directed, as the annexation of Cuba and the Philippines by the United States, the latest island-acquisitions of Germany in the South Seas, and the English struggles in Sudan and South Africa sufficiently prove. Expansion is the keynote of imperialism, its true essential trait. The striving after new land-acquisitions equally rules English, American and German imperialist policy; the English customs-union plans are only a local and, on

8. [Cunow then dedicates two pages to describing the economic, political and financial obstacles an imperial customs-union would confront, arguing that it would result in retaliatory measures by other developed states, growing exclusion of England from the world market, and a rise in the production-costs of English industry.]

the whole, secondary ingredient. Moreover, even the English customs-union strivings often find support among English imperialists only because they think that the economic union of England with its colonies will also imply a political community of interests and provide valuable support to England's struggle for the 'partition of the world'. Mr. Cecil Rhodes, the main interpreter of English imperialism, described his creed, not without good reason, as follows:

> My real idea is the solution of the social problem, which, being interpreted, means that in order to keep your forty millions here from eating each other for lack of other victuals, we beyond the seas must keep open as much of the surface of this planet as we can *for the overflow of your population to inhabit*, and to create markets where you can dispose of the produce of your factories and of your mines. The Empire, I am always telling you, is a bread-and-butter question. If you have not to be cannibals, you have got to be Imperialists.[9]

The development, or rather conquest, of new lands is the real goal of imperialism, either to sell the motherland's industrial products or, as one can hear no less frequently in imperialist circles, to procure work for industrial labourers. At the very least, this alleged goal appears to be not quite consistent with that strange care for the workers that Mr. Cecil Rhodes has hitherto shown as representative of the Chartered Company and the De Beers Mining Company – the same care for the workers that his imperialist American coreligionists, Messrs. Rockefeller, Morgan, Spreckels, etc., have evidenced in their gigantic enterprises. In the agitation for expansion, however, it is common to hear the allegation that the conquest of a colony is synonymous with development of its markets for the conquering country's industry, which, under contemporary economic relations, is the most attractive argument [of the imperialists] and is therefore employed again and again. In professorial speeches agitating in favour of enlargement of the German fleet, the need to acquire overseas colonies as sales markets for the powerfully rising German industry also plays, alongside the spectre of a blockade, the leading role. To be sure, most of the speakers are themselves not at all clear about the lack of

9. [Stead 1897, Part I: On the Engaging of an Editor, Chapter I: The Ideas of Mr. Cecil.] Quoted in Beer 1897, p. 304. [Cunow's emphasis.]

foundation for this argument. After the colonies lost their eighteenth-century significance for trade as monopolised sources of supply, they have only been regarded from the point of view of their significance for the motherland's industrial development, especially since blooming English industry found its theoretical expression in the so-called Manchester school at the beginning of the nineteenth century. And this interpretation still continues to have an effect, although in the meantime a new turnabout in the field of colonial economy has taken place that promises to have an economic significance no less important than the previous transformation of the trade-colonies into sales markets for the industrial products of the metropolitan countries.

To this should be added that, even if the decline in Great Britain's exports to its colonial possessions during recent decades is indisputable, in most English colonies this trade is still the largest component part of imports. The temptation was great, therefore, to view England's economic development as being sustained and supported by its colossal colonial empire, although it was not the colonies that were responsible for England's greatness but rather its early development as an industrial state, which enabled it to anticipate its later industrial competitors by half a century. This development would have secured for England a monopoly of world trade and industry even without its colonies. How little England's colonial possessions contributed to its industrial expansion is best shown by the above-mentioned fact that even up to a few decades ago it was precisely English economists and theoreticians of industrial progress who considered the possession of colonies to be a millstone round England's neck.[10]

What colonial possessions really amounted to for industrial development can be seen from the economic decadence of Spain and Portugal, the industrial backwardness of Holland with its large colonies vis-à-vis Belgium, and the decline in France's exports despite its colonial possessions, which have been constantly growing during the last twenty years. The argument that the Anglo-Saxon race now has a peculiar aptitude for colonisation means virtually nothing, because this aptitude itself is nothing but a result of industrial development – a product of the *embourgeoisement* of the English régime, the triumph of industrialism over traditional feudal-bureaucratic forms of adminis-

10. [Letter of Disraeli to his Cabinet colleague Lord Malmesbury, 13 August 1852. Quoted in Malmesbury, 1884, Vol. I, pp. 343–4 and in Beer 1897, p. 303.]

tration. If one traces the formation of English colonial administrative practice, it becomes apparent that most reforms did not arise out of wise foresight but were very simply forced upon England by domestic conditions. It is plainly obvious that England cannot administer Australia or the Cape Colony, for instance, as Spain until recently administered the Philippines, if only because England lacks those feudal and clerical forces upon which the Spanish colonial régime rested.

The statement that the possession of colonies by a state secures their territory as a market for its industrial products is, as can be proven easily by statistical data, completely erroneous. What decides the colonies' imports is not who owns them but rather, in the first place, the quality and cheapness of the industrial products as well as the degree of development of competing industries, followed by the ease of trade, which basically depends again on geographical location and the quality of the means of communication.

Actually, this realisation should today be common knowledge because it can already be found in old Adam Smith. Nevertheless, most imperialist-colonialist arguments are today based on the assumption that whoever acquires a colony simultaneously disposes of its market for foreign products. This view is, indeed, far more common among imperialist/semi-socialist English politicians, who advocate an aggressive world policy, and among their coreligionists, the German national socialists, than among liberals. Among the latter, perhaps, their practical experience in the question of foreign trade acts as a counterbalance to the one-sidedness of their theoretical notions. [...][11]

The preceding examples can be increased by dozens more. They show that *it is not possession of a colony that decides the share in its imports*, but, rather, the condition of competing industries and the ease of trade. It follows from this that the striving to expand foreign markets can best begin at home by strengthening the competitiveness of industry, by creating commercial and industrial educational institutions, by abolishing tariffs on foodstuffs and, last but not least, by improving popular education and the workers' standard of living.

When a colony is shut off from foreign imports by high differential tariffs, this not only provokes the states concerned into levying retaliatory tariffs but

11. [Cunow then provides two pages of examples from English and German colonial statistics.]

also turns the colony, if its products are not granted privileged access to the motherland's markets, into a mere object of exploitation. It is forced to buy the motherland's more expensive products and forbidden to trade with foreign countries; its entire economic development is artificially stunted, and its population becomes antagonistic towards the mother-country. The result of such a commercial policy is illustrated by the decay of the Spanish colonial empire. If, on the contrary, the colony's raw materials are also protected by high differential tariffs in the motherland's markets as compensation, this implies an increase in the cost of foodstuffs and raw materials for industry. There is yet another way of securing exports to the colonies such as cutting shipping rates by means of subventions to shipping companies, paying export-bounties, granting specially reduced rates to the motherland's commodities on colonial railways, etc. Unfortunately, those practices also provoke foreign powers into adopting countermeasures and, moreover, make more or less heavy demands on the public treasury. Our colonies also provide some examples, even if they are only partially valid, of those colonial policy methods. While the total exports to German East Africa from the German tariff-area in 1894–9 amounted to only 10.45 million marks, in the same years the total imperial allowance for administration-costs reached 22 million marks, to which should be added annual subventions of 900,000 marks for the East Africa Company, so that each mark in exports to that market cost approximately three marks in subsidies from the imperial exchequer.

The acquisition of colonies *was thus able to contribute very little to the expansion of German exports*; domestic industry actually had very little interest in it. The situation was different in the case of money-capital seeking profitable investments, which is actually the real driving force behind imperialist expansion efforts. For capital seeking higher profits in foreign undertakings than in domestic ones, it is by no means immaterial to whom this or that territory belongs, because political rule is of decisive significance for the feasibility and security of investments. A state with large colonial possessions can not only grant franchises and subventions for plantations, mines, railways, etc., but the interests of capital invested in those enterprises are also naturally given much more consideration than they would receive under a foreign political régime that is not equally under the influence of the respective financial circles and that regards foreign investments mostly as a source of revenue for the public treasury. Hence, the phenomenon that when foreign capital has become firmly established in a certain area, it subsequently attempts to bring that territory under the political rule of its own state – a fact attested to by the agitation of American planters in Cuba and Hawaii in favour of American annexation, the propaganda of German proprietors in Samoa for German occupation, and the machinations of English mine-owners in the Transvaal republic in favour of English rule. Besides, colonial policy forces the state to make considerable financial expenditures on armaments, fleet-enlargement, coaling stations and the like, incurring debts, issuing new bonds, and thereby offering many business opportunities for money-capital.

When, half a century ago, English economists and trade-politicians saw in the colonies just more or less significant markets for superfluous English industrial products, that view was justified. Since then, however, the economic situation has completely changed. From the accumulation of profits by industrial capital, a constantly growing money-, and finance-capital has rampantly sprung up, looking for profitable employment. Alongside the export of commodities grew capital-exports, and the colonies developed from sales-markets for large-scale industry into investment markets for the superfluous capital of the rich industrial countries. And this, so to speak, *need for employment and expansion on the part of money-capital, is what finds expression in modern expansion and world policy*. One needs only to examine the motives and consequences of the colonial acquisitions made in the name of imperialism during recent years to be clear about that. What drove the United States to annex Hawaii and Cuba was clearly not the prospect of conquering their markets, in which it was annually gaining ground in any case, but, on the one hand, the fear on the part of American capitalists of a decline in the value of their Cuban plantations and railways, and, on the other, their eagerness to exploit the rich planting estates and the usually overlooked iron-mines of Santiago province. The Spanish-American War had hardly finished when the sugar-trust was already buying new plantations and a Cuban mining syndicate was formed in New York.

And the Philippines? Had it only been a question of trade in Luzon and the Bisayas archipelago, the sacrifice of tens of thousands of soldiers [and Filipinos] would have been unnecessary. That goal could have been reached more easily by granting limited autonomy to the Filipinos, especially in Manila Bay and Cebu Island, the central points of Filipino trade. But the real motives that prompted the American government to make those huge financial and human expenditures were different. Even cursory study of the leading American financial and stock-exchange magazines, which expatiate so freely and unabashedly on the prospects of sugar and tobacco-culture in the Philippines, the exploitation of mineral deposits and so on, is enough to recognise the reason for the devastation visited upon the Filipino people.

The picture is the same everywhere. Was the French conquest of Madagascar, the purchase of the Caroline Islands or the conquest of Rhodesia a question of winning sales markets? Where is that motive to be found in the contemporary struggle between England and the Boer states? While Mr. Cecil Rhodes, as head of the British South Africa Company, declared that the goal of imperialism is the development of new sales markets, he did everything possible to hinder trade through his administrative measures and by raising tariffs. The Chartered Company was created merely to exploit the supposed gold-riches of Matabeleland and Mashonaland. But after those exploits proved unprofitable and yielded since 1890 a total deficit of 5 3/4 million pounds sterling, the 'land-developer' Mr. Cecil advocated recognition of Rhodesia as an independent colony and the assumption by the government of the total costs, that is to say, reimbursement of the stock-holders for all their outlays.

The turnabout in economic relations appears most clearly in the changed policy of the diplomatic representatives of the large industrial states in the court of Peking. The previous endeavour to secure open harbours is today replaced by the striving to secure special spheres of interest and to procure railway or mining concessions for some syndicate. Even in our wretched African colonies, the main goal is to establish new colonisation companies. Insignificant as trade with the German customs-area is, a large number of companies have set themselves the goal of bringing to bear 'German capital' and 'German labour' in the German-African colonies. [...][12]

This character of imperialist world policy implies, for the German socialist party, the need to fight against it all the more ruthlessly. Attempts have been made to interest the workers in German capital invested in colonies and foreign lands by arguing that a part of the profits yielded by those investments flows back to Germany, where they go into consumption and, in that way, contribute to the expansion of so-called national production. That this argument is partially correct is indisputable, but expansion of the domestic market

12. [A description of colonial scandals follows.]

by those means is more than compensated by the narrowing of foreign trade. Wherever German beer, musical instruments, metal goods, etc. penetrate, German capitalists establish enterprises to satisfy those needs, and the respective German industries are, in the long run, gradually deprived of those sales-markets. Moreover, as America has learned and as Germany and England are now learning, there is also no expansion-policy without expending colossal sums that in one way or another must be raised by taxes and partially covered directly by the workers' consumption – not to mention the growing danger of military entanglements, the sharpening of the clashes of interests between rival states and the repercussion of those clashes on mutual trade-relations. Surely the industrial worker also has an interest in industrial development, which, under given economic conditions, means the growth of exports; however, that goal cannot be reached by creating an exclusionary customs-area or by conquering new colonial possessions, but rather through a policy of commercial treaties conducted with expertise and energy on the principle of *do ut des*.[13] German industry has reached a stage of development where it can successfully meet competition with more or less favourable treaty-terms. If the dream of a German world empire, whose trade will reach out to all lands and seas, can be realised at all, it is only in that way.

13. [Latin for 'I give, so that you might give' – the principle of reciprocity.]

Chapter Nine

'American Expansionist Policy in East Asia' (June–July 1902)

Heinrich Cunow

1. Early American expansionism[1]

The conquests of Cuba, Puerto Rico and the Philippines are always described in tracts dealing with American imperialism as a new turn, representing a break with the old traditions of American policy. If one understands by imperialism a policy of expansion dictated by capitalist interests, this view does not quite hold water. Shortly after its 'liberation', as soon as it felt its strength growing, the Union began attempts to expand its territory by all possible means – not only through annexation of territories that remained outside the confederation but also through diplomatic intrigues, the purchase of large areas, military provocations and even filibustering expeditions undertaken in peaceful times. The purchase of Louisiana – which then included the Mississippi basin and Missouri – from France for 15 million dollars was followed by the purchase of Florida in 1819, skilfully exploiting Spain's distress, and by the first preparations for the conquest of Cuba. The Pearl of the Antilles aroused the Yankees' exploitative instincts not just recently, but already back then.

1. [Cunow 1902. The subtitles have been added by the editors of this volume.]

In 1823, the then Secretary of State, John Quincy Adams, wrote to the American minister at Madrid: 'It seems scarcely possible to resist the conviction that the annexation of Cuba to our Federal Republic will be indispensable to the continuance and integrity of the Union.'[2]

But, because Cuba proved to be a goal momentarily unattainable, the Florida purchase was followed by expansion of the United States to the Pacific coast; an expansion marked by the bargaining with England over the Oregon region, the fomentation of the Texan landowners' attempts to secede from Mexico, the provocation of Mexico into war and, after its defeat, the annexation of Texas, California, New Mexico and the Northern part of Sonora to the Union's territory.[3] The young republic had hardly taken possession of the Pacific coast when it already began to look out to the Pacific Ocean for new acquisitions, and, in 1852, it dispatched Commodore Perry in an expedition to Japan that opened up that land to American trade through the treaty of 1854. At the same time, under the leadership of James Buchanan,[4] the American diplomats in London and Southern planters' ruthless agents resumed the intrigues for the acquisition of Cuba, which, failing all other methods, they hoped to attain through an audacious invasion. And Buchanan actually knew how to instigate the American diplomats in Paris and Madrid, because in 1854, at the Ostend Conference, they submitted to the American government a plan for the seizure of Cuba.[5] The following year witnessed William Walker's

2. [Morse 1898, p. 131.]

3. [In 1846, under a treaty with Britain, the United States gained possession of the Pacific coast between the 42nd and 49th parallels. The Republic of Texas successfully seceded from Mexico in 1836. In 1845 Texas joined the United States as a full-fledged state. The Mexican-American War (1846–8) broke out in the wake of the 1845 US-annexation of Texas.]

4. [James Buchanan (1791–1868), Democratic American politician, was the fifteenth President of the United States (1857–61). He served as minister to the Court of St. James (Britain) from 1853 to 1856, during which time he helped to draft the Ostend Manifesto.]

5. [The Ostend Manifesto was a secret document written in 1854 by US diplomats at Ostend, Belgium, describing a plan to acquire Cuba from Spain. On orders from US Secretary of State William L. Marcy, three US diplomats (minister to Britain James Buchanan, minister to France John Y. Mason, and minister to Spain Pierre Soulé) devised a plan to purchase Cuba, for $120 million, for the United States. Further, if Spain were to refuse the offer, the manifesto suggested that America would be 'justified in wresting' Cuba from Spain. The document was then sent back to the US State Department, but news of it leaked out and it was soon made public. The aggressively worded document, and Soulé's advocacy of slavery, caused outrage among Northerners who felt it was a Southern attempt to extend slavery. American free-soilers, just recently stirred by the Fugitive Slave Law passed as part of the Compromise of 1850,

expedition of conquest to Nicaragua, supported by the federal government, to implement the slave-owners' annexation-plans. Walker was a *condottiere*[6] who, some years earlier, had been agitating in California at the service of Southern politicians and who in 1853 – as a true forerunner of Jameson[7] – had undertaken an unsuccessful foray into the Mexican province of Sonora.

Those are just a few characteristic features of the North-American republic's earlier expansionist policy, but they show clearly enough that it takes the whole capacity for self-delusion of a German-American politician like Carl Schurz,[8] with the strangest reminiscences from the movement of 1848, to assert that it was only with the inauguration of the so-called recent imperialist policy that the Union deserted 'the path of righteousness, high principle and glorious destiny'. In his well-known speech for Bryan's election he even said:

> 'Expansion,' then, in the historical and truly American sense, means the extension of our Constitutional system together with the extension of our territorial area. In this sense we are all expansionists, provided the expansion be honorably effected. And if in the course of events our northern neighbors, a people like our own and practiced in self-government, should

decried the manifesto. Thus, Cuba did not become part of the United States. American intervention in Cuba would next surface near the end of the nineteenth century in the Spanish-American War.]

6. [A *condottiere* was a leader of a band of mercenaries common in Europe between the 14th and 16th centuries.]

7. [The Jameson Raid (29 December 1895–2 January 1896) was a raid on Paul Kruger's Transvaal Republic carried out by Leander Starr Jameson and his Rhodesian and Bechuanaland policemen over the New Year weekend of 1895-96. It was intended to trigger an uprising by the primarily British expatriate workers (known as Uitlanders) in the Transvaal but failed to do so. The raid was ineffective and no uprising took place, but it did much to bring about the Second Boer War and the Second Matabele War.]

8. [Carl Schurz (1829–1906), was an American political leader born in Germany, where he participated in the revolutionary uprisings of 1848–9. Compelled to flee to Zürich after the collapse of the movement, he migrated in 1852 to the United States, where he settled in Watertown, Wisconsin, and became a strong supporter of Abraham Lincoln, who appointed him US minister to Spain in 1861. Schurz resigned this position to serve in the Civil War, where he saw action and was promoted to major general. He worked as a journalist and later was elected US Senator (1869–75) from his adopted state of Missouri. In the presidential elections of 1876, Schurz supported Rutherford B. Hayes, whose hard-money views he approved, and from 1877 to 1881 he served as Hayes's Secretary of the Interior. In 1896, Schurz supported the Republican presidential candidate William McKinley because of William Jennings Bryan's currency views, but in 1900 he shifted to Bryan because of his opposition to imperialism, which also led to Schurz's membership in the American Anti-Imperialist League. His most famous anti-imperialist speech is Schurz 1899.]

> express a wish to join this Union – a consummation which our present policy of imperialistic adventure is apt rather to put off than to bring on – we all would welcome them with heart and hand.
>
> But when we annex to this Republic foreign territory, especially territory in the tropics which, owing to climatic conditions, can never be settled by our own or homogeneous people, with the intent and expectation that such territory shall never come into our Constitutional system, but shall as to the civil, political and economic status permanently depend upon the will of our central Government in which they are to have no determining share, those countries thus being vassal provinces, and their people subject populations, that is not mere expansion, in the historic American sense, but that is imperialism.[9]

That is seeing nothing but the externals in the history of American expansionist policy. Even the statement that previous expansion of the Union's territory was always followed by extension of the American constitutional system is not totally correct because Alaska, purchased from Russia in 1867, was ruled like an English crown-colony by an appointed governor. The only difference between the early and the contemporary phase of the American expansionist movement is that, with the exception of Alaska and recently Hawaii, the annexed territories were borderlands that could simply be incorporated into the Union, whereas the Philippines and Puerto Rico are far-off countries, completely different ethnically and climatically, that cannot simply be integrated into the so-called state-organism in the old way. But it was not the 'high principle' of the Constitution that in the past hindered annexation of those distant tropical areas – as the ever-recurring efforts to acquire Cuba and Santo Domingo, as well as the interventions in the struggles of the Spanish-American republics and the occupation of Hawaii show – but, rather, the opposition of those areas to annexation, the threatening conflicts with the European powers, particularly with Spain, the former backwardness of American sea-power and, finally, the fact that there was enough territory within the Union's boundaries whose exploitation initially seemed a much more important task.

To this should be added the fact that in the struggles between the free-trade, slave-owning Southern states and the Northern states, with their farms and

9.. [Schurz 1900, in Schurz 1913, p. 218.]

their developed large-scale industry (a struggle in which, from the election of Andrew Jackson in 1829 until 1860, the Southern states always had the upper hand), each party sought to settle and incorporate into the Union those territories with which it had similar economic interests and from which it could thus expect a strengthening of its influence on the government and Congress. The Southern states, therefore, strove to annex those states and territories where slavery and plantations were the foundation of economic life, or to which the Southern economic system could at least be transplanted, while the Northern states, on the contrary, sought to annex those territories where a farm-economy and the rudiments of industry predominated. For both goals, however, the absorption of borderlands adjacent to the Union was more fitting than the conquest of distant areas.

Those are the political and economic relations that determined the direction of the republic's expansionist policy until the 1870s. But the economic significance of industry and trade grew rapidly after the Civil War and with them the political supremacy of Northern bourgeois interests. Thereupon, other economic factors began to influence American expansionist efforts.

2. Modern American imperialism

When the Northern bourgeoisie took up the struggle with the South in 1860, domestic industry and foreign trade were relatively undeveloped; after the Civil War, however, both experienced rapid growth. [...] Favoured by the high protective tariff of 1861, which made imports prohibitive in many branches of the economy, the developing industry at first endeavoured to conquer the domestic market. Most exports consisted of agricultural products, particularly raw materials for European industrial states; the share of manufactures still amounted in 1880 to no more than 12.5 per cent of total exports. In that year, however, the United States experienced a new industrial impetus, supported in many respects by the McKinley and Dingley [tariff-] bills. A significant export-industry developed, at first limited to certain branches for which the country's wealth in coal, ores, cotton, etc. offered especially favourable production conditions. The more vigorously that export-industry developed within those limits, the more energetically it demanded the winning of foreign markets.

Even more important for the new phase of expansionist policy was the enormous capital-accumulation that took place after 1865. Until then, a constant, strong flow of capital-exports went from England, Germany and France to the United States. All the large undertakings, the great railroads, industrial investments, mining companies, etc. were assisted by English and partially by German and French capital, while the share of Yankee capital in the Central- and South-American undertakings remained for the time being extremely modest. The growing industrialisation and economic development of the country by great railroad-lines, whose tracks were followed by streams of new settlers and led to the creation of new economic territories in areas where previously the prairie or the primeval forest stretched endlessly, brought about a strong growth in wealth. Ever since the end of the Civil War, national wealth has doubled approximately every twelve years. In 1850 it was calculated at 7,135 million dollars and in 1900 at 94,300 millions, while per capita wealth grew from 307 to 1,235 dollars. The demand for capital increasingly receded vis-à-vis the supply, as Charles Conant aptly explained in an article in the *North American Review* of September 1898 concerning the tendencies of American imperialism. The drive to find 'new productive employments for capital' and new investment markets began, and with it the 'turn to countries which have not felt the pulse of modern progress'.[10]

3. American policy in Latin America

In search of such investment and sales markets, American capitalists first turned to Central and South America. A very profitable 'employment' for their capitals appeared in the construction of Mexican railroads. Until the early 1880s, Mexico's railroads were hardly developed; in 1872, the length of track amounted to some 80 German *meiles*.[11] Those railways belonged mostly to English companies. North-American capital then appeared on the scene in order to connect the Mexican railroad-network to the great North-American railway system. In 1890, more than 1,225 German *meiles* were already laid, and, by early 1900, approximately 1,985 *meiles* were in operation, of which at least two-thirds were under the control and administration of North-American capitalists. At the same time, Yankee capital in Mexico turned

10. [Conant 1898, p. 338. On this issue see Parrini and Sklar 1983.]
11. [The *meile* was a traditional unit in German-speaking countries, measuring 7,532.5 metres. *Mile* refers most commonly to the *international mile* of 1,609.344 metres.]

to industrial undertakings, particularly the construction of spinning mills and cotton-weaving mills, because several land-tracts, especially Laguna de Torreón, supplied good raw materials, and the mountainous country had easily exploitable water-power. In 1899, approximately 467,000 spindles and 14,000 looms were already in operation. In the Mexican mining industry, much American capital is employed as well. But it is especially in the field of banking that American capital completely outstripped English capital. During recent decades, American banks sprang up in all the large trade-centres and ports, introducing American banking practices and capturing an ever-growing share of the banking business. The small Central-American republics have fallen no less massively under the influence, or more correctly the domination, of North-American high finance, to which they owe huge sums and which therefore received all kinds of land, mining, railway and trade concessions.

But the picture changes if we look at South America. No matter how many efforts North-American finance made during the last two decades in order to extend its control over the South-American states, English capital has been able to maintain its dominant position in Colombia and Venezuela, and that is even truer of Peru, Ecuador, Chile, Argentina and Brazil. In the latter states, and particularly in Chile, German capital invested large sums and in many regions has driven back English capital through competition. The industrial undertakings of the two Chilean provinces of Valdivia and Lanquihue, which are industrially the most highly developed in Chile, are almost totally in German hands. The German (Hanseatic) merchant-houses likewise gained first place in export- and import-trade, and even a large share of the banking and money-business is gradually going over to German banks, among which the branches of the German Overseas Bank and the German-Chilean Bank are the most significant. And we also find German capital, though not on such a large scale as in Chile, invested in industrial undertakings, plantations, trade, railways and banking in several Brazilian provinces, particularly in Sao Paulo, Rio de Janeiro, Parana, Minas Gerais and Rio Grande do Sul.

As a market for sales by United States industry, Latin America has also not become very important.[12]

12. [Some statistical examples follow.]

The causes of this meagre success of North-American capital and the export-trade in South America cannot be examined more closely here. The most important are the mistrust of the Spanish-American countries towards the policy of Uncle Sam; the special nature of their import-trade, which often consists of commodities that North-American industry cannot supply; the backwardness of American shipping; and finally the Union's new tariff-policy.

4. American policy in the Pacific Area

If the capitalist conquest of South America and the winning of its markets only advanced painstakingly against overwhelming obstacles, in the archipelagos and countries on the other side of the vast ocean – which its discoverer, Balboa, called 'pacific' – a much more favourable field of activity presented itself for American energy and the spirit of enterprise. Here, English and Hanseatic businessmen had not yet seized the largest share of the booty; everything was still fluid and in the making, and there was a world to win. China and Japan, now for the first time open to trade, offered not only good sales markets but still more favourable investment markets for surplus American capital as soon as the economic development of the huge Middle Kingdom, with its dense population and its rich natural resources, had begun. And not only China and Japan came into consideration, but also Korea, the Philippines, South-East Asia and the entire rich island-world of the Pacific Ocean, which the whole economic development of recent decades points to increasingly as the great field where the decisive battles for economic supremacy will be fought. Moreover, this battleground lay so much closer to the United States that American capitalists had an advantage from the outset over their European competitors, an advantage that will be even greater when the planned inter-oceanic canal permits easy and rapid connection between the eastern coast of the United States and East Asia.

The clever Yankee businessmen discerned this advantage early on. The young republic had hardly reached the Pacific coast when it was already preparing itself to gain access to the China-trade, and, in 1844, it concluded a treaty with the Middle Kingdom that secured a number of important rights for the Union. That was followed by a protest against the course of action of England, which had taken possession of Greytown (Nicaragua) in order to take over the project of building an isthmoid canal – which naturally, being built with English money and under English suzerainty, would have meant strengthening English vis-à-vis American trade in anticipation of American plans for the future. The means were lacking for proceeding directly against England, so the American representative in Nicaragua appealed to the local government and was granted certain transit-rights over the isthmus. England gave in and agreed in 1850 to the Clayton-Bulwer Treaty in which both parties pledged not to secure sovereignty over any part of the Central-American coasts or ever to claim control over a trans-isthmus canal. As is generally known, that treaty held until last year, when the United States declared it no longer binding because it stood in the way of their plans to build a fortified canal completely under their own control. After long negotiations with England a new treaty was concluded [in 1902], the Hay-Pauncefote Treaty, which granted to the United States much more extensive rights than they were ready to grant to England a century ago. And, just two years after the Clayton-Bulwer Treaty, [in 1852] a further enterprise was already undertaken to establish American influence in the 'Mediterranean of the future'; namely, the expedition of Commodore Perry to Japan, which, as already mentioned, ended in the conclusion of the Treaty of Kanagawa, opening the ports of Simoda and Hakodade to the ships of the United States and securing for them free trade as well as all privileges that Japan might in future grant to other nations.

In the following years, internal struggles and the Civil War naturally diverted the United States' attention from enterprises in the Pacific Ocean. But, after the country recovered and industrial production reached new heights, the United States continued to go along the previously traced path. As early as 1851, the North Americans had a growing influence over the Sandwich Islands,[13] which lay approximately half way to the southern part of East Asia and offered an excellent base for further expansion. First of all, they attempted to bind the archipelago economically to the United States. That goal was reached through the reciprocity-treaties of 1875, which provided for free trade between both

13. [The Sandwich Islands was the name given to the Hawaiian Islands by Captain James Cook when he discovered them on 18 January 1778. The name was given in honour of one of his sponsors, John Montagu, 4th Earl of Sandwich, who was at the time the First Lord of the Admiralty and Cook's superior officer. During the late 19th century, the name fell into disuse. The Sandwich Islands should not be confused with the South Sandwich Islands, an uninhabited British dependency in the southern Atlantic Ocean.]

countries. The Union further received the exclusive right to build a marine station in Pearl Harbour – a concession that actually meant *de facto* control of the Hawaiian government by the United States.

Those attempts to pave the way for a grandiose expansion-policy in the Pacific Ocean, however, emanated from a far-sighted circle of great capitalists and politicians; in ordinary, everyday politics, they were hardly noticed. Not until the rapid increase of industrial production in the 1880s and early 1890s, the growing opposition of Hispanic America to the Union despite all pan-American congresses, the difficulties of increasing commodity-exports to South America and, last but not least, the growing significance of the export and import trade with East Asia, Oceania and Australia, did public opinion turn more and more to the West, to the opposite shore of the vast ocean. And then the opportunity for yet another coup presented itself.

On 17 June 1893, under the leadership of the American representative in Hawaii and under the protection of American warships, the monarchy was declared abolished in the Sandwich Islands, a provisory government was set up and a plenipotentiary representative was sent to Washington to negotiate the annexation. President Harrison, as a politician appointed by the plutocracy, was perfectly willing to satisfy their demands despite all the filth-ridden intrigues. On 15 February 1894, just a few weeks before the end of his presidency, he submitted to the Senate an annexation-treaty bill. But the next president, Grover Cleveland, an opponent of the annexation-policy, immediately withdrew the project and did not enable its further submission to the Senate during his term of office. McKinley proved more willing to oblige; in June 1897, he submitted a new treaty that was ratified the following year. In August 1898, the United States representative in Hawaii formally assumed sovereignty over the archipelago.

Hand in hand with those efforts to gain a base for further annexations in the Pacific Ocean went endeavours to expand trade with that area – and with greater success than in South America. [American imports from South America surpassed American exports to that area.] But the United States' trade with East Asia and Oceania shows an expansion that can only be the envy of other nations. While England's exports to those areas pretty much stood still and even suffered partial setbacks, the United States has been able to increase its exports to East Asia (China, Hong Kong, Japan) in the past four years from 19.3 to 52.9 million dollars, and to Oceania from 17.2 to 43.4 million – a success with which North-American trade and capitalism could have been completely satisfied if American expansionist policy were not dictated much more by the search for new investment markets to employ surplus-capital profitably than by the need to win new commercial outlets. The agitation among Cuba's native population, which was keenly fomented by the North-American capitalists involved in Cuban plantations, mines and industrial enterprises, provided a welcome pretext for satisfying the long-entertained lust for the Pearl of the Antilles and, in addition, for making some giant steps forwards in the Pacific region. Spain had to pay for the 'liberation' of Cuba with the loss not only of its West-Indian possession but also of the Philippines and the Marianas (Ladrones) Islands.

5. The Philippine-American War and the open-door policy in China

Contrary to the promises of autonomy made to the rebellious Tagalogs, the Philippines were simply declared an American possession, and a war of extermination was launched against the native Malayan population, a war in which perhaps even more bestialities were committed than under earlier Spanish rule.

There is hardly any clearer evidence of the American movement's imperialist tendency than the war against the Filipinos. Had it just been a question of winning new sales markets for American capital, of commercial expansion, then the bloody war in the Philippines, the sacrifice of tens of thousands of American soldiers and Tagalogs, and the waste of public funds, would have been completely superfluous. The foreign trade of the Philippines has long been concentrated at certain points: the trade of Luzon in Manila, that of the Visayas Islands in Cebu. Just as almost all German trade with America passes through Hamburg and Bremen, so the foreign trade of the Philippine Islands passes through Manila and Cebu; and the occupation of Cebu Island and of Manila Bay, with their surrounding coastal areas, would have been sufficient to usurp trade, particularly since the North-American government would have reserved to itself the protectorate over the archipelago and the construction of the railroad from Manila to Northern Luzon over Cagayan to Aparri. Besides, due to the racial antagonisms and contradictory interests between the native tribes, which would quickly have led to the ruin of the

Tagalog elements, the whole group of islands would probably have fallen into the hands of the Americans anyway. But the Yankee expansionist politicians had no intention of waiting; together with the great capitalist press, which carried enthusiastic reports about the mineral riches, fertility and favourable geographical location of the islands, they demanded immediate annexation, whose consequence was a struggle against the local population that continues even today.

But the real issue, which is admittedly only hinted at here and there, was the winning of a strong foothold, a military and naval base for later expeditions to China and perhaps also to the Indian archipelago. That is clearly shown by the grandiose harbour-construction works in Manila Bay, finished in the autumn of last year, which serve both commercial and military purposes and were recently employed in the attack [against China]. But, for the time being, the government held back because agitation against the American usurpers continued in the interior of Luzon, and it was only by maintaining numerous troop-detachments that the American occupation-government was painstakingly able to maintain some order. Moreover, the harbour and fortification works required at least three to four years. American policy in the Philippines therefore temporarily restricted itself to granting as many privileges as possible to American capitalists.

American policy in the Pacific area otherwise limited itself to preserving the so-called integrity of China and maintaining the status quo, that is to say, to intervening against the granting of concessions to foreign powers by the Chinese government – as it recently intervened, for instance, against the granting of mineral rights to Russian subjects in the province of Kirin. This tactic had three advantages: it made the American government appear concerned about Chinese imperial glory, it hindered the granting of privileges that American expansion could later find inconvenient, and it held everything in suspense – until the time for intervention arrived. Besides, it fitted American diplomacy – which, in the motherland, kept the doors carefully shut and in the colonial possessions only opened them to the extent required by American interests[14] –

14. In conformity with its promises, the government of the United States was admittedly forced to implement the tariff-law for the Philippines endorsed by the President on 8 March 1902 and accepted by the Philippine Commission on 17 December 1901, which provides that commodities exported from the United States to the Philippines should pay customs as if they had come from foreign states; but trade between the archipelago and the United States was indirectly granted all sorts of advantages that

to appear enthusiastic for the time being about the 'Open Door' in China. Secretary of State John Hay's course of action in this regard is well known. On 6 September 1899, the American *chargés d'affaires* in Berlin, London, Paris, Petersbug, Rome and Tokyo were commissioned to solicit the consent of the respective governments to a declaration that they would not modify under any circumstance the treaty-ports or meddle with the vested interests lying in their concessions or in one of the so-called spheres of influence – an empty demonstration of friendliness that later American world politicians, especially members of the Asiatic Association, would find highly amusing.

The riots that broke out in China in May 1900 quite embarrassingly got in the way of that policy. The Chinese people's uprising made intervention by the great powers inevitable. Considering the contradictory interests and mutual jealousy, who could predict how that event would unfold? Naturally, the United States also had to take part in the expedition.[15] But, soon after the troops occupied Peking, the American government beat a retreat and later worked for return of the Court, complete departure of all troops and reduction of the compensations demanded by European governments. 'Henceforth no other conflict' was the *leitmotif* of their efforts. In some newspapers, this behaviour was described as springing from humanitarian considerations – a remarkable conception of American expansionist policy and the capitalism driving it. While American diplomacy was proving so 'humane' in China, the most brutal massacres of women and children were taking place in the Philippines.

make foreign competition difficult. For instance, agricultural and industrial products imported from the Philippines to the United States pay a tariff approximately 25 per cent lower than the same products from other countries, and inasmuch as an export-duty has been levied at the shipping in Filipino ports, that tariff is deducted from the import-duties of the United States. Besides, commodities produced in the United States and exported to the Philippines are not only exempted from the customs-duties on imported raw stuff and semi-manufactures but also from internal taxes, which otherwise would have been collected. And, finally, foreign ships coming from the Philippines to the United States ports have to pay the same fees as if they had come from a colony not belonging to America. If one adds to that all sorts of little obstacles in the levying of customs, the legalisation of factures, etc. it is easy to see whether one can still speak about an 'open door.'

15. [The China Relief Expedition (1900–2) was the United States military term for the military force sent by the imperialist countries to China to suppress the Boxer Rebellion. The focus shifted from rescuing diplomatic personnel and missionaries to suppressing the uprising. By 1902, at least in the city of Peking, the Boxer Rebellion had been effectively controlled.]

That American imperialists regard the Philippines merely as a base for further acquisitions in China and elsewhere gradually became evident from hundreds of occasional, more or less cryptic utterances in their press and political writings. The American imperialists consider contemporary Chinese relations a transitory phase and think that, if no unexpected events take place even earlier, then those relations will result in a further delimitation of spheres of influence and will eventually lead to annexation of the Chinese coastal regions in one form or the other. And it is clear in their minds, at least among the most far-seeing ones, that this struggle over the control of East Asia will be fought out between the United States and England – even if they are not usually as candid as the well-known imperialist Brooks Adams, who in his writing on *America's Economic Supremacy*[16] described the Philippines as a base for coming struggles in that area. As regards relations between the Union and England, he suggested that they could result in 'a conflict which probably is as inevitable as that with Spain'.[17] As the American State Secretary Shaw recently declared in a banquet-speech in Pittsburgh, sovereignty over the Pacific Ocean must pass over from the Union Jack to the Stars and Stripes.

6. The driving forces of American expansionist policy

The ordinary view in German newspapers is precisely the opposite. They argue that the United States has the same commercial interests in China as England and Japan have (Germany, too, is often mentioned in this context), i.e., the same interest in keeping the Chinese door open – as opposed to Russia, which wants to annex and monopolise. Consequently, the United States, England and Japan must conclude an alliance against Russia. This view may have some justification for the next couple of years. As long as the United States continues with its current tactic of preserving the so-called integrity of China, it will tend to reject Russia's claims and, as previously, exploit the situation by playing one great power against the other. But, for the rest, this kind of argument shows that they have not understood the essence of American expansionist policy. They assume that it is just a question of promoting commodity-exports, while actually the American expansionist

16. [Adams 1900.]
17. [Adams 1900, p. 23.]

policy is driven much more by finance-capital than by commercial capital. The approaching struggle will not at all be merely a question of a somewhat greater or lesser share in Chinese imports, but of *the overall economic and political supremacy* in East Asia and, therefore, also in the northern part of the Pacific Ocean. Today, that area is England's domain; if the United States wants to have the upper hand there, it must drive England out of its current position.

What about Russia? For a long time yet, it will not be a serious rival for the control of East-Asian waters, and even less will it be a regional commercial and financial power. Its entire exports to China amounted to 6 million marks annually in 1898–9. It may annex additional territories to its East-Siberian possessions in the north, seize Manchuria and Shangking, and perhaps even the northern part of the Chihli province [now Hebei], but the South-Eastern coastal provinces and the Yangtze region are more important.

And the chances of the North-American republic in those incipient struggles for predominance are constantly increasing. After establishing a good base of operations through the appropriation of Hawaii and the Philippines, they are now energetically pursuing construction of a fortified inter-oceanic canal and creation of a large navy and commercial fleet. It is characteristic of their goals that the shipping-subventions bill, approved by the Senate in March, privileged shipping in the Pacific Ocean by giving an equal share of the subsidies to ports on the Atlantic and Pacific coasts. The law further stipulates that each subsidised ship must be placed at the disposal of the government in case of war.

By contrast, England is dissipating its capital and forces. Despite defeating the Boers and swallowing the South-African morsel, it will suffer from digestion problems for a long time to come. In a way, one can deplore this weakening of England, because genuinely capitalist and brutal as English imperialism is, vis-à-vis American imperialism it is, after all, the lesser evil. Consideration for the different interests of its colonies and the clinging to old traditions and institutions impose on English imperialist policy a certain reserve, while, over there in Dollarland, those counterbalances are almost totally lacking.

To be sure, the best defence against the brutal capitalist expansionary policy of a large state is growth of a strong Social Democracy in its midst. One must hope, therefore, that the rise of American Social Democracy will keep pace with the rise of American imperialism. Unfortunately, it is not up to us to decide what path development will follow.

Chapter Ten

'Social Democracy and Imperialism' (May 1900)

Eduard Bernstein

In the history of European Social Democracy, Eduard Bernstein's position was unique. In his famous collection of essays, *The Preconditions of Socialism*, he was one of the first followers of Marx to dispute the most essential themes of Marxism. His critical commentary began with the proposition that 'the materialist conception of history' must 'take full account of the legal and moral concepts, the historical and religious traditions of every epoch, geographical and other natural influences, which include the nature of man himself and his intellectual dispositions'.[1] He then proceeded to forget 'the materialist conception of history' and to argue instead that Marx had helped to clarify the laws of economic development, thereby also implying the possibility of controlling their effects if only 'the conflict of interests' between various elements of society could be overcome.[2]

The principal themes of Bernstein's book can be summarised briefly: 1) Marx's labour-theory of value was mistaken, since the rate of profit had not fallen nor had unemployment significantly increased;[3] 2) the emergence of trusts and cartels facilitated

1. Bernstein 1993, p. 16.
2. Bernstein 1993, pp. 18–19.
3. Bernstein 1993, pp. 53–4.

more rational control of economic phenomena, thereby diminishing the prospect of a general crisis of capitalism for 'purely economic' reasons;[4] 3) joint-stock ownership also contributed to social stability by expanding the number of members of the possessing classes 'both absolutely *and* relatively';[5] 4) greater economic stability and the extension of ownership discouraged class-consciousness;[6] and 5) if socialism was, therefore, neither economically nor politically inevitable, it could only come about by virtue of its ethical superiority over capitalism. Bernstein concluded that universal suffrage represented the alternative to violent revolution, for in a democracy

> ... the parties, and the classes supporting them soon learn to recognise the limits of their power and, on each occasion, to undertake only as much as they can reasonably hope to achieve under the circumstances. Even if they make their demands rather higher than they seriously intend in order to have room for concessions in the inevitable compromise – and democracy is the school of compromise – it is done with moderation.[7]

In all things, Bernstein's watchword was moderation, a trait he greatly admired in the English tradition, with its pragmatism and compromises such that even the feudal monarchy and the Lords had been bridled by constitutionalism: 'The state,' he once declared, 'is a product of development. Its form at any time is partly determined by the past. It is impossible to jump out of the state: we can only hope to change it.'[8]

Holding the political in much higher regard than the economic, he treated the issue of imperialism with the same scepticism as he did Marxist economic theory. He believed it was simply folly to regard imperialist reactions as economically inevitable, much less as the dying gasp of capitalism. Imperialism was a phenomenon as old as history itself, and, among its contemporary variants, some were more and others less reactionary. Indeed, Bernstein emphasised that the emergence of modern British imperialism had actually coincided with expansion of workers' rights alongside growth of self-determining democracy in the settlement-colonies. French imperialism, on the other hand, was more centralised and less enlightened, while German imperialism

4. Bernstein 1993, p. 96.
5. Bernstein 1993, p. 61.
6. Bernstein 1993, p. 104.
7. Bernstein 1993, p. 144.
8. Bernstein quoted in Gay 1962, pp. 249–50.

typified militarist aggressiveness. The key to these differences lay in the *political traditions* of the respective countries: France, unlike England and true to its own centralising traditions, afforded its colonies 'little or no self-government', while in Germany imperialist expansionism was inseparable from rule by the Hohenzollern Emperor with support from the reactionary Junkers and business interests.

As Bernstein commented in the article translated here, 'there is imperialism and imperialism', and he was convinced that Great Britain's efforts to create an imperial federation deserved the support of progressive parties, unlike German imperialist efforts in Africa and elsewhere, which were thoroughly reactionary, due to the autocratic character of the German government.

Bernstein's foreign-policy views were characterised by Anglophilia, a Cobdenite defence of free trade that was common in British radicalism, and strong Russophobia. He therefore advocated a 'League of the West against the East': a triple alliance of Britain, France and Germany, i.e., of the 'civilised world' against barbarism. These convictions would later lead him to break with the protectionist and Anglophobic tendency within the revisionist camp represented by Richard Calwer, Karl Leuthner, Max Schippel, Gerhard Hildebrand, Ludwig Quessel and other *Sozialistische Monatshefte* writers.[9] As early as 1900, Calwer advocated the creation of a 'Greater Germany [*Alldeutschland*]', an autarkic German world empire, through a Franco-German understanding directed mainly against Great Britain, as the largest colonial empire in the world and the traditional enemy of European integration. The members of this camp were increasingly opposed to Bernstein's support of disarmament as a concession to England.[10] Bernstein's pacifism would ultimately lead to a rapprochement between him and Karl Kautsky after the latter's break with the left wing to become the theoretical leader of the SPD 'Centre'.

In an article published shortly after the current item, called 'Socialism and the Colonial Question', Bernstein praised 'the advantages of colonisation' and denounced the 'kolonialpolitischen Nihilismus' of the 'orthodox', calling for 'support of colonial enterprises'.[11] He argued that 'all other conditions being equal, the higher culture always has the greater right vis-à-vis the lower; if

9. Fletcher 1984, p. 40.
10. For an assessment of the split in the revisionist ranks between ardent nationalists and Anglophile pacifists such as Bernstein, see Hilferding 1909.
11. Bernstein 1900b, pp. 559, 561.

necessary, it has the historical right, even the duty, to subjugate the former'.[12] He elaborated upon these ideas seven years later, on the occasion of the debate on colonialism at the International Socialist Congress in Stuttgart and at the SPD-congress in Essen: 'Humanity is not yet advanced enough to forgo the application of force under all circumstances. Where two civilisations clash, the lower must give way to the higher. This law of evolution we cannot overthrow, we can only humanise its action. To counteract it would mean to postpone social progress.'[13] In all these comments, he believed that socialists must recognise the need for 'a certain guardianship of the cultured peoples over the non-cultured peoples'.[14]

* * *

'Social Democracy and Imperialism'[15]

'I must say that I hate the word.' Thus spoke one of the few Gladstonian-Liberal Peers, the Earl of Kimberley [John Wodehouse], a few weeks ago at a dinner of the radical Eighty Club. The word that sounds so hateful to the current leader of the Liberals in the House of Lords is the much-quoted, much-discussed word: imperialism.

An ominous word indeed. The idea most closely associated with it is that of Roman Caesarism: an empire built on brute force, based upon and held together by a brutal Praetorian guard, with a Nero or Caligula as Emperor and simultaneously its idol and instrument. Who does not shudder before this picture?

Or let us take a more modern example, France under the two Bonapartes. What were the First and Second Empires? Tyranny, Byzantinism, foreign wars and adventures that always resulted eventually in humiliating disasters for the country.

Even the example of the first German Empire [the Holy Roman Empire] was not exactly appealing. Its glamorous days were few and expensively paid for. Each period of asserting its world-conquering power – and they were

12. Bernstein 1900b, p. 551.
13. Bernstein 1907a, quoted in Fletcher 1984, p. 160.
14. Bernstein 1907b, p. 989.
15. Bernstein 1900a.

always brief – was followed by renewed separations and disruptive inner turmoil. Exorbitant in its demands and aspirations for world power, it destroyed today what it created yesterday, in order finally to waste away in miserable enfeeblement. These excesses, which were also inherent in the world empires of the East, thus seem to be inextricably linked to imperialism and were its undoing in every case. But the people had to bear the costs.

There is nothing easier than to charge imperialism with a catalogue of sins that secured hatred and contempt for it from every friend of the freedom and progress of peoples. History is not lacking in curses against it.

But despite all of those experiences, and despite all the curses, again and again it arises anew. Indeed, it has become universal. Today, we are witnessing imperialist tendencies on all sides. With the exception of Austria and Turkey, those remnants of a great imperialist past that are now in complete disintegration, there is today no large state that does not exhibit a strong imperialist current. If we abstract from the form of government, the Third French Republic is no less imperialistic than the English monarchy, and the giant republic of the United States is no less imperialistic than the huge empire of the tsars. With regard to imperialism, the current French Republic differs from the second Bonapartist Empire only in the fact that it pursues an imperialist policy in more practical terms than the former did – or, we should say, in a more businesslike manner, for it is quite doubtful that all its conquests and acquisitions are very practical. In any case, it aims at material gain, whereas Louis Bonaparte struggled to realise the Napoleonic 'ideas'. Its imperialism is realistic and has achieved successes, whereas Louis Bonaparte's was, to a large extent, sentimental and collapsed for that reason. In America, the United States wields a protective power and supremacy similar to that of Russia in Asia. The Monroe Doctrine acts there as a substitute for the so-called Testament of Peter the Great, and has been gradually expanded in a similar way. On the question of the Panama or the Nicaragua Canal, the Monroe Doctrine was applied to Central America; on the Cuban question it was extended to the Central-American archipelago; and, on the Venezuela question, its sphere of application was transferred to South America. On the other hand, Samoa and the Philippines show that the strength of the United States has only a very moderate effect as a factor of self-restraint.

No doubt, we are in the midst of an era of imperialist urges. How are we to explain them, and what position should we adopt towards them?

One view, quite widespread within Social Democracy, sees imperialism as a final, desperate attempt of the bourgeoisie to prolong its rule, or, rather, to delay the moment of its downfall. For adherents of that view, it is therefore a question of 'the world policy of dying capitalism', a symptom of the decay of the bourgeois world, a more or less skilfully disguised piece of reaction.

The basic ideas upon which this view is based are well-known. They are handed-down theorems, in which one piece of historical reality has received an epigrammatic form. Moreover, since they also stem from intelligent and knowledgeable thinkers, one only has to write into the conventional sentences new names and new data over and over again in order to apply them to all possible situations. Anyone who regards the bourgeois world as about to die will be easily led into seeing only death-signals, last gasps and the like in all its doings.

However, history does not unfold according to the scheme of epigrams, or it only does so over long epochs. What is correct *sub specie aeternitatis* [from the standpoint of eternity] can be very mistaken *sub specie diei* [from the standpoint of a day]. From any particular moment onwards, our life is a continuous process of dying, but, long after that moment, our action will remain a preparation for life, not for death.

It was recently asserted in Parvus's correspondence for the German socialist journals[16] – amidst a torrent of abuse against the writer of these lines and with reference to Brentano – that imperialism in England also entails 'the most brazen reaction, the incitement of the population'. Admittedly, Brentano allows himself to be duped very easily by newspaper-reports, but I consider it unthinkable that he would have made an allegation that flies so directly in face of all the facts.

One may regard English imperialism as reaction. The word is ambiguous; Marx once ironically referred to its use by certain politicians, saying that, for them, reaction was the 'night, wherein all cats are grey'. And, in fact, it serves more often to obscure than to illuminate a political phenomenon. Every movement is a reaction insofar as it moves away from a previous movement and represents the antithesis to it. Modern English imperialism is a countercurrent to the 'Little-England' movement preached in England during the

16. [*Aus der Weltpolitik* (*From World Politics*), a weekly bulletin of articles issued by *Parvus* in Munich from 1898 to 1905.]

middle two quarters of the nineteenth century; it is also a 'reaction', therefore, against those who professed it. But not a single curtailment of the political rights of the British workers, not a single statutory restriction on their right of assembly, and not a single prosecution of political views has up to now marked the era of the imperialist tide. The last quarter of the nineteenth century brought [English] workers extension of their rights in central, county and local administration, in the management of schools and assistance to the poor, while their trade-union and co-operative organisations are stronger than ever. To be sure, there are politicians and economists who regard all this with fear and anger and would like to turn the clock backwards, but their influence is far too weak to change anything in that direction.

At the end of February of this year, a conference of trade-unionists and socialists was held in London with the purpose of creating a workers' electoral alliance. In addition to socialists, it was attended almost exclusively by advanced trade-unionists – the conservative trade-unionists were absent. Despite that fact, an overwhelming majority rejected a resolution submitted by the Social-Democratic delegates, who wanted to commit candidates to the class-struggle and collectivisation of the means of production and exchange.

The reason for that rejection was opportunistic in nature: people did not want to weaken the attractive power of the electoral alliance. Mind you, it was a question of its attractive power among workers, not among the bourgeoisie. But would that restraint be so pervasive if England were in an era of 'incitement'? 'We recognise class-differences, but not class-struggle,' said the representative of one of the organisations of unskilled workers (bricklayers). One can see this merely as moderation or as an example of the hostility to abstraction that is typical of the English mentality, but can one really believe that such moderation would pervade the workers' minds if they were under the influence of incitement? Certainly that would not be true among English workers; in any struggle they are the last ones to mince words.

No, in a broad historical sense, British imperialism may mean reaction or retardation – suspension of social progress that would otherwise have taken place and expenditure of social forces in the wrong places – but it does not mean actual reaction, manifesting itself in oppressive measures and the deprivation of rights.

However, even if the first situation were actually the case, it would clearly be sufficient [grounds] for Social Democrats [to oppose imperialism]. For the party of those who suffer under current conditions, one of the most important considerations is that social progress should unfold as quickly as possible and that all delaying measures or proposals be resisted.

But is that currently the case? Is imperialism a retarding factor for England?

One should not identify the policy that led to the current war in South Africa – or more accurately, the policy that was held responsible for that war – with imperialism. If that policy is imperialism, then imperialism is an ancient phenomenon. As an English socialist recently put it very well: 'British boasting is by no means something new, but there is a new element in British imperialism.'

But then there is imperialism and imperialism. One can thus lose sight of the fact that certain superficial similarities are in each case declared to be its essential [traits], while their inner differences are proclaimed inessential. However, the famous equation of Monmouthshire with Macedon – because they both start with 'M' and are crossed by a river – suits brave Captain Fluellen well, but not the representatives of a doctrine that calls itself scientific socialism.[17]

With regard to this point, I have elsewhere quoted Marx's sentence in *The Civil War in France*: 'It is generally the fate of completely new historical creations to be mistaken for the counterparts of older, and even defunct, forms of social life, to which they may bear a certain likeness,'[18] and I have also referred to *The Eighteenth Brumaire*, where Marx protested against the equation of modern with ancient Caesarism, remarking that, given the great differences between modern and ancient society, the one could have no more in common with the other than the Archbishop of Canterbury has with the High Priest Samuel.[19] Now, one might hold against me passages from both books that sound fiercely anti-imperialist. Thus [Marx] says, for instance, in *The Civil*

17. [Fluellen was a comic character in Shakespeare's play *King Henry the Fifth*, who compares the young King Harry of Monmouth to Alexander the Great, arguing that Harry was from Monmouth and Alexander from Macedon, and that there are rivers in both places, and that salmon swim in both the rivers.]

18. [Marx 1977b, p. 72.]

19. ['The difference between the material, economic conditions of the ancient and the modern class struggles is so complete that the political figures produced by them can likewise have no more in common with one another that the Archbishop of Canterbury has with the High Priest Samuel.' Marx 1978a, p. 5.]

War in France: 'Imperialism is, at the same time, the most prostituted and the ultimate form of that state power which nascent bourgeois society had commenced to elaborate as the instrument of its own emancipation from feudalism, and which full-grown bourgeois society has finally transformed into an instrument for the enslavement of labour by capital.'[20] But this sentence is aimed at the Bonapartist Empire, and one can raise the question of whether, by generalising it, one does not go beyond the limits set by the above-quoted sentence regarding the assessment of historical phenomena. If one reads through the passage closed by that sentence, one finds not just superlatives, which do not bear close scrutiny given the state of contemporary knowledge,[21] but also the likewise overly-generalised sentence: 'In reality, it (the Empire) was the only form of government possible at a time when the bourgeoisie had already lost, and the working class had not yet acquired, the faculty of ruling the nation.'[22] Thirty years of the [Third French] Republic have shown that a different form of government could also satisfy the needs of the nation at least as well as the Empire, and that the question was not at all the one formulated [in Marx's writings]. It is not just a question of the bourgeoisie and the working class, but of a whole series of relationships in the living conditions and interests of various differentiated classes or strata, of which, however, no single one is strong enough to rule the nation, so that the question today is: either command of all by a power standing over them and leaning upon the sabre, or government on the basis of coalitions and compromises.

For a fairly long time to come, this will continue to be the hallmark of the problem of government in France, and the Workers' Party of France must

20. [Marx 1977b, p. 69.]

21. ['Under its sway, bourgeois society, freed from political cares, attained a development unexpected even by itself. Its industry and commerce expanded to colossal dimensions.' Marx 1977b, p. 69.] The degree of expansion that France's industry had reached in 1870 appears quite modest to us today. In 1870, France was still a predominantly agricultural country, and small and medium-sized enterprises played by far the main role in its industry.

Superlatives are, even in the best publicistic writings, always suspicious. Reading the two above-quoted works, one comes across sentences, amidst their truly elastic remarks, that turn out to be anticipations of a development that has not yet taken place even today. In *The Eighteenth Brumaire* the peasant land-holdings of France are portrayed as outlived 'parcels', oppressed by mortgages and waging a 'mortal combat' for their 'survival'. Today, two generations later, the overwhelmed parcels still are not breathing their last. Incidentally, Marx already gives in *Mr. Vogt* a much more realistic picture of the agrarian population of France.

22. [Marx 1977b, p. 69.]

therefore be prepared and determined to join such a coalition government [*Comprömissregierung*] whenever this can happen under decent conditions that imply no renunciation of fundamental rights and demands. It is a categorical imperative in political life to exploit all the means at our disposal in order to promote the cause we represent. It is in this sense that the writer of these lines once replied with wholehearted and principled assent to the survey from French socialists concerning the entry of Millerand into the Waldeck-Rousseau ministry, and it seems that even many of those who at the time doubted the correctness of that step now rejoice that it was made.

But if France, as I said, is no longer Caesarist-Bonapartist, it is still imperialistic – even more imperialistic than the Second Empire. Its extensive colonial possessions and protectorates impress upon it the stamp of an empire that is only partially built upon equality of customs and institutions – not to mention community of race and nationality – while resting partly on relations of dominion. France is an Empire not because of its form of government, but due to its composition [*Zusammensetzung*]. French socialists have fought against the policy that led to this situation, but if the opportunity arrives for them to undo its results, they would probably think twice about doing so and make a distinction [between different types of colonies]. In any case, the contemporary Republic has no intention of relinquishing its colonies.

But to expound upon the colonial problems of France falls beyond the framework of this article. As far as England is concerned, it has long been an imperialist state in the most highly developed sense. English usage, which is always striving for accuracy, strictly distinguishes between the United Kingdom – which only includes England and Wales, along with Scotland and Ireland – and the British Empire, which encompasses the United Kingdom together with all its overseas possessions. In 1876–7, Disraeli symbolised the latter when he crowned the Queen of England with the imperial crown of India.

At the same time, however, the perception prevailed in England that precisely the English settlement-colonies constituted only a temporary appendage of the British Empire; and this appendage was felt by many British statesmen and economists to be not a very beneficial possession but rather a burden – 'a millstone round our necks',[23] as Disraeli once said. It was gen-

23. ['These wretched colonies will all be independent, too, in a few years, and are a millstone round our necks.' Letter of Benjamin Disraeli to his cabinet colleague Lord Malmesbury, 13 August 1852. Quoted in Malmesbury 1884, Vol. I, pp. 260–1.]

erally assumed that the example of the United States furnished the typical model for the political development of all English colonies; that is, that each one of them, once it was sufficiently developed, would sever its connection with the mother-country.[24]

This view, which sprang from the then dominant doctrine of Manchesterism [*laissez-faire* liberalism], is also attributable to the fact that, for generations, not the slightest attempt has been made to combine the colonies organically with the mother-country. This is one of the characteristic differences between French and English colonial administration. France gives its colonies little or no self-government, but a number of them are represented by their own deputies in the French Parliament. In the English Parliament, which can rather be called the imperial parliament, there is no representative of the imperial colonies; only the Colonial Secretary has an authoritative voice regarding the colonies (or to be precise, the Secretary of State for India and, for certain crown-colonies, the Secretary of State for Foreign Affairs). But the English colonies with a strong white population have such far-reaching self-government that the need for them to be represented at the Westminster Parliament is minimal. The relationship involves as loose a federalism as can possibly be imagined.

But it is also a thoroughly inorganic, unsystematic federalism, the product of extreme opposition to the French propensity for schematisation. If anything has followed a zigzag course, it is colonial policy in England. It is only due to the incompetence, disintegration and weakness of the continental powers that this zigzag course did not lead to defeats and disasters in every corner. But now the time is past when England could afford to commit colonial blunders.

Contemporary English imperialism is partly a matter of resistance against the expansionist and exclusionary tendencies of the protectionist great powers, and, to that extent, it is self-defence in favour of free trade – a struggle that would otherwise have to abandon free trade and embrace protective tariffs or duties on grain imports. On the other hand, English imperialism is partly a reaction against administrative Manchesterism in colonial administration,

24. John Morley said it was most unlikely that the Australian colonial federation would come into being in the foreseeable future, if ever, or that the Australian cattle-ranchers and the timber-merchants of Canada would ever spend even a penny for imperial purposes in South Africa. The present situation shows how premature was this prophecy of the Manchester positivist.

that is, a movement to set up a rational, systematically organised imperial federation.

The methods by which Great Britain has tried to achieve the first objective naturally require the closest scrutiny on the part of socialists, although, in principle, one cannot say much against them because England is seeking to reserve the widest possible area of the unappropriated world for free trade. In recent years, socialist criticisms, especially of the undertakings falling within this category, have therefore been quite half-hearted. We are abstracting, of course, from the few eccentrics who imagine that by stopping this development we can bring about a great collapse of the current social order.[25] For instance, the consolidation of settlements on the Niger into a veritable example of an imperial colony has met with little or no opposition from the English socialists.[26] Faced with the choice between capitalist concessional enterprises in the colonies (so-called Chartered Companies) and imperial colonies – and that today is the real alternative – socialists everywhere would today give preference to the latter because in them, unlike the economy of capitalist conquistadores, the imperial administration does not advocate political principles and administrative methods hostile to development.

The other side of modern British imperialism, the movement for organic connection of the Empire with its self-governing colonies, is entitled to a sympathetic judgment on the part of Social Democracy for several reasons.

Admittedly, one can doubt whether it will be possible to bring colonies so different in social composition and economic tendencies successfully into a lasting and closer connection with the Empire. However, this doubt refers mostly to the idea of an imperial customs-union, which different people did, indeed, originally connect with the idea of an imperial federation, but which now has been removed from the agenda. The current programme of the imperial-federation movement includes the issues of unifying the highest administrative and judicial bodies, a better distribution of tasks between the Empire and the colonies, as well as direct representation for the colonies in the imperial parliament.

---

25. [A veiled reference to Bernstein's polemics with Ernest Belfort Bax. See Bernstein 1988a, Bax 1988a, Bax 1988c, Bernstein 1898, Bax 1898.]

26. [The Royal *Niger* Company built its headquarters at Lokoja, in present-day Nigeria. This British settlement regulated trade in the rivers Niger and Benue in the nineteenth century.]

All of this lends to contemporary British imperialism a strongly democratic, freedom-affirming character, since the colonies in question represent more developed democracy and a more progressive social policy than the mother-country. Even on the far Left, among radical social reformers and socialists, it has resolute supporters. Others are opposed to it in principle, in the same way that Social Democracy opposes trusts; that is, critically but not in a totally negative way. They see expansion of the big states' sphere of power as an inevitable product of modern development and particularly of modern transport facilities, much like the extension of purely business enterprises. Finally, however, there are also many people who merely see in imperialism the nurturing of militaristic tendencies, fearing that it will have politically reactionary, anti-democratic repercussions, and therefore thinking that they must fight against it in any form – a view that I believe can only be held as long as Social Democracy is too weak to have any decisive influence in actually shaping events.

As with its attitude towards economic trusts, the attitude of Social Democracy towards imperial federations may also differ with the circumstances and have to adjust to their forms, legal bases and methods. Assuming that this will be the case, what will its position be with regard to contemporary German imperialism?

This question was thoroughly and forcefully discussed in a document recently published by Friedrich Naumann, the famous founder and leader of the National-Social Union in Germany.[27] Mr. Naumann wants to persuade German democracy, especially its strongest wing, Social Democracy, of the need to support the imperialist policy of the German Emperor in general, and the current naval bills [*Flottenvorlage*] in particular. It must be admitted that he does that with extraordinary skill. It is a highly plausible work, which in a beautiful, well-ordered and clear presentation contains pretty much

27. Friedrich Naumann, *Demokratie und Kaisertum: Ein Handbuch für innere Politik*, Berlin-Schöneberg: Buchverlag der Hilfe, 1900. [Friedrich Naumann (1860–1919) was a German politician and Protestant parish-priest. In 1894 he founded the weekly magazine *Die Hilfe* to address the social question from a non-Marxist, middle class point of view. In 1896 he also founded the National-Social Association in an attempt to provide a nationalist, social-liberal alternative to the Social Democrats. Having failed to establish a political party based on his Association, in 1903 he joined the Freisinnige Vereinigung (Free-Thinking Union), which later merged with the Progressive People's Party, and in 1907 he was elected to the Reichstag. In 1919 he was one of the founders of the Democratic Party and served as the Party's leader until his death.]

everything that can be said in favour of the socialist *Realpolitik* proposed by its author. It is set out with impressive warmth, free of rhetoric, and is just as full of inspiring ideas as of instructive factual material. All this justifies its claim to a thorough discussion.

The basic thesis of Mr. Naumann is that if the imperial government and its head, the German Kaiser, still rest today upon support from the Conservatives, and if the class of Prussian Junkers, playing an increasingly oppressive role in the nation's economic life, also has a decisive influence in determining the policy of the federal government and even more that of the largest German state, Prussia; and if Germany's political development does not keep pace with its economy but rather lags behind it (indeed experiences setbacks); and if, in contrast to industrial progress, political stagnation or regression prevail – all this is largely attributable to the negative attitude of the democratic parties in Germany who are opposing the requirements of a strong and far-sighted foreign policy. This policy of the democratic parties – which Naumann regards as doctrinaire and negative – compels the Kaiser, who must attend to broad national interests, to purchase support from the Junkers and their henchmen that can be had only at the price of reactionary domestic measures and burdening the popular masses in favour of those classes. No defeat of reaction can be expected in Germany until this policy is changed. Hence national socialism! It is up to the imperial government, however, to make such national socialism possible by renouncing all petty obstruction and harassment of the workers' movement.

One has to be blind to ignore the fact that there is a kernel of truth in this whole line of reasoning. However, this kernel of truth still does not warrant accepting the whole argument along with its conclusions. It only demands the most careful scrutiny.

One may readily believe Mr. Naumann's statement that the Kaiser wants to win over German workers for his national policy and would be willing to make some concessions for that purpose. It would be absurd to assume the contrary. The question here is not his goodwill, but his power to introduce social reforms and the number and nature of the counterclaims. Is what the Kaiser may give to the workers proportionate to what he claims or may claim from them? To create a democratic policy, friendly towards workers, the Kaiser would have to do more than just break with the Junkers in East Prussia. By doing so, he would turn conservative party supporters of the Junkers –

who are economically reactionary – along with the big industrialists and their followers, against him. The reason is that such a policy, if it is to be more than mere palliatives, should be resolutely directed to social progress in all areas, not just in narrowly defined social policies but also in education, in the distribution of political rights, as well as in financial, customs and other administrative policies. But this is beyond the power of the Kaiser, and not just because of the social force that the coalition of the above-mentioned social strata would represent! Should the occasion arise, they would actually be confronted by a coalition of socialists, democrats and other friends of reform who could very well stand up to them as a 'progressive mass'.[28] The greatest difficulty does not lie there. Germany's social composition and its level of intellectual development are no more unfavourable to such a coalition than is the case in France and other countries. Yes, in this respect, Naumann is quite correct, in my opinion, to say that establishment of such a cohesive coalition may be a vital issue, under certain circumstances, for the development of freedom in Germany – to put it bluntly, the question may be either genuine reaction, against which the current alignment of the Junkers and obscurantists is just child's play, or playing *va banque* in the street. However, if the elements for such a party of the Left were to get together, would the Kaiser govern with them, on their terms – and indeed could he? Even if his sympathy were on their side in nine-tenths of their economic programme, he still could not go along with them. He does not stand above the parties and the classes like a prince descended from the sky. He belongs to a class himself, he represents the traditions of a class, and that class is more intimately related to the East-Elbian Junkers than to anyone else. In his consciousness as a ruler, he may rise ever so far above their narrow horizon; he may feel only lukewarm sympathy for their economic ailments; he may simply shrug at most of their idiosyncrasies – but there is still a point at which he feels himself completely to be their natural ally. His decrees, his speeches, and his mottos clearly enunciate the fact that, as a Hohenzollern, he is first of all representative of the personal régime, a prince, the most aristocratic representative of the Junker-nobility. No matter how modern the terms in which he may otherwise think, he clings

28. [A paraphrase of Ferdinand Lassalle's observation that vis-à-vis the working class, all other classes constituted a 'reactionary mass'.]

to this heritage with all the fibres of his being, and, for that reason, any lasting alliance between him and the Left is impossible.

I will admit it openly – for me, a republic, as a mere form, is not so exalted that I could not conceive a Social Democracy friendly towards the government in a monarchy. But then, at least, the essential institutions of the country, and the constitution, would have to be built upon republican, i.e., upon democratic foundations. This is almost totally lacking today in Germany. Even the army is sworn in by the person of the emperor and king, rather than by the constitution and the parliament. Decisions of parliament that do not suit the government still end up in the trash-bin. The Empire is still a federation of governments, which themselves may be as undemocratic as they wish. It is a republic not of peoples or parliaments but of princes, presided over by a hereditary prince, in whose state it is impossible for the working class to send its own representatives to parliament in entirely free elections. In the first state of the German Empire [Prussia], the most reactionary of all franchises is in force, keeping the working class in a position of political helots.[29]

A party of privileged persons can quietly grant instruments of power to a government as long as it receives in exchange the assurance that the government will protect or respect their privileges. But things are not so simple for the working class. Its position can worsen considerably through submissiveness in these matters, for we can be sure of one thing: the moment Social Democracy shows itself ready to grant appropriations for the army and the navy, the complaints of the Junkers and their henchmen against those demands will stop at once. They would show – indeed, they would have to show – that they are at least as good patriots as the socialists, and as soon as the latter raised a

29. [A helot was a state-owned serf of the ancient Spartans. The helots were, in a sense, state-slaves, bound to the soil and assigned to individual Spartans to till their holdings; their masters could neither free them nor sell them.

The Prussian three-class franchise system [*Dreiklassenwahlrecht*] was introduced in 1849 by the Prussian king Friedrich Wilhelm IV for the election of the Lower House of the Prussian State-Parliament. Those eligible to vote were men over the age of 24, and they were divided by their direct tax-revenue into three classes. Voting took place orally and in public; there was no secret ballot. It was also indirect; representatives known as electors [*Wahlmänner*] were voted for, with each class electing a third of all the electors. The classes contained widely differing numbers of people, even though the number of electors was the same for each. This distribution meant that a first-class vote had several times the value of a third-class vote. This electoral system was only completely abolished in 1918.]

demand that would seriously shake the essence of the semi-absolutism transferred from Prussia into the German Reich, the friendship of the government with the Right would immediately be restored again.

Naumann denies that this must necessarily be the case. He argues that the sharp eye of the Emperor, whose milieu is not at all so composed of Junkers as people think, has revealed to him that the future of his house [the Hohenzollern house] does not have to be with the large landowners. But this is a conjecture that collapses when one realises that, in a situation such as we have assumed here, the services of the Junkers could be had for much less than relinquishing the world-trade interests of German industry.

No, under the current political circumstances, German Social Democracy cannot compete with the parties of capitalists and large landowners in granting appropriations for the army and navy. Imperialism in Germany is missing the element of democracy that is inherent in the current British imperialism; and when, in its efforts to promote Germany's international trade, it represents a cause conducive to social progress, it does something that every capitalist entrepreneur does in his own way. But this does not bar him from being politically reactionary.

Certainly, it is not a matter of indifference for the main representative of imperial power that a party with two million voters behind it should be opposed in principle to his policies, especially on questions concerning the army and navy. Despite the recent polemics with Erich Rother, the truth is that, on this point, Social Democracy supports demands related to protection of the soldiers, but, other than that, its policy is primarily determined by political and not by military-technical considerations. Otherwise, it would be paradoxical to uphold, on the question of the navy, a standpoint that recognises as justified only expenditures for coastal defence, which is the ultimate defence. It would be the most preposterous thriftiness in the world.

As I make this point, I would like to add – in order to avoid giving occasion for yet another misunderstanding – that, on essential points, I differ from Rother, and that I do not consider Naumann's remarks on behalf of the current naval bills to be sound. I do not proceed from any vague cosmopolitanism but from the standpoint that I developed in my book on *The Preconditions of Socialism*, i.e., that a healthy internationalism is only possible on the foundation of recognition of national communities, and that, consequently, one can very well be a nationalist without necessarily being, for that reason, a bad internationalist. The national units of large nations, which we know as empires, are today, in the era of transport and communications, more than ever necessary as bearers of economic progress, for they are the precursors for realising the idea of a free union of peoples. It is well known that even the Roman Empire of the Caesars brought great historical progress from this point of view. For Social Democracy, in my opinion, the German Reich is also not merely an actual fact to which it must acquiesce, but also a very worthy phenomenon as a broad community. At the same time, I do not ignore the fact that, even today, we are not so far advanced as to expect the preservation of peace merely from the insight and fraternal attitude [of other nations], and that we must also secure it through the preservation of [Germany's] defence-capability.

In defending the naval plans, Naumann describes dangers that do not actually exist. The development of German world trade is not at all dependent upon adoption of plans to increase the navy. German world trade has developed to its present strength without a large navy and will therefore also grow in the future, even if it has just a modest war-fleet behind it. It is not in a defensive position, and it has nothing to fear from England – not because Englishmen have a particularly noble nature and are exceptionally sympathetic towards Germany, but because England is not in a position to initiate an era of trade-restrictions injurious to Germany. 'Where power is, there goods flow,' says Naumann. This may be true of mere conquest, but never of modern trade-relations built on the basis of industry. 'If England has the leadership of world trade, it takes our work and pays us for it at its pleasure,' Naumann continues, to which we could respond with the catechismic question: 'How does this happen?' If England ever did rule international trade in such a way, those times are gone forever. And though Naumann further conjures up the spectre of England possibly closing or taxing the sea-routes through Gibraltar and the Suez Canal, this argument loses all force when we remember that all nations are equally interested in the freedom of these trade-routes, and that England will not be allowed to turn them into its monopoly – quite apart from the fact that no one in England ever thought of doing so.

The cause for concern lies precisely with the entire modern German fleet-movement, which is directed above all against England, i.e., against that sea-power whose trade and colonial policy uphold the most liberal and progressive principles. This must puzzle every friend of free development from the outset. I do not want to idealise England or disregard the fact that many conflicts may arise with it, in which appeal to formal law is not enough. But the danger of such conflicts is smaller, not greater, than the danger of a conflict with any other commercial power; and through a prudent, progressive trade-policy, it may be reduced to a minimum by appropriate treaties.

Naumann's arguments in favour of the current naval plans are so unconvincing that one cannot shake off the idea that such a judicious man must have other reasons for supporting those plans, which, for some reason – as far as I am concerned, some totally honourable reason – he does not want to state. It is certainly no supposition made up from thin air that he and his friends, for instance, would have been very happy to see an intervention by Germany's 'armoured fist' in favour of the Transvaal Boers; and other friends of the fleet have pronounced themselves on this matter with all desirable clarity. I will also confess frankly that I could rather understand support for the Boers on national grounds than on the ground of democratic legal conceptions.[30]

However, with this question, we are entering an area where the granting of instruments of power to a government is a matter of confidence – confidence not only in its good will to promote the nation's industrial and commercial progress but also in its ability to avoid letting itself be carried away by precipitousness and political adventures once these instruments of power are available in sufficient measure. Whether German Social Democracy is entitled to place its trust in the German imperial government is a question that Naumann himself can be left to answer.

Social Democracy is ultimately a party of peace; it would be unfaithful to one of its foremost tasks if it gave up its role of being the guardian of peace and *the mutual confidence of peoples*. In a country where the personal régime is still so strong, how could it fulfill this task if it supported the armament-bills, which are regarded at least by a large and influential part of the nation as means to other purposes – particularly when it lacks any legal means to prevent such use? The current naval bills exceed the needs of a policy solely

30. It is downright funny when, for example, people who otherwise cannot stress enough how revolutionary they are, compete with the most conservative newspapers in their indignation over the Jameson Raid. It is no less contradictory when socialists and radicals applaud those British workers who said that they would have received good wages in the Transvaal, and *consequently* would have had no interest in electoral rights and civil liberties.

directed towards preservation of peace; they are aimed, as Naumann himself explained, at the expansion of naval power. Power can be a factor for peace, but it need not necessarily be so.

Naumann argues that the navy, and the army too, should become democratic institutions – which, formerly, was precisely a demand of democracy. Certainly, you cannot use the navy against the people in the same way as the army. But, for exactly this reason, the navy defies democratic control more than the army, for it is more subject than the army to the personal instructions of the supreme military authorities.

The German Empire is responsible for representing the nation to foreign countries. As long as it still remains undemocratic in its very nature, national policy – in the sense that Naumann understands it – means relinquishing democracy for the sake of potential small advantages that are by no means certain. Social Democracy cannot allow this to happen. Its task is to fight for democracy. And it will only be able to address foreign policy more freely to the extent that it is able to expand its influence on the leadership of the country by means of democratic institutions, to the extent that it becomes a guiding rather than a restraining influence. In the meantime, it can only exert a preventive influence on imperial policy, and that is the yardstick, insofar as it does not abandon its general principles, by which it measures the naval plans and similar requirements of German imperialism.

Chapter Eleven

'The South-African War and the Decadence of English Liberalism' (July 1901)

Theodor Rothstein

Theodor Aronovich Rothstein (1871–1953) was a Russian émigré who settled in England in 1890. In 1895, he joined the Social-Democratic Federation and became part of its left wing. A strong supporter of the Bolsheviks following the 1903 split in Russian Social Democracy, he also took an active part in English political life. He supported the unity process that led to formation of the British Socialist Party in 1911, involving a merger between a number of socialist groups and the SDF (which had become the Social-Democratic Party in 1907). After the outbreak of the First World War, Rothstein took a prominent part in the move to oust Hyndman and his 'patriotic' national clique in the BSP in 1916, and later participated in the foundation of the British Communist Party. He returned to Russia in 1920 and became increasingly involved in the USSR. From 1921 to 1930, he was engaged in diplomatic work and later took a position with the Soviet academy. Rothstein was a frequent commentator on imperialism, particularly British imperialism, for the international socialist press. His articles, written for the English socialist journals *The Social Democrat*, *Justice* and *The Call*, have been collected and are available online at the Marxist Internet Archive. He is also the author of a book on the history of British socialism.

* * *

'The South-African War and the Decadence of English Liberalism'[1]

Numerous observers of English life have for a long time regarded it as a banal truth that England, of all the countries of Europe, was the one that enjoyed the most normal development. Unlike France, Germany and the rest of the continental states, where the social processes took place at an often changing tempo, now slowly, now quickly, and where they often overtook each other and mutually paralysed each other, in England, it was thought, social development proceeds gradually and at a measured pace, never hastily but always decidedly and firmly. Slowly, but systematically, one advance followed the other; development was never suddenly interrupted; old institutions never departed before the new ones had fully materialised. And, as they appeared, existing arrangements died out as soon as their usefulness turned into uselessness and the detrimental effects were perceptible.

This view of English life was long held, as we said, as a banal truth; it was even accepted in the social sciences. England is a country developing in a completely normal way, and whatever happens in it corresponds to the direction of its social life; it is just a specific episode resulting from and illustrating the general course of its evolution. No wonder that, when the South-African War broke out many people were astonished. For generations, England has been synonymous with democracy, progress and freedom – and now suddenly that War, that shameless filibuster raid on two free republics,[2] undertaken and led in the most disgraceful way for the sake of a handful of money-makers *sans foi, sans loi* [faithless and lawless]. What horror, what a painful surprise! Had the English people perhaps suddenly fallen victim to a blinding sickness; were they perhaps afflicted by a mind-numbing disorder?

---

1. [Rothstein 1908. Note by the editors of *Die Neue Zeit*: 'The article was written before the conflict that broke out in the Liberal Party over the motion of Lloyd George, but it could not be published earlier due to lack of space.' On 17 June 1901, the House of Commons debated the use of concentration-camps for Boer civilians, on a motion from Liberal MP David Lloyd George denouncing their management. The motion was defeated by 253 to 154, with almost 50 liberal imperialists abstaining.]

2. [The reference is to two independent Boer republics of the Orange Free State and the South-African Republic (Transvaal Republic).]

Those who have had the opportunity of observing and studying English public life during recent decades will presently find the solution to that tragic mystery. Even if the War at first surprised them as well, they will soon recognise that it was just as little a fortuitous incident as the appearance of spots in a decomposing body. The outbreak of the War appeared so accidental precisely because in England's social body those processes took a peaceful course without visible external effects. But, if one studies its development in the context of all the changes that have taken place in English political and social life during the last quarter of a century, it actually appears 'inevitable', as Chamberlain and his satellites have not hesitated to declare. Yes, inevitable; but not in that fatalistic sense in which the determinists look upon social phenomena *à outrance* [in the extreme]; and also not in that sense in which the initiators of the War use that word to shift the blame for the crimes committed against the two republics, but rather in a simple scientific sense as the symptom of an illness appears inevitable. And that illness of England is the growth of imperialism and the decline of liberalism accompanying it.

During almost three quarters of a century, England enjoyed undisputed supremacy over the world market. Thanks to its situation and natural riches, as well as its momentous early entry into the industrial and commercial arena, it easily conquered one market after the other, and soon every inhabited area of the world was either a consumer of our industrial products or a supplier of raw materials. To employ the expression that Cobden was fond of using to describe his ideal, England became the 'workshop' of the world, the ruler of capitalist industry, whose sceptre was seen everywhere. It could therefore afford to be progressive, liberal, and generous. Why should its rich, powerful and independent ruling classes be worried? They needed neither the power of the state to help them with industrial organisation nor the support of military power to secure for them the possession of foreign markets. Its economic superiority was forceful enough. Even more: if the workers demanded reforms, let them have those reforms. We, they thought, are well off enough to be able to spare ourselves quarrels with our 'hands'. If some oppressed nation fights somewhere in the world for its freedom, then let us by all means support it. The progress of nations can only be advantageous for us as commodity-producers. Will our great overseas colonies finally become free and independent from the motherland? Why not? Indeed, as we only gained from the loss of the United States of America, we can also gain if we get rid of our colonies. In that way, we will not have to worry about their administration while we will still have them as consumers. In short, freedom, progress, and democracy were the watchwords of the English middle class, especially the part that in politics took the name of the Liberal Party, which in the economic field represented the interests of English capitalist industry.

But the transformation that has taken place during the last twenty to twenty-five years in England's economic situation has also brought about a transformation in the views of the English bourgeoisie. With habit comes contempt, and the upper classes disregarded the preservation of their apparently secure position. Conscious of England's monopolistic industrial position, they fell into an ossifying routine and did not see that, supported by their respective states, by science and modern methods of organisation, new rivals had appeared in the industrial arena. The English capitalist class initially ignored the consular reports that warned it about the coming danger from all parts of the world; it dismissed such certainly superficial but nevertheless characteristic warnings as the cry about 'Made in Germany'. But facts began to speak for themselves more and more loudly until the death-knell [for English industry] began to be heard. What was to be done? 'Change your business methods,' advised some. 'Organise a national system of technical education,' argued others. 'Drop your free-trade system', proposed a third group. But realisation of all those proposals and plans implied a complete transformation in the customary industrial methods of the country. Instead of the old *laisser faire, laisser aller*, which deluded the country into a false feeling of security and misled it into resting on its laurels, the state, as the organised power of the ruling class, had to come to the rescue – and not only the state of the British islands but also of the entire English-speaking world, or at least of the British colonies. Why should England and its sister-states across the seas lead an isolated economic and political life? Why should they not combine into a powerful union, bound together by a common protective tariff and perhaps by a common central government for the purpose of defence and attack? The days of ruling as an industrial monopoly on the old individualist foundations were over; the mere power of economic superiority could no longer be trusted, therefore, as a weapon in the international struggle over sales markets. What if we could win back our previous monopolistic position and supremacy by the united physical power of the Empire? This idea became pervasive. Exaggerated in the most laughable and theatrical way by Lord Beaconsfield, and seriously elaborated by Sir Charles Dilke, Lord (then still Mr.) Curzon and many others, it soon became common knowledge and circulated from hand to hand and from class to class.

Like the revolutionary ideas in France in the eighteenth century, the imperialist idea in England immediately became a sort of plaything, with which men fell in love and flirted. Not that the English people suddenly became hypocrites; rather, one must assume that the masses, as in so many similar cases, did not see that the idea would turn into a monster that would devour old England. For them, it was actually just a development of the liberal ideal, expanded beyond the British islands to the entire Anglo-Saxon world. How could a more glorious enterprise be conceived, what could possibly have more beneficent effects on the entire civilised world than the union of England, the mother of freedom, with the colonial states founded by it and also living in freedom? It is no exaggeration to say that the whole country (even among the ranks of socialists, and not just the Fabians but also the Social-Democratic workers) talked about imperialism, about a 'Greater Britain', about an infusion of younger, more forcefully pulsating blood in the ageing body of the motherland, etc. Unfortunately, the good men did not see that their lyrical and sentimental transports actually reflected the sober impulse of economic life, which one fine day would assert itself in all its nakedness and sweep away all the glittering rubbish with which imperialism had decorated itself.

Then came the War, which, in all its essential features, is the brutal but logical expression of the imperialist spirit in its aggressiveness, its supremacy of the Union Jack, its pan-colonial actions. Would the good people now beat a retreat? What did they think? Did they just talk and mean nothing by it? No, they had said ABC, and now felt bound to say XYZ. Besides, many thought that despite everything some truth lay hidden in the phrase 'Imperialism means business'. They therefore turned their backs on the previously revered shadowy products of their imagination and went down on their knees before the real, living and all-absorbing imperialism.

That was the official declaration of bankruptcy of the liberal creed. Liberalism was doomed as a political principle the moment the first rivals entered the world-industrial arena. It suffered its first incurable wound in the mid-1880s, when part of the Liberal Party split from it over the home-rule question, which was, at bottom, a question of whether Britain would dissolve into its constituent elements or whether these elements should be brought closer together in order to create a compact Empire. Liberalism then degenerated completely over the next decades because it yielded to the imperialist lust bred by Lord Rosebery, which silently but effectively undermined the party organism even under Gladstone's eyes. The Liberal Party finally stood aghast at the spectacle of its own decay. The last prophet of the Cobdenite creed died with the knowledge that everything was lost and that the once so splendid party structure was more and more crumbling to pieces.[3]

And, precisely at that moment of confusion and insecurity, the War broke out with a bang. The elements that had long professed the new creed (Rosebery, Fowler, etc.) were glad at having the opportunity to side openly with imperialism. Others, who were still insecure and wavering (Asquith, Herbert Gladstone), were swept away by the general imperialist flood-tide. Only a small part of the Gladstonite old guard (Harcourt, Morley) maintained their former position or drew back full of disgust. Only ruins and nothing but ruins remain – a veritable burnt offering of old principles and avowals. Only some small columns still stand out from the rubbish heap and remind one of the former splendour.

That is the result of the South-African War. Fortuitous only externally, it actually represents a dividing line in English history. It is the flowing Styx, which separates the land of light and freedom from the land of darkness and reaction, and from which, as from Hades, there is no return. Even if the opportunity were to present itself, there would be no return. In the House of Commons, the Liberal Party still occupies the seats of the opposition and there is a nucleus of Gladstonites. Among journalists, one still finds people like Massingham, the former editor of the *Daily Chronicle*, who do their best to bring the sheep back to the flock. Even among the broad masses of the people, there are still many radical ideologists, like Mr. Thompson of *Reynold's Newspaper*, for instance, who carry out a real liberal agitation. But all that is actually meaningless and cannot improve the prospects of liberalism.

In Parliament, the Liberal Party offers an image of hopeless dissolution. Without a programme or a distinct policy, it is often deprived of the help of the Irishmen, who were compelled by the all-absorbing imperialism and the abandonment of the home-rule question to create their own political camp. The unity of the Liberal Party is merely a question of words, as the frequent conflict between its speeches and resolutions shows, and their leadership

3. [William Gladstone died on 19 May 1898.]

lies in the hands of a vulgar Gladstonite of the neither-meat-not-fish variety, Sir Henry Campbell-Bannerman, who is an object of general derision. Their entire opposition is a makeshift work, not a question of principle. It springs solely from the intention of preserving for the Party a physiognomy different from that of the Conservatives and keeping it intact for the prospect of returning to the ministerial posts, but even that is mostly a wasted effort. The real situation breaks through again and again despite all the manoeuvres to deceive public opinion. Nothing shows this better than the recent election of Sir Henry Fowler, the worst warmonger, to reject the budget bill. Even if they manage to convince public opinion that the Liberal Party is once again something different from the Tories, and even if they succeed in occupying the vacant ministerial chairs after the collapse of the present ministry under the burden of its own sins, one thing is sure: not many years will pass, if any at all, until the Liberal government collapses in turn; and that will be its last exit from the political stage.

That is the situation in Parliament, and in the country Liberalism does no better. Mr. Massingham is now touring Ireland, attempting to bring about something like a fresh liberal public opinion concerning the home-rule question, thus providing the party with a new, if already stale, slogan as well as with a political alliance – to be sure, always a costly one. That will not happen. The efforts of the National Democratic League are no more promising. Launched amidst trumpet fanfares that even found an echo in the breast of Tom Man, it rattled noisily for some time with its tricolour wings but now lies flat on the land like a paper-dragon. Thus nothing remains to save liberalism. Under the pressure of economic relations, the middle classes exchanged it for imperialism, and the latter now marches triumphantly with its bodyguards, militarism and reaction, to the conquest of the Anglo-Saxon world.

Chapter Twelve

'Reflections on England's Decline' (March 1901)[1]

Max Beer

Three events dominated the end of the nineteenth century: the American Civil War, the Franco-Prussian War and England's decline.[2] All three were momentous and assumed world-historical dimensions. They released boundless energies, and their positive and negative effects find their expression in contemporary history: in the conscious, all-surpassing struggles of peoples for purely material interests, in the decline of bourgeois democracy, and in the standstill of the socialist movement.

The American Civil War opened up a rich and fruitful continent to the world market and threw highly developed characters, reared in puritanical self-discipline, onto the path of industry. Emerson's ideal heroes and Whitman's democrats, animated by a stormy thirst for action, were followed by bold economic organisers. The ideal evaporated in the fire of competition and real personality remained. With John Brown and Abraham Lincoln, the last representatives of Puritanism went to their graves, and the Huntingtons and Rockefellers occupied their place.

1. Beer 1901a.
2. Sources: Giffen 1880–6; Adams 1895; Adams 1900; Bureau of Foreign Commerce, Department of State 1900–1; *The Economist* 1900.

The effects of the Franco-Prussian War were deeper and more direct because its arena was the hearth of European civilisation. It shattered a radical, enthusiastic petty bourgeoisie that had put a check on the reactionary flood and pledged to tame the tyrants. The War turned tsardom into the arbiter of the world and enabled it to lay hands on Asia. It filled industrial Germany with self-confidence and millions, but it also invigorated the social-fermentation process, inflamed the class-struggle and accelerated the awakening of a new world-view, which, slowly but surely, conquered a place alongside the others. In the historical sciences, its influence is tangible. One of its most remarkable spiritual products is, alongside German socialism, modern German drama. The initial stages of a process of social dissolution have always been rich in dramatic conflicts and therefore favourable to the rise of dramatic literature. So it happened in Athens during the fifth century and in Rome during the second century BC; likewise in England during the sixteenth, in France during the seventeenth and in Germany at the end of the eighteenth century.

In the midst of these powerful upheavals on the European continent and in America, the Britons rested on the riches that had been supplied to them from the four corners of the world by the raids against India, the industrial revolution and free trade ('war, trade and piracy', as the rude Mephisto was fond of saying). In the century between 1770 and 1870, England reached an economic level that no people had seen before. Excluding the campaign against the United States, it succeeded in everything. That was the heyday of the English spirit: Smith, Ricardo and Mill; Burns, Byron and Shelley; Scott, Dickens and Thackeray; Lyell, Wallace and Darwin. Soon afterwards, the period of exhaustion set in. Weariness took possession of the once untiring seafarers, merchants and mechanics.

* * *

Until approximately the year 1875, England ruled absolutely over the world-market. Trade and industry yielded a profit-rate that today seems fabulous. 'We count our percentages in thousands', said the Lancashire manufacturers. The surpluses that domestic enterprises could no longer absorb flowed as loans to other continents: to the United States, Argentina, Australia and India. There, they stimulated and awakened the slumbering agricultural and industrial forces that soon stood up as rivals of England. The effects [of the rise of England's rivals] were twofold: they arrested the development of English exports and caused a general fall in prices, which was made even more painful by the dethronement of silver in Germany. European agriculture was the first to be affected, and English agriculture became totally unprofitable. Thus it happened that England was forced to make ever-greater outlays for foodstuffs when its industrial energies began to decline. In 1860, England imported 68 million pounds sterling in foodstuffs; in 1870, 91; in 1880, 60; in 1889, 154; and in 1899, 205 million pounds sterling. The increasingly unfavourable English balance of trade must be largely attributed to these growing outlays on foodstuff-imports.

[The nominal deficit in England's balance of trade grew from 40.2 million pounds sterling in 1850 to 232.1 million pounds sterling in 1900]. In order to appreciate those numbers correctly, it is necessary to stress that, until 1889, about 85 million pounds sterling in interest from overseas loans and approximately 60 million pounds sterling in ships' freights were included among the imports, so that the [real-goods] deficit was unimportant. Since then, however, the situation has changed considerably. In order to cover the growing deficit, England was forced at about that time to begin the liquidation of its foreign assets. The pressure on creditors grew yearly. The United States, which, in the meantime, had made great progress and concentrated its industry more and more, paid promptly, but Argentina broke down under the pressure and dragged the Barings [Bank] along with them into the abyss (1890). Australia followed in 1891 and 1892; and, in 1893, the United States was shaken by a violent crisis. The capital-deprivation completely ruined the weakest of the creditors, emaciated India, which was apparently abandoned to famine. Extremely sensitive and complicated as the mechanism of modern finance is, a single push was enough to spread the shock everywhere. Enormous sums of English capital invested in those countries perished in the crisis. Those liquidations and losses have obviously reduced the favourable financial components of English imports. Incomes shrink, but life is increasingly refined, costly and dependent on foreign imports. In 1898, the influx of American payments did not suffice to cover the surplus of American imports. And, in 1900, the roles were inverted: New York became the creditor, and London the debtor!

In England, people were still unconscious of the real situation in 1897. Most of them saw only the pomp of the world empire. But instincts were on the alert. In the bourgeoisie, they manifested themselves in the drive to control the gold-mines of Transvaal, in the glorification of problematic characters like [Barney] Barnato, [Leander Starr] Jameson, and the leaders of the

South-African Chartered Company. Politically, and in literary terms, in terms of public opinion, those instincts manifested themselves in imperialism, which inevitably turned towards South Africa. The English interests in Asia were disregarded, and the foreign policy of Disraeli, which turned entirely on the Anglo-Russian conflict of interests, was declared antiquated. England's bourgeois-cultural mission lay at present in other parts of the world.

* * *

The struggle over Transvaal, whose conquest was meant to be the keystone of a powerful empire, [actually] accelerated England's decline. I do not have the military expertise to pass judgement on English warfare. However, three events attract attention in a general survey of the South-African campaign: the Englishmen's quick retreats after suffering small losses; the numerous surrenders of strong detachments not facing serious resistance; and the absence of the bourgeoisie in the army. In Magersfontein, Methuen lost among dead and wounded about 8 per cent of his troops; in Colenso, Buller lost only 5 per cent. What are those losses compared to those of Gettysburg in the American Civil War, where the army of the North lost in the field 27 per cent and that of the South 36 per cent of its men, or compared to those of Pleven [the battle of Plevna, during the Russo-Turkish War of 1877–8], where 18,000 out of 60,000 Russian soldiers fell! The Frenchmen, who were then regarded as decadent, lost 12 per cent of their troops in the battle of Gravelotte. [...] Most striking was the surrender in Lindley, where 400 soldiers of the Imperial Yeomanry, the flower of the English race, laid down their weapons and, led by *eight* Boers, walked resignedly into captivity.

Of even greater social significance is the absence of the bourgeoisie from the South-African battlefields. As far as we know, the sons of the old nobility and the military families put up a good fight. The proportion of fallen officers is uncommonly high, and their contempt for death is, from the English standpoint, still the brightest side of this war. The poor Tommies,[3] the poorest of

3. [A long established nickname for a British soldier has been 'Tommy Atkins' or 'Tommy' for short. The origins are obscure but most probably derive from a specimen army form circulated by the Adjutant-General Sir Harry Calvert to all units in 1815, the blanks being filled in with the particulars of a Private Thomas Atkins, No 6 Company, 23rd Regiment of Foot. Rudyard Kipling published the poem *Tommy* (part of the *Barrack Room Ballads*, which were dedicated 'To T.A.') in 1892, and in 1893 the music-hall song *Private Tommy Atkins* was published with words by Henry Hamilton and music by S. Potter. In 1898, William McGonagall wrote *Lines In Praise of Tommy*

the poor, flocked to the standard. Here and there, one also finds a name from high finance. But where were the sons of the middle class, which, according to the arithmetic of our thoughtful savants, should be continuously increasing![4] All the volunteers counted at most 11,000 men – that is all the 'broad middle classes' were able to supply. A truly eloquent piece of social statistics!

The financing of the War showed at least the same slackening. It was said in New York that, after the battle of Colenso, something like a panic seized haughty Lombard Street, and that the Bank of England was menaced with a run. The government had to look out for gold. Not for nothing did Balfour, the Conservative leader of the House of Commons, invite the Rothschilds for advice on the eve of the War, to the great annoyance of our comrade Hyndman (*Justice*, beginning of October 1899). Balfour had a clear insight into the financial situation of England. The government raised two small loans, totalling 40 million pounds sterling; something the foremost financial power in the world should have done easily. Yet the Chancellor of the Exchequer considered it more prudent to raise the second loan in New York, in order to redress somewhat the English shortage of gold. A small loan of approximately 11 million pounds sterling was finally negotiated here [in New York].

A people seeing in success the only proof of virtue must have been deeply shaken by the events of the latest period. '*Strength*, well understood, is the measure of all worth,' says Carlyle in *Heroes and Hero Worship*. 'Give a thing time; if it can succeed, it is a right thing.'[5] No wonder that the English people is at present seized by a despondency that is perhaps as extreme as its former arrogance, for England is still enormously rich and has very important capitalist interests everywhere in the world. But the time is past when Cobbett could exclaim: 'Who will say that an Englishman ought not to despise all the nations in the world? For my part I do, and that most heartily.'[6] Today, Lord Rosebery holds up the Americans and Germans before his people as an example. And Kaiser Wilhelm II marched in triumph through the streets of London. What Englishman, what observer of English life, would have predicted that even a few years ago? William Clarke's article on 'The Social Future of England' in

---

Atkins, which was an attack on what he saw as the disparaging portrayal of Tommy in Kipling's poem.]

4. [A reference to Eduard Bernstein's argument in the revisionist controversy that the middle classes were increasing in numbers as a result of industrial concentration.]

5. [Carlyle 1890, p. 192.]

6. [Quoted in Bulwer 1868, Vol. II, p. 136.]

the *Contemporary Review* of December 1900 is very instructive.[7] He points out England's economic decline, the anti-democratic tendencies of the population and the growth of the servant-classes, and sees a future England as a playground for American and Australian millionaires, whom the Englishmen will serve as lackeys, waiters, doormen and schoolmasters. Lord Rosebery also remarked upon this tendency and lamented it in his great rectorial speech (Glasgow, 16 November, 1900). A deep sadness permeates his *Questions of Empire*, as that masterpiece of English rhetoric is called.[8]

* * *

The exhaustion is today more noticeable among the working classes than among the ruling classes. Without intellectual training, political goals or broad economic perspectives, they fall into passivity more rapidly than the bourgeoisie, who can draw on richer spiritual reserves. And the passivity of the English proletariat has pernicious effects on the rising and advancing international Social Democracy. The dependence of the latter on England's economic and political theories, and its respect for the English labour-organisations, deprive the young, inexperienced international Social Democracy of the boldness necessary to shove aside those paralysed masses. Even more: sometimes the question creeps up on us as to whether the English masses are not, in their 'statesmanlike calmness', a living refutation of our theories. At international labour-congresses, which we attend in the hope of getting new encouragement and enthusiasm, the attitude of the representatives of the English proletariat always has confusing and depressing effects. Socialist thought recoils from those immutable and unmovable masses, or else it shipwrecks on Fabianism, whose lack of illusions, hyper-critique and self-irony can only be the product of a stagnating people.

Today, it is clearer than ever to me that contemporary England represents not a normal and healthy but an exhausted and declining state of affairs. And to this country many of us have wandered, studying and wondering at its social relations, much like our forerunners made pilgrimages to Paris some fifty or sixty years ago. There they found humanitarian élan, revolutionary enthusiasm and critical social thought. In England, we found an extremely rich and dazzling culture, cold reflection, meticulous analysis, and practical

7. [Clarke 1900.]
8. [A reference to Rosebery 1900.]

shrewdness – an imposing but burnt-out volcano. And many of us succumbed to those influences. Revolutionary exiles, who in their motherland bore witness to their spirit of sacrifice, here modified their views and became prudent and cautious. One could give dozens of names, but the question dealt with here is too serious and objective to become personal.[9]

It is difficult to rise above our familiar surroundings; it is even more difficult to deal critically with a new environment belonging to a higher cultural stage. And it would be silly to blame it for being unable [to be as we would like it]. But it is worthwhile to stress those facts emphatically.

The ruling classes have no idea how much they owe to cautious, common-sense England. It did for the existing social order at the end of the nineteenth century what the tsarist régime did five decades ago with the force of arms. The exultation of the European bourgeoisie over the South-African fiasco was a testimony to its ignorance, to its narrow social and political horizon.

Social progress has nothing more to expect from England. And yet, only social progress can preserve from degradation the Britons, who gave to the world the modern political and social alphabet. To fall back on petty-bourgeois agriculture is impossible for them. By contrast, large-scale agricultural enterprises are perhaps possible there, but they should be preceded by a nationalisation of the land because English workers are no longer ready to work as farm-labourers. Such a sweeping reform would make the country independent of imported foodstuffs and redress the swelling deficit in its balance of trade. But where is the class able to carry out that heroic task?

At a certain cultural level, socialism will become an organic, constructive vital force. Woe to those who tame and stifle it.

* * *

Let us outline briefly the probable effects of England's decline, a task made easier today by the fact that the decline is already strongly felt in world politics, which hitherto possessed a certain balance. Momentous shifts are taking place before our eyes: the commercial centre is moving to New York while the political one is moving, more than ever before, to Petersburg. England's prestige, its brilliant position between the Dual Alliance and the Triple Alliance,[10] kept

9. [A reference to Eduard Bernstein, who gave up his revolutionary views in England under the influence of the Fabian Society. See Bax 1988a (7 November).]

10. [The Dual Alliance (*Zweibund*), also called the Franco-Russian Alliance, was a political and military relation between France and Russia that developed from friendly

Russian ambitions in check for a long time. As this prestige fades, Russia no longer has any reason for restraining itself. Its independent course of action in China – the seizure of Manchuria – sufficiently illustrates this state of affairs. To be sure, it was prepared by the Franco-Prussian war, which threw France and its finance into the arms of Russia. The Trans-Siberian Railroad, which brought Russia to Peking, was built with French millions. Incidentally, the railroads, from which our old liberals expected at least as much as good Catholics did from their missionaries, have currently become chains to subjugate foreign peoples. The construction of German railroads in Asia Minor is destined to play that same role with regard to Turkey.

The United States, with its ruthlessly protectionist tariff-policy, vast territories and endless energies, is proving to be the most powerful rival of England and Germany. These latter two countries, with their restricted territories, saturated industries and internal restraints, look not only for overseas *markets* but also for overseas *possessions* in order to exploit their natural resources and cheap workforce. The goals of their policy are not foreign-trade agreements but foreign undertakings [*Gründungen*: establishments]. Their imperialism has *financial* motives. The capitals that find no employment in the motherland flow to China, Asia Minor, South America and South Africa. (Germany has investments of approximately 7.5 billion marks in those lands.) Their governments are therefore forced to protect their 'national' capitals against the uncivilised – that is to say, anti-capitalist – governments of those places. The most effective method for doing so is to establish protectorates; hence the aggressiveness of financial imperialism, and the association of England and Germany in China. The United States, on the contrary, still has enough opportunity and space to employ its capitals at home, and it requires for the time being only sales markets for its overproduction, which grows continuously. In 1890, they imported 823,395,000 dollars and exported 857,000,000;

---

contacts in 1891 to a secret treaty in 1894, which became one of the basic European alignments of the pre-World War I era. The Triple Alliance (*Dreibund*) was an alliance between the German Empire, Austria-Hungary, and Italy, established in 1882. Its basis was the understanding that, if two or more great powers attacked one of the parties, the other two would come to its assistance. It was additional to the secret Dual Alliance between Germany and Austria-Hungary signed in 1879. Its original duration was for five years. It was renewed in 1887, 1891, 1896, 1902, 1907, and 1912. The Triple Alliance was brought to an end in 1914 by the refusal of Italy to enter into hostilities with the powers then at war with Germany and Austria-Hungary.]

in 1900, their imports stood at 827,800,000 and their exports at 1,478,050,000 dollars. Those enormous commodity-surpluses push outwards. Hence their [open-door] peace policy in China, for only a united, independent China can offer its markets to the United States. Americans are compelled by their economic interests to appear disinterested towards China.

Different economic stages produce different interests that give imperialism a specific character. English and German imperialism is financial; American imperialism is industrial; Russian imperialism is fiscal. The seizure of Manchuria had no other purpose than securing for the government of a country impoverished by oppression, a government that is expensive and in permanent financial straits, rich territories in order to obtain new mortgages. The China-policy of Russia is simply a robbers' policy. It is naturally much more pleasant to have as a neighbour old, run-down China rather than England and Germany. Hence the Russian *chamade*.[11]

The outcome of this is the following world-political constellation: a) England and Germany with their allies; b) a compromise between the United States and Russia, with France as mediator of their petty sugar-conflicts. For deceived France, this apostolate of peace would be more than sufficient compensation for its two billions.[12]

---

11. [Defintition of *chamade*: (Mil.) A signal made by drum or trumpet inviting an enemy to parley: 'They beat the *chamade*, and sent us *carte blanche*.' (Addison).]

12. [Probably a reference to the bankruptcy of the Panama Company (*Compagnie du canal interocéanique*) headed by Ferdinand de Lesseps, builder of the Suez Canal. The company collapsed in February 1889. Three years after the collapse of the company, the largest corruption scandal of the nineteenth century shook the French Republic. The Panama affair was one of the major political crises of the Third Republic in France (1870–1914) and resulted in the fall of two cabinets. In 1892–3 French nationalists accused a large number of ministers (including Clemenceau) of taking bribes from de Lesseps in 1888 for the permit of the lottery issue. This resulted in a corruption trial held in 1892 against Ferdinand de Lesseps and his son Charles. At the same time, 510 members of parliament – including six ministers – were accused of bribery by the Panama Canal Company in connection with the course of events concerning the permit for the lottery-issue (1888). Large bribery-sums were also paid to the press, banks and private persons. Ferdinand and Charles de Lesseps, members of the management as well as the entrepreneur Gustave Eiffel were at first given long jail-sentences, which were later annulled. In the bribery trial, the former city-development minister, Bethaut, received five-years imprisonment, three of which he had to serve. Baron Reinach – the financial adviser of the Canal Company and exerciser of the various bribes – committed suicide. Other defendants fled to England. The remaining investigations into the Panama affair were abandoned in 1894. On 7 December 1894, Ferdinand de Lesseps died. The investigations into the Panama affair were resumed in 1897; however, the defendants were acquitted. Approximately 1.5 billion francs were lost affecting 800,000 investors.]

Chapter Thirteen

'Social Imperialism' (8 November 1901)

Max Beer

In this article, Max Beer examines Fabian ideas on social reform as the domestic counterpart of support for imperialism abroad – a stance he characterised as 'social imperialism'. The Fabian Society, a socialist educational organisation founded in London in 1884 by a group of middle-class intellectuals, rejected the Marxist theory of class-struggle and promoted a capitalist welfare-state. The Fabian influence on Eduard Bernstein was evident as early as 1896[1] and recurred throughout his book *The Preconditions of Socialism*.

In 1899, the outbreak of the Boer War in South Africa led to a clash between two tendencies within the Fabian Society. A minority faction, led by Ramsay MacDonald, argued that Britain had to educate subject-peoples towards self-government, while the pro-imperialist majority, led by Sidney Webb and George Bernard Shaw, advanced an intellectual justification for central control by the British Empire, arguing that existing institutions should simply work more 'efficiently'. The majority criticised Gladstonian Liberalism both for its individualism at home and for its lack of enthusiasm for imperialism

1. Bax 1988a. A good selection of documents on the first phase of the revisionist controversy, i.e. before the publication of books by Bernstein and Kautsky, is found in Tudor and Tudor (eds.) 1988.

abroad. They favoured a national minimum wage in order to induce British industries to invest in capital-equipment rather than lowering wages; slum-clearances and a health service in order to breed 'even a moderately Imperial race', which would be more productive and militarily superior to recruits drawn from malnourished slum-dwellers; and a national education system because 'it is in the class-rooms that the future battles of the Empire for commercial prosperity are already being lost'.[2]

Beatrice and Sidney Webb first met Lord Rosebery, former Liberal Prime Minister, in March 1900.[3] Trying to promote Rosebery's political resurrection, in September 1901 Sidney Webb published an article called 'Lord Rosebery's Escape from Houndsditch', in which he appealed to the Liberal imperialists to discard the last vestiges of Gladstonian policies and create a vital opposition based upon a political programme that would promote 'the national minimum' in all fields. Webb rejected 'Irish Home Rule and Boer independence' as 'obsolete hypocrisies about peoples' "rightly struggling to be free"', demanding instead 'virility in government – virility in South Africa'.[4] But, by the beginning of 1902, Rosebery abandoned his desire to create a new 'national' party or to re-invigorate the parliamentary opposition. Although the Webbs 'continued to pay court to Liberal Imperialists', they grew increasingly exasperated with the ambivalence of Rosebery's position.[5]

---

2. E.J.T. Brennan's introduction to Webb 1901 (September), in Brennan 1975, p. 60.
3. Archibald Philip Primrose, 5th Earl of Rosebery (1847–1929), was a British Liberal politician who, as foreign Secretary in Gladstone's last two governments (1886 and 1892–4), supported policies of imperial expansion, notably in Uganda and South Africa. When Gladstone retired in 1894, Rosebery became his successor as Prime Minister, to the disgust of Sir William Harcourt, the Chancellor of the Exchequer and leader of the more left-wing Liberals. His selection was largely the consequence of Queen Victoria's dislike for the other leading Liberals. Rosebery's government was, for the most part, unsuccessful. His designs in foreign policy, such as expansion of the fleet, were defeated by disagreements within the Liberal Party, while the Unionist-dominated House of Lords stopped the whole of the Liberals' domestic legislation. On 21 June 1895, Rosebery resigned after a minor defeat in the House of Commons, leading to a ten-year period (1895–1905) of Tory governments under Lord Salisbury and Arthur Balfour. Rosebery also resigned as leader of the Liberal Party on 8 October 1896, to be succeeded by Harcourt. He gradually moved away from the mainstream of the Liberal Party, finding support among members of the imperialist wing such as Herbert Asquith, Edward Grey and R.B. Haldane. During the Boer War (1899–1902) Rosebery became estranged from most of the Liberal Party because of his enthusiasm for the British Empire; and, late in 1905, a few weeks before the Liberals returned to power, he completely broke with them by declaring his opposition to Irish home rule. The Earl of Rosebery died in 1929.
4. Webb 1901, in Brennan 1975, pp. 68 and 83.
5. Webb 1901, in Brennan 1975, p. 61.

* * *

'Social Imperialism'[6]

'It is beginning to be hinted that we are a nation of amateurs.'

(Lord Rosebery, *Rectorial address at Glasgow University*, 16 November, 1900.)[7]

The last stage of the Fabians

The Fabians proved to be the amateurs of English socialism. The socialist doctrines, as they found them in *Capital*, had a great appeal for these spirited writers. That is easily explicable. The liberal principles and axioms of philosophical radicalism had been fully acted out between 1775 and 1875. Already [John Stuart] Mill, one of the best of this species, stood at the cross-road between two worlds. Only Gladstone[8] remained – a giant amongst the ruins of Liberalism. Incidentally, it is instructive to know that he was to some extent conscious of this situation. According to Lord Tweedmouth,[9] the 'great old man' said that he spent the last twenty years of his life, from 1878 to 1898, 'patching up old clothes'. The patched up old clothes were apparently good enough for the workers. The fate of the English workers seemed to be to satisfy their spiritual and material needs in second-hand shops. But the

---

6. Beer 1901b.
7. Quoted in Bartlett 1919, p. 827.
8. [William E. Gladstone (1809–98) was a British Liberal statesman and prime minister. He studied at Oxford, and entered parliament in 1832 as a Conservative, working closely with Peel. From 1834, he held various junior posts, becoming President of the Board of Trade (1843–5). A firm supporter of free trade, he was Chancellor of the Exchequer in Aberdeen's coalition (1852–5) and again under Palmerston (1859–66). In 1867 he became leader of the Liberal Party, and soon after served his first term as premier. He disestablished and disendowed the Irish Church, and established a system of national education (1870). Frequently in office until his resignation in 1894, he succeeded in carrying out a scheme of parliamentary reform (the Reform Act, 1884) that went a long way towards universal male suffrage. In his last two ministries he introduced bills for Irish home rule, but both bills were defeated. Gladstone's policies followed his strong religious convictions and his liberalism. He resisted imperialist expansion, and his mistrust of socialism was reflected in a belief that government alone cannot solve social problems.]
9. [Edward Marjoribanks, 2nd Baron Tweedmouth (1849–1909) was a British Liberal-Party statesman. He was Comptroller of the Household in 1886, and Parliamentary Secretary to the Treasury from 1892 to 1894. As Baron Tweedmouth, he was Lord Privy Seal and Chancellor of the Duchy of Lancaster from 1894 to 1895, First Lord of the Admiralty from 1905 to 1908, and Lord President of the Council from April until October 1908.]

young men who came to London in the 1880s from the universities of Oxford, Cambridge or Dublin wanted to have the new intellectual products. And thus they found Marx, who, during the past thirty years, gave to European social and political thought its direction.

But Marxism in England could not have the immediate significance that it had, for instance, in Germany. In the first place, the English economy is more mature for a socialist transformation. Its need for reform is more evident and also makes itself felt in different ways among the middle classes. It no longer takes the class-instinct of the proletariat to feel that something is rotten in the state. It is, therefore, more difficult to become conscious of the class-line separating the bourgeoisie and the proletariat. The slogan 'we are all socialists now',[10] which was born before the onset of imperialism, did not just arise from hypocrisy. Besides, in England, the revolutionary effect of the capitalist mode of production found its conservative, conciliatory counter-effect in emerging democracy. The two most important elements of modern democracy – *the cabinet as a committee, as the executive organ of the parliamentary majority*, and *the loose connection between central and local government* – already exist in England. They are the viable, promising political product of the entire previous development, while, in Germany, the arousing blows of a police-state, which originated in a completely different period, further strengthen the revolutionary effect of the economic system. Finally, and this is the most important factor, while, in Germany, sweeping, systematic and therefore revolutionary thought is a native product, which makes the contradiction between doctrine and life appear much more evident, the curse of the English people is their tendency to shun sweeping thought, to avoid thoroughgoing reform and to remain amateurs in most areas of thought and action. In England, knowledge of the contradictions that are the most powerful spur to spiritual progress has been far too long in coming. And the wretched conditions of the primary schools attended by the workers have prolonged that waiting period. *On the continent, knowledge is in advance of actual relations, while, in England, it lags behind them.* But a great, historical class-struggle, as Marx understood it, can only break out from the clash between a class demanding its rights out of knowledge

10. [A statement by Sir William Harcourt (1827–1904), a Liberal member of Parliament, in 1888, in a speech to the House of Commons.]

of the nascent social relations, and another class in unshaken possession of handed-down privileges and refusing to grant it those rights. However, in the years 1880 to 1899, the situation in England was such that one class lacked the necessary knowledge while the other class could no longer uphold the unshaken possession of its privileges, because advancing political democracy did not allow it to do so.

These conditions, with their numerous accompanying phenomena, are the source of the disappointments and mistakes of the English Social Democrats and their friends. For the amateur socialists they were completely catastrophic. George Bernard Shaw told me once in 1895:

> At first we were totally fascinated by Marx. A new world opened up before us. However, practical agitation showed us that Marx is dated for contemporary England. His analyses originate in the England of 1840 to 1850. We stand today at a higher cultural stage. The workers and the bourgeoisie are anxious to accommodate the new conditions. The appeal to the class-struggle can only harm that accommodation-process. The drive to reforms is there; the democratic means and ways to bring them about already exist. Our task can only be to show where and how the reform work has to begin. In short, our policy is to penetrate all the available popular strata with socialist ideas and realisable reform proposals.

At bottom, that change of direction was due to the circumstances described above: the apathy of the workers, the presence of democratic institutions, and the need for reform arising out the ripeness or perhaps over-ripeness of economic life. Deeply discouraged, the Fabians finally took leave of the radicals, as they had done before of the Marxists, and threw themselves into the arms of the Liberal imperialists. By doing so, they shot the last arrow from their quiver. The radical *Speaker* of 7 September 1901 told them this bitter truth [retranslated from the German]: 'If there is an even more conspicuous phenomenon than the weakness of the parliamentary opposition in recent years, it is the decadence of the school of Sidney Webb as a political factor.' The external and domestic reaction of the last two years [marked by the Boer War] led to utter disarray among the amateur socialists. Their set phrases about higher cultural stages and general accommodation lost even the appearance of a justification.

Webb's disavowal of radicals and socialists

Webb's essay in the September issue of *Nineteenth Century*, entitled 'Lord Rosebery's Escape from Houndsditch',[11] marks this last stage of the Fabian Society.[12] Webb first argues thoroughly with Liberalism, for an Englishman far too thoroughly, because he polemicises completely in the spirit of the German *Kathedersozialisten*, who understandably could have no idea about the historical tasks of Liberalism – the liberation of the individual and of national individuality. It took the Fabians twenty years to reach the standpoint of Schmoller in 1872.[13] Webb writes:

> The political force of this old [Gladstonian] Liberalism is spent. During the last twenty years its aspirations and its watchwords, its ideas of daily life and its conceptions of the universe, have become increasingly distasteful to the ordinary citizen as he renews his youth from generation to generation. Its worship of individual liberty evokes no enthusiasm. Its reliance on 'freedom of contract' and 'supply and demand', with its corresponding 'voluntarism' in religion and philanthropy, now seems to work out disastrously for the masses.... Its very admiration for that favourite Fenian abstraction, the 'principle of nationality', now appears to us as but Individualism writ large, being, in truth, the assertion that each distinct race (which it never is, by the way), has an inherent right to have its own government, and work out its own policy, unfettered by any consideration of the effect of this independence on other races, or on the world at large.[14]

It is impossible to read this excerpt calmly. The Englishman presents the right to national self-determination, for which Europe has been fighting for fifty years, as merely an abstract principle of the Fenians.[15] The representative of

---

11. Houndsditch is the London equivalent of the *Mühlendam*, a street in which old clothes are traded – a hint at Rosebery's separation from Gladstone, the tailor of old clothes.

12. Webb 1901 (September), in Brennan 1975, pp. 59–84.

13. Schmoller instinctively realised that years ago. In his newest monumental work, Webb is honoured as one of the *Kathedersozialisten* and naturally placed high above Marx. [Gustav von Schmoller (1838–1917) was the leader of the 'younger' German historical school of economics. He was a leading member of the *Kathedersozialisten* (socialists of the chair), and a founder and long-time chairman of the *Verein für Socialpolitik*, the German Economics Association. Beer refers to his magnum opus: Schmoller 1900–4.]

14. Webb 1901, in Brennan 1975, pp. 62–3.

15. [The name Fenians was first applied by John O'Mahony to the members of the Irish-nationalist organisation that he founded in America in 1858. The Fenians, both

a nation practising national oppression uninterruptedly for two centuries, which, in Asia, interferes with brute force in the fate of half of humanity, complains about the recklessness of other peoples. For the rest, Webb has done us a great service with his essay. As long as the Fabians limited themselves to social and political questions of detail, one could delude oneself about them. But this illusion disappears the moment they afford us an opportunity to survey their general world-view. The same, I think, is true of other reformers. Webb continues:

> During the last twenty or thirty years we have become a new people. 'Early Victorian' England now lies, in effect, centuries behind us. Such things do happen. The processes which make one generation differ from another operate sometimes slowly and imperceptibly, sometimes quickly and even suddenly.... Such an epoch of transformation we now recognise, to cite only one instance, in the reign of Elizabeth. We note, within a single generation, a distinct change in the content of men's minds. Their standpoints are shifted. Their horizons are suddenly enlarged. Their whole way of considering things is altered, and lo! a new England. In the same sense, the historian of the future will recognise, in the last quarter of the nineteenth century, the birth of another new England. Elizabethan England changed because Englishmen became aware of new relationships. They saw themselves linked, almost suddenly, with the past in classic antiquity, and with the future in America. The England of this generation is changing because Englishmen have had revealed to them another new world of relationships, of which they were before unconscious. This time it is not a new continent that the ordinary man has discovered, but a new category. We have become aware, almost in a flash, that we are not merely individuals, but members of a community, nay, citizens of the world.[16]

---

the Fenian Brotherhood and Irish Republican Brotherhood, were fraternal organisations dedicated to establishment of an independent Irish Republic in the nineteenth and early twentieth century. O'Mahony, who was a Celtic scholar, named the American wing of the movement after the Fianna, the legendary band of Irish warriors led by Fionn mac Cumhaill. The term is still used today, especially in Ireland and Scotland, where its original meaning has continued and expanded to include all supporters of Irish nationalism.]

16. Webb 1901, in Brennan 1975, pp. 64–5.

Webb declaims all these things earnestly, as if he were the forerunner of a new philosophy of history. And, except for the small circle of English Marxists, his approach actually is more or less new in England. In the English press, the artistic and personal handling of historical processes is still prevalent. But one should not think that Webb uses the expression 'citizens of the world' in its democratic sense. Due to his false perspective, democratic internationalism and the imperialist stranglehold on the peoples are for him identical concepts. Webb then describes how the workers' future depends on the trade-unions and social legislation, how the merchants' wealth depends on a good community and state-policy, and how the manufacturers' prosperity depends on the prestige of their government in the eyes of the other peoples.

> In short, the opening of the twentieth century finds us all, to the dismay of the old-fashioned Individualist, 'thinking in communities'. Now the trouble with Gladstonian Liberalism is that, by instinct, by tradition, and by the positive precepts of its past exponents, it 'thinks in individuals'.... This same atomic conception of society, transferred from the State at home to the British Empire as a whole, colours the Liberal propaganda of Home Rule for Ireland, and in its latest metamorphosis, the demand for the independence of the Transvaal.[17]

The antithesis between the thought of the old and the new England constitutes the basic idea of the critical part of the essay. According to Webb, due to their lack of a foreign policy, the Social Democrats have also proved to be a part of the old England.

His view of English socialism is quite interesting; it is the quintessence of Fabianism:

> Democratic Socialism, as a theory of economic and political State organisation, has at least the double merit of being based on the latest political science, and in accord with the aspirations of the new England of today. Indeed, we can now see that the rise of the organised Socialist movement in England after 1880 was only one symptom of the political change of heart which the nation was experiencing. Just for this reason the propaganda of practical Socialism has, during the last twenty years, had a great effect on English thought.... But, looking back on the last two decades, we see that

17. Webb 1901, in Brennan 1975, pp. 65 and 67.

> this effect has come, not so much in causing people to abandon their political parties, or to abstain from using party watchwords, as in forcing upon their attention an altogether novel criticism, and in changing their whole way of looking at things. What hinders the formation of a separate Socialist party in England is always that the increase of Socialism is so much faster than that of professed and organised Socialism. The effect of the Socialist propaganda on our matter of fact nation is like the overflow of a flooded river. It extends horizontally with a certain rapidity, but vertically only with extreme slowness, perhaps never reaching any high point. It first wets everyone's boots, and then steals unobtrusively over the ankles and knees, producing an amphibious condition in which the elector or statesman, whilst strongly objecting to being called a Socialist, or to join any avowedly Socialist organisation, nevertheless becomes convinced that an enlightened and progressive interpretation of his traditional political creed, Conservative or Liberal, demands the addition of collectivist items to the party programme. But by the time the professed Socialists were weaned from their primitive policy of the 'conversion of England' and the formation of an all-powerful Socialist party, to a policy of permeating the existing parties, the political horizon was widened by the rise of Imperial questions, and the advent of modern world politics. The Socialists, having no definite views of their own on foreign policy, immediately found their boom of 1885–1891 collapsing; and for a time they could only account for this by 'the apathy of the working classes'. When the [Boer] war came the secret was out. Outside the two spheres of labour and local government the majority of the Socialist leaders proved to be, notably with regard to the British Empire, mere administrative Nihilists – that is to say, ultra-nationalist, ultra-Gladstonian, old-Liberal to the finger-tips.... On the issues of 'nationalism' and the Empire, Mr. Hyndman and Mr. Keir Hardie find themselves, in fact, by honest conviction, on the same platform as Sir Wilfred Lawson and Mr. Labouchère.[18]

This summary equation of the foreign policy of Social Democracy with that of Liberalism is as untrue as the reproach of the Liberals that Social Democracy agrees in domestic policy with the Conservatives, because sometimes both come close to each other in legislation for the protection of the workers. Both

18. Webb 1901, in Brennan 1975, pp. 70–1.

argumentations are false. They rest on the generalisation of some superficial phenomena. For the rest, we concede to Webb that Social Democracy does not have and cannot have what people commonly call a foreign policy. Modern socialists cannot outwit diplomatic secrecy, before which the Philistines and the Fabians stand in awe, for the same reasons that they are so good at labour and domestic policy. One of the best means to judge the spiritual and moral condition of a state is the relation between its domestic and foreign policy. The domestic policy of the civilised peoples has, in theory, the purpose of letting the classes, groups and individuals fight out their struggles within certain legal limits and with spiritual weapons. Foreign policy recognises no legal limits and is, in fact, the art of deceiving and cheating the opponent, ultimately bringing him down by violent means. The imperialist Tommy Atkins knows about that. He sings in one of Kipling's *Barrack-Room Ballads*:

> Ship me somewheres east of Suez, where the best is like the worst,
> Where there aren't no Ten Commandments an' a man can raise a thirst;
> For the temple-bells are callin', an' it's there that I would be –
> By the old Moulmein Pagoda, looking lazy at the sea.[19]

The more developed the domestic policy of a state, the more moral, and therefore weakening, will its effect be on foreign policy; the more undeveloped the domestic policy, the more strongly it suffers the brutalising influence of foreign policy. The former strives towards democracy, the latter towards absolutism. The management of domestic policy is very difficult. It requires moral and spiritual qualities of the first order, such as sincerity and impartiality. The management of foreign policy is easier. It only requires moral and spiritual qualities of a lower order: cleverness, pliancy, good manners, ability to identify the intentions of the opponent and to exploit his weaknesses, unscrupulousness, and self-possession. No wonder that the aristocracy and Catholic priests, as well as the Jews, supply so many suitable diplomats, while good domestic politicians, wise statesmen, are so scarce. Bismarck, the successful diplomat, failed ingloriously as a domestic politician. Russian absolutism pursues an astonishingly successful foreign policy, admittedly at the expense of domestic policy – in other words, its domestic policy is pursued with the same means as foreign policy. But the more democratic a

19. [Kipling 1893, p. 193. First Series (1892), 'Mandalay'.]

state, the higher its moral and intellectual level, the weaker will its foreign policy be, taking the word in its contemporary sense. The moment the states are placed on Social-Democratic foundations, the whole of diplomatic secrecy will be brought to an end. The legal provisions and moral foundations determining domestic policy will also be applied to foreign policy, to the traffic between peoples. The modern state has a Janus head, looking with one face to barbarism and with the other to civilisation. Socialism will abolish that contradiction.

Those are, in short, the reasons for the lack of a foreign policy in Social Democracy. It is certainly not my duty to defend Gladstone's foreign policy as regards the Transvaal and Ireland, but it does not take a sharp eye to recognise that it was a clever one. Gladstone withdrew from Transvaal after the English defeat at Majuba Hill in 1881.[20] Had he not done so, we would not have been able to occupy Egypt in 1882. The Nile country, which Englishmen nowadays treasure so much, would likely have fallen into French hands, as Manchuria has today fallen into Russian hands. Gladstone reckoned with the lengthiness of a South-African campaign, and in the end he also proved to be far superior to Salisbury and Chamberlain[21] as a diplomat. And, had his Home Rule Bill [for Ireland] been approved, England would not have had to suffer today such an ignominious diplomatic defeat at the hands of the United States on the question of the Nicaragua canal.[22] The Irishmen, who remain hostile towards the English government, rule as journalists and readers of the

20. [The battle at Majuba Hill (near Volksrust, South Africa) on 27 February 1881, was the main battle of the First Boer War (16 December 1880–23 March 1881). It was a resounding victory for the Boers. Of the small British force, 92 died and 134 were wounded, while Boer casualties were trifling. Although small in scope, the battle is historically significant because it led to the signing of a peace treaty and later the Pretoria Convention between the British and the newly created South-African Republic, ending the First Boer War.]

21. [Robert Cecil, 3rd Marquess of Salisbury (1830–1903) and Joseph Chamberlain (1836–1914).]

22. [In 1901 the United States and the United Kingdom signed the Hay-Pauncefote Treaty. This agreement nullified the Clayton-Bulwer Treaty of 1850 and gave the United States the right to create and control a canal across Central America, connecting the Pacific Ocean and the Atlantic Ocean. The British, recognising their diminishing influence in the region and cultivating friendship with the United States as a counterweight to Germany, stepped aside in the treaty to permit a canal run solely by the US This occurred under President Theodore Roosevelt. The treaty was negotiated under the table by United States Secretary of State, John Hay, and the British Ambassador to the United States, Lord Pauncefote.]

sensationalist press in the great American cities. During the Boer War, they created an aggressively anti-English public opinion that forced the government in Washington ruthlessly to tear to pieces the Clayton-Bulwer treaty. That was the revenge of the 'Fenians'. Incidentally, the only foreign policy adapted to the modern mode of production was suggested precisely by a Liberal, by Richard Cobden. Webb sees nothing of all this. The spiritual horizon of the imperialists is that of Kipling's Tommy Atkins: the Old Testament minus the Ten Commandments.

The social programme of imperialism

Thanks to his socialist studies, Webb's social policy is better than his foreign policy. Despite his belief in the higher cultural stage of progressive England, he sees the decay in the efficiency of the ruling classes and the mental enfeeblement and pauperisation of the masses. His confessions, written with great warmth, have greater value for us than the sharpest criticisms of revolutionary writers. He asks: What are the best elements of the English people thinking about today? And he answers:

> They are not thinking of Liberalism or Conservatism or Socialism. What is in their minds is a burning feeling of shame at the 'failure' of England – shame for the lack of capacity of its governors, shame for the inability of Parliament to get through even its routine business, shame for the absence of grip and resourcefulness of our statesmen, shame for the pompous inefficiency of every branch of our public administration, shame for the slackness of our merchants and traders that transfers our commercial supremacy to the United States, shame for the supineness which looks on unmoved at the continued degradation of our race by drunkenness and gambling, slum life, and all the horrors of the sweated trades.... Today, in the United Kindgom, there are, Sir Robert Giffen tells us, not fewer than *eight million* persons, one-fifth of the whole population, existing under conditions represented by a family income of less than a pound a week, and constituting not merely a disgrace, but a positive danger to our civilisation....[23] This sense of shame has yet to be transmitted into political action. Lord Rosebery's quick politi-

23. Webb 1901, in Brennan 1975, pp. 72–3. [Beer interpolated this quotation from the following page of Webb's article into the main one.]

> cal wit seizes this fact, and rightly pronounces that 'the country is ripe for a domestic programme', which shall breathe 'new life into the administrative dry bones of our public offices'.[24]

Webb's burning shame concerning England's decline is a consequence of the South-African War. Before the War, that feeling burned only among the little circle of English Marxists. Here lies the cultural and historical significance of this campaign. It tore apart the deceptive cover hiding England's exhaustion. The absence of a strong Social-Democratic movement, therefore, does not have its cause in the rapid growth of socialism [outside the Social-Democratic ranks], but in the general decline [of English society], which understandably makes much more difficult the task of gathering the energies necessary to create a revolutionary movement. When I wrote the last section of my 'Reflections on England's Decline' for this journal, I had no idea that such a classical witness as Sidney Webb would be found for each remark. Had he still been a socialist, he would have seen that regeneration of the English people requires thoroughgoing reform, beginning with nationalisation of the land and the railways. But the Fabians have long ceased to be even amateur socialists. There should be no doubts about that in Germany, because it is not impossible that we shall see Sidney Webb as a member of a Liberal-imperialist ministry, perhaps as president of the Local Government Board. Rosebery has announced his willingness to return to the political arena after five years of retirement. I would not be surprised at all if the programme with which he returns were drafted by Sidney Webb. His whole article looks like an exegesis of the coming Liberal imperialist programme, whose outlines are laid down in the above-mentioned article.

Webb asks: what is England lacking? National efficiency. How can it be attained? Through the implementation of a reform programme containing a national minimum. He quotes a sentence from Mr. Asquith, the ablest follower of Lord Rosebery.[25] The sentence reads: 'Every society is judged and

---

24. Webb 1901, in Brennan 1975, pp. 71–2.
25. [Herbert Henry Asquith, 1st Earl of Oxford and Asquith (1852–1928), was elected to Parliament in 1886 as the Liberal representative for East Fife, in Scotland. He achieved his first significant post in 1892, when he became Home Secretary in the fourth cabinet of Gladstone. He retained his position when Archibald Primrose, 5th Earl of Rosebery, took over in 1894. The Liberals lost power in the 1895 general election and for ten years were in opposition. In 1898, Asquith was offered and turned down the opportunity to lead the Liberal Party. After the Conservative government of Arthur Balfour fell in December of 1905, the Liberal Party formed a new cabinet and

survives, according to the material and moral minimum which it prescribes to its members.'[26] Webb then unveils the contents of the national minimum:

Factory legislation:

> The statesman who is really inspired by the idea of National Efficiency will stump the country in favour of a 'National Minimum' standard of life, below which no employer in any trade in any part of the kingdom shall be allowed to descend. He will elaborate this minimum of humane order – already admitted in principle in a hundred Acts of Parliament – with all the force that eloquence can give to economic science, into a new industrial charter, imperatively required, not merely or even mainly for the comfort of the workers, but absolutely for the success of our industry in competition with the world. With the widespread support which this policy would secure, not only from the Trade-union world and the two million organised co-operators, but also from ministers of religion of all denominations, doctors and nurses, sanitary officers and teachers, Poor Law administrators and modern economists, and even the enlightened employers themselves, he would be able to expand our uneven and incomplete Factory Acts into a systematic and all-embracing code, prescribing for every manual worker employed a minimum of education, sanitation, leisure, and wages as the inviolable starting-point of industrial competition.[27]

Healthy housing:

> Why does not the Local Government Board undertake a systematic harrying up of the backward districts, regularly insisting, for instance, that all those having death-rates above the average of the kingdom shall put themselves in order, improve their drainage, lay on new water supply, and insure, by one means or another, a supply of healthy houses sufficient to enable every family to comply with the formula of 'three rooms and a scullery', as the minimum necessary for breeding an even moderately Imperial race?[28]

Asquith became Chancellor of the Exchequer under Henry Campbell-Bannerman. The Party won a landslide victory in the 1906 general election, but Campbell-Bannerman resigned due to illness in April 1908 and Asquith succeeded him as Prime Minister. He served as Liberal Prime Minister of the United Kingdom from 1908 to 1916.]

26. Webb 1901, in Brennan 1975, p. 73.
27. Webb 1901, in Brennan 1975, pp. 73–4.
28. Webb 1901, in Brennan 1975, pp. 74–5.

Reform of poor relief:

> What an energetic President (of the Local Government Board) would take in hand would be... vigorous insistence on the humane treatment of the aged, the most scientific provision for the sick, and, above all, the best possible rearing of the 'children of the State'.[29]

Education:

> What stands between us and a really effective National Minimum of education is a strong Education Minister who really knows his business, who is backed by his Cabinet against the natural resistance of the Chancellor of the Exchequer.[30]

Good local administration:

> The Local Government Board has necessarily to be always coercing its local authorities to secure the National Minimum.[31]

Miscellaneous reforms:

> The reorganisation of the War Office and the substitution of a system of scientific fighting for our present romantic and incapable 'soldiering'; the energetic rehandling of the Budget (which now yields no more per head than it did a hundred years ago), so as to assert the claims of the State as the sleeping partner in the unearned increment both of urban land values and the huge gains of monopolised industry; the reform of local taxation on the lines of an assessment according to site-value instead of the present penalising of the building and improving of houses; the rescue of our present 'tied' refreshment houses from the tyranny of the brewer, and the adjustment of their number and hours of business to the actual needs of each locality; the reform of the House of Commons by confining all ordinary speeches to a quarter of an hour, and the increased devolution of business to committees – all these are but points in the same policy of National Efficiency.[32]

Webb's programme is not only a 'patching up of old clothes' but also a dangerous attempt to tear apart parliamentary freedoms. Against the congestion

29. Webb 1901, in Brennan 1975, p. 75.
30. Webb 1901, in Brennan 1975, p. 81.
31. Webb 1901, in Brennan 1975, p. 78.
32. Webb 1901, in Brennan 1975, pp. 82–3.

of parliamentary work and the resulting standstill of the parliamentary machine, there is only one democratic means: *home rule and decentralisation*. For Webb's imperialist-bureaucratic mind, the idea is unbearable.

Webb's essay closes with a call to Lord Rosebery to come out of his reclusion and gather around him men able to elaborate and implement that programme. Before these lines appear in the press, we will probably hear Lord Rosebery's reply. It is, moreover, not excluded that already the first months of the coming year will bring us new ministerial combinations that will give him the opportunity of getting closer to Webb's programme. That possibility admittedly depends on the new South-African developments. However, a ministry headed by Rosebery will come sooner or later. England is growing more and more accustomed to the idea of expecting light and leadership from him in the difficult crisis. Whether he will brace himself for reform actions is, of course, a different matter. Until now, Rosebery has appeared as a modern Hamlet: profound, rhythmic monologues and weak willpower.

Chapter Fourteen

'Party Projects in England' (January 1902)

Max Beer

In his essay on 'Party Projects in England', Max Beer turns from the Fabian ideas of Sidney Webb to proposals from John Hobson to create what Beer calls a party of 'socialism *sans doctrines*' – a fusion of socialist, radical and labour groups into a single, centre-left party. Beer's account of the economic ideas behind Hobson's project is in some ways reminiscent of Eduard Bernstein's thinking in *The Preconditions for Socialism*. In particular, Hobson and Bernstein both rejected Marx's labour-theory of value. Bernstein thought Marx could account neither for the distribution of incomes in modern society nor for the growing contribution to prosperity by service industries,[1] while, for Hobson, 'true surplus-value', or 'disguised profit', was simply the excess that any party to a bargain acquired through shrewd negotiating or superior power.

Bernstein reviewed three of Hobson's early works in *Die Neue Zeit: The Evolution of Modern Capitalism, Problems of Poverty* and *The Problem of the Unemployed*.[2] He was enthusiastic about Hobson's ethical convictions, but he disputed his emphasis on

1. Bernstein 1993, pp. 47–56.
2. Hobson 1894, 1891, 1896.

underconsumption.[3] According to Bernstein, Hobson borrowed his theory of underconsumption from Thomas Robert Malthus's explanation of trade depressions. Bernstein denied that capitalism *necessarily* entailed underconsumption, even citing Marx's point that crises typically began when workers acquired a larger share than usual of the commodities intended for consumption.[4] Hobson's remedy for unemployment was to increase the consumption of the masses through taxing unearned income, shortening working time and raising wages. Disagreeing with Hobson in theory, Bernstein saw no reason for opposing 'such a "Progressive" consumption policy', since 'Any way to fight unemployment that does not hinder social progress – and none of Hobson's proposals can be accused of doing that – will not be opposed by Social Democracy.'[5]

This article by Max Beer appeared in *Die Neue Zeit* shortly before publication of Hobson's most famous work, *Imperialism: A Study*. Beer attributes Hobson's sympathies with labour both to his ethical commitments – as distinct from the Fabians – and to his conviction that labour's *bargaining power*, in both political and economic terms, must be strengthened in order to address the maldistribution of income that Hobson would soon cite as a key factor in his explanation of imperialism.[6]

* * *

'Party Projects in England'[7]

Among the different attempts to form new political parties in England, those of John A. Hobson and James Keir Hardie deserve a closer look. They are – like the party project of Sidney Webb – characteristic of many phases of current social and political thought. As we pointed out in a previous article,[8] Webb's endeavours are aimed at uniting the Liberal imperialists – without

3. Bernstein 1894, a review of Hobson 1894.
4. See Marx 1978b, pp. 486–7.
5. Bernstein 1897, a review of Hobson 1896a and Hobson 1891.
6. For an excellent short summary of Hobson's economic theories and moral concerns see Richmond 1978.
7. Beer 1902a. The last section, called 'Keir Hardie's inspirations' (pp. 434–6), has been left out.
8. [Beer 1901b. See Chapter 13.]

doubt the most educated elements in English politics – the trade-unionists and the reformers into a single party in order to replace bankrupt individualism with state-regulation. Hobson seeks the fusion of all socialist, radical and labour elements into a democratic party. Keir Hardie strains after an alliance between socialists, workers, radicals and Irishmen. All these projects have a common principle: socialism *sans doctrines*; a principle that Leroy-Beaulieu learned in his study trip to Australia and then put into circulation for the anti-Marxist politicians of Europe. The antagonism in the socialist camp becomes more and more clear. It finds its sharpest expression in the struggle between *scientific socialism* and *empirical socialism*. The latter is essentially a product of the English conditions and thought of the last twenty years.

Class-struggle and theories of value

According to the best English bourgeois historians of economics, the old economists (Petty, Adam Smith and Ricardo) were chiefly concerned with *production, the accumulation of commercial wealth*, while the new economists (Cairnes, Cliff Leslie, Jevons and Marshall) turned their attention to *distribution, consumption and the satisfaction of human needs*. The old economists examined mostly the inception of commodity-circulation, while the new ones study its conclusion. The former have dehumanised economics, while the latter have humanised it.

Apart from the phrase on humanising, the shift in standpoint is clearly described. It is significant because it reflects the period of overproduction, stagnant markets and crises that opened up after the closing of classical political economy. The question of production was completely solved for the bourgeois world. That was the result of the Industrial Revolution. On the other hand, consumption, the successful conclusion of commodity-circulation, became a problem of greater significance. It threatened the existence of the bourgeois world. The growing contradiction in economic life separated the economic theories. The socialists, as the living expression of menace to the bourgeois world, turned to research the causes of overproduction and crises, developing economic theory accordingly, while the neoclassical bourgeois economists, following the feelings and thoughts of their milieu, abstracted from production and with it necessarily from the labour-theory of value, which is intimately connected with production and its theoretical expression – classical political economy. They proclaimed consumption to be the main object of economic science and, instead of the value-theory of production, introduced the price-theory of consumption. Political economy dwindled into a psychology of consumers.

Böhm-Bawerk emphasised forcefully that Marx was one of the few people who did not accept unquestioningly the labour-theory of value but subjected it to an examination. That is nothing but remarkable. Marx did not shrink back from the contradictions of economic life. These contradictions were indeed his living element. As a revolutionary thinker, he had to begin with production and its labour-theory of value. Analysing it, he found the key to understanding economic life as it has manifested itself since the end of classical political economy, and with it also the possibility of integrating the particular critical results of his socialist predecessors with developing economic theory. The theory of value showed him the economic contradiction between exploitation and acquisition; in overproduction and crises, it showed him the revolutionary tendency towards a new economic form and towards the abolition of economic contradictions. In the theory of value, he discovered the real basis of the theory of class-struggles, and in the economic tendencies he found the political goal of class-struggles – socialism. Hence the huge, sometimes excessive mental energies he dedicated to the theory of value. And, even if, like other theories, it does not manifest itself directly in practice, if in economic life value appears as production-price, we still have got, on the whole, after the research of production and consumption, a deep, systematic view of modern civilisation; we have discovered the source of profit, the origin of capital and poverty, and identified the necessity of creating and educating a social-revolutionary workers' party. In short, with the help of the theory of value, we arrived at scientific socialism, while the marginal-utility theory, which, at bottom, says that prices depend on the costs of production, remained totally isolated and fruitless.

How widely apart both theories remain in their theoretical and practical consequences! If we ask the supporters of consumers' psychology about the causes of social dynamics, about the mainsprings of economic life, they refer us with an inarticulate hint to empirical facts: there are poor people and rich people. The political consequences of the marginal-utility theory must logically lead to the formation of a poor people's party, a party of improvement and justice. The creation of a social-revolutionary party resting on the class-struggle loses any *raison d'être*. After all, there are unionists who own shares and house-owners burdened with mortgages, well-paid workers and bankrupt businessmen. And, in fact, the supporters of consumers' psychology instinctively abhor the watchwords: class-struggle, value-theory, workers' party, and scientific socialism, because they belong to a completely different world-view. They demand an association with all the politically and economically progressive elements. Progress, movement, and reform are, for them, solid, tangible and comprehensible things; the final goal can have no meaning for them because it finds no support in the marginal-utility theory. It is characteristic, for instance, that Jevons traces crises back to sun-spots. The marginal-utility theorist does not see the great, pervasive contradiction between capital and labour, but, rather, a series of disconnected particular social questions in whose solution all the poor and the just can work together harmoniously. Such socialism is tailor-made for Anglo-Saxon liberals, democrats and nonconformists. If we add to this the social, political and spiritual conditions that we described in a previous article,[9] we have the programme: socialism *sans doctrines*, empirical socialism *contra* scientific socialism. Altogether: marginal-utility theory, party of the poor, and progress *contra* theory of value, class-conscious workers' party and socialist goal. The former grows out capitalist embarrassment and the analysis of consumption; the latter springs from revolutionary knowledge and the investigation of production.

Hobson's teachings and politics

John A. Hobson is a major publicist and one of the most fruitful economic and political writers of our time.[10] Although akin to the social politician Sidney Webb, one should not include Hobson among the Fabians. The difference

9. [Beer 1901b. See Chapter 13.]

10. His major works are: *Problems of Poverty* (Hobson 1891), *The Evolution of Modern Capitalism* (Hobson 1894), *The Problem of the Unemployed: An Enquiry and an Economic Policy* (Hobson 1896a), *John Ruskin: Social Reformer* (Hobson 1898), *The Economics of Distribution* (Hobson 1900a), *The Social Problem* (Hobson 1901a), *The War in South Africa* (Hobson 1900c), *Psychology of Jingoism* (Hobson 1901c), 'Economics of Imperialism' (a series of articles in *Speaker*, 1901) [Hobson 1901d, 1901e, 1901f, 1901g, 1901h, 1901i]. In addition, he published numerous articles and brochures, and was active as a speaker in the ethical movement. [Hobson's books are available online at the Marxist Internet Archive.]

between them is less political than economic. Disappointed with the events of the last two years in English life,[11] the most prominent leaders of the Fabian Society turned, by way of Nietzsche, to imperialism, and saw in the suppression of universal freedom the means to a regeneration of their people. By contrast, Hobson remained loyal to his democratic principles and, driven by a deep ethical conviction, sees England's remedy in the curtailment of imperialism, which he considers a sinister conspiracy of international high finance. The economic views of Hobson and Webb are rather close, although their starting point was different. The leaders of the Fabian Society were awakened to systematic economic thinking by Marx. But since, in England, the class-struggle in its political form did not exist, they logically threw the Marxist theory of value overboard and accepted the marginal-utility theory of Jevons and its modified form by Marshall.

Hobson, on the contrary, was from the very beginning under the influence of the new economists, although he also read Marx's *Capital*. The chapters on the effects of modern technique on the workers seem to have appealed especially to him, and he occupies himself with them in his work *The Evolution of Modern Capitalism*. An economist by profession, he could not be satisfied with the marginal-utility theory. After long research, he came to the conclusion that it is only a theory of the determination of prices by production-costs. It could therefore give him almost no information on the problem of poverty, with which he was deeply concerned as an ethicist. In his *Problems of Poverty*, there is indeed very little theory. He rather accepted poverty in its different forms as a fact, showing its effects on social life without, however, making an earnest attempt to determine the ultimate causes of poverty. He therefore did not occupy himself with the workers as a class, but rather with the less-skilled and unskilled workers, and with empirical questions of detail.[12] His *Evolution of Modern Capitalism* likewise belongs to descriptive economics.

---

11. [A reference to the second Boer War (11 October 1899–31 May 1902).]

12. His conception of the notion of poverty deserves to be quoted: 'To give a clear meaning and a measure of poverty is the first requisite.... But since dependence upon wages for the support of life will be found closely related to the question of poverty, it is convenient to throw some preliminary light on the measure of poverty, by figures bearing on the general industrial condition of the wage-earning class. To measure poverty we must first measure wealth. What is the national income, and how is it divided? These will naturally arise as the first questions.... If by poverty is meant the difference between felt wants and the power to satisfy them, there is more poverty than ever. The income of the poor has grown, but their desires and needs have grown more rapidly.

Hobson first set out his own theory of value (which also claims to be a theory of prices and to explain the inception and conclusion of the circulation of goods), in his strongly theoretical *Economics of Distribution*. The title is already significant. He makes a significant concession to Marx but soon gets lost in a theory of mutual cheating, which significantly should also be capital-forming. Hobson says:

> Karl Marx was right in his insistence upon the fundamental importance of recognising the idea of surplus value. He was wrong in regarding the surplus value as exclusively the product of labour-power taken by capital in the process of bargaining for the sale of labour-power. He failed to explain why labour, alone of the factors, should be conceived as making all the 'value' of material marketable goods. He failed also to explain what the nature of the power was by which capital took the surplus value made by labour; and, finally, he failed to show how any individual capitalist who took it was not compelled to relinquish it under the stress of competition with his fellow-capitalists.
>
> The surplus value here described issues, not merely from one class of bargains (between capital and labour power), but from every class; it represents the economic might of the stronger in every market.[13]

Hobson's objections only show that he read the first volume of *Capital* partially, and the other two not at all. The objections have, however, deep causes. It is the theory of class-struggles, so deeply bound up with the theory of value, that does not allow him to reach a full understanding of the latter. The same reasons led to its rejection by the Fabians. Hobson's ethics are perhaps also a significant factor in this regard. He continues:

> Surplus value, then, is not something which emerges in the dealings of capital with labour or of land with labour; it emerges in every competitive bargain and adheres to the stronger bargainer; it is only because in modern industry the owner of capital, land or business capacity is normally found to be the stronger bargainer, that he obtains most of the surplus[14]…. Thus

(Hence the growth of a conscious class hatred, the "growing animosity of the poor against the rich", which Mr. Barnett notes in the slums of Whitechapel.)' Hobson 1899, p. 28.

13. [Hobson 1900a, pp. 353–4.]
14. [Hobson 1900a, p. 357.]

> emerges the true surplus value, derived not from some vague, unintelligible idea of tyranny, but from the various hindrances to perfect equality of bargaining-power in the owners of the various factors of production.[15]

Different theories and practical proposals are classified according to how they intend to remove those hindrances. The liberals believed that the goal could be achieved through a *laisser-faire* policy. Since the free play of forces proved inadequate, the stronger must be allowed to pocket the surplus-value, which Hobson calls 'disguised profit', in order then to take part of it away from them through taxation for the good of society. If this taxation-policy is ineffective, as in the case of great monopolies, then they must be nationalised in the interest of economic progress.

The development of this theory of value reads like an extremely feeble popularisation of the misunderstood Marxist theory of value. The haggling and mutual cheating, which the new English economists with so much boasting call 'bargaining', was already known to old Adam Smith as the 'higgling of the market'.[16] But what, in Smith, Ricardo and Marx is objectively determined, the new economists regard as subjective, psychological strivings and operations. Bargains and agreements can distribute profits and determine prices but cannot generate profits – a fact that, to be sure, is not at all easy to recognise under the rule of overproduction and general competition. With the tendency to eliminate individual competitors, with the concentration of production and trade, with the creation of trusts and department-stores, people should finally stop speaking about 'bargaining'. The trusts determine in secret meetings not only production-prices but also retail-prices, and not according to the narrow law of supply and demand but according to the well-known principle: 'what the trade will bear', what the public is able to pay. Under such conditions there is no longer elbowroom for 'bargaining' and consumers' psychology. These are, theoretically speaking, obsolete viewpoints.

Only one class of 'bargaining' remains: between organised capital and the organised proletariat over the mass of surplus-value. And the English capitalists now set out to wipe out that 'bargaining'. That is why Hobson was thrust

15. [Hobson 1900a, p. 360.]

16. ['(Value) is adjusted...not by any accurate measure, but by the higgling and bargaining of the market, according to that sort of rough equality which, though not exact, is sufficient for carrying on the business of common life.' Smith 1776, p. 77.]

into the arena of labour politics. The crisis in trade-unionism, created by the judicial decision of the House of Lords, prompted him to step forward with two articles containing practical political proposals. One of them appeared in *New Age* and the other in *Echo*. Here are some quotations from the latter:

> What is the question that forced itself on the leaders of the labour-movement in the Anglo-Saxon world? The steel-strike in America and the subsequent great strike in England were surely reminders to the thinking workers of America and their bourgeois supporters about the conflict between employers and workers, which in the Australian colonies was already understood. A series of union-struggles, led according to the English model, which found their climax in the great spinners' strike of 1890, showed to the Australian colonists the hopelessness of the organised worker vis-à-vis organised capital. Since then all trade-unions over there have become political and employ their votes and political power to attain goals which they could not reach by purely union-methods. Through their direct parliamentary representation, as well as through organised pressure on the liberal party in New Zealand, they have made much greater steps towards achieving the eight-hour day, minimum wages, old-age pensions and the abolition of sweatshops than they could have made in forty years through costly and grinding union-struggles. In the United States, trade-unionism can have no real prospects of success. Already weak and spasmodic in action during ordinary times, American unionism can accomplish little in such a large country, with its different races, interests and ideas, against the united forces of the ablest and best organised capitalists of the world.... The Australian remedy is not fit for the Americans.... The rule of organised capitalism over politics is there as absolute as its rule over economics. According to very moderate observers, the American impasse can only be broken through a workers' revolution.[17]

Hobson then discusses the situation in England, as created by the decision of the House of Lords in the case of Quinn v. Leatham,[18] and comes to this conclusion:

---

17. [Retranslated from the German version.]

18. [In 1901, in the case of Quinn v. Leatham, it was ruled illegal to strike or threaten to strike in order to press an employer to dismiss non-union labour. Leatham, a butcher, had refused to replace his employees with union-members. Quinn and other union-organisers threatened to strike at the business of one of Leatham's customers unless he stopped doing business with Leatham. The customer acceded to this demand,

> The pessimistic judgement of Frederic Harrison is in close conformity with the facts. Attempts to escape from the net of laws made by the judges cannot succeed because the ultimate weapon of capital is not law but lawsuits. The inevitable consequence of this volte-face must be: labour politics.... There was never a time riper than this. The old Liberal Party is burnt out to the core.

Hobson therefore summons the ILP and the SDF to lay aside for the time being the final goal in order to build the core of a reform party for workers and radicals – a party of 'socialism *sans doctrines*'. The common programme would be: high taxes on urban and rural landed property, nationalisation of railways and mines as well as of all monopolies harmful to the public welfare, extension of municipal socialism, housing reform, old-age pensions, industrial legislation, decentralisation, home rule, and limitation of the power of the House of Lords.

causing financial loss to Leatham, who filed suit and won damages. The House of Lords upheld this result and ruled that unions should be liable in tort for helping workers to go on strike for better pay and conditions. This riled workers so much that it led to the creation of the British Labour Party.]

Chapter Fifteen

'Imperialist Policy' (December 1902)

Max Beer

In this article, Max Beer continues to explore the origins of imperialism, turning from British domestic issues to the forces behind capital's worldwide drive to acquire and control new territories. Beer's account of imperialism is succinct and perceptive. In the first paragraph, he states his theme that modern productive forces have outgrown the boundaries of existing national states (an idea that Kautsky and Trotsky later came to when anticipating a United States of Europe). He notes that capital-exports are becoming more important than commodity-exports, and, in his analysis of world politics, he cites Germany's late arrival in the competition for territories as the principal destabilising factor. Relating imperialist rivalries to domestic circumstances, he concludes that, in all its manifestations, imperialism 'represents an attempt of the bourgeois classes to escape from socialism'.

* * *

'Imperialist Policy'[1]

The rapid growth of the productive forces beyond the boundaries of capitalist markets is the basic fact of our time. The capitalist countries produce more than they consume. Riches grow more quickly than the possibility of transforming them into capital.

The distinguishing *economic* features of this period are: a) the outflow of capital towards foreign, backward lands, and the return flow of dividends and interest to the home-country – hence the apparently unfavourable balance of trade of the capitalist countries (the growth of imports over exports); b) the growing domination of finance over production; c) the concentration of production in syndicates and trusts; d) the feverish hunt for consumers; e) the incipient theoretical attention to the significance of the home market. To this should be added in Europe a secondary but no less important fact: the growing supremacy of the United States in iron- and coal-production, by which European industry feels threatened.

The distinguishing *political* features of this period are: a) the drive to expand the national economic area and create state-federations; and b) the conquest of overseas colonies, dependencies and spheres of influence.

Thus congestion of capitals, concentration of the most important instruments of production, and the search for consumers constitute the economic basis of our time, while imperialism is its bourgeois-political superstructure.

* * *

Imperialism drives the national states towards: 1) a broadening of the national state in a union of states, and 2) an overseas world policy.

[As for the first point,] the capitalist national state,[2] which developed through the absorption of local, independent organisations, now shows the

1. Beer 1902b.
2. The national state began to develop with the decline of the middle ages. It was built upon the ruins of serfdom, the autonomous municipalities and the guilds, as well as in struggle against the universal church and the universal monarchy. Its economic policy was mercantilism: prohibition of bullion-exports, protective tariffs, the favourable monetary balance (the strong preponderance of exports over imports), and colonial policy (which was entirely aimed at the creation of a favourable monetary balance and at the promotion of metropolitan production). The material basis of the national state was the *development of capitalist production* and with it also of the bourgeoisie as the carrier of that mode of production. See Kautsky 1888 [English version: Kautsky

tendency to enclose all the surrounding and culturally related nations and countries. The productive forces unchained within the national state need more space. This is the prosaic meaning of the racial fantasies about Anglo-Saxondom, pan-Germanism and a Latin union. England strives for a federation with Canada, Australasia and South Africa; Germany, for a customs-union with Holland, Denmark and Austria-Hungary; and France, for a union with Italy and Spain. The United States was instinctively formed in that way and is justly called the imperial republic.

* * *

The second characteristic of imperialism is the drive towards colonies, protectorates and spheres of influence, in short towards a world policy. Only those states that engage in a world policy are great powers. The essence of the world policy can be best understood through a comparison with the national state and mercantilist colonial policy. The latter served above all the demands of production in the mother-country, the creation of a favourable monetary balance, the largest possible exports of metropolitan commodities to foreign lands and the smallest possible imports from foreign countries. The world policy has other purposes: it serves above all the interests of investment-capital and loan-capital through the opening up of territories for surplus-capitals, the extraction of tribute from foreign races, and the creation of a 'favourable' balance of trade. It further serves to dispose of the surplus intelligence and energies of the ruling classes, and finally to extract raw materials, especially iron, coal and bullion. The European world policy towards the Far East is above all aimed at the mineral riches of China: the European countries hope that those riches will help them hold their ground against American competition. The development of Chinese mineral wealth by Germany or England would easily unsettle the industrial supremacy of the United States, which rests on iron and coal; that is the reason for the American policy of peace towards China.[3] Hence also, to a certain extent, the impossibility of the alliance with the United States so ardently desired by Germany. On

1927]; Mehring 1893; Mehring *Die polnische Frage* and Karl Marx *Die Bilanz der preussischen Revolution*, in Mehring 1902, Vol. III: Von Mai 1848 bis Oktober 1850.

3. [A reference to the so-called 'open-door' policy in China, by which America opposed China's partition into spheres of influenced separated by tariff-barriers.]

the other hand, the United States cares very little about a Russian occupation of Manchuria because it will be a long time before Russia has the industrial spirit of enterprise necessary to develop China economically.

The wars of the mercantilist period were aimed at facilitating sales. In [modern imperialist] world policy the sale of commodities plays a secondary role, because the export of commodities to non-capitalist countries is relatively small and can by no means cover the expenses of the world policy. The English radicals and the German liberals, who believe they can fight against the world policy with the help of export-statistics, have no idea of its current meaning. The mercantilist colonial policy strove to occupy effectively the conquered overseas areas and to rule directly over the entire population. The financial world policy contents itself with controlling the native rulers. The rulers and governments of China, Siam, Afghanistan, Persia, Turkey and North Africa lie under the always vigilant control of the imperialist classes of Europe. The Asiatic and African rulers are trained to deceive and exploit their own peoples in the interests of the Europeans, and to repress any attempt at a [national] regeneration. Only Japan and Abyssinia have – thanks to their military capabilities – preserved their independence and developed at present as national states. In world policy, the fleet and the army are the only signs of the maturity of nations. But now, European imperialism, which broke out with instinctive violence, has robbed most Asian and African nations of the opportunity to reach that maturity. China may perhaps still have some hope of becoming independent if it lets itself be guided by Japan.[4]

4. [It is hard to recall today, after the atrocities of Japanese imperialism in China during the 1930s and the Second World War, that Japan was seen as a liberating force in Asia at the beginning of the twentieth century. In 1922, Karl Radek wrote in a commentary on the Versailles Treaty: 'When in 1905, Tsarist Russia was beaten by young Japanese Imperialism, an exultation caught hold of the various sections of the yellow race, who were regarded as a sort of human manure, but who desired to be regarded as a part of mankind. Their exultation sprang from the fact that the victory of military, semi-feudal and capitalist Japan over the Tsarist government was a victory of the yellow man over the white "superman". This victory was the starting point of the revolutionary movement in China, where, after the victory of the Japanese, a 300 million-strong population said, "I shall likewise be victorious." It gave a new impetus to the revolutionary movement of India, where over 300 million people are striving for freedom. From that victory sprang the revolutionary surge, the waves of which are rolling forth and, before they reach the shore, are increased and strengthened by the rising waves behind them.' See Radek 1922, p. 33.]

Japan is presently making remarkable attempts to turn the Far East into a yellow empire. All other states (Siam, Afghanistan, Persia, Asiatic Turkey, Egypt, Tripoli and Morocco) are bound to Europe, and their destinies will be decided in the foreign offices of Europe if capitalism still has the upper hand for a long time.

The dynamics of world policy have already achieved certain regularity. The only disturbing element is Germany. The course of all the other great powers can be foreseen with a certain degree of certainty. *England's* policy is the status quo. The conquest of the Boer republic was the keystone of the British Empire. It can absorb no more and therefore wants a tranquil digestion, a development in Asia and Africa as peaceful as possible. *The United States* has its Monroe Doctrine for America; it seeks further to control the Pacific Ocean and have a safe commercial intercourse with the East. *It ultimately regards itself as heir of the British Empire*, for whom it will therefore stand up in a moment of danger. The United Sates already has a major secret influence on British world policy. *France* aspires, as leader of the Latin peoples, to possession of the entire Western half of the Mediterranean. It intercedes in Tripoli on behalf of Italy and in Morocco on behalf of Spain. That is the reason for its great expenditures on the naval stations of Biserta [Benzert], Ajaccio and Toulon. In Asia, France sides with Russia against England. Simultaneously with Russia's accelerating drive to Northern India via Afghanistan, France is driving from Indochina to Burma via Siam. By the same token, France will be on Russia's side in the conflict between Russia and Germany over Syria and Persia. *Russia* regards Asia as its hinterland and strives to possess the Bosporus and the Dardanelles in order to secure the coastline of the Black Sea and the capacity to develop Southern Russia into an industrial centre. This economic motive is associated with historic-sentimental ones about the conquest of Constantinople, making it more than ever one of the ruling principles of Russia's world policy. With the further economic development of Southern Russia, the old oriental question will enter its final, decisive phase.

On the other hand, nothing certain can be said about *Germany's* world-policy. Its glance rambled over South America, South Africa, Turkey, Persia and China, without finding a firm resting point. On the horizon of world-policy, Germany appears as a comet among fixed stars. Hence the uneasiness it calls forth everywhere. In the course of the last decade, it has thrice changed the direction of its world policy: from about 1890 to 1895, it was Anglophile;

from 1895 to 1900, it sought an alignment with the overseas policy of the Dual Alliance and was Anglophobe.[5] It went along with Russia and France against Japan, stirred France into a conflict with England over Egypt, and supported Russia in China. In 1900, a new period began. Germany's world policy drew nearer to Anglo-Saxondom. Only at one point did the clouds of Germany's world policy condense and begin to assume definite shape: in *Asia Minor*. From then on, German world policy started to have a direction.

On the oriental question, Germany is beginning to take the position that England had until approximately 1880. It will become the watchman of Turkey's territorial integrity. It will therefore clash with Russia on this point and be forced to take the side of England in Asia. The German railway from the Bosporus to Kuwait in the Persian Gulf [the so-called Baghdad Railway] is a Turkish defensive barrier, guarded by Germany against Russia and France. Through the railway concession to Wilhelm II, Abdul Hamid proved to be a great diplomat. German world policy would be covered with ridicule if Germany were to abandon Turkey in a moment of danger. Moreover, Austria-Hungary acquired a new significance for Germany. Its territorial integrity has become a condition for the success of German diplomacy. In the same way, Austrian influence on the Balkan Peninsula, or even the Austrian occupation of Macedonia, have become necessary for Germany to secure access to the ports of the Adriatic and Aegean seas and to rule over Asia Minor. This oriental policy will bring Germany into a certain contradiction with Italy, which lays claims to Albania. On the other hand, it is in England's interest that Germany should gain a foothold in the Orient: first, because in that way the world policy of Germany will be diverted away from the British possessions and into Turkey, where England has no vital interests to defend; secondly, because England will then receive the help of a European great power in its struggle against Russia. The English interest in Germany's oriental policy will lead sooner or later to a swap of Cyprus against some German-African possession, because ever since France secured the Mediterranean for itself by means of the naval stations in Biserta, Ajaccio and Toulon, this route lost its

5. [The Dual Alliance (*Zweibund*), also called Franco-Russian Alliance, was a political and military pact that developed between France and Russia from friendly contacts in 1891 to a secret treaty in 1894; it became one of the basic European alignments of the pre-World War I era.]

strategic significance for England. Egypt could just as well be defended from the Red Sea.

* * *

It is more difficult to determine the policy that could lead to a transformation of the national state into a union of states. To all appearances, this process can only take place with the help of liberal principles. Where liberalism is absent as a living factor, the imperial-state tendencies will hardly assert themselves. The imperial union cannot be established by the same means that welded together the national state. The nation-state was based on the army, because its mission was to centralise the internal regions. The imperial union must lean upon the navy because it must have a wide seacoast and preserve commercial intercourse with the overseas protectorates. Commercial ships and warships, commercial harbours with nearby military harbours, maritime coaling stations and bases, in short, sea-power is the instrument of imperialism. Sea-power is less dangerous for popular liberty than the army. The national state needed military and police automata and bureaucrats; the imperial union needs men with free initiative, with great executive capabilities; it needs organisers and administrators. Such men do not thrive in a police and bureaucratic state, where young people's backbones are broken early. Great administrative talents only develop in a free political climate and in countries with autonomous local administrations. No emperor, even if he were an organisational genius of the first order, could realise his plans without the help of an imperialist nation, that is to say, a nation accustomed to governing. The national state, whose economic basis was the development of production, needs docile proletarians; the imperial union, whose economic basis is the widening of consumption, must have a prosperous, well-paid population as well as a quite free working class. Finally, the tariff-system of the national state was intended for the defence of production, while the aim of the tariff-system of the developed capitalist countries is the defence of the home market or, as in England, the delimitation of the imperial union.

Germany presently stands at the crossroads between those two state-forms. Imperialist researchers therefore regard it with deep theoretical interest. An extension of the national state into a central-European customs-union will not take place if the interests of the landowners, the absolutist traditions of Prussian royalty and the reactionary factors of a bygone period prevail. Germany would thereby close its market to the agricultural products of Hungary, Galicia and Romania, that is to say, it would shut itself off through a high tariff-wall from access to Trieste and Salonica and therefore to Asia Minor. Then Holland and Denmark would be thrown by German reaction into the arms of the Dual Alliance.

In the United States, internal expansion always meant freedom.[6] The Constitution was automatically carried over to the territories. On the other hand, its overseas policy, which it entered into in 1898, is as unfree as the overseas policy of the Europeans. The Supreme Court in Washington ruled in its decisions from 1900–1 that the Constitution could not follow the flag everywhere. This means an almost complete break with the political past of the United States. England behaved likewise. By far the largest part of the population in the overseas possessions of Great Britain stands outside the imperial union of the Anglo-Saxon race, founded on freedom.

Incidentally, for England imperialism means a regression. The economic facts that today drive the capitalist countries to imperialism were already noticeable in England after Waterloo. The task of the national state – development of production – was already solved. But, instead of turning to imperialism and expanding further the national state, England removed all national barriers and regarded the entire world as a single economic territory. That was the meaning of free trade, as elaborated by David Ricardo in the seventh chapter of his *Principles*.[7] English economic policy no longer turned on the favourable balance of trade, which, in the mercantilist period, had led to wars. Ricardo believed that, without state-interference, production would divide itself over the entire world in such a way that each nation would produce, in its own interest, only such commodities as it was best fitted to produce by nature and education. Each nation would consequently produce cheaply, that is to say, with the least possible expenditure of labour-power, and buy cheaply, i.e., it would only trade in commodities for whose production it needed a greater [domestic] expenditure of labour-power [than required abroad]. Nations would in that way mutually benefit [from commercial exchange and the international division of labour].

---

6. [Max Beer, like Kautsky, had a blind spot for European settler-colonialism. They probably took this idea from the English progressives (the so-called 'New Liberals') such as John A. Hobson.]
7. [Ricardo 1821, Chapter VII: On Foreign Trade, pp. 131–61.]

Mercantilists thought that someone's profit was someone else's loss. The advocates of free trade believed that trade brings profits to all parties concerned. Mercantilism stood for jealousy and war; free trade, on the contrary, for respect and peace. With mercantilism, England also gave up the principle of the balance of power, the so-called European equilibrium, and recognised the right of every nation to an independent development and *home rule*. This peculiar period lasted a few generations until the closing decades of the nineteenth century. Since then, a slow reversal has been taking place in all areas. England returned to state-demarcation of an economic territory; it created the Anglo-Saxon Empire and surrounded it with low customs-barriers; it resisted *home rule* [in Ireland] (this question gave the death-blow to the Liberal Party); it rehabilitated the principle of the balance of power (naval armaments, army-reform and the alliance with Japan); it restricted popular education and the right of association (ecclesiastical school-laws and judicial functions of the House of Lords). In order to complete this regression, the professors of political economy are now busy refuting Ricardo's theory of international trade.

* * *

Let us sum up: modern production has reached a point where its further expansion is inhibited by the narrow barriers of consumption. The productive forces drive towards a state-expansion of the economic area. Politics become imperialist. Imperialism breaks down into two parts: a liberal imperial-union policy and a barbaric overseas world policy. The national state can be transformed into an imperial union only with the help of liberalism. At bottom, imperialism represents an attempt of the bourgeois classes to escape from socialism, because the economic basis on which modern imperialism rests also offers the possibility of liberating the working class. Modern imperialism and scientific socialism are two class-expressions of the same economic facts, but, for the time being, the latter will be exploited in the interest of the class that holds political power.

Chapter Sixteen

'Imperialist Literature' (December 1906)

Max Beer

This article by Max Beer was originally a review of four books, from which we have extracted his comments on John Hobson. As previous articles by Max Beer in the collection indicate, he disagreed with Hobson's economic theory, although, he admired his ethical concerns on the matter of income-distribution. After an intensive review of the SPD, periodicals, this is the only reference that Hans-Christoph Schröder could find to Hobson's book on imperialism in the German socialist press.[1] As we stated in the main introduction to this book, Hobson's *Imperialism* quite probably attracted Lenin's attention during the period of his London exile, which coincided with the publication of the first edition of the book (1902).[2] All the quotations from Hobson's *Imperialism* were taken from Part I: The Economics of Imperialism, Chapter V: The Economic Taproot of Imperialism.

* * *

1. Schröder 1968.
2. Krupskaya 1959, Part I: Life in London, 1902–3.

'Imperialist Literature'[3]

John A. Hobson, Imperialism: A Study, *London: James Nisbet, 1902*

Imperialism is one of the basic tendencies of contemporary life. It is impossible to know from the French and German writings what this tendency consists of. One is treated by them to all sorts of philosophical and biological speculations about the will to power, about the instinct of sovereignty, about ruling races or simply with outbursts of brutality, but one can learn nothing definite from them about the meaning of imperialism, its practical-political significance and its social sources. That means that, in those countries, an imperialist practice is lacking. For instance Seillière, an otherwise gifted and very well-read writer, instead of offering us an explanation of the political stage known as imperialism gives us a history of the psychology of the lust for power.[4] That is just as little an answer to our question as, for instance, the history of aesthetic sense can be an answer to the question: Where did the Gothic style originate and where did it survive longest?

In England, where people do not speculate about imperialism but practise it, the term is defined more or less as follows: imperialism is the expansion of the political power of the original or national state to other countries. As long as the ancient city-state waged war, or the modern national state wages war, just to strengthen its borders and consolidate itself, one cannot speak of imperialism. Those are only patriotic or national strivings, which belong to the preliminary stages of imperialism. The highest stage of imperialism is overseas expansion, the combination of land- and sea-power. The basic distinguishing mark of imperialism is, therefore, the expansion of the original state beyond the city-boundaries (as in antiquity) and beyond its national boundaries (in the modern era). [...]

Only when imperialism is brought down from the philosophical or biological clouds to the political and economic ground, and regarded as a definite historical stage of development, can the term be understood and made use of.

* * *

3. Beer 1906.
4. Seillière 1903–8.

Hobson's book is one of the best studies of imperialism. It is, admittedly, often written from the point of view of a humanitarian morality, but its author is also a politico-economic writer of significance and therefore pays sufficient attention to the historic and economic elements.

The first thing that draws attention in modern imperialism is the number of imperialist powers competing with each other. Those states first entered the imperial arena in the last thirty years. Since 1871, England has brought under its rule in Europe, Africa and Asia an area of 4,754,000 square-miles, with 88 million inhabitants: in Europe, Cyprus; in Africa, Zanzibar and Pemba, the Eastern-African protectorate, Uganda, Somaliland, British Central Africa, Zambia, Ashanti, Egypt, the shores of the Nile, Sudan, Griqualand West, Zululand, Botswana, Rhodesia, Transvaal, and the Orange Free State; in Asia, Hong Kong, Weihaiwei, Socotra, Upper Burma, Beluchistan, Sikkim, Rajputana, Burma, Dschama, and Kashmir, the Malaysian protectorates, North-Borneo, Sarawak, British New Guinea, and the Fiji Islands. In order to understand better the significance of the conquests made in the last thirty years, let us add that the area of the German Reich amounts to approximately 209,000 square-miles, while the area of the United Kingdom (Great Britain and Ireland) is only 121,000 square-miles.

Since 1884, Germany has acquired colonies in Africa, Asia and the Pacific Ocean with an area of 1,027,820 square-miles and a population of 13.5 million people. Since 1899, there has been a standstill in German expansion. Since 1880 France has once again had an active colonial policy. In that period, it has acquired African possessions almost three times as large as those of Germany. Italy has colonies in Africa with an area of around 188,500 square-miles. The United States of America has 172,000 square-miles [of colonies] in America and Asia. Japan acquired Formosa [Taiwan], Korea and half of Sakhalin.

We are therefore dealing with a universal phenomenon. Where does it come from? According to Hobson, the economic taproot of imperialism lies in the economic conditions of our times [characterised by underconsumption and oversaving].

> Over-production in the sense of an excessive manufacturing plant, and surplus capital which cannot find sound investments within the country, force Great Britain, Germany, Holland, France to place larger and larger portions of their economic resources outside the area of their present political domain, and then stimulate a policy of political expansion so as to take

> in the new areas. The economic sources of this movement are laid bare by periodic trade-depressions due to an inability of producers to find adequate and profitable markets for what they can produce. The Majority Report of the Commission upon the Depression of Trade in 1885 put the matter in a nut-shell. 'That, owing to the nature of the times, the demand for our commodities does not increase at the same rate as formerly; that our capacity for production is consequently in excess of our requirements, and could be considerably increased at short notice; that this is due partly to the competition of the capital which is being steadily accumulated in the country.'[5]

And that applies to all the capitalist countries. Hobson continues:

> Every improvement of methods of production, every concentration of ownership and control, seems to accentuate the tendency. As one nation after another enters the machine economy and adopts advanced industrial methods, it becomes more difficult for its manufacturers, merchants, and financiers to dispose profitably of their economic resources, and they are tempted more and more to use their governments in order to secure for their particular use some distant undeveloped country by annexation and protection.[6]

But is this expansion absolutely necessary? Are there no other means of bringing about harmony between supply and demand?

> It is not industrial progress that demands the opening up of new markets and areas of investment, but mal-distribution of consuming power which prevents the absorption of commodities and capital within the country [...] Many have carried their analysis so far as to realise the absurdity of spending half our financial resources in fighting to secure foreign markets at times when hungry mouths, ill-clad backs, ill-furnished houses indicate countless unsatisfied material wants among our own population [...] The most convincing condemnation of the current economy is conveyed in the difficulty which producers everywhere experience in finding consumers for their products: a fact attested by the prodigious growth of classes of agents and middlemen, the multiplication of every sort of advertising, and the general increase of the distributive classes. Under a sound economy the pressure would be reversed: the growing wants of progressive societies would be a

5. Hobson 1902b, p. 86.
6. Ibid.

> constant stimulus to the inventive and operative energies of producers, and would form a constant strain upon the powers of production.[7]

The best means against imperialism are thus 'Trade-unionism and Socialism'.[8] But the politicians who reject those methods have recourse to protective tariffs and imperial federations in order to secure for the local capitalists a wider and safer market and to continue with the old system within this area. Modern imperialism is thus bound up with the protectionist system.

7. Hobson 1902b, pp. 91–2.
8. Hobson 1902b, p. 96. [The complete sentence reads: 'Trade Unionism and Socialism are thus the natural enemies of Imperialism for they take away from the "imperialist" classes the surplus incomes which form the economic stimulus of Imperialism.']

Chapter Seventeen

'An Essay on Imperialism' (April 1904)

Paul Louis

In this essay, Paul Louis expresses more systematically the conception of imperialism that he first set out in his article of March 1899, 'Anglo-Saxon Imperialism'.[1] Here, Louis views imperialism as a worldwide phenomenon, entailing the threat of war not only in colonial regions but also within Europe itself. Attributing imperialism to underconsumption – 'production surpasses, everywhere and always, the demand for commodities', and 'overproduction has become inevitable and permanent' – Louis enunciates essentially the same economic theme as John Hobson. Unlike Hobson, however, he argues that, ultimately, one or the other, imperialism or socialism, must triumph, for the contradiction between them is the defining characteristic of the modern age.

* * *

1. See Chapter Four.

'An Essay on Imperialism'[2]

Imperialism is a general phenomenon of our epoch. It is one of the characteristic features of the beginning of the twentieth century, and very few peoples have been able to escape its action.

The world is currently going through the era of imperialism just as it previously suffered the crises of liberalism, protectionism, and colonialism; just as it experienced the collective effort of nationalities; and just as it witnessed in the last ten years the universal spread and increasing growth of socialism. Besides, all these elements, all these aspects of the life of mankind, are closely linked, and imperialism and socialism to a very large extent constitute the fundamental opposition of our age. To lay down this contradiction practically amounts to defining the essential principles of both.

Just as socialism is spreading in both old and new countries – in America, where formidable industrial equipment creates unprecedented production and overproduction, and where hundreds of thousands of proletarians are concentrated in the service of a single enterprise; in Russia, where the first strikes are taking place; and in the Balkan states, where it is still little more than a hypothesis – so imperialism also triumphs indiscriminately in England and the United States, in Japan and Russia, in Germany, France and Italy. Like socialism, imperialism is also more or less coherent depending upon conditions, its energy being greatest where industry is mature and where it can gather up pre-existing aspirations and link them to its cause.

Imperialism appears everywhere as capitalism's supreme effort to preserve its wealth, political domination and social authority. This involves territorial conquests, the violent or peaceful extension of [colonial] possessions, the closure of markets and the creation of a closed empire. That is why imperialism awakens old historical factors that are not yet totally eliminated, such as dynastic aspirations, military appetites and national covetousness. But imperialism has galvanised those factors while also depriving them of any independent force. It has linked them to an ideology that is overtaking them; it lets

2. Louis 1904. This essay was reviewed by Lenin in his *Notebooks on Imperialism*, where the title of the article, probably retranslated from the Russian, is rendered 'Outline of Imperialism'. Lenin 1964, Vol. 39, Notebook γ (gamma): Paul Louis, 'Outline of Imperialism', *Le Mercure de France*, Paris, Vol. 50, April 1904, pp. 100 et seq.

them operate to the extent that they serve imperialism; it shuts them down as soon as they threaten its interests.

It is not difficult, therefore, to distinguish the current phenomenon from previous modes of expansion. Long before the British Colonial Secretary Joseph Chamberlain came up with his idea of an Anglo-Saxon *Zollverein* [customs-union], or the Russian Tsars Alexander II, Alexander III and Nicholas ordered their generals to conquer Central and Eastern Asia, immense empires had already been erected and collapsed all over the world. History records a whole series of more or less lasting formations leaving a more or less powerful mark: examples abound from Xerxes and Genghis Khan to Charlemagne and Napoleon. But in the erection of those colossal domains, the purely economic element was juxtaposed to others no less important. If, even in barbaric times, subsistence-needs and the wish to annex more fertile lands played a role, to this element were also added the personal ambition of the monarch, the excitations of his avid entourage, and the more or less well-understood feelings of a people.

Generally speaking, at the beginning of the twentieth century, the dynastic spirit has been relegated to a secondary role. That decline is largely due to revolutions that shattered the structure of the state. In some places, monarchy has been abolished; in others, it has been deprived of its main prerogatives and its role has been cut down to that of a simple executive power; while in others, although still semi-absolutist, it is restrained by the apprehension of public opinion, by constant fear of revolt, and by the wish to preserve its current status. If we look at the recent wars that have desolated the world – the Sino-Japanese War (1894–5), the Spanish-American War (1898), the Greco-Turkish War (1897), the Second Boer War (1899–1902), and the Russo-Japanese War (1904–5) – we see that dynastic interests have not been the sole or even the main cause of those conflicts.

National feelings have also lost somewhat their stirring power. This attenuation can easily be explained by its own victories. Many of the unsettling factors at work in Europe in the period 1820–48 have been at least partially eliminated by the formation of large national states in Germany and Italy, and by the creation of secondary kingdoms or principalities in the East. If a series of ethnic designs, more or less confined, still await their consummation, and if Austria-Hungary and the Balkans continue to witness eternal discords, [in Europe] the field of national struggles has lost three fourths of its extent.

A third factor, not unknown in the past, needs to be mentioned because it has caused and could still cause further attempts at brutal expansion: namely, the policy of diversions. Many times in the course of the nineteenth century, governments have provoked continental or colonial wars in order to distract public opinion and turn it away from subversive ideas and to consolidate the existing system of social domination. Imperialism certainly does not exclude this quite natural and simple idea; it rather includes it in its own arsenal, just as it does the dynastic spirit and national feelings, but it rests upon a much stronger foundation of universal value and appeals to less contestable and transitory arguments.

Imperialism appears as the result of an economic revolution, as the product of capitalism, industrialism, free competition and the universal struggle for markets. One can say that, like proletarian socialism, it had to result inevitably from all the phenomena caused by the growth of production and exchange in the last century, and that is why it is so engaging, general and appealing. If a people lapses into the imperialist conception, or, rather, if its leaders try to inculcate in it the imperialist spirit, that is a certain sign that the ruling class, which exploits and oppresses that people, feels threatened in its fortune and hurt in its interests. Now, in which country are the bourgeoisie, the oligarchy of landowners and industrialists sure of their future and income?

In the past, each market was national, in the sense that the products manufactured within a state were mostly consumed within that state. Australian and Canadian commodities, goods from Argentina and Egypt, for instance, could not crowd out French national production. The means of communication were too slow, difficult, and expensive for a merchant from Melbourne or Wellington to try to transport his eggs, butter and poultry to Europe; and American wheat did not reach Paris, Berlin, and Milan to depreciate the harvest of Beauce, Prussia or Lombardy. But, as the nineteenth century passed, exchange was internationalised, markets became global, and competition, formerly limited to a single country or section of a continent, became universal. This phenomenon, one of the most interesting of our age, will have incomparable consequences and is already causing great apprehension among the large manufacturers and landowners.

At the same time, production grows incessantly due to the substitution of machinery for labour-power and the adoption of more modern methods of production. Although needs, and with them consumption, also increased, manufacturing activity grew far beyond them: production surpasses, everywhere and always, the demand for commodities. People even congratulated themselves – some ministers did it publicly in France and elsewhere – on poor harvests. If in agriculture the succession of weak, average and disastrous years reached a certain equilibrium, in industry the most absolute disorder prevails and overproduction has become inevitable and permanent. Thus, the world stumbles from one crisis to another, and the growing conquest of new markets, their seemingly indefinite enlargement, appears as a vital necessity.

The bourgeoisie, the wealthy class, cannot therefore be satisfied with the territorial *status quo*. If it does not want to perish under the accumulation of wealth that it cannot sell, being struck down by its own weapons, it must find new customers at any cost. It will either monopolise the domestic market by law (protectionism) or else carry out annexations beyond its borders by force or cunning (colonialism). Imperialism combines colonialism and protectionism; it can even lead to war in so-called civilised territory because there is always the possibility of a colonial enterprise having deep repercussions within old Europe.

France, Germany, the United States, Great Britain, and many other countries are suffering from this overproduction. All are complaining about the attempts by other countries' industries to penetrate their own market. Finally, all of them have a surplus population that they cannot feed under the present conditions of wealth-distribution and must inevitably send off abroad. Demographic growth, which under a different economic structure would be a blessing, becomes a public danger under the capitalist system. It entails new threats for its leaders; indeed, it increases the risks of subversion because the growth of unemployment draws the hour of revolt nearer. Even countries where the birth- and death-rates tend to balance each other out, such as France, behave as if they were suffering from overpopulation. How much more necessary must imperialism therefore appear to those who – like Japan, England, Italy and Germany – feel their narrow framework creaking under the weight of their growing population.

From these considerations, one can clearly see the character of contemporary imperialism. It should be studied above all in Great Britain, for there it has found its promised land. There it is the programme of a large party that has turned it into a doctrine and is struggling desperately against public opinion – against the proletarian masses – in order to turn it a living reality.

The United Kingdom has long been the foremost industrial and trading state of the world. The products of its coal-mines and industry have flooded the two hemispheres; its fleet has monopolised transportation on all the seas; and its colonies, above all India, have furnished it with abundant and undisputed markets. It could regard with *hauteur* and *sang-froid* all the changes taking place throughout the world, for its wealth was incomparable and nobody dared to predict that it would one day vacillate under the attack of competitors recently equipped and similarly aggressive but possessing a superior organisation. This exceptional development gave to the British bourgeoisie an apparently unbeatable social power. Socialism never quite took root beyond the English Channel; and, if the trade-unions, gathering hundreds of thousands of workers, have coverage unrivalled elsewhere, their moderate demands did not worry the textile-industrialists of Leeds and Manchester or the ship-owners of London and Liverpool. Moreover, the British employers secured their supremacy by granting to the working class higher wages than those prevailing on the European continent. The supplementary sacrifices they were ready to make secured the continuity and stability of their opulence, snatching the revolutionary weapon from the hands of the workers. At the same time, free trade enabled the English masses to purchase all kinds of commodities at low prices, raising the national standard of living as a whole. This economic position was suddenly shattered during the final years of the nineteenth century. England, which previously had to face only moderate competition from France, came up against Germany, the United States and even Japan. England, which had not previously experienced any disappointment in the traditional colonial markets, suddenly found rivals there, not only from Europe but also among the indigenous producers themselves. England, which had been ruler of the oceans and sole distributor of the world's riches, now saw its commercial fleet threatened by other imposing merchant-navies. Imperialism arose from these three causes.

The speeches that Joseph Chamberlain delivered this winter after his resignation [from the post of Colonial Secretary], and that he now wants to deliver in other Anglo-Saxon communities in order to convert them to the idea of imperial federation – those speeches are backed up by innumerable statistics. It is a balance-sheet having imperialism as its underlying thesis. One cannot accuse him of lack of frankness, because the supporters of imperialism deal as merchants do with a commercial issue.

Some have contested Chamberlain's statistics before attentive audiences, but the popular element was lacking. It is true that Chamberlain denounced a situation already known and now partially changing. It is true that recent years have been better for British foreign trade than those picked up by Jingoist propaganda. But it is also undeniable that the United Kingdom is declining. If British foreign trade has grown, that of Germany and the United States has done so much more quickly. If British exports to the colonies have retained their level or even increased, their share as a proportion of the total colonial imports is shrinking without respite. Objectively considered, the fundamental data of imperialism cannot be contested because England no longer plays that essential, preponderant and unique role in world economic activity that it was accustomed to playing for more than a century.

The idea of imperial federation follows from those facts. The United Kingdom, India, Australasia, South Africa, and the Dominion of Canada will join in a single economic unit, setting up a homogeneous market with the same tariffs. Restoration of the tariffs abolished in 1846 will secure colonial agricultural products to Great Britain's customers, and to the customers of the colonial possessions it will secure the industrial products of the metropolis. At bottom, imperialism wants to resuscitate the [British Empire of the past], only replacing constraint by free agreement between the Anglo-Saxon communities.

That is the doctrine. Is it utopian and chimerical, as Chamberlain's adversaries argue? Will it amount to a dangerous practice, risking the complete ruin of the United Kingdom? Will it triumph or, on the contrary, collapse before the sharp opposition that has already manifested itself in the elections of South Devon, Norwich and elsewhere? We shall not deal with those questions because our goal here is to denounce the bases of imperialism.

The demonstration applying to Great Britain also applies to the United States, Russia, Germany and Japan.

The United States, despite the immensity of its territory and the enormity of its population, also suffers from dreadful chronic overproduction. It has tried to regulate production by setting up the trusts, which could limit economic anarchy, but they have to keep occupied their formidable industrial equipment, which develops incessantly. The financial powers that control the trusts exert themselves in America more freely and insolently than anywhere else, and they find almost open assistance in a debased and discredited Congress.

They have, therefore, determined a new foreign policy. The United States, which professed the Monroe Doctrine but boasted of discarding any idea of conquest, embarked some years ago [after the outbreak of the Spanish-American War in 1898] on a career of annexations: Cuba, Puerto Rico, Hawaii, and the Philippines are the first possessions of an empire that will surely grow and not remain purely insular. Imperialism at Washington is but the supreme resort of the capitalist bourgeoisie against threatening bankruptcy, and here too it combines exaggerated protectionism and intemperate colonialism.

Germany, suddenly transformed in the aftermath of the Franco-Prussian War of 1870–1 and raised to the rank of a great industrial state, quickly experienced the evils inseparable from industrial expansion. Hence the multiple attempts to acquire possessions first by private companies, then with the government's support, and finally at the government's initiative. Hence the colonial programme deliberately adopted after Bismarck's downfall in 1890, and the world policy pursued by Wilhelm II, marked by the 'leasing' of Kiaotschau [Jiaozhou] in 1898, the acquisition of the Caroline Islands in 1899 and the interventions in Asia Minor and Mesopotamia.

Russia, foreseeing the time when its new industry in Poland and the Donets river basin will experience a crisis, did not wait for its capitalists to succumb under the weight of accumulated inventories. Its efforts in the Transbaikal region and in Manchuria were aimed above all at penetrating the Chinese market in order to secure the future of Russian industry. But Russian imperialism clashed with Japanese imperialism, which results both from the economic situation of the island and from its overpopulation. Therefore, an armed clash in the Far East became inevitable, and the result was the Russo-Japanese War of 1904–5.

Thus, at the basis of all the imperial enterprises undertaken by states, whatever their political form, appear the same elements. The ruling class wants to reserve for itself the domestic market as well as to expand wherever possible its outlets, which are too narrow. World competition drives it to abuse the law and resort to force. By violent means, it assimilates populations of other races in whom it inculcates the vices and needs of the white men. The exploitation of those races imposes intolerable burdens on the proletariat; in exchange, the ruling class offers it resounding words, bellicose exultation and the illusory satisfaction of national greatness. Psychologically, nationalist sentiment is a direct product of the imperialist idea. Never before did the peoples show such an irritable disposition, such an exasperated notion of collective dignity. Each human group pretends to have a monopoly of loyalty, bravery and intelligence, not only arrogating all virtues and qualities to itself but also denying them to others. Europe is nothing but a juxtaposition of overexcited patriotisms, which are all the more inflammable because they are undermined by corrosive forces whose effects grow daily.

The talent and ability of the ruling classes to link up the popular masses sentimentally to their selfish and coldly calculated interests are evident in the press reports, parliamentary speeches and public celebrations. The idea of the fatherland, jealous and closed, hostile to other countries, scornful towards anything outside it, armed and vigilant, and forgetful of the possibility of pacific greatness, has never been championed more vigorously. The more precarious and staggering the idea of the fatherland appears before the deep, organic and fatal revolution that the world is undergoing, the more the bourgeoisie, hiding behind monarchic dynasties or republican façades, devotes its interest and fallacious argumentation to the fatherland.

Nationalism, which merges with imperialism or is its diffuse and demagogic expression, is spreading all over Europe and America with a rapidity and an authority backed everywhere by the wretched state of public education, by ignorance of the most elementary facts, and by the prestige of the aristocracy of wealth in the eyes of the disinherited. It raises above humanity the spectre of perpetual threats of conflagrations with incalculable consequences. Nationalism has awakened savage passions of destruction and massacre. It has tried to erect impenetrable barriers between neighbouring countries that would prevent not only the exchange of products but also of ideas; it wants to turn each nation into a religious community obsessed with its flag, a congregation hidden in sombre vaults and obstinately shutting out the sounds and glimmers from outside.

But imperialism has its remedy in itself. If it must breed war, everything indicates that the armed conflicts of the future will, immediately or gradually, deal irreparable blows to the social institutions of the participating countries. The conflicts of the nineteenth century – the Crimean War (1853–6), the campaigns in Italy, Bohemia and France – already left behind them bloody traces, and if a Caesarist dictatorship can arise as a consequence of military victory in some great republic, the defeat of a militarist monarch could also lead to a proletarian triumph and bring down a military caste.

If imperialism awakens latent national feelings, if it re-excites sleeping passions, then the nation it tries to create by combining hitherto separated economic interests will have to operate in a less narrow framework. It leads, therefore, to the constitution of vaster political groupings. The continents will have a new physiognomy if six or seven great empires, like the Anglo-Saxon *Zollverein* or Russia, that will divide up the surface of the globe among themselves. In that sense, imperialism is the final and necessary stage between the small-scale geographical expressions of the nineteenth century and the future human family.

Finally, imperialism is, in our opinion, the essential and omnipotent instrument of the proletarian eruption. Imperialism increases public expenses by its logical tendency to strengthen armies, navies and the military apparatus of the state, and consequently it imposes greater burdens on the wage-earners for the benefit of the wealthy oligarchy, thus aggravating the discontent of the masses. German socialism received renewed impetus from the continuous growth of military expenditures, and Crispian[3] megalomania has recruited an incalculable number of supporters of democracy in Italy.

Raising all tariff-dues and with them the cost of living, and reducing in its petty foreign policy the foreign markets, imperialism on the one hand puts pressure on the proletariat for the benefit of capital and, on the other, reduces its chances of employment. In that way it will have a more efficient effect than the most subversive propaganda on the evolution of the working class. Imperialism, which is the last card of the capitalist world, which seems to it the last refuge against bankruptcy and the spontaneous disintegration that increasingly threaten to engulf it, is also a wonderful and incomparable artisan of revolution.

---

3. [Francesco Crispi (1819–1901) was an Italian politician instrumental in the country's unification. He served as Premier from 1887 until 1891 and again from 1893 until 1896. A deputy to the Italian parliament from 1861, he was at first a republican but later became an outspoken monarchist. He became minister of the interior (1877–8) in the Depretis cabinet. A charge of bigamy hindered his political career for the next nine years, but he returned to the cabinet in 1887 and became premier upon Depretis's death. He strengthened Italy's commitment to the Triple Alliance with Germany and Austria-Hungary, but thereby helped cause Italian relations with France to deteriorate still further, leading to a tariff-war between the two countries from 1888 to 1892. He also pressed a forward policy in North-East Africa and organised the colony of Eritrea. He was overthrown in 1891 by Giolitti, but returned to power in 1893 and was re-elected by an impressive majority in 1895. However, resentment over his reactionary policies and, above all, the terrible defeat suffered at Adwa (1896) by Italian forces seeking to expand into Ethiopia, forced him out of office.]

Chapter Eighteen

'English Imperialism' (4 October 1904)

Julian B. Marchlewski (Karski)

Julian Balthasar Marchlewski (1866–1925) was a Polish Social-Democratic and later Communist activist and publicist. He was also known under the aliases Karski and Kujawiak. In 1889, he was one of the co-founders of the Polish Workers' Union, and four years later, together with Rosa Luxemburg, he founded the Social-Democratic Party of the Kingdom of Poland, which was dissolved in 1895 after massive arrests. Marchlewski was arrested himself and served time in prison. After 1900, he became a member of the Social-Democratic Party of the Kingdom of Poland and Lithuania and participated in the Russian Revolution of 1905 in the Polish territories. After failure of the Revolution, he migrated to Germany, where he joined the anti-revisionist camp and later the left wing against the Kautskyist centre.

At the 1907 International Socialist Congress, held at Stuttgart, Marchlewski, then a delegate from the Polish SDKPiL, argued that the socialist colonial policy advocated by the revisionists was a contradiction in terms, since 'one can speak just as little about a socialist colonial policy as about a socialist state'. He also shared Rosa Luxemburg's analysis of the Russian Revolution, disputing the commonly held view 'that every nation must go through capitalism'.[1]

1. International Socialist Congress (7th) 1907, pp. 32–3.

During World War I, Marchlewski was again jailed from 1916–18, this time for participating in the German revolutionary-socialist movement. He belonged to the Berlin Internationale group, together with Rosa Luxemburg, Karl Liebknecht and Franz Mehring, and was co-founder of the Spartakus group (Spartacist League). After being exchanged with Russia for a German spy, in 1919 he took part in negotiations with Poland arising from the Polish-Soviet War. During the Red Army's counterattack in Poland under Mikhail Tukhachevsky, he headed the Polish Provisional Revolutionary Committee in Białystok, which planned in 1920 to declare a Polish Soviet Socialist Republic. After a year in Moscow, he returned illegally to Germany and became a member of the Central Committee of the German Communist Party. From 1922 until his death in 1925 (during a vacation in Italy), he served as President of International Labour Defence, known in Great Britain as the International Class-War Prisoners' Aid.

We have included in this anthology two of Marchlewski's journalistic articles – 'English Imperialism' and 'A Victory of Imperialism'. We have also included two works that are more theoretical: his review of Hilferding's *Finance Capital* and his main work on imperialism in the 1912 brochure *Imperialism or Socialism?*, which we have translated for the first time into English.[2] Readers will note that, in the present article, Marchlewski took Rothstein to task for emphasising England's need to maintain markets for sale of goods and, instead, gave primacy to the need to export capital in response to a falling rate of profit. However, in his later review of *Finance Capital*, he changed his perspective and criticised Hilferding for dismissing underconsumption as the major cause of crises.[3] In this respect, Marchlewski's later views were closer to those of Rosa Luxemburg in *The Accumulation of Capital* (1913).

* * *

'English Imperialism'[4]

The political season has begun in England, and in coming months the propaganda for imperialist ideas will be pursued with redoubled zeal. The

2. Marchlewski 1912, reprinted in Marchlewski 1978, pp. 167–86. See Chapter 35.
3. Marchlewski 1910, reprinted in Marchlewski 1978, pp. 100–10. See Chapter 28.
4. Marchlewski 1904a, reprinted in Marchlewski 1978, pp. 51–6.

time has come, therefore, to remind readers of the main issues that will be decided there.

Chamberlain's imperialist plans have two main goals: a closer union between Great Britain and its colonies to create a uniform empire, and a break with free trade to introduce protective duties. Those protective tariffs should first and foremost serve to chain the interests of the colonies to England: the future empire should be a powerful economic unit, a completely self-sufficient economic organism. That was the starting point. But, in the course of time, the question, as often happens, has substantially shifted, and part of the English bourgeoisie has begun to take to the idea of protective tariffs that should secure higher profits for English industry. The significance of protective tariffs for imperialism has therefore receded to the background. The agitators for imperialism thus got bogged down in protectionism, and it seems that the decision will be made pre-eminently over the question of protectionism or free trade.

Naturally, in a country like England, which advocated the principle of free trade for so long and with such glaring success, it is not easy to agitate for protective tariffs. The main argument of the political string-pullers is that English industry is declining and losing its competitiveness, that it will not only be driven out of the countries that surrounded themselves with tariffs but that it is also losing ground in neutral markets. Free trade has brought about the decline of British industry; in order to save that industry, and with it the existence of the British people, the country must break with that principle.

If the decline of British industry were actually proven, it would still be necessary to prove that protective tariffs are a means of redressing that evil. The analogical conclusion, according to which the United States and Germany, England's two most powerful rivals, adopted protective tariffs and developed their industry extremely rapidly, and that England must therefore also switch to protectionism, is in every respect illogical. Undoubtedly, protective tariffs have, for some time, had a favourable influence on industrial development in the United States and Germany, but they were just one of several factors and not even the most important. There are, after all, countries with even higher tariffs than Germany whose industry has made no particularly great progress, France for instance. On the other hand, England's transition from free trade to protectionism would certainly hurt a series of industries, namely, those depending on the importation of semi-manufactured products.

Meanwhile, the main question of whether we can actually speak about a decline of British industry has by no means been decided. Export-statistics say something completely different. [...] [The export of iron-wares from England grew from 4,760 million marks in 1884 to 5,932 million marks in 1903]. We cannot, therefore, speak about a general decline in the last twenty years. Production-statistics also show a constant rise.

Yet the idea that British industry is declining is very widespread even among people who are decided opponents of both imperialism and protectionism. A year ago, for instance, an English party comrade, Theodor Rothstein, published in *Justice* and *Die Neue Zeit* a series of articles asserting that decline.[5] He stated that one cannot speak about an absolute decline but that: 1) England's production has not expanded as rapidly as that of its rivals; 2) England's share in the import of industrial products of individual countries did not shrink absolutely but relatively. Both observations are correct. England has today less iron-ore than the United States and Germany; it produces less pig-iron than the United States, and it is also falling behind it in coal-production. But that only means that the production of the United States and Germany, countries that developed much later than England, is still capable of expansion, while England's development has reached a climax where its tempo must necessarily be slower. England's ores can be compared with

5. ['What, then, is the genuine Imperialism, that Imperialism which is to rule the future?.... Throughout the last quarter of the nineteenth century, while capitalist England was resting on her oars, the other states – more especially Germany and America – were using the whole of their collective efforts to work out the various problems of industrial organisation and to forge, in the shape of protective tariffs, export-premiums, national systems of technical, commercial and general education, model factories, effective consular services, experimental laboratories, etc., such weapons as could with advantage be used by their respective capitalist classes in the struggle for the world's market.... And so the idea of the state began to make way in the minds of the public. The more the economic peril that was threatening England became realised, the deeper and the wider the conviction grew that the atomistic theory and practice in industry and commerce is a failure, and that under modern conditions it is the whole of the consolidated forces of the state that must be brought to bear on the question of economic survival, let alone supremacy. The Liberal Party, the party of *laisser faire*...began, as a consequence, to rot...and a new current, fed by the new requirements, began to make itself felt both among the leaders and the rank and file. That this current has given itself and still wears the name of imperialist is very natural, seeing that it is the question of consolidation or non-consolidation of the Empire that has hitherto had the occasion – first and feebly in Egypt, then stronger in Ireland, and now, strongest of all, in South Africa – to assume an acute form and to bring to consciousness the differences between the old and new parties.' Rothstein 1901b, pp. 359–63.]

those of the United States in their richness, but the comparison is misleading [given the very different sizes of the two countries]. The second observation is also correct.... [England's share in Germany's imports did decrease from 13 percent in 1893–95 to 12 per cent in 1898–1900]. England's share in France's imports also remained stationary, while imports from the United States grew, etc.

But what does that prove? Only that, as trade specialises more and more, the sources of supply become more numerous. For instance: if, thirty years ago, a textile-factory was erected somewhere in the world, it was almost self-evident that the machines would come from England. Today, on the contrary, one finds in a modern establishment of that sort English machines alongside German, Swiss and French ones. Specialisation goes so far that today England supplies steam-engines to Germany and vice versa. And it is not only technical specialisation that brings that about; commercial development also leads to the exchange of a whole range of products that can be produced everywhere. Clothes, leather-goods and furniture, for instance, go from England to Germany and vice versa. It is a platitude that England has ceased to be the only supplier of industrial goods; and therefore its share in the commodity-supply of different countries must naturally also shrink. But, as long as it is not proved that England's production is actually decreasing or stagnating, one cannot speak about a decline of English industry. Relative figures cannot prove that. What is the meaning, for instance, of the comparison with the United States? They have an area of 9.16 million square-kilometres and a population of 76 million, while the United Kingdom has an area of 244,820 square-kilometres and a population of 21 million. America's industrial development necessarily had to find greater elbow-room for the productive forces given the larger size of the country.

Comrade Rothstein asserts that English industrialists lately display an outspoken disregard for science, and that, in general, England's entire capitalist class has stagnated spiritually. That may be true; on the other hand, the 'decline of British industry' has become a slogan for the imperialist agitators to bait the masses. For England's working class, the decline of English industry would undoubtedly be a fearful danger, and that is why the slogan is doubly dangerous.

The real reason why part of the bourgeoisie has taken up protectionist plans with such a suspicious zeal is, however, completely different: English capital, like capital in other developed countries, lacks today employment-opportunities. The mass of capital grows, the mass of profit accumulates, but the profit-rate sinks. If a customs-union were set up according to Chamberlain's plans, if the colonies were closed to foreign goods and opened up to English capital and goods, a colossal field of activity for English capital would be created in those colonies. The consequence would be *an era of reckless financial speculation,*[6] *of capitalist orgies such as the world has never seen*. Industries would spring up hothouse-like in the colonies and profits would grow – until the next crash. On the other hand, it is certain that English workers, as consumers, have very much to fear from the impending protectionist era.

Recently, an English agitator in the constituency of Thanet [a district in the county of Kent] enlivened the elections for the House of Commons with an act of genuine English wit: at a meeting, he produced a bottle with dog-meat and a label with the words 'dog-slaughterhouse'. He wanted to say to the workers: vote for the imperialist candidates and you will get protective tariffs, which mean more expensive foodstuffs as in Germany, where agrarian tariffs have raised the price of meat to such an extent that workers eat dogs, so that in Germany there are dog-slaughterhouses. [...] The 'pure consumers' standpoint' is today certainly an object of ridicule, particularly among politicians, but the English workers should nevertheless give some thought to the argument of that agitator from Thanet.

Chamberlain and company now, of course, are solemnly declaring that they do not want to introduce any tariff on foodstuffs; on the contrary, they promise the abolition of existing tariffs on tee, coffee, etc. Those promises, however, should not be taken seriously because the future tariffs are conceived above all as means of economic struggle, and a commercial struggle with agrarian countries is impossible if tariffs on foodstuffs are left out of consideration.

If the role of commercial policy in the struggle over imperialism has moved to the forefront of agitation, it is not the only – or even the most important – issue that has to be decided. Imperialism necessarily leads to an adventurous policy of conquest, the expansion of the military system and the strengthening of state-power, all of which must, sooner or later, be dangerous for the

6. [*Gründerära*: A reference to the German *Gründerjahre*, referring to the years of financial speculation following the Franco-Prussian War of 1870, which can also be translated as 'speculative phase'.]

proletariat. Admittedly, there are socialist politicians, like Eduard Bernstein, who deny this connection, see in the Boer War just a vile trick of Chamberlain, and are unable to find any danger for the English working class in the whole modern frenzy of conquest in England.[7] The development of affairs in Transvaal, however, should have opened the eyes of even the politically dullest workers to the actual course of imperialist policy.

To all appearances, the decisive hour is approaching, and the workers of England will perhaps have to decide as early as the near future. In the camp of the bourgeoisie, the politicians seem to have come to an agreement. Balfour's latest speech, at any rate, shows that the former opponent of Chamberlain is disposed to make peace with him. Balfour has changed his position on the question of protectionism and has also met halfway Chamberlain's plans to convene a conference of colonial representatives. Admittedly, the contradictions of the different groups of interests will not be disposed of so easily, and if the [colonial] conference meets it may well turn out that the bourgeoisie in the colonies is not at all disposed to risk such a dangerous experiment. The final decision, however, will have to be made by the workers. Whether the first step towards realisation of the imperialist plans is made or not will depend on their political maturity.

7. [Bernstein 1900. See Chapter 10.]

Chapter Nineteen
'A Victory of Imperialism' (10 November 1904)

Julian B. Marchlewski (Karski)

This article by Marchlewski-Karski is remarkable for its emphasis on the creation of a conservative labour-aristocracy as a result of imperialism – an idea he probably took, as Lenin did later, from the Socialist Labor Party of Daniel De Leon, an American socialist who famously called the American Federation of Labor leaders 'labor lieutenants of the capitalist class'.

* * *

'A Victory of Imperialism'[1]

As expected, the presidential elections in the United States of America resulted in a splendid victory for [Theodore] Roosevelt. He obtained a larger majority than any of his predecessors. Voter turnout was also the highest in the history of the United States: the number of voters surpassed 14 million. And yet the excitement was not particularly great in America or anywhere else in the world. Only in Colorado, where the capitalist camorra established a gruesome reign of terror a year ago, and where dynamite and revolvers in the hands of 'Pinkerton detectives' are

1. Marchlewski 1904b, reprinted in Marchlewski 1978, pp. 56–8.

constantly imposing new sacrifices on the workers – only there and in Kentucky did the elections lead to bloodshed and human sacrifices.[2] Everywhere else, they took place quite peacefully, and, even in New York, the announcement of the electoral result did not produce special disturbances.

We have already referred to that phenomenon and explained that this time nothing substantial was really at stake in the election. The decision between Roosevelt and [Alton] Parker was merely a question of choosing between whole- and half-hearted imperialism. Despite all the Democratic proclamations, imperialism itself was no longer in question. And, in the interest of historical progress, it is certainly preferable that whole-hearted imperialism should be raised along with Roosevelt to the presidential chair.

Imperialism means historical progress insofar as it is the political expression of a more developed form of capitalism, and, in this sense – indeed, only in this sense – it is also to be welcomed by the working class. In the political field, imperialism gives as sharp an expression to robbery of the people as the trusts do in the economic field, and it is no coincidence that the development of politics into imperialism was accompanied by the development of industry into the trust-system. The connection between the two developments is especially clear in America, and Roosevelt's significance lies in the fact that both tendencies meet in his person. One should not be misled by his tirades against the trusts. They belong to his profession; if one does not take the field against trusts at American meetings, he does not stand a chance of making a

2. [The incidents usually referred to as the Colorado Labor Wars involved a struggle between the Western Federation of Miners (WFM) and the mine-operators, particularly the Cripple Creek Mine-Owners' Association, during the years 1903–5. A WFM drive for the eight-hour day, supported by a majority vote of Colorado citizens, was thwarted first by the judiciary and then by the state government. In the summer of 1903, the WFM called for a sympathy-strike among miners to support a smelter workers' strike for an eight-hour day. By the end of October, the call for action at the mining town of Cripple Creek succeeded, and operations in the gold-mines ground to a halt. Eager to resume mining and break the union, the mine-owners turned to Governor Peabody, who on 23 November 1903, sent the state militia into Cripple Creek to crush the union. Soldiers rounded up union-members and sympathisers, including the entire staff of a pro-union newspaper, and imprisoned them without charges. In June 1904, a WFM member, Harry Orchard, blew up a railroad-station, killing 13 strike-breakers. This turned public opinion against the union, and the mine-owners were able to arrest and deport the majority of WFM-leaders. By midsummer the strike was over, but the WFM did not die as a result of the Colorado Labor-Wars. A number of WFM-miners and leaders, such as William 'Big Bill' Haywood, travelled to Chicago in June 1905 to help launch the Industrial Workers of the World.]

political career, let alone of being elected president of the republic. The trusts value those vehement declamations for what they are, political palaver, and if one cannot be president without thundering against the trusts, he can even less be president without the support of the magnates of capital. Roosevelt is also a tool of the trusts.

It is clear that the sort of world policy that Roosevelt conducts did not spring out of his own brain, as bourgeois journals often say, and that the world politician is also ultimately only a manager serving those capitalist organisations. The youthful elasticity of American capitalism has become flesh and blood in the figure of the 'Rough Rider', who seeks out the quarrels of this world rather than shunning them – at least as long as business can be expected from them – and who nurtures the specific weapon of imperialism, the navy, with loving care. No state in the world has so many warships in reserve as America, whose navy is the second largest in the world.

It is possible that, due to its geographical location, America will be protected from the niceties of fully developed militarism, but its navy must consequently increase all the time. And the huge burdens that a strong navy means for the American working class must also sooner or later be politically noticeable. To be sure, we have no illusions about the strength and spirit of the American workers' organisations. An incidental feature of the trust-system is that it brings a stratum of workers who, through the quality of their work and the level of their wages, rise above the mass of the workers and, as a consequence, come into a certain contradiction with their own class. This contradiction is strengthened by the lack of proletarian solidarity, a phenomenon common to all the Anglo-Saxon working class. The danger that the relatively well-paid workers of the trusts will turn into defence-troops of capitalism is nowhere greater than in America. But Social Democracy is making great progress. It received 15,000 votes in New York City, 50,000 in the state of New York, 45,000 in Chicago, and 17,000 in Milwaukee. The complete collapse of the Democratic Party would surely be to its advantage. William Hearst, the Populist candidate Watson, and Bryan have already declared that they want to found a new party out of the wreckage of the Democrats, and the future will tell whether this new edition of bourgeois radicalism is a serious danger for socialist ideas in America or not.

The German bourgeois press, regardless of party differences, hailed the election results, and Wilhelm II insisted upon sending to Roosevelt an

English-Latin congratulation, which surely must have given the Rough Rider as much pleasure as the monument that Old Fritz sent over there in his day.[3] There was also jubilation in England, although, in our opinion, there is little reason for celebrating in London. The *Neue Preussische Zeitung* quite correctly pointed out that the election results will initially lead to co-operation between America and England, but, before long, they will bring about a break between the two countries – namely, when the American navy becomes so powerful that it no longer needs English crutches. Thus, the victory of imperialism in America opens up ominous perspectives for English imperialism. But we know that the shattering of imperialist ideas in Great Britain is a precondition for the triumphal march of the *socialist* movement in the oldest and strongest industrial country of the world.

3. [Friedrich II (1712–86), King of Prussia (1740–86) from the Hohenzollern dynasty. He became known as Frederick the Great (*Friedrich der Große*) and was nicknamed *der alte Fritz* ('Old Fritz').]

Chapter Twenty

'On British Imperialism' (January 1907)

Otto Bauer

Otto Bauer (1881–1938) was a leader of the left wing of Austrian Social Democracy and one of the foremost thinkers of Austro-Marxism and of the centrist tendency within the Second International. The term 'Austro-Marxism' is used to describe a group of Viennese intellectuals belonging to the Austrian SDAP (Sozialdemokratischen Arbeiterpartei) that included, in addition to Bauer, Karl Renner, Max Adler, Friedrich Adler, and Rudolf Hilferding. Gustav Eckstein and Karl Kautsky, two socialist leaders active in Germany, and the historian of socialism Karl Grünberg, also had strong links with this tendency.[1]

The son of a prosperous Viennese-Jewish textile-manufacturer, Otto Bauer earned a Ph.D. in Law at the University of Vienna and in 1907 published his major book, *The Question of Nationalities and Social Democracy*. In that work, he defended 'cultural-national autonomy' rather than national self-determination (up to and including separation), as advocated by Russian Social Democracy. In 1907, Bauer also founded *Der Kampf*, the theoretical journal

1. Leon Trotsky, who lived in Vienna from October 1907 to August 1914, was strongly influenced by some aspects of Austro-Marxism, but he ultimately dismissed the school itself as 'an erudite and stilted theory of passivity and capitulation'. See his assessment of Austro-Marxism in Trotsky 1920, Chapter 9: 'Karl Kautsky, His School and His Book', pp. 177–87.

of the Austrian Social-Democratic Party, and, from 1907 to 1914, he was party secretary. Captured on the Eastern Front in the early months of the World War I, he spent three years as a prisoner of war in Russia, returning to Austria in 1917.

Following Victor Adler's death in 1918, Bauer became leader of the Austrian Social-Democratic Party. From November 1918 to July 1919, the Austrian Social Democrats formed a coalition government with the Christian-Social Party, with Otto Bauer serving as Minister of Foreign Affairs. When Engelbert Dollfuss, with the assistance of elements of the Christian-Social Party and the Heimwehr, installed an authoritarian corporatist dictatorship in 1933, Austrian Social Democracy was severely repressed. After the Social Democrats' failed attempt at an uprising in February 1934, Otto Bauer was forced into exile. He continued to organise the resistance, first from Brno, Czechoslovakia, and later from Paris. He died in Paris on 4 July 1938, aged 56, just four months after Austria became part of Hitler's Reich.

* * *

'On British Imperialism'[2]

> Gerhart von Schulze-Gaevernitz, *Britischer Imperialismus und englischer Freihandel zu Beginn des zwanzigsten Jahrhunderts*, Leipzig: Duncker & Humblot, 1906.

Mr. Schulze-Gaevernitz has recently published a book on British imperialism, but the bulky volume contains little valuable material for those who want to write its history. However, it will not be completely useless to future historians, because it shows the cultural currents prevalent among the German bourgeoisie at the beginning of the twentieth century.

The ruling ideas of each age have always been the ideas of its ruling class.[3] But, in the great transitional epochs of history, the class-ideology of the ruling class is often defeated by the world of ideas belonging to the revolutionary class that it rules, even before the rising class conquers political power. Thus, the political victory of the bourgeoisie was preceded by the

2. Bauer 1907.
3. [*Communist Manifesto*, Chapter 2: 'Proletarians and Communists'.]

victory of its science, art and philosophy over the world of ideas of absolutism and feudalism.

Fifteen years ago, it looked as if something similar was going to happen in our time. Many people thought then that perhaps proletarian ideology would defeat bourgeois science and art even before the proletariat conquered state-power. Bourgeois ideology seemed to have come to terms with proletarian ideology: *Kathedersozialismus*[4] bloomed, Marx's method of historical research was applied by many bourgeois historians, and poetry and the visual arts discovered the life of the proletariat. But the victorious career of proletarian class-ideology is not a straight line. As the 'era of social policy' was followed by the era of high tariffs, colonial corruption, attempts at anti-union legislation and anti-worker class-justice, the pro-worker stirrings of bourgeois science and art were quickly followed by reaction. People wanted to escape from the Marxist method, whose iron logic inevitably led to unwanted consequences, and, for that purpose, they revived forgotten philosophy. The theory of knowledge had to prove that the method of the natural sciences could not be applied to the 'cultural sciences'. The bourgeois state had to be fortified with the power of religious ideology, and the attention of science was therefore turned again to religious problems. The exploitation and oppression of the proletariat, and the violent practice of capitalist colonial policy (which sacrificed entire nations to the profit-drive of the capitalists), had to be justified, and for that purpose the will to power[5] and the struggle for existence were romanticised, turning them from concepts for the explanation of reality into commandments of an allegedly superior morality. World history was rewritten as a drama of racial conflict. And those who were unable to bear all this fled from the grim reality of class-struggles into the illusory world of empty aestheticism. Werner

4. [A tendency in German political economy in the last third of the nineteenth century that supported state-intervention in the economy and adoption of a progressive social policy in order to mitigate class-contradictions. Their name was given to the *Kathedersozialisten* by their liberal opponents; actually, they were not socialists but social reformers. Their scientific centre was the Verein für Sozialpolitik, established in 1872. It counted among its members A. Wagner, G. Schmoller, and L. Brentano].

5. [The 'Will to Power' (German: *Der Wille zur Macht*) is a prominent concept in the philosophy of Friedrich Nietzsche. Historically, the concept was also appropriated by the Nazis, who used it to justify their imperialist quest for power and world-domination. The phrase was used as the title of a posthumously published book, compiled from Nietzsche's notes by his sister, Elisabeth Förster-Nietzsche. Nietzsche 1914, Vol. 14.].

Sombart admonished intellectuals to cultivate an 'apolitical mind'. In that way, many people who some years ago posed as socialists now dedicate their musing hours to the 'study' of modern furniture.

Undoubtedly, many valuable works owe their existence to that movement. Of course, knowledge of the social roots of a philosophical, scientific or artistic work does not determine its truthfulness or beauty. As a whole, however, the entire shift in bourgeois awareness has meant nothing but an escape from science, at least from the *law-governed science*[6] of social life, which became suspicious when people realised that it inevitably leads to Marxism. The devastation that this whole ideological reaction has brought about is clearly reflected in Schulze-Gaevernitz's work.

The economic train of thought of this voluminous work is very poor. English free trade was the economic policy of the exporting industrial state. Great Britain, however, is more and more turning from an industrial state into a *rentier*-state. The newly accumulated capital does not flow to domestic production in order to export goods to foreign countries, but is rather invested in other continents. It builds railways in America and canals in Egypt; it develops gold mines in South Africa. England annually invests abroad no less than a billion marks! The more rapidly England turns in that way into a creditor-state, the more England's wealth is based on its rule over foreign countries and on political power. If the citizens of an industrial state are interested in free trade, the inhabitants of a creditor-state are inclined to imperialism. The struggle between English free trade and British imperialism is a manifestation of the antagonism between the industrial and the *rentier*-state.

Undoubtedly, this train of thought is partially correct. The subjection of foreign countries continually opens up for capital new investment spheres with a higher profit-rate; the navy and the colonial governments are a world police force that enables capital to invest safely all over the world and, in that way, to subject the whole world to the law of the equalisation of the rate of profit.

Nevertheless, this explanation of imperialist policy is fragmentary. Behind imperialist policy stand not only the stock-exchange, great banks and holders of foreign and colonial bonds, but also great industrial capitalists, especially

6. [*Gesetzwissenschaft*, as opposed to *Geschichtswissenschaft*, or purely descriptive historical science.]

the heavy-iron industry. Industrial protective tariffs are meant to make it easier for them to create powerful cartels and trusts; the investment of British capital in remote corners of the world enables them to secure the sale of rails, locomotives, machines, etc.; and the British customs-union is meant to protect them from the competition of foreign industry. The struggle over economic policy hides not only the antagonism between finance-capital and industrial capital, but also the contradictions within industrial capital; the struggles between free-traders and imperialists reflect not only the antagonism between London and Manchester, but also between Birmingham and Manchester.

Finally, economic and political struggles are rooted not only in the contradictions of interests within the capitalist class but also in class-contradictions. Capital everywhere strives for investment in those branches of production and regions where the profit-rate is highest. 'National' policy ought to enable them to transfer their funds to those production areas. *Ubi bene, ibi patria* [Where he is well off, there is his country]. In capitalist terms: where the profit-rate is high, there is my investment sphere. The 'national' policy of imperialism serves the economic cosmopolitanism of capital. The interests of the working class, however, clash with that policy. What interest could British workers have in facilitating the flow of accumulated sums of surplus-value to foreign continents; in opening up the door for capital to flow out that could be invested at home and employ British workers? Should British workers rejoice at a policy that took away millions in English capital from the domestic labour-market to South Africa, where Chinese slaves could be employed? Actually, the attitude of the British workers (not only of the Labour Party, but also of those workers who still follow the Liberals) led to the defeat of Chamberlain in the last elections.

Schulze-Gaevernitz has not solved the problem of understanding the struggle over imperialism as a class-struggle. That requires an analysis of the diverse and mutually contradictory effects of imperialist policy on the labour-market. Such a task can only be undertaken by a 'discursive', that is to say mathematical, economics based on the theory of value, which is as alien to Schulze-Gaevernitz as it is to the whole historical school. He must therefore restrict himself to describing imperialism as the ideology of finance-capital and the *rentier*-class, and free trade as the policy of industrial capital. Following the fashion of our time, he attempts to disguise the poverty of this line of reasoning by embarking upon a broad ideological disquisition.

According to Schulze-Gaevernitz, the struggle over imperialism is rooted in moods and inclinations that have their ultimate foundation in a great crisis in English spiritual life. He describes that crisis as follows: the most important event of the nineteenth century was the world rule of the Anglo-Saxons. The matchless supremacy of the English nation was historically based on the fact that England begot sooner than any other people the strong state and the strong man. However, the strong man, the creator of British capitalism and British democracy, of the British world empire, of English science and philosophy, was the product of a specifically English spiritual culture, particularly Puritanism and Enlightenment. On him rested England's political democracy and English empiricism; he created that self-control and methodical way of life without which England's economic, political and cultural greatness would have been impossible. But, today, those foundations of English culture have been theoretically overcome. Hence the cultural crisis that manifests itself in neo-Malthusian practice, in the displacement of austere work by idle *rentier*-existence, and in the intellectual and moral scepticism of the modern English writers. English culture rests on Puritanism and the Enlightenment, but these cannot withstand the assault of modern natural and historical examination and of modern philosophy. It is not the German navy and American trusts that jeopardise England's greatness, but rather the decomposition of the ethical basis of English culture. England must base its culture on new knowledge and new ethics. England can only receive that new basis of cultural greatness from German idealism, which alone can continue the social disciplining that Puritanism formerly provided. In order to do that, England must be culturally germanised. Not British imperialism, but only German idealism can put an end to English cultural decomposition.

Here, the reader can see at work that ideological reaction that we spoke of at the beginning. To criticise that line of reasoning a few lines will suffice.

Undoubtedly, Puritanism was intimately connected with England's economic and political development. The new men created by capitalism, and the modern state growing out of that capitalist basis, could not be satisfied with the ideology of the feudal epoch, based on a natural economy. They therefore created Puritanism and the Enlightenment. If one discovers in that system of ideas those ethical values required by the economic and political development of England, that is easily explicable: the men formed under the pressure of capitalism are now the creators and carriers of that world of ideas.

If, today, England's old ideology is tottering, that is not due to the fact that it was overcome theoretically. The thoughts of a quiet scholar refuting a handed-down system of ideas are powerless if they do not sink into the consciousness of the people, who are chained to hard work and excluded from the full possession of modern culture; and they cannot prevail if they clash with class-interests and ideologies born out of the position of individuals and classes in society. Puritanism was already refuted theoretically when it was born. If, today, its strength is actually declining, that cannot be explained by its refutation but only by the changed conditions of social life that made that refutation sink into the consciousness of the masses and, generally speaking, imbued them with new ideas.

It is doubtful whether the decomposition of the old English ideology has progressed as far as Schulze-Gaevernitz argues. One certainly cannot infer that from the works of modern English writers who express the mood of a thin stratum of intellectuals. Whoever wants to judge the spiritual condition of England from the writings of Shaw and Wilde acts as imprudently as that German historian who, at the end of the nineteenth century, wanted to discover the psyche of the German people in the dramas of Hermann Bahr. Finally, consider the remedy that Schulze-Gaevernitz recommends to the Englishmen! What an odd idea to want to renovate the culture of a great nation by means of German classical philosophy, which, in its most consummate form, no longer describes a particular knowledge but cognition of the conditions of all knowledge; no concrete imperative, but only cognition of the essence of any imperative![7]

Certainly, British imperialism has its own powerful ideology. As long as the English bourgeoisie saw in free trade the best means of finding markets for its goods and opening up spheres of investment for its capital, it enthused over the peace and freedom of all nations. But, in the age of great banks and capital-exports, of cartels and trusts, it realises the 'moral' significance of war, and its ideologists turn the subjection and exploitation of foreign peoples first into the right and then into the duty of the 'superior race'. This ideological metamorphosis reflects the development of capitalist productive forces, which have changed the tools of capitalist economic policy. Schulze-Gaevernitz has

7. [Probably a reference to Kant's *categorical* imperative – universal moral *knowledge* as distinct from the *theory of knowledge*.]

not tried to derive this new ideology from the changes that took place in social being, nor even to assess its value with the methods of critical philosophy, which is closest to him. Such an examination would, admittedly, not have superseded or decided the class-struggle, but it could perhaps have helped many intellectuals and perplexed people to escape the influence of an alluring class-ideology, and to form an opinion about the great struggles of our time. Instead of doing that, the professor took flight into aimless talk about religion and philosophy, art and science, which, to be sure, includes many insightful remarks, but it does not answer the concrete economic and political questions that the classes and interested groups are striving to answer. The Englishmen ask: 'Should we introduce a protective tariff or not?' 'Study Kant and Fichte!' answers the German professor. And people who in that way evade the duty of adopting a position on social questions talk about the primacy of practical reason!

It is very characteristic that, in the most voluminous work on British imperialism so far to appear in the German language, the interaction between German economic policy and British imperialism was hardly mentioned. And yet British imperialism is a frightful danger for Germany; it wants to deprive German industry of its most important markets! Moreover, the imperialist movement in England draws constant nourishment from German tariff-policy, from the export policy of the German cartels, and from the naval and world policy of the German empire. Was it not the duty of a German writer dealing with British imperialism to answer this question: How must Germany conduct its economic and foreign policy in order to ward off the unparalleled danger that threatens the German people as a result of British imperialism? Let us hope that, on election day, German workers will answer the question that 'national' bourgeois scholars shun. British workers defeated British imperialism in the last elections and, in that way, momentarily eliminated an awful threat to the German people. German workers will defeat the much less successful – but also much more dangerous – German imperialism, and, in that way, they will also weaken the imperialist movement in Great Britain.[8] While

8. [Otto Bauer's hopes were dashed: this article was written immediately before the so-called 'Hottentot elections' in Germany, held on 25 January 1907, in which a wave of imperialist chauvinism resulted in the SPD losing nearly half of its seats in the Reichstag. The elections resulted in the formation of a new imperialist governing coalition, known as the Bülow Bloc after Chancellor Bernhard von Bülow].

the working class of each country fights for its own interests, it also fights at the same time for the interests of its class-comrades beyond the channel. Both here and there Chamberlain's phrase holds: the decisive struggle will be fought out between imperialism and socialism.

Chapter Twenty-One

'Before the "Hottentot Elections"' (January 1907)

Parvus (Alexander Helphand)

Parvus's book *Colonial Policy and the Breakdown* was a collection of four brochures written around the time of the so-called *Hottentottenwahlen*, held on 25 January 1907. The Reichstag elections of 1907, carried out in what Rosa Luxemburg described as 'a paroxysm of imperialistic enthusiasm' and an atmosphere of 'spiritual pogrom', resulted in a dramatic fall in the number of Social-Democratic representatives in the Reichstag from 81 to 43.[1] In the words of Carl Schorske, the main historian of pre-WWI German Social Democracy, 'The elections raised a crucial issue which the party had previously been able to ignore: its relationship to state and nation in the era of imperialism.... Kautsky felt that the ruling class had found the political answer to the vision of socialism in "the fascinating effect of the colonial state of the future".'[2] According to Schorske, 'The election of 1907 brought home to the party the power of the imperialist ideology, the state's principal weapon against the socialist threat.'[3]

1. Luxemburg 1915b, p. 40.
2. Kautsky 1907a, p. 588, quoted in Schorske 1970, p. 63.
3. Schorske 1970, p. 88.

For Parvus, the root cause of imperialism was capitalist overproduction and the protectionist drive to monopolise markets for the export of both commodities and capital. In earlier periods, colonial riches had been the objects of imperialist plunder. Now that relationship was changing. Capitalist industry, he wrote, 'forcefully demands an expansion of the market', yet each capitalist state, by seeking to monopolise and protect its own markets, was simultaneously dividing the world market into smaller units. This, for Parvus, was the main contradictory effect of imperialism: 'Each industrial state wants to have its own *colonial empire*, from which all other industrial states will be excluded or driven back as much as possible.'[4] Emphasising the contradiction between the scale of modern industry and the restrictive effects of protectionism, Parvus warned German workers that empire-building would only occur at the expense of their own wages. In response to the 'imperialistic enthusiasm' described by Rosa Luxemburg, he called for democratisation of Germany's political system and the economic unification of Europe, first through removal of all economic barriers and ultimately through socialist revolution: 'Demokratie, Einigung Europas, Freihandel [Democracy, Union of Europe, Free Trade]' were his watchwords.[5]

Reviewing Parvus's book in 1907, Rudolf Hilferding spoke of it as an 'important contribution' to understanding the 'driving factors' behind German politics and capitalist expansionism. Hilferding shared Parvus's conviction that imperialist protectionism ultimately narrowed markets rather than expanding them, with the consequence that the workers' interests were actually better served by free trade. Division of the world into colonial empires would ultimately mean 'technological decline and a growing pressure on the workers' wages'. Hilferding concluded:

4. Parvus, 'Vor den Reichstagswahlen 1907,' in Parvus 1907, p. 17.

5. Parvus 1907, p. 30. The 'United States of Europe' slogan was embraced by the Austro-Marxists like Otto Bauer: 'The *United States of Europe* will thus be no longer a dream, but the inevitable ultimate goal of a movement that the nations have long since begun and that will be enormously accelerated by forces that are already becoming apparent.' Bauer 2000, p. 414. In 1911, Karl Kautsky adopted the 'United States of Europe' slogan, but Rosa Luxemburg dismissed it as imperialist and racist: Kautsky 1911a (April), Luxemburg 1911a (6–8 May). For an English version of Rosa Luxemburg's article see Chapter 28.

Parvus shows in detail how the connection between colonial policy and protectionism, arising out of the community of interests between large landowners, cartelised industry, bureaucracy and militarism, stands in contradiction with the requirements of the development of capitalist production itself. He demonstrates very well how tariff-protection ultimately becomes the enemy of European capitalism, which, through the division of the European economic territory into little areas separated by tariff-barriers, will be abandoned to the superior strength of North-American competition. The free-trade policy of the proletariat, far from hindering the development of production, will on the contrary strongly accelerate it, and with it also the triumph of the proletariat.[6]

* * *

'Before the "Hottentot Elections": The Capitalist Drive to the Colonies'[7]

The drive to expand Germany's naval power and colonies has already stood at the foreground of German colonial policy for several years. People aim at creating a *German colonial empire*. But the other capitalist industrial states display the same striving for colonial possessions. The phenomenon must therefore have general causes. Indeed, these are readily apparent: they lie in *capitalist overproduction* and *capitalist competition*.

People have long argued in the economic literature over whether there is overproduction. It has been said that there is no overproduction but rather underconsumption, because the people do not even remotely consume what they need. But that is just a squabble over words. If someone wants to understand by overproduction a surplus over *popular needs*, then there is certainly no overproduction because the great popular masses lack even the most

6. Hilferding 1907a, p. 687. By 1910, however, Hilferding's view had changed. In *Finance Capital*, he argued that the workers' interest lay neither with free trade nor with protectionism, only with socialism: 'The proletariat avoids the bourgeois dilemma – protectionism or free trade – with a solution of its own: neither protectionism nor free trade, but socialism.' Hilferding 1981, p. 366. At that point, Eduard Bernstein criticised Hilferding for abandoning the fight for free trade. See Bernstein 1911a, p. 951.

7. Parvus, 'Vor den Reichstagswahlen 1907', in Parvus 1907, pp. 11–17. The current title was provided by the editors of this anthology.

necessary goods for their vital needs. But that is not the point. Capitalist overproduction arises from the *surplus of the propertied classes' revenues over their expenses*. That surplus is certainly enormous. And that is precisely the dreadful contradiction: *while the popular masses starve, a few capitalists have so much that they do not know where to place their wealth*.

The workers have the need, but not the means to buy the commodities; the capitalist class has the money, but not the need. Thus a part of the annual production is left over. What to do with it?

In the first period of a country's capitalist development, when capital-accumulation is not yet large, it is understandable that the contradiction appears less acute. It also does not assert itself very strongly so long as industry confronts a significant stratum of craftsmen, at whose expense it can expand. The capital-surplus is then employed for the expansion of industry, which creates for itself a market by displacing the independent producers. To an even larger extent, capitalist industry, in that early period, makes room for itself by destroying the natural economy in the countryside and turning the peasants into buyers of commodities – and thereby, of course, also into commodity sellers. The spinning room must give way to the cotton-spinning mill, the hand-weaver to the cloth-mill, and, like them, the shoemaker and the tailor must make way for the shoe and textile-industries. In the meantime, capitalist production grows and with it the capital-surplus constantly looking for new employment.

At the same time, ever more powerful means of production are set into motion. The colossal initial capital-investments that they require conceal for a while the contradiction of overproduction immanent in capitalist production. The most conspicuous example in this respect is railway-construction. As long as the railway-network is being built, the capital-surplus finds in it abundant employment – indeed, capital is raised abroad for development of the railway-network. Whole branches of industry develop in connection with railway-construction. However, when the country is saturated with railways, it regularly suffers an economic crisis because the capital-surplus can no longer find employment.

Hence industry's drive into foreign markets, which already appears at a quite early stage of its development. *Instead of enabling the local population to satisfy its own needs through higher wages, the capitalists seek with might and main to dispose of the surplus abroad*.

In each new country selected by capitalist industry as a market, the same process repeats itself. It happened in England, France and Germany, in the whole of Europe, in Russia and the United States. Everywhere capital has awakened enormous productive forces, and everywhere the result has been growing overproduction. Now they all crowd together, seeking new markets.

Germany is a huge industrial state. Its capital-accumulation has reached colossal dimensions, and its surplus-capital is therefore correspondingly colossal.

Germany's capitalist magnates have built for themselves castles surpassing the homes of princes in splendour and wealth – palaces, compared to which the old knightly castles appear as beggarly barracks. The luxury-industry reaches dimensions that dwarf anything of which people could have dreamed. Pleasure-retreats in the four corners of the world, special railway- and steamer-lines, a whole population of lackeys, waiters and hotel-workers stands at the service of the international aristocracy of money. And, yet, what the capitalist class consumes is minuscule compared to the surpluses it annually gets from exploitation of the workers.

To the extent that the capitalist class pays taxes, part of it goes to the state and municipalities. However, the popular masses must pay even more money through excise-duties [indirect taxation]: while the capitalist class pays yearly just 300 million marks in taxes, the popular masses have to pay more than 2,000 million marks! That means a curtailment of their income, which reduces their purchasing power in the same proportion and consequently increases the unsaleable commodity-surplus, the overproduction!

The more difficult it becomes for the capitalist class to invest its surplus-capital into production, the more willing it is to invest that surplus in public bonds. The enormous growth of the state-debt of the German Empire is in this respect proof of the growth of capitalist overproduction. The public debt of the federal government and of the four main states of the German Empire (Prussia, Bavaria, Saxony and Württemberg) amounts to 12,556 million marks. A part of that debt is placed abroad, but on the other hand an incomparably larger amount of German capital is also invested in foreign state-securities. *While the German people thus live a miserable existence, a stream of gold pours out of Germany over the entire world.*

The state-debt bears interest. The federal government and the four main states of the German Empire each year pay 464 million marks as interest, which flow into the pockets of the capitalist class and once again increase its surplus-wealth.

On the other hand, taxes and debts admittedly increase state-consumption. If the state spent that money for the benefit of the people, one could not object. But the state uses it mainly for war, armaments, naval outlays and colonial policy. [...] [The German Empire spends over a billion marks each year for those purposes]. To this should be added the huge amount of labour-power unproductively wasted every year in the military: in 1906 there were 614,363 people in the army and 43,669 in the navy; i.e., 658,032 persons taken away from production who had to be fed by the people.

But capitalism needs this huge waste of men and goods; it tempts, provokes and, if necessary, forcefully drives the state to this end because it can no longer control the productive forces it has brought into being.

While the German capitalist class worries about where to put its enormously growing surplus-wealth, a constant demographic surplus arises. In the last twenty years, *more than a million Germans emigrated* – 1,063,000 to be more precise. *The capitalists do not know where to place their money, nor the masses how to make a living.*

And overproduction increases constantly! *Colonies* are needed precisely in order to create an outlet for them.

The drive to the colonies, caused by capitalist overproduction, is heightened by *capitalist competition*. When the capitalist industry of a country creates a market for itself by exploiting the workers, the sales-potential appears boundless to the single capitalist enterprise because it counts on the prospect of driving the other producers out of the market and obtaining an outlet at their expense. It therefore strives to expand on and on. Moreover, it is compelled to do so because competition, whose main weapon is cheap prices, forces it to expand. Production, therefore, cannot be stabilised; industry must either develop or break down! Continuously growing expansion of production or...an economic crisis! The whole development of the capitalist commodity market resembles an ice-field, in which individual ice-floes pile up, dash into each other and gather into icebergs, while ever-growing masses of ice push from below, and all together are carried away in a furious stream.

Thus people go to the colonies not in order to fetch something there – that comes at a later phase – but because capitalist development forces them to dispose of the country's surplus-capital. Capital looks for investment opportunities. The capitalists look for some faraway place where they can unload the wealth they have extracted from the workers. The colonies are there not in order to draw money from them, but in order to put money into them. That is the crux of modern capitalist colonial policy. Look at the German-African colonies! These are wastelands, deserts, but that does not matter: all the more capital can be plugged into them! People want to build railways through primeval forests, to cultivate rocky soils. German capital will do wonders in Africa just in order to deprive German workers of the opportunity of benefiting from the wealth they have created in their own country.

First of all, of course, the state must assume the burdens of colonial policy. It must begin by sending to the colonies *civil servants* and *military personnel*, who must be paid by the people. They are followed by the steamship lines set up with *state-subventions*. Then people begin to advance to the interior of the colonies; and, the more they push in, the more they make the indigenous population rebellious because no primitive people has yet submitted to capitalist exploitation willingly. Thus begin the *colonial wars*. But that is precisely what was lacking: colonial wars bring the colony straight away to a higher level of development, because they increase state-expenses enormously, and money consequently flows to the colony *en masse*. That is the stage of development reached at present by the German-African colonies. Now, after their soil has been fertilised with German blood and paved with German gold, a *liberal-capitalist colonial policy* can be stage-managed. It starts with the *railways*. Dernburg's memorandum formally inaugurates this new era.[8] It reaches the following conclusion: 'The sacrifices that we had to make until now for our dependencies rest only secondarily on economic grounds, and to a much larger extent on military grounds.... The experiences of all colonial peoples confirm that large colonial areas without railways remain uncertain possessions that are impossible to develop economically.' Thus, we cannot do without railways. Moreover, their construction has already started. More appropriations are therefore required for railway-construction, and their approval by the majority parties, including the Centre, has already been

8. [A reference to Bernhard Dernburg (1865–1937), a financier and public official in Wilhelmine Germany, who served as colonial director (1906) and colonial secretary (1907–10), and later as finance minister in the Scheidemann cabinet (1919) and Reichstag deputy (1920–30). Among his published lectures delivered on the occasion of the 'Hottentot elections' can be mentioned Dernburg 1907a, 1907b and 1907c.]

secured. Now, one railway will follow another. Their end is not in sight, and they will cost *billions*.

It is in the nature of things that trade and production will also, to a certain extent, develop in connection with the huge sums the state overspends. But the whole colonial economy is unprofitable because it costs the people far too much. Today, there are already German farms in South Africa. But each glass of milk produced on an African farm is more expensive for German taxpayers than a glass of champagne. That is precisely the crux of the matter: whether German industry and wealth must be used to transplant the capitalist mode of production to Africa with might and main, so that the surplus-wealth of the capitalist class can be increased even more – or whether it should rather be *used within the country to increase the welfare of the people*.

That the colonies will never cover their costs, that the people will therefore always have to throw good money after bad, is conceded by the German government itself. The best possible scenario is that, with time, perhaps, the colonies will cover their own *administrative costs*, but not the large military and infrastructure-costs. [...] [Parvus provides statistics showing the outlays and income of the French state in the colony of Algiers, which Dernburg had taken as his model, during the years 1830–1900: tax-revenues covered only 30 percent of expenditures during those seven decades]. Those are the financial prospects of the colonies that the government memorandum itself holds up to us.

It has been calculated that Germany has already spent *one billion marks* in its colonies, not including naval outlays. That billion will rapidly be forgotten in face of the *many new billions* that German colonial policy will require. That is its real course!

Finally, the continuation of colonial policy is depicted as a matter of 'national honour'. What is the purpose of colonial policy? It serves to deprive the people of the wealth they created and that they require for the satisfaction of their own needs; to take it away from them and waste it. It also serves for the bourgeoisie to exploit its own as well as foreign peoples. If there is any matter of national honour involved, then in our opinion it can only be to keep our hands off these disgraceful proceedings.

Chapter Twenty-Two

'Colonies and Capitalism in the Twentieth Century' (June 1907)

Parvus (Alexander Helphand)

'Colonies and Capitalism in the Twentieth Century' is the third part of Parvus's book on *Colonial Policy and the Breakdown*, a collection of four essays written on the occasion of the so-called 'Hottentot elections' to the German Reichstag on 25 January 1907 (see also the previous document). This essay consists of seven sections, of which we have translated sections four to six.

Many of the earlier articles that we have included in this anthology were preliminary attempts, often journalistic accounts of current events, to define modern imperialism. In that sense, they were tentative and hypothetical. This essay by Parvus is of an entirely different order. No longer is imperialist expansion associated with contingent historical events or the whims of individual statesmen in Europe or America; instead, Parvus makes a first attempt at a systematic exposition of modern imperialism in terms of the laws of capitalist development that Karl Marx explained in *Capital*. For Parvus, modern capitalism has become a *world system* of interconnected 'national' economies, and *capital* itself has grown beyond its particular manifestations in production and exchange to merge in the form of *finance-capital*.

With his emphasis upon the *global* process of capital-accumulation, Parvus anticipated the work of Rosa Luxemburg in her famous book *The Accumulation of Capital*; and, by exploring the mediating role of banks in that process, he also anticipated both Hilferding's *Finance Capital* and Lenin's essay on *Imperialism: the Highest Stage of Capitalism.*

In place of the personal proclivities or political stratagems of a Cecil Rhodes or Joseph Chamberlain, in Parvus's account the principal forces at work are the tendency of the falling rate of profit and the effects of capitalist production on the distribution of social income, both of which were compelling developed capitalist states to sustain profit-rates through foreign investments and to realise commodity-values through exports to foreign markets. Parvus ties together the loose ends in previous accounts of imperialism and weaves them into a coherent Marxist tapestry that attempts, for the first time, to provide a comprehensive picture of the global order emerging at the outset of the twentieth century.

The first section of 'Colonies and Capitalism in the Twentieth Century' ('Cultural Work in South Africa'), deals with the Herero and Namaqua genocide. Some 65,000 Hereros were massacred by German troops from 1904 to 1908 in German Southwest Africa (modern-day Namibia), whose southern region was inhabited by the Nama, or Hottentot, people. Out of 80,000 Hereros, only 15,000 survived the war and German concentration-camps. Parvus wrote that 'with the Herero War, in which a whole people were massacred', the Reichstag for the first time gained 'deeper understanding of the great social drama taking place in South Africa'.[1] Describing slave-hunting expeditions as 'the first *capitalist cultural work* in Africa', he showed how the natives' lands were seized by white settlers, while food-shortages and alcoholism were used 'to turn the savages into wage-workers'. This, Parvus ironically remarked, was the sort of 'capitalist cultural work' now being applauded by Eduard Bernstein, 'a former spokesman for socialism'. There is no need to translate here Parvus's entire account of this 'cultural work', for much more detailed studies are today available.[2] We will only summarise by noting that, according

1. Parvus 1907, p. 63.
2. Drechsler 1980.

to Parvus, the iniquities perpetrated by Germany against the natives were a hundred times worse than those perpetrated by England against the Boers.[3]

Section Two ('The Colonies and the Development of Capitalism in Europe') offered an overview of the primitive-accumulation process that Marx had described in the first volume of *Capital*, including references to mercantilist legislation, the rise of colonial plantation-slavery, the expropriation and proletarianisation of European peasants, etc. The most remarkable passage in this section involves the distinction drawn between exploitation-colonies in the tropical and subtropical regions and work colonies in the temperate regions, a taxonomy also developed by Kautsky in several of his articles and particularly in his book *Socialism and Colonial Policy*.[4] Both Parvus and Kautsky used that distinction to highlight the significance of the United States for the future of capitalism, although, in practice, this approach led to a rather tolerant attitude towards settler-colonialism that might well be considered racist by modern standards.

Section Three ('The Colonies and the Developed Capitalist World Market') dealt with the economic development of the United States in the nineteenth century, and particularly with the role of American food-exports in bringing down European ground-rents and provoking the call for agrarian protection by European landowners. Among other things, Parvus noted that Canada and Australia, following the pattern of the United States, had also become virtually independent, with the implication that this was a general tendency that would lead to replacement of colonial policy by commercial policy.

Parvus then turned to an explanation of the search for markets characteristic of modern colonial policy. Perhaps the most surprising aspect of his analysis of imperialism was his emphasis on the exploitation of metropolitan workers rather than of the colonial countries, with a consequent transfer of material values from imperialist centres to the colonies rather than the other way round. While German proponents of imperial conquests promised benefits to German workers, Parvus replied that imperialism resulted from limitations on working-class consumption and that these could only intensify:

3. Parvus 1907, p. 75.

4. Parvus 1907, pp. 82–3. 'In my article of 1883 I named two types of colonies: "Work-Colonies" and "Exploitation-Colonies". I still hold these descriptions to be valid today.' Kautsky 1907b, p. 24.

> The development of production requires an expansion of the demand for commodities, which can only be achieved by increasing the number of consumers among the popular masses and the volume of their consumption, i.e., through the social advance of the *working class*. But the proletariat is today much more hindered in its social rise by capitalist private property in the means of production than the bourgeoisie was in its day by feudal property in land and the political privileges of the aristocracy. As long as that fundamental cause is not removed, the contradiction between the development of capitalist production and the development of the capitalist commodity market assumes ever-sharper forms. Hence the feverish *search for sales markets*, which is most characteristic of modern capitalist development in general and of *modern capitalist colonial policy* in particular. A complete reversal of circumstances has taken place: people first looked to the colonies for treasures and rare articles like spices, and then for mass-consumption articles and raw materials to further domestic production; but today all that recedes before the wish to find in the colonies *buyers for European products*.[5]

The parts of this brochure most relevant to the origins of the theory of imperialism are Sections Four to Six, which are translated below and elaborate Parvus's argument that colonial policy results principally from domestic overproduction (or underconsumption) and that monetary and industrial capital have coalesced in search of a higher rate of profit in foreign lands. In the final section of the work, ('Colonies, Technical Development and Wages') Parvus predicted that the future of European industry lay not in colonies but in Europe's own economic integration. He was among the first to claim that the most lucrative opportunities lay in exchange of goods *between advanced economies themselves*, whereas a sustained commitment to colonial exploitation would entail both technological decline and further intensification of the problem of markets due to steadily rising taxation of workers in support of imperialist adventures.

* * *

5. Parvus 1907, p. 86.

'Colonies and Capitalism in the Twentieth Century'[6]

The motives of modern colonial policy

We have already pointed out that the main driving force of modern colonial policy is the search for *markets*. The governments are definitely aware of this motive power, but they confuse it and mix it up with motives carried over from earlier phases of capitalist colonial development. Let us look at the main reasons that have been alleged for the need to hold colonies and then examine them on the basis of colonial development and the current state of the matter. We have already emphasised that we must distinguish between *overseas trade* and *overseas colonies*:

1.) *Settlement-areas*: We know from the history of America that *agriculture* provided the broad foundation for European immigration. On the other hand, the capitalist revolution in Western Europe created the preconditions for the great outflow of emigrants by proletarianising the peasantry. The great stream of immigrants to America now comes from Eastern Europe, especially Russian Poland and Galicia, as well as from Italy. It goes to the United States and Argentina, which, for the foreseeable future, can still absorb growing numbers of immigrants. The attempt to divert the emigration flow to Africa is an absurdity; and besides, it is totally impossible to implement. The workers who emigrate from Central Europe are moved to do so by the development of American industry. Insofar as Africa comes into consideration for those emigrants, they will not go to the colonial possessions of Germany and other European states but rather to the mining districts with urban populations, i.e., the area of Cape Town and the former Boer republics, which already find themselves in the transitional stage from a colony to an independent state.

Naturally, for us socialists, the fundamental issue is that the formation of a 'surplus'-population cannot be prevented by deporting it across the ocean. That is a problem whose solution presupposes abolition of the capitalist form of property.

2.) *Supplying countries*: Let us now look at *Germany's* commodity-imports. Germany is an industrial state; it is also one whose government argues that

6. Parvus, 'Die Kolonien und der Kapitalismus im XX. Jahrhundert', in Parvus 1907, pp. 92–105, 110.

the establishment of a colonial empire has become a vital necessity. [...] The cheap production of raw materials can no more be the goal of modern colonial policy than the cheap production of foodstuffs, because the actual preconditions for that are lacking. But colonial policy was not meant for that purpose at all. Even if Germany actually succeeds in raising a considerable cotton-crop in Africa, the first consequence – assuming that no fundamental change takes place in its commercial policy – will be the imposition of *import-tariffs* on cotton produced outside the colonies. Just as foodstuffs were made dearer by tariffs, and as tariffs were imposed on cotton-yarns even though they served the production-needs of the weaving mills, so also will tariffs be introduced, to the detriment of the German textile-industry, on raw-cotton imports in order to promote colonial cotton-cultivation. Protective tariffs and colonial policy go hand in hand, and Europe's colonial policy can therefore only be understood if it is seen in connection with its tariff-policy. We will return to this point later.

3.) *Markets*: German industry finds its markets mainly in Europe itself, followed by the United States, South America and Asia. Those destinations taken together receive 97 *per cent* of German commodity-exports. If we look specifically at exports to Asia, we find that they go mainly to East India, China and Japan. What does this mean?

The more advanced the economic, political and cultural development of a country, the larger the market it represents for industry. The contradiction between industrial countries and industrial sales markets no longer exists. The main markets for industry are today the industrial countries. Thus 18 per cent of German commodity-exports go to England, 9 per cent to the United States, and 23 per cent to France, Belgium Holland and Switzerland.

The statistics speak clearly enough, but they could only do so after other industrial states developed alongside England, because, until then, actual relations in the world market were different. England drew its raw materials from the colonies and its foodstuffs from the European continent, and it used Europe as a market in which to sell its manufactured products. But this special position of England was conditioned by the scarce development of industry and the world market, and by the backwardness of Europe's social development. The nineteenth century thoroughly did away with the conditions for England's industrial supremacy. It placed industrial technique on a scientific basis and turned it into a common good of all nations; it established the capitalist social order in Europe and America and, above all, it created the free proletariat required for the development of industry. It also created the conditions for development in Asia; it mutually linked the nations through the construction of railways and steamship-lines; it created great cities that have become the nodal points of an international culture; it centralised money-capital, transplanting it all over the world, organising it and placing at its disposal a world communication-service. From London or Berlin today, by pressing an electric button, capital can command armies of workers in all continents.

At the same time, industrial development has quite obliterated the distinction between raw materials and manufactured products: capital no longer regards this distinction as one between different objects, but as one between the different positions occupied by these objects in the circulation-process. Cotton-yarns are a manufactured product, but they are also raw material for the weaving mills. The import of cheap railway-tracks means competition for the iron-industry, but it also favours the development of railways, which increase iron-consumption and first make possible the development of a modern iron-industry. The import of cheap cotton ousts peasant linen-weaving, creating the conditions for development of the cotton-industry. We have ahead of us the completion of a world-market development that contradicts its starting point: it is not the old but rather the new industries that today have the competitive advantage, because they can be set up according to new technical conditions. Any new industrial state, whether in America or in Asia, that is able to base its industry and transportation on electricity by exploiting favourable natural conditions will drive all others from the world market.

The development of the world market has not only equalised the technical and social conditions of production in Europe, America and partly in Asia, but has also brought, as commercial statistics show, the industries of all countries into the deepest and broadest connection and interaction. It can be stated as a principle that the development of an industrial country depends above all on the development of its trade with the other industrial countries.

The development of the world market pushes towards an ever-increasing amalgamation of the industrial countries; it creates a *world production* that is striving after corresponding political forms. The commercial policy of capitalist governments is not the result of that development of production but rather its antithesis.

The struggle of capitalist production against inherited state-formations has a long history. Capitalism tore down feudal barriers, built the centralised state, and later created the national state. The capitalist class was the revolutionary carrier of this development. Now, the development of production, with the corresponding degree of development of the world market, once again encounters political barriers. The capitalist class, however, no longer furthers this development but rather hinders it, because capitalist development has reached a stage where the capitalist form of property finds itself in permanent contradiction with the development of production. The agent of this new development can only be *the proletariat*.

Capitalist overproduction – that is, the contradiction between capitalist production and the capitalist distribution of goods resulting from the capitalist property form – drives capital in the individual countries to obtain a special place in the world market through the state's instruments of power. That is the meaning of the protectionist system as it developed at the end of the nineteenth century. The domestic market is for 'national' capital – and the foreign market too! But by barricading themselves in that way, countries mutually cut themselves off from markets. Then they try mutually to undermine their tariffs through *export-bounties* – a crazy trade policy leading to bankruptcy. Simultaneously, efforts grow all the more to secure in the colonies the markets that industrial states prevent each other from finding in their mutual exchange. The drive to the colonies is a flight of capital away from its own tariff-system, which capital itself, however, has carried over to the colonies. That is *imperialism*: the combination of an industrial state and a colonial empire, and their common separation from the rest of the world by a tariff-wall! If this ideal is indeed realised in practice, the contradictions of capitalist development leading to this capitalist *imperium* will, for the first time, really assert themselves. But it cannot be attained, because the connections of world-market development cannot be torn apart. Again, we see a reversal of circumstances that is very characteristic of the current degree of development of capitalist economy: while the policy of the proletariat gains more and more real ground, the policy of the capitalist class turns to fantastic and groundless plans. But, since the capitalist class is in possession of state-power, the utopian policy of capital is a danger to the peoples, since the attempt to thwart the development of the world market by force must lead, and moreover has already led, to catastrophes in the world market and to outbreaks of political violence.

English imperialism

In order to understand in their concrete form, the colonial – or rather imperialist – struggles with which the twentieth century has begun, we must consider *England*'s commercial relations with the protectionist countries. [...] [Parvus here quotes figures showing the growth of Great Britain's foreign trade since 1854.] England [...] long benefited from Europe's industrial development: it increased its exports to Europe as well as its imports from it; and indeed this is, as we have explained, the normal consequence of the development of the world market. But, ever since 1880, i.e., since the beginning of the new protectionist era on the European continent, a sharp turn has taken place: England's imports from Europe grew continuously, but its exports to Europe grew much more slowly. [...] [Parvus quotes statistics showing that a relative drop in England's exports vis-à-vis its imports had also taken place in its commercial relations with the United States, and that if that tendency continued England would ultimately import more manufactured products than it exported.] And yet, until the middle of the nineteenth century, it was argued that England was 'the workshop of the world'! The demise of England's exceptional position is again a normal result of world-market development, but its outcome was shifted and distorted to England's disadvantage by the protectionist tariffs of the other states.

While the European industrial states kept back English imports through protective tariffs, they also exploited England's free-trade policy to penetrate the English colonies. That is suggested by the growing figures of English re-exports. This intermediary trade above all benefited *Germany*, which also did not neglect to carry on direct trade with the English colonies. That trade developed all the more quickly, the more those colonies were on the road to their economic and political independence.

English imperialism clearly emerged as an antithesis to the protectionist systems of the other industrial countries. In this respect, it is a political reaction of world-market development to the commercial policy of states running contrary to it. One incongruity generated another – in that manner, capitalist development corrects itself. But the phenomenon also has another side. English imperialism is not just the reflection of European and American tariff-policy; it is also, at the same time, the political reaction of the English capitalist class to the social development of its colonies.

We know that the development of the capitalist colonies leads to their detachment from the mother-country. This process is accompanied by an ever-stronger expansion of the colonies' commercial relations with other countries to the detriment of the mother-country. The commercial policy of the great English colonies provides us with quite clear evidence of this. [...] [Parvus quotes figures showing a decrease in English exports to the colonies expressed as a percentage of their total imports.]

English capital, which in its struggle against the protectionist industrial states is seeking to secure a monopoly-position in its colonies, must, in the process, enter into an ever-increasing conflict with the development of production of the colonies themselves, which requires, on the contrary, an ever-growing development of their international commercial relations.

The capitalist development of production, leading to an equalisation of technical and social conditions of production over the entire world, at the same time brings to bear once more the geographical and natural conditions of production it previously rendered ineffective. Thus, we see a process of economic consolidation in America, and another one in East Asia. This social amalgamation, borne by the development of the world market, must become increasingly powerful. English imperialism is trying to disentangle the colonies from this process – colonies that are scattered all over the world and increasingly interrelated with their surroundings and with the non-English world by their economic development – and to combine them into a world-unit with the help of state-power. In that sense, it is completely irrational.

English imperialism does not mean the strengthening but rather the death convulsions of the British Empire. It is not the beginning of a development but the end. Imperialist ideas ruled at the beginning of English colonial policy.[7]

7. England, in the seventeenth and eighteenth centuries, repeatedly enacted prohibitions to its colonies to import commodities otherwise than in English ships with English captains and sailors; it prohibited direct exports from the colonies to foreign countries; it drew up a special list of articles whose export was possible only to England or to other colonies, including sugar, cotton, and tobacco (the list was continuously extended, so that it finally included all significant colonial export-articles); prohibitive tariffs for non-English exports were repeatedly imposed; not content with

Like the other European colonial powers, England did not dream of granting independence to its colonies and opposed that development with all its military power. But English imperialism received a death-blow at the end of the eighteenth century with the American Revolution. Since then, Great Britain, through a policy of adaptation and concessions, has managed to sustain a more-or-less loose political connection with its settlement-colonies. Today, that development has reached such a point that the British Empire is threatened from all sides with disintegration. Thus we see English capital making a desperate attempt at the last moment to keep its colonial empire together by the most unsuitable means – all the more unsuitable as it has to wage a difficult struggle at the same time for its position in the world market. That is modern English imperialism.

But the more difficult it becomes for English capital to sustain a monopoly-commercial position in the progressive colonies, and the more it must expect competition from industries developing in the colonies themselves or in geographically privileged places, the more it also looks around for backward colonial areas. Thus Africa also appears to them as the object of their desire.

Banks, cartels and colonial policy in Africa

In his speeches glorifying colonial policy, the German colonial director Dernburg[8] mentioned as an important reason the fact that during the past 22 years German 'national wealth' has grown 'by at least 30 billion' and that the deposits in savings banks amount to 700 million marks annually. That is supposed to prove, firstly, that because the wealth of the bourgeoisie grew, it is ingratitude and presumptuousness on the part of the workers to complain about the taxes that cut down their meagre wages. But, in the mind of the man appointed to carry over the business practice of the banks into the politics of the German Reich, those figures have another fundamental significance: they are, for him, capital in search of investments, capital that must find employment by any means and by force if necessary. He portrayed as a great

that, England was anxious to nip in the bud any independent commercial activity in its colonies by means of tariffs and direct interdictions, and it arbitrarily burdened the colonies with taxes. It [English mercantilism] was an *imperialism* such as nobody dares to dream about today, and it led to the collapse of the system even back then.

8. [See the previous chapter, footnote 8.]

mistake the fact that Germany did not embark earlier upon a far-reaching colonial policy and declared: 'Today we are compelled to do so, much more than before, by *the expansion needs of our industry*.' Finally, he even referred to the judgement of a French writer: 'Contemporary Germany must either sell overseas or perish.'

It is not Germany but *the rule of capital* that stands before its doom, and this holds not only for Germany!

It is enough to establish at this point that the leader of German colonial policy lumps together overseas trade with colonial trade, so that commercial intercourse with America, which is prevented by protective tariffs, serves to justify the subventions for steamers trading with Africa.

For us, it is important to recognise in the above-mentioned official justification of German colonial policy the real driving force of modern capitalist colonial policy that we ascertained earlier. Admittedly, it confronts us today in a parodied form, generated by the confusion of capitalist development as a class-phenomenon with the social development of nations. By growing 'national wealth', we must understand the growing *capital-accumulation* that gives rise to the 'expansion needs of our industry'. But just why the expansion needs of industry do not generate a corresponding expansion of the *domestic market* is a problem falling beyond the capitalists' ken. We know that this contradiction arises as a result of capitalist overproduction because the capitalist form of property stands in the way of the expansion of demand in the capitalist commodity market. Hence capital's striving to win foreign markets over and beyond the domestic market, a striving that has also been enormously boosted by the growing interrelations of world production. The capitalist statesmen may not be able to explain this phenomenon, but the very fact imperiously forces itself upon them and they therefore accept it as a natural necessity.

Mr. Dernburg speaks in stock-exchange jargon. This much, however, emerges from his exposition without further ado; namely, that modern colonial policy is less a question of economic benefits from the colonies and more one of the *inner necessity of capital*, which forces it to look for colonial areas wherever possible and by any means. That driving force manifests itself in the growing accumulation of money-capital, although this by no means gives the full measure of its size.

The nineteenth century witnessed a colossal concentration and accumulation of money-capital in the banks. [...] [Parvus gives statistics showing the growth of banking capital in England.] The visible amount of circulating money-capital thus grew in the nineteenth century because of growing capital-accumulation, but also because the congestion points of money circulation were eliminated, because manufacturers and merchants deposited circulating money in banks or invested it in commercial paper, so that the cash-reserve in their coffers was reduced to a minimum. The development of bank-clearing also reduced the number of cash settlements, replacing them by accounting transfers. At the same time, the banks and saving banks capitalised the money of peasants and craftsmen, the income of social strata standing outside the production-process such as the liberal professions (physicians, lawyers, etc.) and civil servants, and even the wages of workers and maidservants before their use as means of payment for the purchase of goods. The growth of money-capital, which arises automatically in the capitalist class due to the excess of surplus-value over the demand required for the upkeep of that class, is artificially engendered in other classes of the population through the limitation of their consumption, through 'thrift'. The effect of the much-praised savings banks is thus a reduction of demand and an increase in the 'expansion-power of our industry'. This strengthens and sharpens more than ever capitalist overproduction, or the contradiction between the development of production and the form of property.

To this should be added a fact based on a law of capitalist production development ascertained by Marx, which the capitalist class perceives not in its causal connection but in its effect as a growing drive to expand production. That law is the falling tendency of the rate of profit. In order to understand it, one must recall that with the development of technique the worker is able to tend complicated machines and process ever-larger amounts of raw materials; the result is that capital-investment per worker, insofar as it is a question of outlays on raw materials, machines and similar factory equipment, greatly increases. Thus, for instance, according to the *Statistischen Jahrbuch für das Deutsche Reich*, one worker processed on average 51.3 tons of pig-iron in 1885 and 80 tons in 1904, while, during the same period, the total value of the commodities produced on average by a worker grew from 5,200 to 7,000 marks. The *surplus-value* extracted from the workers by the capitalists also grows, but not in the same proportion; it can remain stable or even diminish. The growing surplus-value of the entire annual production of society is thus spread over capital that is growing at a faster pace, thus resulting in a lower profit-rate. The law of the falling tendency in the rate of profit is then transmitted to the credit system and manifests itself in the declining interest-rate. Thus, for instance, the average interest-rate of the Bank of England decreased from 4.5% in 1801–50 to 4.1% in 1851–60 and to 3.3% in 1881–8.

But wherever the banks' growing inflow of money may originate, whether in growing capital-accumulation, in the generalisation and facilitation [of credit transactions], in overcoming the weak points of monetary circulation or in the restriction of the consumers' demand, and whatever may determine the fall of the interest-rate, be it the law of the falling rate of profit arising from production or the excessive accumulation of money-capital – in any case, the result will be construed by the banks, or rather by the capitalist class, as a 'shortage of capital-investments' that they will try to redress through the expansion of industry.

Attempting to escape the law of the falling tendency of the rate of profit through the expansion of industry, which is bound up with technical revolutions, the capitalist class ultimately causes an even greater fall in the profit-rate. Inasmuch as it actually succeeds, by means of a hothouse-like development of industry, in raising the interest-rate for a short period of time, it is unable to explain the final result – an ever-stronger fall in the interest-rate – and it repeats the same process again.

Driven to relentless expansion by the general laws and inner connections of capitalism's contradictory development, capitalist industry seeks to avoid the obstacles that the restriction of consumption imposes upon it – a restriction that is caused by the exploitation of the worker – by increasing the *production of means of production*. Each new instrument of production is for it a welcome means to eliminate the old instruments of production, to drive factories to bankruptcy in order to erect new industries in their place. Each technical change is also immediately transplanted to all countries; and wherever any industrial activity begins to develop, it is immediately promoted by the industrial states that supply machines and semi-finished products. The consequence is that, since the end of the nineteenth century, a change has developed in the technical conditions of European industry that has great influence on the development of its market in the twentieth century. *The iron and machine industry* moved to the foreground of industrial production in place of the textile-industry. Whereas people formerly imported cheap cotton from foreign countries, now they look for areas where they can build up entire industries, actually transplanting railways and cotton-mills to Asia for that purpose.

We see that *railways* also move to the forefront of colonial policy in Africa. If one wants to look for an economic explanation of that phenomenon, it will be found less in Africa's economic development and more in the development of *the iron-industry in Europe and America*. After the building of railways in the industrial states, it was the iron-and-machine industry that crucially pushed for the forced construction of *armour-plated vessels* and is today pushing for the building of *railways in Africa*.

This development was facilitated by cartels, syndicates and the concentration of banks.

This subject has already acquired fundamental significance for contemporary capitalist development. Here, we can naturally offer only a brief outline in connection with our real subject.

The concentration of money-capital in the banks led to the concentration of banks. Industrial concentration grew out of technical development and capitalist competition, but it was significantly encouraged by the concentration of money-capital – in the banks as well as in individual hands. In the cartels and syndicates, we see a concentration of industrial capital that partly goes beyond the technical concentration of enterprises and partly presupposes it. On the other hand, the barriers between purely monetary capital and industrial capital have fallen down: the banks own the shares and financial obligations of industrial enterprises, which, in turn, own shares of the banks and have members on their supervisory boards. The whole system is ruled by *industrial cartels and banking syndicates*. The *capitalist state* appears as a third partner whose budget represents the greatest concentration of industrial as well as monetary capital. Through the technical transformations of the modern military and the public debt, the state is intimately bound up with private capital.

Following the laws of development of a capitalist world market that is driving it towards world production, concentrated capital has long ago deserted the soil of the 'national' state and found bases in the most distant parts of the world. [...]

Thus, we see *industrial cartels* (particularly in the *iron-industry*), *banks* and the *state* all cooperating in sweet harmony. This trinity rules capitalist policy. If one recalls this fact, one is no longer surprised by the collaboration between banks and government during the last elections. While people in the Reichstag argued with the government about the application and limits of political force, the cartels and banks outside the Reichstag subjugated the government and turned it into the instrument of their policy. The 'Hottentot' elections of 1907 have shown this dramatically. It was not merely a question of colonial policy but of the entire policy of the state in all areas, even if *colonial policy*, and particularly the *building of railways in the colonies*, is the immediate goal for which the cartels and banks are striving.

Chapter Twenty-Three

'German Imperialism and Domestic Politics' (October 1907)

Rudolf Hilferding

Rudolf Hilferding (1877–1941) was, like Otto Bauer, born in Vienna into a prosperous middle-class Jewish family. He joined the Austrian Social-Democratic Workers' Party (Sozialdemokratische Arbeiterpartei Österreichs or SDAP) in his student days. Whereas Bauer earned a Ph.D. in Law, Hilferding studied medicine at the University of Vienna. By 1902, however, his brilliance in economics was such that Karl Kautsky invited him to become a contributor to the SPD's theoretical journal *Die Neue Zeit*.

In 1904, together with socialist friends from university days – Max-Adler, Otto Bauer and Karl Renner – Hilferding founded a socialist publishing enterprise called the *Marx-Studien* [Marxist Studies] series. This joint effort was the foundation of what later came to be known as Austro-Marxism, a socialist point of view midway between Russian Marxism and the reformism of the Social-Democratic parties during the first three decades of the twentieth century. The first published volume of *Marx-Studien* was Hilferding's reply to Eugen von Böhm-Bawerk's *Karl Marx and the Close of his System*.

Unlike Bauer, who stayed in Vienna, Hilferding moved in 1906, at Kautsky's initiative, to Berlin, where the taught political economy at the SPD's party school. He was forced to give up this job because of a law forbidding the employment of teachers without German citizenship, but he remained in Berlin as editor of the SPD central daily paper *Vorwärts* and a regular contributor to both *Die Neue Zeit* and *Der Kampf*. There he completed his major work, *Finance Capital*, which was published in 1910. The work appeared initially as the fifth volume in the series of *Marx-Studien* and was later published separately as a book. A major theme of Hilferding's thinking concerned the institutional changes that had transformed the competitive capitalism of the mid-nineteenth century into a new form dominated by big banks together with industrial trusts and cartels – 'organised capitalism' – which enjoyed the active support of the capitalist state in a programme of imperialist expansion. At the time, *Finance Capital* was widely regarded as one of the most important publications in Marxist economics since *Capital*, a reputation that it still enjoys a century later.

In his biography of Rudolf Hilferding, F. Peter Wagner states that

> although *Finance Capital* was not published until 1910, the work 'was ready in its main outlines' by 1905, as Hilferding later admitted in the preface. These outlines can be traced in two of his early essays of the period: 'The Functional Change of the Protective Tariff,' published in 1902, and 'German Imperialism and Domestic Politics,' published under the pseudonym of Karl Emil in 1907.[1]

In his 1902 article, Hilferding had argued that by the turn of the century tariffs no longer fulfilled an 'educative' role of protecting nascent industries against foreign competition; instead, they now enabled local capitalists to form a cartel in order to finance 'dumping' in the world market and win out over competitors. Hilferding continued:

> ...this sharpening of the struggle for the world market cannot remain without consequences for the foreign policy of the capitalist nations. They will increasingly aspire to appropriate pieces of the world market where competition is increasingly more difficult, costly and insecure, in order to annex them to the domestic market, eliminate foreign competition by political means and monopolise them for the native capitalist class. The consequence is an aggressive colonial and world policy. The interests of high finance,

1. Wagner 1996, p. 72.

> whose business thrives best under the protection of the home state, are joined by those of industrial capital, organised in cartels, which now also follows a policy of expansion and exclusion towards foreign countries and wants to get rid of foreign competition by conquering foreign and neutral markets.[2]

Competition between the capitalist classes was increasingly carried out by political means, making victory dependent on instruments of power at the disposal of the state. The role of the capitalist state had to expand in order both to hold down the popular masses, whose standard of living was increasingly threatened by rising tariffs, and also to serve the interests of domestic capitalists in struggles over the world market. Hilferding warned that 'increase in armaments, growth of the navy, internal reaction, violence and threats to peace in foreign relations, those are the necessary consequences of the newest phase of capitalist commercial policy'.[3] In the final paragraph of the article from 1902, Hilferding wrote that modern commercial policy had

> ...ushered in the last phase of capitalism. In order to check the fall in the rate of profit – that law of motion of capitalism – capital did away with free competition, organised itself and, by means of that organisation, was able to place the state-power directly at the service of its exploitative interests. It is no longer the workers alone, but the entire population, who are subordinated to the desire for profit of the capitalist class. All the instruments of power available to society are consciously mobilised and converted into means by which capital can exploit society. It is the immediate precursor of socialist society because it is the complete negation of that society; a conscious socialisation of all the economic potentialities of modern society in a form that does not benefit society as a whole, but is intended to increase the rate of exploitation of the entire society to an unprecedented degree.[4]

Hilferding's later article on 'German Imperialism and Domestic Politics', which we have translated here, appeared two months after the Seventh International Socialist Congress, which met at Stuttgart in August 1907 and adopted the famous resolutions on colonial policy and militarism. Leon

2. Hilferding 1903a, p. 278.
3. Ibid.
4. Hilferding 1903a, pp. 280–1.

Trotsky judged the article to be 'Excellent!',[5] and Hilferding's biographer, Wagner, confirms its importance with the comment that *Finance Capital* can actually be read as his 'general commentary to the Stuttgart resolution'.[6]

A draft resolution initially proposed for the Stuttgart Congress by Henri van Kol and supported by the majority of the German delegation had declared that 'socialism strives to develop the productive forces of the entire globe and to lead all peoples to the highest form of civilisation. The congress therefore does not reject in principle every colonial policy. Under a Socialist régime, colonisation could be a force for civilisation.' After prolonged debate, the final resolution adopted an entirely different tone, declaring that imperialism led to 'enslavement' and 'extermination' of colonial peoples and that capitalism's claim to a civilising mission was merely 'a veil for its lust for conquest and exploitation'.[7] Rudolf Hilferding's article came to the same conclusion. Seven years before World War I, his study of German economic history convinced him that 'The colonial expansion of Germany is impossible without a European war'. The sole alternative to imperialism and war was democracy, and democracy in Germany was 'identical with Social Democracy'.

* * *

'German Imperialism and Domestic Politics'[8]

I

It is, at first sight, an amazing fact that, while the developed capitalist countries of Europe dispose of large colonial empires, some of which are very valuable for the capitalists, Germany, where capitalist economy has experienced the greatest and most intensive progress since the middle of the nineteenth century, has no comparable colonies, and the few that it does own were acquired very recently. It is understandable that the German capitalist class should regard that as a bitter contradiction. But we are interested, first of

---

5. Letter from Trotsky to Hilferding, no date, no year (possibly 1907): article by Hilferding on imperialism judged by Trotsky 'Excellent!' ['Ausgezeichnet!']. Wagner 1996, p. 88, note 29.
6. Wagner 1996, p. 84.
7. International Socialist Congress (7th) 1907. English passages in Riddell (ed.) 1984.
8. Hilferding 1907b.

all, in knowing why that happened, for the answer can perhaps shed some light on the character and future destiny of what we have become used to calling German imperialism.

The economic development of Germany is distinguished from that of the southern and western states of Europe because it remained for the longest period under the conditions of natural economy. The ultimate reason for this is that while Italy, Spain, France and England, partly under the influence of the Romans and their legacy, outgrew a purely agrarian culture, Germany found broad opportunity for nourishment of the surplus population generated by the agrarian-production conditions of that time first by clearing the primeval forests of the motherland and later through colonisation of the Slavic regions, whose scattered inhabitants, dwelling in sparsely populated and secluded villages, were driven back by force or partly assimilated in that vast colonisation-work that won for Germans the lands in the east and southeast.

But natural economy excluded all possibility of a strong, centralised power. Holders of public functions could only be rewarded for their services with gifts of land. The sovereign rights of the state were, so to speak, accessories to a certain landed property and were handed down together with the latter. All attempts of the royal central power to create a centralised administrative organisation came to nought due to economic conditions. The state was not a unitary organisation animated by a *single* state-will, but an aggregate of boisterous diminutive states, each one with its own will, and they only coalesced into a single will on special occasions, mostly under the compulsion of external necessity.[9]

9. The possibility of creating a homogeneous state-will, to which, as a result of the balance of power between the different classes of capitalist society, all classes of this society submit at any one time, is the condition that modern constitutional institutions must fulfill. The curiae-parliament of Austria was shipwrecked in the first place because it brought to bear the special interests of the particular classes and strata of bourgeois society in a way that made impossible the emergence of such a general state-will. This became apparent in the chronic obstruction that finally forced the introduction of equal suffrage under the pressure of the working class on the one hand and of state necessity on the other. Also in Germany, the shortcomings of its constitutional arrangements asserted themselves in the modern period. On the one hand, there is the distribution of electoral districts, which increasingly shifts to the disadvantage of city-dwellers and especially the working class, distorts the force of the urban population in the Reichstag, and therefore the resultant of the class-relations in terms of the state-will – not to mention the overdone division of power between the Federal Council [upper house of the German parliament] and the Reichstag. Further friction results from the fact that the political balance of power as expressed in the Reichstag, and

Monetary economy first generated the need and the opportunity for a single centralised state-power. The advent of commodity-production developed the cities, which supported the endeavours for state-unity and at the same time gave to their representative, the royal power, the means for creating the instruments of state-power: a bureaucracy and an army of mercenaries who no longer strove for land, and therefore for independence, but were paid with gold and thus were always dependent on the central power. But the time at which monetary economy developed, and the pace at which it unfolded its counter-tendencies to natural economic development, was of crucial importance for the development of that central government. The dissolution of the original central power into a series of feudal lordships and their centralisation into a sovereign territory was a centuries-long historical process. Monetary economy set in much earlier and developed much more rapidly in southern and western Europe than in Germany. Consequently, England and France succeeded in establishing central state-power, while Italy – where a monetary economy developed earliest and most quickly but foreign influences prevented development of central power – disintegrated into a series of city-states that rushed ahead of the great states of that time in terms of economic and therefore political power, as shown by the history of Venice, Florence and Genoa.

The driving force of the expansionary policy of those city-states was capital in commerce and usury, which developed very early in the pores of medieval society. While domestic trade still had, to a large extent, a 'handicraft' character, both as regards the size of its turnover and its manner of operation, a kind of commercial undertaking began to separate out of it and develop first as occasional but later as professional trade, above all as overseas trade, which was combined with piracy and the robbery and enslavement of overseas territories. The interests of this trade were what led to the first period of colonial economy. But colonial economy presupposed for its realisation the existence of a strong centralised state-power able to place the material and

therefore the will of the German nation, confronts the will of Prussia, the largest section of the nation, which is again determined in a completely different way. It is, on the one hand, the contradiction between the political will of Germany and that of Prussia, and, on the other, the contradiction in the formation of the Prussian state will itself, where 85 per cent of the population has not influence at all on the formation of the resultant, that turned the introduction of equal suffrage into a necessity if development is to proceed peacefully and constitutionally.

personal forces of the entire people at the service of colonial policy. Thus there arose at the same time as monetary economy and the development of commercial capital an interest in colonial policy and the possibility of implementing it. This naturally began where the development of commercial capital was strongest, in Italy. The Genoese and Venetians had already made the greatest gains from their participation in the Crusades, not only by supplying transport and financing the campaigns, but also through extensive land-acquisitions. From that time on, their whole endeavours were directed to expansion of their territories. Sombart correctly says that 'The systematic exploitation of the Mediterranean peoples through forced labour was the foundation upon which the primacy of Venice and Genoa arose.'[10]

The Italians discovered the Canary Islands in the fifteenth century and were the first to look for a sea-passage to the East Indies. Still later, they were mostly Italians who led the Atlantic peoples in voyages of discovery. 'Christopher Columbus,' says Burckhardt, 'was only the greatest in a whole series of Italians who travelled to foreign seas at the service of the Western peoples.'

The interests of commercial capital were what led to those discoveries, and their driving force, above all, was the search for a direct passage to the East Indies in order to bypass the commercial monopoly of the Arabs, who were taking the lion's share of the profits away from the European traders, and also to find an alternative to the trade-routes through Central Asia, which were disrupted by continuous struggles.

Those endeavours were also initiated by Italians. They were followed by the Portuguese, who finally found the sea-route to the West Indies and at the same time broke the Arabs' commercial monopoly by means of force. The struggles of nations entering the capitalist period broke out over India and later over newly discovered America; and, along with them, began the [Pope's] arbitrations of colonial possessions. Germany, however, was left out of those struggles. The reasons for this lay not only in the development of German *trade*. To be sure, it developed first as landed trade and, above all, as intermediary trade. South Germans mediated the trade of the Nordic countries with the Italian cities, which brought the riches of the East to Europe. The trade of Lower Germany mediated the exchange between East and West, between England and the Netherlands on the one hand and Scandinavia and the Slavic

10. Sombart 1902, p. 332.

East on the other. It was a trade dependent for its development on the progress of Italian and English trade. Nevertheless, on those foundations developed a commercial capital whose interests went well beyond those of intermediary trade and peremptorily demanded that Germany participate in partitioning the new world. Houses of the size and power of Fugger and Welser[11] supported a German colonial policy. But their endeavours failed due to lack of a strong central power, which alone would have been able to mobilise the vast resources required for such policy. A central power did not exist because development based on natural economy had long ago disrupted the Empire's unity. Development based on monetary economy came too late for the central government to be able to pluck its fruits. The grandees of the Empire had already usurped all state-powers, and, once in possession of power, they were the ones who knew how to use development based on monetary economy for the establishment and consolidation of their own territorial domains. Germany's participation in the new world empires foundered upon the German princes, those primitive relics of the natural-economic period in our history.

The Fuggers vainly sought to bring about at least a personal union of Germany with Spain, the great colonial power, through partnership in the affair of the German imperial election. But, after some initial successes, the great South-German commercial house finally went bankrupt in the wake of Spain's bankruptcy.[12] Financing the Habsburgs was a speculative failure.

For the Low-German cities, however, the main obstacle was their geographical location. Because the central power broke down, their isolation precluded from the outset any active participation in colonial policy. That policy was tied to control of the new commercial routes, above all those of the Atlantic Ocean, which, after Spain's decline, passed on to the Hanseatic League's old rivals in the Netherlands and England.

11. [The Fugger and Welser families were prominent bankers and merchant-capitalists from the fifteenth to the early seventeenth century.]

12. [The Fugger banking house financed the bribes needed for the Habsburg Charles I, King of Spain, to be elected as Charles V, Holy Roman Emperor, in 1519. Spain's bankruptcy took place in 1575. Bankruptcy of the Welser house occurred in 1611, and the Fugger house terminated its Spanish businesses in 1643.]

It was a peculiar sight: on the face of things, no other state was better qualified for the new policy required by geographical discoveries than the kingdom of Charles V, upon which the sun never set.[13] Spain and the Netherlands were the acknowledged strongholds for controlling the oceans as the new commercial routes. German trade was still powerful and significant, and the Emperor's influence in Italy was great. All the conditions for the emergence of a powerful world empire, in which capitalism could have developed boundlessly, seemed to have been fulfilled. But those conditions became ineffectual without a unified central power. Territorial interests were stronger than the needs of German urban development. The former triumphed, and the Empire split into impotent sections. The peripheral areas, which were indispensable for the development of colonial power, broke away. The Netherlands seceded, imperial influence withered in Italy, and capitalist development bypassed Germany; the country was left behind in the misery of national disunity and natural-economic retrogression. Germany played no part in the first partition of the world. Germany's capitalist development was set back for centuries by the hostile policy of the German princes. The first decision on German imperialism had been made.

To imperial enthusiasts, this may look like a tragic element in that epoch of German history: all the conditions seemed to have been met more completely than could ever happen again. Almost the entire continent had been united under the authority of a single emperor, to whose share had also fallen large parts of the new continent with its endless treasures. But all that outward pomp came to ruin, due to internal weaknesses resulting from a process that is also the proudest and most honourable page of our historical development: our colonisation of the East, which presupposed a long development based on natural economy and therefore the independence of the princes, and thus made formation of a strong central power impossible.

13. [As Holy Roman Emperor, Charles V (1500–58) ruled over Austria, the Habsburg Netherlands and Spain and its colonies until abdicating in 1556.]

II

Colonial policy – the robbery of natural treasures (above all of precious metals) and the enslavement of natives – was the most powerful lever of that primitive accumulation from which *industrial* capitalism developed in Europe. But, as long as industrial capitalism was still incipient, the interests of commercial and interest-bearing capital were dominant. Commercial capital passed over into capitalist production, initially in the form of rural cottage-industry and manufactures, in order to obtain the products for overseas and colonial trade that the old methods of production were unable to guarantee in sufficient quantities, and to increase its commercial profit by appropriating surplus-labour from numerous producers. Since the new methods of socially combined labour simultaneously increased its productivity, commercial capital obtained the products needed for exchange more cheaply than in the case of handicraft-products. But capitalist production in the form of manufactures appeared only as an auxiliary agent, an accessory of trade (above all overseas trade), and as a way of increasing profits that still originated chiefly in trade and the exploitation of the colonies. This was the epoch of mercantilist economic policy, a period marked by the incessant commercial wars of the great European nations in which their share of the booty was settled. Disunited Germany stood outside that settlement.

A change in attitude towards the colonies first took place with the rapid development of industrial capitalism after the introduction of modern machinery. That produced a shift of interests within the capitalist class. Industrial capital increasingly predominated over commercial and interest-bearing capital, which now assumed the form of banking capital. Both forms fell more and more under the sway of industrial capital. But, for the latter, the decisive thing was no longer colonial trade. The cheapening of production by machinery created for it closer, more important and broader outlets. Production based on machinery displaced rural cottage-industry, ruined the handicraft-industries and created, for the first time, a home market. The effects of industry, which first developed in England, made themselves felt in the rest of the European countries, turning them into suppliers of agrarian products to England and then into the most important markets for English capital. Compared to this, the importance of the colonies diminished. The first place was no longer occupied by the profits of colonial *trade* but by *industrial* profit arising out of the exploitation of local wage-workers. The importance of the exploitation of colonial natives decreased vis-à-vis exploitation at home, a development that was partially accelerated by colonial conditions. In America, the native population was less suitable for difficult, assiduous slave-labour and was therefore annihilated. Their place was occupied by blacks, but they only played an important role as workers in the Southern plantations. The Northern states were settled by Europeans, who very quickly saw their interests threatened by the exploiting motherland and were strong enough to shake off its yoke.

For indigenous industrial capital, European trade-channels became increasingly important. Their expansion was served by the free-trade policy, which prevailed completely over mercantilism in England and circumscribed the protectionist policy of other European countries. Indifference towards the colonies grew simultaneously with the free-trade tendency.

For industrial capital, the colonial question is purely one of costs, and it quickly found that money could be better employed in home-industry than in insecure colonial investments with their numerous unproductive outlays. The great possibilities of expansion that young industrial capitalism found in the domestic field, and the great profits made by factories while they still had to face only the competition from old methods of production (European handicraft and peasant cottage-industry), sharply diminished capital's wish for spheres of investment in overseas countries and ultimately generated antipathy towards any colonial policy, even to the extent of wanting to give up the colonies altogether.

However, the development of capitalism once again changed the attitude of the capitalist class towards colonial policy. English industrial capitalism completely drove other economic forms from the field, and its labour productivity increasingly determined prices. The high surplus-profits that the industrialists pocketed – so long as they had to compete at home and abroad with products whose prices were higher due the low productivity of more backward production techniques – came to an end. The rate of profit fell. English products increasingly encountered those of European industry, and old markets became more and more saturated. This development was accelerated by the protectionist tariff-walls with which European countries surrounded themselves; tariffs that first and foremost hindered the sale of English commodities and lowered the rate of profit for English capital. The newly emerging continental capitalism, however, had less elbow-room from the outset. Only the home market was partially secured for it through protective duties, but, if industry reached the stage of export-capability and had to enter the world market, it faced English capital, which was already there in advance as its most powerful competitor. The period of high profit-rates was much shorter for continental than for English capital. Until the most recent period, when the huge expansion of the world market along with high protective duties and cartels modified this trend, the situation of continental industry and its accumulation and concentration of riches were relatively modest compared to the English case. English industry, moreover, had already collected the surplus profits from competition with handicrafts in the European markets. In continental Europe, industrial capitalism had to develop above all in competition not with handicrafts, but rather with the English factory.

But this trend awoke, particularly in English capital, a striving to compensate for the curtailment in Europe, which was relative, to be sure, but still represented a barrier to capital's need for absolute development of all productive forces through opening up new markets. There are special reasons why countries sought to obtain those new markets mainly in the form of colonies.

The primary significance of the first period of colonial policy was that it made possible, for the first time, a powerful expansion of primitive accumulation. The colonies were less significant as markets, even if their provisioning accelerated the development of capitalist manufacture. But, with the development of machine-industry, the colonies became less significant; this was true not only because European markets, as we have seen, became more important, but also because the overseas markets had a colonial character and were politically dependent on the mother-country. At that time, the industries that supplied means of consumption were in the forefront of capitalist production. Sale of their products was secured by their low prices. English industry had secured the monopoly of sales through its technical efficiency and the superior development of the English commercial fleet. Political coercion appeared superfluous, costly and dangerous. It was only important in two senses. First, it had to secure markets that were able to absorb industrial products. Apart from India, the cradles of ancient culture in the Mediterranean and East Asia were particularly important, whereas Africa offered no special prospects. Then it had to secure commercial relations, which required occasional military interventions, but these assumed the character more of commercial than of colonial wars. The textile-industry was not warlike.

Modern colonies have a completely different character. They are not primarily exploitation-colonies with great natural riches that can be stolen and a native population that can be enslaved. They are just as little markets for industries producing means of consumption in the mother-country. The interests at the forefront of European industry today are not those of industries producing means of consumption but, rather, of those producing means of production, and, above all, those of the heavy-iron industry. But it is precisely the latter that see in modern colonies favourable spheres for capital-investment. The colonies are required not in order to export or import capital but, instead, to export from Europe a piece of ready-made capitalism together with the capital itself. And they have to be colonies because technique makes production today more or less the same in the developed states, and it is therefore not price-differences but state-power that determines which country will have the opportunity of profitably investing its capital in foreign countries, i.e., of investing at a higher rate of profit than in Europe. It is primarily means of production that are sent to the colonies, particularly railways and modern means of transportation whose production requires huge capital-sums. The cause of modern colonial policy is the surplus of capital; that is to say, of commodities that by their nature and material properties can only serve as means of production, which today signifies means for the exploitation of alien-labour.

III

Since approximately the last third of the nineteenth century, we have been witnessing a new epoch in capitalist colonial policy. The first country to display the new tendencies was, naturally, England, the most developed capitalist nation and the one where those tendencies made themselves felt sooner than anywhere else. It was followed by France, especially after the loss of Alsace-Lorraine, while the remaining countries of Europe's Atlantic coast re-evaluated their old possessions and partially expanded them at the same time as the United States grabbed the most valuable parts of the Spanish colonial empire. Only Germany was an exception.

The reasons for this are clear. Capitalism developed very late in Germany. Territorial disunity prevented its appearance even after all the other preconditions had long been fulfilled. This political obstacle could only be overcome by political means. The revolution of 1848 was the first attempt. The revolutionary path implied creation of a German state that would have included the German regions of Austria. In that way, Germany would have had access to the Adriatic and Mediterranean seas through Trieste. Just how clear the significance of Trieste was to the Frankfurt Parliament[14] is attested by its declaration that an attack on Trieste would be regarded as an attack on Germany. The triumph of the revolution would also have implied the triumph of democracy. Such a free and therefore powerful state at the centre of Europe would have paved the way for the democratic development of the entire continent, exerting the greatest power of attraction on the smaller states. A close alliance with Holland would have been entirely possible. For the second time in Germany's history, the conditions would thereby have been fulfilled for its participation in colonial policy. Without free access to the Atlantic Ocean, which the Dutch harbours would have offered, and without a foothold in the South such as Trieste, a safe and successful colonial policy was impossible. The fleet alone is useless if it can be easily locked up in the North Sea. It was not the English fleet but free access to the sea and possession of harbours and coaling stations at all the cardinal points of the world's sea-routes that established the maritime supremacy of England and gave it the possibility of safeguarding its overseas conquests. That fact was also very well known to our pan-Germanists, who regarded the fleet only as a first step in the hope that with a bit of luck a victorious war would also have supplied the requisite harbours.

14. [The Frankfurt Parliament (1848–9) is the name of the German National Assembly convened at Frankfurt on 18 May, 1848, as a result of the liberal revolution that swept the German states early in 1848. The parliament was elected by direct manhood-suffrage, and its purpose was to plan the unification of Germany. But conflict among the traditionally separate German states, notably Austria and Prussia, its own fear to take supreme power into its hands and adopt a firm stand on the cardinal questions of the German revolution, and finally the suppression of the revolutionary movement led to the parliament's downfall. In March 1849 the Parliament adopted a federal constitution of the German states, excluding Austria, with a parliamentary government and a hereditary emperor. Frederick William IV of Prussia was chosen emperor but refused to accept the crown from a popularly elected assembly, and the scheme foundered. In June 1849, the Parliament was dispersed by troops of the Württemberg government. Frederick William attempted to substitute a union-scheme of his own, but his efforts were smothered by Austria through the Treaty of Olmütz (1850), which restored the German Confederation.]

But the revolutionary movement was defeated by reaction; the unification of Germany on a democratic basis was frustrated; and the chance of a German imperialism foundered for the second time on the opposition of the princes. While Bismarck exploited the need for German unity in the dynastic interests of the Hohenzollern, he established that unity at the expense of its integrity. National unification under the aegis of Prussia implied the exclusion of Austria and with it loss of the Austrian coastal regions for Germany. Prussia's leadership also meant lack of democracy and, because of its annexation of Alsace-Lorraine, enmity with Western Europe, which has turned Russia for so long into the arbiter of the European continent. Finally, the victory of Bismarck's policy also signified the ultimate defeat of German imperialism. Germany was definitively excluded from the sea-routes to which its fleet must have access if it wants to participate successfully in colonial policy. The weakness and cowardice of the German bourgeoisie in the political field were thus the cause of its backwardness in the field of colonial policy.

Bismarck, with his sharp eye for the real relationship of forces between European states, always realised the impossibility of German imperialism. For a long time, he did not want to hear about participating in the general colonial drive upon which the capitalist nations were again embarking. He saw in France's colonial policy – and this was, admittedly, short-sighted from the point of view of capitalist politics – only a desirable diversion from French interests in Europe. Bismarck was able to maintain that policy without facing opposition at home only because German capital, which was finally free of the barriers that territorial disunity had raised against it, was sufficiently busy in its own country. Meanwhile, however, Englishmen and Frenchmen, and partly also Russians and Italians, divided up between themselves the remaining valuable portions of the world. Nothing was left for Germany but what others scorned.

IV

Apart from the American bourgeoisie, it is the German capitalist class that today has the greatest need for expansion. It is the youngest capitalist class of all the great European states, and its drive for enrichment still far outweighs its concern for pleasure. Protective tariffs have secured its home-market, accelerating cartelisation and raising cartel-profits enormously.

Besides, industry has expanded so much that in years of prosperity it already reaches the limits of the available working population. Further investments of capital at home threaten to lower the profit-rate. In order for newly accumulated capital to yield a rate of profit as high as the old one, it has to be at least partially exported. But, because all European countries are in the same situation, German capital encountered everywhere the competition of foreign capitals, which had to be driven out just as the competition of foreign commodities was driven from the domestic market. Overseas countries had to become German colonies. That also had the advantage of forcing the state to spend large sums on armaments and, in certain cases, even to guarantee the return on exported capital – for instance, capital invested in the construction of railway-lines.

If the interests of the German capitalist class, combined with the interests of military and bureaucratic circles, are a powerful driving force behind Germany's participation in colonial policy, this participation also faces huge obstacles that cannot easily be overcome given the German Empire's geographical configuration within its current political boundaries. Driven, on the one hand, to colonial policy, and, on the other hand, repeatedly encountering the impossibility of its successful implementation, our foreign policy since Bismarck's downfall is necessarily following a zigzag-course characterised by repeated advances and retreats. At one moment, there is boundless optimism and megalomaniacal boasting; at the next, humble Christian resignation and fearful protests of friendship. But this proves that German imperialism is impossible if Germany does not overcome the current situation by violent means, that is, through conquering the necessary harbours in Europe along with valuable colonial possessions belonging to other countries.

On four occasions, German imperialism has made false starts. It was typically banking capital together with heavy industry, which, in Germany, is so closely linked to the banks – above all the electrical, weapons and iron industries – that led this process. First of all, German capital sought to win influence over South America, especially in Brazil. There, it came across the superior economic and political power of the United States. The Monroe Doctrine, expanded into the Drago Doctrine,[15] ruled out all hope of anything

15. [The Drago Doctrine was announced in 1902 by the Argentinean Minister of Foreign Affairs Luis María Drago. Extending the Monroe Doctrine, it set forth the

more than purely economic success in competing for South America. The second attempt was made in East Asia, through Germany's participation in the China adventure and in the intervention against the Japanese in favour of the Russians. The consequences are well known. The Russo-Japanese War secured Japan's ascendancy; and the Anglo-Japanese alliance, which followed the French-Japanese and Japanese-Russian treaties, excluded Germany from any influence over the course of events in East Asia, while at the same time turning Jiaozhou[16] into a pledge of Germany's good conduct in the hands of Japan, behind whom stands England. In the third attempt, Germany, being driven away from the Pacific Ocean, sought to win influence over the Mediterranean countries. The [first] Morocco affair at the same time revealed the great dangers to world peace that colonial policy brings in its wake.[17] The

---

policy that no foreign power, including the United States, could use force against an American nation to collect debt.]

16. [Jiaozhou Bay in China was a German colonial concession from 1898 to 1914. With an area of 552 km², it was located in the imperial province of Shandong on the southern coast of the Shandong Peninsula in northern China. Jiaozhou was romanised as Kiaochow, Kiauchau or Kiao-Chau in English and Kiautschou in German. Qingdao (Tsingtao) was the administrative centre. See Kautsky 1898b.]

17. [Between March 1905 and May 1906 an international crisis over the colonial status of Morocco took place, known as the First Moroccan Crisis, or Tangier Crisis. It was brought about by the visit of Kaiser Wilhelm II to Tangier in Morocco on 31 March 1905. The Kaiser made certain remarks in favour of Moroccan independence, meant as a challenge to French influence in Morocco. France had her influence in Morocco reaffirmed by Britain (through the Entente Cordiale) and Spain in 1904, a move that Germany saw as a blow to her interests and took diplomatic action to challenge. The speech turned the French public against Germany, and with British support the French foreign minister, Théophile Delcassé, took a defiant line. The crisis peaked in mid-June, when Delcassé was forced out of the ministry by the more conciliatory premier Maurice Rouvier. By July 1905, Germany was becoming isolated and the French agreed to a conference to solve the crisis. Both France and Germany continued to posture up to the conference, with Germany mobilising reserve army units in late December and France actually moving troops to the border in January 1906. The Algeciras Conference, lasting from 16 January to 7 April 1906, was called to settle the dispute. Of the thirteen nations present, the German representatives found their only supporter was Austria-Hungary. France had the support of Britain, Russia, Italy, Spain, and the US The Germans eventually accepted an agreement, the Act of Algeciras, signed on 7 April 1906, which appeared to limit French penetration. It reaffirmed the independence of the sultan and the economic equality of the powers, and it provided that French and Spanish police officers be under a Swiss inspector general. But, though France yielded certain domestic changes in Morocco, it retained control of key areas. The real significance of the Algeciras Conference is to be found in the substantial diplomatic support given France by Britain and the United States, foreshadowing their roles in World War I, to which the Moroccan Crisis was a prelude. Continuing German dissatisfaction with the Moroccan situation led to a Second Moroccan Crisis in 1911 against a background of worsening international tensions that ultimately led to World War I (1914–18).]

Moroccan adventure ended in the encirclement of Germany. Apart from Holland – whose sympathies are always with the other side because, despite all official assurances (which today are certainly well-intentioned), it sees itself threatened by the inner logic of German imperialist endeavours – the Mediterranean powers, together with the old colonial powers, are today united against any expansionist endeavour on the side of Germany. This constellation, which became evident in Algeciras, was strengthened by the alliance between England, France and Spain. Finally, the Anglo-Russian agreement, which is significant above all for Central Asia, also increased England's predominance in Europe; that is to say, the power of England against Germany. It is no wonder that today German foreign policy – over which prince Bülow[18] boasts and political children rejoice – has momentarily been immobilised.

Finally, under the leadership of Deutsche Bank, German capital has recently carved out for itself a sphere of interests in the area of the Anatolian railroad [the Baghdad Railway]. Here, too, Germany runs into English spheres of interests. Moreover, this region cannot be held by force because its base of operations is too far away from the fatherland while England controls the sea-routes. An occupation is therefore impossible and certainly unnecessary because the fertile territory at the disposal of German capital [in Turkey] offers sufficient profit-opportunities. By the same token, however, the impossibility of German imperialism, which admittedly was clear from the outset, is also empirically proven. The colonial expansion of Germany is impossible without a European war.

V

It is clear that this situation cannot fail to react upon domestic politics, because the situation, as we have described it thus far, naturally appears in the minds of the ruling classes in a completely different light. Expansion is the vital need of capital; and the form it assumes today, when capital's interests decide everything, is colonial expansion. In capitalist circles, therefore, there is no room for any idea of the impossibility of that expansion. For them,

18. [Prince Bernhard Heinrich Karl Martin von Bülow (1849–1929) was a German diplomat and conservative politician who served as Chancellor of the German Empire from 1900 to 1909.]

that would be admitting that some other way must be found out of the difficulties created by growth of the productive forces in capitalist society, and that way out can only be socialism. Imperialism is today the grand delusion [*Lebenslüge*: vital lie] of dying capitalism, the last, comprehensive ideology at its disposal to confront socialism. To all appearances, the decision between the bourgeoisie and the proletariat will be fought out as a struggle between imperialism and socialism.

What to us appears impossible seems to the bourgeoisie to be the only salvation. Accordingly, the failure of German policy does not seem necessary to them but, rather, accidental and contingent upon the ineptitude of its leaders (in the opinion of the bourgeois opposition), or a result of the people lacking a spirit of sacrifice (according to the government and its supporters). But the more difficult the external situation becomes, the more susceptible will people be to opposition to that policy at home. Among the opponents of imperialist policy are to be found not only proletarians, for whom it means both new burdens in the present and postponement of their final victory, but also the middle strata. In particular the productive middle class, peasants and craftsmen, do not have the slightest interest in seeing their tax-burden increased further by a policy that can only be to the advantage of large-scale capital. No matter how dependent those strata are today, the parties that rely upon them, like the Centre and also, to a certain extent, the Progressive People's Party [Freisinnige Volkspartei][19] can support imperialist policy only cautiously and

---

19. [The German Centre Party (Deutsche Zentrumspartei or merely Zentrum) was a Catholic party during the German Empire and the Weimar Republic. Early in 1871, the Catholic representatives to the new national parliament, the Reichstag, formed a 'Centre' faction. The Party not only defended the Church's liberties but also supported representative government and minority rights in general, in particular those of German Poles, Alsatians and Hannoverians. The Centre Party remained a party of opposition to Bismarck, but, after his resignation in 1890, it frequently supported the following administrations' policies in the Reichstag, particularly in the field of social security. The Party became known for its pragmatism: it was willing to support a wide variety of policies so long as the interests of German Catholics and of the Catholic Church itself were advanced. The Party was also notable for the mixture of class interests it represented, ranging from Catholic trade-unions to aristocrats. The Party dissolved itself on 6 July 1933, shortly before the conclusion of a Concordat between the Holy See and Germany. After World War II, the Party was re-established, but it could not rise again to its former importance as most of its members joined the new Christian Democratic Union (CDU). It was represented in the German parliament until 1957.

The German Free-Minded or Progressive Party (Deutsche Freisinnige Partei) was a liberal party, founded as a result of the merger of the German Progress Party and Liberal Union on 5 March 1884. In 1893, the Party split into the Free-Minded Peo-

with hesitation. To that should be added traditional opposition to the government on the part of representatives of the urban masses, which was kept alive by the government's reactionary tendencies and by permanent injury to all liberal ideologies as well as by the exclusion of those masses from the administration and by the privileging of the aristocracy in all fields. If the situation of the government is thus always precarious externally, it only finds support at home among the representatives of the country-squires [*Junkertum*] and large capital, while the old and new middle classes and their political representatives follow only hesitantly and unwillingly, curtailing the resources that seem necessary to the government and giving it the impression that only lack of support at home is to blame for failures in foreign policy.

Those feelings (and, among the supporters of German policy, it is as likely as not a question of feelings and moods rather than of clear insights) have given rise to the newest phase in domestic politics. The *bloc-policy*[20] is nothing but the wish to gather together all the bourgeois forces amenable to imperialist ideology in support of that policy. That was all the more necessary because, in Germany, that ideology was fought against relentlessly by the largest and most resolute party [the SPD]. This fight must have seemed all the more distasteful to the ruling classes precisely because German imperialism, which demanded considerable sacrifices from the working class, was unable to offer

ple's Party and the Free-Minded Union. The Free-Minded People's Party (Freisinnige Volkspartei), to which Hilferding refers several times in this essay, was a left-liberal party whose most prominent member was Eugen Richter, the Party's leader from 1893 to 1906. On 6 March 1910, the Free-Minded Union, the Democratic Union, and the German People's Party merged into the Fortschrittliche Volkspartei (FVP), variously translated as Free-Minded People's Party, Liberal People's Party or Progressive People's Party. The Party was disbanded after the fall of the Empire in 1918.]

20. [A reference to the Bülow Bloc: In 1900 Bernhard von Bülow replaced Hohenlohe-Schillingsfürst as Reich Chancellor and president of the Prussian State Ministry. He relied on the support of the Conservative Party and the Catholic Centre Party. The government of Bülow was active in foreign policy, and the confrontation with France and Britain over Morocco (1905–6) increased international tension. In 1907, Bülow dissolved the Reichstag after the conflict with the Centre Party. On 25 January 1907, the so-called 'Hottentot elections' took place in which the SPD was defeated on the colonial issue and lost a large part of its parliamentary representation. The elections led to creation of a pro-colonialist government coalition of Conservatives, National Liberals and Left Liberals known as the Bülow Bloc. In October 1908, Bülow's relationship with the Emperor Wilhelm II suffered from the *Daily Telegraph* Affair. After the Bülow Bloc failed to reach an agreement on financial reform, Bülow resigned the chancellorship on 14 July 1909.]

to the masses even those apparent and illusory successes that imperialism was somehow able to grant in the countries bordering the Atlantic. And, because it seemed hopeless to attempt to move the [country's] infernal regions, higher powers had to be mobilised.[21] But, then, two elements opposed each other. In the previous government coalition of the Centre and the Conservatives, imperialist policy was still regarded with misgivings and alarm when what it always requires is *élan*, enthusiasm and an unhesitating drive forwards – especially given the great dangers it implies for Germany. But the Centre had to take into consideration its petty-bourgeois constituency, and the [party] leadership employed that distress, if not to make a virtue out of necessity, then at least to make profits and obtain all kinds of concessions by legislative and administrative means (what was known as the 'collateral government'). But this co-government with the Centre had the further disadvantage of keeping liberalism in the opposition.

German liberalism originated, like any other, in the struggle with absolute monarchy. In other countries, after the defeat of royalty or after reaching a tolerable compromise, liberalism joined the government. As a representative of state-power, liberalism in those places naturally satisfied all the government needs, which, in Prussia, would be called fulfilment of national duties, and gradually became a supporter of imperialist ideas. But, in Germany, victory went not to liberalism but to Bismarck's Caesarism. Liberalism split: the National Liberals, representatives of large capital, made the content of Caesarism – creation of a unified economic territory and the unchaining of capitalist forces – its *leitmotif* and became the true government party, especially in questions concerning the shaping of the capitalist economic order. The Progressives, by contrast, resented the bureaucratic and police-form of Caesarism and remained in opposition, being weakened on the one hand by the apostasy of large capital and on the other by the proletariat, at whose expense this development had to take place. But the Prussian Conservatives were not so much a government party as a ruling party that furnished Prussia with its governmental, administrative and military personnel.

21. [A paraphrase of Virgil's *Aeneid*, Book 7, Line 312: '*Flectere si nequeo superos, acheronta movebo*' – 'If I cannot bend the Higher Powers, I will move the Infernal Regions' (literally: 'I will stir up Acheron.'). An alternative translation reads: 'If I cannot move heaven I will raise hell.']

Naturally, that fact is not disproved by the occasional frictions between government and Conservatives; if Conservatives are the government, then Conservative politicians in public positions are bound by certain imperatives that Conservatives as party men overlook. But not *all* class-demands of the large landed proprietors can be completely realised in industrial states like Saxony and Prussia. Conservative ministers must, therefore, often adopt a policy similar to that of Free Conservatives or right-wing National Liberals. That is why they are somewhat ill at ease with too large a parliamentary representation of Conservatives. It therefore answered a ministerial need when the question of electoral reform in Saxony and Prussia was brought before the government, although, naturally, only if electoral reform were to go no further than to replace impossible Conservatism by possible Conservatism; that is, a reform made much easier by an economic development that has increasingly impregnated the Junkers with capitalist interests and almost completely obliterated the differences between Free Conservatives, National Liberals and pure Conservatives. To this were added the needs of the government, which, by granting an impotent pseudo-representation to the working class, could deceive a little while longer those circles of workers who are still politically indifferent but might easily be won over by Social Democracy through agitation for electoral reform.

Next to the Progressives, the Centre also belonged at first to the opposition. Later, however, it adopted that idiosyncratic, manoeuvring attitude characteristic of all bourgeois parties that are not outspoken class-parties but, instead, represent a conglomerate of class-fractions held together by ideological bonds that gradually become traditional. The Progressives, however, had to continue [the traditions of] the only noteworthy period of German liberalism: the period of struggle against Bismarck's demands. At that time, they fought against military demands and they have continued that struggle ever since – although, naturally, not in a principled way – as opponents of militarism and supporters of a proletarian-democratic army organisation, because no bourgeois party could do that. They fight against militarism by applying to it the standards of an anxious petty bourgeois, always questioning its profitability. They do not repudiate military and therefore naval demands but seek to bargain over them, and in that respect they resemble the Centre, although the Centre are better bargainers and also exploit the conjuncture better. With the appearance of the imperialist trend, the Progressives underwent once again, for different reasons, a process they had already experienced as a result of the triumph of Caesarism. A new split led [in 1893] to departure of the remaining residue of large capital – more commercial and shipping capital than industrial capital – who now incorporated imperialism into their programme along with support for the army, navy and colonial policy. The other section of the Party, under the leadership of Richter, upheld the old traditions in a tedious and nagging way. With Richter's death [in 1906], however, all party traditions died away and thus the last obstacles disappeared in the way of capitulation by the Progressives to imperialism. To that party belong stock-exchange dealers, whose trade has been restricted by legislation; petty-bourgeois small craftsmen and small capitalists threatened by large capital and the trade-union movement at the same time; and [salaried] employees of all sorts in trade and industry, a stratum that has grown rapidly with capitalist development. Those social strata are without pronounced class-interests because some of them can no longer have a distinctive class-policy, while others do not recognise that their own interests lie in the ranks of the proletariat. Social strata with different interests must be held together by an ideology. Liberalism provides one, but only partially, because it represents a certain danger for those purely urban classes. Democracy in the city means that the Progressives will be compelled to wage a struggle with uncertain results for local government. Some petty-bourgeois strata, however, are driven by fear of Social Democracy to an increasingly cautious attitude towards liberalism as well. The liberal bond is too weak, and, here, imperialist ideology presents itself as a welcome reinforcement.

After social development smoothed the path in that way, Bülow was able to succeed where Bismarck and Miquel[22] had failed: in transforming the bourgeois opposition into a pillar of the government without modifying the government's goals in the least. It is characteristic that the coalition

22. [Johann von Miquel (1829–1901) was a German politician and one of the founders of the German Nationalverein. In 1864 he was elected to the Hanoverian parliament as a Liberal and an opponent of the government. He accepted the annexation of Hanover by Prussia without regret and entered the Prussian parliament in 1867. He served as mayor of Osnabrück and Frankfurt am Main, and was the chief agent in the reorganisation of the National Liberal Party in 1887, in which year he entered the imperial Reichstag. After Bismarck's fall in 1890 he was chosen Prussian minister of finance and held this post for ten years until June 1901. He died later that year in Frankfurt.]

of parties necessary to create the [Bülow] Bloc was not the work of those parties themselves, not the fruit of any understanding reached between them, but an event brought about by command from above, which is something almost unprecedented in parliamentary history. At the same time, it is proof of the extraordinary weakness and instability of the bourgeois parties in Germany, a weakness partially flowing from the instability of contemporary party formations that have become completely antiquated. The Bloc was possible, above all, because it represents a transitional stage for a reorientation of bourgeois politics – or, more accurately, for the expression of such a reorientation, which, in fact, had long been announced within the parties themselves.

To begin with, the Bloc offers an important advantage for the government: it won over the non-proletarian urban masses for imperialist policy and therewith also the urban press, or 'public opinion'. By those means, the government got rid of the opposition within the bourgeoisie to military and naval plans and to colonial adventures. The 'national', that is to say imperialist, tasks must be fulfilled without parliamentary compensation and out of a 'sense of national duty'. Not only the 'people's rights' can be ignored, but also any consideration for the parties' wishes; government absolutism is stronger, and the parliament is more impotent and less influential than ever before. But because governmental absolutism is identical with the Conservatives' rule, the latter are also keenly interested in avoiding any disturbance of that policy.

The government has been freed from any consideration for the wishes of the petty bourgeoisie as represented by the Centre. At the same time, it also broke in that way the only bourgeois party still worth mentioning, a party that represented a power outside the government and even against it because it was supported by broad social strata. The new government policy strengthens social contradictions within the Centre: the large capitalist circles in the Centre are supporters of government policy, of imperialism and the struggle against Social Democracy, and they endured opposition status only with difficulty. But opposition status can become even more dangerous for the Centre, precisely because of the existence of opposition-minded circles in its own ranks – above all the workers. If opposition status aligns those workers with Social Democracy, they will, in many cases, have to admit what we have been saying all along. Besides, the Centre, precisely because of its influence on the government, has persuaded its workers that the Party did for them everything it could do in social and political terms because they did not remain in sterile opposition like Social Democracy but, instead, supported the government. Hence their irresolute behaviour, their dislike of opposition, their fear of 'unleashing the popular storm', their ever-recurring attempts to curry favours with the government, and their competitive manoeuvres against the Progressives in their bid for building the fleet.

But the Progressives are themselves trapped. It would be completely ridiculous now if they were to go back into opposition and confess that they were cheated. If not ministers, then political parties at least die of such ludicrousness. Nothing remains to them but an attempt to hold their supporters together for as long as they can by means of imperialist clamour, national demagogy and rabble-rousing against Social Democracy. That kind of opposition party must become the most resolute and unconditional government party.

The Bloc, which is merely a transitional stage, will thus enable the government to reach its goal of gathering together all bourgeois forces to secure its rule against the attacks of the proletariat. If liberalism is sufficiently tamed, the hour will arrive for incorporating the Centre, which even today stands aside, into the government coalition. But that will transform the Centre itself. It will no longer be able to carry out its customary political swings: its traditional fear of the difficulties inherent in opposition status will grow, its demagogy will be aggravated, and its bourgeois-capitalist character will stand out clearly in the alliance with the other parties. The entire strength of the bourgeoisie will then be directed towards imperialism, today's all-encompassing bond, and against the proletariat that is its negation.

To accelerate this trend, while simultaneously diminishing as far as possible its dangers for the proletariat, is the obvious task of proletarian policy in the coming period. But in order to do that, it is not enough to explain theoretically the eventualities of political development; that would only be necessary as a political object-lesson. It is characteristic of German imperialism – and historically necessary, although it increases its great weakness – that it is reactionary at home and must remain so because the working-class opposition to it is already too strong. Here, Social Democracy must begin the counter-offensive. The programme of imperialism opposes free self-determination of peoples at home and goes against democracy in legislation and administration. As a result of historical development, however, the struggle for democracy today focuses on achieving equal suffrage in Prussia. It is only by Social Democracy placing itself at the head of this action and conducting it with all the energy and all the instruments of power at the disposal of a highly developed and splendidly organised proletariat in a modern industrial country that we can demonstrate to those who are indifferent and hesitant that democracy in Germany is identical with Social Democracy.[23]

23. [The concluding paragraph of Hilferding's article was prescient in an unexpected sense: Prussian suffrage did become the focal point of the SPD's attempts to democratise Germany's political system, and the debate over the general strike as a means of achieving equal suffrage in Prussia would lead to the split between the SPD left wing, led by Rosa Luxemburg, and the centre-fraction led by Kautsky. When Luxemburg submitted an article urging the strike as a means of securing universal suffrage in Prussia – while simultaneously posing the demand for a republic in the hope of provoking revolutionary action – Kautsky refused to publish it. This resulted in a severing of his relations not only with Luxemburg but also with Franz Mehring (who was removed from the editorial board of *Die Neue Zeit* in 1912), as well as in a series of bitter polemics in *Die Neue Zeit* with several other leading representatives of Social Democracy's left wing. In the course of these debates, Kautsky developed his so-called 'strategy of attrition (*Ermattungsstrategie*), as opposed to Luxemburg's *Niederwerfungsstrategie*, which called for 'defeating the enemy'. See the introduction to this volume, footnote 198.]

Chapter Twenty-Four

'Austria and Imperialism' (October 1908)

Otto Bauer

In its Brünner programme of September 1899, the Austrian Social-Democratic Party demanded not the right of nations oppressed by Germans and Magyars to secede from the Austro-Hungarian Empire, but rather the right to national-cultural autonomy (setting up self-administered, but not necessarily contiguous, national entities with their own parliaments, schools, etc.) within the framework of a multinational federal state.[1] Otto Bauer's essay on 'Austria

1. Leon Trotsky later commented that the nationality-policy of Austrian Social Democrats in fact made no distinction between oppressor and oppressed nations, with the consequence that 'the Austrian program disclosed nothing but its own weaknesses: it saved neither the Empire of the Hapsburgs nor the Austrian Social-Democracy itself. Cultivating the idiosyncrasies of proletarian national groups, while at the same time failing really to satisfy the oppressed nationalities, the Austrian program merely camouflaged the dominance of the Germans and the Magyars' (Trotsky 1941, p. 156). Roman Rosdolsky had the same view: 'Although the General Austrian Social Democratic Party formally supported the transformation of the Austrian Empire into a federation of nationalities, its German-Austrian components had taken up Karl Renner's idea of resolving the national question by constituting the empire's nations as voluntary national cultural institutions whose activities were not confined to any particular territory. It loudly proclaimed its commitment to internationalism and the right of peoples to self-determination but in practice supported a policy that left "*the decisive positions of state power in the hands of the German minority*"' (Rosdolsky 1987, p. 184, quoted in Kuhn 2007, pp. 27–8, emphasis in the original).

Otto Bauer's credentials on the nationality-question certainly appeared to be compromised by his colonialist fantasy concerning a German *Lebensraum* in Russia:

> Let us assume, for example, that a future socialist society sees that it can increase the productivity of labour in Germany by lowering the number of workers there and can increase the productivity of labour in southern Russia by increasing the number of workers there. It will thus seek to transfer a part of the German population to southern Russia. But Germany will not

and Imperialism' relates the intensifying conflicts between the European great powers to the issue of minorities within Austria-Hungary itself and to the fate of the small nations on its borders, aspiring to independence while squeezed between Austria, Russia and Turkey. Anticipating a conflagration that might be set alight in the Balkans, Bauer's essay provides insight into the fateful dilemma of Austrian Social Democrats as the enfeebled Habsburg Empire, nursing its own territorial ambitions in the Balkans, found itself increasingly embroiled in rivalries between Germany, Russia, England and France.

* * *

'Austria and Imperialism'[2]

The *antagonism between Great Britain and Germany* has been the most influential fact during recent years for development of the foreign policy of all European states. The vigorous development of German industry was first felt in England in the *commodity market*. [...][3] It is understandable why many British industries regarded this development of German foreign trade with little goodwill. German commodities were imported duty-free into England, while Germany imposed heavy tariffs on English imports. Safely protected by a tariff-wall, the German industrialists created powerful cartels that by means of export-subsidies and dumping practices changed competitive conditions in the world market and in England itself to the disadvantage of English industry – which, being unprotected by tariffs, was deprived of those weapons. The agitation of English protectionists made German competition appear unfair in the eyes of the local population.

---

send its sons and daughters to the east without safeguarding their cultural independence. The German colonists will consequently enter the polity of the Ukraine not as individuals, but as a corporation under public law. If the national territorial corporations unite to form an international polity, planned colonisation will give rise to foreign-language associations of persons within the international polity, associations that in some respects will be legally bound to the territorial corporation of their nation, and in others to the polity of the foreign nation whose soil they inhabit. (Bauer 2000, p. 395.)

2. Bauer 1908.

3. [Bauer here provides statistics showing the growth of German exports, particularly to Great Britain and the British Empire.]

But in the *capital-market*, too, German competition drove England out in the struggle over investment spheres because the German banks, strengthened by an exceedingly rapid concentration process, organised German capital-exports.

The competition for sales markets and investment spheres is closely connected with the striving of both states to annex overseas lands to their colonial possessions. Germany's *colonial policy* has no fixed goal. In one place after another, it is arousing suspicion that Germany is pursuing selfish plans, and this is exciting the jealousy of the greatest colonial power. The German emigration law of 1897 provoked suspicion that Germany wanted to subject South America systematically to its influence. In the Middle East, German capital built the Baghdad railway. Germany's relation with Turkey, its position on the Moroccan question, and the travels of the German Emperor to Jerusalem and Tangiers are all evidence of a fantastic plan to incorporate the Islamic regions close to the Mediterranean into German spheres of influence. Since the acquisition of Kiaotschau [Jiaozhou] and the Hun expedition,[4] Germany has been considered a dangerous rival in the Far East. Finally, the imprudent telegram of the German Emperor to President Kruger has not been forgotten in England,[5] with the result that Germany's policy in Africa also seems dangerous to the English imperialists. German colonial policy has created steadily growing alarm in England precisely because Germany did not

4. [*Hunnenfeldzug*: A reference to a famous speech in 1900 by Kaiser Wilhelm II, on the occasion of the departure of the German military expedition against the Boxer rebellion in China, in which he invoked the memory of the 5th century Huns and Atila.]

5. [The Kruger telegram was sent by Wilhelm II to Stephanus Johannes Paulus Kruger, president of the Transvaal republic on 3 January 1896. The Kaiser congratulated the president on repelling the Jameson Raid, a sortie by 600 irregulars from Cape Colony into the Transvaal under the command of Leander Starr Jameson, with the intention of triggering an uprising by the primarily British expatriate workers. The raid ended in a fiasco with approximately 30 raiders killed and the rest surrendering. The Kaiser's telegram read: 'I express to you my sincere congratulations that you and your people, without appealing to the help of friendly powers, have succeeded, by your own energetic action against the armed bands which invaded your country as disturbers of the peace, in restoring peace and in maintaining the independence of the country against attack from without.' This was seen as an endorsement of Transvaal's independence in an area regarded by the British as their own sphere of influence, resulting in further deterioration of relations between Germany and Great Britain. van der Poel 1951, p. 135.]

devote its energies to a definite goal but, instead, intervened simultaneously in all the questions of world policy.

This anxiety found further nourishment in the continuous enlargement of the German *army* and *navy*. Even today, the English population has to make the heaviest sacrifices for the armed forces. Military expenditures per capita are 27.3 marks in England, 21.3 in France and 17.1 in Germany. A strong current of opinion, including not only the Labour Party but also a large part of the Liberal electorate, demands the limitation of armaments. But they can always be effectively dismissed with the argument that Germany is continuously increasing its military forces and rejecting English disarmament proposals.

Finally, *Germany's internal political development* also strengthens British imperialism. The German bourgeoisie has given up any opposition to naval and colonial policy. The entire bourgeois press has joined in the agitation against England. The history of the Reichstag elections shows that the government can overcome any opposition, even from powerful Social Democracy, if it turns a question of military or colonial policy into an electoral slogan.[6] The hope that the German people would itself defeat German imperialism therefore appears futile.

Thus, England and Germany face each other in mutual distrust. The proletarian and democratic opposition against imperialism appears in both cases to be ineffective. To seek allies against Germany now seems to be the natural task of the English government. Germany's Moroccan policy gave England the opportunity of coming to an understanding with *France*. It was then a question of winning over *Russia*, which, since the onset of reaction after the revolution of 1905, again appears to be a valuable ally – if not at the moment, then at least for the future. Austria-Hungary's intervention gave the English politicians the desired occasion.

In the last session of the Delegations,[7] the minister of foreign affairs announced construction of the Sandschak [Sanjak] railway, which will go from Uva [Uvats], the final point of Bosnia-Herzegovina's railway-network,

---

6. [A reference to the defeat of the SPD in the 'Hottentot elections' of 25 January 1907.]

7. [In Austria-Hungary, Delegations were the legislative bodies dealing with legislation that regulated the common affairs of the two kingdoms. Each of the two Delegations consisted of 60 members, a third of them from the upper house of the Austrian Imperial Assembly (*Herrenhaus*) and two thirds from the lower house (*Abgeordnetenhaus*). The Delegations met annually and alternated between Vienna and Budapest.]

to Mitrovitsa, which is already connected to Thessaloniki by a railway-line.[8] Russia declared that this intervention by the Austro-Hungarian government abrogated the Mürzsteg convention between Russia and the Danube Monarchy on concerted action in the Balkan Peninsula. The British government immediately exploited this favourable situation. Russia and Great Britain submitted to Turkey a reform programme for Macedonia as their joint demand. The English and French press supported Russia in the struggle against the Austro-Hungarian railway-construction plans. In that way, the policy of Aerenthal[9] rendered valuable service to British imperialism. *England supported Russia's policy in the Balkan Peninsula against Austria-Hungary in exchange for Russia's alignment with the Anglo-French coalition against Germany*. The 'encirclement' of Germany is completed.

The commercial and political value of the Sanjak railway has been overestimated in Austria. [...][10] The construction of the Sanjak railway will bring only *very little profit* to our economy; *at all events, much smaller profits than good commercial treaties with the Balkan states would have been able to bring*. That insignificant advantage must be set against its grave disadvantages. The antagonism of interests between Austria-Hungary and Russia over the Balkan Peninsula

8. [A reference to the Sanjak railway crisis. The Sanjak of Novi Pazar (or Novibazar) was an Ottoman sanjak (second-level administrative unit) that was part of the Ottoman province of Bosnia and later Kosovo Province, and included most of the present day Sandžak region as well as northern parts of Kosovo. From the Congress of Berlin in 1878 until 1908, the Sanjak was garrisoned by Austro-Hungarian troops. On 27 January 1908, the Austrian foreign minister, Count Alois Aehrenthal, announced the intention of the Austrian government to build a railway through the Sanjak of Novi Bazar toward Saloniki (from Uvats in Bosnia to Mitrovitza.). The declaration's purpose was to drive a wedge between Serbia and Montenegro, where anti-Austrian agitation was rising. The move was much resented by Russia, who claimed it was a violation of the Austro-Russian entente of 1897, as well as by Great Britain, which regarded it as a rapprochement between Austria and the Ottoman Empire. The Serbians presented a counter-proposal, with the support of Italy and Russia, suggesting a line from the Danube to San Giovanni di Medua. Action was prevented by the outbreak in July 1908 of the Young Turk Revolution. On 6 October 1908, Austria announced the annexation of Bosnia and Herzegovina, enraging Serbia and Montenegro, who had long regarded the two annexed provinces as a future legacy. The Germans supported Austria loyally in order to uphold their alliance, while Russia, Great Britain and France opposed it. In the aftermath of the annexation, Austria, as a concession to the Turks, gave up the right to occupy the Sanjak militarily. Following the Balkan Wars of 1912–13, the territory of the Sanjak was divided between Serbia and Montenegro.]

9. [Count Alois von Aehrenthal (1854–1912) was foreign minister (1906–12) of the Austro-Hungarian Dual Monarchy. His direction of the latter's annexation of Bosnia and Herzegovina in October 1908 provoked the Bosnian crisis of 1908.]

10. [Bauer gives a number of technical reasons.]

is again assuming a threatening character. Since the English government supports Russia, while the [Austro-Hungarian Dual] Monarchy sides with Germany, the Balkan question is closely connected with disputed world-political problems in the diplomatic struggles between German and British imperialism. England abandoned our interests in the Balkans to its Russian ally in order to strike at Germany. *The Danube Monarchy was hit by a blow aimed at German imperialism.* Each world-political complication, including the Moroccan question, which has once again become dangerous due to Germany's intercession on behalf of Muley Hafid, will become dangerous for us as well. It is even conceivable that the fire that English imperialism hopes will finally consume its rival will be ignited in the Balkans.

The *alliance with Germany*, having now acquired a new content, is certainly not one that the peoples of Austria will want to dissolve at the moment. We need Germany's support because tsarism is again being strengthened; otherwise we would be reduced to an alarming relation of dependence upon the genocidal tsarist kingdom, and instead of taking care of the affairs of German imperialism we would have to attend those of British imperialism, which is no less hostile to the people. The reopening of the Balkan question also affects the most sensitive point of our foreign policy: our relations with Italy. We could magnify the ever-threatening dangers from that direction by dissolving the Triple Alliance.[11] But, if we cannot dissolve our alliance with Germany and Italy, we still have every reason to be dissatisfied with their internal development. The Triple Alliance would be thoroughly valuable for us if it made the cultural relationships between peoples closer, but it does not fulfill that task. Although our authority in the alliance has certainly increased as a result of Germany's encirclement, our government is not even able to protect Austrian workers in Germany against disgraceful ill-treatment by the Prussian government – against the identification system of the Prussian Agricultural Workers' Office [Feldarbeiterzentrale], which hands Austrian workers over defenceless to the German employers. The Triple Alliance, which let Austrian citizens be deprived of their freedom of movement in Germany, makes us dependent on the adventurous policy of German imperialism and all the vicissitudes

11. [The Triple Alliance (Dreibund) was a defence-association between the German Reich, Austria-Hungary and Italy. The alliance was formed in 1882, enlarging the former Austro-German Zweibund. It was renewed in 1912 but terminated by Italy in 1915.]

of German-British competition. The British-Russian agreement has turned us into the victim of German imperialism.

The few *commercial* advantages from the Sanjak railway do not compensate for those dangers. It would be completely incomprehensible if Count Aehrenthal had compromised our most important interest, peace, and our most valuable possession, independence from the quarrels of the imperialist world powers, just in order to divert trade with the villagers in Amselfeld from Thessaloniki to Sarajevo. The suspicion creeps in that the Sanjak railway project serves *other interests*, that it represents the first step on the steep path of the old great-power policy of expansion in the Balkan Peninsula. The peoples of Austria must therefore warn the government very forcefully that they *reject any policy of conquest in the Balkan Peninsula* and that they are not ready seriously to imperil peace in exchange for some ridiculously small economic advantage. The situation in the Balkan Peninsula does not allow us to undertake any dangerous experiment, if only because thoughtless military absolutism has already created serious dangers in *Bosnia* from which we cannot be diverted by means of high-treason trials. A democratic constitution, giving majority-representation to the majority of the population in a legislative assembly, would turn the whole attention of the country to its great social problem – the introduction of bourgeois property-rights for the peasants – and would deprive the Greater-Serbian movement of any support. Today, however, conditions in the occupied provinces force us to be doubly careful.

For the time being, an unexpected event has admittedly allayed the threatening danger. Turkey was threatened by the British-Russian agreement even more seriously than Austria and Germany. The Macedonian reform programme [proposed by Great Britain and Russia] would again have curtailed the sovereignty of the Ottoman Empire. All the educated and nationally conscious classes of the Turkish people – the army-officials, the civil servants and the clergy – realised that only a complete political revolution could avert the danger represented by the gradual undermining of national independence. The *Turkish revolution* is thus indirectly a product of the struggle between German and British imperialism.[12] The Young Turks have extricated us from

12. [The Young Turk Revolution of July 1908 reversed the suspension of the Ottoman parliament by Sultan Abdul Hamid II in 1878, marking the onset of the Second Constitutional Era.]

a very serious situation. The British-Russian reform programme had to be abandoned; guerrilla struggles in Macedonia have ceased; and no state can today intervene in Turkish affairs. Neither from Russia nor from Italy's side are we today threatened by any immediate danger.

But the dangers have by no means disappeared on that account. Even in the case of a decisive victory of the Turkish revolution, military entanglements in the Balkan Peninsula remain possible. The Macedonian struggle among nationalities will not be solved so quickly, and the army-officers who have seized power in Turkey will not follow a peaceful policy at any price, as witnessed by the conflict with Bulgaria. It would be even worse if the rule of the Young Turks were short-lived; the disappointment of the nationalities in Macedonia would then give rise to portentous imbroglios. Since the peaceful development of the Balkan peoples is thus by no means yet secure, it seems to us doubly necessary to warn the Austro-Hungarian government against that dangerous Balkan policy of which the Sanjak railway project seems to be the first step.

The proletariat is the only militant opponent of imperialism in every state. In Austria, too, the working class must oppose any policy of conquest and anything leading to such a policy. Certainly we have to fulfill great tasks among the Romanians and the Southern Slavs. We must bring those peoples culturally closer to us by helping their fellow countrymen gain national self-government in Austria-Hungary and furthering their cultural development, by giving a democratic constitution to the population of Bosnia and freeing them from the fetters of Turkish feudal laws. We must overcome the agrarian tendencies in our commercial policy in order to improve our relations with the Balkan peoples. But we find it very alarming to see even party comrades talk about a mysterious Austrian 'mission' in the Balkan Peninsula and our 'protectorate' over the Balkan Slavs, as comrade Schulz did in the last issue of *Der Kampf*.[13]

Unlike imperialism in other states that are homogeneous, the Austrian great-power policy cannot appear as representing a common national interest. However, since it involves us in international disputes, one is actually promoting its cause by confusing the imperialist tendencies of the great capitalist *states* with the striving of *nations* for freedom, unity and greatness. For

---

13. [Schulz 1908.]

that reason, we are bound to teach the Austrian workers to see through the deceit of that confusion. The German working class in Austria certainly feels part of the great German people, but it cannot do business with German imperialism, which is the mortal enemy of their brothers in the German empire. In the same way, the Slavic workers in Austria must stay away from rejuvenated pan-Slavism, which has no function other than providing an ideological cover for tsarist imperialism, which has imprisoned even the largest Slavic nations with iron shackles. Only if we keep the working masses totally away from *any* imperialist ideology can we harness their energy for the policy that will keep us away from the struggles of the imperialist world powers and secure peace for ourselves.

The International [Socialist] Congress in Stuttgart has made the struggle against perpetually bellicose and genocidal imperialism the duty of the proletarians of all countries. In that struggle, the working class of all the nations of Austria has an important role to play. By opposing Austria's great-power policy, we also support our comrades in the German Empire, as well as in France, Russia and England, in their difficult struggles against the imperialist tendencies of the governments and capitalist classes of their own countries.

Chapter Twenty-Five

'National and International Viewpoints on Foreign Policy' (September 1909)

Otto Bauer

This is Otto Bauer's major theoretical essay on imperialism (with the exception of the relevant chapters of his book *The Question of Nationalities and Social Democracy*).[1] Most noteworthy is the rationale that he provides to support German Social Democrats in advocating mutual limitation of armaments between the major European states.[2] A year and a half after this essay, in March 1911, Bauer wrote an article on the Turkish Revolution and the resulting threat of a war between Italian and Austrian imperialism over the Balkans. He concluded it with a section called 'Social Democracy and Imperialism' that reads as follows:

> The sharpening of the antagonisms between Austria-Hungry and Italy brings Social Democracy onto the scene. It is our duty to oppose the policy of imperialism.

1. Bauer 1907, pp. 370–415. Bauer developed his theory of imperialism (which he called 'capitalist expansionism') in Chapter 6.
2. See the main introduction to this volume. The call for an international limitation on naval armaments played a key role in dividing Social Democracy into factions of the Left, Right and Centre.

We fight against *armaments*, which impose unbearably heavy burdens on the peoples and deprive all cultural tasks, above all social welfare, of the necessary means.

We tear the popular mask away from imperialism's face. We will not tolerate the competitive struggle between Italian and Austrian capitalists in the Balkan Peninsula being portrayed to the popular masses as a struggle for popular national goals – in one place as a struggle for the redemption of 'unliberated Italy', in another as a struggle for the world status of the German nation, and elsewhere for the creation of a South-Slavic empire or for the liberation of Poland.

We want to resist whatever may provoke the frightful danger of a *war*. The question of whether Austrian or Italian capitalists should build railways in the Balkans is not worth the life of a single Tyrolese rifleman.

We do not want any *conquests* in the Balkans. The right of national self-determination that we demand for ourselves, we also accord to the Balkan peoples.

We demand that railway-construction in the Balkans be *internationalised*. The railways should further the development of the productive forces of the Balkan countries; they should not be the point of departure for imperialist campaigns of conquest.

We do not want the antagonism between Austria and Italy to push democratic Italy into the arms of *tsarism* and turn the peoples of Austria into involuntary followers of *German imperialism*. In the interests of the democratic development of Europe we demand that the alliance between Austria-Hungary and Italy be supplemented by a treaty committing both kingdoms to suspend their armament, to reach an understanding about the Balkan railways and to renounce any plans for conquest.

The development of capitalism works against us. With its railways, it penetrates into the Eastern countries, releasing all their internal contradictions, shaking the foundations of the entire political order, and turning the countries of the East into an object of struggle between the capitalist states. A world war is capitalism's last word.

We resist that development. If capitalism eventually brings about a world war, it will have to be conducted against our will and opposition. Capitalism will have to bear responsibility for the sacrifices of that war on the day of battle as on the day after the peace settlement.

If the Turkish Revolution leads to a war in Europe over Turkey, the European revolution will be the inevitable effect of the European war.[3]

* * *

'National and International Viewpoints on Foreign Policy'[4]

The family and the village, the mark[5] and the manor – that was the world of the peasant in the feudal period. He was full of local feeling and humility before the hereditary lord of the land; national consciousness and feeling were foreign to him. To be sure, he thought that his small native country was part of a great international community that united the whole of Christendom under the world empire and the world church. But that great cosmopolitan community was dashed to pieces in the early stages of bourgeois society by the development of [national] territorial sovereignty and the state church. The rising bourgeoisie was thus pitted against the small states that had grown out of feudal society. As obstacles to bourgeois economy, those states restricted bourgeois personal freedom and opposed the claims arising from bourgeois spiritual development. In the struggle against those relics of a bygone age, the bourgeoisie again discovered *humanity*. However, the bourgeoisie no longer regarded humanity as the community of Christendom that would bring all true believers under the rule of one emperor and one Pope, but rather as the carrier of the general laws of human reason, valid for all times and all peoples, under which (laws) the bourgeoisie disguissed its demands against the hostile legal order. The bourgeoisie no longer regarded the narrow communities, where the peasants spent their lives, as branches naturally growing out of the tree of humanity but looked instead to the big *nations*.

This intellectual world appears very clearly in Fichte's *Addresses to the German Nation*. He turned against peasant regionalism and feudal particularism, exhorting the 'radiant spirit' to turn away from 'earthly patriotism, which clings to the soil, the rivers, and the mountains' and turn instead to 'where there is light and justice'. The narrow communities handed down

3. Bauer 1911, p. 251.
4. Bauer 1909.
5. [In this context, the *mark* refers to a parcel of land held by the Teutonic village-community and farmed by the three-field system.]

from feudal society had to give way before the natural organisation of mankind into nations: 'The separation of Prussia from the rest of the Germans is artificial, founded on arbitrary and accidental arrangements, while the separation of the Germans from the other European nations is founded on nature.' He summoned Germans to struggle for free self-determination in a free community, 'for a free German republic, without princes and hereditary aristocrats'. But this national community received its right from a supranational determination. Its mission was not to rule over other peoples: 'May the Germans' favourable fate protect them from having any share in the plunder of other worlds!' The mission of the German people was also 'not to assert some special national peculiarity'. Rather, it should live its free national life in order to accomplish a great task in the service of the whole human race: its destiny was 'to realise in practice freedom for the citizens [*Bürger*: commoners]'. That is how the great awakener of the German youth pointed out the national mission to his people from a supranational point of view. His nationalism was embedded in a universalistic, cosmopolitan world of ideas. Meinecke[6] can, to be sure, show in his instructive book about the history of German national political ideas how the national and international ideas of the young German bourgeoisie grew out of the same roots and were inextricably mixed.

This unity of national and international ideas is founded on the whole development of the rising bourgeoisie. If Germany supplied its philosophical rationale, the English bourgeoisie justified it with economic doctrines. *English liberalism* was certainly national, even in the narrowest sense: its leading idea was not the great British world empire but the particular interests of Little England. It believed, however, that the national interest could best be protected by a great international division of labour; a large community of free peoples, encompassing the whole world, without protective tariffs, trade-privileges, colonies, or war; a community of nations peacefully exchanging their goods, in which everyone would be the richer, the better things were for the others.

The unity of national and international thoughts, the legacy of German philosophy and English economy, became the possession of European democ-

6. [Friedrich Meinecke (1862–1954) was a liberal German historian who in his book *Cosmopolitanism and the National State* (1908) traced the development of national feelings in the nineteenth century. Meinecke 1908.]

racy, which had fought the battles of the bourgeois revolution. The idea of international cultural unity, of international communities of states and an international division of labour, in which each nation would fulfill its specific historical task, live its own independent political life, and increase its national affluence, merged with the idea of the *international revolution*, whereby each nation would gain its free national existence in a free national state, in the *national republic*, by fighting (over the ruins both of the small states that divided the nation and of the multinational states that chained nations to each other).[7] Thus, for instance, the October [1848] revolution in Vienna was, according to its cause, an uprising for the Magyar revolution, a heroic manifestation of international solidarity, while, in essence, it was also a struggle for the national unity and freedom of the Germans, for the great German republic; and Friedjung[8] could well say that the capture of Vienna made a purely national development of Central Europe impossible.

Frightened by the revolt of the proletariat, the bourgeoisie sought refuge in the midst of the revolution behind the bayonets of the historically existing state-authorities. Therewith ended the revolutionary epoch of the bourgeoisie. Its national ideas now ceased to be revolutionary. The German bourgeoisie no longer hoped for a 'revolution from below' in order to realise its national goals but rather sought to obtain its national state by means of a 'revolution from above'. Detached from revolutionary ideas, the bourgeoisie became

7. This community of the international revolution encompassed, to be sure, only the great historical nations (Germans, Italians, Poles, Magyars), not the little nations without history, about which Lassalle said even in 1859 that they had no 'independently developing *Volksgeist* [special national spirit] able to keep pace with the cultural progress of mankind as a whole'. Today, the nations without history are also rising, one after the other, to historical existence. If they remained on the sidelines during the 1848 revolution, in the near future their awakening can become a driving force for great upheavals. When, in spite of that, some comrades who otherwise are quite distant from Marxism, think they are able today to back their antipathy against those nations by appealing to Marx, Engels and Lassalle, we Marxists have every reason to scoff at 'orthodoxy' and 'dogmatic beliefs'.

8. [Heinrich Friedjung (1851–1920) was an Austrian pan-German historian and journalist of Jewish extraction. He participated in writing the Linz Programme in 1882 and edited a periodical, *Deutsche Wochenschrift*, from 1883 to 1886. In 1886–7, Friedjung was editor-in-chief of the party organ of the German National Party, *Deutsche Zeitung*, but he was excluded from the Party due to his growing anti-Semitism. Friedjung served as municipal councillor in Vienna from 1891 to 1895. In 1904, he was publicly disgraced for using forged sources, although he did so in good faith. During the First World War, he supported a greater-German *Mitteleuropa*; after 1918, he supported the annexation of Austria to Germany.]

narrowly national; its national goals could only be realised to the extent that the historically existing state-authorities were able to accomplish them; and they were in practice incompletely achieved even in the Great-Prussian Empire by completely giving up eleven million Germans under the Habsburg sceptre. At the same time, national ideas were detached from international ones: the national state was not obtained through an international revolution but through the wars of the German princes against other nations.

But, as the German bourgeoisie made its peace with the princes, with their bureaucrats and their armed power, building its national aspirations on that power, the proletariat continued to support revolutionary ideas. It remained faithful to the idea of complete *national unity and freedom*. If comrade Leuthner[9] deplores today as a crime against the German nation the fact that German Social Democracy did not silence its criticism even during the events of 1866 and 1870, he completely forgets that that criticism was made in the name of the *great German republic*. Social Democracy does not confront the national problems with obtuse indifference: it was, indeed, created during a demonstration for Poland's freedom; fighters for Italy's freedom sat in its councils; and its concern for Germany's freedom is proved by the writings of its founders and leaders during the great German crisis of 1859.[10] But it did certainly inscribe on its banner the *international solidarity* of the proletariat: national freedom should be achieved through the international proletarian revolution! And, no matter how those ideas may have faded in the decades of stagnant development, as soon as a period of upheavals begins in Europe, the idea that the

9. [Karl Leuthner (1869–1944) was a right-wing Social-Democratic politician, journalist, and a frequent contributor to *Sozialistische Monatshefte*. From 1895 to 1934, Leuthner was foreign and military-policy editor of the newspaper *Arbeiterzeitung*. From 1911 to 1918, he was a member of the House of Deputies in the Austrian parliament (Abgeordnetenhaus), from 1918 to 1919 of the Provisional National Assembly, from 1919 to 1920 of the Constituent National Assembly, and from 1920 to 1934 of the National Council (Nationalrat), one of the two houses of the Federal Assembly of Austria.]

10. [A reference to the Austro-Italian war or Austro-French Piedmontese War of 1859. The Austrians suffered two major defeats at Magenta and Solferino and concluded peace. The Battle of Solferino (24 June 1859), the last engagement of the Second War of Italian Independence, was fought in Lombardy between an Austrian army and a Franco-Piedmontese army and resulted in the annexation of most of Lombardy by Sardinia-Piedmont, thus contributing to the unification of Italy. The monarchy gave up Lombardy and kept Venetia but, more importantly, it lost its influence in Italy. The Habsburgs had no say in the events of 1860 and 1861 that led to the proclamation of a unified Italy under the rule of the kings of Sardinia.]

international revolution also comprises the realisation of national tasks, and that it appointed us to fulfill those tasks, will awaken to a new life. For that reason, our considerations about the problems of foreign policy must proceed even today from the question: How do we serve the great revolutionary work that the whole revolutionary proletariat, the entire international community of Social Democracy is called upon to accomplish?

Marx and Engels answered that question for their time by seeking to mobilise all the forces of European democracy *against Russia*. War against Russia should have been for the European revolution what the wars against the united princes of Europe were for the French Revolution. Marx called on Germany in 1848, and on England and France in 1853, to wage war against Russia; and, even in 1888–90, Engels set his hopes on a war of Germany and Austria against Russia. As a matter of fact, tsarism actually was the most powerful protector of all reaction.

Russia reached its heyday under Nicholas I.[11] Its army had defeated Turkey and Persia and suppressed Poland's uprising; the Hungarian revolutionary army laid down its weapons before Russian troops. Austria's forces were tied down by the struggles in Italy and Germany; it had to let Russia have its own way in the Balkans. In Germany, Nicholas was the arbiter between Prussia and Austria. In both states, the powerful reactionary party stood on the side of Russia, the mortal enemy of the revolution. As in Prussia, the squires [*Junker*] and the generals – in Austria Windischgrätz, Liechtenstein, Schwarzenberg, and Radetzky – saw in Austria the 'palladium of lawfulness',[12] the natural head of the counterrevolution. Prussia was, as Bismarck said, 'a Russian vassal state in all the European constellations from 1831 to 1850'. Friedjung has vividly described how the Tsar gave orders to the Austrian ministers as if they were servants. Even at the beginning of the Crimean War, the Tsar treated Austria as a vassal-state: he demanded Austria's armed support and offered in return to guarantee its territorial integrity. Then it seemed as if the dissolution of Turkey [i.e. of the Ottoman Empire] was to lead to a vast increase in the power of the tsars. In 1853, the Tsar offered Egypt and Crete to the English envoy Seymour, in exchange for which England was to

11. [Nicholas I, known as one of the most reactionary of the Russian monarchs, was Tsar of Russia from 1825 until 1855.]
12. [The reference is to a wooden statue of Pallas believed to ensure the safety of Troy.]

recognise Russia's suzerainty over Moldavia and Walachia, Serbia and Bulgaria, while admitting the occupation of Constantinople by the Tsar as 'Europe's trustee'. Such an enormous expansion of the power of tsarism had to appear as the worst danger to European democracy. As the reactionaries in Berlin and Vienna wanted to put the armed power of their states unconditionally at the service of the head of the counterrevolution, democracy welcomed as its ally every opponent of tsarism. 'There are only two powers in Europe: Russia and absolutism, the revolution and democracy,' wrote Karl Marx at the time.[13] Whoever unsheathed the sword against Russia was the ally of democracy, even Louis Napoleon, even Turkey, which was stained with accumulated blood-guilt.

And, even after the Crimean War,[14] those ideas survived for a long time. Bismarck recounts in his *Gedanken und Erinnerungen* [*Memoirs*] that even after 1871 he still considered the possibility of concluding an alliance with Russia and Austria 'directed against what, I feared, was the approaching struggle between the two European tendencies which Napoleon called the republican and Cossack ones, and which in contemporary parlance could be labelled, on the one hand, the system of order and monarchical foundations and, on the other, the social republic, to whose level the anti-monarchical movement tends to sink either slowly or by leaps and bounds'. This state of affairs explains why Marx and his followers made a war against Russia the first maxim of the proletariat's foreign policy. One can admit that, in the passion of this struggle, they judged many things unilaterally, incorrectly and unfairly, and one certainly should not any longer call today, as they did, for a war against Russia out of hostility towards tsarism, because Russia has long experienced the revolutionary illness in its own body and has long been too weak to threaten democracy in West and Central Europe. But, even today, and more than ever since the revolutionary uprising of the proletarians of Russia and Poland, anyone who has the interests of European revolution close to his heart must consider it one of his most important duties to deprive tsarism of any support and bring it into disrepute. Important tasks spring from this consideration,

13. [The reference here should be to Engels 1853. This article was published in the collection *The Eastern Question* (Marx 1897), which gave Marx as the author of the article. However, it was later discovered that 'The Real Issue in Turkey', as well as 'The Turkish Question' and 'What Is to Become of Turkey in Europe?', were written by Engels.]
14. [The Crimean War took place from March 1854 to February 1856.]

especially for the Slavic comrades in Austria and the Balkan Peninsula, whose nations are exposed to all the temptations of newly dressed up pan-Slavism.

The relation of our teachers to *militarism* must also be understood in the context of their attitude towards the problems of international politics. They took over opposition to the standing army from bourgeois democracy and even deepened its criticism: on the one hand, by proving that the standing army is not only an instrument of power of the princes against democracy but also reflects in its all organisation the class-structure of capitalist society and the class-rule of the bourgeoisie and, on the other hand, by showing that the development of modern tactics and modern weapons leads to the transformation of militarism into the militia. The militarist army organisation thus appeared as a hindrance for the development of the army to its highest possible capability, although it was retained because the rulers preferred to have less efficient weapons to fight against the 'external enemy' rather than relinquish the most effective weapons for fighting the 'internal enemy'. Social Democracy therefore demanded a democratic army-organisation that would unchain the forces of the peoples for internal struggles against their oppressors and for external struggles against the powers of reaction. Its objectives were war rather than peace, the arming of the people rather than disarmament, and the militia system rather than international agreements and arbitration-courts.[15] Today, other considerations are certainly relevant to the criticism of militarism besides those formulated by Friedrich Engels. But we still retain from his works the criticism of militarism and the insight into its developmental tendencies as valuable possessions. If, today, under completely changed circumstances, the struggle for peace is our most important task, this struggle must be waged as part of our struggle against imperialism – not in a plaintive-sentimental style *à la* Tolstoy or Suttner, which does not suit a party of irreconcilable struggle, but with full awareness that war, which today is a means of imperialist oppression, can once again become a means of proletarian liberation.

15. [Peace, disarmament, international agreements for the limitation of armaments and international arbitration-courts would become the main watchwords of the Marxist Centre, headed by Kautsky and the Austro-Marxists, against the left wing of the SPD and international Social Democracy, headed by Rosa Luxemburg, Karl Radek and Anton Pannekoek, who called for the replacement of standing armies by militias and the transformation of the inevitable imperialist war into a socialist revolution.]

The further development of our views on foreign policy (apart from the far-reaching effects of the rise of the nations without history) was brought about by the development of *imperialism* in the great capitalist states. The girding of economic territories with high tariffs, under whose protection powerful cartels and trusts were formed; the systematic direction of the competitive struggle towards the duty-free markets, which is made possible by the rich surpluses of the domestic cartel-economy; the systematic promotion of capital-investments in foreign, still non-capitalist countries, and the direction of the competitive struggle for investment opportunities by the states, whose monarchs and ambassadors appear in foreign lands as agents of the great banks; the expansion and plundering of colonial regions, the intervention of capitalist states in the internal affairs of the most distant lands in order to prepare the conditions for later colonial acquisitions; the huge increase in armaments on land and sea; the constant recurrence of threats to resort to arms in the capitalist competitive struggle; the war-atmosphere and the war-danger constantly engendered anew by those threats; the contagious infection of broad popular masses by a cynical nationalist master-ideology, which flies in the face of any ethics, betrays all cultural values, and has nothing in common with the old national ideas but the name – these are the most important features of the tendencies that we sum up under the notion of imperialism. They have led to a grouping of states completely different from what Marx could have imagined in 1853, or Bismarck in 1871. We see today the whole of Europe divided into two hostile armed camps: imperialist Great Britain and the imperialist German Empire, each with its own allies.

In all states, the working class is waging the fiercest struggle against imperialism. Its protective tariffs reduce the buying power of wages; capital-exports diminish the demand for labour-power in the domestic labour-market; armaments burden the working class with oppressive taxes; imperialist ideology militates against the ethic of the working class, proletarian ideology, which condemns any exploitation and recognises the right of all labourers to their share in cultural life; and finally, imperialist policy endangers the working-class youth, who have to sacrifice their lives for a foreign cause they hate. For those reasons, the working class everywhere struggles against imperialism – the French Socialists, the English Labour Party, even the proletarian voters of the English Liberals, just as Social Democracy does. Against imperialist enmity, incitement and exploitation of nations, the proletarian International now stands not only as the fighter for the people's freedom but also as the defender of the people's peace.

Entirely new specific tasks spring from this new attitude of Social Democracy towards the problems of international policy. An example will illustrate them graphically.

British imperialism is waging a hard struggle against Little-English, liberal ideology, which is still very strong in England and behind which the interests of those classes that are hostile to imperialism today entrench themselves. Free trade, self-government for the colonies, low taxes, disarmament, peace with the neighbouring nations, and support for freedom-struggles everywhere – those are today, as in Cobden's time, the ideals of a very large part of the English people. Nothing is more mistaken than the idea that every Englishman is a Jingo! But imperialism has often known how to abuse liberal ideology in order to make it serve its own interests. It therefore asks for protective tariffs, ostensibly in order to force other states to give up their own protective tariffs and thus bring about free trade for the first time! It portrays every imperialist campaign of conquest as a struggle for the true freedom of foreign peoples – for instance, the incitement against Germany and Austria-Hungary as a struggle for the freedom of the Balkan peoples. It offered Germany an agreement on naval armaments, knowing that Germany would decline, in order to draw from that refusal new material for warmongering and to shift the blame for naval armaments onto Germany.

Today, when English taxpayers feel very heavily the frightful burden of naval armaments, and English imperialists very skilfully exploit that ill-feeling to agitate against Germany, nothing can be more useful than confronting those intrigues. For that reason the Social-Democratic fraction in the Reichstag put forward a motion for the allied governments[16] to reach an agreement on naval armaments with Great Britain. Had they done that, had they taken the British government at its word, British imperialism (and with it German imperialism) would have lost the best part of their force. In that way, German Social Democracy rendered the best service to the *international*

16. [A reference to the Triple Alliance (Dreibund), a defence-association between the German Reich, Austria-Hungary and Italy. The alliance was formed in 1882, enlarging the former Austro-German Zweibund. It was renewed in 1912 but terminated by Italy in 1915.]

struggles against imperialism: an agreement between Germany and England would have removed the greatest danger to peace and deprived the imperialists of their most effective weapon of agitation. But the motion of the Social-Democratic fraction in the Reichstag was, at the same time, also a *national* action in the best sense of the world. One need only consider the actual implementation of Chamberlain's ideas on an imperial customs-union to realise that there is no greater danger to Germany's economy, power and peaceful development than the strengthening of British imperialism. By showing to Germany the way of wresting from British imperialism its most powerful weapon in the struggle for the consciousness of its own people, German Social Democracy rendered a true service to the German people.[17] Its motion was nothing but an attempt to make impossible the abuse of liberal disarmament ideas by British imperialism, to strengthen the power of liberal ideology in England in the struggle against imperialism, and to unite democratic England with proletarian Germany in the struggle against imperialism. The whole German party press thus justifiably rejected in a forceful way the improper criticism that Comrade Leuthner levelled against that motion.

But this example also shows us how the struggle against imperialism has changed in relation to militarism. *It is today no longer just a question of army-organisation* – a standing army or a militia – *but also of military burdens*, of armaments or disarmament. The huge armaments worsen the living standards of the working class to the extent that they are paid for by means of indirect taxes, and they impede the growth of capital, the expansion of enterprises, and the increase of working opportunities insofar as they lead to a rise in direct taxes; in both ways, they hinder the advance of the whole economy, which is exhausted by militarism and naval expenditures. They engender a hostile atmosphere towards other nations because the taxpayers of each country are told that the armaments of the other states make those of their own country necessary, and, in that way, they breed and increase the war-danger. The working class cannot accept such tremendous sacrifices for extraneous and inimical goals. Therefore, the struggle for reduction of military expenses must be a constituent part of its military policy. Today, we cannot allow the

17. Actually such an agreement was recommended even by conservative and national politicians in Germany – according to Harden, even by Holstein!

increase in the military burdens and the growth of armaments, even if they are bound up with a democratic army-organisation.

Those are, broadly sketched, the main features of the development of our attitude towards foreign policy and militarism. What we can learn from those international developments will have to be considered by the party congress of Austrian Social Democracy that will deliberate on these questions.

In order to remove the grounds for a hostile mood towards Austria on the part of neighbouring peoples and thus to eliminate the causes of the war danger, we must create for the Italians, South Slavs, and Romanians within the Danube Monarchy the conditions for national and cultural development; within Austria, we must grant the right of national self-determination to Poles and Ruthenes [Little Russians] in order to strengthen the forces of the revolutionary-national movements in Russia and thus to weaken tsarism. The first rule of our international policy is *national autonomy*.

Secondly, we must bring down the barriers between us and the Balkan peoples erected by agrarian selfishness. *Free trade with the East!* That is the second rule of our international policy.

Thirdly, we must struggle energetically against any attempt at a policy of conquest in the Balkan Peninsula and oppose the madness of an arms-race with Italy. That is our *struggle against Austrian imperialism*.

Fourthly, we must also oppose any attempt to place the forces of the peoples of Austria at the service of *foreign imperialism*. We cannot demand the dissolution of the Triple Alliance because that would completely cut up the already very loose tie that unites us with Italy, increase the danger of a war with Italy, drive the German Empire, the strongest military power in Europe, to Russia's side, and therefore strengthen tsarism. But we must certainly demand that the Triple Alliance be kept limited to its original goal – defence against a Russian attack – rather than place us at the service of German imperialism, which is the mortal enemy of the German working class.

If the Reichenberg party congress contributes to educating the German workers in Austria in those ideas, it will thereby render a vital service to the German and therefore also to the international proletariat.

Chapter Twenty-Six

'Imperialism and Socialism in England' (January 1910)

Otto Bauer

In this article, Otto Bauer provides a perceptive description of British imperialism but also a whimsically optimistic assessment of the socialist and anti-imperialist character of the Labour Party. These illusions were characteristic not only of Austro-Marxism but also of the wider centrist current it represented within the International, whose radicalism and often brilliant historical analyses were marred by equivocal political conclusions, leading in practice to an adaptation to the reformist trade-union and party bureaucracy.[1]

Bauer's article was written immediately before the United Kingdom's general election of January 1910, held from 15 January to 10 February. It produced a hung parliament in which no political party had an outright majority. The Conservative Party, led by Arthur Balfour, received the largest number of votes, while the Liberals, led by Herbert Asquith, returned two more MPs than the Conservatives. The Labour Party, whose election manifesto did not even raise

1. See, for instance, the debate between Karl Radek and Karl Kautsky over the Labour Party's tactics: Radek 1909 and Kautsky 1909a.

the question of imperialism,[2] received 505,657 votes and 40 seats (11 more than in the previous election). Otto Bauer's assessment of the results of the British general election of January 1910 was sombre but simultaneously hopeful:

> Reaction triumphed in England; the Lords and capitalism, the landed proprietors and protectionists have triumphed; imperialism has triumphed. But imperialism cannot prevail without awakening forces that it cannot master. During recent years, we have seen at work in Eastern Europe the driving forces of the great upheavals of the future.[3] Today we see in the highly developed West the ripening elements of the coming revolutions.[4]

In the article translated below, Otto Bauer elaborated the political forces at work in England that he hoped would eventually culminate in a Labour-victory.

* * *

'Imperialism and Socialism in England'[5]

The development of capitalist society places first one and then another corps of the great proletarian army at the forefront of the class-war. In 1905, Russian and Polish workers were the pioneers of the entire International. For a moment, our own struggle for voting rights and our electoral victory brought Austria to the foreground. In recent months, the great electoral victories in Germany and the mass-strike in Sweden drove the German and Swedish workers into the front line of battle. Now, all eyes are turning to the English workers. As so often in the past, this time too our wishes and hopes accompany the workers of Great Britain in their momentous struggle.

England has the oldest constitution, and the oldest and strongest political traditions of all the European states. On this historical soil, each political development assumes forms that are determined by a centuries-long development. For that reason, it is not easy for the workers of the continent

2. See the January 1910 Labour Party General Election Manifesto in Dale (ed.) 2000, pp. 12–13.
3. [A reference to the first Russian Revolution of 1905.]
4. Bauer 1910c (February), p. 209.
5. Bauer 1910a.

to understand the political struggles of England. We will try to reveal to Austrian workers the historical roots of the great struggle for which the powerful island-kingdom has today become the arena.

British imperialism

Capitalist industry developed more rapidly in England than in any other country. In the first half of the nineteenth century, English industry did not have to fear foreign competition. It needed no protective tariffs for its industrial products, but the protective duties on agrarian products raised the prices of raw materials for industry and foodstuffs consumed by the people. For that reason, the English bourgeoisie, after a great struggle, succeeded in abolishing the Corn Laws and all protective duties (1842 to 1860). England became the classical country of *free trade*. The English example also led other states to reduce their tariff-rates and conclude commercial treaties. But, since the crisis of 1873, a transformation has taken place. Bismarck led the German Empire into strict tariff-protection. Other states followed suit. Only England remained true to free trade. In recent years, however, a movement demanding the reintroduction of protective tariffs has grown stronger over there as well.

The powerful development of German and American industry has broken the absolute power of England over the world market. Germans and Americans are also competing with English businessmen in the English market itself, while the markets of those countries are protected by high tariffs against the penetration of English goods. German cartels and American trusts sell their commodities in the English market much more cheaply than in their home country, where tariff-duties protect them. Powerful branches of industry in England feel seriously threatened by the dumping practices of foreign cartels. They demand the adoption of tariffs to protect themselves against foreign competition.

In the struggle over protective tariffs, the affected industrialists courted the votes of the workers. The economic situation of English workers has undoubtedly worsened during the past decade. Wages have risen more slowly than commodity-prices, and there is vast unemployment. English workers no longer know first hand the effects of protective tariffs; it is therefore possible to portray the actual effects of capitalism as the effects of free trade.

Powerful capital-sums flow each year from England to foreign countries, where they employ foreign workers: the protectionists argue that tariff-duties, by guaranteeing higher profits to domestic industry, will retain English capital in the home-country, encourage the establishment of new undertakings and the expansion of existing ones, and increase demand in the labour-market. The huge naval armaments are a burden on English taxpayers: the protectionists say that tariffs are a means of 'taxing the foreigners' and shifting the costs of the English fleet to Germans and Americans.

Those endeavours, however, face powerful opponents. The iron-industry may want a rise in the price of German iron-imports, but the machine-industry and shipbuilding do not want to dispense with the cheap iron that foreign iron-syndicates bring to England duty-free. Cheap raw materials guarantee to English industry its competitiveness in the world market; the great export-industries, the powerful textile-industry above all, therefore stand for free trade. They are joined by the overwhelming majority of the petty bourgeoisie and the working class, who rightly fear that tariffs will increase the prices of foodstuffs and other basic commodities that they consume.

But, in the struggle against those opponents, the propaganda for protective tariffs finds a powerful ally in England's great concern for preservation and consolidation of its world empire. At the time of the great free-trade victories, concern for the colonies was not so great. England's trade with independent foreign states was then incomparably greater than its colonial trade. Commercial treaties with the European states, therefore, appeared more important than extension of the colonial empire. The colonies appeared to be poor customers that could only be preserved at a high cost. For that reason, the old free-traders were 'Little Englanders' and opponents of *colonial policy*. England's wealth did not seem to them to depend on the size of the British world empire. They granted complete autonomy to those colonies inhabited by white populations, reduced the English colonial army, and, for decades, effectively resisted expansion of the colonial empire.

In recent decades, however, the attitude of the English bourgeoisie towards the colonies has changed significantly. Foreign states are hindering the import of English products through high tariffs; they are offering dangerous competition to English industry in the world market; the colonies, by contrast, have become rich customers and important investment fields for English capital.

The more the English bourgeoisie began to appreciate the value of the colonies, however, the more its possessions seemed endangered. The colonies settled by white populations (Canada, South Africa, Australia, New Zealand) are independent states with independent parliamentary governments and independent legislation. In order to accelerate the development of their own industry, they also locked in their markets with high protective tariffs against English commodities. But the other colonies (India, the crown-colonies and protectorates) are ruled in an absolutist way from London; their legislation and administration serve the interests of English capital at the cost of hundreds of millions of people who are subjected to the British world empire. Yet the revolutionary movements in India and Egypt do not let the English bourgeoisie enjoy those possessions peacefully. The awakening of the peoples of Asia and the opening up of huge territories by new railway-lines affect the interests of the world-encompassing empire. Could it possibly be the case that naval construction on the part of the German Empire was now contesting England's absolute rule over the ocean, or that in the Far East a new great power, a second England, was rising in the islands of Japan?

This world-historical context makes it comprehensible why a part of the English bourgeoisie should want to strengthen the loose structure of the great world empire. Here, the protectionists came forward again. The protective duties, at first only of interest to some branches of English industry, would become a means for imperial politics to glue together the diverging parts of the British Empire.

The passage to the protectionist system would, first of all, change the relation between England and those colonies enjoying complete self-government. Canada, South Africa and Australia supply England with foodstuffs and raw materials. Those commodities are today imported duty-free whether they come from the colonies or from foreign states. Protective duties would make it possible for England to grant privileges to the colonies vis-à-vis other states: colonial products would pay lower duties when imported into England than the products of other states. By contrast, the colonies should pledge themselves to levy lower duties on English goods than on the goods of other countries. In that way, England would be bound more closely with the Anglo-Saxon colonies on the other side of the ocean by the strong tie of economic interests. An economic union should strengthen the political one. Through the system of tariff-privileges, a closer constitutional connection should be brought about between the motherland and the colonies, just as the German customs-union previously paved the way for German unification.

England's world rule is confronted by a serious threat. A large part of the propertied classes in England is convinced that the Empire must increase its navy and colonial army even more rapidly than before, and that the threatening danger can only be met through an aggressive policy, especially against the German Empire, so that even the prospect of a decision through world war must be fearlessly contemplated.

This policy, however, demands heavy financial sacrifices. The tariffs should also be useful in that respect. They would be a new source of income for the state treasury. And, through the granting of tariff-privileges, the colonies would be enticed into placing their military forces at the disposal of the motherland and would contribute to paying the armament-cost. Thus 'tariff-reform', or the introduction of protective tariffs, appears as one means of *imperialist policy* among others – including the system of alliances that England has erected against Germany – together with the construction of dreadnoughts, those formidable gigantic warships; the efforts to introduce general conscription; and all the arts that England employs to rule over the greatest empire known to world history and to make its influence felt throughout the world. The persuasive power of *national* thought; the idea of world rule by the Anglo-Saxon race; the great traditions of the nation that created its unequalled wealth through subjugating entire continents; and the hatred directed against foreign rivals – all of these factors speak for protectionism. All economic misgivings are dashed by the admonition: 'Learn to think imperially!'[6] 'Do not think about your petty particular interests, worry about the immeasurable world empire!'

The plans for this great system are nothing new. Disraeli first sketched them. The Imperial Federation League disseminated them. But they only became a burning question of English daily politics in recent years. The last two economic crises; the growth of German and American imports in the English market; the intensified competition in the world market; the rise of tariff-rates in the protectionist states; German naval armaments; the revolutionary move-

6. [In English in the original. A motto of Joseph Chamberlain (1836–1914), Liberal MP and Colonial Secretary (1895–1903), who allegedly first used it in 1895.]

ments in Asia; the Moroccan crisis and the Balkan crisis – in short, everything that concerns Great Britain's economy and political power has been exploited by the imperialists with great skill. *Joseph Chamberlain*, the colonial minister of the last Conservative government, led the *Conservative Party* into the camp of protectionist imperialism. Until recently, it could hope to conquer the majority in the next elections. Their victory would be a serious danger for European peace and for the economy of those countries that furnish the English market with their products.

English socialism

The first independent political mass-movement of the English proletariat was the *Chartist movement* in the 1830s and 1840s. Its immediate goal was universal and equal suffrage. The Chartists led the struggle for voting rights in great demonstrations that grew into an attempt at a political mass-strike. They were defeated, but their struggle showed the English bourgeoisie the dangers that threatened it. Far superior to its sisters on the continent in terms of wealth, insight and cleverness, the English bourgeoisie knew how to appease the discontent of the working class through concessions timely granted. In that way, it succeeded in preventing the English proletariat from uniting into an independent political party. The English workers were able to develop their trade-unions, co-operatives and relief-funds undisturbed by state-power. Shrewdly preventing a popular movement rather than being driven by it, the bourgeoisie gave workers the suffrage in 1867 and 1884. The great transformation in local administration offered workers the possibility of advancing their interests in economic matters and public welfare through autonomous self-governing bodies. The occupational-safety legislation of England anticipated and was far in advance of that in other European countries. By those means, the English bourgeoisie managed to instil in the English working class the belief that it did not need an independent political party.

The whole history of England seems to confirm this view. Since the [Puritan] Revolution, Liberal and Conservative parliamentary majorities have alternately formed the government and ruled the country. The Liberal and Conservative parties were originally aristocratic parties. The bourgeois revolution did not take place in England through the bourgeoisie creating an independent political party that defeated the two aristocratic parties, but, rather, through bourgeois elements breaking into both aristocratic parties and gradually overwhelming the feudal elements within them. The conclusion seemed to be that the working class, likewise, could not smash both historical parties but, instead, had to win a gradually growing influence within them and finally to conquer their leadership, because, following the electoral reform, the parties could not do without the proletarian voters. English workers, therefore, always gave their votes to whichever of the two historical parties was inclined to fulfill an actual demand of the working class. There seemed to be no place for an independent proletarian party.

Under such circumstances, the English socialists had an exceedingly difficult task. They took part in the construction of trade-unions and co-operatives and in the reform-activity of the municipalities, and their propaganda fertilised England's whole political life with many socialist ideas. But being incapable of uniting the broad masses of the English working class into a great political party, the English socialists were only able to build small propaganda-groups: the SDP (Social-Democratic Party), which propagated the ideas of Marxian socialism; the ILP (Independent Labour Party), which lagged far behind the SDP in theoretical clarity but knew better how to adapt its agitation to England's special conditions and to impart socialist ideas to the broad masses; and, finally, the Fabians, a society of a couple of hundred intellectuals who advocate a reformist socialism.

No great transformation took place until the past decade. The economic situation of the working class has deteriorated. The slow progress of occupational-safety legislation did not satisfy its needs. The opposition of the bourgeoisie to the unions' activity increased. The years-long work of the socialists began to have an impact. Under the impression of judicial decisions that threatened the very existence of the unions, the union-leaders finally gathered up enough courage to act. They created the great new Labour Party, which was joined by the trade-unions, the ILP and the Fabians. For the time being, the SDP remained outside the Labour Party because it believed it was better able to conduct its propaganda-work in complete independence.

The new Labour Party set itself the task of providing independent representation of the working class in parliament, separate from the Liberals and Conservatives. They want to represent the class-interests of the workers in parliament. The young party has not adopted a programme or declared the socialisation of the means of production to be its final goal, but many socialists work in its ranks. Comrade Keir Hardie, the leader of the socialist ILP, stands at their head. Last year, the International Socialist Bureau in Brussels decided to admit the party to the [Socialist] International.[7]

The difficulties that the new party has to face are not small. It was not joined by individual union-members but by the unions as organised bodies. Consequently, it can by no means count on the votes of all unionised workers. Thousands of workers still follow the Liberals or the Conservatives, even though they belong to a trade-union that joined the Labour Party. For decades, the English workers were under the influence of both bourgeois parties. The Labour Party lacks the most important propaganda-means needed to free them from that influence: an independent press. To that should be added the difficulties that the English electoral law causes to a proletarian party. For instance, in England, the parties must meet not only the agitation-costs but also the costs of the electoral process, which almost everywhere else are borne by the state. The English MPs receive no allowance from the public exchequer; the representatives of the Labour Party must therefore be supported by the party. In England, the elections are decided by relative majorities: whoever receives the most votes is elected – even if he failed to get half of the votes. The English electoral system knows no second ballots. For that reason, the Labour Party cannot nominate candidates everywhere: if it takes away part of the Liberal votes in a constituency, without obtaining a relative majority for itself, the Conservative imperialist is elected – even if the Liberals and the Labour Party have more votes together than he does. The greatest precaution is therefore necessary in the nomination of candidates; otherwise the effect of the party's agitation would be that instead of the least dangerous, the most dangerous among the bourgeois opponents would be elected.

---

7. [Admission of the Labour Party to the Second International was the cause of the first major clash between Lenin and Kautsky on international issues. At the October 1908 meeting of the International Socialist Bureau, Lenin criticised Kautsky's resolution supporting the affiliation of the Labour Party. He agreed to admit it, but since it was not a socialist organisation pursuing a class-policy independent of the bourgeoisie, Lenin proposed an amendment describing it as 'the first step on the part of the really proletarian organizations of Britain towards a conscious class policy and towards a *socialist* workers' party'. He argued that the Social-Democratic Federation's sectarian errors could not be remedied by giving 'even a shadow of encouragement to *other, undoubted and not less important* errors of the British opportunists who lead the so-called Independent Labour Party'. Lenin 1908, pp. 235–7.]

Despite those difficulties, the Labour Party achieved great successes by participating in the last general elections: 29 representatives of the Labour Party were elected [in the general elections of 1906]. The bourgeois parties see how the working class is beginning to break free from their leadership and are greatly concerned.

The counterblast of the Liberals

In the elections of January 1906, the Liberals achieved a great majority. Chamberlain's new protectionist propaganda frightened away many voters. The importation of Chinese wage-slaves into South Africa, where they were placed at the service of international gold-mining capital, was an affront to the British workers. Had the sons of the people sacrificed their lives in the struggle against the Boers so that white workers could be displaced by coolies in the conquered country? The rise in taxes and the increase of the state debt due to the Boer War provoked the displeasure of the electorate. The non-conformists (supporters of the free churches that stayed separate from the state church) were particularly dissatisfied with the school-legislation and the alcohol-legislation. The Liberals, therefore, achieved a great success in the last elections. But they could not rejoice at their success, because the growth of the Labour Party, on the one hand, and the strengthening of protectionist imperialism, on the other, threatened their rule.

Apprehension at the defection of its proletarian voters to the Labour Party forced the Liberal parliamentary majority to make great concessions to the working class. In the period between 1906 and 1909, the following political reforms were implemented: a trade-union law that secures the unions against any serious attack; a law providing for compensation of occupational accidents, which extends the responsibility of the employers over eight million workers and equates occupational diseases and occupational accidents; old-age pensions for workers at the public exchequer's expense even if they did not make financial contributions; the legal eight-hour workday for mining; a minimum wage for those employed in cottage-industry; the creation of a fund for the occupation of the unemployed; a law providing for the creation of state-run employment-agencies; broadening of the factories' and mines' inspection; a law providing for the feeding of poor schoolchildren; and the abolition of Chinese slavery in South Africa. All that in four years!

On the other hand, the Liberal majority was compelled by the noisy nationalist agitation of the Conservatives to make concessions to imperialism. They were elected in order to reduce public expenses, preserve the peace, and mitigate the oppressive colonial policy; instead, they had to step up naval armament, follow a foreign policy that during the Moroccan crisis and the Balkan troubles threatened to lead to war, and govern India by means of martial law.

But while the Liberal majority had to make great concessions, on the one hand, to the Labour Party and, on the other, to the Conservatives, its own plans were shipwrecked by opposition from the House of Lords. While the Liberals dispose of a vast majority in the House of Commons, the Conservatives have the majority in the House of Lords. Twenty Liberal bills were rejected or fundamentally altered in recent years by the House of Lords. To this should be added the fact that old-age pensions and the construction of dreadnoughts compelled the government to introduce new taxes for which the Liberal majority naturally had to answer before the voters, while the severe economic crisis strengthened both protectionist agitation and the workers' discontent. The Liberals faced a difficult situation. Each by-election brought Conservative successes. It was expected that the Liberal majority would disappear in the next general election. The only issue in doubt was whether the Conservatives would win the majority or whether neither of the two historical parties would be able to form a government without the support of the Labour Party. In this hopeless situation, the Liberal government decided to deliver a bold counterblast that has completely changed the political situation.

New taxes had to be imposed to cover the deficit in English public finances. According to the budget that the Liberal government submitted, something more than a fourth of that deficit would be covered by a rise in indirect taxes on spirits and tobacco, while almost *three fourths* would be covered through *property-taxes*. The budget raised income-taxes on great incomes, death-duties, fees for sale and lease contracts, the stock-exchange tax, fees for the production and sale of alcoholic drinks, and transportation-taxes. Large capital and large landed property were outraged, but the Liberal Party could boast of having submitted a 'poor man's budget', one that imposes most new burdens on the propertied classes. Should the deficit be covered by taxes on the propertied classes or by tariffs that increase the prices of the workers' foodstuffs? That is the question that the Liberal budget set against the protectionists.

The most important part of the budget, however, involves the *taxes on landed property*. They include: an incremental value-tax on urban real estate; reversion-taxes, which the landowner has to pay when the leased land reverts to him at the expiration of the leasing contract; a building-lot tax, levied on unimproved urban land; and a mine-tax, levied on the rents that mines have to pay to the landowners. The large landed proprietors offered the strongest resistance to the new taxation-plans of the Liberal government. The establishment of a cadastre [land-register], which would be necessary for introduction of the new taxes, would show what huge wealth the large landed proprietors dispose of and how well they have managed to evade the taxes levied on them so far by local organs of self-government. Hence the Lords' commotion! The English people, however, rejoiced at the taxation-plans.

The largest part of England's soil belongs to the large landed proprietors, not only in the countryside but also in the cities. In the countryside the landowners lease it to tenants for cultivation. In the cities, they lease it for a number of years, and the houses that the tenants have built on alien ground devolve on the landowners at the expiration of the leasing contract. Four thousand families own half of the English soil; they draw from it a huge unearned income. London alone pays 480 million Austrian crowns to 20 large landowners. For that reason, the idea of land-reform is exceedingly popular among all classes of the English population. The old principle, according to which land-reform is 'the socialism of the enlightened bourgeoisie', is nowhere so true as in England. While the agrarian question causes great difficulties even to the Social Democrats in countries where the land belongs to small peasants, in England, the classic land of large landed property and the lease-holding system, no demand of socialism is as popular far beyond the circle of the working class as the socialisation of the land. Since a government has finally dared to impose somewhat higher taxes on idle large landed property (admittedly, only on urban real estate!), and since the noble Lords put up a fight against this plan, the persuasive power of the idea of land-reform and the hatred of the popular masses for the large landed proprietors, to whom they must pay huge rents as tenants both in the countryside and in the cities, militates in favour of the government.

With the land-taxes, the Liberal government has taken up the fight against the large landowners. The bulwark of the large landed proprietors is the House of Lords, controlled by the Conservatives. The House of Lords rejected the budget, which imposes new taxes on its members, by a large majority. Thereby the question of taxation was turned into a *constitutional question.* Ever since the time of the revolution (1642 to 1688), and even more clearly since the first of the three great electoral reforms (1832), there has been a contradiction in England between the form and the essence of the constitution. According to the form, the king appoints the prime minister; both houses of parliament have equal rights; and each law requires the consent of House of Commons, the House of Lords and the king. In fact, however, the great revolution brought about a completely different distribution of power. The king appoints the prime minister, but he must appoint the candidate selected by the majority of the House of Commons. The laws require the sanction of the king, but he cannot refuse his sanction to any law that has been approved by both houses of parliament. The House of Commons alone, however, decides the budget and taxation. In addition, the budget formally requires the consent of the House of Lords and the king, but they must agree to any the budget that the majority of the House of Commons has resolved upon. That is the actual English constitution and the great achievement of the revolution, sanctified by three centuries of usage and cemented by the democratic electoral reforms. The Lords have now infringed that constitution in order to evade the new taxes. They attempted to turn their duty of giving formal approval to a budget resolved upon by the House of Commons into a right to approve or reject that budget. The House of Lords has rejected the budget. The government has now dissolved the House of Commons and put the question to the mass of the voters: Will you tolerate one of the great achievements of the revolution, which for centuries has been the undisputed foundation of our unwritten constitution, according to which popular representation should alone decide taxation and public finances, being violated by the House of Lords because the large landowners would rather infringe the constitution than pay new taxes?

The struggle over the budget has therefore changed the entire political situation. The Liberals can go now to the elections as fighters against indirect taxes and tariffs and for property-taxes, as fighters against the privileges of the large landowners, as fighters for democracy who are defending the right of popular representation against the arrogance of the Lords. They now feel so strong that they have even dared to take up the demand most hated by English nationalism: the demand for home rule (self-government) for Ireland.

Until recently, the Conservatives hoped to regain a majority in the next elections. Today, their situation has deteriorated. They must appear before the voters as accomplices of the Lords, as advocates of indirect taxes, as custodians of large landed property, as defenders of the arrogance of the House of Lords against freely elected popular representation.

But the Labour Party is also compelled to enter the electoral struggle under rather unfavourable circumstances. Admittedly, its consistency and determination in the fight over the budget was greater than that of the Liberals. 'The Liberal government,' said comrade Keir Hardie recently, 'wants to tax mining rents by 5 per cent; the Labour Party claims 100 per cent of the mining rents for the community.' The Liberals want to reform the House of Lords, while the Labour Party wants to abolish it. But, despite all that, the current situation is not favourable for the Labour Party. Its programme is for the complete independence of the working class against both bourgeois parties, but, today, it is forced to wage the struggle alongside the Liberals. Its most important task is to win over several hundreds of thousands of workers who constitute a significant part of the Liberal electorate, but, today, it cannot fulfill that task because it must struggle shoulder to shoulder with the Liberals against the landowning class.

But the inauspiciousness of the moment must not conceal from us the hopeful prospect of a great future for English socialism. This election campaign is a turning point in England's history. It will bring to light forces that will powerfully advance the cause of English socialism.

The English population has today learned a great course on capitalist economy. In countless meetings, Conservatives speak about the competitive struggle in the capitalist world, the Liberals about land-monopoly and land-reform, the socialists about the antagonism between the propertied and the propertyless. The liberal taxation-policy had an explosive effect on the traditional parties: it pushed proprietors, who, until recently, were Liberals, into the arms of the Conservatives; and the petty bourgeoisie and workers, who were hitherto Conservatives, into the Liberal camp. New ideas are emerging in the election meetings: people are now talking about the abolition or reform of the House of Lords, its transformation into an elected Senate, an electoral reform for the House of Commons with female suffrage and proportional representation, and a written constitution. The rigid party system is tottering; a tidal wave of new social and political ideas is sweeping over the country. Thus, the soil is broken in which socialism will plant its seed.

The Liberals are playing a bold game. In order to save free trade, part of the English bourgeoisie has taken up the class-struggle against the landowners. In that struggle it has borrowed weapons from the arsenal of socialism – a dangerous beginning inspired by despair! The Liberal Party cannot go to the end of the path it has entered upon without repelling the propertied classes and turning into a party of workers and the petty bourgeoisie. On the other hand, the Liberal Party cannot desert that path without succumbing and leaving the arena to the two powers that one day will fight the decisive battle against each other: the Conservatives and the Labour Party, imperialism and socialism. The Liberal Party had to enlist social ideas in its service if it did not want to succumb to the persuasive power of imperialist ideas, but it cannot hold on to those social ideas without ceasing to be a bourgeois party. That is the great dilemma they will soon have to face. With giant steps, England is approaching the decisive struggle between imperialism and socialism.

For that reason, the working class of all countries follows with the most vivid interest the struggle that England's workers are waging today. The current English struggle over tariffs and taxes, over a warlike or pacific policy, over the right of popular representation, etc., affects not only our daily interests; it also gives us great hope for the future. The rigidity of the historical party system in England and the weakness of English socialism are even today weak points in the forward march of the international proletarian army. Today, England stands at the threshold of a period of political transformations that will set an example for the entire Anglo-Saxon world, above all for the United States. Let us hope that the political upheavals in England will pave the way for socialism in the great Anglo-Saxon world, which will lead the working class of the most mature and powerful peoples of the world into the camp of the International. Only then will the circle be closed. And then, for the first time, we will be prepared for decisive struggles against the capitalist world.

Chapter Twenty-Seven

'*Finance Capital*' (June 1910)

Otto Bauer

Otto Bauer's review of *Finance Capital* outlines some of the principal concepts that made Rudolf Hilferding's work so celebrated. Bauer was one of many who thought *Finance Capital* read 'almost like an additional volume of *Capital*'. In particular, his review examines Hilferding's account of 'fictitious capital' and its connection with the process of concentration and centralisation predicted by Marx. This was a vital point, for many revisionists believed that joint-stock organisation had achieved a 'democratisation' of capital through widespread shareholding. Eduard Bernstein declared that 'by virtue of its form the joint-stock company tends to be a very significant counterweight to the centralisation of wealth through the centralisation of business enterprises. It permits an extensive division of already concentrated capital.'[1] The implication appeared to be that it was 'quite wrong to suppose that the present development shows a relative or indeed absolute decrease in the number of property-owners.... The number of property-owners increases.... If the activity and the prospects of Social Democracy depended on a decrease in the number or property-owners, then it

1. Bernstein 1993, p. 58.

might indeed "go to sleep".'[2] Hilferding, to the contrary, explained that share capital was typically 'fictitious' capital, i.e., nothing but the sum of 'titles to income that are traded by the capitalists'. Meanwhile, the banks enriched themselves through 'founder's profit', transforming joint-stock ownership into 'an ingenious financial technique whose goal is to control alien capital with as little as possible capital of their own'. Bauer concluded that

> Hilferding's book...shows us the most important facts of the most recent development of capitalism. What Marx was able to sketch only in broad outlines in his doctrine of the concentration of capital, of the developmental tendencies of capitalism, becomes here a vivid picture of our times. What once was bold prophesying has now turned into a reality.

* * *

'Finance Capital'[3]

Marxist economics made little progress after Karl Marx's death. Marxists rightly considered the popularisation of Marx's doctrines and their defence against the attacks of opponents as their most important task. Little time remained to us for the upgrading and continuation of Karl Marx's economic teachings. Ultimately, the work of popularisation also began to suffer from this situation. The capitalism described in most of our propaganda-literature is that of the 1860s and 1870s, not the capitalism of our own day. The newest phenomena in economic life were certainly dealt with in many valuable articles and brochures, but we lacked a systematic theoretical presentation. Even in the most significant and independent economic work hitherto produced by the Marxist school, apart from those of Marx and Engels themselves, even in Kautsky's *Agrarian Question*, the immediate political purpose and the needs of popularisation thrust the historic-descriptive exposition into the foreground and the theoretical part into the background.[4] Meanwhile, a new world has arisen in the economic life of all developed nations: the old presentations of the developmental tendencies of capitalism no longer suffice. The gaps result-

2. Bernstein 1993, p. 61.
3. Bauer 1910b.
4. [Kautsky 1988.]

ing from this situation have now finally been filled at least in part. Rudolf Hilferding's *Finance Capital* gives us what we have long needed.[5]

The newest phenomena in economic life are Hilferding's subject. The latest economic literature, including periodical literature as well as the newest cartel, banking and stock-exchange surveys, furnished him the raw material he has elaborated. He accomplished this work as a Marxist: his tools are Marx's economic concepts, and he placed the latest facts of economic development in the framework of Marxist economics. To be sure, Hilferding confronts Marx with complete freedom. In the theory of money and credit, in the presentation of the joint-stock company, and in the theory of crises, he goes considerably beyond Marx; he combats and corrects the views of the master in the theory of the interest-rate. But, even if Hilferding does not accept the results of Marx's work without a proof, he has completely appropriated Marx's method. And, together with Marx's method, he has also adopted the manner of presentation – even the language ridden with anglicisms! This appropriation of Marx's manner of presentation is not completely harmless. As always happens in the redefinition of a science, Marx developed a whole system of vivid images and comparisons, of metaphors, tropes and symbols, in which he clothed his concepts and laws. We often forget that we speak in *images* when we say, for instance, that the value of the means of production is 'transferred' to the commodities, that value finds its 'expression' in price, or that the law of value 'manifests itself' in the movement of prices. Goethe said, in a similar context, that 'people think they speak pure prose, but they actually speak in tropes'. Now, the whole science of our times shows a tendency to shift its manner of presentation away from colourful images and towards abstract concepts. Marxism must not avoid that tendency. The satisfaction of that need is important, not so much because Marx's metaphorical language, which originated under the influence of Hegel's metaphorical language, has induced many authors (for instance Koppel and Hammacher)[6] to reinterpret Marxism in

5. Hilferding 1910a [English version Hilferding 1981]. The work appeared simultaneously in the third volume of *Marx-Studien, Blätter zur Theorie und Politik des wissenschaftlichen Sozialismus* edited by Max Adler and Rudolf Hilferding. The volume also includes the beautiful work of the comrade Tatiana Grigorovici, *Die Wertlehre von Marx und Lassalle*. We already reviewed this work in *Der Kampf* when it appeared as the author's doctoral dissertation. [See Bauer 1908a and Grigorovici 1910.]

6. [Koppel 1905 and Hammacher 1909.]

the sense of an idealist metaphysic, but, above all, because this manner of presentation is not the manner of science in our own day, and because it therefore constitutes an obstacle to the triumphal progress of the content of Marx's system. Hilferding's work does not satisfy that need because he leans on Marx too closely in the manner of presentation. On the other hand, precisely that close following of Marx is again a great merit of this work. With the exception of Engels's writings, there is no other economic work so completely filled by Marx's spirit, so purely cast in Marx's forms of presentation and so wholly written in Marx's own language. Hilferding's work reads almost like an additional volume of *Capital*. And, yet, with those means, he has mastered the newest economic phenomena – facts that were totally unknown to Marx. This connection, this complete mastery of the new facts through the old concepts and terminology, clearly shows the fruitfulness of Marx's doctrine, its living efficacy beyond the lifetime of its creator, and its undiminished vitality. For that reason, despite all our reservations, we must thank Hilferding for having declined to replace Marx's manner of presentation by a new, original one.

The foundation of the whole work is the *theory of money* and *credit*. Hilferding sets out from Marx's theory of money. On that foundation, he attempts to explain the latest monetary phenomena, particularly the peculiar development of Austrian, Dutch and Indian currencies. This attempt led him to develop further Marx's theory of money on essential points. It is precisely in this development that the fruitfulness of Marxist economics clearly manifests itself. Hilferding has succeeded in explaining phenomena that remain a riddle for bourgeois economics.

The theory of money is the most complicated part of political economy. It would seem that, on this field, we deal exclusively with opposing theoretical views that are completely independent from the social position of their authors. And yet the whole of social development is also reflected in the theory of money! The old theory of money was filled with the spirit of liberalism. Since vulgar liberal economics considered all categories of capitalist society as natural categories, seeing in each intervention by the state an improper disturbance of natural harmony, it also regarded money as a thing whose character as money was assigned to it by nature itself, whose value was necessarily intrinsic, while the paper currency issued by the state could only produce dangerous disturbances in economic life. However, the more the capitalist class moved away from liberalism, the more it regulated economic life through the conscious action of great organisations and put the state into its service as the most inclusive and powerful of those organisations, the more it came to consider money also as the direct product of state law. The time was ripe for a 'state-theory of money'. The Marxist theory of money, by contrast, stands midway between liberal 'metallism' and Knapp's 'chartalism'.[7] Because Hilferding sees in money the material mediation of social relations, he can show how those social relations, which are usually mediated by a precious metal, can also be established by a worthless piece of paper that owes its standing to a fiat of the state as an organ of society. In that respect, Hilferding's theory of money borders upon Knapp's chartalism. On the other hand, though, we also know that the necessity of materially mediating social relations is rooted in the anarchy of commodity-producing society, which sets limits to the displacement of this material mediation by the conscious intervention of the state. Hilferding's theory of money thus gives its due likewise to the old metallism.

Hilferding's theory of money is important in itself because of the light it sheds on the currency and banking policy problems of our time. In the context of his work, however, it appears as the foundation upon which he builds up his *theory of finance-capital*. We will attempt to outline the leading ideas of this most important and original part of the work without entering into the many valuable details it contains.

The *development of the productive forces* controls the development of human society. In our age, the relations of working people with the tools of labour and the raw material of their work change exceedingly quickly. The system of machines that a given number of workers operate and the amount of raw material they work up are always increasing, and the same holds for the immense system of means of transportation and communication that supplies them with those raw materials. That technical upheaval finds its capitalist expression in the *change in the composition of capital*: constant capital (material capital) grows much more rapidly than variable capital (capital invested in wages); and fixed capital (stationary capital such as buildings, machines, ships, railways, etc.)

7. [Chartalism is an early twentieth century monetary theory advocating the use of fiat-money instead of commodity-money. Its developer was the German economist Georg Friedrich Knapp (1842–1926), who claimed that money must have no intrinsic value and must strictly be used as government-issued tokens, i.e. fiat-money. Knapp was author of *The State-Theory of Money* (Knapp 1905, English version Knapp 1924).]

grows much more rapidly than circulating capital (revolving capital in the form of wages, raw materials and auxiliary supplies, etc.). The struggle for the highest possible profit forces each capitalist enterprise to accumulate part of its annual profit and to change the composition of its capital constantly in the direction of this general developmental tendency. However, the increase of capital through accumulating the profit yielded by each enterprise occurs too slowly for the enterprises to be able to expand and transform their production apparatus quickly enough in that way. The demand for credit therefore grows constantly. Concentration in banks of all the available fragments of capital creates the possibility of expanding credit.

Together with the technical transformation, the *relation of banks to industry* also changes. The larger is the proportion of fixed capital, the less adequate will it be for industrialists to borrow only circulating capital. But, if fixed capital is also used to secure credit, the capital that is being loaned out can only be returned with great difficulty, so that the bank acquires a lasting interest in the enterprises to which it grants credit; it wins influence and power over the enterprises that depend upon it.

But even the growth of bank-credit is not enough to free industrial enterprises from the limitations of individual property. The *joint-stock company* can accomplish that goal much more perfectly. In terms of providing capital, it serves the individual enterprise better because it involves not just individual capitalists but the entire capitalist class. It is also better for accumulation-purposes, because the creation of a reserve-fund and the increase of capital are independent of the living and luxury-needs of the capitalists as well as of the fates of family and inheritances. Since its energy for growth is greater, the joint-stock company can expand without disturbance and according to technological needs. In that way, industrial concentration is detached and made independent from individual-property concentration. The destinies of individual capitalist families no longer affect the industrial undertakings but only the movement of shares as property.

The capitalist as a shareholder is no longer an industrial entrepreneur but now a money-capitalist. He therefore does not claim the average rate of profit. If an industrial undertaking in which 1,000,000 crowns are invested, yielding an average profit of 150,000 crowns (50,000 crowns interest and 100,000 crowns of enterprise profit), were turned into a joint-stock company, then, given an interest-rate of 5 per cent, 3,000,000 crowns in shares can be issued, because 3,000,000 crowns at 5 per cent yield an interest of 150,000 crowns. The

bank undertaking this conversion can thus sell shares to the sum of 3,000,000 crowns, even though only 1,000,000 crowns were invested in the enterprise that it is turning into a joint-stock company. It thus obtains a *founder's profit* of 2,000,000 crowns.[8] Because the shareholders, as money-capitalists, only draw interest, the issuing bank appropriates the founder's profit at the time of the foundation.[9] The capitalised profit of the enterprise, appropriated by the bank, is the founder's profit. The amount of share-capital is thus equal to the profit of the enterprise capitalised at the average interest-rate. While profit, according to the law of the average profit-rate, is determined by the amount of capital, the size of the share-capital is determined, on the contrary, by the amount of profit. In addition to the functioning capital, which is invested in the enterprise and determines the sum of profit, there now appears *fictitious capital*, which is actually nothing but the sum of revenue-claims, i.e., of titles to income that are traded by the capitalists and determined by the sum of profits.

Those income-titles are traded on the *stock-exchange*. The speculative profits obtained there are not a share of the surplus-value but purely differential profits ('profit upon alienation')[10] resulting from the different valuation of income titles. The function of the stock-exchange is to reduce the price of those income-titles to the profit capitalised at the interest-rate. While the equality of profit-rates of functioning capitals is all the more difficult to attain the larger is the fixed capital (because equal profit-rates can only be attained through the outflow of capital from branches of production with lower profit-rates and the inflow of capital to branches of production with higher profit-rates) the equality of interest-rates for fictitious capital is achieved through the formation of share-prices.[11] The production-process itself remains unaffected. What is traded on the stock-exchange are property-claims detached from the function of the entrepreneur. The stock-exchange is the market for the 'circulation of property in itself'.

---

8. Actually, the founder's profit is smaller, because the profit to be distributed among the shareholders is reduced by higher taxation, bonuses and higher administration-costs.

9. [Foundation (*Gründung*) also means 'launching; or 'flotation'. Founder's profit (*Gründergewinn*) can also be translated as 'floater's' or 'incorporator's gain'.]

10. [In English in the original.]

11. [*Kursbildung* can also be translated as 'formation of rates'.]

The separation of property from the entrepreneur's function accelerates the concentration of capital. On the one hand, the concentration of business[12] is detached from the concentration of property as the former proceeds more rapidly than the latter. On the other hand, a rapid *concentration of property* also takes place through the accumulation of founder's profit and more lastingly through the effects of speculation, which is a means for larger capitalists to dispossess smaller ones, or the 'public'. Larger capitals, especially the banks, speculate with entirely different prospects of success than smaller ones: they are better informed about particular companies thanks to their links with industrial enterprises; their capital-strength allows them to buy and sell at the most favourable moment and, even by themselves, to bring about desired changes in share-prices. The share form, moreover, allows them to *concentrate economic power* even beyond the concentration of property. It is by no means necessary to own the whole of the share-capital, or even most of it, in order to control a joint-stock company; the banks developed an ingenious financial technique whose goal is to control alien capital with as little capital of their own as possible.

If the stock-exchange is the market for fictitious capital, trade with fictitious commodities develops on the *commodity-exchange*.[13] Since the use-value of wares traded on the commodity-exchange is assumed to be of a standard type, they are dealt with as pure exchange-values. If money is usually the representative of commodities, on the commodity-exchange commodities are nothing but representatives of money. If money usually functions in the circulation of commodities only as a means of calculation, that is precisely the function of commodities in the differential business of the [commodity-] exchange. If values are usually exchanged in commodity-trade that represent a multiple of the existing money supply, in the [commodity-] exchange sums of commodities are exchanged that represent a multiple of the existing commodity supply. This speculation opens up new opportunities to apply banking capital; it also leads to control of the most important branches of world trade by the banks.

---

12. [*Betrieb* can also be translated as 'undertaking', 'establishment', 'factory', 'plant', 'firm', etc.]
13. [*Warenbörse*: also can also be translated as 'produce-exchange'.]

We call this whole development the *mobilisation of capital*. Sums of money, which, in the hands of their owners, cannot serve as productive capital, are placed at the disposal of industry and trade through the mediation of the banks. They are, on the one hand, sums of money that occasionally step out of the circuit of industrial capital – the size of these sums grows with the development of fixed capital – and, on the other hand, they are fragments of capital belonging to non-productive classes and savings of small capitalists, peasants, workers, etc. – whose size grows with the concentration of all fragments of money-capital in the banks. The composition and extent of these sums change constantly. But there always remain in the employment of the industrial and commercial capitalists sums of money at the disposal of the banks. Industry and trade thus function with a capital larger than the total capital belonging to the industrial and commercial capitalists. Hilferding calls bank-capital, capital in money-form that is in that way transformed into industrial and commercial capital, *finance-capital*. A growing share of the capital employed in industry and trade is finance-capital, capital at the disposal of the banks being used by industrialists.[14] The larger this share, the larger is the power of banks over industry.

The banks take advantage of this power in order to strengthen the tendencies towards the *limitation of free competition*. These tendencies originate in industry itself. The larger is the mass of fixed capital, the more obstacles there are in the way of the equalisation of profit-rates. The profit-rate sinks especially in the sphere of the largest capitals, where capital-influx was exceedingly facilitated by the share-form [i.e. by joint-stock companies] and outflow was made much more difficult by the large extent of fixed capital, and likewise in the sphere of the smallest capital, where all capitals that are no longer competitive in the more developed spheres crowd together. Besides, in the fluctuations of the business-cycle, perceptible differences in profit-rates emerge between enterprises producing raw materials and those processing them: in times of prosperity, the higher prices of raw materials curtail the profits of those working them up, while, in times of depression, the lower prices of raw materials reduce the profits of their producers.

In presenting the development of finance-capital, Hilferding adds a chapter dealing with *economic crises*. In contrast to previous presentations of the

14. [Here Bauer is quoting Hilferding's definition. See Hilferding 1981, p. 225.]

Marxist theory of crises, including my own,[15] Hilferding provides compelling evidence that 'the pure accumulation of money at the level of society as a whole is impossible on the assumption of reduced or stationary production'.[16] For the rest, Hilferding's presentation touches on mine in the decisive points. The presentation of how the fall in the profit-rate asserts itself is new, as well as the description of the changes effected in credit conditions and the interest-rate by the fluctuations of the business-cycle – a discussion that also answers important questions about central-bank legislation. Bernstein's illusions are finally disposed of by Hilferding's presentation of the modification of crises by finance-capital. Yet we still miss much in this section; in particular, the effects of international integration of economic areas on the business-cycle are not thoroughly developed. Thus, for instance, the rise in corn prices results in great international shifts in value. The cereal-exporting countries are enriched at the expense of the importing areas. Western and Central-European workers are able to buy fewer domestic industrial products, while Western and Central-European landowners are able to buy more American shares. It is obvious that these and similar international value-shifts have a strong influence on the business-cycle. The systematic presentation of such influences would have filled many gaps in Hilferding's work.

The work closes with a presentation of modern *economic policy*. What is original here, above all, is the theoretical presentation of capital-exports. By contrast, in the discussion of changes in commercial policy, in class-structure and class-struggles, in the trade-union struggle and in the critique of imperialism, Hilferding closely follows much of what has already been explained by others, especially by Kautsky, Parvus, Cunow and even by Hilferding himself in *Neue Zeit*,[17] as well as by me in *The Question of Nationalities*.[18] Yet those chapters are also very important because they are the most popular of the whole book, and their argumentation will be an effective weapon for us in the struggle against democratic, free-trade and revisionist illusions. No doubt, it would have been desirable also to have a discussion of modern state-capitalism and the creation of private monopolies by direct political intervention,

15. [Bauer 1904.]
16. Rudolf Hilferding, *Finance Capital*, p. 352.
17. [A reference to Hilferding 1907b. See Chapter 23.]
18. [Bauer 2000, pp. 370–415.]

as has been attempted by the German potash bill, by Bilinski's plan for an 'oil-monopoly', by the Austrian sugar-law of 1903 or by the Brazilian coffee-valorisation. It is characteristic that today the working class, in its struggle against state-capitalism, is, in many respects, resuming the traditions of liberalism; for instance, in the struggle against protective tariffs, against certain capitalist tax-privileges such as the alcohol-quota, against state promotion of private monopolies, etc. In the struggle against imperialism, we can also appeal to the arguments of the 'Little Englanders'. A discussion of that peculiar swapping of roles by the classes would have made very clear the complete change in the whole economic and political situation. Our literature is full of criticisms of old Manchester-liberalism. The opponents being fought against in that literature are now dead. Until now, we have lacked a systematic presentation and criticism of the new opponents who have appeared in recent decades. Hilferding's book is the most valuable building stone for such a discussion!

Hilferding's book thus shows us the most important facts of the most recent development of capitalism. What Marx was able to sketch only in broad outlines in his doctrine of the concentration of capital, of the developmental tendencies of capitalism, becomes here a vivid picture of our times. What once was bold prophesying has now turned into a reality. A vast image of the development of society opens up before us. We see how capitalism, in its restless transformation of the whole of economic life, creates the conditions for its own overcoming. The way to socialism, in turn, appears clearly before our eyes. And, in the face of such an overwhelming picture of world-historical upheaval, we feel ashamed at the despondency that sometimes seizes us when confronted with the troubles of everyday work. Marxist knowledge lifts us up from the miseries of daily struggle by turning our gaze to the driving forces that, unaffected by the undulations on the surface, drive us forward in restless motion, forward at an ever-quickening pace, irresistibly forward.

Our most important task is to bring to the masses this certitude that theory gives us. Hilferding's book is a difficult work requiring arduous study. But it sets new tasks for our work of popularisation; it should and will enrich our press, our pamphlet-literature, our lectures, and our whole propaganda-work. To fulfill this task seems to us more important than many noisy actions and many laborious parliamentary struggles. Only theory can be the conscience of the proletarian masses, only theory frees us from the confusing influence of the bourgeois surroundings and will prop us up when the changing experiences of the day make us faint-hearted. For that reason, any theoretical achievement, even if it directly influences only a few, is nevertheless a fruitful deed for us all in its long-range effect, because 'theory itself becomes a material force when it has seized the masses'.[19]

19. [The whole quotation from Marx reads: 'The weapon of criticism cannot, of course, replace criticism by weapons, material force must be overthrown by material force; but theory also becomes a material force as soon as it has gripped the masses.' Marx 1844.]

Chapter Twenty-Eight

'Rudolf Hilferding's *Finance Capital: A Study of the Latest Phase of Capitalist Development'* (27 August 1910)

Julian B. Marchlewski (Karski)

This review of Rudolf Hilferding's *Finance Capital* was first published in one of the two main organs of the SPD left wing, the *Leipziger Volkszeitung*.[1] Unlike Otto Bauer, who shared Hilferding's view of economic crises as the product of disproportionalities due to unplanned investments, Marchlewski suggests that underconsumption was the principal casual factor: 'the overwhelming majority of the population, the proletariat, gets back only a small share of the product of its labour in the form of consumption articles of every kind'. He objects that Hilferding failed to explain either the periodicity of crises or why 'they follow immediately after a period of prosperity, indeed, almost always after a period of the highest tension in the productive forces'. The misgivings expressed here also reappeared later. As a member of the Berlin Internationale group led by Rosa Luxemburg, Marchlewski would be one of the few Marxist theoreticians with any economic expertise who greeted Luxemburg's theory of a

1. See also the reviews in the second left-wing daily, the organ of the Bremen left organisation: Nachmison 1910a and Nachmison 1910b.

chronic problem of markets as a major contribution to the explanation of imperialism.[2]

In fact, Hilferding attributed both cycles and crises to changes in the rate of profit: a crisis presupposed a decline in the profit-rate 'until a point is reached where new capital-investment ceases and there is an evident slump in sales'. Among factors contributing to this outcome, Hilferding listed labour-shortages and the consequent rise in wages, which secured for workers a temporarily larger share in the distribution of consumer goods:

> At the peak of prosperity labour time per unit of output may increase as a result of the shortage of labour, especially skilled labour, to say nothing of wage disputes which are usually more widespread during such periods.... During prosperity the demand for labour power increases and its price rises. This involves a reduction in the rate of surplus-value and hence in the rate of profit.[3]

The other salient issue that Marchlewski raises in this review concerns the effect of finance-capital upon class-relations. Whereas Bernstein thought joint-stock ownership entailed expansion of a property-owning middle class, Marchlewski replies that Hilferding proved 'precisely the opposite'. If cartelised industry temporarily benefited from new forms of organisation, it was largely at the expense of small-scale production so that 'the growing power of finance-capital leads to acceleration of the concentration process and destruction of the middle classes'. The result was that small capitalists, in a futile attempt to avoid ultimate proletarianisation, had become the 'leaden weight of reaction'. The ensuing intensification of class-conflict affirmed Hilferding's conclusion that 'In the violent clash of these hostile interests the dictatorship of the magnates of capital will finally be transformed into the dictatorship of the proletariat.'[4]

* * *

2. Marchlewski 1913 and Mehring 1913. [The references suggest this should be Marchlewski 1913, not 1913a.]
3. Hilferding 1981, p. 260.
4. Hilferding 1981, p. 370.

'Rudolf Hilferding's *Finance Capital: A Study of the Latest Phase of Capitalist Development*'[5]

Since Karl Marx wrote his ingenious analysis of the dynamics of capitalism, the development of capitalist economy has proceeded at a frantic pace. The direction of this development was in the main foreseen by Marx, but, obviously, the complexity of these processes results in dozens of problems whose solution is only possible on the basis of a precise knowledge of factual material. Thus the task is either to seek a solution to those problems in harmony with the general theories of Karl Marx or, for Marx's opponents, to advance a solid theory explaining them. This second alternative has not even been attempted by bourgeois political economy. To be sure, reams of material are written on economic matters. One could fill a freightliner with the products of scholarship thrown into the market every month, but theoretical research is very poorly served by this jumble of books. The only attempt to advance a new theory, emanating from the school of Eugen von Böhm-Bawerk, foundered on its own shortcomings, and today the best minds and ablest workers among bourgeois economists occupy themselves with purely descriptive treatments of economic matters in which hardly any mention is made of theoretical clarification. Many of those people have more or less openly plundered Marx and seek to hide their own spiritual poverty with intellectual garments they owe to the study of *Capital*. From this situation emerge works with outward finery but without any real essence, such as those by Mr. Werner Sombart.[6]

And what of the Marxists? The real disciples of Marx learn one thing from the master above all else – the absolute necessity of struggling against capitalist rule – and the result is that they are mostly lost to the study-room. It takes a very rare combination of circumstances for a Marxist to have the opportunity to devote years of painstaking study to writing a theoretical work. Rudolf Hilferding has just given us such a work.[7] To come straight to the point, it is a work of the greatest significance that nobody wishing to write on economic theory can ignore.

5. Marchlewski 1910.
6. [Probably a reference to Sombart 1902. See the review by Hilferding 1903b.]
7. Hilferding 1910a. [English version: Hilferding 1981]. The work appeared simultaneously in the third volume of *Marx-Studien*, which also includes the work of Tatiana Grigorovici, *Die Wertlehre von Marx und Lassalle*. [Grigorovici 1910.]

Hilferding set himself the task of explaining the new phenomena of capitalism on the basis of Marxist theory. 'The most characteristic features of "modern" capitalism,' he argues, 'are those processes of concentration which, on the one hand, "eliminate free competition" through the formation of cartels and trusts, and on the other, bring bank and industrial capital into an ever more intimate relationship.'[8] Through this relationship, capital assumes the form of finance-capital. The present phase of economic development is characterised by the dominance of this form just as earlier phases were characterised by commercial capital, which made the whole world the playground of its buccaneering forays, and later by industrial capital.

Bank-capital is money-capital, and it participates in the world of profit making through credit transactions. Consequently, an accurate knowledge of the essence of money and credit is the precondition for understanding money-capital. Now, some things have changed since Marx set out his theory of money. Above all, developments in two states have been a hard nut for economists to crack: the silver currencies of Austria and India. In Austria, the free coinage [of silver] was discontinued; [Austrian money] consists of a 'credit-currency', and it became evident that circulating paper money played the role of measure of value. In India, free coinage [of silver] was also suspended, and it became apparent that the market price[9] of the silver rupee, which is the legal means of payment, remained completely independent of the value of the silver [content of a coin][10] and of the price of silver. The rate of exchange of the rupee remained 16 English pence, although the metal value contained in it amounted to 8.87 pence. In Hilferding's opinion:

> Monetary theorists are still plagued by the question: What constitutes the standard of value when coinage is suspended?[11] Obviously it is not silver (nor gold, when gold coinage is suspended).[12] The exchange rate[13] of money

8. Hilferding 1981, p. 1.
9. [*Kurs*: also exchange-rate.]
10. [*Silberwert*]
11. [*bei der gesperrten Währung*: literally 'with an inconvertible currency', i.e. when the currency is not convertible into gold or silver (bullion).]
12. [*bei gesperrter Goldwährung*: with an inconvertible gold currency. Hilferding probably refers to a nominal gold currency, when gold is no longer in circulation but is only used as reserve and kept in the central bank's vaults.]
13. [*Kurs*: also market price. It is not clear why the translators of Hilferding's book rendered this term as 'value'.]

> and the price of bullion follow completely divergent courses.... Finally, it is impossible to establish a relation between a mass of bullion on one side and a mass of commodities on the other.... It is equally useless to invoke the power of the state as an answer to the question. In the first place, it remains a complete mystery how the state can possibly confer a purchasing power on a piece of paper or on a gram of silver which wine, boots, shoe polish, etc., do not have.... Naturally, commodities are still expressed in money terms or 'measured' in money, [as they were before the suspension of coinage]. And as before, money continues to serve as 'measure of value'. But the magnitude of its value is no longer determined by the value of the constituent commodity, gold, or silver, or paper.[14]

The mystery can only be solved on the basis of Marx's theory of value: commodities have an objective value, determined by the amount of socially-necessary labour [time]. Only by keeping that in mind is it possible to explain why [paper] money that has no value in itself can be in circulation within the boundaries of a state. Outside that state, the paper money, or depreciated metal-money, naturally cannot play its role as measure of value and means of payment. Also, paper money within the state cannot serve as a means for permanently storing value. Hilferding rightly remarks: 'The impossibility of an absolute paper currency is a rigorous experimental confirmation of the objective theory of value, and only this theory can explain the peculiar features of pure paper currencies, and more particularly, of currencies with inconvertible coinage.'[15] The appearance of [paper] currencies with inconvertible coinage thus results in some modifications in Marx's theory of

14. Hilferding 1981, pp. 46–7. [The quoted paragraph continues: 'Instead, its "value" is really determined by the total value of the commodities in circulation, assuming the velocity of circulation to be constant. The real measure of value is not money. On the contrary, the "value" of money is determined by what I would call the *socially necessary circulation value*. If we also take account of the fact that money is a medium of circulation... this socially necessary circulation value can be expressed in the formula:

$$\frac{\text{total value of commodities}}{\text{velocity of circulation of money}}$$

plus the sum of payments falling due minus the payments which cancel each other out, minus finally the number of turnovers in which the same piece of money functions alternately as a means of circulation and as a means of payment.' Hilferding 1981, pp. 47–8].

15. Hilferding 1981, p. 58. [The expression *bei gesperrter Prägung* was rendered by the English translators as 'with suspended coinage'.]

paper money, for which Hilferding gives an account. But it is impossible for us to go into that here.

Hilferding then proceeds to offer a thorough analysis of credit. In this field, very important transformations have taken place during recent decades; capital has, so to speak, been increasingly mobilised, and from this follows the necessity of reviewing most particularly Marx's remarks on the circulation-process of capital. As Hilferding remarks, in the second volume of *Capital* 'we have a prevision of the dominance of the banks over industry, the most important phenomenon of recent times, written when even the germ of this development was scarcely visible'.[16] He undertakes to explain how the development of the production-process necessarily had to bring about this result. At first, the bankers played only a secondary role. They stepped in when the industrialists needed cash, either because the production-process had not yet been completed but new purchases of means of production were already needed, or else when the production-process was indeed finished but the circulation-process had not yet been completed and the manufactured commodities had not yet been sold and reconverted into money. The bankers therefore lent money. The socioeconomic conditions of these credit transactions are naturally very numerous, and the most different circumstances exert their influence here. The turnover-period of commodities comes into consideration, as well as the ratio between fixed and circulating capital and many other factors. That makes the investigation of these phenomena extremely complicated. The circumstance that changed the relations between banks and industry completely was the growing use of credit for fixed capital. The personal capital of individual industrialists is not enough to build the huge production establishments of gigantic modern enterprises. The raising of share-capital was not sufficient to overcome these difficulties, and banks began to lend out capital that was employed as fixed capital. In that way, however, the industrial enterprises were bound up with the banks. The former credit relation, which was easily terminated, became a lasting one, and the banks began to control the

16. Hilferding 1981, p. 385, note 21. ['...the greater the disturbances, the greater the money capital that the industrial capitalist must possess in order to ride out the period of readjustment; and since the scale of each individual production process grows with the progress of capitalist production, and with it the minimum size of the capital to be advanced, this circumstance is added to the other circumstances which increasingly turn the function of industrial capitalist into a monopoly of large-scale money capitalists, either individual or associated.' Marx 1978ba, p. 187.]

enterprises. Furthermore, even if fixed capital is not individual property but was raised by means of shares, or stock, the banks still dominate the enterprises; indeed, they do so to a much higher degree because the banks, as a result of the credit mechanism, seize control over external capital. The technique of credit transactions also results in tendencies that influence the concentration of banking capital, and the course of capitalist development thus irresistibly leads to a small number of banks gaining control over industry.

The question of the interest-rate plays an important role in the treatment of credit. Here, Hilferding not only applies Marx's theory to the new phenomena of capitalist development but also feels compelled to make essential corrections. First, the assumption of a constant fall in the interest-rate, which Marx shared with the experts of his time, turned out not to hold water. Above all, practice failed to show a fall in the interest-rate. During the decade from 1897 to 1906, which included years of both prosperity and crisis, the interest-rate was, on average, higher than during the two previous decades. Hilferding, therefore, gives a rule for changes in the interest-rate that is somewhat different from Marx's. Marx assumed that [variations in] the rate of interest (all other circumstances being equal) depend on the supply of loan-capital, 'i.e. of capital lent in the form of money, in metal or notes; as distinct from industrial capital that is lent as such, in the commodity form, by commercial credit among the reproductive agents themselves'.[17] Hilferding objects that this raises the question of how large the amount of banknotes can be. In England, this question is certainly not important, because the sum of banknotes was determined in proportion to the coins in circulation by the so-called Peel Act.[18] But that does not apply to other countries. In general, one can say that fluctuations in the interest-rate depend on the amount of loanable money. Loanable

17. Marx 1992, p. 631.

18. [The Bank Charter Act 1844 was an Act of the Parliament of the United Kingdom, passed under the government of Robert Peel, which restricted the powers of British banks and gave exclusive note-issuing powers to the central Bank of England. This marked the beginning of the classic gold-standard of the nineteenth century. Under the Act, no bank other than the Bank of England could issue new banknotes, and issuing banks would have to withdraw their existing notes in the event of their being the subject of a takeover. At the same time, the Bank of England was restricted to issuing new banknotes only where these were fully backed by gold. The Act served to restrict the supply of new notes reaching circulation and gave the Bank of England an effective monopoly on the printing of new notes. The Act was a victory for the British currency-school, whose members argued that the issue of new banknotes was a major cause of price inflation.]

money, however, is money that is not in circulation but flows into the banks' vaults. Part of these hoards must be kept in reserve (how much is determined by experience), while the rest can be loaned. The demand [for credit] fluctuates with the business-cycle. But, since most of the credit is commercial credit, i.e., credit determined by commodity-circulation, supply and demand rise and fall evenly. In times of prosperity, the demand for credit is great, but credit is also easily granted; in times of stagnation, the demand decreases, but credit is also more difficult to obtain. The banks intervene and do not raise the discount-rate until the gold-reserve is threatened. Hilferding concludes from this analysis that 'the rate of interest would show a downward tendency only if it could be assumed that the relation of the existing gold stock to the demand for loan capital is always becoming more favourable, that is to say, that the gold stock increases more rapidly than the demand for loan capital'.[19] Such a tendency, however, is unverifiable and therefore cannot be theoretically postulated. This view seems to me to be correct. On the other hand, further research into the question along these lines seems necessary. With the growth in power of the large banks, they begin to exert a decisive influence on credit supply. The money market (where the private bank discount, to which the interest-rate generally conforms, is determined by supply and demand), is more and more overshadowed by those large banks, and the question arises concerning the extent to which the interest-rate can be artificially raised through the banks' monopolistic position. It should be emphasised that, if a fall in the interest-rate is denied, the law of the declining tendency of the rate of profit is not thereby affected. The profit-rate can fall even if the interest-rate remains high, but the former cannot sink lower than the latter. A falling profit-rate, with a constant interest-rate, means that the share of total profits appropriated by the owners of money-capital, or more accurately, by those who are in command of that money-capital, is relatively larger. That is one of the factors increasing the superiority of finance-capital vis-à-vis industry.

The first part of Hilferding's book [dealing with money and credit] closes with the chapter on the rate of interest. Because it contains abstract theoretical analyses, one should not wonder that it makes for quite difficult reading. Such research naturally demands a presentation that can never be totally popular. However, one cannot but reproach the author for having done nothing on his

19. Hilferding 1981, p. 103.

part to facilitate the readers' work. Indeed, one can even say that he made it much more difficult. Hilferding flirts with Marx's style, and one often has the impression that one is reading the most difficult chapters of *Capital*. That is certainly explainable: one who occupies himself intensively with Marx's works for a long time falls under his spell, and the way of thinking and even mode of expression are influenced by him. Yet there is no doubt that it would have been advantageous for the book if the author had taken the trouble of making the presentation as clear as possible in the final revision. Whoever is not thoroughly at home in Marxist economic theory will find it very hard to master the first part of the book.

The following two parts are devoted to analysis of the phenomena of contemporary capitalist development. They are entitled 'The Mobilisation of Capital [fictitious capital]' and 'Finance Capital and the Restriction of Free Competition'.

The second part deals with the joint-stock company, the stock-exchange and the banks. The author analyses the nature and role of the joint-stock company, describes the procedures for financing those companies, the methods for undertaking the founder's operation [i.e. the floating of shares],[20] and the banks' influence on the joint-stock companies. Those who still believe in Eduard Bernstein's assertions about the decentralising effect of the joint-stock company, for which he certainly furnished no proof, should read this chapter. They will find in it evidence that the case is precisely the opposite; that share-capital was actually one of the preconditions for accelerating the process of concentration of capital. This demonstration is conducted by means of a careful theoretical analysis of economic events and illustrated with a rich volume of factual material. Hilferding also analyses the mechanism of the stock-exchange and the banking business.

The third part is dedicated to analysis of the monopolistic tendencies of modern capitalism. It deals above all with cartels and trusts. It begins with a chapter on 'surmounting the obstacles to the equalisation of rates of profit', which yields very valuable insight. Each capitalist strives for the highest possible profit; and, from those strivings, results a tendency towards establishment of an equal average profit-rate for all capitals. Capital flows out of the investment spheres where profit is low and into those where profit is high.

---

20. [*Erzielung der Gründertätigkeit*: the realisation of the incorporators' operation.]

But this inward and outward flow is made more difficult as capitalist development proceeds. Capitalism tends to replace human labour by machines. The precondition of this process is that constant capital – capital invested in buildings, machines and raw materials – must grow at the expense of variable capital, or capital spent on wages. But, among the component parts of constant capital, the one that grows relatively most quickly is fixed capital, which is tied down for a long time in the production equipment. The 'freedom of movement' of capital is therefore impaired. It is not easy to invest in the iron-industry capital that is already invested, let us say, in the textile-industry, even if the former yields a higher profit than the latter. That, however, hampers the formation of an equal rate of profit. The concentration of capital itself also has the same effect: large-scale enterprise have the upper hand, but it is difficult for enterprising capitalists to raise as much capital as that required in order to set up gigantic modern enterprises able to compete successfully with the existing ones. Those are obstacles to the equalisation [of the profit-rate]. On the other hand, however, there is a simultaneous tendency to overcome those obstacles. To the extent that capital is mobilised, differences in profitability between particular enterprises and branches of industry tend to disappear for the individual capitalist. Wherever share-capital dominates, this occurs through changes in the market value [of shares], which is determined by the rate of return of the particular enterprises. If an enterprise yields [a revenue of] 5 per cent, and the stock-exchange value[21] of its share is 100 per cent, while the market value of the share of another enterprise, yielding [a revenue of] 10 per cent, is 200 per cent, the owners of both shares, if they bought them at those market prices, are on a par: capital yields a revenue of 5 per cent for each one of them. The equalisation is thus effected without actually transferring capital from one sphere of investment to the other. In the same way, the mobilisation of capital makes it possible to overcome the other barriers [to the equalisation of returns]. The fact that huge capitals are required to found new competitive enterprises is less significant if raising capital in the amount of hundreds of millions through the issue of new shares becomes commonplace.

To this should be added the fact that the concentration of capital itself also brings about an equalisation of the profit-rate in related industrial sectors. If,

---

21. [*Kurs*: stock-price, market price.]

for instance, the profit-rate is higher in weaving than in spinning, spinning companies will combine with weaving ones and vice versa. The 'combined enterprises' will have only one average profit [-rate].

Finally, the banks' influence operates in the same sense. The banks are interested in a large number of enterprises in the same industrial sector. In case of an all-out competitive war between those enterprises, in which some may win extra profits but others will face ruin, the banks are threatened with losses because capital invested in the latter is endangered. The banks are therefore interested in doing away with competition; they work towards eliminating the competitive struggle and the fusion or cartelisation of those enterprises. Cartels are, to a certain extent, suitable for equalising the profit-rates of the enterprises belonging to them. At the same time, the power of the banks is so great that they can force a company to join a cartel even against the will of its director. Even in Germany, we have had striking examples of that phenomenon. In his analysis, Hilferding gives a detailed explanation of the consequences of these tendencies.

In the following chapters, Hilferding offers an excellent analysis of cartels and trusts. Bourgeois writers have gathered a large amount of factual material on these economic formations, but little has yet been done to understand the pertinent phenomena. Apart from some essays in the Marxist camp, which could not possibly exhaust the subject, Hilferding's work is the first containing a systematic theoretical analysis of trusts and cartels.

The fourth part is devoted to the study of crises. For the most part, Hilferding leans upon the analysis in the second volume of *Capital*, where Marx analysed the conditions under which the reproduction-process takes place and pointed out in numerous places the obstacles necessarily emerging from this process. Fundamental here is the well-known diagram according to which the production of society as a whole breaks down into two departments: production of new means of production and production of means of consumption. The circumstance that in each department capital breaks down into variable and constant capital, and that the latter breaks down again into fixed and circulating capital; that each one of these component parts must furthermore be replaced in the process [of capitalist production as a whole: *Gesamtprozess*]; and that, in addition, the resulting surplus-value has to enter again in different proportions into the sphere of production in order to serve for new capital-accumulation, means that, in the anarchical [capitalist] economy, disturbances must take place [in the accumulation-process]. On the other hand, it is characteristic of capitalist development that the productive forces grow extremely quickly, while the overwhelming majority of the population, the proletariat, gets back only a small share of the product of its labour in the form of consumption-articles of every kind. That much is clear about crises. However, there is a series of problems that have not yet been solved. For instance, the periodicity of crises has not yet been elucidated, and theory does not sufficiently explain why crises follow immediately after a period of the highest prosperity. Hilferding looks for the causes of crises in the fall of the profit-rate:

> As we already know, the organic composition of capital changes. For technological reasons, constant capital increases more rapidly than does variable capital, fixed capital than circulating capital. The relative reduction of the variable component of capital results in a fall in the rate of profit. A crisis involves a slump in sales. In capitalist society this presupposes a cessation of new capital-investment, which in turn presupposes a fall in the rate of profit. This decline in the rate of profit is entailed by the change in the organic composition of capital, which has taken place as a result of the investment of new capital. A crisis is simply the point at which the rate of profit begins to fall.[22]

Why, however, do crises appear suddenly? Why do they follow immediately after a period of prosperity, indeed, almost always after a period of the highest tension in the productive forces? Hilferding asks the question directly in the above-quoted passage, but he offers no direct and clear answer. In the following pages, he dwells on the factors influencing and accelerating changes in the organic composition of capital and the reduction of the profit-rate. A sudden, sharp change in the profit-rate, however, is only possible through a fall in commodity-prices. This certainly happens in crises. But that is not the cause, only one of the symptoms of crises; and, besides, it is a symptom that regularly appears only after some time. The first period of a crisis is characterised much more by a stagnation in sales, which, quite naturally, results in complications in monetary circulation, rather than by a fall in prices.

---

22. Hilferding 1981, p. 257.

All of the arguments adduced by Hilferding for his thesis are excellent. The tendency of the profit-rate to fall is certainly one of the causes of crises. It is equally correct that changes in the organic composition of capital have an impact not only on the formation of prices but also on the [relative] diminution of circulating capital; and that, in consequence, at the beginning of a period of prosperity, [certain] factors already assert themselves that could lead to disturbances [in the accumulation-process]. But the outbreak of crises must always be traced directly back to actual overproduction. Hilferding denies this argument categorically, but he does not refute it. This peculiar misunderstanding makes his theory of crises one-sided. A complete explanation can only be attained by including the effects of the previously mentioned factors,[23] such as the phenomena of commodity-production, on the reproduction-process of capital.

In the following chapters of Part Four, Hilferding deals with the changes appearing in the course of the business-cycle due to the altered credit-conditions, speculation, the large banks and cartels. As regards the last point, Hilferding reaches the conclusion that cartels cannot prevent crises but they do modify their effects by shifting their burden onto non-cartelised industries. His conclusion is correct, but we cannot completely agree with his argumentation; namely, where he argues that, if we trace crises back to overproduction, cartels could actually prevent them by curtailing production. That is false for the simple reason that cartels do not at all have the power to prevent overproduction, but, on the contrary, contribute to it in the same proportion, indeed, under certain circumstances, even to a higher degree, than non-cartelised enterprises. Cartels, therefore, aggravate the danger of crises. Unfortunately, we cannot discuss this issue in greater detail for reasons of space.

The fifth and final part of *Finance Capital* is dedicated to the economic policy of finance-capital. It provides evidence that there is a causal link between the growing domination of finance-capital and monopolistic strivings in industry on the one hand, and the policy of imperialism and protectionism on the other. According to Hilferding, the antagonisms between rival groups have been to a large extent abolished. Industry and trade have combined their strivings under the leadership of finance-capital, and, in that way, they have acquired unheard-of political power.

---

23. [*Vorgänger*: forerunners, predecessors]

Protective tariffs become the universal watchword. Pretexts are abandoned along with talk about 'educative tariffs', and the goal of plundering the domestic consumers undisturbed is openly proclaimed. Cartels and protective tariffs offer the possibility of making extra profits.

On the other hand, the drive to acquire spheres of influence becomes even greater under the influence of finance-capital. It is not commodity-exports but capital-exports that are the decisive motive in commercial policy towards other countries. This drive can be satisfied most easily in capitalistically backward countries, and that is the main reason for the policy of colonial robbery and the adventurist policy towards the Asian countries.

On the other hand, the growing power of finance-capital leads to acceleration of the concentration-process and destruction of the middle classes.

Persuasive as these remarks are, we cannot agree with them completely. Above all, here Hilferding overlooks the fact, which he emphasises elsewhere, that cartels and trusts do not bring about a peaceful understanding between cartelised enterprises at all, and that within these monopolistic associations a frantic struggle also rages between the members. It is enough to recall the striking example of the struggle between the 'pure' and 'mixed' firms in the mining industry.

Hilferding's argument that the contradiction between large-scale capital and small enterprises has become less significant also seems to us false. It may be true that contemporary large-scale capitalists are completely indifferent towards the craftsmen's demand for special protection for their industries. But the contrary is not true. Small entrepreneurs, such as craftsmen, cannot under any circumstances be indifferent towards monopolistic cartels – above all because, as Hilferding himself emphasised, cartelisation curtails the profit-rate of craftsmen and small producers through the tribute that cartels impose upon them (the rise in prices of semi-finished goods is not always completely compensated by the rise in prices of finished goods). The only difference from the previous period is that these middle classes are no longer capable of being a *constructive* political power because their position is already hopeless. The process of proletarianisation of crafts has not yet ended; small and middle enterprises in industry and trade are constantly being undermined; the antagonisms of interests are [therefore] as sharp as before, perhaps even sharper. But, because the social classes that represent these small enterprises no longer have any hope, they also no longer have any political *élan*. Only rising classes have political ideals and know how to defend them; declining classes are just a dead weight. But that does not hinder them from playing a decisive role in politics. They dominate in parliament; the press serves them; they constitute 'public opinion'. They are the explanation of the reaction that is now a leaden weight upon Europe.

In that respect, Hilferding is perfectly correct: what reigns in those classes is a most frantic hatred of the proletariat. The rate of profit is falling, and the small entrepreneur has only one means of preventing it: to compensate himself by plundering the workers to the hilt as producers and consumers. In their hatred of the workers, those classes furnish assistance to large-scale capital and even hurt themselves in their blind fury (see the tariff-policy, taxation, colonial policy and imperialism). The concluding remarks of Hilferding's book are therefore apodictic:

> Finance capital, in its maturity, is the highest stage of the concentration of economic and political power in the hands of the capitalist oligarchy. It is the climax of the dictatorship of the magnates of capital. At the same time it makes the dictatorship of the capitalist lords of one country increasingly incompatible with the capitalist interests of other countries, and the internal domination of capital increasingly irreconcilable with the interests of the mass of the people, exploited by finance capital but also summoned into battle against it. In the violent clash of these hostile interests the dictatorship of the magnates of capital will finally be transformed into the dictatorship of the proletariat.[24]

24. Hilferding 1981, p. 370.

Chapter Twenty-Nine

'Peace Utopias' (6–8 May 1911)

Rosa Luxemburg

In this article, Rosa Luxemburg criticises socialists who supported the idea of a European Union in the framework of capitalism and imperialism. On 28 April 1911, Kautsky published an article called 'Peace and War: Considerations on May Day', supporting the Reichstag fraction's second disarmament and arbitration proposal, submitted on 30 March 1911.[1] Kautsky argued that 'the aversion to war increases rapidly not only among the popular masses, but also among the ruling classes',[2] so that 'the immediate task is to support and strengthen the movement of the petty bourgeoisie and bourgeoisie against war and the arms-race. One should not underestimate this movement.' Kautsky continued:

> ...we should under no circumstances confront the demand for international agreements to preserve peace or limit armaments, for example, with the remark that war is closely linked to the nature of capitalism and therefore inevitable. The matter is not so simple. And when proposals are made from the bourgeois side for the preservation of peace or the limitation of armaments,

1. Kautsky 1911a.
2. Kautsky 1911a, p. 99.

> which are to some extent feasible, we have every reason to support them and to force governments to state their position on them. When our parliamentary fraction did that recently in the Reichstag, it acted in a completely correct way.[3]

But, while international agreements for arms-limitation and the establishment of international arbitration-courts advocated by the bourgeois peace movement had to be supported, they were, at bottom, only palliative measures. As Kautsky added:

> The implementation of those agreements still offers no guarantee for a lasting duration of peace that banishes the ghost of war forever. For that there is only one way today: the union of the states of European civilisation into a federation with a common commercial policy, a federal parliament, a federal government and a federal army – the formation of the *United States of Europe*.[4]

Kautsky depicted the establishment of a future European Union in glowing terms as the inauguration of the era of 'permanent peace'.[5]

The slogan of a European Union had originally been raised by Otto Bauer and Parvus in 1907. In *The Question of Nationalities and Social Democracy* Bauer wrote: 'The *United States of Europe* will thus no longer be a dream, but the inevitable ultimate goal of a movement that the nations have long since begun and that will be enormously accelerated by forces that are already becoming apparent.'[6] In *Colonial Policy and the Collapse*, Parvus opposed the prospect of colonial wars and arms-race between imperialist powers with the watchwords: 'Democracy, European Union, Free Trade'.[7] During the First World War, however, the slogan was bluntly rejected by Lenin, who argued that 'from the standpoint of the economic conditions of imperialism' – the export of capital and the division of the world by the colonial powers – a United States of Europe was, under capitalism, 'either impossible or reactionary' because it was 'tantamount to an agreement on the partition of colonies'. A European Union could only be an imperialist consortium to compete with the

3. Kautsky 1911a, p. 101.
4. Kautsky 1911a, p. 105.
5. Kautsky 1911a, p. 106.
6. Bauer 2000, p. 414.
7. Parvus 1907, p. 30.

more dynamic American and Japanese imperialism. Yet, even such a reactionary agreement would still be unstable because 'uneven economic and political development' was 'an absolute law of capitalism' causing periodic disturbances of the equilibrium between imperialist powers and making new wars necessary to test the real might of each state.[8]

Lenin's polemics were directed against not only Karl Kautsky but also Leon Trotsky, whom he regarded at that time as a left Kautskyist, prone to conciliation with the centrists. In this conviction, he was supported by other fractions of the resolute Zimmwerwald Left, such as the Dutch Tribunists, with whom Lenin otherwise disagreed on basic issues such as support for the right of national self-determination. In his book *Imperialism, the World War and Social Democracy*, published at the outbreak of the First World War, Hermann Gorter rejected as 'pseudo-Marxist chatter' Trotsky's argument, in *The War and the International*, that 'The policy of imperialism is above all a proof that the old state has become obsolete and now presents itself as an unbearable obstacle to the development of the productive forces.' On the contrary, Gorter argued:

> Instead of a rebellion of the forces of production against capitalism's current nation-state form of exploitation, the war is the means by which some nations will become stronger, larger and more unified, it is the means utilised by some nations for the development of world capitalism and to allow the struggle between these nations to contribute to a renewed strengthening, extension and intensification of capitalist production. Imperialism and this war show that the great nation-state is not yet obsolete, that it still possesses gigantic forces which allow it, in its struggle against other nation states, to spread capitalist production and to make it the global mode of production.

For that reason, Gorter concluded, 'the practical proposals – the right of every nation to self-determination, a United States of Europe, without monarchies, without standing armies, without reigning feudal lineages and without secret diplomacy – which Trotsky bases on this perspective and which he formulates as the proletariat's proposals for after the peace, are...equally false.'[9]

Finally, the 'Theses on the Tasks of International Social Democracy', adopted at a conference of the Internationale group on 1 January 1916, which

8. Lenin 1915b, pp. 340–2.
9. Gorter 1915.

were added as an appendix to Rosa Luxemburg's brochure *The Crisis of Social Democracy* (*The Junius Pamphlet*), also rejected the call for a United States of Europe. Thesis number 8 read:

> World peace cannot be secured by the international arbitration courts of capitalist diplomats or by diplomatic agreements on 'disarmament', on so-called 'freedom of the seas' or by 'European federations', 'Central European customs unions', 'national buffer states' and such-like utopian or at bottom reactionary projects. Imperialism, militarism and wars cannot be eliminated and contained as long as the capitalist classes exercise their undisputed class domination. The only safeguard and the only support of world peace are the revolutionary will and the capacity for political action of the international proletariat.[10]

* * *

'Peace Utopias'[11]

Our party has freshly and eagerly begun to agitate everywhere for the Reichstag elections.[12] The general and happiest possible beginning was the splendid May Day celebration, which, despite all the resistance and crippling influence of circles that regard it as a 'worthless crock', turned out to be an imposing mass-strike and demonstration.[13] It showed again what militant

10. Luxemburg 1925.
11. Luxemburg 1911a.
12. [The Reichstag election to which Rosa Luxemburg refers took place on 12 January 1912. Social Democracy increased the number of its parliamentary mandates from 43 in 1907 (the time of the 'Hottentot elections') to 110, thus becoming the strongest fraction in the Reichstag.]
13. ['May Day was labour's high holiday of defiance. According to international socialist tradition it could be properly celebrated only by a one-day strike. The German radicals adhered with great tenacity to this annual ritual sacrifice in which the workers risked real economic privation to demonstrate their loyalty to their faith. For them May Day was an important factor in strengthening class consciousness.... The leaders of the trade unions, whose political thought centred upon the immediate material interest of the workers, had long rankled under the sacrifices which the May Day strike had often cost the unions.... At the Amsterdam congress of the International in 1904, the German trade union representatives had tried in vain to have a May Day observance changed from a strike to an evening demonstration.... At long last a formula was found in the creation of May Day funds on a regional rather than a local basis. On trade union insistence the funds had to be collected separately for this purpose; general funds were to remain untouched. This agreement, with more protest

enthusiasm and self-sacrificing idealism is to be found in the working masses. All the more urgent, therefore, is the Party's task of turning the agitation for this year's parliamentary elections not just into a struggle for the greatest possible number of votes and mandates, but primarily into a period of intensive education in the principles and whole world-outlook of Social Democracy. Naturally, one of the central points of the election campaign and the agitation will again be the *question of militarism*. And, in this regard, clarification of our position on this matter, linked with the recent debate in the Reichstag, takes on lasting and far-reaching significance.

If the question under discussion were simply whether our Reichstag fraction acted correctly in bringing forward a motion demanding that the German government conclude agreements for the purpose of reducing armaments, the controversy would have awakened no real interest. Since we use the parliamentary tribune as one of the most effective means of agitation, it appears to be a simple duty of the socialist deputies to exploit every opportunity to counterpose the party's views concerning the most important phenomena of public life to those of the ruling classes. Committed to parliamentary terms, the Reichstag fraction naturally must have recourse to interpellations, motions and the like. And it is undoubtedly very meritorious of our Reichstag group that it has seized the opportunity to secure a great debate on the question of militarism, forcing the representatives of the ruling classes to state their view clearly. The wording of the motion submitted by the socialist deputies, as such, played a rather minor role. The position of the Party was expressed not in the formulation of the motion, but in the reasons given for it and in the speeches of our fraction. The parliamentary motion must often be the hook that supports our agitation in the parliamentary tribune.

The real question, one that is significant for the broad circles of the Party, is whether our party, in the debate that it initiated, was able to champion the principled standpoint of Social Democracy clearly and consistently and whether, through this debate, it helped to disseminate among the masses the

than approval from the floor, was accepted by the party congress of Leipzig in 1909. Under the new plan, the May Day celebration, made safe and sane, could limp along until the outbreak of the war.' Schorske 1970, Part II: The Consolidation of the Right, Chap. IV: The Extension of Trade Union Influence, ii. The Destruction of a Symbol, pp. 91–7.]

socialist view of the nature of militarism and of the capitalist social order in order to win those masses over to socialism.

The answer to this question depends on which aspect of our attitude towards militarism one considers the most important and decisive. If the position of Social Democracy amounted to nothing more than demonstrating to the whole world, at every opportunity, that our party is an unconditional supporter of peace and an ardent opponent of armaments, while the government is to blame for the arms-race, then we could be fully satisfied with our performance in the recent Reichstag debate. But this alone would hardly be a sufficient result for this large and important action. Our task does not consist merely in vigorously demonstrating at all times Social Democracy's love of peace; our task is, first and foremost, to make clear to the masses the nature of militarism and to bring out sharply and clearly the principled differences between the standpoint of Social Democracy and that of bourgeois peace-enthusiasts. Wherein does this difference lie? Certainly not merely in the fact that the bourgeois apostles of peace are relying on the influence of fine words, while we do not depend on words alone. Our very points of departure are diametrically opposed: the friends of peace in bourgeois circles believe that world peace and disarmament can be realised within the framework of the present social order, whereas we, basing ourselves on the materialist conception of history and on scientific socialism, are convinced that militarism can only be abolished the world over with the destruction of the capitalist class-state. From this follow our opposing tactics in propagating the idea of peace. The bourgeois friends of peace are endeavouring – and from their point of view this is perfectly logical and explicable – to invent all sorts of 'practical' projects for gradually restraining militarism, and they are, naturally, inclined to consider every apparent outward sign of a tendency toward peace as the genuine article, to take every expression in this vein by the ruling diplomacy at its word, and to exaggerate it into a basis for earnest activity. The Social Democrats, on the other hand, must consider it their duty in this matter, as in all matters of social criticism, to expose bourgeois attempts to restrain militarism as pitiful half-measures, to expose the expressions of such sentiments on the part of the governing circles as diplomatic make-believe, and to oppose the bourgeois claims and pretences with a ruthless analysis of capitalist reality. This was the attitude of our party, for example, towards the [Second]

Hague Conference.[14] While the opportunists of various countries, with the usual petty-bourgeois optimism, praised it as a beneficial approach to world peace – two years ago, Comrade Treves, in the Lower House in Rome, made a proposal in a bold speech to honour the Hague Conference in celebration of its tenth anniversary – German Social Democracy has always regarded the charming creation of the bloody Tsar and his European colleagues with well-deserved scorn as an impudent farce.

From this same standpoint, the task of Social Democrats with regard to declarations of the kind made by the British government[15] can only be to show up the idea of a partial *limitation* of armaments in all its impracticability as a half-measure, and to endeavour to make it clear to the people that militarism is closely linked up with colonial politics, with tariff-politics, and with world-policy, and that the present states, therefore, if they really seriously and honestly wish to call a halt on the arms-race, would have to begin by disarming in the field of commercial policy and by giving up colonial predatory campaigns and the world policy of spheres of influence in all parts of the globe – in a word, in their foreign as well as in their domestic policy, they would have to do the exact contrary of everything that the nature of the present politics of a capitalist class-state demands. And, in that way, the kernel of the Social-Democratic conception would be clearly explained: that militarism in all its forms – both as war and as armed peace – is a legitimate child and logical result of capitalism, which can only be overcome with the destruction of capitalism, and that whoever honestly desires world peace and liberation from the tremendous burden of armaments must therefore also desire socialism.

14. [The Second Hague Conference took place between 15 and 18 October 1907. Representatives from 47 countries participated. The imperialist great powers refused to reduce their armaments or accept mediation by courts of arbitration. The First Hague Conference was convened in May 1899 and attended by twenty European powers, along with the United States, Mexico, Japan, China, Siam (Thailand) and Persia (Iran). It originated in an initiative of Tsar Nicholas II, who, in August 1898, called for an international conference to discuss disarmament. The Russian proposal for freezing armament-levels was defeated, but the Convention did agree on rules of warfare and established a Permanent Court of Arbitration, which later became the International Court of Justice].

15. [Ever since the First Hague Conference, Great Britain repeatedly proposed to Germany the limitation of armaments on the basis of keeping a superior or equal fleet. Those proposals were rejected by the German government].

Only in this way can real Social-Democratic enlightenment and recruiting be carried on in connection with the armaments debate.

This work, however, will be rendered more difficult, and the attitude of the Social Democrats will become obscure and vacillating if, by some strange exchange of roles, our party tries, on the contrary, to convince the bourgeois state that it can quite well limit armaments and bring about peace, and that it can do this from its own standpoint, from that of a capitalist class-state. Admittedly, it is true that our Reichstag fraction in the recent debate did not admit the possibility of a complete abolition of militarism and war within the framework of the bourgeois order. Comrade Ledebour entered rather strong caveats against this conception. But precisely those caveats showed that the simultaneous eager support for partial disarmament is a strange compromise-position, standing midway between two viewpoints, that of the bourgeois apostles of peace and that of Social Democracy; a position that denies the possibility of completely overcoming militarism in today's society but considers it plausible that an era of peace is drawing near in the midst of the capitalist world – and yet still adheres to the idea of the inevitability of social revolution.

Until now, it has been the pride and the firm scientific basis of our party that not only the general lines of our programme but also the slogans of our practical everyday policy were not invented out of odds and ends as something desirable, but that, in all things, we relied on our knowledge of the tendencies of social development and made the objective lines of this development the basis of our attitude. For us, the determining factor until now has not been the possibility of implementing our demands from the standpoint of the relation of forces within the state, but the possibility of doing so from the standpoint of the tendencies of development of society. If we demand again and again the statutory eight-hour workday, even though this requirement is completely without prospect in today's parliaments, it is precisely because it is in line with the progressive development of the productive forces, of technology, and of the international competition of capitalism. It is just because the eight-hour day would also be an enormously revolutionising step forward in the education and organisation of the working class that the bourgeoisie opposes it with all its forces. Economically, however, introduction of the eight-hour day, far from hindering the development of capitalism, would raise it to its highest and most advanced stage. The limitation of armaments, the retrenchment of militarism, is not in line with the further development of international capitalism; it could only arise from the *stagnation* of capitalist development. Only those who wish for a standstill in world policy (and this is the highest and last stage of capitalist development) can consider a standstill in the progress of militarism to be a probability. World policy and the militarism serving it on land and sea, in times of war or peace, is nothing but the specific capitalist method to develop and settle international antagonisms. With the further development of capitalism and the world market, these antagonisms grow and increase immeasurably, together with domestic class contradictions, until they become intolerable and bring about the social revolution. Only those who believe in the mitigation and blunting of class antagonisms, in the possibility of checking the economic anarchy of capitalism, can believe that these international conflicts could somehow be slackened, mitigated and wiped out. The international antagonisms of the capitalist states are but the complement of class-antagonisms, and world-political anarchy is but the reverse side of capitalism's anarchic system of production. Both can only grow together and be overcome together. 'A little order and peace' is therefore impossible; it is just as much a petty-bourgeois utopia with regard to the capitalist world market as to world policy, and the same applies to the limitation of crises or the limitation of armaments.

Let us cast a glance at the events of the last fifteen years of international development. Where do they show any tendency towards peace, disarmament, and the settlement of conflicts by arbitration?

Here is what those fifteen years have brought: in 1895, the war between Japan and China, which was the prelude to the East-Asiatic period of world-policy; in 1898, the war between Spain and the United States; in 1899–1902, the British Boer War in South Africa; in 1900, the campaign of the European powers in China; in 1904, the Russo-Japanese War; in 1904–7, the German Herero War in Africa; then there was the military intervention of Russia in 1908 in Persia; and, at the present moment, we are witnessing the military intervention of France in Morocco, not to mention the incessant colonial skirmishes in Asia and in Africa. Hence, the bare facts alone show that, for a decade and a half, hardly a year has gone by without some military activity.

But more important still are the repercussions of these wars. The war with China was followed in Japan by a military reorganisation that enabled it ten years later to undertake the war against Russia and made Japan the predominant military power in the Pacific. The Boer War resulted in the military reorganisation of England and the strengthening of her armed forces on land. The war with Spain was the starting point for reorganisation of the US navy and has turned the United States into a colonial power with world-political interests in Asia, thus creating the germs of an antagonism of interests between the United States and Japan in the Pacific Ocean. The Chinese campaign was accompanied in Germany by a thorough military reorganisation, notably the great Navy Law of 1900, which marks the beginning of the naval competition of Germany with England and the sharpening of antagonisms between these two nations.

But there is another and extremely important factor besides: the social and political awakening of the hinterlands, of the colonies and 'spheres of interest', to an independent life. The revolutions in Turkey and Persia; the revolutionary ferment in China, India, Egypt, Arabia, Morocco and Mexico; all these events are also the starting points of world-political antagonisms, tensions, military activities and armaments. During the course of these fifteen years, in which the points of friction in international politics have increased to an unparalleled degree, a number of new states have stepped into active struggle on the international stage, and all the great powers have undergone a thorough military reorganisation. The antagonisms arising from all these events have reached an acuteness never known before, and the process is continuing because, on the one hand, the ferment in the Orient is increasing from day to day, and, on the other hand, every settlement between the military powers inevitably becomes the starting point for fresh conflicts. The Reval Entente between Russia, Great Britain and France,[16] which Jaurès hailed as a guarantee of world peace, led to the sharpening of the crisis in the Balkans, accelerated the outbreak of the Turkish Revolution, encouraged Russia to military action in Persia and led to a rapprochement between Turkey and Germany that, in turn, rendered the Anglo-German antagonism more acute. The Potsdam agreement[17] sharpened the crisis in China, and the Russo-Japanese agreement had the same effect.

---

16. [The Anglo-Russian Entente, aimed at encircling Germany, was signed in September 1907].

17. [On 4–6 November 1910,a meeting was arranged between Nicholas II of Russia and Wilhelm II of Germany in Potsdam. This move was intended to chastise the British for their perceived betrayal of Russia's interests during the Bosnian crisis. The two monarchs discussed the Baghdad Railway, a German project widely expected to give Berlin considerable geopolitical clout in the Fertile Crescent. Against the background of the Persian Constitutional Revolution, Russia was anxious to control the prospec-

Therefore, a mere reckoning with the facts demonstrates that one must wilfully close one's eyes in order to refuse to realise that these facts give rise to anything but a mitigation of international conflicts, or to argue that there is any sort of disposition toward world peace.

In view of all this, how is it possible to speak of tendencies toward peace in bourgeois development that are supposed to neutralise and overcome its tendencies toward war? Where are they expressed? In Sir Edward Grey's declaration and that of the French Parliament?[18] In the 'armament-weariness' of the bourgeoisie? But the middle and petty-bourgeois sections of the bourgeoisie have always been groaning at the burden of militarism, just as they groan at the devastation of free competition, at economic crises, at the unscrupulousness of stock-exchange speculation and the terrorism of cartels and trusts. The tyranny of the trust-magnates in America has even called forth a rebellion of the broad masses of the people and a protracted campaign against the trusts on the part of the state-authorities. Did Social Democracy interpret this as a symptom of the beginning of limitation on the development of trusts, or did it rather sympathetically shrug its shoulders at the petty-bourgeois rebellion and smile scornfully at the state campaign? The 'dialectic' of the peace-tendency of capitalist development, which was supposed to cut across its war-tendency and overcome it, simply confirms the old truth that the roses of capitalist profit-making and class-domination also have thorns for the bourgeoisie, which it prefers to bear as long as possible round its suffering head, despite all the pain and woe, rather than get rid of them, along with its head, along the lines of the well-meant advice of Social Democrats.

To explain this to the masses, to smash ruthlessly all illusions about the peace attempts made by the bourgeoisie, and to proclaim proletarian

---

tive Khanaqin-Tehran branch of the railway. The two powers settled their differences in the Potsdam Agreement, signed on 19 August 1911, giving Russia a free hand in Northern Iran. The first railway connecting Persia to Europe would provide Russia with a lever of influence over its southern neighbour. Notwithstanding the promising beginning, Russo-German relations disintegrated in 1913 when the Kaiser sent one of his generals to reorganise the Turkish army and to supervise the garrison in Constantinople, remarking that 'the German flag will soon fly over the fortifications of the Bosporus', a vital trade-artery that accounted for two fifths of Russia's exports].

18. [When the Liberals returned to power in Britain in 1905, Sir Edward Grey (1862–1933) became Foreign Secretary, a position in which served for eleven years. Before the outbreak of the First World War, he oversaw the completion of the Entente with Russia in 1907, the peaceful settlement of the Agadir Crisis, and the joint mediation for the end of the Balkan Wars.]

revolution as the first and only step toward world peace – that is the task of Social Democracy with regard to all disarmament antics whether they occur in Petersburg, London or Berlin.

To tell the plain truth to oneself and others is always the best practical policy for the party of the revolutionary proletariat; and that is doubly our duty in beginning the agitation for the Reichstag elections if we want to increase not only the extent but also the depth of our power and influence.

II

The utopianism of any standpoint that expects an era of peace and retrenchment of militarism in the present social order is plainly revealed in the fact that it is having recourse to designing projects, for it is typical of utopian strivings that, in order to demonstrate their practicability, they hatch 'practical' recipes with the greatest possible details. In this category also belongs the project of the 'United States of Europe' as a basis for the limitation of international militarism.

> We support all efforts within capitalism, [said Comrade Ledebour in his speech in the Reichstag on 3 April 1911] aiming at the elimination of predatory influences. We want to strengthen all the economic forces working within capitalism itself in the direction of peace by bringing about a union of states with a common economic and cultural development, in order to abolish even today, in the era of capitalism, the pretexts for the incessant increase in military outlays. We demand the economic and political union of the European states. I am firmly convinced that, while it is certain to come during the period of socialism, it can also come to pass before that time that we will live to see the *United States of Europe* just as we face today the competition of the United States of America. In the interest of the capitalist development of Europe itself, and so that later, in the global competition, Europe will not be totally beaten, we demand from capitalist society, from the capitalist statesmen, that they prepare this merger of European states into the United States of Europe.[19]

---

19. Reichstag 1911, II. *Legislaturperiode*. II. *Session*, Bd. 266, pp. 6142–3. [*Debates of the Reichstag*. XII Legislature, Session II, Vol. 266, Stenographical reports, Berlin 1911, pp. 6142–3].

And in the *Neue Zeit* of 28 April 1911, Comrade Kautsky writes:

> The implementation of those agreements still offers no guarantee for a lasting duration of peace that banishes the ghost of war forever.
>
> For that there is only one way today: uniting the states of European civilisation into a federation with a common commercial policy, a federal parliament, a federal government and a federal army – the formation of the *United States of Europe*.
>
> Were this to succeed, then a tremendous step forward would be achieved. These United States would possess such a superiority of forces that without any war they could compel all other nations that did not voluntarily join them to liquidate their armies and give up their fleets. Therewith all necessity for arming the new United States themselves would disappear. They could not only relinquish all further armaments, give up the standing army and all offensive weapons at sea, which we are demanding today, but also give up all means of defence and the militia system itself.
>
> Thus the era of permanent peace would be certainly established.[20]

First of all, it must be said that this idea is entirely new, at least in party-agitation. Our minimum-programme contains no mention of any such construction; our party congresses and the international congresses never concerned themselves with it, nor has it ever been seriously discussed in the party literature. And it would certainly be unfortunate if such improvised, *ad hoc* vagaries, which have all the features of being the product of an embarrassment, were officially advocated from the parliamentary tribune on behalf of the whole Party. In that way, those views would be advanced not only before bourgeois opponents but also in socialist circles abroad as the official position of German Social Democracy, which, to speak in purely formal terms, the Reichstag fraction is certainly not entitled to do.

Plausible as the idea of the United States of Europe, as a peace-arrangement, may seem to some at first glance, on closer examination, it has nothing in common with the method of thought and the standpoint of Social Democracy.

As adherents of the materialist conception of history, we have always adopted the standpoint that modern states, as political structures, are not artificial products of creative fantasy, like, for instance, the Duchy of

20. Kautsky 1911a, pp. 105–6.

Warsaw of Napoleonic memory,[21] but, rather, historical products of economic development. Although dynastic interests from the middle ages onwards have decisively influenced the shaping of the boundaries and the composition of today's states, such as the Austro-Hungarian monarchy, capitalist development later intervened and created economic links between the loose medley of countries and provinces, and the common class domination of the bourgeoisie determined the political maturity of the state. The United States of America in its present form, as an enormous economic territory and political power, is also the product of a century of capitalist development within common national borders.

But what economic foundation lies at the bottom of the idea of a European State-Federation? Europe, it is true, is a geographical and, within certain limits, an historical-cultural conception. But the idea of Europe as an economic unit contradicts capitalist development in two ways. First of all, the most violent competitive struggles and antagonisms exist within Europe among the capitalist states, and they will continue to operate so long as these states themselves exist. Secondly, the European states can no longer get along economically without the non-European countries. As suppliers of foodstuffs, raw materials and manufactured goods, and also as consumers of the same, the other parts of the world are linked in a thousand ways with Europe. At the present stage of development of the world market and economy, the conception of Europe as an isolated economic unit is a sterile concoction of the brain. Europe no more forms a coherent special unit within the world economy than does Asia or America.

And if the idea of a European union in the economic sense has long been outstripped, this is no less the case in the political sense. It is, at bottom, only a democratically embellished version of the idea of the concert of European powers as the moving centre, the central sun of the political universe, which would determine the course of world history. But the times when the centre of gravity of political development and the axis around which capitalist con-

21. [The Duchy of Warsaw was a Polish state established by Napoleon Bonaparte in 1807 from the Polish lands ceded by the Kingdom of Prussia under the terms of the Treaties of Tilsit. The Duchy was held in personal union by one of Napoleon's allies, King Frederick Augustus I of Saxony. Following Napoleon's failed invasion of Russia, the Duchy was occupied by Prussian and Russian troops until 1815, when it was formally partitioned between the two countries at the Congress of Vienna.]

tradictions crystallised lay on the European continent are long gone. At the beginning of the nineteenth century, and traditionally until the March [1848] Revolution, the area of partitioned Poland, on the German-Austrian-Russian border, was the centre of international politics. In the 1850s, it shifted to the Bosporus. In the 1870s, the Franco-Prussian War created a new focus around which the Dual and Triple Alliances grouped as pillars of European equilibrium. At that time, the utopia of a European Federation at least made some historical sense. With the 1880s began a whole new era in international politics: colonial conquests set in with renewed force, followed in the 1890s by the general race of world politics towards overseas spheres of influence, and in the last decade by the general awakening of the Orient. Today, Europe is only a link in the tangled chain of international connections and contradictions. And what is of decisive significance: European antagonisms themselves no longer play their role simply on the European continent but in every corner of the world and on all the oceans.

Only if one were suddenly to lose sight of all these processes and shifts, and to transfer oneself back to the blissful times of the European concert of powers, could one then say, for instance, that, for forty years, we have had uninterrupted peace. This standpoint, which only considers events on the European continent, does not notice that the very reason why we have had no war in Europe for decades is the fact that international antagonisms have grown infinitely beyond the narrow confines of the European continent, and that European questions and interests are now fought out on the oceans and not in the by-corners of Europe.

Hence the 'United States of Europe' is an idea that runs directly counter, both economically and politically, to the course of development, and that takes absolutely no account of the events of the last quarter of a century.

That an idea so little in accord with the tendency of development can fundamentally offer no progressive solution, despite all radical disguises, is confirmed by the fate of the slogan of the 'United States of Europe'. The idea of a European Union has been raised every now and then not by Social-Democratic parties but by *bourgeois* elements. Each time, this has involved a clearly *reactionary* tendency. It was, for instance, the well-known enemy of socialism, Prof. Julius Wolf, who propagated the idea of a European Economic Community. It meant nothing but a customs-union for *commercial-political wars against the United States of America*, and it was understood and criticised as such by the socialists. Every time bourgeois politicians have championed the idea of Europeanism, of the union of European states, it has been with an open or concealed goal directed against the 'yellow peril', the 'dark continent' or the 'inferior races' – in short, it has always been an imperialist abortion.

And if we, as Social Democrats, were now to try to fill this old skin with fresh and apparently revolutionary wine, then it must be said that the advantages would not be on our side but on that of the bourgeoisie. Things have their own objective logic. And the solution of the European Union within the capitalist social order can *objectively*, in the economic sense, only mean a tariff-war with America, and, in the political sense, only a colonial-patriotic race-war. The Chinese campaign of the united European regiments, with World Field-Marshall Waldersee at their head and the gospel of the Hun as our standard – that is the actual and not the fantastic, the only possible expression of a 'European State-Federation' in the present social order.[22]

But are we still generally for the 'United States of Europe' in the capitalist world?

That is the difficulty of the whole business. One the one hand, it is a question of a federation of states 'with a common commercial policy, a federal parliament, a federal government and a federal army', and thus it is doubtless a bourgeois creation. Comrade Ledebour expressly required the contemporary statesmen to prepare this European Union as being in the best interest of capitalism itself. But, on the other hand, if we ask about the possibilities of realising this project, Comrade Kautsky says that the only way of doing this would be – a European *revolution*. Now, as everybody knows, today the proletariat,

---

22. [The Boxer Rebellion in China in 1900 was put down by the Eight-Nation Alliance, which included Austria-Hungary, France, Germany, Italy, Japan, Russia, the United Kingdom, and the United States. The military contingent from the United States was called the China Relief Expedition; in Germany it was known as the *Hunnenzug*, or 'Hun campaign'. When a regiment of German troops was sent to China after the murder of the German ambassador, the Emperor Wilhelm II, in a speech of 27 July 1900, exhorted these troops: 'Just as the Huns under their king Etzel created for themselves a thousand years ago a name which men still respect, you should give the name of German such cause to be remembered in China for a thousand years.' This exhortation became known as *Hunnenrede*, or the 'Hun speech'. Alfred Graf von Waldersee (1832–1904), a German general, served as Chief of the Imperial German General Staff from 1888 to 1891. When European troops were dispatched to China, it was agreed that Count Waldersee should have supreme command of the joint forces as *Weltmarschall*. However, he arrived at the front too late to lead his troops to the assault of Peking.]

under the leadership of Social Democracy, is the only class that could make a revolution. The realisation of the 'United States of Europe', which is proposed as a practical way to limit today's militarism, would therefore only be made possible by the victory of the revolutionary proletariat, i.e. after the social revolution! We do not know what is more wonderful in this idea: the rule of the socialist proletariat with a federal government and a 'federal army', or the invitation to the present politicians to prepare the social revolution 'in the best interests of capitalism itself'.

If the idea of a European union of states thus betrays its utopian nature by insecurely wavering between the capitalist and the socialist world, it is also totally useless as an agitation slogan to convey a more concrete representation of the basic principles of proletarian policy. The idea of a European cultural community is completely alien to the world of ideas of the class-conscious proletariat. Not European solidarity, but *international* solidarity embracing all parts of the world, races and peoples is the cornerstone of socialism in the Marxist sense. Any partial solidarity is not a step towards achieving genuine internationalism, but its contrary, its enemy, an equivocation out of which peeps the cloven hoof of national antagonisms. Just as we always fought against pan-Germanism, pan-Slavism and pan-Americanism as reactionary ideas, we must also reject the idea of pan-Europeanism.

Our agitators would therefore do well in the forthcoming election campaign not to make further use of the slogan of the 'United States of Europe', which has been introduced so suddenly and unexpectedly. It is only fit to blur and water down the clear guidelines of our policy and of our international revolutionary propaganda for peace. But we also do not need such truly innovative vagaries. Our current views have until now served us well; they gave us our reputation among our opponents and the confidence of millions. We have no reason to destroy them with daring new 'ideas'.

'The Word they still shall let remain.'[23]

23. [*Das Wort sie sollen lassen stahn*: A quotation from Martin Luther's hymn 'A Mighty Fortress Is Our God' (*Ein' feste Burg ist unser Gott*), written in 1529.]

Chapter Thirty

'Morocco' (August 1911)

Rosa Luxemburg

This article by Rosa Luxemburg provides a short introduction to the Agadir affair, involving a German attempt to challenge French rights in Morocco by sending the gunboat Panther to Agadir in July 1911. The action incited the Second Moroccan Crisis, which contributed to the tensions in Europe that led to the outbreak of the First World War and played a major role in sharpening the polemic between the centre and left wings of the SPD on the question of imperialism and disarmament. It also anticipates Rosa Luxemburg's later argument, developed at length in *The Accumulation of Capital*, that the driving force of imperialism was capitalism's need for 'third parties' outside capitalist society (i.e. in the colonies) to realise surplus-value. In her book, Luxemburg argued that capitalism was trapped in an inescapable contradiction: incorporation of the non-capitalist milieu through imperialist expansion was imperative in pursuit of immediate profit, but it also simultaneously erased the 'third-party' markets upon which the system depended for its survival. In the article translated here, the same thought occurs: 'The Nemesis of capitalism lies in the fact that the more sections of the world it swallows in order to prolong its life, the more it undermines its own foundations.'

* * *

'Morocco'[1]

A dark imperialist cloud is hanging over the capitalist world. Four European great powers – France, Germany, England and Spain – are directly implicated in an affair in which first of all the fate of Morocco and then that of even vaster regions of the 'dark continent', which have been mentioned in the deliberations as 'compensations', are at stake. Every day brings new reports about the state of the negotiations, and, with them, hopes and fears rise and fall in rapid succession. Will the lightning of a murderous war on two continents flash down from the new thundercloud, or will the threatening thunderstorm dissipate so that its end will 'just' be a 'peaceful' haggling to transfer some shred of the world from one iron fist of European militarism to the other? That is the question that today stirs millions of people. To find an answer, all eyes turn with anxious expectation to the closed door of a room in which two 'statesmen' are conferring together: the French Ambassador [Jules] Cambon and the German Foreign Minister [Alfred von] Kiderlen-Wächter. Everyone knows that neither 'statesman' can be credited with having any superpowers; indeed, they are just poor puppets whose little arms and heads are moved automatically by strings whose ends, in both cases, are in the hands of some clique of great capitalists. War or peace, Morocco for Congo or Togo for Tahiti, those are questions in which the life and death of thousands, the weal and woe of entire peoples are at stake. The political clerks of a dozen greedy captains of industry bargain and deliberate over these questions as people haggle in the market about mutton and onions; and the civilised peoples wait with anxious restlessness for the decision, just like lambs led to the slaughter. It is an image so shockingly brutal and crudely vile that it must fill everyone not directly interested in the haggling with the deepest anger. But moral indignation is not the criterion and the weapon with which to approach phenomena such as capitalist world politics. For class-conscious proletarians, it is above all a question of *understanding* the Moroccan affair in its symptomatic significance in order to appreciate its intimate connections

1. Luxemburg 1911b.

and its consequences. The newest world-political adventure is rich in lessons for the political enlightenment of the proletariat.

The Moroccan crisis is, above all, a merciless satire of the disarmament farce enacted some months ago by the capitalist states and their bourgeoisie.[2] In England and France, statesmen and parliaments spoke with sonorous phrases as late as January [1911] about the need to reduce the outlays on instruments of murder and to replace barbaric war by the civilised means of arbitration proceedings. In Germany, the Progressives enthusiastically joined in the peace chorus. Today, those same statesmen and parliaments are backing a colonial political adventure that brings peoples to the brink of the abyss of a world war, and the Progressive hosts in Germany are enthusing over this warmongering adventure as much as they formerly did over peace-declamations. The sudden change of scene shows, once again, that the disarmament proposals and peace demonstrations of the capitalist world are nothing but painted scenes, which may, at times, be fit for some political comedy but are cynically cast aside once the affair is serious. To expect some peaceful tendencies from this capitalist society, and to rely earnestly upon them, would be the most foolish self-deception on the part of the proletariat.

Moreover, the Moroccan affair clearly shows again the intimate connection of world policy with internal political conditions in Germany. The Moroccan adventure, which is threatening to push Germany into a bloody war, and whose final result will in any case be a profound change in its foreign relations and colonial possessions, is taking place, just as the China campaign did eleven years ago and later the Algeciras affair, during a parliamentary recess.[3] The supreme representation of the German people, the Reichstag, is completely excluded from the most important and momentous events and decisions.

---

2. [In February 1911, the French Chamber of Deputies called on the government to include the question of arms-limitations in the agenda of the next peace conference. The motion was supported in the House of Commons by the English government, while naval allocations were simultaneously raised.]

3. [References to the repression of the Boxer rebellion in China in 1900 by the Eight Nation Alliance (Austria-Hungary, France, Germany, Italy, Japan, Russia, the United Kingdom, and the United States) and to the Algeciras Conference (16 January–7 April 1906), an international conference of the great European powers and the United States, held at Algeciras, Spain, to discuss France's relationship to the government of Morocco. The conference was the climax of the First Moroccan Crisis.]

The personal régime along with its handymen – themselves just irresponsible instruments in the hands of an irresponsible clique – does what it wants with the destinies of 64 million Germans, as if Germany were an oriental despotism. The Kaiser's speeches in Königsberg and Marienburg have become flesh and blood:[4] the instrument of heaven does what he pleases autocratically – or, rather, a couple of rapacious capitalist cliques do what they please through him and on the people's backs. Monarchism and its main props, the warmongering conservative Junkers, are first of all to be blamed for the Moroccan adventure.

But the brazen intervention of German diplomacy in the Moroccan affair also shows the driving force of reckless military and naval armaments. It is the brutal pressure of cannons and armoured vessels, amassed over decades because they are allegedly necessary as bulwarks of peace, which makes those driving German foreign policy so bold and bellicose. Above all, we have to thank those bourgeois parties who, by their support of incessant armaments, have directly pampered German imperialism for this 'panther leap' of world-policy, which may have an ultimate outcome with the most calamitous consequences for the German people. With the mark of blood on its forehead, the hypocritical Centre Party marches at the head of them all – the party that, in 1900, used the memorable doubling of the German navy in order to saddle up as government party. No less responsible, however, is wretched Liberalism, whose gradual political decay over a quarter of a century can be measured directly in the number of military bills it supported. The miserable end of bourgeois Liberalism is total collapse in the face of advancing militarism – which treads upon and crushes democracy, parliamentarism and social reform.

But precisely because the most recent world-political course, together with the current adventure, is merely a logical consequence of the internal economic and political development of bourgeois class-society, it has, as does the whole development itself, a revolutionary reverse-side that makes itself felt along with the immediate wretchedness and contemptible character of its momentary manifestation. The historical reason for the conflict over Morocco, reduced to its simplest and crudest expression, is the competitive struggle

4. [Wilhelm II called himself a king by the grace of God at his speeches in Königsberg (25 August 1910) and Marienburg (29 August 1910).]

among the representatives of European capitalism over who must be first to jump at the northwest corner of the African continent in order to devour it for capitalism – that is the significance of this piece of world-political development. But the nemesis of capitalism lies in the fact that the more sections of the world it swallows in order to prolong its life, the more it undermines its own foundations. At the same moment as capitalism prepares to introduce capitalist 'order' over the primitive conditions of the isolated shepherd-tribes and fishing villages of Morocco, the order that it has already created is breaking up everywhere else in the world. The flames of revolution are ablaze in Turkey, Persia, Mexico and Haiti, and they are silently consuming the state-machinery in Portugal, Spain and Russia. Everywhere we look, we see anarchy and the rebellion of the vital interests of the peoples, of the powers of progress and development, against the negligent patchwork of capitalism. The latest campaign of capital for new conquests will therefore merely lead it to the field where it will meet its fate. The Moroccan adventure, like every world-political thrust, will, in the long run, be merely a step towards the acceleration of capitalist collapse.

The class-conscious proletariat is called upon to be more than simply a passive observer in the final development of bourgeois society. The conscious realisation of the inner meaning of world policy and its consequences is not abstract philosophising for the working class, but rather the spiritual foundation of an energetic policy. In itself, the moral indignation of the masses is certainly not a weapon against the criminal economy of capitalism; but it is, as Friedrich Engels said, a crucial *symptom* that the ruling society has entered into contradiction with the sense of justice and the interests of the popular masses. The duty and task of Social Democracy today is to express this contradiction as clearly as possible. Not only the organised vanguard of the proletariat, but also the broadest strata of the working people must unleash a storm of protests against the new thrust of capitalist world policy. The only effective means of fighting against the crimes of war and colonial policy is the spiritual maturity and determined will of the working class, which will turn a world war, contrived by infamous capitalist interests, into a revolution of the exploited and oppressed for the realisation of world peace and the socialist brotherhood of peoples.

Chapter Thirty-One

'Petty-Bourgeois or Proletarian World Policy?' (19 August 1911)

Rosa Luxemburg

This polemic of Rosa Luxemburg with Eduard Bernstein over the Second Moroccan Crisis is a good example of the growing schism in the attitude towards imperialism between the left and right wings of the SPD. It is also notable as a stepping stone in Rosa Luxemburg's developing view of capitalism as a search for 'third-party' markets outside the capitalist world to realise surplus-value ('the innermost essence, the core, the whole meaning and content of the policies of the imperialist capitalist countries is the continuous and incessant tearing apart of all countries and peoples so that they can be gradually devoured and digested by capitalism') and as a defence of the native peoples' rights in their fight against imperialism – a matter of secondary concern to most European socialist politicians, who were worried above all about preventing the outbreak of a war between the major imperialist powers.

* * *

'Petty-Bourgeois or Proletarian World Policy?'[1]

The mass-action organised by the Party against the Moroccan policy had hardly begun when already a well-meant but nonetheless quite mistaken attempt was made to steer this action into the wrong channels. In two articles in *Vorwärts* – which the editorial staff of the central organ printed without comment on the first page[2] – Comrade Bernstein analysed the concrete solution that our protest movement against the Moroccan affair should advocate. He obviously wants to adopt a 'practical policy'. Bernstein thinks it is the duty of Social Democracy to advance 'positive' proposals for the solution of world-political problems. As Social Democrats, we should now find a way out that we should then recommend to the capitalist states as the 'best' and most practical settlement of the Moroccan Crisis. How could Social Democracy fulfil such an alien task and prepare recipes for capitalist diplomacy and its cabinets? Bernstein tries to show how to do just that. Since he, as a Social Democrat, is also dabbling in a craft foreign to him, the result is something quite remarkable. He lifts from the floor a scrap of paper he found under the table of the diplomats, smoothes it down on his knee with all care, and then waves it joyfully in the air as the single best solution to the Moroccan conflict – the only policy in the spirit of 'peace and equality of rights', in the spirit of the 'highest commandments of humanity', as well as in the best material interests of the peoples and the only solution worthy of Social Democracy and the twentieth century: the Act of Algeciras.[3] Who could possibly avoid crying – or laughing?

The Act of Algeciras was the expression of an international situation in which France could not yet openly claim Morocco as a colony, while the other powers did not want to and could not undertake warlike actions for Morocco's sake. The international guarantee for the sovereignty of Morocco's Sultan, i.e., for the formal independence of the country, which all the states then underwrote 'in the name of the Almighty', expressed a certain momentary

1. Luxemburg 1911c. In this and other sources of the period, the term 'world policy [*Weltpolitik*]' is used as synonymous with 'imperialism'.
2. Bernstein 1911b.
3. [The Act of Algeciras of 7 April 1906, ended the First Moroccan Crisis. The treaty guaranteed Morocco formal independence, but it also solidified the influence of France in the country by stipulating that the country should remain for five years under French and Spanish control.]

balance of power among various geopolitical interests. Translated from the knaves' language of diplomatic offices into ordinary German, the 'Declaration of Sovereignty' of Morocco's Sultan means the following: for the time being, that puppet may sit on his little throne and serve as a figurehead of Moroccan independence because Morocco's partition does not suit us for the moment and we have other concerns. Time will tell; see you again at the next opportunity!

The sovereignty of the Sultan and the independence of Morocco were already a stale farce at the moment of signing the Algeciras Act, which nobody in the wide world took seriously except for Bernstein. The fact that the Sultan is a mere puppet of French and German stock-exchange sharks, and that Morocco is one of the satrapies of European, primarily French, capitalism, is now something that everyone can see. Since then, however, the situation has gone even further in the same direction. France has tightened its grip on Morocco, whose 'sovereignty' is now more than ever a joke. And the other powers, especially Germany, quietly let France do that because they believe that the issue is already ripe and the time has come for finally bartering away the country. The Algeciras Act has done its work, now it can go.[4] It was made obsolete by the same trend of development that gave it birth. It has become a worn-out shoe in the house of diplomacy that can be thrown onto the trash-heap.

Eduard Bernstein now raises this precious object as the banner of socialist world policy. He has discovered a wonderful guiding principle for capitalist world policy: the Algeciras Act was 'moral', its violation is immoral; it is a breach of the law. And he expands on the issue of morality and immorality; his entire article drips with morality. 'Germany would have behaved infinitely more honourably,' he says, 'had it stated: No haggling, but contractual rights.' By behaving as it did, Germany morally 'humiliated itself'. But England's morals, Bernstein finds to his sorrow, are also not entirely flawless. 'When official England shouted at Germany apropos of Agadir and its hinterland, hands off!, it had in our eyes forfeited every moral right to do so because it allowed France, again and again, to smack the provisions of the Algeciras Act in the face in the largest and most civilised part of Morocco.' Bernstein

4. [A reference to Friedrich Schiller, *Fiesco, or the Genoese Conspiracy*, in Schiller 1849, p. 189.]

gradually discovers that, in fact, all states behaved immorally there, and he works himself up into a rage. Full of moral solemnity, he stares behind his glasses at Mr. Kiderlen-Wächter[5] and, with a raised index, admonishes him: 'Kiderlen, you are a dealer in stolen goods; yes, a dealer in stolen goods!' (Bernstein says it twice in his article.) 'Kiderlen, you better be honest, honourable, and moral!' We fear that Mr. Kiderlen will impatiently just turn his head and in his laconic way grumble: 'Mr. Bernstein, get lost!'

Indeed, what pointless absurdity it is to importune someone with demands he never met and could never possibly meet. Capitalist imperialism should be 'moral'. That is roughly the same as asking prostitution to be 'moral'. And, if someone could only say of prostitution that it is 'immoral', he would show exactly the same depth of social understanding that Bernstein demonstrates towards imperialism. The innermost essence, the core, the whole meaning and content of the policies of the imperialist capitalist countries is the continuous and incessant tearing apart of all countries and peoples so that they can be gradually devoured and digested by capitalism. It is also – if one wants to regard the historical process from a formal-legalistic and ethical side – nothing else, from its very beginning, but a continuous breach of the law and an act of violence turned into a principle. The battle over these scraps of foreign countries and peoples is the only content and purpose both of the armed clashes and of the open and secret treaties, which are only a further method of imperialist warfare and represent but a momentary determination of the mutual relationship of forces in this battle. What political child does not know today that these treaties are made only in order to be broken with the appropriate shift of power? Where is there ever to be found an international treaty of imperialist character that would not be broken? The unchangeability and inviolability of the international treaties of capitalist countries can only be counted upon by someone who does not realise that the international situation is in constant flux and that the law is therefore also subject to constant shifts, appearances and disappearances, development and change. This international world-political development is nothing but the reverse-side of the inner development of capitalism, upon which our desire for a socialist revolution is based.

5. [Alfred von Kiderlen-Wächter (1852–1912) was the German Foreign Minister at the time of the Second Moroccan Crisis (1911).]

And, precisely *now*, Social Democracy is to turn the sanctity of international diplomatic treaties, which are always points of departure for new antagonisms and struggles, into its slogan! It should convert the capitalist world to 'morality'!

But, we ask again, what kind of morality and right does Bernstein advocate here? According to him, the Algeciras Act was 'legal'; its violation is a 'breach of the law'. Bernstein only noticed in the Algeciras Act the equal right of all 'trading nations' in Morocco, and he quite strangely overlooked the fact that, besides European traders, there is still another factor, which also has, as it were, certain 'rights': the native people, the tribes of Morocco, who are now rebelling. He did not notice that, by guaranteeing the sovereignty of Morocco's Sultan, the Algeciras Act trampled underfoot the rights of the indigenous people and threw upon their back a despicable and homicidal leech that European trading nations use to suck the blood of the Moroccan tribes, which then flows into the pockets of stock-exchange sharks. Yes, it is our moral preacher here who shows lax morals. With *sangfroid* he says:

> There [in Morocco] it can only be a question of the operation of European capitalist enterprises, where Africans are employed as workers. German entrepreneurs are legally entitled to operate plantations and mines in different areas; the Algeciras Treaty grants them the same rights in Morocco as English and French entrepreneurs. To demand the strict fulfilment of this treaty, signed by all interested powers, is not only the *most honourable* and *humane* but also the *cheapest* way of helping *Germans* wanting to do business in Moroccan trade and industry; they can demand [the implementation of the Algeciras Act] with honour and reason.[6]

'With honour and reason' Krupp and Mannesmann should demand that African workers be delivered to them as leather to be tanned! 'The right' to rush African workers to their deaths in mines and plantations for capitalist profit – for Bernstein, that is the 'honourable and humane way'! Oh morality-preacher! But it always happens to our 'practical politicians' that, out of a statesmanlike urge to stand on 'positive ground', they end up fidgeting with their feet in the air and their finest parts on the floor.

6. Bernstein 1911b.

Bernstein's bad luck just proves that he approached the whole issue from the wrong angle. One cannot gauge phenomena such as modern imperialism with 'law' and 'morality'. To *understand* its tendencies, roots and historical significance as the final period of capitalist development – that is the task of Social Democracy. The inseparable connection of imperialism with capitalist development, whose legitimate child it is despite its daunting ugliness, or rather precisely in its daunting ugliness – that is what we must teach the working class to understand. And, consequently, the working class must draw the conclusion that imperialism, war, plundering countries, haggling over peoples, breaking the law, and the policy of violence can only be fought against by fighting capitalism, by setting social revolution against global genocide. Looking *within* imperialist policy for remedies and solutions to its conflicts, wanting to oppose its *Sturm und Drang* by trying to scale things back to past conditions, is not a proletarian but a petty-bourgeois policy, a hopeless policy that boils down to a constant defence of the imperialism of yesterday against the imperialism of today.

Moral indignation does play a major role in our protest movement against world policy. It will only become a political factor if it is connected with an *understanding* of the laws of this historical phenomenon, if it is directed not against its external forms but against its essence, not against its consequences but against its roots; in a word, if it is the revolutionary outrage of a mass ready to take by storm the capitalist social order as such.

Chapter Thirty-Two

World Politics, World War and Social Democracy! (August 1911)

Karl Kautsky

This document was originally published as a broadsheet by the Central Committee of the Social-Democratic Party of Germany in mid-August 1911, on the occasion of the Second Moroccan conflict, also known as the Agadir crisis (1 July–4 November 1911). It should be read together with the next item in this anthology, a sharply critical response from Rosa Luxemburg.[1] The paragraphs that provoked Rosa Luxemburg's condemnation were those suggesting that imperialism (or world policy, as Kautsky called it, following the old nomenclature) was not in the interest of most sections of the German bourgeoisie. Kautsky thought arms-expenditures were 'actually detrimental to large numbers of the possessing classes'. He claimed that

> It is in the interest not only of the proletariat but of the entire German people, and even the mass of its propertied classes, to prevent the government from continuing its world policy, which

1. See the debate on the Moroccan policy of the Parteivorstand at the SPD-congress in Jena (10–16 September 1911) in *Sozialdemokratische Partei Deutschlands 1911, Bericht der Kontrollkommission*, pp. 204–70. For an assessment of the debates by the SPD left wing, see Anonymous 1911a and 1911b.

> saddles the people with unheard-of burdens and brings ever closer the risk of a devastating war without any benefit except for a few monopolists and speculators.

In this conviction, Kautsky would soon find himself increasingly at odds with those who attributed imperialism to strictly economic imperatives of the capitalist system as a whole. Lenin saw imperialism as an objectively necessary consequence of the law of 'uneven development'; Luxemburg saw a compulsive need for 'third-party' markets; even Hilferding linked colonial expansionism with the concentration and centralisation of capital. For those on the Left, imperialism was inseparable from capitalism – it was certainly not a matter of political choice in which 'large numbers of the possessing classes' might oppose what Kautsky called 'a small minority of officers, public officials, armour-plate manufacturers, suppliers and speculators' who profited directly.

* * *

World Politics, World War and Social Democracy![2]

The peoples of Europe see themselves, unexpectedly and overnight, threatened by all the horrors of a world war. Thanks to the loving efforts of its neighbours to maintain its integrity, the Moroccan kingdom seems about to collapse; and the quarrel of those who reported themselves as its heirs is temporarily assuming dimensions that could set the whole of Europe ablaze.

Apparently, it is France that got itself into a dangerous contradiction with the other powers, particularly Germany, but, actually, the greatest danger to world peace comes not from the antagonism between France and Germany but from the antagonism between Germany and England. The current clash is only an accompanying phenomenon, a part of the great antagonism between the two powers that has been emerging since Germany, a dozen years ago, began its new world and naval policy. That antagonism has been deepening and growing from year to year.

Morocco had a different importance for England than for Germany and France. For the latter, Morocco is important as a missing link to round off

2. Kautsky 1911d.

its North-African possessions and to turn them into a huge, contiguous area. Besides, French and German capitalist groups are striving to control the country, with the help of state-violence, in order to monopolise the rich mineral resources of its soil. Some of those groups tend to co-operate in order to reinforce their position, but others come to blows, turning their clashes into national antagonisms and presenting advocacy of their own monopolistic desires as the most pressing interest and point of honour for the state.

For the Englishmen, on the contrary, Morocco is significant because of its geographical location, which dominates both access to the Mediterranean and the traffic on the Atlantic Ocean, especially to South Africa and South America.

Through Morocco pass the two sea-routes to the East Indies, that huge area with three hundred million people and inexhaustible natural wealth on whose possession and exploitation rests the colonial policy of England, a policy that was and still is incredibly profitable by comparison with that of other capitalist states, whose colonies have become sources of constant losses and sacrifices. The possession of India and the naval supremacy that secures it are today the most important foundations of England's social system and of the existence of its ruling classes.

For that reason, Great Britain has been striving ever since the eighteenth century to dominate the sea-route to the East Indies. To secure the entrance to the Mediterranean, it occupied Gibraltar and fortified it to the utmost. It will never tolerate a hostile naval power crippling those arrangements.

It was inevitable, therefore, that the appearance of a German cruiser off of Agadir should evoke the liveliest protest from the British government and bring us to the brink of war. Once again, our imperial government has wounded the nerve-centre of England's ruling classes at its most sensitive spot – and again without any apparent interest to the German people.

It is probable that, this time again, we will be spared the horrors of war. The interests of the German capitalists are the government's main concern in Morocco, and probably the antagonism of interests between the French and German capitalist groups over there are not powerful enough in themselves, from a capitalist point of view, to warrant all the terrible devastation and tremendous risk of a war – and that is quite apart from the interest of the people, for which the ruling class cares little.

But, even if war can once again be avoided, the situation responsible for the war-threat remains and worsens from year to year. A war is becoming increasingly difficult to avoid so long as the German Reich continues its current world policy and its related arms-race with England – a policy intended simply to curtail England's prestige and power but one which, in current circumstances, really threatens the existence of England's ruling classes. No class and no nation allows itself to be peacefully expropriated; and thus our current world policy is inevitably driving Germany into a bloody conflict with England, or rather with England's ruling classes.

The English working classes do not want war. Like all workers, they do not live from the exploitation of others but by the product of their own hands. This product, like that of all wage-workers, does not even entirely devolve on them: they have to leave the lion's share in the hands of their rulers and exploiters. They do not have the slightest interest in sacrificing their wealth and blood to prolong their exploiters' conditions of existence; instead, they have every interest in cutting the ground from under their feet. The collapse of England's naval supremacy and colonial empire could perhaps harm them temporarily, but, in the long run, it would benefit them because it would exacerbate class-contradictions in their country; and, given the vast power of the British workers, that could redound to their benefit. Continuation of their exploitation would be impossible from the moment they become conscious of their power and of the contradiction between their interests and those of the ruling class.

That is why the socialist-minded part of the proletariat in England is even today actually one of the strongest guarantors of peace. It must be thanked, above all, for the fact that the British government has not yet confronted German naval armaments by warlike means.

But we cannot rest on this guarantee of peace alone. No matter how great the love of peace on the part of the socialist section of English proletarians, the exploiting classes are still the ones who rule in England as they do elsewhere. They dispose of all the instruments of state-power as well as of the means of information with which to influence the masses. A provocative policy on Germany's part would quite likely give them the opportunity, at least temporarily, of carrying along in their wake a large part of the British proletariat as happened during the Boer War.

We should not, therefore, impose the duty of preserving world peace on English socialism alone. We in Germany also have to do our part in vigorously countering a policy that inflicts the worst sacrifices upon us in times of peace and is making a world war inevitable, namely, the world policy based on the arms-race with England.

In this respect, we are far better off than our British brethren, for, in Germany, not even the interests of the propertied classes call for this type of world policy. In England, there are few families of the propertied classes that are not in one way or another interested in England's colonial possessions and hence in its naval supremacy. But, in Germany, after thirty years of colonial policy, the number of members of the propertied classes that today benefit from posts or possessions in the colonies is very small.

Then again, in England, the rich profits from the colonies mitigate class-contrasts, albeit to a constantly decreasing extent. In Germany, on the contrary, the colonies and the naval arms-race require rising taxes, which have become a steadily growing burden on the working classes, in part directly and in part by increasing the cost of foodstuffs, thereby sharpening class-contradictions. However, the expenses of the arms-race and colonial wars are even today assuming such dimensions that it is impossible to shift them perpetually onto the working classes alone. The propertied classes must shoulder part of the burden. Colonial policy and naval construction thus not only yield no profit, but are actually detrimental to large numbers of the possessing classes. Only a small minority of officers, public officials, armour-plate manufacturers, suppliers and speculators benefit from it.

To be sure, people refer us to the future of the colonies, and we must admit that everything we do is determined more by the future than by the present, more by our expectations and fears than by our current circumstances. That applies not just to Social Democrats: Liberals and Conservatives also have their own 'state of the future' that they describe in the most glowing terms. And that 'state of the future' is precisely the colonies. For the sake of this colonial state of the future, we are asked not only to bear the crushing burden of the arms-race but also to accept all the dreadful horrors and devastations of a World War; as if the danger of the whole of Europe being as desolated as Germany was in the aftermath of the Thirty Years' War is not too expensive a price to pay for the colonial state of the future.

Those expectations are based on the brilliant results of English colonial policy. People think that as soon as England's supremacy at sea is broken, Germany will be able in the twentieth century to draw as much wealth from colonial possessions as England did in the eighteenth and nineteenth centuries.

But the times for that kind of colonial policy are gone forever, because it was based on the defencelessness of the non-European nations vis-à-vis European war-technology, and on their backward state-organisation. Since then, the old cultured peoples of Asia and the Islamic countries have awakened; they are taking possession of European knowledge, techniques and institutions. With giant steps, they are hastening to achieve their independence if they have not already achieved or maintained it.

Let us assume the best possible case for German world policy: that it actually manages to break England's naval supremacy. What would that achieve? Could Germany seize China or even part of it? That could have been dreamt of a dozen years ago, when the new German world and naval policy were inaugurated. The desire to be able to seize a good morsel in the seemingly impending partition of China probably provided the impetus for that policy. But, since then, China has become stronger and made gigantic progress; and it would today be quite impossible for such a far-away country as Germany to occupy a major part of the Middle Kingdom and retain it for long – not to mention the fact that, alongside China itself, America and Japan would also energetically veto such a policy even if England were no longer able to do so.

Would it be possible to appropriate England's colonial wealth by conquering its colonial possessions? A fortunate war of Germany against England could very well lead to the East Indies, Egypt, and South Africa breaking away from England, but never to them becoming German possessions. If England manages even today to hold its own there only with difficulty – even though those areas have been its possessions for many years and in some cases for more than a century, and even though it has anchored its domination through many organisations as firmly as possible – it would be completely impossible for a new foreign invader to establish itself as ruler and exploiter in any of those countries after they have conquered their freedom.

No, colonies like those of the seventeenth and eighteenth centuries, when one could easily win exuberant wealth, are today no longer at hand. That kind of colonial policy has come to an end. The English propertied classes, indeed, have everything to lose from destruction of England's naval supremacy, but those of Germany have nothing to win.

It is in the interest not only of the proletariat but of the entire German people, and even the mass of its propertied classes, to prevent the government from continuing its world policy, which saddles the people with unheard-of burdens and brings ever closer the risk of a devastating war without any benefit except for a few monopolists and speculators.

Nevertheless, in Germany, there is only one party today that offers vigorous resistance to that world policy as well as to the naval arms-race: Social Democracy.

The Conservatives and National Liberals have always championed world-policy because they represent those strata who, unlike the rest of the people, derive benefit from it: they dispose of the officers' and civil servants' posts, and they are dominated by the war-mongers who fabricate the armour-plated vessels and cannons, place loans, speculate in colonial lands, and provide supplies to the government.

For the most part, the Progressives and the Centre were formerly opponents of world policy, but they have since given in, partly due to servility and careerism and partly because, according to the traditions of the German bourgeoisie, political power is not won by wresting it from the current rulers but by becoming their servant and making oneself indispensable to them. Currently, the Centre has become, through this servile role, the darling of a government dominated by Conservatives.

However, the enthusiasm for world policy also stems partly from ignorance. People see only the happy example of England and feel annoyed because their own colonies do not make progress and because they cannot profit from them as England did, and still does, from its colonies. People do not know that the barrenness of contemporary colonial policy is inevitable and deeply grounded in the circumstances, and they believe that everything will be better if they are able to bring England down.

The bourgeois politicians certainly do not want a war against England. They are anxiously concerned for peace; and, even among Conservatives and National Liberals, the number of unscrupulous persons longing for a war must be small.

But this merely proves the groundlessness of their policy: they recoil from the inevitable consequences of their own actions and yet clamour against Social Democracy, which opposes those actions. They desire peace and abhor war, but they encourage and urge a policy that will necessarily lead to war if the Social-Democratic parties on either side are not strong enough to prevent it.

Social Democracy is the only true peace party; the only party that not only wants peace and abhors war, but also digs out the roots of war and works against the causes leading to it.

The stronger Social Democracy and the organisations supporting the proletarian class-struggle, the more determined will they be to mobilise all their power to maintain peace, and the more secure the peace will be.

To strengthen those organisations is therefore the duty of everyone wishing to work for the preservation of peace.

Whoever wants to strengthen the only force that seriously serves peace must therefore read the socialist press, attend socialist meetings, join a Social-Democratic organisation, affiliate with a free [Social-Democratic] trade-union if he is a wage-worker, and elect Social-Democratic candidates whenever possible.

A biblical proverb says: 'The fear of the Lord is the beginning of wisdom.' [Psalms 111: 10].

Today we can say: the beginning of the wisdom of governments is their fear of Social Democracy.

Chapter Thirty-Three

'Our Broadsheet on Morocco' (26 August 1911)

Rosa Luxemburg

The previous document in this collection, *World Politics, World War and Social Democracy!*, was published anonymously but written by Karl Kautsky. The title of the article promised a comprehensive examination of the war-threat, which implied an account of the fundamental connections between the capitalist system and imperialistic adventures such as the Moroccan affair. Certainly, this was what Rosa Luxemburg expected. While Luxemburg later claimed that she was unaware that Kautsky authored the brochure,[1] she was clearly alert to its conceptual confusion and resulting political implications. She condemned the article on two grounds: first, it narrowly conceived the threat of war in terms of rivalry between England and Germany, rather than attributing imperialism to the economic imperatives of capitalism as such; and second, by denying a necessary economic causality, it also implied that imperialism resulted from little more than a mistake in judgement on the part of the propertied classes, most of whom would derive no direct economic benefit. In that case, Kautsky's article suggested that the 'idiocy' of imperialism required Social Democracy merely to explain

1. Kautsky 1911d. See Chapter 32.

to the bourgeoisie, most of whom were already 'anxiously concerned for peace', that colonialism was 'a *bad bargain* for everyone'. Kautsky's conclusion, Luxemburg noted, was that a 'harmony of interests' existed 'between the proletariat and "the mass of the propertied classes"' – a judgement that she considered 'comical' in its simplicity and alarming in its implication that war might be averted by enlightening 'everyone' with clever 'antiwar slogans'.[2]

* * *

'Our Broadsheet on Morocco'[3]

It was surely a source of satisfaction to many comrades that our party, after finally deciding to organise a mass-action against the Moroccan affair, also immediately issued a broadsheet on that subject.[4] Brochures are less exciting than public assemblies, but they are much more lasting in their effects; they are meant to enlighten the broad popular masses and – for those circles not yet politically active enough to come to our meetings – to acquaint them with our views. As trailblazers opening our way to circles not yet won over, and as a means of consolidating our hold over those who are already sympathetic towards the Social-Democratic world-view, brochures are extraordinarily important weapons for us, and the Party must pay the greatest attention to writing them.

But anyone who sees the broadsheet on the Moroccan affair cannot help but be reminded of the saying: Nothing good is done in a hurry! If the decision to organise mass-actions against warmongering had not first been delayed and then made in such haste, and if the broadsheet had not been drafted overnight, we probably could have done something useful. Unfortunately, in its present state, this broadsheet, having been distributed in a hundred thousand copies, is almost a wasted effort.

The first thing one would expect from a broadsheet elucidating the Moroccan affair from a Social-Democratic point of view is surely a description of

2. Kautsky answered Luxemburg's criticism in a note in *Vorwärts*. See Kautsky 1911e.
3. Luxemburg 1911d.
4. Luxemburg 1911e.

the connection between world policy and capitalist development. The masses must first of all be taught what contemporary world policy is. The title of the broadsheet itself reads: 'World Policy, World War and Social Democracy'. Its first task therefore should have been to elucidate the essence of world policy and to examine its connection with the advanced maturity of contemporary capitalism. In historical terms, this connection is the only means with which to anchor our attitude towards world policy as well as the latter's link with socialism. Apart from this, all that remains is 'ethical' indignation at the inhumanity of war, or else a kind of shopkeeper's narrow-mindedness to the effect that we workers have nothing to gain from world policy. But the party broadsheet contains not a word about the nature of world policy and its connection with capitalism, which are the alpha and the omega of our point of view. It says nothing at all about world policy as a world phenomenon. The broadsheet begins straightaway with the antagonism between Germany and England, and it regards the whole problem exclusively from that point of view. England and Germany, Germany and England – thus runs the whole broadsheet; and the result, together with its generally dreadful shallowness, is more likely to give the impression of a litany of socialist platitudes than a Social-Democratic analysis of great problems.

In our opinion, one would also have expected the broadsheet at least to touch upon the connection of world policy in general, and the Moroccan affair in particular, with Germany's *domestic* development: with militarism, the naval arms-race, financial and taxation-policy, the standstill and reaction in social policy, and the untenability of the whole internal political situation. But we find not a single word about all that in the brochure. When Germany's arms-race is mentioned, it is merely from the point of view of the antagonism with England, and especially its role as the *source* of that antagonism. But the origin of the arms-race and the drive for world power in Germany, as well as in all the other states, remains a mystery and is not even mentioned.

We know very well that a broadsheet is not a learned treatise; it must be brief and popular. But there are no circumstances in which that relieves us from explaining our most important and fundamental views on the problems under discussion, even if only in a few words. In the broadsheet under review, there is no mention of those views; and that happens not because of lack of space but because the whole issue was put together on a false basis. Instead of regarding the Moroccan affair as an attendant phenomenon of international world policy in general, as the title promised to do, the broadsheet insists on the antagonism between Germany and England. The result is that, instead of explaining world policy as a necessary product of capitalist development, it strives instead to portray it the whole time as an absurdity, as an *idiocy* even from the viewpoint of capitalist society. Led by this original vagary, the broadsheet then attempts to prove at every turn that world and colonial policy is no asset but rather a burden even for the propertied classes. The Party thereby finds itself not only in a bizarre contradiction with the commonly known fact that today the whole of the ruling classes in Germany, as well as in the other states, are of a colonial-patriotic, militaristic and nationalistic mind; it also places itself in the comical situation of pretending to know the interests of the bourgeois classes better than those classes do themselves, while, as a rule, it is just the other way round. The Party thus undertakes to struggle against *capitalist* world policy and militarism, not from the point of view of the proletarian class-struggle, but rather in the name of an alleged harmony of interests on this point between the proletariat and 'the mass of the propertied classes'! And, in order to prove this fantastic harmony of interests, the broadsheet goes so far as to say that the bourgeois classes are not at all bellicose and patriotic but are 'anxiously concerned for peace'. The broadsheet explains the bourgeoisie's enthusiasm for world policy partly as the product of mere *ignorance* (thus giving Social Democracy the task of enlightening first and foremost the bourgeois classes about their true interests, rather than the proletarians) and partly as a result of 'servility' and 'careerism'! The depth of understanding with regard to Germany's domestic political development corresponds entirely with this profound analysis of its world-political development.

What is the final great secret, ignorance of which misled German bourgeois society into its mistaken enthusiasm for world policy, and knowledge of which is the key to the Social-Democratic position? It is the fact that the 'brilliant results of English colonial policy' are, once and for all, beyond the reach of other states because the high times of world policy are over. English colonial policy rested on the fact that non-European nations were militarily defenceless and backward in terms of state-organisation. Since then, however, European technique and institutions have been introduced everywhere in the East, and, for that reason, colonial rule is no longer possible. And that exhausts the problem of world policy! It would take the whole length of the broadsheet just to discuss all the historical obliquity contained in this short formulation of the problem. In any case, it can only be a source of confusion to declare, as the broadsheet does, that bourgeois parties are ignorant on world-political questions. But the most important thing is that, in this tangle of historical wrong-headedness, something else comes to light, and that is the fundamentally mistaken angle from which world policy is tackled. The subject is handled exclusively from the point of view of a scheme that claims colonial policy is a *bad bargain* for everyone. Accordingly, we only fight colonial policy because it does not pay; and we provide evidence to the masses in order to make them ill-disposed towards a colonial policy that cannot, indeed, yield any further profit. The other side of this conception is that the interests of the bourgeoisie in world policy are identified directly with monetary profit, with naked cash-interests, from which it follows that, in the whole of bourgeois society, there are only a handful of navy-suppliers who support world policy – which otherwise is suspended in the air – while all the exaltation of the possessing classes is based on ignorance, servility and other such purely psychological foundations.

Added to this is the fact that the whole broadsheet says not a single word about the native peoples of the colonies, about their rights, interests or sufferings as a consequence of world policy. It refers repeatedly to the 'brilliant results of English colonial policy' without ever mentioning the periodic outbreaks of typhus due to hunger along the Indus River, the extermination of Australian aborigines or the whipping of the Egyptian fellahs. Furthermore, there is no mention in the broadsheet of the disgraceful situation of the German people, who waited like children for a decision from Kiderlen on the Moroccan question; nor is there any word concerning the wretched role of the Reichstag and its need to be convened,[5] nor about the personal régime of the monarchy and its role in world policy, and finally – not even a word about socialism and its goals!

We know very well that it is easier to criticise than to write, and easier to write an article for a periodical than for a popular broadsheet. The author of the broadsheet on Morocco surely had the best intentions. But it seems indisputable to us that we have not fulfilled our duties with *that* particular

5. [The Second Moroccan Crisis took place during a parliamentary recess.]

broadsheet, and that we could have had one much more suitable and better thought out had the effort been undertaken with calmer deliberation, with thoroughness and critical examination, rather than being done hastily and abruptly.

In any case, this official brochure, as well as the fact that Bernstein's article[6] appeared unchallenged in the central organ of our party, proves that the Moroccan affair and world policy also require clarification within our own ranks and cannot be disposed of with some antiwar slogans: the party-congress must deal with these questions seriously and thoroughly.[7]

6. [Bernstein 1911b. See Rosa Luxemburg's criticism of this article in Luxemburg 1911c (for an English version see this Chapter 31.]

7. [A reference to the second Jena party congress of the SPD, held on 10–16 September 1911.]

Chapter Thirty-Four

'The Party Congress and Foreign Policy' (September 1911)

Rudolf Hilferding

The background to this document was the Agadir Crisis, also called the Second Moroccan Crisis (1 July–4 November, 1911), in which Germany provoked international tension by deploying the gunboat *Panther* in the Moroccan port of Agadir. Germany intended to intimidate France into an alliance and to enforce claims for compensation after accepting French control over the area. France's preeminence in Morocco had been upheld by the 1906 Algeciras Conference following the Tangiers (or First Moroccan) Crisis of 1905. Germany finally accepted France's position in Morocco, which was turned into a French protectorate by the Treaty of Fez (30 March 1912), in return for territory in the French Equatorial African colony of Middle Congo (now the Republic of the Congo). This territory of 275,000 km², known as Neukamerun, became part of the German colony of Kamerun and of German West Africa until they were captured by the allies in World War I.

The conclusion of Hilferding's article, calling for 'international disarmament', placed him squarely in the developing centrist tendency within the SPD and the Second International, led by his mentor Karl Kautsky. During the First World War, Hilferding revised his former revolutionary perspective and endorsed the possibility of achieving 'organised capitalism'.[1] In 1918, he joined the Independent Social-Democratic Party of Germany (USPD), where he belonged to the right wing that supported a rapprochement with the SPD. At the peak of the hyperinflation, he served as German Minister of Finance from August to October 1923. In May 1924, he was elected to the Reichstag, where he served as the SPD chief spokesman on financial matters until 1933. Between 1928 and 1929, he again served as finance minister. After the Nazis' rise to power, Hilferding escaped from Germany but was later murdered by the Gestapo in Vichy France in 1940.

* * *

'The Party Congress and Foreign Policy'[2]

The party congress is meeting in Jena at a critical time.[3] While representatives of the working class prepare for the coming electoral struggle, in Berlin [the German Foreign Minister Alfred von] Kiderlen-Wächter and [the French Ambassador] Jules Cambon are holding a private conference whose outcome will decide on peace and war. This is a forceful reminder to the proletariat that however important and significant parliamentary action is, and however decisive the result of the coming elections may be for the scale and intensity of future struggles, decisions concerning the fate of peoples and the most momentous events in their history will not be made in the speakers' tribunes and assembly-halls of parliaments.[4] The German, French and English parliaments are adjourned, and a small number of leading ministers hold in their own hands the uncontrolled power of decision over the vital questions of their nations. The popular representatives wait patiently to be confronted with the *faits accomplis.* The only unique feature of German absolutism is that in the selection of leading figures the Reichstag was completely ignored and the personal role of the monarch stands out much more prominently.

1. Hilferding 1915.
2. Hilferding 1911.
3. [The second Jena congress of the German Social Democratic Party (*Parteitag*) was held on 10–16 September 1911. See Sozialdemokratische Partei Deutschlands 1911.]
4. [See Hilferding 1905b. Original version: Hilferding 1905a.]

But, in England and France, too, the parliamentary representatives have let themselves be quietly shoved aside. As soon as the rulers of the capitalist states face vital decisions, the *leitmotif* of their policy becomes an appeal to the *ultima ratio* of violence; and the representative institutions, provided by constitutions, are superseded by governing committees of the ruling classes.

This is the second such warning for the German working class. The first also came at a party congress held in Jena, and the lessons there were fruitful for proletarian policy.[5] At that time, six years ago, the Russian Revolution [of 1905] was at its peak, and its powerful thunder echoed in the deliberations. The party congress realised that the period of stormy development that all the leading capitalist states had entered was making greater claims on proletarian tactics. By recognising the significance of direct actions by the masses themselves, it did not deprive its previous [electoral and parliamentary] methods of their significance. On the contrary, it secured against violent interference the tireless small tasks of organisation and agitation, the tenacious struggles to conquer even insignificant positions in administration and the legislative bodies, and finally parliamentary action itself. By setting an appeal to the direct social power of the masses against the ruling classes' hope of driving the workers out of the parliamentary arena by violent means in case of an emergency, the first Jena party congress posed universal and equal suffrage as the sharpest weapon of the proletariat, one that involved no risk of breaking down precisely when it became dangerous for the enemy.

Back then, in Jena, important political lessons were thus drawn from the great struggles in Russia. The great consequences of those powerful events for the international situation are now manifesting themselves in the second Jena party congress.

---

5. [The first Jena congress of the German Social-Democratic Party was held on 17–23 September 1905. Against the decision of the Cologne trade-union congress of 22–7 May 1905, which rejected the mass-strike as a political tactic and prohibited even propaganda for this means of struggle, the first Jena congress approved in principle the use of the political mass-strike in the fight for electoral and democratic rights, though, at the insistence of Bebel, the general strike was also described as a defensive tactic against an expected assault by the bourgeoisie on the growing gains of the socialist movement. See Sozialdemokratische Partei Deutschlands 1905, 6. Der politische Massenstreik und die Sozialdemokratie. Berichterstatter: A. Bebel, pp. 285–354. Hilferding fails to mention, however, that on 16 February 1906, the SPD-executive and the General Commission of Free (i.e. Social-Democratic) Trade-Unions of Germany held a secret conference that resulted in an agreement by which the party leaders pledged to prevent a mass-strike, if possible, and to assume the sole burden of leadership should it break out.]

In terms of the tsarist kingdom's authority, the Russian Revolution completed what defeat at the hands of the Japanese had begun. It dealt a death-blow to the already shaken and disorganised Russian army and turned it from an aggressive power into a demoralised corps of bodyguards directed solely against the internal enemy. The defeat of the Revolution also made impossible for a long period any reorganisation of the military establishment. The reinstatement in power of a corrupt and rotten bureaucracy left in place all the causes that made the Russian army unfit for a serious war and that hinder even the most capable administration from accomplishing the huge work of rebuilding the broken army and the annihilated fleet. State-power in Russia is strong enough to ward off the internal enemy – but only at the expense of losing its foreign authority.

The downfall of Russian power also meant a decisive turning point for European politics.

The new era of imperialism announced itself with the [First] Sino-Japanese War and the Spanish-American War.[6] It is characteristic that both wars were begun by the youngest capitalist powers with the stormiest economic develop-

6. [The First Sino-Japanese War (1 August 1894–17 April 1895) was fought between the Qing Dynasty in China and the Meiji dynasty in Japan over the control of Korea. It would come to symbolise the degeneration and enfeeblement of China, demonstrating how successful modernisation had been in Japan since the Meiji Restoration as compared with the Self-Strengthening Movement in China. The principal results were a shift of regional dominance in Asia from China to Japan and a fatal blow to the Qing Dynasty that would later result in the 1911 Revolution. By the Treaty of Shimonoseki, signed on 17 April 1895, China recognised the total independence of Korea (which was turned into a Japanese sphere of influence) and ceded the Liaodong Peninsula (in the south of present-day Liaoning Province), along with Taiwan/Formosa and the Pescadores Islands, to Japan 'in perpetuity'. China was to pay reparations to Japan, and it also signed a commercial treaty permitting Japanese ships to navigate the Yangtze River and allowing the Japanese to operate manufacturing facilities in treaty-ports and to open four more ports to foreign trade. The Triple Intervention, however, forced Japan to give up the Liaodong Peninsula.

The Spanish-American War (25 April–12 August 1898) began after Spain rejected the American demand for a peaceful resolution of the Cuban fight for independence. Strong expansionist sentiment in the United States motivated the government to target Spain's remaining overseas territories: Cuba, Puerto Rico, the Philippines, Guam and the Caroline Islands. Only 109 days after the outbreak of War, the Treaty of Paris ended the conflict and gave the United States ownership of the former Spanish colonies of Puerto Rico, the Philippines and Guam, while also establishing a *de facto* protectorate over Cuba. On 14 August 1898, 11,000 US ground-troops were sent to occupy the Philippines. When American troops began to take the place of the Spanish in controlling the country, warfare broke out between US forces and the Filipinos. The Philippine-American War lasted from 4 February 1899 to 2 July 1902].

ment. The first war was waged against the oldest cultured state in the world, whose old Asiatic mode of production had remained unchanged for millennia; the second, against the oldest capitalist power after [the city-states of] Northern Italy. The most valuable parts of Spain's remaining colonial possessions, stemming from the beginning of the colonial era, were easily taken over by the United States. But victory also brought the victors [Japan and America] into a mutual antagonism that contains the germs of future entanglements.

In its second stage, imperialist policy spread over the European states. England waged the Boer War in order to secure its South-African possessions, to conquer the last large African settlement area and to annex the alluring gold-mines and diamond-fields.[7] China's weakness united the large European states, the United States and Japan in the glorious Hun campaign.[8] But, because they were united by greed, the booty falling to the share of each one of them was small. The significant result [of the repression of the Boxer Rebellion] was to show Russia and Japan that a conflict between them, as the powers most interested in China's fate due to geographical reasons, had become inevitable. A war ensued. Japan's victory set Asia in revolutionary motion, and its most immediate consequences have been the Turkish and Persian Revolutions and the strengthening of India's independence-movement.[9]

Russia's elimination as an actual great power led to the third stage of imperialism. Decisions shifted to the European centre of the capitalist world. The issue is no longer one of conflicts on the periphery of capitalism as in the first stage; no longer colonial campaigns of conquest by the European states, as during the second stage; today, we are witnessing a decisive struggle between

---

7. [A reference to the Second Boer War (11 October 1899–31 May 1902).]

8. [The Eight-Nation Alliance (which included Austria-Hungary, France, Germany, Italy, Japan, Russia, the United Kingdom, and the United States) put down the Boxer Rebellion in China in 1900. The military contingent from the United States was called the China Relief Expedition. The customary designation in Germany is *Hunnenzug*, or the 'Hun campaign'. After the murder of the German ambassador during the Boxer Rebellion, a regiment of German troops was sent to China. In a speech of 27 July 1900, Emperor Wilhelm II exhorted the troops: 'Just as the Huns under their king Etzel created for themselves a thousand years ago a name which men still respect, you should give the name of German such cause to be remembered in China for a thousand years.' This exhortation became famous in German history under the name of *Hunnenrede*, or the 'Hun speech'.]

9. [Hilferding refers to the Russo-Japanese War (10 February 1904–5 September 1905), the Young Turk Revolution of 1908 and the Persian Revolution of 1909.]

the great European powers that cannot end simply in a colonial war but threatens instead to hurl the European states themselves into a world war.

Ever since Bismarck's downfall, Germany has found itself in a transition to the new political tasks arising from imperialism. Foreign policy is acquiring an unsteady and erratic character, and fumbling attempts are being made everywhere. Glances turn to South America, Africa, Asia Minor, and China. The German Empire appears to be a Johnny-on-the-spot in all the alleys of world policy. Successes are few; Germany encounters everywhere the opposition of the old colonial powers. But, meanwhile, the state works feverishly to produce those weapons without which imperialist policy cannot be pursued: in a relatively short space of time, Germany has become the second naval power of the world and has set out to challenge England's supremacy.

Russia's defeat meant a complete shift in the hitherto prevailing foreign relations. The old antagonism between England and Russia, which had previously dominated a large part of world policy, lost its significance. Russia ceased to be dangerous to England. Its place was taken by the antagonism between an old power, England, and the new and rapidly developing power, Germany – an antagonism that has grown out of the latest economic developments and cuts across all state relations. After a short period of wavering, a reorientation of English policy took place (although, for a while, Chamberlain considered concluding an alliance with Germany directed against Russia and France).

All the states with old colonial possessions, with France at their head, united with England against German imperialism. Russia, driven back from East Asia, sought to compensate itself in the wake of England and France through an active Balkan policy. And the small states, which were not compelled by colonial troubles to take England's side, opted in favour of the organisation of Western powers due to its superior fleet. The encirclement-policy [against Germany] seemed to be totally successful.

The Moroccan question already emerged twice during this period and endangered peace. Both times, Germany beat a retreat. But then, the crisis of the Bosnian annexation burst the bubble. In the gravity of that decision, the facts came into their own.[10]

---

10. [The Bosnian Crisis of 1908–9 was caused by the annexation of Bosnia and Herzegovina by Austria-Hungary in October 1908. Article 25 of the Treaty of Berlin

It is a fact that, since Russia's defeat, Germany and Austria exert a [virtual] military dictatorship over Europe. Against their united power, the Triple Entente[11] is impotent – that was the lesson of the Serbian crisis. The states that have more to fear from the enmity of a [continental] military power than from a sea-power, at least those in the second rank, began to draw back from following England. Russia, despite the 'humiliation', went to Potsdam and promised to keep peace in Persia in exchange for a rich gratuity.[12] In Italy, people once again began to take seriously the Triple Alliance,[13] for so long a laughing stock, and to ask themselves whether it might be possible to get more in Africa by siding with Germany than with the Western powers. And, even

---

(13 July, 1878) gave Austria-Hungary the right to occupy and administer the two provinces of Bosnia and Herzegovina. The annexation of Bosnia became an urgent matter for Austria-Hungary when, in 1908, the Young Turk Revolution convinced many that the Ottoman Empire could regain its former power in the Balkans. When the Austrian foreign minister, Count Alois Lexa von Aehrenthal, announced the annexation, the Serbians were outraged and demanded a Russian intervention, calling for either a return to the *status quo ante* or compensation. By early February 1909, the Serbian army was mobilised. Germany immediately declared its support for any action by Austria-Hungary, while the Serbs asked for support from Russia. Clearly not prepared for a war against both Germany and Austria-Hungary, Russia was forced to abandon its Serbian allies. Without Russian support, the Serbs were forced to agree to the annexation. Austria's annexation of Bosnia and Herzegovina increased tensions amongst the Great Powers and led to international complications, which, for several weeks early in 1909, threatened to end with a general European war and ultimately contributed to World War I].

11. [The Triple Entente was the name of the agreement between the United Kingdom, France and Russia – made after the signing of the Anglo-Russian Entente in August 1907 – to oppose the Triple Alliance of Germany, Austria-Hungary, and Italy].

12. [On 4–6 November 1910, a meeting was arranged in Potsdam between Nicholas II of Russia and Wilhelm II of Germany. This move was intended to chastise the British for their perceived betrayal of Russia's interests during the Bosnian Crisis. The two monarchs discussed the Baghdad Railway, a German project widely expected to give Berlin considerable geopolitical influence in the Fertile Crescent. Against the background of the Persian Constitutional Revolution, Russia was anxious to control the prospective Khanaqin-Tehran branch of the railway. The two powers settled their differences through the Potsdam Agreement, signed on 19 August 1911, and giving Russia a free hand in Northern Iran. The first railway connecting Persia to Europe would provide Russia with a lever of influence over its southern neighbour. Notwithstanding the promising beginning, Russo-German relations disintegrated in 1913 when the Kaiser sent one of his generals to reorganise the Turkish army and to supervise the garrison in Constantinople, remarking that 'the German flag will soon fly over the fortifications of the Bosporus', a vital trade artery that accounted for two fifths of Russia's exports.]

13. [The Triple Alliance (*Dreibund*) was a defensive association between the German Reich, Austria-Hungary and Italy. The alliance was formed in 1882, enlarging the former Austro-German Double Alliance (*Zweibund*). It was renewed in 1912 but terminated by Italy in 1915.]

a small state such as Spain could make an adventurous attempt to exploit the Anglo-French antagonism in order to emancipate itself from France's policy. German imperialism already made its first breakthrough. Turkey, threatened by Russia and England, sought Germany's protection; and construction of the Baghdad Railway, German imperialism's old child of sorrow, will consequently continue despite the opposition of the Western powers.

In this changed situation, Germany availed itself of France's move in order to raise the question of Morocco for the third time. And, this time, the demeanour of German imperialism is totally different. It is defiantly demanding its share and making clear reference to its powerful army and imposing fleet. And, this time, unlike before, it did not have to fear an outright rejection of its demands. France immediately opened negotiations.

This is not the time or place to go into specific questions about Morocco's significance and possible compensations. Only two observations seem necessary in this context. First, to the extent that it is even possible, given the obscurity surrounding the negotiations, we must attempt to give some account of the most urgent issue, the preservation of peace; and then we must consider some of the results [of the Agadir affair] that, in our opinion, can already be recognised.

The opening of the Moroccan action by the dispatch of a warship to Agadir immediately turned the situation into a crisis because it appeared as if Germany wanted to gain a footing on Morocco's Atlantic coast, and this must naturally rouse England's opposition. Those who did not foresee those developments failed completely to appreciate the significance of the German-English antagonism. English imperialism cannot tolerate such a German foothold [on the Moroccan coast], any more than German imperialism can renounce the continuous strengthening of its position at sea. For this reason, if the dispatch of warships was anything more than simply a display of power aimed at forcing negotiations, the conflict seems insolvable.

This behaviour must awaken in German imperialist circles the hope that it will finally be possible to achieve a resounding success and seize part of Morocco. To these circles, any other outcome must look like a defeat and a retreat. To that end, a wild agitation began and found an echo in all the bourgeois parties. This heightens the danger, however, that the government will be pressed to go further than it perhaps intended at the beginning of the action. Taking into consideration the precarious domestic political situation in which the government and the parties find themselves, it appears that we actually find ourselves now in a very dangerous situation.

On the other hand, one cannot fail to recognise that, on the German side, too, there are important reasons for avoiding a war. Apart from everything else, the relative weakness of the German navy is one circumstance that presently argues for the preservation of peace. From the standpoint of German imperialism, the potential loss of the German navy would be a momentous event for which even a victory on land could not compensate because, for a long period, it would consolidate the English ascendancy at sea, which is the strongest obstacle to German imperialist plans. On the contrary, German imperialism hopes to overtake this English lead and somehow obtain England's consent to its colonial expansion. It is characteristic that the circle of big merchants (admittedly, almost on their own) energetically opposed the agitation over Morocco and came out in Hamburg emphatically for peace. This split in the ranks of the managers of our economic policy must influence the policy of the government and the bellicose mood of the country, undoubtedly mitigating the current war-danger. Precisely in this situation, however, the proletarian peace actions, which hinder the rise of nationalist madness, are revealing their great significance and immediate practical effectiveness. We must hope, therefore, that, despite the slight interest that many imperialist circles display in the settlement of the conflict, peace will be preserved unless some incalculable event intervenes. Thus, even now, a series of remarkable insights follow for proletarian policy.

First, the Moroccan conflict is typical of the most recent foreign policy. The youngest capitalist states have sought to emancipate themselves from England's supremacy through protectionist tariffs. They have split up the world market into separate parts and sought to create, as far as possible, monopolistic positions for national industry. These processes resulted in the growth of state antagonisms that have become increasingly acute due to expansionist capitalist efforts – driven by cartels, trusts and the controlling large banks (finance-capital), all of which have in turn been powerfully stimulated by protective tariffs. The resulting colonial policy seeks to reserve the newly acquired areas for national capital and to exclude foreign capital from them as much as possible. Thus, colonial policy, the necessary result of protectionist economic policy, has become a continuous and effective cause of warlike developments between the great capitalist states.

A 'socialist colonial policy', therefore, remains a mere phantom. This idea could only originate in a small country removed from the centres of world-politics and with colonial possessions acquired long ago, such as Holland, where some people call 'socialist' the struggle for the alleviation and humanisation of exploitation in the colonies – a struggle that is necessary and natural for all socialists – in order to hide the unbridgeable contradiction between socialism and capitalism.[14] The Moroccan affair is a striking and classic example of harsh reality. The question in dispute is not the administrative régime of the old colonies or the degree of protection for the natives. The natives are not an issue at all, and the shelling by Frenchmen and Spaniards, along with the burning of villages to the ground, are self-evident actions about which nobody argues. It is, rather, the acquisition and repartition of colonial possessions that rules foreign policy, demanding a continuous increase of the army and navy budgets and pushing nations towards world war as its natural consequence. We cannot set a 'socialist' and philanthropic colonial policy – which differs from the real one only by being inconsequential and unfeasible – against a policy that arises from the very nature of capitalist development. This capitalist policy can only be replaced by a proletarian policy – not by a socialist colonial policy but by socialism.

And just as little can the proletariat set against the international conflicts arising from this policy the 'international law' that the capitalist states themselves drew up only yesterday in order to violate it today. This would mean that in opposing today's power-relations the proletariat would appeal to the power relations of yesterday, whose fitting expression was the outlived and violated agreement. [The capitalist powers] want to get rid of the old 'international law' in order to create a new one more suited to the real conditions. The foreign policy of the proletariat would not only become totally unreal but would actually amount to an attempt to preserve old and untenable relations. The proletariat would thus become directly entangled in struggles of interests on the part of the capitalist classes, and, instead of taking up the struggle in each country against its own rulers, who are all equally responsible and guilty, would have to side first with one capitalist group and then with another. Instead of international solidarity, which is the only real foundation

14. [A reference to the Dutch delegate Hendrick van Kol, who, at the 1907 Stuttgart Congress of the Socialist International, advocated a 'socialist colonial policy'.]

of proletarian peace policy, and, instead of their own class-interests, the proletarians would have to study the acts of diplomatic congresses in order to discover the foundations of their policy. The only advantage of the Moroccan affair is that it put an end to all such illusions.

Still another point must at least be mentioned, and that is the lack of influence by parliaments on foreign policy. This phenomenon must not be misunderstood: for the most part, it is due to the voluntary collaboration of the bourgeois parties, which was not wrung from them by force. It is simply another manifestation of the strength of the imperialist tendencies that have swept the capitalist world and are increasingly drawing it into their ominous vortex.

Foreign policy is also increasingly determining the development of our domestic relations. The contradiction between capitalist and proletarian policy is here totally irreconcilable. Precisely because of the war-danger, the ruling classes are most sensitive to internal opposition. Hostility towards Social Democrats is growing, and the political struggle is sharpening, while the demands of world policy on taxation are simultaneously causing the economic situation to deteriorate at a time when the international cost of living is high. It is clear that all of these factors, which are mentioned here only briefly and fragmentarily, require a profound and thorough discussion before the forum of a party congress. That is all the more necessary because we must expect foreign policy to be brought before the masses by our opponents themselves. It is therefore natural that a series of motions have been submitted to include foreign policy on the agenda of the party congress. It seems that, on this occasion, the party congress will not have sufficient time for an exhaustive debate. Bebel will certainly refer to the main political repercussions of the most recent phase in his report. Nevertheless, an official declaration concerning the Moroccan adventure should obviously be made by the representatives of German workers, restating our will for peace as manifested in our protest movement.[15] However, a more extensive discussion of imperialist policy requires such thorough preparation, including exhaustive debate in the party press, that it should be assigned as one of the most urgent tasks for

15. [The SPD-resolution against the imperialist policy in Morocco can be found in Institut für Marxismus-Leninismus 1975, Band 4: März 1898–Juli 1914, 1975, document nr. 216, pp. 369–70.]

the next party congress.[16] Perhaps, as a result of the debate, German Social Democracy will want to put imperialism and foreign policy on the agenda of the next international congress,[17] for, along with growth of the war-danger must also grow the preparedness of the proletariat and the effectiveness of its *international* actions, which alone make possible the development of proletarian strength.

This time, the party congress will do its best work for peace by preparing for the coming elections; in that effort, it will also deal with decisions directly affecting foreign policy. The most important thing that can be done for peace just now is to strengthen the party that clearly recognises the workers' interests by rejecting protectionism and colonial policy, fighting against militarism, demanding international disarmament and refusing the capitalist system a single man or a single penny.

The war-danger and the high cost of living – these are the gloomy signs under which the representatives of the strongest party in the world are meeting. While they do not frighten us, they do show capitalist society its own destiny.

---

16. [See the debate and resolution on imperialism at the Chemnitz Congress, held the following year (15–21 September 1912): Sozialdemokratische Partei Deutschlands 1912, pp. 403–34. See this volume, Chapter 42.]

17. [A reference to the Vienna Congress of the Second International, scheduled for 23–9 August 1914, which failed to meet due to the outbreak of the First World War on 1–3 August 1914. See Georges Haupt: 'On Imperialism: The Debate which Failed', in Haupt 1972, pp. 135–60.]

Chapter Thirty-Five

Imperialism or Socialism? (1912)

Julian B. Marchlewski (Karski)

In the first part of her work *The Crisis of Social Democracy* (also known as *The Junius Pamphlet*), Rosa Luxemburg quotes the closing paragraph of this document with its admonition that 'History is approaching great decisions' and that only the proletariat might 'spare humanity the abominations of a world war'. Luxemburg spoke of Karski's '*Imperialism or Socialism?*' as 'an official pamphlet published by the Party [and] distributed in hundreds of thousands of copies a few years ago'.[1]

In this powerful essay, Karski provides one of the most comprehensive summaries of the forces within capitalism that press continuously in the direction of imperialist warfare. Modern industry, he notes, presupposes an expanding market; but, given the limits to domestic consumption, capital is driven to conquer and monopolise foreign markets for the export not merely of commodities but also increasingly for capital-investments. '*Capital-exports,*' he observes, 'have become the most important economic means for the conquest of the world by capital.'

1. Luxemburg 1919.

Karski also ties the modern primacy of capital-exports directly to the domestic problem of markets. The capitalists, he notes,

> seek to expand the market; not, however, the domestic market by means of wage-hikes, but rather foreign markets. Then they do not have to relinquish part of their profits to the working class as wage-increases but can export it abroad as capital. Therefore the capitalists' commercial policy always has in mind foreign markets, while that of the workers focuses on the domestic market and centres above all on *wage-policy*. The capitalists, on the contrary, cling to tariff-policy.

The result is that capital 'strives to turn the whole earth into its field of exploitation and increasingly transforms the world into a single economic territory' at the same time as 'protectionist policy simultaneously divides this territory once more into isolated areas whose exploitation should be reserved as the monopoly of particular national capitalist classes'.

Apart from socialist revolution, the only conceivable outcome must be a world war. Written less than two years before the conflagration of World War I, Karski's brochure cites the powerful warning delivered by August Bebel to the German Reichstag in November 1911: 'The great order to march will be given, sending to the battlefields sixteen to eighteen million men, the flower of European youth, equipped with the best tools for murder and turned against each other as enemies.' In a moment of high drama, Bebel evoked Wagnerian imagery to warn the bourgeoisie of a new 'twilight of the gods.... [M]ass bankruptcy, mass misery, mass unemployment, the great famine.... Then things will come to pass that you certainly do not want, but they will necessarily take place, I repeat, through no fault of ours, but because of you. *Discite* [*iusticiam*] *moniti*! ('You have been warned, learn justice!' Virgil, *Aeneid*, VI, 620.).'[2]

Karski's document also shows that, in the debate over disarmament vs. the call for a citizens' militia, in which Kautsky defended the former against Lensch, Pannekoek and Radek, not all left-wing critics of militarism foreclosed the possibility of disarmament. Karski, who, together with Rosa Luxemburg,

---

2. August Bebel: *Rede auf der 201. Sitzung des Deutschen Reichstages, XII. Legislaturperiode. II. Session, gehalten am 9. November 1911*. [August Bebel, Speech at the German parliament, 9 November, 1911]. In Reichstag 1911, Band 268, Stenographische Berichte, p. 7730D.

had been one of the founders of the Social-Democratic Party of the Kingdom of Poland and would later become a supporter of the Bolsheviks and co-founder of the Spartacus League in Germany, initially backed Kautsky's position on disarmament[3] while, at the same time, repudiating Radek's accusation of being a supporter of the Reichstag fraction because of his support for disarmament.[4] The break between Kautsky and Karski took place late in 1912, after the publication of this brochure.

* * *

Imperialism or Socialism?[5]

1. *Economic and social transformations*

Beginning in the mid-1890s capitalism entered a period of 'Sturm und Drang'.[6] Until then, economic development had proceeded comparatively slowly and gradually, following the world crisis of 1873: it was basically a constant expansion of capitalist production – as it had developed in England, the ruler of the world market – into the states of the European continent and the United States of America. In social terms, this development meant the complete displacement of handicrafts by capitalist production, the proletarianisation of small producers and the creation of an increasingly numerous class of wage-workers. The intensive economic upswing that began in the [second half of the] 1890s, the rapid succession of booms interrupted only by short crises, announced the end of this economic period of mainly *internal capitalist development* of the leading states and the beginning of a new period characterised by the deepest changes in the internal structure of capitalist production and in property-relations, and also by a new, incomparably more intensive, *conquest of the world* by capital.

If the previous period was characterised, above all, by the struggle of capitalist production with backward modes of production, now large-scale capital completed its victorious struggle against small and mid-sized capital

3. [Marchlewski 1911a].
4. [Radek 1911b.] Marchlewski 1911b.
5. Marchlewski 1912.
6. [See Parvus, 'The "Sturm-und-Drang" Period of Capital', section 4 of Parvus 1901.]

and established its absolute rule over the economy. Industrial leadership is no longer in the hands of the industries producing means of consumption, which supply the immediate necessities of life, but, instead, belongs to those branches of production supplying raw materials and means of production. The textile-industry, with small and mid-sized capital in contemporary terms, long ago had to surrender its former pre-eminence to the highly capitalistic branches of the coal, iron, engineering, chemical and electrical industries.

The organisational forms of industry have also changed completely. The independent capitalist, owning his own enterprise, is steadily disappearing. His place is taken by the *corporation*,[7] in which employees are paid by capital to manage production. Corporations enormously facilitate raising even the largest sums of capital, and thus they make it possible to bring enterprises to the highest standards required by the level of technology. At the same time, their formation offers the opportunity of making huge foundation-profits;[8] in that way, together with stock-exchange speculation by shareholders with insider-knowledge, they effectively boost concentration of the largest capitalist fortunes.

The corporation also makes it much easier to combine previously separate and independent enterprises into a single entity; and this striving for unification is characteristic of modern large-scale industry. As with single entrepreneurs, the previously separate enterprises steadily disappear. Companies seek to unite and combine all the successive stages of production, from raw-material extraction to the finished product. Thus, one enterprise unites coal and steel-production, including the production of pig-iron and its conversion into steel, the processing in steel-mills into beams and rails, sheet-plates and wires, and the transportation of these products. The size of capitalist enterprises grows continuously, and their union gives birth to the gigantic enterprises that have today become typical of so-called heavy industry.

Simultaneously with the enormous concentration of industry, the relations between banking and industrial capital become ever closer. The *banks* gather the momentarily idle money of industrialists and other classes of the population and place it at the disposal of the enterprises. The larger the enter-

7. [*Aktiengesellschaft*: joint-stock company or incorporated company.]

8. [*Gründungsgewinnen*: a reference to Hilferding's term *Gründergewinn* or founders' profit, which can also be translated as 'floaters' or 'incorporators' profit'.]

prises, the more important it is for them, generally speaking, to have access to bank-credit in order to exploit quickly every favourable turn of the market. Corporations also intensify this influence on the part of the banks. The banks issue and place shares, control the price-level on the stock-exchange, and finally, as shareholders or representatives of many shareholders, exercise voting rights and dominate the general meetings [of shareholders]. The larger are the industrial enterprises, however, the larger must the bank be in order to work with such enterprises. And thus we see a concentration of banking taking place, which occurs simultaneously with the concentration in industry and eventually reaches far beyond it, so that today six large Berlin banks, each with a capital of more than 100 million marks, are the real rulers of the German economy. *Finance-capital* thus increasingly unites in its own hands the economic power of bourgeois society.[9]

But the larger are the enterprises, the greater are the potential dangers of competition for them. If a factory that is rich in capital and technologically better equipped confronts one that is weaker and more backward, the outcome of the competition is clear, and the larger factory will have no reason to shun the struggle. Indeed, following its victory it will acquire the market of its former competitor. But the situation is different when large enterprises, approximately equal in strength, confront each other. In that case, the result is in doubt and the only certainty is that the struggle will be protracted and extremely costly for all concerned. Thus originates the striving to eliminate competition, to avoid struggle and come to an agreement in order to determine jointly the scale of production, to force up prices and rule the market monopolistically. This striving by large-scale industry is boosted by the large banks because, for instance, a bank that provided credit to a series of ironworks must fear being affected by the damages caused through competitive struggle. It will, therefore, employ its vast influence over the factories in order

9. [Marchlewski took this idea from Hilferding: 'The socializing function of finance capital facilitates enormously the task of overcoming capitalism. Once finance capital has brought the most important branches of production under its control, it is enough for society, through its conscious executive organ – the state conquered by the working class – to seize finance capital in order to gain immediate control of these branches of production.... Even today, taking possession of six large Berlin banks would mean taking possession of the most important spheres of large-scale industry, and would greatly facilitate the initial phases of socialist policy during the transition period, when capitalist accounting might still prove useful.' Hilferding 1981, pp. 367–8.]

to make even potential competitors reach an agreement. Thus, the striving to eliminate competition and to replace it by capitalist monopoly becomes the final result of the capitalist competitive struggle. *Cartels* and *trusts* increasingly rule economic life. The times of free competition are past for the decisive industries within capitalist states. Monopolistic exploitation by capitalist magnates yields huge profits. The concentration of capital is progressing with tremendous rapidity. Three dozen men in the United States dominate the immense production of that gigantic republic; and according to the competent testimony of Rathenau,[10] 300 men, all of whom know each other, are the rulers of European economic life. This rule is concentrated in a small number of organisations. Behind the powerful cartels, which above all supply the means of production of modern society and thus increasingly subject all other branches of industry to their domination, stand the modern large banks; and the chief managers of the large Berlin banks are today those who first and foremost rule German economic life and with it, to a large extent, the German people.

If the 300 capitalist magnates were replaced by representatives of the proletariat, production could be managed without further ado in the interests of the working class rather than of capital, and the transition to socialist organisation of the economy would begin. That is how far capitalist spadework has already advanced even today.

2. *The economic policy of imperialism*

Naturally, the profound economic changes that we have just mentioned have the greatest influence on the economic policy of capitalist states. Above all, they determine the character of modern *commercial policy*. Until the beginning of the 1870s, free-trade policy – which was perfectly suited to old English industries that did not have to fear any competition – seemed to make continuous progress. But the opposition of continental capitalists to free trade, which exposed their still infant and defenceless industries to the much more

10. [Walther Rathenau (1867–1922) was a German industrialist, manager of the Allgemeine Elektrizitäts-Gesellschaft (AEG), writer and politician, who served as Foreign Minister of Germany during the Weimar Republic. Rathenau argued that '300 men, each knowing all the others, together control the economic destiny of the Continent'. This sentence appeared in an article he published in the *Neue Freie Presse* (Vienna) on 25 December 1909. Henderson 1951, p. 98.]

powerful English industry, grew steadily. European industrialists had no intention of bearing the costs of English competition themselves. With the help of protective tariffs, they wanted to shift those costs onto the shoulders of the masses of continental consumers. A tariff-wall would protect backward German industry from its overwhelming rivals until it was strong enough to enter the struggle for the world market without state help. Those were supposed to be educative tariffs, aimed at facilitating the transition-period. The powerful crisis that swept over the capitalist world in 1873 strengthened the protectionist tendency in industry.

The industrialists soon found powerful allies in the *landowners*. Germany turned from a corn-exporting into a corn-importing country; and the overseas competition began that would cause a falling tendency in corn prices for many years to come. From being the most enthusiastic free-traders, large landed proprietors turned into increasingly desperate supporters of protectionism. To this should be added the fiscal interest in developing new sources of income. This transformation took place in 1879, when Bismarck began the so-called national economic policy. Free trade, which, for a while, seemed to conquer the world, suffered a decisive defeat.

The further development of capitalism gradually changed the meaning of industrial tariff-policy. German industry grew much stronger and, from an economic-technical point of view, was perfectly capable of confronting any other industry in the world market. For a while, it seemed as if, for this reason, the protectionist policy would gradually be abandoned and replaced by a policy, if not of totally free trade, then at least of long-term commercial agreements with low tariff-duties. Caprivi became a supporter of this policy, whose principles were reflected in the commercial treaties of 1893.[11]

Yet a growing opposition immediately developed against this policy. Overseas competition had admittedly been blunted, but corn prices remained at a relatively modest level. The reduction of agricultural tariffs would have caused a fall in land-prices, and the landowners felt injury to their main

---

11. [Count Georg Leo von Caprivi (1831–99) was a German major general and statesman, who succeeded Otto von Bismarck as Chancellor of Germany. Caprivi served as German Chancellor from March 1890 to October 1894. Under him, the antisocialist law was abrogated and military service was shortened from three to two years. Favouring industrial over agrarian interests, he negotiated (1892–4) a series of reciprocal trade-agreements to stimulate industrial exports. The agreements reduced duties on agricultural products and aroused agrarian opposition that contributed to his dismissal.]

interest. The raising of agricultural tariffs became the battle-cry by which the large landed proprietors rallied all classes of the countryside around their Agrarian League.[12]

And industry again came to their help. It was precisely the representatives of the strongest and most developed industries that now took the field for high tariffs. Experience had taught them that protective tariffs, by excluding foreign competition, were an excellent means of facilitating cartelisation. Today, cartels can easily adjust the relation between supply and demand in the internal market in such a way that the prices of protected commodities are permanently maintained above the world-market price by approximately the amount of the tariff. Protective tariffs had become superfluous as educative tariffs for industry, which had already been strengthened long ago, but they were turned into *enrichment-tariffs*, the best means of promoting in hothouse-fashion the creation of cartels and of allowing monopolistic industry to collect an indirect tax from all consumers amounting to the height of the tariff on their goods. Such enrichment-tariffs had to unite the cartel-magnates with the agrarian collectors of ground-rent. From this union arose a usury-tariff whose consequences could no longer be concealed due to the enormous rise in the cost of living.

Protectionist policy tore apart what free trade had united. It split the world-market into isolated economic territories and increased the antagonisms resulting from the capitalist expansion-drive. Monopolisation through protective tariffs was too convenient for national capital to restrict its application to the national economic area. The protectionist countries increasingly sought to reserve for themselves pieces of the world market. The strivings of all capitalist countries were thus increasingly aimed at acquiring new colonies and locking them up against foreign competition.[13]

---

12. [The Agrarian League, or Bund der Landwirte, was an extra-parliamentary organisation active in the German empire from February 1893. Formed to combat the free-trade policies initiated in 1892 by Chancellor von Caprivi, it worked for farmers' subsidies, import-tariffs, and minimum prices. The Agrarian League grew from 200,000 members in 1893 to 330,000 in 1913.]

13. [Marchlewski summarises here an idea first advanced by Hilferding in his article 'The Functional Change of Protective Tariffs', published in 1903. Hilferding 1903a.]

3. *The capitalist expansion-drive*

The period of 'Sturm und Drang' that capitalism is going through also means a huge *increase in production,* which requires [new] markets. The following statistics of coal and iron-production from 1890 to 1910 give an idea of that increase.

Coal-production in 1,000 metric tons			
Year	1890	1900	1910
Germany	89,281	149,788	222,302
England	184,529	228,795	268,700
United States	143,127	244,653	455,000

Pig-iron production in 1,000 metric tons			
Year	1890	1900	1910
Germany	4,658	8,521	14,794
England	8,031	9,103	10,547
United States	9,350	14,011	27,737

At the same time, this enormously increasing production means a huge accumulation of wealth in the hands of concentrated large-scale capital, cartels and trusts. However, sales on the domestic market are limited because capital holds the masses of the population in its grip. It seeks to restrict the workers' [consumption] to the necessities of life. A socialist society would immediately employ the huge means of production in order to produce *within* the state the items required by the popular masses. But capitalists prefer to look for new markets, new sales and areas of exploitation abroad in order to sell their products with the highest possible profit.

This expansionist drive has always dominated capitalist policy, but it is now much more intensive. The capitalists are no longer satisfied simply with selling their product – calico, for instance – to the inhabitants of India or South America. They would rather export their commodities as *capital.* They transplant capitalism even to previously closed parts of the world, building mines and factories on the largest scale and equipping them with the most modern means of production. This capitalisation of the whole world provides the necessary markets for the enormously increasing production of the old capitalist states. And, by spreading capitalist production, capital transforms all traditional conditions, destroying backward modes of production, ruining and proletarianising their representatives, completely overturning all social relations and thus creating the economic as well as political conditions for revolutions in all the countries it penetrates. *Capital-exports* have become the most important economic means for the conquest of the world by capital.

4. *The imperialist ideal*

While capital thus strives to turn the whole earth into its field of exploitation and increasingly transforms the world into a single economic territory, protectionist policy simultaneously divides this territory once more into isolated areas whose exploitation should be reserved as the monopoly of particular national capitalist classes. Protectionist economic policy thus increases the antagonisms between states. Since each seeks to exclude the others from the world market, they all try to annex by force as large a share of the world market as possible. Thus, the capitalist expansionist and protectionist policies turn into a single policy of colonial conquest. The outcome of all this is the capitalists' ideal of turning their [colonial] empire into a world empire at the expense of all others, making it an *imperium* so vast that all the economic needs of capital would be satisfied within its boundaries. Since the capitalists, due to their ever-tightening economic and political organisation, dominate state-power ever more absolutely, and since the bureaucracy and the military protect their interests and increase their power through imperialist policy, it is imperialism that increasingly rules over all the capitalist states. The idea of eternal peace, which English free trade once promised to realise throughout the world, is ridiculed, scoffed at and replaced by the glorification of war and violence. The *conquest of colonies* increasingly becomes the substance of foreign policy.

But the goal of foreign policy is no longer to acquire settlement-colonies to which surplus population might flow – the role played, for instance, by the United States for England in the eighteenth century – because a surplus population no longer exists in the advanced industrial states. Capitalist development increasingly brings *demographic growth*, that important drive of cultural progress, to a halt. We are witnessing, in all the industrial states, a rapid diminution in the number of births. Only the decline in mortality figures has so far prevented demographic stagnation in those states, and this at a time when the rapid expansion of production always requires new troops of workers. *Emigration from Germany* has, accordingly, become insignificant. In 1910, some 25,000 people left Germany, while 1.5 million foreigners are brought in yearly by German capital as a cheap labour-force for its exploitation-needs. Emigration has virtually nothing to do with modern colonial policy, as proved by the fact that emigrants take good care to avoid the German colonies. In 1910, for instance, no fewer than 22,773 Germans migrated to the United States. Yet, during the whole of the last decade, exactly 596 Germans went to Asia and Africa! It is therefore an impudent demagogic lie to say that colonial policy provides new homesteads for German workers and farmers. Colonial policy actually pursues completely different and purely capitalist goals.

The great capitalist upswing since the mid-1890s has greatly raised the prices of industrial raw materials, especially metals and cotton; and the cartels and trusts, on the one hand, together with stock-exchange speculation on the other, have increased prices even more. The capitalists seek to develop new sources of supply in the colonies. Their goal is to find states where mineral resources can be turned into the monopoly of large capitalist enterprises or where commercial crops, above all cotton, can be produced for the world-market by the enslaved natives. The watchword is no longer the creation of settlement-colonies but of *exploitation-colonies*.[14] The development of colonies also provides large-scale capital with the required markets for its products. Entrepreneurs build railways, whose returns must be guaranteed by the tax-payers. Ports are constructed, new shipping lines are established and richly subsidised by the state, mines are developed, the lands of the natives are taken away from them in order to set up plantations, and this entire process is accompanied by wild speculation in real estate and on the stock-exchange. The final result is that a small number of magnates of capital dispose of the new riches. But, in order to exploit the colonies as much as possible, capital must rule absolutely. Above all, it must dispose of the lands and labour-power of the natives as freely as possible. For that reason, the natives are robbed of their rights; their land is taken away from them, they are rapidly and suddenly proletarianised and forced to submit defencelessly, as propertyless workers, to the most burdensome terms of capitalist exploitation. And, if they do not

14. [A distinction first advanced in Kautsky 1883, and developed at length in Kautsky 1907b.]

submit willingly – if, driven to desperation, they want to defend themselves – then state-power intervenes and the European workers, as soldiers, must put down the 'rebellion', and as taxpayers they must pay the costs of the glorious colonial wars. These *violent methods* pertain to the essence of colonial policy, which would lose its capitalist meaning without them. The presumption that colonial policy can be pursued but its violent methods can be done away with cannot be taken seriously. It is just as little possible as wanting to do away with the proletariat while preserving capitalism.

The capitalist class of each country seeks to reserve for itself its own colonies and to exclude foreign capitalists from them. The free-trade principles of the open door are increasingly being given up, and colonies are drawn into the area closed off by tariff-walls. Thus, each colonial acquisition by a great power awakens the jealousy and opposition of the others. In that way, colonial policy, which is the necessary result of protectionist tariff-policy, becomes a perpetually effective cause of warlike entanglements between the great capitalist powers.

5. *The imperialist politics of violence*

We have seen how capital-exports became the economic means of conquering the world. Let us now see how politics have been placed at the service of capital.

While bourgeois parties in the developed capitalist nations increasingly join forces against the forward movement of the working class, while they declare ever more loudly their abhorrence of revolution and would like best to blot out from their history-books any remembrance of the bourgeoisie's great revolutionary period, capitalism itself continues to be a great revolutionary [force] and *violence* has once again become the midwife of new developments.

Violence operates in two ways: as revolution and as war. Capitalism penetrates ever more deeply into the old agrarian states of the Orient; it disintegrates the old social relations and creates a modern bourgeois class that becomes the carrier of revolutionary transformations, either by turning against the old state-power as in Japan, Turkey, Persia and China, or by acting as a national movement against foreign rule as in India or Egypt. At the same time, the disturbances that revolution inevitably entails offer to the large capitalist powers the opportunity of exploiting the temporary weakness of those states for pillaging or annexing them outright. Alongside the deep antagonisms within the capitalist world, these revolutionised states thus constitute new *sources of crises* that heighten the war-danger or themselves lead to wars.

Indeed, this period of economic transformations is, at the same time, to an extremely high degree a *period of wars*.

In 1894 the Sino-Japanese War announced to the world the awakening of Asia, showing that capitalism in the Far East, among the despised yellow race, had led to the appearance of a new state, a national state according to the European model, with the technology of European industry, the murderous technology of European weapons and all the exaggerations of European nationalism and chauvinism.

In 1898, the United States of America, the country with the youngest and most concentrated capital, waged its first great colonial war [the Spanish-American War] and deprived Spain of the most valuable parts of its colonial possessions. The occupation of the Philippines turned the United States into an interested party in all decisions concerning the Asian Far East. In diplomatic negotiations, the United States forced England to renounce construction of the Panama Canal; it seized the territory of the isthmus and is now working with feverish zeal to complete the joining of the Atlantic with the Pacific Ocean in order to enable its rapidly growing navy to have a say in all the great decisions in both areas. At the same time, American trust-capital set out to conquer Central and South America economically, crushing any opposition against its interventions by financing 'revolutions' in the reluctant states, which it could then exploit according to its own needs.

The old great power of capitalism, England, followed the example of the youngest capitalist power. In 1899 began the Boer War, which was carried out for the sake of gold and diamond-fields and turned South Africa into an English colony.

The whole of Europe was shaking with the fever of colonial conquest. Japan had revealed not only its own strength but also China's weakness, thus giving birth to the idea of partitioning China. Germany, England, Russia, France and Japan occupied parts of the Chinese kingdom and divided it into the spheres of interest that paved the way for its future partition. Those actions awakened national opposition in China. The Boxer Rebellion[15] pointed out

15. [The Boxer Rebellion (literally 'The Righteous and Harmonious Society Movement') was an anti-imperialist revolt in northern China that took place from November 1899 to September 1901. The Boxers attacked foreigners as well as Christians, who were held responsible for the foreign domination of China. In June 1900,

this danger to the intruders. The infamous repression of the rebellion was then undertaken by the Eight-Nation Alliance.[16] The troops of the European great powers, Japan and the United States marched into Peking led by 'World Marshal' Count Waldersee.[17] Their ravages showed the humiliated Chinese the dangers that threatened them. The reform movement, which strove to follow Japan's example and transform China into a modern military state, grew rapidly and finally turned into *revolution*.[18] European capitalism performed a new revolutionary feat: the oldest and most conservative state in the world, which, for millennia, had experienced almost no development, entered world history and became a new factor in historical progress, including that of the European peoples.

But, in the meantime, the other state of East Asia, Japan, had already decisively intervened in European history. It halted Russia's advance in East Asia in the most violent war of modern times.[19] It defeated the astonished Russian army and destroyed the Russian navy. And the [historical] law that wars are followed by revolutions now became effective in Russia. What the Japanese

---

the Boxers invaded Beijing and killed 230 non-Chinese. Tens of thousands of Chinese Christians, Catholic and Protestant alike, were killed mostly in Shandong and Shanxi Provinces as part of the uprising. The government of Empress Dowager Cixi was helpless as diplomats, foreign civilians, soldiers and some Chinese Christians retreated to the legation quarter and held out for fifty-five days while a multinational coalition rushed 20,000 troops to their rescue. The Chinese government was forced to indemnify the victims and make many additional concessions. Reforms implemented after the crisis of 1900 laid the foundation for the end of the Qing Dynasty and the establishment of the modern Chinese Republic.]

16. [The Eight-Nation Alliance (which included Austria-Hungary, France, Germany, Italy, Japan, Russia, the United Kingdom, and the United States) put down the Boxer Rebellion in China in 1900. The military contingent from the United States was called the China Relief Expedition. The customary designation in Germany is *Hunnenzug*, or the 'Hun campaign'.]

17. [Alfred Graf von Waldersee (1832–1904) was a German general who served as Chief of the Imperial German General Staff from 1888 to 1891. When European troops were dispatched to China to quell the Boxer insurrection in 1900, it was agreed that Count Waldersee should have supreme command of the joint forces as *Weltmarschall* (World-Marshal). However, he arrived at the front too late to lead his troops to the assault of Peking.]

18. [The first Chinese Revolution of 1911 (also known as Xinhai or Shinhai Revolution), began with the Wuchang Uprising on October 10, 1911 and ended with the abdication of Emperor Puyi in 1912. The primary parties to the conflict were the Imperial forces of the Qing Dynasty (1644–1911) and the forces of the Revolutionary Alliance (Tongmenghui). Although the monarchy was briefly restored twice in the course of the revolution, the final outcome was that the Republic of China formally replaced the Qing Dynasty on 12 February 1912.]

19. [The Russo-Japanese War (10 February 1904–5 September 1905).]

war-machine had left in place was now lost in the long and cruel civil war.[20] Russian despotism triumphed once again, but only at the price of the impotence of the country, whose foundations are rotten.

If Japan's victory attested to the awakening of Asia, it also aroused new forces in other nations suffering the inroads of European powers. Repulsed from East Asia, Russia sought to compensate itself where the least opposition was to be expected. Allied with England it began to advance against Turkey. The response was the Turkish Revolution.[21] The Asiatic despotism of Abdul Hamid had proved incapable of offering resistance to the European advances. The army officials, who wanted to strengthen the old [Ottoman] Empire externally, placed themselves at the head of the revolution. The Sultan was compelled to grant a constitution, and was dethroned and imprisoned. And Persia then followed the Turkish example.[22]

6. *England and Germany*

We see that warlike events and revolutionary developments flare up on the periphery of world affairs and approach ever more closely the European centre; and we know that, for years, the great European states have faced the growing strain of the war-threat. The most immediate and powerful cause of this war-threat is the *antagonism between Germany and England*. England, for a long time the absolute ruler of the world market, is, at the same time, the greatest colonial power. Germany, ever since the establishment of the [Second] Empire,[23] has caught up with the English economic lead by giant

20. [The civil war that followed the outbreak of the first Russian Revolution on Bloody Sunday (22 January 1905). For Marxist commentary on the first Russian Revolution see Day and Gaido (eds.) 2009.]

21. [The Young Turk Revolution of 1908 reversed the suspension of the Ottoman parliament by Sultan Abdul Hamid II in 1878, marking the onset of the Second Constitutional Era.]

22. [A reference to the Persian Revolution of 1905–9. Persia was beset by internal political violence and rebellions against the tyrannical rule of Shah Muhammad Ali. Actual warfare broke out in 1908 with a rebellion in the city of Tabriz. The Shah's forces besieged Tabriz, but the rebellion did not end until an intervening Russian army brutally seized the city in March 1909. While this was occurring, other rebel factions marched on Tehran and captured the capital city on 12 July 1909. The Shah abdicated his throne, and his son Ahmad Mirza, an eleven-year-old boy, became the new Shah.]

23. [The Second Reich (German Empire) was formed in 1871 and terminated in 1918. Since 1815, Germany had consisted of 39 states known as the German Confederation. The two largest states were Prussia and the Austro-Hungarian Empire. Immediately

strides; its industry is today second to none, not least due to the excellence of its science and the intelligence of its working class, educated by Social Democracy and awakened to a higher spiritual life. But, as one of the youngest capitalist countries, politically impotent at the time when the decisions over the [division of the] world were made, Germany has no colonial possessions worthy of the name. And Germany, as a colonial power, is outdone not only by England and France but also by smaller states like Belgium, Holland, Portugal and Spain. Yet, we already know that capitalism never pushed more than it does today for the extension of markets, the violent opening-up of foreign territories, their acquisition and annexation.

This striving has dominated German foreign policy ever since Bismarck's downfall.[24] The results up to now have been meagre. Meanwhile, however, Germany has been feverishly busy producing those weapons without which imperialist policy is impossible: in a relatively short span of time, it became the second naval power of the world and set about challenging English hegemony. As the dominant force in foreign policy, the German-English antagonism was increasingly pushed to the foreground by Russia's extreme weakening due to the Russo-Japanese War and the Revolution [of 1905], which eliminated it for a long time as a militarily significant great power. But this circumstance also did away with the old antagonism between England and Russia. As long as Russia was strong, both Germany and England had to be prepared to grant it the final decision in any conflict between them. Indeed, once Russia joined one of the two sides, it decided the struggle and could dictate the peace-terms. That is no longer possible. Russia can conduct its foreign policy only by exploiting the German-English antagonism; and it is forced by geographical circumstances to lean mainly on England, whose navy is of decisive military significance in those regions where Russian expansionism is most active. Alongside Russia, the other old colonial powers, above all France, have also taken England's side. The old Triple Alliance[25] of Germany, Austria-Hungary and Italy, has to face the Triple Entente of England, Russia and France.

---

after France's defeat in the Franco-Prussian War, the Prussian king Wilhelm I was proclaimed Emperor of Germany at the military headquarters in Versailles on 18 January 1871. Bismarck was appointed the new empire's first imperial Chancellor.]

24. [Bismarck resigned at the insistence of German emperor Wilhelm II on 20 March 1890, to be succeeded as Chancellor of Germany and Minister-President of Prussia by Leo von Caprivi.]

25. [The Triple Alliance (*Dreibund*) was a defensive association between the German Reich, Austria-Hungary and Italy. The alliance was formed in 1882, enlarging

Russia and England exploited the Persian Revolution in order to rob the country of its independence and share in its control. Austria proclaimed the annexation of the former Turkish provinces of Bosnia and Herzegovina.[26] The Triple Entente protested and the danger of war became acute, but Russia's military weakness vis-à-vis the superior Austro-German forces prevented its outbreak. The crisis passed away only to be replaced by a new one, the [second] Moroccan Crisis. That conflict, which led to the brink of a world war, ended in a compromise but increased the antagonism between England-France and Germany even further, giving rise to a new acceleration of the arms-race. Its immediate result was the Italian raid on Tripoli.[27] The Italo-Turkish War reopened the Eastern Question with all its dangers because in Tripoli all the rivalries of the great powers run into each other. But Constantinople is one of the most important strategic points. Constantinople is coveted by England and Russia, Thessaloniki (Salonica) by the Austrians, the Albanian coast by the Italians; in Asiatic Turkey, German, English, French and Russian interests collide; and the Balkan states are fighting each other

the former Austro-German Double Alliance (*Zweibund*). It was renewed in 1912 but terminated by Italy in 1915].

26. [The Bosnian Crisis of 1908–9 was caused by the annexation of Bosnia and Herzegovina by Austria-Hungary in October 1908. Article 25 of the Treaty of Berlin (13 July, 1878) gave Austria-Hungary the right to occupy and administer the two provinces of Bosnia and Herzegovina. The annexation of Bosnia became an urgent matter for Austria-Hungary when, in 1908, the Young Turk Revolution convinced many that the Ottoman Empire could regain its former power in the Balkans. When the Austrian foreign minister, Count Alois Lexa von Aehrenthal, announced the annexation, the Serbs were outraged and demanded a Russian intervention, calling for either a return to the *status quo ante* or compensation. By early February 1909, the Serbian army was mobilised. Germany immediately declared its support for any action by Austria-Hungary, while the Serbs asked for support from Russia. Clearly not prepared for a war against both Germany and Austria-Hungary, Russia was forced to abandon its Serbian allies. Without Russian support, the Serbs were forced to agree to the annexation. Austria's annexation of Bosnia and Herzegovina increased tensions amongst the Great Powers and led to international complications, which for several weeks early in 1909 threatened to end with a general European war and ultimately contributed to World War I.]

27. [The Italo-Turkish or Turco-Italian War (also known in Italy as *guerra di Libia* or Libyan War) was fought between the Ottoman Empire and Italy from 29 September 1911 to 18 October 1912. Italy seized the Ottoman provinces of Tripolitania and Cyrenaica, together forming what became known as Libya, as well as the Isle of Rhodes and the Greek-speaking Dodecanese archipelago near Anatolia. Although a minor confrontation, the war was an important precursor of the First World War as it sparked nationalism in the Balkan states. Seeing how easily the Italians had defeated the disorganised Ottomans, the members of the Balkan League attacked the Empire before the war with Italy had ended.]

over the rest of European Turkey until they become themselves the booty of the victorious great powers.

In the Far East, revolutionary China is another source of crises. The European and American banks want to exploit the financial distress of the giant country to subject it to debt-slavery, which can later lead to political interventions. Japan and Russia reached an agreement over the extension of their spheres of influence in China in order to bring the huge territories of Manchuria and Mongolia under their control.

Thus wars and revolutions again have become everyday events in the world, and the main content of bourgeois politics seems to be the preparations for war – for a *world war over global dominance.*

7. *Imperialism and domestic politics*

Foreign policy has become increasingly decisive for the development of our domestic conditions. We have seen how intimately imperialist policy is bound up with the protectionist system (only England constitutes a temporary exception due to specific historical reasons). But protectionism means a *rise in the cost of living* for the working masses, and this at a time when prices for the main foodstuffs are constantly rising in any case. The rapid development of capitalism favoured above all, as we have seen, the highly capitalistic industries that supply means of production. But the development of agriculture did not keep pace with industry. We therefore see in all countries an ever-growing increase in the prices of foodstuffs and industrial raw materials. Overseas competition, which, in the previous period, brought down corn prices, has long ceased to have a deflationary effect. But agrarian tariffs, which exert an intolerable pressure on the standard of living, have remained in place and even increased. At the same time, industrial tariffs have greatly promoted the creation of cartels that exploit the tariffs in order to force up prices, thus joining together industrial and agrarian price-gouging. The protectionist solidarity of interests between big landowners and large industrialists has also united these classes politically, binding them into a common resistance to the proletarian struggle against the rise in the cost of living.

The burdens of protective tariffs are accompanied by the tremendous *burdens of war-preparations* and the *costs of colonial acquisitions*. Since colonial policy is a policy of violence, all capitalist states seek to strengthen their armies as much as possible. The consequence is an unprecedented and continuously accelerating *arms-race*. To the growing expenditures for militarism on land and sea are now added the costs of the air-force with its rapidly growing demands. At the head [of this process] stand England and Germany. Each increase [in military expenditures] by one of them brings about a corresponding increase by the other. It is an endless vicious circle. The arms-race swallows billions and billions. In 1911, Germany alone spent over 1,700 million marks on armaments, if one adds the interest on public debts contracted for that purpose. But this enormous sum is too little according to our government! Amidst cheers and complete lack of criticism, in 1912 the bourgeois parties approved the new military bill that throws 650 million more marks into the jaws of militarism until 1917. And England immediately answered with a preliminary strengthening of its battleship-construction from 16 to 21 new dreadnoughts over the next five years.

The bourgeois writer Fried calculated that, in the decade 1899–1910, Germany's military and naval outlays amounted to 11,867 million marks, i.e., almost 12 billions![28] The annual military expenses of the European states, as supplied by the official military budgets and therefore not counting invisible and indirect outlays, amounted to approximately 9–10 billion marks in 1910. Twenty years ago, they were merely half that sum. Those states spend 40 per cent of their income on militarism, only 5.6 per cent on public education, and only 2.1 per cent on the administration of justice!

No money remains for cultural tasks; social policy stands still; the government declares in the Reichstag that reduction of the retirement-age from 70 to 65, a merely half-adequate provision for the widows and orphans of workers fallen in the battlefields of industry, and for supporting the hungry veterans themselves, is impossible on financial grounds; and the bourgeois parties consider themselves satisfied. The Moloch of militarism devours everything![29]

28. [A reference to Alfred Hermann Fried (1864–1921), an Austrian-Jewish pacifist, publicist, journalist, co-founder of the German peace movement, and winner (with Tobias Asser) of the Nobel Prize for Peace in 1911. The data were probably taken from Fried 1911.]

29. [Moloch: ancient Middle-Eastern deity to whom children were sacrificed. The laws given to Moses by God expressly forbade the Israelites to sacrifice children to Moloch, as the Egyptians and Canaanites did. By extension, a 'Moloch' is something that has the power to exact extreme sacrifice.]

But, since the capitalists rule the state and practise colonial policy in order to increase their profits, constantly increasing the size of armies for that purpose, colonial policy would no longer be profitable for them if they had to pay for it themselves. Therefore, the workers exploited by capital must always be those who pay for armaments and foreign-policy adventures. The billions for the arms-race are not raised by means of property-taxes, not from the rich, but by means of *indirect taxes and tariffs*, by duties on the most necessary commodities consumed by the broad masses – in other words, they are taken out of the pockets of the poor. This has been proved again by the latest financial reforms, which imposed on the working masses a new and enormous burden of almost half a billion marks.

All of these things are inseparably connected: the protectionist system, the rise in the cost of living, colonial policy, the arms-race, the standstill in social policy, the ever-increasing pressure of indirect taxes and the growing danger of war!

8. *Growing contradiction between capital and labour*

The vital interests of the proletariat compel it to take up the fight against this policy with all its power, because the proletariat's economic policy always stands in basic contradiction with the capitalists' policy. The struggle of the wage-workers is, at first, a struggle within the bourgeois social order for a larger share in the new value created by labour. Imperialist policy, however, tends to reduce that share and impede its increase. It strengthens the power of heavy industry, where cartels and trusts prevail. That also means strengthening the employers' organisations against the trade-unions. The unions' struggle and the raising of living standards are made more difficult, and this at a time when inflation reduces the purchasing power of money and makes a rise in wages necessary simply in order to keep pace with the rise in the cost of living. At the same time, the economic power of business, concentrated in the cartels and trusts, dominates the state ever more publicly, subjecting the government completely to its will, hindering social and political progress and placing the whole administration and policy of the state in service of the struggle against the trade-unions and the political organisations of the working class.

In *commercial policy*, the interests of the workers demand, first and foremost, expansion of the *domestic market*. The higher the wages, the larger is the workers' demand for commodities. This demand brings about a rapid expansion of industries producing finished products, which employ a relatively large amount of labour. In that way, the position of the workers in the labour-market is made relatively more favourable, the trade-unions' power grows, and the prospects of victory improve in the struggles to raise wages. But, for the capitalists, that means a fall in their profits, a slowing down in their accumulation of wealth. For that reason, they also seek to expand the market; not, however, the domestic market by means of wage-hikes, but rather foreign markets. Then they do not have to relinquish part of their profits to the working class as wage-increases but can export it abroad as capital. Therefore the capitalists' commercial policy always has in mind foreign markets, while that of the workers focuses on the domestic market and centres above all on *wage-policy*. The capitalists, on the contrary, cling to tariff-policy. If protectionism means a further rise in the cost of living for the workers, for the capitalists it means easier, more rapid and solid cartelisation and exploitation of the masses of domestic consumers through monopoly-prices. The higher the tariff and the larger the area protected by it, the larger will monopoly-profits be, but also the sharper will be the contradiction between the capitalist classes of the different states and the more fervent their strivings to expand their tariff-area by violent methods in order to make competition in the world market more difficult for other capitalists. The protectionist system thus becomes the foundation of imperialist policy, and the struggle over commercial policy acquires a new, momentous significance. It is no longer just a struggle of the working class in defence of free trade and against the rise in prices for foodstuffs, a struggle against the plundering of consumers by the monopoly-profits of large landowners and cartel-magnates. The struggle against protective tariffs is now also a struggle for the preservation of peace. The decision over the future course of commercial policy has thus become, to a large extent, also a decision concerning the question of war or peace.

As in commercial policy, the contradiction between proletarian and capitalist interests stands out ever more acutely [in other fields]. In *taxation-policy*, the proletariat offers an ever-growing resistance to the plundering of the masses by means of indirect taxes, which the propertied classes must take into account. The proletariat also develops a tireless agitation *against the armaments-race*, unmasking national slogans as deceitful phrase-mongering that provides an ideological cover for the great capitalists' profit interests.

The proletariat struggles ever more intensively against absolutism in foreign policy, demanding both the full implementation of democracy and, above all, that *the decision over war and peace be left to the people.*

9. *The struggle against the war-danger*

All bourgeois parties stand today in the camp of imperialism. Not only the Conservatives and National Liberals, who represent the interests of large landed proprietors, great capital and high bureaucracy, but also the Centre and Progressives have given up any movement against colonial policy, against militarism on land and sea. As they fulfill unconditionally the wishes of large-scale capital, they are betraying the interests of their small-peasant and petty-bourgeois voters for whom imperialism only means greater burdens. That is how strong the domination of concentrated capital over all strata of the bourgeoisie and their public representatives has become!

The proletariat, therefore, stands essentially alone in the struggle for the preservation of peace. Not only is the economic and political significance of the proletariat constantly growing but also its military significance, because the proletarian element increasingly predominates in the modern conscript-army. The morale of the army, the enthusiasm with which it goes to war, is significant in a double sense. The army's morale is an essential element for victory. The individual man, his endurance, bravery and willingness to make sacrifices, are increasingly significant in deciding the course of modern war. But these will be all the greater, the more he is convinced of the necessity and justice of the struggle. The judgement of the masses thus becomes increasingly significant. It is ever more difficult to wage war against the will of the masses. That is why they must try to understand the essence of imperialism. If the masses learn to recognise the essence of this policy behind imperialist phraseology and nationalist slogans, if they see through them to the capitalist profit-interests and are conscious of the sacrifices that this policy imposes on the working class in times of peace – and, to an infinitely larger extent, in times of war – they will be immune to all the imperialist wiles, they will remain sober when others are muddled by imperialist drunkenness, and the rulers will be unable to bring forth that war-mood among the people without which they would not dare to ignite a war. And they would be all the more unable to start a war because they would not know how the masses, who want peace, would behave if their rulers were to drive them to a catastrophe.

Let us hear what Bebel said to the ruling classes on this subject during the debate on the Moroccan affair. After showing how the arms-race implies the danger that, at some point, one of the two sides will prefer an end with horror over horror without end, he shouted to the bourgeois world:

> Then the catastrophe will come. The great order to march[30] will be given, sending to the battlefields sixteen to eighteen million men, the flower of European youth, equipped with the best tools for murder and turned against each other as enemies.
>
> But, in my opinion, the great slaughter will lead to a great crash....[31] It will not come because of us [the Social Democrats] but because of you. You are carrying matters to extremes, you are driving us to a catastrophe, and you will live to witness what we have so far seen only on a very small scale.... You will be reimbursed for your expenses and harvest what you have sown. The twilight of the gods of the bourgeois world is coming. Be sure of that: it is in the offing! Today you are about to destroy your own political and social order. And what will be the consequence? Behind this war stand mass bankruptcy, mass misery, mass unemployment, the great famine. [Protests from the Right]. You want to deny that?.... Anyone surveying events objectively cannot deny the veracity of this statement. What has the little Moroccan affair already shown this summer? The well-known run on saving banks, collapse of the stock-exchange, alarm in the banks! That was just a small beginning; as a matter of fact, it was nothing! What will happen when things become really serious? Then things will come to pass that you certainly do not want, but they will necessarily take place, I repeat, through no fault of ours, but because of you. *Discite* [*iusticiam*] *moniti*! ('You have been warned, learn justice!' Virgil, *Aeneid*, VI, 620.)[32]

---

30. [*Generalmarsch*: A German military alarm-signal meaning 'Attention! Assemble at your positions!', 'To the Colours', or 'Get ready', given at the sound of drumbeats rather than bugle-calls.]

31. [*Kladderadatsch*: bang, mess, chaos.]

32. August Bebel: *Rede auf der 201. Sitzung des Deutschen Reichstages, XII. Legislaturperiode. II. Session, gehalten am 9. November 1911*. [August Bebel, Speech at the German parliament, 9 November 1911]. In Reichstag 1911, Band 268, Stenographische Berichte, p. 7730D.

The *fear of a social revolution*, fear of the socialist proletariat, is today the surest guarantee of peace. Without this fear of its heirs, the bourgeois world would have let loose the furies of war long ago.

The most important task of the proletariat is thus to watch over the foreign policy of the bourgeoisie incessantly and, as soon as war-danger threatens to become acute, to evince its will for peace, its consciousness of international solidarity, by means of powerful demonstrations, setting against the bourgeoisie's national disunity its own international unity. At the same time, however, the representatives of the proletariat in parliament must make every possible effort to check absolutism in foreign policy, fearlessly and decisively opposing the nationalist incitement, always supported by the actions of the masses themselves outside parliament.

The proletariat's struggle against imperialist policy proceeds uninterruptedly and permanently. We have seen how the arms-race can become a direct cause of war. The proletariat has always fought against the armament-policy. It has always rejected any increase in the army and navy, demanding transformation of the standing army into a popular militia in order to turn it from a possible means of attack into a pure means of defence, from a means of class-rule into a lever for liberation. The navy has long ago outgrown its role in defence of the coasts and become a means for capitalist colonial conquests. In particular, its constant growth increases the antagonism between England and Germany and constitutes an immediate danger. Therefore we demand an *international agreement for the limitation of naval armaments* as a momentary means of prevention, together with abolition of the barbaric legislation for goods captured at sea,[33] which will add the horrors of famine to the horrors of war. To the ruling classes' demand for a constant increase in armaments, we oppose unremitting agitation to limit their burden and to use the tax-revenue for social and cultural policy. By fighting for these demands, we show the rulers the way out of their war-policy. If they do not follow us, they will answer for the consequences.

By fighting against imperialist policy, we are increasingly opposed to the ruling classes in all fields. We set against their chauvinism the demonstration of international solidarity; against their isolationist and exclusionary policy,

33. [*Seebeuterecht:* the combatants' right to seize foreign ships and goods in an area of naval war.]

the demand for freedom of international trade; and against their policy of colonial conquest and rape, and their flight from socialism into ever-new areas of exploitation, the struggle for the elimination of capitalist exploitation everywhere.

10. *The struggle for power*

The contradiction between the proletariat and bourgeoisie thus grows continuously in the era of imperialism. *Class-contradictions sharpen*, trade-union and political struggles grow in intensity and extent, and the fight widens to include ever more important and momentous decisions. At the same time, capitalist development has reached its highest degree of maturity. Capital centralises all of the weapons at the disposal of society. It organises production in cartels and trusts, unites its power into employers' associations, by means of its organisations rules the political parties as well as the governments, and places state-power at the unconditional service of its exploitative interests at home and its expansionist needs abroad. Thus capital gathers together all the economic powers of modern society – not, however, in the interest of society itself but in order to increase exploitation to a hitherto unknown degree. But the open and obvious character of these circumstances is precisely what makes their continuation impossible. Against the actions of the capitalist class, in which concentration of the means of production has brought about an increasingly growing unification of its will and action, they awaken the actions of the proletariat, which only needs to be conscious of its power in order to become an irresistible force.

The more integrated are the actions of the ruling classes, the more the particular measures are all directed towards one goal: to escape from socialism by fleeing into new areas of exploitation. All the separate political questions are therefore more intimately connected than ever before. The working class must be made aware of this context, in which each specific question is placed, in order to understand that the whole process is at issue and that this phase of capitalism can only end with the conquest of political power by the proletariat.

The struggle against imperialism is thus growing more and more into *a decisive struggle between capital and labour*. The war-danger, the high cost of living and capitalism on the one side, versus peace, abundance for everyone and socialism on the other – that is how the question is posed. History is approaching great decisions. The proletariat must work untiringly in order to fulfill its world-historical tasks, to strengthen the power of its organisations and the clarity of its understanding. Whatever may happen – whether the proletariat's strength enables it to spare humanity the abominations of a world-war, or whether the capitalist world goes down in history as it was born, in blood and violence – the historical hour will find the proletariat ready, and *readiness is everything!*

Chapter Thirty-Six

German Imperialism and the Working Class (March 1912)

Karl Radek

Karl Bernardovich Radek (1885–1939) was born Karl Sobelsohn in Lvov (then in the Polish part of Austria-Hungary) to a Jewish family. He was active in socialist circles from the age of sixteen, joining the Social-Democratic Party of the Kingdom of Poland and Lithuania. In 1904, he moved to Switzerland, but, the following year, he returned to Poland to participate in revolutionary activity in Warsaw. After a brief prison-term, Radek spent the next decade working as a Social-Democratic publicist in both Poland and Germany. Together with Anton Pannekoek, he became one of the two main spokesmen of the Bremen left wing grouped around the *Bremer Bürger-Zeitung*. His criticisms so irritated leading socialists that he was successively expelled from the Polish and the German Social-Democratic Parties. During the First World War, Radek returned to Switzerland, where he became Lenin's main ally in the Zimmerwald Left.

After the overthrow of the Tsar in February 1917, Radek accompanied Lenin in the 'sealed train' across Germany, but was not allowed to enter Russia. He then spent several months in Stockholm organising Bolshevik support among European socialists, and, after the Bolshevik Revolution in October 1917, he moved to Moscow. There, he became responsible for foreign-language propaganda, accompanying Leon Trotsky to Brest-Litovsk although he opposed the treaty and supported the Left-Communist opposition. At the end of 1918, after the collapse of the imperial régime in Germany, Radek returned to Berlin in order to help organise the German Communist Party. Though he counselled against a putsch, the Spartacist uprising of January 1919 led to his incarceration for almost a year.

After returning to Moscow, he was assigned major roles in the Communist International and also became head of the Central-European Section of the Soviet Commissariat of Foreign Affairs. He helped to organise the founding congress of the German Communist Party in December 1918, and, the following year, he was elected to the Bolshevik Party's Central Committee and became the Comintern secretary. However, Grigorii Zinoviev used the collapse of the German Revolution of 1923 to exclude Radek from the Comintern and high party posts. Radek's support for Trotsky's left opposition to Stalin's régime led to his expulsion from the Bolshevik Party in 1927 and subsequent exile to Siberia. After recanting in 1929, he became a fervent Stalinist and a foreign-affairs commentator for *Izvestiya* (1931–6). In 1936, Radek was one of the co-authors of the new Soviet constitution. However, later that year, he was arrested for treason, and, in the so-called Trial of the Seventeen, in January 1937, he was convicted of being a Trotskyist agent and sentenced to ten years of imprisonment. Radek died in a prison-camp sometime in 1939.[1]

Radek's brochure on German imperialism, written in the aftermath of the Second Moroccan Crisis, was 82 pages in length and divided into eight chapters, of which the first two are translated here. The other six dealt with the history of German colonial policy; the transition from a continental to a world foreign policy and the corresponding growth of the German navy; the transformation in world politics brought about by the growing Anglo-German antagonism (which would later lead to the outbreak of the First World War); German interventions in China, Turkey and Morocco; German imperialism and the situation of the working class (especially the influence of imperialism on social reform and democracy); and the relationship between the struggle against the arms-race and the struggle for socialism. In Chapter Five ('Ten Years of German Imperialist Policy'), Radek offered the following definition of imperialism: 'Modern imperialism is not a chase after phantoms, after a purely

1. The standard biography in English is Lerner 1970.

Platonic world rule, but a policy of capitalism in its deepest phase, which seeks spheres of investment for capital threatened by the sinking profit-rate.' See also the definition of imperialism in the last paragraph of this selection.

In his review of Radek's book, Otto Bauer described it as 'a very useful introduction to the questions of foreign policy'.[2] According to Jean-François Fayet, Rosa Luxemburg recommended Radek's book to Kostja Zetkin in a letter sent shortly after its publication.[3] See also the repeated references to it in one of the two main organs of the SPD left wing, the *Bremer Bürger-Zeitung*.[4]

Shortly after publication of his brochure on German imperialism, Radek entered into a polemic with Georg Ledebour, the official speaker of the Reichstag fraction and a prominent member of the Kautskyist Centre, who argued that there was a struggle over foreign policy between different bourgeois strata and that the true interest of capitalism lay in disarmament. Radek rejected Ledebour's characterisation of imperialism as the policy of particular groups of capitalist interests rather than the policy of capitalism as a whole in its mature stage. He argued that the call for 'disarmament' was utopian because support for imperialism among the bourgeoisie was much more widespread than the Reichstag fraction assumed: imperialism was the main manifestation of contemporary capitalism, and imperialism and the arms-race were indissolubly linked with modern capitalism.[5]

* * *

German Imperialism and the Working Class[6]

In an Era of Acute War-Danger

The clang of arms resonates all over the world. Forty years have passed since the Franco-Prussian War brought to an end the wars that marked the formation of national states in Western Europe. Peace, it is said, has characterised

2. Bauer 1912.
3. 'Pour l'essentiel, les vues de Radek sur ces questions étaient partagées par les radicaux, R. Luxemburg recommandait d'ailleurs la lecture de la brochure de Radek sur l'impérialisme. (Lettre de R. Luxemburg à Kostja Zetkin du 31.3.1912. R. Luxemburg, *Gesammelte Briefe*, Bd. 4, p. 191).' Fayet 2004, p. 80, note 82.
4. Anonymous 1912a, 1912b and 1912c.
5. Radek 1911c. Andreucci 1988, pp. 252–3.
6. Radek 1912a.

this period, even if an armed one. Explaining this state of affairs, many bourgeois politicians have gone so far as to assert that war among civilised nations is no longer possible. Actually, the last four decades have been a period of rapid *expansion of the European colonies* and subjugation of entire peoples in various parts of the world. 'The percentage of territory belonging to the European colonial powers, among which we include the United States,' writes the geographer A. Supan,[7] [has grown as follows]:

	1876	1900	Increase or decrease
In Africa	10.8%	90.4%	+ 79.6%
In Polynesia	56.8%	98.9%	+ 42.1%
In Asia	51.5%	56.6%	+ 5.1%

This expansion, which primarily meant *the partitioning of Africa* and *the end of China's seclusion*, took place amidst *uninterrupted colonial wars.* In 1873, the Russians occupied the city of Khiva, and the English the Fiji Islands; in 1874, the Japanese sent an expeditionary force to Formosa [Taiwan]; in 1876, Fergana became Russian; in 1877, Great Britain annexed Transvaal; in 1878–80, the Second Anglo-Afghan War took place; in 1879, Bosnia was occupied; in 1881, Transvaal regained its independence after the First Boer War, and Tunisia became a French protectorate; in 1882, England occupied Egypt; in 1884, German colonial policy officially began and the Sino-French War broke out; in 1885, Upper Burma became English after the Third Burmese War, and the Italians occupied Massawa; in 1889, Rhodesia was founded, etc. – to mention only the main events, which found their most striking expression in the [First] *Sino-Japanese War* of 1894–5, the [Second] *Boer War* of 1899–1902 and the *Russo-Japanese War* of 1904–5. But the public opinion of arrogant capitalist Europe, for which all non-capitalist peoples are just the object of politics – as the brazen Junker Jordan von Kröcher[8] once said of the German working class – was not disturbed by these bloody wars and profound changes because they could

7. Supan 1906, p. 254. [Lenin quoted this statistical table, without mentioning Radek's book, in Lenin 1970, p. 90.]

8. [Jordan von Kröcher (1846–1918) served as President of the Prussian House of Representatives and Privy Council.]

not drag the European nations into battle against each other. This legend of peaceful capitalism was not even destroyed by the fact that the colonial expansion of the capitalist states in Africa and Asia gave rise to *antagonisms between European powers* such as the Anglo-Russian and the Franco-English antagonisms, which could, at one time or other, end in war.

This belief in the indestructible European peace, which appeared to be threatened only by the Franco-German antagonism, blurred any awareness that *Europe has entered into an era of acute war-danger* at the very time when *Germany's turn to imperialism* has manifested itself in the construction of a war-fleet and England, the oldest colonial power, has begun to tremble at the imminent danger from Germany. The *German-English antagonism,* the antagonism between the old, rich capitalist robbers and the young, hungry ones, destroyed in no time the absurd fairy-tale about capitalist pacifism. When Russia's defeat in the war with Japan weakened the Anglo-Russian antagonism in Asia, because it paralysed the Russian thrust [to the East], the German-English antagonism at once came back to the forefront. And, since then, *the war-danger* has not abated for a moment. Wherever a conflagration threatens to break out – whether in Morocco or in Turkey – Germany and England, the two civilised powers, step to the foreground armed to the teeth; and nobody can predict whether the fight of wild Berber tribes against their Sultan (who treats them like old trousers when dealing with foreign countries), or the struggle of the Turkish troops against the Arabs (which should demonstrate the level of Young-Turkish culture through the excellence of Krupp's cannons), will not end in an Anglo-German war. Through an extensive system of alliances, Germany and Great Britain have ensured that that their confrontation will turn into a world war. The German-Austrian-Italian Triple Alliance and the Anglo-French-Russian Triple Entente – those are the camps into which the capitalist world is divided, and any day they can become war-camps. The war-clouds never scatter for long, and, from time to time, a lightning-bolt proves that devastating storms are brewing. Twice already, the *Moroccan conflict* has kept Europe in suspense; the *turmoil in Turkey* has threatened to unleash a world conflagration; and there are, in addition, many other war-centres.

The capitalist world faces these dangers with undisguised apprehension but is unable to ward them off. Like blind men, they draw nearer to the abyss. The *proletariat* looks at these heinous proceedings, whose results will vastly increase its misery and suffering, with growing indignation. But, unlike the bourgeoisie, it will not let things take their course. It has learned to forge its own fate in its struggle against capitalism, and it will also attempt to overcome the war-threat. From its struggle against capitalism, the proletariat knows that one can overpower and control only those elements whose sources and driving forces are known. It therefore seeks first of all to understand the reason for the relentless war-danger. Even the most superficial glance at the history of recent decades tells the workers that *the cause of conflicts* threatening peace has been the *striving to occupy undeveloped countries (colonies)* distant from Europe and inhabited by totally alien peoples. These awakened the appetite of the capitalist states, which were not interested in annexing sections of their own people standing under foreign rule but, rather, in subjugating foreign peoples and turning their free lands into areas where European capitalism could have *carte blanche*. What explains this urge to fight over undeveloped foreign countries, this obsession to turn them into capitalist colonies? The answer to this question will also show why the *proletariat must adopt a distant, indeed a hostile attitude towards these strivings.*

The Nature of Imperialism

1. *Capitalist attempts at obfuscation*

It is clear that this general struggle for colonial possessions, which is being restlessly pursued and poses a constant threat to peace, must have general causes. Capital and its supporters mention a series of such causes: they talk about the *overpopulation* of the old capitalist countries, about the need to secure a supply of *raw materials* without which industry could not exist. And, where these arguments do not catch on, they have recourse to more high-sounding clichés. They speak about the right, indeed the duty of *higher civilisation* to educate the undeveloped countries. It is enough to examine briefly the validity of these arguments to see that they are merely *pseudo-arguments* meant to obfuscate the true causes of the capitalist exploitation-drive....[9]

9. [Radek provides statistics showing that only an insignificant number of German emigrants moved to the German colonies and a similarly small portion of German raw-material imports came from those colonies.]

Even if these two 'justifications' of colonial policy were nothing but mystification, their rebuttal nevertheless required us to go into the underlying facts. The third argument from the proponents of colonial policy – the appeal to the right *of higher civilisation*, which is brought in at particularly solemn moments – can be quite summarily dismissed. Capitalist states are organisations to keep the people down and prevent them from rising to a higher culture. Nobody knows that better than the German working class, which has made every single cultural advance through its struggle against the capitalist bearers of culture; and the workers also know that the culture that German capital will bring to the wild peoples implies exploitation and oppression. Peters, Arenberg, and General von Trotha:[10] these are the carriers of German culture in the colonies. In view of these facts, the appeal of the advocates of colonial policy to the law of higher civilisation sounds like mockery in the ears of workers. With this assertion one might mislead some youngsters, but not the German working class, to whom decades of serious, painful struggle for culture have given much insight into the nature of capitalism. The workers know that, if the capitalists begin to speak about culture, that is a sure sign that they are trying to conceal a particularly profitable business.

The capitalist advocates of colonial policy only obscure its real character. This brief examination of the arguments from proponents of colonial policy in general, and of German colonial policy in particular, as given by bourgeois writers, shows that the roots of colonial policy are not to be found in the *general interests of society and even less in those of the popular masses.* That is precluded by the fact that the carriers of colonial policy are precisely the worst enemies of the working class. It is the manufacturers who wage lockouts,

10. [Karl Peters (1856–1918) was a German explorer in Africa, one of the founders of the German East-African protectorate of Tanganyika, now a part of Tanzania. In 1885, he formed the German East-Africa Company and, six years, later became imperial high commissioner for the Kilimanjaro district. Ultimately, his brutal behaviour against the local population provoked an uprising that cost him his office. Peters has been called 'the first agent of German imperialism'. Adrian Dietrich Lothar von Trotha (1848–1920) was a German military commander who took part in the repression of the Boxer Rebellion in China as Brigade-Commander of the East-Asian Expedition Corps and was later noted for his conduct during the Herero Wars in South-West Africa. As Commander in Chief of German South-West Africa, he issued a *Vernichtungsbefehl*, or extermination-order, against the Hereros, whose population dropped from 80,000 to 15,000. He was also responsible for the killing of approximately 10,000 Nama people. The actions of Trotha have been called 'the first genocide of the twentieth century'.]

the bread-usurers[11] and the bureaucrats who bully the people at every turn, the army that on every occasion clamours for crushing the 'revolutionary canaille' – in short, it is the élites of capitalist society that push most fervently for colonial policy. Are its roots, therefore, not to be found in the interests of these same classes? We will find the answer to this question most easily if we visualise the developmental tendencies of capitalism as it freely unfolds today.

2. *The driving forces of imperialism*

The unprecedented development of capitalism, which, in the second half of the nineteenth century, conquered one country after another in Europe and gradually transformed the United States of America from an agricultural into an industrial country, was based on a development of productive forces whose limits are impossible to predict. One technical invention after another helped put the forces of nature at the service of production. Capitalist industry, equipped with these means, defeated the craftsmen and rural household-workers. It enlisted proletarianised craftsmen into its army of slaves, added the proletarianised peasants, eradicated the remains of natural economy and created an internal market. Capital triumphed. There is no longer any God on earth except capital; and all the old powers make deals with it and serve it.

But it soon became apparent that the altar of the capitalist Baal is perched upon a volcano and that its priests might easily blow up. *The forces of production grow more rapidly than the market*, which must provide customers for the products of capitalist industry so that the surplus-value created by the working class might return as pure gold to the pockets of the high priests of capital – and that is the sole object of capitalist desire. The purchasing power of the workers, who toil for stingy wages, grows very little because the situation of the workers, despite all capitalist blather, is always bad if not totally discomforting. The larger the section of society constituted by the working class, the narrower are the bounds of market-expansion so long as capitalism continues to *develop technology* with no consideration for these needs of capital.

11. [In the electoral campaign of 1903, the SPD raised the slogan 'Down with the bread-usurers (*die Brotwucherer*)' to denounce the adoption of agrarian protectionist tariffs causing a rise in food-prices.]

Before a new invention is properly exploited, a second one appears – and woe betide those capitalists using the old one: they will produce too expensively and sell at a loss. The vastly increased forces of production flood the market with goods that find no buyers. But it is impossible to predict what mass of goods the market can absorb and how much will be produced, because there is no organisation of production, which is conducted in an increasingly haphazard way – the more the better – because given the growing *competition*, production-costs can only be reduced through increased levels of output.

This development leads to *crises*. Production is anarchically conducted, more is produced than the market can absorb, and, therefore, at a certain point, stagnation must begin. Goods find no outlets, their prices fall and credit becomes more expensive. The destruction of immense masses of values paves the way for further development of production. Bankrupted small companies that could not survive the crisis, and vast suffering among the workers who found no work and starved while industry could not find consumers for its goods – all this testifies to the fact that in capitalist society economic development is not controlled by men but by blind forces. The sufferings of the workers have been the last concern of capital. The working class was still weak, unenlightened, unorganised and saw its affliction as a natural event foreordained by God. But the other consequences of crises, which the capitalist class felt in its own pockets, drove it to defend itself. Capital sought to bring about an *organisation of production* in order to prevent overproduction, and, if that did not work, to maintain high prices despite overproduction. It created associations that divided up the market among its individual members, determined price-levels and imposed heavy penalties on any manufacturers daring to sell more cheaply than the others.

But, here, the capitalist class met a serious obstacle. How could the creation of *trusts and cartels* help if foreign capital, due to increasingly cheaper transportation-costs, could penetrate its domain? If foreign capital is able to penetrate the domestic market, the creation of cartels and trusts would only be a means of leaving the domestic market open to import of foreign commodities. Capital therefore cried out for *protective duties* in order to erect a tariff-wall to ensure the territory it exploits – which it lyrically calls the old fatherland – against the irruption of foreign goods. Wherever protective duties were still in place, dating from a time when they were meant to protect less-developed [domestic] industry against competition from stronger foreign industries, the capitalists demanded to keep and raise those duties even though domestic industry was now fully prepared to meet foreign competition. Protective duties now had only one role: to give capital the opportunity of increasing prices at its own discretion. Thus, cartels and trusts led to the imposition and increase of protective tariffs, which, in turn, made possible increased exploitation.

But even this only helped for a time. Technical development and the accumulation of ever-larger capitals pushed for the expansion and broadening of production. What to do with the products? Capital dumped them at cheap prices, sometimes without any profit, in foreign markets. In that way, it was able to reduce production-costs and compensate, through high prices in the domestic market, for the profitless *waste* of a portion of the products in foreign markets. But this policy of the cartels likewise did not always help. Foreign capitalist classes defended themselves using the same means; they too learned to surround themselves with protective tariffs and to squander the products of the workers' sweat in foreign markets. It was necessary to find other ways of securing high profits to the ever-growing capital.

A solution to this problem was found in the *export of capital*. Capitalist magnates lent money to the governments of less-developed, capital-poor countries so that they could create armies, build railways and set up a modern administration after the model of the big states. Russia, the Balkans, the South-American countries, Turkey, China; all of them dug deeply into the pockets of Western-European capital at huge interest-rates, committing themselves to equip their armies and supply their railroads only through their creditors. Exported capital thus returned, in the form of interest-rates and orders for goods, to the pockets of European capital, tremendously expanding its power. Capital turned to the state to represent its interests abroad, safely counting on its help.

The *states* of Western Europe, whose economic life underwent this evolution, did not, in the meantime, remain unchanged: they changed together with capital. Whereas they were previously ruled by big landowners, by dynasties that were at the same time the largest landowners in the country and availed themselves of capital for their own purposes, they are now only servants of the great capital that rules the country. The vast majority of the population is now dependent not on land but on capital. Most of the population works in its factories. The state depends on it because, without its help, the state-machinery cannot move. Technical development, which each year revolutionises the means of production, also dominates development of the *army*, the main instrument of the state's power. The old murder-machines, like any other machine, must therefore quickly be replaced by new, better and more expensive ones, and the competition of the major powers in this area is even greater than that between manufacturers. The costs of equipping a modern army grow continuously, and the army itself is growing at the same pace as the population. Ever since the French Revolution threw mass-armies into the battlefields in order to defend its achievements from feudalism, one state after the other abandoned the system of mercenary armies in favour of a more-or-less consistently implemented system of general conscription.

This change in the character of armies is also accompanied by transformation of the second means of power of the capitalist states: the *bureaucracy*. The state now reaches into every corner of business life. It has become active and diverse; all its parts interlock with each other, calling for regulation. The tasks of the bureaucracy are growing enormously. If it is not equal to them, if the bureaucracy does not control the whole of social life, it loses its power.

Thus society pushes in the direction of ever-faster growth while the army of the bureaucracy swells continually.

The maintenance-costs of the army and the bureaucracy become increasingly unaffordable. Although the modern state seeks to tax everything and the tax-burden grows more and more, it must still resort to *loans*. The *national debt* grows and with it the dependence of the governments on capital, which buys their bonds.

Profitable as these bonds are for capital, it gets even more out of them than just the profit: it also wins power over the state. No matter how feudal the government may still be, or how much contempt the higher bureaucracy may feel for bourgeois upstarts, it cannot manage without capital and must therefore be subservient to them. And the capitalists are not embarrassed to make use of government power: they employ it to hold down the working class, and they consider its most important task to be that of guarding their interests against the numerous weaker bourgeois strata.

As enforcer of the will of capital inside its boundaries, the capitalist *state* also becomes *the guardian of capitalist interests outwardly*. We have already described those interests. What responsibilities do the West-European capitalist states assume vis-à-vis those capitalist interests abroad? They depend on the nature of the borrowing state and the conditions in which its subjugation by foreign capital occurred. First, the undeveloped state that is borrowing money must regard it as a sacred duty to pay the interest to foreign capital on time even if all its obligations towards its own subjects are left unfulfilled. It must not only pay them on time, but also procure the goods it needs from them. And, if it wants foreign capital to be happy, it also has to squander its country's riches at ridiculous prices. But the government of a half-developed country cannot always fulfill these obligations: the growing fiscal pressure, and the exploitation by strangers who crawl throughout the country like vermin, sucking its juices, set in motion the masses of the native population who previously lived quietly; they resist their own government by refusing to pay taxes and, finally, through armed rebellion. At that point, European capital becomes alarmed; it demands that its government protect its economic interests in the foreign country and occupy it.

Here is another situation. Capital has nestled in a less-developed country. It has lent money to its government on usurious terms and now feels at home there. With that money, the government succeeded in increasing its instruments of power and securing its position vis-à-vis the population. It now wants to exploit that situation. It has taken a look at the world and knows what usurious interest it pays to foreign capital. In order to lighten its burden somewhat, it begins to make difficulties for foreign capital and, by copying its methods, tries to obtain better conditions through a declaration of bankruptcy. Foreign capital, seething with indignation, calls on its own government to put pressure on the treacherous barbarians and teach them that civilisation consists primarily in the observation of commitments towards foreign capital.

Here is yet another case. Foreign capital is a general term; in reality, it is *national* groups of Western-European capitalists that do business with the governments of undeveloped countries. German, English, and French capitalists want to place their money in a country craving for capital. They compete with each other and try to eliminate their rivals. Each national group of capitalists demands that its government support their own offer with all its power. The government must convey to the borrowing government how unpleasant it would be if the offer from the group of capitalists in question were not accepted; and it does this by drawing attention to its military forces and the services they could render to the borrowing government against other powers.

In all these cases, the government of a capitalist country must represent the interests of its own capitalists against the borrowing state. In one case the matter ends in diplomatic pressure; in another, with a military demonstration; in yet another, with occupation of the country and its annexation by the creditor-country. Thus, the export of capital to foreign, undeveloped countries – so-called peaceful expansion – often leads to their occupation. Through golden snares, they are drawn nearer to the creditor-state and exploited; and, if they rise against the overwhelming burden and are defeated, their independence is taken away from them and they are turned into *colonies*. The capitalists then assign to their own government the role that the foreign government could not or did not want to fulfill.

But that is not the only way colonies are formed. Often, capital must make the government of its own country first occupy a patch of vacant land before it can be invested there. Capital-export means the construction of ports, cities and railways in an undeveloped country. But, if the country is at such a low level of development that there is absolutely no state-organisation, or if it is so weak that it cannot be trusted with the protection of borrowed capital, the capitalists must first carry over there a separate state-organisation; that is to say, they must subjugate the population and appropriate its land. That is how, for example, all the German colonies originated.[12]

Now we can see just what forces stand behind the conquest of colonies, that is to say, imperialist policy. But, in order to grasp its nature better, it is also necessary to investigate more closely the interests that lie behind this policy and the classes that support it.

3. *Imperialism and the bourgeoisie*

We have shown that the interests of cartelised, trustified capital, as well as those of the banks exporting capital to foreign countries, are behind the creation of colonies. Regarded more closely, those are primarily the interests of the iron-magnates and the large banks. Since the capital lent to the

12. Of course, history does not develop in every capitalist country in the same way, but the object of this presentation is not to describe the emergence of imperialist policy in a particular country – we will describe the history of German imperialism in detail later – but the analysis of the general driving forces of imperialism. They are best described by Rudolf Hilferding in his *Finance Capital* (Hilferding 1910a, pp. 374–477 [of the German edition]), Otto Bauer in *The Question of Nationalities and Social Democracy* (Bauer 2000, pp. 355–93 [of the English edition]), Parvus in *Colonial Policy and the Breakup* (Parvus 1907), and Kautsky in *Socialism and Colonial Policy* (Kautsky 1907b).

governments of undeveloped countries is spent mainly to buy guns and rifles, to construct fortifications, railways and so on, it also supplies orders to the magnates of metallurgical plants, cannon-factories, etc. Since the capitalist state whose capitalists export capital must always be ready to come to their succour, it must also have a strong *navy.* That again provides employment to the same branches of industry, creating an ever-increasing goods market that is all the more remunerative for them because they can dictate its prices. The governments of countries subjugated by foreign capital must accept the prices of orders as determined by those industries – otherwise they would not get the loans. The home-government also pays what those industries demand for their ships and guns. If they were to turn to factories elsewhere, capital would sound the alarm, arguing that they were endangering the country's security. To set up competing companies is not easy, given the enormous capital needed, and [for the governments] to produce for themselves all the things necessary for militarism and the naval arms-race is not so easy either, because the prices of the products of bureaucratic enterprises are even higher than Krupp's. *Thus heavy industry, iron-producers, arms-manufacturers and shipping companies are the strongest group of beneficiaries of imperialist policy.* Billions of marks are thrown into their huge enterprises. But that is not the only reason for their strength, because, despite their size, they are only a section of German capital. [In addition to their size] they are consolidated and have long-lasting relationships with the government through the provisioning of the army.

To this should be added the fact that, behind them, stands *finance-capital,* to which the government is deeply indebted due to its public-debt policy. But finance-capital also backs them because it is deeply involved itself in heavy industry, whose scope is too large to be the property of individuals. The capital requirements of heavy industry grow so rapidly, so enormously, that they cannot be met by the surplus-value generated by its own workers. It must have a continuously growing capital-inflow, and the large banks take care of that. They are, therefore, interested in the development of heavy industry. Thus, finance-capital's own interests also make it one of the most avid supporters of imperialism. First, imperialist policy compels the capitalist state to become ever more indebted, which is very welcome for the big banks; and, second, they are the brokers of capital-exports to foreign countries. What a handsome profit they make out of it can be shown by a few examples.

Theodor Rothstein used the following example to assess the loans of the last Egyptian Khedive[13] that later led to the occupation of Egypt by Great Britain.[14] The loan of 1873 was allegedly 32 million pounds sterling (640 million marks) at 7 per cent interest and 1 per cent amortisation. The banks that placed this loan gave the Khedive only 20.7 million pounds and kept the remainder, roughly 12 million, as a guarantee against risk. Not satisfied with this, they also forced him to accept in payment 9 million in notes of his own floating debt at a rate of 93 pounds sterling, although the loan was meant precisely to pay back this debt and the banks had bought the notes at a rate of 65 pounds sterling.

To take an example from more recent times, the banks that financed the Baghdad Railway earned 100 million francs for their intermediation and 180 million francs in savings on excessive construction-costs that had been charged to Turkey. That is how the business looked according to English calculations; according to the director of Deutsche Bank, the 'savings' in construction-costs were admittedly smaller, but the brokers' profit was nevertheless estimated at 138 million francs.[15] From the loan of 62 million franks contracted by the Sultan of Morocco in 1909, the banks pocketed 14 million; from the loans amounting to 110 million francs, which they had placed in previous years, they 'earned' from their intermediation 71 francs for every 500-francs bond.

When one considers how great the power of the large banks is, and how much the bourgeois press and parties depend on them, one can realise the force with which they advocate imperialist interests and try to turn them into the general interests of capitalism and, indeed, of the nation as a whole. But, behind imperialist policy, there are interests even vaster than heavy industry and finance-capital. When finance-capital equips the armies of barbaric states or builds railways in Anatolia and China, it weaves around these companies, primarily to the benefit of heavy industry, a wreath of business from which various branches of manufacturing industry profit. It tears part of the indigenous population away from work on the land and makes them build roads;

13. ['Khedive' was the title granted in 1867 by the Ottoman sultan to the hereditary pasha of Egypt. It was replaced by the title sultan in 1914, when Egypt became a British protectorate.]
14. Rothstein 1910, p. 40.
15. *The Nineteenth Century*, June 1909.

to be sure, it pays them meagre wages, but, with that money, the natives buy European goods. Merchants follow the railways and buy from the farmers their products, dragging them too into the chaos of commodity-exchange. Thus the circle of industrial parties who are interested in imperialism expands.

But imperialist policy finds supporters in even broader circles. It finds its most avid defenders in *military circles,* to whom it opens broader fields of activity. That attracts the *small gentry,* who were not originally sympathetic towards colonial policy, because it was pursued primarily in the interest of big business. But noble sons, as army-officers, are interested in imperialist policy. The hope of working their way up with even a small capital in the colonies, where the state has dumped millions, beckons the younger sons of the lesser gentry. At home, they would only divide up the family-estate and could not make ends meet with the little paternal rat-shop.

This exhausts the circle of parties directly interested in colonial policy. The *wider circles of manufacturing industries and trade,* working for the internal market or drawing their profits from exchange with foreign capitalist countries, have no interest in it. Their numbers are far greater than those in the sections of industry working for the colonies and uncivilised countries. Imperialist policy hampers their development because it perpetuates tariff-protection, increases the military burden, and, time and again, upsets the world market by the threat of war.

But they are not capable of resisting imperialist policy, because it seems to them to be the policy that will correspond to their interests *in the future.* Today, five-sixths of German exports go to developed capitalist countries. But all strata of the bourgeoisie are asking: What will the next day bring? All countries are developing their own industry; will they not provide them with ever-diminishing markets? Even if the colonial lands are today so little developed, is it not imperative to develop them so that they will later become a ready market for domestic industry? Of course, the bourgeoisie will not incur costs today out of deference to its future interests, but these considerations are sufficient to make it sympathetic towards colonial policy – all the more so since the colonial burdens are for the most part not borne by them. The popular masses cover most of the budget of the capitalist states through indirect taxes.

And, finally, how can the bourgeoisie manage without the colonial dream; what can it set against the popular masses' ever-louder calls for socialism?

Some decades ago, it could still disregard socialism and ridicule it as a utopia. What can the bourgeoisie set against the proletariat today – when the socialisation of work through the progressive domination of industry by finance-capital, and the elimination of individual entrepreneurs and their displacement by impersonal corporations, point to the development of production under social management, i.e. to socialism, and when the ever-growing power of the working class also proves that the forces that can take up this task are mature? Is there any other excuse for the bourgeoisie but the fact that it still faces the great historical task of introducing capitalism, with its wonders of technology, into the uncivilised countries? How can the bourgeoisie reply to the proletariat if it points out that the narrowing of markets will confront the old capitalist countries with crises and shocks in which the workers, tormented by misery, will implement a different organisation of production? It has no other refuge except belief in the viability of the colonies. Consequently, although broad circles of the bourgeoisie may derive no direct benefit from the colonies, and even if imperialist policy actually causes them difficulties, they will still tow behind it.

For the *educated classes*, who have no share in production and live on crumbs falling from the bourgeoisie's table, imperialism is also the only possible ideology, if they are forced by the impact of important political events to leave the quiet corners of their indifference and intervene in politics. Adoration of the ruthless and strong personality: that is the most common world-view among these circles that can only make their mark through personal efficiency. Where else, however, does bourgeois 'personality' find a more ruthless expression today than in the colonies? And, if grey bourgeois life disgusts the intellectual, where does he see people who do not shrink from adventures and who live life 'to the full', regardless of the customs, laws and hypocrisy of the homeland? In the colonies! Thus imperialism captures one bourgeois stratum after another; it fastens them to its wagon and celebrates its triumphal procession throughout the world.

From the countries of developed capitalism – from England, France and Germany – imperialism penetrates into countries where capitalism is weak, where there is still room for its further development, and wins hearts there as well. Italy, Austria and even sick Spain see how the old capitalist countries are taking possession of one piece of Asia and Africa after another. Soon, there will be nothing left to steal. If they console themselves with the idea that, for decades, they will have their own issues to deal with, will they not have to face later the same difficulties that are at this stage threatening to bar the way of the old capitalist countries? The imperialist fever is seizing them as well and making them take upon themselves burdens under which they will surely collapse.

Thus we see in imperialism a policy corresponding to the interests of modern heavy industry and a section of the manufacturing industry as well as of finance-capital; a policy that appears to capital as the only salvation from the difficulties threatened by its own further development and one that attracts the educated strata of the bourgeoisie as the only 'total' world-outlook. *Imperialist policy is not associated with the interests of the people, but with those of capital in its last stage of development.*

Chapter Thirty-Seven

'Our Struggle against Imperialism' (May 1912)

Karl Radek

This article, written against the background of the Second Moroccan Crisis, is a polemic against Karl Kautsky's theory of imperialism as advanced in his two May Day articles of 1911 and 1912[1] and in his essay 'World Politics, World War and Social Democracy', published in August 1911 and included in this volume. Kautsky believed that imperialism only directly benefited a small clique of major capitalists but was clearly not in the interest of most of the German bourgeoisie: 'colonial policy and naval construction,' he wrote, '...are actually detrimental to large numbers of the possessing classes'. Kautsky hoped that broad sections of the bourgeoisie would be led by their own self-interest to join with workers in opposing the 'small minority of officers, public officials, armour-plate manufacturers, suppliers and speculators' who profited personally from arms expenditures and imperial conquests.

In 'Our Broadsheet on Morocco', also included in this volume, Rosa Luxemburg responded to Kautsky by denying that any 'harmony of interests' was possible between the proletariat and 'the mass of the propertied classes' – a prospect that she considered

1. Kautsky 1911a. Kautsky 1912c.

'comical' in its simplicity and alarming in its implication that war might be averted merely by enlightening 'everyone' with clever 'antiwar slogans'.

In March 1912, Karl Radek turned to these same questions in his pamphlet *German Imperialism and the Working Class*, the preceding document in this collection. He agreed with Kautsky that finance-capital, together with 'heavy industry, iron producers, arms-manufacturers and shipping companies are the strongest group of beneficiaries of imperialist policy'. He also agreed that

> The wider circles of manufacturing industries and trade, working for the internal market or drawing their profits from exchange with foreign capitalist countries, have no interest in it.... Imperialist policy hampers their development because it perpetuates tariff-protection, increases the military burden and time and again upsets the world market by the threat of war.

But, on the main issue in dispute, Radek clearly sided with Luxemburg when he added that these bourgeois groups were 'not capable of resisting imperialist policy because it seems to them to be the policy that will correspond to their interests in the future'. This was a theme Radek picked up from Kautsky himself. In 'World Politics, World War and Social Democracy', Kautsky had written that 'everything we do is determined more by the future than by the present, more by our expectations and fears than by our current circumstances. That applies not just to Social Democrats: Liberals and Conservatives also have their own "state of the future" that they describe in the most glowing terms. And that "state of the future" is precisely the colonies.' Radek turned this observation back on Kautsky by commenting that the real future of capitalism necessarily involved an intensified struggle for markets, with the consequence that all sections of the capitalist class must ultimately subscribe to the 'colonial dream'. Without the fantasies of imperial conquest, he demanded, how could the ruling class possibly respond to 'ever-louder calls for socialism' from the popular masses?

In the article translated below, Radek makes these same arguments even more forcefully. He insists that imperialism is not a contingent policy of the bourgeoisie, a matter of choice, but rather '*the* policy of capitalism in the age of finance-capital': 'It promises to the bourgeoisie room for continued development of the productive forces, thus overcoming the threat of social revolution. It opens up, in the era of growth of the material power and spiritual decay of the bourgeoisie, the prospect of a display of power that fills it with rapturous delight. There is no other policy but imperialist policy for the capitalism of our days.' Denying any possibility of a multi-class alliance against imperialism, still less an inter-imperialist agreement for peaceful division of the world, Radek shared Luxemburg's concern to emphasise the immediate and urgent necessity of socialist revolution as the only conceivable response by the working class.[2] The threat of imperialist war made 'all or nothing' the only practical options for Social Democracy. 'The choice,' Radek wrote at the end of this essay, 'should be easy!'

* * *

'Our Struggle against Imperialism'[3]

Imperialism as the policy of capitalism

The foundation of all the differences in our relationship to imperialism is *the question of its character*. What is imperialism, and what is its relationship to capitalist development in general and to world-economic expansion in particular? Is it *the* foreign policy of crashing capitalism,[4] or simply *one* of the forms still possible for capitalist display of power? The importance of these questions has become clear to the German proletariat only gradually in recent years. For a long time, imperialism seemed to it to be a legitimate policy of *British capital*, one that was imposed on Great Britain by geographical conditions and became, as it were, a national peculiarity.

2. [Although Radek does not mention Kautsky by name, probably because his article was meant for publication in *Die Neue Zeit*, there is clearly no doubt that Kautsky was the principal addressee. For an excellent introduction to the debate on disarmament in the SPD in 1911–12, see the classic article by Ratz 1966; also Radek 1912a. For a selection from the first, theoretical part see the previous item in this anthology. Radek's article 'Our Struggle against Imperialism' was written after the foregoing book and prior to Kautsky's polemics with Paul Lensch on the militia and disarmament. For that debate, see Kautsky 1912c, Paul Lensch 1912a, Kautsky 1912d, and Lensch 1912b. For an English version of the last item see this volume, Chapter 38.]

3. Radek 1912b.

4. [A phrase used by Franz Mehring in 1900 to describe the new imperialist turn in world politics. He argued that, with the demise of Manchesterism in the late nineteenth century, the bourgeoisie 'erased from its banner free trade and peace and wrote instead monopoly and war. The world policy of large-scale industry turned into the world policy of crashing capitalism.' Mehring 1900, p. 427. 'Die Weltpolitik des krachenden Kapitalismus' is also the title of Section VI of that brochure, pp. 428–32.]

Since English world policy boasted of such 'successes' as the burgeoning, self-governing states of Canada, Australia and New Zealand, people tried to defend even the English exploitation of India against the 'doctrinaire' condemnation of a Hyndman; and, even if the Boer War showed the robber's face of English imperialism, it was later concealed by the concessions England made to the defeated in granting them self-government. *French* imperialism was only regarded from a special angle, as a product of the obsession to compensate for the defeat of the year 1871 by means of 'glorious' feats on colonial terrain. And, when *German* foreign policy gradually began to turn from a continental into a world policy, when its main means of power, the navy, began to expand, this most important process in the history of the new German Reich seemed to be more *the product of a bizarre Caesarist delusion than a historical need* to which we must oppose the higher need of socialism, although it is vital to study and understand it if the fight against it is to be properly conducted.

But, when the 'insanity' became a system, when the German Empire stumbled from one 'adventure' to the other, when it began to devour billions and give rise to war-threats, the common foundations of the whole imperialist policy of capitalism became clear to the Party, and even five years ago its main features were properly recognised by Kautsky and Parvus. But, until now, we have lacked not only a through knowledge of the developmental trends of German imperialism but also a *consistent application of the analysis of the driving forces of imperialism* (as put forward by Parvus and Kautsky in their commendable, if unevenly worked out, brochures on colonial policy and then deepened by Hilferding and Otto Bauer[5]) *in the daily agitation of the Party*, in its statements on concrete questions of imperialism.[6]

The theorists of Marxism depicted imperialism as *the* policy of capitalism in the age of finance-capital. They described the overseas expansion of capital as a result of its escape from the declining profit-rate in the countries of developed capitalism, and they depicted imperialism as a consequence of this development that is just as necessary as cartels and the policy of tariff-

5. [*Hilferding* 1910a, pp. 374–477 (of the German edition), Bauer 2000, pp. 355–93 (of the English edition), Parvus 1907 and Kautsky 1907b.]

6. Whoever bothers to browse through the speeches of our Reichstag deputies on the foreign-ministry budget as well as on the military and naval budgets of the last twenty years, will see that we are actually dealing here with the stages of development of the knowledge of imperialism in the Party. The study of the treatment of these questions by our main journals will only confirm this judgement.

protection that serves them. The development of overseas capitalist expansion led to colonial policy, to the striving for overseas areas virtually reserved for national capital and legally bound to the mother-country – i.e., to imperialist policy. *All overseas policy now serves imperialism.* Even if national capital cannot turn all the overseas territories it economically 'develops' into colonial possessions, and even if that is not always its goal – in the field of world policy, as elsewhere, capitalist states must concentrate on certain goals and cannot grab every desirable object – economic expansion in all countries that could eventually become colonies serves imperialist policy. Through the expansion of its economic influence in various places of the earth that it does not intend to occupy, the imperialist state is economically strengthened to pursue its main goals. And, as the masses of profit and interest accruing to capital increase, the imperialist state acquires economic resources with which to impose its will in the targeted areas, thus holding all the cards to enforce its goals. The economic arrangement in Morocco secured millions from the exploitation of Moroccan farmers to German finance-capital; but, even more, it gave the German government the possibility of demanding compensation from France in Congo, which opened up the whole Central-African question.

The penetration of German capital into Persia, although only in its infancy, gave Germany the means to do away with the obstacles posed by Russia to the Baghdad Railway and even led to the loosening of relations between Russia and Britain, which strengthened the general objectives of German world policy. The connection between capital's 'peaceful' overseas policy and its eventually violent overseas policy – that is to say, imperialism – is even greater. In certain circumstances, a country's goal of peaceful expansion can turn violent under the pressure of circumstances: riots by the 'peacefully' exploited population, or a collision with other powers that want to win the area in contention for their own exclusive expansion through less peaceful means, can, under certain circumstances, easily turn peaceful expansion into a warlike one, even if a given state had not previously chosen a conscious path of world policy. That was one of the risks of German interference in the Moroccan affair, although it is our firm conviction (confirmed by the new, penetrating studies by bourgeois world politicians)[7] that the German government had no warlike intentions at the outset.

7. Oncken 1911.

In many cases, however, peaceful expansion is first possible as a result of violent expansion. What is the main purpose of overseas expansion? Certainly not the export of products of daily use, textiles, etc., whose demand is very small in colonial lands and can only be developed if a state-power is located on the spot, giving trade the required security. Such power does not exist in undeveloped areas, and therefore cannot pave the way for the peaceful economic expansion of the capitalist countries through regular legal relationships or transport routes. This makes the construction of railways and other means of communication by finance-capital in the undeveloped countries a precondition for 'peaceful' development, which again requires the occupation of these areas. And the export of capital for the construction of means of communication, which follows the grafting of the state-mechanism onto backward countries, is the main element of 'peaceful' economic expansion.

Given all that, one must vigorously reject the view, widespread even among some radicals, that *Social Democracy is a firm opponent of colonial policy but that it advocates the peaceful overseas expansion of Germany.* This view is totally wrong because it overlooks the link between peaceful and violent expansion. One could let it quietly disappear as a vestige of the days when free-trade views influenced the intellectual life of Social Democracy if it did not have very significant consequences for our agitation: namely, that *it breaks the backbone of every consistent struggle against colonial policy and imperialism.*

The foundation of this view is the assumption that overseas expansion is in the interest of the working class because it creates new jobs. If this view is recognised as correct by Social Democracy, the imperialist press only has to prove – which it can do very successfully – that the time for peaceful overseas expansion in colonial areas is gone, and that whoever regards economic expansion overseas as an interest of the working class must also stand for the means of securing its development, that is to say, for the navy and imperialism in general. Someone regarding peaceful expansion as an interest of the working class therefore loses all ground in the struggle against imperialism. But if, at the same time, he wants to retain a negative attitude toward imperialism, he is then left with a single alternative: *he must not deal with imperialist policy as the foreign policy of crashing capitalism but, rather, try to prove that another foreign policy is possible for capitalism, one that is also in the interest of bourgeois society.* The implication is that only lack of understanding by the masses of the propertied classes prevents them from realising this, and this lack of understanding is exploited by a small clique of self-seeking interested parties who mislead the masses of the bourgeoisie.

This kind of treatment of imperialism, which also has some representatives in the camp of German Marxism, drives our knowledge of imperialism back by decades by *taking as the point of departure for the analysis not imperialism as it actually is, but a totally different world policy, namely, that of the long-vanished era of English industrial capital*, whose theoretical expression came in the writings of the English free-trade economists. They pointed out that colonial markets were captured by the quality of products rather than by cannons, and that any colonial policy was therefore evil. It was only necessary to tear down the Chinese walls and leave the rest to the penetrating power of the capitalist economic system. But, leaving aside the fact that this theoretical propaganda never led to the abandonment of a single colony, this view was based on the dominance of English industry and the belief in the saving effect of free competition.

In 1774, the well-known English writer Josiah Tucker justified the opinion favourable to the [independence of the North-American] colonies in the following characteristic words:

> The colonies, we know by experience, will trade with any people, even with their bitterest enemies...provided they shall find it their interest so to do. Why then should any man suppose that the same self-interest will not induce them to trade with us?....Granting, therefore, that North America was to become independent of us, and we of them, the question now before us will turn on this single point: can the colonists, in a general way, trade with any other European state to greater advantage than they can with Great Britain? If they can, they certainly will; but if they cannot, we shall still retain their custom, notwithstanding we have parted with every claim of authority and jurisdiction over them....[As regards] the native commodities and merchandise of North America, which are the most saleable at an European market...there is hardly one of these articles, for which an American could get so good a price anywhere else, as he can in Great Britain and Ireland....Let us now consider their imports....It is evident, that the colonies could not purchase such goods at a cheaper rate at any other European market....The second objection against giving up the colonies is that such a measure would greatly decrease our shipping and navigation, and consequently diminish the breed of sailors. But this objection has been fully obviated already: for if

> we shall not lose our trade, at least in any important degree, even with the Northern colonies...then it follows, that neither the quantity of shipping, nor the breed of sailors, can suffer any considerable diminution.[8]

Much has changed since then. No single national bourgeoisie has a monopoly of the world market. A terrible battle rages over the world market, demanding such a rapid development of the productive forces that it threatens to turn the capitalist world upside down. The watchword of capital is no longer free competition but monopolies, including monopolisation of foreign markets through the creation of colonies. Indeed, even if the principle of the open door and equal tariff-treatment for all goods should prevail in these colonies – which is often necessary due to the colony's finances or international treaties – the possession of political power gives the bourgeoisie of the country owning the colony the required advantage over its competitors. The common language with the colonial authorities, their connections with the national capital, the financial dependence on the mother-country – all this turns the colony into an area for monopolistic exploitation by the colonising country.

Whoever thinks it possible to recommend the world policy of English capital at the beginning of the nineteenth century to the monopolistic capital of our era, will be totally unable to understand and successfully fight against imperialist policy.

The belief in the possibility of a policy different from the imperialist world-policy of finance-capital leads to further mistakes. From it follows the view that imperialist affairs should be presented, in the agitation against imperialism, as products of the intrigues of a small clique, against which the broad strata of the bourgeoisie can take a sharp stand. Since they do not do so, the attitude of the bourgeoisie on imperialist questions is represented as a comedy of errors. The result of such an approach for the policy of our party is that it is unable to appreciate coolly and correctly the causes of the imperialist turnabout in bourgeois strata, which leads to a whole set of fallacies, particularly on the question of the fight against imperialism, to which we shall later return at length.[9]

---

8. Zimmermann 1905, p. 41. [Quoting Tucker 1776, pp. 203–4, 206, 209.]
9. [Radek 1912c.]

In order for our attitude against imperialism to acquire an unshakeable foundation, it is necessary to eradicate from the intellectual life of the Party *the remnants of old ideologies* that once had a partially realistic basis but now are misleading because they no longer correspond to the facts.

Imperialism is *the only possible world policy of the present capitalist era.* It admittedly benefits a narrow layer of leading capitalist circles, the banks and heavy industry, but, behind it, stand the widest circles of the bourgeoisie because it opens up prospects for them that, even if unrealisable, have an insuperable force for the bourgeoisie. It augurs the creation of monopoly markets in which the bourgeoisie would be free from the worries of the world market. It promises to the bourgeoisie room for continued development of the productive forces, thus overcoming the threat of social revolution. It opens up, in the era of growth of the material power and spiritual decay of the bourgeoisie, the prospect of a display of power that fills it with rapturous delight. There is no other policy but imperialist policy for the capitalism of our days.

Means in the struggle against imperialism

The above-mentioned differences in the treatment of imperialism lead to very significant *differences in how one views the struggle against imperialism.* Whoever does not see in imperialism the policy of capitalism but only the policy of capitalist cliques, which anti-imperialist tendencies within the bourgeoisie can balance, or at least oppose with some prospect of success, will entertain the hope that the proletariat, together with the anti-imperialist bourgeois strata, will be able to remove imperialism's most poisonous fangs. This hope seems to be confirmed by facts from time to time. In Spain, the petty bourgeoisie took part in the proletarian uprising against the colonial adventure,[10] and, in England, it stands for mitigation of the Anglo-German antagonism. Whoever

10. [*Riffabenteuer*: It is not clear to which event Radek is referring. The Rif is a region of north Morocco stretching from Cape Spartel and Tangiers in the west to the Moulouya River in the east, and from the Strait of Gibraltar in the north to the river of Ouargha in the south. By the Treaty of Fez (30 March 1912), Sultan Abdelhafid gave up the sovereignty of Morocco to the French, making the country a protectorate. Spain gained possession of the lands around Melilla and Ceuta in Northern Morocco, which became known as El Protectorado de Marruecos (1912–56). The Rif War of 1920, fought by Spain and France against the Moroccan Rif and J'bala tribes, led to creation of the Republic of the Rif in September 1921. It was dissolved by Spanish and French forces on 27 May 1926.]

looks only at the surface of events can see in these occurrences signs of a growing bourgeois opposition to imperialism. But a real rebellion of the petty bourgeoisie against imperialism, such as in Spain, is only possible in totally undeveloped capitalist countries where imperialism has not yet coalesced with the interests or aspirations of other bourgeois strata and really is just an adventure of a small court-clique.

Where the élite of the bourgeoisie is interested in imperialist business, where the banks dominate the press (even in economically relatively backward countries, standing only at the threshold of the transition from an agrarian to an industrial state, such as Austria, Japan and Italy), there is no notable bourgeois opposition to imperialism. There, the bourgeoisie and petty bourgeoisie join the imperialist wagon and believe that they are thus championing their own future interests, preventing the old capitalist countries from completely dividing up the world among themselves. The annexation of Bosnia and Herzegovina awakened no anti-imperialist opposition among the petty bourgeoisie although it brought Austria to the brink of war and badly damaged its finances. The same happened in Italy. A big defeat such as the [First] Italo-Abyssinian War[11] usually produces a state of despondency, but, a few years later, imperialist ideology again dominated Italian public opinion. Perhaps the aftermath of the Tripolitan adventure[12] will again lead to disillusionment among the petty bourgeoisie, but that would clearly have no influence on the Tripolitan booty that is temporarily shut under lock and key. And, by the time Italy gathers forces for new adventures, this despondency will also have disappeared.

11. [The First Italo-Abyssinian War (also referred to as the First Italo-Ethiopian War) was fought between Italy and Ethiopia in 1895–6. It was one of the very few instances of successful armed African resistance to European colonialism in the nineteenth century. Italy was forced to recognise the independence of Ethiopia in the Treaty of Addis Ababa signed in October 1896.]

12. [The Tripolitan War or Italo-Turkish War (known in Italian as guerra di Libia or Libyan War) was fought between the Ottoman Empire and Italy from 29 September 1911, to 18 October 1912. Italy seized the Ottoman provinces of Tripolitania and Cyrenaica, together forming what became known as Libya, as well as the Isle of Rhodes and the Greek-speaking Dodecanese archipelago near Anatolia. Although minor, the war was an important precursor of the First World War as it sparked nationalism in the Balkan states. Seeing how easily the Italians had defeated the disorganised Ottomans, the members of the Balkan League attacked the Empire before the war with Italy had ended.]

What about the supposedly anti-imperialist bourgeois movement in England? We leave aside its weakness. Recently, the *Daily News* rightly asked: how can anti-imperialist articles and speeches by left-wing MPs help if they are followed by imperialist deeds? It is a big mistake to see in the 'German-friendly' behaviour of the English petty bourgeoisie and part of English commercial capital – note the attitude of *The Economist* – any opposition to British imperialism. It is a movement for the preservation of British world domination with cheaper methods, because the large naval expenditures are a heavy financial burden on the petty bourgeoisie. The cry for 'Understanding with Germany!' therefore does not mean 'Down with Imperialism!' but, rather, securing British imperialism against power-shifts favourable to German imperialism. And, finally, to assess the attitude of the large parties of the bourgeoisie and petty bourgeoisie towards imperialism, German Social Democracy must first of all consider its own experience. The complete alignment of all the German bourgeois parties in the imperialist camp during the last five years, and especially during the Second Moroccan Crisis, must dispose of all speculations concerning a bourgeois opposition to imperialism.

But the hope for a bourgeois opposition to imperialism is not the only consequence of this underestimation of imperialism or even its most important one. Whoever does not regard imperialism in its connection with the cartelisation of industry and the protective tariff-policy, i.e., as a necessary result of the last phase of capitalist development, will easily succumb to the temptation of *underestimating imperialist antagonisms*. If imperialist interests are not seen as *the* interests of the bourgeoisie but merely of particular cliques, the hope arises that the warring imperialist camps could be forced by the pressure of the proletarian-bourgeois opposition to make mutual concessions and reach a compromise. This hope is all the greater because, first, the governments as a whole represent the general bourgeois interests against the special interests of the cliques, and second, because they must fear the masses' reaction to an imperialist collision.

This view, of course, has a legitimate core: where no major economic interests of capital are at stake, and when the general world-political objectives of a state promote momentary compromise, the crisis does not end in a collision but in haggling. Naturally, one cannot doubt the possibility of such compromises. Only two things are questionable about them: first, *whether one can deduce from these compromises a trend towards the mitigation of imperialist antagonisms*, and second, *what attitude the proletariat should assume towards this trend as well as towards particular instances of imperialist haggling*. If one studies the business of European finance in China and Turkey during the last few years – the story of the latest Turkish-French loan and of the international loan currently being negotiated for China can be regarded as textbook-cases – two facts are clear: the agreement of international finance on a joint course of action is very difficult, first because it is difficult to dissuade particular national financial groups from trying their luck against other national groups in order to associate for a joint international foray, and, second, because it is very difficult to balance the interests of different national groups. The distribution of the spoils takes place according to power relations that are neither easy to determine nor immutable. *For that reason* – and this is the second fact of the matter – *a union of national capitalist groups in some overseas financial businesses is absolutely no incentive to reduce armaments and mitigate imperialist trends.* Each national capitalist group is eventually ready to assert itself against the others based on the power of its own state.

Even if doubts were factually raised about these developmental trends, the fact that large sections of the Party fail to keep a distance from imperialist agreements, seeing them as a welcome result of our struggle against imperialism – indeed, as the beginning of a convergence of peoples – shows a total lack of careful analysis on the question of our attitude toward imperialism. Even if such compromise-agreements were international and did not result in new groupings of great powers, i.e., in the replacement of old antagonisms by new ones – as has always been the case – that would not be the result we are striving for. An international agreement of imperialist powers, naturally, could not bring about anti-imperialist results; it would end in the partition of the earth as has already happened several times. Such a situation, which would open up free space for colonial activities to countries so far blessed with few colonies, cannot, precisely for that reason, be for us a goal of the proletarian struggle, because we are principled opponents of colonial policy. But the question looks even worse if one does not deal with it in the vacuous realm of abstraction but on the ground of reality and in light of the geographical, economic and political factors deciding the course of world-politics. The world is very unevenly distributed among the great powers. A table compiled by G. Hildebrand concerning the [demographic and territorial] ratios between the metropolises and the colonies shows that very clearly:

	Census-year	Inhabitants per square kilometres of the mother-country	Ratio of colonial territory to mother-country
Belgium	1910	255.2	80.9:1
Netherlands	1909	177.0	61.84:1
Portugal	1900	58.5	22.58:1
France	1906	73.8	12.86:1
England	1910	145.0	99.39:1
Germany	1910	120.0	4.91:1
Austria-Hungary	1910	75.8	–
Italy	1910	121.0	1.71:1

The disadvantaged imperialist states can gain free space for their economic expansion only *at the expense of third parties.* If that happens through show-downs between the imperialist powers, it will clearly result in new antagonisms that would be more acute than the current ones. But, even if an agreement is reached, for instance, between England and Germany on the Belgian and Portuguese colonies, ending in a monetary compensation for the states being robbed, in the long run, that would introduce an *element of unrest* in world politics: a mad arms-race would become the watchword of the weakest powers and, in their wake, of the stronger ones, because nobody would feel safe from a new 'compromise-agreement' concluded at their expense. *Not only new colonial burdens but also new military burdens would be the result of such an agreement.* For that reason, the only possible attitude of Social Democracy is *to unmask the anti-popular goals of these agreements, pointing out to the working class that it has nothing to expect from them and that its only task is to wage a resolute struggle against the entire international policy of imperialism.*

It has often been argued against this position that we cannot cross our arms in face of the steadily worsening German-English antagonism; that we must try to reduce it and eliminate from it the danger of armed confrontation. Whoever, starting from this assumption, supports, even if only in principle, the 'compromise-agreements' of the imperialist states, arrives at a completely different goal from the one he originally intended, because our inhibiting effect on imperialist schemes grows in proportion to the suspicion felt by the popular masses against imperialist policies and their leaders, i.e., in proportion to the anti-imperialist mood and action of the working class. Only fear of the proletariat increases the caution of the government in its advocacy of imperialist interests. But what can weaken the active force of the working class more than the hope – and, as we have seen, a totally unfounded one to boot – for agreements between imperialist powers? What can lull to sleep the workers' sharp antagonism towards imperialism better than a tactic that boils down to weakening the struggle against new colonial acquisitions out of consideration for the alleged abatement of both imperialist antagonisms and the arms-race that is to be achieved by colonial haggling?

We pose the question of our relationship to the imperialist agreements in general terms and decline at present to offer a concrete description of the current phase of the German-English antagonism, the role of the armaments question in it and the treatment of these issues by our press. Our present goal is to identify the main standpoints from which proletarian tactics in the struggle against imperialism can be established.

Because imperialism is the policy of capital in our day, one that has swept up all the bourgeois strata in the developed capitalist countries and is ever creating new antagonisms between the states, *a permanent mitigation of the imperialist danger is impossible*. Current attempts to mitigate it, as proposed by the major powers, bring about the purely imperialist results of shifts in colonial possessions among the imperialist countries – which, arising out of power-shifts, lead to ever-increasing imperialist displays of power. In view of this fact, the task of Social Democracy cannot be simply to apply ointment on the wounds inflicted by imperialism but, rather, to wage a principled struggle against imperialism, rejecting and fighting its combinations.

Socialism versus imperialism

The struggle against imperialist adventures is gathering strength in the whole proletarian world. In Germany, during the [Second] Moroccan Crisis, it reached an extent that until recently nobody could have expected. The very successful meetings organised by Social Democracy showed that imperialist agitation had not succeeded in hiding the goals of capitalist imperialism from the masses and falsely presenting them as national goals. Whoever had the opportunity of speaking on German world policy during the electoral campaign, even in small towns, must have noticed with the greatest joy a lack of nationalist emotions in the working masses. This fact makes it unnecessary to go specifically into the *question of the limits of our struggle against imperialism*. What matters is the constant agitation that widens and deepens the gap between imperialism and the working class and shows the objective contradiction between imperialism and the interests of the working class. From these facts, it follows that in the grave situation into which, by hook or crook, imperialism will drive us, it will not find the working class on its side.

Most of the errors undermining the struggle against imperialism, even among its principled opponents, stem from the *nature of German imperialism*. The geographical position of Germany meant that German imperialism had to be strongly anchored in continental policy. It had to take into account the fact that every major political decision can cast the dice on the continent, and that its diplomatic deployment must therefore always begin with creation of a favourable political constellation on the continent. It awakened in the German bourgeoisie, finally, the urge to unite continental and world politics by simultaneously expanding the army and the navy. The contradiction between both tendencies in German policy has not been completely eradicated even today, but, in the past, this world-political tendency had to pave its own way very laboriously. It was fought against by the Junkers, who looked upon it suspiciously as an effect of the industrialisation of Germany, and it awakened the envy of the army-officers, who are a branch of the tree of Junkerdom. The liberal bourgeoisie were also no friends of world policy. Long after Germany's commercial policy had become protectionist, on the issues of world policy the liberals in the National Liberal camp – witness Bamberger's attitude towards colonial policy[13] – adhered to free-trade views on the superfluity of world policy.

In view of the cold shoulder given to German imperialism by the bourgeoisie, how could it be regarded by representatives of the working class as anything but an exotic plant, in the struggle against which they could count upon allies [among other classes]? And the fact that this struggle was undertaken

13. Interesting material on this issue, if not very profound, can be found in the well-documented work of Dr. Kurt Herrfurth, *Fürst Bismarck und die Kolonialpolitik* (Herrfurth 1900).

[Ludwig Bamberger (1823–99) was a German politician, economist, banker and journalist. An ardent liberal, he took part in the Revolution of 1848 and was forced to live in exile until 1866. After being granted an amnesty he was elected to the Reichstag. As a member of the Reichstag (1871–93), he was chiefly responsible for adoption of the gold-standard by Germany and for the founding of the Reichsbank. He worked for the unification of Germany, and, as a leader of the National Liberals, he supported Otto von Bismarck until he was alienated by the Chancellor's turn to protectionism.]

on a modest scale and not waged forcefully on the basis of principles must also be ascribed to a large extent to the character of German imperialism. The long years of total *morass in German colonial policy* led to anything but a principled struggle against imperialism as the last refuge of capital before socialism. It was much easier to fight against it with the figures of colonial trade and the colonial budget, a struggle in which one could also count upon support from a large part of the bourgeois press.

The development of German imperialism affected our struggle against it much like the morass in German colonial policy and the bourgeoisie's colonial weariness. Now, after twenty years of imperialist policy, one can, on the basis of study, clearly recognise its guidelines.[14] But they are not the product of an effort consciously made from the beginning by the German government. The imperialist course underwent many fluctuations; it was tugged in all directions by various influences, until it stabilised somewhere. These errors and confusions gave the impression of a zigzag-course; they were sharply attacked from the bourgeois side. And, although the bourgeois criticism of German foreign policy exhibited even less the signs of a carefully thought-out tendency, and even more the character of a zigzag-course than official policy, one that ultimately, under the pressure of objective conditions, found the right path – from the imperialist point of view! – this bourgeois discontent with the first steps of imperialism aroused hopes in the bourgeoisie of pushing Social Democracy away from the path of a principled struggle against imperialism as capitalist policy and instead into a struggle against imperialism as *bad* capitalist policy.

The rapid development of German imperialism, which concealed its 'normal' developmental tendencies, also resulted in an aberration of tactics that we have not yet mentioned. Precisely because the goals of the imperialist policies of other countries were clearly drawn out, while German imperialist policy seemed to float in the air, in the battle against German imperialism its absurdity was often set against the logical character and relative merit of English and French imperialism. As a consequence, not only did the struggle on the basis of principle suffer, but we also revealed our weakness to our oppo-

14. I tried to describe them in my brochure *German Imperialism and the Working Class*, Bremen: *Bremer Bürgerzeitung* Publishers, 1912. [Radek 1912a. See this volume, Chapter 36.]

nents and made more difficult the fight of our sister-parties abroad against their own imperialism, something that can be attested by documents.

If the source of a number of shortcomings in our struggle against imperialism is to be sought in the nature of German imperialism, the cause of other errors lies in *the intellectual life of the Party, which did not keep pace with the tempo of capitalist development.* While this stormy development prepared Germany's soil for socialism, ripening the material conditions for the social revolution, this maturity of the material structure did not correspond with the spread of socialist education among the masses, who did not yet realise that imperialism is the last card of capitalism. Not only the broad masses – those beyond the influence of Social Democracy, those lacking faith in their own power, groaning under the yoke of capitalism and still knowing nothing of socialism – but even broad strata of Social Democracy take the appearances of imperialism as proof that socialism is still a matter for a very distant future. The fact that socialism can only triumph as a movement of the vast majority of the people closes their eyes to a second fact: that a major part of the working class can get rid of their indifference, their distrust in their own power, and become socialist only in the process of the struggle for power by the Social-Democratic workers, and that, therefore, the road to power and the struggle for power must not begin only after the overwhelming majority gathers under the banner of Social Democracy.

The lack of understanding that, with the level and severity of class-contradictions currently existing in Germany, the era of mass-struggles has already begun, and that the possibility of imperialist conflicts, as well as of economic and political conflicts between the forces of reaction and the working class, can set the ball rolling at any moment, had serious consequences for our struggle against imperialism. *Because socialism is not a 'current' issue for wide circles of the Party, it is not deemed a concrete answer to the imperialist questions.* Socialism is not set as a rallying cry against the imperialist war-cry, but, rather, answers are sought in terms of *Realpolitik*. People do not care about the fact that these are totally fantastic answers as well as purely bourgeois ones, or that they are advocating purely imperialist combinations such as an 'English-German agreement', etc. They have the advantage of remaining in the framework of capitalism, and those who prove that this 'advantage' will be outweighed by 'disadvantages', that these measures do not curb but rather promote imperialism, are accused of advocating the policy of 'all or nothing' rejected by the Party long ago.

They forget that *the alternative of all or nothing – of socialism or the raging of the imperialist furies – is not an alternative of watchwords that one poses when favourably disposed to 'anarcho-syndicalism' and laughs at if one is a Realpolitiker. It is an objective alternative posed by capitalism.* Capitalism plays *va banque*, and it cannot be deterred from playing this risky game by good advice, because capitalism is driven to do so by its whole situation. If it does not want to allow the free development of social forces, that is to say, of socialism, it must attempt to fetter them through syndicates, trusts, protective tariffs and colonies, i.e., through imperialism. In doing so, capitalism creates antagonisms that can blow it to pieces. Since it cannot go back, only one thing remains for us: to strengthen our struggle against imperialism by struggling for *democracy*, and to prepare ourselves, through agitation and action against imperialism, for the moment when, after imperialism is knocked down by the explosion, we will be able to break its neck.

The aversion to the policy of 'pure negation' in the question of imperialism draws strength in radical party circles from two sources. The first is the tradition of *Marxist foreign policy;* the second is an analogy with our *reformist activity* in domestic questions. It has often been objected that the fathers of scientific socialism always sought concrete solutions to foreign-policy issues; that they took a position for or against Italy, for this or that solution to the Oriental question. This objection, however, ignores the fact that the conditions in which our old masters formed their opinions have changed in every respect. The working class, at that time, hardly existed as a class that was conscious of its special historical tasks; and the opinions of Marx, Engels or Lassalle on issues of foreign policy should not, in any case, determine the strategy of proletarian action. They were written to show bourgeois democracy the direction in which it should influence the course of events. The works of our old masters, written for that purpose, were often published anonymously in bourgeois journals. And the subject of their opinion was completely different. In the era of struggles for the creation of national states in Central and Southern Europe, the question was not the subjugation of other peoples, as it is now in the imperialist countries, or burdening the working class and creating the possibility of temporarily hindering the free development of the productive forces. On the contrary, the question was one of creating the terrain for the struggle for socialism. And it is questionable whether the proletariat would have actually implemented the foreign policy advocated by Marx if it had then been an independent social force, because then it would not have been necessary to fulfill a bourgeois task such as creating the terrain for the development of the proletariat. That foreign policy, therefore, undoubtedly bears no relation to the tasks now facing the proletariat of the developed capitalist countries. As interesting as Marx's foreign-policy views are for historical research, under no circumstances can they serve as a guide for our position on imperialism.

The analogy with the tactics of Social Democracy on domestic issues is even less conclusive than the reference to Marx; it is, rather, a hindrance to the development of proletarian tactics on the question of foreign policy. We fight for reforms in the area of domestic politics, but only insofar as they are feasible within the framework of capitalism. We have always rejected the fight for unrealisable reforms even if they were momentarily very effective for agitation. Neither the 'right to work' nor a general state guarantee for the minimum wage were advocated by Social Democracy, because it regarded these reforms as incompatible with the existence of capitalism. If you want to be secure against unemployment and poverty, fight capitalism: that was the response of Social Democracy to the magical recipes of social quacks who wanted to heal the incurable wounds of capitalism. Imperialism is an incurable disease of capitalism, threatening the world with general infirmity. References to other curable diseases cannot be regarded as valid arguments against those who declare with regard to imperialism: *Ignis et ferrum sanat!* [*Iron and fire will be the cure!*][15]

The test by the coming test

The German government has once again approached the German nation with enormous *armaments proposals* that today require half a billion of new spending and tomorrow will require half a billion of new revenue and bring international antagonisms to a head. It is unnecessary to insist that an action must be undertaken against this gigantic new thrust of German imperialism. How it will be launched must be decided upon by the responsible party bodies. We

15. [A paraphrase of Hippocrates's dictum: *Quae medicamenta non sanat, ferrum sanat. Quae ferrum non sanat, ignis sanat!*: What medicine cannot cure, the iron will; what the iron cannot cure, fire will!]

only wish to show by this practical example what *content* the action can have, depending on whether uniform, properly thought-out tactics are pursued or whether we let our opinion be influenced by the intellectual remnants of a bygone era.

In the first case, we show the masses the goals of imperialism and ask them: Will you endure new burdens and new dangers for the sake of these capitalist idols? We show them the consequences of this imperialist policy and appeal to their desire for liberation, strengthening their faith in themselves. In the second case, we try to prove to the masses that this new thrust of German imperialism was unnecessary, even from a bourgeois standpoint, and that bourgeois Germany can get on well with England by means of an agreement. In this case, we not only run the risk of the imperialists replying to us, rightly from their point of view, that the shortest path to an agreement with England passes through an increase in armaments ('with the tip of the spear one takes the gift', as the *Song of Hildebrand* says),[16] but we will also tie our hands in the principled agitation against colonial policy, even though the main goal of the new arms-outlays is to clear the way for it. In the first case, we are clear for action; in the second, we get entangled in a maze of contradictions, forcing ourselves – we, the party of *Realpolitik* – to close our eyes to the real situation and to enter the struggle with a broken spear and under a foreign banner.

The choice should be easy!

16. [*The Song of Hildebrand* (line 37) in Wood (ed.) 1914, p. 5.]

Chapter Thirty-Eight

'Militia and Disarmament' (August 1912)

Paul Lensch

In 1912 the author of this article, Paul Lensch (1873–1926), was one of the main anti-revisionist spokesmen of the Left, whose positions he had defended at party conferences in Essen (1907), Jena (1911) and Chemnitz (1912). From 1908 to 1913, Lensch served as chief editor of the *Leipziger Volkszeitung*, and in 1912 he was elected to the German Reichstag for the SPD. He opposed war-credits in October 1914 but later changed his view. In 1915, the Lensch-Cunow-Haenisch group was formed with the purpose of endorsing German imperialism on Marxist grounds, especially through their organ *Die Glocke* ('The Bell'), edited by Parvus. As an Anglophobe, Lensch regarded Germany as the 'revolutionary' side in the conflict, with England as the 'counter-revolutionary'.

When the SPD split in October 1917, Lensch became one of the journalistic spokesmen of the SPD-majority grouped around Friedrich Ebert. In November 1918, he played an important role as a contact-man between the Council of People's Representatives and the military leadership. Lensch then withdrew from party politics and, in 1919, received a professorship of economics at the University of Berlin through his friend, the Prussian Minister of

Culture Konrad Haenisch. He also worked as a foreign-policy correspondent for the *Deutsche Allgemeine Zeitung*, a journal belonging to the concern of Hugo Stinnes. In 1922, Lensch left the SPD and became increasingly associated with conservative opponents of Social Democracy until his death in 1926.[1]

The article translated here dates from Lensch's radical early years, when he challenged Karl Kautsky for proposing disarmament agreements as the appropriate tactical response to imperialism. On 29 March 1909, the SPD Reichstag fraction submitted a resolution calling for an international agreement to limit naval armaments. The resolution was a response to Germany's rejection of informal disarmament initiatives by the British government. It referred to decisions of the Hague conferences of 1899 and 1907, which had been approved by the German government, and called upon Germany to take the necessary steps 'in order to bring about an international understanding of the great powers for the mutual limitation of naval armaments'.[2] Almost two years later, on 30 March 1911, the Reichstag fraction widened that demand into a proposal for a general limitation of armaments.[3] Both resolutions were rejected by the bourgeois majority in the Reichstag.

By this time, Karl Kautsky, who, as early as 1898, had called for the standing army to be replaced by a people's militia – he then ridiculed disarmament as nothing more than '*reduction of the standing army* to dimensions that will still enable [governments] to hold down their own people'– revised his own position and sought to justify the course taken by SPD Reichstag deputies.[4] In the dispute that followed, Kautsky's main opponents were Lensch, as chief editor of the *Leipziger Volkszeitung*, together with Anton Pannekoek and Karl Radek, both representatives of the Bremen left wing grouped around the *Bremer Bürger-Zeitung*. Lensch opened the quarrel with an article describing the disarmament motion as a utopia that was unrealisable within the framework of capitalism.[5] This was the first in a long series of articles by Lensch, Radek and Pannekoek.[6] Rosa Luxemburg also became involved in 1911 with her

1. Ascher 1961, Sigel 1976, Lensch 1918.
2. Reichstag 1909, XII. Legislatursperiode, I. Session, Bd. 236 (29 March 1909), p. 7822A (for Ledebour's speech see pp. 7818A–7825C). See also Ledebour 1909.
3. Reichstag 1911, XII. Legislatursperiode, II. Session, Bd. 266 (30 March 1911), p. 5982B (for Scheidemann's speech see pp. 5978C–5983D).
4. Kautsky 1898c, p. 743.
5. Lensch 1911. See also Radek 1911a.
6. Radek 1911a, Pannekoek 1911, Radek 1911b, and Radek 1911c.

article on 'Peace Utopias', which we have included in this volume.[7] In resisting his critics, Kautsky was supported by Georg Ledebour, who approved of both the Reichstag fraction and the disarmament slogan.[8]

Following Kautsky's May Day article in 1912,[9] Lensch condemned support for disarmament as a mere 'improvisation' with no foundation in theory. He summarised as follows:

> The idea of a limitation of armaments is foreign to our programme as well as to our theoretical literature. Up to now, it was considered a reactionary swindle or ridiculous pacifist babbling. It sprang up among us simply because of a parliamentary improvisation arising from the agitation needs of our Reichstag fraction. The first, and so far the only, attempt to harmonise this improvisation with the fundamental views of scientific socialism was put forward in Kautsky's May Day article.[10]

To emphasise Kautsky's inconsistency, Lensch highlighted the following excerpt from the closing chapter of Kautsky's book *The Road to Power*:

> So long as world policy continues, the madness of the arms-race will accelerate until complete exhaustion is reached. Imperialism, however, as we have already seen, is the single hope, the single ideal for the future that still beckons present-day society. Otherwise, there is only one alternative: socialism. Consequently, this madness will increase until the proletariat gains the power to determine the policy of the state, to overthrow the policy of imperialism and substitute the policy of socialism.[11]

Lensch claimed that Kautsky's analogy between the building of economic cartels in the domestic market and the creation of political cartels in world-politics, for the pacific division of colonial spoils between the great imperialist powers, was both formal and unrealistic. He emphasised that, under imperialist conditions, disarmament must remain impossible because imperialism, for economic reasons (especially the need to export surplus-capital), could not help but pursue the colonial policy that gives birth to militarism.

---

7. Kautsky 1911a. See Luxemburg 1911a, English version in this vol., Chapter 29.
8. Ledebour 1911 and 1912.
9. Kautsky 1912c.
10. Lensch 1912a, p. 313.
11. Kautsky 1909b, p. 98.

It is of some historical interest to add that, while Lenin took no part in the debate on centrism within the SPD, according to Trotsky he privately tended to side with Kautsky. According to Trotsky's testimony:

> In Rosa Luxemburg's struggle against Kautsky, especially in 1910–14, an important place was occupied by the questions of war, militarism, and pacifism. Kautsky defended the reformist programme: limitations of armaments, international court, etc. Rosa Luxemburg fought decisively against this programme as illusory. On this question, Lenin was in some doubt, but at a certain period he stood closer to Kautsky than to Rosa Luxemburg. From conversations at the time with Lenin, I recall that the following argument of Kautsky made a great impression upon him: just as in domestic questions, reforms are products of the revolutionary class-struggle, so in international relationships it is possible to fight for and to gain certain guarantees ('reforms') by means of the international class-struggle. Lenin considered it entirely possible to support this position of Kautsky, provided that he, after the polemic with Rosa Luxemburg, turned upon the right-wingers (Noske and Co.).[12]

Lenin's respect for Kautsky, and his detachment from the internal SPD-debate, were the main reasons why the capitulation of German Social Democracy on 4 August 1914, took him totally by surprise – he actually believed that the issue of the *Vorwärts* that carried the patriotic declaration of the Social-Democratic Reichstag fraction was a forgery by the German general staff. After the outbreak of the First World War, however, Lenin broke with Kautsky and ended up supporting Lensch on countless occasions, most notably in his 1916 article on 'The "Disarmament" Slogan'.[13]

* * *

'Militia and Disarmament'[14]

I would like to make just a few comments on the campaign that Comrade Kautsky launched against his own past in Nos. 39 and 40 of *Die Neue Zeit*.[15]

---

12. Trotsky 1932.
13. Lenin 1916f.
14. Lensch 1912b.
15. [Kautsky 1912d.]

First, I would like to rectify briefly one of Kautsky's assertions, by means of which he hopes to be able to dismiss the contradiction that I pointed out between his current position on the question of disarmament and his previous one. He writes:

> Lensch can provide the exact date when the despicable improvisation of my break with party traditions took place: 'We can indicate even the day when the idea of a limitation of armaments made its entry in our ranks. It was not "always" there but exactly since the 29th of March 1909.' In order to provide support for this new idea, says Lensch, I had to renege on everything I said in my book *The Road to Power* and in the second edition of my brochure on commercial policy concerning the inevitability of imperialism, armaments and the world war.[16] But when did my *Road to Power* appear? In May 1909, and therefore *after* the 29th of March, the date of my apostasy from my old beliefs.... If Lensch's arguments were correct, people would have witnessed the curious spectacle of me simultaneously deserting an old belief and resolutely professing it. Strange, is it not?

On 29 March 1909, it was not Kautsky who carried out 'the despicable improvisation of breaking with the party traditions' but the *Reichstag fraction*. On that day, it introduced the resolution on disarmament. Kautsky did not then deal with this question at all. *The Road to Power*, however, did not appear in May 1909, but earlier. If comrade Kautsky had taken a look at his brochure, he would have discovered that the preface is dated Christmas 1908. The *Leipziger Volkszeitung* published a review of it as early as on 22 February 1909. Why Comrade Kautsky gives May 1909 as the date of appearance of his book is incomprehensible to me. In itself, it is completely inconsequential when it appeared, before or after 29 March 1909. Kautsky's contradictions will not go away because of that; but, for a date to be able to prove anything, it must be correct.

Yet another small correction. Kautsky is scandalised because I 'dared' to assert that the party conference held in Stuttgart ridiculed the disarmament-proposal advanced by the tsar in 1898.[17] However, Kautsky's indignation is purely the product of a misreading. I wrote:

---

16. [Kautsky 1909b and 1911f.]

17. [The SPD *Parteitag* in Stuttgart was held on 3–8 October 1898. After Alexander III died in 1894, his 26-year-old son Nicholas II came to power. In August 1898, Nicholas

> People ridiculed the tsar[18] and called his *disarmament proposal* a *confirmation* that the resolute opposition, which the Social Democracy of all countries had so far raised against the mad armaments-race, had been totally justified.

Thus, it is clearly stated here that people ridiculed the tsar as an unbidden pioneer of the idea of disarmament (Kautsky himself lampooned him at that time as a 'high-minded youngster on the tsarist throne')[19] but that his disarmament proposal was greeted as an unintended corroboration of the correctness of Social-Democratic military policy. In order to prove that assertion, I quoted Bebel's resolution at length. Kautsky turns the ridicule of the tsar into a ridiculing of his disarmament proposal and, indignant over my impudence, quotes exactly the same passages from Bebel's resolution. To be sure, he can only hope to use these passages against me because he had previously, in the above-mentioned quotation from my article, where they were literally reproduced, picked out some sentences and replaced others by ellipses!

In any case, the facts remain the same: the disarmament proposal of the tsar did not make the Reichstag fraction submit a disarmament bill, and this is more telling than any moral indignation. But there is still another fact that is perhaps even more characteristic. Kautsky set forth to defend the 'traditional' position of Social Democracy on a militia and disarmament against the

---

called for an international conference to discuss disarmament. He was worried because Austria was re-equipping her artillery with modern field-guns that Russia was unable to match due to the inability of his country to stand the financial strain of the arms-race. The Conference was convened at The Hague in May 1899. Twenty European powers attended, along with the United States, Mexico, Japan, China, Siam (Thailand) and Persia (Iran). The Russian proposal to freeze armament levels was defeated, but the Convention did agree on rules of warfare, and it established a Permanent Court of Arbitration that later became the International Court of Justice. The Court did not, of course, prevent the catastrophe of 1914.]

18. [Literally *Väterchen*: 'dear old father'.]

19. [Kautsky 1898c. In this article, Kautsky wrote: 'Disarmament accomplished by contemporary governments can mean neither the *abolition of the standing army* nor its replacement by the *militia*. It can mean only one thing: *reduction of the standing army* to dimensions that will still enable them to hold down their own people. It means disarmament against the external enemy but not against the *internal* one; it means *disarming the people*, not the *arming of the people*.... Disarmament would allow them to replace the army raised through general conscription by a *praetorian guard*, an army of hired lumpenproletarians, whose diligent care will preserve the sacred products of our culture.... Social Democracy demands *complete* disarmament or the arming of the people, not the creation of a praetorian guard; it demands disarmament at sea as well as on land; it demands world peace, not just peace on the European continent. That is what we understand by disarmament.' Kautsky 1898c, pp. 743 and 746.]

'friends of mass-instincts',[20] and now he finds himself compelled to give up the demand for a militia and to uphold only [the demand for] disarmament. The 'youngest youngsters'[21] declared: we stick to our party programme, which only knows the demand for a militia but not for disarmament. Kautsky, on the contrary, was forced to give up the programmatic demand and proclaim the disarmament idea, which is completely unknown to our party programme, as the only truth in order to defend the Reichstag fraction's improvisation. Thus, he wrote in his article on May Day:

> During the last two decades the navy has played an ever-larger role. And in the navy, the idea of the militia fails completely. If we limit ourselves in our agitation to that demand and drop the demand for disarmament, we cannot oppose any agitation [of our own] to the agitation for enlargement of the navy.[22]

In his June article, Kautsky elaborated on the 'complete failure' of the demand for a militia. There he wrote: 'If the demand for a militia fails already in the army as a means of reducing the military budget, it is completely meaningless for the navy.'[23]

Thus, while, in the first article, the idea of a militia was preserved for the army and only 'completely' rejected for the navy, in the second article, it was repudiated for both – not 'completely' however, but only as means of reducing the military budget. But 'completely' or not, Kautsky argues, the demand for a militia recedes absolutely into the background, and in the foreground

20. [A reference to the leaders of the SPD Left, notably Rosa Luxemburg and Anton Pannekoek, who championed the mass-strike and similar extra-parliamentary direct actions as opposed to one-sided dependence on electioneering tactics. Kautsky accused them of syndicalist (anarchist) leanings. See Kautsky 1912a, Pannekoek 1912a, Kautsky 1912e, and Pannekoek 1912b.]

21. [A reference to the opposition by the 'youngsters [*Jungen*]' to the Social-Democratic executive in the years 1890–4. In 1890, there was a major debate in the SPD about the tactics it would choose after the lifting of the Anti-Socialist Laws. A radical oppositional wing known as Die Jungen (The Young Ones) developed. While the party leaders viewed parliament as a means of social change, Die Jungen thought it could, at best, be used to spread the message. They were unwilling to wait for the collapse of capitalist society and wanted, instead, to start a revolution as soon as possible. This wing was strongest in Berlin, Magdeburg, and Dresden. The 'Young Ones' were expelled from the SPD at the party congress held in Erfurt on 14–20 October 1891. Some of the expelled members turned to anarchism and established an organisation called the Association of Independent Socialists.]

22. [Kautsky 1912c.]

23. [Kautsky 1912d.]

there appears only the demand for arms-limitations. We must wait and see whether, at the Chemnitz party conference,[24] Kautsky proposes a corresponding change in our party programme – which, as we said, includes the demand for a militia but does not even hint at a limitation of armaments.

This turn on the question of the militia is highly characteristic. The idea that the demand for a militia fails in the army but is completely meaningless for the navy has already emerged at one time in the history of our party. That was in the year 1898. Then Schippel defended that point of view, while Kautsky rejected it in a brilliant polemic.[25] In the meantime, however, the situation has changed completely. Today the navy-budget is the main point. And here [according to Kautsky] the demand for a militia breaks down completely: it is 'totally meaningless'. The consequence of this new insight is the demand to abandon the old programmatic demand for a militia and to replace it by something new that the International had never heard of until the Copenhagen Congress,[26] the demand for international agreements for the purpose of gradually reducing armaments: the warships must be gradually dismantled and the regiments and the army-corps gradually disbanded.

Actually, the comrades who now suddenly recommend the gradual reduction of armaments abstain from offering any explanation on how the implementation of their proposal should proceed. Should Germany and England pledge themselves not to make any invention in the field of naval armaments,

24. [The SPD held a party conference (*Parteitag*) at Chemnitz on 15–21 September 1912. Kautsky did not take part in it for health reasons, and the same happened with Rosa Luxemburg. Lensch was the main speaker for the Left, together with Pannekoek and Cohen.]

25. [Kautsky 1899a, Kautsky 1899b, and Kautsky 1900b. Max Schippel (1859–1928) was a leading revisionist author and member of the Reichstag.]

26. [The Second (Socialist) International held its eighth Congress at Copenhagen from 28 August to 3 September 1910. The resolution adopted by the Copenhagen congress against militarism read: 'Socialist parliamentary representatives have repeatedly affirmed their duty to refuse funds for armaments and to use all their strength to combat them. The congress stands by this position and expects these representatives: a) continually to reiterate the demand for compulsory international courts of arbitration in all conflicts between states; b) continually to renew proposals aimed at general disarmament and, first and foremost, at an agreement for limitation of naval armaments and abolition of the right of seizure at sea; c) to demand the abolition of secret diplomacy and the publication of all the existing and future treaties and agreements between governments; d) to intervene in favour of the peoples' right of self-determination and in their defense against armed attack and forcible subjugation.' Riddell (ed.) 1984, p. 70.]

or at least not to employ them? Should they build no more warships but only upgrade old ones? And should this upgrading be practised only on obsolete types of ships? Alternatively, should both countries every year 'disarm' an equal percentage of their already existing ships? That is, after all, the meaning of armaments 'reduction'. And the same should naturally hold for the other countries. No more improvements in weaponry. The present condition of infantry and artillery-weapons would be fixed by international agreements, alongside military-aviation technique. Then the signatory states would gradually proceed to disband their brigades and army-corps – naturally, always in the same percentage and during the same lapse of time – until the army is turned into a praetorian guard, or militarism on land and sea vanishes in a contractual way.

One only has to represent concretely the demand for gradual disarmament in order to see its utopian character and realise why the International never and nowhere admitted it. We have no reason to change our party programme for the sake of this utopia.

What about the irreconcilability between the demand for a militia and modern development of the navy? This much is clear: if a militia and the navy are irreconcilable opposites, then the contradiction existed even when the war-fleet was small, as the German navy was until 1893. Therefore, nobody should have supported the demand for a militia even back then. However, as we have already mentioned, when Schippel pointed out in *Die Neue Zeit*, back in 1898, the incompatibility between a militia and the navy, Kautsky bluntly rejected the idea.

Kautsky does not say why a militia and the navy are incompatible. He proclaims it as an obvious fact. One can perfectly well agree with that without accepting his conclusion: abandonment of the demand for a militia. The militia system is the military constitution of a democratic state that should guarantee the safety of the country both outwardly and inwardly. A militia is quite unsuitable for wars of conquest, and it is for precisely that reason that we advocate it. If the militia system is unsuitable for the navy, that happens because the modern navy is an avowedly offensive weapon. It serves to conquer foreign countries rather than to protect the national coasts, which, as the German Navy Office once explained, can defend themselves. The colossal development of this offensive weapon during recent decades is a natural epiphenomenon of imperialism, of that epoch in the development of capitalism whose quintessence is the struggle for new colonial areas and for division of those countries that are not yet capitalist between the leading large states of international capitalism.

It is obvious why the militia system, which was calculated solely for the purpose of defence, is unsuitable as an offensive weapon. But we must not conclude from this that the militia has become completely meaningless and that we must look for a new expedient. On the contrary: the sharper the dialectical contradiction between imperialism and the proletariat, the more incompatible are their mutual demands. For imperialism, the navy is a vital necessity; socialism aims at depriving imperialism of its vital conditions. The specific weapon of imperialism, the high-sea fleet, is an offensive weapon *par excellence*, while the military programme of the proletariat is defensive *par excellence*. The application of the defensive military programme of Social Democracy to the special offensive weapon of imperialism would certainly be 'completely meaningless'.

There are two ways of facing this dilemma. One is to drop the demand for a militia in order to develop imperialism; the other is to retain the demand for a militia because it is absolutely opposed to imperialism and the navy. Kautsky follows the first course. He abandons the demand for a militia and replaces it by the demand for 'reduction of armaments'. He declares that only then would imperialism be able to develop completely, and that the capitalists could 'tap, in a far more vigorous and untrammelled way than before, the whole area of at least the Eastern Hemisphere'. The other way leaves it to the capitalist classes to care about the further development of imperialism. Supporters [of this second way] stick to the demand for a militia, which is only useful for the army, because they do not want to adapt their defensive military programme to the needs of a purely offensive weapon. They want to retain or create an organisation for the defence of the country outwardly and inwardly, that is to say, a militia. There is no place in the programme of Social Democracy for a navy. It does not need one and cannot possibly need one. It is, therefore, not a sign of the weakness but, on the contrary, of the soundness of the demand for a militia as the military programme of Social Democracy, if it is 'completely meaningless' for such an avowedly offensive weapon as the navy.

* * *

The whole debate over 'disarmament' is only a part of that larger debate [on centrism] that has already been going on for two years. It began with the essays of Comrade Luxemburg on the mass-strike and was continued by the articles of comrade Pannekoek on mass-actions.[27] The substance of this debate is the question: *what tactical attitude should Social Democracy adopt towards imperialism*? The answer to this question depends on what people understand by imperialism. One will adopt a different attitude towards it depending on whether one regards the arms-race and the division of colonial areas as a passing episode of development, which may have a particular form but could also assume a different one, or whether one regards imperialism as the last phase of capitalist development as a whole, inevitably leading to socialism.

Within scientific socialism, insofar as it has occupied itself with these contemporary problems, imperialism has always been described as the last and highest stage of capitalist society. For approximately twenty years, international capitalism has experienced an unprecedented prosperity, only briefly interrupted by crises that were rapidly overcome. The productive forces have grown everywhere to a gigantic extent and with them the capitalists' wealth. The workers' wages, despite absolute increases, have remained far behind the increased productivity of labour. The question, therefore, arose for the entrepreneurs: what to do with the wealth? They could not consume it themselves, and the working class, whose wages are only a fraction of the value it produces, is out of the question in this respect. The valorisation-needs of capital led to subjection of all the categories of society that were not yet directly subjugated by the capitalist mode of production. The obliteration of the middle classes, small craftsmen and peasants was one of the consequences; the concentration of capitals in the banks, cartels and syndicates, the other. The stream of gold grew and grew, and with it the need to find investment opportunities for the surplus-capitals. Then capital began to flow abroad in order to complete the process it had begun at home. It looked for new markets all over the globe. The huge surplus-capitals, which [the bourgeoisie] did not know what to do with, built railroads and roads, mines and harbours in tropical and subtropical areas, in Siberia, Mesopotamia, South Africa, America, East Asia; they introduced electrical energy, gas and oil, built factories and even entire cities and, last but not least, poured upon humanity the blessings of modern weapons, from small-calibre [rifles] to dreadnoughts. In other words,

27. [For the first round of the debate see Kautsky 1910a, Luxemburg 1910c, Kautsky 1910b, Luxemburg 1910d, and Kautsky 1910c. For the second round see See Kautsky 1912a, Pannekoek 1912a, Kautsky 1912e, and Pannekoek 1912b.]

capital pushed into the maelstrom of capitalist development the last areas of the earth that were not yet subjugated by it. It seized the last reservoirs from which it could still draw vital energies in order to prolong its life. Once they are exhausted, the final hour of capitalism will come. The productivity of labour grows and grows, and the colonial countries themselves are turned into capitalist areas looking for investment opportunities for their own surplus-capitals. Yet the possibilities of valorising these capitals dry up. Capitalism chokes on its own fat. Wage-labour, the condition and foundation of the capitalist mode of production, turns into an intolerable fetter for the continuation of production. Society breaks apart. The working class, which created the surplus-wealth for which the ruling classes can no longer find employment opportunities, seizes state-power in order to carry out the great revolutionary measures arising from [capitalist] development itself.

We thus see that imperialism actually means the era of revolution, that it is the last word of capitalism. The past eight years [1904–12] give us an idea regarding the tempo of its development. The Russo-Japanese War [1904–5], the Russian Revolution [of 1905], the Young Turk Revolution [1908], the revolutions in Persia [1909] and China [1911], the partition of Africa, the events in Mexico [the revolution that began in 1910],[28] the break-up of the Ottoman Empire and the partition of Persia: all these profound revolutions took place in the ridiculously short lapse of eight years. The more rapidly the division of the not yet capitalist world proceeds, the stormier has been the arms-race of the great powers scrambling for the booty. The question under dispute (namely, whether they can grab enough territories in which to invest their surplus-capitals) was vital for them. For precisely that reason, the character of modern colonial policy has totally changed – something which, incidentally, Comrade Ledebour has not yet noticed.[29]

While, previously, in the times about which Ledebour speaks, the purpose of having colonies was to extract as much out of them as possible, either

28. [The Mexican Revolution began in November 1910 as an effort to overthrow the 30-year dictatorship of Porfirio Díaz. Some of the fundamental goals of the revolution were incorporated in the 1917 constitution, although widespread factional fighting continued until 1920. The two most famous rebel leaders – Francisco 'Pancho' Villa and Emiliano Zapata – supported the growing demands from the lower classes for major social and economic reforms, such as agrarian reform. Others sought curbs on the social control and political influence exercised by the Catholic Church.]

29. [Ledebour 1912.]

through fraud or by fleecing the natives today colonies are sought in order to invest in them as much as possible. People no longer seek to cheat the natives out of valuable objects in exchange for a couple of glass beads. Thus, today the value of colonies for imperialism is not as sales markets for European textiles or similar commodities, but, rather, as areas in which it can employ the huge surplus-capitals looking for valorisation-opportunities. The goal of colonising capital today is to build railroads, bridges and highways; in other words, investments running into the hundreds of millions. Obviously, capital will not venture into such costly enterprises if it is not certain that they will yield returns. It therefore seeks to influence foreign states in order to create 'orderly' conditions, so that state-power becomes a policeman for foreign capital. But downright annexation is admittedly the simplest way by far. That path was taken, therefore, without any procrastination. Capital then rules absolutely over the country and does not have to fear foreign competition. Hence the tendency of imperialist states not only to invest capitals abroad, but also to subject foreign states to its own power, either completely or as far as possible. The open-door policy is increasingly abandoned. Accordingly, the struggles of the imperialist powers over the rest of the globe become struggles of the great powers against each other. And, precisely because this is a question of being or not being for the powers overflowing with capital, precisely because they *must* have [new] areas in order to employ their surplus-wealth, the struggle [over them] becomes a question of life and death. The arms-race is its most evident accompanying symptom; and the huge increase in military outlays during the last decade, not only in Germany and England but everywhere, is further proof of how strong the difficulties have become, arising out of the contradiction between the extremely developed productive force of labour and the increasingly narrow opportunities of employing the surplus-capitals. The wish to fight this arms-race with the fanciful idea of mutual agreements for the gradual limitation of armaments is, and will remain, utopian. No one has demonstrated this more clearly, convincingly and irrefutably than Comrade Kautsky.

Whoever wants to accomplish this gradual limitation of armaments must seek a parliamentary majority for that purpose, since the whole idea historically originated in the parliamentary arena. Kautsky thus appeals to the bourgeoisie, describing on the one hand, and in gruesome detail, the horrors of wars resulting from the arms-race, and on the other the alluring image of the 'energetic and untrammelled' continuation of the imperialist policy of robbery. Strangely, nobody in the bourgeois world reacted either to his horror-cries or to his siren-songs. Both the German and the English parliament turned a deaf ear on disarmament proposals. And one must admit that the bourgeoisie of both countries has, from an imperialist point of view, good reasons for doing that. English imperialism wants to remain the ruler of the world, and it is ready to discuss arms-limitation only on condition that its absolute rule remains undisturbed. The German bourgeoisie cannot agree to that because the troubles of German capital stem precisely from that supremacy of the English Empire. And it doubts for very good reasons that English capital, with its superior navy, will be ready to grant willingly, only because of a mere piece of paper, an equal share in those global investment opportunities that it wants for itself – precisely now, when English capital is noisily complaining about German competition. And if [after an agreement is concluded] England shreds this piece of paper and violates the agreement, should the German proletariat take to the field in defence of the threatened exploitation opportunities of German capital in East Asia or elsewhere?

The German bourgeoisie realises very well that, through the armaments-race, the superior position of England at sea is being increasingly undermined despite all English navy bills. The latest debates on the fleet in the House of Commons furnish proof of that. For years already, England has no longer been able to maintain its previous position of 'splendid isolation'. It must conclude alliances and enter into the Entente Cordiale with France. This is the political manifestation of a phenomenon that has already been going on for two decades in the economic sphere: the gradual undermining of English hegemony. What that means for international socialism, especially for the political awakening of the English workers, was explained at one time by Engels himself with these words:

> The truth is this: during the period of England's industrial monopoly the English working class have, to a certain extent, shared in the benefits of the monopoly. These benefits were very unequally parcelled out amongst them; the privileged minority pocketed most, but even the great mass had, at least, a temporary share now and then. And that is the reason why, since the dying-out of Owenism, there has been no Socialism in England. With the breakdown of that monopoly, the English working class will lose that privileged position; it will find itself generally – the privileged and leading

> minority not excepted – on a level with its fellow-workers abroad. And that is the reason why there will be Socialism again in England.[30]

The powerful ferment in the English working class, which manifests itself in unprecedented mass-struggles and has already been troubling the sleep of the English bourgeoisie for years, is a confirmation of Engels's insights. The ever-increasing misery of unemployment among the English proletariat, due to the decline of English industrial superiority, forces the English bourgeoisie to seek new investment possibilities all over the world for the huge masses of surplus English capital – by any means possible and on pain of the most violent domestic commotions and workers' revolts. And, precisely at this moment, the international armaments-race threatens the omnipotence of its fleet. It is no wonder that the English bourgeoisie came up with the idea of proposing to the weaker states a limitation of armaments; a proposal about which the leader of the Conservatives, Bonar Law, said openly in Parliament: 'If I were a German, I would not have accepted it either!'[31]

These statements show clearly enough how we must wage the struggle against the arms-race. We have to fight it not as a phenomenon separate from imperialism, as a special illness for which we have a special medicine (the Party always rejected that nonsense), but in its connection with the whole of imperialist development.

30. [Engels 1943, Preface to the English edition, p. xviii.]

31. [Andrew Bonar Law (1858–1923) was a Canadian-born leader of the British Conservative Party and Prime Minister of the United Kingdom from March 1921 to October 1922.]

Chapter Thirty-Nine

'Imperialism and Arms-Limitation' (September 1912)

Gustav Eckstein

After Radek, Pannekoek, and Lensch criticised Kautsky from the left, the Austro-Marxist Gustav Eckstein (1874–1916) came to Kautsky's defence in this article published in *Die Neue Zeit* in September 1912. Like Kautsky, Eckstein disputed the left-wing thesis that imperialism and the arms-race were indispensable for the economic development of what he called 'high capitalism'. Following Hilferding's lead, he attributed imperialism to disproportions between different branches of production.[1] Whereas Hilferding also associated disproportions with *cyclical* crises, however, Eckstein thought in terms of a *chronic* tendency towards heavy-industrial overproduction. Imperialism addressed this problem in two ways: part of the output of heavy industry was consumed by the state through militarism and the arms-race; another part was shipped abroad through foreign investment. Chronic overproduction in heavy industry, relative to more labour-intensive branches of the

1. Unlike Kautsky, Hilferding considered the conflict of interest among the imperialist powers economically necessary; he agreed, however, that Social Democracy should work for Anglo-German understanding and not content itself with protesting against imperialism as a whole. Hilferding 1913.

economy, was the driving force behind imperialist rivalry over colonies and territories for capital-exports.

In the article translated here, Eckstein concluded, as Kautsky had done, that the only strata of the bourgeoisie with a direct interest in imperialism were those engaged in the most capital-intensive branches. It followed that any constraints imposed upon militarist expansionism would have the effect not of paralysing capitalism as such, only of altering its course by slowing accumulation in heavy industry and accelerating the development of other branches, including agriculture. In opposing state-expenditures on militarism, the proletariat could therefore win support from other strata of the bourgeoisie, whose interests objectively favoured arms-limitations through inter-governmental agreements. Eckstein believed that this was an eminently more responsible policy than that proposed by Pannekoek and his comrades on the Left, who appeared increasingly to be moving towards anarcho-syndicalism through espousing extra-parliamentary mass-actions and the general strike.

In another article on 'Militarism and the Economy', published the following year, Eckstein distinguished his own view from Rosa Luxemburg's thesis of a chronic problem of markets. Following the lead given by Otto Bauer's criticism of Luxemburg,[2] he concluded: 'the allegation that militarism is unconditionally necessary to sell the products of industry is unsustainable'.[3] Bauer's commentary on Luxemburg affirmed the possibility, already demonstrated by Marx's reproduction-schemes in Volume II of *Capital*, of capitalism creating its own market – provided, Marx added, that the conditions of proportional reproduction were assumed in advance. Marx regarded this assumption as a methodological abstraction, and Eckstein gave his own understanding of how real disproportionalities emerge and might be overcome. Capital, he wrote, tended

> to flow always into industrial branches with a higher organic composition, particularly into mass-production industries. There is, therefore, always a tendency for industrial mass-articles, especially those of heavy industry, to be produced on too large a scale, while those that are predominantly hand-made, above all agricultural and mining products, are produced on too small a scale. If the economy of a capitalist state were actually, as the

2. Bauer 1913, English version: Bauer 1986. See this volume, Chapter 45.
3. Eckstein 1913a, p. 168.

> reproduction-diagrams assume, secluded from the outside world, that disproportionate expansion of mass-industries would lead to a continual reduction in the prices of their products and a rise in prices of the products of manual labour, above all agriculture and mining, thus restoring the equilibrium.[4]

Eckstein thought changes in prices, in the absence of foreign trade, would necessarily curtail the growth of capital-intensive industry, with a regressive equilibrium being restored through heavy-industrial contraction. Foreign trade averted that regressive outcome by enabling industrial countries to

> export surplus mass-articles and exchange them against the products of mainly manual labour, against agrarian products and luxury-articles. In that way, the division of labour, which is necessary in capitalist economy for the maintenance of economic equilibrium, is overridden, and the capitalist country turns into a large factory, which draws its raw materials and consumption goods for its workers to a large extent from foreign countries that are still undeveloped from a capitalist point of view, and exports its industrial products.[5]

This analysis led to the conclusion that *foreign trade* was obviously beneficial to capitalist development, although *militarism*, just as obviously, was not. Militarism hindered accumulation: it slowed the expansion of capitalist production by impoverishing workers and taking away large numbers of able-bodied youth from the workforce. Moreover, it helped 'to fence off a part of that world market for the exclusive exploitation of the capitalists of the land in question. Hence the striving of capitalist states to reserve for themselves the largest possible agrarian areas for exploitation, shutting them off against competition by other capitalist states – [in other words,] imperialism.'[6] Like Kautsky, Eckstein believed that

> militarism is not an economic necessity for the development of capitalism, but it facilitates and accelerates, together with foreign trade, colonial policy and capital-exports, the development of mass-production at the expense of branches where manual labour predominates, and offers to the large

4. Eckstein 1913a, pp. 168–9.
5. Eckstein 1913a, p. 169.
6. Ibid.

> bourgeoisie a convenient and profitable, even if not indispensable, market. The bourgeoisie as a whole is, therefore, not at all interested in the development of militarism.... Export-trade, imperialism and militarism facilitate the overgrowth of high-capitalist mass-production.[7]

The political implications appeared to be equally clear: 'Although the real interests of the bourgeoisie do not at all lie in the direction of militarism, the bourgeoisie has nevertheless today become, under the influence of the mass-producing industries, and especially the powerful groups of military suppliers and their minions, incapable of offering independent and energetic resistance to it.'[8] To redress this bourgeois weakness, Eckstein agreed with Kautsky's political conclusion. The organised workers, he wrote, must drive the 'progressive and pacifist bourgeoisie' away from the magnates of heavy industry and into a broadly-based movement in favour of peace and disarmament.[9]

* * *

'Imperialism and Arms Limitation'[10]

I

Comrade Pannekoek, in his article 'The Essence of our Present Demands' (*Neue Zeit*, XXX, 2, No. 48), distinguishes between demands whose fulfilment is today precluded for political reasons and those whose implementation is economically impossible because they are incompatible with the *essence* of capitalism. He declares the really controversial question to be whether agreements between great powers for the limitation of armaments belong to the first or the second category.[11]

He and his friends think these agreements are incompatible with the essence of capitalism, and they support this allegation by referring to 'the force and inner necessity of imperialist policy for the bourgeoisie'. Comrade Lensch dealt with this question, in more detail than Pannekoek has done, in his article

7. Eckstein 1913a, p. 171.
8. Eckstein 1913a, p. 170.
9. Stargardt 1994, pp. 120–1.
10. Eckstein 1912b.
11. [Pannekoek 1912c. A polemic with Eckstein 1912a.]

'Militia and Disarmament'.[12] Lensch tried to prove that imperialism is the inevitable result of highly developed capitalism and that, consequently, the great powers '*must* have [new] areas in order to employ their surplus wealth'. If they do not want to 'choke on their own fat', they must wage a struggle to the death [over colonial territories].[13]

Comrade Lensch evidently wished to demonstrate that imperialist colonial policy is the natural and inevitable result of highly developed capitalism and that the arms-race is a natural and inevitable accompaniment of that colonial policy. Comrade Pannekoek emphasises these assertions and concludes that it is utopian, and therefore a waste of energy – indeed a misleading of the proletariat – to attempt to check this course, because 'any attempt to stop the development of capitalism and to force it into its old forms must necessarily fail'.

The objection that naturally arises from this point of view is that we are wrong in rejecting the colonial and navy-budget, because if we actually succeeded in depriving the state of the means for continuing its imperialist policy (and that can be the only serious goal of our attitude), we would oppose the natural development of capitalism even more than with the proposal to restrict armaments by agreement. Comrade Pannekoek seeks to dispose of this objection by arguing that it is not our task to further imperialist policy, which we would do by approving the colonial and navy-budget. But only the forms of our parliamentary life enable Pannekoek to hold this opinion. What would happen if the government did not simply submit demands to the parliament, which the latter can only answer with a 'yes' or 'no', but the parties themselves had drawn up the budget? Should Social Democrats submit a motion to abolish the allocation for colonies and the navy? According to their point of view, Comrades Pannekoek and Lensch should answer decidedly in the negative [because that would be an 'attempt to stop the development of capitalism and to force it into its old forms']. But this shows that, in order to be consistent, they should not reject the budget allocations in question. However, in their revision of our political tactic, they shrink back from going so far as to draw the final consequences from their own doctrines.

12. See the previous document in this volume.
13. [Lensch 1912b, pp. 770–1. For an English version see this volume, Chapter 38.]

It is not only the absurdity of the conclusions following from these ideas that shows the feebleness of the axiom about the intrinsic impossibility and harmfulness of the demand for arms-limitation. The indefensibility of Comrade Pannekoek's point of view can be demonstrated precisely according to the standard he himself set.

The only way to prove that the demand for limitation of armaments is impossible would be for Pannekoek to demonstrate that the economic policy of high capitalism is impossible without the arms-race. That would certainly be the case if the construction of warships, military harbours, etc. were necessary as market outlets for the existence of capitalist industry. To my knowledge, no party writer has made that assertion so far, even if the importance of these sales outlets and the significance these considerations for the imperialist mood of our heavy industry have rightly been emphasised.

More important is the second possibility, namely, that the arms-race is indispensable for the realisation of imperialist colonial policy, and that this again represents a vital necessity for high capitalism. That is also, as we have seen, the standpoint of Pannekoek and Lensch.

What is the role of the arms-race in modern colonial policy? One can divide the inhabited areas of the globe into the following groups of territories: 1. States with high-capitalist military establishments, such as Europe, the United States and Japan. 2. The colonial areas of the military great powers. 3. The colonial areas of small European states, such as Portugal, Belgium and Holland. 4. The nominally still independent, non-European states with insufficient military establishments, such as the Ottoman Empire, Persia, China, the South American republics, Mexico, etc.

Wars to shift European boundaries are unlikely, and navies would probably not have great significance in them. Attempts to influence European tariffs by military means are also not to be expected. Tariff-wars are much more effective in this case. The great powers do not need a large navy for the capitalist exploitation of their own colonies; the colonial troops are sufficient for that.

But the case is different with the impending division of territories belonging to the third and fourth categories. Struggles over them can and will take place. It has been shown by the events in Morocco and Congo and the exchange of colonial possessions, as well as by the almost completed partition of Persia, that in those struggles the rivals do not necessarily have to draw their swords; rattling them can suffice. But the share of each great power in the booty depends essentially on the military power at its disposal.

Let us assume, for instance, that we succeed in obtaining an international agreement between the great powers, stipulating that for the next twenty years the extent of the navy budget cannot be exceeded by any of the signatory states; that it must stand, for instance, in a certain ratio to the average navy allocation of the last five fiscal years. How would high-capitalist development in the signatory countries be disturbed by such an agreement? Not even their imperialist policy has to be hindered by it. Such an agreement,[14] for instance, would not at all bar England, Germany and France from dividing the African possessions of Portugal and Belgium, [nor would it] prevent the partition of Persia or even impede the initiation of Turkey's partition. One may consider these events probable or not, one may greet or abhor them, but their eventuality would not be precluded by a limitation of armaments through international agreements. In the struggles [between colonial powers], the relation of forces prevalent at the time of the agreement would more or less prevail. But, in any case, a regulation of the military budget would prevent a further increase in the tax-burden. Technical improvements in weaponry do not have to be hindered within this framework.

II

The arms-race is thus not indispensable for the development of high capitalism, and its containment does not have to hinder the further development of imperialist policy. Even if imperialist policy were necessary for the development of capitalism, that still would not prove the indispensability of the arms-race for the economic development of high capitalism. But this assumption about the indispensability of imperialism for the economic development of high capitalism is not even correct in the sense that capitalism would be deprived of its conditions of life if imperialist policy were brought to a standstill.[15] Since the opposite assertion has been made time and again, it would perhaps not be superfluous to go briefly into that question as well.

---

14. The supervision of this agreement would naturally be in the hands of parliaments, which would have to check budget estimates and the [final] statements of accounts. Abuses would be forestalled by the control of the workers' parties of the different countries.

15. The fact that imperialist policy is the natural result of high capitalism is an entirely different question and should by no means be denied. It is a 'necessary' accompaniment, but it does not have to be necessary for its existence and development.

Comrade Lensch tried to prove in his article 'Militia and Disarmament' that the development of imperialist economic policy is a vital necessity for heavy industry. He wrote: 'The question, therefore, arose for the entrepreneurs: what to do with the wealth? They could not consume it themselves, and the working class, whose wages are only a fraction of the value it produces, is out of the question in this respect.'[16]

Overproduction would be the cause, therefore, of the export of commodities and then of capitals. This theory of capitalist overproduction, resulting from the fact that wages constitute an ever-smaller share of the product of labour, was first advanced and advocated by Rodbertus. It has, however, been refuted long ago by Marx, who in the last chapters of the second volume of *Capital* demonstrated that an equilibrium between production and consumption, even if constantly more unstable, is possible with any extension of capitalist production, because the causes of crises do not lie simply in 'overproduction' but must be sought in factors that disturb or prevent the preservation of that equilibrium. Above all, there are two factors at work here as the causes of crises, which disturb the proportionality of production. In addition to Marx, Hilferding in his *Finance Capital* and Kautsky in his series of articles on 'Finance-Capital and Crises' have pointed out one of these factors: the differences in the turnover-periods of capital.[17] A second factor, however, which is of special significance precisely for this question, has not, in my opinion, been given the attention it deserves.

Under the conditions of simple commodity-production, production is regulated in a simple way by prices. If they fall below production-costs, the production of the articles in question is curtailed. Other branches of production are therefore stimulated, and production is thus always adapted to social needs. These simple conditions were fundamentally altered by the introduction of machines and other labour-saving procedures. The single manufacturer, who introduces a newly invented machine, does so in order to pocket an extra profit. As long as that machine is not generally in use, the old market price remains fairly unchanged. The manufacturer who first introduced the new methods of labour can thus underbid his competitors and make a considerably larger

16. [Lensch 1912b. See the previous chapter in this volume.]
17. [Hilferding 1981, pp. 239–98. Kautsky 1911b, partial English version in Kautsky 1911c.]

profit than they do, although, in doing so, he depresses prices below general production-costs. The result of all this is precisely the opposite of what happened under simple commodity-production. The large profits made by the [innovating] manufacturer tempt and, indeed, force others to adopt the new methods of production. Competitors thus do not curtail their production, but rather expand and accelerate it by introducing new machines. This process continues until prices fall to the level of the production-costs resulting from the application of the new machines and even below them. That is inevitable because, as we said, prices have lost their immediate regulatory function and therefore cannot prevent production from exceeding the mass of social needs. The final result of all this process, if it proves impossible to find new marketing opportunities, is a crash. This is not an isolated phenomenon, but one that repeats itself in all areas of production where machines can be employed and the turnover-period shortened. It must, therefore, make itself felt all the more strongly, the more widespread is the use of the new methods of labour in a branch of production, and the higher the organic composition[18] of the capital in question. It is thus inevitable that a continual relative overproduction should be the rule in those branches of production. That does not mean that too much is produced because the workers do not have sufficient buying power. It means that the production of those commodities is not in correct proportion to the production of branches with lower organic composition and slower capital-turnover, where a relatively large quantity of manual labour is employed. There are too many [mass-produced] factory goods in proportion to the products of [labour-intensive] manufacture and agriculture.

That is the reason why large-scale capital pushes for exports to countries with backward modes of production. Simple overproduction would not be relieved by such exports, because manufacturers are not willing to give away their goods in those countries, preferring instead to sell them at a profit and receive other goods in return. In that case, overproduction would only be increased by foreign trade. But if the goal is to exchange surplus manufactured goods for goods requiring much manual labour, whose prices at home are therefore relatively high (because capital, as we already mentioned,

18. By the 'organic composition' of a given capital, we mean the ratio between the value of the means of production and the wages of labour. The greater this ratio, the fewer workers are employed in proportion to a given capital and the higher is its organic composition.

withdrew from those branches of production), in that case exports to economically undeveloped countries would be the correct thing to do. Raw materials, agricultural products, the products of handicrafts and manufactures would then willingly be exchanged for manufactured products, and the equilibrium between the branches of production would be restored.

This factor plays a large role in export and colonial policy even today. But, as soon as industrial capitalism takes possession of a country and displaces manual labour with machinery, that country becomes unsuitable for this kind of exchange. The question then arises with even greater urgency: what to do with the products of large-scale industry? Domestically, as we have seen, they can no longer be exchanged against the products of capitals with lower organic composition and slow turnover; or they can be exchanged only on very unfavourable terms. Because regulation by prices has lost its old effectiveness in the era of machines, it works only from time to time through violent revolutions [in the process of production], which capitalists try to avoid at all costs. Exports to high-industrial countries thus offer no relief, while the once undeveloped countries, which were good buyers, are beginning to develop their own large-scale industry. What is to be done, then, with the products of large-scale, especially heavy, industry?

The question was to find buyers ready to pay well for these manufactured products although there is no social need for them; buyers who would not first have to sell products of capitals with lower organic composition in order to buy the products of heavy industry, and who would not make productive use of the latter but merely consume and destroy them. The magnates of capital found these remarkable buyers mainly in the workers of their own country, who certainly would not have entered into this quite unfavourable business willingly but were forced to do so by the state. A considerable share of their wages is confiscated in the form of indirect taxes, and with this money warships, uniforms, etc. are bought and unproductively wasted; military fortresses and harbours are built, but also railways, mines, etc. in foreign countries, which admittedly, to the extent that they do not serve purely military purposes or were undertaken for totally absurd reasons, are not unproductive but (like mines) supply products with lower organic composition or (like railways) open up new lands that are more backward in economic development.[19]

19. I advanced this argument in a popular form in the *Arbeiter-Jugend*, Jg. 1912, Nr. 11, 14 and 15. From the point of view of use-value, this policy of great industrialism

Thus it can be easily explained why the representatives of large-scale industry, especially of heavy industry standing at the highest capitalist level, are so enthusiastic about the armaments-race at sea and on land, and why the actual supporters and advocates of imperialist policy must be sought in their ranks. As long as the exchange of goods with backward countries sufficed to dispose of the products of large-scale industry, this industry was an enthusiastic supporter of the 'Open Door'. But when it became a question not just of simple exchange, but rather of huge capital-investments in backward countries, capitalists sought to protect [their investments] through the political power of their own state, ruled by the financial aristocracy. Modern imperialist policy is the expression of that endeavour.

From this analysis it follows, first, that *not* all strata of the bourgeoisie are directly interested in imperialist policy, but mainly large-scale industry working with capitals with a high organic composition; and second, that containment of this policy must by no means necessarily lead to the paralysis of capitalist economic development.[20] The checking [of imperialist policy] would slow down capital-accumulation in heavy industry and thus hamper its development; on the other hand, it would accelerate the development of other industries, especially agriculture. Capital would turn to other branches of production, which would experience rapid development. Agriculture, in particular, would finally be practised by completely capitalist methods. Certainly, the checking of imperialism would produce deep changes in the economy; but the development of capitalism [as a whole] would not be hindered [as a result]; it would only be forced into different channels.

But even if, contrary to what comrades Lensch, Pannekoek, etc. argue, the containment of imperialist policy is by no means economically impossible, it nevertheless constitutes a political impossibility under the current relations of political forces. The interests behind imperialist policy are today still

---

appears only as a chase after raw materials for production and foodstuffs for the workers. Certainly, this chase is stimulated by the greater opportunities for exploitation existing in those countries without proletarian movements, but the export of industrial goods and capitals has already been going on for a long time, and not just because the purchase of foreign products at less than their values and the exploitation of coloured labour are especially profitable; these exports are forced by the impossibility of realising the profits of large-scale industry in other way.

20. Why other strata of the bourgeoisie stand under the influence of imperialist ideology, and how far this influence goes, have been shown by Hilferding in *Finance Capital* and by Kautsky in his broadsheet on Morocco [Kautsky 1911d. See this volume, Chapter 32.]

incomparably stronger than the proletariat, and one can only count to a very limited degree on the co-operation of that part of the bourgeoisie not directly interested in imperialist policy. That is why, in the immediate struggle against imperialism, we can do little more than reject the colonial and navy-allocations [in the state budget] – even if we are unfortunately still unable in that way actually to prevent military expenditures – as well as vote against the protective tariffs. At the same time, it is obvious that we have to take action against the policy of high capitalism, explaining its ominous effects to the proletariat and setting our socialist programme against this policy.

The question of disarmament or arms-limitations is different. Since the arms-race, as we have already shown, is not even necessary for the continuation of imperialist policy; since, furthermore, the burdens of the arms-race make themselves felt immediately on broad strata of the bourgeoisie and especially on the peasantry; and since, at the same time, the ideology that today props up and glorifies imperialism does not extend with the same force over the arms-race as such – it appears by no means excluded that a united exertion of the international proletariat may succeed in checking the arms-race and eventually in bringing about a standstill in the growth of military budgets, at least for a certain period, by means of international agreements between governments. Whether the proletarian actions in parliaments or on the streets succeed [in doing that], or whether both kinds of methods should be combined, is a tactical question depending on actual political circumstances and has nothing to do with the question at hand. If hindering the arms-race were an economic impossibility, as Pannekoek and Lensch argue, then it could not be induced by mass-actions any more than by parliamentary actions.

III

For Pannekoek and his present like-minded comrades, the slogans 'mass' and 'mass-action' have such a magical appeal that they believe they can attain anything by those means. Just as bourgeois democrats formerly spoke about the wonder-working 'people', the 'people's will', etc., so today [left radicals] speak about the 'masses'. That is an old idolatry before a new altar. The class-differences arising from the roles in production disappear in the 'mass', that is to say, the multitude of the poor and the disinherited, whatever their social function. In that way, representatives of this view sink back into the old conceptions of anarchism, which were overcome long ago and have always been blind to actual class-antagonisms, seeing only the struggle between the rebellious and disinherited and the sated proprietary classes. Comrade Pannekoek reproaches me with gratuitously accusing him of anarchism. I think he totally misunderstood me. I only wanted to point out that he is about to plunge headlong into that current, and to warn the comrades trusting his leadership that they are approaching the same fate.

If additional proof of the kinship between the current ideas of Pannekoek and anarcho-syndicalism were required, the conclusion of his article provides it.[21] For the syndicalists, the trade-union struggle means above all a kind of military exercise for the impending general strike, in which the proletariat, gathered in union-organisations, abolishes the capitalist mode of production and itself carries on production. To awaken and keep alert the fighting spirit is the essential task of the union-action, and to strengthen the organisation for the decisive struggle in the form of the general strike is the first duty of the trade-union. Fighting over momentary successes is only to be greeted to the extent that it introduces proletarians to the organisation, hardens them in the struggle and consolidates [the union]. But the immediate successes of the struggle, according to the old but still almost completely anarchist conception of the syndicalists, were more prone to lull the fighting spirit and turn the revolutionary proletarian into a comfortable petty bourgeois.[22]

Karl Marx had a completely different notion of the role of the trade-unions in the liberation-struggle of the proletariat. Already in 1846, he compared the trade-unions with the old municipalities, the centres of the class-struggle of the bourgeoisie against feudal aristocracy, and the same comparison reappears in a resolution of the Geneva congress of the International.[23] Were the bourgeois municipalities simply organisations for the overthrow of feudal society; did they do nothing else but brace themselves for the struggle? Step by step, the bourgeoisie, in tenacious, costly fights, gained ground, winning economic and political rights. When it came to a revolutionary decision, the

21. [Pannekoek 1912c.]
22. See my introduction to Louis 1912. [A translation of Louis 1911.]
23. [Marx 1977a, pp. 166–75. The International Workingmen's Association (IWA), sometimes called the First International, held its first congress in September 1866 in Geneva.]

bourgeois municipalities were the centres and main sources of strength of the bourgeoisie precisely because they had conquered all those rights.

But we do not need to draw historical parallels. Even if one were to accept Pannekoek's standpoint, the question boils down to the strength of the organisations: how long would trade-union organisations remain alive if they did not deliver any success in the daily struggles? But, apart from that, is the shortening of working time, which first made spiritual life and political union possible [for the workers], not the most necessary precondition for the development of proletarian power? And does Comrade Pannekoek embrace the standpoint of the syndicalists, according to which abundant strike-funds are not a means of struggle but rather of neutralising the fighting spirit? How could such strike-funds be raised if wages remained at miserable levels? Certainly, an improvement in living conditions can paralyse the spirit of the class-struggle in some individual workers and turn them into petty bourgeois. But to generalise this observation and turn it into the foundation of our views about the trade-union struggle, as Pannekoek does, means steering with full sails into the camp of syndicalism. In France, these conceptions are giving way more and more to the spirit of actual proletarian class-struggles. They cannot be transplanted into Germany.

Chapter Forty

'Ways and Means in the Struggle against Imperialism' (14 September 1912)

Karl Radek

The best introduction to the debate on the 'disarmament controversy' in the SPD is the article by Ursula Ratz in the *International Review of Social History*. This is what she said about this essay by Radek, which was originally meant for publication in *Die Neue Zeit*:

> The mood of irritation that developed in connection with the disarmament controversy actually led to an editorial verdict, as shown by the refusal to publish Radek's article 'Ways and Means in the Struggle against Imperialism' in *Die Neue Zeit*. Admittedly Gustav Eckstein, who declared Radek's article to be 'very confused and extremely brazen', accepted it for publication (letter to Kautsky, 15 July 1912, *Kautsky-Archiv* DX/65). But the editors of *Die Neue Zeit* used the coincidence of the planned publication with the beginning of Radek's expulsion process as a pretext to reject his article (see the letters on 'Radek's case' in the *Kautsky-Archiv*). The Karl Kautsky Papers at the International Institute of Social History in Amsterdam also contain the corrected proofs of Radek's article, which finally appeared in the *Bremer Bürger-Zeitung* on 14 September 1912.[1]

1. Ratz 1966, p. 223, note 4.

The editors of the *Bremer Bürger-Zeitung* remarked:

> We cannot accept the standpoint of the editors of *Die Neue Zeit* and, given the fact that the question of imperialism is one of the most important ones that will come up for discussion at the Chemnitz party congress [15–21 September 1912] and that Comrade Radek, besides, seems to us the most competent person to orient us on this question, we rather consider it imperative to publish this prominent article before the party congress.[2]

Radek had already been expelled from the Social Democracy of the Kingdom of Poland and Lithuania (SDKPiL) at Rosa Luxemburg's request. His status in the German Party was discussed at the Chemnitz Congress and decided a year later, at the second Jena Congress in September 1913, when he was expelled from the SPD. The decision of the Congress was protested against by the Bremen organisation, which continued to provide Radek with an outlet for his writing in its newspaper.

* * *

'Ways and Means in the Struggle against Imperialism'[3]

The discussion in *Die Neue Zeit* concerning our struggle against imperialism has already led to a result: it has sharply highlighted the existence of two opposing views on imperialism and our struggle against it. Now, it is possible to identify clearly the nature of this difference, its sources and its consequences, because only complete clarity about actually existing differences of opinion can avoid unnecessary friction and allow the Party to assess their importance. This article, in the form of a polemic against comrade Kautsky, is an attempt to describe in detail the positions that Pannekoek, Lensch and I have been holding for several years on the question of the struggle against imperialism. As our individual starting points correspond to the contradictory nature of the issue, there are differences of opinion on partial questions between my remarks and those of the individual comrades referred to, which we have no reason to hide since their clarification can only strengthen our fundamental agreement.

2. Schüddekopf 1969, p. 469.
3. Radek 1912c.

Two methods of investigation and two views of imperialism

Kautsky holds the arms-race to be the expression of a policy of the propertied classes, which, although based on the interests of very influential strata of capital, is not a vital necessity for capitalism.

> Factors – he writes in the *Die Neue Zeit*, 1912, pp. 106–7 – that are vital elements of the capitalist production-process, without which it cannot exist, can, of course, only be removed with capitalism itself. But it is a gross misconception to consider every phenomenon resulting from the capitalist production process as a vital element without which it can not exist.
>
> The extraction of surplus-value is a vital element of capitalist production. It generates the drive for extension of the working day. But the latter is not a vital element of capitalism, which may also flourish, and do so even better, on shorter working hours. The striving to increase surplus-value is merely steered into other channels by restriction of the working day. The shorter the working hours, for example, the stronger the desire to replace manpower by machines.
>
> So, too, *the constant expansion of the market is a vital necessity for capitalism.* At a certain level of its development, the most convenient method of achieving this expansion appears to be the acquisition of colonies and spheres of influence, which leads to the arms-race. *But if this method is blocked, that would not imply the collapse of capitalism but only the need to apply other methods of expansion.*
>
> The arms-race is often based on economic reasons, but not on an economic necessity. *Its cessation is not at all an economic impossibility.*[4]

That is the basic view of Comrade Kautsky, and upon it he builds his theory.

Because imperialism is only *one of the methods* by which the vital needs of capitalism can be satisfied, not only is the fight against the arms-race as a product of imperialism possible, which no one denies, *but disarmament is also possible.* Since Social Democracy must advocate all reforms that lighten the burden on the working class and facilitate the conditions of the class-struggle, it must also advocate disarmament.

To buttress his argument, Kautsky is not satisfied with asserting that 'our agreement with the bourgeois advocates of disarmament is based…on a

4. Kautsky 1912c, pp. 106–7.

commonality of interests between the bourgeois world and the proletariat on this issue' (which would be a very comforting finding in the 'new period of revolutions')[5] but he also writes:

> *The immediate task is to support and strengthen the movement of the petty bourgeoisie and the bourgeoisie against war and the arms-race.* One must not underestimate this movement. It arises, just as the opposite movement does, out of real motives, and we have every reason to strengthen it against the latter.... And when proposals are made from the bourgeois side for the preservation of peace or the limitation of armaments, which are to some extent feasible, we have every reason to support them and to force governments to state their position on them.[6]

Thus [wrote] Kautsky. I met with total silence a year ago when I tried to figure out, in the *Bremer Bürger-Zeitung* of 29 April 1911, just which developed capitalist country was noteworthy for its petty-bourgeois and bourgeois movements against war and the *armaments-race* (rather than against armaments *sans phrase*) and had made proposals for armaments-limitation that were feasible even to some extent. One will also look in vain in Kautsky's current remarks for any example of such a movement. He must excuse us, but we cannot take seriously his appeal (in *Die Neue Zeit* of 6 September 1912)[7] to the 'substantial bourgeois disarmament movement' in Britain, represented by the British government, which 'surely' finds hearing and support even in French government circles. This is the case not only because the consent of France to the alleged British 'disarmament movement' is a state secret revealed only to Comrade Kautsky, which no other mortal has ever heard about, but also because, as we will further demonstrate, the British government supports neither disarmament nor a general limitation of armaments. And this is where the revision of Kautsky's views on imperialism must begin. For it is clear *that a view unable to show a single historical fact* on which it could lean – and there is no bourgeois movement against war and the arms-race actually supported by a social class – *can be nothing more than a lifeless speculation.*

5. [A reference to the last chapter of Kautsky 1909b.]
6. Kautsky 1912c, p. 101.
7. [Kautsky 1912d.]

If you imagine capitalism in the abstract, based upon a schema for all time, from the beginning of capitalist commodity-production to the present day, then capitalism has only one vital necessity: the production of surplus-value and its realisation as profit. But this general scheme is not enough even for *representation* of the general laws of capitalism, let alone for understanding [their operation] in the various countries and periods.

If one looks at the development of capitalism in individual countries, or at its international development in concrete periods when deep transformations in its policy raise the question of its laws, it becomes apparent that *next to its general vital necessities, capitalism has others of more limited historical significance that are just as important as the former, because the general vital necessities of capitalism can only assert themselves in concrete forms.*

For reasons of space, I must refrain from illustrating this assertion with examples of the vital necessities of capitalist development in particular countries. Consideration of these vital necessities, for instance, turned Austrian Social Democracy into an opponent of the demand for Bohemian statehood, and Polish Social Democracy into an opponent of the demand for the independence of Poland, although neither of these demands collides with the vital necessities of capitalism so abstractly formulated by Kautsky. I must dwell a little longer on the question of the international vital needs of capitalism, which in a given historical situation may dominate its policy, because the matter under dispute today, the nature of imperialism, embodies precisely that question.

Kautsky's argument, that imperialism is one of the many methods by means of which capitalism's need to expand may assert itself, has two main shortcomings: one relates to the history of capitalism, the second to its foreseeable future, whose trends can be determined even today on the basis of facts. As for the past, it is clear that capitalism in England, France and Germany, when it arrived at a certain stage of development, adopted the establishment of colonies as its main form of expansion. I leave aside the question of whether, in each of the three countries, colonial policy was equally necessary for the capitalists as a class already at the beginning; but the fact that capital in all these countries kept on pursuing that policy, even though it conjured up the greatest threats for capitalism, should be seen as a symptom that colonial policy corresponded to a historical vital necessity of capitalism. This vital necessity consists of *the conflict, worsening with capitalist development, between the capitalist law of wages and the capitalist necessity to expand production and enlarge its markets*. Even if the law of wages today were totally different from the past, and real wages oscillated around a stable level, the fact remains, nevertheless, that despite the resistance of the organised working class against the oppressive tendencies of capitalism, labour-productivity is growing much more quickly than the share of the working class in social income. The bigger the working class is compared to the other social classes, therefore, the greater is capitalism's need to expand into non-capitalist states by exporting commodities. This historically necessary development has further consequences: the need to graft a state-organisation onto countries that do not have one, the need to fight against non-capitalist countries opposing the spread of capitalism and, finally, the need to arm against the expansionist drive of other capitalist states.

Thanks to these links – which we can merely outline because they are assumed to be well known (they are best described in Hilferding's *Finance Capital* and Bauer's *The Question of Nationalities*,[8] although the analysis of imperialism given in those works is not exhaustive and must be pursued further) – *imperialism became a vital necessity of the present historical phase of capitalism.*

To deny *imperialism* the character of a policy corresponding to one of the vital necessities of capitalism listed by Kautsky – *the need to expand* – he must undertake a task that would be very attractive to a devotee of unhistorical, purely rationalist speculation but has nothing in common with the tasks of a Marxist. Kautsky tries to prove that stubborn lady, History, could have behaved more properly had she found a wise counsellor in her younger years. Unfortunately, that is beyond repair: the lady has had several mishaps, which in some countries have driven her onto the imperialist path even before the above-mentioned contradiction, which constitutes the main driving force of imperialism, was acutely felt, while, in other countries, she was pushed at a faster pace onto the track of imperialism by different, secondary factors. Instead of the movement of the petty bourgeoisie and bourgeoisie detected by Kautsky, a growth of the imperialist mood in all classes of capitalist society – with the exception of the proletariat – can be observed in Western Europe.

He does not attempt to determine the real tendencies of imperialism, which are demonstrable by the facts, but rather jumbles them together.

8. [Bauer 2000, Hilferding 1981.]

In his article on May Day of this year (in the last volume of the *Die Neue Zeit*, pp. 107–8) he writes:

> What for the past two decades increasingly rules the relationships between firms, will now begin to apply to the relationships between capitalist states. They all strive for expansion, they all increasingly bother each other, disrupt and hinder each other, and for that reason increase their armed forces and the costs of business expansion in such a way that all profits from it go down the drain. Nevertheless, this method continues as long as some countries still believe that they will be able, through armaments, to beat the competition and monopolise the world market at tom's point.[9] The more that prospect diminishes, the clearer it becomes that continuation of the competitive struggle ruins all parties, and the closer we come to *the stage where the competitive battle between states will be neutralised by their cartel relationship.* This does not mean abandonment of the expansion of domestic capital, *it only means the transition to a less expensive and dangerous method....*
>
> The capitalists of Germany and England, for instance, would not lose in the least if the two countries reached an understanding over foreign policy *and, as a result, restricted their armaments.* Both countries together would then be able to bring at least the other countries of Europe to join in the agreement and to *disarm*, and then their capitalists could tap, in a far more vigorous and untrammelled way than before, the whole area of at least the Eastern Hemisphere.[10]

We do not want to deal here with the practical application that Kautsky makes of these considerations with regard to our position on the armaments question, or to raise the question of whether Social Democrats, given the harsh consequences of free competition, ever demanded or promoted its abrogation by the trusts. Here, we only want to ascertain that Kautsky finds these developmental trends of imperialism *in his own imagination alone,* as it would be quite difficult for him to point out even a single *fact* on which he could base his comments. The facts from the last ten years of imperialist development indicate that in capitalist countries there are many capitalist elements that are generally interested in peace – for example, shipping capital and others – whose interests place them in concrete capitalist opposition to bellicose

9. [A *tom* is a long naval gun mounted amidships.]
10. Kautsky 1912c, pp. 107–8.

developments. (Thus, for example, the heavy industry in Rhine-Westphalia has been almost consistently opposed to a war over Morocco since a merger was reached between Thyssen Krupp & Co. and Schneider-Creusot.) These facts indicate that some capitalist groups do consider the dangers of a war between Europe's major powers to be so great that they will do their utmost to get out of its way. Finally, they indicate that competing groups of capitalists with imperialist business (foreign-government bonds, etc.) are inclined to agree on the division of the loot, which, incidentally, is not easy. *But I was not able to discover in any modern state* – with the exception of England, the main naval power, which can only expect a further deterioration of its position from the arms-race and therefore stands for preservation of present conditions in the *North Sea* (only in the *North Sea!*) – *one of those strata interested in peace that is actually opposed to the arms-race, despite a zealous reading of the relevant literature and press.* Notwithstanding their fear of war, they all support armaments not only because they have material interests in them – orders, shares in the industries involved in naval construction, etc. – but also because they possess in armaments a measure of their influence on imperialist business.

I have already demonstrated all of this in a more detailed way in *Die Neue Zeit* without receiving any reply from Comrade Kautsky.[11] Thus, his remarks about other methods of expansion open to capital float completely in the air, which is an unwanted admission of the fact that imperialism is a vital necessity for capitalism. Kautsky considers the expansion of capitalism to be one of its vital necessities, but he is unable to point out among the developmental trends of capital any other way for it to expand except through imperialism, which thus remains a vital need for capitalism.

To conclude this section, we must point out one further fact: even if there were some tendencies pointing to a common way for European capital, their enforcement would entail – in order to be lasting – such consequences as a common commercial policy of the European countries, a joint army to struggle against the awakening Orient (even if weapons were laid down between European countries) and a joint federal government. All of this, however, would require getting rid of so much inter-state plunder that only the iron broom of revolution could suffice. In his May Day article of last year,[12] it was

11. Radek 1912b, reprinted in Radek 1921: 156–176. See this volume, Chapter 37.
12. Kautsky 1911a, pp. 105–6.

precisely Kautsky who dealt with the slogan of the *United States of Europe* and reached the conclusion that it would be a very good idea – which, however, could only be realised by *means of a revolution*. In Western Europe, that means *social revolution*. That idea was elaborated very aptly by Kautsky in his book *The Road to Power*:

> More and more it becomes evident that the only possible revolution is a proletarian revolution. Such a revolution is impossible as long as the organised proletariat does not form a body large and compact enough to carry the mass of the nation with it under favourable circumstances. But when the workers become the only revolutionary class in the nation, it necessarily follows that any breakdown of the existing government, whether of a moral, financial or military nature, must involve the bankruptcy of all capitalist parties, which are held accountable, because in that case the only régime that could take over from the existing one would be a *proletarian* régime.[13]

To make a long story short: expansion is a vital necessity for capitalism. However, the only way in which it can expand is imperialism. Even if any other method were possible (and nothing suggests that this is so), it could only be enforced by means of a revolution. But the revolution is today only possible as a proletarian revolution, and it would result in the destruction of capitalism, the source of imperialism, thus depriving capitalism of the ground for other methods of expansion. Capitalist expansion is, therefore, only possible today as imperialist expansion, or else it is impossible.

The difference between the two views of imperialism thus proves to be a result of *different ways of applying the Marxist method of investigation. For us, it serves to study the development that is really taking place, to detect its trends. For Comrade Kautsky, it is only a springboard for intellectual summersaults, a means to harp on an interesting theme: It could be nicer, and what would happen it if were?*

We leave it to the reader to judge who has the right to speak about a misunderstanding regarding the nature of economic necessity and to dress himself in Marxist clothes.

* * *

13. Kautsky 1909b, p. 18.

It is now necessary to examine what conclusions must be drawn from this analysis for our tactics in the struggle against imperialism, i.e., what means we must use against it. But before doing so, we must dispose of one of Kautsky's misunderstandings, which is completely incomprehensible to me. Kautsky writes:

> *The struggle against the arms-race is absurd as long as capitalism rules* – that is the latest, let us say, improvisation of our 'youngest young ones'.[14]
>
> It is just as little the case today as in the past that the indispensable needs of 'bourgeois industry' must appear as necessary commandments for the proletariat, which it can resist only by means of a socialist revolution and *not already within capitalist production. The proletariat does not adjust its demands to the needs of the capitalist class but to its own needs, and these needs of its own are what force it to demand disarmament.*[15]

On this subject, I must say that neither I nor Pannekoek nor anyone else associated with us in this matter ever wrote a word that could be construed in that sense; *our efforts and strivings were always aimed at subjectively and objectively strengthening our struggle against imperialism and the arms-race.* If we had held the fight against the arms-race to be an absurdity within the framework of capitalism, what sense would there have been in our agitation for mass-actions against imperialism?

Militia and disarmament

We have seen that Kautsky reckons on the support of a part of the bourgeoisie in the battle against imperialism and the arms-race because he accepts the possibility of a further expansion of capitalism without imperialism. As he reached that conclusion on the basis of pure speculation, his slogans in the struggle against the arms-race do not grow out of an investigation of reality but out of a totally arbitrary abstraction from that reality. His speculations do not even have the character of a single train of thought: their constituent parts are contradictory, just as his intellectual construction as a whole contradicts actual development.

14. Kautsky 1912d, p. 467.
15. Kautsky 1912d, p. 519.

According to Kautsky's analysis, the militia slogan was 'sufficient' until the arrival of the [modern] navy. As the arms-race turned to the seas and it became apparent how terribly expensive it is, we cannot just content ourselves with the demand for a militia. First, because the idea of the militia failed completely in the navy; secondly, because it has been shown that the militia is not cheaper than the standing army, and in the navy this is of even greater importance because the cost of warship-construction is much greater than the expenditure on naval personnel.

Let us examine Kautsky's attitude in light of its underlying assumptions. He claims that we advanced the militia demand for political reasons in order to weaken the power of the government over the professional army, while now the disarmament demand must be supported for economic reasons.

His assertion, to the extent that it relates to the demand for a militia, is correct although incomplete. The scientific supporters of a militia in the ranks of Social Democracy – primarily Engels, whose military writings are an excellent introduction to military studies for all Social Democrats even today – did not support the militia idea just because its achievement would be politically useful for the working class, but because it is *in line with military progress. Engels's attitude towards militarism was analogous to his attitude towards all capitalist institutions.* We take militarism and capitalism as facts, *on whose ground* we must stand if we want to fight them. The capitalist state and all its institutions exist and are organs of the bourgeoisie's rule; this applies to militarism no more and no less than to the parliamentary system. Because they are institutions of bourgeois class-rule, we fight against them in principle, but we cannot stand outside them by setting against them institutions that would abolish their functions.

We go to parliament in order to represent the workers' interests. But we do not say: we must replace parliament by a people's parliament that would represent popular interests against the bourgeoisie. That would be a Platonic protest, not a struggle on real ground. We take the same attitude towards militarism. It is an organ of class-rule internally and of capitalist expansion externally. We fight it on principle, but we cannot ignore it. We say: a militarism that is neither externally nor internally an organ of class-rule is impossible in a capitalist society. No, *the militia idea was only intended to strengthen the elements within militarism itself that prevent a smooth fulfilment of the functions assigned to it by capitalism and that facilitate the struggle of the working class against militarism.*

This objective assessment of the nature of our demand for a militia stands in contrast to many subjective views on this subject that the Party has made its own. In my article 'The Militia Idea' (1912),[16] I tried to depict the historical causes that give the demand for a militia a character that no other requirement of our minimum-programme has: the character of a purely anti-capitalist institution that impairs *in advance* the functions of the capitalist army within the framework of capitalism. It was a legacy of the *petty-bourgeois worldview,* which we took over from the petty bourgeoisie together with the militia-demand. The petty bourgeoisie saw in the militia a real *people's army* and in a democracy the rule of the people. We were very critical towards democracy, but not towards the militia idea. In the first case, France and America showed the real meaning of democracy within capitalism, while, in the second, an experiment carried out on a vast scale was lacking.

Just as we participate in capitalist parliaments although we are in principle hostile towards capitalist parliamentarism as an organ of class-rule, and just as we can do so because parliament requires representatives of the working class to be able to exercise its functions, thus enabling us to struggle in parliament against capitalism, so we [take a similar] stand vis-à-vis democratic reconstruction of the army-organisation. *And the same factors enable us here, as with the parliamentary system, to strengthen the anti-capitalist trend in a capitalist institution.*

The parliament makes the whole nation, including the working classes, assume responsibility for the state economy. It thus seeks, in order to make the people more docile, to give them the impression that they also have an influence on that economy. It is the institution representing the central interests of the propertied classes against particular interests; that is why parliament, by attracting representatives of the popular classes, tries to make it impossible for the particular interests to base themselves upon the people. Parliament is an institution for the preservation of class-domination, but it also seeks to be an outlet for the dissatisfaction of the people. All of this facilitates the struggle for universal suffrage, making its abolition more difficult if the bourgeoisie feels threatened because the working class tries to use it to transform the function of parliament, advancing its proletarian interests and

16. Radek 1912d.

attempting to transform the parliamentary tribune from an organ of class-rule into one of proletarian-revolutionary agitation.

We see the same trends in modern militarism. It is an organ of class-rule, but its function is exercised by the people in arms. The people cannot be excluded from the army in the age of general conscription, but they are made submissive by means of the drill and by erecting a wall between the army and the civilian population. We cannot abolish the army as long as capitalism exists, although we oppose it in principle, as we demonstrate by voting against the military budget. But, since we cannot abolish militarism, we try to strengthen within the army the elements that make it more difficult to enforce its function as an institution of class-domination internally and capitalist expansion externally. We are doing this through our entire socialist agitation among the workers, who, each year, account for a larger part of the army; we are doing so especially through our anti-militarist action, which reveals the character of the army. Finally, we are doing so by demanding abolition of the wall separating the army from the people, the long service period, the drills, and military justice. Is this a Platonic demand? Absolutely not. *Our militia demand is based on tendencies already existing within capitalism and militarism themselves.* Compelled to abet the spread of education among the popular masses, capitalism, even against its will, makes possible a short period of service. By sharpening the antagonisms between states, capitalism requires the recruitment and training of growing masses of soldiers, thus strengthening the tendency – at least in states experiencing demographic growth – to implement universal military service, whose cost again strengthens the trend to shorten the service-time. The capitalist states will not do that by themselves because other tendencies counteract this one, such as the traditional views of the officer-caste, the bourgeoisie's fear of the effects of shortening the period of service, etc. It is possible that full implementation of a democratic military constitution will shipwreck on this resistance,[17] but because it is linked to real living trends, it can find

17. In this sense, a full implementation of the militia idea, the conversion of militarism into a real people's army, is unfeasible within the framework of capitalism, much as full *sovereignty of the people* is impossible in capitalism, where private ownership of the means of production rules over the people. In that respect, Comrade Pannekoek is right in his article against Grimm (*Leipziger Volkszeitung*, 7 July, 1912) when he speaks about the unfeasibility of the militia in the framework of capitalism. But not an iota further, because the democratisation of the military organisation is just as feasible as any other democratic measure in the framework of capitalism.

an echo in the masses and educate them about the nature of militarism, thus strengthening again the anti-capitalist tendencies in the army. The result of our struggle, whether it manifests itself in partial or full implementation of the militia idea or just in the agitation and education of the masses, will be to *strengthen the anti-capitalist tendencies in the army,* thus making more difficult *the carrying out of its capitalist functions.* While it would be utopian and unhistorical to hope that, even after the introduction of the militia, the army would immediately cease to be an organ of class-rule internally and capitalist expansion externally, the more vigorously we conduct the struggle for a militia among the broad masses of the people, and the greater its results, the more difficult will it be for capitalist governments to use the army as an instrument with no will of its own. Although no ruling class ever abdicated or turned into its opposite for fear of its own downfall, capital will also, when the water reaches its neck, play *va banque,* and then the contrast between the functions allotted to the army by capital and the proletarian content of most of its ranks will emerge. It would be idle to examine here whether that will happen by means of fierce internal revolutionary mass-struggles or through external conflicts. *The main thing is to realise the link between the militia demand and our struggle against imperialism and the arms-race.*

If we assume that imperialism cannot be replaced within the framework of capitalism by some other method of capitalist development, then the function of the army cannot be abolished by some other organisation. But the developmental tendencies of the army strengthen the contradiction within it between the working class and imperialism. *By translating this contradiction into the political demand for democratisation of the army organisation, that is to say, for the militia, we wage our battle against imperialism on a real basis, not on the basis of some speculation.*

Kautsky does not reject the demand for a militia. His view of the connection between its gradual realisation, or the fight for it, and imperialist development is not clear. He even said during the discussion on the militia, as opposed to disarmament, that the demand is not up to date. In his May Day article of this year,[18] he goes even further and says that *the militia idea breaks down in the navy.* This claim, in which he is in solidarity with Matthias Erzberger, has been made in our party literature for the very first time. In a footnote to my article

18. [Kautsky 1912c.]

'Our Struggle against Imperialism', published two months ago in *Die Neue Zeit*, I asked Kautsky about the reasons for his opinion since it is of great importance for the discussion.[19] However, I removed this footnote at the request of the editors, for Kautsky would have been forced to respond immediately, which would have disrupted the course of the debate. I hoped that Kautsky would unveil his reasons later. But he keeps silent to this day on this issue; he just meekly writes: 'How much the period of service would be reduced by it [the implementation of the demand for a militia] *eludes me.*'[20]

But, since the shortening of service-time is the most important prerequisite of the militia, this means that whether the militia idea fails in the navy escapes Comrade Kautsky – unless he wants to endorse the brilliant idea of Erzberger that the militia fails in the navy for another reason, namely, because the soldier cannot carry his ship home. But then the demand for a militia also fails in the artillery, because the soldiers cannot go home with their cannons, as well as in the infantry, because the thirty cartridges that the soldiers take home with them – as is done in Switzerland – are only enough for them to defend themselves for a few minutes while machine-guns last rather longer. In short, if the militia idea fails in the navy due to the impossibility of taking a warship home, then it also fails in the army. But, since Kautsky wants to keep the militia demand for the army, only one possible conclusion remains: *Comrade Kautsky assumed on the 26th of April that the militia idea fails in the navy due to the impossibility of reducing the period of service, but on the 28th of June he converted to Socratic wisdom: I know nothing except the fact of my own ignorance.*[21] He leaves the question of the period of service in the navy open.

I leave it to the comrades to determine what value can be claimed for a general view of the disarmament question based on such 'self-denying

19. Radek 1912b, reprinted in Radek 1921: 156–76. See this volume, Chapter 37.
20. [Kautsky 1912d, p. 467.]
21. This is not the only point in this polemic where knowledge of the facts eludes Comrade Kautsky. When he writes in his last article of 6 September that 'Germany has an unlimited human material to expand its navy, while England finds it increasingly difficult to man its new ships,' or when, in the same article, he says that neither Africa nor Asia faces great territorial shifts, it must be said that the factual data elude him. These statements must be ascertained on factual grounds. It is clear that even a man like Kautsky, to whom the Party owes so much, must not and indeed cannot possibly master all areas of policy with the same thoroughness. The debate over new phenomena requires thorough study, however, because without knowledge of the facts it can only lead to political platitudes.

knowledge' of very important factual data, and I affirm, on the basis of the rich material available,[22] that we have absolutely no reason to vouch for the truth of Mr. Tirpitz's[23] assertion about the impossibility of shortening the period of service: *a notable reduction of the service-period in the navy* is possible, and since the abolition of military justice is naturally just as possible in the navy as in the army, the main objection against the possibility of democratising the navy-organisation remains the isolation of sailors by life aboard ship.

But since, despite this seclusion, revolts break out again and again in the French Navy, and given the sailors' role in the Russian Revolution [of 1905], it is clear that this seclusion, if the service-period is shortened, could not choke the socialist spiritual life of the sailors, who are recruited partly from the crew of the commercial fleet (mariners) and partly from skilled industrial workers and who are, therefore, accessible to socialist agitation. *The idea of democratising the military organisation is thus as feasible in the navy as in the army. The militia idea is a unified notion, methodologically and politically uniform and encompassing the whole disarmament issue. Methodologically, because democratisation of the army is not a Platonic demand for the purpose of greater symmetry in the party programme, or a pure invention [adopted] because of its [propagandistic] advantages, but one that rests upon real developmental trends of capitalism. Politically, because the militia demand illuminates one of our goals: to strengthen the influence of the working class on the main organs of imperialism in order to create within it the conditions for its breakdown during the decisive battle between the working class and imperialism, thus accelerating the social revolution.* Of course, that does not mean that the degree of democratisation of the naval organisation can and must be the same as in the army. In the navy, the operation of modern machinery plays the biggest role. The factory-proletarian can learn to operate it in a short time, and that is why reduction of his service is possible, but, the longer he serves, the more experienced he becomes in handling the machines. The reduction of service-time in the navy is thus doubtless possible, but it is not required by the development of the navy itself. In addition, the importance of democratising the navy, for social development as a whole, is not as great as in the case of the

---

22. Since I have already exceeded the allowed length of my article, I must refrain from illustrating this question by means of statistics, etc.

23. [Alfred von Tirpitz (1849–1930) was a German Admiral and Secretary of State of the Imperial Naval Office, the administrative branch of the Imperial Marine, from 1897 until 1916.]

army. The navy cannot intervene as much as the army does in class-struggles, nor can the spirit inspiring the masses of the proletariat in the decisive battles manifest itself in the navy as much as in the army, because the sailors are not concentrated in such large masses and because the dead element of machinery plays a greater role in the navy than in the army. Probably these factors led Comrade *Lensch*, for example, to come round to Comrade Kautsky's view that the militia idea fails in the navy. For us, accounting for these factors is only a warning against a stereotyped appraisal of the militia idea for the army and the navy. But, since we assume that we can reduce the period of service in the navy, as well as [implementing] other measures in order to democratise its organisation, and since we regard democratisation of the navy as an anti-imperialist factor, we believe that we can and must retain the militia idea also for the navy.

The idea of disarmament, which Kautsky considers a complement to the militia idea, is directly opposed to it methodologically and politically. The militia idea is feasible due to the development of the military system. It ties in with the trends created by that development. *The disarmament idea would be a total departure from that development* and yet it would remain on the ground of capitalism. Kautsky's disarmament idea is *an invention* in the best or worst sense of the word because, as we have seen, he could provide no proof of the existence of any bourgeois tendencies caring for disarmament. In view of that fact, one could abandon it to its fate, had it not found a certain diffusion in recent years. Therefore, we want to examine it more closely. Methodologically, it contradicts, as I said, the way in which such a programmatic demand can be posed: it is not a product of the analysis of real trends but of speculation about the sins and errors of capitalism in the past, as well as about all the possible and impossible courses that could be followed if a revolution were so kind as to clear up the mess of capitalist national divisions without abolishing capitalism.

This methodological miscarriage corresponds to the political character of the disarmament idea. It is unfeasible not just because the bourgeoisie does not want it, but *because the arms-race is a product of the contradictions tearing apart capitalist society, which it cannot overcome.* It would only be *possible to stop the arms-race* if there were other tendencies in operation that were able to do away with these contradictions. Disarmament is impossible not because the bourgeoisie does not want it, but because it cannot want it. If that is the case, it is irrelevant how Kautsky portrays the merits of this idea. Whether it reduces the financial burdens that the masses must bear or not, this cannot help its viability. But, if it is true that Social Democrats must advocate disarmament because it can bring great economic relief to the masses, *why stop at the navy?* Does the army cost so little? Is it to be ruled out that new major transformations in arms technology – Kautsky can follow in the military press the issue, now under discussion, of the introduction of the automatic rifle – will require hundreds of millions in the short term? Even more: according to Kautsky's statements, disarmament in the navy would be feasible because it would enable the replacement of imperialist competition by the reconciliation of capitalist states.

If that is the case, then the army also loses one of its functions – that of a fighting body directed outwards – because contemporary antagonisms between capitalist states, despite their old historic forms (revenge in France [for the Franco-Prussian War], etc.) are of an imperialist nature. So, away with the militia and long live disarmament all along the line!

One could argue that the army also has a second function: to hold down the working class. However, according to the view that Kautsky championed in 1898 in his polemics against Schippel, this function disappears with transformation of the contemporary army into a militia.[24] Up to now, Kautsky has not revised this view; he must, therefore, draw the necessary conclusions from it. If imperialism disappears and the militia takes the place of militarism, then capital loses any interest in it. But even if, under the influence of Comrade *Grimm's* interesting remarks *on the militia in Switzerland* (*Die Neue Zeit*, Nr. 37/38),[25] Kautsky came to the conclusion that the bourgeoisie, after the

24. [Kautsky 1899a, Kautsky 1899b.]

25. [Grimm 1912.] Grimm's article makes a clean sweep of many petty-bourgeois illusions that Social Democracy took over, together with the militia idea, from the petty bourgeoisie. I do not understand why he turns his polemic against me, because – as he must admit – my articles were farther from the popular illusions about the wonders of the militia than any others in the party press. If I cannot agree with the too-narrow position of Comrade Grimm in assessing the power-shift that the development of a militia would bring about in Germany – which would also influence social policy – that happens for this reason: Grimm examines the [Swiss] militia as it is turning, under the influence of the development of military technology and capitalism, from petty-bourgeois into capitalist, while, in Germany, one must study how democratic tendencies assert themselves in capitalist militarism under the pressure of the proletariat. These different perspectives give rise to the apparent difference of opinion between my view of the militia and Grimm's. The difference would be serious if, after the bankruptcy of the petty-bourgeois militia hopes, he had developed illusions about disar-

transformation of the standing army into a militia, will still be able to employ it for some time to hold down the proletariat, how could he replace the demand for a militia by a different programmatic demand? Kautsky correctly writes:

> *The proletariat does not adjust its demands to the needs of the capitalist class but to its own needs, and these needs of its own are what force it to demand disarmament.*[26]

Now then! Revise the party programme, Comrade Kautsky, eliminate the demand for a militia. In your opinion, it is idle and only scrapes a living thanks to our allegiance to good old ideas. But some ideas do not harmonise, even if one would like to leave them stand peacefully together: the new, because they correspond to a new situation; the old, because people do not want to have the reputation of being a revisionist of the Right, Left or any other kind.

The result of our investigation is therefore as follows: the question under dispute is not whether two slogans [militia and disarmament], arising in different historical situations but having the same objective – the struggle against imperialism – supplement or circumscribe each other. *The two ideas are the product of two different views of imperialism developed in different ways.* We now want to examine the political consequences of both, but first it is necessary to answer still another attempt to obscure the issues under dispute.

The limitation of armaments

An attempt to blur the contradiction between a militia and disarmament has often been made lately in the party press and at rallies, where some comrades have declared that general disarmament is impossible but *partial, temporary* disarmament would be to the benefit of the proletariat. Sensing that his argument failed concerning the possibility of replacing the current imperialist policy by a *general* agreement of imperialist states for the purpose of joint action in the colonies, Kautsky clings in his May Day article of this year to this attempt [to advocate at least partial and temporary disarmament] and writes in *Die Neue Zeit* (1912, p. 108):

---

mament speculation, illusions that, in his case, would be forgivable due to the special Swiss conditions but are objectively unacceptable.

26. [Kautsky 1912d, p. 519.]

> Just as an association of entrepreneurs cannot eliminate competition forever, so an agreement between capitalist governments, clearing away all conflicts for all time, is impossible. *Therefore, no agreement between them can possibly bring about complete disarmament.* Nevertheless, it would already be an enormous accomplishment if it were possible to substitute for the present situation, in which a world war is inevitable in the near future, a condition in which *war would certainly not be excluded forever but would at least be postponed.* That could even mean the final demise of major wars between European states, because the European proletariat is growing in power every year and bringing its influence to bear against such a war.[27]

Kautsky did not notice that his *support for a modification of current imperialist policy, in order to make it peaceful, quickly turned into a recognition of that policy* because, if his sentence has any meaning, it is simply this: if nothing else is possible, then for the time being we will content ourselves with *agreements* between capitalist states that will turn the war-threat from a daily occurrence into a rare event. The fact that he linked this 'momentary' reconciliation with the capitalist alliance-policy to the hope that the proletariat will, in the meantime, become so strong that it will make wars between major powers impossible (and a colonial war against China, would that be in order?) testifies to his hopes but also to his *horrendous confusion of ideas.*

What has the question of the possibility of imperialist agreements to do with the question of abolishing imperialism within the framework of capitalism? And what has the question of disarmament to do with Kautsky's hypothesis about a situation in which war *'would certainly not be excluded forever but would at least be postponed'*? The fact is clear that such 'a condition' [see the quotation from Kautsky above] has nothing to do with disarmament but rather with the question of a *limitation of armaments.* But this is an entirely different question. Imperialist agreements between great powers are not only possible but also belong to the essence of imperialism.

Because the risk of war in the age of imperialism is enormous, the powers with secondary antagonisms straighten things out and concentrate on the main ones, for whose warlike or peaceful solution they arm themselves. Within this diplomatic constellation, agreements on armaments under certain

27. [Kautsky 1912c, p. 108.]

circumstances can lead to *acceleration* of the arms-race, in others to its temporary *delay*, but they are always, to use the expression of Kautsky's previous May Day article, 'palliatives' that can be disposed of at any moment. Their palliative character depends on the economic-political upheavals changing the relationships between the states as well as on the development of weapons-technology. Obviously if a government, on the basis of an agreement with another power, slackens its arms-race for a while, we welcome it. But we must demonstrate to the working class the palliative character of these measures and the factors that threaten to wreak havoc with them. In any such case, we will refuse to take responsibility for such temporary measures and will assign it to the propertied classes.

This intrusion of another question in place of the one that has occupied us here – of an ordinary parliamentary question [like arms-limitation agreements] instead of the principled question about the character of our foreign policy – is no coincidence and deserves a brief comment. Kautsky refers to the issue [under dispute] several times with this formula: he is a supporter of reforms in all fields, including the field of imperialism, while his opponents are revolutionaries who want all or nothing. And this reform of imperialism would also imply agreements between capitalist countries. Were that in fact the case, such agreements would be a beginning of the end of bellicose imperialism, finally giving Kautsky some ground under his feet. However, since those agreements are just means to put aside the smaller antagonisms in order to gather forces for the big battles, it would be a total disregard of their character to see in them a departure from imperialism. They are the *practice* of imperialism.

Kautsky's final saving leap from the clouds is thus a leap onto the ground of imperialism. What he sees as the reform of imperialism is actually its strengthening. But, while the reforms advocated by the proletariat usually strengthen the proletariat, the policy of alliances between great powers cannot become an objective of the workers without weakening their cause. Were the proletariat of two countries to draw breath for a moment and work together for a 'reconciliation' of their imperialist governments, that could not happen without the agreement being based on a common standpoint of *the imperialist governments*. Imperialist agreements mean haggling over colonies. Without accepting this colonial haggling, the working class cannot play the role of an *'honest broker'* between governments – to use the expression of Comrade Ledebour, which is the best, even if unconscious, condemnation of this policy (he used it in his Reichstag speech on the Foreign Office budget in May of this year) – because a broker must offer something of value to both sides. The result of that policy could only be the recognition of colonial policy; that is to say, acceptance of the capitalist position by the proletariat, because one cannot advocate 'reconciliation' and reject the only way leading to it under the given circumstances.

But, if a reform advocated by the proletariat leads away from the class-struggle, then it is not a reform that the proletariat can accept or even support. It is a *yellow reform*, to use Rappaport's expression against Millerand. The fact that Kautsky accepted it is, in view of his general position, yet another proof that he fails to notice the momentousness of the issue in dispute, and that he can no longer notice it due to the consequences of the policy he has pursued in recent years.

The sources and the consequences

Investigation of the differences between a part of the radicals and Comrade Kautsky on the issues of our foreign and defence-policy has shown that they are based on a difference in application of the Marxist method. However, it would be incorrect to assume that this is the ultimate root of those differences. We do not want to investigate here whether Kautsky always studied and explained our present policy in this speculative manner, because this is not a personal confrontation, although Kautsky sees the source of the differences in my zeal as an unhappy inventor and in the fact that I succeeded in seducing an innocent, unsuspecting country-wench like Paul Lensch. The fact that Kautsky formerly saw imperialism with rather different eyes, and that his position on this issue is supported by comrades who gave us excellent analyses of the driving forces of imperialism, as well as by others who do not bother about theory but rather support disarmament for purely political reasons,[28] shows that the actual source of the differences lies in a totally different place. It must be sought in the *general tactical differences* that have arisen during recent years within the camp of German Marxism. Kautsky's method only clarified the nature and consequences of the general tactical position shared by him and a part of the radicals on the peculiarities of German imperialism,

28. [A reference to Georg Ledebour and Hugo Haase.]

which I tried to outline in my article 'On Our Struggle Against Imperialism' in *Die Neue Zeit*.[29] Kautsky's standpoint on this issue found support among a part of the comrades who, on general tactical questions, have nothing in common with his position.[30]

What scandalised Kautsky most in our position is that it describes the situation with the formula: Here imperialism – there socialism; that it sees in imperialism the last phase of dying capitalism; that it rejects all illusions about the possibility of reforming imperialism; that it sees a major task of the working class in organising mass-actions against imperialist practice at moments when it is really stirring the masses. He sets against this policy a different one: the fight against imperialism and against the arms-race; not, however, as an independent struggle of the working class but as a joint struggle with the petty bourgeoisie, indeed, together with a part of the bourgeoisie, which, in this matter of life and death for capitalism, allegedly has common interests with the proletariat. What is this other than the slogan: Against the *black-blue bloc!* as the political basis of the *runoff election-agreement*, which Comrade Kautsky, at the expense of method and the facts, defended this winter with the same zeal as the disarmament slogan?[31] Kautsky does not set a principled rejection of mass-actions against the policy [of the radicals], which, in view of the dangers of imperialist policy, regards raising the activity of the masses as the only task of Social Democrats on this issue; indeed, he even declares (in *Die Neue Zeit*, XXIX, 2, p. 103) that the success of a mass-strike in such a situation is not excluded. Yet, some sentences later, he declares:

> If the people see the cause of a war not in their own government but in the viciousness of their neighbours (*and what government is not trying, with the help of its press, its parliament, its diplomats, to impress this idea upon the mass of the population?*), under such circumstances they go to war because the whole population is unanimously convinced of the pressing need to secure the borders against the evil enemy, to protect them from its invasion.
>
> *Then they all become first of all patriots, including the internationally minded,* and if some individuals had the *superhuman courage* to rebel against this and

29. Radek 1912b, reprinted in Radek 1921: pp. 156–76. [See this volume, Chapter 37.]
30. [Karl Liebknecht and Julian Marchlewski, for instance, supported disarmament.]
31. [The black-blue bloc was an alliance of the Conservatives and the Centre.]

> wanted to prevent the military from hastening to the border and being massively equipped with war-materiel, *the government does not have to lift a finger to render them harmless. The angry crowd would kill them itself.*
>
> The political mass-strike is a tremendous enterprise that only comes about and can succeed where a whole series of extremely favourable circumstances come together. To want to apply it as a means of preventing defence of the borders against a foreign invasion is to bring it about when all the circumstances, without exception, make it impossible and when, at best, it can be nothing but *heroic madness.*[32]

What kind of government will not try, in a conflict with another, to play the innocent lamb? Kautsky himself admits that every government will act that way. In what wars will the enemy not be at the border? And who really believes that a capitalist government would 'frivolously' attack if it were perceived to be devoid of justice by its own people? Every war would present all the conditions necessary to make the mass-strike hopeless if, as Kautsky assumes, *class-contradictions disappear from the consciousness of the masses at the moment of war, and the forty-years-long work of Social Democracy could, and indeed should, be blotted out* – even if only temporarily.

We have no wish to deal with this issue in detail (that was already done by Pannekoek)[33] because we are not interested here in refuting Kautsky's assertions on this point, only in establishing the facts of the case. It is clear that if anyone fears that a mass-action against imperialism must collapse miserably, he must turn against a theoretical analysis that ascertains the whole helplessness of parliamentary action against imperialism by showing it to be the last card of capitalism. Although we do not believe that the masses in every war-situation can brace themselves for defensive action, or that every defensive action must be successful, we do regard it as the task of Social Democracy, in all its daily agitation against imperialism, to disseminate among the masses the knowledge that the whole bourgeoisie supports imperialism, and that there is no means against it but the action of the working class, which is entrenched in all positions, even in the fortress of imperialism, in the army,

---

32. [Kautsky 1911a, p. 103]
33. The article was written before the publication of the article by Comrade Pannekoek on mass-actions. [Pannekoek 1912a.]

which must therefore be democratically reconstructed as far as possible in the interest of the struggle against imperialism.

That position seems to Kautsky to be an agitation for 'heroic madness', and *that is the source of his efforts* to avoid seeing what is actually taking place. *He revised his view of imperialism* because he fears the consequences of the analysis of imperialism for his 'attrition-strategy', *just as two years ago he revised his theory of the mass-strike out of consideration for the attrition-strategy.*[34]

The fact that he describes Lensch – who proved this revision for any unbiased observer to see – as a very bad fellow is only a counterpart to his assertion that Comrade Luxemburg falsified quotations to prove his departure from his old views on the mass-strike. If we mention this rather comic side, it is just because it leads to very serious questions about the political consequences of Kautsky's policy.

It is the same with the policy of Social Democracy as with any other: if you do not move forwards, you go backwards. Whoever closes his eyes out of a (not necessarily conscious) fear of the consequences of stating what is, has not only failed to fulfill his Social-Democratic duty to say what is but will also be forced to say what in reality does not exist, to spread *illusions*. Any misunderstanding of reality leads to *confusion*.[35]

The fact that these illusions manifest themselves in an individual trying to prove that it is not he who has changed but others, is not very important; however, that would lead to a wavering policy in the Party that would weaken its agitational force. This should be taken into account first and foremost by the comrades engaged in practical activity, by those who declare that disarmament is impossible but that it constitutes a stirring *agitational* slogan, and that arms-limitation agreements would be a temporary measure but would have a greater impact upon the masses as a *concrete achievable* goal and be better able to mobilise them than general agitation – no matter how correct this view may be in itself. We leave aside the fact that the struggle for democratisation of the army, waged in a concrete form, is an even more realistic goal that we could

34. [*Ermattungsstrategie*: 'attrition-strategy'. See Rosa Luxemburg 1910c.]
35. This confusion occurs most glaringly in the articles by Comrade Eckstein in *Die Neue Zeit* – for instance, his recent article on the feasibility of the contemporary demands of Social Democracy in capitalist society [Eckstein 1912a] – as well as in those of Spectator [Miron Isakovich Nachimson] in the *Dresdner Volkszeitung* on the same topic.

link to our daily struggle against imperialism, and that the imperialist threats always offer a specific target. We only wish to emphasise that Social Democrats must never adapt their agitation to the illusions of the masses; that they must, on the contrary, try to free them of all illusions by telling them in every action what is the case. But the practical politicians, who assume that belief in the possibility of disarmament and in the benefit of agreements between capitalist governments have become established among the masses, are poor observers. At the meetings, nothing leaves the masses more indifferent than remarks about agreements between the 'cultured nations' and the possibility of limiting armaments, and nothing draws such applause from them as the appeal to solidarity in the actions of the proletariat against the policy of these 'cultured states', who are shaking hands with the tsar so that he will help them to cut each other's throats. Nothing arouses greater enthusiasm in the crowds than the observation that imperialism leads capitalism to the abyss, and that it is the historical role of the working class to shove it there. All this will ultimately happen because it is based on the knowledge, which is instinctively making its way into the working class on account of the whole nature of its struggle, that no class resigns or changes its nature without first having risked everything, and because that knowledge is based on the feeling by the working class that its power to achieve victory over capitalism is growing every year. That is why the disarmament slogan and all its accoutrements, which some of the practitioners advocated for agitational reasons, will do anything but strengthen agitation.

That is also why we are certain that, although at the party congress in Chemnitz, given the still scarcely clarified nature of the problem, the majority of the Party declared itself in favour of the position of the Reichstag group, for which Kautsky provides a theoretical justification, that victory will be very short-lived. With fantasies one may make poems; with speculation, bad philosophy; but a fight requires a sword, and iron can be found only in the hard rock of reality.

Chapter Forty-One

'Social Democracy and Foreign Policy'[1] (9 December 1912)

Paul Lensch

The events of recent weeks – the war-danger, proletarian peace demonstrations, the Basel Congress,[2] the debates at the Reichstag in Berlin and at the military committee of the Austrian House of Representatives – have shown that Social Democracy is increasingly forced to expand its role in shaping foreign policy.

Not that the socialist parties previously left this question unattended. Marx already indicated, in his concluding sentences of the inaugural address of the

1. [Lensch 1912c. This article appeared as an unsigned editorial. We have attributed it to Paul Lensch because he was the chief editor of the *Leipziger Volkszeitung*. The journal also included among its editors Rosa Luxemburg and Julian Marchlewski (Karski).]

2. [In the context of an increasingly disturbed diplomatic situation (war between Italy and Turkey, and the Balkan War of 1912), the International Socialist Bureau decided to convene a congress of the Socialist International in an extraordinary session, which was held at Basel, Switzerland, on 24–5 November, 1912. A single item was on the agenda: action against the threat of war. The Congress recommended creation of a Balkan Federation, took exception to any Austrian intervention aimed at bringing Serbia under its control, and refuted Russian claims to pose as protector of the Slav peoples. The Manifesto adopted by the Extraordinary Congress stated: 'The overcoming of the antagonism between Germany on the one hand and France and England on the other would eliminate the greatest menace to universal peace, undermine the powerful position of tsarism which exploits this antagonism, render an attack by Austria-Hungary upon Serbia impossible, and assure peace to the world. All the endeavours of the International, therefore, are to be directed primarily toward this goal. The Congress notes that the entire Socialist International is at one on these principles of foreign policy. It invited the workers of all countries to oppose the power of the international solidarity of the proletariat to capitalist imperialism.' Manifesto of the Extraordinary International Socialist Congress, Basel, 24–5 November 1912, in Hess Gankin and Fisher (eds.) 1940, p. 84.]

[First] International, the necessity of mastering the secrets of foreign policy.[3] But the power of Social Democracy was still too undeveloped to be able to confront the historical process with more than impotent protest. However, the more acute social antagonisms become, the more imperialism strengthens and the competitive struggle over the world market threatens world peace, the more unavoidable has the necessity become for the international proletariat to bring its influence to bear on shaping foreign policy. That is especially valid for the German proletariat; not only because Germany's political and trade-union organisations are the strongest and the power of the organised proletariat is relatively the greatest, but also because the economic development of the German Empire has placed the German proletariat in the front ranks of the struggle against imperialism. No other state in the world is so restless and indefatigable, so hungry for world-political power, as the German Empire. German imperialism is a constant source of anxiety in world politics. The activity of the German bourgeoisie is ubiquitous precisely because German imperialism is still in its youthful phase. It intrudes everywhere, and everywhere it is repelled. The other predatory powers, being older, have long ago taken possession of the last corners of the earth. That is the cause of the German-English antagonism, and that is why the main danger of war lies in Germany, the *parvenu* of imperialism. And precisely for that reason, the struggle against imperialism must be taken up most keenly in Germany, for the decision lies here.

The expanded role of the German proletariat – to lead the struggle against the final, the most dangerous and, at the same time, the most powerful organisation of capitalism – has naturally forced German Social Democracy to shoulder greater responsibility. The German example of how to fight imperialism has been eagerly followed by the foreign sister-parties and readily adopted

3. ['If the emancipation of the working classes requires their fraternal concurrence, how are they to fulfil that great mission with a foreign policy in pursuit of criminal designs, playing upon national prejudices, and squandering in piratical wars the people's blood and treasure?.... The working classes [have] the duty to master themselves the mysteries of international politics; to watch the diplomatic acts of their respective governments; to counteract them, if necessary, by all means in their power; when unable to prevent, to combine in simultaneous denunciations, and to vindicate the simple laws or morals and justice, which ought to govern the relations of private individuals, as the rules paramount of the intercourse of nations. The fight for such a foreign policy forms part of the general struggle for the emancipation of the working classes.' Marx 1864, p. 13.]

as a rule of conduct. Moreover, the bourgeoisie of other countries is attentively watching the attitude of the German proletariat in this world-historical struggle.

What is our position? In our comments on foreign policy, we must take greater notice than before of the international character of socialism. There is general agreement on the need to give up the old, comfortable and easy habit of praising the policy of foreign states in order to criticise more forcefully one's own government. This method had the unwanted effect of making it more difficult for our foreign comrades to criticise the conduct of their own governments.

But there are also other methods that quite recently have been applied more frequently and give rise to serious misgivings. We mean the fact that socialists have often declared their agreement with alliances and treaties of capitalist states on whose design we had no influence, whose content we never know exactly and fully, and, most importantly, which were concluded, despite all the talk about their 'purely defensive character', in order to turn against other states. Thus, for instance, the Triple Alliance was concluded as 'an alliance of peace and mutual defence'. But the inner logic of this Triple Alliance gave rise to its counterpart: first the Dual Alliance and later the contemporary Triple Entente. Today, the whole of capitalist Europe is divided into two armed camps: here, the Triple Alliance, there, the Triple Entente. And the 'purely defensive' character of the Triple Alliance is shown by Austria's demeanour. Strengthened by the alliance with Germany and Italy, Austria plundered Bosnia three years ago in a period of peace (Italy did exactly the same in Tripoli a year ago), and today its brawl with Serbia threatens to unleash a world war.

For a socialist to support the Triple Alliance, as Comrade David[4] did last Tuesday during the budget debates, is completely inadmissible and would ultimately lead to the break-up of the International. If one supports the Triple Alliance, one cannot blame our comrades in France, England and Russia for taking the side of the Triple Entente, which is ultimately as 'purely defensive' as the Triple Alliance. And this attitude in favour of the Triple Alliance cannot

4. [Eduard David (1863–1930) belonged to the revisionist right wing of the SPD. During the Weimar Republic he was the Minister of the Interior from 21 June 1919, to 3 October 1919.]

be justified by referring to Russia. In this regard, David stated in his speech to the Reichstag on 3 December 1912:

> We know very well that in Russia there is a pan-Slavist war-party at work, whose expansive endeavours also extend to the West. It follows from our whole attitude towards Russia that we are in no way inclined to assist those expansionist strivings. When we speak about Russia, we do not mean the Russian people, but the system of tsarism, that régime of blood and plunder, that system which, with knouts and gallows, hinders a healthy domestic development and continually seizes new areas with insatiable rapacity and lust for power. We are obviously of the opinion that nothing should be done to give the tsar a taste for attacking Germany or Austria. What our attitude would be in the case of a provocative attack by Russia, was stated clearly enough by my party Comrade Bebel, who some years ago declared that in such a case he would be ready to take the rifle upon his back.[5]

According to a telegraphic report of the *Vorwärts* from Vienna, Comrade Renner[6] expressed himself similarly in the military committee of the Austrian House of Representatives:

> Unfortunately, Social Democrats still do not decide and there are still wars: aggressive and defensive wars. If we, through your serious fault, are driven

5. ['But if Germany's existence were at stake in a war, in that case – I give you my word – we will all, to the last man, even the oldest amongst us, be ready to take the rifles upon our backs and defend our German soil. . . . We live and struggle in this soil, for this fatherland, which is as much our fatherland, perhaps even more so, than yours.' August Bebel's speech to the Reichstag of 7 March 1904. Reichstag 1904, XI. *Legislaturperiode*. I. *Session, erster Sessionsabschnitt*, 1903/1904, zweiter Band, p. 1588C. For the full text of Bebel's speech see pp. 1583C–1592A.]

6. [Karl Renner (1870–1950) was an Austrian Social-Democratic politician. He joined the Austrian Social-Democratic Party (SPÖ) in 1896 and represented the Party in the Reichsrat beginning in 1907. After the defeat of the Austro-Hungarian Empire in the First World War, the country was dismembered, and the peace treaty of St. Germain, signed in 1919 by the victorious Allies, declared Austria to be a republic. Renner became Chancellor of Austria and Minister of Foreign Affairs from October 1918 to July 1920, and he was President of the Representative Assembly from 1931–3. He always pleaded for the annexation of Austria by Germany but distanced himself from politics during the Second World War. In April 1945, just before the collapse of the Third Reich, the defeat of Germany and the end of the war, the elderly Renner set up a Provisional Government in Vienna with politicians from other three parties SPÖ, ÖVP and KPÖ, which was recognised by the Four Powers. Renner served as first post-war Chancellor of Austria from April 1945 to 20 December, 1945, when he became the first President of the Second Austrian Republic until his death in December 1950.]

> into a defensive war, we (and our comrades in other countries – Bebel left no doubt about it in the Reichstag) will obviously not overlook the fact that our own people will be threatened most. We do not need your patriotic fairy-tales for that. We are – I say it expressly so that there will be no mistake – very far from answering for the incalculable ramifications of your policy, and yet we can resolutely repeat what we said in Basel and what is the long-standing legacy of European democracy: if the meagre rights and freedoms that we have won (and that even today the government is trying to curtail) were to be threatened by tsarism, we would all be compelled and ready to take up the defence.

In both utterances, as well as in the reference to Bebel, the differentiation between aggressive and defensive wars re-appears; but, already at the party congress in Essen, Kautsky remarked that the distinction between aggressive and defensive wars is meaningless and impossible.[7] Who was the aggressor in 1870? Was it Bismarck, who falsified the Ems dispatch,[8] or Napoleon, who let himself be manoeuvred into a situation where he had to declare war? Nothing is easier than to provoke an adversary into an 'aggressive' war. As for Bebel's utterance, one should remember that it was made before the Russian Revolution [of 1905] and was rendered obsolete by that world-

7. [Opposing Noske's and Bebel's support for a war of national defence in Germany, Karl Kautsky told the SPD party congress, held at Essen on 15–21 September 1907: 'Some day the German government might make the German proletariat believe they were being attacked; the French government might do the same with its subjects, and then we should have a war in which the French and German workingmen would follow their respective governments with equal enthusiasm, and murder each other and cut each other's throats. Such a contingency must be avoided, and it will be avoided if we do not adopt the criterion of the aggressive or defensive war, but that of the interests of the proletariat, which at the same time are international interests.' Quoted in Trotsky 1918, pp. 150–1.]

8. [The Ems dispatch was a communication between King William of Prussia (later German Emperor William I) and his premier, Otto von Bismarck. In June 1870, the throne of Spain was offered to Prince Leopold of Hohenzollern-Sigmaringen, a relative of King William. Leopold at first accepted the candidacy, but withdrew it in July after the French government of Napoleon III had protested. During these transactions, William and Bismarck were taking the waters at Ems, Germany. There, the French ambassador Comte Benedetti, in an interview with the king, requested William's guarantee that the candidacy of Leopold to the Spanish throne would never be renewed. William rejected the request. Bismarck, intent on provoking war with France, made the king's report of the conversation public on 13 July in his celebrated Ems dispatch, which he edited in a manner certain to provoke the French. France declared war on 19 July, and the Franco-Prussian War began.]

historic event. Today, the strongest guarantee that Russian tsarism will not provoke a world-war is exactly the same one applying to Germany and the governments of all capitalist states; namely, fear that the beginning of a world war will be the beginning of a world revolution. Since Bebel's remark, the decomposition of the Russian empire has advanced so far, as the events of 1905–6 have shown, that Russia's position is no longer an exceptional one for the International. If, even today, we want to proclaim: 'Against Russian despotism all Social Democrats must take up weapons, because Russian tsarism is the worst danger!', Polish Social Democrats could declare with the same right: 'If German despotism wages a war of aggression against Russia, we will all take up weapons, because German despotism is the worst enemy of Poland!' The International would be torn apart in that way.

Actually, capitalist Europe is organised into two state-cartels ready to attack each other: the Triple Alliance and the Triple Entente. The international proletariat has nothing to do with either of them: it stands above them both as the International of world peace. The struggle against the despotism of a given country is the cause of the Social-Democratic party of that particular country. To pick out one country and label it the common enemy of all the other countries, against which all socialists should take up weapons, is today not only an obsolete position but also a dangerous one to the highest degree, which can only harm rather than further the idea of world peace. How much what we have just said applies to David's speech is shown by the attitude of the bourgeois press, which drew from it the quite soothing conclusion (for the capitalists) that they can go calmly to war because the German working class will not stir. Can that be the effect we hoped for from the International Socialist Congress at Basel?

Chapter Forty-Two

SPD Party Congress at Chemnitz, 'Debate and Resolution on Imperialism' (15–21 September 1912)

Hugo Haase et al.

The SPD held its annual party congress at Chemnitz in September 1912, just weeks before an Extraordinary International Socialist Congress was to convene at Basel.[1] The party meeting occurred against the background of a triumph in the Reichstag elections of 12 January 1912. Social-Democratic candidates received approximately 4,250,000 votes (34.8 per cent of the total), dramatically increasing the party's representation from the 43 Reichstag members of the 1907 'Hottentot elections' to 110 deputies. This victory served to reinforce the hope of centrists and

---

1. The interest generated by the Chemnitz congress can be gauged by the fact that it drew commentary from as far away as America. The *New York Times* predicted a 'bitter fight' and reported that a 'miracle' would be required to save the SPD from its 'warring factions': the revisionist wing was intent on imposing 'more practical common sense' in its struggle against 'extreme radicals on the left', while stalwarts of the middle ground, including Bebel, were struggling to 'maintain a semblance of peace'. See 'German Socialists in a Bitter Fight; Annual Congress, Which Opens at Chemnitz To-day, Likely to Tear the Party Apart. Three Groups Now Exist. Marxists, Revisionists and Extreme Radicals so Antagonistic that Union Seems Impossible.' *The New York Times*, 15 September 1912.

The Extraordinary International Socialist Congress convened at Basel on 24–5 November 1912, shortly after the outbreak of the first Balkan War in October 1912. Attended by 545 delegates from 22 countries, it was more significant in the history of socialism than the Chemnitz congress of the SPD but added little to development of the theory of imperialism and is therefore less relevant for the purposes of this book. See the preparatory documents of the congress at *Quellen zur Entwicklung der sozialistischen Internationale (1907–1919): Der X. Internationale Sozialistische Kongress in Wien* on the Bibliothek der Friedrich Ebert Stiftung website.

revisionists alike that the imperialist drive towards world war could be thwarted by proletarian activism, including co-operation with bourgeois pacifists in promoting limitations on the arms-race.

The principal theoretical support for this view came from Rudolf Hilferding's *Finance Capital*, which many party leaders understood to mean that capitalism's next step would be formation of international cartels to avoid war and jointly exploit foreign markets. That theme recurs throughout the speeches that we have translated here and was only decisively challenged, on the level of general theory, by Rosa Luxemburg's *Accumulation of Capital*, which appeared in the spring of 1913. For that reason, the following four documents that we have included in this volume are reviews of Luxemburg's work.

Several issues were debated at Chemnitz, but the most contentious was a proposed resolution on imperialism. The *rapporteur* on this subject was Hugo Haase, chairman of the Reichstag delegation, who, together with Friedrich Ebert, a prominent member of the Kautskyist Centre, later co-chaired the SPD after Bebel's death in August 1913.[2] Haase condemned imperialism as the

2. Hugo Haase (1863–1919) was born in Allenstein (Olsztyn), a Province of Prussia, the son of a Jewish shoemaker. He studied law in Königsberg (now Kaliningrad), was the first Social Democrat in the Königsberg city council, and became a Reichstag deputy in 1897. Haase belonged to the 'centre' wing of the party, led by Karl Kautsky. In July 1914, he organised the antiwar rally of the SPD, and on 31 July and 1 August he fought unsuccessfully against the SPD-majority's decision to support the war-credits. Haase's plea to reject the credits was rejected by a vote of 78 to 14. Haase became increasingly vocal in resisting the policies of the SPD-faction and was forced to resign as a party chairman in 1916. In March 1916, he took over the leadership of the Sozialdemokratische Arbeitsgemeinschaft, founded by war-critics in the SPD. In 1917, he became chairman of the newly founded Independent Social-Democratic Party of Germany (USPD), which split the so-called 'Majority Social Democrats' group and advocated immediate peace negotiations. With the German Revolution of November 1918, Haase and Friedrich Ebert (leader of the majority Social Democrats) headed the provisional government known as the Council of People's Representatives. After the violent repression of the Revolution, Haase and the two other USPD-representatives, Wilheim Dittman and Emil Barth, abandoned the government on 29 December 1918. The Haase-led USPD received only 7% of the vote for the Weimar National Assembly on 19 January 1919. On 8 October 1919, Haase was shot by Johann Voss, a leather-worker who apparently was mentally ill. Voss was severely injured and died on 7 November 1919.

Leon Trotsky's assessment of Haase can be found in the sixteenth chapter of his autobiography:

> Bebel's fond hopes for a successor centred in Haase. The old man was doubtless attracted by Haase's idealism – not broad revolutionary idealism, which Haase did not possess, but a narrower, more personal, everyday sort of idealism; one might

drive 'to acquire *new spheres of power and influence* in other countries, especially the *annexation* of overseas countries to one's own state'. While he warned of the potential for 'ever-new conflicts', Haase hoped that the peace movement might yet succeed. Capitalism was responsible for imperialism, but it also gave rise to counter-tendencies, among which he cited international cartels, the economic interdependence of nations, and the increasing strength of socialist parties, all of which suggested the possibility of international agreements to restrain the arms-race.

Speaking for the left wing, Paul Lensch replied that a programme of 'international agreement for general arms-reduction' was simply 'utopian'.[3] Anton Pannekoek added that, although it could be demonstrated that 'imperial ism damages the interests of broad strata even of the bourgeoisie', the fact remained that the entire capitalist class supported armaments due to the interconnections of finance-capital and the emotional appeal of imperialist ideology. For Pannekoek, mass-actions were the proper response to imperialism, not illusions concerning disarmament. Max Cohen took a similar view, claiming that agreements between some imperialist powers merely exacerbated contradictions with others. Referring to the case of China, Cohen claimed that so-called peaceful penetration of backward areas would itself lead to armed confrontations.

From the right wing, Eduard Bernstein supported Haase's resolution although he wished to broaden it by including a call for international arbitration-courts. Bernstein's foreign-policy views were characterised by Anglophilia and a Cobdenite defence of free trade, together with pronounced

---

instance his readiness to sacrifice a rich legal practice at Königsberg to party interests. To the great embarrassment of the Russian revolutionaries, Bebel referred to this not very heroic sacrifice even in his speech at the party congress – I think it was in Jena – and insistently recommended Haase for the post of second chairman of the party's central committee. I knew Haase fairly well. After one of the party congresses we joined each other for a tour of some parts of Germany, and saw Nüremberg together. Gentle and considerate as he was in personal relations, in politics Haase remained to the end what his nature intended him to be: an honest mediocrity, a provincial democrat without revolutionary temperament or theoretical outlook. In the realm of philosophy he called himself, somewhat shyly, a Kantian. Whenever the situation was critical, he was inclined to refrain from final decisions; he would resort to half-measures and wait. No wonder the party of the independents later chose him as its leader. (Trotsky 1930, pp. 167–8.)

3. Lensch's tirade against disarmament, as a manoeuvre of the British bourgeoisie to maintain its world supremacy, had an Anglophobic tinge that foretold his later somersault to the extreme nationalist right wing of the SPD. See Lensch 1918.

Russophobia. Elsewhere, he advocated a 'League of the West against the East' – a triple alliance of Britain, France and Germany, i.e. of the 'civilised world, against barbarism'.[4] These convictions later led him to break with the protectionist and Anglophobic tendency within the revisionist camp, represented by Richard Calwer, Karl Leuthner, Max Schippel, Gerhard Hildebrand, Ludwig Quessel and others associated with the journal *Sozialistische Monatshefte*.[5] Bernstein's support for disarmament, and Kautsky's break with the left wing to become theoretical leader of the SPD 'centre'-fraction, ultimately led to a rapprochement between them and to Bernstein's renewed collaboration with *Die Neue Zeit* after the outbreak of the First World War.

Karl Liebknecht, who later became one of the most famous leaders and martyrs of the revolutionary Left, also sided on this occasion with the Centre. Picking up Haase's theme, Liebknecht objected that Pannekoek and Lensch remained 'trapped in a rather mechanistic view of society and its development' that denied capitalist 'counter-trends against warlike tendencies and the arms-race'. Lensch, in particular, had 'constructed an inherent contradiction between disarmament and a militia' that, in Liebknecht's opinion, simply did not exist.

Although the left wing scored a minor victory when Gerhard Hildebrand, one of the main SPD-spokesmen for social imperialism, was expelled, the historian Carl Schorske summarised the Chemnitz congress as a clear triumph 'of the centre', whose policy 'was anti-war, but not revolutionary – an extension of Social-Democratic domestic policy into the sphere of foreign affairs'.[6] The speeches that we have translated exemplify both the achievements and the impending failure of Social Democracy. On the one hand, the Party was the only political force in Europe that clearly anticipated and might

4. Fletcher 1984, p. 40.

5. For an assessment of the split in the revisionist ranks between ardent nationalists and Anglophile pacifists such as Bernstein, see: Hilferding 1909. As early as 1900, Calwer had advocated the creation of a 'Greater Germany [*Alldeutschland*]', an autarchic German world empire, through a Franco-German understanding directed mainly against Great Britain as the largest colonial empire in the world and the traditional enemy of European integration. Members of this camp were increasingly opposed to Bernstein's support of disarmament, which they viewed as nothing more than a concession to England.

6. Schorske 1970, p. 264. For left-wing assessments of the Chemnitz party congress see the following articles in the *Leipziger Volkszeitung*: Anonymous 1912d, 1912e and 1912f. For a right-wing view, see Schippel 1912b.

have stood in the way of world war. Yet the ideas expressed at Chemnitz also portended Social-Democratic limitations when imperialist expansionism took the guise of patriotism, national honour, and defence of economic interests that supposedly affected the workers themselves in terms of wages and employment.

* * *

Reporter Hugo Haase:[7]

Comrades! At present there is hardly a word that buzzes so frequently throughout the political world and rings so often in its ear as the slogan of *Imperialism*. To the question of what must be understood by imperialism, we get different answers. Many understand it to mean creation of an economically self-sufficient empire so extensive that within its own territory all raw materials can be obtained and all industrial products can be manufactured and sold in one's own market. I do not think I have to spend many words on this idea, because all those images of economic self-sufficiency and so-called autarchy are but fanciful speculations; all such self-sufficient political and economic national territories are chimerae. As protective tariffs rose more and more in America and the countries of continental Europe, an agitation for protectionism was also triggered in England that promoted the imperialist tendency, whose goal was to consolidate the different parts of the English Empire into a united whole, to incorporate all the members of the empire, including the colonies, into a great *imperium*, an imperial customs-union. This protectionist agitation, conducted especially by Chamberlain, suffered shipwreck because the different parts of the English world empire have separate interests and because the finances of the great self-administering colonies [Australia and Canada] depend on their customs-revenue. But everywhere the striving to acquire *new spheres of power and influence* in other countries, especially the *annexation* of overseas countries to one's own state, has become dominant. This imperialist idea has currently seized the whole world, America

7. Sozialdemokratische Partei Deutschlands 1912, pp. 403–34. English version of the resolution on imperialism and of selected passages of the debate in Riddell (ed.) 1984: pp. 80–3.

and Japan as much as the European countries. It springs from the economic development of the great capitalist states.

Production has increased phenomenally, as I will show in a few figures. World trade has doubled during the last twenty years. Germany's share in the growth of world trade and of the world economy is considerable. The value of exports in special trade[8] in 1880 amounted to 2.95, i.e. almost 3 billion marks; it grew to 3.317 billion in 1891, thus experiencing within those 11 years only a relatively small growth. But, in 1900, it already amounted to 4.61 billion, and by 1910 it grew abruptly to 7.47 billion. [*Hear! Hear!*] Imports experienced a similar development. The value of imports alone in Germany's special trade amounted to 2.86 billion in 1880, grew to 4.12 billion in 1891, by 1900 had already reached 5.77 billion, and in 1910 reached the enormous sum of 8.93 billion. [*Hear! Hear!*] That means German imports have doubled during the last 20 years and exports have increased even more.

We have a yardstick to measure *the expansion of world traffic* in the number and extent of the means of transportation on land and sea. In 1890, Germany had a railway-system of 42,800 kilometres; by 1909, its range had already expanded to more than 60,000 kilometres, and the same development took place in all the countries of Europe and the world. In Europe, the railway-system grew from 223,000 to 329,000 kilometres [between 1890 and 1910]. In the United States of America, it grew from 268,000 to 381,000 kilometres; and, if we look at the states of the Far East, because of their special significance for the immediate future, it turns out that the railway-system of Japan and Korea grew from 2,233 to 9,281 kilometres, and in China, which until recently was excluded from world trade by the Chinese Wall, the railway-system grew from 200 to 8,224 kilometres after the wall began to break down. [*Hear! Hear!*] Since that time, those areas of the Far East have experienced an even more rapid development.

Merchant-shipping fundamentally comes into consideration for sea-transportation, which, in Germany, experienced a really extraordinary development. The tonnage of German merchant-ships amounted to approximately 982,000 registered tons in 1871, rising to 1,500,000 in 1896 and 2,903,001 in 1911. A similar development took place in all countries. In the United States

8. [*Spezialhandel*: The traffic of goods within the German tariff-zone and from it to foreign countries, not including the so-called free-trade zones in Germany.]

of America, the volume of maritime commerce was 3,340,000 net tons in 1901 and 4,459,000 tons in 1910. The volume of Great Britain and Ireland's merchant ships amounted to more than 9 million net registered tons in 1901 and 11.5 million in 1910. It also follows from this that England, which according to the well-known saying is no longer the workshop of the world, is still by far its largest carrier. [*Very good!*] England still has more than half the tonnage of the entire world.

And, everywhere, the first signs of a *powerful upswing in world traffic* are visible. The Baghdad Railway is nearing completion. Built by the Deutsche Bank with the blessing of the German government, the Baghdad Railway, after completion of the line from Konya to Kuwait, will be almost as long at the line from Berlin to Constantinople [Istanbul].[9] The economic significance of that railway, if it is extended to the Persian Gulf, is beyond dispute. The English engineer Willcocks, who won his spurs in Egypt as an outstanding hydrological engineer, was commissioned by the Turkish government to investigate what could be done economically with the area between the Euphrates and the Tigris, the old Mesopotamia. In his memorandum, *Irrigation of Mesopotamia*,[10] he came to the conclusion that some five million hectares, which currently lie in waste, can be cultivated once again after their original fertility is fully restored, and that wheat, barley, and leguminous plants can thrive wonderfully, in addition to rice and apparently also cotton.

---

9. [In the late nineteenth and early twentieth centuries, the Ottoman Empire planned to construct a Baghdad Railway under German control. The Baghdad Railway consisted of the already constructed Orient Express line, linking Paris to Constantinople, and the newer Constantinople-Baghdad line through Turkey, Syria and Iraq. The Germans' ultimate goal was to establish a port on the Persian Gulf. The Ottoman Empire, in turn, desired to maintain its control of Arabia and to expand its influence across the Red Sea into Egypt, which was controlled by Great Britain. The railway became a source of international disputes during the years immediately preceding World War I. In 1903, the Ottoman Government gave permission to the German-controlled Baghdad Railway Company to build a railway-line from Konya (a city in Turkey, on the central plateau of Anatolia) to Baghdad. There was concern in Russia, France, and Britain as the implications of the German scheme to construct a Berlin-Baghdad railway became apparent. A railway linking Berlin to the Persian Gulf would provide Germany with a connection to her colonies in Africa, i.e., with German East Africa and German South-West Africa (present-day Tanzania and Namibia), as well as strengthen the Ottoman Empire and its ties to Germany, shifting the balance of power in the Middle East. Despite obstructions at the diplomatic level, work began slowly on the railway. Both geographical and political obstacles prevented the completion of the Baghdad Railway before World War I commenced in 1914.]

10. [Willcocks 1911.]

While our ruling classes enthuse over the policy of overseas expansion, as if hypnotised by Cecil Rhodes's slogan that 'expansion is everything',[11] one section of them, our agrarians, who formerly backed this policy enthusiastically together with the representatives of heavy industry and finance-capital, are now seized with terror at the idea that imperialism could lead to the importation of grain and foodstuffs from foreign countries into Germany, which could palliate the [inflationary] state of emergency. [*Lively applause*]

I can only quote a few facts in order to show what perspectives open up for world trade. The Hejaz Railway[12] from Damascus through Medina to Mecca, 1,320 kilometres long, is [virtually] finished, and the Indian government, whose trade depends on the Gulf of Aden, intends to establish a connection from Aden to a remote point 3,000 kilometres away. What transformations will take place if the railway from Cape Town to Cairo is built, not to speak of the railway project from Alexandria to Shanghai! Australia will be traversed by a railway-line. We see further that the Panama Canal, that technical marvel that will become the centre of world trade, will soon be inaugurated. In that way, America will have even closer commercial ties with East Asia than it presently does. India will be 3,000 nautical miles closer to New York through the Panama Canal than it was through the Suez Canal. Europe will lie 2,500 miles further away from China and Japan than New York will. The Panama Canal will open up the markets of entirely new corners of the world, which were until now hardly, if at all, touched by modern civilisation.

But not only commodities for personal consumption are exported by highly developed industry; *an export of means of production, an export of capital,* is also taking place at an ever-growing scale. Even if the colonies are not suitable

---

11. ['Expansion is everything.... The world is nearly all parcelled out, and what there is left of it is being divided up, conquered, and colonized. To think of these stars that you see overhead at night, those vast worlds which we can never reach. I would annex the planets if I could; I often think of that.' Cecil Rhodes as quoted in Liebson Millin 1933, p. 138.]

12. [The Hejaz Railway was a narrow-gauge railway running from Damascus to Medina, through the Hejaz region of Arabia, with a branch line to Haifa, on the Mediterranean Sea. The main purpose of the Hejaz Railway was to establish a connection between Istanbul, the capital of the Ottoman Empire and the seat of the Islamic Caliphate, and Hejaz in Arabia, the site of the holiest shrines of Islam and the city of Mecca, which is the yearly pilgrimage destination of the Hajj. The Hejaz Railway was eventually able to reach no further than Medina because the construction-works were interrupted due to the outbreak of World War I.]

for agriculture and cattle breeding, even if they supply few raw materials, they are still valuable for capital because roads and railroads are built, bridges erected, and cities founded on them, and, for this purpose, means of production and transportation are exported there. If the costs of the colonies are covered mostly by indirect taxes, so that they are not primarily met by the propertied classes, the bourgeoisie involved in the profitable export of means of production does an excellent business. *Capital accumulates in such vast proportions that it pushes for new valorisation-opportunities*. Money-capital is virtually forced onto foreign states, not only to obtain commissions and interest-payments from the debtor-states but also in order compel them to use most of the sums that are lent in order to buy goods and means of production from the creditor-states. Thus, not only do the large banks get what they came for, but since they are closely linked to heavy industry, the latter also get their money's worth with the emigration of loan-capital. To give an idea of the *size of capital-exports* we need only refer to the following facts.

England has invested approximately 70 billion marks abroad, half of it in the colonies, mainly Canada, India and Australia. Outside the colonies, its main debtor is America: in the United States alone, England has invested 13.5 billion. England's income from interest amounts to roughly 100 million pounds annually. According to the experts, in 1905 Germany had already invested a capital of some 20 billion marks abroad; currently, probably at least 35 billion marks. People reckon that Germany, France and England alone supply the world yearly with some 6 billion in capital, which serves to tap the natural wealth of the world – naturally, not for the mass of the people but for large-scale capital. As a result of all this, *countries* previously totally excluded from industry, with a natural economy producing at the *lowest level*, have been dragged into *large-scale capitalist business*, developing industries that later compete with those of the countries from which capital originally came.

Within the framework of this report, I do not want to go into colonial policy; it is a part of imperialist policy, and one of its driving forces is likewise often the *demand for raw materials* that constitute a vital need for industry. It is precisely colonial policy that displays the features eminently characteristic of imperialism – especially violence. When we recently read that, in Peru, 30,000 Indians were slaughtered in a bestial manner without any qualms, merely in order to obtain 400 tons of rubber, we were reminded of Marx's descriptions of colonial atrocities in the chapter of *Capital* dealing with the 'Genesis of the

Industrial Capitalist'. The words with which Marx closed that chapter prove to be true even today: 'If money, according to Augier, "comes into the world with a congenital blood-stain on one cheek," capital comes dripping from head to toe, from every pore, with blood and dirt.'[13]

In the chase by highly developed industrial states after new markets, after countries supplying raw materials and areas for investment, *entanglements* must inevitably develop within the countries marked out for plunder as well as between rival states aiming at the same booty. Large-scale capital, which controls the state, does not shrink from violence if it appears necessary to achieve its goals. Under the rule of imperialism, violence is an 'economic power' of the first rank. Imperialism increases the *sources of friction between states* and produces ever-new *conflicts*. It puts its stamp on the foreign policy of the modern states. The struggle of the United States of America with Spain, their appropriation of Cuba, Puerto Rico, the Philippines and Hawaii, and their advances in Central and South America; England's struggle with the Boers; the repression of the Boxer Rebellion in China; the Russo-Japanese War; Japan's annexation of Korea; the partition of Persia between Russia and England; Morocco's penetration by France; Germany's intervention in the Moroccan affair and its economic penetration into Turkey; Austria's annexation of Bosnia and Herzegovina; Russia's and England's thrusts into Asia; Italy's plundering raid into Tripoli – these are just some of the stages in imperialist policy.

Bismarck mainly pursued a European policy; only timidly did he undertake in 1884 the first attempts towards a colonial policy. He was delighted when France became involved in Africa, because, in that way, it could not turn its gaze to the East, to Germany. Caprivi often stated that the government would think about whether it wanted to hang on to [the German colony of] South-West Africa. The idea of giving up the colonies was then common in the ruling circles. How totally different the situation became after 1896! It was on 18 January 1896, at the celebration of the twenty-fifth anniversary of the creation of the [Second] Reich, that Kaiser Wilhelm II gave a speech in which he advocated for the first time the idea of imperialism. He said on that occasion:

> The German Empire has become a world empire. Everywhere in distant parts of the world live thousands of our fellow countrymen. German goods,

13. Marx 1976, p. 926.

> German knowledge, German activity are going over the ocean. The values that Germans have taken over the seas amount to hundreds of millions. Upon you, gentlemen, falls the serious obligation of helping me to bring this larger German Empire even closer to our own domestic Reich.

Here, a Greater Germany, the annexation of other parts of the world to the German Reich, was proclaimed as a goal. A year later [on 18 June 1897], the Kaiser delivered in Gürzenich zu Köln (Cologne) his 'trident speech', similar in tone to the previous one:

> The sea-god, with the trident in his hand, is a symbol [of the fact] that, ever since our great Kaiser pieced our empire together again, we also have other tasks in the world; German citizens in all sorts of places, whom we have to look after, German honour, which we also have to preserve abroad. The trident is in our fist.

When the Kaiser, on 16 December 1897, gave a farewell-speech in Kiel to his brother Prince Heinrich, who sailed for China [to take part in the repression of the Boxer Rebellion], he said: 'If someone ventures to violate our rights or tries to injure us, then go there with an armoured fist [*mit gepanzerter Faust*].'

The armoured fist became the symbol of the new imperialist policy. This view came to light even more clearly in the Kaiser's farewell-speech to the troops sent to China in 1897 to join in the retaliation-campaign [against the Boxer Rebellion]. Then he said:

> The ocean is vital for Germany's greatness; but this also demonstrates that no major decision should be made about it and the distant lands beyond it without [consulting] Germany and the German emperor.

Thus it was announced to the whole world that *Germany* wanted to be consulted about the *partition of the world*; that it wanted to take part in *world policy* and have a share of its fruits. In his Hammer and Anvil Speech before the Reichstag, the Chancellor of the Reich, Prince Bülow, said on 11 December, 1899:

> If the English speak of a 'Greater Britain', if the French speak of a 'Nouvelle France', if the Russians open up Asia, then we, too, have the right to a Greater Germany.

Thus, the idea of a *Greater Germany* was advanced among the German people from a responsible position in the Reich. The situation is often described as if each utterance of the Kaiser were merely the product of an absolutist disposition. Outwardly, that appears to be the case, and it is true that the outer aspect [of the situation] arises from the absolutist spirit; but behind it hides a changed political outlook that grew out of a completely transformed economic situation. When the Social-Democratic party congress met at Mainz in 1900 and debated world policy, Comrade Schoenlak, in a very effective speech that followed the report submitted by our late Comrade Singer, described the whole situation as if it were just a question of driving back absolutism. But, already, the next speakers, Ledebour, Fähndrich and Luxemburg, pointed out that the question under discussion was much greater – namely, the onset of a new phase of capitalist development.

If the states pursue a policy of conquest and plunder, it is self-evident that they will try to strengthen their military power in order to be superior to the others. As a consequence, *armaments*, the *arms-race*, developed on an ever-larger scale. I do not need to expand here on the dimensions reached by the arms-race. During the last elections, we have all described to the voters in dozens of speeches the really staggering amounts the states spend on the army, the navy and the air force. Since then, the arms-race has accelerated.

The new Reichstag approved a bill of more than 650 million marks for naval and military appropriations. We had foreseen those bills, but the rapidity with which they were submitted surprised even us. The English government promptly answered the Reichstag's resolution with an additional appropriation for the fleet. The minister [actually First Lord of the Admiralty] Churchill explicitly stated that the English government was bound to request 990,000 pounds sterling, i.e. 19,800,000 marks, for that purpose due to Germany's course of action. In July of this year France approved a one-time outlay of 3 million and a permanent outlay of 14 million for military purposes. Austria increased its peacetime army to 520,000 men and established a recruitment-quota of 213,000 men. It strengthened its navy and built strategic railways in Bosnia to position itself favourably for the partition of Turkey. Due to the importance of the [military] bills for the ruling régime, Hungary does not hesitate to breach rules of procedure and legal regulations in order to muzzle the opposition by force. Russia, which after its defeat in the Russo-Japanese War seemed to have been excluded for a long time from the circle of the great powers, has been recently granted by the Duma one billion marks that should be spent on the navy until the year 1917, and behind that 'small'-fleet programme stands the large one that will require some 3 billion roubles from the year 1918 to 1930. How much of that will flow into other pockets is another question. In any case, Russia, whose military budget in 1911 already reached 543 million roubles, is taking an active part in the general arms-race in a big way, and it is especially significant for us that, in the discussion of the navy bill, it was explicitly stated that the fleet was necessary against Germany. The costs that have been sacrificed to the Moloch of militarism are not yet the last or the largest. Hardly had the Reichstag approved the new army and navy appropriation bills when the Admiral of the Fleet, von Köster, said in a speech at the Düsseldorf Navy League that a navy commensurate with the great German Reich does not exist. [*Hear! Hear!*] We must therefore expect even greater demands to be made again soon.

With the ruling imperialist system and the international tension, the stimulus to increase armaments everywhere has become much stronger, and the question arises for us (there are differences of opinion about it in our ranks): 'Can the arms-race be checked on the foundations of capitalist society or not?' Is the arms-race a *vital necessity* for capitalism, so that capitalism must cling to it in order to escape self-annihilation? An important factor for assessment of this question is the fact that the *capital invested in the arms-industry* is enormous. According to a table published in the *Morning Leader*, 6 corporations producing war-matèriel in England have a share-capital of 352 million marks and bonds worth 203 million marks. If the capital invested in those industries were to lie idle, that would certainly have strong repercussions on economic life. The arms-race has become for capitalism a means of prolonging prosperity and weakening the possible effects of a crisis. But it would be totally wrong to contemplate only the valorisation-needs of the capital invested in those industrial branches and to disregard all other facts. I must, in discussing this issue, recall the words that Engels wrote for the *Berliner Volksblatt* in a letter dated 5 October 1895, to Comrade Paul Ernst:

> Whoever is unable, in assessing an economic or political situation, to consider impartially the relative equilibrium of the facts at hand or the strength of the forces at play, will force upon the party a completely insane tactic.

If we try to ascertain the relative equilibrium of all the facts at hand, we come to the conclusion that, with the great influence that the powerful groups of armaments-interests and the cliques associated with them have on the state, the struggle against the arms-race is exceedingly difficult. But it cannot be said that the outcome has been decided in advance. England's population increases by only 400,000 people annually, France has almost no demographic growth, and both countries have almost reached the limits of their capacity. It is obvious, therefore, why the idea of arms-limitation begins to sink roots there. A quite remarkable article in the *Times* of 15 June reads:

> We have been told that the German navy is there to repel an English attack, but we know that such an attack is unthinkable for many reasons, above all because in a *war* with Germany we would be *gambling with our own life*, while the German Empire does not even have to lose its great power status on the European continent.[14]

If the burden of the arms-race is shifted onto the shoulders of the propertied classes, as partly happens already in England, the bourgeoisie will feel it so deeply that it will rather reduce it than prodigiously enrich a small group of capitalist magnates. It is an historic fact – I wonder how it could have been contested lately – that the *English government*, in all probability acting in concord with the French government, has attempted to bring about a *limitation of armaments*. If that is true – and it cannot be disputed – then even the critics of my views must concede that proof has been furnished that the arms-race cannot be a *vital condition* of capital. Because what capitalist government could possibly want to undermine the vital conditions of its own bourgeoisie? When the previous English Minister of War, [Lord Richard Burdon] Haldane, came back from his last trip to Germany and handed over his war-ministry portfolio, he declared in a speech that dwelt repeatedly upon the military credits:

> We have spoken in the most friendly manner to the only power that is our rival, and we made known our commitment that, whatever efforts they may make, they can count upon the fact that we will strive even harder than they do. We have said also in Berlin that we have no intention of attacking Germany but only of securing our naval supremacy, which for us is a question of life and death.[15]

This proves that Haldane has undoubtedly made proposals in Berlin to stop the arms-race. Some comrades wonder how the limitation of armaments would take place. I think that is a totally idle question. It is the governments'

---

14. [Retranslated from German.]

15. [Retranslated from German. Haldane's detailed account of his discussions in Berlin was reprinted in the *New York Times* on 2 June 1918: 'Why Lord Haldane Failed At Berlin; Report On His Mission in 1912 Made Public in London'.]

business to make feasible proposals, and when Haldane was sent for that purpose to Berlin it surely was not without any practical suggestion.

It follows from this that the proposals for the *limitation of armaments*, made and championed in the most effective manner by our fraction in the Reichstag on 17 March 1910, and 30 March 1911, were *correct* [*Quite true!*], and that our parliamentary fraction did what the situation demanded. I remind you all of the joy with which our audiences reacted during the last elections when we told them that the Social-Democratic Party was the only one that made a motion for the limitation of armaments, and the only one that attempted to bring about an agreement between England and Germany. The masses have understood us, and those who place such special value on their feelings should also not pass them by heedlessly in this case. [*Very good!*]

That the arms-race already entails a serious war-danger is clear to us all, and I am not going to repeat what we have all often said. The competition in the arms-field must ultimately lead either to a world war or to a financial collapse. People, even ministers, now say that the war does not actually have to break out; already, the mere development of naval and military power guarantees that result – a very dangerous statement. The English minister [First Lord of the Admiralty] Churchill, in a great speech about armaments delivered on 11 March 1912, said the following:

> The most hopeless explanation that people can give for this peculiar phenomenon is that competition at sea and on the land is the *modern substitute* for what would have been in earlier times *real war*, and that just as credit in our days has to a large extent replaced cash settlements, the jealousy and quarrels between nations will more and more be settled through the possession of armaments without the need actually to employ them. If that were true, one could perhaps think that the *great stupidity of the twentieth century* bears a less unpleasant appearance. But we cannot fail to recognise the fact that we live in an *age of incipient violence* and strong, deeply rooted unrest. The usefulness of a war, even for the victor, must in most cases be an illusion. Surely no war, of whatever kind, can be of any profit to the British Empire, but if war breaks out, it will be no illusion – people will feel even a single bullet as a very real fact.[16]

16. [Retranslated from German.]

The minister thus confirms that we do not live in an age of 'peaceful expansion', of 'pénétration pacifique', but in an *age of violence*; that the arms-race is not a substitute for war, but we are threatened by war itself. Even if the arms-race is not an absolute need of capitalism, is not *world war* the unavoidable undoing of the imperialist states? There is no doubt: imperialism is not peaceful, it has the *tendency towards bellicose* conflicts. But those who argue that a war between competing industrial states is an *inevitable* fate abandon the ground we should stand upon as Marxist-educated comrades. [*Very true!*]

Marx and Engels always rightly warned us against embracing a fatalist conception of history. Certainly, we must not underestimate the fact that *imperialism has a violent character*, but the tendency to hasten the predatory states into a war with each other is *thwarted by other tendencies*. Those phenomena are not something new; such a view of economic and political processes is familiar to us. Capitalism certainly has the tendency to impoverish the proletariat, to prolong working time and reduce wages. The proletariat, however, does not regard those tendencies as an inevitable fate with which it must come to terms; it has successfully counteracted those ominous tendencies through its trade-union and political movement. Marx called the achievement of the ten-hour workday the triumph of a principle. Moreover, the warlike entanglements that capitalism brings forth find their restraints.

The *capitalist groups* of the most different countries are in many ways *internationally* linked and interconnected with each other. They consider it more advantageous to divide the markets of the world among themselves than to wage exhausting struggles whose outcome is uncertain and represents a threat to their profits. That has already been pointed out on the basis of the international rails-syndicate, which was joined by the German, English, American, Belgian, French, Austrian, Hungarian, Spanish and Russian manufacturers. The members of that syndicate have divided up the world among themselves, letting each one of those states have a certain territory as its booty. In this respect, I would like to recall that last year in Brussels the international steel-association was launched, and its godfathers were Krupp, Thyssen and Schellenbrandt. If the great magnates of the mining industry reached an international agreement, then what is taking place on the great stage of the world is the same thing that we have witnessed within individual states: competition, based on the capitalist mode of production, has been partially neutralised by cartels, trusts and employers' associations. Last year, when we stood on the brink of war because of wretched Morocco, there were two entrepreneurs of the first rank among those who worked for peace: Creuzot and Krupp, who had consolidated the exploitation of Morocco's coal-riches. This fact cannot simply be brushed aside with a wave of the hand.

In the monthly *Nord und Süd*, two well-known great German industrialists, Stinnes and Thyssen, have recently suggested a similar co-operation of English and German capital on the world market as the best means to alleviate the English-German antagonism. Stinnes declared:

> If both nations see it as their main task to make the *rest of the world liable to pay* for their industriousness, then a conflict will hopefully be avoided, because it would leave even the *victor* exceedingly *weak* and promote to world predominance powers that will surely use this position to the detriment of both England and Germany.

And Thyssen also stressed that in the economic sphere an association of both peoples would be *'to the advantage of both'*, that and 'each one of them can develop its idiosyncrasy and its strength next to the other'. A statement of the National-Liberal member of the Landtag [legislative assembly of a German state] vom Rath deserves attention in this connection. He turned in strong words against the agitators for the navy, saying: 'The commercial and industrial competition, as a cause of *military* conflicts between Germany and England, is and will remain a malicious and tendentious invention of the agitators for the navy.' The commercial relations between Germany and England are actually so close and diverse that the outbreak of a war between these states must bring about a really devastating crisis. In 1911, we exported commodities to Great Britain to the value of 1,139 million marks, that is, 15 per cent of our total exports, and we imported from them 808 million marks in commodities, i.e., 8 per cent of our entire imports. Thus, *economic dependence is a factor restraining the warmongers.*

But even stronger than the cohesion of international capital is the firmly established solidarity of the fraternal international proletariat. [*Very true!*] German Social Democracy has always voted on principle against the arms-race, and, in July of this year, the English Labour Party proclaimed in the English Parliament, through its leader MacDonald, that on this question the English workers stand shoulder to shoulder with the German workers because they have sided with their comrades in Germany and opposed the increase in the navy. Could the power of the international proletariat actually be so small that it carries no weight in the scales of war and peace? If our peace demonstrations mean nothing, then we must conclude that we should not organise any more demonstrations for peace at all. [*Very true!*] If we must declare that a war between England and Germany is inevitable, that it is a vital condition of capitalism, which is ruthlessly driving the peoples to a war, then what are the demonstrations for peace supposed to mean?

Let us not forget that the governments, especially in those states where Social Democracy is strong, are very worried about *what a future war will look like*, for none of them knows whether a profit or a loss will come from it. [*Approval*] All the military writers agree on the fact that precisely modern war requires a high degree of devotion and enthusiasm from the soldiers. The governments can force the proletarians to go to war, but they cannot force them to practise the art of war with devotion and enthusiasm. The governments must also worry about what will become of them if the war ends in defeat. Social Democracy has always warned the people about imperialism and its dreadful accompanying phenomena. Would not the overwhelming majority of the people, in case of a defeat, see Social Democracy as their saviour in the hour of distress? Would not the hour arrive for Social Democracy to seize political power and replace the ruling classes? Should these ideas not occur to the statesmen and make them cautious in their decisions? It would surely be a pernicious illusion if we were to cease to regard, even for a moment, the dangers associated with imperialism.

All the bourgeois parties are under imperialism's spell, from which they expect rich fruits for the whole bourgeoisie and the landowners [*Junkertum*]. A part of its supporters will soon recognise how they were duped. However, imperialism still has power over the intellectual and emotional world of broad circles of the bourgeoisie, who, completely devoid of ideals, have made an idol out of it that they will worship until it breaks down.

It is our duty to reach clarification on the essence of imperialism, but also to champion *understanding between the peoples*, to organise mass-demonstrations in support of peace as much as we possibly can. It is true that we cannot prevent every war, but we could in particular cases check the destruction. World peace is and remains the ideal of the proletarians of all countries. [*Bravo!*]

We must follow up the labyrinthine paths of our *foreign policy* to be able to intervene in a timely manner in the interests of the proletariat. I can only deal briefly with this subject. When the [Austro-Prussian] war of 1866 broke out, Kaiser Wilhelm I wanted by all means to take away from the Austrians parts of their country, pieces of Silesia and Bohemia. Bismarck opposed that policy resolutely, considering that there would always remain resentment in Austria if parts of the country were taken away from it. He ultimately imposed his view with the support of the crown-prince.

This clever policy, however, was not followed in the [Franco-Prussian] war of 1870. Germany committed not only the crime but also the mistake of taking away Alsace-Lorraine from France and annexing it. In that way, France was pushed to Russia's side, and, ever since then, the antagonism between us and England has sharpened as the Franco-Russian alliance became the Triple Entente,[17] by which Russia associated itself with the United Kingdom and France. The Russian system, with its blood-stained hands, the Russian régime that only functions through gallows and hangmen and is inwardly thoroughly rotten, has become a factor of the greatest significance in world policy despite its defeat by little Japan [in the Russo-Japanese War of 1904–5].

Russia has become has become the centre of European and Asian politics. Kaiser Wilhelm II travelled to Baltic Port,[18] the Japanese Prime Minister Taro Katsura followed his trail, the French Prime Minister Poincaré hastened to get to Russia, and all made a bow to the Tsar. Thus wooed, the Russian régime acquired a significance that is inversely related to its worth. It has not been officially stated what was agreed upon at Baltic Port.[19] Semi-official newspapers have reported that the German and Russian governments have agreed upon their position on Turkey and Italy. Saint Petersburg's newspapers speak about an agreement on a common intervention by Germany and Russia on the Turkish question. The understanding reached between both emperors at their meeting of November 1911 in Potsdam[20] was, to be sure, corroborated:

---

17. [The Triple Entente was the name of the agreement between the United Kingdom, France and Russia – made after the signing of the Anglo-Russian Entente in August 1907 – to oppose the Triple Alliance of Germany, Austria-Hungary, and Italy.]

18. [Балтийский Порт: The official name of the Russian city of Paldiski in Estonia in 1783–1917.]

19. [In 1912, Tsar Nicholas II held several political interviews on Russian territory. His first visitor was Kaiser Wilhelm II, who arrived at Baltic Port in his yacht *Hohenzollern* in June 1912.]

20. [On 4–6 November 1910, a meeting was arranged in Potsdam between Nicholas II of Russia and Wilhelm II of Germany, intended to chastise the British for their perceived betrayal of Russia's interests during the Bosnian crisis. The two monarchs

Germany gives Russia a free hand in Persia, in exchange for which Russia commits itself not to get involved with any alliance of an aggressive character against Germany. But, at the same time, the chief of staff of the Russian navy, Admiral Prince Lieven, and the chief of staff, Chilinski, prepared in Paris the conclusion of a naval convention with France and secured Russia's loyalty to France. The Russian Foreign Minister, Sazonov, announced his visit to London, where he will probably hold talks with the English government not only about the Chinese and Persian questions but also about Turkey's partition.

Turkey can be set ablaze at any moment. The Serbs, Bulgarians and Greeks have joined forces in a common course of action. Russia, which will enforce free passage of the Dardanelles, is just waiting for a favourable opportunity. Austria has announced, through its foreign minister Count Leopold von Berchtold, that it also has interests in the Balkans: it would like [to grab] Thessaloniki (Salonica) [from Greece]. Italy has turned its gaze to Albania, and Germany has great economic interests in Turkey. *The situation is thus extremely tense*. Just how unscrupulously the policy of conquest was pursued has been described through Persia's example by the American Morgan Shuster, who was expelled as Persia's treasurer-general due to pressure from Russia and England:

'Only the pen of a Macaulay,' he writes,

> or the brush of a Verestchagin could adequately portray the rapidly shifting scenes attending the downfall of this ancient nation, – scenes in which two powerful and presumably enlightened Christian countries played fast and loose with truth, honor, decency and law, one, at least, hesitating not even at the most barbarous cruelties to accomplish its political designs and to put Persia beyond hope of self-regeneration.[21]

discussed the Baghdad Railway, a German project widely expected to give Berlin considerable geopolitical influence in the Fertile Crescent. Against the background of the Persian Constitutional Revolution, Russia was anxious to control the prospective Khanaqin-Tehran branch of the railway. The two powers settled their differences through the Potsdam Agreement, signed on 19 August 1911, giving Russia a free hand in Northern Iran. The first railway connecting Persia to Europe would provide Russia with a lever of influence over its southern neighbour. Notwithstanding the promising beginning, Russo-German relations disintegrated in 1913 when the Kaiser sent one of his generals to reorganise the Turkish army and to supervise the garrison in Constantinople, remarking that 'the German flag will soon fly over the fortifications of the Bosporus', a vital trade-artery that accounted for two-fifths of Russia's exports.]

21. [Morgan Shuster 1912, pp. xiii–xiv.]

Wherever peoples are defenceless, this shameless robbers' policy for the greater glory of capital is pursued as soon as rich profits beckon. In *China*, whose partition began after the Sino-Japanese War,[22] and where we, following a modern imperialist method, did not seize Kiaotschau [Jiaozhou] and its hinterland but 'leased' it for 99 years, Japan, Russia, America and the European states are lurking in order to pursue their policy of plunder at the first favourable opportunity. Katsura reached an agreement in Saint Petersburg for the partition of Manchuria and Mongolia between Japan and Russia, while England should get Tibet as a 'sphere of influence'. Probably, this robbery will not take place smoothly: the Chinese people have awakened from their slumber; they have overthrown the old government by means of a revolution.[23] This revolution would not have succeeded if, already in the short period of time since China's foreign trade opened up, a [Chinese] bourgeoisie had not sprung up that needs a modern state for the development of its capitalist interests. [*Very true!*]

If we by no means underestimate the dangers threatening us, all the same they can only be a stimulus to increase our strength more and more in order to preserve peace amidst all this turmoil and violent developments. [*Bravo!*] We all know how disastrous the *domestic* effects of imperialism are. One of its accompanying phenomena is the *high cost of living*, whose effects are heightened among us by protectionist policy, that powerful sponsor of imperialism. [*Very true!*] Imperialism increases the *power of the industrial warmongers*, our most vicious enemies. Among those industrial warmongers, those most eager for profit and power aim at concentrating more and more capital and do not shy away from curtailing the workers' right of association in order to hinder their rise and block all progress in social policy. The protectionist system, in full blossom among us, has led to *suppression of the workers' standard of living*, narrowing the home market and increasing the craving to dump the surplus commodities into the world market. The proletariat struggles against

22. [A reference to the First Sino-Japanese war (1 August 1894–17 April 1895).]
23. [The first Chinese Revolution of 1911 (also known as Xinhai or Shinhai Revolution), began with the Wuchang Uprising on 10 October 1911, and ended with the abdication of Emperor Puyi on 12 February 1912. The primary parties to the conflict were the Imperial forces of the Qing Dynasty (1644–1911) and the forces of the Revolutionary Alliance (*Tongmenghui*). Although the monarchy was briefly restored twice in the course of the revolution, the final outcome was a republican form of government: the Republic of China formally replaced the Qing Dynasty on 12 February 1912.]

this protectionist system, which serves for the enrichment of the magnates of capital and the large landowners, and will not rest until it is dropped and freedom of world trade is secured. [*Bravo!*]

The proletariat reiterates its resolute determination to do everything in its power to prevent a world war. For this purpose, it will cultivate international relations between workers, strengthening the power of the international proletariat. Our goal can only be reached if we consolidate our political and economic organisations ever more powerfully, if we never tire of gathering new troops for our great cause. If the danger of war and the exploitation of the masses will only be abolished together with capitalism itself, we still recognise it as our task even now to minimise its devastating effects.

Imperialism drives the capitalist system to its highest stage;[24] it is ready to make room for another system, the socialist one. The proletariat is destined to be its heir, and the workers will come into that inheritance with the conviction that *peace, freedom, independence and prosperity of all peoples* will flourish under the banner of the mature, rising proletariat! [*Stormy and prolonged applause.*]

Dr. Paul Lensch (Leipzig)

First I would like to express a wish. I think it would be very useful if resolutions like the one submitted here on imperialism were published a month before the party congresses. Otherwise, the party press is unable to express itself with sufficient detail on the questions under debate. A detailed discussion in the party press is absolutely necessary, particularly on a question so important as imperialism, which I consider by far the most significant of the whole party congress. Only in that way can we make clear to the working masses the significance of the problem at hand. [*Very true!*]

I must also express my sincere regret that two such outstanding party members as Comrades Kautsky and Rosa Luxemburg are not among us at this time because of ill health. They are the most competent to have a say on this question, and all of us would have gladly wished them to be able to stimulate and animate our exchange of ideas by participating in the debate for the good of the Party. [*Bravo!*] I personally regret the absence of Comrade Kautsky. Some of you are perhaps unaware that a debate on the subject

24. [*Stufenleiter*: ladder, stepladder.]

of imperialism has been held on the pages of *Die Neue Zeit*. Since Comrade Kautsky cannot be present here, I think it is an obvious duty of loyalty on my part not to go back to that debate.

Although I have many reservations regarding the proposed resolution, I must forgo submitting an alternative one; first, because the time at my disposal to speak makes it impossible to develop my ideas in adequate detail; second, because I consider the party press the most suitable place for the discussion of such issues; and third, because I am convinced that it can only be a question here of beginning the debate on imperialism, and that the coming years will force us to discuss this issue often enough.

My misgivings chiefly concern the passage in the resolution dealing with arms reduction; not so much because it could mislead the Reichstag fraction into a more or less false step or proposal – because a poorly formulated parliamentary motion hardly deserves many words – but, rather, because our differences of opinion on the evolution of imperialism are most clearly expressed precisely on the disarmament question. Let there be no mistake. By no means do I consider a temporary agreement between two capitalist states on questions of armament policy to be excluded. On the contrary, I have always stressed this possibility. But that is something completely different from what the resolution calls for and what was earlier proposed by the Reichstag-fraction.[25] Here, it is a question of an international agreement for general arms-reduction. And I, as before, certainly consider that to be utopian.

Comrades! How did the international arms-race that we have witnessed these last ten years come about? Is it really just a case of an international misunderstanding that could be resolved by an international agreement? That would mean that world history has made a mistake, as it were; that capitalism is also feasible without resort to force, without colonies and fleets. No doubt that is true, but only in a vacuum! Perhaps in your imagination, or on

25. [On 29 March 1909, the SPD Reichstag fraction submitted a resolution calling for an international agreement to limit naval armaments as a reaction against the German government's rejection of informal disarmament initiatives by the English government. The resolution referred to the decisions of the Hague conferences of 1899 and 1907, which had been approved by the German government, asking it to take the necessary steps 'in order to bring about an international understanding of the great powers for the mutual limitation of naval armaments'. Almost two years later, on 30 March 1911, the Reichstag fraction widened that demand into a proposal calling for an agreement for a general limitation of armaments. Both resolutions were rejected by the Reichstag.]

paper, you can conceive of capitalism without violence. But we are dealing with real capitalism here on earth. Our task cannot be to correct world history's homework and say: 'Dear world history, here is your work back! It's swarming with mistakes. I marked them all for you in red. In the future I expect better work from you!' [*Laughter*] That is not how it works! We must deal with capitalism as it is, and in so doing we must admit that the arms-race grows naturally and inevitably out of the given economic relations.

Protected by tariffs, imperialism has shut out free competition in the internal market and replaced it with monopoly. In the process, it has demolished the economic foundations of liberalism – an event of great political importance! – but only to unleash free competition all the more in the world market. The struggle for the world market brings as its necessary complement the international arms-race. The one is unthinkable without the other. War is the continuation of politics by other means, says Clausewitz. By the same token, the international arms-race is the continuation of international economic competition by other means.

I never said that a war is absolutely inevitable under all circumstances. Up until now, that has also always been the conception of Social Democracy. I could give you dozens of proofs from our literature, but I cannot do that out of time-considerations. Some people say: imperialist development is admittedly driving us to a world war, but it also brings about strong counter-tendencies, and it is our duty to support them. First of all, I must point out that the resolution says nothing about those counter-tendencies. On the contrary, it contains the sentence: 'The bourgeois parties are completely under imperialism's spell and approve without resistance all appropriations for the army and navy.' I find this sentence to be the best in the resolution. One can even speak about a strongly increasing imperialist contamination of the bourgeoisie. The outlays for the arms-race are growing in all the states of the world, but opposition among bourgeois parties to the growing burdens generated by this policy has steadily diminished and has today become totally silent. Only among the ranks of the proletariat is this opposition continually growing, and that gives us an indication as to how we must assess the 'counter-tendencies' to the arms-race. Those counter-tendencies against imperialism are nothing other than counter-tendencies against capitalism as a whole – namely socialism! Social Democracy! Those counter-tendencies are in their essence revolutionary, they lead beyond the existing social order. It is them we must support! But they have nothing in common with disarmament.

Next to them there are admittedly other, reactionary counter-tendencies, and some people now appeal to them in support of disarmament. What are these hopes pinned on? In the first place, some people say, on the British government. They made a great fuss about the fact that the English government made disarmament proposals [to Germany]. Our Reichstag fraction proceeded in 1909 by referring to those proposals. It goes without saying that our parliamentary representatives had to exploit those English disarmament proposals and their point-blank rejection by the German government for agitation purposes; not, however, by making the English proposal their own – supplemented by a motion for abolishing the legislation concerning goods captured at sea[26] – but by presenting England's proposals as proof of the total helplessness of the capitalist states; as proof, moreover, that reveals how unbearable the arms-race is, the awful dangers they face (Lloyd George spoke about the impending rebellion of the English workers), and the fact that despite all that they can see no way out of the blind alley other than a bloodless utopia. [*Very good!*] Because, by stepping forward with such disarmament proposals, the English government declares itself to be precisely in such an historic and economic situation.

The English bourgeoisie feels threatened in its previous security by imperialist competition. It finds itself more and more in transition to a rentier-state – see Sartorious von Waltershausen[27] – and has, like all rentiers, only one wish: to keep things exactly as they are. But it must see, to its sorrow, how the other capitalist states are more and more overtaking it. Even its previously absolute naval supremacy has been shattered by the arms-race. In this situation, it came upon the idea of persuading other states to suspend the arms-race. Thus, its naval supremacy would be secured forever! Why the other powers did not join in this initiative is clear. Here we can see not only its utopian, but also its reactionary cloven hoof! The English bourgeoisie wants to seize historical development by its coat-tail and drag it back to the past in order to perpetuate existing relationships. We, on the contrary, fight against imperialist development by trying to drive it beyond itself. The gradual disruption of English naval supremacy, caused by the arms-race, is a necessary consequence

26. [*Seebeuterecht:* The combatants' right to seize foreign ships and goods in an area of naval war.]
27. [Probably a reference to von Waltershausen 1907.]

of the disruption of English industrial supremacy, which undeniably has already set in.

The English bourgeoisie is making futile attempts through free trade to keep the other nations in a state of agricultural economy in order to make England's position as the only industrial power in the world last forever. It is seeking just as vainly, through the idea of disarmament, to sentence the other capitalist states – and especially a strong, young, and lusty capitalist state like the German Empire – to perpetual naval inferiority, thereby preserving forever England's naval supremacy. But international socialism has not the slightest cause for helping to perpetuate this lasting supremacy of one capitalist state over all others. In that way, the conditions of victory for socialism would just be artificially worsened and delayed.

Remember how Friedrich Engels estimated the great significance that disruption of the English industrial monopoly would have for the spread of socialism in England. He said:

> During the period of England's industrial monopoly the English working-class have, to a certain extent, shared in the benefits of the monopoly. These benefits were very unequally parcelled out amongst them; the privileged minority pocketed most, but even the great mass had, at least, a temporary share now and then. And that is the reason why, since the dying-out of Owenism, there has been no socialism in England. With the breakdown of that monopoly, the English working-class will lose that privileged position; it will find itself generally – the privileged and leading minority not excepted – on a level with its fellow-workers abroad. And that is the reason why there will be socialism again in England.[28]

But a very important means of preserving this privileged position of England in the world market is the absolute superiority of its fleet, with which it shores up and strengthens its world-political and therefore its economic rule. Of course, the ways in which England's naval supremacy is being worn down within capitalist society, such as the awful arms-race, are abhorrent to us, and it is our self-evident duty to oppose them with all our power. But, within capitalist society, almost all progress takes place in ways that are unwelcome to us. Capitalism's mightiest achievement, the fabulous increase in the produc-

---

28. [Engels 1943, p. xvii.]

tivity of labour, without which the organisation of a socialist society would be unthinkable, takes place through the sacrifice of hundreds of thousands of people, through the poverty and misery of the masses, which we try to counteract as much as we can without failing, on that account, to recognise that this bloody march of capitalism ultimately leads to socialism. So the highly objectionable swelling of military forces into modern mass-armies also has one good aspect for us: the fact that the army more and more encompasses all the people fit for military service, thus sending all revolutionary elements into that bulwark of the enemy. Capital must always, whether it likes it or not, ultimately work for us, even where it is apparently just crushing underfoot the interests of humanity, as in the case of the arms-race. [*Very true!*] [...]

By pressing even the last able-bodied man into its service, the arms-race creates the material conditions for our programmatic demand for a militia. If disarmament were feasible, those conditions would lead to the development of praetorian guards – the absolute opposite of the militia. On this issue, too, we have no reason to stop the wheel of historical development. The world must be ours! I shall confine myself to these allusions.

In our fight against imperialism, we cannot view the arms-race as an isolated phenomenon. We have no special weapons against it, only the great but simple slogans: agitate and organise! We say to the masses that imperialism is the final expression of the existing society that opens up all the well-springs of social revolution. By subjugating the entire earth to its domination, imperialism taps the last reservoir of the earth's life-giving springs and blocks up the channels through which the powerfully increased productive forces can be discharged. Even at home, it drives all contradictions to the breaking point. While the tables of the capitalist magnates groan under the weight of their gold, the spectre of hunger haunts the alleyways of the working people. The class-struggle sharpens visibly; and in the colossal struggles of the modern unions, the organised classes stand so close to each other that they can see the whites of their opponents' eyes.

We are approaching a time of great mass-struggles and acute conflicts that will make the highest demands on the understanding and energy of proletarian organisations. We must arm ourselves for these struggles. I completely agree with Haase's conclusion that if we extend our organisation, our political education, if we prepare ourselves – then all we must do is be ready! [*Lively applause*]

Eduard Bernstein

I would like to say a few words, first and foremost, not only to recommend that you adopt the resolution but also to applaud it as an impressive political demonstration of Social Democracy. We all agree that the question of imperialism constitutes the focus of the present political struggles, in which the lines of separation between the parties are becoming manifest. Here, indeed, lies the dividing line for politicians – in how they confront the question of imperialism and the related question of the massive arms-race. For me, it was quite characteristic, when I had to speak some time ago in the Reichstag's budget commission against the naval bill, that a speaker of the party closest to us, and undoubtedly one of its best and most sympathetic representatives, said after me [*Ledebour: who is that? Gothein?*]:[29] 'I totally subscribe to what Mr. Bernstein said, but we must approve the naval budget because it is a practical imperative.' But why should it be a practical imperative to continue this endless arms-race? Is this statement not a declaration of the bankruptcy of contemporary society if its representatives proclaim themselves powerless vis-à-vis the boundless arms-race, that horror without end?

Some people actually uphold the same view when they say, as [the left wingers] just did, that on the basis of modern society the arms-race is an absolute necessity. Why should such a necessity exist? Admittedly, we have a powerful combination of capitalist interests before us, as Haase has admirably shown us with imposing statistics. But this development also has a reverse side that is becoming evident in a definitely oppressive way not only for the working classes but also for the bourgeoisie.

We now live at a time of a high cost of living. [Inflation] is an international phenomenon brought about and boosted precisely by capitalist expansion. [*Very true!*] That expansion means an endless waste of means of production. Not only have the prices of foodstuffs risen, but also those of products that

29. [Georg Gothein (1857–1940) was a German mining engineer and politician belonging to the Freisinnige Vereinigung, a left-liberal progressive organisation. In 1901, he was elected to the Reichstag and was successively re-elected until 1918, when he became one of the founders of the Deutsche Demokratische Partei (DDP). In the Reichstag, he fought against German militarism, particularly the Kaiser's naval policy. In 1919–20, he was elected to the Weimar National Assembly. From 13 February until 20 June 1919, Gothein was Minister of the Treasury in Scheidemann's cabinet. Subsequently, he became a Reichstag deputy again until 1924. In 1921, he also became President of the Verein zur Abwehr des Antisemitismus, an association for combating anti-Semitism.]

are the basis of modern industry: iron and metals. We hear a lot about the prosperity of the mining industry, but that prosperity did not result from the fact that today vast quantities of metal are squandered in the boundless arms-race, as well as in the construction of railways that perhaps some day will pay, but whose extent today is grossly excessive. Some industries are prospering at the expense of the masses of the population. I remember an article in the last issue of *Nautikus* that enumerated how many industries were set in motion by militarism and the naval arms-race. Apparently that is correct. However, the building of pyramids, organised by the despots in ancient Egypt, also set in motion large masses of workers, but the people were thereby impoverished and [society] did not experience any development. [*Very true!*] Alongside the mining industry, there are other industries that employ much larger numbers of workers – think about Chemnitz and its surrounding area with its textile industry. It is of little use to them if undeveloped lands are occupied in Africa or some other place where the local population will long be unable to consume its products. But those industries will be hurt if the prices of foodstuffs rise and the tax-revenue taken from the people is spent on all sorts of armaments purposes.

Admittedly, among the big nations today there are all sorts of problems; more disputes and conflicts of interest arise than in previous periods. But one should not say that they cannot be settled in any other way than through the arms-race and war. Many controversial issues have already been settled in a different way – otherwise we would have war every day. The matters under dispute would also be solvable if we had international courts of arbitration.

If anything is missing for me in Comrade Haase's resolution, it is a reference to international courts of arbitration. But resolutions cannot be exhaustive. I hope that Haase's report will be handed over to us as a pamphlet. What is necessary today is to organise stronger protests against the arms-race and to strengthen the internationality of workers' interests – and not only the interests of the workers but also those of the great masses of citizens in all the developed nations – a protest against protectionism and a demonstration for peace, freedom and free trade between nations. Then we will have history on our side. Parties that do not stand up for this are reactionary, blinded or weakened by half-measures.

I would rather not bring polemics into this debate, but it is impossible to keep silent at the remarks of Comrade Lensch. What he said may seem plausible, but it is nevertheless flawed to the highest degree, and many remarks will be given a warm welcome by people whom Lensch certainly does not want to serve – the people of the *Post* and its consorts. [*Very true!*] I regret that he ascribed England's disarmament proposals so exclusively to the egotistic interests of the English bourgeoisie. Do not forget that Campbell-Bannerman,[30] the person who, when he came to power, made the first step to seek an understanding with Germany, is the same person who, when England waged the Boer War, was one of the few who dared to protest decidedly against it, and that it was his government that gave their self-government back to the Boers.

We are clear in our minds about the old free traders and their faults, yet they were different from what Lensch argued. I will only mention Richard Cobden. Once someone pointed out to him that free trade would make England dependent on foreign countries. And what did he reply? That's right, that's precisely the good thing! He was much more internationally minded than people think today; he was a true man of peace. At the time of the Crimean War, he was, together with Bright, one of the champions of the struggle against the War and organised great protest demonstrations against it. At that time, Marx, who was still young, sneered at him. But only a few years passed and Marx recognised as an interest [of the working class] that Cobden and Bright should triumph in the elections. They stood manfully on the side of those who protested against the planned persecution of the French [Communard] exiles. They were always where it counted, advocating the peoples' rights and international freedom.

Germany has become an industrial state; it even has colonies. Its industry has powerfully developed. Even before it built its navy, it spent large sums on armaments. I could say many things about the idea that what we are demanding today, namely disarmament, is utopian and reactionary. World history has often taken false paths, peoples have often suffered from political self-delusion; whole cultures have often decayed. We want organised society to intervene consciously not only in the process of production but also in the international antagonisms. We hold up for humanity the goals that the greatest reformers of all times had in mind. We stand up for the words of the founder of Christianity, which were forsaken by his followers, as well as for those of

30. [Sir Henry Campbell-Bannerman (1836–1908) was a British Liberal politician who served as Prime Minister from 5 December 1905, until resigning due to ill health on 3 April 1908.]

a Matthias Erzberger,[31] who today is one of the worst agitators for militarism – the slogans that the Centre has betrayed: 'Glory to God in the highest, and on earth peace, good will toward men.'[32] We must never rest in our efforts to make sure that society develops unhindered towards general welfare, towards equality of rights for nations by means of international agreements and disarmament. At least the working class of Germany, like that of the other developed nations, is resolved to leave no stone unturned in working for that goal and to struggle [until it is reached]. [*Stormy and prolonged applause*]

Anton Pannekoek (Bremen)

Naturally, this discussion can only be a preliminary debate to ascertain the points of difference and awaken interest [on the issue of imperialism] among broad circles. I will therefore intervene only in order to clear some false views out of our way.

We regard imperialism as a necessary or, even better, as an inevitable form of the development of capitalism, not in the sense that some other form could not be conceivable or construed, but in the sense that this path was the one actually pursued. We can demonstrate that imperialism damages the interests of broad strata even among the bourgeoisie. But the fact remains that the whole bourgeoisie supports this policy. We do not affirm that imperialist policy is necessary in the sense that, otherwise, a collapse, crises and unemployment would ensue. Haase referred to the military industries in which unemployment would develop as a result of disarmament, [arguing] that those considerations cannot be decisive for us. But we have not only the arms-industry to fight. The circle of those with direct interests at stake is much bigger. All large-scale capital and finance-capital have a stake in imperialist policy and

31. [Matthias Erzberger (1875–1921) was a prominent German politician in the Centre Party. He was elected to the Reichstag in 1903. Erzberger belonged to the left wing of the Centre Party and attacked the way in which Germany treated the African people in its colonies. He initially supported the country's involvement in the First World War, but, by 1917, was calling for a negotiated peace. On 11 November 1918, Erzberger headed the German delegation that signed the Armistice. In June 1919, Erzberger became finance minister and endorsed the Treaty of Versailles. His liberal views made him unpopular with right-wing nationalists, and, in March 1920, he was forced from office. Erzberger was murdered in Baden by members of the right-wing *Freikorps* on 26 August 1921.]

32. [Luke 2:14, *King James Bible*.]

consequently in the arms-race. Therefore, imperialism is more than a simple policy-interest of the bourgeoisie; it is, rather, a way of thinking, an ideology. It is only a policy-interest for large-scale capital. The mass of the bourgeoisie allows itself to be taken in tow for many material and ideological reasons. We often hear talk of imperialism as some sort of mental derangement of the bourgeoisie. In the party congress issue of the *Chemnitzer Volksstimme*, Bernstein speaks of a spiritual epidemic. But we should not conceive of it in such an un-Marxist manner, as if it were an accident. Our literature lays bare the many threads that tie each bourgeois group to that policy. That is why we consider it utopian to count on its reversal.

People counter by referring us to the English disarmament proposals. Before the arms-race, England had, as it were, an imperialist monopoly – a monopoly that it can only lose through the arms-race. [*Bernstein: Without disarmament, even more!*] It was natural that it should make disarmament proposals, but it was equally natural that the German government should ignore them. [*Hear! Hear!*] Natural [that is], from the point of view of large-scale capital – from the standpoint of the proletariat, it is precisely the opposite. Our Reichstag fraction represented the latter point of view through its rejection of the budget and its conduct at each military bill. But, if it wants to proceed by asking the German government to agree to the British [disarmament]proposals, it must be said that they are not achievable.

The ruling class cannot adopt that course because it is an exploiting class, because the politics of looting and brutality are part of its nature. Thus, the different powers want to take part in it as far as possible. Power alone determines the outcome of their conflicts. Even if it does not lead to war, the arms-race is not useless for large-scale capital, because it can be used to force concessions from its competitors elsewhere, from the other world powers. That is why the arms-race is pursued so zealously. Haase mentioned how the capitalist magnates are already organising internationally, but he added that this process will not eliminate wars. If that is so, and if the capitalists know that wars are unavoidable, then the arms-race will not disappear either. [*Haase: Ending the arms-race is not the same thing as disarmament!*] Our standpoint, therefore, has nothing to do with the vindication of that [armament] policy. We emphasise the inevitability [of the arms-race] in order subsequently to organise our struggle against imperialism. We want to struggle as brusquely as possible against this brutal, dangerous form of capitalism, but not by trying to drive capitalism back to an earlier form. That is impossible. There is only one way: beyond imperialism to socialism.

People object to this: must we therefore feed the popular masses, who are heavily oppressed by taxes as a consequence of the arms-race, merely with hopes about the state of the future? That's not the point! Let us take in comparison a scenario in which dock-labourers are suddenly threatened by the introduction of machines, by corn-elevators throwing thousands of workers into the streets. The idea would then spring up: couldn't we fight against it with our trade-union power? But Social Democracy would answer: that's impossible, we cannot fight against progress; make sure that the machines fall into your own hands. [*Hear! Hear! and objections*] Otherwise, we would really be feeding the workers with promises about the future. It is not at all true that our standpoint means that we cannot fight today against imperialism and that we content ourselves with pointing to the state of the future. The working class can struggle in practice against imperialism, it must do so, and that struggle is simultaneously a struggle for socialism.

The struggle against the high cost of living provides a good example. It is an imperialist phenomenon. Gold-production, cartels, protective tariffs, closing of frontiers, domestic reaction and employers' associations – they all make the high cost of living so oppressive. They drive the masses to revolt and they revolutionise people's minds. But they also drive the masses into the streets, as happened last Sunday in Stuttgart. Under the slogan 'Convene the Reichstag, Open the Borders!' the masses will ineluctably move forwards to ever more powerful demonstrations until the goal is reached. These mass-actions are, at one and the same time, a struggle for an immediate goal, the alleviation of distress, and a struggle for socialism, because the power, the confidence, the unity of the masses are increased by them. The struggle against domestic reaction is a similar case: mass-actions are the main weapon in the struggle for universal equal suffrage in Prussia.

The danger of war will also inevitably bring in its wake the intervention of the working class in order to lessen its consequences, and mass-actions will play a large role in it. Our standpoint against imperialism also means a very determined struggle, relentlessly and continually pursued in parliament but also, at a certain point, through actions of the masses themselves. We therefore emphasise that, in the struggle against imperialism, the workers must not primarily count on some possible anti-imperialist tendencies of the bourgeois world but solely on their own forces. In themselves they will also find the strength to win. [*Applause*]

Salomon Grumbach (Colmar)[33]

I would like first of all to emphasise that this morning the party congress approved the parliamentary report, which states our position on disarmament as follows: 'A reduction of armaments through agreements is possible and realisable.' Given the arguments that have lately been brought forward, on the one hand by Pannekoek and Lensch and on the other by Kautsky, we must ask ourselves: are there tendencies at work in international capitalist life that could support our peace strivings? If we answer positively, it is our duty to support those tendencies, even if counter-tendencies are noticeable from the other side; even if, as is doubtlessly the case within capitalism, there are tendencies driving towards war. Even if only the shadow of a tendency in favour of peace exists within capitalism, our task is to strengthen it. [*Very true!*] Those peace tendencies do exist, and numerous causes prompt modern capitalism to want peace in every way. [*Very true!*]

There is a close connection between the capitalists of all countries – to put it visually, there is a cobweb of capitalist threads – which could be so disrupted by a warlike blow that all national capitalisms would be badly affected by it. There is nothing in the relations between France and Germany or between Germany and England forcing those countries to go to war. A false view has been advanced for years, according to which Germany's industrial rise has hurt England's industrial prosperity badly. English exports have grown more strongly than German exports in absolute terms, if not relatively. In

33. [Salomon Grumbach (1884–1952) was an Alsatian politician and journalist. Closely associated with the SPD and the French Section of the Workers' International (SFIO), he particularly strove to improve German-French relations. At the Chemnitz party congress, Grumbach spoke as a delegate from Colmar in support of Kautsky's views. During the First World War, he became a French social-chauvinist. In 1918, he adopted French citizenship. Within the SFIO, he belonged to the right-wing minority that opposed co-operation with Communist parties. Grumbach later supported the Popular Front governments under Léon Blum and Édouard Daladier. After the Second World War, he was elected in mid-December 1946 to the Council of the Republic, to which he belonged until 1948. At the end of 1948, Grumbach became a member of the French delegation to the United Nations.]

any case, English [foreign] trade has grown by many billions along with German trade.

On the other hand, we see that Germany and France are not fundamentally separated by any imperialist question. It is not an economic problem that constantly renews the antagonism between the two countries, which have so many economic interests in common, but the question of Alsace-Lorraine, which belongs to the domain of 'national honour' and international law. [*Very true!*] The French nationalist deputy Delafosse[34] has recently expressed this view clearly in the *Echo de Paris*. But, if we know that no imperialist question separates both countries, that the economic antagonism between England and Germany is not that great, and that the conflict between the two countries must necessarily result in either a war or the collapse of one of them, we must come to the conclusion that this is one of those points where we can apply leverage in favour of the peace movement.

You can see that the great powers are not willing to break the peace, to take a recent example, from the outbreak of the Panama conflict between America and England. The English newspapers of all tendencies wrote: it should not occur to England to start a war because of that conflict, for in that way we would only hurt ourselves. Actually, every country has today [invested] so much capital in the other that it must hurt itself by a war. [*Very true!*] Even our 'hereditary enemy', France, has already invested in Germany a capital of more than a billion [marks] in all sorts of enterprises. Consequently, within the capitalist world itself, there must therefore be a strong need to preserve peace. One has only to look at the stock-exchange reports in order to realise that the stock-exchange sections of the newspapers sing a very different tune from the leading articles, where [journalists] believe they must give as warlike and heroic expression as possible to the idea of national honour.

If we look at the current situation, we realise how totally false is Pannekoek's statement that precisely finance-capital has an interest in the arms-race. No, it is precisely finance-capital that has an interest in stopping the arms-race. I am not talking about the arms-industry. That the arms-industry has an interest in the arms-race is obvious, but despite its expansion it does not encompass the largest part of finance-capital. The managements of the great banks in Berlin,

34. [A reference to Jules-Victor Delafosse (1841–1916), a right-wing, Bonapartist member of the Chambre des Députés for Calvados from 1877 until his death in 1916.]

Paris and London will doubtless not provoke a world war but will rather do as much as possible to preserve peace by diplomatic means.

You laugh, Comrade Henke?[35] You have no reason, for those strivings are well established. Finance-capital displays a special kind of activity that was brilliantly explained by Comrade Hilferding in his superb book *Modern* [sic] *Finance Capital*. We must not be deceived by certain external gestures of the representatives of finance-capital suggesting that it has an interest in the arms-race.

Dr. Lensch said: Capitalism without an army hovers in the air. That is correct, and it is especially true for the beginnings of capitalism. But we also see that, at a certain stage [of its development], capital has an interest in bringing that military advance to a standstill. We are not utopians asking capitalism to disband its army completely. For the time being, we demand only a reduction of the arms-race rather than further disarmament. If the arms-race is a natural consequence of great-capitalist policy, it is certainly no longer an absolute necessity at a certain stage. In my opinion, to argue that it is hopeless to advocate the limitation of the arms-race because that is an inevitable phenomenon is to uphold a conservative-fatalistic, ideological-Marxist view. [*Laughter!*] No, that is not the case, because the arms-race is [not] a natural necessity, and because we cannot fight against it without working together with reactionaries and ideological pacifists. We fight with other weapons and

35. [Alfred Henke (1868–1946), was a cigar-maker from Bremen who was active in the left wing of the SPD from the mid-1890s. Henke belonged to the tobacco-workers' union and was a delegate to their congresses. From 1900 to 1919, he was editor of the left-wing newspaper *Bremer Bürger-Zeitung* together with Heinrich Schulz. Henke took part in many SPD party conferences and international socialist congresses. From 1906–22 he was a member of *Bremer Bürgerschaft* (the parliament of the Free Hanseatic City of Bremen) and from 1912–18 a Reichstag deputy. At the SPD party congress in Jena in 1913, he voted for the mass-strike resolution of Rosa Luxemburg. At the start of First World War, Henke joined the minority of the Reichstag group opposed to granting war-loans. In March 1916, he was excluded from the SPD Reichstag fraction together with the other opponents of the war-loans and became a member of the Sozialdemokratische Arbeitsgemeinschaft. In 1917, he was one of the founders of the USPD, on whose advisory committee he served until 1920. During the German Revolution of November 1918, Henke became Chairman of the Workers' and Soldiers' Council in Bremen and, from January–February 1919, was Chairman of the Council of People's Representative of the Bremen Soviet Republic. Elected to the National Assembly in Weimar, Henke succeeded Hugo Haase as one of the co-chairs of the USPD fraction. He rejected the union of the USPD with the KPD. Until 1922, he was a member of the advisory committee of the minority in the USPD and took part in its party conferences. With the merger of the SPD and the USPD in that year, Henke rejoined the SPD. Subsequently he was elected again as Reichstag deputy until 1932.]

other arguments than the bourgeois peace supporters do, and we cannot at all be mistaken for them.

Above all, comrades, think what the effect abroad would be if German Social Democracy were to adopt Pannekoek's and Lensch's arguments and abandon the demand for disarmament. Everywhere out there, in other countries, we find armies of our bourgeois opponents who are just waiting to be able to say that German Social Democracy is looking for theoretical reasons not to have to fight anymore against the 'arms-race desired by the German people'. [*Very true!*] Today, Jaurès in the French Chamber of Deputies, Keir Hardie in the English House of Commons, and Pablo Iglesias in the Spanish Cortes, can always argue that, in Germany, there is a living, one-million-strong army of socialists, whose most eloquent spokesmen stand up time and again for cessation of the arms-race. We must think practically if we want to deal with this practical question.

The most dangerous thing we can do would be to follow the tactic of Pannekoek and Lensch. We would strike a very hard blow at the peace movement, insofar as it is conducted by socialists, if we were to suggest the possibility of eventually removing the disarmament demand from our programme or were even seriously to contemplate doing that. Our view on that issue is nothing other than the practically applied basic view, also shared by the trade-unions, that wherever possible, within bourgeois society and on the ground of the capitalist social order, we must contain its excesses, minimise them and bring them to a standstill. In that sense, the conclusions from Pannekoek's views, which boil down to the idea that the disarmament demand is a utopia, are indeed not utopian at all but rather very dangerous.

Today, German Social Democracy, the most renowned and powerful section of the socialist International, should loudly declare: Just as we have always struggled for disarmament, we further want to do everything possible to strengthen the trends, existing within capitalism and the capitalist social order, against world war, with the extraordinary force of the popular masses standing behind us. (*Stormy and prolonged acclamation and applause*)

Dr. Karl Liebknecht (Berlin)

I dare to remind you, without being immodest, that the two international youth-conferences, held in 1907 and 1910, discussed at length the questions dealt with here, and I think they also fully discussed all the ideas advanced today and earlier in the press debates.[36] Undoubtedly, there is a contrast between the views of Comrades Lensch and Pannekoek, on the one hand, and Kautsky and his supporters on the other. But it does not seem to me to be a conflict so tragic as to make our hair stand on end. [*Laughter*] I think Pannekoek and Lensch did not think through to the end the train of thought pointed out by Marxism. They remain half-way, trapped in a rather mechanistic view of society and its development. [*Lively: Very true!*] It is very strange that Lensch, who is otherwise such a keen observer of the antagonistic nature of our social order, has so completely failed [to notice it] here. Surprisingly, he ignores the fact that, in capitalist society, there are admittedly necessary trends, but no absolute necessity in any direction, and that necessary tendencies everywhere face just as necessary counter-tendencies. And, when Lensch says we have to take capitalism as it is, we can retort, borrowing one of his own expressions, that we must not take capitalism in isolation, placed under a glass bell as it were and cut off from the simultaneous anti-capitalist forces and impulses. It belongs to the tendencies of the capitalist period of development that everything is necessary only temporarily and impermanently. We need only think about capitalist competition – I am not speaking about international competition – and how it assumed various characters in different periods. Existing trends are necessary only to the extent that counter-trends do not develop to bring about alterations and modifications.

The same happens with the question occupying us here. It is not true that, in capitalism, there are no counter-trends against warlike tendencies and the arms-race. The resolutions of the international youth-conferences have dealt with this issue thoroughly.[37] And, a year ago, at the party congress in Jena, Bebel described in striking and forceful words precisely the international connections speaking against the war-madness even from the standpoint of capitalism.

Lensch has constructed an inherent contradiction between disarmament and a militia. I deny that this contradiction exists. At the youth-conference in Copenhagen in 1910 – excuse me for enlarging on this issue, perhaps you are inwardly smiling at it, but I think it is important – we wanted to demand, in

36. [A reference to the first and second International Conferences of Socialist Young People's Organisations, held in Stuttgart on 24–6 August 1907 and in Copenhagen on 4–5 September 1910.]

37. [Internationale Verbindung sozialistischer Jugendorganisationen 1907, and International Conference of Socialist Young People's Organisations (Copenhagen), 1910.]

accordance with the German party programme, the militia, the general arming of the people, as one of the objectives of the anti-militarist movement. But we found vigorous opposition from the Scandinavians, to whom the militia appears as a worsening of their current situation. The issue therefore stands as follows: we do not aim at a militia for its own sake; we do not want to arm the people if they do not need to defend themselves against the dominant and oppressive domestic powers and against foreign enemies. A militia is not always and in all cases the best thing compared to existing conditions; it can also be, under certain circumstances, an aggravation; it is only the lesser evil vis-à-vis the greater evil, above all standing armies, compared to which the militia is less dangerous in both international and domestic conflicts. There is, therefore, no contradiction in principle between a militia and disarmament.

Imperialism, you could say briefly, is a capitalist business, and because of that it is better to encapsulate the essence of the struggle against it in a commercial formula. [*Very good!*] From a business point of view, the historic mission of the proletariat with respect to imperialism is to increase, through its politics of class-struggle, the social, political and economic risk of the war-like form of international competition to the ruling classes of the participating countries, so that the ruling classes, likewise from a business point of view, will consider a peaceful understanding in international competition, through trustification for instance, to be the most advisable policy. We are not giving up any Marxist principle by looking at the issue from that perspective.

The main tendency against imperialism is the proletarian one of solidarity between all peoples, of waging the class-struggle within particular countries and in the International against the circles whose business is imperialism. We need to continue to work in exactly the direction in which Social Democracy and the international socialist congresses have done thus far; we do not have to change one iota from what we have said and done. And, if the Social Democracy of all countries continues to work in that direction, mobilising all its power, it will do everything humanly possible to prevent imperialism's military adventures.

To strengthen and fortify international proletarian solidarity, to pursue the class-struggle with ever-mounting intensity and zeal, to be ready to fight against imperialism whatever the cost – that, in my opinion, is a very good and safe defence against the incitement of the masses by the ruling classes. We can do no better against the war-threat than to leave no doubt in the minds of the ruling classes regarding the mighty economic, political, and social perils they would conjure up by setting off a world conflagration in face of the advanced intellectual development of the proletariat and of the workers' resolve to carry on the class-struggle come what may.

For us the old maxim still holds: *si vis pacem, para bellum* – if you want peace, prepare for war. If we want peace among nations, we must prepare and advance the class-struggle, fomenting it more and more on an international scale. We cannot afford to stray from the line we have adopted at previous congresses. We just need to rally together unanimously and enthusiastically against imperialism, for international solidarity and for recognition of the important and meaningful role of proletarian power against the powers of imperialist capitalism. In a time so filled with explosive material as this, it is impossible to slur over this issue in a socialist congress. And it is equally impossible to claim any serious disagreement over the call that we issue to the world proletariat: 'We want to be a single nation of brothers, not to be separated by misery and danger!' [*Great applause*]

Max Cohen (Leipzig)[38]

Since I did not participate directly in the polemic between Lensch and Kautsky, I think I am not going against any practice of the party congress if I include Kautsky's views in my argument. I will limit myself to what is strictly necessary, but it is impossible simply to pass them over. Both Kautsky and Lensch have remarked to each other that their respective views are new. Kautsky

38. [Max Cohen (1876–1963) was a German journalist and Social-Democratic politician. The son of a Jewish businessman, he received a merchant's training. In 1902, he joined the SPD where, beginning in 1904, he worked as a journalist and belonged to the left wing. From 1912 to 1918, he was a Reichstag deputy for the Principality of Reuss ältere Linie. From 1908 to 1914, he was also a member of the city council of Frankfurt am Main. During the First World War, Cohen served in the army and shifted to the extreme right wing of the SPD. According to Abraham Ascher: 'Max Cohen, who had supported Lensch and Pannekoek in 1912, belonged to this ("radical imperialist") group after 1914.' (See Cohen 1915a, 1915b and 1915c.) Parvus, the editor of *Die Glocke*, a journal of the SPD-imperialists during the War, was also a radical. Probably the most ardent expansionist of all these radicals was Konrad Haenisch. (See Haenisch 1915a, 1915b and 1919.) (Ascher 1961, p. 574, note 43.) Cohen filled official posts during the Weimar Republic. He left Germany at the beginning of the Nazi rule and never returned permanently to his homeland. After 1945, he worked as a correspondent for various German newspapers and, from 1947 to 1951, served as official representative of the SPD in France.]

emphasised that the International always upheld the idea of disarmament. Lensch denied this and Kautsky pointed out, in this case rightly, that in 1907 he published an article in the *Leipziger Volkszeitung*, separately published in Leipzig as a brochure,[39] which argued that governments could disarm if only they wanted to. But that proves nothing against Lensch's views; first, because the *Volkszeitung* must doubtless also have published opinions countering his own, and second, because he has nothing to do with the *Leipziger Volkszeitung* printing office, so that the edition of Kautsky's brochure by the Leipziger Buchdruckerei cannot be used against him.[40] It may well also be the case that Lensch has become much cleverer since 1907 and no longer holds the same views.

Indeed, I think that Lensch sees further here than Kautsky, and that he furnished proof that the idea of international disarmament leading to world peace was not formerly advanced in the International. An example will show Liebknecht how impractical it is to refer to Bebel's statements, even one made at the Jena party congress. There, Bebel said: 'We will no longer separate in the future disarmament and the questions connected with it. Besides, the watchword for bourgeois Europe in the future will not be disarmament, but the arms-race. I believe that this arms-race can only end with a great catastrophe.' Bebel did not mean by this that he wished for the arms-race and catastrophes, only that they *must come*. Lensch and Pannekoek are not saying anything different.

Grumbach made the enormous mistake of limiting imperialism only to the relations between Germany, England and France. Show me a passage from Lensch, Pannekoek, Luxemburg and others denying the idea that the present war-danger could be temporarily eliminated by an agreement between Germany and France. That is not the main issue.

Actually, we face a new and acute danger: that the consequences of an agreement between Germany and England could be felt almost certainly in the not too distant future. The goal of an agreement between those two powers would be to enable them to act together imperialistically vis-à-vis everyone else, particularly to take away those parts of other countries about which they may perhaps reach an agreement. The danger of an arms-race against

39. [Kautsky 1907c.]
40. [Paul Lensch then worked as editor of the left-wing *Leipziger Volkszeitung*.]

other countries would therefore always exist. I cannot believe a Social Democrat could seriously imagine that one could possibly reconcile all countries.

I was very much surprised when Bernstein called the possibility of a great war a declaration of the bankruptcy of contemporary society. It would only be so from an ethical point of view, and he must first show that development must take an ethical-moral path. Unfortunately, there can be no such declaration of bankruptcy from the point of view of development, because the latter can also take a bloody and warlike path. Bernstein has also spoken about [international] arbitration-courts. None of us believes that arbitration-courts would not be a good thing on particular issues, but all Social Democrats reject the idea that arbitration-courts could have the final say on the vital questions of the peoples. When Bernstein further argued that by such a rejection we serve the work of reaction, he used the method that was always employed against us by the Progressives [*Freisinnigen*] when they wanted us to change our position. We have never let those considerations prevail or prevent us from doing something we considered correct [*Very true!*]

Kautsky first pointed out in his book *The Road to Power* that, as long as world policy lasts, the insanity of the arms-race must also increase until the proletariat accumulates enough power to overcome capitalism and replace it by socialism. Pannekoek and Lensch say the same thing; they are not arguing that we should not fight against imperialism. But it is false to pin our hopes on an understanding between Germany and England, or between the whole of Western Europe, because America's interests do not coincide with those of the Western-European states, neither do those of East Asia, etc. And if the Reichstag fraction had contented itself with saying that an agreement between Germany and England could reduce the immediate war-danger and dispose of an important dispute, no one would have objected. But I consider it utopian to pin hopes on securing world peace through international agreements as the resolution does.

Haase asserted that capital's tendency to imperialism could be offset by our counter-tendency [to preserve peace], just as capital's tendency to impoverish the workers was halted [by the trade-union struggle]. But he must prove that; it is not enough just to state it. By making this analogy, he also made a logical *salto mortale*. He aligned himself with Kautsky's argumentation, according to which there are also other methods besides the arms-race, namely, peaceful penetration [of backward areas] by capital. The peaceful penetration of East Asia by Western-European capital is, however, the germ of grave catastrophes. If China or some other country decides to stop depending on Western-European capital and to set itself free, the Western-European powers will have to arm themselves more than ever in order to defend the interests of their capitalists in East Asia.

If you understand by disarmament that a temporary mitigation [of the war-threat] could be brought about by an agreement [of Germany] with other countries, we have nothing against that. But think about tariff-agreements, which people consider the Alpha and Omega of a peace instrument. They simply postpone the decision.

For all of these reasons, it is impossible to support that part of the resolution that sees in international agreements the chance of world peace. We could not associate ourselves with them. Agreements between some nations will not hinder any catastrophe. On the contrary, they mean the cutting off of other countries, against whom it would then be doubly necessary to arm. International peace can only be guaranteed by socialism, not by agreements between some powers or groups of powers, which can spring from some momentary situations but which, in the changing course of things, can only be transient phenomena.

Ludwig Quessel (Darmstadt)[41]

I certainly have the rare pleasure of expressing my agreement with the views of Comrades Lensch and Pannekoek, insofar as I think that what has been said today about the problem of imperialism can only be regarded as the beginning of a debate. Above all, I miss in the resolution a consideration of the commercial and industrial side of imperialism. During the elections, I was repeatedly reproached by our opponents that, on the Moroccan question, our party abandoned industry and with it the vital interests of the German people. I referred to Bebel's statement that we must, under all circumstances, demand equality of rights for our industry in the world market. But I miss the fact that

41. [Ludwig Quessel (1872–1931) was born into a working-class family in Königsberg (present-day Kaliningrad) and worked until 1897 as an assistant watchmaker. In 1890 he joined the SPD, where he became a prominent member of the right wing, working as foreign-policy editor for the revisionist theoretical journal *Sozialistische Monatshefte*. In addition, he worked as a journalist for newspapers in several German cities. In 1912, he was elected to the Reichstag and successively re-elected until 1930. From 1919 to 1920, Quessel was a member of the Weimar National Assembly.]

Bebel's statement at Jena, which all of us then received with a thunderous applause, and which has rendered us exceptional service during the elections, finds no expression in the resolution.

We support freedom of world trade. But what answer must we give if our opponents ask us how we want to uphold it? According to our hitherto prevailing views, we should answer: we always want to have the 'Open Door'. But closer investigation of the question of commercial policy has convinced me that the 'Open Door' does not always achieve what we socialists hitherto believed. We deal with our colonies as foreign countries; no industry is encouraged there by protective tariffs, not even German industry. According to the official memorandum, the German metal-industry sold 34 times more in the German colonies than in the English ones, but the export of products from the British metal-industry to India in 1909–10 amounted to 152 million, while German exports amounted to only 5.8 million – that is to say, in precisely the reverse proportion to our colonies.

For the solution of a problem, it is extremely important that people should first of all be conscious of the difficulties. We can, naturally, have no immediate, fixed and ready solution for the issue that has become especially topical lately. But it must be emphasised that it is a vital problem for the German proletariat. A partial solution certainly lies in sticking to the principle of asserting our power everywhere, of securing as much as possible the freedom and political independence of the peoples everywhere. That applies to Persia as well as to the Chinese and Turkish peoples. Also in the Moroccan affair, which already belongs to the past, we could have advocated more energetically the country's independence vis-à-vis rapacious French imperialism.

But from this also follows the need to stand behind the German government wherever it actually champions the equality of rights for our industry. That lies in the interest of the proletariat, exactly as we stand behind the government when it really tries to conclude favourable commercial agreements. It is necessary for the ultra-radicals, revisionists and Marxists to state their positions on the question of the 'Open Door'. [*Ledebour laughs*] It doesn't matter that you laugh. Often facts are laughed at because the people concerned have not occupied themselves thoroughly enough with them. I know that Bebel considers this question extremely important. A year ago at Jena,[42] I still

42. [A reference to the second Jena party congress of the SPD, held on 10–16 September 1911.]

held the view that the 'Open Door' sufficed to secure equality of rights for German industry. I have now abandoned that opinion, and anyone examining the commercial statistics objectively will likewise have to abandon that view. For the time being, I cannot provide a solution to this difficult question; however, I have given important indications for elucidation of the problem in the *Sozialistische Monatshefte*.[43]

Georg Ledebour[44]

Quessel's statistical reservations on the open-door policy were first expressed some months ago in the *Sozialistische Monatshefte*. They awakened then the same amusement as they do today. He thinks he has delved especially deeply

43. [See, for instance, Quessel 1912a, 1912b and 1912c. Quessel argued at Chemnitz that 'the goal of the whole article was to show that the bourgeois imperialists are not fantastic dreamers but are, on the contrary, driven by purely egoistic motives, by the profit interests of imperialist policy'. He also denied that he had in any way advocated the capitalist colonial policy of the contemporary German government. 'I hold the view that we need a civilising colonial policy, as comrade Bebel formulated it in his day to the jubilation of the [Reichstag] fraction, and which has rendered us good services at the elections.' Sozialdemokratische Partei Deutschlands 1912, pp. 432–3.]

44. [Georg Ledebour (1850–1947) was born in Hanover and served as a paramedic during the Franco-Prussian War of 1870–1. From 1876 to 1882, he worked as a foreign correspondent in London for left–liberal newspapers. In 1882, he joined the German Progressive Party, but, in 1891, he left it to join the SPD, where he originally belonged to the left wing. From 1900 on, he was a member of the editorial staff of the *Vorwärts* and then of the *Sächsischen Arbeiterzeitung* in Dresden. From 1900 to 1918, he was also a prominent member of the SPD Reichstag fraction. During the First World War, Ledebour took part in the Zimmerwald and Kienthal conferences and supported opponents of both the War and the *Burgfrieden* policy (of party truce) within the SPD, who from 1915–17 either left the Party or were expelled and formed the USPD in 1917. During the German Revolution of November 1918, Ledebour served as a member of the executive of the Workers' and Soldiers' Council in Berlin. In January 1919, he took part in the Spartakus uprising and was a member of the Revolutionary Committee. After the suppression of the uprising, he was arrested, but, in June of the same year, was acquitted. As chairman of the USPD, he sat again in the Reichstag from 1920 to 1924. Ledebour spoke out against an association of the USPD exclusively with the KPD or the SPD and called for the unity of all socialist forces. After most USPD-members joined one of the two competing parties, Ledebour remained in the USPD rump until the end of 1923, later joining a splinter-group known as the Sozialistischer Bund. In the second half of the 1920s, Ledebour participated in KPD front-organisations such as the World League Against Imperialism and the International Workers' Aid (IAH). In the autumn of 1931, he joined the newly formed Socialist Workers' Party of Germany (SAP), which unsuccessfully attempted to make all the German workers' parties endorse him as their common candidate for the presidential elections of 1932. In 1933, he fled from the Nazis to Switzerland, where he worked as a journalist against National Socialism. In 1946, he one again tried to bring about a merger of the SPD and the KPD in the Sozialistische Einheitspartei Deutschlands (SED) but died shortly thereafter.]

into that question. From the fact that English export figures to the English colonies are higher than the German ones, he wants to draw the conclusion that only England's sovereignty [over its colonies] has brought about that result. That is incorrect, because those English export figures doubtless also include German products. Such a profound researcher must know that commodities arrive in the English colonies mostly through England, even if they were produced in other countries. But those are the ways of trade. The circumstance that the export of metal-wares from Germany to its colonies is, on the contrary, relatively very large is due to the fact that the German colonies are, at present and for a long time to come, not exactly culturally developed areas. What is sent there as metal-wares from Germany are particularly railway-tracks and all sorts of materials required for railway-construction, which were directly exported by German entrepreneurs with German subventions. Those are completely artificial [commercial] relations, totally unsuitable for drawing a general conclusion. Quessel has carefully walked around the question of the 'Open Door'. When I read his article in the *Sozialistische Monatshefte*, I might have thought it had been written by a Paasche or some other National Liberal had it not been for the fact that I read the name of a Social-Democratic Reichstag deputy under it. [*Hear! Hear!*] We must unconditionally advocate the open-door policy.

The source of the views separating Lensch, Pannekoek and other comrades from us is a sentence in Pannekoek's speech. He argued that the German government has, from the point of view of the interests of capital, the right to pursue by violent means the capitalist policy of plunder. Lensch's speech sounded the same note. Both proceed from the assumption that the doubtless existing tendency of capitalism to plunder other countries can only be earnestly pursued *by violent means*. The arms-race is therefore something that must naturally grow to ever-larger proportions – always from the standpoint of the capitalist governments. Lensch also pointed out, in this connection, that the English disarmament proposals, which gave occasion for our [parliamentary] motion, can actually be ascribed to the fact that England wants to condemn other countries to permanent naval inferiority. From this follows the view that this policy of plunder by violent means is something absolute and that [its tendencies] prevail absolutely, without other capitalist tendencies counteracting it.

Grumbach and Liebknecht have already pointed out why such views are wrong. I would like to supplement [their criticism] by pointing out another tendency at work in capitalism. You know that competition is an essential element of the capitalist mode of production. At the beginning of the capitalist mode of production, competition ruled absolutely almost everywhere. The single capitalist tried to grab his profit by all means at his disposal, fair or foul. In its further development, capital went beyond that absolute competitive struggle. The capitalists finally united for the common exploitation of the workers and the consuming public. That is the role of cartels and trusts. The originally competing capitalists joined together into great exploiting trusts [*Konzernen*]. In the end, to speak like Marx, the expropriators were themselves expropriated. European and American capitalism has already come so far that the cartelisation-needs assert themselves between states as they previously did among the capitalists of individual countries.

From this general point of view, I understand England's [disarmament] proposals as a symptom of the cartelisation-needs of English capitalism with other state-capitalist organisations for common exploitation of the world market. Lensch has already pointed out very correctly the reasons why that symptom first came to light precisely in England. The English capitalists, who actually require for their exploitation the instruments of state-power, are, as it were, the fat rats, and the German capitalists are the hungry rats. The fat rats realise that they have achieved what they could with the previous way of exploiting other countries through the instruments of state-power, but that, from now on, they can only maintain or even increase that exploitation if they join forces with their competitors in other countries to form great, world-encompassing exploiting trusts [*Konzernen*]. Naturally, this comparison should not be taken literally; I am sure you understand what I mean.

Generally speaking, if one traces all these phenomena back to their economic causes, that is what the state, as organ of the cartels, is trying to do at present in the economically advanced nations of the world: to reach agreements with other states in order to bring about a reduction of armaments. We have every reason to strengthen that trend, which is naturally counteracted by other trends, not only in order to facilitate general economic development, which is leading beyond capitalism to socialism, but also because it corresponds fully with our will to preserve peace. [*Very true!*] When that symptom manifested itself in England, we therefore immediately seized upon it and submitted our [parliamentary] motion, which I drafted myself, and which I still uphold, because it was not just a momentary inspiration but a consistent step in pursuit of a socialist world policy. [*Bravo!*]

To conclude the debate, a motion was brought forward and approved.

Hugo Haase (closing words)

The material on imperialism is so vast that I was able to give you only a short excerpt. I am therefore not astonished that some speakers found that much was missing in my report. I can only reply briefly to the objections raised.

Insofar as Quessel had to be refuted factually, Ledebour did it completely in the sense of my own views. We could have supported Quessel's argument that the bourgeois imperialists are not fantastic dreamers but egoists in search of profits, if only he had properly expressed those ideas. By the way, I am astonished that he, being known as a thorough worker, gave rise to misunderstandings in his articles and in his speech today that could have been avoided by taking even a superficial look at the statistics.

Cohen has made things very easy for himself by proceeding as lawyers do when a situation becomes uncomfortable for them. His duty was to adduce proof for the views advanced by him and by his friends, Lensch and Pannekoek. However, he tried to shift the burden of proof onto others by asking me to prove that their ideas are incorrect. It can only be a question of probabilities here; and the most probable course of development is the one I pointed out. Nobody can supply mathematical proof of that.

I must cause a little pain to Bernstein. He wanted the resolution to contain something on arbitration-courts. We all want [international] arbitration-courts; we demanded them in the Erfurt programme,[45] but we cannot share

45. ['Proceeding from these principles, the German Social-Democratic Party demands.... Education of all to bear arms. Militia in the place of the standing army. Determination by the popular assembly on questions of war and peace. Settlement of all international disputes by arbitration.' Sozialdemokratische Partei Deutschlands 1891, *Protokoll über die Verhandlungen des Parteitages der Sozialdemokratischen Partei Deutschlands abgehalten zu Erfurt vom 14. bis 20. Oktober 1891*, pp. 3–6.]

the exaggerated significance that Bernstein seems to attach to them, as can be shown from a recent example.

In 1850, England and the United States signed the Clayton-Bulwer Treaty, by which America was not authorised to build a Panama Canal[46] without England's consent. Under pressure from the Boer War, England agreed in 1901 to sign the Hay-Pauncefote Treaty, granting America the right to build the Panama Canal alone with the proviso that open passage should be granted to the ships of all nations without distinction.[47] You know that America, in a really thoughtless way, flouted that treaty and committed an egregious breach of the agreement.[48] When the English government demanded that the issue be settled through arbitration-court proceedings, the American president Taft refused to do that – the same president who two years ago celebrated eternal world peace with such fanfare, announcing that he wanted to conclude a treaty binding the signatories to recognise the verdicts of an international arbitration-court on any question that could not be regulated by treaties, regardless of what the question might be, whether it involved honour, territory or money. The same man who, so solemnly and under all circumstances, wanted to submit to arbitration-court proceedings has abandoned that standpoint at the first opportunity given to him to prove that he stuck by his word. [*Bernstein: But that proves nothing against arbitration-courts!*] But it does speak against your exaggerated appreciation of that idea.

46. [The agreement actually addressed a project for an inter-oceanic canal across Nicaragua.]

47. [In 1901, the United States and the United Kingdom signed the Hay-Pauncefote Treaty. This agreement nullified the Clayton-Bulwer Treaty of 1850 and gave the United States the right to create and control a canal across Central America, connecting the Pacific and the Atlantic Oceans. The British, recognising their diminishing influence in the region and cultivating friendship with the United States as a counter-weight to Germany, stepped aside in the treaty to permit a solely US-run canal. This occurred under President Theodore Roosevelt. The treaty was negotiated by US Secretary of State John Hay and the British Ambassador to the United States, Lord Pauncefote. The Hay-Pauncefote Treaty, though it handed all canal-building power over to the United States, provided that all nations would be allowed freely to use and access the canal, and that it should never be taken by force.]

48. [A reference to the Panama Canal Tolls Controversy: in 1912, the United States passed a bill exempting American ships from payment for use of the Panama Canal. Great Britain opposed the move, saying it violated the 1901 Hay-Pauncefote Treaty. After some dispute, the United States eliminated the exemption-clause in 1914. See Miller and Freehoff 1914, and Coker 1968.]

We all agree, however, on one thing: that we must muster all our forces to act against the war-danger and war-mongering, and that we must mobilise for that purpose all the strength the proletariat is able to deploy. I believe that the rest of the party comrades will also agree if I state as our common understanding that imperialism reveals a great ripeness of capitalism. Imperialism will be the gravedigger of the capitalist mode of production; capitalism changes at the height of its development into socialism. We must make sure that when that hour arrives, we are ready and armed to fulfill the task assigned to us by history.

The resolution proposed by Haase was accepted by the delegates with only 3 votes against and 2 abstentions. [The following is the text of the resolution]:[49]

Given the exploited proletariat's stunted standard of living, the enormous expansion of capitalist production requires an extension of its markets, and the immense accumulation of capital is driven to find new areas of investment and new valorisation-possibilities.

With the growing exports of commodities and capital, of means of production and transportation, world trade grows even more and the world economy expands. The employers' organisations, cartels, and trusts, strongly reinforced by the tariff-system, increasingly dominate economic life and use their influence on their countries' governments to harness the powers of the state in their drive to expand, to enclose large parts of the world's productive areas in their spheres of influence and power, and to exclude foreign competitors. They willingly resort to the most brutal violence whenever it promises to bring success. The consequence of these imperialist strivings for expansion is an unscrupulous policy of robbery and conquest, which was already denounced at the Mainz congress [of the SPD] in 1900. To carry out their plundering expeditions successfully and bring the booty back safely, the imperialists perfect and stockpile their weapons of murder as never before.

Between the states whose capitalist classes have this need to expand and who employ the same means to satisfy it, deep antagonisms and severe

49. Sozialdemokratische Partei Deutschlands 1912, *Protokoll über die Verhandlungen des Parteitages der Sozialdemokratischen Partei Deutschlands agbehalten in Chemnitz vom 15. bis 21. September 1912*, pp. 529–30. English version in Riddell (ed.) 1984, pp. 82–3.

entanglements emerge that further augment and intensify the arms-race to the point of madness.

The resulting danger of a devastating world war is further increased through shameless incitement by the capitalist magnates and the Junkers, who have a special interest in the provision of war-materiel and in the expansion of the state bureaucracy and the officer-corps.

Imperialism strengthens the power of the war-mongers, endangers the right of association, and hinders the further development of social reform. Military expenditures place an unbearable burden on the masses of the people, while the increasing cost of all necessities undermines their health.

The bourgeois parties are completely under imperialism's spell and approve without resistance all appropriations for the army and navy. Social Democracy most emphatically opposes all imperialist and chauvinist endeavours wherever they appear and, with firm resolve, nurtures international proletarian solidarity, which never entertains hostile feelings toward another people.

Even if imperialism, which is a product of the capitalist economic system, can only be completely overcome along with it, nothing must be left undone to lessen its dangerous effects.

This congress proclaims its resolute will to make every effort to bring about an understanding among the nations and to maintain the peace.

The congress demands international agreements to put an end to the arms-race, which threatens the peace and is driving humanity into a terrible catastrophe.

The congress demands freedom of world trade instead of the greedy policy of conquest, as well as abolition of the tariff-system, which only serves to enrich the capitalist magnates and big landlords.

The congress expects that party comrades will work tirelessly to build the political, trade-union, and co-operative organisations of the class-conscious proletariat in order to fight against brutal imperialism with greater force until it is overcome. It is therefore the task of the proletariat to transform capitalism, now brought to its highest stage, into socialist society, thus securing lasting peace, independence, and freedom for the peoples.

Chapter Forty-Three

'Review of Rosa Luxemburg: *The Accumulation of Capital: A Contribution to the Economic Explanation of Imperialism*' (January 1913)

Anton Pannekoek

Following publication of Hilferding's *Finance Capital* in 1910 and Luxemburg's *Accumulation of Capital* in 1913, a clear distinction of emphasis developed among writers on imperialism concerning the relative importance of capital-exports and commodity-exports. Anton Pannekoek thought Hilferding was correct to give primary importance to capital-exports, and, for that reason, he disputed Luxemburg's thesis that capitalism invariably depended upon commodity-sales in third-party markets (chiefly colonies) for the realisation of surplus-value. Pannekoek noted that capital and commodity-exports were 'intimately linked', but the question of emphasis was *politically significant*. If capitalist production depended primarily on commodity-exports, then workers' jobs would also appear to depend directly on imperialist expansion, 'an idea that bourgeois politicians willingly advertise in order to turn attention away from capital's greed for profit'. In the document preceding this one, Ludwig Quessel, a right-wing Social Democrat, also alluded to exactly this concern at Chemnitz when he emphasised the need to protect German export-opportunities and 'to stand behind the German government wherever it actually champions the equality of rights for our industry. That lies in the interest of the proletariat, exactly as we stand behind the government when it really tries to conclude favourable commercial agreements.'

Pannekoek's assessment of this question was shared by Lenin. In his own early debates with Russian Narodniks, Lenin had anticipated Luxemburg's thesis and come to a conclusion exactly the opposite of her view in *The Accumulation of Capital*. Lenin wrote that 'Marx proved in Volume II [of *Capital*] that capitalist production is quite conceivable without foreign markets, with the growing accumulation of wealth and without any "third parties".'[1] 'Pure capitalism' was abstractly conceivable, but, in reality, Lenin, like Hilferding, also associated capitalist expansionism with a falling rate of profit and the need to correct disproportionalities in the domestic economy resulting from lack of coherent planning. In his later writing on *Imperialism, the Highest stage of Capitalism* (first published in 1917), Lenin directly associated this theme with the compulsive export of capital and reformulated Hilferding's thesis as *the law of uneven development*:

> The uneven and spasmodic development of individual enterprises, of individual branches of industry and individual countries, is inevitable under the capitalist system.... [T]he accumulation of capital has reached gigantic proportions. An enormous 'surplus of capital' has arisen in the advanced countries.[2]

Pannekoek's criticism of Luxemburg, in the article translated here, was endorsed by Lenin, who, shortly after its publication, sent Pannekoek a letter asking 'if you could send me the two issues of *Bremer Bürger-Zeitung* in which you published a review on Rosa Luxemburg's book'. He added:

> I am very pleased to see that on the main point you come to the same conclusion as I did in the polemic with Tugan-Baranovsky and the *Narodniki* 14 years ago, namely, that the realisation of surplus-value is possible also in a '*purely* capitalist' society.[3]

1. Lenin 1894, pp. 498–9.
2. Lenin 1970, p. 72.
3. Lenin 1913a, Lenin refers to his essay 1899c.

Pannekoek argued that, in theoretical terms, Luxemburg was mistaken to see capitalism as dependent upon third-party markets, although he agreed that, in practical terms, such a dependence did exist by virtue of the historical fact that capitalist production originated in the context of foreign trade:

> In reality, capitalism exchanges its products with non-capitalist producers because it developed in an environment of such producers. That existence of non-capitalist buyers and suppliers is *a practical fact*, albeit *not a necessity* without which an emerging capitalism could not exist.

Lenin replied by repeating that Marx's analysis of reproduction explicitly excluded foreign trade:

> I have not yet seen Rosa Luxemburg's book, but *theoretically* you are quite correct on this point. It seems to me, though, that you have placed insufficient emphasis on a very important passage in *Capital*, Vol. II, where Marx says that in analysing annually produced value, foreign trade should be entirely *discarded*.... The 'dialectics' of Luxemburg seem to me (judging also from the article in *Leipziger Volkszeitung*)[4] to be eclecticism.[5]

In a letter to Kamenev in March 1913, Lenin returned to this idea:

> I have read Rosa's new book *Die Akkumulation des Kapital*. She has got into a shocking muddle. She has distorted Marx. I am very glad that Pannekoek and Eckstein and Otto Bauer have all with one accord condemned her, and said against her what I said in 1899 against the Narodniks. I intend to write about Rosa for No. 4 of *Proveshcheniye*.[6]

According to the editors of his *Collected Works*,

> in March and April 1913, Lenin was working on an article to be called 'Rosa Luxemburg's Unsuccessful Addition to Marxist Theory.' He drew up a plan of the article, compiled statistical tables and copied quotations from Marx's *Capital*, but the article was never published.

However, the outline of the article has been preserved and reads as follows:

---

4. Probably a reference to Mehring 1913a. See also Marchlewski and Mehring 1913.
5. Lenin 1913a, p. 332.
6. Lenin 1913b, p. 94.

I. 14 years ago. Narodniks versus Marxists. Legal Marxists and Social Democrats
II. Distortion of R. Luxemburg.
III. State of theoretical problems.
IV. Rosa Luxemburg's Criticism. Anti-Criticism.
V. Rosa Luxemburg's 'addition'. Failure
V. bis. German Social-Democratic Press and the 'Trouble-maker'.
VI. Dialectics and Eclectics
VII. Imperialism and realization of surplus-value (Rothstein etc.)[7]

In his article for the *Granat* encyclopedia, Lenin recommended three reviews of Rosa Luxemburg's work: the one below by Pannekoek, Gustav Eckstein's in *Vorwärts*[8] and Otto Bauer's in *Die Neue Zeit*, which is the only one so far translated to English.[9] Lenin's marginal notes to Rosa Luxemburg's book have also been translated into English.[10] Anton Pannekoek's review of Rosa Luxemburg should also be read in conjunction with his later criticism of Henryk Grossman's *Das Akkumulations und Zusammenbruchsgesetz des Kapitalistischen Systems* [*The Law of Accumulation and Collapse of the Capitalist System*], which Pannekoek similarly rejected as a refurbished version of the 'breakdown theory'.[11]

* * *

I. 'Review of Rosa Luxemburg'[12]

In the preface to her bulky work, 446 pages in length, the author explains how she came to write it. In the process of writing a popular introduction to political economy [for the SPD party school in Berlin], she came across difficulties in the presentation of the capitalist reproduction-process. As she delved further into this question, she came to the conclusion not only that Marx's presentation in the second volume of *Capital* remained incomplete in

7. *Leninskii Sbornik* 1933, pp. 347–8.
8. Eckstein 1913b. See this volume, Chapter 44.
9. Bauer 1913, English version: Bauer 1986. See this volume, Chapter 45.
10. Lenin 2000.
11. Pannekoek 1934.
12. Pannekoek 1913a.

its form, but also that there was a substantial gap here, a problem that Marx had not solved. The work under review would provide the solution to this problem. While Marx's economic theory would in this way be substantially supplemented, the work would also provide a theoretical foundation for the modern forms of capitalism's manifestation, which we identify with the name of imperialism.

Let us first explain the problem. As is well known, the value of the product of each capitalist breaks down into three parts: 1. Replacement of the consumed means of production and raw materials, whose value was transferred to the product; 2. reimbursement of the wages paid to the workers, which constitute a part of the new value created by their work; 3. surplus-value, which constitutes the rest of this new value. If the capitalist sells his product, with those revenues he can replace the means of production consumed, and once again he has money to pay for new wages as well as for his personal consumption (and eventually for accumulation). He can thus produce again; his capital is reproduced, and production becomes an ever-repeated cycle. In order for each capitalist to find the necessary elements in the market, the whole social production must satisfy certain conditions: precisely as much of each commodity must be produced as is required for the renewal of all the elements of production. If we look at nothing but the two great departments of means of production and means of consumption, as many commodities of the first kind are necessary as the amount represented by the first of the above-mentioned three parts; and from the second, as many as the amount of wages and surplus-value put together. Marx's diagrams for simple reproduction provide an example of that.

> The production of means of production amounts to:
>
> I. 4,000 c + 1,000 v + 1,000 s = 6,000 product
>
> The production of means of consumption amounts to:
>
> II. 2,000 c + 500 v + 500 s = 3,000 product

In this example, we assume that the consumed constant capital is four times as large as the variable capital (this proportion is determined by the level of technique) and that the rate of exploitation is 100 per cent; that is to say, that the surplus-value is equal to the variable capital (this proportion is determined by actual circumstances). In order for the above ratio between both spheres of production to be met, 4,000 in Department I and 2,000 in Department II are necessary for renewal of the constant capital, which is precisely the sum of the total product of 6,000. Necessities [means of consumption] must be available for 1,000 v + 1,000 s in Department I and 500 v + 500 s in Department II, which corresponds exactly to the total product of 3,000. Through mutual exchange between capitalists, in which money serves as the means of circulation, all commodities are brought from the producers into the hands of those who need them. If this ratio is maintained, all producers will dispose of their products and each will find what he needs in the market. This ratio must ultimately always assert itself through all the fluctuations of real, planless production.

But capitalists do not consume all of their surplus-value; they accumulate part of it, i.e. turn it into capital, therefore also buying both elements of production – constant capital and labour-power. But that no longer corresponds to the above diagram. Marx offered some examples of this situation that suffer from the defect of not fitting well with actual conditions; Comrade Luxemburg begins her criticism with them. Marx assumed that the capitalists of Department I accumulated half of their surplus-value; from the figures assumed for Departments I and II, it can then be calculated how much of their surplus-value the capitalists of Department II must accumulate and how much they must consume. In Marx's presentation, this appears as if the capitalists of Department I decided arbitrarily and the capitalists of Department II had to submit to them. In reality, both can regulate [the rate of accumulation], since both of them have to conform to the ratio between the two Departments of production. Let us take Marx's first example (*Kapital*, vol. II, p. 487),[13] where he assumed for Department I a ratio of $c : v = 4$; let us assume for Department II a ratio of $c : v = 2$; in the second year, we meet the following proportions:

I. 4,400 c + 1,100 v + 1,100 s = 6,600 product
II. 1,600 c + 800 v + 800 s = 3,200 product

Marx assumed that the capitalists of Department I accumulated and turned into capital half of their surplus-value, and those of Department II 30 per cent of theirs; therefore, s breaks down into:

I. 1,100 = 550 consumed + 550 accumulated (= 440 c + 110 v)
II. 800 = 560 consumed + 240 accumulated (= 160 c + 80 v)

13. [See Marx 1978bb, pp. 510–13.]

Thus 4,400 + 1,600 are necessary for the replacement of means of production and 440 + 160 for the production of new ones – together 6,600, precisely the total product of Department I. In terms of necessities [means of consumption] 1,100 + 550 + 800 + 560 are required for the capitalists and the old workers, and 110 + 80 for the newly employed ones – together 3,200, precisely the total product of Department II. Each one sells his product and everyone finds the elements for expanded production in the market. The growth of v and c in both Departments is 10 per cent; the capitals grow by 10 per cent, and in the following year production takes place on a scale expanded by 10 per cent.

I. 4,840 c + 1,210 v + 1,210 s = 7,260 product
II. 1,760 c + 880 v + 880 s = 3,520 product

The same process repeats itself so that accumulation can always continue in this way. Comrade Luxemburg did not recognise the regularity of the figures assumed by Marx in this example (the figures she gives on p. 95 of her book are partially incorrect),[14] and she therefore believes that Marx let accumulation in Department II be determined by accumulation in Department I.

This criticism, however, just paves the way for the real question, because even if those conditions are met by a well-fitting diagram, and even if the will to accumulate exists, that is not enough.

> A further condition is required to ensure that accumulation can in fact proceed and production expand: the effective demand for commodities must also increase. Where is this continually increasing demand to come from, which in Marx's diagram forms the basis of reproduction on an ever rising scale?[15]

Not from the capitalists' consumption, which is served by the other part of the surplus-value; accumulation means non-consumption of the whole surplus-value. Who consumes the production of the accumulated part of surplus-value? Department I produces more means of production.

> And who requires these additional means of production? The diagram answers that Department II needs them in order to produce means of

14. [See Luxemburg 1963, p. 122. In the table on this page, the figure for consumption in the second year should be 560 (not 660); and the figure for accumulation in the third year should be 264 (not 254).]
15. [Luxemburg 1963, p. 131.]

> subsistence[16] in increased quantities. Well then, who requires these additional consumer goods? Department I, of course – replies the diagram – because it now employs a greater number of workers. We are plainly running in circles. From the capitalist point of view it is absurd to produce more consumer goods merely in order to maintain more workers, and to turn out more means of production merely to keep this surplus of workers occupied.[17]

The natural growth of population cannot provide the required demand, because the source of the demand of the popular masses is not a need independent of production, but rather variable capital. The other strata of the population also cannot help, because their income derives either from *s* or from *v*, as fellow-consumers of the surplus-value or parasites of the proletariat. Foreign trade remains a way out, but this only transfers the difficulty from one country to another.

Marx tried to solve this difficulty, but was actually unable to do it. [According to Comrade Luxemburg], in the last chapter of the second volume of *Capital*[18] Marx dealt with the problem from all sides, but always came across the question of where does the money come from required for circulation of the growing masses of products. He asked this question clearly enough, but in doing so he lost sight of the actual problem. Who buys the commodities in which the capitalised surplus-value lies hidden? Not the capitalists themselves, even if they have enough money in their pockets, because through accumulation they became 'non-buyers of their surplus-value'. Where, therefore, are to be found the customers without whom surplus-value cannot be realised? [According to Rosa Luxemburg] it is not surprising that Marx did not deal with this question, if one considers that the second volume of *Capital* was put together out of many incomplete manuscripts, many of which were just drafts and first revisions, which therefore do not constitute a complete whole. These chapters were manifestly incomplete and fragmentary, only first drafts for self-clarification, and for that reason the theory must be supplemented and completed on this point by the work of his disciples.

---

16. [*Lebensmittel*. In the English version of Luxemburg's book this term is rendered as both 'consumer goods' and 'means of consumption' indistinctly.]
17. [Luxemburg 1963, p. 132.]
18. [Marx 1978b, pp. 489–523.]

II. Criticism

Thus did Rosa Luxemburg pose the problem, for which she then tried to provide a solution. Before everything else we must ask ourselves: is there a real problem here? The question posed here is this: Where are the buyers of the products in a simple abstract case of capitalist production with accumulation, as presented in the diagram [for reproduction on an enlarged scale]? The answer is provided by the diagram itself in the simplest way, because *all the products find there a market. The buyers are the capitalists and the workers themselves.* The capitalists need 6,000 in means of production to replace those that were consumed, and they need an additional 600 in means of production for the newly invested capital to be able to expand production. Besides the amount of necessities [consumed in] the previous year (1,900 + 1,110),[19] 190 in means of consumption are required for the newly recruited masses of workers, so that therewith the whole production of necessities will be consumed. If the capitalists and workers, as the diagram shows, buy all the products themselves, then there are no more products for which a demand must be sought elsewhere. There is, therefore, no problem at all to be solved.

When Rosa Luxemburg asks: Who consumes the increased means of production and necessities [means of consumption], the question should actually be: Who buys them, who purchases them? And the answer is already given. What she calls an absurdity from the capitalist point of view because it would represent an aimless circular motion – to produce more and more means of consumption in order to feed more workers, who would produce more and more means of production that serve for the production of those means of consumption – only appears to be absurd because the decisive factor was left out of consideration. The goal of producing more and more is to extract and accumulate more and more surplus-value, but those accumulated masses of capital can only fulfil their goal of producing new surplus-value by being thrown again and again into the whirlpool of production. The self-valorisation of capital in the creation of profit, the transformation of profit into new capital, is the driving force giving sense and a goal to that alleged absurdity: the apparently aimless, always expanding circuit of production. This 'absurdity' shows the inner nature of capitalism, which exists not for

19. [There is a typographical error in the original text of Pannekoek's review, giving the figure of 1,360 for capitalists' consumption rather than 1,110.]

the purpose of production but rather uses production as a means in order to produce surplus-value and capital.

One difficulty admittedly exists: that with which Marx occupied himself concerning the role of money. One could formulate it as follows: the capitalists of Departments I and II, when they both replaced the elements of capital in the previous expansion, must remain with the products in which the surplus-value is materialised, because the capitalists must sell them to each other, but each can only buy (that is spend the realised surplus-value as capital) after having realised the surplus-value, that is after having sold it; thus each must wait for the others, making no headway. But this difficulty actually is, as Marx showed, [only] an apparent one, and it is practically solved through the role of money as hoard and means of circulation; we do not have to go into that here, because it plays no role in Rosa Luxemburg's arguments.[20]

We thus come to the conclusion, in complete contradiction with her, that no problem exists here that eluded Marx and for which we must now seek a solution. But perhaps her opinion might be due to the fact that the diagram does not correspond with the reality of capitalism? That would be a second reason, different from the first one, which was derived from the diagram. Comrade Luxemburg seems to want to base her thesis also on this second argument, because now and then she sarcastically remarks that on paper everything may fit together nicely, if one just tailors the figures properly, but in reality…! Such an appeal to reality, however, is out of place here. The question is to give simple abstract examples in order to let the basic conditions [of a given phenomenon] operate undisturbed [by other factors] in such a way that one can recognise their consequences. By then adding more and more of such conditions, the image can be made increasingly similar to reality. Only in this way can the effects of different forces and phenomena be identified. The question for any example, therefore, is whether the essential conditions are contained in it. The above example shows the following: if we assume definite quantities for $c : v$, for $s : v$, and for the division of the surplus-value into consumption and accumulation funds, so that they might correspond with reality, a ratio can be found between the extent of production in Departments I and II whereby production and demand coincide with each other and production

20. [For Marx's discussion of the role of hoarded money, see the appendix to this volume. For more detail, see Day 1980.]

expands constantly. The answer to the question – For whom do capitalists produce, who are the customers? – is that the capitalists and workers themselves are the buyers.

But let us address the second issue. The diagram is, no doubt, only an extremely abstract and simplified representation of production:

> If we examine critically the diagram of enlarged reproduction in the light of Marx's theory, we find various contradictions between the two. To begin with, the diagram completely disregards the increasing productivity of labour.[21]

Actually, the ratio between *c* and *v* certainly grows gradually as a result of technical progress, while the ratio between *s* and *v* also gradually rises. If one takes this into consideration, Comrade Luxemburg says,

> [on the basis of what is actually happening, namely a greater yearly increase of constant capital as against that of variable capital, as well as a growing rate of surplus-value,] discrepancies must arise between the material composition of the social product and the composition of capital in terms of value.[22]

She then gives as an example a diagram in which the quantities actually do not fit together, but yield a growing deficit in means of production and an excess in means of consumption. But what does that prove? Examples that do not work out can be drawn up without any problem; Marx's first reproduction-diagram also would not work out with other figures. However, that does not prove that simple reproduction is impossible, only that the example is incorrect. Rosa Luxemburg should prove here, if she were right, that it *cannot* work out, and that it is therefore impossible to draw up a diagram in which everything fits together. Her numerical example on p. 307 is therefore completely worthless.[23] It proves nothing, and cannot possibly prove anything, because *her thesis is incorrect*. It is certainly possible to draw up a division of production in which *c* : *v* gradually grows and everything fits together.

Let us assume, to avoid unnecessarily complicating the calculations, that both departments initially have the same ratio between *c* : *v*, namely 4 : 1. Let

21. [Luxemburg 1963, p. 335.]
22. [Luxemburg 1963, p. 336.]
23. [Luxemburg 1963, p. 337.]

us assume further that the capitalised half of the surplus-value, that is the capital-increase, is divided in a ratio of 9 : 1 between constant and variable capital. The calculation shows that the ratio between the two departments must be 89 : 21.[24] If the capitals are 8,900 and 3,100 then

I. 7,120 *c* + 1,780 *v* + 890 *s* + 890 *ss* = 10,680 means of production
II. 2,480 *c* + 620 *v* + 310 *s* + 310 *ss* = 3,720 means of consumption
Total 9,600 *c* + 2,400 *v* + 1,200 *s* + (1,080 *c* + 120 *v*) = 14,400 product

9,600 + 1,080 = 10,680 in means of production are necessary, as well as 2,400 + 1,200 + 120 = 3,720 in means of consumption, both of which are available. Now the constant capital has grown in a proportion of 80 to 89,[25] the variable of 20 to 21,[26] the ratio *c* : *v* grew from four times[27] to 89 : 21,[28] and we assume that this holds true for both departments. In the second year, the ratio of both spheres of production must also change; the new capital of 1,200 must be divided in a new proportion between Department I and Department II. It is also clear that the relative share of Department I in the entire production must always grow, because [variable] capital is always transferred from Department II, where it is produced, to Department I; for the capitalists, it is a matter of indifference where their capitals are invested. If half of the surplus-value is again accumulated and divided in the same way, it follows that the capital in Department I must be 9,920 and in Department II 3,280, so that from the new capital of 1,200, 1,020 must be invested in Department I and 180 in Department II. The following schema thus results for the second year:

I. 8,026 *c* + 1,894 *v* + 947 *s* + 947 *ss* = 11,814 means of production
II. 2,654 *c* + 626 *v* + 313 *s* + 313 *ss* = 3,906 means of consumption
Total 10,680 *c* + 2,520 *v* + 1,260 *s* + (1,134 *c* + 126 *v*) = 15,720 product

10,680 + 1,134 = 11,814 in means of production are necessary, as well as 2,520 + 1,260 + 126 = 3,906 in means of consumption, both of which are available.

---

24. [The reference to the 'ratio between the two departments' should be to the ratio between the totals for the two types of capital, constant and variable; that is, 10,680c/2520v.]
25. [9,600/10,680 = 80/89]
26. [2,400/2520 = 20/21]
27. [9,600/2,400 = 80/20 = 4]
28. [10,680/2,520 = 21]

In this way, production can always continue. If in the first year $c : v = 80 : 20$, it is now

in the second year = 89 : 21
in the third year = 98.45 : 22.05
in the fourth year = 108.37 : 23.15 etc.

This shows that an increase in the organic composition of capital is possible, taking place alongside accumulation, without the appearance of a contradiction in the form of a deficit or surplus in products. Therefore, when Comrade Luxemburg says of the contradiction she discovered that '[t]hese results are not due to mere chance',[29] the reply must be that these results are just the product of incorrect calculations in the examples supplied by her and are, therefore, worthless. In a similar way, a gradual change in the rate of exploitation can also be accounted for.

Rosa Luxemburg adduces some other reasons why the diagrams could not correspond with reality, but they are as immaterial as the previous one. For instance, that, according to the diagram, the capitalists *ought to* be dictated to by the production of the previous year as to how the following year's production should be technically organised[30] (in doing so, she overlooks the fact that the stocks of commodities enable them to choose within certain limits). Or, that the role of the money hoards is not taken into consideration [by Marx][31] – which, in principle, has no significance for this question. Or, that the diagram does not correspond with the contradictions of the law of the falling rate of profit: 'According to the diagram, there is no inherent contradiction between the production of the surplus-value and its realisation, rather, the two are identical.'[32] Quite right, but the question here does not involve the causes of crises, in which that contradiction appears. Crises do not prove that the diagram of enlarged reproduction does not correspond to reality; on the contrary, the crises themselves must be explained on the basis of this diagram and by means of additional factors.

29. [Luxemburg 1963, p. 339.]
30. [Luxemburg writes: '...the technological shape of enlarged reproduction is...strictly prescribed by the material form of the surplus product'. Luxemburg 1963, p. 339, also pp. 340–1.]
31. [Luxemburg 1963, p. 341.] Our appendix includes Marx's account of money hoards.
32. [Luxemburg 1963, p. 345.]

Therefore, an internal contradiction of that kind, according to which capitalist production in its expansion through accumulation must necessarily produce a surplus or deficit in commodities, does not exist. There is simply no problem affecting the very foundations and the essence of capitalism as a whole that has been left unsolved by Marx. Indeed, if such a problem had existed and Marx had overlooked it, that in itself would be a most remarkable fact.

III. Historical controversies

Rosa Luxemburg argues, however, that the alleged problem she came across played an important role in the history of political economy. Her detailed presentation of those controversies is extremely interesting – even if, in our opinion, their significance is different from what she asserts. The first debate took place in 1819–21 between Sismondi on the one hand and Ricardo, McCulloch and Say on the other.[33] Classical-bourgeois political economy had begun to analyse scientifically the social production-process. What was once a disorderly crowd of private persons, manufacturers, merchants, workers, landowners, peasants, etc., each chaotically pursuing his own private gain, revealed itself before their eyes as a whole with internal laws, a peculiar order with a life of its own. Full of enthusiasm, they praised the internal harmony hidden under the apparent chaos. In doing so, however, by means of simplification they traced monetary economy back to simple commodity-economy, and capitalist exploitation back to primitive commodity-production. The farmer who produces 1,000 sacks of corn exchanges them against 1,000 yards of fabric produced by the manufacturers; through technical progress, these masses grow to 1,100, 1,200, etc.; exchange constantly increases, and with it grows also the comfort of the producers. In this primitive way, Ricardo expounded his basic idea that in capitalism the growing masses of commodities can be mutually exchanged without difficulties, and that the consequence is growing universal welfare. In contrast, Sismondi was the critic of capitalism who saw its contradictions, emphasised them and strove to find a solution for them. The first crisis, in 1815, had already shown that something was wrong with the internal mechanism of capitalism. Sismondi pointed out the workers'

33. [Luxemburg 1963, Chaps. 10–13.]

poverty, their displacement by machines, the driving out of small business by competition and overproduction, but he did not go further theoretically. At a certain point, he put the question of markets in these terms: the production of this year must be bought with the income of the previous year, and accumulation and expanded reproduction are therefore impossible. But, in the course of the debate, in which his opponents confronted him with their primitive examples in which production and exchange fit together perfectly, he let himself be cheated and shifted the argument to the field of ethics, where he analysed the effect of luxury and the growth of production on the craftsmen and workers.

We leave aside here the debate between Kirchmann and Rodbertus, which dealt with the same questions.[34] The 'third round',[35] which took place in Russia, is more interesting, above all because, by then, Volumes II and III of *Capital* had already appeared and the debaters were familiar with their arguments. The motive of this debate was the question of the future of capitalism in Russia; the Narodniki ['Populists'] regarded it as a foreign product, which could only have impoverishing and dissolving effects but not a future of its own, while the 'Marxists' saw it as a natural phase of development that was replacing the old order. [The Populists] Vorontsov and Nikolayon therefore stressed that capitalism could not last on its own or manage without markets for sales, without foreign demand, because it undermined its own foundations by impoverishing the peasantry. By contrast, the [legal-Marxist] professors Bulgakov and Tugan-Baranovsky emphasised that capitalism creates its own demand, that Marx's diagrams of expanded reproduction proved that growing production could find its markets without difficulties. Tugan-Baranovsky even built on this basis a theory according to which consumption becomes increasingly unimportant under capitalism and production rises enormously by itself alone, in ever increasing circles, independently of consumption. In their optimism about the future of capitalism in Russia, they proved more than needed to be proved – namely, the possibility of the eternal duration of capitalism – and in that way came close to the old bourgeois doctrines of harmony on the part of Say and Ricardo.

34. [Luxemburg 1963, Chaps. 15–17.]
35. [For Luxemburg's discussion of the 'third round', see Luxemburg 1963, Chaps. 18–24.]

IV. The solution of the problem

For Comrade Luxemburg, therefore, there is a contradiction in capitalism that makes it impossible for capitalist society, left to itself, to expand on an ever-larger scale. This contradiction manifests itself in the question of who will buy the commodities in which the expansion of production, and therefore the accumulated surplus-value, is materialised. Her answer is:

> Realisation of the surplus-value is doubtless a vital question of capitalist accumulation. It requires as its prime condition – ignoring, for simplicity's sake, the capitalists' fund of consumption altogether – that there should be strata of buyers outside capitalist society.[36]

Actually, capitalist society is in constant exchange with non-capitalist peoples who supply it with their raw materials and buy its products. In these exported products, a larger part of total production may lie hidden than the part represented by surplus-value. But the realisation of surplus-value makes this enlistment of foreign markets necessary. In the realisation of the surplus-value

> outside consumers *qua* other-than-capitalist are really essential. Thus the immediate and vital conditions for capital and its accumulation is the existence of non-capitalist buyers of the surplus-value, which is decisive to this extent for the problem of capitalist accumulation.[37]

From this arises the significance for capitalism's own existence of its activity in other parts of the world. It cannot exist without non-capitalist buyers and must therefore create them for itself. The struggle *against natural economy* – which is particularly aimed at taking possession of productive forces and natural resources, freeing the labour-forces, introducing commodity-economy and separating agriculture from industry – is dealt with in detail in the last chapter of Comrade Luxemburg's work. This struggle also determines the political intervention of capitalist state-power in the fates of foreign continents. The author thus finds in her economic theory also a theoretical foundation for imperialism.

---

36. [Luxemburg 1963, p. 351.]
37. [Luxemburg 1963, pp. 365–6.]

We have seen that her theory is wrong, that the problem does not exist, and that the contradiction found by her in capitalist accumulation is likewise spurious. Capitalism, left to itself, would be able to expand continuously – assuming a growth of capital and the labour-force – without coming across the impossibility of sales. There is no theoretical need for non-capitalist buyers [to realise surplus-value].

Are the further analyses of Comrade Luxemburg worthless for this reason? Is the struggle she describes against natural economy fortuitous, devoid of any internal necessity? No, but the causes lie elsewhere than where she looked for them. In reality, capitalism exchanges its products with non-capitalist producers because it developed in an environment of such producers. That existence of non-capitalist buyers and suppliers is *a practical fact*, albeit *not a necessity* without which an emerging capitalism could not exist. Since the existence of non-capitalist buyers is a fact, the expansion of capitalism at the same time requires *an expansion of non-capitalist production* with which it exchanges its products. Therefore, their area must be constantly increased, often forcibly; here lies the real cause of the struggle against natural economy. It is not fortuitous; it has an economic cause, even if it is entirely different from the one Comrade Luxemburg thought she found. And that is why her detailed description of the praxis of capitalist expansion is not a superfluous presentation of casual events, but the illustration of the practical realisation of an economic necessity.

She deals first with the dissolution of the old Indian peasant-communities by British rule, which, through complete neglect of the old irrigation-system, the technical foundation of agriculture, and through tax-oppression and usury, destroyed the old millenarian welfare. She then proceeds to describe the destruction of the old natural economy of the Arabs in Algeria, where the Frenchmen plundered and pauperised the natives by means of legislation and the tyranny of state-officials under the name of introducing private property. The opening up of China by means of the Opium-War of 1839–42 and additional wars is also treated within this framework. Valuable is the analysis of the development of American agriculture, the prostration and subjugation of the farmer by large-scale capital, which secured for itself huge land tracts as railway-capital. The more corn-production developed for the market, the more the farmers pushed first to the West and then to the North, to Canada, 'with the railways in the van, and ruin in the rear; that is with capital simultaneously playing the role of leader before them and of murderer behind them'.[38] The conquest of Transvaal by the Englishmen [in the Boer War, 1899–1902], owing to the gold-industry in Johannesburg, constitutes an additional chapter in this expansion. The construction of railways on foreign continents and international loans are important means in this expansion of capitalism; their significance is illustrated by the example of Egypt, which was completely subjugated by European capital through the loans forced upon it. The author adds to this example some observations on Turkey and the Baghdad railway.

V. Imperialism

Those examples lead us into capitalist world policy, which, together with the whole internal policy accompanying it, we identify by the name of imperialism. Rosa Luxemburg believes, as the preface and title of her book show, that she made a contribution to the economic explanation of imperialism. But we must distinguish [between two aspects of the problem]. We disregard now the fact that her economic analysis is incorrect and that it can therefore prove or explain nothing, because the thesis that she built upon it is correct, although for a completely different reason: expanding capitalism does need a constant expansion of markets for sales, of areas of non-capitalist production. This necessity has always been a driving force in the world policy of the capitalist states, and this world policy, based on *the necessity of ever newer markets for sales*, is as old as capitalist production, or at least as large-scale industry. But what people usually understand by imperialism is a modern phenomenon that is not simply identical with the capitalist world policy of the whole nineteenth century. Naturally, we must pick up a name as best as we can, and occasionally any striving towards overseas conquests, from the Spanish conquest of America onwards, has been called imperialism. However, that does not serve to explain but only to conceal the peculiarities characterising capital's modern world policy. We would, therefore, like to denote by imperialism the striving of modern capitalist powers to bring the largest possible areas of foreign continents directly or indirectly under their

38. Luxemburg 1963, p. 410. [The translation has been corrected against the original.]

political control and to combine them into a world empire. *This* imperialism finds its economic explanation not in the necessity of new markets for sales or in the interests of *selling commodities,* but in *capital-exports*. Rosa Luxemburg's analysis, even if it were economically correct, makes no contribution to understanding the economic roots of this imperialism; in this sense, the title of her work is somewhat misleading. Comrade Luxemburg did not refer to the real economic problem we are dealing with here, namely, the export of accumulated capital to primitive lands – it is Hilferding's *Finance Capital* that contributed most to the understanding of this problem.

This must be emphasised so that there will be no misunderstanding as to whether modern imperialism revolves around the question of selling commodities – an idea that bourgeois politicians willingly advertise in order to turn attention away from capital's greed for profit. But it is clear that the side of the question stressed by Comrade Luxemburg is not in itself unimportant. That is why we said above that the title of her work is 'somewhat misleading', because she did not deal with the essential factor but with a circumstance that does, however, come into consideration. The driving force of the old world-policy continues to work today; capital-exports and sales of commodities are intimately linked; and capital-export is, in practical political questions, inseparable from the supply of commodities. In the world policy of the European states, one finds both sides [of the question] mixed together; the cases dealt with by Comrade Luxemburg also run from pure sales policy (as in the Opium War) to pure capital-export policy without sales being involved (as in Egypt). But capital's drive to look for *investments* in other continents increasingly constitutes the most important driving force of imperialist world policy.

Chapter Forty-Four

'Rosa Luxemburg's *The Accumulation of Capital*: A Critique' (16 February 1913)

Gustav Eckstein

Rosa Luxemburg's famous work on imperialism was rejected by Lenin as a return to Narodnik theories about the impossibility of late-capitalist development.[1] Nevertheless, it has inspired a long line of Marxist theoreticians, including Fritz Sternberg and Roman Rosdolsky, and it continues to attract attention today as witnessed by one of the best-known recent works on the subject, David Harvey's *The New Imperialism*, which builds on her theory for its description of neoliberal policies as 'accumulation by dispossession'.[2]

In his article on Marxism for the *Granat* encyclopaedia, Lenin recommended three critical reviews of Luxemburg's work: one (the preceding document in this volume) by Anton Pannekoek, a Dutch Tribunist and prominent member of the SPD left wing in Bremen;[3] the second (the next document in this volume), by the Austro-Marxist Otto Bauer;[4] and the third, the essay translated here and written by Gustav Eckstein. Although Eckstein's work claims

1. See the introduction to the previous document in this volume.
2. Harvey 2003.
3. Pannekoek 1913a.
4. Bauer 1913, English version: Bauer 1986. See this volume, Chapter 45.

none of the fame of Rosa Luxemburg's, at the time he was widely respected for both his political convictions and the breadth of his knowledge. In an obituary following Eckstein's death in 1916, Leon Trotsky spoke of him as 'one of the most outstanding Austro-German Marxists'. Trotsky continued:

> All Comrades who have followed *Neue Zeit* and *Kampf* over recent years will know this name and will recall with gratitude his numerous articles from which we have learnt a great deal.
>
> Eckstein possessed an exceptionally many-sided erudition: he combined a profound learning in the field of the natural sciences and ethnography with a serious education in the field of history and political economy. He wrote and spoke in the simple clear language of the propagandist which gave the most complex thoughts a generally comprehensible form: in this sense he belonged to Kautsky's school, with whom he was generally linked by a close ideological friendship in the course of the last, most fruitful period of his life.
>
> From the start of the war and of the crisis in German Social-Democracy to which it gave birth, Eckstein took up the position of an internationalist – on the left flank of *Neue Zeit*. We do not know in what relation he stood to the left wing of Social-Democracy in his contributions to party meetings, where he subjected the official line of the party to criticism and, in particular, mercilessly unmasked the myth of a 'democratic' war against Tsarism.[5]

Rosa Luxemburg's estimate of Eckstein was, predictably, more dismissive than Trotsky's. In her *Anti-Critique*, she reserved her most detailed comments on Eckstein's review for a long footnote:

> The reviewer of *Vorwärts*, Eckstein, of all my critics, has understood least what it is all about. He belongs to the category of journalists who came up with the growth of the working-class press. He can write anything about anything: Japanese family laws, modern biology, the history of socialism, ethnography, culture, economics, tactical problems – whatever is needed at the time. These universal writers move about in every sector of knowledge with such scrupulous safety that they are the envy of any serious scientist. Where they have no understanding of the matter, they replace it by becoming impudent and tough. Here are two examples:

5. Trotsky 1918.

> Let us recognize here and now (says Eckstein at one point in his review) that the author has misunderstood the meaning and purpose of Marx's analysis, and this recognition is confirmed by the remainder of her book. Above all, she is completely incapable of understanding the technique of these models. This is already quite clear on p. 100[6] of her book.

There I am dealing with the fact that in his models Marx includes the production of money in the Department of means of production. I criticize this in my book and attempt to demonstrate that, since in itself money is *not* a means of production, this confusion must inevitably result in great difficulties for a precise treatment of the subject. Eckstein carries on impudently:

> Comrade Luxemburg objects that Marx incorporates the production of money-materials, i.e. gold and silver, in row I and calculates it with the production of means of production. That is supposed to be incorrect. *For this reason she adds a third row to those constructed by Marx, which is supposed to represent the production of money-materials.*

And now he is bitterly disappointed!

> In the model constructed by Comrade Luxemburg the difficulty is . . . not only very great, it is insuperable. . . . She herself does not make the slightest effort to portray these 'organic tangles'. The very attempt would have shown her that her model is not feasible. . . .

But the 'model constructed by Comrade Luxemburg' on p. 100 was not 'constructed' by me at all – but by Marx! I simply wrote down the figures given in *Capital*, Vol. II, p. 470,[7] in order to show that, *according to Marx*, it is impossible to incorporate the production of money, as I explained explicitly in the following:

> Besides, a mere glance at Marx's model of reproduction demonstrates what inconsistencies must follow from confusing means of exchange with means of production.

And along comes Eckstein to blame me for Marx's model, which I criticize, and to scold me because of this model, like a stupid hussy, for having completely failed to understand 'the technique of these models'.

6. [Luxemburg 1963, p. 100.]
7. [Marx 1978b, p. 470.]

Another example: on p. 510 of *Capital*, Vol. II,[8] Marx constructs his first accumulation model, in which he allows the capitalists of the first Department always to capitalize 50 per cent of their surplus-value, but lets it happen any old way in the other Department, with no visible rules, purely according to the need of the first Department. I attempt to criticize this assumption as an arbitrary one. Then along comes Eckstein with the following effusion:

> The mistake lies in the very way she has made her calculations, and this shows *that she has not grasped the essence of Marx's models.* She thinks that these are based on the requirement of an equal rate of accumulation, i.e. she assumes that accumulation always proceeds equally in both main Departments of social production. But this assumption is quite arbitrary and contradicts the facts. In reality there is no such general rate of accumulation and it would be a theoretical nonsense.

Therein resides the 'scarcely comprehensible error of the author, which shows that she is completely puzzled by the *essence of Marx's models'*. The real law of equal rate of profit stands 'in complete contradiction to the fictitious law of equal accumulation' and so on with that meaty thoroughness, salted and peppered, with which Eckstein ensures my destruction. If indeed…then indeed. But *five pages later*[9]…Marx gives a second example of his accumulation model, the real and fundamental model, which he then uses exclusively till the end, whilst the first one was merely an attempt, a preliminary sketch. And Marx continually assumes the *equal rate of accumulation,* 'the fictitious law', *in both Departments* in this second and definitive example! The 'theoretical nonsense', in 'complete contradiction to the real law of equal rate of profit' – these capital offences and capital crimes can be found in their entirety on p. 513 of *Capital,* Vol. II, and Marx is unrepentant right up to the last line of the volume. Thus the effusion goes all over the unfortunate Marx, who was obviously 'completely puzzled' by the 'essence' of his own models. At least he does not have to share this hard luck with me alone; Bauer, too, takes his fair share of it, since in his own 'incontestable' models he similarly stated his explicit assumption 'that the rate of accumu-

8. [Marx 1978b, p. 510.]
9. [Marx 1978b, pp. 513ff.]

> lation is equal in both spheres of production'.[10] ... And to think that one is treated to such insolences by a fellow who has not even read Marx's *Capital* properly! It is characteristic of the domination of the two central organs of Social Democracy by the 'Austro-Marxist' school of epigones that such a 'review' could even appear in *Vorwärts*. If God grants that I am alive to see the second edition of my book I shall not be robbed of the opportunity to save this pearl for posterity by printing it in full in an appendix![11]

Paul Frölich, Rosa Luxemburg's biographer and the first editor of her collected works in German, fulfilled her wish and reprinted Eckstein's essay, translated here into English for the first time, as an appendix to the 1923 edition of *The Accumulation of Capital*.[12]

* * *

'Rosa Luxemburg's *The Accumulation of Capital*: A Critique'[13]

I. The relation between social production and consumption in Marx

The theoretical understanding of any commodity-producing economy is based on knowledge of the law of value. Only when one understands the laws that regulate the exchange of commodities can the secrets of that economic form be unravelled. In capitalist society, the value of a commodity is determined by the labour *socially* necessary to produce it. But, irrespective of technique, which does not concern us here, only that labour is socially necessary that suffices to satisfy the social need for the commodity in question. When, for instance, at a certain moment, more hats or steam-engines are brought to the market than corresponds to the social need, then the labour embodied in those supernumerary wares was not socially necessary, and, for that reason, it created no value and the commodities remain unsaleable. How large, however, is that social need for a certain kind of commodity, and on what does its extent depend? This is one of the fundamental questions of

10. [See the next item in this volume (Bauer, before the heading 'The Realisation of Surplus-Value').]
11. Luxemburg 1921, pp. 87–9, note.
12. Luxemburg 1923.
13. Eckstein 1913b.

political economy. The so-called subjectivist school of political economy, the representatives of the 'marginal-utility' doctrine, want to answer the question through psychological considerations. But what is the good of the finest psychological views about my vital need for a hat when I have no money to buy it, and how can psychology determine how great is the need of a manufacturer for a steam-engine of 100 horse-power? It is clear that social needs are determined by the size and distribution of incomes in society, as well as by the possibility of making a profit through the application of means of production. It is also clear that these two determinants stand in the most intimate reciprocal connection. The need for steam-engines is determined by the possibility of producing, with their help, commodities that can be sold at a profit. But how many commodities [must be produced], and at what price they can be sold, depend in turn on how much is paid as wages, profit, ground-rent, etc. The size of those categories of income depends, in turn, on production-relations and conditions. One can see that the solution to the problem under consideration is by no means simple or easy.

It is one of the most brilliant achievements of Karl Marx not only to have clarified this question for the first time, but also to have answered it in the most ingenious way. The third section of the second volume of *Capital*, in which that occurs, is one of the deepest but also most difficult parts of the entire work.

Marx first examined the question of the interdependence between production and consumption in capitalist society when no accumulation takes place, that is to say, when the capitalists consume all the surplus-value and leave nothing for increasing their capitals. That is, admittedly, a case that constitutes a rare exception in the real world, but that is the only way for science to move forward: by first tracing the most complicated phenomena back to their simplest forms, studying the latter thoroughly, and only then examining the influence exerted by the factors purposely left out of consideration at the beginning. Marx used the so-called 'method of abstraction' in his entire masterpiece, but he perhaps did it in the most masterly manner precisely in the sections under consideration. He divided the entire social production into two groups: the production of means of production, such as machinery, raw materials, factory-buildings, etc., and the production of means of consumption, such as foodstuffs, dwelling houses, in short, all the products that are not employed again in production but go into the unproductive consumption of society. Then he examined the interdependence between both departments of production. Should production, according to the assumptions [of simple reproduction], remain at the same scale – that is to say, should it continue without expanding – then the means of production in both departments must first be replaced to the extent that they are worn out in annual production; and, secondly, means of consumption must be produced for the workers and capitalists, who consume their entire surplus-value. The way in which this consumption takes place – for instance, if the capitalists employ a large domestic staff, purchase works of art, erect splendid buildings or rather build warships – is, at first, a matter of indifference for the question under consideration. The way in which surplus-value is extracted from the workers is equally a matter of indifference – whether it be when wages are paid out, or, perhaps later, through the sale of foodstuffs at monopoly-prices, or through protective customs or indirect taxes. The essential thing is to show the intricate ways in which the different parts of the produced value and of the total production of society are exchanged against each other. Marx illustrated this procedure in numerical rows in the famous diagrams of the second volume of *Capital*.

After he examined the relations in simple reproduction (that is to say, without accumulation), Marx moved on to the even more difficult task of studying the influence of accumulation on the distribution of products between the different groups and on production itself. Here also, the exposition, of course, does not correspond immediately with reality but rather makes quite strong simplifications. The matter was precisely to delineate in their simplest outlines the intricacies of the circulation-process as a whole and the relations of reciprocal dependence. In doing so, the above-mentioned departments, the production of means of production and of means of consumption, naturally could not be considered independently of each other precisely because the question was to study their reciprocal dependence. When, therefore, it is assumed, for instance, that, in one of the two departments, the capitalists used on average half of the surplus-value to increase their capitals, one cannot assume offhand that accumulation in the other department takes place in the same proportion. Rather, one must make a complicated calculation. First it must be determined how wages in both departments, as well as the part of surplus-value destined for immediate consumption, are exchanged against the product of the second department, which exists in the form of means of consumption. Then one must determine how the means of production in both departments are not only replaced but also expanded in such a proportion that the equilibrium in production between the two departments is maintained. Despite all the simplifications made by Marx, this is quite a difficult and complicated problem that is, however, of the greatest importance and significance. The study of those equilibrium-conditions in production made it possible for the first time to understand the disturbances in that equilibrium, much as physicians must first thoroughly research the processes in healthy bodies before they can reach an understanding of illnesses. Marx's research on the laws of simple and expanded reproduction, on the mutual dependence of both departments, on the reciprocal exchange of particular groups of values and products, and, finally, on the money-transactions that mediate this exchange, have enabled us to get to grips with the problem of crisis on which the whole of bourgeois economics has broken its teeth in vain.

II. Marx's diagrams and the crises

The Russian professor, Tugan-Baranovsky, in particular, emphasised the significance of Marx's diagrams; however, he misconceived their interrelation.[14] He re-calculated Marx's diagrams, experimentally changing different presuppositions, with the result that equilibrium was always preserved with progressive accumulation. There seemed to be no room for disturbances in the diagrams drawn up by Marx, and Tugan-Baranovsky therefore concluded that such disturbances, including crises, were not at all necessary but were only casual epiphenomena of capitalist accumulation, which could proceed peacefully and undisturbed if only the proper proportions were maintained in production.

This conclusion, which was the subject of passionate discussions among Russian and German Marxists, was due to a misunderstanding of the aim and significance of Marx's diagrams. These were not meant to illustrate how capitalist accumulation actually happens, but rather how, under the presupposition of capitalist accumulation, a condition of equilibrium between production and consumption is conceivable, and how the social need for both means of production and means of consumption takes shape under capitalist

14. [Tugan-Baranovsky 1901. Two chapters translated by A. Ramos-Martínez: Chapter 1: The Fundamental Causes of Crises in the Capitalist Economy, and Chapter 7: Marx's Theory of Crises, in Zarembka (ed.) 2000.]

accumulation. The calculations of Tugan-Baranovsky, therefore, only proved the excellence of Marx's diagrams, but did not under any circumstance justify his [Tugan's] conclusion. If one wants to study the problem of crises, one must first of all ask the question: What is the relationship between the reality of capitalist accumulation and Marx's equilibrium-diagrams, which show only the *possibility* of equilibrium?

That raises the question of how the relations described by Marx will be maintained. The producers themselves, naturally, have no idea about those diagrams and would look down with sovereign disdain upon the whole hair-splitting brain-wrecking business, which is incomprehensible to them. Who, therefore, regulates production? [The answer is] prices. Capitalist commodity-producers know only one goal: they want to obtain prices that will secure for them the greatest possible profit.

Under conditions of simple commodity-production for familiar customers, as they are known to this day by village-tailors or boot-makers, the survey of production and social needs was relatively simple; and, even when people began to turn to production for the market, it could easily be regulated by prices. If many units of a particular commodity were produced, prices sank immediately; production then decreased, and equilibrium was soon re-established. The circumstances are very different under the conditions of a developed capitalist mode of production. Here, the 'market', i.e. social need, becomes quite obscure and complicated, especially because the investments in large-scale enterprises usually take years, in the course of which the entire production- and consumption-conditions of society can change completely, and, furthermore, because a substantial reduction of production in those enterprises is almost impossible, while, on the other hand, its expansion often promises high momentary gains at the expense of weaker competitors. Thus, it has become almost impossible for particular producers to know beforehand the social need for the commodities they bring to the market; at most, they can be assumed, indeed guessed at, and the wildest speculation rules over production.

Marx's diagrams show how capitalist production must proceed if equilibrium is maintained, and how great is the actual social need for different kinds of products. But production is managed only with a view to the highest possible profit, thus deviating quite significantly from social needs. The adjustment takes place from time to time violently in the form of crises.

Prof. Tugan-Baranovsky misjudged the essence of Marx's analysis inasmuch as he believed that he was able to deduce from it that crises are not necessary but are only casual phenomena on the surface of capitalist accumulation. To be sure, this misunderstanding must be attributed, above all, to the fact that Marx did not have the opportunity to develop his theory of crises on the basis of his diagrams.

Comrade Luxemburg, however, misunderstood the essence, purpose and significance of Marx's analysis much worse than did Tugan-Baranovsky.

III. The conception of the problem in Rosa Luxemburg

In the first six chapters of her book, Rosa Luxemburg offers, in close connection with Chapters 18 to 21 of the second volume of *Capital* (but with some deviations, to which we will partially return later), an outline of the problem of distribution of the annual social production in relation to the overall circulation of social capital, as it appears in the works of Quesnay, Adam Smith and Marx. In the sixth and seventh chapters, in particular, she deals with the above-mentioned Marxian diagrams of expanded reproduction and begins her critique. The decisive sentences can be found on pages 131–2 and again on pages 334–5 of her book.[15] Those sentences are the kernel of her comments and characterise her standpoint. Her remarks are purely abstract and therefore force the critics who want to respond to them to follow her into those regions.

Rosa Luxemburg complains that it is not clear in Marx's diagrams where the constantly growing demand that underlies the progressive expansion of production comes from. If this reproach were true, it would demonstrate that Marx's entire analysis is false and absurd, because the purpose of his diagrams, as we have seen, was precisely to discover the laws that regulate this exchange of different groups of values and products and that bring about the equilibrium between production and consumption. Comrade Luxemburg sarcastically criticises and disparages Marx's analysis, which she quotes with the addition of numerous expletives (see for instance pp. 120ff;[16] this scornful criticism pervades especially Chapters 8 and 9 of her book). What do the

---

15. [Luxemburg 1963. These page references are to the 1963 edition by Routledge and Kegan Paul.]
16. [Luxemburg 1963, Chapter 7 of the English edition, where the added exclamation marks were removed.]

arguments with which Rosa Luxemburg confronts Marx consist of? She says on pages 131–2:

> Where is this continually increasing demand to come from, which in Marx's diagram forms the basis of reproduction on an ever rising scale? It cannot possibly come from the capitalists of Departments I and II themselves – so much is certain right away – it cannot arise out of their personal consumption. On the contrary, it is the very essence of accumulation that the capitalists refrain from consuming part of their surplus-value which must be ever increasing – at least as far as absolute figures are concerned – that they use it instead to make goods for the use of other people.... But what of the remaining surplus-value, the part that is accumulated? For whom can it be destined? According to Marx's diagram, Department I has the initiative: the process starts with the production of producer goods. And who requires these additional means of production? The diagram answers that Department II needs them in order to produce means of subsistence [*Lebensmittel*] in increased quantities. Well then, who requires these additional consumer goods? Department I, of course – replies the diagram – because it now employs a greater number of workers.[17]

Apart from the fact that, in the final sentences, the capitalists' consumption is forgotten, and that it is not only a question of consumer goods but also of means of consumption (and, therefore, also of private and public palaces as well as cannons, barracks, warships, etc.), this exposition corresponds not only to Marx's diagrams but also to reality. The capitalist mode of production is governed by the quest for profit. The question, therefore, is whether Marx's diagrams show how that profit is realised for the capitalists. That is absolutely the case. In the diagrams that Comrade Luxemburg is fond of quoting, the surplus-value accruing to the capitalists actually grows quite quickly. It amounts in the first year to 1,285; in the second to 1,399; in the third to 1,515; and in the fourth to 1,642 (approximately a million marks, although the numbers are arbitrarily chosen and only meant to illustrate the ratios). The process therefore makes perfect sense for the capitalists as well. But Comrade Luxemburg continues:

17. [Luxemburg 1963, pp. 131–2, Chapter 7: Analysis of Marx's Diagram of Enlarged Reproduction. The translation has been amended, as it rendered *Lebensmittel* as both 'consumer goods' and 'means of consumption' indistinctly.]

> We are plainly running in circles. From the capitalist point of view it is absurd to produce more consumer goods merely in order to maintain more workers, and to turn out more means of production merely to keep this surplus of workers occupied.[18]

It is difficult to fathom the relevance of those words to Marx's diagrams. The aim of capitalist production is profit, and the capitalists acquire it in the process described, which is therefore anything but an absurdity from their point of view. On the contrary, from their point of view it is the very embodiment of reason, i.e., of the striving after profit.

This train of thought is the core around which Rosa Luxemburg's entire book was written. It contains everything she has to say on the question of accumulation.

IV. The application of the diagrams by Rosa Luxemburg

Let us recognise here and now that the author has misunderstood the meaning and purpose of Marx's analysis, and this recognition is confirmed by the remainder of her book. Above all, she is completely incapable of understand-

18. Luxemburg 1963, p. 132. [On pp. 334–5 Luxemburg makes a similar comment: The growing consumption of the capitalists can certainly not be regarded as the ultimate purpose of accumulation; on the contrary, there is no accumulation inasmuch as this consumption takes place and increases; personal consumption of the capitalists must be regarded as simple reproduction. Rather, the question is: if, and in so far as, the capitalists do not themselves consume their products but 'practise abstinence', i.e. accumulate, for whose sake do they produce? Even less can the maintenance of an ever larger army of workers be the ultimate purpose of continuous accumulation of capital. From the capitalist's point of view, the consumption of the workers is a consequence of accumulation, it is never its object or its condition, unless the principles (foundations) of capitalist production are to be turned upside down. And in any case, the workers can only consume that part of the product which corresponds to the variable capital, not a jot more. Who, then, realises the permanently increasing surplus value? The diagram answers: the capitalists themselves and they alone. – And what do they do with this increasing surplus value? – The diagram replies: They use it for an ever greater expansion of their production. These capitalists are thus fanatical supporters of an expansion of production for production's sake. They see to it that ever more machines are built for the sake of building – with their help – ever more new machines. Yet the upshot of all this is not accumulation of capital but an increasing production of producer goods with no purpose whatever. Indeed, one must be as reckless as Tugan Baranovski, and rejoice as much in paradoxical statements, to assume that this untiring merry-go-round in thin air could be a faithful reflection in theory of capitalist reality, a true deduction from Marx's doctrine. (Luxemburg 1963, pp. 334–5, Chapter 25: Contradictions within the Diagram of Enlarged Reproduction.)

ing the technique of these models. This is already quite clear on p. 100[19] of her book. There, she deals with simple reproduction, that is to say, reproduction without accumulation, without capital-growth. Comrade Luxemburg objects that Marx incorporates the production of money-materials, i.e. gold and silver, in Row I and calculates it with the production of means of production. That is supposed to be incorrect. *For this reason, she adds a third row to those constructed by Marx, which is supposed to represent the production of money-materials.* That is certainly admissible, but one wonders how the reciprocal exchange between the three rows should take place. In Marx's diagrams, there are always only two rows, and whoever has taken up their study will agree that their mutual intertwining is often very complicated and difficult enough. In the model constructed by Comrade Luxemburg, the difficulty is not only very great; it is insuperable. A cursory look at her schema shows that the total amount of wages and surplus is 3,010, while only 3,000 of means of consumption are available. Within the framework of simple reproduction, the exchange is simply impossible. To be sure, she explicitly stated in the preceding page that

> We can only obtain a comprehensive diagram of the essential points of capitalist production if we show the *organic interweaving* between the production and reproduction of money and the two other Departments of social production.[20]

But she herself does not make the slightest effort to portray these 'organic tangles'. The very attempt would have shown her that her model is not feasible.

She reveals the same incapacity to work with Marx's diagrams in Chapter 25 ('Contradictions within the Diagram of Enlarged Reproduction'), where she once again attempts to refute Marx's exposition. Besides the arguments already quoted, she also attempts to prove mathematically the deficiency of Marx's diagrams. She wants to include among her presuppositions the growth of the proletariat as well as the circumstance that the value of the means of

---

19. [Luxemburg 1963, p. 100.]
20. Luxemburg 1963, p. 99 of the English edition, Chapter 5: The Circulation of Money, Eckstein's emphasis. [The English version reads: 'if we demonstrate the original relationship', but that is a paraphrase. In the English version of Rosa Luxemburg, *The Accumulation of Capital – An Anti-Critique*, the expression *organischen Verschlingung* is rendered as 'organic tangles'.]

production in the course of capitalist development grows more rapidly than the total amount of wages paid. Sure enough, the calculations show that production and consumption no longer coincide, and she announces that result quite arrogantly. Actually, that is simply a result of the fact that her calculations are completely wrong.

The mistake lies in the very way she has made her calculations, and this shows that she has not grasped the essence of Marx's models. She thinks that these are based on the requirement of an equal rate of accumulation, i.e., she assumes that accumulation always proceeds equally in both main departments of social production. But that assumption is quite arbitrary and contradicts the facts. In reality, there is no such general rate of accumulation and it would be a theoretical nonsense. Marx's diagrams themselves show that very clearly, and Comrade Luxemburg states it explicitly on page 122 of her book. But she thinks she has found an argument against the correctness of Marx's diagrams: she says

> There is no rule in evidence for accumulation and consumption to follow [in Department II]; both are wholly subservient to the requirements of accumulation in Department I.[21]

That is absolutely true. It is precisely the task of the diagrams to show how accumulation in one of the rows depends on accumulation in the other. If Comrade Luxemburg's views were correct, then no change at all could take place in the reciprocal relationships between the different branches of production; any adjustment would be out of the question. In reality, there is no such general rate of accumulation, and it would also be an absurdity from a theoretical point of view. When Comrade Luxemburg asserts on page 340 that 'Marx's diagram, where strict conformity of the two Departments is axiomatic, precludes any such fluctuations in the rate of accumulation in either Department',[22] she makes a scarcely comprehensible error, which once again shows that she is completely puzzled by the essence of Marx's models.

Accumulation in different branches of production results from the prospect of employing capital in them profitably. And this prospect is by no means

21. Luxemburg 1963, p. 122, Chapter 7: Analysis of Marx's Diagram of Enlarged Reproduction.
22. Luxemburg 1963, p. 340, Chapter 25: Contradictions within the Diagram of Enlarged Reproduction.

the same in all branches of production. The real law of an equal rate of profit stands in complete contradiction to the fictitious law of equal accumulation. The calculation method of Comrade Luxemburg is all the more remarkable because she could have asked herself the obvious question: Why did Marx employ such an intricate and complicated method of calculation as the one that appears on pages 513 and 518[23] of the second volume of *Capital*, if such a simple and primitive method as the one employed by her would have served his purpose?

The most astonishing results, however, arise from the calculations in the last chapter of her book. Rosa Luxemburg assumes there that an amount of 100 is taken away from the workers of both departments, and only from them, through indirect taxes for military outlays. Actually, that would only mean that in Department II, where means of consumption are produced, more uniforms, barracks and armoured ships would be produced, and fewer workers' clothes, apartment-buildings and foodstuffs. This shift could react on Department I only indirectly. Military equipment belongs, in any case, to the means of consumption. In the question under consideration, as we have already mentioned, it makes no difference in principle whether the 'means of consumption' are consumed by capitalists. Comrade Luxemburg, however, argues that there is an opposition between those two kinds of consumption. At once, she turns 'means of consumption' into 'foodstuffs' and argues that an arms-race must have special consequences for the total circulation of capital, reaching, in that way, the most astonishing results. According to her calculations, when workers have to pay a sum of 100, the value of total annual production decreases by 171.5, i.e., almost twice as much as the entire amount of tax. How that happens is mysterious. But she calculates further and finally reaches the conclusion that in total production, even if one allows for the fact that the 100 [taken away from the workers as taxes] were employed in the production of war-materiel, wages decrease by 34.75 and the value of means of production going into annual production decreases by 51. What happened to those 51 is also a mystery.

23. [The page numbers refer to Marx 1978bb.]

V. The circulation of money

The above-mentioned diagrams also play a great role for Marx in another respect. It is clear that, for accumulation [to take place], ever-greater sums of money are necessary, because each investment-seeking capital appears first in the form of money-capital. Money-hoards are of the greatest significance for the entire economy because they constitute the foundation of the entire credit system, which can only be understood when one grasps the mechanism that governs the circulation of money, and particularly of those hoards (compare *Capital*, Vol. III, Chapters 30 to 32 dealing with 'Money-Capital and Real Capital'). Marx therefore dedicates special attention to the investigation of this question, particularly in the chapters mentioned.

Strange to say, Comrade Luxemburg completely misunderstood Marx's remarks. Beginning with the false premise that the diagrams leave open the question of 'where does the always growing demand come from', she mistakes Marx's analysis of the origin of the money that the capitalists must hoard in order to apply it to accumulation for an analysis of where the money for buying the surplus-products comes from; that is to say, of who will be the buyers of those products. Naturally, for that reason, she is also unable to find in Marx's analysis any answer to the question, which Marx certainly answered in his diagrams but is not at all dealt with in the chapters under consideration. But she does not realise her mistake and lashes out at Marx for having posed the question [of consumers in enlarged reproduction] 'in a perverted form as the question of additional money sources'.[24] Actually, it is a question of real demand, of the use of commodities, not of money-sources for their payment. Just how completely she misunderstood Marx's point is especially clear in the following sentence:

> As to money as a means of circulation: when considering the reproductive process as a whole, we must assume that capitalist society must always dispose of money, or a substitute, in just that quantity that is needed for its process of circulation.[25]

24. Luxemburg 1963, p. 300, Chapter 22: Bulgakov and His Completion of Marx's Analysis.
25. Luxemburg 1963, p. 155, Chapter 9: The Difficulty Viewed From the Angle of the Process of Circulation.

Marx was not satisfied with making this assumption, but instead undertook the investigations so thoroughly criticised by Comrade Luxemburg.

VI. The solution of the problem

If Comrade Luxemburg overlooked the problems where they actually are and found them where they do not exist, the solution that she offers is even more astonishing than the problem itself. She formulates the great question that her book seeks to answer as follows: '*if, and in so far as, the capitalists do not themselves consume their products but "practise abstinence", i.e. accumulate: for whose sake do they produce?*'[26] We have seen that Marx's diagrams answer this question, but Comrade Luxemburg is not satisfied with that answer. And what is her answer? This is what she writes on page 366:

> the immediate and vital conditions for capital and its accumulation is the existence of non-capitalist buyers of the surplus-value, which is decisive to this extent for the problem of capitalist accumulation.[27]

Then she proceeds to describe in long historical expositions how capital pushes for export to non-capitalist countries, destroys the old economic forms everywhere, exploits the people, often plunders by violence what it cannot get through trade, but thereby lays the foundations for the development of capitalism in all countries. Thus capitalism digs its own grave into which it will ultimately plunge. The question 'for whom do the capitalists produce?' receives therefore the remarkable answer: for the small peasants in Europe and China, for the blacks in Central Africa, in short, for the non-capitalist countries and social strata. Strange! But the thing is even more astonishing when it is looked at closely. Comrade Luxemburg showed precisely how those non-capitalist countries and popular strata are frightfully exploited by capitalism, and the same has already been described by many other authors. But exploitation consists of the fact that someone takes away from the exploited more value than he gives to them. The question then arises as to where the surplus-value goes that is thrown into the market year after

26. Luxemburg 1963, p. 334, Chapter 25: Contradictions Within the Diagram of Enlarged Reproduction (Eckstein's emphasis).

27. Luxemburg 1963, p. 366, Chapter 26: The Reproduction of Capital and Its Social Setting.

year as a result of capital-accumulation. Comrade Luxemburg answers that this surplus-value is disposed of by selling among non-capitalist peoples and classes that give a much greater value in exchange. How the alleged difficulty should be redressed by those means is totally incomprehensible; it would rather be considerably intensified in that way.

Actually, a violent import of commodities [into the non-capitalist countries] does take place, and Luxemburg's portrayal of the process is essentially correct, but the economic causes of those exports, which I cannot examine more closely within the framework of this review, are totally different from the ones described by her.

Comrade Luxemburg thinks that with her book she has made a contribution to the economic explanation of imperialism.[28] In fact, she deals with the actual problems of imperialism only in Chapter 30, 'International Loans', which, however, contains nothing new. Generally speaking, the book has so little to do with the new phenomena of today's pulsating economic life that it could have been written just as well twenty or more years ago.

Together with the theoretical foundations, fall the practical conclusions, above all the theory of catastrophes, which Comrade Luxemburg constructed on the basis of her doctrine concerning the necessity of non-capitalist consumers.

It is painful to pass such a harsh judgment on a book that was meant to contribute to the advance of the proletarian movement. But as Comrade Mehring rightly said in a similar case:

> It is, to be sure, no pleasant task to judge the book of a comrade in arms so unfavourably. However, if we did not criticise such works just as sharply, we would lose every right to scrutinise the bourgeois literature on Marx as carefully as we usually do. And even that is not the main reason. Such works must be rejected not only out of consideration for our opponents, but also out of respect for our own party.

28. [That is the subtitle to the original German edition of Rosa Luxemburg's book, which was left out in the English translation: *A Contribution to the Economic Explanation of Imperialism*.]

Chapter Forty-Five

'*The Accumulation of Capital*' (1913)

Otto Bauer

Of all the critical responses to her *Accumulation of Capital*, the one that most infuriated Rosa Luxemburg came from Otto Bauer. She devoted four of six chapters of her *Anti-Critique* to the article translated here. Although she dismissively spoke of Bauer's commentary as a theoretical 'disgrace' and a 'scandal for Social Democracy',[1] she also acknowledged that, on first reading, the work might appear reflective and erudite, incorporating 'long and detailed calculations with four tables [ten, in fact], with wide, lengthy, oval-bracketed and four-storied formulae',[2] including not merely prose and arithmetic but even 'a few Greek letters'.[3] The problem, she claimed, was that Bauer committed the elementary logical error of assuming in advance what had to be proven. Marx's schemes in Volume II of *Capital* had given an arithmetic illustration of crisis-free expanded reproduction in the absence of foreign trade and capital-exports. Taking the issue to be settled, Bauer merely reformulated Marx's models without once questioning whether capitalism actually did require third-party markets. Luxemburg replied with this analogy:

1. Luxemburg 1921, p. 135.
2. Luxemburg 1921, p. 68.
3. Luxemburg 1921, p. 67.

> In olden times, people believed in the existence of all kinds of fabulous creatures: dwarfs, people with one eye, with one arm and leg, and so on. Does anybody believe that such creatures really existed? But we see them drawn in precisely on the old maps. Is that not *proof* that those conceptions of the ancients corresponded exactly with reality?[4]

Although his introductory paragraphs appeared to paraphrase elements of Luxemburg's own thesis, mentioning the limits to consumption in capitalist society and their connection with periodic crises, Bauer believed that, ultimately, the expansion of capitalist markets was pre-determined by the need for accumulation to match the natural tendency of population-growth. This empirical context, he believed, was the decisive element missing from Marx's abstract models in Volume II of *Capital*. If capitalist society were able rationally to anticipate and make advance provision for population-growth, then no crises would be possible; capital-accumulation would proceed smoothly without any reference to the export of either commodities or capital. In that case, accumulation would be planned and would achieve exactly the goals intended for socialism. The key for understanding economic growth in any social system was the relation between population and accumulation.

The problem, as Bauer saw it, was that capitalism had to make the necessary adjustments in a spontaneous manner, driven by individual capitalists' pursuit of their own individual profits, so that any achievement of 'equilibrium' must be strictly fortuitous. Yet, the principal theme of his argument remained the conviction that 'equilibrium' and crisis-free accumulation, at least in theoretical terms, were completely possible in a self-contained capitalist economy. The central purpose of his essay was to explain how

> accumulation takes place without disturbance so long as it maintains a definite quantitative relationship on the one hand with population-growth, on the other with the development of productivity which expresses itself in the progress towards a higher organic composition of capital.

Of course, there would always be spontaneous deviations from the required pattern. In some cases, there would be underaccumulation; variable capital (wage-payments) would grow too slowly, resulting in unemployment and

4. Luxemburg 1921, p. 69.

the industrial reserve-army. At other times, there would be instances of over-accumulation, when the growth of variable capital would occur too quickly. But, in both cases, Bauer thought accumulation must ultimately revert to the required 'equilibrium'. In the event of underaccumulation, a fall in wages would objectively shift income-distribution in favour of the capitalists, thus increasing the social rate of accumulation until variable capital grew once more at the same rate as the work force; in the case of overaccumulation, higher wages and falling profits would precipitate a crisis as the means to restore the necessary quantitative relationships. Bauer concluded that capitalism had a built-in mechanism of mean reversion, '*a tendency for the adjustment of the rate of accumulation to the growth of the population*'.

How, then, could the reality of imperialism be explained? For Bauer, the answer had nothing to do with Luxemburg's claims concerning the impossibility of capitalist growth in the absence of third parties. The role of imperialism was to mitigate the inevitable crises by widening the systemic limits to continuous accumulation. Imperialism was a *complement* of capitalism, not an inherent *necessity*. Recourse to external markets made more labour available for exploitation, helped to acquire necessary 'material elements' from abroad, aided in the resolution of crises through commodity-exports, and was of principal benefit to the most capital-intensive industries. On the international scale, imperialism was a further manifestation of the objective need to maintain a certain relationship between capital-accumulation and population-growth. As Bauer wrote,

> The tendency for accumulation to adjust to population-growth also dominates international relations. Each year countries with continuous overaccumulation invest a large and growing part of their accumulated surplus-value overseas. Examples: France and England.

He concluded that, despite its propensity towards crises, capitalism remained essentially a self-equilibrating system within the limits imposed by population-growth:

> Of course, again and again, the development of accumulation pushes ahead of these limits; but, again and again, accumulation is brought back within them through periodic recurrent crises. The result of our investigation is thus (i) that the accumulation of capital is possible even in an isolated capitalist economy, so long as it does not exceed a fixed limit at any particular

> time, and (ii) that it is brought back automatically to this limit through the mechanism of the capitalist mode of production itself.

Rosa Luxemburg was appalled by this argument. She considered it a fantasy that flew in the face of both Marxist theory and obvious facts. In the first place, Bauer implied that, despite the reality of exploitation, capitalism was actually *good* for the proletariat. Notwithstanding temporary deviations, the system objectively tended to match growth of wage-payments with growth of the work-force; and, taking into account the effect of technological progress in reducing the value of necessary goods, the result must actually be a secular trend of steadily rising living standards. Luxemburg protested that

> if the rise in the workers' standard of living is so strong that the variable capital (sum of money wages) must grow year after year in exactly the same proportion as the working population, then this means that all the technological progress is for the benefit of the workers alone.[5]

While Bauer denied that his theory was an 'apology' for capitalism, Luxemburg thought he had crudely misunderstood the implications of his own statements.

Moreover, Bauer's work was an egregious affront to Marx, who posited a relation between accumulation and population that was exactly the reverse of what Bauer described. Instead of mean-reversion and gradual adjustments of accumulation to population-growth, Marx saw secular expansion of the industrial reserve-army, punctuated by periods of prosperity and acute crisis, as an objective prerequisite for all capital-accumulation. Few passages in *Capital* were as famous as Marx's ringing declaration that capital-accumulation was impossible without social catastrophes and ruthless exploitation:

> ...a surplus of labouring population is a necessary product of [capital] accumulation.... a condition for the existence of the capitalist mode of production. It forms a disposable industrial reserve army, which belongs to capital.... a mass of human material always ready for exploitation.... The mass of social wealth, overflowing with the advance of [capital] accumulation...thrusts itself frantically into old branches of production, whose market suddenly expands, or into newly formed branches, such as railways, etc.... In all

5. Luxemburg 1921, p. 108.

> such cases, there must be the possibility of suddenly throwing great masses of men into the decisive areas.... The path characteristically described by modern industry, which takes the form of a decennial cycle (interrupted by smaller oscillations) of periods of average activity, production at high pressure, crisis and stagnation, depends on the constant formation, the greater or less absorption, and the re-formation of the industrial reserve army or surplus population. In their turn, the varying phases of the industrial cycle recruit the surplus population, and become one of the most energetic agents for its reproduction.[6]

As Luxemburg remarked,

> This is the culminating point of the first volume of *Capital*.... Along comes Bauer, who [then] turns this whole edifice upside down and tells the world that the entire movement of capital results from the tendency to adjust to the increase of the working population! In terms of content Bauer's theory is a soap bubble.[7]

Whereas Bauer made capital-accumulation dependent on population-growth, Luxemburg replied:

> What about France, for instance? There population growth has steadily decreased.... The population growth is slowly coming to a standstill, perhaps even an absolute decrease is ahead. In spite of that, capital in France happily carries on accumulating: so well that France can provide the whole world with its capital reserves. In Serbia population increases twice as fast as in England; but, as is well known, capital accumulation is much stronger in England than in Serbia. How does that make sense?[8]

As for the relation between accumulation and population on a world scale, here capitalism's effects were even more problematic for Bauer's thesis:

> In fact, the capitalist method of producing a world market goes hand-in-hand with decimation and even extermination of whole tribes. This process, still going on, has accompanied capitalist development since the discovery of America: the Spanish in Mexico and Peru in the sixteenth century, the

6. Marx 1976, p. 785; Luxemburg 1921, p. 132.
7. Luxemburg 1921, p. 134.
8. Luxemburg 1921, p. 111.

> English in North America in the seventeenth, in Australia in the eighteenth century, Dutch in the Malay Archipelago, French in North Africa, English in India in the nineteenth century, Germans in South West Africa in the twentieth century. The wars of European capital to 'open up' China have also led to periodic mass slaughter of the Chinese population.... [T]he expansion of the base of accumulation in non-capitalist countries is linked with the partial extermination of the populations....[9]

But, apart from these questions of economic theory and historical fact, Luxemburg also saw in Otto Bauer's work something more sinister. Exactly his kind of thinking was the ideological basis for 'a distinct political tendency' that, before 1914, encouraged the illusion that imperialism was simply a *policy*, not a *necessity* for expanded reproduction, and that the policy itself served only the interests of minority sections of the capitalist class, particularly heavy industry and finance-capital: 'The logical conclusion of this idea is to look on the phase of imperialism...as the wicked intervention of a small group of people who profit from it.' If that were the case, then, as Karl Kautsky and others had argued, the main duty of Social Democrats would be to avoid social clashes and form 'a bloc of the proletariat with broad sections of the bourgeoisie in order to "moderate" imperialism'. In place of revolutionary struggle, Marxists would pursue the 'utopia of historical compromise'. They would 'educate' sections of the bourgeoisie, work for 'disarmament treaties', and ultimately strive for a 'peaceful federation of democratic nation-states...against the struggle of the great powers for world domination'. Karl Kautsky thought this tactic was 'the road to power'; Rosa Luxemburg acidly replied that it was 'the road to impotence' and 'a policy of "abstention" on epoch-making decisions of world history'.[10] She concluded that Otto Bauer's essay typified the kind of literature that debilitated revolutionary Marxism and crippled effective resistance to imperialist war.

* * *

9. Luxemburg 1921, p. 112.
10. Luxemburg 1921, pp. 148–9.

'The Accumulation of Capital'[11]

I

Accumulation and capacity to consume

Every year the capitalists convert part of the surplus-value they have obtained into capital. They use part of the surplus-value to extend existing factories and establish new ones, thereby expanding their productive capacity and increasing the labour-force at their command. Marx calls this conversion of part of surplus-value into capital the *accumulation of capital*. The further capitalist development progresses, the smaller becomes the part of surplus-value consumed by the capitalists, and the larger the part which they accumulate. The *rate of accumulation*, the ratio of accumulated to total surplus-value, rises.

While the accumulation of capital is boundless, the productive capacity of society expands, and the mass of commodities produced in the capitalists' factories increases massively, narrow limits are set to the *capacity to consume* of capitalist society. The purchasing power of the *working class* grows more slowly than capital; for, as the value of labour-power falls with the development of the forces of production, the share of the working class in the value of the social product declines. But the purchasing power of the *capitalist class* also grows more slowly than capital. The more the capitalists accumulate, the less they can consume. Thus the *capacity to consume* of capitalist society falls further and further behind the boundlessly developing forces of production. This internal contradiction of the capitalist mode of production leads to the *decline in the rate of profit* that becomes apparent in disastrous crises, in which the mass of commodities thrown onto the market by the expanded productive capacity searches in vain for purchasers.

The explanation of crises in terms of disproportionality between the accumulation of capital and society's power to consume was first developed by *Sismondi*, followed by *Malthus, Chalmers*, and *Rodbertus*. For Sismondi, it

11. Bauer 1913. This English version was translated by J.E. King and first published in the journal *History of Political Economy*, Vol. 18, No. 1 (Spring 1986), pp. 87–110. We would like to thank Prof. King – who is the co-author, together with Michael Charles Howard, of *A History of Marxian Economics* in two vols. (Princeton University Press, 1989–92) – for his kind permission to reproduce it here.

formed an essential component of his critique of capitalism; for Malthus and Chalmers, it was an assumption behind their demonstration that capitalist society needs 'third persons' to be able to sell its commodities at all – third persons who consume without producing.

The explanation of the decline in the rate of profit in terms of disproportionality between the accumulation of capital and the growth of the work force was first provided by the 1821 *pamphlet* [*The Source and Remedy of the National Difficulties, Deduced from Principles of Political Economy*],[12] *Hodgskin*, and *Ramsay*.

The defenders of capitalism have attacked this theory. They deny the possibility of general overproduction, arguing that with the growth of commodity-production, the purchasing power of the producers would also increase. Crises could arise only from disproportionality between the sectors of production, not from general overproduction. And none of this could be altered by the fact that the worker has to share the value of his product with the capitalist. For the less the workers can consume, the greater becomes the purchasing power of the capitalists. The demand for commodities thus remains unchanged in total, whether the workers' share in the value of the product rises or falls. Exactly the same applies to the rate of accumulation: if it increases, proportionally fewer consumer goods are indeed purchased, but more means of production. So argued *Ricardo, MacCulloch, Say*.

No more than crises is the decline in the rate of profit to be explained by overaccumulation. The rate of profit falls only because the growing difficulties in supplying food increase the value of labour-power and reduce the rate of surplus-value. The decline in the rate of profit is thus attributed to inevitable natural laws: to overpopulation and the diminishing fertility of the land. So argued especially *Ricardo* and *John Stuart Mill*.

Marx finally disposed of this objection from the Ricardo-Say school, but at the same time he also gave an entirely new version of Sismondi's teaching concerning the internal contradiction of capitalist accumulation. He divided capitalist production into two parts: *the production of means of production and the production of consumer goods*. He demonstrated that the reproduction of capital can take place only if definite quantitative relations exist between the

12. [Bauer here refers to an anonymous pamphlet entitled *The Source and Remedy of the National Difficulties, Deduced from Principles of Political Economy: In a Letter to Lord John Russell*, published in London in 1821 and praised by Marx in Volume III of *Theories of Surplus Value* (Marx 1968–72, Vol. III, pp. 238–41, 252–7).]

two branches of production. But in capitalist society this harmony cannot be established except as a 'result of the process of dissolution of the existing disharmonies'.[13] Hence crises appear not as accidental phenomena caused by chance disproportionalities in production, but as unavoidable phases in the reproduction of capital, because only through crises are the necessary quantitative relations established between the two branches of social production. The decline in the rate of profit, however, occurs even with full proportionality in production, not as a result of inevitable natural laws but as the effect of the fact that capital grows faster than the labour-power it sets in motion, which alone produces surplus-value.

The models in the second volume of *Capital*, in which Marx presented the conditions for equilibrium between the two branches of production, powerfully influenced the *Russian economic literature*. The latter discussed the question whether capitalism was a 'transitional necessity' also for Russia; whether, as the *Zapadniki* ('Westernisers') believed, Russia too must accept the economic, social and political institutions of western and central Europe or whether, as the *Slavophiles* thought, she could preserve her national individuality and originality. Put in socialist terms: whether in Russia, too, concentration of capital, proletarianisation of the mass of the people, class-conflict between bourgeoisie and proletariat are the preconditions for socialism, as the *Social Democrats* taught; or whether Russia could construct a socialist community on the basis of the *mir*, the peasant village commune, without having to go through capitalism, as the *Narodniki* ('Populists') and their followers, the *Social Revolutionaries*, supposed. Now in this controversy the question was raised as to whether capitalism could establish itself outside the area of western and central Europe; whether the development of capitalistic production in the East must not founder upon the impossibility of selling the commodities produced by its expanded productive capacity. In the battle against the Narodniki the Marxists showed, using Marx's models, that capitalism could expand further and further, that productive capacity could be increased more

13. [Here, as elsewhere, Bauer apparently cites Marx but does not give a source. In Chapter 18 of *Theories of Surplus Value*, the passage referred to is translated as follows: '...how is it possible to achieve the necessary balance and interdependence of the various spheres of production, their dimensions and the proportions between them, except through the constant neutralisation of a constant disharmony? This is admitted by those who speak of adjustments through competition, for these adjustments always presuppose that there is something to adjust, and therefore that harmony is always only a result of the movement which neutralises the existing disharmony.' See Marx 1968–72, II, p. 529.]

and more powerfully, without the capitalists lacking a market for their commodities, and thus that equilibrium between the output of means of production and of consumer goods is constantly re-created through the capitalistic mechanism itself.

The controversy between the Marxists and the Narodniki in Russia was decided by history. But now *Rosa Luxemburg* takes up the thesis of the limitedness of capitalism once more, admittedly for a quite different purpose. Her book, *The Accumulation of Capital: A Contribution to the Economic Explanation of Imperialism* (Berlin: Vorwärts, 1913),[14] poses a new version of the problem which has appeared, over and over again, since the days of Sismondi.

We first assume simple reproduction: the entire surplus is consumed, and none of it is accumulated. According to Marx the total production can be presented in this case as follows:

I. Means-of-production industries
   Constant capital (c) + variable capital (v) + surplus-value (m)

II. Consumer-goods industries
   Constant capital (c_1) + variable capital (v_1) + surplus-value (m_1)

The *means-of-production industries* must buy food from the consumer-goods industries: (i) to feed their workers, amounting to v; (ii) for consumption by their capitalists, amounting to m; thus $v + m$ *in total*.[15] On the other hand the *consumer-goods industries* have to buy c_1 means of production, from the industries which have produced them, to renew their constant capital. The exchange between the two groups takes place without disturbance if $c_1 = v + m$. This is the equilibrium-condition in simple reproduction.

It is different with reproduction on an extended scale. Here the total production can be set out in the following model:

I. *Means-of-production industries*
   Constant capital (c) + variable capital (v) + the consumed part of surplus-value (k) + the accumulated part of surplus-value (a)

II. *Consumer-goods industries*
   Constant capital (c_1) + variable capital (v_1) + the consumed part of surplus-value (k_1) + the accumulated part of surplus-value (a_1)

---

14. [Luxemburg 1963.]
15. [In German, 'surplus-value' is 'Mehrwert', so that in this translation the designation 's' is replaced by 'm' standing for surplus-value.]

Difficulties arise here. The means-of-production industries buy food amounting to $v + k$, and the consumer-goods industries buy the same quantity of means of production to renew their constant capital. But what happens to a and a_1? First of all, a takes the form of means of production: who can buy them? And a_1 is embodied in consumer goods: where are they sold? Here Rosa Luxemburg seizes upon the old hypothesis of 'third persons'. She believes that *the part of surplus-value which is to be accumulated cannot be realised at all unless capitalist production can sell its excess-values outside its own sphere, to non-capitalistically producing petit bourgeois and small peasants*. This explains the pressure of capital for the extension of its markets. Hence the effort to destroy natural economy, to transform simple commodity-production everywhere into capitalist production, to make the whole earth into a market-area for capitalist industry: hence *imperialism*! But once the market-area can be expanded no further, capitalism can no longer sell a large part of its commodities. It suffocates in the wealth which it has produced. Its last hour approaches. This is the fundamental idea in Comrade Luxemburg's work. We must now examine whether it is correct.

Accumulation and population-growth

Every society with a growing population must extend its productive capacity each year. This will be just as necessary for the socialist society of the future as for the capitalist society of the present, exactly as it was for the simple commodity-production or the peasant-economy of the past, which produced for its own needs.

Let us assume that in a socialist society the population grows at 5 per cent each year. Next year, society will have 5 per cent more people to feed than this year. Thus society must (i) produce this year the consumer goods which the extra population will need next year; thus, for example, it must build enough houses for the total housing stock to be increased by 5 per cent, and grow enough grain for the supply of bread after the next harvest to be increased by 5 per cent, and so on; (ii) produce this year enough means of production for the necessary workplaces and instruments of labour to be placed at the disposal of the 5 per cent larger labour-force next year. Every year society must devote a part of its labour to the production of the consumer goods and the means of production which will be needed by the extra population in the following year.

Now capitalist society must do the same. But here the extension of productive capacity and food-supplies is bound up with the accumulation of capital. A part of surplus-value is converted into capital, and indeed one part of the accumulated surplus-value is added to variable and another part to constant capital. The capitalists carry out this accumulation in order to increase their profit; but the social consequence of accumulation is to supply the consumer goods and means of production required by the increase in population. The growth in variable capital represents the supply of food, and the growth in constant capital the provision of workplaces and instruments of labour for the increase in population.

But, while, in socialist society the social organs responsible for the planning of production ensure that the expansion of productive capacity and food-supplies keeps pace with population-growth, capitalist society has no such organs. Here the accumulation of capital depends upon the decisions of the capitalists. Hence accumulation can lag behind population-growth or run ahead of it. We now wish to discover, first, *how the accumulation of capital must take place in order that it may remain in equilibrium with population-growth.* Once we know this we will understand without any difficulty what effects the disturbance of this equilibrium-condition must bring about.

We assume that the population grows at 5 per cent per annum. If equilibrium is to be maintained, variable capital must also grow at 5 per cent each year. Constant capital increases faster than variable capital; how much faster is determined by the state of technical development attained at any given time. We will assume that constant capital grows at 10 per cent per annum. Thus we obtain, for example, the series:

Table 1

	Constant capital	Variable capital
Year 1	200,000	100,000
Year 2	220,000	105,000
Year 3	242,000	110,250
Year 4	266,000	115,762

To simplify the investigation we assume for the time being that the rate of surplus-value remains unchanged, at 100 per cent.[16] Every year the mass of

16. [This critical assumption is not in fact relaxed later in the article. A constant rate

surplus-value is exactly equal to that of variable capital. Which part of surplus-value is accumulated, which part consumed? That part is accumulated which allows variable capital to grow at 5 per cent and constant capital at 10 per cent. For example, in the first year, surplus-value amounts to 100,000. To increase constant capital (from 200,000 to 220,000) 20,000 is required; to increase variable capital (from 100,000 to 105,000) 5,000 is needed. Thus in total 25,000 is accumulated and 75,000 consumed. Over four years the process can be represented as:

Table 2

	Total surplus-value	Consumed [surplus-value]	[Surplus-value] added to constant capital	[Surplus-value] added to variable capital
Year 1	100,000	75,000	20,000	5,000
Year 2	105,000	77,750	22,000	5,250
Year 3	110,250	80,539	24,200	5,511
Year 4	115,762	83,374	26,600	5,788

First of all, 5 per cent of surplus-value is withdrawn each year from capitalists' consumption and used for the expansion of variable capital. But in addition part of the surplus-value must be used to increase constant capital. Since surplus-value grows at the same rate as variable capital, but constant capital grows faster than variable, that part of surplus-value added to constant capital must increase from year to year. The rate of accumulation (the ratio of the accumulated part of surplus-value to the total surplus-value)[17] is thus:

Table 3

	Approximate rate of accumulation
Year 1	25 per cent
Year 2	26 per cent
Year 3	27 per cent
Year 4	28 per cent

of surplus-value and rising labour-productivity imply increasing real wages, but it is not clear whether Bauer recognised this.]

17. [By 'rate of accumulation', Bauer thus means the capitalists' savings ratio and not the rate of growth of total capital, which he later defines as the 'social rate of accumulation' in contrast with the 'capitalist rate of accumulation'.]

On the assumption of an unchanged rate of surplus-value, reproduction on an extended scale with an increasing organic composition of capital is thus possible only if the rate of accumulation rises from year to year. *If accumulation and population-growth are to remain in equilibrium, the growth of the rate of accumulation must bear a definite quantitative relationship to the growth of population and the increase in constant capital.* The numbers in our example show this to be the case. Anyone accustomed to thinking in terms of abstract numbers will find no difficulty with the equation which expresses this quantitative relationship in general terms.

Up to now we have looked at the growth of total capital. We will now investigate how this total capital must be divided between the two great branches of production, the output of means of production and that of consumer goods. We assume that production in the first year can be represented:

Table 4

	Means-of-production industries (I)	II. Consumer-goods industries (II)	Total production
Constant capital (*c*)	120,000	80,000	200,000
Variable capital (*v*)	50,000	50,000	100,000
Consumed part of surplus-value (*k*)	37,500	37,500	75,000
Accumulated part of surplus-value:			
Added to constant capital (κ)	10,000	10,000	20,000
Added to variable capital (β)	2,500	2,500	5,000
Total	220,000	180,000	400,000

Now, how must the capital be divided in the second year? It is impossible for the surplus-value accumulated in the two departments of production to be invested productively in the same departments in the following year, for the progress to a higher organic composition of capital requires a movement of capital from the consumer-goods industries into the production of means of production. Thus we must calculate *what part of the surplus-value accumulated in the consumer-goods industries must be transferred to the production of means of production* to be used for their expansion.

According to Tables 1 and 2 we have, in the second year:

Table 5

Variable capital	105,000
Consumed part of surplus-value	77,750
That part of surplus-value added to variable capital	5,250
Total	188,000

In the second year the value of the products of the consumer-goods industries must thus amount to 188,000, for the consumer goods can only be exchanged against these sums of value.

In the first year in the consumer-goods industries 10,000 κ (constant capital) and 2,500 β (variable capital) are accumulated. Now, if the value of the products of these industries in the second year amounts to 188,000, only 5,334 κ and 1,333 β of the surplus-value accumulated there in the first year can be invested in the consumer-goods industries. The remainder must be transferred to the means-of-production industries.[18] Consequently we have for the second year:

Table 6

	Means-of-production industries (I)	Consumer-goods industries (II)	Total production
Constant capital (c)	134,666	85,334	220,000
Variable capital (v)	53,667	51,333	105,000
Consumed part of surplus-value (k)	39,740	38,010	77,750
Accumulated part of surplus-value:			
Added to constant capital (κ)	11,244	10,756	22,000
Added to variable capital (β)	2,683	2,567	5,250
Total	242,000	188,000	430,000

18. These numbers were calculated in the following way. In the second year, the value of the products of the consumer-goods industries amounts to $c + v + m = 188{,}000$. As the rate of surplus-value is 100 per cent, so that v = m, it follows that: $c + 2v = 188{,}000$. The growth of constant capital in the production of consumer goods between the first and second years is $(c - 80{,}000)$, and the growth of variable capital is $(v - 50{,}000)$. If a similar proportion of κ and β are to be transferred to the means-of-production industries, we have:

$(c - 80{,}000) : (v - 50{,}000) = 10{,}000 : 2{,}500$.

Solving these equations we obtain $v = 51{,}333$ and $c = 85{,}334$.

By the same calculations, we can ascertain the quantities for the following year, obtaining the series:

Table 7

	c	*v*	*k*	κ	β	Total
Year 1						
I	120,000 +	50,000 +	37,500 +	10,000 +	2,500	= 220,000
II	80,000 +	50,000 +	37,500 +	10,000 +	2,500	= 180,000
	200,000 +	100,000 +	75,000 +	20,000 +	5,000	= 400,000
Year 2						
I	134,666 +	53,667 +	39,740 +	11,244 +	2,683	= 242,000
II	85,334 +	51,333 +	38,010 +	10,756 +	2,567	= 188,000
	220,000 +	105,000 +	77,750 +	22,000 +	5,250	= 430,000
Year 3						
I	151,048 +	57,576 +	42,070 +	12,638 +	2,868	= 266,200
II	90,952 +	52,674 +	38,469 +	11,562 +	2,643	= 196,300
	242,000 +	110,250 +	80,539 +	24,200 +	5,511	= 462,500
Year 4						
I	169,124 +	61,738 +	44,465 +	14,186 +	3,087	= 292,600
II	98,876 +	54,024 +	38,909 +	12,414 +	2,701	= 204,924
	266,000 +	115,762 +	83,374 +	26,600 +	5,788	= 497,524

The numbers which Marx uses in the second volume of *Capital* in his presentation of the reproduction-process are arbitrarily selected and not without contradictions. This is easily explained by the fact that Engels found this part of Marx's work unfinished in his literary remains. But because Marx did not present his train of thought impeccably, it does not follow that this train of thought is false. Rosa Luxemburg is content to demonstrate the arbitrary nature of the Marxian models, and she seems to believe that without the arbitrariness the models would be entirely untenable. We prefer to look for a satisfactory clarification of Marx's train of thought and to conduct our own investigation with a model which is free from arbitrariness. Hence we have presented here *models which, once one accepts the assumptions, have nothing else arbitrary about them, and whose magnitudes are actually derived, one from the other, with compelling necessity.*

Only the assumptions made in the first year are arbitrary: that constant capital amounts to 200,000 and variable capital to 180,000; that variable capital is divided equally between the two departments of production; that the rate of surplus-value is 100 per cent; and that the rate of accumulation is the same in both departments. Also arbitrary is the assumption that constant capital grows at an annual rate of 10 per cent, and variable capital at 5 per cent. But if these assumptions are accepted, all the magnitudes presented in the model follow from them with mathematical necessity. Development cannot proceed differently, so long as the rate of surplus-value remains unchanged and the rate of accumulation stays the same in both departments. With our model we thus obtained an impeccable basis for investigating the problem posed by Comrade Luxemburg.

The realisation of surplus-value

From Table 7 above we now wish to discover whether the mass of commodities in which the accumulated part of surplus-value (κ + β) is embodied can be sold within the capitalist world itself, or whether, as Comrade Luxemburg believes, it can find a market only outside the capitalist world.

To begin with we investigate the sale of commodities in the first year. In the means-of-production industries, commodities with a value of 220,000 are produced in the first year. Who buys these commodities? First of all, the capitalists in the means-of-production industries themselves need new means of production. They meet part of this requirement by using means of production from their own factories for the renewal or extension of their factories. Thus the coal-mines themselves need coal to heat their steam boilers, and the ironworks themselves require iron to renew or extend their productive capacity. Another part of the requirements is met by purchases inside the means-of-production industries. Hence ironworks buy coal from the mines, the mines buy machines from the machine-factories, and the machine-factories buy iron from the ironworks. Now, how large is the total requirement of the means-of-production industries for new means of production? The constant capital used up in production must first be replaced: to this end the capitalists in the means-of-production industries have to use means of production with a value of 120,000. In addition, however, the capitalists wish to use the surplus-value which they accumulated in the first year to extend their existing factories or to establish new ones. If in the next year they wish to employ a capital which is 12,500 larger, they must this year build new workplaces, buy new machines, and increase their stocks of raw materials, so that the labour-force which they will engage at the beginning of the next year will find the necessary instruments of labour ready for them. To this end they must buy from each other means of production with a value of 10,000. Thus of the means of production produced in Department I (with a value of 220,000) a total of 130,000 are sold within this department itself: (i) 120,000 for the renewal of productive capacity; (ii) 10,000 for the extension of productive capacity for the next year. But what happens to the remaining means of production, with a value of 90,000?

First, the capitalists in the consumer-goods industries have to buy means of production with a value of 80,000, in order to renew the means of production used up in the first year. But in addition the capitalists in the consumer-goods industries must this year build workplaces, buy machines, and expand their stock of raw materials, because they wish to carry on production next year on an extended scale. To this end, Department II buys from Department I means of production with a value of 5,334. Thus in total the capitalists in the consumer-goods industries buy means of production, for the production of consumer goods, amounting to 85,334. Hence, only 4,666 worth of means of production remain unsold. Where do they find a market?

The capitalists in the consumer-goods industries transfer part of the surplus-value accumulated in the first year to the means-of-production industries – either by themselves establishing factories for the production of means of production, or by transferring part of their accumulated surplus-value, through the mediation of the banks, for use of the capitalists in the means-of-production industries;[19] or through buying shares in companies which produce means of production. If the productive capacity of Department I is to be extended in this way in the next year, the elements of this productive capacity (workplaces, machines, raw materials) must already be purchased this year. Thus the means-of-production industries buy commodities with a value of 4,666 with that capital which was accumulated in the consumer-goods industries but is to be invested in the means-of-production industries. And so the capitalists in the consumer-goods industries buy, in addition to means of production with a value of 85,334 for use in the production of consumer goods,[20] additional means of production with a value of 4,666 destined for the production of means of production.

19. [The original reads 'consumer-goods industries'.]
20. [The original reads 'means of production'.]

Thus, all in all, the means of production produced in the first year are sold in this manner:

Table 8

1. To capitalists in the means-of-production industries:	
a. For the renewal of productive capacity in I:	120,000
b. For the extension of productive capacity in I:	10,000
Total	130,000
1. To the capitalists in the consumer-goods industries:	
a. For the renewal of productive capacity in II:	10,000
b. For the extension of productive capacity in II:	5,334
c. For the extension of productive capacity in I:	4,666
Total	90,000

And so the whole mass of commodities produced in Department I is sold, in its entirety.

Now, how does the sale of consumer goods take place? To simplify our investigation, we first assume that the entire working class lives in company houses (houses owned by the industrial capitalists) and do all their shopping in company-stores (stores owned by the industrial capitalists). In this case all the consumer goods which are produced come into the hands of the industrial capitalists: one part to be consumed by them, the other to be sold by them to the workers.

In the first year the value of the commodities produced by the consumer-goods industries amounts to 180,000. A part of these commodities is used in the consumer-goods industries themselves. First, commodities with a value of 37,500 are consumed by the capitalists of the consumer-goods industries themselves. In addition the capitalists in the consumer-goods industries must supply part of their commodities to their company-stores, so that they can be sold to the workers in Department II. Now, how large must this part be? The income of the workers in II amounts to 50,000 in the first year and to 51,333 in the second year. Thus the capitalists in II must supply 51,333 out of the product of the first year to their company-stores, so that the necessary stock of food will be ready for the workers in the second year. Hence, from the product of Department II, 37,500 + 51,333 = 88,833 are sold within this Department itself.

The capitalists in the means-of-production industries must buy commodities from the consumer-goods industries. For their own needs they require consumer goods with a value of 37,500. Apart from this they need to buy commodities for their company-stores. In the first year the income of the workers in Department I amounts to 50,000. This will be increased to 52,500 in the second year through the addition of the accumulated surplus-value. The capitalists in I must thus buy 52,500 from the first year's product of II for their company-stores, so that the latter can supply the needs of the workers in the second year. Thus the total requirement of the capitalists in the means-of-production industries amounts to 37,500 + 52,500 = 90,000 consumer goods.

Finally the capitalists in II use part of the surplus-value they have accumulated for the construction of new factories, in which means of production are produced. These factories too must establish company stores, which have to buy part of the consumer goods produced in the first year in order to supply the requirements of the workers employed in the new factories in the second year. They purchase consumer goods with a value of 1,167.

Consequently the consumer goods purchased in the first year are sold as:

Table 9

1. To capitalists in the means-of-production industries:	
a. For their own needs:	37,500
b. For the company-stores:	52,500
Total	90,000
1. To the capitalists in the consumer-goods industries:	
a. For their own needs:	37,500
b. For the company-stores in II:	51,333
c. For the company-stores in I:	1,167
Total	90,000

Thus the entire mass of commodities produced in Department II is sold. At the same time we see from this description that the capitalists in the consumer-goods industries buy means of production with a value of 90,000 from the means-of-production industries and sell them consumer goods with the same value. The transactions between the two departments consist of the exchange of consumer goods with a value of 90,000 for means of production of 90,000. In consequence the entire value of the product of both departments, and hence also the total surplus-value, is realised.

Up to now we have assumed that the sale of commodities is undertaken by the industrial capitalists themselves; that the industrial capitalists themselves accumulate stocks of commodities and sell them to the workers. But in essence nothing changes in the entire process if this function is taken over by a special capital – if *commercial capital* takes the place of the commodity capital of the industrial capitalists. In this case the following changes occur: (i) merchants rather than company-stores buy the commodities, and (ii) part of commodity capital is in the hands of the merchants rather than the industrial capitalists, who share their surplus-value with them; to the extent to which this occurs, the demand of the merchants replaces the demand for commodities from the industrial capitalists. The total consumer power of society remains unaffected by this. In this case too the entire surplus-value is realised.

In the same way, one can convince oneself, using Table 7, that not only in the first year but also in every subsequent year the entire value of the product of both departments is sold without any disturbance, and the total surplus-value is realised. Comrade Luxemburg's hypothesis that the accumulated part of surplus-value could not be realised is thus false. How was it possible for Comrade Luxemburg to arrive at this false hypothesis?

We have assumed *that in the first year the capitalists buy those means of production which will be set in motion by the growth of the work force in the second year, and that they buy in the first year those consumer goods which they will sell in the second year to the additional work-force.* Hence a part of the product of labour in the first year will be sold for use in the second year as additional productive capital. If we do not accept this assumption, the realisation in the first year of the surplus-value produced in that year would in fact be impossible, and sales would then be as shown in

Table 10

Sales of means of production	
To renew constant capital in I	120,000
To renew constant capital in II	80,000
Total	200,000
Sales of consumer goods	
To the capitalists in I	37,500
To the workers in I	50,000
To the capitalists in II	37,500
To the workers in II	50,000
Total	175,000

In this case, in fact, means of production amounting to 20,000 and consumer-goods amounting to 5,000 remain unsalable. It would actually be precisely that part of surplus-value destined for accumulation (κ + β) which could not be realised.

Rosa Luxemburg believes that the accumulated part of surplus-value cannot be realised. In fact it cannot be realised *in the first year*, if the material elements of additional productive capital (new workplaces, machines, raw materials, consumer goods for the increased labour-force) are sold only in the second year. But they *must* finally be sold, if not in the first then certainly in the second year; for otherwise the extension of productive capacity and the productive investment of the newly formed capital is impossible. And as soon as they are sold, the hitherto only latent part of the surplus-value produced in the first year will be realised.

Marx presents the circulation of capital in the following way:[21]

$$G - W \begin{cases} Pm \\ A \end{cases} \ldots P \ldots W_1 - G_1$$

Now we can divide W_1 into three parts: $W_1 = W + w + w_1$, where W is equal to the cost-price ($c + v$), w to the consumed and w_1, to the accumulated part of surplus-value. We then obtain the following picture:

$$G - W \begin{cases} Pm \\ A \end{cases} \ldots P \ldots \begin{pmatrix} W \\ + \\ w \\ + \\ w_1 \end{pmatrix} - \begin{pmatrix} G \\ + \\ g \\ + \\ g_1 \end{pmatrix}$$

After the conclusion of the production-process, circulation is divided into three partial processes. And of course the time required for the conversion of the produced commodities into money can be divided only between these three partial processes. So long as only the process $W - G$ is concluded, absolutely no surplus-value is realised, but only the cost-price. Once the process

21. [The capitalist begins with a sum of money (*G*: Geld). He purchases commodities (*W*: Waren) of equivalent value, consisting of means of production (*Pm*: Produktionsmittel) and labour-power (*A*: Arbeitskraft). In the course of the production-process (*P*: Produktion) they are converted into qualitatively different commodities of greater value (W1>W). Finally, they are sold for a sum of money equivalent to their value (G1>G). The standard English notation (with *C*, *M*, etc.) has not been adopted here, to avoid confusion with symbols used by Bauer elsewhere in the article.]

$(W + w) - (G + g)$ is completed, the consumed but not the accumulated part of surplus-value is realised. The accumulated part of surplus-value can be realised only in the instant in which *w1* is converted into *g1*; in other words, only in the instant when those commodities are sold in which the accumulated part of surplus-value is embodied – those commodities, that is, which constitute the material elements of the additional productive capital for the next production period.

Thus, it can actually occur that only the consumed and not the accumulated part of surplus-value is realised; it will occur if $(W + w)$ *has already been converted into* $(G + g)$*, but w1 has not yet been converted into g1*. But this phenomenon is only *a transient phase* in the whole circulation-process. To the extent to which the productive investment of newly formed capital takes place, the accumulated part of surplus-value will be realised. Thus, if $(W + w)$ is converted into $(G + g)$ in the first year, while *w1*, produced in the first year can be changed into *g1* only in the second year, then of course only the consumed part of surplus-value can be realised in the first year. That part of surplus-value produced in the first year and destined for accumulation is not, however, unrealised; it too will be realised, but only in the course of the second year.

The *surplus-product* which is produced in the first year consists of two parts: (i) *consumer goods* for the capitalists, and (ii) *the material elements of additional productive capital*. As soon as the first component is sold, the consumed part of surplus-value is realised; as soon as the second component is sold, the accumulated part of surplus-value is realised. It is impossible to realise that part of surplus-value denoted by *k* first, and only later to supply consumer goods to the capitalists: the realisation of *k* takes place precisely through the sale of the first component of the surplus product. It is equally impossible to realise the $(\kappa + \beta)$ part of surplus-value *first*, and only later to buy the material elements of additional productive capital: the realisation of $(\kappa + \beta)$ occurs precisely in the sale of the second component of the surplus product. Thus it is not at all strange that Rosa Luxemburg cannot realise $(\kappa + \beta)$ in the first year, for she assumes that capitalists buy the material elements of additional productive capital only in the second year. Realisation of $(\kappa + \beta)$, and productive use of the surplus-product in which $(\kappa + \beta)$ is embodied, are two aspects of the same phenomenon. They can only occur *simultaneously*. The whole difficulty arises only if it is assumed that the selling period of the commodities in which the accumulated surplus-value is embodied is longer than the selling period of the other commodities. In reality, of course, the circulation time of individual capitals and its division into purchase-, production-, and selling periods varies considerably. Marx had to ignore these differences and assume the annual product to be sold within each year, so that he could set out the reproduction of capital in a simple model. But even if we disregard this assumption of the Marxian model, we obtain no other result than the unsurprising conclusion that part of the surplus-value produced each year is realised only in the course of the following year.

Comrade Luxemburg believes that the commodities in which (κ + β) is embodied must be sold outside the capitalist world for the realisation of the surplus-value contained in them to be possible. Well, what sort of commodities are they? They are the very means of production which the capitalists need to expand their productive capacity, and the very consumer goods which are required to feed the growth in the work-force. If these commodities were to be ejected from the capitalist world, production on an extended scale in the following year would be altogether impossible; there would be neither the necessary means of production for the extension of productive capacity nor the food supplies required to feed an increased work force. *The withdrawal of this part of the surplus-product from the capitalist market would not, as Rosa Luxemburg believes, make accumulation possible; on the contrary, it would make any accumulation impossible.*

In reality the accumulated part of surplus-value is also realised within capitalist society. Of course this realisation generally comes about step by step. For example, the food used in the second year to feed the additional work-force is probably as a rule produced in the first year and sold by the producers to wholesale capital; a part of the surplus-value embodied in this food is thus already realised in the first year. The realisation of the other part of this surplus-value then occurs only in the course of the second year, with the sale of the food by wholesalers to small shopkeepers and by the latter to the workers. Naturally the model cannot include all the details of this process. But these details alter nothing in the process as a whole. Whatever the idiosyncrasies in the circulation of individual capitals, the fact remains that the realisation of (κ + β) takes place simultaneously with the productive investment of the newly formed capital. Expressed more clearly, the former occurs in and through the latter. To that extent our model gives a true picture of reality. It proves that the accumulated part of surplus-value can also be realised within the capitalist sphere itself.

Underaccumulation and overaccumulation

Our model (Table [7]) assumes that (i) the work force grows at 5 per cent per annum, (ii) variable capital grows at the same rate as the work-force, and (iii) constant capital grows faster than variable, to the extent required by technical progress. On these assumptions it is not surprising that no difficulty arises in realising surplus-value. The workers' capacity to consume grows in this case at the same rate as their numbers. The capacity to consume of the capitalists grows equally fast, for with the number of workers, the mass of surplus-value also grows. Thus, the capacity to consume of the whole society increases at the same rate as the value of the product. Accumulation changes nothing in this; it means only that less of consumer goods and more means of production are needed than in simple reproduction. The extension of the area of production, which is a precondition of accumulation, is here given by the growth of the population.

However, this equilibrium-condition between accumulation and population-growth can be maintained only if the rate of accumulation grows sufficiently rapidly that, despite the increasing organic composition of capital, variable capital increases at the same rate as the population (Table 3 above). If the increase in the rate of accumulation falls behind this requirement, the growth of variable capital will lag behind the increase in those seeking work. The condition which then arises can be termed *underaccumulation*.

The first effect of underaccumulation is the formation of an *industrial reserve-army*. Part of the increased population remains unemployed. Unemployed proletarians exert pressure on wages. *Wages fall and the rate of surplus-value rises*. Since in a society consisting only of capitalists and workers the unemployed proletarians can find no source of income other than wages, wages must fall and the rate of surplus-value must rise, until the entire working population finds employment despite the relatively reduced variable capital. The change in the distribution of the value of the product which thus occurs is brought about by the fact that, with the increase in the organic composition of capital in which technical progress is expressed, *the value of labour-power has declined*, so that *relative surplus-value* has been created.

If, with an unchanged rate of accumulation, the rate of surplus-value has increased, then the accumulated part of surplus-value will also have risen. Thus the mass of surplus-value used to increase variable capital grows too. It must continue to increase on this course *until equilibrium between the growth of variable capital and the growth of population is restored*.

I term the ratio between the accumulated part of surplus-value and the total surplus-value the *capitalist rate of accumulation*, and the ratio between the accumulated part of surplus-value and the value of the total product (variable capital plus surplus-value) the *social rate of accumulation*.[22] We can thus present in the following way the mechanism through which underaccumulation is repeatedly generated. If the social rate of accumulation is too small, an industrial reserve-army comes into existence. Wages fall and the rate of surplus-value increases. Hence the social rate of accumulation also increases, even with an unchanged capitalist rate of accumulation; for, with the same capitalist rate of accumulation, the social rate of accumulation grows with the rate of surplus-value. Under the pressure of the industrial reserve-army the rate of surplus-value increases and with it the social rate of accumulation, until the latter has become large enough for variable capital to grow at the same rate as the work-force, in spite of the increasing organic composition. Once this occurs, the industrial reserve-army is absorbed and equilibrium between accumulation and population-growth is restored.

Thus the capitalist mode of production contains within itself the mechanism which, when accumulation lags behind population-growth, adjusts it to population-growth once more. But this adjustment takes place at the expense of the working class. It comes about through an increase in the rate of exploitation. Again and again the progress to a higher organic composition of capital causes underaccumulation; again and again it is overcome by the increase in the rate of surplus-value. It is a *periodically recurring* but always only a *transient phase in the industrial cycle.*

Eventually the rising social rate of accumulation reaches a point at which variable capital grows faster than the population. We term the situation in which this occurs *overaccumulation*. But, like underaccumulation, overaccumulation too is always just a transient phase in the industrial cycle.

Marx describes the situation of overaccumulation in the following way:

> Once capital grows so fast that neither the absolute labour time nor the relative surplus labour time performed by this population can be increased (the latter would anyway be impossible in a case where the demand for labour was so strong that wages tended to rise); thus where the increased capi-

22. Up to now, when I have referred to the rate of accumulation, I have always meant the capitalist rate of accumulation.

> tal can produce only the same or even a lower mass of surplus-value than before, absolute overproduction will occur. In other words, the increased capital C + ΔC will produce no more profit, or even less, than before its expansion by ΔC. In both cases there will be a sharp and sudden fall in the general rate of profit, but this time because of a change in the composition of capital due not to the development of productivity but to an increase in the money value of variable capital (on account of increased wages) and the corresponding decline in the ratio of surplus to necessary labour.[23]

This point indicates the *absolute limit of accumulation*. When it is reached, the adjustment of accumulation to population-growth results in a devastating crisis with massive unemployment of capital, wholesale destruction of values, and a sudden fall in the rate of profit.

In reality the adjustment can take place before the absolute limit described by Marx is reached. If the rate of accumulation is too large, the reserve-army is quickly absorbed, wages rise, the rate of surplus-value falls, and with it the social rate of accumulation, thereby slowing down the growth of variable capital once more and achieving the adjustment of accumulation to population-growth.

Moreover in a situation of overaccumulation the rate of profit falls very quickly. The rate of profit declines as a result of the progress towards a higher organic composition of capital, even if accumulation and population-growth are in equilibrium. It falls even faster if the progress towards a higher organic composition of capital is accompanied by a declining rate of surplus-value, as is the case with overaccumulation. In the moment 'in which the above-mentioned tendencies for the rate of profit to decline assert themselves against the tendencies which, because of increasing demand, have caused a rise in prices and profits, the crisis begins.'[24] In the crisis and the resulting industrial depression, the rate of accumulation is drastically reduced and the growth of variable capital once again lags behind population-growth.

Like underaccumulation, overaccumulation is also generated again and again by the mechanism of the capitalist mode of production itself. There exists, in the capitalist mode of production, *a tendency for the adjustment of capital-accumulation to the growth of population*. This adjustment has occurred as

23. Marx 1962, pp. 246–7.
24. Hilferding 1910a, p. 823.

soon as variable capital grows at the same rate as the work-force; but constant capital grows faster to an extent required by the development of productivity. In a socialist society the social organs responsible for the control of production would ensure, consciously and according to a plan, that the growth of population is provided for. This adjustment must also occur in capitalist society, but here it can take place only by means of great crises, with unemployment, wage-reductions, and increasing exploitation on the one hand, and unemployment of capital, destruction of values, and a declining rate of profit on the other.

The tendency for accumulation to adjust to population-growth also dominates international relations. Each year countries with continuous overaccumulation invest a large and growing part of their accumulated surplus-value overseas. Examples: France and England. Countries with continuous underaccumulation attract capital from abroad and send labour overseas. Examples: the agrarian countries of Eastern Europe. *The expansion of productive capital within a country itself is always restricted by the available work-force.* In the long run variable capital can grow no faster than the population, while constant capital always grows faster than variable to a degree determined by the stage of development of the forces of production. Thus one can appreciate the anxiety of the capitalists over the declining birth-rate: decelerating population-growth narrows the limits to the growth of their capital.

Viewing the capitalist world economy as a whole, the tendency for accumulation to adjust to population-growth is apparent in the industrial cycle. Prosperity is overaccumulation, which destroys itself in the crisis. The ensuing depression is a time of underaccumulation which also brings itself to an end, inasmuch as the depression itself produces the conditions for renewed prosperity. *The periodic alternation of prosperity, crisis, and depression is the empirical expression of the fact that the mechanism of the capitalist mode of production automatically generates overaccumulation and underaccumulation, with the accumulation of capital adjusting again and again to the growth of population.*

The individual capitalist believes that it depends only on his 'abstinence' as to what part of surplus-value he 'saves'. In reality capitalists are taught in every crisis that objective limits are set to their accumulation; that capital can be increased only to the extent that society is able to increase its productive capacity. Given the stage of development of the forces of production, the objective limit to accumulation is determined by the growth of the work-force.

Accumulation presupposes an expansion in the area of production; and the area of production is increased by population-growth. 'An *increasing population* appears to be the basis of accumulation as a continuous process.'[25] If population-growth were to cease altogether, variable capital could no longer be permanently increased; accumulation would then be possible only to the extent that the development of the forces of production required additional constant capital to employ an unchanged labour-force.

Comrade Luxemburg knows that there are objective limits to the accumulation of capital. But she sets these limits incorrectly. Comrade Luxemburg believes that the accumulation of capital would be altogether impossible in a capitalist economy which could not sell its commodities in peasant or petit-bourgeois areas. This view is false. Every society with a growing population must extend its productive capacity. Under the capitalist mode of production the extension of productive capacity assumes the particular form of the accumulation of capital. This accumulation takes place without disturbance so long as it maintains a definite quantitative relationship on the one hand with population-growth, on the other with the development of productivity which expresses itself in the progress towards a higher organic composition of capital. Of course, again and again the development of accumulation pushes ahead of these limits; but again and again accumulation is brought back within them through periodic recurrent economic crises. The result of our investigation is thus (i) that the accumulation of capital is possible even in an isolated capitalist economy, so long as it does not exceed a fixed limit at any particular time, and (ii) that it is brought back automatically to this limit through the mechanism of the capitalist mode of production itself.

This formulation cannot be interpreted as an apology for capitalism, for while the apologists for capital want to demonstrate the unbounded nature of accumulation – capacity to consume rises automatically with production! – we uncover the limit to accumulation. While the apologists wish to prove the impossibility of general crises, we show that the laws of accumulation can only operate through general crises and the consequent unemployment, wage-reductions, increasing mass-suffering, and growing bitterness and indignation among the mass of the workers.

25. Marx 1968–72, II, p. 477.

The explanation of imperialism

Comrade Luxemburg explains imperialism in the following way. In an isolated capitalist society, the conversion of surplus-value into capital would be impossible. It becomes possible only if the capitalists constantly extend their market in order to sell, in areas where there is not already capitalist production, that part of the surplus-product in which the accumulated part of surplus-value is embodied. Imperialism serves this purpose.

As we have seen, this explanation is incorrect. Accumulation is also possible, and necessary, in an isolated capitalist society. And that part of the surplus-product in which the accumulated surplus-value is embodied cannot be sold to the peasants and petit bourgeois of the colonies, because it is needed in the capitalist motherland itself to extend productive capacity.

But a kernel of truth is concealed in the false explanation. While accumulation in an isolated capitalist society is not impossible, it is nevertheless confined within limits. Imperialism does in fact serve to widen these limits.

Accumulation is limited, first, by the growth of the work-force. Now imperialism greatly increases the working masses who are compelled to sell their labour-power to capital. It does so by undermining the old modes of production in colonial territories, thereby forcing millions of people either to emigrate to capitalist areas or to work in their own homelands for the European or American capital invested there. Since – with a given organic composition of capital – the extent of accumulation is fixed by the growth of the available work-force, imperialism is thus in fact a means of further expanding the limits of accumulation.

Besides the growth in population, the extent of accumulation is determined by the development of the forces of production, by the progress to a higher organic composition of capital. Imperialism can also stimulate this development: firstly, since it gives special encouragement to those branches of production with an above-average organic composition of capital; secondly, since it places at the disposal of capital material elements of production situated outside its homeland and thereby powerfully accelerates the development of the forces of production and the increased productivity of labour.

The adjustment of accumulation to population-growth is accomplished through periodic crises. In every crisis huge masses of commodities are unsalable, and a large part of productive capital lies fallow. Crises are more easily overcome if it is possible to sell vast quantities of commodities in new sales areas. Imperialism seeks to make this, too, possible for capital.

If imperialism is not a means of making accumulation possible in the first place, it is however a means of stretching its limits and facilitating the overcoming of the crises which periodically result from overaccumulation. This effort is in fact one root of imperialism, though not the only one.

In Comrade Luxemburg's view capitalism could not exist at all without continuous expansion. If a barrier were set to the growth of its markets a large part of surplus-value could not be realised, and it would break down of its own accord.

In our opinion capitalism is conceivable even without expansion. But with or without expansion, capitalism itself causes its own downfall. If its expansion is possible, it arouses indignation among the working masses through an arms-race, through increasingly oppressive taxation, and through catastrophic wars. If its expansion is prevented, the limit to accumulation is narrowed and crises become more frequent, longer, more devastating. In either case, a growing part of the popular masses recognise that their life interests are incompatible with the continuation of the capitalist mode of production.

Capitalism will not founder on the mechanical impossibility of realising surplus-value. It will succumb to the indignation to which it drives the masses. Capitalism will break down, not when the last peasant and the last petit bourgeois on the entire earth are converted into wage-labourers, so that no extra market is open to capitalism. It will be brought down much sooner, by the growing 'indignation of the working class, constantly increasing, schooled, united, and organised by the mechanism of the capitalist production process itself'.[26]

26. [In Chapter 32 of the first volume of *Capital*, 'The Historical Tendency of Capitalist Accumulation', Marx wrote: 'Along with the constant decrease in the number of capitalist magnates, who usurp and monopolize all the advantages of this process of transformation, the mass of misery, oppression, slavery, degradation and exploitation grows; but with this there also grows the revolt of the working class, a class constantly increasing in numbers, and trained, united and organized by the very mechanism of the capitalist process of production.' Marx 1961, p. 763. Marx 1976, pp. 784–5.]

Chapter Forty-Six

'Review of Rosa Luxemburg, *The Accumulation of Capital: A Contribution to the Economic Explanation of Imperialism*' (1914)

Franz Mehring

Unlike Rudolf Hilferding's *Finance Capital*, which was greeted with almost universal acclaim (with the exception of the revisionist right wing of Social Democracy), Rosa Luxemburg's *Accumulation of Capital* was favourably reviewed only by the tiny fraction of SPD left wingers that later grouped around the Berlin Internationale group, notably Julian Marchlewski-Karski, Franz Mehring and Paul Lensch.[1] Most reviewers dismissed her main argument as erroneous; they included prominent representatives of the centre-fraction in Germany and Austria, such as Gustav Eckstein and Otto Bauer, but also some of the main figures of the international left wing – notably Anton Pannekoek and Lenin. Franz Mehring's review in *Grünbergs Archiv* was little more than a summary of the controversy over Luxemburg's work, though he distinctly took her side, describing her book as 'the most significant phenomenon in socialist literature since Marx and Engels took up the pen'.[2] He returned to his subject, in a less restrained mood, in the notes to his biography of Marx, first published in 1918:

1. Mehring 1913a, Marchlewski 1913, Marchlewski and Mehring 1913.
2. Mehring 1914, p. 356.

> The huge literature about this classic work [*Das Kapital*] is more remarkable for its volume than for its content, and this applies not only to Marx's opponents. The nearest approach to the original in breadth of knowledge, brilliance of style, logical incisiveness of analysis and independence of thought, while at the same time extending scientific knowledge beyond its limits, is Rosa Luxemburg's *The Accumulation of Capital: A Contribution to the Economic Explanation of Imperialism* (Berlin, 1913). The way in which this book has been attacked, particularly by the so-called Austro-Marxists (Eckstein, Hilferding, etc.), represents one of the crowning achievements of Marxist priesthood.[3]

* * *

'Review of Rosa Luxemburg, *The Accumulation of Capital: A Contribution to an Economic Explanation of Imperialism*'[4]

Although the book is only a few months old, it already has its history and a very eventful one. Written from a Marxist point of view, it has become the object of spirited debates in Marxist circles. While some reject the work as a complete failure, even denouncing it as a worthless compilation, others consider it the most significant phenomenon in socialist literature since Marx and Engels took up the pen.

This reviewer belongs completely to the second group. He sees in this book a work that, in terms of breadth of knowledge, brilliance of style, logical incisiveness of analysis, and independence of thought can stand more than any other right alongside the works of Marx and Engels. However, he considers it his duty to report in these pages about the controversy around Rosa Luxemburg's work by letting the author and her most noteworthy antagonists speak with their own words as far as possible.

The book deals with an old problem of political economy, which has been discussed often and from many sides for a hundred years in France, England, Germany and Russia. How does the accumulation and enlarged reproduction of the entire social capital take place?

Neither simple nor enlarged reproduction is a peculiarity of capitalist society. Both take place in any human society, as soon as men's mastery of nature

3. Mehring 1918, p. 548.
4. Mehring 1914, pp. 356–61.

reaches a level enabling a regular cycle of production and consumption. When a production-period elapses, the raw materials, tools and labour-power must be there for a new production-period to begin. And this new production-period must proceed on an enlarged scale if historical development is to take place.

But, in capitalist society, simple and enlarged reproduction assume a special form. Under capitalism, production is not at all carried out for social purposes and according to a plan. Instead, countless individuals produce on their own initiative, not in order to satisfy social wants but in order to obtain surplus-value. The production of surplus-value is the driving force of the capitalist mode of production. The single capitalist throws a certain amount of capital into the production process in order to extract surplus-value. He employs that surplus-value partly in order to satisfy his own wants and partly to add to his capital, to produce surplus-value on a larger scale. That is by no means left to his own discretion, but is a question of life and death for him. In the general competitive struggle, the individual producers can only survive through constant expansion of their production: a standstill would be economic death for them.

That is how the accumulation of capital, which, in capitalist society, constitutes the foundation of enlarged reproduction, takes place, and, in this respect, there is no dispute, at least among Marxists. But, then, the question arises: Who are the buyers for the accumulated surplus-value? Although the satisfaction of social needs is not the goal of capitalist production, it is, nevertheless, its premise. The capitalised part of the surplus-value initially consists of goods that must be sold, turned into cash, if it is to be invested again in the production-process. From the point of view of the entire social capital, neither the capitalists nor the working class can provide the necessary buyers. The capitalists will not do it, because that is precisely the part of the surplus-value that they do not want to consume, but to capitalise. The workers cannot do it (even if the goods that the individual worker buys from the capitalists turn part of the surplus-value into cash), because even with the highest wages they cannot, as a class, pay back to the capitalists a single cent more than what was advanced to them by the capitalists from their capital.

Some people have attempted to solve this problem by pointing out the mass of 'third persons' – those strata of the population that are to be found in capitalist society alongside capitalists and proletarians: the liberal professions, physicians, lawyers, artists, priests, civil servants, soldiers and the like. 'King, priest, professor, prostitute, mercenary', as Marx, who already disposed of this objection himself, said in his dramatic way.[5] All those social strata cannot furnish the necessary demand for the enlargement of production, because they are themselves fed by capitalist society: they are joint consumers either of the surplus-value or of the wages.[6] Nor does reference to foreign trade answer the question; it only displaces it from one country to the other. This difficult problem has occupied political economy for a century. The author describes the history of the problem in a clear and attractive way in the second section of her book: the clashes in France and England between Sismondi and Ricardo and the Ricardians, in Germany between Rodbertus and Kirchmann, in Russia between the 'Populists' Vorontsov and Nikolayon on the one hand and the 'legal Marxists' Struve, Bulgakov and Tugan-Baranovsky on the other. She herself begins her exposition in the first chapter of her book with the solution that Marx thought he had found to this problem.

In order to grasp the problem in its pure form, Marx proceeded from the assumption that the capitalist mode of production ruled exclusively over the earth and that, accordingly, the only representatives of social consumption were the capitalists and the workers. Marx then separated capitalist production into two departments: the production of means of production and the production of consumption goods, and he tried to demonstrate by means of mathematical diagrams that the reproduction of capital can take place if certain quantitative proportions exist between both departments of production. Those proportions would be established by crises, which Marx did not consider a consequence of accidental disproportions between both departments, but, rather, inevitable phases in the reproduction of capital, because only through those crises could the necessary quantitative proportions between

5. Marx 1978b, p. 372.

6. ['All such "third persons" who are certainly not lacking in any capitalist society are, as far as economics is concerned, joint consumers of the surplus value for the greater part, in so far, namely, as they are not also joint consumers of the wages of labour. These groups can only derive their purchasing power either from the wages of the proletariat or from the surplus value, if not from both; but on the whole, they are to be regarded as joint consumers of the surplus value. It follows that their consumption is already included in the consumption of the capitalist class, and if Struve tries to reintroduce them to the capitalists by sleight-of-hand as "third persons" to save the situation and help to realise the surplus value, the shrewd profiteer will not be taken in. He will see at once that this great public is nothing but his old familiar retinue of parasites who buy his commodities with money of his own providing. No, no, indeed! Struve's "third persons" will not do at all.' Luxemburg 1921, p. 295.]

both departments of social production be established. It must be remarked, however, that the chapter in the second volume of *Capital* dealing with this question consisted only of fragments, of annotations for self-reflection, of drafts that Marx himself described as 'very much in need of revision'.[7]

The author then demonstrates in detail that Marx actually could not overcome the difficulties of the problem. She objects to Marx's diagrams that, even if they were correct mathematically, they would not necessarily be correct economically. She believes that the solution of the problem does not depend on mathematical equations, which can produce astonishingly smooth results on paper, but on the concrete social conditions in which the accumulation of capital takes place. The author argues that the question, in the way Marx put it, cannot be solved. Capitalism would be impossible under the premise that the capitalist production-process rules everywhere and that capitalist society is divided into two sharply demarcated classes, wage-workers producing surplus-value and capitalists appropriating it. As an economic form ruling absolutely on its own, capitalism would be unthinkable because it would lack the possibility of turning into cash the surplus-value contained in the products.

The author thinks that she found the solution of the problem (in contradiction with a single chapter in Marx's *Capital* but in harmony with the rest of his teachings, as well as with historical development and the daily experience of the capitalist mode of production) in the dialectical contradiction by which capitalist accumulation requires non-capitalist formations as its environment: accumulation takes place in constant metabolism with these surroundings and can only exist if it finds them. The existence of non-capitalist buyers of the surplus-value is thus, according to Rosa Luxemburg, a direct primary condition for the existence of capital and its accumulation; as an historical process, capital-accumulation depends, in every respect, on non-capitalist social forms and strata.

In the third section of her book, the author draws the proof of her thesis from history. She distinguishes three phases: the struggle of capital against natural economy, its struggle against peasant-economy, and its competitive struggle on the world stage over the remains of the conditions for accumulation.

7. ['The third section which treats of the reproduction of total capital is merely a collection of fragments which Marx himself considered to be "very much in need of revision".' Engels's introduction to the second volume of *Capital*, quoted in Luxemburg 1921, p. 169.]

The fate of the Indians, of Algiers, Egypt, America and China shows how capital-accumulation carves out for itself ever-larger elbowroom (as indeed it must do according to its conditions of life) by breaking down non-capitalist social forms, either destroying them by force or disintegrating them through commodity-imports, indebtedness, and the establishment of factories – therewith, however, digging its own grave.

The third phase is the historical period of imperialism. Its specific procedures are: foreign investments, railway-construction, revolutions and wars. The last decade, from 1900 to 1910, is characteristic of the world motion of capitalism, particularly in Asia and in the parts of Europe adjacent to Asia (Russia, Turkey and Persia), as well as in Japan and North Africa. The author summarises her views as follows:

> Imperialism is the political expression of the accumulation of capital in its competitive struggle for what remains still open of the non-capitalist environment. Still the largest part of the world in terms of geography, this remaining field for the expansion of capital is yet insignificant as against the high level of development already attained by the productive forces of capital; witness the immense masses of capital accumulated in the old countries which seek an outlet for their surplus-product and strive to capitalise their surplus-value, and the rapid change-over to capitalism of the pre-capitalist civilisations. On the international stage, then, capital must take appropriate measures. With the high development of the capitalist countries and their increasingly severe competition in acquiring non-capitalist areas, imperialism grows in lawlessness and violence, both in aggression against the non-capitalist world and in ever more serious conflicts among the competing capitalist countries. But the more violently, ruthlessly and thoroughly imperialism brings about the decline of non-capitalist civilisations, the more rapidly it cuts the very ground from under the feet of capitalist accumulation. Though imperialism is the historical method for prolonging the career of capitalism, it is also a sure means of bringing it to a swift conclusion. This is not to say that capitalist development must be actually driven to this extreme: the mere tendency towards imperialism of itself takes forms which make the final phase of capitalism a period of catastrophe.[8]

8. Luxemburg 1921, p. 446.

Those are the leading ideas of Rosa Luxemburg's book – of course, only in their most general outlines. The refutations it met with are, for the most part, untenable from a Marxist point of view. The objection that imperialism is not an internal necessity of the capitalist mode of production but a fortuitous fact amounts to a repudiation of the Marxist world-view as a whole. To be sure, some critics conversely proceeded from a Marxist point of view, denying that the capitalist machine will work until the last petty bourgeois and the last peasant are turned into wage-workers and then suddenly come to a halt, but the long paragraph quoted above already shows how far the author is from that automatic-mechanistic or, as she herself said, pedantic view. The hottest debate, however, turned around Marx's diagrams, which, it has been argued, should be calculated in a thoroughly correct way. That may or may not be the case, but the controversy has not dealt with the question of whether those mathematical equations, even if they are correct on paper, offer a true picture of potential and actual economic conditions.

Among the Marxist adversaries of the book, Otto Bauer judged it most calmly and objectively.[9] He admitted that Marx's diagrams are not free from contradictions and drew up new ones. Moreover, he did not content himself with that troublesome calculation, but tried to demonstrate that the accumulation of capital could also take place without disturbances in an isolated capitalist society, as long as certain quantitative proportions are maintained between, on the one hand, demographic growth and, on the other hand, the development of productivity, which manifests itself in the growth of the organic composition of capital. He granted that the development of accumulation tends to go beyond those limits, arguing that it is led back to them by the periodic crises that always bring in their wake unemployment, wage-cuts, rising mass-poverty and the growing exasperation and rebellion of the working masses.

Otto Bauer therefore considers the explanation of imperialism by Rosa Luxemburg to be false, but he concedes that it contains a kernel of truth. Imperialism is, admittedly, not at all a means of making the accumulation of capital possible, but, rather, of stretching its boundaries and facilitating the overcoming of crises periodically arising from accumulation. That quest [to facilitate

9. Bauer 1913, English version: Bauer 1986. See this volume, Chapter 45.

accumulation] would actually be one of the roots of imperialism, if not the only one. To be sure, in his conclusion Otto Bauer unjustly reproaches the book for its 'mechanical' outlook.

It is now to be expected that the author, as she herself announced, will answer her critics in a special work.[10]

10. [Rosa Luxemburg did write an elaborate response to her critics, entitled *The Accumulation of Capital, or What the Epigones Have Made of Marx's Theory: An Anti-Critique*. (Luxemburg 1921).]

Chapter Forty-Seven
'Imperialism' (September 1914)
Karl Kautsky

In his book *The Socialists and the War*, published in 1915 and comprising a collection of statements by major figures of the Second International on imperialism and the approaching world war, the American socialist William English Walling offered excerpts from this article by Kautsky and remarked that it

> sums up an enormous amount of Socialist discussion which has been going on for years in Europe, and especially in Germany. It has to be noted, however, that Kautsky here renounces the widely prevalent Socialist belief ... that capitalism necessarily means war, or that permanent peace must wait for Socialism. He takes the contrary view.[1]

Kautsky wrote the article prior to the outbreak of the First World War and published it immediately after hostilities began. He explained in an editorial note:

> The article below was completed several weeks before the outbreak of the War. It was intended for the number [of *Die Neue Zeit*] that was to have greeted the planned Congress of the

1. Walling (ed.) 1915, p. 18.

> International.[2] Like so much else, this Congress has been brought to nothing by the events of recent days. Yet, although purely theoretical in nature, the article has not lost its relevance to the practice that it sought to help explain. We publish the article with the omission of passages that related to the International Congress and the addition of some considerations on the War.[3]

While Kautsky was not responding directly to Rosa Luxemburg, his article nevertheless had a clear connection with her *Accumulation of Capital.* Luxemburg explained imperialism by reference to 'third parties' and their role in realising the surplus-value to be accumulated by capitalists; Kautsky pointed to a logically prior relation between agriculture and industry. His theme was that agricultural production tends everywhere to lag behind the growth of capitalist industry. If domestic agriculture could not keep pace with industry, the obvious response was to maintain the necessary 'proportions' by exporting industrial goods in exchange for agricultural products. From this perspective, imperialism had precisely nothing to do with the problem of realising surplus-value: 'It consists of the drive of every industrial capitalist nation to conquer and annex an ever-greater *agrarian* zone, with no regard to what nations live there.'

Imperialism was merely a *contingent form* of an *objectively necessary* exchange between agriculture and industry. It had replaced free trade when growing capital-investments in agrarian regions required protection by a state-force, but it could just as easily be supplanted *by a cartel-form* of joint capitalist supervision over agrarian regions. To Kautsky, the implication was contrary to everything Luxemburg had argued: a stage of *ultra*-imperialism would be a perfectly sensible extension of the 'organised capitalism' Hilferding had already portrayed in domestic capitalist economies. 'Ultra-imperialism' would be organised capitalism on a global scale. In Kautsky's words,

> The frantic competition of giant firms, giant banks and billionaires forced the great financial groups, who absorbed the small ones, to come up with the notion of the cartel. In the same way, the world war between the great

2. A reference to the 10th International Socialist Congress, which was scheduled for Vienna in 1914 but failed to meet. The documents of the Congress have been compiled in Haupt (ed.) 1972.

3. [Karl Kautsky,] Editorial Note, *Die Neue Zeit*, Vol. 32, No. 2, 11 September 1914, p. 908.

> imperialist powers can result in a federation of the strongest among them, who would thus renounce their arms-race.
>
> Hence, from the purely economic standpoint, it is not impossible that capitalism may still live through yet another phase, the transfer of cartel-policy into foreign policy: a phase of ultra-imperialism, against which, of course, we must struggle as energetically as we do against imperialism, but whose perils would lie in another direction, not in that of the arms-race and the threat to world peace.

Kautsky thought imperialism had obvious economic causes – *foreign trade* was a necessity for industrial capitalism – but there was no necessary connection between trade, protectionism, and the use of military force. In 1912, he had written that

> Imperialism is not synonymous with the naturally necessary aspiration of capital for expansion, to open up new markets and investment possibilities, it constitutes only a certain method of accomplishing that aspiration, the method of violence.... Violence is by no means a necessary condition of economic progress.[4]

By collapsing Luxemburg's argument concerning the inevitability of imperialist warfare into the anterior question of proportionality between agriculture and industry, Kautsky provided a theoretical case for the Marxist 'centre' that effectively dismissed the arguments of the revolutionary 'Left' and anticipated the prospect of 'peaceful' interimperialist collaboration.

Rosa Luxemburg regarded Kautsky's argument as a betrayal not merely of the working class, but even of civilisation itself. In her *Junius Pamphlet*, published in 1915, she declared that proletarian revolution was the only plausible defence of civilisation against imperialist barbarism.

> Friedrich Engels once said: 'Bourgeois society stands at the crossroads, either transition to socialism or regression into barbarism.' What does 'regression into barbarism' mean to our lofty European civilization? Until now, we have all probably read and repeated these words thoughtlessly, without suspecting their fearsome seriousness. A look around us at this moment shows what the regression of bourgeois society into barbarism means. This world

4. Kautsky 1912f, pp. 850–1.

> war is a regression into barbarism. The triumph of imperialism leads to the annihilation of civilization. At first, this happens sporadically for the duration of a modern war, but then when the period of unlimited wars begins it progresses toward its inevitable consequences. Today, we face the choice exactly as Friedrich Engels foresaw it a generation ago: either the triumph of imperialism and the collapse of all civilization as in ancient Rome, depopulation, desolation, degeneration – a great cemetery. Or the victory of socialism, i.e. the conscious active struggle of the international proletariat against imperialism and its method of war. This is a dilemma of world history, an either/or; the scales are wavering before the decision of the class-conscious proletariat. The future of civilization and humanity depends on whether or not the proletariat resolves manfully to throw its revolutionary broadsword into the scales. In this war imperialism has won. Its bloody sword of genocide has brutally tilted the scale toward the abyss of misery. The only compensation for all the misery and all the shame would be if we learn from the war how the proletariat can seize mastery of its own destiny and escape the role of lackey to the ruling classes.[5]

Lenin criticised Kautsky in similar terms. In December 1916, he published 'Imperialism and the Split in Socialism', arguing that imperialism was 'a specific historical stage of capitalism' whose 'fundamental economic feature' was 'the supplanting of free competition by monopoly'.

> Advancing this definition of imperialism brings us into complete contradiction with K. Kautsky, who refuses to regard imperialism as a 'phase of capitalism' and defines it as a *policy* 'preferred' by finance capital, a tendency of 'industrial' countries to annex 'agrarian' countries. Kautsky's definition is thoroughly false from the theoretical standpoint. What distinguishes imperialism is the rule *not* of industrial capital, but of finance capital, the striving to annex *not* agrarian countries, particularly, but *every* kind of country. Kautsky *divorces* imperialist politics from imperialist economics, he divorces monopoly in politics from monopoly in economics in order to pave the way for his vulgar bourgeois reformism, such as 'disarmament', 'ultra-imperialism' and similar nonsense.'[6]

5. Luxemburg 1915b, pp. 18–19.
6. Lenin 1916g, p. 107.

* * *

'Imperialism'[7]

I. The proportionality of production

First of all, we must be clear about what we understand by imperialism. This word is used all the time today, but the more people talk about it and discuss it, the more indefinite it becomes, which of course makes understanding very difficult. By now, the meaning of the word imperialism has expanded so far that all the manifestations of modern capitalism are included in it – cartels, protective tariffs, the domination of finance, as well as colonial policy. In that sense, naturally, imperialism is a vital necessity for capitalism. But that knowledge is just the flattest tautology; all it says is that capitalism cannot exist without capitalism.

If we take the word not in that general sense, but in its historical determination, as it originated in England, then it signifies only a particular kind of political endeavour, caused, to be sure, by modern capitalism, but by no means coincident with it.

For about a generation, the English have understood by imperialism, on the one hand, the drive to bring all the parts of their enormous colonial empire together with the motherland into a unified empire and, on the other hand, the drive to extend that empire more and more. In other states, apart from 'Greater Britain', only the latter quest comes into practical consideration as imperialism because no other empire possesses independent colonies such as England has.

But not every drive for the territorial expansion of a state should be described as imperialism. Otherwise, we would have to say that imperialism is as old as written history. The drive to enlarge an empire through annexation of neighbouring areas inhabited by members of the same nation is not imperialism, but nationalism. That is why it is totally wrong to talk about Serbian imperialism, for instance. We can just as little consider this drive, which characterises the greater part of the nineteenth century, as imperialistic, as the aspiration,

7. Kautsky 1914b.

very strong particularly in the eighteenth century, to obtain very rich, highly industrial areas.[8]

Imperialism is a product of highly developed industrial capitalism. It consists of the drive of every industrial capitalist nation to conquer and annex an ever-greater *agrarian* zone, with no regard to what nations live there.

To comprehend this drive, we must above all be clear about the exchange between agriculture and industry within the capitalist mode of production. In order to simplify the discussion, we will leave out of consideration the extractive industries – mining – that occupy a middle position between agriculture and the processing industries.

Quesnay, in his *Tableau économique*, established the two great categories of industrial and agricultural production and analysed how the exchange between both must take place in order for each of them to receive all the means necessary for continuation of the production-process.

He regarded this circulation-process, however, not only as a process of circulation of *commodities* but also of *capital*. He analysed not only how the exchange between agricultural and industrial products takes place but also how the surplus-value is appropriated in the process. Ingenious as Quesnay's *Tableau économique* was, it suffered from the error of considering only agricultural labour as productive of surplus-value.

When Marx analysed the circulation-process of capital, he had to disregard at first the distinction between agriculture and industry, because in both branches of production labour produces value and surplus-value if it is employed capitalistically.

However, even in his analysis of the circulation of the entire social capital, Marx did not disregard the special material form of its particular constituent parts.

For the purposes of this analysis, he differentiated between means of production and means of consumption – a distinction that is not peculiar to the capitalist mode of production. Capitalism, like any other mode of production, also produces for consumption or, to put it more correctly, under capitalism the producers also produce in order to consume. But, under capitalism, the

8. [The reference here is, presumably, to areas of highly developed craft-industries as Kautsky subsequently speaks of 'craftsmen' and 'industrialists' interchangeably at an early stage of development.]

particular producer does not directly produce those goods that he will consume himself, but, rather, goods for other producers in order to receive goods for himself in exchange.

In order for society to be able to continue existing in its previous form, sufficient means of consumption must be available for its members – that is to say, as many as they need and are able to exchange against the values at their disposal. If more means of consumption are produced, then their sale, and with it also their production, comes to a standstill.

But, in order for the volume of means of consumption necessary for the preservation of society to be produced, the necessary amount of means of production must also be available. If more means of production are produced than are required by the production of means of consumption, part of them will become unsaleable and their producers will be deprived of the possibility of exchanging them for means of consumption. If, on the other hand, too few means of production are produced, then the production of means of consumption will come to a standstill. In order, therefore, for the whole production-process to go ahead without disturbances, the production of means of production and of means of consumption must always stand in a certain proportion to each other, which changes with technical and social conditions but is defined under the given circumstances. If actual production deviates from those proportions, they assert themselves through price-fluctuations and crises.

It is clear that the correct proportions must exist not only between those two groups. One can go into even more detail, for instance, by dividing the means of consumption into necessary means of mass-consumption and items of luxury, or by undertaking some other arrangement. But that would simply be useless work that would hardly result in any new knowledge about the capitalist production-process.[9]

The only exception would be the arrangement that Quesnay already proposed, namely, distinguishing between industry and agriculture. Certainly, the special way in which the physiocrats applied that distinction to the reproduction-process is incompatible with the Ricardian and the Marxist

9. [Possibly a reference to Rosa Luxemburg, who, in her book, *The Accumulation of Capital* provisionally spoke of a third and separate department for the production of money.]

theory of value and was disposed of by Marx for good. But that does not mean that much new knowledge cannot be gained from that distinction.

I already alluded to it back in 1910, in my review of Hilferding's *Finance Capital*, in a special chapter on 'industry and agriculture' that begins with the words:

> In order to realise how it is possible, in spite of all this, to reconstitute again and again an equilibrium between production and consumption, it is necessary still further to subdivide the commodities produced according to their kind. To the division into means of production and means of consumption, and the division of the latter again into luxury-items and means of mass-consumption, must be added the subdivision into industrial and agricultural products.[10]

At about the same time, in my book on growth and development in nature and society (Chapter 14: 'Agriculture and Capitalism'), I developed from a different perspective the distinction between industry and agriculture in the modern mode of production.[11]

II. Simple commodity-production

We can understand the relation between industry and agriculture most easily if we first analyse it in its simplest form, in simple commodity-production, where the worker owns his means of production and the products of his labour and brings his products ready to the market or directly to the consumers, his customers.

Even before that stage, industrial activity was originally carried out as part of agricultural activity; or, rather, the nature of each singular economic organism was as much industrial as agricultural. It produced foodstuffs and raw materials and manufactured them into means of production and means of consumption. In doing so, a division of labour between the individual members of the economic unit was already possible. Some could occupy themselves mainly with tending cattle, while others took up farming, spinning

10. [Kautsky 1911b, pp. 838–9. English version: Kautsky 1911c, II. The Crises, (b) Industry and Agriculture.]

11. [Kautsky 1910d, pp. 196–224. 14. Kapitel: Landwirtschaft und Kapitalismus (Agriculture and Capitalism).]

and weaving, the processing of wood and metals into working tools, etc. This division of labour was confined, however, to specific boundaries, beyond which it could not go unless the economic organism expanded its size and membership. By contrast, the division of labour and its economic advantages could develop much more rapidly if the individual producers, namely, the processors of raw materials, left the economic unit and, instead of producing for it alone, worked for several units from whom they bought raw materials and foodstuffs in exchange.

That is how the separation between industry and agriculture arose. Therewith, however, the uninterrupted continuation of the reproduction-process was made dependent on a constant supply of the agricultural products needed by industry.

The point of departure and foundation of the whole process is always agriculture, forestry included. It must supply the necessary foodstuffs as well as a large part of the raw materials before industrial activity can take place. Then again, agriculture probably could do without industry for a while, at least under primitive conditions, but industry could not dispense with agriculture. The agricultural production-process can be carried out in the previous way for a certain time, even if the tools and the workers' clothes have not been renewed. By contrast, the industrial production-process would immediately come to a standstill as soon as the supply of raw materials and foodstuffs was even momentarily suspended.

There are two ways of securing this supply for industry. Where industrialists (craftsmen) and farmers (peasants) face each other as free and equal agents, the industrialists will obtain their raw materials and foodstuffs only through commodity-exchange based on the law of value. They will only get the required raw materials and foodstuffs if they find buyers for their industrial products among the peasants. The peasants, in turn, must buy industrial products from them for a sum of values as large as the value of the agricultural products that the industrialists need.

That will only happen if a certain proportionality exists between what is produced by both groups.

There is only one other way of supplying industry with its required raw materials and foodstuffs: by confiscating them from the peasants without compensation. That procedure played a large role historically and is even today applied in colonial policy. However, we want to restrict our analysis to purely economic factors.

The proportionality between industry and agriculture is necessary under any circumstances, but it is always in danger of being violated, first by migration from the countryside to the cities, which deprives agriculture of labour-power in order to supply it to industry, and, secondly, through the development of knowledge and technique in the cities, by means of which the productivity of industry is easily increased. Industrial production also has the tendency to develop more rapidly than agricultural production, because the number of producers and their average productivity grows more quickly in the former than in the latter.

But this tendency seldom assumed dangerous forms under simple commodity-production. The development of handicrafts, the growth of their productivity, proceeded slowly. And the tendency to increase production through overwork did not yet exist in handicraft-production, because the craftsmen themselves would have had to do that work.

The increase in the number of urban workers through the flow of agricultural workers to the cities was partially arrested by the high mortality of the urban population prevalent during that period. But, wherever the death-rate did not limit the increase in urban population, a limit was set by the growing difficulties in securing agricultural supplies. The growth of urban population depended on the state of means of communication, which determined how broad the area could be from which the city dwellers could obtain their raw materials and foodstuffs. The smaller this area, the smaller the city-size had to be. Formerly, the means of communication were, as a rule, dreadful; even the waterways were often unsuitable given the insufficient development of navigation. The area from which urban industry could draw its sources of life was therefore very limited.

The growth of commodity-exchange between the city and the countryside also quickly found its limits. The *drive* to expand industrial production by increasing the work burden of the craftsmen was weak, and the *possibility* of expanding it by increasing the number of urban workers was limited.

III. Capitalist production

Industrial production first received a strong impetus for more rapid expansion from the development of the system of wage-labour and the substitution of capitalist production for simple commodity-production.

The capitalist – as capitalist – does not himself work in his establishment. The obstacles that independent craftsmen set to the excessive expansion of labour-time are nothing to him. It should be borne in mind, of course, that we are referring here to the craftsmen of the time when handicraft-production was at its height, before capitalist competition forced them, including their women, children and apprentices, into extravagant overwork.

The capitalist has his men working for him. Their discomfort is nothing to him. His appetite for their work grows the longer it lasts, because all the larger in that case will be the surplus-value that they produce beyond their wages, and therefore also the profits of the capitalist and his own income.

But the individual capitalist cannot increase production simply by extending the working time. The increase in labour-time has definite physical limitations, no matter how ruthlessly it may be handled. But no such limitation exists in regard to the *number of workers* that an industrial capitalist can employ. Whether he employs 10 or 100 or 1,000 depends entirely on the extent of his capital. And every additional employee means an increase of the mass of his profits and, therefore, also of his own income.

To be sure, the form in which the capitalist employs his workers is not left to his own discretion, but depends on technical and social conditions. If he exploits a thousand workers, he may, at first, be forced to act as a putter-outer,[12] leaving each of them to work in his own cottage as a house-worker. But, as soon as he simultaneously employs many workers, the possibility also arises of gathering them all – or at least part of them – into a single workplace and making them work together. Therewith the preconditions also come into being for capitalist large-scale industry based on the division of labour, which first becomes [small-scale] manufacture, then the factory, and, finally, the modern gigantic enterprise. In the process, at least until now, the number of workers employed in a single enterprise also grows increasingly, but the size of the means of production (buildings, machines, raw materials) of the individual enterprise grows even more rapidly, as well as the amount of capital required to employ a worker.

---

12. [The domestic system, also called the putting–out system, was widespread in seventeenth-century Western Europe. Merchant-employers 'put out' materials to rural producers who usually worked in their homes but sometimes laboured in workshops or in turn put out work to others. Finished products were returned to the employers for payment on a piecework or wage basis.]

To the extent that the sum of profits of the individual capitalist increases, so too grows the percentage of this sum that he must not consume but lay aside and accumulate if he wants to increase further the sum of his profits. However, the possibilities of accumulating capital are by no means as extensive in agriculture as in industry. The smaller possibilities of accumulation must not be understood, of course, in the sense that the capitalist farmer and the large landowner have less possibility of amassing capital than the industrialists. But not every capital thus accumulated by a farmer will immediately become agricultural capital. It can also be invested in industrial shares, in railway-construction, etc. Within a given territory, the possibilities of employing the amassed capital in agriculture and of expanding capitalist production in that field are smaller than the possibilities of capitalistically expanding industry in the same region. The causes of that phenomenon lie in a series of technical and social factors.

Agriculture has to do with the production and reproduction of living organisms, and this cannot be arbitrarily accelerated or extended by increasing the amount of work employed. Industry, on the contrary, can always be enlarged if it disposes of enough raw materials and labour-power.

Then again, to increase the number of workers in a single establishment is much more difficult in agriculture than in industry, because the latter is much more detached from the land than the former. If an industrial capitalist disposes of the necessary amount of money, he will have hardly any difficulty in finding the necessary space to enlarge his enterprise, which formerly occupied ten workers, so that it will be able to employ one hundred. As a rule, he will always find as much land as he needs in order to expand his factory or build a new one. The situation is completely different with the farmer. If he wants to employ ten times more workers than he did previously, he must, with an unchanging mode of operation, increase by ten times the amount of land he has at his disposal. In doing so, however, he comes across the private property of his neighbours, whom he must oust if he wants to enlarge his establishment. He will usually find it impossible to do so, but, even if he succeeds, the land-area and therefore the number of workers of his neighbours will be reduced (as we said, with an unchanging mode of operation) in the same proportion as his own establishment grows. As a result, the total number of workers employed in agriculture within the state will not grow. A simultaneous increase in the size and number of individual agricultural undertakings and in the number of workers employed in agriculture as a whole is impossible in an already settled country with an unchanging mode of operation. Industry, on the contrary, can very well simultaneously increase the average size of the enterprises, the number of enterprises and the total number of workers employed, even with an unchanging mode of operation.

Technical development, again, affects industry and agriculture differently. In both cases, it tends to reduce the number of workers in proportion to production and to the amount of capital invested. In industry, however, this reduction has until now only been relative, never absolute. Instead of a decrease in the number of industrial workers, the effect of technological development has been a much more rapid increase in the invested capital and in the amount of production than in the number of occupied workers.

In agriculture, on the other hand, the decrease in the number of workers caused by technical advance has often been not only relative but absolute.

Besides, the impact of those differences was increased by another circumstance that was already alluded to in the analysis of simple commodity-production. With the separation of industry from agriculture, the latter remained the basis of the whole economic mechanism. Without the constant supply of new agricultural products, we could not go on living. By contrast, we could endure for a period the absence of a number of industrial products. In the cities, we could hardly subsist for a day without new supplies of flour and milk, meat and vegetables. But we would not perish if we were forced to wear our old coats and hats a little longer. Thus, for instance, the manufacturer of cotton goods could not get on without new cotton supplies, but if his spinning machines are old he can perhaps make do with them for another year – to be sure, only with the greatest difficulty – if new ones are not yet available.

But this is not all.

The mass-products of agriculture are less diverse than those of industry, and their use-value is more constant. Grain and milk, meat and potatoes are everywhere the chief means of subsistence; they are not subject to varying fashions. But, if you want a new coat, you will have to choose among countless models. And how rapidly their fashions change! The spinner who needs a new machine has a choice among many designs, and technical progress constantly brings to light new and better ones.

The effect of all this is that, in capitalist industry, there is a powerful factor at work that is scarcely of any significance in agriculture even under capitalist management: *competition, the struggle of various enterprises among themselves for their sales.* The industrial capitalists must struggle far more vigorously than the farmers in order to sell their products. To the extent that the latter have difficulties selling their products, the difficulties fall more upon the middlemen than upon other farmers.

And the situation changes constantly to the disadvantage of industry the more rapidly its capital accumulates, the more agriculture lags behind it, the more the industrial population grows and demands increased quantities of food supplies and raw material, and the smaller, by contrast, is the agricultural population and thus the more limited is the collective demand for industrial products.

In the competitive struggle, however, the larger and technically more efficient enterprises have better prospects of holding their ground than the smaller ones. The sharper competition becomes, the greater is the necessity of each enterprise to grow, enlarge its plant and improve its equipment.

Thus far we have viewed the accumulation of capital only from the point of view of its *convenience* for the individual capitalist, who can this way increase his profits and, with them, also his consumption. We must now look at it from a different point of view. Accumulation is not just an advantage for the industrial capitalist, who may or may not do so at will, or who may even renounce it at his own discretion. It is increasingly a *necessity* for him that he cannot avoid. The constant expansion of his enterprise and growth in the sale of his products now become for him a necessary condition of life. The increase of his production is no longer just a question of the natural increase of domestic demand. The individual capitalist must now constantly increase his production under all circumstances, and, if domestic demand does not naturally grow in the same proportion, then he must employ all the forces at his disposal to enlarge that demand artificially and to broaden the market.

The intensity of industrial competition results from the fact that the drive and the possibility to accumulate capital and increase production are far greater in industry than in agriculture. This fact, resulting from the differences between industry and agriculture, in turn becomes one of the most powerful factors causing the distinction between them to grow.

This situation presents an important problem.

Industry must develop very rapidly under capitalist conditions or else society will be plunged into the greatest misery. Agriculture is constantly turning out workers. Even where the number of agricultural workers remains stationary, the increase in population is sent to the cities. Industry is constantly attracting growing numbers of workers. Massive unemployment develops as soon as industry does not grow rapidly enough. On the other hand, the fiercer competition becomes, the more the capitalists are forced to expand and improve their enterprises. Any slackening in the corresponding expansion of sales is accompanied by devastating bankruptcies.

But, if industry is to expand, agriculture must increase its production and its population in the same proportion; it must produce larger quantities of raw materials and foodstuffs in the same proportion as industry's demand for them increases; and it must also consume, in the same proportion, the industrial products with which agricultural products are purchased.

How is that possible if the accumulation of capital goes on much more rapidly in industry than in agriculture?

What Malthus regarded as a *natural law of population*, the fact that it has the tendency to increase more rapidly than foodstuffs – the former growing geometrically, that is, in the progression 1, 2, 4, 8, 16, etc., and the latter arithmetically, that is, in the progression 1, 2, 3, 4, 5, etc. – turned out to be an *economic* law of capitalist *accumulation*. It is, however, no less tantalising, for in accordance with it the industrial population of a region increases in proportion to the series 1, 2, 4, 8, 16, while the agricultural population remains stationary or decreases. And, at the same time, the total production of an industrial worker increases much more rapidly than that of an agricultural worker. While it is not impossible, the accumulation of capital would actually be much made more difficult and would be restricted to narrow confines if the industry of a city, industrial region or state were limited to the same area as the suppliers and buyers whom it originally served. Capitalist accumulation in industry can only proceed unhindered and develop freely if the agricultural regions it serves as supplier and buyer expand constantly, which requires a constant extension and improvement of the means of communication.

IV. Accumulation and imperialism

We have seen that the undisturbed advance of the production-process presupposes that the different branches of production all produce in the correct proportion. Yet it is also evident that, within the capitalist mode of production, there is a constant drive towards the violation of this proportion, because within a specific zone the capitalist mode of production tends to develop industrial production much more quickly than agricultural production. On the one hand, this is an important reason for the periodic crises, which are always industrial crises, and which restore the correct proportions between the different branches of production. On the other hand, the drive to expand the agricultural area that supplies industry not only with foodstuffs and raw materials but also with customers is all the greater, the more powerful is the expansion of activity by capitalist industry.

Since the importance of the agrarian zones to industry is a dual one, the disproportion between industry and agriculture may also be expressed in two ways. Firstly, the sales of industrial products in the agrarian zones may not grow so quickly as industrial production, which appears as *overproduction*. Secondly, agriculture may not provide the quantities of foodstuffs and raw materials needed for the rapid growth of industrial production, which takes the form of *the high cost of living*.[13]

These two phenomena may seem mutually exclusive, but, in fact, they are closely inter-related insofar as they derive from the disproportion between industrial and agricultural production and not from some other causes such as, for instance, fluctuations in gold-production or changes in the power of producers vis-à-vis the power of consumers through cartels, commercial policies, fiscal policies, and the like. One of the two phenomena, overproduction or the high cost of living, may easily pass over into the other, because they both derive from the disproportion in question. An increase in prices has always foreshadowed the beginning of a crisis, which emerged as overproduction and brought with it a price-collapse.

On the other hand, the constant drive of the industrialised capitalist countries to extend the agricultural zones involved in trade-relations with them takes the most varied forms. The demonstration that this drive is one of the conditions of existence of capitalism is still far from being a proof that any one of these forms is an indispensable necessity for the capitalist mode of production.

---

13. [The high cost of living was one of the items on the agenda of the Vienna International Socialist Congress. See Otto Bauer's report at the Bibliothek der Friedrich-Ebert-Stiftung website (Bauer 1914).]

One particular form of this tendency is *imperialism*. Another form preceded it: *free trade*. Half a century ago, free trade was seen as the last word of capitalism, just as imperialism is today.

Free trade came to dominate because of the superiority of England's capitalist industry. Great Britain's aim was to become the workshop of the world, and therefore to turn the world into an agrarian zone that would buy England's industrial products and provide her with foodstuffs and raw materials in exchange. *Free trade* was the most important means by which this agricultural zone could be expanded continuously in accordance with the needs of English industry, and all sides were supposed to profit from that arrangement. In fact, the landowners of the countries that exported their products to England were as inveterate free traders as England's industrialists.

But this sweet dream of international harmony quickly came to an end. As a rule, industrial zones overwhelm and dominate agrarian zones. This was true earlier of the city vis-à-vis the countryside, and it is now true of the industrial state vis-à-vis an agrarian state. A state that remains agrarian decays politically and usually economically, too, and loses its autonomy in both respects. The efforts to maintain or win national independence or autonomy therefore necessarily generated everywhere within the circle of international capitalist circulation the striving to establish an autonomous [national] heavy industry, which must, under present conditions, be a capitalist one. The development of the sales of foreign industrial products in the agrarian state itself created a series of preconditions for this. The sale of foreign industrial products destroys the domestic precapitalist industry, thereby releasing a large quantity of labour-power that is at the disposal of capital as wage-labour. These workers emigrate to other states with growing industry if they can find no employment in their home-country, but otherwise would rather stay at home, where they facilitate the development of a capitalist industry. Foreign capital itself flew into the agrarian country, first to open it up by building railways and then in order to develop its production of raw materials, which included not only agriculture but also extractive industries – mining. The possibility of adding other capitalist enterprises to these grew. Whether an autonomous capitalist industry developed then depended primarily on the political power of the state.

At first, it was the areas of Western Europe and the eastern regions of the United States that developed from agrarian into industrial states in opposition to English industry. They imposed protective tariffs against English free trade; and, instead of the world division of labour between the English industrial workshop and the agricultural production of all other zones, which was England's aim, they wanted a division of those zones of the world that still remained free – as long as they could not offer resistance – between the great industrial states. England reacted to this. That was the beginning of imperialism.

Imperialism was particularly encouraged by the system of capital-export to the agrarian zones that emerged at the same time.

The growth of industry in the capitalist states today is so rapid that a sufficient expansion of the market can no longer be achieved by the methods that had been employed up to the 1870s. Till then, the primitive means of transportation that existed in the agrarian zones sufficed, particularly the waterways, which formerly made possible the mass-transportation of foodstuffs and raw materials. Until then, railways had been constructed almost exclusively in highly industrialised and heavily populated zones. Now, they became a way to open up thinly populated agrarian zones, making it possible to take their products to the market but also to increase their population and production.

But these zones did not possess the means to build those railways themselves. The capital necessary for this, as well as the managers and overseers, were provided by the industrial nations. They advanced the capital, thereby raising their export of railway-materials and increasing the ability of the newly opened up areas to buy the industrial products of the capitalist nations with foodstuffs and raw materials. The material exchange between agriculture and industry was thus greatly increased.

But if a railway in the wilderness was to be a profitable business, if it was even to be possible, if it was to obtain the labour-power necessary for its construction and the security necessary for its operational demands, there had to be a state-authority strong and ruthless enough to defend the interests of the foreign capitalists, one that would even yield blindly to their interests. Naturally, this was best done by the state-power of those capitalists themselves. The same rule also applied when there was a possibility of mining richer ores or raising the production of commercial crops such as cotton by constructing vast irrigation-works – undertakings that were also possible only through the export of capital from the capitalist countries.

Thus, together with the drive to increase capital-export from the industrial states to the agrarian zones of the world, grew also the tendency to subjugate these zones under their state-power.

To this should be added another important factor: the effects of capital-exports on the agrarian zones to which they are directed may be very different. We have already pointed out how badly off the agrarian countries are in this respect, and how they must aspire to become industrial countries in the interests of their own prosperity or even autonomy. In agrarian states that had the necessary strength to protect their autonomy, the capital imported was used not only for the construction of railways but also for the development of their own industries – as in the United States or Russia. In such circumstances, capital-exports from the old capitalist states only furthered their industrial exports temporarily. They soon crippled them by fostering strong economic competition in the agrarian zone. The desire to thwart this process was another motive for the capitalist states to subject the agrarian zones directly as colonies, or indirectly as spheres of influence, in order to prevent them from developing their own industry and force them to restrict themselves entirely to agricultural production.

Those are the main roots of imperialism, which has replaced free trade.

Does it represent the last possible phenomenal form of capitalist world-policy, or is another still possible? In other words, does imperialism offer the only possible remaining form of expanding the exchange between industry and agriculture within capitalism?

That is the question.

There can be no doubt that the construction of railways, the exploitation of mines, and the increased production of raw materials and foodstuffs in the agrarian countries have become necessities of life for capitalism. The capitalist class is no more likely to renounce them than it is to commit suicide, and this also applies to all the bourgeois parties. Rule over the agrarian zones, and the reduction of their populations to slaves with no rights, are too closely bound up with this tendency for any of the bourgeois parties sincerely to oppose these things. The subjugation of these zones will only come to an end when either their populations or the proletariat of the industrialised capitalist countries have grown strong enough to throw off the capitalist yoke.

This side of imperialism can only be overcome by socialism.

But imperialism has still another side. The striving to occupy and subjugate the agrarian zones has produced sharp contradictions between the industrialised capitalist states, contradictions that turned the arms-race, which was previously only a race for land-armaments, into a naval arms-race as well, and that have in the last analysis been the cause of the actual outbreak of the long prophesied world war. Is this side of imperialism also a necessity for the continued existence of capitalism, one that can only be overcome together with capitalism itself?

There is no *economic* necessity for continuing the arms-race after the world war, even from the standpoint of the capitalist class itself, with the exception of, at most, certain armaments-interests.

On the contrary, the capitalist economy is seriously threatened precisely by the contradictions between its states. Every far-sighted capitalist today must call on his fellows: Capitalists of all countries, unite!

For, first of all, there is the growing opposition of the more developed agrarian zones, which threatens not just this or that imperialist state but all of them together. This is true of the awakening of Eastern Asia and India as well as of the pan-Islamic movement in the Near East and North Africa.

This upsurge is accompanied by the growing opposition of the proletariat of the industrial countries to every new increase of their tax burden.

To this should be added the fact that even before the War, ever since the Balkan War, it was clear that the arms-race and the costs of colonial expansion had reached a level that threatened the rapid advance of capital-accumulation and thereby capital-export, i.e., the economic foundations of imperialism itself.

Industrial accumulation at home still advances continuously, thanks to technical progress. But capital no longer rushes into export. This is visible in the fact that, even in peacetime, the European states had difficulties in covering their own loans. The rates of interest they were forced to grant rose.

This is revealed, for example, by the average market prices of [securities]:[14]

	3% German imperial loans	3% French annuities
1905	89	99
1910	85	97
1912	80	92
Mid-1914	77	83

14. [The falling prices of these securities indicate steadily rising yields for the purchasers, paid out by the borrowers.]

After the War, this trend will get worse, not better, if the arms-race and its demands on the capital market continue to grow.

Imperialism is thus digging its own grave. From a means of developing capitalism, it is becoming a hindrance to it.

Nevertheless, capitalism need not yet be at the end of its tether. From a purely economic standpoint, it can continue to develop as long as the growing industries of the old capitalist countries can generate a corresponding expansion of agricultural production. This becomes more and more difficult, of course, as the annual rate of growth of world industry increases and the still unopened agrarian zones become fewer and fewer.

So long as this limit has not been reached, capitalism may be wrecked against the rising political opposition of the proletariat, but it does not need to come to an end through an economic collapse.

On the other hand, just such an economic bankruptcy would occur prematurely as a result of a continuation of the present policy of imperialism.

This policy of imperialism, therefore, cannot be continued much longer.

Naturally, if the present policy of imperialism were indispensable for continuation of the capitalist mode of production, then the above-mentioned factors might make no lasting impression on the ruling classes and would not induce them to give a different direction to their imperialist tendencies. But this change will be possible if imperialism, the striving of every great capitalist state to extend its own colonial empire in opposition to all the other empires of the same kind, represents only one among various modes of furthering the expansion of capitalism.

What Marx said of capitalism can also be applied to imperialism: monopoly creates competition, and competition, monopoly.[15]

The frantic competition of giant firms, giant banks and billionaires forced the great financial groups, who absorbed the small ones, to come up with the notion of the cartel. In the same way, the world war between the great imperialist powers can result in a federation of the strongest among them, who would thus renounce their arms-race.

---

15. [Marx wrote: 'In practical life we find not only competition, monopoly and the antagonism between them, but also the synthesis of the two, which is not a formula, but a movement. Monopoly produces competition, competition produces monopoly. Monopolists are made from competition; competitors become monopolists.' Marx 1977a, p. 152.]

Hence, from the purely economic standpoint, it is not impossible that capitalism may still live through yet another phase, the transfer of cartel-policy into foreign policy: a phase of ultra-imperialism, against which, of course, we must struggle as energetically as we do against imperialism, but whose perils would lie in another direction, not in that of the arms-race and the threat to world peace.

This analysis was completed before Austria surprised us with her ultimatum to Serbia. Austria's conflict with Serbia did not arise from purely imperialist tendencies. In Eastern Europe, nationalism still plays a role as a revolutionary driving force, and the present conflict between Austria and Serbia has nationalist as well as imperialist roots. Austria tried to implement an imperialist policy by annexing Bosnia and threatening to include Albania in its sphere of influence.

This aroused the nationalist opposition of Serbia, which felt threatened by Austria and is now a danger to the existence of Austria on its own account.

The World War did not come about because imperialism was a necessity for Austria, but because Austria, by its own structure, endangered itself with its own imperialism. Imperialism could only have driven an internally homogeneous state that attached to itself agrarian zones far beneath it in cultural terms. But, here, a nationally divided, half-Slavic state wished to pursue imperialism at the expense of a Slavic neighbour whose culture has the same origins as the culture of the neighbouring regions of its opponent.

Of course, this policy could only have such unexpected and vast consequences because of the contradictions and discord that imperialism has created between the other great powers. All the consequences ripening in the womb of the present world war have not yet seen the light. Its outcome may still be that the imperialist tendencies and the arms-race will at first be sharpened – in which case, the subsequent peace would be no more than a short armistice. From the purely economic standpoint, however, there is nothing further to prevent this violent explosion from finally replacing imperialism by a holy alliance of the imperialists. The longer the War lasts, the more it exhausts all the participants and makes them recoil from an early repetition of the armed conflict, the nearer we come to this last solution, however unlikely it may seem at the moment.

Chapter Forty-Eight

'The Collapse of the International' (20–2 October 1914)

Anton Pannekoek

Social Democrats were remarkably perceptive, first in conceptualising imperialism, and then in desperately attempting to awaken workers and even bourgeois politicians to the menace of imperialist war. During the entire decade prior to 1914, the socialist press sounded the alarm throughout Europe, yet these efforts ultimately ended in a political catastrophe diminished only by the scale of the War itself – the collapse of the Second International.

On 1 August 1914, Germany declared war against Russia, followed, two days later, by the opening of hostilities with France. Thereafter, declarations of war spread across Europe. For Social Democrats, the most shocking consequence was the patriotic zeal with which workers rallied to the colours in the name of national 'honour' and 'self-defence'. The workers of the world, whom Marx had summoned to defend each other against a common class-enemy, instead chose 'fatherland' and 'flag'.

Most deplorable of all was the fact that many Social-Democratic parliamentarians, the same people who had been warning for years of the impending disaster, one after another declared support for the War. Their reasons were varied: some hoped to protect workers' organisations built up with such effort in the prewar years; others thought military victory would either ensure democratic rights already won, or else bring democratic 'rewards' from grateful rulers once the War ended. But, no matter how the paralysis of socialist parties might be explained or rationalised, the inescapable fact was that August 1914 ended the great era of prewar Social Democracy.

In the spring of 1913, Anton Pannekoek had already denounced a foreboding precedent when 52 SPD deputies out of 96, with 7 abstentions, had contrived to support the Kaiser's demand for credits with which to expand Germany's armed forces. The crucial factor on this occasion was that the government proposed to finance the expenditure with direct, rather than indirect, taxes. Two bills were therefore under discussion: an armament bill and an appropriation bill. Once the first measure was passed in the Reichstag, despite SPD-opposition, the majority of SPD-deputies then acceded to the appropriation bill on the grounds that they were merely voting on the *form* of taxation, and the Party had always favoured direct taxes because they fell more heavily on the wealthy.[1]

Pannekoek and Luxemburg both denounced this ruse as a fundamental abandonment of principle. In September, Luxemburg wrote 'After the Jena Congress', an article considered so radical in its denunciation of reformism that it was not published until 1927. 'What,' she demanded, 'has been expressed by this "new era" of the property tax in Germany? Nothing more than the fact that in its advance, German militarism has even abandoned its convoluted indirect taxation system and now demands that the bourgeoisie be partially drawn in to cover its costs.'[2] If the operative formula had now become approval for military funds through direct taxation – provided it could 'be represented as the sole means of avoiding the placing of a burden on the people through more adverse taxes' – then the Party had implicitly given 'carte blanche for all budget approvals', since any budget could 'be portrayed as the "prevention" of another, more adverse one'.[3] Luxemburg argued that the only proper response to 'the immense military bill' would have been to

1. On the debate over funding for the military budget [*Deckungsfrage*], i.e. the approval of taxes for military purposes by the SPD-representatives in the Reichstag in 1913, see Walling (ed.) 1915, pp. 64–81.
2. Luxemburg 1913c, p. 348.
3. Luxemburg 1913c, p. 350.

focus party attention on the revolutionary mass-strike.[4] Pannekoek took the same view in an article on 'Taxation and Imperialism':

> *The goal of the struggle against imperialism is not to arrest its development, but to mobilise the masses against it.* Our party, with every advance, should fight against imperialism over every inch and offer the most tenacious resistance to it, thus mobilising the broadest popular masses, drawing them into the struggle and enlightening them. The masses, made rebellious by imperialist oppression, will gather around our party, which will become the leader and will show them the way to a successful struggle. *The organised mass-power that will do away with capitalism is thus formed in the struggle against imperialism.* On these fundamental ideas rests the criticism directed against the party leadership and the Reichstag fraction on the occasion of the military bill. The argument that the approval of the military bill was inevitable, and therefore all forces had to be concentrated on the question of financing, is untenable from this point of view. On the contrary, everything possible should have been done to hinder and impede the approval of the army bill, because only in that way would the enlightenment of the masses have been as vast and lasting as possible.[5]

Karl Kautsky had portrayed imperialism as serving the interests only of a minority of capitalists, the heavy industrialists and financiers, but Pannekoek saw a more urgent threat in the power of imperialist ideology to transcend differences within the ruling class and to propagate bourgeois self-assurance:

> *The policy of the bourgeoisie is thus not simply negative, limited to a defence against socialism, but has positive forward-looking goals,* the goals of world policy. It therefore drives the ruling classes to intense action and inspires the intelligentsia with the ideology of world power, of mastery and forceful development. The necessity of this world-power policy for modern large-scale capital is so irresistible that all reasoning from the time of small-scale capitalism is powerless against it. The slogans of peaceful competition between states, rational social reform for the preservation of internal peace, securing of world peace through treaties, and the absurdity of the arms-race no longer have anything substantial behind them in the bourgeois world.[6]

---

4. Luxemburg 1913c, p. 346.
5. Pannekoek 1913d, p. 114, emphasis in the original.
6. Pannekoek 1913d, p. 113, emphasis in the original.

Pannekoek repeated his conviction that imperialism *'mobilises the popular masses against capitalism much more quickly and thoroughly than would otherwise have been the case'.*[7] The mobilisation he had in mind involved *mass-action*, not merely amassing votes. To the majority of the SPD, however, mass-action seemed to be more of a threat than support for the Kaiser's war-credits. If history was on the side of socialism, what sense did it make to provoke the government on momentary issues? To many, it seemed far better to endure small setbacks in order to maintain the prospect of ultimate success.

The attitude of most party officials was typified by another document dating from the final week of August 1914, when armies were already on the move. Hugo Haase submitted a report (for an intended International Socialist Conference in Vienna that failed to meet on account of the War)[8] proclaiming that

> The International will do all in its power to prevent the people from becoming a plaything in the hands of the diplomats, who carry on their work...by...secret agreements.... It demands that any difficulties arising between different peoples be referred to, and all cases settled by, arbitration-courts. The alleged insult to the honour or injury to the life interests of a nation, to which the diplomats always refer when they wish to incite and encourage war, is no reason for refusing the method of arbitration-courts.[9]

In this document, which repeated conclusions drawn by the SPD-executive in June, Haase summarised the remarkable illusions that fed Social-Democratic compromise: 'The feelings of enmity,' he declared,

> which existed between Great Britain and Germany and which the Basel Congress, in 1913, regarded as the greatest danger to the peace of Europe, have now given way to a better understanding and feeling of trust. This is largely due to the ceaseless efforts of the International and also to the fact that at last the ruling classes in both countries are gradually coming to realise that their interests are best served by bridging over the differences.[10]

---

7. Pannekoek 1913d, p. 114, emphasis in the original.
8. On this issue, see Georges Haupt: 'On Imperialism: The Debate which Failed', in Haupt 1972, pp. 135–60.
9. Haase 1914. See Haase's report at the Bibliothek der Friedrich-Ebert-Stiftung website.
10. Haase 1914.

The first major Marxist theoretician to react to the betrayal of internationalism by the leading parties of the Second International, and particularly by the SPD, was Anton Pannekoek in the following article, 'The Collapse of the International', which was originally published in German on 20–2 October 1914 and also circulated widely in English, Dutch and Russian versions. Lenin responded to the article by declaring that Pannekoek was 'the only one who has told the workers the truth'. Pannekoek's words were 'the only socialist words. They are the truth. Bitter, but the truth.'[11]

* * *

'The Collapse of the International'[12]

I

Exactly half a century has passed since the International Workingmen's Association was founded in London under the leadership of Karl Marx. It fell to pieces after the Franco-Prussian War of 1870 and the Paris Commune. Exactly a quarter of a century ago, at the Congress of 1889 in Paris, the new International was founded. This year, the Congress at Vienna was to celebrate the double anniversary. But, just a month before it was to take place, the firebrand of international war was tossed into Europe from Vienna. With the outbreak of the European War, the new International, too, is disrupted.

When the old International was founded (1864), capitalism in Europe, with the exception of England, was still in its first stages. Its political form, the bourgeois state, was as yet only partly developed. Only in England was the bourgeoisie already in absolute control of the government. There, modern industrial methods and large-scale production had produced a proletariat that had, to be sure, lost all revolutionary spirit in the remarkably prosperous period following 1850, but that had, nevertheless, built up strong organisations by means of which it fought bitter struggles in the sixties in order to realise some of its immediate demands.

In France, on the other hand, the old system of small-scale production was still in vogue, though here, too, it was already being hard pressed by the

11. Lenin 1914b, p. 168.
12. Pannekoek 1914a. English version: Pannekoek 1914b.

hot-house like growth of capitalist industry. In Germany, the factory-system began to grow strongly only in the sixties. It did away with the old system of handicrafts, impoverished the craftsmen and drove them into the factories.

In these countries, the working class was still wholly under the influence of the ideals and thoughts of the age of individual enterprise. Their feeling of enmity toward capital was not the hatred of the exploited worker against his exploiting master. It was, rather, the resentment that the unfortunate, miserable master must feel for his stronger competitor, and this is proven by the fact that co-operative associations for production, rather than the trade-unions, occupied the centre of popular interest.

Their supporters hoped, by means of these societies, to place machine-production in the hands of the worker and thus to render him able to compete with the manufacturer. Lassalle's proposal for productive associations supported by state-loans, and the prevalence of Proudhon's ideas in France, both bear witness to the popularity of this idea.

The bourgeoisie, having yet to acquire political mastery in these countries, formed a strong radical opposition party that strove, above all, to unite the various provinces into a national whole. Its middle-class wing, true to the ideals of 1848, aspired to political democracy and meddled with the labour-movement, confusing the minds of many workers with its empty phrases.

The workers of Western Europe were unanimous in their determination to defend their democratic institutions against European reaction under the leadership of Russian tsarism. Thus, the Polish Revolution in 1863 gave the impetus that led to organisation of the International.

The history of the old International was one of constant struggle between the middle-class ideals of the handicraftsmen and the spirit of the modern working-class movement produced by the development of capital. The new spirit – coming from England, defended at the congresses by English delegates, and provided with a general theory by Karl Marx – gradually pushed the petty-bourgeois ideals of the past into the background. Thus, the International became a school for the propaganda of fundamental Marxian theories. The more progressive groups of the working class became class-conscious and gained the insight into social problems that was to determine their tactics in the period that followed. Recognition of the necessity of industrial organisation in the struggle against capitalist masters, and of independent political warfare to secure control of the government, with communism as the ultimate goal – that was the abiding result of the internal struggles of the old International. But the organisation itself was doomed to destruction. The European wars, coming to a close in 1870, fulfilled the national ideals of the bourgeoisie. In Central Europe, larger nations such as Germany and Italy, which were necessary for the further development of capitalist industry, had come into existence. These nations, together with the older France and England, were the battleground upon which the coming struggles of the proletariat were to be fought. The internationalism of a general organisation, governed by an executive in London, had become impossible. The workers of each nation had to shape their own struggles according to local political conditions. The collapse of the International, therefore, was inevitable once the Paris Commune proved 'that the working class could not simply lay hold of the state machinery and wield it for its own purposes' (Marx). In other words, the proletariat was still in its first infancy from the point of view both of intellectual development and of organisational power.

II

Twenty-five years after the foundation of the old International, representatives from the working-class organisations of twenty nations met in Paris. The fact that the congress was recruited from representatives of socialist parties as well as from labour-organisations linked the New International to the Old and proclaimed the theoretical postulates of the latter as a great practical force. The seed had sprouted. Everywhere, the workers had embraced the socialist idea and were carrying on the political struggle with steadily increasing success. With new industrial conditions, a new generation had awakened with new ideals. Capitalism had gained full control of industrial life; it had spread to the ends of Europe in the East and to America in the West. Everywhere, it had done away with small-scale production and handicrafts and had cast the great mass of the people into the class of wage-proletarians. But, even in the hour of its full development, it produced the germs of its own destruction. The long years of business depression after 1875 aroused doubts as to the stability of the capitalist order even in bourgeois circles, while, in America, the newly arisen monsters, the trusts, proclaimed the end of the era of free competition. Middle-class opposition disappeared; the proletariat was arrayed face to face against the ruling class. The old middle-class illusion, that matters might be mended with the simple expedient of co-operative organisations, died out. The new problem stood out clearly and distinctly: the proletariat must obtain control of society so that it might master the whole mechanism of production. Conquest of political power was recognised as the immediate aim; parliamentarism was the means, prepared and supplemented by the conquest of universal suffrage, which, at that time, was the most important factor in the political struggles of a number of nations. Hand in hand with the political struggle went the efforts to found and build up trade-unions in order to secure better conditions. The congresses of the new International were deliberative conferences of independent and autonomous parties of various countries. After the last remnants of the earlier anarchism were thrown out, these congresses were chiefly occupied with the discussion of parliamentary tactics.

Another twenty-five years passed. Capitalism grew and spread even more rapidly than in the preceding period. Favoured by the period of unparalleled prosperity, which began in 1894 in Germany and, interrupted only by short crises, spread out over the other nations, capitalism had taken possession of the earth. It revolutionised every continent; it broke down the rigid immobility of immense empires that had resisted change for thousands of years; it seized the treasures of the world; it exploited men of every race and colour. And, everywhere, the socialist spirit, hatred against capital, took root in the minds of exploited workers, often combined with the aspiration for national freedom.

Socialist organisations arose in China and New Zealand, in Johannesburg and Honolulu, in Alaska and Arabia. Capitalism and socialism were flooding the whole earth.

More important still were the internal upheavals. Capital had won complete mastery over the industrial and political life of nations. All classes, even those that were apparently independent – farmers and small businessmen – became its servants; but, in the same measure, ever greater masses of men became its foes. Gigantic factories, filled with the latest machinery, put millions of workers under the power of a few magnates. Organisation, growing steadily more perfect, took the place of anarchistic competition. Twenty-five years ago, the first trusts were but the weak beginnings of that concentration of capitalist power that now placed the whole of industrial life and the treasures of the earth into the hands of a few hundred kings of production. In Germany and America, this development occurred with the utmost vigour and rapidity. But, while, in America, the great expanse of territory made possible the broadest development, in Germany, where all activity is crowded into a small space, the antagonism between classes and conditions became exceedingly acute.

These conditions have changed the attitude of the working class. They no longer believe that social supremacy can be won casually by parliamentary legislation. Parliament has become a mere machine for granting appropriations to defray the cost of the new governmental functions, and, at best, a stage upon which the protests of labour may find utterance.

The proletariat is pitted against the colossal power of the state, which must be attacked and vanquished. But the strength of the proletariat, too, has grown. The socialist idea has taken possession of large minorities of the people in all capitalist nations. Greater still is the growth of trade-unions; insignificant in 1889, they have taken rapid strides forward in the years of prosperity. Everywhere in the trade-unions, there are great armies firmly organised, bound to each other by strong ties of solidarity and confronting the mighty power of the magnates of capital.

But, within this struggling mass of workers, progressive and conservative elements are fighting for supremacy.

III

The policies and theories that comprise the spirit and nature of modern capitalism may be summed up under the name of imperialism. Capital is eager to spread out over distant continents, to start railroads, factories, plantations and mines in order to realise high profits. To this end, it is necessary that these foreign regions be controlled politically by the home-country. Each government strives to conquer or control the largest possible part of the earth for its own bourgeoisie, so that it may be in a position to protect the interests of its capital. Each government, therefore, strives to secure the greatest possible amount of world power and arms itself against the others in order to impart the greatest possible weight to its demands and to force the others to recognise its claims. Thus we see each European nation striving to become the centre of a world empire consisting of colonies and spheres of influence. To a greater or lesser extent, this policy of 'imperialism' nowadays controls the political life of all nations and the mental attitude of the bourgeoisie. It has given to the possessing classes, who hitherto had nothing to oppose to the socialist ideals of the working class, a new ideal: to make the fatherland great and mighty among the peoples of the earth. The intellectuals, who formerly flirted with socialism, now became enthusiastic supporters of the bourgeoisie; the old ideals of world peace, progress and democracy were supplanted by the ideals of world power, patriotism, racial prejudice, and the admiration of force and brutality. All doubts as to the ability of capitalism to persist indefinitely and in full vigour have disappeared, while socialism is now regarded [by bourgeois intellectuals] as a feeble humanitarian sentimentalism that unfortunately puts the working class in opposition to national aims. An insane competition in the increase of naval and military armaments eats up billions of dollars, piles heavy taxes upon the masses of the people, and makes drastic social reforms impossible. In all lands, it has become apparent that a small but powerful clique of capitalists and bureaucrats controls political life, not only in the semi-absolute monarchies of Germany and Austria but also in democratic France and in parliamentary England. To enable it to cope with the problems of the great world struggle, the centralised power of the state has tremendously increased.

On the other hand, the forces of resistance in the proletariat were also growing. The ever-increasing taxes and military burdens aroused the bitterest opposition in ever-widening circles, as was plainly evidenced by the electoral victories of Social Democracy. Spontaneous outbreaks among the masses revealed possibilities of new methods of working-class warfare other than parliamentarism and trade-unionism. They showed the weapons at the disposal of the proletariat in the struggle against imperialism; mass-actions, in which the working masses demonstrate their opposition on the streets or seek to impose their will upon governments by means of political general strikes. Thus, the political and industrial struggles of the workers flow together into one united struggle against the government and organised capital. To be sure, such actions demand of the proletariat a strength, a firmness of organisation, a willingness to make sacrifices, a solidarity, a clear socialist understanding, and a revolutionary energy such as are now to be found only inadequately and can only grow in the course of the struggles themselves. But these first struggles already open before us a vista of the coming period of revolutionary assaults upon the state by the proletariat, a period that is destined to supersede the preparatory period of peaceful parliamentarism and trade-unionism.

But, at the same time, the elements of weakness also become more apparent. The rapid growth of party and trade-union organisations has produced an army of parliamentarians, functionaries and officials, who, as specialists of a sort, became representatives of the traditional methods of warfare and obstructed the adoption of new methods. As Social Democracy grew in parliamentary strength, the tendency to join hands with portions of the capitalist class for the purpose of winning reforms became more marked. The middle-class idea of making capitalism more tolerable by means of small reforms was adopted in place of the revolutionary struggle for power. This reformism, which refused to have anything to do with the class-struggle of the proletariat, gained the upper hand in the Social Democracy of most of the West-European nations – in France, Belgium, Holland and Denmark, while, in England, the Labour Party showed the same tendency without using socialist phrases. In Germany, as a direct result of reactionary pressure from above, the tactics of the class-struggle maintained their ascendancy; but, here too, similar reformist tendencies made their appearance with the growth of organisation. It is true that organisation is a condition, a necessary instrument for the victory of the proletariat; but, as it becomes stronger, there is a dangerous tendency to regard it as the end instead of a means to an end; its maintenance becomes the highest aim, and, in order to safeguard the organisation, serious struggles are carefully avoided. This tendency is furthered by the numberless officials and executive heads of the party and the trade-unions. In recent years, the struggle between these two opposing tendencies in German Social Democracy came to a head upon several occasions. But, each time, those who called for revolutionary tactics against the increasing strength of imperialism, and pointed to the necessity of mass-actions, were in the minority. In the main, this was due to the fact that, among the workers themselves, there was little revolutionary energy. This, again, is a direct result of the prosperity that furthered capitalist expansion as well as the growth of labour-organisations. For, in good times, there is little unemployment, wages rise, and the labouring masses are comparatively satisfied; they are not driven to rebellion by hunger and unbearable misery. This is the underlying cause for the growth of reformism in Europe, for the indifference of the masses, for their unwillingness to adopt revolutionary measures, for the stagnation of the entire labour-movement.

In such circumstances, the International itself was bound to degenerate. The congresses, which were, at one time, the scene of passionate discussion on tactical questions, degenerated into bureaucratically organised theatrical performances staged by reformist politicians and bureaucrats. There was but one force that could make of this international union of Social-Democratic parties a living, necessary thing. That was the international policy of imperialism with its ever-growing menace of world war.

Unlike the Old International, whose centre of gravity lay in the international policy of the proletariat, the New International lacked a clearly defined international policy. It was concerned with questions of domestic politics, with questions and struggles caused by the development of capitalism in each individual country. This had to change when imperialism raised its head, with its militaristic armaments, its endless conflicts among the various states, its ever-present menace of war. The new international policy had to be entirely different from that of Marx and Engels. At that time, the aim of the International was defence of European democracy against tsarism. Today, after the Russian Revolution [of 1905–6], it could only be to defend the proletariat against world war, to preserve world peace. The International should, therefore, have become a firm union of the working-class parties of all countries against war. The party has always striven toward this end and has always emphasised this phase of its activity. The highest expression of this effort was reached at the International Congress in Basel [in 1912], when Social-Democratic representatives from all countries protested against war and declared that they would do everything in their power to prevent it. But, behind this declaration, there lay much more fear of war than firm determination to take up the fight against it. Its outward form – the session in the church,[13] the ringing of bells, the avoidance of all discussion as to how and with what means war was to be prevented – all these things betrayed an effort to mesmerise the governments with words and outward appearances instead of trying to organise the real strength of the proletariat and preparing it for such a struggle requiring so many sacrifices. And, when finally the governments really wanted war, there was neither the strength nor the courage to take up the fight. Internationalism went up in smoke, and the International lay in ruins.

IV

Austrian Social Democracy has always ranted vigorously over the stupidity of the ruling politicians in Vienna, because they could not win the confidence

13. [The Congress met in the mediaeval Basel Cathedral.]

of Balkan peoples by adopting a sensible policy towards the various nationalities. Yet, in theory and in practice, it supported nationalism itself, and, instead of fighting nationalistic passions, in reality it supported them. Thus, when the conflict between Austria and Serbia broke out, the *Vienna Arbeiter Zeitung*, rather than vigorously attacking its own government, took up the cudgels against the Serbian government and played into the hands of the warlike Viennese government. Naturally, anti-war demonstrations in Vienna were entirely out of the question. The despised Serbians, on the other hand, were the only ones who loyally did their duty as Social Democrats – although, if anywhere, a nationalistic attitude on the part of the Balkan workers in their desire to uphold the independence of their awakening nations would be perfectly intelligible. Comrade Lapshewitz declared that, while the attack by Austria was an outrage, he was yet of the opinion that the Serbian government was partly to blame because of its policy; Social Democracy, therefore, as an unalterable opponent of this policy, must protest against it by voting against all war-credits. This is an example of courage that may well be compared with the memorable stand taken by Bebel and Liebknecht in 1870.

Through its organisation and socialist education, the German working class has been the strongest cohort of the International. Here, if anywhere, it should have been possible to arouse an energetic opposition to the war-plans of the government. Beyond a doubt, the government, as well as the bourgeoisie, were, at first, somewhat uneasy as to the attitude of the German workers. But this uneasiness was soon dispelled. The Party was not willing to fight the government and immediately used the argument employed by the government itself to create a war-sentiment among the people: 'We have been unwillingly forced into a war of defence against Russia, which has insolently attacked us and threatens our culture.' And the Social-Democratic press showed that the war against Russia was a sacred bequest from Marx. In its ignorance of the imperialist character of modern war, together with the fear of taking up the fight against the terrible power of the militaristic state, the German proletariat has allowed itself to be harnessed to the cart of German imperialism. The Social-Democratic parliamentarians voted war-credits for the government; long years of socialist opposition against militarism were thus wiped out.

This determined the course of socialists all over Europe. True, the Russian socialists refused to vote war-credits, and, in England, the Labour Party – in accordance with ancient pacifist-liberal tradition – bitterly attacked the government for its interference. But, in Belgium, Emil Vandervelde, former Chairman of the International Bureau, was made a member of the cabinet; and, in France, that old uncompromising fighter of the class-struggle, Jules Guesde, who always championed the German radical tendency, accepted a place in the cabinet. In a manifesto published by the French Party, the workers are called upon to defend the democracy and socialism of France against 'German imperialism' – as if the French armies were not fighting for French and English imperialism! Not one whit better are the syndicalists and anarchists, whose hatred of German Social Democracy has now become a fertile ground for jingoism. Thus, at the burial of Jean Jaurès, Jouhaux expressed himself in a purely nationalistic sense. German Social Democrats are now going to the neutral countries as commissioners, so to speak, of the German government, in order to soften the hostility of socialists against the German government; thus, Südekum in Sweden, Scheidemann in Holland, and a whole deputation in Italy. And, everywhere, they are repulsed, not because they have violated their socialist duty to the International but because they speak in the interests of a Germany that is feared by the middle class of all other nations. In Sweden, Branting spoke as if he were the representative of the Swedish middle class: 'We can never forgive you for violating the neutrality of Belgium.' While the proletarian masses, obedient to the rulers, dissolved into national armies and are slaughtering one another in the service of Capital, international Social Democracy has broken up into groups of jingoistic politicians who bitterly attack one another.

The Second International is dead. But this ignoble death is no accident; like the downfall of the First International, the collapse of the Second is an indication of the fact that its usefulness is at an end. It represents, in fact, the downfall of the old fighting methods of the epoch – not in the sense that they will disappear or become useless, but in the sense that the whole world now understands that these methods cannot bring the revolution. They retain their value as preparation, as auxiliary means. But the conquest of power demands new revolutionary forms of struggle. To have pointed these out, to have placed before us the new problems that it was incapable of solving itself – this is the bequest to us of the Second International. These will be fully developed by the new capitalist world that will grow out of this world war – a world of mightier capitalist development, increased oppression of the proletariat, and more pronounced antagonism of the three great world powers, Germany,

England and America. And, out of these new conditions, a new International of Labour will grow, more firmly founded, more strongly organised, more powerful and more socialist than the one that has now perished. Looking beyond the terrible world-fire, we revolutionary socialists are boldly erecting upon the ruins the standard of the new, the coming internationalism:

C'est la lutte finale,
Groupons nous, et demain
L'Internationale
Sera le genre humain.

This is the final struggle
Let us gather together, and tomorrow
The International
Will be the human race.

Chapter Forty-Nine

'National State, Imperialist State and Confederation' (February 1915)

Karl Kautsky

From a Marxist perspective, one can read this essay by Karl Kautsky and make countless critical notations. Whether Kautsky could still be considered a 'Marxist' by 1915 is a matter for dispute. Rosa Luxemburg certainly considered him by this time to be a dangerous renegade, and, in the article that follows this one, she ruthlessly ridiculed the work translated here. On the other hand, Leon Trotsky, in 'The Nation and the Economy' just as obviously read Kautsky's work favourably, particularly his comments on the linguistic community, the national state it facilitated, and the need to go beyond the *economic limitations* of the state by way of a United States of Europe.

The central issue that separated Kautsky from left-wing critics was whether imperialism was inevitable or simply a policy-choice. Kautsky's answer – that imperialism was 'a question of power, not an economic necessity' – is explained at length in this work. He was convinced that *industrial* capital was interested merely in making a profit from selling commodities. When a textile-product was exported from Europe, the transaction ended at the point of sale. Things were different with a railway constructed in a foreign territory that had no state-institutions in the European sense. *Fixed capital-investments* demanded protection, and the imperialist state projected its own power for that purpose. Kautsky thought the way to restrain finance-capital was to exploit differences within the capitalist class. If movement towards freer trade could satisfy industrial capital, interested only in the export of commodities, then resources could be diverted from the arms-race into technological progress, enabling increased productivity, higher living standards and gradual social reform.

With this prospect in view, he had no interest in revolutionary violence or mass-action. While he spoke the language of class-struggle, his immediate interest by 1915 lay in counting ballots. Throughout this essay, democracy is treated as the original and even natural form of social organisation. Its essential modern attributes were 'parliamentarism, the press, and large party organisations encompassing the entire country'. He admitted that there was nothing easier than to criticise those institutions, but he added that 'nothing is more impossible than to do without them in a modern democracy'.

The conclusion of this work can be summarised in a brief formula: combine democratic *political* states in an *economic* federation to eliminate tariffs, and the result would be to alleviate imperialist contradictions. Numerous critics regarded this as a naive and facile simplification. Rosa Luxemburg's 'Perspectives and Projects' was withering in its ridicule. Anton Pannekoek's 'The Prehistory of the World War', also included in this collection, was no less damning. Lenin's responses, just as hostile, are included as footnotes to this translation. The common theme shared by all of Kautsky's critics on the Left was that beyond the national state and the imperialist state lay socialist revolution and the workers' state – not the fantasy of a peaceful federation of free-trading bourgeois democracies.

* * *

'National State, Imperialist State and Confederation'[1]

I. Some remarks on democracy and the national state

Unfortunately, we have once again entered one of those periods when we must begin with the ABCs in order to achieve some clarity. A number of

1. Kautsky 1915.

comrades are finding that everything we previously knew has turned out to be humbug or become outdated, that it corresponded to circumstances that no longer exist and today belongs with the 'liberal inheritance' in 'the junk-room of historical curiosities'.

The principle that the Reichstag fraction upheld in its declaration of 4 August 1914, 'that each people has the right to national self-determination', is also referred to as one of those obsolete views.

That principle is today being attacked by party comrades. We must take stock of it because it will play a great role in the coming peace negotiations.

In an article published in the Chemnitz *Volksstimme* of 8 December 1914, Comrade Winnig[2] declared that that principle was not 'originally a socialist principle, but was inherited by the labour-movement, like so many others, from the spiritual armoury of the bourgeois-revolutionary period of the nineteenth century'. He further argues that the demand has nothing in common with scientific socialism.

> Socialism can make neither the contemporary boundaries nor the unconditional right of every nation to absolute self-determination the foundation of the world political layout. To the extent that socialism can influence the rearrangement after the war, it must, in this matter as in any other, derive its course of action from the general developmental tendencies and the interests of the proletariat.
>
> The development of politics, however, is today unmistakably proceeding in the direction of the large state.

Winnig does not say how this large state, to which we must aspire according to the 'general developmental tendencies', will appear, but it is clear that it should be a state going beyond the scope of the national state.

---

2. [August Winnig (1878–1956) was one of the organisers of the German masons' union. He edited its organ *Die Grundstein* from 1905 and was elected its vice-president in 1913. During the First World War, Winnig belonged to the 'social-imperialist' wing of the SPD. In 1917–18, he was appointed Minister Plenipotentiary to the Baltic Provinces and Reich-Commissioner for East and West Prussia. In 1919, he became Oberpräsident of East Prussia. The following year, he was removed from office and expelled from the SPD for his participation in the Kapp Putsch. In 1933, he welcomed the Nazis as providing the 'salvation of the state' from Marxism, but his Lutheran convictions led him to oppose the neo-pagan tendencies of the Third Reich and to withdraw from politics into 'inner emigration'. Wistrich 2001, p. 177.]

This view has met with applause from the Right and the Left, from Karlsruhe and Halle. Thus, the Karlsruhe *Volksfreund* reprinted an article from the [left-wing] Halle *Volksblatt*. It says among other things:

> In his brochure concerning the Italian war of 1859, Lassalle said that without the independent national state no democracy is possible.[3] It is difficult to see why not. Why could a state like Germany, where in addition to German nationals also live Poles, Danes and Frenchmen, not be democratically administered? Why could a state like Germany – in its contemporary and not purely national existence – be unable to attain democracy even if the twelve million Austrian Germans stay out of it? Today it is class-differences, not national differences and antagonisms, that hinder the attainment of democracy as the complete equality of rights for all citizens.

On that basis, the author from Halle further argues that Lassalle's view in 1859 was not absurd at the time; it was justified because Germany and Italy needed a unified state. Since then, however, capitalism has grown tremendously and increased its productive forces

> ...to such an enormous extent that the framework of the national state has become too narrow for them. For years, the worldwide predominance of states has been the great mainspring of politics. That means that each large state strives to go beyond its boundaries, and indeed *must* strive to do so, because in the capitalist system further economic progress and growth of the productive forces is no longer possible.

In the last sentence, the author has evidently forgotten to add the words 'within the current boundaries' or 'within the framework of the national state' before the words 'is no longer possible'.

All these remarks contain many correct ideas. But, for that reason, there is all the more danger that the great mistakes they conceal, which can be extremely harmful for our propaganda, should pass together with them unheeded.

In order to define these mistakes, we must go into rather more detail and discuss first the essence of democracy.[4]

---

3. [Lassalle 1859.]

4. Cf. on this issue my essay on 'Nationality and Internationality' (Kautsky 1908a). [Lenin remarked: 'K. Kautsky finds fault with the right-winger (Winnig) and a left-winger of Halle (from the Halle *Volksblatt*), who say that the principle of "the right

Democracy is as old as humanity. Its first organisations were the hordes that administered their affairs partly through convention and habit, partly through the decisions of experienced and freely elected leaders, and partly through the decisions of their assembled members. It is self-evident that all horde-members were able to understand each other, that they spoke the same language. When, here and there, female captives spoke a foreign language, they were not part of the democratic community. Insofar as democracy existed, it was for the language-community. That is to say, all those belonging to the same democratic commonwealth spoke the same language. The contrary was not true, however: not all those who spoke the same language were united in a community. That was not the case for by far the largest part of human history.

As long as reading and writing had not been invented and the masses were not familiar with them, while, at the same time, the means of transportation were scarcely developed, democracy could only function through verbal agreement. For that purpose, certain boundaries were drawn for the area and the population of the single democratic communities that could not be trespassed. The popular assembly was the highest democratic authority, and the community's area could not be expanded so far as to hinder part of its members from attending the assembly regularly. On the other hand, the assembly could not be so numerous as to prevent part of its members from being able to follow the proceedings. No primitive community, therefore, ever went beyond the boundaries of the village-community [*Markgenossenschaft*][5] and the township.

At that stage, a larger state usually evolved through an especially strong or favoured community (whether a tribe or a strong city) subjugating other tribes or communities and turning them into tributaries. However, the subjugated peoples usually retained their self-government in all domestic

of every nation to national self-determination" (p. 5 in the declaration of August 4) is out-of-date. Kautsky favours the centrist position on this issue, and chews over all the old stuff about the link between democracy and the national state.' Lenin 1939, Notebook "η" ("Eta"): K. Kautsky, *The National State, the Imperialist State and the Alliance of States*.]

5. [In his *Communism in Central Europe in the Time of the Reformation*, Kautsky spoke of the *Markgenossenschaft* as 'the primitive society of the members of a commune holding land in common' (Kautsky 1959, p. 38). Engels also wrote an appendix to *Socialism, Utopian and Scientific* that was published separately as *The Mark* (Engels 1902).]

issues. The democracy of communities can thus become the foundation of despotism in the state, as is often the case in the East to this day. Engels already pointed out that Russian absolutism is based upon the democracy of village communities.

Since each community continues to regulate its own internal affairs, it is not necessary for all the communities united under a single state to speak the same language. It is enough for a couple of representatives in each community to speak the language of the rulers. The community of language holds within the area of the singular democratic organisations. The dictatorship that keeps them together stretches over territories with different tongues. For the expansion of a state at that stage there is thus no other limit than those imposed by the strength of the conquering community. Besides, there is no other possible way of keeping the communities together. Only the warlike strength of the ruling community can build the state, which, as a result, can rapidly experience enormous growth. If that strength diminishes, it can just as quickly fall apart. Even in recent times, we saw examples of such a state's expansion. The rapid advance of Russia to the East and South since the seventeenth century, as well as the rapid conquest of the largest part of India by England in the eighteenth century, would have been impossible in both cases if the primitive democracy of the community had not prevailed, above which a military tyranny arose as the element holding the state together. In that way, Russia acquired more than twice the area of Europe, and it is basically thanks to India that the population of the British Empire almost equals that of Europe. Europe has 443 million inhabitants; the British Empire has 418 million, of whom three quarters live in India. Russia encompasses approximately 150 nationalities, and the languages of India are even more numerous.

But, during the period when both giant empires were formed, the material conditions also developed to realise democracy in a state going beyond the area of the community, or the *Markgenossenschaft*, thus replacing primitive by modern democracy. That was achieved by the development of transportation, by printing and the generalisation of reading and writing. Now the means existed for all those who spoke the same language to communicate without having to come into personal contact. The significance of spoken understanding gradually receded vis-à-vis the significance of written and particularly printed communication. An intensive spiritual community now developed not only for an upper stratum of educated persons but also for the masses of those who spoke the same language. This community further reduced the diversity of dialects through a common written language, in that way increasing even further the extent and intensity of the linguistic community. At the same time, the modern large state arose with a centralised bureaucracy and customs-barriers. At first, it strengthened central political power, which was absolute. But the development of exchange and the press made it increasingly possible for the population of the entire state to know the deeds and omissions of the central power, to discuss and criticise them. The demeanour of the central power, at the same time, became increasingly important for the individuals the more its scope grew. The urge appeared, therefore, to have an influence on it through a system of representatives elected and controlled by the masses. In that way, modern democracy developed, whose essential traits are parliamentarism, the press, and large party organisations encompassing the entire country. Nothing is easier than to criticise those institutions, and nothing is more impossible than to do without them in a modern democracy. People are more and more up in arms about parliamentarism. The assertions that it has outlived itself and must be replaced by a more perfect democratic system are almost as old as parliamentarism itself. But, upon closer examination, this alternative system appears as a form of primitive democracy. That is true both of direct legislation by the people and also of its more assertive variant, the mass-strike. If the mechanism of parliamentarism someday grinds to a halt, both can have significant historical effects, but only as supplements to parliamentarism or as an impetus for it; they cannot replace it.[6] The most resolute opponents of parliamentarism, the anarchists, are consistent enough to want to get rid of it by going back to the communities and dissolving the state into a sum of sovereign communities. Thus, they strikingly demonstrate how primitive any democracy is that wants to give up the representative system, and how reactionary are the attempts to establish such primitive democracy.

The organ of politics and of all social action is language. I can only influence my party if I speak its language; I will influence it all the more easily (all other conditions being equal) the better I master that language. If different languages are spoken within a state, it is almost impossible for a politician, a newspaper or a party to speak to the entire people; each one will only speak to

6. [Kautsky is summarising here the views developed by Bebel when he defended the compromise on the mass-strike with the German trade-union bureaucracy in 1906.]

part of it. Even a party as international as Social Democracy is split in Austria-Hungary into different parties unable to understand each other, and each of these acts only on a part of the proletariat within the state.

The contributor to our party organ in Halle asks why full democracy cannot be achieved in Germany with its Poles, Danes and Frenchmen. A Polish politician, a Polish newspaper or a Polish book may well speak to us very vividly, convincingly and significantly in their own language, and they will perhaps have an impact on Poles, including those living outside Germany, but not on the German people. However, the essence of democracy consists in acting on the people and through the people.

In a democratic state, with a uniform language, all politicians and parties have only *one* possibility of increasing their influence on the state: by propagating their ideas among the people, by winning supporters among them. In a multinational state [*Nationalitätenstaat*], no one can influence the entire people, and the propaganda of each is limited by the number of members of his own language-community. The larger that number, the more promising his propaganda and the greater his power in the state. That is why, in multinational states, the development of democracy and the struggle of parties for propagation of their ideas are joined by the efforts of the party organisations of different nations to bring into their own nationality – that is to say, into their language community – as many people as possible from the general population, particularly through appropriate school facilities. Democracy is adulterated, disrupted and weakened in relation to the central political power by the struggle of nations within the state.

Yet another aspect of democracy comes into consideration here. Democracy does not mean simply control of the state-power by the popular masses but also equality of the rights of individuals in relation to state-power. This equality of rights is likewise impaired in a multinational state. Every modern state requires a uniform administration and therefore also a standard language. There is no modern state without an official language that must be understood and mastered at least by all the higher public authorities. The United States of America comprises countless nationalities; it is not even a centralised state. It has, however, a single official language: the English tongue. Indeed, even the two multinational states united by personal union into the Habsburg monarchy [of Austria-Hungary] each have an official language – Hungary has the Magyar language, Austria in fact has the German language.

It is certainly not to the benefit of Austria that German is an official language only incompletely. If necessary, a small state can have two official languages. More official languages in a single state are practically impossible.

It is clear that democratic equality is badly impaired by the diversity of languages within a state. Whoever speaks the official language has a powerful advantage over those who do not master it. The defendant is discriminated against if the judges and attorneys do not understand his language; the pupil, if he is taught and examined in a language that he speaks only painstakingly. State-officials who do not speak the language of the bureau are removed from their posts. A speaker in parliament is seriously impaired in his function if he has to speak a language with which he is he is not familiar, or if he speaks a language that is understood by only a part of the persons present. An isolated foreigner in the country can put up with that situation. But, as members of a strong nation within a state, the individuals rebel against the discrimination they have to suffer due to their nationality. The stronger the democratic consciousness, the stronger also is the urge to fight for equality of rights for their nation within the state. National opposition thus comes into growing contradiction with the conditions of life in the state.

The class-struggle is also weakened by that national opposition. If one nation is injured by another within a state, all classes of the oppressed nation all too easily feel solidarity in relation to the oppressors. Class-antagonisms are blurred or distorted, finding no expression or only an aberrant one, and the solidarity of members of the same class is impaired, especially among the members of the exploited classes, whose class-consciousness is, as a rule, naturally not as developed as that of the exploiters.

All those difficulties are avoided where the entire mass of the people in a state speaks the same language, i.e., in a national state. In old multinational states, created before the rise of modern democracy, the difficulties are somewhat lessened by habit and the adaptation of the population, which has not yet experienced the advantages of the national state. They are completely unbearable if a state forcefully annexes alien elements for whom political action in the framework of modern democracy has already become second nature. The striving for a national state appears simultaneously with the striving for modern democracy and is intimately bound up with it. Nothing is more mistaken than the idea that Austria-Hungary simply needs democracy in order to become viable. All the democratic attempts to regenerate Austria amount to transforming the unitary state into a federation of national states. The national autonomy demanded by peoples living on the outskirts of the Russian Empire amounts to the same thing. It is within each of those national states that full – not just formal but real and efficient – democracy is possible.

Social Democracy has taken over from bourgeois democracy the aspiration towards a national state. True, we are not bourgeois democrats, but we do not distinguish ourselves from them by regarding democracy as something less important or even superfluous. As the lowest class in the state, the proletariat cannot assert itself otherwise than through democracy. But we do not share the illusions of bourgeois democrats that the proletariat will come into its own simply by attaining democracy. That only constitutes the ground on which the proletariat can struggle for its rights. In a democracy, the proletarian emancipation-struggle does not cease, it just assumes different forms.

It is precisely for the proletariat, rather than for the bourgeoisie, that democracy is a vital necessity. The bourgeoisie has today abandoned its democratic ideals and, with them, the idea of the national state. It throws this 'liberal inheritance' into 'the junk-room of historical curiosities'. But that is truly no reason for us to do the same. We must not understand the materialist conception of history as if the 'general developmental tendencies' of the bourgeoisie, because they are determined by economic relations, must therefore also be accepted by the proletariat. The proletariat has its own developmental tendencies, which are no less economically determined and which it has to follow regardless of whether they differ from those of the bourgeoisie or even contradict them.

Admittedly, it is just a question of *tendencies* that must be understood and followed attentively, not of absolute models. That should be obvious. And, yet, some people believe that by criticising the stereotyped application of models they have proved the tendency to be false. That is the position of [the right-winger] Winnig and of the [left-wing] comrades from Halle.

First of all, the demand for a national state should not be regarded as an absolute obligation to unite all persons speaking the same language in a common state. The idea of the national state only says that democracy thrives best and can be most fully implemented if the entire mass of the population within a state speaks the same language. Another state with the same language can very well appear next to it. Why should that contradict the needs of democracy? If the official language of the United States is English, of Brazil Portuguese, and of the other states of South America Spanish, nobody will see in the separation of those states from England, Portugal and Spain an infringement of the principle of nationality.

Certainly, the quest to establish national states is, in many cases, equivalent to the striving to unite all people speaking the same language within a single state-organism. That is only possible for areas inhabited by a compact mass of members of the same nationality and bordering upon each other.

Under those conditions, there are three reasons that bring forth the drive towards national unity. The first and most immediate is the wish to make the national state as great and strong as possible, a striving that is certainly compatible with democracy if that strength is not used to oppress others but only for self-protection against foreign intervention. The second reason is the wish, springing from the growth of capitalist exchange, to do away with any sectionalism, to abolish internal tariffs and achieve uniform business conditions such as a single currency and uniform legislation. These two motives are joined by a third, which is particularly strong among the lower strata of the population if the compatriots in neighbouring areas are discriminated against or even mistreated because of their nationality. The stronger the democratic consciousness and solidarity, the stronger will be the need to set those compatriots free.

Our comrade from Halle would perhaps have been less energetic in repudiating 'the dissolution of Austria-Hungary in order to allow the twelve million Germans living there to join Germany' if, for instance, the Magyars completely dominated Austria, if only Hungarian could be spoken at the Vienna parliament, if the schools and universities taught only in Hungarian, and if every public official had to master the Hungarian language. He would then perhaps have understood how much democracy and national independence have to do with each other.

We must mention still another point regarding Winnig's attempts to ridicule the quest for a national state by presenting it as a stereotyped model, as an 'absolute right'. Language is an important means of communication and of union between people, but it is not the only one. People speaking different tongues can also communicate with each other even if they have to do so through an interpreter. Within every state, economic, familiar, and political relations are established that, under certain circumstances, can be stronger than the bond created by a common language. None of the modern great states developed straightaway as a national state; all began as multinational states, and most of them bear today the traces of their multinational origins. For that reason, close relations have developed here and there between groups of different nationalities within the historical states, whose termination could be painful and, indeed, could imply downright economic or political degradation if it took place by force, through conquest. If someone simply wants to take up a language-map of Europe and organise the reconstruction of our continent on that basis, he would meet energetic opposition in some places. Let us recall how vehemently the Alsatians protested in 1871 against their incorporation into Germany, although they were more familiar with the German tongue than with the French. The French Swiss do not want to become Frenchmen but rather prefer to remain together with the German Swiss. In addition, there are Italians who fear that Trieste will face economic decay if it is detached from Austria, etc.

If we recognise all this, what becomes of the nationality-principle? Winnig argues that, in that case, we will reach the *status quo*, which is as unacceptable as the principle of nationality.

> One could argue that the nationality-principle can be understood to mean that the *contemporary* state-arrangement cannot be altered, and that, above all, Germany and Austria cannot annex any alien peoples to their territories. But that means nothing but to turn the famous *status quo* into the world-political system of socialism . . . as well as to renounce all future development by the perpetuation of current borders.

Naturally, the *status quo* is not the ideal world-political system of Social Democracy. Nor do we ask that the idea of the national state be implemented unconditionally and that all existing borders that do not correspond to it be overthrown. That alone would be enough to reassure Winnig and our friend from Halle that we do not demand the disintegration of large states into countless little national states. Besides, we will see later that there are means of uniting little national states into larger communities.

Under no circumstances are we interested in preserving the *status quo*. But we are interested in the way in which it will be changed.

Democracy and the idea of the national state, which is closely related to it, require that the *status quo should not be altered without the support of the affected peoples*. We are opposed to the forced annexation of population to a state purely on the basis of the right of conquest. Nobody can oppose the *status quo* more decidedly than Social Democracy. And nobody rejects the right of conquest as a method of changing the *status quo* more decidedly than Social Democracy. If we uphold this standpoint, the changes in the *status quo* that we support will represent further approximations to the ideal of the national state rather than new infringements of that idea.

Nothing could be worse for the German people than to have this war result in the transformation of Germany from a national into a multinational state, i.e., if the German state were to expand to include non-German nations. Those who want this to happen have not worked in a multinational state and do not know how much it distorts and oppresses democracy.

Are we not thereby setting ourselves against economic necessity? Does the latter not force the modern state 'to go beyond its boundaries, because, otherwise, the further growth of the productive forces is no longer possible'?

2. The necessity of the imperialist state

We have already remarked that the ideas of democracy and the national state have lost their power of attraction for the bourgeoisie. At a certain stage in their development, all the capitalist states strive to go beyond their boundaries even if, in the process, they annex elements alien to the nation. But that does not mean that this reveals a tendency to change from a national into a multinational state.

The new driving force that creates this expansionist drive among the developed capitalist states is *imperialism*. It is not my intention to repeat here what has already been said countless times. What, in general terms, had to be said about the causes and phenomena of imperialism has already been sufficiently stated. In my article on imperialism,[7] I said whatever I might add. There I gave the reasons for this definition:

> Imperialism is a product of highly developed *industrial* capitalism. It consists of the drive of every industrial capitalist nation to conquer and annex an ever greater *agrarian* zone, with no regard to what nations live there.'[8]

7. Kautsky 1914b. See Chapter 47.
8. Kautsky 1914b, p. 909.

The decisive thing for imperialism is the antagonism between *industrial* and *agrarian* areas. The agrarian countries that the capitalist states are eager to annex are economically backward. But they are also backward politically. They still stand at a stage of primitive communal or associational[9] democracy and are still incapable of developing a modern, national democracy encompassing the whole state – not because of any racial characteristics, but because they have not developed the material preconditions for that democracy. They are not like children needing guardianship, incapable of protecting their own interests or of managing their own affairs, but they are still unable to do so within the framework of a large state.

To conquer and subjugate such communities is very easy for a centralised European state, not only where the communities and village-associations[10] have remained completely independent but also where they have been united into a primitive state. In those places, European despotism just replaces local despotism.

Through that sort of state-expansion, no national state can be established, only a colonial state. The newly annexed elements have neither the force nor the will to take part in the political life of the state or to influence it in a democratic way. They merely want to be left in peace. This increase in state-territory does not create domestic political difficulties for the metropolitan state.

Nonetheless, it contradicts the democratic feelings and the international solidarity of the proletariat, whose conditions for emancipation are incompatible with any exploitation and oppression. Even when they are not affected directly, their exploiters and oppressors are indirectly strengthened. And the proletariat cannot free itself by letting some of its elements, in certain trades or areas, become the beneficiaries of exploitation and oppression. That rather means a weakening of its position.[11]

For the bourgeoisie, of course, these scruples do not exist. If, some day, it decides to enlarge the national state into a multinational state, this tendency finds no limits other than opposition from the other colonial powers.

9. [*Markgenossenschaftlichen*: mark-like, corporate.]
10. [*Markgenossenschaften*: village-communities.]
11. [Lenin commented on this statement: 'And not a word of conclusion from this!! The sophist!' Lenin 1939, Notebook "η" ("Eta"): K. Kautsky, *The National State, the Imperialist State and the Alliance of States*.]

The will to establish a national state has certain limits. Even if it is militarily victorious, a state that has already reached the national stage encounters growing difficulties in the endeavour to expand beyond its boundaries by means of conquests.

The striving to expand a national state by annexing to it, against their will, alien peoples who have a developed modern democracy or are at least aspiring to it, and who have an active national life, encounters resistance from the annexed population that will be all the greater and more invincible the greater its numbers and the higher its economic and political development. Even the Russification of alien-western elements in Russia encounters growing difficulties. In developed modern states, even very small national minorities have managed to oppose absorption and preserve their peculiarities. Even the greatest military successes are no longer able to change that.

The endeavour to acquire or expand colonial possessions is totally different. It does not give rise to the same difficulties as the multinational state. To be sure, though, the colonial state also does not display the solidity and closeness of the national state. Colonial possessions can as easily be lost to other colonial powers as won from them; they can be bought and sold. A lasting resistance from the native population to such changes is not to be expected. Here, only the military balance of power between the colonial powers is decisive. On the other hand, the expansion of a colonial empire also finds its limits only in the military power of the state vis-à-vis other colonial powers.

Through the strong democratic life of its inhabitants, on the contrary, the national state offers the most energetic and lasting, almost insuperable resistance to any curtailment or change that may be imposed in its territory by a foreign conquering power. On the other hand, that state finds its limits in the extent of the contiguous area of the nation, which it cannot overstep without injuring itself. All this makes the force of its democracy more important for its existence than the force of its army, which must have a purely defensive character in a cohesive national state if it wants to remain cohesive. The idea of the militia develops simultaneously with the idea of modern democracy and the national state.[12] They are all three supported by the same parties and popular classes.

12. [The text mistakenly reads 'multinational state'.]

The period of imperialism, by contrast, which began approximately a generation ago, set in with complete abandonment of the militia idea by all the bourgeois classes and became a period of feverish arms-race not only on land but also, and particularly, at sea.

Winnig and the Halle comrade say nothing about this. They simply declare that the expansion of the state beyond its previous boundaries is inevitable and absolutely necessary, because otherwise 'further economic progress and growth of the productive forces is no longer possible'. They declare the imperialist impulse to be not only economically based, which is beyond any doubt, but also, for that reason, essential.

It is remarkable how the extremes meet in this question. The extreme Right and the extreme Left of our party declare that imperialism is a necessity for the existing mode of production. But the former conclude from this that we must support imperialism, while the latter say that imperialism is inevitable in the capitalist system. Therefore, if we do not want imperialism, [according to the left wing] we must counter it with socialism; that is, not simply propaganda for socialism, with which we have opposed all forms of capitalist rule for half a century, but also its immediate implementation.

This looks very radical, but it is only suitable for driving those who do not believe in the immediate practical implementation of socialism into the camp of imperialism. It is grist for the mill of those socialists who say: We want socialism, but as long as we do not have it we must be imperialists, because a good Marxist must not oppose the 'general developmental tendencies'. [These socialists argue that] under the given circumstances imperialism is an economic necessity for capital and therefore also for the proletariat, which thrives all the better the more rapidly capitalism develops, and which suffers most when the capitalist production-process stagnates.[13]

If one operates with the concept of economic necessity, one should above all beware of conceiving the economic process as a rigid mechanism. Society is not a mechanism but an organism. The concepts of elasticity and adaptability are therefore present from the outset. The social organism has those properties

13. [Lenin called these passages 'a swindling distortion of the position of the Lefts', adding: 'This is followed by the most banal prattle about society being an organism and not a mechanism, and similar childish nonsense (with hints about the strong "national sentiments" among the workers).' Lenin 1939, Notebook "η" ("Eta"): K. Kautsky, *The National State, the Imperialist State and the Alliance of States*.]

to an ever-greater degree because its elements are not cells that unconsciously react to any stimulus but thinking men, who, between the stimulus and the action it triggers, can in many cases interpose deliberations in which, partly consciously and partly unconsciously, not only their own personal experiences but also the experiences accumulated during millennia by the whole society, which sediment in our brains in a more or less imperfect form, assert themselves. The effects of this sediment on the individuals are much too complicated and diverse for us always to be able to predict them with the means at our disposal. Insofar as they are unpredictable, the will appears to be free, although actually it is necessarily conditioned as with all natural phenomena. The entire social process is the result of the action of countless individual wills, which partly reinforce each other if they operate in the same direction or else paralyse and abolish each other if they are antithetic.

Despite all individual differences in ability and experience, all men are in fundamental terms equally ordered, and to that extent they react in the same way to similar stimuli under the same circumstances. That comes to light whenever we look at great masses in processes that repeat themselves regularly. From these observations arose the concept of law-governed processes in human society, which assert themselves as a natural necessity. Of course, this presupposes that we accurately know all the factors operating under those circumstances. If some of them have changed without our knowledge, or if we evaluated that change wrongly, the masses will behave differently from what we predicted.

One of the factors most difficult to calculate is the *balance of power* between the classes. A theoretical analysis can define clearly enough the *interests* of each class but not their *power* at any given moment. In the process, many so-called imponderables come into consideration, spiritual influences that cannot be determined statistically and can easily change with changing circumstances. Thus, for instance, the class-antagonism between capital and labour can be clearly identified on purely economic grounds; the workers can be made conscious of it relatively easily, and, on that basis, it is possible to organise a special workers' party with anti-capitalist goals.

But, in questions where no immediate economic interests are directly involved, that does not eliminate the influence of the ruling classes upon the working class through religious organisations and customs or through national feelings existing from time immemorial. One should not, for instance, imagine that everyone voting for Social Democracy advocates each point of the Social-Democratic programme with the same intensity. Some of these points will be closer to their heart while others will lie further away, and some may even displease them. Thus, the strength of Social Democracy can vary widely according to changes in the situation that place special emphasis on different points of its programme. If the main issue of a parliamentary election is, for instance, new taxes, the masses will rally around us in much larger numbers than if the struggle turns around militarism and colonial policy. One only has to compare the 'Hottentot elections' of 1907 with the elections after the financial reform of 1912.

Independence of thought on the part of a class – a well-grounded and firm conviction that is not shaken by moods or momentary interests – is a power-factor of the first rank. Nothing is more mistaken than the opinion that historical materialism traces every political power back to the wallet. It ultimately traces all political and social phenomena back to material *conditions*; not, however, in all circumstances, to material *interests*. The thirst for knowledge that distinguishes the urban proletarian from the small peasant must be traced back to the peculiarities of his conditions of life, not to his economic interests; and the same is true of the possibility of satisfying that striving. If we expect better results from the class-struggle of the modern proletariat than from the struggles of the working classes of previous times, the essential reason is the greater thirst for knowledge and the greater educational opportunities of the modern workers.

Historical materialism is not at all incompatible with the idea that the first condition for a successful class-struggle is liberation of the struggling class from the ideological influence of the enemy-class. But precisely that factor is difficult to ascertain accurately, and illusions can easily creep in. Despite all the progress in economic theory and statistics, the balance of power between classes and parties is hardly predictable, especially in abnormal situations.

Shifts in that balance of power are to be traced back ultimately to changes in economic relations. On the other hand, power-shifts can, in turn, bring about economic changes, which, under certain circumstances, can radically transform the entire mode of production or, under other circumstances, merely compel it to a slight adjustment to the new relations.

Bourgeois economists have muddled up economy and technique, seeing in economic relations the relations between men and the things created by them, and in capital and the wage-fund an accumulation of things, thereby taking the size of capital and the level of wages under certain conditions as given. Marx showed that economic relations are relations between men mediated by things; he showed the elasticity and adaptability of the capitalist mode of production and its various forms, as against the bourgeois economists who declared that any intervention in the production-process was the worst threat to society. Marx showed how often precisely the intervention of a regulatory power, for instance the state-power or the trade-unions, not only did not impair the production-process but rather lifted it to a higher stage. That was the case, for instance, with the compulsory reductions of the hours of work that the entrepreneurs prophesied would bring about the ruin of industry.

Since then, the elasticity and adaptability of production have not diminished but instead have grown considerably, as the current war clearly proves. That must be attributed, on the one hand, to the fact that convention and habit in industry are more and more being superseded by science, which is constantly revolutionising the production-process. On the other hand, it is due to the centralisation of enterprises, their organisation in cartels and trusts, their growing domination by a few great banks and the increasing economic significance of state-power. Instead of countless individual wills, which, in a new and unprecedented situation, find it difficult to unite into a single collective will, a few potentates appear who are all interested in and accustomed to reaching a mutual understanding. It is easier for them to impart a new direction to the entire process.

This growing elasticity and adaptability of production does not at all mean a growing viability of capitalism. Capitalism owes to them the fact that it approaches more and more those forms of production characteristic of the socialist mode of production. But it remains faithful to its capitalist nature: profit continues to be its driving force. The profit-interests stand, as before, in contradiction with the interests of the working class; the mode of production is forced to increase the mass of its products more rapidly than the growth in the mass of its labour-forces.[14] These traits are indissolubly attached to capitalism,

---

14. [*Arbeitskräfte*: manpower, workforce, labour-force. The usual rendering of *Arbeitskraft* in the English versions of Marx's *Capital* is 'labour-power'. The passage evidently refers to the slower growth of effective demand vis-à-vis total production due to the limited consumption of the working masses.]

and they awaken ever-greater opposition among the propertyless classes of society, setting limits to its continuity. The growing elasticity and adaptability of capitalism do not enable it to exist and grow *ad infinitum*. They only mean that even a shift in the balance of power between classes, one so deep that it leads to a political and social catastrophe, will not necessarily lead to an economic catastrophe, and [at the same time] they mean that the transition from capitalism to socialism can take place without an economic collapse.

If one takes into consideration this already extensive elasticity and adaptability of capitalism, one will no longer conclude offhand, from the fact that imperialism finds its powerful economic driving forces in capitalism, that imperialism is inevitable as long as the capitalist mode of production exists or that it is absurd to want to oppose it within the framework of that mode of production.

Given the already inevitable expansion of capital, the question is whether there are any social strata and classes interested in choosing means other than expansion of the colonial empire, which, from now on, can be accomplished by individual powers only by means of another world war. The further question is whether those social strata and classes are strong enough to oppose the imperialist tendencies.

That those social strata exist and have the most urgent *interest* in world peace and disarmament is beyond doubt and requires no proof. The petty bourgeoisie and small peasants, indeed, even many capitalists and intellectuals, have no interest in imperialism that could possibly be greater than the injuries they suffer from war and the arms-race. In the proletariat, those reasons for struggling against imperialism are joined by democracy and internationalism.

The *power* standing behind that interest [in peace and disarmament] is admittedly impossible to measure. The social elements interested in imperialism not only dispose of the strongest material instruments of power; they also exert a powerful economic and spiritual influence on broad strata of the population, including the working class.

Whether the opponents of imperialism have the power to contain it is thus by no means assured. But the opposite is also not certain. We have seen that precisely the balance of power is something impossible to predict. That is especially true of a period such as the present one, which entails completely new situations.

It is true that the party of international-proletarian interests has not proved strong enough to prevent the War in the circumstances in which it broke out. But one can doubtless argue that opposition to the War would have been stronger if it had shown more clearly its imperialist character, and if it had not been perceived everywhere as a struggle for the independence and integrity of the nation.

We do not know how the course of the War will affect imperialist moods and tendencies. In any case, to argue that imperialism is indispensable for capitalist production in its current stage, and as long as such mode of production lasts, is not the suitable means to counteract it. Whatever intentions people may have in making these statements, they are actually serving the imperialists' interests, raising their spiritual influence on the popular masses and in that way increasing their power.

Actually, imperialism is just a question of power, not an economic necessity. Not only is it not necessary for capitalist economic life, but its significance for capitalism has in many cases been exaggerated beyond all measure.

One can demonstrate, first, that imperialism is not the sole driving force of the expansionist movement of states. Second, that colonial policy itself, precisely in its most important manifestations, does not have imperialist origins. Third, and finally, that the power-politics of imperialism, far from being indispensable for the economic development of capitalism, are even today the most costly and dangerous but by no means the most effective method of capitalist expansion, and that other methods can be employed alongside them that have far greater economic importance.

3. Causes of the expansionist thrust of states

The characteristic feature of imperialism is the combination of finance-capital with industrial capital.

Whoever wants to recognise the historical effects of capital must clearly distinguish its different categories. That was done for the first time by Marx in the third volume of *Capital*, where he distinguished between industrial, commercial and monetary capital.

Developing those ideas, in 1898 I investigated how the different types of capital related to colonial policy; and, in the series of articles on 'Old and New Colonial Policy' and on 'Jiaozhou', I showed in what sense this new imperialist policy differed from the previous colonial policy.[15] I supplemented those observations in the course of a lengthy polemic I waged in 1900 with Max Schippel, who then supported the naval bills because, among other reasons, 'today pretty much every Englishman is a pirate at heart, much as every Prussian is a gendarme'.[16] My brochures *Commercial Policy and Social Democracy*, which first appeared in 1901, and *Socialism and Colonial Policy* (1907) followed the same train of thought.[17] In those works, I developed in greater detail arguments that I can only mention briefly here.

Today, it is generally recognised that the first exhaustive and therefore essential exposition of finance-capital on a Marxist basis – of its economic roots, conditions and tendencies – was accomplished by Hilferding in his *Finance Capital* (1910).[18]

Industrial capital, the class of industrial entrepreneurs, shows, from the outset, completely different tendencies from those of commercial and financial capital. It tends towards peace between peoples, limitation of the absolute power of the state by parliamentary and democratic institutions, and austerity in the national budget; it is always against protective tariffs on foodstuffs and raw materials. It even regards industrial tariffs as mere educative tariffs born of industrial backwardness that should disappear with economic progress.

By contrast, finance-capital, the class of great money-lenders and bankers, tends to support absolute state-power and the violent assertion of its claims domestically and externally. It has an interest in great state-expenditures and public debts as long as they are not so large as to bring about the bankruptcy of the state. It is on good terms with large landed proprietors, and it has no objections to their preferential treatment through agrarian tariffs.

Economic development brought to power monetary capital and the policy corresponding to it much earlier than industrial capital. But, in the nineteenth century, industrial capital came to power and increasingly curtailed the influence of money-capital on the state. However, that was only a tem-

15. Kautsky 1898a and 1898b.
16. Kautsky 1900b.
17. Kautsky 1911f and 1907b.
18. Hilferding 1910a.

porary stage. It was finally overcome by another stage in which the form of the joint-stock company, which had already acquired great importance for commercial and money-capital, took hold of industrial capital. In that way, the largest and strongest part of industrial capital united with money-capital while, at the same time, initiating its rapprochement with large-scale landed property. Trusts and centralisation of the great banks carried this development to extremes.

The statist tendencies of finance-capital now became the general tendencies of the entire ruling economic classes in the most developed capitalist states.

That is one of the distinguishing features of the current period, which people have called the imperialist period.

The second distinguishing feature of the contemporary imperialist period is the fact that the export of commodities has assumed a new character. From its very beginning, capitalist production has been directed not only to satisfaction of the domestic demand of the state but also to export. The first theoretical principle it raised [mercantilism] was to sell as many as possible of its own products abroad and to buy as little as possible from the outside. Those exported products, however, served only the consumption of foreign countries. In the imperialist period, that kind of export is not enough to provide sufficient occupation for the productive forces of developed capitalist states. Now, it became necessary to export means of production that serve as capital in foreign countries, for instance, material for the construction and operation of railways by means of which agrarian territories were opened up, machines for the operation of mines, of plantations, and finally even of industries, etc.

This second kind of tendency is certainly irresistible and will exist as long as the capitalist economy exists. Its containment would only be possible by curtailing and crippling economic development. But it is another question whether all the tendencies of the first kind, the political methods employed by finance-capital, are inevitable and can likewise only be restrained by means leading to economic decay.

The most conspicuous of these methods is colonial expansion. It has given its name to the whole direction of state policy controlled by finance-capital. That policy has been called imperialism, the striving to establish a great *imperium*, a world empire, whose agrarian parts are large enough to absorb the surplus-capitals of the mother-country and employ them in its interests. When people speak today about the expansionist need of states, they always think about imperialism. On the one hand, imperialism is seen as the cause of all expansionist endeavours; on the other hand, imperialist expansion is considered to be the only remaining way of further developing the capitalist mode of production.

Let us begin by analysing the first assumption. If we follow up in detail the expansionist endeavours of the different capitalist states in recent times, we will discover that the imperialist tendencies, characterised by the fusion of industrial and finance-capital and the need to export capitals, were by no means the only cause of these expansionist efforts. Alongside them other, more primitive tendencies were also at work; the imperialist tendencies are only the newest and most striking ones and therefore those of greatest interest to the theoretician. The theoretician can analyse in depth the imperialist tendencies, as in the case of any other phenomenon, only to the extent that he analyses them on their own, abstracting from all disturbing accidental circumstances. That does not prove, of course, that these circumstances do not exist. The theoretician must also take them into consideration when he analyses the process as a whole.

Not every expansionist striving of the state has economic motives even if they are always affected by economic conditions. The quest for power and security can also influence them.

The most primitive of all expansionist tendencies is the tendency violently to appropriate the products of someone else's labour, not just once, temporarily, through robbery, but to do it over and over again by means of a permanent tribute. That tendency can be traced back as far as written history goes. It is closely connected, as we have seen, with primitive *markgenossenschaftliche* or communal democracy. As long as the methods and means of modern bureaucracy have not developed, the foreign lord is only able to extract tribute or raise taxes from the communities [*Gemeinde oder Genossenschaft*], not from their individual members. Power-relations, therefore, often become a means of preserving, cementing or remodelling primitive communism.

Thus, Russian despotism was until recently based on village-communism, much as the 'benevolent, enlightened' despotism of the Jesuits in Paraguay was in the seventeenth and eighteenth centuries. In British India, a widespread taxation-system was built by the state on the basis of this communism, and, in the Dutch East Indies, the whole compulsory system of agricultural labour on behalf of the foreign exploiter was also erected by the state on the same basis.

The only precondition for such a state-expansion is military superiority. No kind of economic need, such as the promotion of industry, is at play here. It is no more than primitive robbery turned into a system.

By contrast, expansionist policy springs from a real economic need wherever it originates in a demographic surplus of the mother-country. That kind of expansionist policy played a large role in the history of mankind, but not in the age of capitalist colonial policy. This policy was accompanied in the seventeenth and eighteenth centuries by constant complaints about demographic deficits in the European states and continual attempts to increase their population. To be sure, there was a strong emigration from many areas, but it was not brought about by an excessive increase in population but by the political oppression of emerging absolutism as well as by the economic oppression resulting from expropriation of the agricultural population, which swelled the number of propertyless people.

And the situation did not improve in the nineteenth and twentieth centuries. The regions that today supply emigrants almost exclusively also export foodstuffs together with their population. Therefore, that emigration is by no means due to a narrowing food-supply [*Nahrungsspielraum*: scope for getting food].

Nothing is more misleading than the view of modern colonial politicians, according to whom colonies are necessary in order to absorb the demographic surplus of the industrial countries. The countries experiencing emigration are today agrarian countries, such as Russia, the Balkan states, Ireland and India. The densely populated industrial countries actually absorb immigration.

Among the agrarian classes, it is again much less the peasant than the large landed proprietor who pushes for the expansionist policy. The peasant does not want more land than that he can cultivate with his family. The large landed proprietor, who does not cultivate land with his own labour but with wage-workers or bound labourers, can never have enough land. Wherever the feudal aristocracy disposes of the necessary military power, it pushes for expansion of the state-territory, which it naturally wants to become its own territory. Thus, the nobility in the middle ages was the soul of the German expansionist policy in the Slavic areas; in Spain and France it was, alongside absolutism, the strongest driving force of colonial policy in the sixteenth and seventeenth centuries. In America, the Spanish and French conquerors established new feudal institutions. Spanish America and European Spain are suffering even today from the consequences of this expansionist policy, which meant anything but an encouragement of economic progress. It strengthened absolutism and feudalism in Spain, while simultaneously involving that country in constant wars that finally ruined it, despite the proud victories that Spanish weapons achieved for a long time on the battlefields.

The *latifundia*-system that the Spaniards brought to their possessions in America also hindered Latin America's economic growth and political consolidation. Mexican conditions are the result of the unchecked rule of large-scale landed property, and those conditions are not improved by the Mexican landowners now selling off the interests of the state to American and European speculators.

France was less badly affected by its American colonial policy in the eighteenth century because it lost its colonies to England. They did not strengthen absolutism and feudalism as in Spain; their failure rather contributed to the weakening and downfall of those powers [i.e., absolutism and feudalism] and to the French Revolution, as a result of which France, free from colonial burdens, experienced a new, powerful revival.

In the United States it was mainly the great Southern slave-owners who pushed for an expansionist policy. Their mode of production involved such reckless predatory cultivation that it quickly exhausted the soil and awakened the drive to appropriate ever more territories suitable for the cultivation of tobacco and cotton. At their prompting, the great expeditions of conquest were undertaken by the United States against Mexico, which led to the annexation in 1844–8 of Texas, California, and New Mexico, a territory almost three times as large as that of Germany.

When the Civil War, which began in 1861, saw the industrial capitalists, proletarians and peasants of the North break the power of the slave-owners, the expansionist thrust of the United States came to an end for a long time, very much to the advantage of its economic development.

Commodity-production develops new factors that from time to time bring about an expansionist thrust of the state. The most primitive among them is the discovery in certain areas of a commodity in great demand. This immediately generates the desire to possess that territory. The most powerful impulse is naturally generated by the commodity that means power and wealth under any circumstances because everybody wants it, anybody takes it, and nobody ever has enough of it: the money-commodity, gold and silver.

That was the first bait that lured the Spaniards to America; the establishment of *latifundia* followed only later. In California, it was gold that raised the value of *latifundia* and drew in countless immigrants. Australia, likewise, first gained significance for England thanks to its gold.

To this day, wealth in gold is one of the driving forces of colonial and expansionist policy, as the Boer War at the end of the nineteenth century has shown. It was precisely in that war that the distinguishing features of the new imperialism were revealed with particular clarity. For the first time, it strikingly brought forward, before England's popular masses, the contradiction between imperialism and socialism. And, yet, it was not imperialistic in the strictest sense of the word.

Let us not forget that imperialism is understood by some of our comrades as a necessity for further *industrial* development. There, supposedly, lies its significance for the working class. By that they have in mind the *industrial* side of imperialism – on the one hand, the amalgamation of financial and industrial capital, and on the other the necessity of growing capital-exports. Both played only a minor role in the Boer War. It was less industrial capital turned into finance-capital than purely financial capital that strove after possession of the gold and diamond-mines [in South Africa]; it was less the desire to obtain gold through growing exports than the desire to obtain gold without commodity-exchange that led to opening up the country. Those were the same driving forces that animated the Spaniards in the sixteenth century, only in this case they did not benefit absolutism and feudalism but a few financial magnates.

It is true that new gold and silver treasures can give a great boost to industry, but they do not necessarily have to do it in the state that owns the gold- and silver-producing lands. Spanish America's rich yield in bullion served, even more than its *latifundia*, to strengthen absolutism and feudalism as well as the church of the mother-country vis-à-vis the bourgeois classes. The great treasures were squandered to import luxury-articles, and especially to wage endless wars that depopulated and desolated the country, though it did not suffer from foreign invasions for a long time.

Less significant than gold and silver, but still important as a source of expansionist strivings, were other products characteristic of certain areas. Costly furs played a particularly important role. They drove the English and French to occupy North America, and they attracted the Russians to Siberia.

Spices, much sought after in the sixteenth century, were one of the most expensive commodities, driving first the Portuguese and then the Dutch to the West Indies. Modern medicine and chemistry put an end to the power of attraction of these limited areas.

Another commodity that Africa produced especially well – conveyable and saleable labour-power – contributed much to its so-called 'colonisation'. The profitable slave-trade prompted the most diverse states, even Germany, to appropriate African territory for slave-hunting and trade in the sixteenth and seventeenth centuries.[19] Today, it is especially ivory and rubber that turn Central Africa into a colonial area.

As a rule, this kind of driving force of expansionist policy is very short-lived because it leads to exhaustion of the products supplied by nature, not to their planned production by men. But, precisely for that reason, it leads to rapid actions and the opening up of ever-new areas, as in the predatory cultivation of the plantation-economy of the Southern states in the United States. The gradual extermination of fur-bearing animals induced the Russians to traverse and annex the whole of Siberia incredibly quickly. The equally rapid extermination of elephants and rubber-trees was a strong driving force for the very rapidly accomplished opening up and annexation of tropical Africa. A constant and lasting supply of the coveted products, however, requires the confinement, not the furthering, of that expansion of overexploitation. The danger of exhaustion of those products, which were acquired for so long through hunting or lumbering in ever-new areas, makes all the more necessary their production in a planned way in certain limited areas.

The drive to loot costly products and to appropriate the areas holding them naturally presupposes trade. The trapper does not hunt fur-bearing animals because he needs furs (his personal needs are soon satisfied) but because the trader buys from him as many as he can trap.

---

19. [Although the claims made in this sentence appear dubious, this is a literal translation of Kautsky's text.]

The need for expansion characterises trade from the beginning. It is first foreign trade and then domestic trade. The first form of commerce is trade between different communities, which is older than trade within the same community. The need for expansion goes together with the need for monopolisation, but also simultaneously with competition – monopoly for oneself, competition for others. [The monopolist's] driving force is profit, which he makes by buying cheaply and selling dearly. He buys most cheaply if he is the only buyer in the market and the number of sellers is very large. He likewise sells most dearly if he is the only seller and the number of those who need his goods is very considerable. The merchant, therefore, seeks early on to keep competitors away from the market, which is only possible, as a rule, by violent means. He usually does not have the power to do that by himself; the state has to intervene on his behalf. The merchant, therefore, presses for a strong state-power devoted to his aims, for the expansion of its territory and, wherever possible, for special privileges within that area. He is best able to get that by uniting with powerful finance-capital, a union that is much older than that between industrial and finance-capital.

Trade-companies, or joint-stock corporations that were granted commercial monopolies by the state, played a large and continuously growing role in the whole of European colonial policy since the sixteenth century. They contributed powerfully to the development of capitalism. Yet they also became an obstacle to its further development, which could only proceed after the appearance of economic and political powers strong enough to break the monopoly of those companies and to contain their expansionist policy.

It is true that the industrial capitalist is, at bottom, a merchant as well. His driving force is also profit; he also has an interest in buying cheaply and selling dearly. But the most important source of his profit is labour-power, which has the gift of producing more value than it costs. To be sure, his profit does not depend only on that. If he errs in the purchase of raw materials, buying too dearly or purchasing bad machines, that can slash his profits. The same can happen if he incorrectly estimates demand and if the goods he has produced remain unsold for a long time or find no outlet at all. In that respect, he does not differ from a merchant. However, what, for the merchant, is the content of his whole profit-seeking, is, for him, only an accompanying phenomenon. The main thing for the industrial capitalist remains to buy labour-power cheaply and exploit it as much as possible.

To that extent, he also wants monopoly for himself and competition for others, namely for the workers. The employers' associations have always been considered sacrosanct, while workers' organisations have long been regarded as the work of despicable agitators.

However, the industrial capitalist wants competition not only for the workers but also for the traders who sell him his raw materials and sell his workers their foodstuffs, as well as for the merchants who want to buy his goods.

The more of these merchants appear on the market, the better for him; hence away with trade-monopolies, away also with the exclusion of foreign traders from the market, and full freedom for traders of all nations.

This view triumphed thanks to industrial capital, thereby making possible its rapid development but also bringing about a complete revolution in international relations.

The monopoly that merchants or trading companies tried to gain for themselves could only be imposed by force, their own or that of the state. As long as this monopolistic economy lasted, each trading ship was a warship; and, if not every Englishman, then every trader, of whatever nationality, was 'a pirate at heart', and the traders of enemy-nations were chased away from the seas permanently, not just temporarily. During that period, the slogan held true that 'trade follows the flag', i.e., the naval ensign. Then, through the power of its navy, England's maritime trade reached its predominant position in the world; or, rather, both phenomena were tightly correlated, because the English navy could not have achieved its superiority without the abundance of bold and skilled sailors created by the rise of maritime trade and the ocean-fisheries. The building of warships, by itself alone, means nothing.

Since the nineteenth century, with the end of the era of commercial monopoly, the slogan 'trade follows the flag' has become an anachronism. Today, peace is the normal condition for trade, and its driving force is not monopoly protected by cannons or torpedoes but profit. People buy from those who sell most cheaply, not from those who have the most warships.

All the chatter about trade depending on the status of the navy is completely untrue. After England and Germany, the strongest commercial fleet in Europe belongs to tiny Norway, amounting to 1,646,000 registered tons in 1911. It is larger than the commercial fleet of the largest European maritime power after England and Germany – greater than France's, which has only 1,462,240 tons, than Italy's with 1,107,190 registered tons in 1910, or even than Russia's with

756,600 registered tons in 1913. The fleets of Sweden, Norway and Denmark together were almost as strong as the German commercial fleet, which in 1913 had a gross registered tonnage of 3,153,724, while the joint commercial fleets of the Scandinavian countries amounted to 2,990,290 registered tons.

But then, and this is also contrary to the usual chatter, the maritime trade of a country is not at all dependent on the status of its commercial fleet. Traders can also freight their goods in foreign ships. In that way, the country loses shipping profits, but that need not hinder the development of industry. The commercial fleet of the United States is negligible, while its maritime trade is the largest in the world after England. In 1912–13, ships with a gross of 50.6 million registered tons arrived at its harbours, while the harbours of Great Britain and Ireland received 76.2 million and those of Germany, 25.2 million registered tons.

The most conspicuous example of how independent the expansion of maritime trade is from the fleet is supplied by Belgium. Its navy is almost nil, while its commercial fleet had 195 ships with 181,600 registered tons in 1912. In 1912–13, however, ships arrived at Belgian harbours with a gross registered tonnage of 16.4 million, of which 14.5 were foreign and 1.9 its own.

Even if the Englishmen had the intention and power to destroy the German commercial fleet – both of which are equally implausible – that would not mean the destruction of German trade and industry. Naturally, it would harm German prosperity greatly, as would any other defeat of the same magnitude such as the damage land warfare has caused, for example, in East Prussia, or the injury the payment of war-reparations would cause.

Trade would be badly hit by the destruction of so many means of transportation – but that would be the whole of international trade, not just German trade. On the other hand, German trade would also be badly affected if, on the contrary, the international commercial fleet were reduced to half its current capacity by destruction of the British fleet.

Leaving aside the coastal trade, German ships with 13 million registered tons (exactly 12,960,273) arrived at German harbours along with almost as many foreign ships (12.5 million registered tons, exactly 12,529,776), half of which were British (6 million registered tons, exactly 5,957,123).

In 1651, England could still enforce the Navigation Acts, which provided that goods could only be carried in English ships or in the ships of the country that produced those goods. After 1815, those laws had to be given up one after the other, partly because foreign powers set restrictions on English trade, including countries without a considerable navy but with strong commercial ties to England (first the Americans, then the Prussians), and partly because English trade itself suffered as a consequence of them. Finally, the Navigation Acts were completely abolished in 1849. Since then, international trade has developed so far that a similar law would be totally unfeasible because it would disrupt trade completely, and, for that reason, nobody thinks about similar regulations even he is still very much a pirate at heart.

To be sure, during recent decades, a new spirit of monopoly appeared as a result of the growing union between finance and industrial capital. But it no longer aspires to national monopolies or wages wars to protect that monopoly and destroy the trade of the enemy. The new monopolistic strivings aim at economic control of the great means of transportation and the sources of means of production. To the extent that they encompass maritime trade, they must, given the contemporary extension and nature of that trade, be international from the outset. In the shipping trusts or pools that they set up, German and English ship-owners work peacefully together to keep up freight rates.

Trade, however, regardless of all the chatter, does not have the slightest interest in the success of those monopolistic strivings, which only restrict it as well as industry.

Next to the aspiration to set up a commercial monopoly and expand its area, there is yet another expansionist urge that sprang from emerging commodity-trade and today has only historical effects but is frequently labelled imperialistic even though it appeared long before the age of imperialism: the quest to have seaports.

Water-transportation has long been the cheapest way of transporting goods. For bulk-goods such as corn, timber or minerals, it was the only way to carry those products to the market. Even today, when railways have made mass-transportation possible by land and cheapened it dramatically, it proves to be superior for the transportation of goods whose sale does not depend on prompt delivery and strict observance of deadlines.

But the advantages of free access to the sea, in order to participate in world trade, are not exhausted at that point: the sea is the only way that is open to everybody and can be used without conditions, at least in time of peace. A country cut off from the sea always remains dependent on the tariff-policy of its neighbours as well as on the condition of their roads, canals and railways, which were not designed according to its needs but often to thwart them. Only a country with seaports is always in direct connection with the world market. As soon as the latter becomes significant for a state, as soon as its imports and exports become a vital interest, the need also arises to extend its area in some way to the sea.

Today, Serbia still stands at that stage in which creation of a national state not only lies at the heart of its democratic strata but is also a need for its ruling classes. But the drive to acquire a seaport led it to violate the nationality principle in its war against Turkey, when it demanded Durrës in Albanian territory. If an independent Poland arises out of the current war, it will naturally strive to acquire a port on the Baltic Sea. Among other ports, the maritime city of Danzig belonged to the old Polish republic.

When Peter the Great decided to link Russia with world trade, he immediately sought to expand to the sea. He succeeded in pushing Russia to the Baltic Sea, and Catherine II expanded the Russian Empire to the Black Sea. But both the Baltic Sea and the Black Sea are actually lakes, and traffic through them to the ocean can be interrupted at any moment. Hence the Russian longing for Constantinople, which controls the exit from the Black Sea and makes Russia's most important export, the grain of its southern provinces, dependent on the will of the ruler of the Bosporus.

If Russia's trade had been the only consideration, its drive to Constantinople would have found no opposition among the capitalist nations of the West, who are equally interested in the prosperity of trade with Russia, which is also why, to the great annoyance of Marx and Engels, the English free traders and industrialists, and even the radicals among them, were always Russophiles.

But Russia is also a colossal military power. Until now, it was the only state able to jeopardise the English possessions in India, and it would also have threatened the Mediterranean powers, France and Italy, if it had won a basis in Constantinople allowing it to control Greece, Asia Minor, Syria and Egypt.

For that reason, those powers have always opposed Russia's drive to Constantinople. Russia's military power was much more a means of keeping it away from Constantinople, through the mistrust it awakened, than of furthering its advance in that direction. It is not the only example in world history of the exceptionally strong military power of a state achieving the opposite of what it was meant to do because of the suspicion it aroused among other states, which induced them to unite against the power they regarded as a common danger.

The need for a direct link to the sea was felt by all classes with an interest in world trade: the more they controlled the whole economic process, the more it became a national need also among peasants and industrialists.

In yet another way, industrial capital can be interested in an expansionist policy even in the pre-imperialist era. Conditions in many countries are so unfavourable for capitalist industry that they are totally unable to compete in the world market. To these unfavourable production conditions belongs, first and foremost, the backwardness of the working class. People are the foremost means of production, and their quality is crucial for the prosperity of industry. The state can do no better to promote industry than by caring about the physical and spiritual welfare of the workers, and it cannot damage industry more than by lowering the standard of living of the working class.

The more the workers are pressed down, decaying and becoming unable to perform their job properly, the more industry becomes dependent on extensive protective tariffs in order that it might withstand international competition. But any capitalist industry must also grow and expand its markets. If it is unable to step out into the world market, it tries to expand its [domestic] outlet by raising protective tariffs as well as by extending the territory of the state.

At present, Russia is again the most conspicuous example of this process. Its industrial proletariat, burdened with the traditions of serfdom, forcibly kept in ignorance by the state, barred from organising, and abandoned to overwork and alcoholism, is not even remotely capable of performing work such as that of the Western European worker.

But those conditions, which are so degrading for the worker and lower his productivity so much, also reduce the consumption-capacity of the Russian peasants, i.e., not their needs but their ability to buy the poor and expensive products of Russian industry. In order to expand the market for Russian industry, the easier and most immediate way thus seemed to be to expand Russian territory, not to the west with its well-armed national states, its modern democracy and its developed industry, but to the east, towards backward areas with primitive democracy and the Oriental despotisms built upon it, which are also devoid of military force. Thus, Russia overran the Caucasus, penetrated into

Central Asia as far as the Himalayas, gained a foothold in Manchuria, and, to this day, is trying to take possession of Mongolia and Persia.

Naturally, in all these cases, the needs of capitalist industry were not the only determining factor. Even more powerful was the primitive expansionist drive characteristic of Oriental despotism that we witness from the beginning of history: the desire to increase tribute and the tributary areas, which, in modern terms, appears as the quest to increase the number of taxpayers and the amount of taxes paid, to secure for finance-capital new supplies and objects of exploitation, to increase the number of well-paid positions for officers and bureaucrats, and in that way to increase absolutism's instruments of power.

It would have been more useful for Russia's industry to curtail the influence and income of those classes. With the costs of that expansionist policy and the wars it caused over centuries, the Russians could have built countless schools, improved their transportation-facilities dramatically, notably increased the production of peasant-agriculture, and, in that way, they would have been able, on the one hand, to increase rapidly the consumption-capacity of the agricultural classes as well as the productivity of industrial labour, and, on the other, to raise to a higher level the competitiveness and sales of Russian industry.

The method of increasing the state-territory was admittedly the handiest, not only because it required less thinking but, above all, because it met no opposition from the ruling clique, receiving instead its support. That method prevailed merely due to power-relations, not to economic necessity. Economic development would have proceeded much more quickly if those power relations had been overturned.

If the productivity of Russian industry is now approaching more closely to that of Western-European industry, that is not due to the expansionist policy of the state but to the influx of foreign capital and the upsurge that the labour-movement finally experienced despite all obstacles.

All the expansionist strivings we have so far reviewed are, properly speaking, not of an imperialist nature. There is, however, hardly any imperialist tendency that is not steeped in the expansionist strivings of the pre-imperialist forms we have summarised here.

Each one of these strivings is economically caused; most of them, however, are not only economically unnecessary but even harmful: they are the product of powers that do not promote industrial development but, rather, hinder it.

The more people manage to drive them back, the better economic development is able to proceed.

4. Different types and objects of imperialism

a.) *The British commonwealth*[20]

Among the colonial powers of the seventeenth and eighteenth centuries, England is the only one whose industrial development was furthered by colonial policy. It is true that, at the beginning of that policy, a monarchy aspiring to absolute power, and an aristocracy striving for feudal landholding, took part in it. But England's maritime power and its colonial possessions first acquired great significance at a time when the capitalist classes had become economically and politically strong enough to get their share in the fruits of that power and of those possessions, thus further developing trade and industry. England first attained naval supremacy in and through the bourgeois revolution. That revolution triumphed in the middle of the seventeenth century and found its definitive conclusion in the 'Glorious Revolution' of 1688, which handed over power to a monarchy and an aristocracy that were loyal, indeed subject, to the capitalist interests, and which accepted the higher capitalist strata as co-regents in Parliament. England's colonial policy took shape in the eighteenth century no less peculiarly than in the nineteenth century. It rests on two pillars that no other colonial power disposes of or could dispose of. If those pillars ever cast off England's supremacy, no other state will be in a position to subdue them, and the conditions to create something similar are nowhere to be found.

One of these two pillars of the British colonial empire is its three great agrarian colonies of European culture: Canada, South Africa and Australia. To be sure, their population is small as a proportion of the total population of the British Empire, which amounts to approximately 400 million people. But they represent a great economic and political force. Their inhabitants have not only gone beyond the stage of primitive democracy; they are completely imbued

20. [The British Commonwealth formally appeared with the Statute of Westminster (1931). Here Kautsky uses the expression 'Der britische Staatenbund', meaning 'commonwealth', 'federation of states', or 'confederation'.]

with the spirit of modern democracy – indeed, even more so than a European population, because, like the United States, neither in their constitutions nor in their way of thinking did they have to drag along ruins from the time of feudalism and absolutism.

And, economically, these colonies have, as both buyers and sellers for the world market, the greatest significance that a modern, vigorous agriculture, unencumbered by great burdens, could possibly have.[21]

[...] The importance of Canada and Australia, as well as of South Africa, for England's industry and capital is surely great and constantly growing. But that importance does not rest on their status as colonies. Strictly speaking, they are not really colonies. They are independent states with a modern democracy, i.e., national states with greater freedom than any European country with the exception of Switzerland. They are not actually territories subject to England but have a federative relationship with it; all together, they form a federation of states [*Staatenbund*], rapidly growing in population and therefore in strength not only through natural increase but also through immigration, which was especially strong during recent years, particularly in Canada. It amounted to 147,000 people in 1909 and 354,000 in 1912. In that way, not only a considerable part of English emigration remained in the British Empire, but in addition a considerable part of non-British emigration was led into the Empire.

That federation certainly represents a kind of state that has a great future. And, if one wants to see in it the distinguishing feature of imperialism, we would hardly have any reason to object to it.

However, it is not imperialism that established and brought together the states forming the British colonial confederation.[22] England possessed them long before the imperialist period without suspecting their future significance.[23]

[...] What matters here is this: the United Kingdom, which itself became a federation after granting Home Rule to Ireland, forms together with three other federative states a confederation [*Staatenbund*] that within its area still offers many possibilities for the expansion of British capital. Imperialist needs

21. [Statistical data on Great Britain's foreign trade with its colonies and capital exports to them have here been omitted.]
22. [Kautsky's text reads 'den britischen kolonialen Staatenbund'.]
23. [A short overview of the origins of Australia, Canada and South Africa follows but is omitted here.]

have certainly played a role in its formation, but the acquisitions of territory on which it was built, with the exception of the Boer republic, were made a century before the era of imperialism, and the close connection of this confederation was not imposed upon the English possessions with the imperialist method of violence. On the contrary, it became a necessity for all parties concerned due to the force of attraction of democracy and, as we have already remarked, the free trade of the motherland.

That confederation of states is surely a formation with a great future; it also offers important lessons precisely for our era of imperialism. But it cannot simply be copied in colonial areas because, outside of the tropics – that is, in regions that can be inhabited by European manual workers without damaging their health – there are no more areas to be seized by the European powers.

This pillar of the British colonial empire cannot, therefore, be replicated by any other colonial empire. England can perhaps lose it in the future, but it will never support another empire. Canada may one day find it more advantageous to become part of the United States of America instead of belonging to the united British nations;[24] South Africa may one day become the starting point for an independent empire of Africans; but these territories will never agree to become colonies of some other power.

b.) *India*

The second pillar of the British colonial empire, which has no equal, is India.[25]

[...] The striving of the Indian nationalists is [...] initially not to liberate themselves from England but to obtain more freedom within the English commonwealth[26] – a parliamentary representation both for the provinces and for the entire country with legislative powers and control over taxation. Their ultimate goal is a constitution, like Australia's for instance, and they believe that when they reach that goal they can only derive advantages from belong-

24. [Kautsky's text reads 'der Vereinigten britischen Staaten', paraphrasing the name of the USA (*Vereinigte Staaten von Amerika*).]

25. [Here, Kautsky provides a short overview of India's colonisation, its significance for British capitalism and the birth of the Indian National Congress, highlighting the relatively easy burden that English rule supposedly represented compared with the prospect of civil wars between warring national and religious groups after obtaining independence.]

26. [Here the text reads: 'des britischem Staatsverbandes'.]

ing to the British commonwealth. Their goal is an Indian federal state – the United States of India, which, together with the United States of Canada[27] as well as those of Australia and South Africa, will unite around Great Britain to form a federation of states such as the world has never seen.

This is actually a grand goal that can have the greatest significance for the political and economic development of the world. The question, however, is whether it will be reached. The greatest danger threatening it does not come from foreign powers but from the violent policy of the British imperialists. They do not want to give up willingly the huge booty they extract yearly from India. So far, they have answered the growing national opposition with ever more oppressive measures. [...]

It is [...] not excluded that the United States of India, as part of a British world empire, will become a reality. If that happens, it will not be thanks to imperialism but to its overcoming by the forces of democracy in England and India.

It is natural for the imperialists of other countries to want to acquire or create a similar world empire. But if it is not totally certain whether England's world empire will become a permanent institution, it nevertheless is certain that no other nation will be able to obtain one like it. There is only one India. It can cease to be an English possession, but it will not fall as a united country into the hands of any other foreign power.

c.) *Africa*

When the era of imperialism started approximately a generation ago, being characterised by colonial acquisitions, capital-exports, and a system combining agrarian with industrial protective tariffs, the initiative was not seized by England although it was the most highly developed capitalist state. To be sure, it wanted to increase its exports of commodities and to open up agrarian areas by exporting capital, but powerful interests, above all the workers and ship-owners, both of whom are stronger in England than anywhere else, prevented the shift to protectionism, forcing industrial capital to pursue its further expansion with the methods of free trade even though it inclined to imperialist methods due to the growing connection with finance-capital.

27. [The correct reference would be to the United Provinces of Canada.]

Furthermore, the two great areas it already possessed, India and the settlement-colonies, offered England a large scope for exporting capital so that it had no imperative reason to undertake new conquests by violent methods.

The impulse for the new colonial policy did not come from England but from France. But this initial push, likewise, did not at first bear a truly imperialist character. We have already seen that, next to imperialism, there are other motives for state-expansion, among which the most primitive is the quest to increase the territory of the state, which, through the tribute extracted by violence, secures for the ruling classes a direct increase in their consumption and instruments of power without the needs of any mode of production playing a role in this process. We have further seen that this drive to extend exploitation to areas that are in the stage of primitive democracy is likewise a mere matter of power.

We have shown that this has been a very powerful force in Russia's expansionist drive. It influenced no less strongly the expansionist strivings of French Bonapartism at the beginning of the nineteenth century. Napoleon leaned first and foremost upon the army and the bureaucracy and was not constrained in his omnipotence, as feudal absolutism was, by a privileged feudal aristocracy and church. To keep the army and bureaucracy in good humour was one of Napoleon's main concerns. He had to make sure that they always acquired new sources of enrichment, new booties, new posts, new supplies, whereby finance-capital also thrived. This drove him to ever-new conquests. [...]

Despite the relatively insignificant weight of most African possessions for the industry of the mother-state, it was precisely competition over African territories that played an important role in the arms-race of the European states and brought them several times to the brink of world war. But, at the decisive moment, all the powers involved always found that the object was not worth the enormous sacrifices caused by a world war and they reached an understanding. Such was the case in 1898, when the Frenchmen occupied Fashoda in Sudan and confronted the Englishmen over it. Immediately afterwards, it appeared as if the Boer republic would lead to a war between England and Germany. Finally, in 1911, the antagonisms between the three great world-powers reached such tension over Morocco that a world war over this disputed territory seemed inevitable. All the same, war was also avoided this time. At present there is no clash of interests in Africa that could justify a world war, even from the capitalist-imperialist standpoint. The only economically valuable areas for imperialism at the moment are South Africa and Egypt, as well as Algiers. The first has already reached the stage of modern democracy and can only be taken and kept by democratic methods, not by violence. Egypt is rapidly approaching that stage. If circumstances intervene that enable it to shake off the English yoke, Egypt will know how to avoid carrying any other yoke. The same is true of Algiers. These areas no longer come into consideration as objects of imperialist dispute, as nations without a will of their own that the victors can dispose of at pleasure.

d.) *China*

If we abstract from South Africa, Egypt and Algiers, into which the French state has put more money since 1830 than it had to pay Germany as war-reparations in 1871, and which to this day continues to demand high subsidies from the mother country, we find that China is by far the most important area for the world market and for capital-exports coveted by the imperialist policy of conquest. [...]

One cannot overrate China's importance for the further expansion of capitalism. But an imperialist policy there is increasingly impossible for any European power. Japan's attempt to win a controlling position in China could easily amalgamate Japan with China into a common people.

e.) *Turkey*

Apart from those already mentioned, the only objects of imperialism are Turkey and Persia. In order to avoid overextending our presentation, we will abstract from the latter as we avoided looking more closely at Egypt and Algiers in our analysis of Africa. In the same way as much of what we said about India applies to a certain extent to Egypt and to a lesser degree to Algiers, so what we will say here about Turkey also applies to some extent to Persia. [...]

At first, it seemed that the Balkan wars had to spark a world war, but it was deferred once again. Albania, which first appeared as a terrible tragedy, became a comical operetta. Instead of igniting a general world conflagration, the war against Turkey created a situation that made a peaceful agreement between Germany and England easier because it severed the direct territorial connection between Turkey and Austria. Between the two countries, a barrier of independent states was now formed. In that way, the Baghdad railway and the activities of German capital in Turkey altogether lost their threatening character even for the most anxious Englishmen. We know today that an agreement was almost concluded between Germany and England that would have swept away all the Turkish points of contention. The current war prevented it from being signed. It broke out at a moment in which there existed no single imperialist point of contention [*Streitpunkt*: controversial subject].

The starting point of the War was the antagonism between Austria and Serbia, which was supported by Russia. No strong imperialist motive underlay this antagonism. Serbia is still far from any imperialist tendency; it is still situated at the stage of a nascent national state. We know that Russia's expansionist strivings are also of a pre-imperialist nature: they are those of Oriental despotism, of the military and bureaucratic state, of an industry incapable of competing in the world market, of the wish for a harbour on the Black Sea. One cannot speak about capital-exports from Russia; it is still very much in need of capital-imports. It is more the object than the subject of the expansionist strivings of capital in the old capitalist states.

But Austria also still needs capital-imports. It is true that its industry strives for new markets and temporarily developed something that could be called an imperialist drive by supporting Austria's expansion to Salonika. But that thrust is already spent. It is not the needs of exporting industry but much more those of the agrarians that created the antagonism with Serbia.

One is therefore entitled to say that the Eastern-European starting point of the war is not an imperialist one. Eastern Europe is not yet sufficiently developed for its policy to be governed by imperialist needs.

However, Western Europe was [also] not split at the time of the outbreak of war by any imperialist point of contention. They were all regulated [*geregelt*].

f.) *The World War*

At first sight, the current world war is thus not an imperialist one. And yet it is an imperialist war, but only in a final sense [*in letzter Linie*]. Imperialism is responsible for the war-catastrophe to the extent that it was the driving force behind the arms-race, which ultimately cast a spell over all the great powers whether they were driven by imperialist motives or not. The uninterrupted arms-race necessarily had to become a cause for war even if the powers had succeeded in disposing of all the imperialist controversies through peaceful understandings.

Actually, if we follow the history of the day separating the Austrian ultimatum to Serbia from the outbreak of the War, we find that the bellicose spirit was not awakened by any particular territorial or economic demand advanced by one of the sides and rejected by the other but simply by the fact of mutual *mobilisation*. The question of war-guilt thus becomes a question of the date and character of the individual mobilisation-orders. The splendid armies that the states had created to secure peace dragged them into war at the first attempt to employ them.

This peculiar origin of the War gave it an unusual character. Had it broken out because of a particular imperialist point of contention, for instance Morocco, the peoples' war-fever would have been limited, and opposition to the War would have been considerable. It is for this reason that, until now, no imperialist difference was able directly to spark a war. It is otherwise with the consequences of the arms-race. For a long time, it has already been stirring up a rising fury against foreign countries through its growing burdens on the popular masses insofar as they were not explained to them. Along with the extent of the arms-race, however, the mistrust against the alliance of expected enemies also grows, for how can they accumulate such vast instruments of power if they are not contemplating complete extermination of the opponent? Mobilisation and war then made that mood reach the boiling point. Precisely because of the lack of any certain demand on any side, each side feared the worst in case of a defeat, thus giving rise to ardent support for the victory of one's own army.

Initially, this mood was not a product of enthusiasm for imperialism, whose relation to the War was not evident to the masses, but it indisputably fostered the spread of imperialist tendencies even in the ranks of our party, though, admittedly, the rudiments have existed for years.

In the peculiar origins of the War, [which broke out] purely as a result of the arms-race and mobilisation, lie not just the reason for the general war-fever but also the great difficulty in ending it.

Usually a war breaks out because two sovereign states are unable to reach a peaceful understanding over certain demands so that the power of weapons must decide.

In the Crimean War, the problem was whether the Western powers and Austria would allow a further expansion of Russia at the expense of Turkey. In the [Franco-Austrian] war of 1859, it was a question of whether Austria wanted to maintain its position in Italy or was ready to give it up. The [Danish-Prussian] war of 1864 was waged over whether Schleswig-Holstein would continued to be a Danish possession; the [Austro-Prussian] war of 1866, over who should control Schleswig-Holstein, as well as over whether the house of Habsburg could still meddle in the affairs of the German states or Prussia was going to be the only great power among them. Finally, the [Franco-Prussian] War of 1870 was, actually if not formally, waged over the question of whether the French Empire would have the power to impede the unification of Germany. That issue was settled after a few weeks when the French Empire collapsed. The Republic had neither the power not the will to hinder Germany's unification. A new object of struggle now appeared: the [German] demand for the cession of Alsace-Lorraine.

Those were clear war-aims, openly proclaimed from the start.

Today (at the end of February), this war is already in its eighth month and none of the struggling governments has yet given even the slightest hint about its demands. They are all fighting for victory, for a lasting peace, but not yet for a definite aim.

Thus things are today taking a course that counters the usual one. Usually states first formulate their demands and, only then, declare war and mobilise their troops. This time, the mobilisation was not declared because of the war, but war because of the mobilisation; and determination of the goals for which the war should have been waged, and whose granting people want to impose on the enemy, has been made dependent on the outcome of the war.

How is it possible to reach peace this way? As long as the struggle is not waged over definite goals but only out of vague fears knowing no limits, each side will do its utmost to avoid defeat. If everybody knew precisely what the opponent wants, they would perhaps find that continuation of the war, even if they eventually won it, would be more harmful than an understanding over the demands advanced by the opponent.

Until now, we only hear private voices from single countries regarding the conditions under which peace could be concluded. Among those voices, we are particularly interested in the socialists. Many of them proceed from the assumption that a foreign invasion could bring freedom to a people. French comrades believe that a victorious France would give Germany a democratic régime; and, by the same token, German comrades think that a German victory would bring about the collapse of tsarism. They offer previous wars as models, especially the Franco-Prussian War of 1870, in which the French Republic was born out of France's defeat.

But this was not brought about by the victor. Bismarck did not bid the French Republic welcome by any means. It was created to wage the struggle against the foreign invader more energetically, and it was popular for that reason. If a victorious Germany had forced the republic upon Frenchmen in 1871, it would have appeared as a tool of the country's enemies. Nothing could have discredited the republic more.

It is true that in his 1892 article 'Socialism in Germany',[28] which is often quoted lately, Engels thought that a victorious invasion of Germany by France, allied with Russia, would likely have caused a turnabout in favour of Social Democracy – but only if the Social Democrats, like the *sans-culottes* in 1793, could have organised a defence against the invading foreigners more energetically than the bourgeois parties.

This time, we cannot count on that possibility. An intervention in the internal affairs of any of the belligerent states by the others, as a peace condition or as the purpose of victory, should be out of the question for us.

Actually, it is quite different with the peace conditions formulated by the great majority of the socialists of all countries who have pronounced themselves on this issue. They were never repudiated by any socialist party. This unanimity shows most brilliantly how strong the inner ideological cohesion of the International still is. The common advocacy of a common peace-programme must therefore become the best means of strengthening that cohesion even further.

The peace programme of the International naturally does not proceed from the power-relations of the warring parties or from the momentary or expected war-situation, but from the permanent and common needs of the movement of the entire proletariat and those of social development. The two coincide. From this point of view, the peace programme of international socialism, which so far has been stated most clearly in the belligerent states by the Independent

28. Engels 1892.

Labour Party, centres on two points: *no annexations*, that is, no territorial changes without support from the population affected, and *disarmament*.

On the first point, we have hardly anything to add. It needs no commentary. We certainly do not uphold the standpoint of the *status quo*, and we do not believe that boundaries, as they were shaped in the course of historical development by the convergence of multifarious interests and power-relations, must forever remain untouched.

But our democratic standpoint forbids us to aspire to changes in the conditions of existence of nations in any other way than through democracy. We have already remarked what serious drawbacks, indeed dangers, it entails to force a population into a state against its will and to retain it there, particularly if that population has gone beyond the stage of primitive democracy and participates actively and fully in political life. A state that tries to do that arouses the energetic and tenacious resistance of the annexed population and also the mistrust, indeed, the hatred of all democratic nations and of all democratic sections of the people in every nation. In that way, it worsens both its domestic and its external situation most ominously. Such an annexation damages even more the class-struggle of the proletariat, partly by dimming class-antagonisms and partly by distorting them, as we have already seen.

The rejection of annexations thus arises from the democratic character of our party as well as from the daily-increasing force that democratic feelings have already acquired in modern popular life.

By contrast, the demand for disarmament arises as a logical consequence of the war. The war is a product of the arms-race, as we have already remarked. The arms-race was already a most serious financial burden on all states before the War. This burden will become doubly unbearable after the War, even if it does not increase, simply by virtue of the enormous financial expenditures that the War entails and that recovery from the war-damages will bring in its wake. The burdens of the arms-race, however, will not remain as they were before the War but will rather increase if the whole system is not discontinued. And the greater the burden of the arms-race, the closer the danger of the next war.

This perspective is so terrible that there is hardly any government that does not intend to set conditions in the peace agreement providing for disarmament. But disarmament assumes another character if it is unilaterally imposed on the defeated rather than being a general measure resulting from mutual agreement. As a demand of the first kind, disarmament awakens the utmost resistance of the weaker side, and it means a continuation of the war until the most absolute ruin. Willingness to reach an agreement on disarmament, on the contrary, can make possible the most rapid conclusion of peace and put an end to the horrific murder and devastation. And only a general agreement on disarmament can have a lasting character. Unilateral and forced disarmament, on the contrary, results in a permanent urge of the vanquished to shake off the degrading duty as quickly as possible and by whatever method or alliance. In that case, peace would be just a ceasefire and preparation for the next war.

Naturally, by disarmament [*Abrüstung*] we do not mean complete disarmament [*Entwaffnung*]. If some of our comrades in the small states demand complete disarmament, that is due to the peculiar conditions of their country that make any resistance to a foreign invasion hopeless. How far that demand is to be recognised depends on assessment of the special conditions of that state and has nothing to do with our basic principles. The programme of our party does not demand abolition of the army but a 'militia in the place of the standing army'.[29]

The disarmament demand is first and foremost an economic one. It demands the reduction of state-expenditures on the army. Such a reduction can be determined by means of agreements between all the states; for instance, through a general reduction by half of the army and navy budgets with which each state entered the War. That would mean an enormous easing of the burden on states without making them defenceless. They do not even have to stop their arms-race, only give it another form. The course of the arms-race would no longer be determined by the biggest purse but by the brightest minds, those able to accomplish more, technically and organisationally, with limited means. In that way, the worst sting would be taken out of the arms-race, namely, the growing financial burden that embitters all peoples.

Admittedly, that would not completely secure peace. We must not expect that to happen within the framework of a mode of production based on

29. ['3. Education of all to bear arms. Militia in the place of the standing army. Determination by the popular assembly on questions of war and peace. Settlement of all international disputes by arbitration.' Erfurt Programme, in Sozialdemokratische Partei Deutschlands 1891, *Protokoll des Parteitages der Sozialdemokratischen Partei Deutschlands: Abgehalten zu Erfurt vom 14. bis 20. Oktober 1891*, pp. 3–6.]

contradictions. But one of the strongest causes of war would be removed, the maintenance of peace for the classes interested in it would be facilitated, and recovery from the war-damages would become possible.

For years, therefore, Social Democracy has laid greatest stress on the demand for disarmament. It can only be implemented through the avoidance of imperialist methods.

5. Commercial treaties

Whatever shape power-relations may assume in the course of this war, and whatever forms the peace conditions resulting from them may take, one thing is certain: imperialism has reached a crisis. Only two options exist: either [the peoples] succeed in mastering the crisis and shaping the peace conditions in the above-mentioned sense, or else the imperialist factors prove stronger and shape the peace-conditions in their own sense. In the latter case, the world would be divided up among the capitalist powers and imperialism would enter a new stage. Until now it strove for expansion in the so-called non-appropriated areas, that is, areas of primitive democracy not yet annexed by any capitalist power. That kind of appropriation entailed the possibility, if not the necessity, of coming into conflict with other capitalist states and thereby igniting a world war.

If all the 'non-appropriated' areas are divided up after the War, the further expansion of any capitalist state will only be possible by appropriating the possessions of others, i.e., through war. From then on, each imperialist pursuit would mean pursuit of war from the outset. War will no longer be, as previously, a perhaps unwished-for consequence of that pursuit, but, rather its immediate goal.

That would mean continuation of the arms-race on a limitless financial basis as well as an enormous increase of the war-danger. If these tendencies are victorious at the end of the War, they will create conditions in which wars will only be interrupted by periods of the deepest exhaustion, and each recovery would bring about a new war.

Only these two alternatives remain! Either increased safeguarding or increased imperilment of world peace; either a long-lasting peace or a chronic condition of war. A mere return to prewar conditions is no longer possible, only an improvement or a deterioration. In view of this prospect, it does not seem out of the question that the tendencies working in the first direction will find greater echo among the masses of the population. We have absolutely no reason to weaken our cause by arguing from the outset that no other ending of the War is possible than a chronic condition of war, and that any other scenario is an illusion.

And, however, the War may end, our party will be all the more able to win the trust of the masses and to organise international solidarity, the more energetically it champions its peace programme regardless of prospects for its realisation.

To argue that, by so doing, we will set ourselves in opposition to the needs of economic development, is completely groundless. The above remarks have demonstrated that clearly enough.

We have seen that the expansionist strivings of modern states are by no means solely determined by the needs of industrial capital; and, further, that they are best promoted in the most important areas for capital, the agrarian territories, not by the violent methods of imperialism but through peaceful democracy.

One should further add that state-expansion is by no means the only or the most important means of increasing the exports of commodities and capital. In the case of Germany's African possessions, we have already shown what small share the exports of industrial products to and imports of raw materials from its colonies have in the development of German foreign trade. The figures for all the German colonies show the same. [Some statistics follow.] One can see which is more important for Germany's industry: trade with its colonies or with the British Empire.

But the same is true, even if not in the same conspicuous way, for British industry, although the British colonial empire is not only the most extensive but also encompasses by far the most important colonial areas of the world for industrial imports, for the supply of raw materials and for capital-exports. [Some statistics follow.]

At the same time, England's empire, as we have seen, is a completely exceptional formation. Precisely those of its possessions that consume the majority of its industrial products, supply most of the raw materials and import most of the capital are actually federal states and cannot be compared with the colonies of any other state. They must be left out of consideration if one wants to investigate the effects of colonies on metropolitan industry and capital in general.

Yet another thing must be taken into consideration. When we refer to commercial statistics with regard to the colonies, it does not in any way mean that this trade takes place just because they are colonies, and that they must be possessed as such in order for trade with them to be possible. [Some statistics follow.]

England's trade with Egypt thus grows more slowly than its overall trade. We have no reason to assume that, without the military occupation of Egypt, it would have grown any less through the sole weight of economic factors.

There can be no question of a state, by means of colonies, becoming independent of foreign countries in the supply of raw materials for its industry as well as in its outlets. Imperialists who are nourishing that hope just bear witness to their own crass ignorance. The more mightily a country's industry develops, the more it depends on all regions of the world for obtaining raw materials as well as for selling its products. Even England, with its vast colonial empire, could not continue its industrial production without obtaining raw materials and foodstuffs from lands that no power in the world could turn into colonies, such as Russia and the United States. [Some statistics follow.]

If any capitalist industrial state strives to acquire a colonial empire large enough to make it independent from the supply of raw materials by foreign countries, it will unite against it all the other capitalist states and entangle itself in endless, exhausting wars without coming any closer to its goal. That policy would be the surest way of driving the whole economic life of the country into bankruptcy.

Conquests are not the way to ensure as much as possible the supply of raw materials for industry. That can only be done through more rapid development of the productive forces of agrarian countries, the most important of which cannot be turned into colonies – neither Russia nor Argentina nor the United States, nor also Australia or Canada, and just as little, in the foreseeable future, China, while India and Egypt will not tolerate changing hands but will only exchange English rule for complete independence.

Capital-export to these areas, not to the real colonial areas, and construction of railways, irrigation-works, promotion of a higher, more intensive agriculture – those are the most important methods to increase their productivity and thus to meet as far as possible capitalist industry's growing need for raw materials.

No less important for that industry is establishment of the most active exchange-relations between their production-sites and the agrarian areas, and good agreements to facilitate the export of industrial commodities and capital to those areas as well as the supply of raw materials from them. The best way to do that is through *trade-agreements* as close as possible to free trade: no agrarian tariffs here to increase the price of raw materials for industry and bring down the workers' real wages, thus lowering their productivity; and no industrial tariffs there to raise the price of means of production for agriculture.

Trade-agreements of this sort are the best means to promote economic development, but they also prove to be most effective in bringing about and securing world peace.

Naturally, it was an illusion of bourgeois free traders to think that free trade would eliminate the economic antagonisms called forth by capitalism. Free trade is as unable to do that as democracy. But we all have an interest in these antagonisms being fought out in forms demanding as few sacrifices and as little suffering from the working masses as possible, and that is much more the case under free trade and democracy than under agrarian tariffs and a police-state.

The demand for trade-agreements and the greatest possible lowering of tariff-barriers belongs in the peace programme of Social Democracy next to the rejection of any violent annexation forced upon the peoples and a striving for the most sweeping disarmament.

6. Customs-union and federation of states

The tariff-question will assume yet another meaning after the conclusion of peace. With this we come back to the starting point of our reflections, to the question of state-expansion. As we have already remarked, this has become an urgent task for the European states. The framework of national states no longer suffices for them.

There is a large element of truth in this observation. Powerful state-formations have arisen, such as the British Empire, the Russian Empire and the United States of America. How can the states of Central Europe hold their ground alongside them?

The size of each of the three empires mentioned, to which the Chinese Empire will soon have to be added as an equal, is of the greatest importance for the growth of their industry – not, as people think, because any of these areas is economically self-sufficient (none of them is able to achieve that) but because every one of them offers a huge domestic market for its industry, which provides the foundations for organising gigantic corporations able to face the competitive struggle both within and outside the state with the greatest financial power and with the industrial superiority of gigantic enterprises. The industry of Central Europe also needs such an expansion of the domestic market as its firmest foundation in order to be able to face foreign competition in conditions of equality. Until now, Germany's domestic market was enough to provide it with the foundations for a successful economic struggle in the world market. That is beginning to change. Here, and not in the acquisition of new colonies or spheres of influence, lies the current problem for industry not just in Germany but also in its neighbouring states.

Does the solution of this problem lie in expansion of the national state into a multinational state? This would mean that the needs of further capitalist development contradict those of democracy, which, as we have seen, can only find most perfect expression in the national state. The proletariat can only come into its own on the foundation of democracy, and it cannot give it up under any circumstances. However, it would face a terrible dilemma if it had to aspire to obstruct economic development, or if it could only further it by arresting political development.

Fortunately, however, that is by no means necessary. The expansion of the national state into a multinational state, by conquering neighbouring areas belonging to another nationality, is only one of the ways of expanding the domestic market – the one involving the greatest costs and dangers, standing in the most absolute contradiction with the democratic needs of the great masses, hindering political development, and creating increasingly more internal and external opposition the further it proceeds.

The national state did not come into being by one community growing all the while and absorbing neighbouring communities, but by different communities combining into a single one in which all had equal rights and retained self-government in their internal affairs.

The best and most promising means of expanding the domestic market is not the expansion of the national state into a multinational state, but the centralisation of several national states into a confederation with equal rights. *The federation of states rather than the multinational state or the colonial state: that is the form for the great empires required by capitalism to reach its final, highest form in which the proletariat will seize power.*

Such a federation can assume multiple forms; it can be a confederation of federations. As such, it represents the most elastic political form that is capable of endless expansion up to the final world federation.

The United States of America created the first federation of this kind. The British Empire owes its strength to the timely transformation of its mightiest and most rapidly emerging colonies into federative states. The transformation of the Russian Empire into a democratic community will necessarily be accompanied by its metamorphosis from a centralised unitary state into a federation of autonomous national states.

Austria stands before a similar problem. But all the European states between England and Russia have a growing need of tighter centralisation.

A customs-union [*Zollverein*] of the German Empire with its neighbours could provide the point of departure for a United States of Europe.

A joyfully welcome goal, but how can it be reached? People refer to the German customs-union, which, since 1833, paved the way for the German federal state under Prussian leadership. But contemporary supporters of a Central-European customs-union as a rule forget to remark that the German customs-union was only possible because it operated on the foundations of free trade. The tariffs it established were minimal; its great impact on the development of German industry was not due to the exclusion of foreign countries but to the removal of all barriers and obstacles to internal trade, thus creating the broad area of a domestic market required by German industry.

And only on the foundations of free trade could the German customs-union come into being.

Any higher tariff on a product means not only an advantage for its producers but also a disadvantage for its buyers, as well as for other branches of production if it is a means of production. Each tariff heading [*Zollposition*] thus brings about the demand from branches of production affected by it for compensation through higher tariffs for their own products. The adoption of such a protectionist tariff thus generates a race of individual branches for the favour of the legislature. It is completely impossible to satisfy all branches simultaneously. The politically most influential branches, which are for the most part the economically stronger ones, usually get the best of the bargain. That is true of individual production branches but also of individual districts whose prosperity depends on this or that branch of production. In this case, too, the strongest and most influential have the best prospects. The protective tariff, which should protect the weakest, actually privileges the strong at the expense of the weak.

Thus each tariff that raises customs-duties creates contradictions that prevent a voluntary agreement and can finally be overcome only through the power of the state.

For that reason, the German customs-tariff was impossible on a protectionist basis.

Simultaneously with Prussia, its counterpart, Austria, also tried to create a customs-union encompassing the whole of Germany and Austria but on a protectionist basis. The plan miscarried for that reason. Austria was forced to create a protectionist system for itself alone, in that way shutting itself off from the rest of Germany and paving the way for its political exclusion from the German federal state.

Things are no different today. To use an expression often repeated since the outbreak of the War, Germany certainly faces a decisive hour. It needs an expansion of its domestic market, that is, the abolition of all tariff-barriers and obstacles to trade between itself and its neighbours. But if that is possible, it is so only on the basis of a free-trade tariff [-policy]. Only on the basis of free trade can small European states make up to some extent for lack of a large domestic market. They cannot give up that basis under any circumstances.

However, free trade is not the end of the matter. Experience teaches (and it would be easy to demonstrate why it must be so) that, in an age of growing democracy, a lasting integration of different states into a community is only possible on the foundations of democracy – democratic aspirations and conditions in all the states concerned. When the American colonies broke away from England at the end of the eighteenth century, they could only unite into the voluntary community of a federal state because the parts and the whole were democratically organised. We have seen how the commonwealth of federal states of Greater Britain[30] was only possible on these foundations. Its expansion depends on the extent to which the democratic elements of the

30. [The phrase here is: 'der Staatenbund der Bundesstaaten des grösseren Britannien'.]

mother-state succeed in controlling their imperialist politicians and their violent methods [*Gewaltpolitiker*].

For its formation, Germany required not only preparation through a free-trade customs-union but also the democratic concession of universal and equal suffrage [in 1867].[31]

Today, realisation of the longed-for Central-European customs-union or federation also depends on the force that those classes and parties will have who champion the cause of free trade and complete democracy in the member-states, and particularly in those of the core around which all will rally. Imperialist policy is the worst obstacle to that progress, which is urgently necessary for Germany's industrial development.

Domestic politics react on foreign policy and vice versa. Each can force the other to change. Although the world war has already meant a massive transformation and its consequences can bring still others, it need not change anything in the policy of Social Democracy. On the contrary, all demands whose implementation could lead to a lasting peace at the end of the war, providing all the peoples concerned with room for further development, will raise Germany and its neighbours to a higher stage of political life. Social Democracy has always championed those demands, and it also upholds them today with full force. No policy of conquest but disarmament and democracy – these are the true foundations of Social-Democratic thought and will. We merely need to remain true to ourselves in order to aspire to the best that can be desired for Germany and the peoples of the earth at the conclusion of this war.

Our success does not depend on us alone but also on power-relations at the end of the War. But whatever forms the real peace may assume, we will win the trust of the working class and of all those aspiring to a lasting peace and prosperity of the peoples the more firmly we adhere to our programme, and we will alienate them all the less, the more energetically we champion it.

One should not be bewildered by the apparent contradiction that the historical task of Social Democracy reveals. Its task is to defend the interest of the proletariat against capitalism, to struggle against it, but, simultaneously, also to further economic development, which, as long as society is not socialistically arranged, necessarily means the furthering of capitalist development.

31. [The reference is to male suffrage. Female suffrage came in 1918.]

We must simultaneously fight against and promote capitalism. How is that possible?

The possibility lies in the fact that there are different ways of furthering capitalist development. The driving force of capital is profit: an increase in profits is the capitalist watchword. That increase can be brought about in two ways. One way is to raise the productivity of labour; the more the worker produces, the greater the surplus created by him above his maintenance-costs and the greater the profit. The other way is simply to take more away from him without raising his productivity. Of these two ways, the second is the easiest, readiest and cheapest. It requires neither new expenditures nor much headache: it only takes power. This way includes wage-reductions, the prolongation of working time, the raising of foodstuff-prices by indirect taxes or agrarian tariffs, the raising of house-rents, and also the raising of agricultural rent insofar as the arable land is not cultivated by capitalist tenants but by workers for their own consumption.

To the first way belongs the introduction of new machines, better organisational forms of production and distribution, replacement of lower by higher operational forms, such as small-scale cultivation by large-scale cultivation, construction or improvement of means of transportation, better education and physical invigoration of the workers, and scientific structuring of the production-process.

The second way can momentarily further economic progress through a more rapid increase of capital, but it must finally obstruct it by atrophying the most important means of production: the workers. By contrast, the first kind of measures can also momentarily cause great suffering to the working class, but they prepare the material foundations without which liberation of the workers is impossible. The second way must harm the workers under any circumstances; the first way, by increasing the productivity of labour, makes it possible to improve the material conditions not only of the capitalists but also of the workers despite the increased exploitation.

We cannot and must not hinder the introduction of measures of the first kind. We must only strive for their implementation in a way that does not hurt the workers but rather enables them to share in the advantages of the innovations.

By contrast, we must struggle under all circumstances and with all our powers against measures of the second kind. The more powerful the resistance of the workers, the more insuperable the obstacles they set in the way of capital, the more it will be forced to turn to the only way still open to increase its profits, namely, raising the productivity of labour.

In this way, Social Democracy solves the apparent contradiction of its historical tasks, simultaneously struggling against and also promoting capitalism.

We must apply the same method in the question of imperialism. We have shown that imperialism doubtlessly belongs to methods of the second type insofar as it seeks to subjugate and exploit the workers of agrarian countries by violent means. This course of action can momentarily further economic development, but, eventually, it becomes an obstacle to it.

The danger that imperialism represents for the working class is not diminished by the fact that it is openly directed not against the workers of its own country but against those of foreign countries – on the one hand, against those of the occupied colonies, and, on the other, against the workers of other industrial countries that imperialism depicts as competitors for possession of those colonies. Imperialism tells the workers of its own country that they will profit from increased exploitation of their brothers in the colonies, that their comrades in other industrial countries envy them for that reason, and that they must therefore regard them as enemies who must be dealt with by force. Nothing is more fallacious than the prospect of drawing this advantage from colonial possessions. Instead, the workers expropriated in foreign countries come as scabs to the capitalist states. As such, they face the danger of being hostilely received by the workers of these states. For the allegedly privileged workers of the old states, too, the ultimate goal of imperialism thus means only increased pressure on wages and splitting the working class into enemy-camps, i.e., inhibition of the class-struggle. Imperialism alienates the workers from their socialist ideals and tears up their international unity with the pretence of small advantages, which, if they exist at all, are of a temporary nature and must end in weakening and imposing a heavier burden on the working class.

For that reason, the same rule that applies to wage-reductions, to prolongation of working time, to the raising of prices on foodstuffs by indirect taxes or agrarian tariffs etc. also applies to imperialism: a resolute struggle must be waged against it, not to hinder economic progress but, rather, to force the capitalist class to seek the increase of its profits, the expansion of its area of exploitation, the increased exportation of industrial products and importation of foodstuffs and raw materials, no longer through the more proximate and cheaper methods of imperialism but through the methods of democracy and free trade, which, admittedly, require more intellectual capacity but also open the broadest paths for economic development, thereby also strengthening the proletariat physically, intellectually and politically.

Nothing is more mistaken than the opinion that the materialist conception of history forbids us to oppose imperialist methods for as long as capital rules. It rather makes this opposition one of the most important tasks of the working class in our times.

Chapter Fifty

'Perspectives and Projects'[1] (1915)

Rosa Luxemburg

The newest essay by Karl Kautsky, 'National State, Imperialist State and Confederation',[2] partly recapitulates and partly supplements the analysis of the present war that he has offered in different articles in *Die Neue Zeit*.

Kautsky begins by describing the essence and historical role of the national state and then proceeds to say a number of things about it that nobody has heard before. We learn, for instance, that the national state is as much an inevitable logical consequence of the 'modern great-state democracy' as it is, conversely, its indispensable foundation. Thus, national state and 'modern democracy' are an inseparable pair. We further learn that Austria, for instance, can only be democratically regenerated by dissolving into a federation of national states, that such dissolution is also 'required' of 'the peoples on Russia's periphery', etc. According to the conception that prevailed until now in Social Democracy, the whole national phraseology, in Austria as much as in Russia, Germany and everywhere else, served primarily to protect the interests of the bourgeoisie and its class-rule by confusing the class-struggle. Yet, Kautsky tells us

1. Mortimer [Rosa Luxemburg] 1915a.
2. Kautsky 1915.

that national struggles in contemporary states spring only from 'democratic feelings' and are all the more prominent, the stronger those feelings are.

Kautsky thus completely disregards the conception of the national state as a transitory and historically determined phase of bourgeois class-rule, a phase long overcome by imperialism and most clearly buried precisely in the present world war. For Kautsky, the national state is a formula of modern democracy; as such, it is, simultaneously, the ideal of the future, indeed, the programme of Social Democracy! 'Social Democracy has taken over from bourgeois democracy the aspiration towards a national state,'[3] Kautsky tells us, although not a single known Social-Democratic party has thus far written such an 'aspiration' into its programme; on the contrary, until now the task of Social Democracy was considered to be one of welding together proletarians from each state for a common class-struggle – with a common programme and without distinction of nationality – in opposition to petty-bourgeois national strivings. According to the formulation of the International Socialist Congress held in London in 1896, Social Democracy certainly recognises 'the right of every nationality to self-determination'. But, between that formula and the 'aspiration towards a national state' lies precisely the whole abyss that separates socialist principles from bourgeois political programmes. Kautsky was able to make his amazing discovery by simply identifying the abstract notions of national state and democracy in his own head. And, since Social Democracy, of course, 'aspires' to 'democracy', it follows quite obviously, as a natural conclusion, that we must also 'aspire' to the national state.

But what actually is that 'modern democracy' that should be the object of our aspirations? The answer can be found, the reader will say, in the minimal programme of Social Democracy. Far from it! What Kautsky calls 'modern democracy' is actually...contemporary bourgeois parliamentarism! According to this schema, the current Prusso-German semi-absolutism, for instance, should appear to us as 'modern democracy'.

Kautsky further tells us:

> But during the period in which both giant empires [Great Britain and Russia – R.L.] were formed, the material conditions also developed to realise democracy in a state going beyond the area of the primitive community,

3. Kautsky 1915, p. 11.

> thus replacing primitive by modern democracy. That was achieved by the development of transportation, by printing and the generalisation of reading and writing.... At the same time arose the modern large state with a centralised bureaucracy and customs-barriers. At first it strengthened central political power, which was absolute. But the development of exchange and the press made it increasingly possible for the population of the entire state to know the deeds and omissions of the central power, to discuss and criticise them. The demeanour of the central power, at the same time, became increasingly important for the individuals the more its scope grew. The urge therefore appeared to have an influence on it through a system of representatives elected and controlled by the masses. *In that way developed modern democracy*, whose essential traits are parliamentarism, the press, and large party organisations encompassing the entire country.[4]

We have literally transcribed this fine specimen of materialist conception in order for the reader to see how nicely the formation of the bourgeois 'constitutional state' can be explained from the development of 'communication and the press', without the complicated apparatus of class-interests, economic upheavals and the like. 'Modern democracy' appears in this way – like its worthy complement, the national state – not as a prosaic piece of bourgeois class-rule, with all the traces of its limited earthly existence and clear signs of decay, but wrapped up in the thick fog of abstraction and in the everlasting existence of the ideal. We indeed live, as Kautsky says in another part, in 'the age of growing democracy'.[5] Admittedly, our 'modern democracy' first becomes an ideal when we have the pure national state. 'Full democracy', therefore, cannot be realised at all in Germany 'with its Poles, Danes, Frenchmen', because

> A Polish politician, a Polish newspaper or a Polish book may well speak to us very vividly, convincingly and significantly in their own language, and they will perhaps have an impact on Poles, including those living outside Germany, but not on the German people. However, the essence of democracy consists in acting on the people and through the people.[6]

4. Kautsky 1915, p. 8. Emphasis added by Rosa Luxemburg.
5. Kautsky 1915, p. 77.
6. Kautsky 1915, p. 9.

Therefore, it is first 'within each of those national states [into which contemporary large State must break up – R.L.] that *full – not just formal but real and efficient – democracy is possible*'.[7] Do you still believe your eyes, dear reader?

But that charming pair of twins also has a little sister who is inseparable from them: the militia!

> Through the strong democratic life of its inhabitants... the national state offers the most energetic and lasting, almost insuperable resistance to any curtailment or change that may be imposed in its territory by a foreign conquering power. On the other hand, that state finds its limits in the extent of the contiguous area of the nation, which it cannot overstep without injuring itself. All this makes the force of its democracy more important for its existence than the force of its army, which must have a purely defensive character in a cohesive national state if [the 'if' is splendid – R.L.] it wants to remain cohesive. The idea of the militia develops simultaneously with the idea of modern democracy and the national state.[8] They are all three supported by the same parties and popular classes.[9]

Incidentally, Kautsky himself does not belong to those parties and popular classes because, some pages later, when he attempts to draw up the peace programme of Social Democracy, he completely forgets his militia and demands – 'disarmament' of the standing army to half its current strength.

Once again, dear reader: do you still believe your eyes? One wonders where on earth there are now, or have even been, all the lovely things that Kautsky tells us? Perhaps Germany since 1870 is that 'national state' with a defensive militia and growing democracy? Is Switzerland, the most democratic state in Europe and the one that has come closest to the militia, a national state? Is the most democratic non-European state, the United States of America, a national state? One wonders whether Marx's ideas have not acted 'on the people and through the people' in countless lands, even though he only spoke 'his language'. Finally, one wonders: has Social Democracy not always affirmed that 'full – not just formal but real and efficient – democracy' is first conceivable when economic and social equality, that is to say, a socialist economic order,

7. Kautsky 1915, p. 11. Emphasis added by Rosa Luxemburg.
8. [Kautsky's text mistakenly reads 'multinational state'.]
9. Kautsky 1915, pp. 16–17.

is realised, whereas the 'democracy' of bourgeois national states is always, in the final analysis, more or less humbug?

But let us leave aside the national state and democracy, together with the militia; it is impossible to say whether Kautsky portrays them as actually existing historical phenomena or just the rosy products of his fantasy. They are, in any case, just a preparation for the analogous treatment of imperialism.

What is imperialism? Imperialism is merely a beastly 'method'. That is to say, imperialism is a method to achieve, through violence and similarly hateful and reprehensible methods, what is legitimate and necessary in itself but can be achieved 'much better' through other methods, namely, 'democracy'. Kautsky considers the expansionist drive of capital a legitimate need of modern development; he only wants to do away with the means, with the imperialist methods, and thus to remove the 'worst sting' of imperialism, the arms-race and colonial policy.

But, when we examine the case closely, it is almost impossible once again to find imperialism, because either what today appears as such is *not yet* imperialism, or else it is already a thing of the past.

England? Well, its colonies were conquered 'long before the imperialist period'; and today, for instance, the South-African, Canadian and Australian federations rest on pure democracy. Against such a 'state-type' we can hardly 'object'.

South Africa, Egypt, Algeria, and Persia are approaching more and more 'the stage of modern democracy', and therefore those regions can 'no longer' be regarded as objects of imperialism.[10] Russia? Naturally, it cannot 'yet' be driven by imperialism, for it still needs capital-imports itself. Austria? Strictly speaking, it cannot 'yet' pursue imperialist goals because it too still needs capital-imports itself; but, at the same time, it has already moved beyond those goals – its 'temporary' imperialist drive to Salonika 'is already spent' long ago. Its conflict with Serbia by no means has an imperialist character. Proof: its underlying causes were agrarian interests, while Serbia, for its part, is 'still far from any imperialist tendency'; it stands at the stage of the 'national state'. China? It is also approaching with seven-league boots the 'stage' of modern democracy, alias the national state, and therefore 'any imperialist

10. Kautsky 1915, p. 54.

policy is impossible' there too – something that right now the blinded Japanese, who do not read *Die Neue Zeit*, evidently do not suspect at all.

In a word, wherever we look, there is either no trace of imperialism or else its days are numbered, because everywhere it is being driven out by growing 'democracy'. But wait, there is Turkey! Certainly that is an object of imperialism, namely German imperialism. Turkey also threatens to become a storm-centre of the imperialist war. But, in this case, too, everything was 'regulated' just before the outbreak of the current war. It broke out at a moment in which there was 'no single imperialist point of contention'.[11]

Thus, if imperialism did not exist at all before the War, it will more than ever cease to exist after the War – so Kautsky prophesied already in September of last year. 'The export of capitals from the industrial states, that source of imperialism and therewith the ultimate cause of the war, will cease, at least for the time being.' Because, on the one hand, the European industrial states will 'have other worries' than practising imperialism after the War; and, on the other hand, the agrarian states are more and more 'eluding' exploitation by imperialism (*Neue Zeit*, Nr. 23, p. 970).[12] Thus, the whole of imperialism, and especially the present world war, were basically 'much ado about nothing'. How did the War break out, for all that? Well – it was just a result of the arms-race and mobilisation![13]

You may wonder, dear reader, why all these gymnastics? Why so much sweat and toil to contradict well-known facts that today are common knowledge? Kautsky answers us with the following discovery: whoever argues 'that imperialism is indispensable for capitalist production in its current stage' is actually 'serving the imperialists' interests... raising their spiritual influence on the popular masses and in that way increasing their power'.[14] Kautsky therefore 'asserts' the opposite. He 'asserts' that imperialism is not at all economically necessary but is just 'a question of power', that the expansion of capital would be 'best' furthered not by the violent methods of capitalism but 'through peaceful democracy'.[15] How simple and enlightening! Marx asserted that the rule of capital at a certain stage would be an inevitable eco-

11. Kautsky 1915, p. 63.
12. [Kautsky 1914c.]
13. Kautsky 1915, p. 65.
14. Kautsky 1915, p. 22.
15. Kautsky 1915, p. 70.

nomic necessity of social development, thereby naturally serving the interests of the capitalists, increasing their spiritual influence and their power. Engels asserted that corporations were an economic necessity of capitalist production, thus serving the stock-owners' interests and probably increasing their dividends. Social Democracy asserted until now that modern militarism is historically necessary as a tool of capitalist class-domination, and therewith serves the militarists' interests, increasing their influence and their power. That is all crystal-clear – and Lassalle, together with his motto of 'stating that which is', can be buried again.[16]

Kautsky only forgot that his saving discovery about imperialism being unnecessary and 'just' a question of power ultimately gives us little comfort. Because, from a broad historical perspective, as Engels once explained to Dühring, 'power' at the same time is an economic factor and has its roots in economic necessity. Kautsky further forgot that the 'method' of imperialism, which he wants to abolish as a totally extrinsic and beastly accessory to contemporary capitalism, is actually essential to it. When he speaks about the violence of imperialist methods, he only sees the noisy, bellicose external appearance of imperialism. He has forgotten that the 'peaceful' and 'democratic' capitalist expansion that he likes better (the construction of railways and the introduction of commodity-exchange in backward countries) is also a process accompanied – only silently – by the continuous violent breakdown of the existing social organisation through the incessant violent interventions of the state. He has also forgotten completely that English free trade, whose great deeds in China he praises and sets against imperialism, opened China's door with cannons and all the cruelties of war, as well as with countless violent measures of robbery and fraud from 1839 to 1900. In a word, the whole Kautskyist distinction between the legitimate economic kernel of imperialism and its hideous 'violent' shell, which one can persuade capitalism to discard as something accidental, is just an idle rumination. In bloody reality, imperialism has neither kernel nor shell, it is a single whole: economic necessity and violent methods go hand in hand and swap places all the time. Both can only be overcome by the elimination of capitalism. Kautsky's plan to civilise

16. ['All major political action consists in stating that which is, and begins with it. All political mediocrity consists in concealing and glossing over that which is.' Lassalle 1863, p. 108.]

contemporary capitalism, to 'democratise' and pacify it, to take 'the sting' out of it, ultimately turns out to be something like David's 'socialist' colonial policy.[17] The utopian character of all those efforts to clip the tiger's claws – to persuade him that 'the best thing' for him, in his own interest, would be to eat honey and vegetables – finally becomes obvious. And, if David laid out his petty-bourgeois utopias many years before the present war, it is much more astonishing to see Kautsky, amidst the lightning and thunder of the great world-historical catastrophe brought about by capitalism, finding occasion today – lively and untiring as a young grasshopper in the weeds – to sing his little song about 'disarmament', the 'national state', 'democratic development' and free trade as the nearest perspective for the future of capitalism 'in its own interest'. A more upside-down historical perspective for orienting proletarians in the present war is hardly imaginable.

But his bizarre historical conception has a very practical side. It is clear that a reawakening of international class-consciousness in the ranks of Social Democracy, in Germany as elsewhere, will only take place if the worker is freed from the spell of nationalist hypnosis to which he was driven in the current war-slaughter by the ruling classes and his own party leaders, and, if he sees clearly the War's imperialist character and the great tasks resulting from it. Kautsky, by contrast, supplies precisely now, in the midst of the nationalist orgies of the war-mongers, an exuberant apology for nationalism, putting the strongest emphasis on the nationalist idea, which he identifies with 'democratic feelings', and, besides, makes imperialism, as an historical phase, disappear in theoretical fumes. And the moral of the story is: a 'peace programme' of Social Democracy, one that next to the rejection of annexations calls for 'disarmament' by half or even a quarter (as he did in the previous September issue of *Neue Zeit*, p. 971)[18] and a European federation or customs-union, including free trade and commercial treaties. More recipes and projects! Instead of action, instead of class-struggle, Kautsky considers that our most important task in this situation is to give advice to bourgeois society,

17. [A reference to the revisionist Eduard David; see especially his speech at the Stuttgart Congress. David's book *Die Sozialdemokratie im Weltkrieg* (David 1915) has been called 'the best general statement of the Majority point of view on the war'. O'Boyle 1951, p. 828, note 13.]

18. *Neue Zeit*, Nr. 23, p. 971. [Kautsky 1914c, p. 971.]

showing it how, by means of democracy, free trade and pretty little defensive wars, its interests can 'best' be looked after, so that in this gently flickering historical fire the proletariat will also be able to cook its own little soup. The fact that he previously described those peaceful postwar prospects – which would 'separate' imperialism from the arms-race – as the opposite of democracy and free trade and, indeed, as an era of reaction (*Neue Zeit* of 11 September 1914, p. 922),[19] is no doubt irrelevant. Kautsky does not seem to be embarrassed by the fact that his federation, alias customs-union, is nothing but a poor imitation of the reactionary protectionist projects – aimed now against the United States of America, now against England – advanced many times over by Prof. Julius Wolf and Max Schippel, and today again by the official heralds of imperialism such as Losch, Liszt, etc.

In his essay, Kautsky attacks the 'right wing' of the Party, the social-imperialists. He wants to pull the rug from under their feet by means of his historical perspectives. At the same time, in order to maintain his position in the 'Centre', he does not refrain from aiming a couple of smashing blows against the 'far Left'. He denounces it, of course, as a bunch of people who in the first place want to 'replace'[20] parliamentarism by the 'mass-strike' and who, moreover, oppose imperialism with socialism, 'that is, not simply propaganda for socialism, with which we have opposed all forms of capitalist rule for half a century, but also its immediate implementation'.[21] Kautsky would find himself in a pretty awkward situation if someone were to call him politely to account and ask him to state exactly who it was, or where and when anyone in the Party wanted to 'replace' parliamentarism by the mass-strike, or to name the crank who demanded the 'immediate realisation' of socialism.

Just as Kautsky, immediately after the outbreak of the War, sounded the alarm against 'obstructionists' by warning against 'eccentricity' and 'criticism' as the worst crimes (*Neue Zeit* of 21 August 1914, p. 846),[22] so now he

19. *Neue Zeit* of 11 September 1914, p. 922. [Kautsky 1914b, p. 922.]
20. 'But upon closer examination this alternative system appears as a form of primitive democracy. That is true both of direct legislation by the people and also of its more assertive variant, the mass-strike.' [Kautsky 1915, p. 8.] The mass-strike as a 'variant' of direct legislation by the people and as such of the primitive community – what nonsense!
21. Kautsky 1915, p. 17.
22. *Neue Zeit* of 21 August 1914, p. 846. [Kautsky 1914a, p. 846.]

gives excellent service to the right wing by drawing out of his own fantasy a vulgar caricature of the views and intentions of the 'obstructionists'.

But his whole theory, which he advocates in his essay as he does in *Die Neue Zeit*, facilitates even more the work of the social-imperialists, whom he wants to combat, by spreading the greatest confusion in the Party regarding the historical situation, its true tendencies and the tasks of the working class. And, for that reason, those broad scintillating theoretical ruminations are more dangerous than the 'reorientation' of Heine, Südekum, Haenisch and the like. While those people put party members on guard by their crude conduct, the Kautskyist theories might take 'the sting' not out of militarism and imperialism, of course, but out of Social Democracy.

For the rest, Kautsky closes his essay with a nice twist. We must 'decisively struggle' against the imperialist 'method'. 'The more powerful the resistance of the workers, the more insuperable will be the obstacles they set in the way of capital',[23] and the more it will be forced, both in the forms of exploitation and in foreign policy, to take the laudable democratic path and change for the better. Whatever the case, it is clear that the 'powerful resistance' to imperialism and the 'insuperable obstacles' must look completely different from the current attitude of the party authorities and from Kautsky's own attitude since the outbreak of the War. Thus Kautsky unexpectedly closes his essay with a sharp judgement against the official tactic of Social Democracy. And this final twist is pretty much the only unobjectionable thing in his entire pamphlet.

23. Kautsky 1915, p. 79.

Chapter Fifty-One

'The Driving Forces of Imperialism' (March 1915)

Karl Radek

Karl Radek's article on 'The Driving Forces of Imperialism', like the preceding one by Rosa Luxemburg, can be read as a response to Kautsky's identification of democracy with the national state. Kautsky thought imperialist contradictions could be overcome by combining democratic states in an economic federation to eliminate tariffs. The significance that Kautsky attached to the state exemplified the thinking that paralysed the Second International. In every country, social-chauvinists found democratic justification for supporting the national war-effort: British and French labour leaders pointed to the threat of postwar reaction posed by Hohenzollern Germany, ignoring the fact that their own countries were allied with tsarist Russia; German and Austrian Social Democrats claimed that an Entente-victory would strengthen Russia, forgetting that defence of their own fatherlands meant war against bourgeois democracies in Britain and France. In every country, support for one's own country's war-effort could be linked with defending democracy against the threat of reaction posed by the opposing alliance.

Karl Radek's essay articulated a different argument: the national state itself was becoming historically redundant. 'The capitalist state-framework,' he wrote, 'is too narrow. Capitalism had to blow it up everywhere.' In Volume III of *Capital*, Marx had said that capitalist industry has an 'immanent need' for constant expansion of the world market, 'so that now it is not trade that revolutionizes industry, but rather industry that constantly revolutionizes trade'.[1] Radek emphasised a similar causality that led from capitalist industry to the depletion of European agriculture; from reliance upon agricultural and raw-material imports to the predominance of heavy industry and railway-construction in opening new territories; and from the financial requirements of heavy industry to the universal predominance of finance-capital in a world economy forged by imperialism.

Radek's views, like those of Rosa Luxemburg, pointed in the direction of a new internationalism. Six months after publication of the article translated here, an International Socialist Conference met in Zimmerwald to oppose the imperialist war. The Conference Manifesto, drafted by Leon Trotsky, condemned socialists who supported their own country's war-effort:

> [They] have invited the workers to suspend the working-class struggle, the only possible and effective means of working-class emancipation. They have voted the ruling classes the credits for carrying on the war. They have put themselves at the disposal of their Governments for the most varied services. They have tried through their press and their envoys to win over the neutrals to the Governmental policies of their respective countries. They have given to their Government Socialist Ministers as hostages for the observance of the national truce, and thus have taken on themselves the responsibility for this war, its aims, its methods. And just as Socialist Parties failed separately, so did the most responsible representative of the Socialists of all countries fail: the International Socialist Bureau.[2]

While the official Zimmerwald Manifesto called for 'peace without annexations or indemnities' and defended 'the right of self-determination of nations', Radek, together with Lenin, Zinoviev and others, proposed on behalf of the Zimmerwald Left a draft that went much further, calling for the overthrow of the capitalist governments as the only way to put an end to wars. For the

1. Marx 1992, p. 451.
2. 'Zimmerwald Manifesto', in Gankin and Fisher (eds.) 1940, p. 331.

Zimmerwald Left, the only response to imperialist war was proletarian revolution: 'Civil war, not civil peace, between the classes – that is our slogan!'[3]

In April 1916, Radek wrote his 'Theses on Imperialism and National Oppression' and summarised more explicitly the conclusion already emerging in the article on 'The Driving Forces of Imperialism'. His theme was that neither a peace without annexations nor national self-determination was possible without first destroying capitalism and imperialism:

> ...imperialism represents the tendency of finance capital *to outgrow the limits of national states*, to seize for national capital transoceanic sources of raw materials and food supplies, spheres for investment and markets, and to form, *in Europe as well, larger state units* by combining adjacent territories that complement each other economically, regardless of the nationality of the inhabitants.... The tendencies of imperialism toward colonial and continental annexations signify an *increase and general extension of national oppression*, which hitherto had existed only in certain states with a heterogeneous population (i.e. with national minorities).[4]

The Zimmerwald Left elected their own executive body, made up of Lenin, Radek and Zinoviev, but, even within this group, differences remained over the tangled issue of the national state and self-determination. Lenin thought Radek and Luxemburg, whose thinking was conditioned by the particular circumstances of Poland, were *too dismissive* in their attitude towards the national state.[5] Since the resulting discussion was complex and protracted – too protracted to include in this volume – for present purposes it will suffice to summarise it briefly in the words of Leon Trotsky:

> The national problem was particularly acute in Poland. The so-called P.P.S. (Polish Socialist Party), headed by [the militant nationalist] Joseph Pilsudski, came out ardently for Polish independence.... Rosa Luxemburg counterposed...the demand for the autonomy of the Polish region as a constituent part of [a future] democratic Russia.... She looked upon 'the right of self-

3. 'Draft Resolution of the Zimmerwald Left' (11 October 1915), in Gankin and Fisher (eds.) 1940, p. 353.

4. Radek 1916, p. 507.

5. See Lenin 1916b (especially thesis number 9: 'The Attitude of Russian and Polish Social-Democracy and of the Second International to Self-Determination') and Lenin 1916c (particularly section 8: 'The Specific and the General in the Position of the Dutch and Polish Social-Democrat Internationalists').

> determination' as an empty abstraction. The polemic on that question lasted for years. Lenin insisted that...even under imperialism, the working class did not refuse to fight for democratic rights, including among them the right of each nation to its independent existence. Moreover, in certain portions of our planet it was imperialism itself that invested the slogan of national self-determination with extraordinary significance.... [I]n Eastern Europe, Asia, Africa and South America the epoch of national democratic movements had not really begun to unfold until the twentieth century. To deny the right of nations to self-determination is tantamount in effect to offering aid and comfort to the imperialists against their colonies and generally against all oppressed nationalities.[6]

* * *

'The Driving Forces of Imperialism'[7]

Through the thunder of cannons and the groans of hundreds of thousands driven to the misery of the battlefield, capitalist society hammers into people's heads that it wants something new and announces to them that it going through labour-pains. In their daily drudgery, in the even steps of their hard lives, the working masses cared little about what their lords and rulers were doing in distant corners of the world. When a Hamburg docker loaded machines to China or cheap textiles to Turkey, he did not think that he was helping to send dynamite to remote worlds, that those machines and textiles would turn masses of people who formerly knew nothing of the world, and about whom the world knew nothing, into factors of world policy, into citizens of the world. And, when the workers heard something about a railway from Constantinople to Baghdad, or from Cairo to Cape Town, they thought least of all that linking the Mediterranean with the Persian sea, or uniting both ends of Africa, would lead to dissolution of the connection between Hamburg and London. The popular masses of the European continent felt secure within the walls of their national states; they struggled to build their homes, and all that happened in distant corners of the world and changed its foundations they regarded as remote events 'far away in Turkey'. [It may

6. Trotsky 1941, pp. 153–4.
7. Radek 1915a.

be] entertaining: the Chinese cut off their pigtails. [It may be] gruesome: general von Trotha let thousands of black men swelter in the desert. But anyway, [it was] remote. *What happened on the stage of 'higher politics' was an object of indignation, protests, and declarations of sympathy, but not something that concerned their own interests.*

Today, the workers of Germany bleed because German capital built a railway across Turkey, because it does not want to let Russia seize Constantinople or Armenia, because it wants to have strongholds for its fleet everywhere in the world. The English bluejackets [naval sailors] are blowing up with their ships because English capital fears that German capitalism, which built a strong fleet out of nothing and buys and sells all over the world, could gain even more strength, dictate its will to its European neighbours, and exploit the ferment among the Indian masses and the Egyptian fellahs to dethrone England as ruler of the world. The French proletariat believes that it bleeds for democracy; the French petty bourgeoisie thinks of Alsace-Lorraine, yet they actually bleed for French financiers to retain their role as financial sharks so that they will not be forced by German capital to hand over a share of their business or even accept a subordinate role in the far corners of the world. And the Russian peasant, fighting for Orthodox religion and the tsar, is actually fighting to enable his torturers, the Russian bureaucracy and usury capital, to exploit Armenian peasants as well, to enable the tsar to intervene in all the quarrels of the world – and to do so, moreover, in the interests of French capital, to which the Russian peasant already pays tribute today.

The War is revealing to the popular masses that they depend on what happens in Bombay and the Orange River [in South Africa], in the Sea of Marmara [in Turkey] and in Shandong [a province of eastern China]; it is revealing to them that *the age of the isolated nation with its separate struggles is gone, and that world rule, world policy, is the fundamental fact.* Even the working class of a *neutral country* such as Switzerland, knowing no other fleet than the one cutting across the waves of the Bodensee Lake or Lake Geneva [*Lac Léman*], feel to their horror that they have become citizens of the world [*Weltvolk*]. English planes violate Swiss neutrality – although England lies far away by the sea – in order to bombard the workshops of Friedrichshafen.[8]

8. [Friedrichshafen is a town on the northern side of Lake Constance (*Bodensee*) in southern Germany, near the borders with Switzerland and Austria. It is best known for

Argentinean and Russian grain is becoming scarce. Tomorrow, Swiss youth may find themselves involved in a bloody struggle against neighbours, and the country may become a second Belgium. There are, today, no longer neutral countries; every country is now part of the world, which has become a reality: the reality of *antagonisms* and *community*. Modern capitalism, which created the national state as the foundation of national economies, has not only woven them together but has also let their tentacles reach out over the seas to countries where there is not yet a capitalist national economy. If the interweaving of capitalist states means antagonisms and community, agreements and struggles, this is a thousand times more the case in relation to the undeveloped countries. No other principle rules the relations between capitalist states more than struggle. Even if an agreement is reached, it is either the result of an earlier struggle or a means for further struggle over position in the world market.

What are the sources of this economic struggle and where does it lead?

I

Modern capitalism created a *transportation-system* that reduced the significance of distance to a minimum. That enabled it to send great masses of men to *America* and to bring to Europe the product of their work, grain. The cheapness of American grain, the product of a land without ground-rent, enabled capital to turn its back on agriculture. That happened most thoroughly in England, the classical land of capitalism. If it could acquire grain much more cheaply from America, why pay tribute to the English landlords? *Russian* absolutism had to take up loans in capitalist Europe if it wanted to keep its militarism up to date in the age of modern monetary economy. In order to pay the interest on those loans, it exported grain, the product of the peasant-economy, forcing the peasants to engage in commodity-production by squeezing them as taxpayers. European agriculture was threatened from two flanks; it tried to adapt itself to circumstances by laying stress on the production of commodities that did not tolerate distant transportation very

having been home to the Zeppelin airship-company and the Dornier Flugzeugwerke, a German aircraft-manufacturer. The Friedrichshafen Airport lays claim to being the oldest airport in the world.]

well, such as meat, dairy and garden products. But it is confined here, too, by the long turnover-period of capital in agriculture, the limits set by private property in land to the concentration-process in agriculture, and the limits set by the fragmentation of landed property to modern technique, all of which hinder the flow of capital into agriculture. Because it can move much more rapidly and freely in industry, capital does not go into agriculture so readily. For that reason, agricultural productivity does not correspond to the possibilities opened up by agronomical science. The cultural retardation in which capitalism keeps the countryside depopulates it. Modern capitalism strives to pull into the large cities everything that is alive in the village. It makes the rural migrants to the cities dependent on rapidly developing industry, turning them into objects of exploitation but, at the same time, into participants in a greater and more intensive cultural life than even a rich peasant could have. The agrarian protective tariffs, arising against the competition of capitalistically undeveloped countries, have, admittedly, protected the booty of the current agrarian proprietors, but, by raising land-prices in conformity with the higher corn-prices, they did not alter the debased conditions of European agriculture. *Capitalist development shifted the relations between city and countryside to the disadvantage of the latter.*

No matter how much the agrarians, exploiting their political power, may try to counteract this tendency, they can only weaken but not abolish it. And so it happened that even the country with the strongest agrarians [the Prussian Junkers] and the highest agrarian protective tariffs, Germany, is highly dependent on the world market to satisfy its need for foodstuffs and raw material. This dependency brought forth two tendencies: first, the tendency to *control* the sea-routes for the supply of foodstuffs, the *remote oceans*, by means of a strong fleet having at its disposal good strongholds in coasts and islands; and, secondly, to seize *agrarian, capitalistically still undeveloped countries* (colonies) to turn them into sources of *foodstuffs and raw materials* for the capitalist country. When a capitalist country buys American or Argentinean corn or American cotton, it certainly opens up a market for its commodities. But, if it manages to turn Mesopotamia, the ancient granary, into a wheat-and-cotton-producing area by making it into its colony, it will have the possibility, thanks to its political power over the country, of imposing on the Mesopotamian peasants low prices for their products and high prices for its own products.

But the tendency to subjugate agrarian countries has its source not only in the antagonism between city and countryside, which capitalism has decided in favour of the city and industry. *Within industry itself*, a more important antagonism sprang up between industries producing industrial raw materials and industries producing semi-manufactured products, between so-called *heavy industry* and *manufacturing industry*. At the cradle of modern capitalism stood the textile and clothing industry, where the factory-system first developed. It stimulated the liberation of the peasants and the creation of a domestic market. Mining, and the iron and steel industry, came only later. They supplied the already developed manufacturing industry, working to satisfy the demand of the broad masses, with coal and machinery. These industrial branches required much more capital, because digging up the earth's treasures is much more complicated and requires far more powerful machines than spinning and weaving. The concentration of capital in heavy industry took place much more quickly than in manufacturing industry. The growth of cities, where growing masses of proletarians increasingly gathered, the building of railways and of a modern commercial fleet, which characterised the period since 1850 – all this increasingly gave heavy industry the upper hand. As Western and Central Europe became relatively saturated at that point, and Europe's railway-system and urbanisation could not develop at the old tempo – in contrast with the relatively decelerating growth of demand for the products of heavy industry in capitalist Europe, its productivity grew more and more thanks to technological development – the question arose for heavy industry: What now? The deceleration of development would have meant heavy losses in investments; it would have been, so to speak, a checkmating of rich productive sources, of the great profit-opportunities for which technical capabilities had opened the way. The large capitals concentrated in heavy industry overcame these difficulties by driving the state over the seas. *Railway-building in Asia and Africa*, with profits guaranteed by the state, created a great new market for sales by heavy industry.

Besides, the opening up of agrarian countries in Asia and Africa in order to obtain raw materials and foodstuffs would have been impossible without the construction of means of communication. If England wanted to force Egyptian peasants to cultivate cotton instead of the old mode of production, if it wanted to turn them from satisfiers of their own needs into producers for the English market, it had to build railways across the country. If Germany wanted to obtain black workers for its Kilimanjaro plantations, it had to lay track along the whole of East Africa. Only in the wake of railways could merchants, civil servants and soldiers reach the remote Rwandan territory in order to undermine there the subsistence economy of the blacks and force them through taxation to migrate and work in Kilimanjaro.

The interest of the capitalist states in transforming the economically undeveloped countries, which they turned into colonies, into sources of raw materials and foodstuffs, coincided here with the interests of heavy industry. Railway-construction, more railway-construction, and yet again railway-construction – that is modern colonial policy. And the necessity of railway-construction imposed itself also on the capitalistically undeveloped great states like *China* and *Turkey*, which the capitalist states were not strong enough to convert into colonies. If China and Turkey each wanted to combine their remote provinces, living in actual economic independence (as in medieval Europe, where each city and the villages lying within a day's travel constituted an independent territory), into a viable state; if they wanted to exploit fully, financially and militarily, the forces of the population of the whole country; if they wanted to reform their administration – they had to tie together their provinces by means of railways. If they do not succeed in doing that, they will become defenceless objects of the capitalist policy of plunder. To escape that fate, to be able to build the railways, they turned to European capital. They took up loans in London, Paris, and Berlin, granting to the capitalist concerns conditions that meant huge profits for *banking capital* and economic exploitation of the worst kind for the borrowers. The banks received huge commissions for their 'arduous' work of interesting additional circles in the capitalist world [in these enterprises].

But it was not just a question of brokers' fees. *Modern bank-capital dominates heavy industry.* The growth of working capital and investment-capital in heavy industry, which has become an inescapable law due to uninterrupted technical development, cannot take place solely through accumulation of the surplus-value produced in individual undertakings. Large as the mass of surplus-value squeezed by Krupp, Stinnes, Thyssen, etc. out of their proletarians may be, it is not enough to cover the expansion-needs of their enterprises, which grow by leaps and bounds. The banks assemble every particle of capital accumulated in the country and place it at the disposal of heavy industry. The enterprises of heavy industry are *joint-stock companies* (*corporations*); they represent collective capitalist property, and the banks that finance them are their true managers. They bring about looser or firmer associations between these enterprises (*syndicates, cartels, trusts*), and they shut down some of them in order to secure greater profitability and better possibilities for development.

The same banks also place loans for the undeveloped countries. And, in that context, they do not content themselves with the *usurious interest of the loan-brokers*. They force these debtor-countries to assign the construction of railways to enterprises they control, thus getting *the best prices* for rails, locomotives, tunnel-construction, etc., and obtaining *concessions* for mining, the draining of swamps, the irrigation of deserts, etc. as ancillary businesses.

In that way, countries hitherto undeveloped in terms of capitalism are dragged into its maelstrom. They owe huge sums to the capitalist countries. In order to pay them, they must extort surplus-labour from the masses of their people and turn it into money. In order to raise the taxes paid by Chinese peasants, without whom China cannot set up an army, railways must be built. The costs of railways increase the sum of necessary taxes; the peasants must eat less and produce and sell more. They become dependent on the world-market price of soybeans and ploughs, which they buy from European capital, in order to increase the productivity of the land. But, at the same time, European capital becomes dependent on the Chinese peasants' mood. If they rebel against increasing exploitation, revolt against new taxes, and tear up the tracks; if tax-collectors force their way into remote villages with soldiers and the peasants gang up against the cities where the state officials, who sold out to the 'white devils', live, then alarm spreads among European stock-exchanges and orders are sent by telegraph from the admiralty in Kiel and London to naval garrisons: the fatherland is in danger, the purses of finance-capital are threatened by Chinese Boxers! And if the government of a capitalistically undeveloped country seems incapable of playing the role of watchdog for European capital vis-à-vis the masses of its own people, its final hour approaches. Each loan placed by the capital of a European state in capitalistically undeveloped countries is a mortgage on the future partition of the land.

II

Imperialism is the striving of the countries of old capitalism to subjugate and exploit capitalistically undeveloped countries. The latter should supply capitalist countries with cheap foodstuffs and raw materials and pay dearly for the products of European industry, especially heavy industry. The capitalist states have already subjugated all the defenceless states in Asia and Africa. In the process, they have annihilated hundreds of thousands upon hundreds of thousands of human lives. They have turned the obliteration of old modes of production into a sophisticated system. Today, they stand before two great states, the products of centuries, indeed millennia of history: *Turkey* and *China*. For half a century, they have been the object of capitalist desires and appetites. During the last twenty years, those appetites have turned into a system of coherent measures increasingly pushing for a 'solution' of the Chinese and Turkish questions. But Turkey, and this can be said ten times more of China – they are both entire worlds. Turkey is the centre of the Islamic world, and China is a continent with 400 million inhabitants. The 'peaceful' penetration of capitalism into these countries, the undermining of their social conditions of existence, would have been *enough to bring about clashes between West and East the likes of which have never been seen since the migrations of peoples* [the invasions of the barbarians at the beginning of the middle ages]. If millions of Chinese peasants were to rise up against exploitation by capital, capitalist Europe would have its hands full to control the fire. But *there is no single capitalist Europe*. And that exacerbates the dangers of imperialism. In its striving to subjugate non-capitalist countries, capital has for many decades thrown Africa and Asia into turmoil and wars which, because they took place far from us without any obvious connection, did not disturb the picture of a 'peaceful' capitalism. New, enormous dangers of great wars have sprung up ever since capitalism turned China and Turkey into objects of exploitation. But before that could come to pass, Europe itself has been overrun by a horrific war.

Capitalism developed in Europe in the form of *particular states*. In order to penetrate an area and transform the whole population into its slaves, in the course of centuries capital formed nations whose common language facilitated its work; it set up [modern] state-power, which became a means for subjugation, a catalyst and promoter of capitalism. Thus, the capitalist states confronted each other. The development of the last fifty years, briefly described above, proved that *the capitalist state-framework is too narrow. Capitalism had to blow it up everywhere*. The *fracturing of capitalism* into national states led them first to try to overcome these difficulties through even *greater separation*. If the productivity of human labour grew more quickly than the market for sales, it was regarded as imperative to protect this market from the penetration of foreign capital through tariffs. But, under the wings of continental protective tariffs, capitalist associations developed that only worsened these difficulties. They exploited the domestic market through monopoly-prices and in that way were able to dump their products in foreign markets on a massive scale. Even if their profits on the commodities sold in the world market dropped, the expansion of production enabled them to reduce costs and thus increase their profits in the domestic market. *The wild struggle over foreign markets increased their desire to separate from the world market any territories where the exclusionary policy could be carried on* through commercial policy or other measures. *Colonies* should become more or less closed areas where 'national' capital found protected markets. Colonial policy, the peaceful or violent subjugation of capitalistically undeveloped countries, was not pursued by capitalism in the abstract but by capitalist *states*. They struggled diplomatically over colonies, over investments and concessions in capitalistically undeveloped countries that were not yet mature for colonial partition. In these diplomatic struggles, *the arms-race on land and sea was their means for understanding*. The states armed in order to reach an understanding over colonial robbery, over the division of concessions. Hinting at their [military] capabilities to assert their 'rights', even without reaching an understanding, was their most important means of pressure. *The military and naval strength of a state was the yardstick of its share in the division of the capitalist world*. The costs of armaments were by no means felt as a burden by the leading capitalist elements. Armaments themselves were a part of colonial policy. They provided heavy industry with a large monopolised market for selling its products. A dreadnought, which costs 50 million, yielded many millions in profit. And the banks that controlled heavy industry got their money's worth in the process, in addition to covering their costs. But, ultimately, the costs were borne by the masses, whose exploitation increased.

The armaments-system, as a means of imperialist understanding, had to break down some day, either deliberately or despite the will of the capitalist governments. Its essence consisted of every diplomatic party involved in a dispute guessing how strong the other party was and whether it could risk replacing diplomatic struggle by armed struggle. Each party had an interest in trying to make the other believe that it was ready to go to war if its interests were not taken sufficiently into consideration. Thus the colonial and concession-arrangements did not mean abolition of imperialist antagonisms but their summation, rounding off and accumulation. They led to new antagonisms, and the arms-race did not stop for a moment. Sooner or later, a moment had to come when one of the parties would make a mistake concerning the willingness of the other to accommodate. Sooner or later, a moment had to come when one of the parties, feeling superior to the other, would hope to get more by the sword than by the feather. That is how the *world war* came about.

It would be ridiculous to prove first that it is an imperialist war. That is so obvious that no serious bourgeois politician disputes it. But the assessment is not enough. *Only evaluation of the significance of the imperialist era in human history, only examination of whether imperialism can solve the main issues of capitalism, reveals the historical significance of the world war.* We will attempt later to answer this question and to show that the world war is not only *a war over capitalist interests* but also *a war against socialism.*

Chapter Fifty-Two

'The Nation and the Economy' (July 1915)

Leon Trotsky

Earlier in this volume, we included two articles by Parvus: Chapter 19 ('Before the Hottentot Elections') and Chapter 20 ('Colonies and Capitalism in the Twentieth Century'). The theme of those articles was that the productive forces of modern capitalism had outgrown the confining limits of nation-state organisation with imperialism as the result. Parvus wrote that 'Each industrial state wants to have its own *colonial empire*, from which all other industrial states will be excluded or driven back as much as possible.' In 1907, Parvus also wrote an article on German trade-policy that contemplated a European union in response to the rising industrial power of the United States: 'There is only one means,' he declared, 'for European countries to withstand America: that is *economic unification of the whole of Europe*.'[1]

Leon Trotsky collaborated closely with Parvus during the first Russian Revolution of 1905. Together, they played a leading role in debates over the theory and tactics of *permanent revolution*.[2] Trotsky also adopted from Parvus the lasting conviction that one of the major purposes of socialism was to free modern forces of industrial production from the tariff-barriers

1. Parvus 1908, p. 31.
2. Day and Gaido (eds.) 2009.

imposed by nation-states. The potential scale-economies of modern industry could not be achieved without access to wider markets. Confined within national limits, and with enormous commitments of fixed capital, large-scale industry would have needlessly high production-costs that would contradict capital's imperative to maximise profit. The inevitable consequence must be imperialist warfare that could only be prevented by international revolution.

As a correspondent covering the Balkan wars for the journal *Kievan Thought*, in 1909 Trotsky wrote that 'Only a single state of all the Balkan nationalities, based on democratic-federative principles – along the lines of Switzerland or the North-American republic – can bring internal peace to the Balkans and create the conditions for a powerful development of the productive forces.'[3] In 1910, he returned to the same theme in an essay on 'The Balkan Question and Social Democracy':

> The only way out of the national-state chaos and bloody stupidity of Balkan life is unification of all the peoples of the peninsula into a single economic-state unit on the basis of national autonomy of the constituent parts. It is only within the limits of a single Balkan state that the Serbs of Macedonia, Sanjak [Bulgaria], Serbia proper and Herzegovina will be able to unite in a single national-cultural community, simultaneously enjoying all the advantages of a common Balkan market. Only the united Balkan peoples will be able to provide a genuine rebuff to the shameless pretensions of tsarism and European imperialism.[4]

With the outbreak of world war in 1914, Trotsky regarded the Balkan conflicts as a microcosm of the global contradictions that now threatened the whole of human culture. In an article on 'Imperialism and the National Idea', published in May 1915, he applied the lessons of the Balkan wars to the new conflict between the Great Powers. 'For petty-bourgeois ideologues,' he wrote, 'two principles are struggling in the current war: the principle of national right and the principle of coercion – of Good and Evil.... For us materialists, the war appears in its imperialist essence as the fundamental striving of all capitalist states for expansion and conquest.' After summaris-

3. Trotsky 1909.
4. Trotsky 1910.

ing the claims and counter-claims of European states, he dismissed them all with a ringing denunciation of imperialism:

> Imperialism represents the capitalist-predatory expression of a progressive tendency of economic development: to construct the human economy on a world scale, having emancipated it from the constraining fetters of the nation and the state. The naked national idea, which stands opposed to imperialism, is not only powerless but also reactionary: it is dragging the human economy backwards into the swaddling clothes of national limitation. Its deplorable political mission, conditioned by its impotence, is to provide ideological cover for the work of the imperialist butchers.
>
> Destroying the very foundations of the economy, the current imperialist war, illuminating and amplifying the spiritual wretchedness or charlatanism of the national idea, is the most convincing expression of the blind alley that development of bourgeois society has led to. It is only socialism that must economically neutralise the nation, having unified mankind in solidarity and co-operation; [it is only socialism] that emancipates the world-economy from national fetters, thus emancipating national culture from the grip of economic competition between nations – only socialism provides a way out of the contradictions that have broken out before us as a terrible threat to the whole of human culture.[5]

In July 1915, Trotsky responded to the ideas set out by Karl Kautsky's ponderous but thought-provoking essay on the 'National State, Imperialist State, and Confederation'. For Kautsky, the natural human community always originated in a common language, and the consequent limits of popular political discourse dictated the impossibility of abandoning the nation-state and its parliamentary institutions. There was, however, a clear alternative to the imperialist ambitions provoked by nation-state rivalries: a federated Europe in which national-democratic communities might be affirmed while at the same time ensuring free access to markets adequate to the productive forces of modern capitalism. For Kautsky, a United States of Europe need not await the international revolution; even within a capitalist framework, abolition of tariff-divisions would allow for a rise in labour-productivity and popular living standards, thereby improving the lives of workers and the conditions

5. Trotsky 1915a.

for Social-Democratic politics. Whereas Trotsky invariably associated the transcendence of nation-states with *international socialist revolution*, Kautsky explicitly referred to federal Europe as the highest form of *capitalism*:

> The best and most promising means of expanding the domestic market is not the expansion of the national state into a multinational state, but the centralisation of several national states into a confederation with equal rights. *The federation of states rather than the multinational state or the colonial state: that is the form for the great empires required by capitalism to reach its final, highest form in which the proletariat will seize power.*
>
> Such a federation can assume multiple forms; it can be a confederation of federations. As such, it represents the most elastic political form, capable of endless expansion up to the final world federation.

Trotsky replied to Kautsky in the article translated here. Although he respected Kautsky's authority and even shared many of his convictions, he again spoke clearly of freeing the productive forces 'from an imperialist blind alley within the broad arena of socialism'. Trotsky took the link between socialism and elimination of nation-state barriers to be self-evident.

Lenin, who, at the time, thought Trotsky was much too close to Kautsky, insisted on being more explicit. While he acknowledged the attraction of the slogan of a United States of Europe, by August 1915 he worried that its implications might in fact be reactionary, signifying, as Kautsky evidently implied, 'a temporary union of the Great Powers of Europe with the aim of enhancing the oppression of colonies and of plundering the more rapidly developing countries – Japan and America'.[6] Lenin regarded the United States of Europe as a variant of Kautsky's projected 'ultra-imperialism'. Under capitalism, a United States of Europe must be either 'impossible or reactionary'[7] and might even have the effect of postponing socialist revolution. On these grounds, Lenin drew the famous conclusion that would bedevil Trotsky for years to come. In the succession-struggle that followed Lenin's death in 1924, Stalin, Bukharin and countless lesser figures ritually condemned Trotsky on the grounds that he thought socialism was impossible in a single country.[8]

---

6. Lenin 1915d, p. 344.
7. Lenin 1915d, p. 340.
8. In reality, Trotsky objected to the Stalinist slogan of 'Socialism in One Country' on the same grounds that he had always cited when condemning the economic limita-

Trotsky was portrayed as a 'pessimist' who doubted the possibility of Soviet Russia holding out and progressing as a single socialist country confined within a hostile capitalist encirclement. Lenin provided the grounds for this charge when he wrote in August 1915 that the slogan of a United States of Europe contradicted the universal law of uneven development:

> Uneven economic and political development is an absolute law of capitalism. Hence, the victory of socialism is possible first in several or even in one capitalist country alone. After expropriating the capitalists and organising their own socialist production, the victorious proletariat of that country will arise against the rest of the world – the capitalist world – attracting to its cause the oppressed classes of other countries, stirring uprisings in those countries against the capitalists, and in case of need using even armed force against the exploiting classes and their states. The political form of a society wherein the proletariat is victorious in overthrowing the bourgeoisie will be a democratic republic, which will more and more concentrate the forces of the proletariat of a given nation or nations in the struggle against states that have not yet gone over to socialism. The abolition of classes is impossible without a dictatorship of the oppressed class, of the proletariat. . . . It is for these reasons and after repeated discussions . . . that the Central Organ's editors have come to the conclusion that the slogan for a United States of Europe is an erroneous one.[9]

* * *

'The Nation and the Economy'[10]

I

The recognition of every nation's right to self-determination, which is included in Russian Social Democracy's programme, traces its origin to the epoch of

---

tions of capitalism. The Stalinists, he argued, were proposing a reactionary industrialisation-strategy of socialism in a *separate* country, shutting the Soviet republic off from the world economy by ignoring the economic benefits offered by the most extensive foreign trade and even capital-imports within the capitalist encirclement. See Day 1973.

9. Lenin 1915d, pp. 342–3.
10. Trotsky 1915b.

revolutionary battles for national bourgeois democracy. In the final analysis, this demand means recognition of each nation's right to state-independence – and thus it obliges Social Democracy to oppose every régime that involves the compulsory cohabitation of nations or fragments of nations and, depending on circumstances of time and place, to assist the struggle of nations and national minorities against the yoke of a foreign nation. But nothing more than that. Contrary to what the most unrestrained social-imperialists would like, Social Democracy by no means abandons the programme of national democracy. It has no wish to tolerate, nor can it, any forms of compulsory inclusion of national groups within large state-forms, a kind of paralysing open-field system within a national state, in the supposed interests of economic development. But, likewise, Social Democracy by no means takes on the task of multiplying the open-field system, that is, it does not transform the national principle into some kind of absolute supra-historical idea.

It is perfectly true that Social Democracy always and everywhere defends the interests of economic development and opposes all political measures that might delay it. However, it does not regard economic development as something self-sufficient in technical-production terms, as an extra-social process, but, rather, as the basis of human society's development, with its class-groupings, its national-political superstructure and so forth. From this point of view, which, in the final analysis, does not lead to guaranteeing local or national capitalism superiority over the capitalism of other places and countries, but, rather, to ensuring the systematic growth of human power over nature – from this broad historical point of view, the class-struggle of the proletariat is in itself the most important factor guaranteeing further development of the productive forces by way of freeing them from an imperialist blind alley within the broad arena of socialism. There is no doubt that a coercive state of nationalities and national fragments (Russia, Austria…) can, during a certain epoch, promote development of the productive forces, creating a wide domestic market for them. But, in giving birth to the cruel struggle of national groups for influence over the state-authority, or by causing 'separatist' tendencies, that is, the struggle to separate from the state-organisation, the coercive multinational state paralyses the class-struggle of the proletariat as the most important force of economic and all historical progress. The proletariat is deeply interested in abolishing all artificial frontier-posts and tariffs and in the widest possible expansion of a free arena for economic development, but it cannot attain this goal at a cost that would above all disorganise its own historical movement and thus weaken and diminish the most significant productive force of modern society. Today's social-imperialists, mainly of the German type, reject the idea of national self-determination as a 'sentimental' prejudice of the past and recommend submission to an iron necessity of economic development as a supra-historical criterion that trumps the historically limited claims of nations; they put forth not some unconditional requirements for economic progress but, rather, its historically limited form that stands before us in the shape of imperialism, which in the current war is revealing its whole contradiction not just with the requirements for further economic progress but also with the most elementary conditions for human existence.

The condition for the proletariat's development, and the sole form in which it can take possession of state-power, is now and will continue to be democracy. Above all, the latter presupposes growth of the cultural-political independence of the masses, their economic and political communication over a wide arena, and their collective intervention in the fate of the country. Thus, a national language, the instrument of human communication, inevitably becomes, at a certain stage of development, the most important instrument of democracy. For this reason, the striving for national unity was an inseparable part of the movement during the epoch of bourgeois revolutions; and, insofar as in backward areas – not only in Asia and Africa but also in Europe – we are witnessing the awakening of historically delayed nationalities, they necessarily take the form of a struggle for national unity and national independence, while coming face to face with the imperialistic effort to overcome the nationally limited confines of the capitalist economy and to create a world empire through military force.

In this process, Social Democracy by no means identifies itself with the internally contradictory imperialist methods of making way for social-historical tasks that have come to maturity. But just as little, if not less, can it counter imperialism – let alone the progressive historical requirements that it is exploiting – with the naked national idea. It would truly be a miserable petty-bourgeois utopianism *à la* Hervé[11] to think that the fate of development in

11. [A reference to Gustave Hervé (1871–1944). Prior to the First World War Hervé headed the extreme Left inside the French Socialist Party. He was elected delegate to the International Socialist Congress in Stuttgart in 1907, where he spoke against

Europe and the entire world will finally be secured if the state-map of Europe is brought into correspondence with the map of nationality, and if Europe is split into more or less complete nation-state cells ignoring geographical conditions and economic ties. In the previous epoch, France and Germany approximated the form of a national state. This in no way prevented either their colonial policy or their current plans to move the border to the Rhine or the Somme. An independent Hungary, Bohemia or Poland will in the very same way strive for an outlet to the sea by violating the rights of other nationalities, as Italy is doing at the expense of the Serbs or the Serbs at the expense of the Albanians. Besides the national democracy that is awakened by capitalism and strives to unite the greatest possible number of a nation's elements in a single economic-cultural community, there remains capitalism itself, which strives, wherever it has sunk roots, to expand the limits of the domestic market as widely as possible, to find the most favourable outlets to the world-market, and to impose its domination over areas with an agrarian type of economy. For national capitalism, the national principle is neither an absolute idea nor the final crown of the structure. It is merely the ladder to make a new leap – in the direction of world domination. If, at a certain stage of development, the national idea is the banner of struggle against feudal-particularistic barbarism or foreign military coercion, later, by creating a self-sufficing psychology of national egoism, it becomes itself an instrument for the capitalist enslavement of weaker nations and an indispensable instrument of imperialist barbarism.

The task is to combine the claims to autonomy on the part of nations with the centralising requirements of economic development.

II

Social-nationalism has astonished everyone, itself above all, with its power: during the first epoch of the War, it took possession of the strongest parties and organisations of the proletariat. But, together with this suddenly

---

militarism. Editor and publisher of the periodical *Guerre Sociale* (*Class War*), he signed his articles with the pen-name *Sans Patrie* (Man without a Fatherland). But, on the outbreak of war, he renamed the paper *Victoire* and supported Clemenceau's policies. After the War, he created the Parti Socialiste National (PSN) and became an admirer of Mussolini.]

demonstrated force, comes its extraordinary and nothing less than shameful ideological wretchedness. Not a single serious attempt to tie the ends together theoretically! Decisions and actions, on which the life and death of socialism depend, are explained and justified by contradictory and accidental considerations in which political impressions play the most important role freed from all theory. The fundamental argument justifying the social-nationalistic policy of a worker's party is the idea of 'defence of the fatherland'. But, until now, not one of the social-patriots has taken the trouble to give a sensible explanation of just what is actually endangered in the fatherland and what is to be defended. A French socialist speaks of the Republic and revolutionary traditions: he defends the past. A German patriot refers to his mighty national industry as the basis for socialism: he defends the present. Finally, our own native social-nationalist, who 'repeats what he hears and tells lies for two', refers to the interest of Russia's further economic development: he defends the future. Each of them is more-or-less resolutely attempting to proclaim his own 'national' interest to be above the international interest of mankind. But such attempts only bring even more hopeless confusion to the matter. One of the two: either the international interest demands defeat of Germany (or Russia), and then there is no point in speaking of defence of the fatherland, because there are indeed some people in the world for whom Germany or Russia is the fatherland. Or else the opposite: defence of the fatherland is the self-sufficient principle of the proletariat's policy, and then any attempt to combine that task with a generally obligatory line in the behaviour of the international proletariat is hopeless, for the defence of one fatherland presupposes destruction by force of another fatherland.

At the beginning of the War, Kautsky made an attempt to define the fundamental good in whose name the proletariat is sacrificing its class-independence on the bloody altar of defence of the fatherland. That good is the national state. In the first article [above], we spoke of what a powerful factor the national-cultural community is in historical development. Thus it has to be said that the state (it is the fatherland) deserves to be defended insofar as it conforms to the type of a national state. That is exactly how Kautsky puts the question. But, then, the question arises: in what sense can and must the proletariat of Austria-Hungary and to an important degree also Russia defend their fatherland? From Kautsky's point of view, the multi-ethnic proletariat of the Danubian monarchy, apparently, has no obligation whatever to the state of the Habsburgs. Kautsky himself hints at such a conclusion. But, with the existing international combinations, defence of Germany presupposes defence of Austria-Hungary and Turkey, while, on the other hand, defence of the national integrity of France presupposes perpetuating the violent bloc of nationalities known as Russia, or the world-colonial power, Great Britain.

Standing together with states comprising both nationalities and national minorities, there are states in which a far from perfect national unity is supplemented, on the one hand, by an alliance with multinational states, and, on the other hand, by trampling the national independence of the colonies.

In terms of the tendencies of development it has revealed, the current war threatens not the nation as such but, rather, the state, which is the historical dwelling place of the nation. Capitalism has no more realised national unity than it has democracy. It has awakened the demand for national unity, but, in itself, it has brought to life tendencies that prevent realisation of that demand. Meanwhile, the nation is a powerful and extremely persistent factor of human culture. The nation will outlive not only the current war but also capitalism itself. In the socialist system, too, freed from state-economic dependence, the nation will long remain as the most important seat of spiritual culture, for the nation has at its disposal language, the most significant organ of this culture. The state is another matter. It was formed as a result of the intersection of dynastic, imperialistic and national interests together with transient relations of material forces. The state is an incomparably less stable factor of historical development than the nation. During the past epoch, economic development found its accommodation within the capitalist state, which, with an enormous stretch, is called 'national'. This same state-fatherland provided the accommodation for cultural development of the almost always divided nation, exploiting or endeavouring to exploit other nations through its state-apparatus. To the extent that capitalist development became cramped within the limits of the state, the latter was supplemented by annexations and colonial extensions. The struggle for colonies, that is, flouting the economic and national independence of backward countries, was the main content of the foreign policy of the so-called national state. The rivalry over colonies led to the struggle of capitalist states between themselves. The productive forces finally became cramped with the limits of the state. If the current 'national' state finds itself endangered, that danger results from the lack of correspondence between its frontiers and the level of development attained by the productive forces. The danger threatens not from an external enemy but from within, from economic development itself, which, in the language of world war, is telling us that the 'national' state has become an impediment to development, that it is time to scrap it. In this sense, the idea of defence of the fatherland, that is, of the national state that has outlived itself, is a deeply reactionary ideology. To the extent that social-patriots link the fate of the nation – which, in itself, by no means paralyses economic development and in no way prevents it from assuming an all-European and world scale – with the fate of a shut-in state-military organisation, we, the internationalists, are bound to take upon ourselves defence of the historic rights of nations to independence and development in opposition to its conservative 'patriotic' defenders.

Capitalism attempted to compress both the nation and the economy within the limits of the state. It created a mighty formation, which, over an entire epoch, served as an arena for development both of the nation and of the economy. But the nation and the economy have come into contradiction – both with the state and with each other. The state has become too narrow for the economy. In the endeavour to expand, it tramples on the nation. On the other hand, the economy refuses to subordinate the natural movement of its forces and means to the distribution of ethnic groups on the surface of the globe. The state is essentially an economic organisation; it will be compelled to adjust to the requirements of economic development. The place of the shut-in national state must inevitably be taken by a broad democratic federation of the leading states on the basis of the elimination of all customs-partitions. The national community, arising from the needs of cultural development, will not only not be destroyed by this but, to the contrary, it is only on the basis of a republican federation of the leading countries that it will be able to find its full completion. The necessary conditions for this presuppose emancipation of the limits of the nation from those of the economy and vice versa. The economy will be organised in the broad arena of a European United States as the core of a worldwide organisation. The political form can only be a republican federation, within whose flexible and elastic bounds every nation will be able to develop its cultural forces with the greatest freedom.

In opposition to German and other social-annexationists, we have no intention of throwing overboard recognition of the right of nations to self-determination. To the contrary, we think the epoch has been approaching when it will finally be possible to realise this right. On the other hand, we are infinitely far from counterpoising the 'sovereign' rights of every national group or tiny groupling to the centralising requirements of the economy. But, in the very course of historical development, we are discovering the dialectical reconciliation of both 'elements': the national and the economic. For us, recognition of every nation's right to self-determination must be supplemented by the slogan of a democratic federation of all the leading nations, by the slogan of a United States of Europe.

Chapter Fifty-Three

'The Prehistory of the World War'[1] (1915)

Anton Pannekoek

The War has turned Europe into a huge battlefield for more than a year already,[2] yet the causes leading to all these horrors are still very little known. This is true not only in the belligerent countries – whose governments raised the slogan of defending the endangered homeland in order to blame the enemy for the War and to prevent by censorship the expression of any other opinion – but even beyond their frontiers, where the same superficial statements prevail. On one side, the blame is placed on predatory German militarism, which, as the tool of a feudal Junker-caste and a domineering dynasty, seeks to enslave free, developed Western Europe. On the other side, 'Perfidious Albion' is the silent instigator of the slaughter: threatened by the preponderance of more efficient German industry in the world-market, England artfully surrounded its emerging rival with a network of enemies who are now assaulting peaceful Germany from all directions. Pacifists of all kinds lament the incomprehensible madness that has seized humanity, believing that, through peace congresses and propaganda, the peoples will better

1. Pannekoek 1915.
2. [This statement indicates that the document was written after July 1915.]

understand and appreciate each other in its aftermath, thus securing a lasting peace.

The actual cause of the war is imperialism, the policy that aspires to possession of foreign territories as the means to world power. Thus, the economic development that has led to this imperialism is at the same time the root cause of the world war.

Imperialism is the most modern, highly developed form of capitalism. To the extent that ever more money from profits and dividends is accumulated as new capital, which must be profitably invested, it becomes increasingly difficult to find good investment opportunities in the domestic market. That is why capitalists cast their eyes on distant, undeveloped countries and foreign continents. Expensive products are there to collect, cultivate, or extract from mines, products that in the European market are worth a great deal as raw materials for industry or as means of consumption: ores, petroleum, rubber, ivory, cotton, coffee, tobacco. Since the right to exploit them is often sold for a song or simply taken by force, vast profits can be made. In countries with a dense, intelligent population (e.g. India or China), factories can be set up that promise to yield high profits due to the frugality of a population that is satisfied with low wages. Where handicrafts and agriculture flourish, railways can carry products to the world market. The construction of railways in foreign continents is always the beginning of capitalist exploitation; and the iron industry, which supplies locomotives and rails, has the greatest interest in promoting this development wherever it can.

Such an extension of capitalist business over the undeveloped world demands, at the same time, extension of the political domination of European nations over those regions. The legal concepts and forms of primitive peoples do not fit with capitalist enterprise and must be replaced by European law; their freer attitudes and way of life do not correspond to the requirements of capitalist exploitation, which elicits a resistance that can only be broken through armed intervention, conquest and subjugation in favour of European capital. In countries that were already united into large states under despotic rulers, the existing governments are used for this political mastery: through loans (whose proceeds are used to buy luxury-products and guns or else for public works) the monarch is made dependent on the European banks, which gradually bring all the tax-revenues of the country under their control as collateral, gaining more and more concessions and influence. In case of a dispute or unwillingness on the part of the monarch, they can count on the support of their own country's warships. Thus, the dependence of the foreign monarch becomes ever more apparent, and his authority serves mainly to pave the way for European capital. That is what happened or is happening in Egypt, Persia, Morocco, Turkey, and China. Where such states are missing, however, as in Africa, the country is simply taken into possession as a colony; and, if the black people are not satisfied, they are either subjected by violent means or eradicated. This expansion of capitalism all over the world means economic progress and preparation for a higher form of human society, but it takes place in the most barbaric forms: violent extermination of native peoples such as the Kaffirs and Herero in South Africa; impoverishment and starvation, as with the peasants in the British East Indies [Malaysia] and Java; destruction of ancient cultures, violent revolutions and cruel oppression as in China and Persia; and bloody wars of conquest as in Aceh [on the northern tip of the island of Sumatra] and Morocco.

Thus the economic expansion of massively swelling capital leads to political expansion. Each capitalist country wants to have as many investment areas in foreign continents as possible or to bring them directly under its influence as colonies. In addition, they act as each other's competitors. Every state tries to gain possession of as much of the world as possible for *its own* capitalist class. This creates a sharp contrast, an eager race in which each country tries to get as much as possible for itself at the expense of the others. Through colossal military equipment, each country attempts to strengthen itself against the others in order to emphasise its demands. This is the reason for the huge armaments of the past twenty years. Billions have been devoured year after year by the construction of ever larger warships, the production of ever more numerous and bigger guns, the training of ever larger armies – billions that are largely raised by means of heavy consumption-taxes on workers, small farmers and citizens. And at the same time, the likelihood of war between the European states increasingly grew. Again and again, conflicts broke out, first over China, then over Turkey or Persia, then over Morocco. Each time, they were successfully settled until finally, in 1914, when none of the parties wanted to retreat, the great, long-awaited and long-prepared war, the war over world power, erupted.

That the pursuit of a world empire had to lead to such a terrible struggle was not understood by all countries in the same way. Some, such as England, the Netherlands, Portugal, and partly France, traditionally had rich and vast colonies that offered their capital wonderful opportunities for good investments. They were very satisfied with the current situation and wished to change nothing. But the phrase *beati possidentes* [blessed are the possessors] does not apply to them.[3]

That is because there were other countries in which capitalism had developed, but they had few or no colonies. They were not satisfied; they too wanted a world empire, and if it was not voluntarily given to them, they were ready to take it by force. And, since each one of them was not strong enough to do so by itself, they allied with each other. Thus, the two triple alliances arose in Europe: the league of the hungry (the Triple Alliance of Germany, Austria, and Italy), who wanted to acquire a world empire, and the league of the satisfied (the Triple Entente of England, France, and Russia), who had large colonial areas, were ready to cede nothing and, if possible, wanted even more.

Germany is the key member of the first group. German development is the driving force of the present world war. Apart from the United States of America, no other country has experienced such rapid capitalist development during the last forty years. In the production and processing of iron and steel, which is the basic element for the industrial conquest of the world, Germany is already far beyond England and lags only behind the United States. But the German population is much more industrial than the American and consists mainly of entrepreneurs, wage-workers and industrial officials. Above all, Germany surpasses England and nearly all other countries of the world through the highly developed organisation of its industry. Because of its large banks (Deutsche Bank, Diskonto Gesellschaft, Schauffhausen and others), its capital is concentrated in vast organisations that largely dominate industry and give it general leadership, whereas, in England, capital is much more fragmented in private hands. Thus, Germany offered the powerful image of a gigantic great-capitalist country that was developing rapidly but had few colonial possessions. The imperialist quest for a world empire and world power, therefore, had to rule both politics and thought there to the highest degree. The leading economic elements of great capital were connected in Germany with the traditionally dominant political classes, the nobility and the imperial

3. [According to legal doctrine, possession is nine tenths of the law; i.e. the law favours the possessor, whereas anyone else must prove his claim.]

dynasty, because the surviving form of a despotic military state is well suited for the purpose of imperialism. Militarism, whose spirit permeates Germany's state and society – and is mentioned so often as a token of German backwardness, leaving no place for civil liberties on the Western-European model – is but a manifestation of capitalism's modern stage of development. Offensive as that mighty state-coercion may seem to Western Europeans, behind it hides the best organisation of all the forces of society under a single leadership and for one goal. The entire possessing classes, from big capital and the nobility to the petty bourgeoisie and the officials, are behind this policy: the feeling that Germany needs world power in order to give free rein to its expansion, to the development of its economic life, dominates wide circles of the population and even a large part of the unionised workers. This explains the enormous force that Germany is displaying in this war.

From 1898 onwards, Germany began building a powerful war-fleet for its world-political purposes. At the same time, it attempted to establish its economic and political hold over different parts of the world. Since the 1880s and the treaty with England in 1890, Germany has only had some islands in Australia and some colonies in Africa – although, in the latter, Germany once hoped to be able to found a large Central-African empire by annexing the Portuguese areas and the Belgian Congo. In China, Germany occupied Kiaotschau [Jiaozhou], a port of the rich Shandong province, where German capital began to reclaim mines and build railways. The main object of German expansion, however, was Asian Turkey. No conquest was necessary here, only fraternal co-operation with the Sultan. The Baghdad Railway, as a continuation of the railway in Anatolia (a joint venture of German and French capital), was no less politically advantageous for the Sultan than it was economically advantageous for German capital, which was assured rich profits by the kilometre-guarantee[4] and by concessions in the adjacent areas. But, in this way, German world policy came into collision with English imperialism. The Baghdad Railway put into German hands the shortest connection between Europe and the richest of the British colonies, India. It opened up before German capital the

4. [Rosa Luxemburg mentioned this as an example of the use of 'force, the machinery of the state, to convert the national real income into commodities; these are turned into cash in order to realise capital plus surplus value. That is the true object of the guaranteed revenue grants (*Kilometergarantie*) for independent enterprises run by foreign capital, and of the collateral in the case of loans.' Luxemburg 1963, p. 443.]

much promising Mesopotamia, which the British reckoned to claim for themselves and to unite with Egypt, Saudi Arabia, South Persia and India into a large English-Mohammedan world empire. The Baghdad Railway also consolidated Turkey, on whose collapse both England and Russia had counted. After a period of acute tension, that dispute was successfully settled because Germany had to give up its plans in Mesopotamia and the building of the terminus of the Baghdad Railway to the Persian Gulf. But the weakening of Turkey by the Balkan War of 1912, which also weakened Germany's position and led Russia to penetrate further into Armenia, turned the situation into a powder-keg. The battle over the Balkans and the Turkish lands – between German imperialism, on the one hand, and Russian expansion and English world power, on the other – is one of the main causes of the current war.

The general causes of the War are therefore clear enough: imperialism and its quest for world power, arising from the huge increase in capital that was searching for profitable investment, brought about the great armament of the last ten years and finally produced the world war itself. However, there are still many social critics, even capable ones, who measure these new phenomena with the yardstick of past situations and forms. For them imperialism, with its armaments-madness, is a kind of mental stupefaction, an impractical way to settle disputes through unnecessary violence and enormous sacrifices – disputes that it would be much better to resolve peacefully. According to this view (of which for many years Karl Kautsky, the most influential theorist of Social Democracy, was the main promulgator), the economic antagonisms between countries need not have been reason for the arms-race, had not the cannon-manufacturers and 'armour-plate patriots' incited public opinion, with a view to their own private profit, to hate other peoples. The expansion into foreign continents was solely in the interest of big business; the mass of the bourgeoisie could therefore be won over for the slogan of disarmament, and the war-threat would have immediately disappeared. This doctrine is one of the reasons why the War took the Social-Democratic workers' parties completely by surprise. Now, when the argument has been reduced *ad absurdum* by the outbreak of the War itself, Kautsky is trying to argue that the current war is not at all an imperialist war. 'It broke out at a moment in which there existed no single imperialist point of contention',[5] since all dis-

5. [Kautsky 1915, p. 63.]

agreements over mining concessions, railways or territory between England and Germany had just been regulated. In other words, it really broke out quite accidentally, as an unfortunate consequence of the enormous armaments, as a result of mobilisation and mutual fear. Hence also the strange spectacle, according to Kautsky, that this war may not end because nobody knows where it is actually leading. If each side knew what the other wanted, it could consider whether it wants to grant those demands rather than fight. But now they are fighting without a direct purpose.

This blunder already proves that the true nature of an imperialist war is completely different from the image that many can have of it, based on a superficial theory. It is a struggle not over some concrete things but over power, over world power; a world struggle in which the contestants' demands will depend on their degree of success. Previous wars were waged because the warring parties wanted a specific object, such as a region, a city, a colony; the negotiations over that object, before and after the war, were decided by the war itself. Today, the objects are numerous and often indeterminate: they are all over the world, and it is impossible to say in advance which one will be the main issue in the long term. Everything has constantly been subject to negotiation, twisting and intrigue: ideas have shifted; agreements have been made or broken regarding China, Persia, Congo, Mexico, Morocco, Saudi Arabia, Abyssinia, the Pacific islands, Armenia; and likewise with railways, loans, concessions, capital-amalgamations, participation in each other's companies, cessions of areas, trade-benefits, and monopolies. The diplomats, bankers and officials, more or less helped by the press, were constantly busy with all this for years in varying conditions of 'cordial relations', 'overall agreement', 'tense situations', a 'reserved attitude', etc. None of these issues in itself was big enough to start a war. And yet the War broke out, a world war leading to colossal destruction compared to those of the past. It came as a decision not about this or that particular dispute, but about all of them together, as a summary of the struggle over all those issues. It seemed that in all negotiations on all points the same conflict occurred again and again: demands, on the one hand, unwillingness to yield, on the other; the will towards greater world power always clashed with the will to keep the current dominance; the tension, the hatred, the bellicose mood grew, until finally the world war broke out, whose result will simultaneously decide the outcome – at least temporarily – of all the issues of world policy.

The practical consideration of a piece of prehistory of the world war, however, can show the essence of imperialism better than any abstract discussion on whether imperialism is necessary or not, or whether the world could also have been otherwise than it is. Everyone knows that the emergence of Germany as the new capitalist power, which demands a world empire and world power for the export of its capital and products, is the deepest cause of the War. Germany's struggle and conflicts with English imperialism were played out in different areas of the earth. The two major objects of dispute that caused the current war were Asian Turkey and Morocco.

[...][6] The German bourgeoisie was furious about the outcome of the whole Moroccan adventure. For a long time, it believed that a good area for business, marketing and investment could be found there. Now that hope went completely up in smoke, and what was brought back home as gains, a piece of forest and swamp in Central Africa, benefitted a few rubber-merchants and nobody else. The government was blamed in bitter words for its weakness. But much fiercer were the attacks against England, which was the cause of the failure, and against whom the hatred was now directed. England, it now became clear, wanted to prevent any expansion of Germany's world power, always obstructing Germany's path wherever it found a good opportunity. If Germany wanted to expand freely, then England had first to be defeated. There was thus only one way out: to speed up the arms-race in order to prepare for a war that inevitably had to come. This mood was clearly expressed in an epilogue that General von Bernhardi added, on the occasion of the Morocco crisis, to his work *Germany and the Next War*, which appeared in 1912. He said this:

> It is quite evident from her whole attitude that Great Britain was resolved to take the risk of a war.... We have probably obtained the concessions made by France only because she thought the favourable moment for the long-planned war had not yet come. Probably she will wait until, on the

6. [At this point, Pannekoek provides a comprehensive 'overview of the international politics of the last twenty years, with their profound changes of course, with the war as their conclusion and final result'. His survey explores numerous contentious issues between the main imperialist rivals, paying special attention to British foreign policy as well as to the Moroccan crises of 1905–6 and 1911, in which French attempts to control Morocco met with German resistance. A convention signed in November 1911 gave France a protectorate over Morocco, with Germany being compensated through acquiring formerly French controlled territory in Congo.]

> one hand, the Triple Alliance is still more loosened and Russia's efficiency by sea and land is more complete, and until, on the other hand, her own African army has been so far strengthened that it can actively support the Rhine army.... [I]t is patent that the whole arrangement [with France] means a lowering of our prestige in the world, for we have certainly surrendered our somewhat proudly announced pretensions to uphold the sovereignty of Morocco.... The worst result of our Morocco policy is, however, undoubtedly the deep rift which has been formed in consequence between the Government and the mass of the nationalist party, the loss of confidence among large sections of the nation.... [F]or in the critical times which we shall have to face, the Government of the German Empire must be able to rely upon the unanimity of the whole people if it is to ride the storm. The unveiling of the Anglo-French agreement as to war removes all further doubt on this point. The existence of such relations between England and France confirms the view of the political situation which I have tried to bring out in the various chapters of this book. They show that we are confronted by a firm phalanx of foes who, at the very least, are determined to hinder any further expansion of Germany's power.... If the Imperial Government was of the opinion that it was necessary in the present circumstances to avoid war, still the situation in the world generally shows there can only be a short respite before we once more face the question whether we will draw the sword for our position in the world or renounce such position once and for all. We must not in any case wait until our opponents have completed their arming and decide that the hour of attack has come. We must use the respite we still enjoy for the most energetic warlike preparation, according to the principles which I have already laid down.[7]

And so it was. New giant armaments showed how the German bourgeoisie and the German government had understood the lesson of the Morocco conflict. They have contributed directly to the war that is being waged today.

7. [von Bernhardi 1912, pp. 281–6.]

Chapter Fifty-Four

'Imperialism and the Tasks of the Proletariat' (January 1916)

Anton Pannekoek

In his 1912 debate with Kautsky over parliamentarism vs. mass-action, Pannekoek postulated a dialectical relationship between imperialism and mass-actions as a counterpoise to the purely electoral and parliamentary tactics of the SPD-Centre:

> We do not have to deal here with the causes and driving forces of imperialism; let us just enumerate its manifestations and effects: world-power politics, the armaments-race (especially warship-building), colonial conquests, growing tax-oppression, war-danger, growing spirit of violence and domination among the bourgeoisie, reaction in domestic politics, discontinuation of social reform, growth of employers' associations, aggravation of trade-union struggles, high cost of living. All this places the working class in a new fighting position. Earlier it could hope to progress slowly but surely, improving working conditions through the trade-union struggle, advancing social reforms and increasing its political rights through its political representation. Today it has to strain all its forces not to be deprived of its current rights and living standard. *Its attack has been turned into a defence.*

> The class-struggle thus becomes sharper and more generalised; its driving force, more and more, is not the allure of a better situation, but the bitter need of the workers to defend their rights from deterioration. Imperialism threatens the masses with new dangers and catastrophes (the petty bourgeoisie as much as the proletariat) and whips them up into resistance; taxes, high cost of living, and the war-danger make a bitter resistance necessary. But these phenomena originate only partially in legislation and can therefore only partially be fought against in parliament. The masses themselves must enter the political arena and exert a direct pressure on the ruling classes. This necessity is joined by the growing ability of the proletariat to assert its power. An ever-growing contradiction develops between the impotence of parliament, including our Reichstag- fraction, to fight against these phenomena and the working class's growing consciousness of its power. Mass-actions are therefore the natural consequence of the imperialist development of modern capitalism and increasingly constitute the necessary form of struggle against it.[1]

Karl Kautsky replied that the goal of the socialist movement was 'the conquest of state-power by winning a majority in parliament and by making parliament the controller of the government'.[2] In 'Imperialism and the Tasks of the Proletariat', Pannekoek rejected long-established traditions of Social-Democratic parliamentarism to emphasise, instead, the priority of revolutionary, mass-struggle. We have chosen to conclude this volume with Pannekoek's article because it effectively summarises the history we have been documenting and the reasons for the final submission of Europe's Social-Democratic parties to the nationalism and imperialist war-hysteria of 1914–18.

We also regard this article as significant in another respect; namely, its anticipation of the issues ultimately posed by Lenin's concept of the 'vanguard-party'. Though the present article was published in a journal issued jointly by the Bolsheviks and the Dutch Tribunists, Pannekoek's emphasis on mass-actions, as against the bureaucratic organisations of class-parties and trade-unions, clearly foreshadows the future break between Leninism and council-communism.[3] Pannekoek saw the enemy of socialism in the rule of

1. Pannekoek 1912a, pp. 541–2, in Grunenberg (ed.), pp. 264–5.
2. Kautsky 1912e, p. 732. For the continuation of the debate see Pannekoek 1912b and 1913b, Kautsky 1913 and Pannekoek 1913c.
3. On council-communism, see van der Linden 2004. On Pannekoek's further political evolution see Gerber 1989, Smart 1978, Bricanier 1978, Pannekoek 1970.

officials, whether they be officials of a parliamentary party or the Secretariat of a tightly centralised vanguard-party. In that sense, his 'Imperialism and the Tasks of the Proletariat' provides equal insight into the fatal afflictions of both the Second International and its successor, the Third (Communist) International.

* * *

'Imperialism and the Tasks of the Proletariat'[4]

I

The outbreak of the first major world war in 1914 luridly illuminated two facts: first, the *enormous force of imperialism,* and second, the *weakness of the proletariat,* especially its vanguard and leadership in the struggle, the Social-Democratic parties of almost all countries.

Imperialism differs from the old capitalism in its striving to bring foreign parts of the world under its domination in order to create new markets for its products, to find new sources of raw materials and, above all, new investment areas for the overflowing masses of capital. The masses of capital increased enormously during the prosperous period of the last twenty years, and the urge to invest them in undeveloped countries with high profits therefore became dominant among the bourgeoisie. As a result, the various bourgeoisies confronted each other as competitors. The young German bourgeoisie, whose rise is recent, looked everywhere for new territories (colonies or spheres of influence), but saw its way obstructed by the old world-ruling states, particularly England, as in Morocco in 1911, while the German bourgeoisie itself prevented Russia's penetration into Asia Minor. All of them armed in order to have a decisive say in the battle for distribution of the world; all strove for as much *world power as possible.* This quest gradually seized the entire bourgeoisie everywhere. The anti-militarist, progressive or radical opposition among the ranks of the bourgeoisie gradually gave in, yielding to the growing military demands or being abandoned by its old following. In England, as in France and Germany, the old bourgeois opposition to the imperialist course increasingly melted down to a few phrases as votes were cast for the fleet, the

4. Pannekoek 1916.

army and colonial outlays. In Germany, the growth of this tendency among the bourgeoisie was most clearly visible because *German imperialism* naturally had to be *aggressive;* it still had everything to gain and felt strong enough for the purpose. In other countries, where imperialism had primarily to defend its possessions, that process was less evident; in those places the growth of imperialist aspirations and resolve became fully apparent only during the war. But, during the past twenty years, imperialism has everywhere become the ruling policy of all the major capitalist states.

Only one force stood apart from imperialism and fought against it: Social Democracy, representing the proletariat. Its resolutions at numerous national and international conferences expressed antipathy towards this policy. The sincerity of these statements cannot be doubted, because the danger drew steadily closer that a war would flare out of these imperialist ambitions, and, for the workers, such a world war meant the greatest disasters – countless victims and material sacrifices, collapse of their international union, and economic decline over long decades. The international congresses, therefore, made the fight against war the main duty of the Social-Democratic parties. Sometimes people even boasted that governments' fear of Social Democracy would prevent a war. But, when the governments really wanted war in 1914, *the resistance of Social Democracy* in the West-European countries *turned out to be an insubstantial shadow.* Social Democracy never acknowledged its impotence while *gnashing its teeth*. Rather, it went along with the War, submitted to the will of the bourgeoisie, became patriotic and approved the war-loans – a complete break with everything it had proclaimed until then to be its principles and tactics.

How was that possible? The answer repeatedly given is that Social Democracy, the proletariat, was *too weak*. This is true, but it can easily be misunderstood. Defenders of the German Party's attitude also said: We were too weak, so we could not resist and had to join in. But had the problem simply been lack of material force, one could have tried to fight and resist to the utmost, as in Italy for instance. It was far worse – *no attempt was made to fight*. The weakness was much more profound: a lack of ability to fight at all, a lack of mental strength, a lack of will to wage the class-struggle. Everyone knew in advance that the [German Social-Democratic] Party could not defeat and crush the bourgeoisie. In the last elections, it received only one-third of all votes, and, in a nation of seventy million, it only had only one million members (the vast majority of whom simply paid dues). But, according to these measures of its external strength, the Party was strong enough to unleash a large movement against the War and to become the core of a powerful opposition movement. The fact that no such attempt was made, and that people laid down their weapons without a struggle, proves that the Party *was rotten from the inside and incapable of fulfilling its new tasks.*

The Social-Democratic parties arose from earlier conditions of a pre-imperialist period; they are spiritually and materially adapted to the tasks of the proletarian struggle in an earlier period. Their task was to fight for reforms during the ascending phase of capitalism – to the extent that they were possible within the capitalist framework – and to rally and organise the proletarian masses for that purpose. Large organisations and parties were thus created, but, in the meantime, the fight for improvements increasingly degenerated into *striving for reforms at any price,* into begging and compromising with the bourgeoisie, into a limited policy for the most immediate minor benefits, no longer paying any attention to the great interests of the entire class and even giving up the class-struggle itself. Under the influence of immense prosperity, which strictly limited the worst misery of unemployment, a spirit of contentment, of indifference towards general class interests, made itself manifest among a section of the proletariat. *Reformism* increasingly dominated Social Democracy and revealed the degeneration and decay of the old methods at precisely the time when the proletariat faced new tasks.

The fight against imperialism embodied these new tasks. One could no longer manage against imperialism with the old means. In parliament, one could criticise its manifestations (such as armaments, taxes, reaction, the standstill of social legislation), but one could not influence its policy because it was not made by the parliaments but by small groups of people (in Germany, the Kaiser along with some nobles, generals, ministers and bankers; in England, three or four aristocrats and politicians; in France, a few bankers and ministers). The unions could hardly ward off the powerful business associations; all the skill of their officers broke apart against the granite-power of the cartel-magnates. The reactionary election laws could not be shaken through elections alone. New means of struggle were necessary. *The proletarian masses themselves had to enter the stage with active methods of struggle.*

It was conceivable that the Party would be able to adapt to these new conditions and tasks in advance and change its tactics accordingly. In order to do so, it was first of all necessary to have a clear conception, an intellectual grasp of imperialism, of its causes, strength and significance. Second, the masses themselves had to be involved in the fight where the power of parliaments was not enough. A small beginning was made in the struggle for the general suffrage in Prussia; the masses took to the streets so vigorously that the party leadership itself recoiled at the scale of the new struggles, which, all at once, seemed to prefigure the immediate future – and thereafter it began to stifle them. A small group of *left radicals* tried to push the Party further along this path of mass-struggles, and a few sought to awaken some understanding of imperialism. But the leading strata of the Party – the leadership, the *party bureaucracy, Kautsky* and his friends – stood in the way of that pursuit. For them, imperialism was just a bourgeois madness about the arms-race, nurtured by a few great capitalists, from which one had to dissuade the bourgeoisie by means of good arguments. They searched for their salvation in the slogan 'back to the old tried and tested tactic', with which they opposed the new revolutionary tactic and sought in vain to drive back revisionism. The *bureaucracy of officials and leaders*, who naturally identified their own *group-interests* in peaceful and undisturbed party development with the interests of the proletariat, used all their strength to oppose the 'anarcho-syndicalist adventures' into which the 'mass-action fanatics' wanted to plunge the Party. Through its press, offices and prestige, the party bureaucracy dominated the Party mentally and physically. Thus, the traditional *party structure*, handed down from previous conditions, *was unable to face the new tasks and reshape itself accordingly*. It had to perish. The outbreak of war was the catastrophe. Taken by surprise, stunned and confused by events, unable to resist, carried away by nationalist slogans, and without spiritual support, the proudest organisation of Social Democracy broke down as an organ of revolutionary socialism. And with it went almost all the Social-Democratic parties of Europe, most of them being long corroded inwardly by reformism. The question must be left to the future as to how, from these ruins and after a new power-struggle, the advent of socialism will take place. From the collapse of the old Social Democracy, we can only draw some lessons concerning the tasks awaiting the proletariat and how it will be able to fulfill them.

II

The struggle of the proletariat against capitalism is presently possible only as a struggle against imperialism, since modern capitalism does not know any policy other than imperialist policy. Nowadays, the class-struggle, the struggle for socialism, assumes the form of the struggle against imperialism. But, as such, it takes on a new, and actually a more promising character. New prospects of victory appear; indeed, we can calmly assert that *only imperialism creates the conditions for a victory of the proletariat, for the attainment of socialism.*

First, imperialism makes the class-struggle more intensive and all-embracing. Imperialism awakens all the forces dormant in the bourgeois world; it gives to the bourgeoisie much energy and enthusiasm for the ideals of world power that carry away large masses. So long as the workers are trapped in the old traditions and do not yet rise to the height of the times, that admittedly means, at first, a collapse of the labour-movement. But the hope of socialism does not lie in the inability and lack of energy of the bourgeoisie, but, rather, in the ability and strength of the proletariat. Pressure creates counter-pressure; the pressure and energy from above finally awaken exasperation, determination to fight, and energy from below. In the old capitalism, the driving force of the struggle was the desire to improve conditions; yet millions lived on in inert satisfaction, and the striving for reforms was not sufficient to awaken the requisite energy. Today, imperialism brings down their living standards, burdens the masses with rising taxes, and demands from them ever greater sacrifices up to their complete destruction; today, the degradation of their lives arouses them and forces them to defend themselves. Today, the masses can no longer say: I do not care about it because I am satisfied. They are forcibly involved in the struggle because imperialism actively attacks the proletariat. And not just the proletariat, but the farmers and petty bourgeoisie as well; formerly, they did not suffer much from capital, but now they have to surrender their property and their lives for the imperialist goals of big business. Everyone is drawn into the fight on one side or the other, and no one can stand apart from it. And, because socialism cannot be won and built by a small core of fighters amid an unconcerned popular mass, but only by the *whole* nation, this generalisation of the struggle by imperialism creates for the first time the conditions for socialism.

Second, imperialism makes new tactical methods necessary. If *mass-actions* are often referred to as a *new* tactic, that is simply because the correct estimation of reality was lost in the age of parliamentarism, when the illusion arose that speeches by leaders were enough to bring a class to victory. Every major social upheaval, every transmission of power to a new class, has been the work of the masses, of the classes themselves that secured the victory. The parliamentary system was crucial during the preparation-period, when the class had first to be organised and the struggle could only be fought with words. Once sufficient forces were gathered to launch active attacks, the old truth came into its own that only the class itself can fight the battle. And that is all the more true when new conditions and new social hardships incite the masses to action. Just as the French Revolution was a result of the rise of the bourgeoisie and the penetration of new ideas, though its outbreak in precisely those years was simultaneously the effect of the greater distress of the masses and of increased political tension, so in the proletarian revolution the slow growth of socialist thought coincides with the stimulating effect of certain social events.

Both their distress and these events are created by imperialism, which in that way drives the masses to spontaneous action. Parliaments can usually do nothing when the policy of the ruling classes leads, so to speak, mechanically and instinctively to the worst harassment or hostilities against the masses, such as inflation, wage-cuts, taxes, unemployment, political reaction and war. In those circumstances, only the masses can do anything. If the masses remain inactive, being confused and uncertain, all the protests in parliament cannot help, and they must helplessly submit to everything. But, if they wish to act, they must do it as masses, exerting direct pressure on the government through spontaneous or planned demonstrations and actions. This pressure appears as a new political factor because the interest of the ruling class is more or less to give in for fear of the further growth of such movements. It has repeatedly happened in recent years and in various countries that a planned attack on the right of assembly was prevented by a mass-action, for instance, a political strike. Had the German proletariat stepped into action vigorously and massively three years ago against the high cost of living, or a year ago against the War, the ruling classes would certainly have been forced to take it more or less into account.

Not only are mass-actions the only means of waging a successful struggle against those hardships and dangers, but important reforms are also impossible to achieve any other way. In the first period of parliamentarism, many reforms were won because the growth of Social-Democratic votes terrified the ruling classes; they felt the foundations of their rule shaking. But, when they realised that it was just a question of elections, of an oppositional attitude followed by no further action, their fear disappeared and with it their willingness to reform. The phrase *'Oderint, dum metuant'*[5] also applies in the class-struggle; red votes do not harm the bourgeoisie if they are not followed by action. The ruling class makes concessions only out of fear that, otherwise, the dissatisfaction, power and rebellion of the proletariat will grow too far. With imperialism, which inspired the bourgeoisie with new self-confidence and assurance, reforms therefore came to an end. Stronger means and mass-actions are now required in order to win reforms; and in Belgium, Sweden and Russia this method of action has already proved its force in the conquest of new political rights.

This means that the contrast between the revolutionary tactics of mass-actions and the non-revolutionary tactics of 'pure-and-simple' parliamentarism must not be understood in any absolute sense. Everything that increases the power of the working class is revolutionary. Thus, parliamentarism was revolutionary thirty years ago, while attempts to carry out subversive actions were fruitless and therefore non-revolutionary. In many cases, parliamentarism now has non-revolutionary effects because it does not strengthen the power of the proletariat but, rather, weakens it – and yet a well-conducted parliamentary fight can continue to have great revolutionary significance. Under imperialism, the unity of reform and revolution still remains the fundamental principle of socialist tactics; the struggle for the direct vital interests of the proletariat against everything that oppresses it is, at the same time, the struggle for socialism. Compared with the past, the difference lies in the fact that, *in the future, great and important reforms can only be achieved with the great means of mass-actions.* Mass-actions are the main and decisive manifestations of the proletariat's power, which it needs against the enormous power of imperialism in order not to be smashed, to hold its ground and to move forwards. Besides this, all the minor means of the daily struggles still retain all

5. 'Let them hate so long as they fear.' (A favorite saying of Caligula.)

their value and necessity. That is why this new period of capitalism, which we call the age of imperialism, will at the same time be *the age of mass-actions.*

III

We see, therefore, how the new character of modern capitalism makes a *new socialism,* a new labour-movement with a new character, necessary – in the sense that this is the only way in which a really successful fight against capitalism is possible. But this new struggle does not only follow as an inevitable necessity from the new capitalism; at the same time, it also constitutes the only way to overcome the domination of capital and represents the only road to socialism.

The rule of the bourgeoisie, like that of all previous ruling classes, is based on the great instruments of power at its disposal. Although it is usually a minority, it disposes of knowledge and skills that make it intellectually superior to the mass of the ruled; through the school, the Church and the press, the class of the owners rules over the thought and feelings of the masses. In addition, its power lies in its strong organisation. A well-organised minority can dominate a majority if the latter is not organised, that is to say, if it possesses no cohesion, no unity of action and will. This organisation of the ruling class is the state-power; through its multi-branched army of public servants, it confronts the fragmented atoms of the people as a body with a unified will. And where the resulting customary authority disappears among the masses and they become rebellious, the state has strong material instruments of power at its disposal, such as the police, the judiciary, and, finally, a well-disciplined and well-equipped army. What can an unorganised mass of individuals do against all this?

During the period of parliamentarism, the illusion was often cherished that we fight against the bourgeoisie over state-power, to take command of the existing organism of the state that controls legislation. The consequence of this idea was the reformist conception that it was only necessary to replace capitalist by socialist ministers in order to enter into socialism with full sails. One might, on the contrary, question whether any substantial change takes place in the world if the persons of the ministers change. One can recall from experience that every Social Democrat who became a minister, at the same time became a servant and trustee of the ruling class. But the decisive thing for evaluating this parliamentary conquest of power is the fact that the ruling class can everywhere make a peaceful seizure of political power impossible in advance by means of the electoral law and the constitution. To make a parliamentary conquest of power possible at all, universal and equal suffrage must first of all be obtained, and that is only possible through the extra-parliamentary actions of the masses themselves. The constitutional conquest of political power by the proletariat consists of two elements: first, the majority of the people must be won over for socialism; and, second, the majority must have command over government and the state. The first requires propaganda, agitation and action, which are generally conceivable within the framework of the parliamentary system; the second implies absolute *political* democracy, which is nowhere available and cannot be realised by means of peaceful agitation and legislative work in parliament. *It can only be achieved by means of a mass-struggle, through mass-actions.* Thus, the centre of gravity in the struggle for political rule increasingly lies in the struggle *for* political rights, which constitute the expression of the popular majority's rule over the state. In this struggle, as in the class-struggle in general, the ruling class sets in motion against the proletariat the state authority with its instruments of power. State-power is not just a neutral object of the class-struggle, but a weapon and fortress of the bourgeoisie, its strongest prop, without which it could never hold its ground. The struggle of the proletariat is therefore first of all a struggle *against state-power.*

What is the significance of mass-actions in this struggle?

All political conditions and situations are determined by the balance of power between classes. Constitutional questions are questions of power. A rising class can seize power only when it becomes stronger than its opponents. The question of socialism is a question of growth in the power of the proletariat. The social power of the proletariat consists of its numerical superiority, which grows by itself due to capitalism; of its spiritual power – class-consciousness, revolutionary thinking, clear comprehension of the nature of the state and society; and finally, of its material or moral force – organisation, solidarity, unity and discipline. Today, all these factors are still present only in insufficient measure, but, through their growth, the power of the working class will finally surpass that of the ruling class. Through its class-consciousness and socialist understanding, the working class will become intellectually independent of the bourgeoisie and eventually intellectually stronger; through its organisation, it will be able finally to withstand the powerful organisations of the bourgeoisie and become more solid than its state-power. And this growth in the elements of the proletariat's power also means transformation of the whole of humanity from a limited, undiscerning mass of isolated and selfish individuals into an organised mankind, guided by a common awareness of their social nature, who will thus become capable, for the first time, of exercising control by themselves and of consciously shaping their production and social life. That same growth in power will enable the proletariat to overthrow the rule of the bourgeoisie as it simultaneously makes the proletariat mature for socialism.

What is it that brings about this growth? The class-struggle. All struggles, regardless of whether they immediately end in victory or defeat, contribute to developing the proletariat's power by clarifying its understanding, strengthening its organisation or doing away with inhibiting traditions. In the previous period, the significance of parliamentarism lay in the fact that it established the first beginnings of proletarian power, brought socialist consciousness to the masses, helped to create organisations, stirred the masses somewhat and, at the same time, undermined the moral prestige of the state. That was not enough to conquer political power, but it did make mass-actions possible. *Mass-actions will be the means to increase the power of the proletariat further, to its highest level, and at the same time to crush the power of the state.*

In mass-actions, the mightiest of which is the mass-strike, the strongest instruments of power of the two classes confront each other. Through its moral and spiritual force, its organisation and its violence, the state seeks to prevent or break the action of the masses in order to avoid having to yield to it. Through press-censorship, false reports, a state of siege, arrests, rifle-volleys, and the prevention of mutual understanding, the authorities seek to discourage, intimidate and divide the workers. Whether these measures will succeed depends then on the firm and clear knowledge, the unbreakable unity and discipline of the masses. If they do succeed, that means a defeat for the workers, who afterwards must try to do the same thing again with new force. But, if they fail, then the government has more or less to give in and the proletariat achieves a victory; its power grows once again, and the power of the state receives a blow. In a mass-strike, the entire organisation of the state can temporarily be thrown out of joint and its functions can devolve upon the organs of the proletariat. In the future, what happened in 1905 in Russia will happen in Western Europe on a much vaster scale. The organisation of the proletariat then showed – at least temporarily – its superiority over the organisation of the bourgeoisie. If the army is used against the masses, that can temporarily lead to a victory for the government; but, therewith, discipline begins to loosen at the same time, and, ultimately, the strongest means of power of the ruling class escapes from its hands. Of course, some of the achievements thus won can be lost again; victories and defeats will alternate, but, in the long run, the insight, organisational power and revolutionary energy of the masses will continually increase while the power of the state will decrease. If the proletariat, and together with it society as such, are not to perish, then only one outcome of the struggle is possible: *the strength of proletarian solidarity and organisation, growing in battle, smashes the power and organisation of the state through mass-actions.* Political power therewith falls into the hands of the proletariat, who can then go on to create the institutions necessary for a new regulation of production.

The historic significance of mass-actions is that, through the hard struggles of the class itself, they will make the proletariat mature for socialism and enable the destruction of bourgeois rule. This is the historic significance of imperialism: it will force the working class to launch this struggle by means of mass-actions and to strike out on the path of freedom.

A new chapter is beginning in the proletarian liberation-struggle. For the first time, this struggle is now rising to the level of its great objectives: the entire force of the proletariat must be used against the enormous power of a massively developed capitalism and an energetic and combative bourgeoisie. In their many millions, the masses themselves must step onto the scene – whipped by hardship and suffering into energetic actions, their hearts full of enthusiasm, their souls full of revolutionary energy – with their glance no longer fixed on the narrow arena of the workplace and small improvements but on the great world struggle of classes. A new International will arise: not one that simply abounds with fraternal feelings towards class-comrades across the border and then immediately collapses before the national frenzy of the rulers, but one [in which the proletariat] will be ready to fight together with proletarians of other nationalities against its own war-mongering bourgeoisie.

At present we find ourselves amidst the ruins of the old International and the old socialism; we only see from afar, only theoretically as it were, how things must and will turn out. *Can we already notice perhaps, in what is happening today, the beginnings of the new development?* Do we already see the new labour-movement, the new International arising from the old?

It has often been said that, after the War, a *split in the socialist parties must take place.* Those who have gathered on the side of imperialism, who have whole-heartedly made common 'national' cause with the bourgeoisie – people like Scheidemann, Heine, Lensch, Vaillant, Sembat, Plekhanov, the liquidators, Tillett – all of them, whatever their previous services to the labour-movement, will no longer be able to remain with the firm fighters against imperialism. But things are not that simple. Certainly, reformism has long wanted to go along with the bourgeoisie, with its colonial policy and imperialism; the War, which has exposed imperialism as the greatest enemy of the working class, merely made it clear that *reformists and revolutionaries,* who, during the period of small reforms, could remain together in the same organisation, no longer belong together but must be *mortal* enemies. But the case is different with the bulk of the German party leaders and its leading circles – whose literary agent is *Kautsky.* They are not friends of imperialism but enemies: they did not go along with the War out of imperialist convictions or clear national consciousness, but partly because they were duped by the watchword of defence, partly because they retained the old ideology of defence of the fatherland, and also out of ignorance and Philistinism, because they did not know how to fight and did not dare to fight against the ruling class. In their case, therefore, we have the prospect of a swing in their mood that is already significantly noticeable; and the same is true of the best part of the French workers, both among those who previously supported Social Democracy and among those who were with the syndicalists. It is conceivable that these masses and their representatives will come out against the bourgeoisie and the war in an increasingly energetic way. Does this not imply hope that the majority, the largest or at least a very large part of the former Social Democracy, will brace itself for a vigorous struggle against imperialism and, disabused by hard experience, will be able to defend itself and apply the new tactical methods, thus building the new International out of the ashes of the old one?

This question is of paramount importance and cannot be predicted here with any certainty. But some important reasons can be cited for making *another* future likely. They lie in the whole nature of a large, fully developed party, of which German Social Democracy is the model. It is an entrenched gigantic organisation, functioning almost as a state within the state, with its own officers, finances, press, intellectual world and ideology (Marxism). The general character of this organisation is adapted to the peaceful pre-imperialist period; the mainstays of this character are the officials, secretaries, agitators, parliamentarians, theorists and writers, numbering several thousand individuals who already constitute a distinct caste, a group with their own interests who thereby totally dominate the organisation spiritually and materially. It is no coincidence that they all, with Kautsky at their head, want to know nothing about a real and fierce *struggle* against imperialism. All their vital interests are opposed to the new tactic, which threatens their existence as officials. Their peaceful work in offices and editorial departments, in congresses and committee meetings, in writing learned and unlearned articles against the bourgeoisie and against each other – this whole peaceful hustle and bustle is threatened by the storms of the imperialist era. Kautsky's theory and tactics are an attempt to secure this whole bureaucratic-learned apparatus against injury in the coming social revolutions. Actually, it can only be saved by setting it apart from the din of battle, beyond the revolutionary struggle, and thus outside of real life. If the Party and its leadership followed the tactics of mass-action, the state would immediately attack and perhaps destroy the organisations (the foundation of their entire existence and life activity), confiscate their funds and arrest their leaders. Naturally, it would be an illusion if they believed that the power of the proletariat would also be broken that way: the organisational power of the workers does not consist in the outer form of institutional bodies but in their spirit of cohesion, discipline and unity, which would enable them to create new and better forms of organisation. But that would be the end for the officials, because that organisational form is their entire world, and without it they can neither exist nor function. Accordingly, their instinct for self-preservation and their future corporate interests necessarily compel them to [adopt] the tactic of evading [the issue of] imperialism and capitulating before it. What took place before the War and at the outbreak of the War is therefore not an abnormal accident. They say now – as they so often did in the past – that such dangerous mass-struggles will ruin the organisation and therefore must not be undertaken wantonly. It follows that organisations led by them will never wage the struggle against imperialism resolutely and with all their might. Their struggle will be a verbal struggle, with indictments, pleas and entreaties, a *sham-struggle* avoiding every *actual fight*. The best proof of this is provided precisely by Kautsky, who, after long wavering, took up the fight against social-imperialism only simultaneously to call the workers' street demonstrations an 'adventure'. Therefore imperialism must be fought with words alone, not by daring to undertake any action!

Therefore, nothing more must be expected from the previous party-bureaucracy other than further rejection of the revolutionary struggle against imperialism. It will attempt to limit the struggle to small quarrels in parliament and the press, to long speeches on small issues, to petty union-battles. Although the reformists are partisans of imperialism and the centrist radicals its opponents, they can remain together on a common line of mere criticism and inaction. They will attempt to turn the party into a bourgeois reform party, into a Labour Party on the English pattern but with some socialist phrases; a party that will vigorously champion the daily interests of the workers but wage no great revolutionary struggle.

The task of showing the workers the importance and necessity of mass-actions against imperialism, and of standing at their head on every occasion, enlightening, helping and leading them, devolves upon the revolutionary socialists. But if this new tactic is only propagated by minorities or small groups that do not yet have the masses behind them, while, at the same time, the great mass-parties want to know nothing about it – will not any mass-action, which is inconceivable without the masses, be a utopia? This contradiction only proves that mass-actions are not possible as conscious, deliberately planned actions, prepared and led by the Social-Democratic Party, as the extreme Left in Germany advocated in its propaganda in the years before the War. They will come as spontaneous actions, erupting from masses who are whipped up by hardship, misery and outrage: in one case, as the unintended consequence of a small struggle planned by the Party that overflows its limits; in another, as an event that breaks out against the will and decisions of the organisations, breaching all discipline but then carrying these organisations along in their powerful swell and forcing them for a time to go along with the revolutionary elements. The possibility cannot be excluded that, if the War continues for some time, something of that sort could soon take place. The symptoms are already discernible.

In the coming period, therefore, the existing organisations (the Party and trade-unions), by virtue of their whole nature and in contradiction with the goals and tasks of the proletarian masses, will probably play above all an inhibiting role. But, if the new tactic is ever more prevalent, and if the power

of the proletariat gradually increases in great mass-struggles, these organisations will no longer be able to play that role. Then the rigid, immovable bodies of the Party and the trade-unions will become an increasingly subordinate part within a broader class-movement and a larger class-organisation, which will bind together the masses – not through its membership-book but through the community of class-goals – into a powerful community of struggle.

Appendix

Rosa Luxemburg and the Accumulation of Capital

In *The Accumulation of Capital*, Rosa Luxemburg took issue with Karl Marx's account of expanded reproduction on the grounds that it 'cannot explain the actual and historical process of accumulation'.[1] Expanded reproduction, she argued, presupposes recourse to effective demand originating in non-capitalist spheres.[2] This appendix explains how Luxemburg's argument and her theory of imperialism resulted from misinterpretation of Marx's work.

Marx's methodology was to begin with the abstract and move to the concrete. As an abstract analysis, the reproduction-schemes were never intended to explain the 'actual and historical process of accumulation', only to explore the requirements of intersectoral proportionality and thus, by implication, to specify the kinds of disproportionalities that contribute to capitalism's cyclical economic crises.

In his reproduction-schemes, Marx assumed a 'pure' capitalist society in which all incomes derive from capitalist commodity-production, and all exchanges are financed by purchasing power put into circulation by the capitalist class. The value of the social product was then divided into three categories: *c*, representing expenditures on constant

1. Luxemburg 1963, p. 348.
2. Luxemburg 1963, pp. 351–2.

capital (machinery, plant, tools and materials); *v*, representing variable capital (wages advanced to the workers during production); and *s*, representing surplus-value (accruing to capitalists after deducting all costs of production). Of these three sums, the first two are automatically realised in order that production might occur: capitalists replace used up means of production, and workers spend their wages to subsist. Part of the third sum is also easily realised as it provides for the capitalists' own consumption. The problem, for Rosa Luxemburg, concerns the remainder of *s* that must be used for reinvestment to expand production.

The commodities represented by the reinvested part of *s* must obviously be bought by the capitalists themselves. In that case, Luxemburg argued, even though production would expand, it could not be capitalist production for profit. All exchanges would be financed from the capitalists' own pockets so that 'accumulation for the capitalist class, cannot take place'.[3] The capitalists would seem to be producing not for profit, but merely for the sake of production. The alternative appeared to be that capitalists must sell the commodities in question in non-capitalist markets. But, as non-capitalist areas were gradually incorporated into the world-capitalist system, the same problem would reappear continuously until capitalism embraced 'the whole globe',[4] at which point, no further expansion was conceivable. Imperialism was only a temporary palliative for capitalist contradictions.

To compare Luxemburg's reasoning with Marx's, we begin with the account of reproduction in Volume II of *Capital*. The scheme for simple reproduction (stability with no growth) is the following:

I.. $c_1 + v_1 + s_1 = w_1$
II.. $c_2 + v_2 + s_2 = w_2$

Department I (responsible for means of production) realises the sum c_1 within itself as capitalists purchase from each other the fixed and circulating capital needed to continue the next round of production. The commodities represented by v_1 and s_1 must be sold to Department II in exchange for consumer-goods for Department I's capitalists and workers. In simple reproduction, v_1 and s_1 are exchanged for c_2, so that the equilibrium condition is $c_2 = v_1 + s_1$.

3. Bukharin and Luxemburg 1972–4, p. 57; cf. Luxemburg 1963, pp. 334–5.
4. Luxemburg 1963, p. 365.

To portray expanded reproduction, Marx reorganised the total value-product this way:

$$\text{I.. } c_1 + v_1 + s_{1c} + s_{1a} = w_1$$
$$\text{II.. } c_2 + v_2 + s_{2c} + s_{2a} = w_2$$

Surplus-value in I is divided into s_{1c} (consumed by capitalists) and s_{1a} (used for reinvestment), with corresponding changes in II. Marx reformulates the numbers so that the total of new means of production, w_1, now exceeds $c_1 + c_2$, leaving a balance of constant capital for expanded reproduction. Conversely, the total sum of wages and surplus-value is now less than w_2, or the total sum of consumer goods. In each department, the capitalists therefore add to both variable and constant capital. Department I adds $s_{1a'}$ to constant capital and $s_{1a''}$ to variable capital, with corresponding allocations of $s_{2a'}$ and $s_{2a''}$ in Department II. As with simple reproduction, Department II's demand for constant capital must equal Department I's demand for consumer goods, so that $c_2 + s_{2a'} = v_1 + s_{1a''} + s_{1c}$.

Luxemburg acknowledged that these are obvious conditions for expanded reproduction, but she saw no *guarantee* that it might actually occur: 'A further condition is required...: the effective demand for commodities must also increase. Where is this continually increasing demand to come from, which in Marx's diagram forms the basis of reproduction on an ever-rising scale?'[5] The apparent problem was that the equations said nothing about the source of the purchasing power required for realising the growing volume of commodities.

We might assume an increasing money supply, in which case the surplus intended for accumulation would pass into the hands of gold-producers (or the government, with a paper currency). But, in that case, industrial capitalists would gain a hoard of cash but no longer have the real capital that they require. If we assume the capitalists have a previously accumulated hoard of money-capital, we must then explain the origins of that hoard. And, even given the existence of such a hoard, the capitalists would still appear not to be producing for profit if they must continue to finance all purchases out of their own pockets. Were they all to behave as real capitalists, endeavouring to sell more than they buy, then planned savings would exceed intended investments

5. Luxemburg 1963, p. 131.

and a corresponding part of the social product, once again, could not be sold without recourse to third-party buyers in a non-capitalist environment.

Marx points out, however, that, in the very first stage of expanded reproduction, the apparent difficulty will not exist for capitalists in Department I. In simple reproduction, these capitalists sold their surplus to II. If some of them (the As) now decide to accumulate money-capital, while others (the Bs) wish to add to productive capacity, then the Bs will simply purchase from the As the constant capital they require, using money that would otherwise have gone to II for consumer goods. But Luxemburg replied that this solution would hold only for a single moment of 'transition from simple reproduction to enlarged reproduction – in short, a moment that has no reference to reality and can only be conceived speculatively'.[6] And, even then, the solution would be illusory. Department II would now be unable to sell the consumer goods previously bought by the Bs, and there would be no new source of demand to absorb the forthcoming expansion of the Bs' output. As Luxemburg commented, 'The solution ... was a mere illusion – the difficulty still persists.'[7]

Yet, according to Marx, there would be no such difficulty. The Bs, he emphasised, would already have a hoard of *previously accumulated* money-capital and could therefore finance their purchases from the As *without curtailing their purchases from II*. Assuming constant labour-productivity, the Bs will also have to buy more from II, in the form of additional wages paid out to their workers.

At this point, Luxemburg raised what appeared to be a decisive objection: the Bs' hoard could not possibly be spent in the way Marx suggested because *it is already committed to eventual replacement of existing fixed capital that is currently being amortised*:

> Owing to its very nature, the accumulated hoard can only cover renewal of the old capital; there cannot possibly be enough to serve further for purchasing additional constant capital. That means that we are still within the limits of simple reproduction.[8]

Marx's argument does require an explanation of how accumulated hoards of money-capital can be used *both* for replacement of existing fixed capital

6. Luxemburg 1963, p. 145.
7. Luxemburg 1963, p. 146.
8. Luxemburg 1963, p. 147.

and for the purchase of new fixed capital. Recall that, in simple reproduction, the scheme was:

I.. $c_1 + v_1 + s_1 = w_1$
II.. $c_2 + v_2 + s_2 = w_2$

in which case, equilibrium requires that $c_2 = v_1 + s_1$. While this implies that the constant capital of both departments is replaced in kind each year, in reality, c_1 and c_2 represent only a single years' depreciation of fixed capital (in addition to circulating capital used in production). The original value of the constant capital is thus many times larger. The decisive point that Marx makes is that not all fixed capital is replaced at the end of every production-cycle because its material elements wear out at various rates:

> ...the commodity value [of constant capital]...contains an element for depreciation of its fixed capital, which cannot be immediately replaced in kind, but has to be transformed into money, its total sum accumulating bit by bit until the time falls due for the renewal of this fixed capital in its natural form. Each year is a mortal one for fixed capital that has to be replaced in this or that particular business or even this or that branch of industry; for a single individual capital, this or that part of its fixed capital has to be replaced (since its parts are of varying life)....Just as each year people functioning in these branches of production die, so each year do quantities of fixed capital reach the end of their life and have to be renewed in kind from the accumulated money fund....This presupposes however that in earlier years the money needed for this replacement was accumulated in the hands of the department II capitalists.[9]

If we now suppose, says Marx, that, in any given year, Department II requires constant capital valued at less than c_2, while I must still sell means of production to the value of v_1+s_1, then there is an obvious danger of a realisation-crisis in I. Department II sells consumer goods to I valued at c_2, but it buys back constant capital of less value and retains a monetary balance. Marx writes that 'In this case, department II would have a money fund against the wear and tear of its fixed capital; on the other side, however, that of

9. Marx 1978b, pp. 528–9.

department I, there would be an overproduction of means of production.'[10] The result would be that part of the surplus-value I 'cannot be realised, or converted from its natural form of means of production into that of means of consumption'.[11]

How, then, can a depreciation-account be built up in either Department without disrupting the circulation of commodities? The answer that Marx gives is that *not all capitalists are accumulating money-capital simultaneously.* While some capitalists are spending their monetary hoard, others are accumulating one. In other words, some capitalists are always buying without selling, while others are selling without buying.[12]

The condition for proportionality then needs to be modified. Whereas we previously said that c_2 must equal v_1+s_1, we must now add that the amount of money-capital currently being accumulated in II (for replacement-purposes) must equal the amount of previously accumulated money-capital being spent on replacement of fixed capital in II. And, because capitalists in I are likewise both accumulating and renewing at the same time, the condition for overall proportionality must be that total new accumulation of money-capital must equal the current total reinvestment of money-capital in new means of production. In other words, total saving must equal total investment.

In more than one place, Luxemburg recognises that capital wears out unevenly, yet she insists that the accumulated hoard can be used solely for replacement of the existing fixed capital.[13] But Marx noted that *the accumulated money-capital, rather than being hoarded until existing capital is physically worn out, is in fact typically re-invested even before that time.* In *Theories of Surplus Value,* he wrote:

> A part of the constant capital which is calculated to be used up annually and enters as wear and tear into the value of the product, is in fact *not* used up. Take, for example, a machine which lasts twelve years and costs £12,000; its average wear and tear, which has to be charged each year, amounts to £1,000. Thus, since £1,000 is incorporated into the product each year, the value of £12,000 will have been reproduced at the end of the twelve years

10. Marx 1978b, p. 530.
11. Marx 1978b, p. 531.
12. Marx 1978b, p. 537.
13. Luxemburg 1963, pp. 85–7, 91–2, 355.

> and a new machine of the same kind can be bought for this price. The repairs and patching up which are required during the twelve years are reckoned as part of the production-costs of the machine and have nothing to do with the question under discussion. In fact, however, reality differs from this calculation of averages. The machine may perhaps run more smoothly in the second year than in the first. And yet after twelve years it is no longer usable. It is the same as with an animal whose average life is ten years, but this does not mean that it dies by one-tenth each year, although at the end of ten years it must be replaced by a new individual.... Hence where much constant capital, and therefore also much fixed capital, is employed, that part of the value of the product which replaces the wear and tear of the fixed capital, provides an *accumulation fund*, which can be invested by the person controlling it, as new fixed capital (or also circulating capital), without any deduction whatsoever having to be made from the surplus value for this part of the accumulation.... This is an important point. It is a fund for the continuous introduction of improvements, expansions, etc.[14]

The capitalist can use his accumulation fund in the way Marx describes if he anticipates sufficient cash on hand to replace the original machine when necessary. To that end, he will employ the funds set aside for amortisation of his most recent additions. Throughout the period of expanded reproduction, the value of newly purchased fixed capital will exceed the total of current depreciation plus the portion of surplus-value currently being monetised with future additions or replacements in mind. In other words, dishoarding (investment) will exceed hoarding (saving). Should any individual capitalist wish to make a purchase that exceeds his available money-capital, he will simply borrow the difference. The As, who are monetising their currently accumulating surplus-value, do not leave these funds idle. Marx notes that surplus-value is 'absolutely unproductive in its monetary metamorphosis.... It is a "dead weight" on capitalist production.'[15] Accumulating funds will, therefore, move from capitalists with no immediate need to those who are expanding production capacity, the relation between the two groups being mediated by the rate of interest.

14. Marx 1968–72, II, pp. 479–80; cf. Marx 1978b, pp. 497–8.
15. Marx 1978b, p. 574.

Rosa Luxemburg misinterpreted Marx on this issue because she analysed capitalist behaviour in terms of the collective capitalist, or the capitalist class as a whole. She assumed that all capitalists accumulate money-capital simultaneously, in which case, a deficiency of aggregate demand would be the obvious consequence. As for the *incentive* to expand constant capital, it has nothing to do with Luxemburg's reference to 'production for production's sake'.[16] The B-capitalists expand their output simply because they expect greater profits. Expansion by the Bs entails a correlative expansion in II, in order to provide the Bs with the requisite consumer goods for their workers. So long as the markets and investment plans of I and II develop *proportionately*, a dynamic balance will be maintained between them, accompanied by steady enlargement of profits.

But, in Chapter 25 of *The Accumulation of Capital*, Rosa Luxemburg objects that one other crucial factor has yet to be taken into account, namely, the increasing productivity of labour, expressed in the rise of constant-capital expenditures relative to variable capital (the rising organic composition of capital). This circumstance, she argues, must cause a growing disproportion between I and II in which a *deficit* of means of production will be accompanied by an unrealisable *surplus* of consumer goods.[17] By revising Marx's second illustration of expanded reproduction to raise the organic composition in successive years, she illustrates deficits and surpluses in chronic and growing form. Were capitalists in I to make good the deficit of means of production by consuming less of their surplus-value, they would merely enlarge the surplus in II, forcing II capitalists to consume more.[18] If technological progress in I were not to be accompanied by retarded accumulation in II, Luxemburg again concluded that the surplus of consumer goods would have to be disposed of in non-capitalist markets in exchange for imports of means of production.

The sole alternative would be for capitalists in II to facilitate technological change by placing a portion of their own surplus-value at the disposal of capitalists in I. Yet this possibility, Luxemburg contended, is obviously foreclosed:

---

16. Luxemburg 1963, p. 333.
17. Luxemburg 1963, p. 337.
18. Luxemburg 1963, p. 339.

> ...this assumption is possible only so long as we envisage the surplus-value earmarked for capitalisation purely in terms of value. [Marx's] diagram, however, implies that this part of the surplus-value appears in a definite material form which prescribes its capitalisation. Thus the surplus-value of Department II exists as means of subsistence, and since it is to be realised only as such by Department I, this intended transfer of part of the capitalised surplus-value from Department II to Department I is ruled out, first because the material form of this surplus-value is obviously useless to Department I, and secondly because of the relations of exchange between the two Departments which would in turn necessitate an equivalent transfer of the products of Department I into Department II. It is therefore downright impossible to achieve a faster expansion in Department I as against Department II within the limits of Marx's diagram.[19]

The first problem with this conclusion is that it makes no allowance for inventory-adjustments. As Marx noted elsewhere, 'What comes into play here is the merchant's capital, which keeps warehouses stocked with goods to meet growing individual and industrial consumption....'.[20] With capitalism's development, Marx anticipated growing inventories as a 'reserve' against production-disproportionalities:

> The greater the capital, the more developed the productivity of labour and the scale of capitalist production in general, *the greater is also the volume of commodities found on the market, in circulation, in transition between production and consumption* (individual and industrial), and the greater the certainty that each particular capital will find its conditions for reproduction readily available on the market. This is all the more the case, since it is in the nature of capitalist production that: 1. each particular capital operates on a scale which is not determined by individual demand (orders etc., private needs), but by the endeavour to realise as much labour and therefore as much surplus-labour as possible and to produce the largest possible quantity of commodities with a given capital; 2. each individual capital strives to capture the largest possible share of the market and to supplant its competitors and exclude them from the *market – competition of capitals*.[21]

19. Luxemburg 1963, pp. 340–1.
20. Marx 1968–72, II, p. 485
21. Marx 1968–72, II, pp. 483–4.

One of several outcomes might therefore be for capitalists in II to realise their surplus-output by selling to merchant-capitalists and then to lend the cash proceeds to capitalists in I who wish to expand. The latter might then return to the market to purchase all or part of their requirements, thus reconstituting the money-capital of the merchants. Marx wrote that '*Credit*... is the means whereby accumulated capital is not just used in that sphere in which it is created, but wherever it has the best chance of being turned to good account.'[22] The effect of these exchanges would then be to slow the expansion of II, relative to I, eliminate the supposed deficits and surpluses, and guarantee increased output in both departments. Far from being impossible, as Luxemburg suggested, the transfer of capital from II to I turns out to be a routine function of the market.

Taking into account the likelihood of price-changes, the dilemma could also be resolved even more directly. In the conditions that Luxemburg associates with a rising organic composition, the commodities produced in I would rise to a price exceeding their value, those produced in II would sell below their value, and, again, the exchanges would be balanced.

Finally, the pattern of price-changes will be influenced by the availability of reserves of fixed capital, especially in I, which, in concrete capitalism, are substantial. At one time, they represent a planned defence against the entry of new competitors; in other circumstances, they represent the 'excess' capacity that precipitates a cyclical crisis. It was the latter issue that concerned Marx, not the prospect of deficits that Luxemburg anticipated for Department I. Rosa Luxemburg did not consider these facts because she dealt with the abstract model of reproduction and was preoccupied with the need for external markets as the basis for her theory of imperialism. The result was that she left the cyclical dynamic of capitalism out of her analysis altogether. Given its pertinence to issues that Luxemburg poses, a few comments on what Marx said about cyclical crises are therefore in order.

In Volume II of *Capital*, Marx explained that, even with simple reproduction, the different rates at which fixed capital wears out dictate the need for current expenditures on fixed capital to equal current accumulation for future replacements. Should the former exceed the latter, excess demand for

22. Marx 1968–72, II, p. 482.

fixed capital could not be satisfied at existing prices. In the opposite case, the result would be insufficient demand and thus elements of fixed capital that could not be sold: 'There would be a crisis – a crisis of production – despite reproduction on a constant scale.'[23] Marx saw that, for avoidance of crises, Department I must *always* create means of production today in anticipation of tomorrow's demand – a condition that could only be guaranteed through rational foresight in a planned economy:

> Once we dispense with the capitalist form of reproduction, then the whole problem boils down to the fact that the magnitude of the part of fixed capital that becomes defunct and has therefore to be replaced in kind varies in successive years....If it is a very large one year (if the mortality is above the average, just as with human beings), then in the following years it will certainly be so much the less....and so the total production of the means of production would have to increase in one case, and decrease in the other. This can only be remedied by perpetual relative over-production [as inventory creation]....Over-production of this kind is equivalent to control by the society over the objective means of its own reproduction. Within capitalist society, however, it is an anarchic element.[24]

The fact that capitalist production is unplanned and typically undertaken for immediate profit – for holding real inventories is no more profitable than an idle cash-hoard – means that, in years when replacement-levels are low, Department I might fail to make preparations for future demand. Given the unplanned immediacy of their decisions, capitalists generally respond to current incentives. The need to expand production of fixed capital is usually strongest in the wake of a crisis, when much existing equipment is suddenly rendered obsolete by falling prices. In order to reduce costs correspondingly, every crisis requires replacement of much fixed capital that is still physically functional: 'Catastrophes, crises, etc. are the principal causes that compel such premature renewals of equipment on broad social scale.'[25]

A post-crisis wave of capital-renovation compels Department I to expand its plant using previously accumulated money-capital. In the form of rising

23. Marx 1978b, p. 543.
24. Marx 1978b, pp. 544–5.
25. Marx 1978b, p. 170.

prices, the law of value, as the sole guide to investment decisions, provides the signal for unco-ordinated expansion. But prices measure the state of the market only at the existing moment, saying nothing of future demand. Thus, when the post-crisis wave of expansion eventually decelerates, Department I comes face to face with excess-capacity and (unplanned) relative overproduction, which is one of the conditions for the next crisis.

This emergence of excess-capacity in I need not be the result of a *contraction* in II, but can be caused even by a mere slowdown following a wave of investments. Many heavy-industrial investments are likely to mature when the expansion that follows the previous crisis is already coming to an end. In that case, a new flow of commodities from I will accentuate the overproduction already beginning to emerge. Because heavy-industrial investments also entail prominent indivisibilities – one cannot construct half of a blast-furnace, and profitability depends on a certain scale of operations – the tendency towards overproduction is all the more acute. Marx illustrated these problems in *Theories of Surplus-Value* by reference to the experience of a single capitalist in Department I:

> Even if the total capital employed in machine-building were only large enough to replace the annual wear and tear of machinery, it would produce much more machinery than required, since in part the wear and tear exists nominally, and in reality it only has to be replaced in kind after a certain number of years. The capital thus employed, therefore yields annually a mass of machinery which is available for new capital investments and anticipates these new capital investments. For example, the factory of the machine-builder begins production, say, this year. He supplies £12,000 worth of machinery during the year. If he were merely to replace the machinery produced by him, he would only have to produce machinery worth £1,000 in each of the eleven following years [assuming the life of the machinery to be twelve years] and even this annual production would not be annually consumed. An even smaller part of his production would be used, if he invested the whole of his capital [and continued to produce £12,000 each year]. A continuous expansion of production in the branches of industry which use these machines is required in order to keep his capital employed and even to reproduce it annually. (An even greater expansion is required if he himself accumulates.) *Thus even the mere reproduction of the capital invested*

> *in this sphere* requires continuous accumulation in the remaining spheres of production [if a crisis of overproduction in I is to be avoided].[26]

Once again, Marx's account of capitalist crises involves the probability of *surplus-production* in I, not the *deficit* projected by Luxemburg. Economic disruptions occur when the growth of demand for fixed capital slackens. Demand emanating from II weakens when its own capacity becomes excessive relative to social consuming power, which, in turn, is restricted at the peak of a cyclical expansion when shortage of labour briefly raises wages, destroys profit-margins, and results in workers becoming unemployed. 'The ultimate reason for all real crises,' Marx wrote, 'always remains the poverty and restricted consumption of the masses, in the face of the drive of capitalist production to develop the productive forces as if only the absolute consuming capacity of society set a limit to them.'[27]

To some, including Rosa Luxemburg, this comment in Volume III of *Capital* implied a theory of *underconsumption*. But, in reality, the remark is fully consistent with the explanation of crises in terms of *disproportionality* elsewhere in Marx's work. In Volume I of *Capital*, for example, Marx notes that with a 'disproportion between capital and exploitable labour-power', which occurs when full employment raises wages at the peak of a cyclical expansion, 'accumulation slackens as a result of the rise in the price of labour, because the stimulus of gain is blunted'.[28]

The essential characteristic of capitalism's dynamic, for Marx, was always its *cyclical* pattern of crisis, recovery, expansion and crisis – not a *chronic* realisation-problem due to underconsumption, as Luxemburg believed. And that cyclical pattern typically results from the *uneven replacement and expansion of fixed capital*. Emphasising the system's dependence on non-capitalist markets to dispose of commodities that otherwise could not be sold, Luxemburg did not recognise that expansion into these markets is frequently due to the need to alleviate periodic inter-industrial disproportions as well as to offset a declining rate of profit in major capitalist countries.

26. Marx 1968–72, II, pp. 480–1.
27. Marx 1992, p. 615.
28. Marx 1976, p. 770.

Taking the abstract models of reproduction as the basis for her theory of imperialism, Luxemburg overlooked and misinterpreted Marx's analysis of concrete capitalism. The abstract models proved the theoretical possibility of expanded reproduction in pure capitalism, but, by specifying the sources of disproportionality, Marx also proved the impossibility of crisis-free capitalism in practice. Attempting to prove the impossibility of continuous expanded reproduction in terms of the schemes, Rosa Luxemburg implied that imperialism – for a time at least, and leaving aside the inevitability of imperialist warfare – would in fact resolve capitalism's contradictions until the system ultimately embraced the entire globe, leaving no new markets to conquer.

References

Adams, Brooks 1895, *The Law of Civilization and Decay: An Essay on History*, New York: Macmillan & Co.

—— 1900, *America's Economic Supremacy*, New York: MacMillan.

Adler, Alan (ed.) 1983, *Theses, Resolutions and Manifestos of the First Four Congresses of the Third International*, translated by Alix Holt and Barbara Holland, introduced by Bertil Hessel, London: Pluto Press.

Adler, Max 1915, 'Zur Ideologie des Weltkrieges', *Der Kampf*, 8: 123–30. English version: 'The Ideology of the World-War', in Bottomore and Goode (eds.) 1978.

Ageron, Charles-Robert 1973, *L'anticolonialisme en France de 1871 à 1914*, Paris: Presses Universitaires de France.

Andler, Charles 1918 [1913], *Le Socialisme impérialiste dans l'Allemagne contemporaine. Dossier d'une polémique avec Jean Jaurès (1912–1913)*, Paris: Bosard.

Andreucci, Franco 1988, *Socialdemocrazia e imperialismo: I marxisti tedeschi e la politica mondiale, 1884–1914*, Rome: Editori Riuniti.

Anonymous 1911a, 'Die Marokkopolitk auf dem Parteitag', *Leipziger Volkszeitung*, 214 (15 September).

—— 1911b, 'Taktisches und Prinzipielles im Kampfe gegen den Imperialismus', *Bremer Bürger-Zeitung* (5, 9 and 11 October).

—— 1912a, 'Der deutsche Imperialismus und die Arbeiterklasse', *Bremer Bürger-Zeitung* (27 March).

—— 1912b, 'Der Kampf gegen den Imperialismus', *Bremer Bürger-Zeitung* (2 April).

—— 1912c, 'Keinen Mann und keinen Groschen', *Bremer Bürger-Zeitung* (17 April).

—— 1912d, 'Der Parteitag in Chemnitz', *Leipziger Volkszeitung* (14 September)

—— 1912e, 'Die Chemnitzer Woche', *Leipziger Volkszeitung* (23 September).

—— 1912f, 'Chemnitz und die Parteipresse', *Leipziger Volkszeitung* (27 and 28 September).

Ascher, Abraham 1961, '"Radical" Imperialists within German Social Democracy, 1912–1918', *Political Science Quarterly*, 76, 4, (December): 555–75.

Aveling, Edward B. 1898, 'Der Flibustier Cecil Rhodes und seine Chartered Company im Roman', *Die Neue Zeit*, 16, 1, Heft 6: 182–8.

Bartlett, John 1919, *Familiar Quotations: A Collection of Passages Phrases and Proverbs Traced to their Sources in Ancient and Modern Literature* Boston: Little, Brown and Co., 10th ed.

Bauer, Bruno 1882, *Disraelis romantischer und Bismarcks socialistischer Imperialismus*, Chemnitz: E. Schmeitzner.

Bauer, Otto 1904, 'Marx' Theorie der Wirtschaftskrisen', *Die Neue Zeit*, 23, 1: 133–48, 164–70.

—— 1905, 'Die Kolonialpolitik und die Arbeiter', *Die Neue Zeit*, 23, 1: 265–9, 411–20.

—— 1907, 'Über britischen Imperialismus', *Die Neue Zeit*, 25, 1 (January): 535–40.

—— 1908a, 'Tatiana Grigorovici 1910, *Die Wertlehre bei Marx und Lassalle*', *Der Kampf*, 1, 6 (March): 285–7.

—— 1908b, 'Oesterreich und der Imperialismus', *Der Kampf*, 2, 1, (October): 17–22.

—— 1908c, 'Sozialdemokratische Friedenspropaganda,' *Der Kampf*, 2, 3 (December): 102.

—— 1909, 'Nationale und internationale Gesichtspunkte in der auswärtigen Politik', *Der Kampf*, 2, 12 (September): 535–41.

—— 1910a, [Heinrich Weber], 'Imperialismus und Sozialismus in England', *Der Kampf*, 3, 4, (January): 158–66.
—— 1910b, 'Das Finanzkapital', *Der Kampf*, 3 (June): 391–7.
—— 1910c, [Heinrich Weber], 'Ein Sieg des Imperialismus', *Der Kampf*, 3, 5 (February): 205–9.
—— 1911, 'Oesterreich-Ungarn und Italien', *Der Kampf*, 4, 6, (March): 245–51.
—— 1912, 'Parteiliteratur', *Der Kampf*, 5, 6 (March): 286.
—— 1913a, '*Die Akkumulation des Kapitals*', *Die Neue Zeit*, 31, 1: 831–8, 862–74. English version: Bauer 1986.
—— 1913b, *The High Cost of Living*, Brussels: International Socialist Bureau, People's Palace, Documents: 2nd Commission: *The High Cost of Living*, 1914.
—— 1927, 'Nach dem Parteitag,' *Der Kampf*, 20, 12 (December): 545–51.
—— 1937, 'Max Adler. Ein Beitrag zur Geschichte des "Austromarxismus"', *Der Kampf* [Prague], 4, 8 (August): 297–302.
—— 1978 [1927], 'What Is Austro-Marxism?' *Arbeiter–Zeitung*, (3 November), in Bottomore and Goode (eds.) 1978.
—— 1986, 'The Accumulation of Capital', *History of Political Economy*, 18, 1 (Spring): 87–110.
—— 2000 [1907], *The Question of Nationalities and Social Democracy*, edited by Ephraim J. Nimni, translated by Joseph O'Donnell, Minneapolis: University of Minnesota Press.
Bax, Ernest Belfort 1896, 'The True Aims of "Imperial Extension" and "Colonial Enterprise"', *Justice*, (1 May): 7–8.
—— 1898, 'Der Sozialismus eines gewöhnlichen Menschenkindes gegenüber dem Sozialismus der Herrn Bernstein', *Die Neue Zeit*, 16, 1 (1898), Heft 26: 824–9.
—— 1899, 'Jews, Boers and Patriots', *Justice*, (28 October): 6.
—— 1900, 'Some Reflections on the Paris Congress', *Justice*, (13 October): 4.
—— 1907, 'The International Congress and Colonial Policy', *Justice* (14 September): 3.
—— 1988a [1896], 'Our German Fabian Convert; or, Socialism According to Bernstein', *Justice* (7 November) 1896, in Tudor and Tudor (eds.) 1988.
—— 1988b [1896], 'The Socialism of Bernstein', *Justice* (21 November), in Tudor and Tudor (eds.) 1988.
—— 1988c [1897], 'Kolonialpolitik und Chauvinismus', *Die Neue Zeit*, 16, 1, Heft 14 (21 December): 420–7. English ed.: 'Colonial Policy and Chauvinism', in Tudor and Tudor (eds.) 1988.
Beer, Max 1897, 'Der moderne englische Imperialismus', *Die Neue Zeit*, 16, 1, Heft 10 (November): 300–6.
—— 1898, 'Die Vereinigten Staaten im Jahre 1898', *Die Neue Zeit*, 17, 1, Hefte 22, 23 (December): 676–80, 708–14.
—— 1899, 'Die Vereinigten Staaten im Jahre 1899', *Die Neue Zeit*, 18, 1, Hefte 15, 16, (19 November): 457–62, 488–92.
—— 1900, 'Some Reflections on the Paris Congress', *Justice* (13 October): 4.
—— 1901a, 'Betrachtungen über den Niedergang Englands', *Die Neue Zeit*, 19, 1, Heft 26 (March): 804–11.
—— 1901b, 'Sozialer Imperialismus', *Die Neue Zeit*, 20, 1, Heft 7 (8 November): 209–17.
—— 1902a, 'Parteipolitische Projekte in England', *Die Neue Zeit*, 20, 1, Heft 14 (January): 429–36.
—— 1902b, 'Imperialistische Politik', *Die Neue Zeit*, 21, 1, Heft 13 (December): 389–95.
—— 1906, 'Literarische Rundschaud: Imperialistische Literatur', *Vorwärts*, 25 December.
—— 1919–25, *Allgemeine Geschichte des Sozialismus und der sozialen Kämpfe*, Berlin: Verlag für Sozialwissenschaft.
—— 1935, *Fifty Years of International Socialism*, London: Allen and Unwin.
——2002, *History of British Socialism*, London: Routledge.
Bernstein, Eduard 1894, 'John A. Hobson, *The Evolution of Modern Capitalism*', *Die Neue Zeit*, 12, 2: 504–7.
—— 1896a, 'Probleme des Sozialismus: 1. Allgemeines über Utopismus und Eklektizismus', *Die Neue Zeit*, 15, 1, Heft 6 (28 October): 164–71.

—— 1896b, 'Eine Theorie der Gebiete und Grenzen des Kollektivismus', *Die Neue Zeit*, 15, 1, (4 November): 201–13.
—— 1897, 'Literarische Rundschau: John A. Hobson, *The Problem of the Unemployed.* John A. Hobson, *Problems of Poverty*', *Die Neue Zeit*, 15, 1 (January): 500–2.
—— 1898, 'Der Kampf der Sozialdemokratie und die Revolution der Gesellschaft', *Die Neue Zeit*, 16, 1: 484–97, 548–57.
—— 1900a, 'Sozialdemokratie und Imperialismus', *Sozialistische Monatshefte*, 4, 5 (May): 238–51.
—— 1900b, 'Der Sozialismus und die Kolonialfrage', *Sozialistische Monatshefte*, 4, 9 (September): 549–62.
—— 1900c, 'Paris und Mainz', *Sozialistische Monatshefte*, 4, 11 (November): 709–18.
—— 1907a, 'German Socialism and the Colonial Question', *The Nation*, 2, 2 (12 October).
—— 1907b, 'Die Kolonialfrage und der Klassenkampf', *Sozialistische Monatshefte*, 11, 12 (December): 988–96.
—— 1911a, 'Das Finanzkapital und die Handelspolitik', *Sozialistische Monatshefte*, 17, 15 (July): 947–55.
—— 1911b, 'Die auswärtige Politik des Deutschen Reiches und die Sozialdemokratie', *Vorwärts*, 188/189 (13/15 August).
—— 1988a [1896], 'German Social Democracy and Turkish Troubles', [Die deutsche Sozialdemokratie und die türkische Wirren], *Die Neue Zeit*, 15, 1, 14 October, in Tudor and Tudor (eds.) 1988.
—— 1988b [1896], 'Amongst the Philistines: A Rejoinder to Belfort Bax', *Justice* (14 November), in Tudor and Tudor (eds.) 1988.
—— 1993 [1899], *The Preconditions of Socialism*, edited and translated by Henry Tudor, Cambridge: Cambridge University Press.
Bock, Hans Manfred (ed.) 1969, *Organisation und Taktik der proletarischen Revolution*, Frankfurt: Verlag Neue Kritik.
Boothman, H.L. 1900, 'Philosophy of Imperialism', *International Socialist Review*, 1, 5 (November): 229–44, 286–303.
Bottomore, Tom, and Patrick Goode (eds.) 1978, *Austro-Marxism*, Oxford: Clarendon Press.
Botz, Gerhard, and Helmut Konrad, 1974, 'Austromarxismus und Imperialismus', *Die Zukunft. Sozialistische Zeitschrift für Politik, Wirtschaft und Kultur*, Heft 13–14: 15–19.
Boudin, Louis B. 1907, *The Theoretical System of Karl Marx in the Light of Recent Criticism*, Chicago: Charles H. Kerr and Co.
Brailsford, Henry Noel 1918 [1914], *The War of Steel and Gold: A Study of the Armed Peace*, London: G. Bell & Sons (original edition: London: Bell).
Brennan, E.J.T. 1975, *Education for National Efficiency: The Contribution of Sidney and Beatrice Webb*, London: The Athlone Press.
Brewer, Anthony 1990, *Marxist Theories of Imperialism: A Critical Survey*, London: Routledge.
Bricanier, Serge 1978, *Pannekoek and the Workers' Councils*, Saint Louis: Telos Press.
Bryan, William Jennings 1900, 'Imperialism: An Address Delivered in Indianapolis on 8 August 1900 in Accepting the Democratic Nomination for the Presidency', in Bryan 1909, Vol. 2.
—— 1909, *Speeches of William Jennings Bryan*, revised and arranged by himself, with a biographical introduction by Mary Baird Bryan, New York: Funk & Wagnalls.
Bryce, Viscount James 1893, *The American Commonwealth*, New York: Macmillan, 2 vols.
Bukharin, Nikolai I. 1929 [1915], *Imperialism and World Economy*, with an introduction by V.I. Lenin, London: Martin Lawrence Limited,.
—— 1971 [1920], *Economics of the Transformation Period, with Lenin's Critical Remarks*, New York: Bergman.
—— 1982, *N.I. Bukharin, Selected Writings on the State and the Transition to Socialism*, translated, edited, and introduced by Richard B. Day; with forewords by Stephen F. Cohen and Ken Coates, New York: M.E. Sharpe.

Bukharin, Nikolai I., and Rosa Luxemburg 1972–4, *Imperialism and the Accumulation of Capital*, edited with an introduction by Kenneth J. Tarbuck, translated by Rudolf Wichmann, London: Penguin.

Bulwer, Henry Lytton 1868, *Historical Characters: Talleyrand, Cobbett, Mackintosh, Canning*, London: Richard Bentley.

Bureau of Foreign Commerce, Department of State 1900–1, *Review of the World's Commerce: Introductory to Commercial Relations of the United States with Foreign Countries during the Years…*, Washington: Government's Printing Office.

Cain, Peter J. 1992 (ed.), *J.A. Hobson: Writings on Imperialism and Internationalism*, London: Routledge/Thoemmes Press.

—— 1999 (ed.), *Empire and Imperialism: The Debate of the 1870s*, South Bend: St. Augustine's Press.

—— 2002, *Hobson and Imperialism: Radicalism, New Liberalism, and Finance 1887–1938*, Oxford: Oxford University Press.

Calwer, Richard 1907, 'Der 25. Januar', *Sozialistische Monatshefte*, 2 (February): 101–7.

Chamberlain, Joseph 1897, *Foreign & Colonial Speeches*, London: George Routledge & Sons, Limited.

Clarke, William 1900, 'The Social Future of England', *Contemporary Review*, 78 (July–December): 858–69.

Cobden, Richard 1886, *The Political Writings of Richard Cobden*, London: Cassell.

Cohen, Max 1915a, 'Das englische Weltreich', *Die Glocke*, 1: 522–4.

—— 1915b, 'Mitteleuropa', *Die Glocke*, 1: 573–83.

—— 1915c, 'Imperialistische Randbemerkungen', *Die Glocke*, 1: 381–92.

Coker, William S. 1968, 'The Panama Canal Tolls Controversy: A Different Perspective', *The Journal of American History*, 55, 3 (December): 555–64.

Conant, Charles Arthur 1898, 'The Economic Basis of Imperialism', *The North-American Review*, 167, 502, (September): 326–341. Reprinted in Conant 1900.

—— 1900, *The United States in the Orient: The Nature of an Economic Problem*, Boston: Houghton, Mifflin.

Craig Nation, R. 1989, *War on War: Lenin, the Zimmerwald Left, and the Origins of Communist Internationalism*, Durham: Durham, NC.

Cunow, Heinrich 1898, 'Zur Zusammenbruchstheorie', *Die Neue Zeit*, 16, 1 (March): 356–64, 396–403, 424–30.

—— 1900, 'Handelsvertrag und imperialistische Expansionspolitik', *Die Neue Zeit*, 18, 2 (May): 207–15, 234–42.

—— 1902, 'Amerikanische Expansionspolitik in Ostasien', *Die Neue Zeit*, 20, 2 (June–July): 388–93, 429–36.

—— 1910, 'Rudolf Hilferding, *Das Finanzkapital: Eine Studie über die jüngste Entwicklung des Kapitalismus*', *Vorwärts* (7 August).

—— 1915, *Parteizusammenbruch? Ein offenes Wort zum inneren Parteistreit*, Berlin: Vorwärts Singer.

Dale, Ian (ed.) 2000, *Labour Party General Election Manifestos, 1900–1997*, London: Routledge.

David, Eduard 1915, *Die Sozialdemokratie im Weltkrieg*, Berlin: Vorwärts.

Day, Richard B. 1973, *Leon Trotsky and the Politics of Economic Isolation*, Cambridge: Cambridge University Press.

—— 1976, 'Dialectical Method in the Political Writings of Lenin and Bukharin', *Canadian Journal of Political Science/Revue Canadienne de Science Politique*, 9, 2: 244–60.

—— 1980, 'Rosa Luxemburg and the Accumulation of Capital', *Critique*, 12, 1 (Winter): 81–96.

——, and Daniel Gaido (eds.) 2009, *Witnesses to Permanent Revolution: The Documentary Record*, *Historicql Materialism* Book Series, Leiden: Brill.

De Leon, Daniel 1904, *Flashlights of the Amsterdam International Socialist Congress*, New York: New York Labor News.

Democratic Party of the United States 1900, 'The Democratic National Platform', *The New York Times*, July 6: 5.

Dernburg, Bernhard 1907a, *Zielpunkte des Deutschen Kolonialwesens: Zwei Vortrage gehalten am 8. Januar 1907 und am 11. Januar 1907*, Berlin: Ernst Siegfried Mittler.

—— 1907b, *Koloniale Lehrjahre: Vortrag gehalten in Stuttgart am 23. Januar 1907*, Stuttgart: Union Deutsche.

—— 1907c, *Koloniale Finanzprobleme: Vortrag gehalten auf Veranlassung der Handelskammer in Frankfurt a.M. am 3. Februar 1907*, Berlin: Ernst Siegfried Mittler & Sohn.

Drechsler, Horst 1980, *Let Us Die Fighting: The Struggle of the Herero and Nama against German Imperialism (1884–1915)*, translated by Bernd Zoellner, London: Zed Press.

Dilke, Charles W. 1890, *Problems of Greater Britain*, London: Macmillan.

Dziewanowski, Marian K. 1953, 'World War I and the Marxist Movement of Poland', *American Slavic and East European Review*, 12, 1 (February): 72–92.

Eckstein, Gustav 1912a, 'Gegenwartsforderungen', *Die Neue Zeit*, 30, 2: 810–17.

—— 1912b, 'Imperialismus und Rüstungsbeschränkung', *Die Neue Zeit*, 30, 2, (September): 907–16.

—— 1913a, 'Militarismus und Volkswirtschaft', *Die Neue Zeit*, 31, 2: 116–25, 165–72.

—— 1913b, 'Rosa Luxemburg: *Die Akkumulation des Kapitals. Ein Beitrag zur ökonomischen Erklärung des Imperialismus*', *Vorwärts*, 40 (16 February), reprinted in Luxemburg 1923.

Edgell, Stephen, and Jules Townshend 1992, 'John Hobson, Thorstein Veblen, and the Phenomenon of Imperialism: Finance Capital, Patriotism and War', *American Journal of Economics and Sociology*, 51, 4 (October): 401–20.

Engels, Friedrich 1853, 'The Real Issue in Turkey', in Marx and Engels, *Collected Works*, Moscow: Progress Publishers, 1979, Volume 12.

—— 1885, 'England 1845 und 1885', *Die Neue Zeit*, 3, Heft 6: 241–45.

—— 1892, 'Socialism in Germany', *Die Neue Zeit*, 19, 1, Heft 1 (January), in Mecklenburg and Stassen (eds.) 1990.

—— 1902, *The Mark*, New York: New York Labor News Company.

—— 1943 [1892a], *The Condition of the Working Class in England in 1844*, London: George Allen & Unwin.

Fayet, Jean-François 2004, *Karl Radek (1885–1939): Biographie politique*, Bern: Peter Lang.

Fiske, John 1902 [1885], *American Political Ideas Viewed from the Standpoint of Universal History: Three Lectures Delivered at the Royal Institution of Great Britain in May 1880*, Boston and New York: Harper & Brothers.

Fletcher, Roger 1984, *Revisionism and Empire: Socialist Imperialism in Germany, 1897–1914*, London: G. Allen & Unwin.

Florath, Bernd 1987, 'Heinrich Cunow. Eine biographisch-historiographische Skizze', *Jahrbuch für Geschichte*, 34: 85–145.

Foreign Office 1895, *Diplomatic and Consular Reports: Annual Series: Spain*, London: Foreign Office.

—— 1897, *Diplomatic and Consular Reports: Annual Series: Spain*, London: Foreign Office.

Fired, Alfred Hermann 1911, *Handbuch der Friedensbewegung*, 2nd ed., Leipzig: Verlag der «Friedens–Warte».

Friedemann, Peter (ed.) 1978, *Materialien zum politischen Richtungsstreit in der deutschen Sozialdemokratie, 1890–1917*, Frankfurt am Main: Ullstein.

Friedjung, Heinrich 1908–12, *Österreich von 1848 bis 1860*, Stuttgart: J.G. Cotta, 2 vols.

Gankin, Olga Hess, and Harold Henry Fisher (eds.) 1940, *The Bolsheviks and the World War: The Origin of the Third International*, Stanford: Stanford University Press.

Gerber, John Paul 1989, *Anton Pannekoek and the Socialism of Workers' Self-Emancipation, 1873–1960*, Dordrecht: Kluwer Academic.

Giddings, Franklin H. 1898, 'Imperialism?', *Political Science Quarterly*, 13, 4: 585–605.

Giffen, Robert 1880–6, *Essays in Finance*, London: George Bell and Sons, 2 vols.

Gissing, George 1897, *The Whirlpool*, New York: Frederick A. Stokes Company.

Gompers, Samuel 1995 [1898–1902], *The Samuel Gompers Papers*, Vol. 5: *An Expanding Movement at the Turn of the Century, 1898–1902*, ed. by Stuart B. Kaufman, Peter J. Albert, and Grace Palladino, Urbana: University of Illinois Press.

Gorter, Herman 1914, *Het imperialisme, de wereldoorlog en de sociaal-democratie*, Amsterdam: Brochurehandel Sociaal-Democratische Partij (September). English version: 'Imperialism, the World War and Social Democracy', *International Socialist Review*, 15, 11 (May 1915): 645–51ff.

Gay, Peter 1962, *The Dilemma of Democratic Socialism*, New York: Collier Books.

Grigorovici Tatiana 1910, *Die Wertlehre bei Marx und Lassalle: Beitrag zur Geschichte eines wissenschaftlichen Missverständnisses*, Wien: Verlag der Wiener Volksbuchhandlung Ignaz Brand & Co.

Grimm, Robert 1912, 'Erfahrungen mit dem schweizerischen Milizsystem', *Die Neue Zeit*, 30, 2: 385–93, 442–49.

Grünberg, Carl (Hg.) 1916, *Die Internationale und der Weltkrieg. Materialien. Erster Abteilung: Vor dem Kriege und während der ersten Kriegswochen*, gesammelt von Carl Grünberg, in *Archiv für die Geschichte des Sozialismus und der Arbeiterbewegung*, Nr. 06, Leipzig: Verlag von C.L. Hirschfeld.

Grunenberg, Antonia (ed.) 1970, *Die Massenstreikdebatte: Beiträge von Parvus, Rosa Luxemburg, Karl Kautsky und Anton Pannekoek*, Frankfurt: Europaische Verlagsanstalt.

Haase, Hugo 1914, *Imperialism and Arbitration*, International Socialist Congress at Vienna (23–29 August), documents, 3rd commission, report, Brussels: International Socialist Bureau. In: Bibliothek der Friedrich-Ebert-Stiftung, *Sources on the Development of the Socialist International (1907–1919)*.

Haenisch, Konrad 1915a, *Der deutsche Arbeiter und sein Vaterland*, Berlin-Karlshorst: Verlag der "Internationalen Korrespondenz".

—— 1915b, *Krieg und Sozialdemokratie: Drei Aufsätze*, Hamburg: Aus dem "Hamburger Echo", Nr. 280, 286 und 303.

—— 1919, *Die deutsche Sozialdemokratie in und nach dem Weltkriege* Berlin: C.A. Schwetschke.

Hammacher, Emil 1909, *Das philosophisch-ökonomische System des Marxismus. Unter Berücksichtigung seiner Fortbildung und des Sozialismus überhaupt dargestellt und kritisch beleuchtet*, Leipzig: Duncker & Humblot.

Hansen, Erik 1973, 'Marxists and Imperialism: The Indonesian Policy of the Dutch Social Democratic Workers Party, 1894–1914', *Indonesia*, 16 (October): 81–104.

Harvey, David 2003, *The New Imperialism*, Oxford: Oxford University Press.

Haupt, Georges 1972, *Socialism and the Great War: The Collapse of the Second International*, Oxford: Clarendon Press.

Hegel, Georg Wilhelm Friedrich 2001 [1837], *The Philosophy of History*, With Prefaces by Charles Hegel and the translator, J. Sibree, M.A. Kitchener, Ontario: Batoche Books.

—— 2003 [1821], *Elements of the Philosophy of Right*, Edited by Allen W. Wood, translated by H.B. Nisbet, Cambridge University Press.

Helphand, Alexander: See Parvus.

Henderson, W.O. 1951, 'Walther Rathenau: A Pioneer of the Planned Economy', *The Economic History Review*, New Series, 4, 1: 98–108.

Herrfurth, Kurt 1900, *Fürst Bismarck und die Kolonialpolitik*, Berlin: Trewendt's Nachfolger.

Hilferding, Rudolf 1903a, 'Der Funktionswechsel des Schutzzolles', *Die Neue Zeit*, 21, 2: 274–81.

—— 1903b, 'Werner Sombart, *Der moderne Kapitalismus*', *Zeitschrift für Volkswirtschaft, Sozialpolitik und Verwaltung*, Vol. 12: 446–53, reprinted in vom Brocke (ed.) 1987.

—— 1905a, 'Parlamentarismus und Massenstreik', *Die Neue Zeit*, 23, 2 (16 September): 804–16.

—— 1905b, 'Parliamentarianism and the General Strike', *The Social Democrat*, 9, 11 (November): 675–87.

—— 1907a, 'Parvus. *Die Kolonialpolitik und der Zusammenbruch*', *Die Neue Zeit*, 25, 2: 687–8.

—— 1907b, [Karl Emil], 'Der deutsche Imperialismus und die innere Politik', *Die Neue Zeit*, 26, 1 (October): 748–63, reprinted in Stephan (ed.) 1982.

—— 1909, 'Der Revisionismus und die Internationale', *Die Neue Zeit*, 27, 2 (May): 161–74.
—— 1910a, *Das Finanzkapital. Eine Studie über die jüngste Entwicklung des Kapitalismus.* Wien: Ignaz Brand.
—— 1911, 'Der Parteitag und die auswärtige Politik', *Die Neue Zeit*, 29, 2, (September): 799–806.
—— 1913, 'Der Balkankrieg und die Grossmächte', *Die Neue Zeit*, 31, 1: 74–7.
—— 1915, 'Arbeitsgemeinschaft der Klassen?', *Der Kampf*, 8, 10 (October): 322–9, reprinted in Stephan (ed.) 1982.
—— 1981 [1910b], *Finance Capital: A Study of the Latest Phase of Capitalist Development*, edited with an introduction by Tom Bottomore, London: Routledge & K. Paul.
Hirshfield, Claire 1980, 'The Anglo-Boer War and the Issue of Jewish Culpability', *Journal of Contemporary History*, 15, 4 (October): 619–31.
Hirst, Paul Q. and Grahame Thompson 1996, *Globalization in Question: The International Economy and the Possibilities of Governance*, Cambridge: Polity Press.
Hobson, John A. 1891, *Problems of Poverty: An Inquiry into the Industrial Condition of the Poor*, 2nd ed., London: Methuen & Co.
—— 1894, *The Evolution of Modern Capitalism: A Study of Machine Production*, London: W. Scott; New York. C. Scribner's Sons.
—— 1896a, *The Problem of the Unemployed: An Enquiry and an Economic Policy*, London: Methuen & Co.
—— 1896b, 'Collectivism in Industry', *Progressive Review*, 1 (October): 38–52.
—— 1898, *John Ruskin: Social Reformer*, Boston: Dana Estes & Co.
—— 1900a, *The Economics of Distribution*, London, Macmillan & Co.
—— 1900b, 'Capitalism and Imperialism in South Africa', *Contemporary Review*, 77 (January–June): 1–17.
—— 1900c, *The War in South Africa: Its Causes and Effects*, London: James Nisbet & Co.
—— 1901a, *The Social Problem: Life and Work*, London: James Nisbet & Co.
—— 1901b, 'Socialistic Imperialism', *International Journal of Ethics*, 12, 1 (October): 44–58.
—— 1901c, *Psychology of Jingoism*, London, G. Richards.
—— 1901d, 'The Commercial Value of Imperialism', *Speaker*, 2 November.
—— 1901e, 'Imperialism as an Outlet for Population', *Speaker*, 9 November.
—— 1901f, 'Economic Parasites of Imperialism', *Speaker*, 16 November.
—— 1901g, 'Imperialism the Policy of Investors', *Speaker*, 23 November.
—— 1901h, 'The Financial Direction of Imperialism', *Speaker*, 30 November.
—— 1901i, 'Imperialism based on Protection', *Speaker*, 7 December.
—— 1902a, 'The Economic Taproot of Imperialism', *Contemporary Review*, 81 (August): 219–32.
—— 1902b, *Imperialism: A Study*, London: James Nisbet.
—— 1909, *The Crisis of Liberalism: New Issues of Democracy*, London: P.S. King and Son.
—— 1976 [1938], *Confessions of an Economic Heretic: The Autobiography of J.A. Hobson*, Hamden: Archon Books.
Institut für Marxismus-Leninismus 1975 (ed.), *Dokumente und Materialien zur Geschichte der deutschen Arbeiterbewegung*, herausgegeben vom Institut für Marxismus-Leninismus beim Zentralkomitee der Sozialistischen Einheitspartei Deutschlands, 2. Auflage, Berlin: Dietz Verlag.
International Conference of Socialist Young People's Organisations (Copenhagen) 1910, *Resolutions*, Bibliothek der Friedrich Ebert Stiftung.
International Socialist Congress 1976–85 [1889–1917], *Histoire de la IIe Internationale*, Geneva: Minkoff Reprint.
International Socialist Congress 1901 [1900], *Cinquième Congrès socialiste international tenu a Paris du 23 au 27 septembre 1900: Compte rendu analytique officiel*, Paris: Société nouvelle de librairie et d'édition.
—— (7th) 1907, *Internationaler Sozialisten-Kongress zu Stuttgart, 18. bis 24. August 1907*, Berlin: Buchhandlung Vorwärts.

—— (8th) 1910, *Internationaler Sozialisten-Kongress zu Kopenhagen, 28. August bis 3. September 1910*, Berlin: Buchhandlung Vorwärts.
Internationale Tagung der Historiker der Arbeiterbewegung (»VIII. Linzer Konferenz«) 1974 [1972], *Die Stellung der internationalen Arbeiterbewegung zum Militarismus und Imperialismus zwischen den Kongressen von Stuttgart und Basel, 1907 bis 1912*, Wien: Europaverlag.
Internationale Verbindung sozialistischer Jugendorganisationen 1907, *Bericht über die erste Internationale Konferenz der Sozialistischen Jugendorganisationen: abgehalten in Stuttgart vom 24. bis 26. August 1907*, Stuttgart: Singer.
James, Harold 2001, *The End of Globalization: Lessons from the Great Depression*, Cambridge, MA.: Harvard University Press.
Jebb, Richard 1905, *Studies in Colonial Nationalism*, London: Edward Arnold.
Joll, James 1974, *The Second International, 1889–1914*, London: Routledge and Kegan Paul.
Joubert, Jean-Paul 1988, 'Revolutionary Defeatism', *Revolutionary History*, 1, 3: *War and Revolution in Europe: 1939–1945*.
Kaarsholm, Preben 1988, 'The South African War and the Response of the International Socialist Community to Imperialism between 1896 and 1908', in van Holthoon and van der Linden (eds.) 1988: Vol. 1.
Kapelusz, Theodor 1897, 'Industrie und Finanz', *Die Neue Zeit*, 15, 2: 374–9, 405–13, 460–8.
Karski: See Marchlewski, Julian.
Kautsky, John H. 1961, 'J.A. Schumpeter and Karl Kautsky: Parallel Theories of Imperialism', *Midwest Journal of Political Science*, 5, 2 (May): 101–28.
Kautsky, Karl 1883, 'Auswanderung and Kolonisation', *Die Neue Zeit*, 1: 365–70, 395–404.
—— 1886, 'Die chinesischen Eisenbahnen und das europäische Proletariat', *Die Neue Zeit*, 4, Hefte 11–12: 515–25, 529–49.
—— 1888, *Thomas More und seine Utopie: mit einer historischen Einleitung*, Stuttgart: J.H.W. Dietz.
—— 1898a, 'Ältere und neuere Kolonialpolitik', *Die Neue Zeit*, 16, 1 (March): 769–81, 801–16.
—— 1898b, 'Kiaotschau', *Die Neue Zeit*, 16, 2 (March): 14–26.
—— 1898c, 'Demokratische und reaktionäre Abrüstung', *Die Neue Zeit*, 16, 2, Heft 50: 740–46.
—— 1899a, 'Friedrich Engels und das Milizsystem', *Die Neue Zeit*, 17, 1: 335–42, 580–88, 613–17.
—— 1899b, 'Schippel und der Militarismus', *Die Neue Zeit*, 17, 1: 618–26, 644–54, 686–91.
—— 1899c, 'Der Krieg in Südafrika', *Die Neue Zeit*, 18, 1 (November): 196–203.
—— 1899d, *Bernstein und das sozialdemokratische programmem. Eine Antikritik*, Stuttgart: J.H.W. Dietz Nachfolger.
—— 1900a, 'Militarismus und Sozialismus in England', *Die Neue Zeit*, 18, 1, Heft 19 (January): 587–97.
—— 1900b, 'Schippel, Brentano und die Flottenvorlage', *Die Neue Zeit*, 18, 1, (March): 740–51, 772–82, 804–16.
—— 1900c, 'Deutschland, England und die Weltpolitik', *Vorwärts*, 105 and 107 (8 and 10 May).
—— 1900d, 'Germany, England and the World Policy', *The Social Democrat*, 4, 8 (August): 230–6.
—— 1902, 'Krisentheorien', *Die Neue Zeit*, 20, 2: 37–47, 76–81, 110–18, 133–43.
—— 1905, 'Die Folgen des japanischen Sieges und die Sozialdemokratie', *Die Neue Zeit*, 23, 2: 460–68, 492–9, 529–37. English version in Day and Gaido (eds.) 2009.
—— 1907a, 'Der 25. Januar', *Die Neue Zeit*, 25, 1: 588–96.
—— 1907b, *Sozialismus und Kolonialpolitik. Eine Auseinandersetzung*, Berlin: Vorwärts. English version: *Socialism and Colonial Policy: An Analysis*, translated from the German by Angela Clifford, Belfast: Athol Books, 1975.

—— 1907c, 'Mein "Gesinnungswandel" in der Kolonialpolitik', *Vorwärts*, 233 (5 October).
—— 1907c, *Patriotismus und Sozialdemokratie*, Leipzig: Verlag der Leipziger Buchdrukkerei Aktiengesellschaft.
—— 1908a, *Nationalität und Internationalität*, Ergänzungshäfte zur *Neuen Zeit*, Nr. 1, Stuttgart: Paul Singer.
—— 1909a, 'Sects or Class Parties', *Social Democrat*, 13, 6 (June): 316–28. [Originally published in *Die Neue Zeit*, July 1909.]
—— 1909b, *Der Weg zur Macht: Politische Betrachtungen über das Hineinwachsen in die Revolution*, Berlin: Buchhandlung Vorwärts.
—— 1910a, 'Was nun?', *Die Neue Zeit*, 28, 2: 33–40, 68–80, reprinted in Grunenberg (ed.) 1970.
—— 1910b, 'Eine neue Strategie', *Die Neue Zeit*, 28, 2: 332–41, 364–74, 412–21, reprinted in Grunenberg (ed.) 1970.
—— 1910c, 'Zwischen Baden und Luxemburg', *Die Neue Zeit*, 28, 2: 652–67, reprinted in Friedemann (ed.) 1978, Vol. II.
—— 1910d, *Vermehrung und Entwicklung in Natur und Gesellschaft*, Stuttgart: J.H.W. Dietz Nachf.
—— 1911a, 'Krieg und Frieden. Betrachtungen zur Maifeier', *Die Neue Zeit*, 29 (April): 97–107.
—— 1911b, 'Finanzkapital und Krisen (Rudolf Hilferding, *Das Finanzkapital*)', *Die Neue Zeit*, 29, 1: 764–72, 797–804, 838–64, 874–83.
—— 1911c, 'Finance Capital and Crises', *Social Democrat*, London, Vol. 15.
—— 1911d, *Weltpolitik, Weltkrieg und Sozialdemokratie!*, Berlin: Paul Singer & Co., (August), reprinted in Institut für Marxismus-Leninismus 1975, Band 4.
—— 1911e, 'Eine Musterkritik', *Vorwärts*, 204 (29 August).
—— 1911f [1901], *Handelspolitik und Sozialdemokratie: Populäre Darstellung der handelspolitischen Streitfragen*, 2. umgearb. Auflage, Berlin: P. Springer (first ed.: Berlin: Vorwärts).
—— 1912a, 'Die Aktion der Masse', *Die Neue Zeit*, 30, 1: 43–9, 77–84, 106–17, reprinted in Grunenberg (ed.) 1970.
—— 1912b, 'Gold, Papier und Ware', *Die Neue Zeit*, 30, 1: 837–47, 886–93.
—— 1912c, 'Der erste Mai und der Kampf gegen den Militarismus', *Die Neue Zeit*, 30, 2: 97–109.
—— 1912d, 'Der improvisierte Buch', *Die Neue Zeit*, 30, 2: 461–7, 513–23.
—— 1912e, 'Die neue Taktitk', *Die Neue Zeit*, 30, 2: 654–64, 688–9, 723–33, reprinted in Grunenberg (ed.) 1970.
—— 1912f, 'Nochmals die Abrüstung', *Die Neue Zeit*, 30, 2 (August): 841–54.
—— 1913, 'Der jüngste Radikalismus', *Die Neue Zeit*, 31, 1: 436–46.
—— 1914a, 'Der Krieg', *Die Neue Zeit*, 32, 2: 843–6.
—— 1914b, 'Der Imperialismus', *Die Neue Zeit*, 32, 2: 908–22.
—— 1914c, 'Wirkungen des Krieges', *Die Neue Zeit*, 32, 2: 937–48, 969–82.
—— 1915, *Nationalstaat, Imperialistischer Staat und Staatenbund*, Nürnberg: Fränkische Verlagsanstalt.
—— 1919, *Die Wurzeln der Politik Wilsons*, Berlin: Verlag Neues Vaterland.
—— 1927, *Thomas More and His Utopia: With a Historical Introduction*, translated by H.J. Stenning, New York: International Publishers.
—— 1953 [1908], *Foundations of Christianity*, New York: Russell and Russell.
—— 1959 [1897], *Communism in Central Europe in the Time of the Reformation*, London: Fisher and Unwin.
—— 1988 [1899], *The Agrarian Question*, London: Zwan Publications.
King, J.E. and Michael C. Howard 1989–92, *A History of Marxian Economics*, Princeton: Princeton University Press.
Kipling, Rudyard 1893, *Ballads and Barrack-Room Ballads*, New York: Macmillan.
—— 1899, 'The White Man's Burden', *McClure's Magazine*, 12 (February). Reprinted in Kipling 1908.
—— 1908, *The Writings in Prose and Verse of Rudyard Kipling*, New York: Charles Scribner's Sons.

Knapp, Georg Friedrich 1905, *Staatliche Theorie des Geldes*, Leipzig: Duncker & Humblot.
—— 1924, *The State Theory of Money*, tr. by H.M. Lucas and J. Bonar, London: Macmillan and Co.
Koebner, Richard and Helmut Dan Schmidt, 1965, *Imperialism: The Story and Significance of a Political Word, 1840–1960*, Cambridge: Cambridge University Press.
Kommunistischen Partei Österreichs (ed.) 1921, *Die Helden der Wiener Konferenz: mit Beitragen von Lenin, Trotzki, Sinowjew u.a.*, herausgegeben von der Kommunistischen Partei Österreichs (Sektion der III. Internationale), Vienna: Arbeiter-Buchhandlung.
Koppel, August 1905, *Für und wider Karl Marx. Prolegomena zu einer Biographie*, Karlsruhe: G. Braunsche Hofbuchdrückerei.
Krupskaya, Nadezhda K. 1959, *Reminiscences of Lenin*, Moscow: Foreign Languages Publishing House.
Kuhn, Rick 2007, *Henry Grossman and the Recovery of Marxism*, Urbana: University of Illinois Press.
Kurata, Minoru 1974, 'R. Hilferding. Bibliographie Seiner Schriften, Artikel und Briefe', *Internationale Wissenschaftliche Korrespondenz zur Geschichte der Deutschen Arbeiterbewegung*, 10, 3: 327–46.
Lair, Maurice 1902, *L'Impérialisme allemand*, Paris: Armand Colin.
Lane, A.T. (ed.) 1995, *Biographical Dictionary of European Labor Leaders*, Westport: Greenwood Press.
Lassalle, Ferdinand 1859, *Der italienische Krieg und die Aufgabe Preussens*, Berlin: Franz Duncker, in Lassalle 1919, 1.
—— 1863, *Was nun? Zweiter Vortrag über Verfassungswesen*, in Lassalle 1919, 2.
—— 1919, *Gesammelte Reden und Schriften*, hrsg. und eingeleitet von Eduard Bernstein, Berlin: Paul Cassirer.
Laufenberg, Heinrich and Fritz Wolffheim 1914, *Imperialismus und Demokratie: Ein Wort zum Weltkrieg*, Hamburg: Dr. H. Laufenberg.
Lecky, William Edward Hartpole 1899, *Democracy and Liberty*, New York: Longmans, Green, and Co.
Ledebour, Georg 1909, 'Die Einschränkung der Seerüstungen', *Die Neue Zeit*, 27, 2: 99–106.
—— 1911, 'Sozialdemokratie und Rüstungsbeschränkung', *Vorwärts*, 82 and 84 (6 and 8 April).
—— 1912, 'Eine parlamentarische Improvisation', *Die Neue Zeit*, 30, 2 (1912): 537–41.
Lenin, Vladimir I. 1895, 'The Economic Content of Narodism and the Criticism of it in Mr. Struve's Book (The Reflection of Marxism in Bourgeois Literature)', in Lenin 1964–72, Volume 1.
—— 1899a, 'J.A. Hobson. *The Evolution of Modern Capitalism*', *Nachalo*, 5 (May), in Lenin 1964–72, Volume 4.
—— 1899b, *The Development of Capitalism in Russia: The Process of the Formation of a Home-market for Large-Scale Industry*, in Lenin 1964–72, Volume 3.
—— 1899c, 'A Note on the Question of Market Theory (Apropos of the Polemic of Messrs. Tugan-Baranovsky and Bulgakov)', *Nauchnoye Obozreniye*, (January), in Lenin 1964–72, Volume 4.
—— 1907, 'The International Socialist Congress in Stuttgart', *Proletarii*, 17 (20 October) in Lenin 1964–72, Volume 13.
—— 1908, 'Meeting of the International Socialist Bureau', *Proletarii*, No. 37, (16 October), in Lenin 1964–72, Volume 15.
—— 1913a, 'To the Editor of *Bremer Bürger-Zeitung*' (January), in Lenin 1964–72, Volume 43.
—— 1913b, 'Letter to L. B. Kamenev' (March), in Lenin 1964–72, Volume 35.
—— 1913c, 'Theses on the National Question' (June), in Lenin 1964–72, Volume 19.
—— 1913d, '"Cultural-National" Autonomy', *Za Pravdu*, 46 (November), 28, in Lenin 1964–72, Volume 19.
—— 1914a, 'The Right of Nations to Self Determination', *Prosveshcheniye*, 4, 5, 6 (April–June), in Lenin 1964–72, Volume 20.

—— 1914b, 'The Tasks of Revolutionary Social-Democracy in the European War,' (6 September 1914), in Lenin 1964–72, Volume 21.
—— 1914c, 'Letter to A.G. Shlyapnikov (October 27), in Lenin 1964–72, Volume 35.
—— 1915a, 'Karl Marx: A Brief Biographical Sketch with an Exposition of Marxism', *Granat Encyclopaedia*, 1915, 28, in Lenin 1964, Volume 21.
—— 1915b, 'The Conference of the R.S.D.L.P. Groups Abroad', *Sotsial-Demokrat*, 40 (29 March), in Lenin 1964–72, Volume 21.
—— 1915c, *The Collapse of the Second International* (June), in Lenin 1964–72, Volume 21.
—— 1915d, 'On the Slogan for a United States of Europe', *Sotsial-Demokrat*, 44 (23 August), in Lenin 1964–72, Volume 21.
—— 1915e, 'The First Step', *Sotsial-Demokrat*, 45–6 (11 October), in Lenin 1964–72, Volume 21.
—— 1916a, 'The Junius Pamphlet', *Sbornik Sotsial-Demokrata*, 1 (April), in Lenin 1964–72, Volume 22.
—— 1916b, 'The Socialist Revolution and the Right of Nations to Self-Determination (Theses)', *Vorbote*, 2 (April) and *Sbornik Sotsial-Demokrata*, 1 (October), in Lenin 1964–72, Volume 22.
—— 1916c, 'The Discussion on Self-Determination Summed Up', *Sbornik Sotsial-Demokrata*, 1 (April), in Lenin 1964–72, Volume 22.
—— 1916d, 'A Caricature of Marxism and Imperialist Economism', (August–October), in Lenin 1964–72, Volume 23.
—— 1916e, 'The "Disarmament" Slogan', *Sbornik Sotsial-Demokrata*, 2 (December), in Lenin 1964–72, Volume 23.
—— 1916f, 'Imperialism and the Split in Socialism', *Sbornik Sotsial-Demokrata*, 2 (December), in Lenin 1964–72, Volume 23.
—— 1917, 'Materials Relating to the Revision of the Party Programme' (April–May), in Lenin 1964–72, Volume 24.
—— 1919a, 'Eighth Congress of the R.C.P.(B.)' (March 18–23), in Lenin 1964–72, Volume 29.
—— 1919b, 'Greetings to Italian, French and German Communists' (10 October), in Lenin 1964–72, Volume 30.
—— 1919c, 'Address to the Second All-Russia Congress of Communist Organisations of the Peoples of the East' (November 2) in Lenin 1964–72, Volume 30.
—— 1920, *'Left-Wing' Communism: An Infantile Disorder* (April–May), in Lenin 1964–72, Volume 31.
—— 1939, *Notebooks on Imperialism*, in Lenin 1964–72, Volume 39.
—— 1964–72, *Collected Works*, Moscow: Progress Publishers.
—— 1970 [1916], *Imperialism, the Highest Stage of Capitalism: A Popular Outline*, Peking: Foreign Languages Press.
—— 2000, 'Marginal Notes on Luxemburg's *The Accumulation of Capital*', *Research in Political Economy*, 18: 225–38.
——, and G. Zinoviev 1915, *Socialism and War: The Attitude of the Russian Social Democratic Labour Party Towards the War* (August), Genf: Sotsial-Demokrat, reprinted in Lenin 1964–72, Volume 21.
Leninskii Sbornik 1933, Moscow: Partiinoe Izdatel'stvo, Volume 22.
Lensch, Paul 1911, 'Praktische Politik?', *Leipziger Volkszeitung* (31 March).
—— 1912a, 'Eine Improvisation', *Die Neue Zeit*, 30, 2: 308–13, 359–68.
—— 1912b, 'Miliz und Abrüstung', *Die Neue Zeit*, 30, 2 (August): 765–72.
—— 1912c, 'Sozialdemokratie und auswärtige Politik', *Leipziger Volkszeitung*, 285 (9 December), reprinted in Institut für Marxismus-Leninismus 1975 (ed.), Band 4. [Published anonymously.]
—— 1912d, 'Die neuen Wehrvorlagen', *Die Neue Zeit*, 30, 2 (August): 68–75.
—— 1918, *Three Years of World Revolution*, London: Constable and Co. Ltd.
Lerner, Warren 1970, *Karl Radek: The Last Internationalist*, Stanford: Stanford University Press.
Leser, Norbert 1968, *Zwischen Reformismus und Bolschewismus: Der Austromarxismus als Theorie und Praxis*, Vienna: Europa Verlag.

Liebknecht, Karl 1907, *Militarismus und Antimilitarismus, unter besonderer Berücksichtigung der internationalen Jugendbewegung*, Leipzig: Leipziger Buchdruckerei Aktiengesellschaft.

—— 1910, *Theses on Militarism*, in International Conference of Socialist Young People's Organisations (Copenhagen) 1910.

Liebknecht, Wilhelm 1900a, 'Down with Imperialism and Militarism', *The Clarion* (2 January).

—— 1900b, 'Beware of Imperialism and Militarism', *The Clarion* (21 March).

—— 1900c, 'On Militarism', *The Clarion* (21 April).

Liebson Millin, Sarah Gertrude 1933, *Rhodes*, London: Chatto & Windus.

Looker, Robert (ed.) 1972, *Rosa Luxemburg: Selected Political Writings*, London: Cape.

Loughlin, Michael B. 2003, 'Gustave Hervé's Transition from Socialism to National Socialism: Continuity and Ambivalence', *Journal of Contemporary History*, 38 4: 515–38.

Louis, Paul 1899, 'L'impérialisme anglo-saxon', *La Revue Socialiste*, 29, 1, March: 257–74.

—— 1900a, 'L'Impérialisme (Angleterre, Etats-Unis)', *La Revue Blanche*, 23, September–December: 145–8.

—— 1900b, 'Die Kolonialpolitik Frankreichs und der Sozialismus', *Die Neue Zeit*, 18, 2, Heft 49: 673–84.

—— 1901a, 'La colonisation contemporaine', *La Revue Blanche*, 24 (1 February): 161–72.

—— 1901b, 'L'Impérialisme américain', *La Revue Blanche*, 24 (January–April): 220–1.

—— 1903, 'Les bases de l'impérialisme', *La Renaissance Latine*, 3, 2 (15 Septembre): 644–78.

—— 1904, 'Essai sur l'impérialisme', *Le Mercure de France*, 50, 172, (April): 100–14.

—— 1905, *Le colonialisme*, Paris: Société nouvelle de librairie et d'édition.

—— 1911, *Histoire du mouvement syndical en France, 1789–1910*, Paris: Alcan.

—— 1912, *Geschichte der Gewerkschaftsbewegung in Frankreich (1789 bis 1912)*, autorisierte Übersetzung von Hedwig Kurucz-Eckstein, herausgegeben und mit einer Einleitung versehen von Gustav Eckstein, Stuttgart: J.H.W. Dietz.

Löw, Raimund 1986, 'Theorie und Praxis des Austromarxismus', in *Der Austromarxismus. Eine Autopsie: Drei Studien*, edited by Raimund Löw, Siegfried Mattl and Alfred Pfabigan, Frankfurt am Main: isp-Verlag.

Luxemburg, Rosa 1899, *Sozialreform oder Revolution?* (*Leipziger Volkszeitung*, Nr. 219–25, 21–8 September 1898, and Nr. 76–80, 4–8 April 1899), in Luxemburg 1972–4, Volume 1/1.

—— 1910a, 'Was Weiter?', *Dortmunder Arbeiterzeitung*, (14–15 March), in Luxemburg 1972–4, Volume 2.

—— 1910b, 'The Next Step', in Looker (ed.) 1972.

—— 1910c, 'Ermattung oder Kampf?' *Die Neue Zeit*, 28, 2: 257–66, 291–305, in Luxemburg 1972–4, Volume 2.

—— 1910d, 'Die Theorie und die Praxis', *Die Neue Zeit*, 28, 2: 564–78, 626–42, in Luxemburg 1972–4, Volume 2.

—— 1911a, 'Friedensutopien', *Leipziger Volkszeitung*, 103–4 (6–8 May), in Luxemburg 1972–4, Volume 2.

—— 1911b, 'Marokko', *Die Gleichheit*, 21, 23: 353–4, (August), in Luxemburg 1972–4, Volume 3.

—— 1911c, 'Kleinbürgerliche oder proletarische Weltpolitik', *Leipziger Volkszeitung*, 191 (19 August), in Luxemburg 1972–4, Volume 3.

—— 1911d, 'Unser Marokkoflugblatt', *Leipziger Volkszeitung*, 197, (26 August 1911), in Luxemburg 1972–4, Volume 3.

—— 1911e, 'Zur Erwiderung', *Leipziger Volkszeitung*, 200, (30 August), in Luxemburg 1972–4, Volume 3.

—— 1913a, 'Die Reichstagsfraktion und die Militärvorlage', *Leipziger Volkszeitung*, 168–73 (23–9 July), in Luxemburg 1972–4, Volume 3.

—— 1913b, 'Nach dem Jenaer Parteitag', (October), first published in *Die Internationale*, 10, 5: 148–53, in Luxemburg 1972–4, Volume 3.

—— 1915, 'Perspektiven und Projekte', *Die Internationale*, 1: 71–7, in Luxemburg 1972–4, Volume 4.

—— 1916, 'Entwurf zu den "Junius"-Thesen' (January), *Unter dem Banner des Marxismus*, 1, 2 (Juli): 417–19, in Luxemburg 1972–4, Volume 4.
—— 1919 [1915], *The Crisis in the German Social Democracy (The "Junius" Pamphlet)*, New York: Socialist Publication Society.
—— 1921, *The Accumulation of Capital – An Anti-Critique, or What the Epigones Have Made of Marx's Theory*, in Bukharin and Luxemburg 1972.
—— 1923, *Die Akkumulation des Kapitals*, Berlin: Vereinigung Internationaler Berlags-Anstalten (*Gesammelte Werke*, Band 6).
—— 1963 [1913], *The Accumulation of Capital*, London: Routledge and Kegan Paul.
—— 1964 [1906], *The Mass Strike, the Political Party and the Trade Unions*, translated by Patrick Lavin, Colombo: Sydney Wanasinghe.
—— 1966 [1918], *Spartacus: Speech Delivered on December 30, 1918 at the Founding Conference of the Communist Party of Germany held in Berlin*, Colombo, Ceylon: Young Socialist Publication.
—— 1972–4, *Gesammelte Werke*, Berlin: Dietz Verlag.
—— 1980 [1910], *'Theory and Practice': also contains 'In conclusion…' from Attrition or Collision*, Detroit: News and Letters Committee.
——2003, *The Accumulation of Capital*, translated by Agnes Schwarzschild, with a new introduction by Tadeusz Kowalik, London: Routledge.
Maehl, William 1952, 'The Triumph of Nationalism in the German Socialist Party on the Eve of the First World War', *The Journal of Modern History*, 24, 1 (March): 15–41.
Malmesbury, James Howard Harris, 3rd Earl of 1884, *Memoirs of an Ex-Minister: An Autobiography*, London: Longmans, Green, and Co.
Mandelbaum, Kurt 1926, *Die Erörterungen innerhalb der deutschen Sozialdemokratie über das Problem des Imperialismus (1895–1914)*, Frankfurt a. M.: Peuvag, reprinted in Mandelbaum, *Sozialdemokratie und Leninismus: Zwei Aufsätze*, Berlin: Rotbuch Verlag, 1974.
Marchlewski, Julian 1904a, 'Der englische Imperialismus', *Leipziger Volkszeitung*, 240 (4 October), reprinted in Marchlewski 1978.
—— 1904b, 'Ein Sieg der Imperialismus', *Leipziger Volkszeitung*, 261 (10 November), reprinted in Marchlewski 1978.
—— 1910, 'Rudolf Hilferding, *Das Finanzkapital: Eine Studie über die jüngste Entwicklung des Kapitalismus*', *Leipziger Volkszeitung*, 198 (27 August), reprinted in Marchlewski 1978.
—— 1911a, 'Praktische Politik', *Leipziger Volkszeitung*, 77 (3 April).
—— 1911b, [J. Karski,] 'Ernste Fragen und nichtige Eitelkeiten', *Bremer Bürger-Zeitung*, 85 (10 April).
—— 1912, *Imperialismus oder Sozialismus?* Berlin: P. Singer, reprinted in Marchlewski 1978.
—— 1913, 'Eine marxistische Untersuchung über den Imperialismus', *Münchener Post*, (24–5 January).
—— 1960 [1918], *Karl Marx: Geschichte seines Lebens*, Berlin: Dietz.
—— 1978, *Imperialismus oder Sozialismus?: Arbeiten über die Entwicklung des Imperialismus und den antimonopolistischen Kampf der Arbeiterklasse 1895 bis 1919*, Frankfurt: Verlag Marxistische Blatter.
——, and Franz Mehring 1913, 'Aus der Partei. Erklärung von Julian Karski und Franz Mehring wegen Luxemburgs Buch', *Leipziger Volkszeitung* (21 February).
Markham, Edwin 1899a, 'The Man with the Hoe', *The San Francisco Examiner*, 15 January. Reprinted in Markham 1899b.
—— 1899b, *The Man with the Hoe, and Other Poems*, New York: Doubleday & McLure Co.
Marx, Karl 1844, *A Contribution to the Critique of Hegel's Philosophy of Right*, in Schirmacher (ed.) 1997.
—— 1864, *Inaugural Address of the International Working Men's Association* (21–7 October), in Marx and Engels 1975–, Volume 20.
—— 1897, *The Eastern Question: A Reprint of Letters Written 1853–1865 Dealing with the Events of the Crimean War*, ed. by Eleanor Marx Aveling and Edward Aveling, London: Swan Sonnenschein & Co.

—— 1968–72, *Theories of Surplus Value*, Moscow: Progress Publishers.
—— 1970 [1848], *Manifesto of the Communist Party*, Peking: Foreign Languages Press.
—— 1973, *Grundrisse der Kritik der Politischen Ökonomie* (*Outlines of the Critique of Political Economy*), Harmondsworth: Penguin.
—— 1976 [1867], *Capital: A Critique of Political Economy*, Volume I, introduced by Ernest Mandel, translated David Fernbach, London: Penguin.
—— 1977a [1847], *The Poverty of Philosophy*, Peking: Foreign Languages Press.
—— 1977b [1871], *The Civil War in France*, Peking: Foreign Languages Press.
—— 1978a [1852], *The Eighteenth Brumaire of Louis Bonaparte*, Peking, Foreign: Languages Press Chapter.
—— 1978b [1893], *Capital: A Critique of Political Economy*, Volume II, introduced by Ernest Mandel, translated David Fernbach, London: Penguin.
—— 1992 [1894], *Capital: A Critique of Political Economy*, Vol. III, introduced by Ernest Mandel, translated David Fernbach, London: Penguin.
—— and Frederick Engels 1975–, *Collected Works*, Moscow: International Publishers.
—— and Engels, Friedrich 1856–9, *Letters: January 1856–December 1859*, in Marx and Engels 1975–, Volume 40.
Mecklenburg, Frank and Manfred Stassen (eds.) 1990, *German Essays on Socialism in the Nineteenth Century: Theory, History, and Political Organization, 1844–1914*, New York: Continuum Publishers.
Mehring, Franz 1893, *Die Lessing-Legende: Eine Rettung; nebst einem Anhange über den historischen Materialismus*, Stuttgart: J.H.W. Dietz.
—— 1900, *Weltkrach und Weltmarkt: Eine weltpolitische Skizze*, Berlin: Vorwärts (April), reprinted in Mehring 1965 (ed.).
—— 1913a, 'Rosa Luxemburg, *Die Akkumulation des Kapitals. Ein Beitrag zur ökonomischen Erklärung des Imperialismus*', *Leipziger Volkszeitung*, (16, 17 and 18 January).
—— 1913b, 'Miliz und stehendes Heer', *Die Neue Zeit*, 31: 553–8, 673–9, 705–12, 85–6, and 909–14.
—— 1914, 'Literaturbericht: Rosa Luxemburg, *Die Akkumulation des Kapitals. Ein Beitrag zur ökonomischen Erklärung des Imperialismus*', *Archiv für die Geschichte des Sozialismus und der Arbeiterbewegung*, 4: 356–61.
—— (ed.) 1902, *Aus dem literarischen Nachlass von Karl Marx, Friedrich Engels und Ferdinand Lassalle: Gesammelte Schriften von Karl Marx und Friedrich Engels*, Vol. III: Von Mai 1848 bis Oktober 1850, Stuttgart: J.H.W. Dietz.
—— (ed.) 1965, *Zur deutschen Geschichte: von der Revolution 1848/49 bis zum Ende des 19. Jahrhunderts* (Mehring, *Gesammelte Schriften*, Band 7), herausgegeben vom Joachim Streisand, Berlin: Dietz Verlag, 1965.
Meinecke, Friedrich 1908, *Weltbürgertum und Nationalstaat: Studien zur Genesis des deutschen Nationalstaates*, Munich: R. Oldenbourg.
Mill, John Stuart 1868, *Principles of Political Economy, with Some of Their Applications to Social Philosophy*, New York: D. Appleton and Co.
Miller, Hugh Gordon and Joseph C. Freehoff 1914, *The Panama Canal Tolls Controversy; or, A Statement of the Reasons for the Adoption and Maintenance of the Traditional American Policy in the Management of the Panama Canal*, Boston: Chapple Publishing Company.
Miller, Susane 1974, *Burgfrieden und Klassenkampf: Die deutsche Sozialdemokratie im Ersten Weltkrieg*, Düsseldorf: Droste.
Mitchell, Harvey 1965, 'Hobson Revisited', *Journal of the History of Ideas*, 26, 3. (July–September): 397–416.
Mittmann, Ursula 1975, 'Das Postulat der innerparteilichen Demokratie. Der Dampfersubventionsstreit 1884/85', *Internationale Wissenschaftliche Korrespondenz zur Geschichte der deutschen Arbeiterbewegung*, 11, 1: 1–29.
Morgan Shuster, W. 1912, *The Strangling of Persia: A Story of the European Diplomacy and Oriental Intrigue that Resulted in the Denationalization of Twelve Million Mohammedans – A Personal Narrative*, New York: Century.

Morse, Jr., John T. 1898, *John Quincy Adams*, Boston, New York: Houghton, Mifflin and Company.
Nachimson, Miron Isakovich [M.N.] 1910a, 'Finanzkapital', *Bremer Bürger-Zeitung* (18 June).
—— 1910b, 'Die Politik des Finanzkapital', *Bremer Bürger-Zeitung* (21 June).
Naumann, Friedrich 1900, *Demokratie und Kaisertum: Ein Handbuch für innere Politik*, Berlin-Schöneberg: Buchverlag der Hilfe.
Nietzsche, Friedrich W. 1914, *The Will to Power*, in *The Complete Works of Friedrich Nietzsche*, London: T.N. Foulis, Vol. 14.
O'Boyle, Lenore 1951, 'The German Independent Socialists during the First World War', *The American Historical Review*, 56, 4 (July): 824–31.
Oncken, Hermann 1911, *Deutschland und England: Heeres- oder Flotten-Verstarkung? Ein historisch-politischer Vortrag, gehalten am 21. Januar 1912*, Heidelberg: C. Winter, reprinted in Oncken 1914.
—— 1914, *Historisch-politische Aufsätze und Reden*, Munich: R. Oldenbourg, Band 1.
Pannekoek, Anton 1911, 'Abrüstungsfragen', *Bremer Bürger-Zeitung*, 84 (8 April), also in *Leipziger Volkszeitung* (8 April).
—— 1912a, 'Massenaktion und Revolution', *Die Neue Zeit*, 30, 2: 541–50, 585–93, 609–16, reprinted in Grunenberg (ed.) 1970.
—— 1912b, 'Kautsky über "die neue Taktik"', *Bremer Bürger-Zeitung*, 19. Jg., Nr. 209–11 (10–12 September), reprinted in Bock (ed.) 1969.
—— 1912c, 'Das Wesen unserer Gegenwartsforderungen', *Die Neue Zeit*, 30, 2 (August): 810–17.
—— 1913a, 'Rosa Luxemburg: *Die Akkumulation des Kapitals. Ein Beitrag zur ökonomischen Erklärung des Imperialismus*', *Bremer Bürger-Zeitung*, 24–5 (29–30 January).
—— 1913b, 'Marxistische Theorie und revolutionäre Taktik', *Die Neue Zeit*, 31, 1: 272–81, 365–73.
—— 1913c, 'Zum Schluss', *Die Neue Zeit*, 31, 1: 611–12.
—— 1913d, 'Deckungsfrage und Imperialismus', *Die Neue Zeit*, 32, 1 (October): 110–16.
—— 1914a, 'Der Zusammenbruch der Internationale', *Berner Tagwacht*, 245, 246 and 247 (October 20, 21 and 22). English version: Pannekoek 1914b.
—— 1914b, 'The Downfall of the International', *The New Review*, 2, 11 (November): 621–30.
—— 1915, *Uit de voorgeschiedenis van ded wereldoorlog*, Zutphen: W.J. Thieme & Cie.
—— 1916, 'Der Imperialismus und die Aufgaben des Proletariats', *Vorbote: Internationale Marxistische Rundschau*, herausgegeben von Anton Pannekoek und Henriette Roland Holst, Nr. 1 (January 1916), pp. 7–19, reprinted in in Bock (ed.) 1969.
—— 1977 [1934], 'The Theory of the Collapse of Capitalism', Capital and Class (Spring), 1: 59-81. First published in *Ratekorrespondenz* (June 1934): (1, 59–81).
—— 1952, 'La politique de Gorter', *La Révolution prolétarienne* (August–September): 13–14.
—— 1970, *Workers Councils*, Cambridge, MA.: Root and Branch.
Parrini, Carl P. and Martin J. Sklar 1983, 'New Thinking about the Market, 1896–1904: Some American Economists on Investment and the Theory of Surplus Capital', *The Journal of Economic History*, 43, 3, (September): 559–78.
Parti Ouvrier Français 1897, *Quinzième congrès national du Parti ouvrier tenu à Paris du 10 au 13 juillet 1897; (suivi des) Principales résolutions des quatorzième et treizième congrès nationaux tenus à Lille, 1896, et Romilly, 1895*, Lille: P. Lagrange.
Parvus 1901, *Die Handelskrisis und die Gewerkschaften*, Munich: M. Ernst.
—— 1907, *Die Kolonialpolitik und der Zusammenbruch*, Leipzig: Leipziger Buchdruckerei Aktiengesellschaft. (Russian ed.: Parvus, *Kolonial'naya politika i krushenie kapitalisticheskovo stroya*, St. Petersburg: D.P. Veisburta, 1907.)
Quessel, Ludwig 1912a, 'Die Furcht vor dem Imperialismus', *Sozialistische Monatshefte*, 9 (May): 549–51.
—— 1912b, 'Die ökonomische Bedeutung des Imperiums', *Sozialistische Monatshefte*, 12t (June): 707–15.

—— 1912c, 'Der Wert unserer Kolonieen', *Sozialistische Monatshefte*, 18 (September): 1124–31.
Radek, Karl 1909, 'The Unity of the Working Class', *Social Democrat*, 13, 6 (June): 268–77 [originally published in *Die Neue Zeit*, 12 March 1909.]
—— 1910a, 'Kritisches über Kopenhagen', *Leipziger Volkszeitung*, 214–15 (15–16 September).
—— 1910b, 'Falsche Waffen im Kampfe gegen den Imperialismus', *Bremer Bürger-Zeitung*, 218 (17 September).
—— 1911a, 'Auf dem Holzwege', *Bremer Bürger-Zeitung*, 78 (1 April). [Published anonymously.]
—— 1911b, 'Die Sozialdemokratie und die Kriegsrüstungen', *Bremer Bürger-Zeitung*, 81–2 (5–6 April), also in *Leipziger Volkszeitung*, (8/11 April). [Published anonymously.]
—— 1911c, 'Sozialdemokratie und Rüstungsbeschränkung', *Bremer Bürger-Zeitung*, 88, 89, 90 and 91 (13, 15, 18 and 19 April).
—— 1911d, 'Zur Frage der Rüstungsbeschränkung', *Leipziger Volkszeitung* (10, 11 and 12 April).
—— 1912a, *Der deutsche Imperialismus und die Arbeiterklasse*, Bremen: Buchhandlung der Bremer Bürger-Zeitung (March), reprinted in Radek 1921.
—— 1912b, 'Zu unserem Kampfe gegen den Imperialismus', *Die Neue Zeit*, 30, 2, (May): 194–99, 233–41, reprinted in Radek 1921.
—— 1912c, 'Wege und Mittel im Kampfe gegen den Imperialismus', *Bremer Bürger-Zeitung*, (July 1912), reprinted in Radek 1921.
—— 1912d, 'Der Milizgedanke', *Leipziger Volkszeitung* (May Day issue).
—— 1915a, 'Die Triebkräfte des Imperialismus', *Neues Leben*, 3 (March): 70–9.
—— 1915b Parabellum, 'Annexionen und Sozialdemokratie', *Berner Tagwacht*, No. 252 (28 October), *Beilage*, p. 1, and No. 253 (29 October), *Beilage*, p. 1.
—— 1915c, 'Das Selbstbestimmungsrecht der Volker', *Lichtstrahlen*, No. 3 (5 December): 50–4.
—— 1916, 'Theses on Imperialism and National Oppression' ['Thesen über Imperialismus und nationale Unterdrückung', *Vorbote*, 2 (April), first issued in Polish in *Gazeta Robotnicza (Workers' Newspaper)*, No. 25 (January 1916)]. English version in Gankin and Fisher (eds.) 1940.
—— 1921, *In den Reihen der deutschen Revolution, 1909–1919: Gesammelte Aufsätze und Abhandlungen von Karl Radek*, Munich: Kurt Wolff.
—— 1922, *The Winding Up of the Versailles Treaty: Report to the IV. Congress of the Communist International*, Hamburg: The Communist International.
Ratz, Ursula 1966, 'Karl Kautsky und die Abrüstungskontroverse in der deutschen Sozialdemokratie, 1911–12', *International Review of Social History*, 11: 197–227.
Reichs-Marine, Amt (ed.) 1900, *Die deutschen Kapitalanlagen in überseeischen Ländern*, Berlin: Reichsdruckerei.
Reichstag 1871–1918, *Verhandlungen des Reichstags: Stenographische Berichte*, Berlin: Druck und Verlag der Norddeutschen Buchdruckerei und Verlags-Anstalt.
Renner, Karl 1915 'Der Krieg und die Wandlungen des internationalen Gedankens,' *Der Kampf*, 8, 1 (January): 8–23.
Retzlaw, Karl 1972, *Spartakus: Aufstieg und Niedergang: Erinnerungen eines Parteiarbeiters*, Frankfurt: Verlag Neue Kritik.
Ricardo, David 1821, *On the Principles of Political Economy and Taxation*, London: John Murray, 3rd ed.
Richmond, W.H. 1978, 'John A. Hobson: Economic Heretic', *American Journal of Economics and Sociology*, 37, 3 (July): 283–94.
Riddell, John (ed.) 1984, *Lenin's Struggle for a Revolutionary International: Documents, 1907–1916: The Preparatory Years*, New York: Monad Press.
Robertson, J.M. 1899, *Patriotism and Empire*, London: Grant Richards.
Roosevelt, Theodore 1886, 'Machine Politics in New York City', *The Century*, 33, 1, November: 74–83.
Rosdolsky, Roman 1987, *Engels and the Non-Historic Peoples: The National Question in the Revolution of 1848*, translated, edited, and with an introduction by John-Paul Himka, Glasgow: Critique.

—— 1989, *The Making of Marx's 'Capital'*, London: Pluto Press.
Rose, John Holland 1898, *The Rise and Growth of Democracy in Great Britain*, Chicago: Herbert S. Stone and Co.
Rosebery, Archibald P. 1900, *Questions of Empire*, London: Arthur L. Humphreys.
Rosmer, Alfred 1936, *Le mouvement ouvrier pendant la Première Guerre Mondiale*, Paris: Librairie du travail.
Rothstein, Theodor 1901a, 'Der südafrikanische Krieg und der Niedergang des englischen Liberalismus', *Die Neue Zeit*, 19, 2 (July): 452–7.
—— 1901b, 'The Coming of the State', *Social Democrat*, 5, 12 (December): 359–63.
—— 1908, 'Max Beer and the Labour Opportunists', *Justice* (December) 5: 6.
—— 1910, *Egypt's Ruin: A Financial and Administrative Record*, with an introduction by Wilfrid Scawen Blunt, London: A.C. Fifield.
Royal Economic Society 1897, *Economic Journal*, London: Macmillan.
Schiller, Friedrich 1849, *The Works of Friedrich Schiller: Early Dramas and Romances: The Robbers, Fiesco, Love and Intrigue, Demetrius, The Ghost-Seer, and The Sport of Destiny*, London: Henry G. Bohn.
Schippel, Max 1891, *Die deutsche Zuckerindustrie und ihre Subventionirten: Ein Beitrag zur Landagitation*, Berlin: Verlag der "Berliner Arbeiter-Bibliothek".
—— 1911, 'Marokkofragen in der Sozialdemokratie', *Sozialistische Monatshefte*, 17, 24: 1511–17.
—— 1912a, 'Imperialismus und Manchestertum', *Sozialistische Monatshefte*, 18, 20: 1101–19.
—— 1912b, 'Der Imperialismus auf dem Chemnitzer Parteitag', *Sozialistische Monatshefte*, 18, 21 (October): 1271–6.
—— 1913, 'Das Grundgeheimnis des Imperialismus', *Sozialistische Monatshefte*, 19, 3 (February): 147–52.
Schirmacher, Wolfgang (ed.) 1997, *German Socialist Philosophy: Ludwig Feuerbach, Karl Marx, Friedrich Engels*, New York: Continuum.
Schmidt, Conrad 1915, 'Rosa Luxemburg, *Die Akkumulation des Kapitals. Ein Beitrag zur ökonomischen Erklärung des Imperialismus*', *Archiv für Sozialwissenschaft und Sozialpolitik*, 39: 256–61.
Schmoller, Gustav von 1900–4, *Grundriss der allgemeinen Volkswirtschaftslehre*, Leipzig: Duncker & Humblot.
Schorske, Carl 1970, *German Social Democracy, 1905–1917*, New York: Russell & Russell.
Schreiner, Olive 1897, *Trooper Peter Halket of Mashonaland*, Boston: Roberts Brothers.
Schröder, Hans-Christoph 1970, 'Hobsons Imperialismustheorie', in Hans-Ulrich Wehler (ed.), *Imperialismus*, 2., durchges. und geringfügig veränd. Aufl., Cologne: Kiepenheuer & Witsch, 1970:.
—— 1975, *Sozialismus und Imperialismus: Die Auseinandersetzung der deutschen Sozialdemokratie mit dem Imperialismusproblem und der Weltpolitik vor 1914*, Bonn-Bad Godesberg: Neue Gesellschaft.
Schüddekopf, Otto-Ernst 1969, 'Der Revolution entgegen. Materialien und Dokumente zur Geschichte des linken Flügels der deutschen Sozialdemokratie vor dem Ersten Weltkrieg', *Archiv für Sozialgeschichte*, 9: 451–97.
Schulz, Hugo 1908, 'Die Zukunft der "orientalischen Frage"', *Der Kampf*, 1, 12 (September): 542–7.
Schurz, Carl 1899, *American Imperialism: The Convocation Address Delivered on the Occasion of the 27th Convocation of the University of Chicago, January 4, 1899*, Boston: D. Estes.
—— 1900, 'For Truth, Justice and Liberty: Address Delivered at Cooper Union, New York City, September 28, 1900, in Opposition to the Reelection of President McKinley', in Schurz 1913.
—— 1913, *Speeches, Correspondence and Political Papers of Carl Schurz*, New York: G.P. Putnam's Sons.
Schwarz, Maria-Theresia 1999, *Je weniger Afrika, desto besser: Die deutsche Kolonialkritik am Ende des 19. Jahrhunderts: Eine Untersuchung zur kolonialen Haltung von Linksliberalismus und Sozialdemokratie*, Frankfurt: Peter Lang.
Seillière, Ernest 1903–8, *Die Philosophie des Imperialismus*, Berlin: Barsdorf, 4 vols.

—— 1907b, *Der demokratische Imperialismus: Rousseau, Proudhon, Karl Marx* (*Die Philosophie des Imperialismus*, Band 2), Berlin: H. Barsdorf.
Shaw, Bernard (ed.) 1900, *Fabianism and the Empire: A Manifesto by the Fabian Society*, London: Grant Richards.
Sigel, Robert 1976, *Die Lensch-Cunow-Haenisch-Gruppe: Eine Studie zum rechten Flügel der SPD im Ersten Weltkrieg*, Berlin: Duncker und Humblot.
Smart, D.A. (ed.) 1978, *Pannekoek and Gorter's Marxism*, London: Pluto.
Smith, Adam 1902 [1776], *The Wealth of Nations*, New York: Collier.
Social-Democratic Federation 1899, 'Current Topics: "Imperialism"', *The Social Democrat*, 3, 3 (15 March).
—— 1900, 'Capitalism and Imperialism in South Africa', *The Social Democrat*, 4, 1 (15 January).
—— 1901, 'Imperialism and the Coming Crisis for Democracy', *The Social Democrat*, 5, 9 (15 September).
—— 1902, 'The Economic Taproot of Imperialism', *The Social Democrat*, 6, 8 (August).
Sozialdemokratische Partei Deutschlands 1890–1959, *Protokolle über die Verhandlungen der Parteitage der Sozialdemokratischen Partei Deutschlands*, Berlin: Vorwärts.
Sombart, Werner 1902, *Das moderne Kapitalismus: Historisch-systematische Darstellung des gesamteuropaischen Wirtschaftslebens von seinen Anfangen bis zur Gegenwart*, Band I: *Die Genesis des Kapitalismus*, Leipzig: Duncker & Humblot.
Spektator: See Nachimson, Miron Isakovich.
Stalin, J.V. 1913, *Marxism and the National Question*, *Prosveshcheniye*, 3–5 (March–May), in *Works*, Moscow: Foreign Languages Publishing House, 1954, Volume 2.
Stargardt, Nicholas 1994, *The German Idea of Militarism: Radical and Socialist Critics, 1866–1914*, Cambridge: Cambridge University Press.
Stead, W.T. 1897, *The History of the Mystery; or, The Story of the Jameson Raid*, London: 'Review of Reviews' Office.
Steinberg, Joseph 1972, 'Die Stellung der internationalen Arbeiterbewegung zu Militarismus und Imperialismus zwischen den Kongressen in Stuttgart und Basel (1907–1912) unter besonderer Berücksichtigung der deutschen Sozialdemokratie', in Internationale Tagung der Historiker der Arbeiterbewegung (»VIII. Linzer Konferenz«) 1972.
Stephan, Cora (ed.) 1982, *Zwischen den Stühlen; oder über die Unvereinbarkeit von Theorie und Praxis: Schriften Rudolf Hilferdings 1904–1940*, Berlin: J.H.W. Dietz.
Supan, Alexander 1906, *Die territoriale Entwicklung der europäischen Kolonien: Mit einem kolonialgeschichtlichen Atlas von 12 Karten und Kärtchen im Text*, Gotha: Justus Perthes.
Tooze, Adam 2006, *The Wages of Destruction: The Making and Breaking of the Nazi Economy*, London: Allen Lane.
The Economist 1900, London: Economist Newspaper Ltd.
Tremlett, Sheila 1995, 'Paul Louis' in, *Biographical Dictionary of European Labor Leaders*, edited by A.T. Lane, Westport,: Greenwood Press.
Trotsky, Leon 1909, 'Novaya Turtsiya', *Kievskaya Mysl*, No. 3 (3 January).
—— 1910, 'Balkanskii vopros i sotsial-demokratiya', *Pravda*, No. 15 (1 August).
—— 1915a, 'Imperializm i natsional'naya ideya', *Nashe Slovo*, No. 82 (6 May).
—— 1915b, 'Natsiya i khozyaistvo', *Nashe Slovo*, Nos. 130 and 135, (3 and 9 July).
—— 1918a [1914], *The Bolsheviki and World Peace (The War and the International)*, (October), New York: Boni and Liveright.
—— 1918b, 'Gustav Eckstein', *Nashe Slovo*, 178 (August 3), reprinted in Trotsky, *Political Profiles*, translated by R. Chappell, London: New Park, 1972.
—— 1920, *Dictatorship vs. Democracy (Terrorism and Communism): A Reply to Karl Kautsky*, New York: Workers Party of America.
—— 1930, *My Life: An attempt at an Autobiography*, New York: C. Scribner's Sons.
—— 1932, 'Hands Off Rosa Luxemburg!' *The Militant* (6 and 13 August).
—— 1938, 'Ninety Years of the Communist Manifesto' (30 October 1937), *The New International*, 4, 2 (February): 53–5, 63.

—— 1939, 'Again and Once More Again on the Nature of the USSR' (18 October), in Trotsky 1966.
—— 1941, *Stalin: An Appraisal of the Man and his Influence*, edited and translated by Charles Malamuth, New York: Grosset & Dunlap.
—— 1966, *In Defense of Marxism*, London: New Park.
Tucker, Josiah 1776, *Four Tracts on Political and Commercial Subjects*, 3rd edition Gloucester: R. Raikes.
Tudor H. and J.M. Tudor (eds.) 1988, *Marxism and Social Democracy: The Revisionist Debate 1896–1898*, Cambridge University Press.
Tugan-Baranowsky, Michael von 1901, *Studien zur Theorie und Geschichte der Handelskrisen in England*, Aalen: Scientia Verlag, 1969. Reprint of the Jena ed.
van Kol, Henri 1904, 'Über Colonialpolitik', *Sozialistische Monatshefte*, 8 (October): 605–17.
van der Linden, Marcel 2004, 'On Council Communism', *Historical Materialism*, 12, 4: 27–50.
——2007, *Western Marxism and the Soviet Union: A Survey of Critical Theories and Debates Since 1917*, *Historical Materialism* Book Series, Leiden: Brill.
van der Poel, Jean 1951, *The Jameson Raid*, Oxford: Oxford University Press.
van Holthoon, Frits and Marcel van der Linden (eds.) 1988, *Internationalism in the Labour Movement 1830–1940*, Leiden: Brill.
van Rossum, Leo 1969, 'Ein unveröffentlichter Brief Trockijs von Anfang 1916', *International Review of Social History*, 14: 251–66.
Vasilevskii, E.G. 1969, *Razvitie vzgliadov V.I. Lenina na imperializm. (1893–1917 gg.)*, Moscow: Izd. Moskovskogo universiteta.
von Bernhardi, Friedrich 1912, *Deutschland und der nächste Krieg*, Stuttgart and Berlin: J.G. Cotta. English version: von Bernhardi 1914.
—— 1914, *Germany and the Next War*, New York, Longmans, Green, & Co.
vom Brocke, Bernhard (ed.) 1987, *Sombarts 'Moderner Kapitalismus': Materialien zur Kritik und Rezeption*, Munich: Deutscher Taschenbuch Verlag.
von Waltershausen, Wolfgang Sartorius 1907, *Das volkswirtschaftliche System der Kapitalanlage im Auslande*, Berlin: G. Reimer.
Wagner, F. Peter 1996, *Rudolf Hilferding: Theory and Politics of Democratic Socialism*, Atlantic Highlands: Humanities Press.
Walling, William English (ed.) 1915, *The Socialists and the War: A Documentary Statement of the Position of the Socialists of all Countries; with Special Reference to Their Peace Policy*, edited by New York: Henry Holt and Co.
Walther, Rudolf 1981, *"–aber nach der Sündflut kommen wir und nur wir": "Zusammenbruchstheorie", Marxismus und politisches Defizit in der SPD, 1890–1914*, Frankfurt am Main: Ullstein.
Washington, George 1810 [1796], *Washington's Farewell Address to the People of the United States*, Troy: Parker and Bliss.
Webb, Sidney 1901, 'Lord Rosebery's Escape from Houndsditch', *The Nineteenth Century and After*, Vol. 295, (September): 366–86.
Willcocks, William 1911, *Irrigation of Mesopotamia*, London: E. and F.N. Spon.
Wilshire, Henry Gaylord 1901, *Trusts and Imperialism*, Chicago: C.H. Kerr.
Wistrich, Robert S. 2001, *Who's Who in Nazi Germany*, London: Routledge.
Yale University 1898, *The Yale Review*, New Haven: Yale University.
Zarembka, Paul (ed.) 2000, *Value, Capitalist Dynamics, and Money: Research in Political Economy*, 18, Greenwich, CO.: J.A.I. Press.
Zimmermann, Alfred 1905, *Kolonialpolitik*, Leipzig: C.L. Hirschfeld.
Zwick, Jim (ed.) 1992, *Mark Twain's Weapons of Satire: Anti-Imperialist Writings on the Philippine-American War*, Syracuse: Syracuse University Press.

Index

www.ingramcontent.com/pod-product-compliance
Ingram Content Group UK Ltd.
Pitfield, Milton Keynes, MK11 3LW, UK
UKHW021853100926
8556IPUK00020B/1213

9 781608 462353